OXFORD REFERENCE

THE CONCISE OXFORD COMPANION
TO THE THEATRE

THE CONCISE
OXFORD COMPANION
TO THE

THEATRE

Edited by
PHYLLIS HARTNOLL

Oxford   New York
OXFORD UNIVERSITY PRESS

Oxford University Press, Walton Street, Oxford OX2 6DP

Oxford New York Toronto
Delhi Bombay Calcutta Madras Karachi
Petaling Jaya Singapore Hong Kong Tokyo
Nairobi Dar es Salaam Cape Town
Melbourne Auckland

and associated companies in
Berlin Ibadan

Oxford is a trade mark of Oxford University Press

Text © Phyllis Hartnoll 1972
Bibliography © Oxford University Press 1972

First published as an Oxford University Press paperback 1972
Reprinted 1978
First published in hardback 1979
Reprinted in hardback and paperback 1981
Paperback reprinted 1983, 1986, 1987, 1990 (three times), 1991 (twice)

Library of Congress Cataloging in Publication Data
The Concise Oxford companion to the theatre
edited by Phyllis Hartnoll.
p.   cm.
1. Theater—Dictionaries. 2. Drama—Dictionaries.
I. Hartnoll, Phyllis
792'.03—dc20   PN2035.C63   1990   89–27936
ISBN 0–19–281102–9 (pbk.)

Printed in Great Britain by
Richard Clay Ltd.
Bungay, Suffolk

CONTENTS

PREFACE

Although *The Concise Oxford Companion to the Theatre* is based on the same editor's *Oxford Companion to the Theatre*, it is something more than a cut and watered-down version of the original. Every article, however short, has been reconsidered, and in most cases recast and rewritten in miniature in such a way as to retain the essential facts and still leave room, where necessary, for new material. The loss of the long articles on individual countries has been offset by the inclusion of more short articles on actors, dramatists, and directors who are important in the theatrical history of those countries, with perhaps a certain bias towards those more widely known in the English-speaking countries. Room has also had to be found for representatives of the younger generation, though no attempt has been made to cover more than a few outstanding examples of the many recent experimental groups issuing from a theatre in ferment whose relevant outlines will not emerge for many years yet. The omission of long articles on technical matters has not meant the exclusion of these subjects, but rather their fragmentation into short notes which, it is hoped, will be helpful to the beginner and to the student whose main interests lie elsewhere. Indeed, it may perhaps be said that this Companion conforms to the *Shorter Oxford Dictionary*'s definition of 'concise' in that, though brief, it is nevertheless comprehensive. The scaffolding of the original work has been retained; only the ornamentation has been removed, a streamlining which should appeal particularly to those whose need is for easily accessible information rather than academic discussion; and to meet this need a (q.v.) or (see . . .) indicates where further information can be found. Names or terms printed in small capitals within the articles are those to which a cross-reference is given elsewhere. Dates following play titles are those of first performance unless otherwise stated.

This is perhaps the last time that a reference book on the theatre will be able to ignore to some extent the allied arts of film, radio, and television. Even now these media are so closely interwoven in the careers of modern actors and dramatists that they have often had to be mentioned. But in future, no doubt, a full biography of any theatrical figure will have to deal as much with his film or television career as with his activities in the theatre. For the present, the editor has here confined herself to the living theatre, with such asides as 'has also appeared in films' or 'has also written for television'. It is often not enough, but it is all there is room for, and all the editor feels qualified to do.

The chief pleasure of writing a preface to a book of composite scholarship such as this is found in the opportunity it gives for expressing one's thanks to those who have helped with its compilation. First a heartfelt word of gratitude to all those contributors to the three editions of *The Oxford Companion to the Theatre* who have allowed the editor to abridge and rewrite their original articles, often extending their generosity to the reading and approving of the new versions. This has been of inestimable value, and a *Concise Companion*, with its need for compression and elimination, could never have taken shape without their co-operation. The excellencies which are retained in the new articles belong to their original authors; any faults are the editor's.

Among the fifty-odd contributors whose work has been used as the basis of this new volume, it would be invidious to single out any individual, since all have been so helpful in volunteering information and replying to queries. My thanks to them all. Fellow-members of The Society for Theatre Research in England and the United States, and of the International Federation for Theatre Research, have also been quick, as ever, to respond to appeals for help. I should like particularly to express my gratitude for help with the American theatre to Mr. Paul Myers, of the Library and Museum of the Performing Arts, Lincoln Center, New York; and for help with the English theatre to Mr. Eric Johns, editor of *The Stage*, London; Mr. Tony Latham, of the Enthoven Collection, Victoria and Albert Museum, London; and Miss Freda Gaye, former editor of *Who's Who in the Theatre*, London. Mr. Paul Valois, of the School of Slavonic and East European Studies, London, has given me valuable assistance with the Russian theatre; Mrs. Janet Heseltine, editor of *The Oxford Companion to French Literature*, with the French; Dr. Giorgio Brunacci with the Italian; Dr. Heinz Kosok with the German; and Mr. George Katalanos with the modern Greek. Four recently published works which I have found invaluable in my revision are Diana Howard's *London Theatre and Music Halls, 1850–1950*; *The Biographical Encyclopaedia and Who's Who of the American Theatre*, edited by Walter Rigdon; *A Shakespeare Encyclopaedia*, edited by Oscar James Campbell and Edward G. Quinn; and *The Reader's Encyclopedia of World Drama*, edited by Edward Quinn and the late John Gassner, the latter a former contributor to *The Oxford Companion to the Theatre* whose death was a great loss to American scholarship. To him, to the other editors mentioned, to their contributors, and to all the theatre historians in every country who continue to publish the fruits of their research the editor of a theatre companion must feel immeasurably indebted.

PREFACE

ix

A more personal word of thanks is due to my tireless collaborators on the staff of the Oxford University Press, who guided me through the intricacies of publication; to my secretary, Mrs. Sylvia Lee, who created order out of chaos; and to Miss Winifred Kimberley, companion to a Companion and provider of creature comforts. Finally, a belated tribute to that great theatre-historian and lover of everything theatrical, George Freedley, who first introduced me to the American scene, and whose support and encouragement I have missed sadly during the preparation of the present volume.

Lyme Regis
1972

PHYLLIS HARTNOLL

A

ABBEY, HENRY EUGENE (1846-96), American theatre manager, one of the first to present good plays and opera outside New York (where he first managed a theatre in 1877), and to engage Continental stars for the United States, among them Sarah Bernhardt and Coquelin (qq.v.). Irving and Ellen Terry (qq.v.) appeared at Abbey's Theatre (see KNICKERBOCKER THEATRE) on its opening in 1893.

Abbey Theatre, DUBLIN, a famous playhouse built by Miss Horniman (q.v.) to house the company of the Irish National Dramatic Society which, under F. J. and W. G. Fay (qq.v.), aimed to provide English-speaking Irish actors to interpret the new plays of the Irish literary movement. The theatre opened on 27 Dec. 1904 with productions of *On Baile's Strand* by W. B. Yeats and *Spreading the News* by Lady Gregory (qq.v.). In the company were Arthur Sinclair and Sara Allgood (qq.v.), who were destined to play a large part in the future development of the theatre. Among important productions of the early years were the plays of J. M. Synge (q.v.), whose *Playboy of the Western World* caused a riot on its first night (26 Jan. 1907) and of Bernard Shaw (q.v.). In 1910, Miss Horniman, who was already deeply committed to her Manchester venture, withdrew, handing over the theatre to the actors, and a year later Lennox Robinson (q.v.) became manager, a position he retained until his death in 1958. It was under his management that the Abbey Players in 1912 paid their first visit to the United States, where *The Playboy of the Western World* again caused trouble. Later visits proved more successful, and both there and in London the excellent ensemble acting of the company was much admired. The troubles of 1916 threatened its existence for a time but it survived to appear in the early plays of Sean O'Casey (q.v.). Although the Abbey Theatre did not develop in the way its founders had hoped, being in later years more inclined to realistic than to poetic drama, it maintained its reputation for good acting, and gradually widened its repertory to include plays from all countries. In 1924, it received a subvention from the newly-founded Government of Eire, thus becoming the first subsidized theatre in the English-speaking world, but it continued to play in English only until the 1940s, when an amalgamation with the state-aided An Comhar Drámúiochta, which had been producing plays in the vernacular for some time, enabled it to insist on its actors being bilingual, and a number of plays in Gaelic have since been performed. On the night of 17 July 1951 the Abbey Theatre, together with an adjoining theatre known as the Peacock, which opened in 1925, was destroyed by fire. The company moved to the Queen's (see DUBLIN) and continued to function there during the erection of a new theatre, visiting London in 1964 to perform O'Casey's *Juno and the Paycock* and *The Plough and the Stars* during the World Theatre Season. The new Abbey Theatre opened on 18 July 1966 with a commemorative programme, *Recall the Years*, and a year later, on 26 July 1967, a new Peacock Theatre, in the basement, opened with a Gaelic comedy. The Abbey company again took part in the World Theatre season when in 1968 they appeared in a revival of Boucicault's *The Shaughraun*, directed by Hugh Hunt (q.v.).

Abbot of Misrule, of Unreason, see FEAST OF FOOLS.

ABBOTT, GEORGE (1887–), American actor and playwright, who became an outstanding director of musical shows. Most of his plays were written in collaboration, and he directed them on Broadway himself. Among them were *Coquette* (1927), which established Helen Hayes (q.v.) as a star, *Three Men on a Horse* (1935), *The Boys from Syracuse* (1938) (a musical based on *The Comedy of Errors*, which was seen in London in 1963, again directed by Abbott), *The Pajama Game* (1954), and *Damn Yankees* (1955). Among the musicals by other writers which Abbott directed were *Pal Joey* (1940) and *High Button Shoes* (1947).

ABBOTT, WILLIAM (1789–1843), an English actor of whom Hazlitt said 'he never acts ill'. He first appeared at Bath in 1806, and by 1813 was at Covent Garden, where in 1816 he played Pylades to the Orestes of Macready (q.v.) in a revival of Ambrose Philips's *The Distrest Mother*. He also created the part of Appius Claudius in Sheridan Knowles's *Virginius* in 1820. He later went to America, but met with no success and died in poverty.

ABELL, KJELD (1901–61), Danish dramatist and artist, who worked as a stage designer in Paris and with Balanchine at the Alhambra Theatre, London, in 1931. His first play, *Melodien, der blev væk*, was produced in Copenhagen in 1935 and at the Arts Theatre, London, a year later as *The Melody That Got Lost*. None of his other plays has been seen in London, though two of them, *Anna Sophia Hedvig* (1939) and *Dronning går igen* (1943) (*The Queen on Tour*, or *The Queen's Progress*, a protest against the loss of freedom produced during the German occupation of Denmark), were published in English translations, as was *Dage på en sky* (1947), as *Days on a Cloud*, in an American anthology.

ABINGTON, MRS. [*née* FANNY (really FRANCES) BARTON] (1737–1815), English actress, wife of a music-master, from whom she soon separated. She made her first appearance on the stage in Mrs. Centlivre's *The Busybody* at the Haymarket in 1755. On the recommendation of Samuel Foote (q.v.) she was engaged for Drury Lane, where she soon found herself overshadowed by Kitty Clive and Mrs. Pritchard (qq.v.). She therefore left London for Dublin, where she remained for five years, returning to Drury Lane at the express invitation of Garrick (q.v.), who disliked her but considered her a good actress. During the eighteen years that she remained there she played a number of important roles, and was the first Lady Teazle in Sheridan's *The School for Scandal* (1777). She was also much admired as Miss Prue in Congreve's *Love for Love*, in which character she was painted by Reynolds. In 1782 she went to Covent Garden, where she remained until 1790. She finally retired in 1799.

Above, see STAGE DIRECTIONS.

Absurd, Theatre of the, see THEATRE OF THE ABSURD.

Accesi, a company of actors of the *commedia dell'arte*, first mentioned in

1590. Ten years later they were under the leadership of Pier Maria Cecchini and the famous Harlequin Tristano Martinelli (q.v.), with whom they visited France. Among the actors were Martinelli's brother Drusiano, Flaminio Scala, and possibly Diana, formerly of the Desiosi. On their next visit to France in 1608 they were without their Harlequin, but were nevertheless much admired by the Court and by Marie de Médicis. Shortly afterwards Cecchini joined forces with the younger Andreini (see FEDELI), but the constant quarrelling of Cecchini's and Andreini's wives caused the two parties to separate. Cecchini retained the old name of Accesi, but little is known of his subsequent activities. Silvio Fiorillo (q.v.), the first Captan Matamoros, was with the Accesi in 1621 and 1632.

ACCIUS, LUCIUS (*c.* 170–86 B.C.), Roman dramatist, and the last important writer of Roman tragedy. His plays, of which the titles of over forty survive, show the flamboyance and melodrama, the continual search for rhetorical effect, and the eagerness to exploit every situation to the full, which are characteristic of Roman tragedy in its decline, before a change in fashion drove it from the theatre. Yet, unlike the closet plays of Seneca (q.v.), they were written to be staged, and Accius was still under the salutary discipline of having to write with production in view. Though they may appear to be only stiff and constrained versions of their Greek originals, they have a far better technique and far more vitality than the purely literary plays of the later Roman empire.

ACHURCH, JANET (1864–1916), English actress, wife of the actor Charles Charrington, who made her first appearance at the Olympic in 1883. She was one of the first actresses in England to appear in Ibsen's plays, being seen as Nora in *A Doll's House* at the Novelty Theatre in 1889. In 1896 she produced *Little Eyolf* at the Avenue Theatre with herself as Rita, Mrs. Patrick Campbell (q.v.) as the Ratwife, and Elizabeth Robins (q.v.) as Asta. She was also seen as Shaw's heroine in *Candida* and as Lady Cicely Waynflete in *Captain Brassbound's Conversion* (both Strand, 1900). Shaw called her 'the only tragic actress of genius we now possess', and some excellent descriptions of her acting can be found in his *Onr Theatres iu the*

Nineties. She retired from the stage in 1913.

ACKERMANN, KONRAD ERNST (1712–71), German actor, who in about 1742 joined the travelling company of Schönemann (q.v.), playing mainly in comedy, and being particularly admired in such parts as Major von Tellheim in Lessing's *Minna von Barnhelm.* A handsome man, with a restless, vagabond temperament, Ackermann was well suited to the life of a strolling player and soon left Schönemann to form his own company, taking with him as his leading lady Sophia Schröder (q.v.), whom he married after the death of her husband. Together they toured Europe, being joined eventually by Ekhof (q.v.) and by Sophia's son F. L. Schröder (q.v.), and in 1767 opened the first German National Theatre at Hamburg. This enterprise, which inspired the *Hamburgische Dramaturgie* of Lessing (q.v.), the cornerstone of modern dramatic criticism, failed because of the antagonism between Ekhof and Schröder, who both left the company, though Schröder returned shortly before Ackermann's death and took control. Ackermann's daughters, DOROTHEA (1752–1821) and CHARLOTTE (1757–74), both played leading roles in his productions, the former being greatly admired as Lessing's Minna von Barnhelm and as Countess Orsina in his *Emilia Galotti,* in which Charlotte, at the early age of fourteen, played the title-role. Dorothea retired on her marriage in 1778, but Charlotte committed suicide at seventeen, driven to it, it was said, by Schröder's harsh treatment and the strain of too many new and taxing roles.

Acoustics, THEATRE. The Greek open-air theatre, built into the hillside, provided a perfect place for sound. So did the Roman, with its towering façade, or *frons scaenae.* The medieval cathedral must have presented difficulties not so apparent in smaller churches, though even there some sounds no doubt got lost in the roof. In the market-place, audibility must have been as chancy as it is today in a flat open space. But the use of rhymed couplets, and a good deal of miming and horseplay, must have helped the action along. In both the classical and the Elizabethan open-air theatres the use of verse helped to carry the voice over the auditorium, and, as far as we can judge, the actors in both countries were well equipped vocally.

Acoustics really became a problem in the theatre when all plays were given indoors, often in rooms acoustically unsuitable for the purpose. Luckily, the development of the Italian opera-house produced in the eighteenth century a building which, repeated all over Europe, provided a good place for the sound of music. Because the tiers of boxes were heavily draped, the reverberation was short. The flat ceilings, without domes, and the plentiful use of baroque ornamentation, diffused the sound and so prevented echoes, and the large amount of wood used in the building meant that the orchestral tone was adequate, in spite of the size of the auditorium. But for the spoken word these theatres were not so well equipped. The theatre built by Vanbrugh in the Haymarket (see HER MAJESTY'S), with its high vaulted roof, concave in shape, was found, on its opening in 1705, to have sacrificed audibility to architecture. It was said that scarcely one word in ten could be heard distinctly, and that the articulated sounds of the speaking voice were drowned by the hollow reverberation of one word upon another. Luckily the smaller, more intimate English playhouses were better suited to spoken drama, and Vanbrugh's theatre became the first English opera-house, being used for a number of operas by Handel from 1711 onwards. The large theatres built at the beginning of the nineteenth century, though preserving the horseshoe auditorium which was good for sound, though not always for sight, adopted the domed ceiling, which led to some notable echoes, focused from a particular stage position. Even when echoes were not noticeable, curved ceilings gave an unequal distribution of sound, so that some seats were better for hearing than others. But the baroque tradition of ornamentation, stage boxes, and heavy drapery was retained, and helped to keep the reverberation short. Unfortunately, in the period between 1919 and 1939, the design of theatres everywhere was radically changed. Baroque ornamentation was replaced by large continuous surfaces in hard plaster, the stage boxes were removed, the auditorium became fan-shaped, and large areas of sound-absorbing velvet drapery were removed. At first the new fan-shaped plan and splayed proscenium were approved of on the grounds that they provided useful reflecting surfaces, and audibility in the rear seats was improved. But it was then discovered that any return of sound from surfaces at the rear, including balcony fronts, ceiling coves, and balustrades, found its way to the front seats. Complaints of inaudibility now came from the occupants of the expensive stalls. It had been too readily assumed that a powerful sound-absorbing material on the rear wall behind the audience would prevent any return of sound; but in practice, commercial sound-absorbents, often covered with paint, were found to be less effective than modern hard plasters on the reflecting walls and ceiling. Another factor which adversely affected the acoustics in the fan-shaped auditorium was the relatively large area occupied by the rear wall, which was too often given the most dangerous curve possible, one struck from a centre near the stage front. Thus, in the absence of ornamentation and drapery, any remainder of sound—and also any noise from the gallery—was focused towards the front of the house. The result was not a complete echo, but a prolonging of word-endings, likely to obscure rapid speech. It was clear that the fan-shape needed modification, and that the rear wall should not be curved on plan, but straight or polygonal: also that in large theatres it was wise to avoid curved parapets, seat risers, and gallery fronts, and to restore the side-boxes and draped proscenium. A large bare forestage also increases the risk of reverberation in the front of the house. The value of the convex curve, instead of the concave, has now been recognized in the profiling of reflecting canopies and in corrugated ceilings, the latter being also stepped instead of splayed. The modern demand for open and arena stages and particularly for theatre-in-the-round has brought with it further acoustic problems. The human voice has a direction, and is not equally well heard behind and at the side, particularly since the old-fashioned projected speech has been discarded in favour of an intimate conversational tone. New techniques are being evolved to overcome these problems, and also those of the all-purpose theatre. Where drapes and carpets and upholstered seats are discarded for the sake of easy convertibility, there is all the more need for good distributed sound-absorbents on walls and ceilings in order to reduce reverberation.

Act. The divisions of a play are known as acts, each of which may contain one or more scenes. Greek plays were continuous, the only pauses being marked by the chorus. Horace was the first to advocate the division of tragedies into five acts, a suggestion adopted at the time of the Renaissance by academic dramatists. The first English writer to use it was Ben Jonson (q.v.). There is no proof that Shakespeare divided his plays thus, and the divisions in the printed copies were probably introduced by the editors in imitation of Jonson. In comedy more licence was allowed to the individual, two or three acts being quite usual, even in Molière (q.v.). Modern drama usually keeps to three acts, as being convenient for actors and audience alike, but two acts are sometimes found, and many Shakespeare revivals have had only one interval in each play. A division into four acts, once usual, is now seldom found.

Act-Drop, the name given in the late eighteenth century to the painted cloth which closed the proscenium opening between the acts of a play (see CURTAIN).

Act-Tunes, musical interludes between the acts of plays. That these were customary in the Elizabethan theatre is shown by their mention in a number of stage directions. In the Restoration theatre the act-tunes became very important, and composers like Purcell were commissioned to write them. The introductory music was sometimes known as the Curtain-Music or Curtain-Tune.

Actor, Actress, Acting. The art of acting, and the profession of actor, is as old as man, showing itself first in ritual dance and song and somewhat later in dialogue. Of the very early actors nothing is known, but in Greece, where they took part in a religious ceremony, they were men of repute. In Rome their status was low and they were often slaves. With the coming of Christianity they were proscribed and sank into obscurity. The medieval minstrels, however, occupied a special place in the social scale, and were welcome at Court and in noble houses, forming themselves into Guilds for mutual help and protection and being assured of at least a decent livelihood (see MINSTREL). They were not actors, but when the revival of the theatre came in Europe, first in the church and later in the market-place (see LITURGICAL DRAMA), they may have given advice and practical help to the big amateur groups that performed the Mystery cycles.

With the emergence of vernacular drama came the professional actor, who established himself in most countries during the sixteenth century, in Italy with the *commedia dell'arte* (q.v.), in Spain under Lope de Rueda (q.v.), in England under Richard Burbage (q.v.), and in France with the company at the Hôtel de Bourgogne (q.v.). Owing to internal dissension and division, it was not until the eighteenth century that German actors came to the fore, and in Russia, whose early theatrical history is as yet imperfectly known, there was no national or professional theatre before the middle of the nineteenth century.

Women did not act in Greece at all, and in Rome only if very depraved. The medieval stage may have employed a few women, but they were still amateurs. The professional actress emerges first in Italy, the best-known being Isabella Andreini (q.v.), and in France appears at the same time as the professional actor. Elizabethan drama employed no women at all, their roles being taken by boys and young men. It was not until the Restoration in 1660 that women were first seen on the London stage. The players of the Far East were also entirely male, originally, though actresses have now emerged in both China and Japan—usually in modern plays.

The position of the actor was for a long time precarious. In Catholic countries he was refused the sacraments. Legally Shakespeare and his contemporaries were classed as rogues and vagabonds, and in England it was not until the nineteenth century that the actor achieved a definite place in society, culminating in the knighting of Irving (q.v.) in 1895.

Fashions in acting change constantly, and the history of the theatre shows one method giving way to another, one convention succeeding another. In the Far East, traditions in acting remained unbroken down the centuries, but are now in a state of flux. In Greece, the tragic actor was static—a voice and a presence; in Rome he was lively, and, in the last resort, an acrobat. The *commedia dell'arte* demanded a quick wit and a nimble body; French tragedy needed a fine presence and a sonorous voice; Restoration comedy must have called for a polished brilliance and a gentlemanly insolence. Later, 'comedian' and 'tragedian' were separate employments. The melodrama of the nineteenth century could only make its full effect when its actors 'tore a passion to tatters', and the intimate drama which replaced it gave little scope for gesture or raised voices. A more recent innovation is improvisation, and there are now signs of the return of the all-round actor, combining singer, dancer, tragedian, and comedian. Much of an actor's art must be born in him; something can be taught. The ideal is a good balance of intuition and hard work, tempered by all-round experience.

Actors' Equity Association, U.S.A., see EQUITY.

Actors' Studio, see METHOD and STRASBERG, LEE.

Actors' Theatre. (1) An American membership group formed in 1922 for the presentation of good classic and new plays. Dudley Digges (q.v.) was one of the directors, and among the plays of the first seasons were Shaw's *Candida* and Ibsen's *The Wild Duck*. In 1927 the group fused with that of Greenwich Village under Kenneth Macgowan (q.v.). (2) Another American group under the same name was formed in 1939, and gave plays at the Provincetown Playhouse. It was intended for the tryout of new plays and young actors. Most of its activities were suspended on the outbreak of war in 1941, but it continued to function intermittently until 1947.

ADAM DE LA HALLE (*c.* 1245–88), a French *trouvère*, nicknamed 'le Bossu d'Arras', and one of the few medieval minstrels about whom anything is known. He was the author of *Le Jeu de la feuillée* (*c.* 1262), which marks the beginning of lay, as distinct from ecclesiastical, drama in France, and for the Court of Robert II, Count of Artois, he wrote a pastoral, *Le Jeu de Robin et de Marion*, which, by virtue of its music—for Adam was a composer as well as a poet—is now considered to be the first French light opera. First printed in 1822, it was played in a modernized version in Arras in June 1896 during a festival in honour of the composer.

ADAMOV, ARTHUR (1908–70), Russian-born French dramatist. His first play, *La Parodie*, was not produced until 1952, though written some years before. Two later plays, *La Grande et la petite manœuvre* and *L'Invasion*, had been performed in 1950. His early work, including *Le Professeur Taranne* and *Tous contre tous* (both 1953), had much in common with the Theatre of the Absurd (q.v.), as had *Le Ping-Pong* (1955), a satire on the world of commerce and politics which in 1959 was given an amateur production in London. With *Paolo Paoli*, an exposure of the corruptions of the French social scene which was first produced by Planchon (q.v.) at Lyons in 1957, Adamov moved into the world of Brecht's Epic Theatre (q.v.), whose influence was even more evident in *Le printemps '71* (1961), a panoramic history of the Paris Commune, and in *La Politique des Restes* (1963).

ADAMS, EDWIN (1834–77), American actor, who made his first appearance at Boston in 1853 in Sheridan Knowles's *The Hunchback*. At the opening performance of Booth's Theatre, New York, on 3 Feb. 1869, he played Mercutio to the Romeo of Edwin Booth (q.v.). His best-known role, however, was Enoch Arden in a dramatization of Tennyson's poem. He toured in it all over the United States, but made his last appearance in San Francisco, shortly before his early death, as Iago to the Othello of John McCullough.

ADAMS [really KISKADDEN], MAUDE (1872–1953), American actress, daughter of the leading lady of the Salt Lake City stock company, with whom she appeared as a child in such parts as Little Eva in one of the many dramatizations of Harriet Beecher Stowe's *Uncle Tom's Cabin*. In 1888 she made her first appearance in New York, and three years later was engaged to play opposite John Drew (q.v.). She first emerged as a 'star' with her performance as Lady Babbie in *The Little Minister* (1897), a part which Barrie (q.v.) rewrote and enlarged specially for her. Her quaint, elfin personality suited his work to perfection, and she appeared successfully in the American productions of his *Quality Street* (1901), *Peter Pan* (1905), *What Every Woman Knows* (1908), *Rosalind* (1914), and *A Kiss for Cinderella* (1916). She was also much admired as the young hero of Rostand's *L'Aiglon* (1900), and in such Shakespearian parts as Viola, Juliet, and Rosalind. In 1918 she retired, not acting again until 1931, when she appeared on tour, in *The Merchant of Venice*, as Portia to the Shylock of Otis Skinner (q.v.). In 1934 she went on tour again as Maria in *Twelfth Night* and then retired for good.

A.D.C., see CAMBRIDGE.

ADDISON, JOSEPH (1672–1719), English politician and man of letters, author of *Cato*, a tragedy on the French classical model seen at Drury Lane in April 1713, which was supported by the Whigs for political reasons, and by the Tories for effect. Written in unrhymed heroic couplets, it contains some fine poetry, but is not theatrically effective. The part of Cato was originally offered to Colley Cibber (q.v.), who declined it, and it was finally played by Barton Booth (q.v.), with Anne Oldfield (q.v.) as Lucia. Addison's only other play was a comedy, *The Drummer; or, the Haunted House* (1716), also performed at Drury Lane, but his dramatic theories and criticisms can be found in several papers of the *Spectator*, which he edited with Richard Steele (q.v.), while the *Tatler*, No. 42 (1709), which he also edited, contains an amusing mock inventory of the properties and furnishings of Drury Lane.

ADE, GEORGE (1866–1944), an American journalist, humorist, and playwright, whose plays of contemporary life were full of homely humour and wit. Among the most successful were *The County Chairman* (1903), *College Widow* (1904), which added a new phrase to the American language, *Just Out of College* (1905), and *Father and the Boys* (1908). Ade was also responsible for the books of several musical comedies, among them *The Fair Co-Ed* (1909).

Adeline Genée Theatre, see GENÉE THEATRE.

Adelphi Theatre. (1) LONDON, in the Strand, originally the Sans Pareil, built by a colour merchant named Scott, who had made a fortune from a new washing-blue, to display the talents of his daughter. It opened on 27 Nov. 1806 with *Miss Scott's Entertainment*. In 1814 it was redecorated and given a new façade. The theatre prospered and, after changing hands in 1819, reopened on 18 Oct. as the Adelphi. Among the successful productions of later years were Moncrieff's *Tom and Jerry; or, Life in London*, based on Pierce Egan's novel, Fitzball's *The Pilot* (1825), based on Fenimore Cooper's novel, and numerous dramatizations of works by Scott and Dickens. In 1840 a new façade was added, and in 1844 Madame Céleste and Ben Webster (qq.v.) took over the theatre, making it the home of 'Adelphi drama', mostly written by Buckstone (q.v.). The original building was demolished in 1858 and a larger theatre built on the site. This opened on 27 Dec. with a pantomime. Among successful productions of succeeding years were *The Colleen Bawn* (1860) and *The Octoroon* (1861), by Boucicault (q.v.), and *Rip Van Winkle* (1865) with the American actor Joseph Jefferson (q.v.). In 1887 the theatre, which had been modernized and redecorated in 1875, was again enlarged, and a series of Adelphi melodramas followed, starring William Terriss (q.v.), who was assassinated at the entrance to the theatre in 1897. During 1901 and 1902 the theatre, which had been rebuilt in 1901—on which occasion the stage door was moved from Bull Inn Court to Maiden Lane—was briefly called the Century, but the old name was restored by popular demand. In 1908, under George Edwardes (q.v.), it housed a series of excellent musical comedies, and in 1930, after rebuilding, opened on 3 Dec. with Benn Levy's *Ever Green* (with music by Richard Rodgers), the first of a series of productions by C. B. Cochran (q.v.). Plans are now (1972) on foot to replace it by an office block incorporating a small theatre.

(2) NEW YORK, on West 54th Street between 7th and 8th Avenues. This opened on 24 Dec. 1928 as the Craig, but with little success, and after standing empty for some time it reopened as the Adelphi on 27 Nov. 1934. Two years later it was taken over by the Federal Theatre Project (q.v.), which retained control until its dissolution in 1939. The most successful production during this time was Arthur Arent's 'Living Newspaper' on housing, *One-Third of a Nation* (1938). In 1947 the Theatre Guild (q.v.) staged a musical version of Elmer Rice's *Street Scene* at the Adelphi, which later became a radio and television studio. When it reopened in 1954 as a playhouse it was renamed the Fifty-Fourth Street Theatre. Among productions since the reopening have been Camus's *Caligula* (1960) in translation and a musical, *No Strings* (1962).

(See also EDINBURGH.)

Admiral's Men, an Elizabethan company which, with Edward Alleyn (q.v.) as their star actor, was the only real rival of the Chamberlain's Men (q.v.), with whom Shakespeare was associated. Their patron was Lord Howard, who became Admiral in 1585, and at Christmas in the same year the 'Admiral's players' made their first appearance at Court. In 1590-1 they were housed in Burbage's Theatre (q.v.) with Strange's Men. After a quarrel with Burbage over finance, the two companies moved to the Rose, under Henslowe (q.v.). When the Chamberlain's Men were formed in 1594 some of the Admiral's Men joined them, while the rest formed themselves into an independent company under Alleyn, with Henslowe as their landlord and 'banker'. They had a large repertory of plays, most of which, except for Marlowe's, have been lost or forgotten. The retirement of Alleyn in 1597 was a great blow, but in 1600 he returned and the company moved with him into a new playhouse, the Fortune, (q.v.). On the death of Elizabeth they lost Alleyn for good and were renamed Prince Henry's Men. Their young patron died in 1612, and was replaced by the Elector Palatine, the company then being known as the Palsgrave's Men. In 1621 the Fortune was burnt down, and all the wardrobe and playbooks were lost. Two years later a new Fortune Theatre opened with practically the same company as before, but after two difficult years the combination of plague and the death of James I proved too much for it. The company disbanded, after a long and honourable career, and its remnants were probably absorbed into other existing organizations.

Advertisement Curtain, an inner curtain or act-drop used mostly in the English provincial and smaller London theatres in the late nineteenth and early twentieth centuries. It was covered with advertisements of local shops and manufacturers, whose payments helped the theatre's budget.

AE [really GEORGE WILLIAM RUSSELL] (1867–1935), Irish poet, an important figure in the Irish literary revival, who was connected with the early years of modern Irish drama through his play, *Deirdre*, which was first performed, probably in Dublin, at Christmas 1901. A longer version was produced by the Fays' Irish National Dramatic Society in St. Teresa's Hall on 2 Apr. 1902. It was probably AE who brought Yeats and the Fays together, and so helped to lay the foundations of the Abbey Theatre (q.v.).

AESCHYLUS (525–456 B.C.), Greek dramatist, born at Eleusis, near Athens, died at Gela in Sicily. He fought against the Persians in the battle of Marathon and possibly at Salamis and Plataea too. He is said to have written ninety plays, and he gained thirteen victories. The titles of seventy-nine of his plays are known: only seven are extant—the *Suppliants* (*c.* 490 B.C.), the *Persians* (472), the *Seven against Thebes* (469), the *Prometheus Bound* (? *c.* 460), and the trilogy known as the *Oresteia* (the *Agamemnon*, the *Choephoroe* (*Libation-bearers*), and the *Eumenides*) (458). About a quarter of his ninety plays must have been Satyr-dramas (q.v.), in which genre he was an acknowledged master. Nothing of these survives except a few fragments.

Aeschylus may reasonably be regarded as the founder of European drama, and no one but Shakespeare (q.v.) can seriously be considered his equal as a dramatic poet. By reducing the size of the chorus and introducing a second actor into the play, he made the histrionic part as important as the lyric, and (as it has been said) turned oratorio into drama. The transition can be seen in his early plays. In the *Suppliants* the chorus is the chief actor; in the *Persians* the chorus still gives the play its formal unity; but the *Seven against Thebes* is clearly dominated by the chief actor. In his later plays Aeschylus used (in a highly individual way) the innovation of the third actor, introduced by Sophocles (q.v.).

Dramatists competing at the Athens festival had to present three serious plays and one satyr-play; Aeschylus normally made the three plays a connected 'trilogy' in which each part, though a complete unity, was a coherent part of a larger unity. This gave his drama an amplitude which has never been approached since— an amplitude which his vast conceptions needed, and which only his magnificent structural sense could control. The normal scheme might be very baldly summarized as the offence, the counter-offence, and the resolution; sin provokes sin, until justice asserts itself. The only complete trilogy which has survived is the *Oresteia*. Of the other plays, the *Suppliants* and the *Prometheus* were the first plays of their trilogies, the *Seven against Thebes* the third of its; and, judging by what has been recovered, the scale of these trilogies was hardly less majestic than that of the *Oresteia*.

These conceptions were matched by a bold dramatic technique, an immense concentration, a wonderful sense of structure, and magnificent poetry. Aeschylus made the utmost use of spectacle and colour; and, in virtue of the beauty and strength of his choral odes, he might well be regarded as one of the greatest of lyric poets, as well as, possibly, the greatest of dramatists. As a unique honour to him, it was enacted in Athens after his death that his plays might be revived at the festivals, to which normally only new plays were admitted.

AESOPUS, CLAUDIUS, a celebrated Roman tragic actor of the first century B.C., much admired by Horace. He was a friend of Cicero, who speaks of him as having great powers of facial expression and fluent gesture. During Cicero's exile Aesopus would often allude to him on the stage, in the hope of swaying public opinion in his favour.

A.E.T.A., see AMERICAN EDUCATIONAL THEATRE ASSOCIATION.

AFINOGENOV, ALEXANDER NIKOLAE-VICH (1904–41), Soviet dramatist, who began writing in 1926. His first important play (translated into English by Charles Malamuth as *Fear* and published in *Six Soviet Plays*, 1936) was performed at the Leningrad Theatre of Drama in 1931. Dealing with the conversion to socialism of a psychologist who has claimed that fear governs the U.S.S.R., it was one of the first Soviet plays to combine good technique and dramatic tension with party propaganda. This fusion was even more apparent in a later play, seen at the Vakhtangov in 1934, which, as *Distant Point*, was produced at the Gate Theatre, London, on 25 Nov. 1937 in a translation by Hubert Griffith. It has been revived several times in London and the provinces and broadcast by the B.B.C. The death of Afinogenov, who was killed in an air raid in Nov. 1941, deprived Soviet Russia of one of her few early dramatists who might have had a universal appeal.

African Roscius, see ALDRIDGE, IRA.

After-Piece, a short comedy or farce, performed after a five-act tragedy in London theatres of the eighteenth century, partly to afford light relief to the spectators already present and partly to attract the middle-class business men and others who found the opening hour of 6 p.m. too early for them. Half-price was charged for admission. The after-piece was often a full-length comedy cut to one act, but many short plays were specially written for the purpose by Garrick, Murphy, Foote, and others.

AGATE, JAMES EVERSHED (1877–1947), English dramatic critic who numbered among his ancestors the actor Ned Shuter (q.v.). From 1923 until his death he was dramatic critic of the *Sunday Times*, succeeding S. W. Carroll and being succeeded by Harold Hobson (q.v.). His weekly articles, many of which were collected and published in book form, were vigorous and outspoken, and always entertaining, in spite of his refusal to admit greatness in any actor later than Irving (q.v.). In a series of volumes entitled *Ego* he published a day-to-day diary of his life from 1932, but he is more likely to be remembered for his dramatic criticism.

AGATE, MAY (1892–1960), English actress, sister of the dramatic critic James Agate (q.v.). She studied for the stage with Sarah Bernhardt (q.v.), on whom she wrote an interesting book, *Madame Sarah* (1945), and with whom she made her first appearances on the stage in Paris and London. In 1916 she joined Miss Horniman's company at the Gaiety, Manchester, and in 1921 appeared in London, where she had a distinguished, though not spectacular, career, making her last appearance as the Duchess Ludoviska in Elizabeth Sprigge's *Elisabeth of Austria* in 1938. With her husband Wilfred Grantham she made an English adaptation of Musset's *Lorenzaccio* as *Night's Candles* (1933), in which Ernest Milton appeared with great success.

AGATHON, of Athens, a tragic poet and a younger contemporary of Euripides (q.v.), who won the first of his two victories in 416 B.C. Few fragments of his work survive, but according to Aristotle (q.v.), he was the first to write choral odes, unconnected with the plot, as entr'actes. Aristophanes (q.v.) laughs at him for effeminacy, but on his death lamented his loss. There is a character sketch of him in Plato's *Symposium*.

AGGAS [also ANGUS], ROBERT (c. 1619–79), English scene painter, much esteemed in the Restoration theatre. He worked for Killigrew (q.v.), and with Samuel Towers painted the elaborate scenery used at Drury Lane for Crowne's *The Destruction of Jerusalem* in 1677, later suing the theatre for payment.

AIKEN, GEORGE L. (1830–76), American actor and playwright, who made his first appearance on the stage in 1848. He is chiefly remembered for his adaptation—the best of many—of Harriet Beecher Stowe's *Uncle Tom's Cabin*, prepared for George C. Howard, who wished to star in it his wife, Aiken's cousin, as Topsy, and his daughter as Eva. It was first given at Troy in 1852 and in New York a year later, and was constantly revived. Aiken, who wrote or adapted a number of other plays, continued to act until 1867.

AINLEY, HENRY HINCHLIFFE (1879–1945), English actor, possessed of a remarkably fine voice and great personal beauty and charm. He made his first success as Paolo, in Phillips's *Paolo and Francesca* (1902), at the St. James's Theatre under George Alexander (q.v.), and soon became known as an excellent Shakespearian and romantic actor. In 1912 he made a great impression as Leontes in Granville-Barker's production of *The Winter's Tale*, and a year later showed his versatility by his playing of Ilam Carve in Arnold Bennett's *The Great Adventure*. He was associated in the management of several theatres, including His Majesty's, where he was seen in Flecker's *Hassan* (1923), which provided him with one of his finest parts. Illness then kept him from the stage for some years, but in 1929 he returned to score an instantaneous success as James Fraser in St. John Ervine's *The First Mrs. Fraser*, which, with Marie Tempest (q.v.) in the name-part, ran for eighteen months. A year later he was seen as Hamlet at a Command Performance, and he finally retired in 1932.

AKIMOV, NIKOLAI PAVLOVICH (1901–68), Soviet scene designer and director, who first attracted attention by his designs for the productions of Ivanov's *Armoured Train 14–69* and Afinogenov's *Fear* at the Leningrad Theatre of Comedy. Moving to Moscow, he worked at the Vakhtangov Theatre (q.v.) and was responsible for the famous 'formalist' production of *Hamlet* in 1932, in which Hamlet faked the Ghost, and Ophelia, a 'bright young thing', was not mad but drunk. This aroused a storm of controversy, and the play was taken off in deference to public opinion. In 1936 Akimov became Art Director of the Leningrad Theatre of Comedy, being responsible for a beautifully staged

Twelfth Night there. In the 1950s he strove to create an original repertory, and fought for the acceptance of new Soviet comedies. From 1955 until his death he was on the staff of the Leningrad Theatrical Institute.

AKINS, ZoË (1886–1958), American poet and dramatist, whose first play, *Déclassée* (1919), provided an excellent part for Ethel Barrymore (q.v.). Among her later plays the most interesting was perhaps the successful *First Love* (1926), but it, and all her other plays, were overshadowed by the popularity of *The Greeks Had a Word For It* (1930), which was equally successful in London when produced there in 1934. In 1935 Miss Akins was awarded a Pulitzer Prize for her dramatization of Edith Wharton's novel, *The Old Maid.* Her last play, produced in 1951, was *The Swallow's Nest.*

ALARCÓN Y MENDOZA, JUAN RUIZ DE (c. 1581–1639), Mexican-born dramatist of Spain's Golden Age, a cripple embittered by the ridicule attracted by his deformities, rival and enemy of Lope de Vega (q.v.). His plays are satiric, well-constructed, and contain some excellent character-drawing. They were more popular abroad than in his own country, the French in particular finding his work much to their taste. Through French translations Alarcón had some influence in England, Foote's *The Liar* (1762) being based on Steele's *The Lying Lover; or, the Ladies' Friendship* (1703), an adaptation of *Le Menteur* (1643) by Corneille (q.v.), who took his comedy from Alarcón's play about a young man who tells so many lies that when he tells the truth he is not believed. This was *La verdad sospechosa* (*Truth Itself Suspect*), which, with *Las paredes oyen* (*Walls Have Ears*), probably represents Alarcón's best work.

ALBEE, EDWARD FRANKLIN (1928–), American dramatist, grandson (by adoption) of EDWARD FRANKLIN ALBEE (1857–1930), who in the 1920s was at the head of a circuit of some seventy vaudeville houses, with an interest in about three hundred others. The younger Albee, one of the few major dramatists to emerge in the United States in the 1960s, had his first play, a one-acter entitled *The Zoo Story*, performed in 1959 in Berlin, where it won a Festival award. A year later it was seen in New York and London. It was followed by several other plays, including

The Death of Bessie Smith (1960) and *The American Dream* (1961). In 1962 Albee scored his first commercial success on Broadway with an emotional melodrama, *Who's Afraid of Virginia Woolf?*, which was equally well received in London in 1964. *The Ballad of the Sad Café* (1963, based on a novel by Carson McCullers) was followed by *Tiny Alice* (1964), which, with Irene Worth and John Gielgud in the leading parts, caused a good deal of controversy, and was declared by six New York critics to be incomprehensible. It was seen in London at the Aldwych early in 1970, again with Irene Worth as Alice. In 1969, the year of the London production of *The Ballad of the Sad Café*, *A Delicate Balance*, first seen in New York in 1966, was also produced at the Aldwych, with Peggy Ashcroft as Agnes, the part originally played in New York by Jessica Tandy.

ALBERY, SIR BRONSON (1881–1971) and JAMES (1838–89), see MOORE, MARY, NEW THEATRE, and WYNDHAM'S THEATRE.

Albion, LONDON, see TROCADERO.

Alcazar, LONDON, see CONNAUGHT THEATRE.

ALDRICH [really LYON], LOUIS (1843–1901), American actor, who, billed as the Ohio Roscius, toured as a child in such parts as Richard III, Macbeth, Shylock, Jack Sheppard (in a dramatization of Ainsworth's novel), and Young Norval in Home's *Douglas*. He was later known as Master Moses, McCarthy, or Kean, and after a break for schooling returned to the stage as an adult under the name of Aldrich. He was for some years in St. Louis and Boston, and from 1873 to 1874 was leading man of the Arch Street Theatre company in Philadelphia, under Mrs. John Drew (q.v.). He then toured for many years in his greatest part, Joe Saunders in Bartley Campbell's *My Partner*, first produced in 1879, which brought him a fortune. He made his last appearance on the stage in New York in 1899, and died suddenly during rehearsals for a further appearance there under Belasco (q.v.).

ALDRIDGE, IRA FREDERICK (1804–67), the first great American Negro actor, who in 1863 became a naturalized Englishman. He had already appeared on the New York stage when in 1826, billed as the African Roscius, he made his London début as Othello at the Royalty Theatre. Regarded as one of the outstanding actors of the day, he was the recipient of many honours, amassed a large fortune, and married a white woman. He was last seen in England in 1865, and then returned to the Continent, where he had first toured in 1853. He was immensely popular in Germany, where he played in English with a supporting cast playing in German. His Lear was much admired in Russia, the only country in which he appeared in the part.

Aldwych Theatre, LONDON. This was opened on 23 Dec. 1905 by Charles Frohman, with Seymour Hicks and Ellaline Terriss in *Blue Bell*, an adaptation of their successful children's play, *Bluebell in Fairyland*, first produced at the Vaudeville in Dec. 1901. The transfer of *Tons of Money* from the Shaftesbury Theatre in 1923, with Tom Walls and Ralph Lynn (qq.v.), inaugurated a series of successful 'Aldwych farces', among them *A Cuckoo in the Nest* (1925), *Rookery Nook* (1926), and *Thark* (1927), all by Ben Travers (q.v.), in which Robertson Hare and Mary Brough (qq.v.) also appeared. During the Second World War the Aldwych housed successful productions of Lillian Hellman's *Watch on the Rhine* (1942) and Robert Sherwood's *There Shall Be No Night* (1945). In 1949 Vivien Leigh (q.v.) gave a fine performance as Blanche du Bois in Tennessee Williams's *A Streetcar Named Desire*. Fry's *The Dark is Light Enough*, with Edith Evans (q.v.) as the Countess Rosmarin, was seen in 1954. In 1960 the Aldwych became the London home of the Royal Shakespeare Company (q.v.), who opened there on 15 Dec. with Peggy Ashcroft (q.v.) in Webster's *The Duchess of Malfi*, and in the summer of 1964 it housed the first of the World Theatre seasons, arranged by Peter Daubeny (q.v.). It is now used exclusively by the Royal Shakespeare Company (who present the World Theatre seasons), Shakespearian productions being transferred from Stratford to join a repertoire which includes old and new plays by other authors, English and foreign, among them Brecht (q.v.). In 1968–9 there took place the first London season of modern American plays, which included Albee's *A Delicate Balance*, while 1970 saw revivals of Boucicault's *London Assurance* and Shaw's *Major Barbara*, as well as a trans-lation of a play by Günter Grass as *The Plebeians Rehearse the Uprising*.

ALEICHEM [really RABINOVICH], SHOLOM (1859–1916), Jewish writer, who in 1888 was owner and editor of a Kiev newspaper. In 1905 he emigrated to the United States, where a number of plays, based on his novels and short stories of life in the Jewish communities of the Ukraine, were performed in the Yiddish Art Theatres, mainly through the efforts of Maurice Schwartz (q.v.). Aleichem's characters, simple, kindly, but shrewd, offer considerable scope to the actor, and gave both Mikhoels (q.v.) in the U.S.S.R. and Muni Wiesenfreund (known in the cinema as Paul Muni) in Germany their first successes. Some idea of Aleichem's work can be obtained from Maurice Samuel's *The World of Sholom Aleichem* (1943). In 1959 his centenary was celebrated by a production at the Grand Palais Theatre—the last surviving Yiddish theatre in London—of his three-act comedy, *Hard to be a Jew*. An adaptation of another comedy, *Tevye the Milkman*, as a musical, *Fiddler on the Roof*, was successfully produced on Broadway in 1964, with Zero Mostel (q.v.) as Tevye, and in London in 1967, with the Israeli actor Topol (q.v.), who was succeeded in the part by Alfie Bass.

ALEXANDER, SIR GEORGE [really GEORGE ALEXANDER GIBB SAMSON] (1858–1918), English actor, and manager of the St. James's Theatre (q.v.) from 1891 until his death. He made his first appearance at Nottingham in 1879 and in 1881 was seen in London. In 1889 he entered into management on his own. His tenancy of the St. James's was both financially and artistically rewarding. He made his greatest success in the dual role of Rudolf Rassendyll and the King in Anthony Hope's *The Prisoner of Zenda* (1896), and was also much admired as Villon in Justin McCarthy's *If I Were King* (1902) and Karl Heinrich in R. Bleichmann's *Old Heidelberg* (1903). Among his important productions at the St. James's were Oscar Wilde's *Lady Windermere's Fan* (1892) and *The Importance of Being Earnest* (1895), Pinero's *The Second Mrs. Tanqueray* (1893) and *His House in Order* (1906), Stephen Phillips's verse-drama, *Paolo and Francesca* (1902), which introduced Henry Ainley (q.v.) to London, and Jerome K. Jerome's *The Passing of the Third Floor*

Back (1908) with Johnston Forbes-Robertson (q.v.). Alexander was knighted in 1911, the year of the coronation of George V.

Alexandra Theatre, LONDON. (1) Highbury Barn, a concert hall in the grounds of an open-air pleasure resort, converted into a theatre in 1861 by Edward Giovanelli, who staged farces and burlesques there. It finally closed, with the gardens, in 1871.

(2) Park Street, Camden Town. This theatre, which cost £20,000 to build, opened on 31 May 1873 with an operetta, *Marguerite*, by Thorpe Pede (who was also the manager) and a play by Robert Reece entitled *Friendship; or, Golding's Debt*. In 1877 a Madame St. Claire leased the theatre, chiefly to show herself off in the part of Romeo, but without success. In 1879 it became known as the Park Theatre, from its proximity to Regent's Park. It was burnt down on 11 Sept. 1881 and never rebuilt. A theatre at Stoke Newington, which opened on 27 Dec. 1897 and closed in 1950, was also known as the Alexandra. It was not used for theatrical entertainments after 1939.

Alexandrinsky Theatre, LENINGRAD. This theatre, which in 1937 was renamed in honour of Pushkin (q.v.), was founded in 1824, the same year as the Maly Theatre (q.v.) in Moscow. It had a fine leading actor in Vasily Karatygin (q.v.), but no authors of the calibre of Gogol and Ostrovsky (qq.v.), then holding the stage at the Maly, and never developed a settled policy. For some time it staged mainly ballet and opera, followed by vaudeville and French melodrama, but later the patriotic dramas of Polevoy and Kukolik were produced, and after a long, blank period the first stirrings of realism came with such plays as Strindberg's *The Father*, in which the actor MAMONT DALSKY (1865–1918) scored a personal triumph. But the theatre's first production of Chekhov's *The Seagull* in 1896 was a dismal failure, the company's old-fashioned technique being unable to convey the subtlety of the author's characterization. Just before the October Revolution, Meyerhold (q.v.) was working at the Alexandrinsky, his last production there being a revival of Lermontov's *Masquerade*. After the Revolution, the Alexandrinsky, like the Moscow Art Theatre, gradually found its feet in the new world under the supervision of the Commissar for Education, Lunacharsky

(q.v.). By 1924 it was ready to include new plays in its repertory, and among the producers who worked on them were Radlov, Solovyov, and Rappoport. In 1937 Meyerhold returned, to produce *Masquerade* again. During the Second World War the theatre was evacuated and went on tour up to the front line, returning to Leningrad in 1944. An interesting landmark in the theatre's history was the successful production of *The Seagull* by Leonid Vivyen in 1954, in which year he also staged *Hamlet*.

ALFIERI, VITTORIO AMEDEO (1749–1803), Italian dramatist, chiefly remembered as a writer of tragedies in verse. But a recent production of one of the half-dozen comedies written towards the end of his life—*Il Divorzio* (1802), revived by the Teatro Stabile dell'Aquila in 1967—shows that he had a remarkable gift for satiric humour which, if exploited earlier, might have changed the history of the Italian theatre. His first tragedy, *Cleopatra*, was performed at Turin in 1775 with great success. Of the other twenty, of which it has been said that 'their action flies like an arrow to its mark', the best are usually considered to be *Saul* (1782) and *Mirra* (1784). Alfieri, who was born in Asti of a noble and wealthy family, had an unhappy childhood, and at an early age left home to travel widely in Europe. He became the devoted lover of the Countess of Albany, wife of the Young Pretender, to whom he left all his books and manuscripts. She gave them to the painter Fabre, by whom they were eventually bequeathed to the University of Montpellier.

Alhambra, a famous London music-hall whose ornate Moorish-style architecture dominated the east side of Leicester Square. It opened on 18 Mar. 1854 under E. T. Smith as the Panopticon, but with little success, and in 1858 was first called the Alhambra (Palace), retaining the name through successive changes of title (Music-Hall, Palace of Varieties, Theatre, etc.). In 1860 extensive alterations were made to the building and a stage was installed so that it could for the first time be used as a music-hall. In 1861 Léotard, the trapeze artist, appeared there. On 7 Dec. 1882 the theatre was burnt down, but was rebuilt and reopened a year later, when it became known for its lavish spectacular ballets, which continued from 1890 to 1910. In 1911 Diaghilev's Ballets Russes company which had earlier in the year made its first appearance in London was at the Alhambra, returning in 1919 and 1931. De Basil's company was there in 1933 and René Blum's in 1936. Other outstanding events were George Grossmith's picture of London life, 'with music by Nat D. Ayer', *The Bing Boys Are Here* (1916), with George Robey (q.v.) and Violet Loraine, and the revue *Mr. Tower of London* (1923), which made Gracie Fields (q.v.) a star. The fortunes of the theatre then declined, and the last production, *Sim-Sala-Bim*, with the Danish magician Dante, opened on 12 Aug. 1936. The theatre closed on the following 1 Sept. and was demolished in November, the Odeon cinema being built on the site.

Alienation, the English term for the *Verfremdungseffekt* aimed at by Brecht (q.v.) with the use of placards, films, strip cartoons, and stylization, all designed to produce in the audience a state of critical detachment from the drama being presented. The actor assists this process by standing outside the character he is portraying, rather than, as in the method employed by Stanislavsky (q.v.), identifying with it.

ALIZON (*fl.* 1610–48), an early French actor, who specialized in the playing of comic, elderly maid-servants, particularly in farces, or of the heroine's nurse in more serious plays. He was with Montdory (q.v.) at the Marais when he first came to Paris, but later went to the Hôtel de Bourgogne. As with his equally popular companion, Jodelet (q.v.), his own name was frequently given to the parts destined for him.

ALLEN, CHESNEY [really WILLIAM E.] (1894–1982), English music-hall comedian who in 1924 joined Bud Flanagan, and with him was a member of the Crazy Gang (q.v.) at the Palladium from 1935 to 1939. He retired in 1946.

ALLEN, VIOLA (1869–1948), American actress, who made her first appearance on the stage in 1882 and was from 1891 to 1898 a member of Frohman's stock company at the Empire, where she gained a great reputation as one of the leading actresses of the day. After leaving Frohman she toured extensively, and made her last appearance in 1916 as Mistress Ford in *The Merry Wives of Windsor*.

ALLEN, WILLIAM (?–1647), English actor, who may have been one of Beeston's Boys (see BEESTON). He became a member of Queen Henrietta's Men (q.v.) at the Cockpit, where he is known to have played a leading part in *Hannibal and Scipio* (1635), by Thomas Nabbes. After the dissolution of the company in 1636 he joined the powerful King's Men (see CHAMBERLAIN'S MEN). He has sometimes been confused with a William Allen who was an army officer in the Civil War.

ALLEYN, EDWARD (1566–1626), Elizabethan actor and the founder of Dulwich College. He was much admired by his contemporaries and considered the only rival of Richard Burbage (q.v.). Plays in which he is known to have appeared include Marlowe's *Tamburlaine the Great* (*c.* 1587), *The Tragical History of Dr. Faustus* (*c.* 1589), and *The Jew of Malta* (*c.* 1590), and Greene's *Orlando Furioso* (*c.* 1591). He was already known as a good actor in 1583 and remained on the stage until the accession of James I in 1603. He married the stepdaughter of the theatrical manager Henslowe (q.v.), and succeeded to most of his property, and to his papers, which are now at Dulwich. His second wife was the daughter of the poet Donne.

ALLGOOD, SARA (1883–1950), Irish actress, whose early career is bound up with the history of the Abbey Theatre (q.v.). In 1903, she joined the Fays' Irish National Dramatic Society and appeared with them in the opening productions at the Abbey. In 1907 she created the part of Widow Quin in Synge's *The Playboy of the Western World*. She was for a time a member of Miss Horniman's company at Manchester, but returned to the Abbey to play Juno Boyle in *Juno and the Paycock* (1924), in which she also appeared in America, and Bessie Burgess in *The Plough and the Stars* (1926), both by O'Casey (q.v.). She made her last appearance on the stage in New York in 1940, and then appeared only in films.

ALMA-TADEMA, SIR L., see TADEMA.

ALPHONSINE [really FLEURY] (1829–83), French actress, daughter of a flower-seller on the Boulevard du Temple. On the stage since childhood, she became the idol of the little theatres, and was nicknamed 'the Déjazet [q.v.] of the Boulevards'. A fine comedienne, never falling into farce or caricature, but always subtle and witty, she was a pretty woman, with an elegant figure, good voice, and abundant high spirits. She was in the company which went from the Palais-Royal to play before the Court at Compiègne on 13 Nov. 1869 —the last time French actors appeared before Napoleon III.

Alvin Theatre, NEW YORK, on West 52nd Street between Broadway and 8th Avenue, a handsome building with an Adam-style interior which opened on 22 Nov. 1927 with *Funny Face*, a musical comedy with music by Gershwin. It took its name from the first syllables of the names of Alex A. Aarons and Vinton Freedley, who retained control of it until 1932, using it mainly for musical shows with such stars as the Astaires, Ginger Rogers, and Ethel Merman, but also for occasional straight plays, among them a revival of *Mourning Becomes Electra* by O'Neill (q.v.) in 1932, of *Uncle Tom's Cabin* with Otis Skinner (q.v.) in 1933, and the first production of *Mary of Scotland* by Maxwell Anderson (q.v.), also in 1933. In 1935 Gershwin's musical version of *Porgy and Bess* was first seen, and in 1937 Kaufman and Hart's *I'd Rather Be Right* inaugurated a series of successful productions, including *The Boys from Syracuse* (1938) (a musical version of *The Comedy of Errors*), and the Lunts (q.v.) in Sherwood's *There Shall Be No Night* (1940). In 1945 Margaret Webster (q.v.) produced *The Tempest* with the Negro actor Canada Lee (q.v.) as Caliban. Later successful productions included Ingrid Bergman in Maxwell Anderson's *Joan of Lorraine* (1946); Sidney Kingsley's dramatization of Koestler's novel *Darkness at Noon* (1951); *A Funny Thing Happened on the Way to the Forum* (1962), a musical based on the plays of Plautus, starring Zero Mostel; and *The Great White Hope* (1968), by Howard Sackler.

Ambassador Theatre, NEW YORK, on 49th Street west of Broadway. This opened on 11 Feb. 1921 with the musical *The Rose Girl*, under the management of the Shubert brothers. Later the same year it scored a success with *Blossom Time*, a play on the life of Schubert with music taken from his compositions, which ran for over a year and was several times revived up to 1938, and, in an adaptation by Rodney Ackland, was seen in London in 1942. The theatre was often used by visiting foreign actors, by Maurice Schwartz (q.v.), and by the company from the Abbey Theatre (q.v.). For a time it was given over to radio and television, but it later reverted to straight plays.

Ambassadors Theatre, LONDON, a small playhouse in West Street, near St. Martin's Lane, which opened on 5 June 1913. It had little success until a year later Cochran staged a series of intimate revues there, starring Alice Delysia (q.v.). From 1919 to 1930 it was leased by H. M. Harwood (q.v.), whose productions included his own play, *The Grain of Mustard Seed* (1920), and Lennox Robinson's *The White-Headed Boy* (also 1920), with Sara Allgood as Mrs. Geoghegan. In 1925 O'Neill's *Emperor Jones* occasioned Paul Robeson's first appearance in London. Sydney Carroll took over the theatre in 1932, and under him Vivien Leigh (q.v.) made her successful West End début in Carl Sternheim's *The Mask of Virtue* (1935), translated by Ashley Dukes. A later success was John Perry and M. J. Farrell's *Spring Meeting* (1938), with the inimitable Margaret Rutherford (q.v.) as Bijou. *The Gate Revue*, transferred from the Gate early in 1939, had a long run, followed by a sequel, *Swinging the Gate* (1940), and the intimate revues *Sweet and Low* (1943), *Sweeter and Lower* (1944), and *Sweetest and Lowest* (1946), the work mainly of Alan Melville. On 25 Nov. 1952 began the record-breaking run of Agatha Christie's *The Mousetrap*, which still (1972) occupies the theatre.

Ambigu-Comique, THÉÂTRE DE L', PARIS. This opened on 9 July 1769 as a marionette and children's theatre on the Boulevard du Temple (q.v.), where it remained until it was destroyed by fire in 1827. From 1797 onwards it was used mainly for melodramas by Pixérécourt, Bouchardy, and others. A theatre of the same name on the Boulevard St. Martin, still in use, opened on 7 June 1828 to replace the old one, whose site was taken over by the Folies-Dramatiques (q.v.).

AMEIPSIAS, a Greek comic poet of Old Comedy, contemporary and rival of Aristophanes (q.v.). His *Revellers* defeated Aristophanes' *Birds* in 414 B.C. One of his plays ridiculed Socrates. Only fragments of his work survive.

American Actors' Equity, see EQUITY.

American Amphitheatre, see BOSTON.

American Company, a small troupe of professional actors which had the elder Hallam's widow as their leading lady and his son Lewis as their leading man (see HALLAM). The name was first used in a notice of the company's presence at Charleston in 1763-4. The American Company played an important part in the development of early American drama, being the first professional group to produce a play by an American—*The Prince of Parthia*, by Thomas Godfrey, in 1767. It was also responsible for the production of several plays by Dunlap (q.v.), under whose management the first Joseph Jefferson (q.v.) joined the company in 1795, moving with it to the new Park Theatre on 28 Feb. 1798. The company's identity was finally lost when, in 1805, Dunlap went bankrupt and retired, the Park Theatre being taken over by Thomas Abthorpe Cooper (q.v.), who had been a member of the company for some years. The American Company had practically the monopoly of acting in the United States for many years, its only rival being Wignell's company in Philadelphia.

American Educational Theatre Association (A.E.T.A.), an organization formed in 1936 as a branch of the Speech Association of America to represent the academic theatre in the U.S.A. Since 1950 it has been a separate organization, with a board of directors and several thousands of members drawn from academic sources throughout the country. It is the official organ of the educational theatre in America, supervises the election of members to the Educational Theatre Panel of the Board of Directors of the American National Theatre and Academy (q.v.), and publishes the scholarly quarterly, *Educational Theatre Journal*.

American Museum, NEW YORK, a Broadway showplace opened by P. T. Barnum (q.v.) in 1842 which by 1849 had become a theatre with a good stock company and some stars, among them the children of the impresario H. L. Bateman (q.v.). On 17 June 1850, much enlarged and embellished, it opened with an excellent company in a highly moral play entitled *The Drunkard*, by W. H. Smith, which had a record run for that time. Barnum sold the theatre in 1855, but in 1860, being once more financially stable, was able to buy it back. Plays were gradually ousted by freaks, baby-shows, and boxing contests, until on 13 July 1865

the old Museum was burnt down. Barnum went temporarily to the Winter Garden (see METROPOLITAN THEATRE), and on 6 Sept. opened a new American Museum, also on Broadway, which Van Amburgh took over with his menagerie in 1867. Plays were evidently still being given there, however, as it was during a run of a dramatization of Harriet Beecher Stowe's *Uncle Tom's Cabin* that on 3 Mar. 1868 the second Museum was burnt to the ground, and never rebuilt.

American National Theatre and Academy (A.N.T.A.). This organization came into being on 5 July 1935 when President Roosevelt signed the Charter which Congress had just enacted. This important document permits the establishment of a nation-wide, tax-exempt institution which, in the words of its preamble, was to be 'a people's project, organized and conducted in their interest, free from commercialism, but with the firm intent of being as far as possible self-supporting'.

The Charter, secured through the efforts of a group of people interested in, but not connected with, the theatre, carried with it no government grant. The existence of the Federal Theatre Project (q.v.), and then the outbreak of war, made it difficult to raise money privately, and little was done, but in 1945 the Board of Directors was reorganized to include leading theatre people and the heads of all such theatre organizations as Actors' Equity and the Dramatists' Guild. In 1948 A.N.T.A. became the U.S. centre of the International Theatre Institute (q.v.) and two years later acquired the former Guild Theatre as its headquarters, renaming it the Anta Playhouse and running it for some years as an experimental theatre. Later it leased it as the Anta Theatre (q.v.) to commercial management as a source of income, retaining part of the building as offices. In 1963, pending the completion of the Lincoln Center for the Performing Arts (q.v.), A.N.T.A. was responsible for the erection of a temporary structure, designed by Jo Mielziner (q.v.), to house the Vivian Beaumont repertory company. This opened on 23 Jan. 1964 with Arthur Miller's *After the Fall*. It was demolished in 1968. In the same year a major re-organization of A.N.T.A. took place. The Anta Theatre was then presented to the nation to serve as a performing arts centre for non-profit-making groups under the government-subsidized National Council on the Arts. It continues to be maintained and operated by A.N.T.A. and also serves as the headquarters of the newly-formed International Theatre Institute of the United States Inc. under Rosamond Gilder (q.v.).

American Negro Theatre, an organization founded in 1940, under the direction of Abram Hill. Its first production, in the New York Public Library Theatre on 135th Street, was Theodore Browne's *Natural Man* (1941), and among its later productions were two plays by Hill, *Walk Hard* (1944) and *On Strivers' Row* (1946), Walter Carroll's *Tin Top Valley* (1947), and, in a programme at the Harlem Children's Center in 1949, Synge's *Riders to the Sea*. The great success of this group was Philip Yordan's *Anna Lucasta*, starring the Negro actor Frederick O'Neal, which, after an initial production at the Library Theatre in 1944, moved to Broadway, where it ran for nearly three years. In 1947 it was seen with equal success in London. In 1953 the American Negro Theatre went on tour in England and Europe, but after its return to the United States apparently ceased to function.

American Opera House, NEW YORK, see CHATHAM THEATRE (1).

American Repertory Theatre, NEW YORK, see CRAWFORD, CHERYL; LE GALLIENNE, EVA; and WEBSTER, MARGARET.

American Theatre, NEW YORK, at 260 West 42nd Street. This opened on 22 May 1893, and had a somewhat chequered career. In 1908 it was renamed the American Music Hall, and became a burlesque house in 1929. On 18 Dec. 1930 it was badly damaged by fire, and it was finally demolished in 1932.

The first theatre opened by Burton (q.v.) (see CHAMBERS STREET THEATRE) was called the American for a season under Davenport in 1857.

(For the American Theatre, Bowery, see BOWERY THEATRE (1).)

AMES, WINTHROP (1871–1937), American theatre director, who used the money inherited from his father, a railroad capitalist, to back non-commercial ventures in the theatre. In 1909 he built and opened the New Theatre (see CENTURY THEATRE (1)) where he made a gallant but unsuccessful attempt to establish true

repertory, as he did in two other theatres which he built in 1912 (see LITTLE THEATRE (2)), and in 1913 (see BOOTH THEATRE). Neither of them was successful, but in spite of many setbacks Ames did good work for the American theatre over a long period of years. Among his productions were a number of Shakespeare plays and other classics, some revivals of Gilbert and Sullivan, and such modern plays as Housman and Barker's *Prunella* (1913), Maeterlinck's *The Betrothal* (1918), Clemence Dane's *Will Shakespeare* (1923), and Galsworthy's *Old English* (1924).

Amphitheatre (AMPHITHEATRUM), a Roman building of elliptical shape, with tiers of seats enclosing a central arena. It was not intended for dramatic performances, which in ancient theatres were always given in front of a permanent back-scene, but for gladiators and wild beast shows, and mimic sea battles. The first amphitheatre was probably that built by Julius Caesar in 46 B.C. The most famous was the Colosseum in Rome, completed in A.D. 80, and said to be capable of seating 87,000 spectators, which is still extant, though in ruins.

(For the Amphitheatre in London, see CONNAUGHT THEATRE; in New York, CHATHAM THEATRE (1).)

ANCEY [really DE CURNIEU], GEORGES (1860–1926), French dramatist, whose plays, produced by Antoine at the Théâtre Libre (q.v.), were popular in their time. The best of them were *Les Inséparables*, in which two friends share the same mistress, and *L'École des veufs*, in which a father and son find themselves in the same position (both 1889). Ancey's plays went out of fashion with the decline of naturalism and have not been revived.

ANDERSON, DAME JUDITH [really FRANCES MARGARET ANDERSON-ANDERSON] (1898–   ), Australian actress, who first appeared on the stage in Sydney in 1915 in Wills's *A Royal Divorce*. She toured Australia for two years, and then went to the United States, where she adopted her present name and, after some experience in stock companies and on tour, made a great success on Broadway as Elise in Martin Brown's *Cobra* (1924). She was later seen in Pirandello's *As You Desire Me* (1931), and in 1936 played the Queen to John Gielgud's Hamlet in New York. A year later she made her first appearance in London, where she gave an outstanding performance as Lady Macbeth with Laurence Olivier at the Old Vic. She played the same part in New York in 1941 to the Macbeth of Maurice Evans. In 1947 she gave a superb rendering of the name-part in Euripides' *Medea*, in a new adaptation prepared by Robinson Jeffers in which she also appeared in Berlin, in Paris, and with the Elizabethan Theatre Trust (q.v.) in Australia. She was seen again at the Old Vic in 1960, as Madame Arkadina in Chekhov's *The Seagull*, and in the Birthday Honours of the same year was appointed D.B.E. for services to the stage. She then toured the United States in a recital of scenes from her most famous parts, and in 1970 embarked on a further tour, playing Hamlet, without much success, at the age of seventy-one in emulation of Sarah Bernhardt (q.v.).

ANDERSON, LINDSAY (1923–), English stage director, formerly a film director and critic. His first work for the theatre was a 'production without décor' at the Royal Court (q.v.) of Kathleen Sully's *The Waiting of Lester Abbs* (1957). Later productions at the same theatre included Willis Hall's *The Long and the Short and the Tall* and Arden's *Serjeant Musgrave's Dance* (both 1959), a musical, *The Lily-White Boys* (1960), and Frisch's *The Fire-Raisers* (1961). In 1960 he also directed *Billy Liar*, by Keith Waterhouse and Willis Hall, at the Cambridge Theatre, and in 1964 was responsible for the production of Frisch's *Andorra* by the National Theatre at the Old Vic. He had in the meantime returned to the Royal Court to direct in 1963 a dramatization of Gogol's *The Diary of a Madman*, which he adapted himself in collaboration with Richard Harris, who played the only character, Aksenti Ivanovitch, and in 1964 was responsible for a new production of *Julius Caesar*. In 1966 he directed Chekhov's *The Cherry Orchard* at Chichester, and in 1969 joined William Gaskill and Anthony Page in the running of the Royal Court, where he has since directed David Storey's *The Contractor* and *In Celebration* (both 1969) and *Home* (1970).

ANDERSON, MARY (1859–1940), an American actress who made her first appearance at the age of sixteen at Louisville, playing Juliet in *Romeo and Juliet*. She toured the United States for some years in a wide variety of parts, being much admired as Julia in Sheridan Knowles's *The Hunchback*, Pauline in Bulwer-Lytton's *The Lady of Lyons*, and Parthenia in Mrs. Lovell's *Ingomar*. It was as Parthenia that she made her first appearance in London, at the Lyceum in 1883, where in 1887 she played in *The Winter's Tale*, being the first actress to double the parts of Perdita and Hermione. She retired in 1889, and was not seen again on the professional stage, though during the First World War she appeared at some charity matinées, notably as Juliet in the Balcony Scene. In 1890 she married Antonio de Navarro, and settled at Broadway in Worcestershire, where she died.

ANDERSON, MAXWELL (1888–1959), American dramatist, whose *What Price Glory?* (1924), written in collaboration with Laurence Stallings, was a great popular hit, portraying realistically and sympathetically the American soldier in action during the First World War. Another outstanding popular success was *Saturday's Children* (1927), by Anderson alone. A realistic play of modern city life, *Gypsy* (1929), preceded a series of historical and pseudo-historical plays, idealistic in conception and on the whole effectively poetic in language. The best of these were *Elizabeth the Queen* (1930), *Night Over Taos* (1932), *Mary of Scotland* (1933), *Valley Forge* (1934), and *The Wingless Victory* (1936; London, 1943). But Anderson was never content to follow any one dramatic or artistic formula. His realistic satires on political subjects are among his most effective works, among them *Both Your Houses* (1933), a savage attack on political corruption which was awarded the Pulitzer Prize. In *High Tor* (1937) and *The Masque of Kings* (1937; London, 1938) he combined poetic drama with formal verse, philosophy, and political commentary, and in *Winterset* (1935) sought to make tragic poetry out of the stuff of his own times. Among his later plays were *The Eve of St. Mark* (1942; London, 1943), *Storm Operation* (1944), *Truckline Café* and *Joan of Lorraine* (both 1946), *Anne of the Thousand Days* (1948), and *The Bad Seed* (1954; London, 1955).

ANDREINI, a family of Italian actors, outstanding in the annals of the *commedia dell'arte* (q.v.), of whom the first, FRANCESCO (1548–1624), was both actor and author. After an adventurous career as a soldier, he joined a travelling company and soon became famous for his playing of the braggart soldier as depicted in the *Bravure del Capitan Spavento* (1607). In 1578 he married ISABELLA CANALI (1562–1604), one of the most famous actresses of her time. They were both with the Gelosi (q.v.), with whom they toured France several times, Isabella dying in childbirth at Lyons on her way back to Italy. Of her seven children the most famous was GIOVANN BATTISTA (*c.* 1578–1654), known as Lelio. He appeared mainly with the Fedeli (q.v.) and was very popular in France. He was twice married, in 1601 to VIRGINIA RAMPONI (1538–*c.* 1627/30), an actress known as Florinda, and after her death to VIRGINIA ROTARI, whose stage name was Lidia.

ANDREYEV, LEONID NIKOLAIVICH (1871–1919), Russian dramatist, who was encouraged in his early days by Gorky (q.v.). He was at first a revolutionary but after the October Revolution emigrated to Finland, where he died. His plays, permeated with a bitter pessimism, as of a lost soul wandering in a cruel and unpredictable world, express the despair and desolation of the period between 1905 and 1917. The only one to have survived on the stage is the theatrically effective *He Who Gets Slapped* (1914), which was produced in New York in 1922 and revived in 1946 and 1956, and was seen in London in 1927 and again in 1947.

ANDRONICUS, LUCIUS LIVIUS (*c.* 284–204 B.C.), Roman dramatist, who in 240 B.C. produced in Rome the first Latin version of a Greek play. Up to this time the Roman stage seems to have known only a formless medley of dance, song, and buffoonery. The introduction of plays with a regular plot was successful, and Andronicus, who is important as a pioneer though his style was uncouth, continued to translate and produce plays taken from Greek tragedy and New Comedy until his death.

ANGEL, EDWARD (*fl.* 1660–73), a Restoration actor, referred to in Wycherley's *The Gentleman Dancing-Master* (1671) as 'a good fool'. He was first with Rhodes at the Cockpit, and later joined Davenant at Dorset Garden, where he paired excellently with that great comedian, Nokes (q.v.). Angel specialized in

parts of low comedy, particularly French valets. He is not heard of after 1673.

ANGELO, F. D' (1447–88), see PARADISO.

ANGLIN, MARGARET (1876–1958), American actress, who made her first professional appearance in 1894 in a revival of Bronson Howard's *Shenandoah*. Her first outstanding success was as Roxane in Mansfield's production of *Cyrano de Bergerac* (1898) and she was later the leading lady of Frohman's stock company at the Empire, New York, where she appeared in a wide variety of parts. Later, on tour, she was seen in new translations of Greek drama and in such Shakespearian parts as Viola, Rosalind, and Cleopatra. She was also excellent as Mrs. Malaprop in Sheridan's *The Rivals*.

ANGUS, ROBERT, see AGGAS.

Annapolis, one of the earliest towns in America to welcome the players, and one regularly visited by the companies of Hallam and Douglass (qq.v.). They had at first to adapt an existing building for their shows, as Douglass did in 1759, when he produced Otway's *The Orphan* and *Venice Preserv'd*, but in 1771 he built a brick theatre holding 600 persons, in which such a number of plays were given, including *Cymbeline*. The first permanent modern theatre was built in 1831.

ANNUNZIO, GABRIELE D', see D'ANNUNZIO.

ANOUILH, JEAN-MARIE-LUCIEN-PIERRE (1910–   ), French dramatist, whose first play, *L'Hermine*, was produced by Lugné-Poë in 1932. Anouilh was later associated with Pitoëff, who produced *Le Voyageur sans bagage* (1937) and *La Sauvage* (1938), and in Sept. 1938, with *Le Bal des voleurs*, began a fruitful collaboration with the director and scene designer André Barsacq which lasted until the production of *Médée* in 1953. The recurring theme of all Anouilh's plays, many of which have been successfully produced in English translations both in England and in the United States, is the loss of innocence implicit in the struggle for survival in a decadent society. His early plays treated this romantically, as in the '*pièces roses*'— *Le Bal des voleurs* (*Thieves' Carnival*) (1938), *Léocadia* (*Time Remembered*) (1940), *Le Rendezvous de Senlis* (*Dinner* *with the Family*) (1941), and *Colombe* (1951)—or with melancholy resignation, as in the *'pièces noires'*—*Le Voyageur sans bagage* (*Traveller Without Luggage*) (1937) and *La Sauvage* (*The Restless Heart*) (1938)—later transmuted into the glittering wit of the *'pièces brilliantes'*—*L'Invitation au Château* (*Ring Round the Moon*) (1947) and *La Répétition, ou L'Amour puni* (*The Rehearsal*) (1950)—or the bitter disillusionment of the *'pièces grinçantes'*—*Ardèle, ou La Marguerite* (*Ardele*) (1948), *La Valse des toréadors* (*The Waltz of the Toreadors*) (1952), and *Pauvre Bitos, ou Le Dîner des têtes* (*Poor Bitos*) (1956). He has also expressed his ideas in plays based on history—*L'Alouette* (*The Lark*) (1953), on Joan of Arc, and *Becket, ou L'Honneur de Dieu* (*Becket*) (1959)—and on classical themes—*Eurydice* (*Point of Departure*, or, in America, *Legend of Lovers*) (1942), *Antigone* (1944), and *Médée* (1953). *Antigone*, produced in German-occupied Paris, with its study of personal loyalties in conflict with authority, was only too appropriate to the moment and aroused much controversy. In recent years Anouilh, who is, more than most modern French dramatists, an all-round man-of-the-theatre, has been active in the direction of his own and other writers' plays, among the latter, in 1962, being a revival of *Victor, ou Les Enfants au pouvoir*, by Vitrac (q.v.), whom, with Molière and Giraudoux (qq.v.), he considers the main influence on his own work. His latest plays are *La Grotte* (*The Cavern*) (1961) and *La Foire d'Empoigne* and *L'Orchestre* (both 1962). In 1965 *La Grotte*, as *The Cavern*, was first seen in Nottingham, and later in London, with Alec McCowan, and in 1966 *Hurluberlu, ou Le Réactionnaire amoureux* (1959), a sequel to *Ardèle*, was produced at the Chichester Festival (q.v.) as *The Fighting Cock*. *L'Orchestre* was seen in Bristol in 1967, as *The Orchestra*, in a double bill with *Monsieur Barnett*, originally written for television.

ANSKY [really SOLOMON RAPPOPORT] (1863–1920), Jewish ethnologist and man of letters, whose researches into folk-lore in Russia, Paris, and Central Europe resulted in the writing of his one well-known play, *The Dybbuk, or Between Two Worlds*, a study of demoniac possession and the Hassidic doctrine of pre-ordained relationship. First seen in Yiddish in a production by the Vilna Troupe on 9 Dec. 1920, shortly after Ansky's death, it was directed two years later in Hebrew by Vakhtangov (q.v.) for the Moscow Habima company. It was first seen in New York in Hebrew in 1925, and has since been revived several times, both in Hebrew and Yiddish. In London it was first presented in Hebrew in 1930 by the Habima Players. In 1966 an English translation by Joseph C. Landis was published in New York.

A.N.T.A., see AMERICAN NATIONAL THEATRE AND ACADEMY.

Anta Theatre, NEW YORK, at 245 West 52nd Street, between Broadway and 8th Avenue. Built by the Theatre Guild (q.v.) to house its own productions, this opened on 13 Apr. 1925 as the Guild Theatre, with Helen Hayes (q.v.) in Shaw's *Caesar and Cleopatra*. During subsequent seasons further plays by Shaw were given, as well as plays by European and new American playwrights. In 1950 the theatre was taken over by the American National Theatre and Academy (q.v.), and as the Anta Playhouse was used for experimental productions. Given its present name in 1954, it reverted to commercial use in 1957, some of the productions there since being Archibald Mac-Leish's *J.B.* (1959), James Baldwin's *Blues for Mr. Charlie* (1964), seen in London during the World Theatre season of 1965, Peter Shaffer's *The Royal Hunt of the Sun* (1965), and a documentary on the assassination of John Kennedy, *The Trial of Lee Harvey Oswald* (1967). In 1968 the Anta Theatre was presented to the nation, but the building continues to house both the American National Theatre and Academy and the American branch of the International Theatre Institute (q.v.).

Anthony Street Theatre, NEW YORK. This famous theatre, in which Edmund Kean (q.v.) first appeared in New York, was originally a circus. In 1812 it opened as the Olympic Theatre and among the plays which were given there during the first season was the first production in the United States of the famous equestrian melodrama *Timour the Tartar*, by M. G. Lewis. In 1813 the theatre was redecorated and renamed the Anthony Street Theatre. It later passed through various hands and was named successively the Commonwealth and the Pavilion, opening only for the summer. After the destruction by fire of the Park Theatre (q.v.) in May 1820 its company moved to the Anthony Street Theatre, which soon proved too small to hold the crowds that flocked to see Kean. He made his first appearance there as guest artist on 29 Nov. 1820, playing the title-role in *Richard III*. When the Park Theatre was rebuilt the company moved back, and the Anthony Street Theatre closed.

Anti-Masque, see MASQUE.

ANTOINE, ANDRÉ (1858–1943), French actor, producer, and manager, and one of the outstanding figures in the theatrical reforms of the late nineteenth century. In 1887 he founded the Théâtre Libre (q.v.) for the production of the new naturalistic drama then coming to the fore in Europe. Here he produced in 1890 Ibsen's *Ghosts*, playing Oswald himself, and followed it with plays by Hauptmann, Strindberg, Bjørnson, Verga, de Curel, Becque, Brieux, and Porto-Riche. Here, too, he revolutionized French acting and inaugurated a new era of scenic design. Inspired by him, Otto Brahm (q.v.) founded the Freie Bühne in Berlin, and Grein (q.v.) the Independent Theatre in London. In 1890 Antoine took over the Théâtre des Menus-Plaisirs, renaming it the Théâtre Antoine in 1906, and making it a centre for many young dramatists. From 1906 until his retirement in 1916, he was director of the Odéon. His influence, not only in France but all over Europe and in America, was incalculable. Among the outstanding figures of the next generation who owed much to him was Jacques Copeau (q.v.), founder of the Vieux-Colombier.

ANZENGRUBER, LUDWIG (1839–89), Austrian dramatist and the first to present realistic peasant life on the modern Austrian stage. *Der Pfarrer von Kirchfeld* (1870) is a plea for the exercise of tolerance in religious matters. In *Der Meineidbauer* (1871), where an old farmer who cheats two orphans of their heritage assumes demonic stature, Anzengruber proved that peasant life can furnish matter for true tragedy. A comic battle for matrimonial supremacy is the theme of *Die Kreuzlschreiber* (1872). Continuing the vein of rustic humour, *Der Doppelselbstmord* (1875) is a farcical village version of *Romeo and Juliet* which ends happily. Anzengruber's last play was *Das vierte Gebot* (1877), in which he deserts the country for the town but remains uncompromisingly a realist.

Apollo Theatre. (1) LONDON, in Shaftesbury Avenue. This opened on 21 Feb. 1901 with a musical comedy, *The Belle of Bohemia*. Although it was a failure, later productions had good runs, and the Apollo, although never the permanent home of a great management, has been a consistently successful theatre. It is well situated and the right size for either musical or straight plays. During the Munich crisis Sherwood's *Idiot's Delight* (1938) had a great success. Among later productions were Emlyn Williams's *The Light of Heart* (1940), John van Druten's *Old Acquaintance* (1941), and Terence Rattigan's *Flare Path* (1942). Other long runs were achieved by *Seagulls over Sorrento* (1950), by Hugh Hastings, and *Duel of Angels* (1958), by Jean Giraudoux. In 1955 there was an interesting production of Giraudoux's *Tiger at the Gates*, with Michael Redgrave as Hector, and in 1962 Marc Camoletti's *Boeing-Boeing*, adapted by Beverley Cross, started a long run. In 1968 Gielgud (q.v.) appeared in Alan Bennett's *Forty Years On*.

(2) NEW YORK, on 42nd Street between 7th and 8th Avenues. Originally the Bryant, used since 1910 for films and vaudeville, this opened as the Apollo on 17 Nov. 1920. A year later it housed an interesting revival of *Macbeth* directed by Arthur Hopkins, with Lionel Barrymore (q.v.) in the title-role and triangular settings by Robert Edmond Jones (q.v.). A series of musical comedies followed, and for many years the house was occupied by *George White's Scandals*. It became a cinema again in 1933.

The 3rd Avenue Variety Theatre was known as the Apollo for a short time in 1885, as were a playhouse on Chuter Street which opened in Oct. 1926 and a burlesque house on 125th Street.

APPIA, ADOLPHE (1862–1928), a French-speaking Swiss artist whose theories on stage design, and particularly on stage lighting, had an immense influence on twentieth-century methods of play production. He rejected the flat painted scenery of the late nineteenth century in favour of a plastic environment suitable for a three-dimensional actor, and employed light (helped in this by the introduction of electricity) as the visual counterpart of music, enhancing the mood of the play and linking the actor to the setting. Appia formulated his ideas so clearly in his *Die Musik und die Inscenierung* (1899), and in his extremely simple but effective designs for plays by Shaw and Ibsen, that the modern theatre has been able to put them into practice without the need for special apparatus. Mobile lighting, which breaks up and diversifies the direction, intensity, and colour of light, has become the basis of modern practice to such an extent that it is used today by many who do not realize that the techniques they are using derive from Appia's experiments.

Apron Stage, see FORESTAGE.

Aquarium Theatre, LONDON, see IMPERIAL THEATRE.

Aquatic Drama, see CIRCUS and SADLER'S WELLS THEATRE.

ARBUZOV, ALEKSEI NIKOLAYEVICH (1908–), Soviet dramatist, who has become well known to English audiences with the production of five of his plays in translation—*The Twelfth Hour* at the Oxford Playhouse in 1964; *The Promise,* also produced at Oxford in 1967 and subsequently in London; *It Happened at Irkutsk,* produced at Sheffield, also in 1967; *Confession at Night,* produced at Nottingham in 1968; and *Old World,* London, 1976. Arbuzov, in whom English critics have found something akin to Chekhov (q.v.), had his first success in the theatre with *Tanya* (1939), and in 1941 helped to organize a Youth Theatre in Moscow where several of his early plays were first produced. One of his most successful plays was *It Happened at Irkutsk* (also known as *The Irkutsk Story*), which was first produced at the Gorky Bolshoi Theatre in Leningrad in 1960, directed by Tovstonogov (q.v.), and was almost immediately staged at a number of other theatres.

Arch Street Theatre, PHILADELPHIA, see DREW, MRS. JOHN.

ARCHER, WILLIAM (1856–1924), dramatic critic and playwright, born in Scotland, who had had some experience of journalism before he migrated to London, where he worked on several important newspapers. From 1894 to 1898 he was dramatic critic of the *World,* reissuing his criticisms in annual volumes. He was also the author of a number of books on the

theatre, of which the most important was *Masks or Faces* (1888). He took the theatre seriously as an art, and was the first to introduce the plays of Ibsen (q.v.) to the London public. His translation of *Samfundets Støtter* (as *Quicksands*) was first seen in 1880; *A Doll's House* in 1889; *Ghosts* in 1891; *The Master Builder* in 1893; and *Little Eyolf* in 1896. In 1906–8 he published the complete works of Ibsen in English in eleven volumes. Archer had an astringent sense of humour which was probably responsible for his long friendship with Bernard Shaw (q.v.) and, like Shaw, he was antagonistic to Irving (q.v.) who, he maintained, had done nothing for the modern British dramatist. He always protested at the critical over-valuation of ancient drama and the under-valuation of modern plays, and, being more interested in drama as an intellectual product than as a vehicle for acting, he upheld the supremacy of the author's script, which he considered was too often used merely as an excuse for the display of the actor's virtuosity. On 6 Sept. 1923 Archer's own play, *The Green Goddess,* which had already been seen in Philadelphia and New York, was produced in London at the St. James's Theatre. This improbable melodrama ran for 416 performances and has since been filmed.

Architecture, THEATRE, see THEATRE BUILDINGS.

ARDEN, JOHN (1930–), English dramatist, whose early plays, *Live Like Pigs* (1958) and *The Happy Haven* (1960), were grotesque comedies of modern life. They were first seen at the Royal Court Theatre (q.v.), as was his historical drama, *Serjeant Musgrave's Dance* (1959). This study of mingled pacifism and violence was originally a failure, but has since been widely revived, and is now regarded as an outstanding contribution to modern European drama. In 1963 a political play, *The Workhouse Donkey* (originally seen for one night at the Royal Court in 1957 as *The Waters of Babylon*), was produced at Chichester (q.v.), where *Armstrong's Last Goodnight* (based on the Scottish 'Ballad of Johnny Armstrong') was seen in 1965. Both plays were subsequently transferred to London, where, also in 1965, *Left-Handed Liberty,* commissioned by the City of London to celebrate the 750th anniversary of the sealing of Magna Carta, was produced at the

Mermaid Theatre (q.v.). *Friday's Hiding* was seen at the Royal Lyceum in Edinburgh in 1966, and a play for children, *The Royal Pardon; or, the Soldier who Became an Actor*, was produced in London at Christmas 1967. In 1968 Arden and his wife, Margaretta D'Arcy, played the leading parts in *Harold Muggins is a Martyr*, specially written for Unity Theatre (q.v.), and shortly afterwards a new one-act play by Arden, *The True History of Squire Jonathan and his Unfortunate Treasure*, was performed at the Ambiance Lunch-Time Theatre Club. In the same year, a musical based on part of Nelson's life, *The Hero Rises Up*, was seen at the Roundhouse, without much success. While holding a Fellowship for Playwriting at Bristol University, Arden wrote several plays for students there, and also translated and adapted Goethe's *Götz von Berlichingen* as *Ironhand* for production at the Bristol Old Vic in 1963.

Arena Stage, WASHINGTON, D.C., see THEATRE-IN-THE-ROUND.

Arena Theatre, see OPEN STAGE.

ARETINO, PIETRO (1492–1556), Italian author and playwright, chiefly remembered for his comedies, which, though written in haste and lacking refinement, are original, amusing, and thoroughly Italian in their realistic and satiric thought and presentation, providing much light on the less creditable aspects of the social life of the day. It has been suggested that Ben Jonson's *Epicœne* (1609) may owe something to Aretino's comedy *Il Marescalco* (1533), which was based on Plautus' *Casina*. His other comedies are *La Cortigiana* (1526), *La Talanta* (1541), *Lo Ipocrito* (1542), a precursor of Molière's *Tartuffe*, and *Il Filosofo* (1546). Aretino's one tragedy, *Orazio* (1546), is perhaps the best of those written at that time.

Argyll Rooms, LONDON, in Upper Regent Street. These were fitted up as a private theatre and run by subscription from 1819 to 1823, for French plays under aristocratic patronage. Performances were given every Friday from March to September. Plays began at 9 p.m. and ended at midnight, when the company adjourned to the public ballroom and joined in the dancing.

The Trocadero Music-Hall (q.v.) was at one time known as the Argyll Rooms.

ARION, of Lesbos (*c.* 625–585 B.C.), considered the first tragic poet, is an important figure in the development of Greek dramatic poetry, since he was the first to give literary shape both to the dithyramb (q.v.) and to the satyr-revel. He is credited with a miraculous escape from death by drowning at the hands of pirates, being conveyed to land on the back of a dolphin charmed by his singing.

ARIOSTO, LODOVICO (1474–1533), Italian poet and playwright, best known for his epic poem, *Orlando Furioso*, published in 1532. He was also one of the first and best writers of early Italian comedy (*commedia erudita*). Though the material of his plays is taken from Renaissance city life, their structure is modelled upon Roman comedy. His first plays, *La Cassaria* (1508) and *I Suppositi* (1509), were given at the Court of the d'Este family, his patrons, in Ferrara in a theatre, built in a classical style under the influence of Vitruvius (q.v.), which survived until 1533. The scenery was by Raphael. Both plays were in prose, but were later rewritten in verse, as was *Il Negromante* (written 1520, prod. 1530). An English translation of *I Suppositi*, by George Gascoigne (q.v.), was performed at Gray's Inn in 1566.

ARISTOPHANES (*c.* 448–*c.* 380 B.C.), Greek dramatist, author of some forty comedies, of which eleven are extant (the only Greek comedies to be preserved in their entirety). These are the *Acharnians* (425 B.C.), *Knights* (424), *Clouds* (423), *Wasps* (422), *Peace* (421), *Birds* (414), *Lysistrata* (411), *Women at the Festival* (*Thesmophoriazousae*) (410), *Frogs* (405), *Women in Parliament* (*Ecclesiazousae*) (392), and *Plutus* (388). Many of these take their titles from the disguises assumed in them by the chorus, which became wasps, clouds, frogs, etc. Aristophanes' direct influence on drama has been slight; the form and spirit of his comedy were so intensely local that they offered no models and little material to comic dramatists of other times and places. On the other hand, his purely literary influence has been great, particularly on Rabelais and Fielding. The earlier plays, which are characteristic of Old Comedy, have very little plot. Instead a farcical situation, having direct reference to some political or social problem of the time, is briefly sketched, and is then exploited in a series of loosely connected scenes. In the *Acharnians*, for example, an Athenian citizen, weary of the war, makes a private treaty with the enemy and consequently enjoys the advantages of trading with them. The iambic scenes develop the ludicrous possibilities of this invention, and enable Aristophanes to hit out right and left at people he dislikes—politicians, busybodies, philosophers, Euripides. These earlier plays are an astonishing mixture of fantasy, unsparing (and often, to our minds, violently unfair) satire, brilliant verbal wit, literary and musical parody, exquisite lyrics, hard-hitting political propaganda, and uproarious farce. The *Frogs* marks the transition to the much quieter Middle Comedy, in which personal and political invective plays a smaller part, and the plot being more elaborate, the chorus is less prominent. Some of Aristophanes' plays, notably the *Frogs*, the *Birds*, and *Lysistrata*, have been successfully produced in English translations.

(For the 'English Aristophanes', see FOOTE, SAMUEL.)

ARISTOTLE (384–322 B.C.), Greek philosopher and scientist, whose *Poetics* analyses the function and structural principles of tragedy—a second book on comedy is lost—in reply to the criticisms of Plato and Socrates. To the latter's complaint (in Plato's *Apology*) that poets are unable to give a coherent account of what they do and how they do it, he opposes a logical theory of poetic composition; and in opposition to Plato's condemnation of poetry and drama because they do not directly seek to inculcate virtue, he defends poetic tragedy because by its representation of a serious action it arouses terror and pity and so leaves the spectator purged and strengthened by *catharsis*. Within the limits imposed by his concentration on the tragedies of Sophocles (q.v.), which he considered representative of the 'mature' form of the art, those of Aeschylus (q.v.) being the immature and those of Euripides (q.v.) the enfeebled stage, Aristotle's criticism is penetrating and in many ways final. Although extensively studied and quoted in modern times, he has, however, been very much misunderstood. The neo-classical critics of the seventeenth and eighteenth centuries, especially in France, were anxious to use Aristotle's authority to support their own doctrines, but of the famous three unities (q.v.)—of time, place, and action—he mentions only one and a half: he insists on the unity of action, and he remarks, parenthetically, that tragedy 'tries as far as possible to confine itself to twenty-four hours or thereabouts'. About the unity of place he says nothing, and several extant Greek plays disregarded it, if it was convenient and plausible to move the chorus from one (dramatic) place to another.

Arlecchino, one of the comic, quick-witted servants of the *commedia dell'arte* (q.v.). The first Italian actor to adopt the name, in its Italian form, was possibly Tristano Martinelli (q.v.). As Arlequin, still a comic servant, the character appears in later French comedy and in the dumb-shows of the fairs, while, in the familiar form of Harlequin, it passed into the harlequinade (q.v.) of the English pantomime, metamorphosed into the young lover of Columbine.

ARMIN, ROBERT (*c.* 1568–*c.* 1611), an Elizabethan clown, pupil and successor of Tarleton (q.v.). He appears in the list of actors in Shakespeare's plays and probably played Dogberry in *Much Ado About Nothing* in succession to William Kempe (q.v.). He was also known as a writer. His *Foole upon Foole; or, Six Sortes of Sottes* appeared anonymously in 1600, but his name is found on an enlarged edition published in 1608 as *A Nest of Ninnies*. He was probably the author of *Quips upon Questions* (also 1600), a collection of quatrains on stage 'themes', or improvisations on subjects suggested by the audience, and is credited with the authorship of one play, *The Two Maids of Moreclacke*, produced in 1609 (see also CURTAIN THEATRE).

ARMSTRONG, WILLIAM (1882–1952), English actor and director, who in 1922, after a theatrical career in England and America, and experience with the Glasgow and Birmingham repertory companies, went to Liverpool (q.v.) as the director of the repertory theatre there, the oldest in Great Britain, where he remained until 1944. His work in Liverpool was of great value both to the repertory movement and to the English theatre as a whole, many of his company going on to become leading players in London. In 1951 he was awarded the C.B.E. for his services to the theatre.

ARNAUD, YVONNE GERMAINE (1892–1958), an actress who, though born and educated in France, spent her entire professional life in London. Trained as a pianist, she toured Europe as a child, but at the age of eighteen, with no previous stage experience, she appeared at the Adelphi Theatre in the musical comedy, *The Quaker Girl*, and was an immediate success, as she was also a year later in *The Girl in the Taxi*. She continued to appear in farce, notably *Tons of Money* (1922) by Will Evans, and Ben Travers's *A Cuckoo in the Nest* (1925), and in musical comedy, her charm and high spirits, added to a most musical broken English–French accent, making her a general favourite. Among her outstanding performances were Mrs. Pepys in Fagan's *And So to Bed* (1926), the Duchess of Tann in his *The Improper Duchess* (1931), Mrs. Frail in Congreve's *Love for Love* (1943), and Denise in Alan Melville's *Dear Charles* (1952). She lived for a long time near Guildford, where a new repertory theatre has been named after her (see YVONNE ARNAUD THEATRE).

ARNE, SUSANNA (1714–66), see CIBBER, THEOPHILUS.

ARNOLD, MATTHEW (1822–88), English poet, educationist, and critic, whose interest in the drama led him, in 1880, to put the case for its official support. His two poetic plays, *Empedocles on Etna* (1852) and *Merope* (1858), were both written on classical lines. His plays are for the study rather than the stage, yet he did a great service to drama by arguing its claims as an important cultural influence. In his essay entitled *The French Play in London* (1882) he said: 'The theatre is irresistible: organize the theatre!' He was for a short time dramatic critic of the *Pall Mall Gazette*.

ARONSON, BORIS SOLOMON (1900–), American scene and costume designer, born in Kiev. Arriving in New York in 1923 he designed scenery for Maurice Schwartz's Yiddish Art Theatre. His early work was influenced by the sets in Cubist-fantastic style designed by Chagall and Nathan Altman for the Jewish Theatre in Moscow. His later sets were more symbolic, restating by use of forms and colours the mood of the play and its characters, as in his set for MacLeish's *J.B.* (1959). He is the inventor of 'pro-jected scenery', a basic permanent set of interrelated abstract shapes made of neutral grey gauze which can easily be 'painted' any desired colour by directing spotlights upon it through coloured slides. This device was first used in Ballet Theatre's production of Saroyan's 'The Great American Goof' (1940).

ARRABAL, FERNANDO (1933–), French dramatist, of Spanish extraction, whose avant-garde plays derive mainly from Beckett and the Theatre of the Absurd (qq.v.). The best-known are *Piquenique en campagne* (1952), and *Le Cimetière des voitures* (1957), which, as *The Car Cemetery*, was seen in London in 1969 in a production by the Tavistock Repertory Company (q.v.). *Oraison* was seen in Paris in 1958, *Le Tricycle* in 1961, and *La Communiante* in 1966. An earlier play, in French and English, *The Labyrinth*, was seen at the Mercury Theatre in 1968, directed by Jerome Savary, and early in 1971 the National Theatre staged in translation *The Architect and the Emperor of Assyria*, with Anthony Hopkins and Jim Dale, directed by Victor Garcia, of the Argentinian theatre. A production of *The Two Executioners* was also scheduled for the first week in Jan. 1971 by the Mount-view Theatre Club (q.v.).

ARTAUD, ANTONIN (1896–1948), French actor, director, and poet, whose work has been one of the great seminal influences on the contemporary French stage. He was actively connected with the surrealist theatre and in 1927 founded with Roger Vitrac (q.v.) the Théâtre Alfred Jarry (see JARRY), where he produced not only Vitrac's surrealist plays, but Strindberg's *Dream Play* and part of Claudel's *Partage de midi*, as well as his own major dramatic work, *Les Cenci* (1935), based on Shelley and Stendhal. In these he put into practice the theories from which he evolved his conception of the 'Theatre of Cruelty' (q.v.), a theatre which by jettisoning language in favour of symbolic gesture, movement, sound, and rhythm, as in the theatres of the Far East, would have the power to disturb the spectator, and impel him to action by the inner force of the material presented on the stage. Having observed that during the great plagues of history men were liberated from the restraints of morality and reason, and returned to a state of primitive ferocity and power, he envisaged the theatre as a similar catalyst, freeing the repressed unconscious and forcing men to view themselves as they really are. In 1938, the year after he was declared insane and detained in an asylum, where he remained until two years before his death, came the publication of *Le Théâtre et son double*, a collection of essays in which he attempted to explain and define his conception of theatre. His influence is widespread in the theatre today, notably in the plays of Adamov, Audiberti, Camus, and Genet, and in the productions of Barrault, Vilar, and the English director Peter Brook (qq.v.).

Arts Council of Great Britain. This body is in essence a continuation of the Council for the Encouragement of Music and the Arts (C.E.M.A.), founded at the beginning of 1940 with the aid of grants from the Pilgrim Trust and from the Treasury on the vote of the then Board of Education, to bring concerts and plays to the crowded evacuation areas. In 1942 the Pilgrim Trust withdrew, leaving the Treasury to provide the whole of the Council's income, and Lord Keynes was appointed Chairman. It was largely due to his enthusiasm and unceasing activity that the Council was put on a permanent basis, the greater part of its income being provided by an annual grant-in-aid from the Treasury. The Arts Council, as it was then called, was created a Body Corporate under Royal Charter on 9 Aug. 1946 'to develop a greater knowledge, understanding, and practice of the Fine Arts, to increase their accessibility to the public, and to improve their standard of execution'. The Council helps the diffusion of drama largely through 'non-profit-distributing' companies in London and in the provinces. Its other activities are summarized in the annual Report and Accounts published by the Council.

Arts League of Service Travelling Theatre, GREAT BRITAIN. This was founded on 28 Apr. 1919 as a drama section of the A.L.S. From the beginning it was linked to an art movement rather than a theatrical tradition, which allowed great freedom in choice of material and experimentation. The members of the company, among whom were the young Angela and Hermione Baddeley (qq.v.), toured the country, giving a varied programme of mimed folk-song, dances, short plays, sketches, etc. Props and scenery were reduced to a minimum, all being comfortably carried in a van which also served for transport. The company, although doing excellent work in bringing varied and wholesome entertainment to remote corners of rural England and Scotland, was always in financial difficulties, in spite of a grant from the Carnegie Trust, and was finally disbanded in 1937. It may be said that its very success was its undoing, for it stimulated local interest in drama, and soon found itself ousted by the amateur companies it had helped to bring into being.

Arts Theatre, LONDON, a club theatre for the staging of unlicensed and experimental plays, which opened on 20 Apr. 1927. In 1942 Alec Clunes (q.v.) took it over, and for ten years made it a vital centre, producing a wide range of plays and achieving, as one critic said, the status of 'a pocket National Theatre'. The theatre changed hands again in 1953, when Campbell Williams took charge. He continued to offer interesting productions, but later standards somewhat declined, and in 1962 the theatre was sold to the film-producer Nathan Cohen. It was leased for six months of that year by the Royal Shakespeare Theatre as a London home for new and unusual plays, opening on 14 Mar. with Giles Cooper's *Everything in the Garden*. This was followed by five new plays and two revivals, Gorky's *The Lower Depths* and Middleton's *Women Beware Women*, of which only the last was a success. The theatre was then used for mixed programmes, including films, and for holiday matinées of plays for children, given by Caryl Jenner's Unicorn Theatre company.

(For the ARTS THEATRE, Cambridge, see CAMBRIDGE.)

ASCH, SHOLOM (1880–1957), Jewish dramatist and novelist, author of several plays in Yiddish, of which the best-known is *God of Vengeance*. This was given its first production by Reinhardt in Berlin in 1907 in German, as *Gott der Rache*. It immediately attracted the attention of the literary and theatrical world to the possibilities of Yiddish drama, and has since been translated and produced in many countries. Some of Asch's Yiddish novels have also been dramatized or adapted for the stage. More than anyone else Sholom Asch raised the standard of Yiddish writing and helped to place it on a literary basis. His works have frequently been translated into other languages.

ASCHE, OSCAR [really JOHN STANGER HEISS] (1871–1936), English actor, of Scandinavian descent, mainly remembered in connection with his own oriental fantasy with music, *Chu-Chin-Chow*. First produced in 1916, this ran for five years, setting up a record for its own day. Asche himself appeared in it, as did his wife LILY BRAYTON (1876–1953), who had made her first appearance on the stage in 1896 with Benson. In 1903 she made a great success as Yo-San in Belasco's *The Darling of the Gods*, and subsequently her career ran parallel with that of her husband. She made her last appearance in 1932 as Portia in *Julius Caesar*, which Asche directed, playing Casca. In 1921 he had followed *Chu-Chin-Chow* with another play of the same type, *Cairo*, which was not, however, so successful. Asche made his first appearance on the stage in 1893, and was for some years with Frank Benson (q.v.), and with Tree (q.v.) at His Majesty's. He was at his best in such forceful parts as Shylock in *The Merchant of Venice*, Petruchio in *The Taming of the Shrew*, Antony in *Antony and Cleopatra*, and Falstaff in *The Merry Wives of Windsor*, all of which he played in London and during his tours of Australia, his birthplace, and South Africa. In 1911 he made a great success as Hajj in Edward Knoblock's *Kismet*. He published his autobiography in 1929.

ASHCROFT, DAME PEGGY (1907–), English actress, who made her first appearance at the Birmingham Repertory Theatre as Margaret in Barrie's *Dear Brutus* in 1926. She appeared in London a year later, first attracting attention as Naemi in Ashley Dukes's dramatization of Feuchtwanger's novel *Jew Süss* (1929), a part in which she showed that simplicity and sense of poetic tragedy which have since made so many of her performances remarkable. Her Juliet in Gielgud's production of *Romeo and Juliet* at the New Theatre in 1935 finally consolidated her growing reputation. Her Nina in Chekhov's *The Seagull* the following year was also a moving experience. She is an excellent player of comedy—Lady Teazle in Sheridan's *The School for Scandal*, Cecily Cardew in Wilde's *The Importance of Being Earnest*, Beatrice in *Much Ado About Nothing*, Mistress Page in *The*

Merry Wives of Windsor. In 1956 she appeared at the Royal Court Theatre in an amazing dual role as the prostitute and the prostitute's male cousin in Brecht's *The Good Woman of Setzuan*. One of her finest roles is undoubtedly Ibsen's Hedda Gabler, which she played in 1954 in London and on tour in Norway. For this performance she was awarded the King's Medal by the King of Norway. She has made several appearances with the Royal Shakespeare Company, of which she is a director, both at Stratford-upon-Avon and at the Aldwych in London, notably as Madame Ranevsky in Chekhov's *The Cherry Orchard* in 1964. She also appeared as Madame Arkadina in his *The Seagull* at the Queen's Theatre, and in 1969 was seen in Albee's *A Delicate Balance* and Pinter's *Landscape*. She was created D.B.E. in 1956 for services to the theatre, and in 1962 a theatre named after her opened in Croydon, where she was born (see below).

Ashcroft Theatre, CROYDON. Named after Peggy Ashcroft (q.v.), this theatre opened on 5 Nov. 1962. It housed the company under Clement Scott-Gilbert which had formerly played at the Pembroke Theatre-in-the-Round, Croydon, and its first production was *Royal Gambit*, a translation of a German play by Hermann Griessieker on Henry VIII and his wives, who are the only characters. The theatre, which is part of the Croydon Civic Centre, was designed by Beatty Pownall. Although an apparently conventional proscenium-arch theatre, seating just over 700, it can be converted into an arena theatre by the use of hydraulic lifts.

ASHWELL [really POCOCK], LENA (1872–1957), English actress who made her first appearance in 1891, and after playing a wide variety of parts, in London and on tour, made a great success in 1900 in Henry Arthur Jones's *Mrs. Dane's Defence*, in which she was also seen in the United States. On her return to England she took over the Kingsway Theatre (q.v.), inaugurating in 1907 a season of successful repertory with Anthony Wharton's *Irene Wycherley*, and remaining in management until 1915, when she left to organize entertainment for the troops in France and later in Germany, for which work she was awarded the O.B.E. She was active in the foundation of the British Drama League (q.v.) and in 1924 took over the Bijou Theatre (q.v.), in Bayswater, renamed it the Century, and produced there several new plays, including her own adaptations of Dostoievsky's novel, *Crime and Punishment*, and R. L. Stevenson's *Dr. Jekyll and Mr. Hyde*. In 1936 she published her autobiography, *Myself a Player*.

Asphaleian System, one of the earliest of the modern elaborate systems controlling the stage floor; in it the whole stage area is divided into individual platforms, upon hydraulic pistons, each of which can be separately raised, lowered, or tipped.

Assembly Theatre, NEW YORK, see PRINCESS THEATRE.

Association of British Theatre Technicians (A.B.T.T.), an organization founded in 1961, under the chairmanship of Norman Marshall (q.v.), to collect and disseminate information on all the technical aspects of the theatre, including machinery, equipment, acoustics, lighting, scenery, and stage-management, with the intention of raising standards all round. In the year of its foundation, the Association played host in London to the Third Biennial Congress of the International Association of Theatre Technicians, when the subject under discussion was 'Adaptable Theatres'. A report on the Congress, edited by Stephen Joseph (q.v.), was afterwards published. The Association has also published *Theatre Planning*, a work intended for the guidance at all stages of construction of those responsible for the provision of places of public entertainment.

Astley's Amphitheatre, LONDON. This curious theatre, immortalized by Charles Dickens, had many names. It began when in 1784 Philip Astley, a retired cavalry man and horse trainer, erected near Westminster Bridge, on the site of an amphitheatre dating from 1770, a wooden building with a stage intended for the display of feats of horsemanship and equestrian dramas. This was burned down in 1794, rebuilt and reopened as the Royal Grove on Easter Monday 1795, and again destroyed by fire in 1803. Astley then moved to the Olympic (q.v.) in Wych Street while he rebuilt yet again, and the new house opened in 1804 with a great equestrian spectacle, for which type of performance it became famous. Having built similar places of entertainment all over Britain, France, and Ireland (nineteen in all), Astley died in 1814, but the theatre, which was for some years known as Davis's Amphitheatre, continued to feature equestrian spectacles, with Gomersal, enshrined by Thackeray in his novel *The Newcomes* (1853/5), as the chief actor. He was succeeded by the famous Andrew Ducrow, who was so illiterate that he seldom played a speaking part, but excelled in riding, stage management, and production. The building was twice destroyed by fire, in 1830 and again in 1841, after which William Batty rebuilt it, and gave it his own name. He was succeeded by William Cooke, who made Shakespeare's *Richard III* into an equestrian drama, giving White Surrey, Richard's horse, a leading part. In 1863 Dion Boucicault (q.v.) turned the Amphitheatre into the Theatre Royal, Westminster, with disastrous results, and was succeeded by E. T. Smith, who reverted to its former name of Astley's and drew all London across the river to see Adah Isaacs Menken (q.v.) in an equestrian spectacle based on Byron's poem *Mazeppa*. In 1871 the building came under the control of the circus proprietors John and George Sanger, and a year later was renamed Sanger's Grand National. In 1893 it was closed as unsafe, and it was finally demolished some time between 1893 and 1895. No trace of it remains, but in 1951 a memorial plaque was unveiled on the site at 225 Westminster Bridge Road.

ASTON, ANTHONY (*fl.* first half of the eighteenth century), commonly called Tony, and known also as Matt Medley, to whom, in default of more precise information, goes the honour of having been the first professional actor to appear in the New World. In the preface to his *Fool's Opera*, printed in about 1730, he refers to his appearances in 'New York, East and West Jersey, Maryland, Virginia (on both sides Cheesapeek), North and South Carolina, South Florida, the Bahamas, Jamaica, and Hispaniola'. He is known to have appeared in Charleston in 1703, and later in the same year in New York, but we have no knowledge of what he played, or whether he was alone or with a company of other actors. He may have given a sort of variety entertainment like the 'Medley' in which he appeared in the English provinces in 1717. He was in Edinburgh from 1725 to 1728, and in 1735 he protested against the proposed bill for regulating the stage. He was still alive in 1749, when Chetwood spoke of him as 'travelling still and as well known as the posthorse that carries the mail'. There are references to him in O. G. Sonneck's *Early Opera in America* (1915), and his life was written by Watson Nicholson.

Astor Place Opera House, NEW YORK, one block east of Broadway, a house built for Italian opera which opened on 22 Nov. 1847. On 4 Sept. 1848 the English actor Macready (q.v.) appeared there. but owing to the jealousy of Edwin Forrest (q.v.), his visit terminated on 10 May 1849 with the anti-British Astor Place riot, in which twenty-two people were killed and thirty-six wounded by shots fired by the militia. The theatre then closed for repairs, and reopened on 24 Sept. 1849 with *Romeo and Juliet*, Jean Davenport (SEE LANDER) playing Juliet. Other actors who came between opera seasons were Charlotte Cushman, Julia Dean, and George Vandenhoft (qq.v.). The theatre was never successful, however, and it finally closed on 4 Apr. 1854, the furniture, scenery, and props being sold at auction.

Astor Theatre, NEW YORK, on Broadway at 45th Street. This opened on 21 Sept. 1906 with *A Midsummer Night's Dream*. The theatre's first successful productions, both 1908, were *Paid in Full*, by Eugene Walter, and *The Man from Home*, by Booth Tarkington and H. L. Wilson. In 1913 George M. Cohan's dramatization of Earl Biggers's novel, *Seven Keys to Baldpate*, was also successful. The theatre's career was then somewhat uneventful and in 1925 it became a cinema.

Astracanadas, see GÉNERO CHICO.

Atelier, THÉÂTRE DE L', PARIS, see DULLIN, CHARLES.

Atellan Farce, a short impromptu entertainment popular in early Roman times. It was named after the town of Atella in southern Italy, and was originally designed to amuse the crowds on market day or holidays. The surviving titles indicate the primitive rustic humour of the plays— *The Farmer*, *The Vine-Gatherers*, *The Woodpile*, *The She-Goat*—which were acted by a small number of stock characters —Bucco, Dossennus, Maccus, Manducus, Pappus—wearing distinctive costumes and masks. These Atellan farces achieved literary status in the first century B.C., when two writers, POMPONIUS and NOVIUS, wrote out in full short farces using the old stock characters and situations for use

as curtain-raisers. But after them the Atellan farce reverted to improvisation, with a perennial and often fatal interest in politics. On the stages of the early Empire its performers, though social outcasts, enjoyed considerable popularity; but eventually the old rustic farce was ousted by the equally vulgar, but more sophisticated mime (q.v.).

ATKINS, ROBERT (1886–1972), English actor and director, whose career was spent mainly in the service of Shakespeare. He made his first appearance at His Majesty's Theatre in 1906 in *Henry IV, Part I*, and in 1915 joined the Old Vic company, where he returned in 1920, after war service. He remained until 1925, during which time he directed and appeared in a number of Shakespeare and other plays, including Ibsen's *Peer Gynt* (1922) for the first time in London, and the rarely-seen *Titus Andronicus* and *Troilus and Cressida* (both 1923). In 1936 he founded the Bankside Players, and with them produced *Henry V, Much Ado About Nothing*, and *The Merry Wives of Windsor* under Elizabethan conditions at the Ring (q.v.). He also directed plays by Shakespeare at the Stratford-upon-Avon Memorial Theatre and at the Open Air Theatre in London's Regent's Park. During Oct. 1940, at the height of the bombing of London, he continued to present Shakespeare at the Vaudeville Theatre (q.v.). Among his best parts were Sir Toby Belch in *Twelfth Night*, Touchstone in *As You Like It*, Caliban in *The Tempest*, Bottom in *A Midsummer Night's Dream*, Sir Giles Overreach in Massinger's *A New Way to Pay Old Debts*, and James Telfer in Pinero's *Trelawny of the 'Wells'*. In 1949 he was awarded the C.B.E. for services to the English theatre.

ATKINSON, (JUSTIN) BROOKS (1894–), American dramatic critic of the *New York Times* from 1926 to 1960 (with a brief leave of absence during the Second World War, when he went to China and later to Russia as a war correspondent). In this position he maintained a fine record for honest and intelligent observation of the American theatre. On his retirement from the *Times* the Mansfield Theatre, New York, was renamed the Brooks Atkinson (q.v.) in his honour.

AUBIGNAC, FRANÇOIS HÉDELIN, ABBÉ D' (1604–76), one of the first important

French writers on the drama. His *Pratique du théâtre*, published in 1657, upheld the unities (q.v.), and criticized with much acerbity those who departed from them. His own plays were intended as models for aspiring dramatists, but were not particularly successful, partly owing to the mediocrity of their style, and partly to the attacks of the many enemies which d'Aubignac's criticisms had made for him.

AUDEN, WYSTAN HUGH (1907–72), English poet (later an American citizen), and in his early days a playwright. His first play, *The Dance of Death* (1935), was produced at the Westminster Theatre in London by the Group Theatre (q.v.), in a double bill with T. S. Eliot's *Sweeney Agonistes.* The same company produced the three plays which Auden then wrote in collaboration with the novelist Christopher Isherwood—*The Dog Beneath the Skin* (1936), *The Ascent of F. 6* (1937), and *On the Frontier* (1939), this last with music by Benjamin Britten. Auden also provided the libretti for several operas, and in 1958 prepared a modern verse adaptation of the medieval music-drama, *The Play of Daniel*, for performance by the Pro Musica Antiqua of New York.

AUDIBERTI, JACQUES (1899–1965), French dramatist whose surrealist world is close to that of Artaud (q.v.). His first play, *Quoat-Quoat* (1946), a satire on nineteenth-century melodrama, was followed by the commercially successful *Le Mal court* (1947), a tale of innocence corrupted by experience, set in the eighteenth century, and by *Les Femmes du Bœuf* (1948), which was produced at the Comédie-Française, as was *Fourmi dans le corps* (1962). Among his other plays are *La Fête noire* (1948), *Pucelle* (1950), a somewhat irreverent treatment of Joan of Arc's life, *La Hobereaute* (1956), set in medieval Burgundy, *L'Effet Glapion* (1959), and, his last work, *L'Opéra du monde* (1965). Audiberti belonged to no particular school of dramatists, but created his own world of fantasy and farce, in which his eccentricities found full scope, though his work was often rendered unintelligible by an excess of verbal dexterity.

Audience on the Stage. The practice, common in the early English and Continental theatres, of allowing members of the audience, usually chattering fops in fine clothes, to buy seats on the stage was a fertile source of disorder and of acute irritation to both actor and dramatist. It is first mentioned in England in 1596 and in France not until 1649, but by both dates the tradition was well established. In France it may have contributed to the disappearance of the old multiple setting. In England its influence on dramatic convention can be seen in the Induction to *The Taming of the Shrew*, and—a final vestige—in Gay's *The Beggar's Opera.* It was the development of the 'machine' play in France which finally made the presence of spectators on the stage intolerable, and Voltaire (q.v.) was responsible for their removal in 1759 from the stage of the Comédie-Française. When Garrick took over Drury Lane he too tried to remove the spectators from the stage, but had to wait until the theatre was enlarged in 1762. In other London theatres the practice lingered on into the nineteenth century, and was remarked on at Grimaldi's farewell performance at Drury Lane in 1828, and again in 1838 and 1840, when Queen Victoria visited Covent Garden.

Audition, a trial run by an actor seeking employment, either to display his talents in general by singing, dancing, and reciting, or to demonstrate his fitness for a particular role by reading some part of it to the director (q.v.) and his associates. In earlier times actors were often engaged for a company merely on hearsay, by a letter of recommendation, or after a private audition by the manager. In modern times leading actors may be specifically engaged for a part on their reputation alone, while the supporting cast is chosen only after a number of auditions have been held.

Auditorium, that part of a theatre building designed or intended for the accommodation of the people witnessing the play— the audience. The word in its present usage dates from about 1727, though Auditory and Spectatory are also to be found. The auditorium can vary considerably in size and shape, placing the audience in front of, part way round, or entirely round, the acting area. It can also be in one entity, or divided, with galleries above the main area.

AUGIER, (GUILLAUME VICTOR) ÉMILE (1820–89), French dramatist and one of the first to revolt against the excesses of the Romantics. After a few plays in verse, he found his true vocation in the writing of domestic prose-dramas dealing with social questions of the moment, of which *Le Gendre de Monsieur Poirier* (1854) is the best-known. Among others which were successful in their day were *Le Mariage d'Olympe* (1855), which paints the courtesan as she is and not as idealized by the younger Dumas (q.v.); *Les Lionnes pauvres* (1858), which shows the disruption of home life consequent on the wife's adultery; and two political comedies, *Les Effrontés* (1861) and *Le Fils de Giboyer* (1862). Under the influence of the new currents of thought running across Europe, he ended his career with two problem plays, *Mme Caverlet* (1876) and *Les Fourchambault* (1879). Augier's plays were well written in the theatrical conventions of his time, and he was more of a realist than either the younger Dumas or Sardou (q.v.).

Augustus Druriolanus, see HARRIS, SIR AUGUSTUS.

Ausoult, JEANNE (1625–62), see BARON, MICHEL.

AUSTIN, CHARLES (1878–1944), a famous music-hall comedian who for many years featured a character of his own invention, Parker, P.C., in a series of sketches built round an amusing member of the police force. Austin was also a well-known figure in pantomime, and was very popular in his profession.

Australian Marie Lloyd, see FORDE, FLORRIE.

Author's Night, see ROYALTY.

Auto Sacramental, the Spanish term for the religious play in the vernacular which derived from the Latin liturgical drama (q.v.). Although its development followed in general that of the English Mystery Play or French Mystère (qq.v.), it had by the end of the sixteenth century come to be recognized as a dramatic restatement of the tenets of the Catholic faith which embodied the preoccupations and ideals of the Counter-Reformation, as the Passion Play did in Germany (see MYSTERIEN-SPIEL). In this form it provided one of the main elements in the celebrations on Corpus Christi (the Thursday after Trinity Sunday), an important feast-day on the Continent. The distinctive feature of the *auto sacramental*, which was sumptuously staged and accompanied by music, was its use of elaborate allegory. The outstanding writer of such plays in the second half of the seventeenth century was Calderón (q.v.), who from about 1650 to his death in 1681 was responsible for all those staged in Madrid. Even after his death his plays were nearly always the ones revived for the festival. They continued to be performed long after the religious drama had disappeared in France and England, and were finally prohibited by a royal edict of 1765.

AVANCINI, NICKOLAUS (1611–86), an important writer of Jesuit drama (q.v.), whose plays were mainly performed in Vienna, where he combined the functions of Austrian Provincial of the Order and Professor of Rhetoric and Philosophy at Vienna University with that of Court Poet to Leopold I. His plays, on subjects taken from the classics, history, and the Bible, were produced with elaborate transformation scenes and stage effects, splendid costumes and scenery, and interludes of singing and dancing. The best-known, due to its publication with nine engravings showing the stage settings, is *Pietas Victrix* (1659), which ends with the conversion of Constantine and a eulogy of Leopold I as his successor.

Avenue Theatre, LONDON, see PLAYHOUSE (1).

Avignon. In the summer of 1947 Jean Vilar (q.v.) appeared at Avignon in an open-air production of Shakespeare's *Richard II*, which had not previously been seen in French. The play was performed without scenery on a platform stage in the courtyard of the Palace of the Popes, music, lighting, and costumes being used to reinforce the text. The success of this venture led to the establishment of an annual drama festival at Avignon, to which Vilar later brought his company from the Théâtre National Populaire (q.v.). Among the outstanding productions of these early years were Corneille's *Le Cid* and Kleist's *Prinz Friedrich von Homburg* (1951) with Gérard Philipe (q.v.), and Beaumarchais's *Le Mariage de Figaro* (1956) with Daniel Sorano (q.v.). In later years the Festival continued its policy of reviving selected European classics, but also featured a number of modern plays, including Pirandello's

Henry IV, Brecht's *Mother Courage*, and Bolt's *A Man for All Seasons*.

Avon Theatre, NEW YORK, see KLAW THEATRE.

AYALA, ADELARDO LÓPEZ DE, see LÓPEZ DE AYALA.

AYRENHOFF, CORNELIUS VON (1733–1819), an Austrian dramatist whose serious dramas, in contrast to the light fare popular in Vienna at the time, were intended to raise the standard of the theatre. They were given at the Burgtheater, under the able management of Joseph von Sonnenfels, but proved unequal to the task of weaning the public from the light diet provided by harlequinade, farce, and operetta.

AYRER, JAKOB (c. 1543–1605), an early German dramatist, successor of Hans Sachs (q.v.) and like him a voluminous author of long Carnival plays and *Singspiele* popular in his own day, some of which were published in 1618. Ayrer, who was much influenced by the English Comedians (q.v.), spent most of his life in Nuremberg, and was probably a Mastersinger. His *Phänicia* (c. 1593) and *Sidea* (c. 1600) are related to Shakespeare's (q.v.) *Much Ado About Nothing* (c. 1595/9) and *The Tempest* (c. 1611) respectively by a common source, but direct influence by the elder dramatist on the younger is now considered unlikely.

B

BABO, JOSEPH MARIUS (1756–1822), see RITTERDRAMA.

Backcloth, a flat painted canvas which hangs at the back of the stage, suspended from the grid. It was formerly widely used in combination with wings to form a wing-and-backcloth scene. This has now been replaced by the box set (q.v.), or by the open stage (q.v.), and is used only in ballet and pantomime.

Backing Flat, see FLAT.

Backstage, a term applied to the parts of the theatre behind the stage, such as the actors' dressing-rooms; visitors going there are said to 'go backstage'.

BACON, FRANK (1864–1922), see GAIETY THEATRE (3).

BADDELEY, ANGELA (1904–76), English actress, sister of Hermione (q.v.). After playing several child-parts at the Old Vic from 1915 to 1916, and Scissors in A. A. Milne's *Make Believe* (1918), she toured with the Arts League of Service Travelling Theatre (q.v.) for a year. She then went to the Lyric, Hammersmith, under Nigel Playfair, playing Jenny Diver during the three-year run of Gay's *The Beggar's Opera* (1920), and subsequently toured Australia for a year in a selection of plays by Barrie. On her return she made a great success as the heroine of Allen Harker's *Marigold* (1927), and after a tour of South Africa was seen with her sister in Zoë Akins's *The Greeks Had a Word for It* (1934). She was later seen in a number of new plays, including Emlyn Williams's *Night Must Fall* (1935), *The Light of Heart* (1940), and *The Morning Star* (1941); Dodie Smith's *Dear Octopus* (1938); Rattigan's *The Winslow Boy* (1946); and Noël Coward's *Relative Values* (1951). She appeared both with the Old Vic and the Stratford-upon-Avon companies in a variety of Shakespeare parts under the direction of her second husband, Glen Byam Shaw (q.v.).

BADDELEY, HERMIONE (1906–86), English actress, sister of Angela (q.v.), with whom she appeared (as Paste) in

A. A. Milne's *Make Believe* in 1918, subsequently touring with the Arts League of Service Travelling Theatre (q.v.). She joined the company of *The Co-Optimists* at the Palace in 1924, and soon made a great reputation in revue, appearing in such successful productions as Cochran's *On With the Dance* (1925) and its sequel *Still Dancing* (1926); *Nine Sharp* (1938) and *The Little Revue* (1939); and *Rise Above It* (1941) and *Sky High* (1942) in both of which Hermione Gingold (q.v.) also appeared. Hermione Baddeley has also made many successful appearances in straight plays, from Florrie Small in McEvoy's *The Likes of Her* (1923) to Mrs. Pooter in Grossmith's *Diary of a Nobody* (1955). One of her most amusing parts was The Infant Phenomenon, Ninetta Crummles, in Nigel Playfair's *When Crummles Played* (1927), based on the theatrical chapters in Dickens's *Nicholas Nickleby*, and she was also much admired as Polaire in Zoë Akins's *The Greeks Had a Word for It* (1934). Among her other parts were Margery Pinchwife in Wycherley's *The Country Wife* in 1940—her one excursion into classic comedy—and Ida Arnold in *Brighton Rock* (1943), based by Frank Harvey on Graham Greene's novel. She made her first appearance in New York in 1961, when she took over the part of Helen in Shelagh Delaney's *A Taste of Honey*, and was later seen in Tennessee Williams's *The Milk Train Doesn't Stop Here Anymore* (1963).

BADDELEY, ROBERT (1732–94), English actor, first seen on the stage in 1760 at Drury Lane. He married an actress, SOPHIA SNOW (1745–86), daughter of the trumpeter Valentine Snow, who made her first appearance in 1764, and excelled in such Shakespearian parts as Ophelia in *Hamlet*, Desdemona in *Othello*, and Imogen in *Cymbeline*. Zoffany painted her as Fanny in Colman and Garrick's *The Clandestine Marriage* (1766). Owing to her extravagance and dissipation her marriage was a failure, and her husband soon left her. She was last seen in London in 1781, and then appeared only in the provinces. Baddeley remained on the stage until his death, being taken ill while dressing for his most famous part, Moses in Sheridan's *The School for Scandal*, which he played on its initial production in 1777. He was the last actor to wear the royal livery of scarlet and gold as one of the King's Servants. On his death he left Drury Lane Theatre a sum of money for a cake and wine to be partaken of by the company in the green room annually, a custom still observed at Drury Lane on Twelfth Night.

BADEL, ALAN FERNAND (1923–), English actor, who had made a few appearances on the stage before joining the army in 1942, after which he appeared several times with the Army Play Unit, notably as Othello. In 1947 he returned to the theatre, and was at Birmingham, Stratford-upon-Avon, and the Old Vic, playing a wide variety of parts, including Romeo in 1952 and Hamlet in 1956. He then made a great success as Hero in Anouilh's *The Rehearsal* (1961), in which he also made his first appearance in New York in 1963. He has directed a number of plays, including Hochhuth's *The Public Prosecutor* (1957), in which he played Fouquier-Tinville, and as part of Ferndel Productions was responsible for the London production of a dramatized version by Marjorie Barkentin of part of James Joyce's *Ulysses* as *Ulysses in Nighttown* (1959), in which he played Stephen Dedalus. In 1965 he appeared as John Tanner in Shaw's *Man and Superman*, and after a long absence from the theatre due to filming and television appearances, he was seen at the Oxford Playhouse in 1970 as Othello, and in Sartre's adaptation of the elder Dumas's *Kean*, which was later transferred to London with great success.

BAGNOLD, ENID [LADY RODERICK JONES] (1889–1981), English author, who was already well known as a novelist when her *Serena Blandish*, published anonymously in 1924 as 'By a Lady of Quality', was dramatized by S. N. Behrman (q.v.) and produced in New York in 1929. It was seen in London in 1938 with Vivien Leigh (q.v.) in the title-role. Enid Bagnold herself then dramatized two of her novels, *Lottie Dundass* (1943) and *National Velvet* (1946), and wrote two new plays, *Poor Judas*, seen in London in 1951, and *Gertie*, which after a short run in New York in 1952 was produced in London a year later as *Little Idiot*. Her most successful play, both in

New York in 1955 with Gladys Cooper and Siobhan McKenna and in London in 1956 with Edith Evans and Peggy Ashcroft, was *The Chalk Garden*. Three later plays, *The Last Joke* (1960), *The Chinese Prime Minister* (New York, 1964; London, 1965), and *Call Me Jacky* (1968), were unsuccessful in spite of excellent casts, the last being seen only on tour in the English provinces. An interesting *Autobiography*, published in 1969, contains some revealing chapters on the writing and staging of her plays.

BAILEY, BRYAN (1922–60), English actor and theatre manager, whose sudden death in a road accident was a great loss to the English theatre. He was at the time director of the newly opened Belgrade Theatre (q.v.) in Coventry, having previously been director for five years of the Guildford Repertory Theatre. He was a man of immense resources, fertile in ideas, and a hard worker. After leaving Oxford he trained at the Royal Academy of Dramatic Art, acted in repertory, and formed a group for the production of new plays. Although destined to remain at Coventry for only two years, he had already shown initiative and a willingness to encourage new authors by staging the early plays of Arnold Wesker (q.v.) (including *Roots*) after these had been rejected by London managements.

BAIRD, DOROTHEA (1875–1933), English actress, who in 1896 married the elder son of Henry Irving (q.v.). She made her first appearance on the stage with the Oxford University Dramatic Society as Iris in *The Tempest*, and was then in the company of Ben Greet (q.v.), playing numerous Shakespearian roles. Her first appearance in London in 1895 was as Hippolyta in *A Midsummer Night's Dream*, but she first came into prominence with her performance as the heroine of du Maurier's *Trilby* (1896), playing opposite Tree (q.v.) as Svengali. She was for some years at the Lyceum with Irving, and also accompanied her husband on tours of the United States (1906) and Australia (1911). She retired in 1913.

BAKER, BENJAMIN A. (1818–90), a well-loved figure in the American theatre, familiarly known as 'Uncle Ben Baker'. He made his first appearance in New York in 1839, and had already written a number of plays, mainly burlettas, when on 15

Feb. 1848 he produced, for his own benefit night, *A Glance at New York in 1848*, in which the actor Frank Chanfrau (q.v.) made a great success as the hero Mose, a New York volunteer fireman. Other 'Mose' plays followed, including *Three Years After* (1849) and *Mose in China* (1850), and soon had many imitators all over the country, their success giving rise to a type of play verging on melodrama, with strong action set against a background of local conditions.

BAKER, GEORGE PIERCE (1866–1935), one of the most vital influences in the formation of modern American dramatic literature and theatre, and the first Professor of Dramatic Literature at Harvard (q.v.), where he was educated and where, in 1905, he instituted a course in practical playwriting. This in turn led to the foundation of his famous '47 Workshop' for the staging of plays written under his tuition. Among the playwrights who attended his special courses were Edward Sheldon, Eugene O'Neill, Sidney Howard, and George Abbott (qq.v.). In 1925, by which time he had had the pleasure of seeing his pioneer work bear fruit in many other centres of learning, often under his own old pupils, Baker left Harvard for Yale (q.v.), remaining there as Director of the graduate Department of Drama until his retirement in 1933. Combining in a rare degree the attributes of the scholar and the practical man of the theatre, he had an immense influence not only in his own country but throughout Europe, and to the end of his life was unremitting in his industry, accuracy, and perseverance on behalf of his students.

BAKER, HENRIETTA (1837–1909), see CHANFRAU, FRANK.

BAKER, SARAH (1736/7–1816), English theatre proprietor, whose activities in Kent covered a period of more than fifty years. The daughter of a touring actress, she married an actor in her mother's company in about 1761, and was widowed in 1769. Left with three small children to support, she went into management on her own account, and from 1772 to 1777 managed her mother's company. The latter having retired, Mrs. Baker formed a new company which regularly visited Canterbury, Rochester, Faversham, Maidstone, and Tunbridge Wells, with occasional forays to Deal, Folkestone, Sandwich, Sittingbourne, and Lewes. At first a portable theatre or any suitable building was used by the company, but from about 1789 onwards Mrs. Baker built her own theatres—ten in all. Among the actors who appeared with her early in their careers was Edmund Kean (q.v.) (see also DOWTON).

BAKST, LÉON (1866–1924), see COSTUME.

BALIEFF, NIKITA (1877–1936), deviser and compère of a Russian cabaret entertainment, La Chauve-Souris, seen in Paris soon after the First World War. It was brought to London in 1921 by Charles B. Cochran (q.v.), and after a slow start became part of the London theatrical scene. In New York its success was instant and unflagging. In both places Balieff, a big burly man with a vast genial moon-face, who must have weighed at least sixteen stone and who eked out his slender store of English with most expressive shrugs and gestures, gained immense personal popularity. His 'turns', costumed and set with a richness reminiscent of the Russian ballet, consisted of short burlesques, and small, often mimed, sketches based on old ballads, folk-songs, prints, engravings, the woodenness of a toy soldier, or the delicacy of a china shepherdess, rendered amusing by very slight and subtle guying of the material.

Ballad Opera, the name given in England to a play of a popular and often topical character, with spoken dialogue and a large number of songs set to existing tunes. The most famous example is *The Beggar's Opera* (1728), by John Gay (q.v.), but excellent ballad operas were written by Henry Fielding (q.v.) and CHARLES COFFEY (?–1745), whose *The Devil to Pay* (1731) (see JEVON), translated into German as *Der Teufel ist los* in 1743, started the vogue for the *Singspiel* which culminated in Mozart's 'Die Entführung aus dem Serail' (1782). The popularity of the ballad opera was revived by the success of *Love in a Village* (1762), by Isaac Bickerstaffe (q.v.), but as it had music specially composed for it by Thomas Arne (1710–78), this and such later examples as Sheridan's *The Duenna* (1775), with music by Thomas Linley (1733–95), are usually classified as comic operas.

BALLARD, SARAH (1817–92), see TERRY, BENJAMIN.

Baltimore, one of the first towns in America to accept theatrical companies, which at first appeared in adapted halls. The first theatre building opened on 15 Jan. 1782 with *Richard II* and Garrick's farce *Miss in Her Teens*. The town continued to be visited regularly by touring companies, and still retains its position as an important date for the best American and foreign companies.

BANBURY, FRITH (1912–), English actor, manager, and director, who made his first appearance on the stage in 1933, and played a wide variety of parts, both in straight plays and revues, before in 1947 he directed *Dark Summer* by Wynyard Browne, whose comedy *The Holly and the Ivy* he also directed in 1950. He has since been responsible for a number of interesting productions, including N. C. Hunter's *Waters of the Moon* (1951); Rattigan's *The Deep Blue Sea* (1952); John Whiting's *Marching Song* (1954); Goodrich and Hackett's *The Diary of Anne Frank* (1956); Bolt's *Flowering Cherry* (1957) and *The Tiger and the Horse* (1960); and *The Wings of the Dove* (1963), adapted by Christopher Taylor from the novel by Henry James. He has also directed plays in New York, and in 1969 was responsible for the production of Peter Nichols's *A Day in the Death of Joe Egg* with the Cameri Theatre in Tel-Aviv and Robin Maugham's *The Servant* in Paris.

BANCROFT, SIR SQUIRE (1841–1926), English actor-manager, who, with his wife MARIE EFFIE [*née* WILTON] (1839–1921), introduced a number of reforms on the British stage and started the vogue for drawing-room comedy and drama in the place of melodrama. Marie Wilton, the daughter of provincial actors, was on the stage from early childhood. She first appeared in London in 1856, where on 15 Sept. she made a great success as Perdita in Brough's extravaganza on *The Winter's Tale*. She continued to play in burlesque, notably at the Strand in H. K. Byron's plays, until she decided to go into management on her own account. On a borrowed capital of £1,000, of which little remained when the curtain went up, she opened an old and dilapidated theatre, nicknamed the 'Dust Hole' (see SCALA THEATRE). Renamed the Prince of Wales's, charmingly decorated, and excellently run, it opened on 15 Apr. 1865. In the company was Squire Bancroft, who had made his first appearance on the stage in the provinces in 1861, and had played with Marie Wilton in Liverpool. The new venture was a success—the despised 'Dust Hole' became one of the most popular theatres in London, and there the Bancrofts (who had married in 1867) presented and played in the plays of Tom Robertson (q.v.). The Bancrofts did much to raise the economic status of actors, paying higher salaries than elsewhere and providing the actresses' wardrobes. Among other innovations, they adopted Mme Vestris's idea of practicable scenery (see BOX-SET). In 1880 they moved to the Haymarket and continued their successful career, retiring in 1885. There can be no doubt that they had a great and salutary influence upon the English stage. Happily married and of congenial temperaments, they commanded the highest respect from their staff and audiences, and the knighthood conferred upon Bancroft in 1897 was a recognition of the services of both to their profession.

Bandbox Theatre, NEW YORK, at 205 East 57th Street. This opened on 23 Nov. 1912, and closed on 28 Apr. 1917, a cinema being built on the site. It was there that the Washington Square Players (q.v.) first appeared in New York in a series of one-act plays.

BANKHEAD, TALLULAH BROCKMAN (1903–68), American actress, equally well known in London, who made her first appearance in New York in 1918, and in 1923 was seen in London as Maxine in Hubert Parsons's *The Dancers*, playing opposite Gerald du Maurier (q.v.). She then played the title role in Knoblock's *Conchita* (1924), and in 1925 achieved a great success as Julia Sterroll in Noël Coward's *Fallen Angels*. She remained in London until 1930, when she was seen in the younger Dumas's *The Lady of the Camellias*, and three years later returned to New York, having in the meantime appeared in a number of films. Among her outstanding parts in the 1930s were Sadie Thompson in Maugham's *Rain* (1935), Regina Giddens in Lillian Hellman's *The Little Foxes* (1939), and, her first classical part, Shakespeare's Cleopatra in 1937. In 1940 she toured in a revival of Pinero's *The Second Mrs. Tanqueray*. She subsequently created the part of Sabina in Wilder's *The Skin of*

Our Teeth (1942), played the Queen in the first American production of Cocteau's *The Eagle Has Two Heads* (1947), and appeared as Blanche du Bois in Tennessee Williams's *A Streetcar Named Desire* (1956) and as Mrs. Goforth in his *The Milk Train Doesn't Stop Here Anymore* (1964). In 1952 she published her autobiography, *Tallulah Bankhead*.

BANKS, JOHN (*c.* 1650–1706), English dramatist, author of eight tragedies, of which the best is probably *Virtue Betrayed; or, Anna Bullen* (1682). Banks, of whose life very little is known, shows traces of pathos and intimate tragedy which mark him as a precursor of Nicholas Rowe (q.v.).

BANKS, LESLIE J. (1890–1952), English actor, who made his first appearance in the provinces in 1911, and in London at the Vaudeville Theatre in 1914. After serving in the army during the First World War, he joined the Birmingham Repertory company, and returned to the West End in 1921, where he soon established a solid reputation as a player of power and restraint in a long series of successful productions. Among his best parts were Petruchio in *The Taming of the Shrew* (1937), with Edith Evans (q.v.) as Katherina, the schoolmaster in James Hilton's *Goodbye, Mr. Chips* (1938), and the Duke in Patrick Hamilton's *The Duke in Darkness* (1942). He appeared many times in New York, notably as Captain Hook in Barrie's *Peter Pan* in 1924 and as Henry in Benn Levy's farce, *Springtime for Henry*, in 1931. In 1950 he was appointed C.B.E. for services to the stage.

Bankside Players, see ATKINS, ROBERT.

BANNISTER, JOHN (1760–1836), English actor, son of the comedian CHARLES BANNISTER (1741–1804), whose modest reputation was made mainly at the Haymarket with Foote (q.v.). John made his first appearance, also at the Haymarket, in 1778, and was then engaged for Drury Lane. Overshadowed by John Philip Kemble (q.v.) in tragedy, it was in comedy that he found his true bent. He was the first to play Don Ferolo Whiskerandos in Sheridan's *The Critic* (1779), and was also good in such parts as Sir Anthony Absolute in Sheridan's *The Rivals*, Tony Lumpkin in Goldsmith's *She Stoops to Conquer*, Scrub in Farquhar's *The Beaux'*

Stratagem, and Doctor Pangloss in Colman's *The Heir-at-Law*. In 1783 he married ELIZABETH HARPER (1757–1849), principal singer at the Haymarket, who retired in 1793, Bannister himself remaining on the stage until 1815.

Banvard's Museum, NEW YORK, see DALY'S THEATRE (1).

BARBIERI, NICCOLÒ (?–*c.* 1640), an actor of the *commedia dell'arte* (q.v.), who came from Milan and played Beltrame, a character somewhat akin to Scapino (q.v.). He is first found with the Gelosi in Paris in 1600–4, and then joined the Fedeli. He later had a company of his own. One of his plays, *L'Incanto, ovvero L'Inavvertito* (1629), was used by Molière (q.v.) for *L'Étourdi* (1655). Barbieri was the author of a volume of memoirs which throw much light on the working of the *commedia dell'arte* and of a history of the stage in his time, *La Supplica*, published in 1634.

BARD, WILKIE [really BILLIE SMITH] (1870–1944), a music-hall star who first appeared in Manchester in 1893, singing coster songs. He then went to London, appearing at Collins's in impersonations featuring the high, domed forehead, modelled on Shakespeare's (whence his stage name of 'Bard'), fringed with sparse hair, and two black spots over the eyebrows, which were thereafter inseparably associated with him. He appeared in pantomime, playing Pantaloon in the harlequinade and, with Will Evans (q.v.), reviving much of its old spirit. As Idle Jack in *Dick Whittington* at Drury Lane in 1908 he started the vogue for tongue-twister songs with his 'She Sells Sea-Shells on the Sea-Shore'.

Barker, a character of the fairground or itinerant theatre company, whose job it was to stand at the door of the booth and by his vociferous and spellbinding patter to induce the audience to enter. He is probably as old as the theatre itself, and was known to the ancient world. He achieved notoriety in sixteenth-century France and in the later fairs and showgrounds of Europe.

BARKER, HARLEY GRANVILLE- (1877–1946), English author, actor, and director, one of the outstanding figures of the progressive theatre at the beginning of the twentieth century. In 1891, he joined the stock company at Margate, and then toured with Waller, Ben Greet, and Mrs. Patrick Campbell (qq.v.), later appearing in such widely diverse productions as Weyman's *Under the Red Robe* with Tree (q.v.) at the Haymarket, and *Richard II* and *Edward II* directed by William Poel (q.v.) for the Elizabethan Stage Society. In 1900 Shaw chose him to play Marchbanks in the Stage Society's production of *Candida*. He continued to act for the Stage Society for several years, appearing in a number of plays by Shaw with his first wife, Lillah McCarthy (q.v.). In 1904 his partnership with J. E. Vedrenne (q.v.) at the Court Theatre made theatrical history. The repertory there included Euripides, Galsworthy, Hankin, Hauptmann, Ibsen, Maeterlinck, Schnitzler, and Shaw (qq.v.) as well as Barker's own play, *The Voysey Inheritance* (1905). It was his experiences at the Court, which were artistically rather than financially rewarding, that led Barker to espouse the cause of a subsidized theatre, which he championed in his book, *A National Theatre: Scheme and Estimates* (1908), written in collaboration with William Archer (q.v.). Barker's approach to the problems of producing Shakespeare was largely conditioned by his association with Poel, and his productions at the Savoy in 1913–14 of *The Winter's Tale*, *Twelfth Night*, and *A Midsummer Night's Dream* were later considered epochmaking in their simplicity and poetic impact. As well as several plays written in collaboration, Barker was the author of *The Marrying of Ann Leete* (1902), *Waste*, which was presented privately by the Stage Society in 1907 but fell foul of the censor and was not publicly performed until 1936, and *The Madras House* (1910). He also made a stage version of Thomas Hardy's *The Dynasts* (1914). He was at the height of his stage career in England when a visit to America directed his activities into fresh channels. Divorced from Lillah McCarthy, he married an American, hyphenated his name, and emerged as the translator (with his second wife) of the plays of Martínez Sierra and the Quintero brothers (qq.v.) and as a serious Shakespeare scholar, publishing between 1927 and 1947 the *Prefaces to Shakespeare* (in five volumes) on which his later fame chiefly rests.

BARKER, JAMES NELSON (1784–1858), American dramatist, author of the first American play on an Indian theme, which was also the first play from America to be performed in England. This was *The Indian Princess*, given in Philadelphia in 1808, and, as *Pocahontas; or, the Indian Princess*, at Drury Lane in 1820. Of Barker's other plays, only three have survived: *Tears and Smiles*, a comedy of manners played in Philadelphia in 1807; a dramatization of Scott's *Marmion*, which held the stage for many years, being last revived in 1848; and *Superstition* (1824), the story of a Puritan refugee from England who leads his village against the Indians, mingled with a tale of intolerance and persecution of witchcraft.

BARLACH, ERNST (1870–1938), see EXPRESSIONISM.

BARNES, CHARLOTTE MARY SANFORD (1818–63), American actress and dramatist, the daughter of JOHN BARNES (1761–1841), who went with his wife MARY from Drury Lane to the Park Theatre, New York. They were both popular players for many years, the husband as a low comedian, the wife in such parts as Rowe's Jane Shore and Isabella in Southerne's *The Fatal Marriage*. Charlotte first appeared on the stage at the age of four in Mark Lewis's *The Castle Spectre*, and in 1834 made her adult début at the Tremont, Boston, in the same play. In 1842 she appeared in London, playing, among other parts, Hamlet, in which she was well received. Four years later she married an actor-manager named Edmond S. Connor, and became his leading lady, being associated with him in the management of the Arch Street Theatre, Philadelphia. Her first play, *Octavia Bragaldi*, written at the age of eighteen, was produced at the National Theatre, New York, with herself in the leading part. Of her other plays, the only one to survive was *The Forest Princess* (1844), one of the many dramatizations of the story of Pocahontas.

BARNES, SIR KENNETH (1878–1957), see VANBRUGH, VIOLET.

BARNES, THOMAS (1785–1841), English editor and critic, educated at Christ's Hospital, editor of *The Times* from 1817 till his death. His love of the theatre is manifest in his early work in the *Examiner* under the name of 'Criticus'. In the same journal, while Leigh Hunt (q.v.) was in prison, he described the famous first appearance of Edmund Kean (q.v.) in *The Merchant of Venice* at Drury Lane on 26 Jan. 1814. His account of this, though much less well known, bears comparison with that of Hazlitt (q.v.).

Barnstormers, a name given in the late nineteenth century to the early itinerant companies whose stages were often set up in large barns, and whose work was characterized by ranting and shouting and general violence in speech and gesture.

BARNUM, PHINEAS TAYLOR (1810–91), a great American showman, who for fifty years provided the world with entertainment, constantly gulling the public yet always finding them ready to be gulled again. His first great enterprise was the American Museum (q.v.), known also as Barnum's, which opened in 1842 and was burnt down in 1865 and 1868. Tom Thumb, Jenny Lind, freaks, giants, and curiosities of natural history were exhibited there impartially, and during most of its history it housed plays as well. In 1871 Barnum started his immense circus—'The Greatest Show on Earth'—which for twenty years began its spring season at Madison Square Garden.

BARON, MICHEL (1653–1729), French actor, son and grandson of strolling players. His father, ANDRÉ BARON [originally BOYRON] (c. 1601–55), was with Montdory at the Marais and later at the Hôtel de Bourgogne (q.v.), and is said to have died of a wound in the foot self-inflicted during a spirited performance as Don Diègue in Corneille's *Le Cid*. André's wife, JEANNE AUSOULT (1625–62), was much admired in breeches parts. Her early death during the run of Mlle Desjardin's *Manlius* was much regretted by Corneille (q.v.), who said he had written a part for her in his next play, probably *Sophonisbe*. Michel, orphaned before he was ten, was acting with the juvenile Troupe du Dauphin when Molière (q.v.) saw him and took him into his own company, giving him small parts to play. Unfortunately Molière's wife took a dislike to the boy, and on one occasion slapped his face, whereupon he ran away and rejoined his former companions. He remained with them until 1670, when Molière asked him to return and play Domitian in Corneille's *Tite et Bérénice*. On Molière's death in 1673 Baron went to the Hôtel de Bourgogne, and later

became the chief actor of the newly formed Comédie-Française (q.v.). He did a great deal to raise the status of actors in his day, and helped many a struggling dramatist by his fine rendering of a poor part. He was himself the author of several comedies, of which the best is *L'Homme à bonne fortune* (1686). He retired in 1691, at the height of his powers, but returned to the stage in 1720. He was taken ill during a revival of Rotrou's *Venceslas*, and died shortly afterwards. He was the last actor who had known Molière to appear at the Comédie-Française. His son ÉTIENNE (1676–1711) was on the stage as a child, made his adult début in 1694, and died young as the result of dissipation.

BARRAULT, JEAN-LOUIS (1910–), French actor and director, who made his first appearance on the stage on his twenty-first birthday, as one of the servants in Jules Romains's translation of Jonson's *Volpone*. He then began the study of mime, which was to be so important in his career, and his first independent production was a mime-play based on Faulkner's novel, *As I Lay Dying*. During the German occupation of Paris in 1940 he was engaged by Copeau for the Comédie-Française, making his début in Corneille's *Le Cid*. In 1946 he and his wife, Madeleine Renaud (q.v.), who was already an established star at the Comédie-Française when he joined it, left to found their own company. Its opening production, at the Théâtre Marigny, was *Hamlet*, on 17 Oct. 1946, in a translation by André Gide. The company remained at the Marigny until 1956, appearing in a mixed repertory of classic and modern works, among them the plays of Claudel (q.v.)—*Partage de midi*, *L'Échange*, *Christophe Colomb*, and *Tête-d'or*—which have occasioned some of Barrault's finest work. The inclusion of some of Marivaux's plays in the company's repertory can be attributed partly to the outstanding acting of Madeleine Renaud in this author's works. On the lighter side the company revived several farces by Feydeau (q.v.), and gave the first performance of such modern plays as Ionesco's *Rhinocéros* (1960). In 1956 Barrault left the Marigny for the Théâtre Sarah-Bernhardt, and later occupied the Palais-Royal. In 1959 he was appointed director of the Odéon (one of the two national theatres, renamed Théâtre de France), but was summarily dismissed in 1968, after the theatre had been occupied by student demonstrators. He then launched out once more on his own with a dramatization of Rabelais, acted in the round on a cruciform stage in an all-in wrestling arena in Montmartre, and subsequently on tour, visiting the National Theatre at the Old Vic in Sept. 1969.

Barrel System, a method of moving scenery (see DRUM-AND-SHAFT).

BARRETT, GEORGE HORTON (1794–1860), American actor, familiarly known from his elegant appearance and gracious manners as 'Gentleman George'. He was the son of an English actor who went to New York in 1796, and of his wife, who as Mrs. Rivers had previously been well known in London. He appeared on the stage at the Park Theatre (q.v.) as a child, playing with his parents in Benjamin Thompson's *The Stranger* and Home's *Douglas*. As an adult actor, he was one of the best light comedians of his day, his finest parts being in Sheridan's plays—Young Absolute in *The Rivals*, Charles Surface in *The School for Scandal*, and Puff in *The Critic*. He was also much admired as Sir Andrew Aguecheek in *Twelfth Night*. He made his last appearance on the stage in 1855.

BARRETT, LAWRENCE (1838–91), American actor and director, who, as a boy actor, travelled the United States with many outstanding companies, including that of Julia Dean (q.v.). In 1857 he was seen in New York in Sheridan Knowles's *The Hunchback* and other plays, and in 1858 he was a member of the Boston Museum company. He frequently played Cassius in *Julius Caesar*, the part in which he is best remembered, to the Brutus of Edwin Booth (q.v.), and in 1871 was manager of Booth's Theatre in New York. While Irving (q.v.) was in America in 1884, Barrett took over the Lyceum in London, and though his visit was not a success financially, he was made welcome and fêted on all sides. Tall, with classic features, and dark, deeply sunken eyes, he was probably at his best in Shakespeare, to whose interpretation he brought dignity, a dominant personality, and intellectual powers somewhat exceptional in an actor at that date.

BARRETT, WILSON (1846–1904), English actor-manager, who had few equals in the melodramatic plays fashionable in his time. His finest parts were Wilfred Denver in Jones and Herman's *The Silver King*, which he produced in 1882 during his tenancy of the Princess's, and Marcus Superbus in his own play, *The Sign of the Cross*. This was first produced at the Grand Opera House, St. Louis, on 28 Mar. 1895, during one of Barrett's American tours. It netted him a fortune, and was equally successful when produced in New York the following May, and in England, first at the Grand, Leeds (which Barrett himself built), in 1895, and then in 1896 at the Lyric Theatre, London. It was also perennially successful on tour. Barrett's brother and nephew were in his company, and his grandson was also on the stage, playing in the Brandon-Thomas companies and establishing repertory theatres in Glasgow and Edinburgh.

BARRIE, SIR JAMES MATTHEW (1860–1937), Scottish novelist and dramatist, whose whimsical children's play, *Peter Pan*, based on one of his own novels, has become a feature of the London theatrical scene at Christmas. It was first produced in 1904, with Nina Boucicault (q.v.) as Peter, a part subsequently played by a long list of distinguished young actresses. Barrie's early plays were unsuccessful, and he first came into prominence with a comedy, *Walker, London* (1892), in which Toole (q.v.) played the lead. The success of *The Professor's Love Story* (1894) and *The Little Minister* (1897) established him as an outstanding playwright, and he consolidated his position with the romantic costume play *Quality Street* (1902) and the social comedies *The Admirable Crichton* (also 1902) and *What Every Woman Knows* (1908). The mixture of fantasy and sentimentality which runs through much of Barrie's work was uppermost in *Dear Brutus* (1917) and *Mary Rose* (1920), both of which invoke supernatural elements in a realistic setting. Among his shorter plays, the one-act *The Old Lady Shows her Medals* (1917) and *Shall We Join the Ladies* (1922), the latter intended as the first act of a full-length murder mystery, have been popular with amateur companies. His last play, on a biblical theme, *The Boy David* (1936), was specially written for the German actress Elisabeth Bergner. It was not a success, and he is more likely to be remembered for his earlier works, especially *The Admirable*

Crichton, whose title has passed into everyday speech to describe a man of all-round excellence, and for *Peter Pan*. A life of Barrie, by Janet Dunbar, was published in 1970.

BARRY, ELIZABETH (1658–1713), the first really outstanding English actress, who excelled in tragedy, and played opposite Betterton (q.v.) for many years. She is credited with the creation of over a hundred roles, including Monimia in *The Orphan* (1680) and Belvidera in *Venice Preserv'd* (1682), both by Otway (q.v.), and Zara in Congreve's only tragedy, *The Mourning Bride* (1697). She made her first appearance on the stage in 1673 in a revival of Orrery's *Mustapha* and retired in 1710.

BARRY, PHILIP (1896–1949), American dramatist, author of a number of plays, of which *Here Come the Clowns* (1938), a mystifying but provocative allegory of good and evil, was much acclaimed at the time of its first production, but has since been forgotten in favour of his light sophisticated comedies—*Holiday* (1928), which deals with the revolt of youth against parental snobbery; *The Animal Kingdom* (1932), which reverses the roles of wife and mistress by making the latter the loyal companion and therefore the true wife; and *The Philadelphia Story* (1939), a deft comedy of manners and character which retains its appeal. Barry left unfinished a comedy, *Second Threshold*, which was completed by his friend Robert Sherwood (q.v.) and presented in New York, with some success, in 1951.

BARRY, SPRANGER (1719–77), Irish actor, first seen on the stage in Dublin in 1744. In 1746 he was at Drury Lane, where he appeared as Othello to the Iago of Macklin (q.v.). When Garrick (q.v.) took over in 1747 he remained in the company, playing leading roles, and arousing much interest when he alternated with Garrick in such parts as Jaffier and Pierre in *Venice Preserv'd*, Chamont and Castalio in *The Orphan* (both by Otway), Hastings and Dumont in *Jane Shore*, and Lothario and Horatio in *The Fair Penitent* (both by Rowe). In 1750 Barry went to Covent Garden and set himself up as a rival to Garrick, not always successfully. Later, having ruined himself by the speculative building of a theatre in Dublin (q.v.), he returned to Drury Lane.

Shortly afterwards his wife died and he married ANN DANCER [*née* STREET] (1734–1801), an actress who excelled in high comedy. After the death of Barry, who was buried in Westminster Abbey, she married a fellow-actor and retired in 1798.

BARRYMORE, ETHEL (1879–1959), one of the leading actresses of the American stage, granddaughter of Mrs. John Drew (q.v.) and sister of John and Lionel Barrymore (qq.v.). She made her first appearance in New York in 1894, and in 1898 was in London, where she appeared with Henry Irving (q.v.) in his son Laurence's *Peter the Great* and in Lewis's *The Bells*, on tour. Returning to New York, she scored her first outstanding success as Madame Trentoni in Clyde Fitch's *Captain Jinks of the Horse Marines* (1901). In 1911 she played Rose in Pinero's *Trelawny of the 'Wells'*, but she was also successful in more serious parts, such as Nora in Ibsen's *A Doll's House* and Paula Tanqueray in Pinero's *The Second Mrs. Tanqueray*. In 1928 she opened the Ethel Barrymore Theatre (q.v.) in New York with Martínez Sierra's *The Kingdom of God*, in which she played Sister Gracia. In New York she was considered outstanding in two English parts—as Gran in Mazo de la Roche's *Whiteoaks* (1938) and as Miss Moffat in Emlyn Williams's *The Corn is Green*, which ran for four years. She also played in vaudeville in Barrie's *The Twelve-Pound Look* and did much film work. In 1909 she married Russell Griswold Colt, and had three children who were all on the stage.

BARRYMORE, JOHN (1882–1942), an outstanding but very uneven American actor, grandson of Mrs. John Drew (q.v.), brother of Ethel and Lionel Barrymore (qq.v.), who became a popular matinée idol and a good light comedian, but in 1916 proved himself a serious actor also by his performance as Falder in Galsworthy's *Justice*. On 16 Nov. 1922 he electrified New York by his Hamlet at the Sam H. Harris Theatre, with Blanche Yurka (q.v.) as Gertrude and settings designed by Robert Edmond Jones (q.v.). This success was repeated in London in 1925 at the Haymarket Theatre, with Constance Collier (q.v.) as Gertrude and Fay Compton (q.v.) as Ophelia. Barrymore gave a fine, meticulous, and scholarly reading of the part, and hopes for his future ran high, but he failed to fulfil his promise and his last years, during which he appeared mainly in films and on the radio, were feverish and unhappy. His daughter by his second marriage, DIANA (1921–60), was also on the stage.

BARRYMORE, LIONEL (1878–1954), American actor, brother of Ethel and John Barrymore (qq.v.) and grandson of Mrs. John Drew (q.v.), under whom he made his first appearance on the stage. After achieving some success, notably in Isaac Henderson's *The Mummy and the Humming Bird* (1902) and the title-role of Barrie's *Pantaloon* (1905), he went to Paris with his first wife DORIS RANKIN (1880–1946) to study art. Returning to the United States in 1909, he reappeared on the stage in Conan Doyle's *The Fires of Fate*, and soon became one of New York's leading actors, being particularly admired in dramatizations of du Maurier's *Peter Ibbetson* (1917) and in Augustus Thomas's *The Copperhead* (1918). He had already appeared in a number of early films, and after about 1925 gave up the theatre in favour of the cinema, where he had a long and distinguished career. In 1951 he published an autobiography, *We Barrymores*.

BARRYMORE, MAURICE [really HERBERT BLYTHE] (1847–1905), English actor, who took his stage name from an old playbill hanging in the Haymarket Theatre in London. He made his first appearance on the stage in 1875, and then went to New York, where he played opposite many leading actresses, including Modjeska (q.v.), for whom he wrote *Nadjezda* (1886). He married in 1876 GEORGIANA DREW (1856–93), actress daughter of Mrs. John Drew (q.v.), under whom she first appeared on the stage at the age of sixteen. After her marriage she appeared with her husband in a number of plays, but her career was much hampered by illness and she died young. Her three children, Lionel, Ethel, and John (qq.v.), were all on the stage.

BARRYMORE, RICHARD BARRY, EARL OF (1769–93), English nobleman, and a great amateur of the theatre, who maintained a private theatre in his house at Wargrave, Berkshire, and another in Savile Row, London, where he engaged professional stars to play with himself and his friends.

BARRYMORE, WILLIAM (1758–1830), not related to any of the above, was an actor-manager who in 1818 opened the Old Vic Theatre (q.v.) as the Royal Coburg with one of his own productions. He was the author of several plays, as was his younger unrelated namesake, WILLIAM (?–1845), a 'sound, useful actor' who, with his wife, appeared both in London and in New York.

Bartholomew Fair, see FAIRS.

BARTON, JOHN (1928–), theatre director, who has been connected with the Royal Shakespeare Company (q.v.) since leaving Cambridge in 1960, where from 1954 he had been a Fellow of King's, directing a number of plays for the Marlowe Society and the A.D.C. His first production at Stratford was *The Taming of the Shrew*, and he has since directed, both in Stratford and London, a number of plays for the Royal Shakespeare Company, of which he became associate director in 1964. But his main work has been done in the adapting of Shakespeare's *Henry VI* and *Richard III* as *The Wars of the Roses* (1963), and in devising the recitals *The Hollow Crown* (1961) and *The Art of Seduction* and *The Vagaries of Love* (both 1962), in all of which he took part himself. In 1969 he prepared for Theatregoround, which is concerned with the Royal Shakespeare Company's work for schools and young people, a shortened version of *Henry IV*, as *When Thou Art King*, which concentrates on the relationship between Prince Hal and Falstaff. He also made a shortened version of *Henry V* as *The Battle of Agincourt*, and in 1970 added to it two more scenes from the history cycle, calling them *The Battle of Shrewsbury* and *The Rejection of Falstaff*.

BASSERMANN, ALBERT (1867–1952), German actor, nephew of August Bassermann (q.v.), who made his first appearance at Mannheim at the age of nineteen under his uncle's management, and was for a time with the Meininger company (q.v.). Under Otto Brahm (q.v.), whom he joined in 1899, he became the outstanding interpreter of Ibsen in Germany. The rise to power of the Nazi party sent him into exile, and in 1944 he appeared on Broadway in his first English-speaking part, playing the Pope in *Embezzled Heaven*, based on a novel by Werfel. He died in

Zürich, having returned to Europe in 1945.

BASSERMANN, AUGUST (1848–1931), German actor, who made his début at Dresden in 1873 and later appeared at the Vienna Stadttheater in such parts as the title role in Pizarro's *Rolla* and Karl Moor in Schiller's *Die Räuber*. In 1886 he was manager of the Mannheim Theatre, where his nephew, Albert Bassermann (q.v.), made his first appearance on the stage under his direction, and from 1904 until his death he was director of a theatre at Karlsrühe. He went to New York several times, and played in the German Theatre there, being much admired in classic and heroic parts, but was never seen in London.

BATEMAN, HEZEKIAH LINTHICUM (1812–75), American impresario, who by his wife, SIDNEY FRANCES COWELL (1823–81), daughter of the English actor Joseph Cowell (q.v.), had four daughters, all on the stage from early childhood, touring the United States and the English provinces with their parents, and later becoming well known as adult actresses in London. In 1871 Bateman leased the Lyceum Theatre in London and engaged Henry Irving (q.v.) as his leading man, allowing him, after some initial disappointments, to put on *The Bells*, which was an immediate success. After her husband's death Mrs. Bateman continued to run the Lyceum until Irving took over in 1878. She then went to Sadler's Wells with her youngest daughter, ISABEL EMILIE (1854–1934), who in 1898 left the stage to join the Anglican Community of St. Mary the Virgin at Wantage in Berkshire, of which she later became Reverend Mother General. Of her elder sisters, ELLEN DOUGLAS (1844–1936) retired from the theatre on marriage, and VIRGINIA FRANCES (1853–1940) married the actor Edward Compton (q.v.), and continued her career. The eldest girl, KATE JOSEPHINE (1842–1917), played opposite Irving at the Lyceum, but retired in 1892 and under her married name, as Mrs. George Crowe, ran a school of acting in London.

BATES, ALAN ARTHUR (1934–), English actor, who made his first appearance in London in 1956, and later the same year attracted favourable notice as Cliff Lewis in Osborne's *Look Back in Anger*, in which he also appeared in New York the following year. He then played Edmund Tyrone in O'Neill's *Long Day's Journey into Night* (1958) at Edinburgh and in London. It was, however, as Mick in Pinter's *The Caretaker* (1960) that he made his first outstanding success, both in London and in New York, where in 1964 he appeared as Richard Ford in *Poor Richard*, by Jean Kerr, a part originally intended for Richard Burton (q.v.). He also appeared as Richard III at the Stratford, Ontario, Theatre in 1967. In 1969 he was back in London, appearing in David Storey's *In Celebration*, and in 1970 was seen as Hamlet at the Nottingham Playhouse in a production which later went to London. He has also had an outstanding career in films and television.

BATES, BLANCHE (1873–1941), American actress, whose parents were both in the theatre. She first appeared on tour in California, from 1894 to 1898, and then made a brief appearance in New York under the management of Augustin Daly. It was, however, as the leading lady in plays by Belasco—*Madame Butterfly* (1900), *The Darling of the Gods* (1902), and *The Girl of the Golden West* (1905)—that she made her reputation. She was also much admired as Cigarette in a dramatization of Ouida's *Under Two Flags* (1901). After leaving Belasco she continued to act, under her own and other managements, but less successfully, until her retirement in 1927.

Bath. The first theatre in Bath was built in 1705. On the passing of the Licensing Act in 1737 it was demolished, and the company moved to a room under Lady Hawley's Assembly Rooms. In 1750 a second theatre was erected in Orchard Street, the shell of which still exists. The two theatres were rivals until 1756, when the companies amalgamated under John Palmer. The Orchard Street Theatre was reconstructed in 1767, and again in 1774–5, a royal patent being obtained in 1768. Mrs. Siddons (q.v.) was a member of the stock company from 1778 to 1782. In 1805 a new theatre in Beaufort Square was erected by Palmer, the city architect, in conjunction with George Dance. In 1817 a long connection with the Bristol theatre was broken, and from 1822 a decline set in. In 1862 Palmer's building was destroyed by fire and a new theatre opened on the same site, which since 1884 has been used by touring companies.

Batten, a length of timber used to stiffen a surface of canvas or boards, as by 'sandwich-battening' a cloth (i.e. fixing the upper and lower edges between pairs of 3″ × 1″ or 4″ × 1″ battens screwed together), or by 'battening-out' a section of boards, or a run of flats, with crossbars. A Light Batten is a row of lights fixed rigidly together. In America this is known as a Strip Light or Border Light.

Batty's Amphitheatre, LONDON, see ASTLEY'S AMPHITHEATRE.

BATY, GASTON (1885–1952), French director, who in 1930 opened the Théâtre Montparnasse under his own name. Here he put on an imposing series of old and new plays, many of them foreign classics, and several dramatizations of novels, of which the best was based on Dostoievsky's *Crime and Punishment*. His own play, *Dulcinée* (1938), was based on an episode from *Don Quixote*. Baty was sometimes accused of subordinating the text of the play to the décor, which led him to substitute pictorial groupings for action, but this resulted in some fine work, most noticeable in his productions of such plays as Gantillon's *Maya*, Lenormand's *Simoun*, and J.-J. Bernard's *Martine*. In 1936 Baty was appointed one of the directors of the Comédie-Française, where his undoubted erudition and impeccable theatrical technique helped to reanimate the classical repertory.

BÄUERLE, ADOLF (1786–1859), Austrian dramatist and the creator, in his *Die Bürger in Wien* (1813), of the comic character Staberl, played by Ignaz Schuster. At first specifically Viennese in his humour, Staberl became the leading character of four more plays by Bäuerle, and was then by the genius of Karl Carl (q.v.) transmuted into a figure acceptable all over Germany. Bäuerle, who wrote about eighty plays, was also a successful provider of Viennese *Zauberstücke*, or 'magical fantasy plays' of which his *Aline, oder Wien in einem anderen Weltteile* (1822) is typical.

BAX, CLIFFORD (1886–1962), English author and playwright, who in 1922, following the success of Playfair's revival at the Lyric, Hammersmith, of Gay's *The Beggar's Opera*, prepared for the same management an adaptation of its sequel, *Polly*. He also translated Čapek's *The Insect Play* (1923), and several plays by Goldoni. His own historical play, *The Rose Without a Thorn* (1932), on Catherine Howard, fifth wife of Henry VIII, is frequently revived by amateur societies. He was one of the founders of the Phoenix Society (q.v.), which did excellent work in the 1920s in reviving masterpieces of Elizabethan and Restoration drama.

BAYLIS, LILIAN MARY (1874–1937), English musician and manageress, and one of the outstanding women of the English theatre. She was appointed Companion of Honour in 1929 and was the second woman outside the university to be given an Hon. M.A. at Oxford (in 1924). In 1895 she gave up a musical career in South Africa (where she had gone with her parents, both musicians) to help her aunt, Emma Cons, run the old Victoria Theatre in London as a temperance hall (see OLD VIC). In 1912, on her aunt's death, she took over the theatre and devoted the rest of her life to it. An intensely religious and single-minded woman, she brought all her forces to bear on the achievement of her object—a popular home for opera and drama. When drama, in the person of Shakespeare, threatened to oust opera, she looked about for another theatre, and took over, re-built, and opened in 1931 Sadler's Wells Theatre (q.v.), where under Ninette de Valois, whom Lilian Baylis, with her usual perspicacity in choosing her collaborators, had engaged as ballet-mistress at the Old Vic in 1928, the popularity of opera was again equalled, if not surpassed, by that of ballet. Under Lilian Baylis's management at the Old Vic all Shakespeare's plays were produced there, from *The Taming of the Shrew* in 1914 to *Troilus and Cressida* in 1923; plays by other dramatists were sometimes included in the programme, among them Ibsen's *Peer Gynt* (1922).

BAYES, NORA (1880–1928), see NORWORTH, JACK.

Bayreuth, a German town near Nuremberg, which Richard Wagner (q.v.) made a festival-centre for the performance of his operas. For this purpose a theatre, the Festspielhaus, was built by the Bayreuth architect Wölfel and the stage machinist

Karl Brandt, for whose use Wagner borrowed from King Ludwig of Bavaria the plans made by Gottfried Semper for an abandoned site at Munich. It had no galleries, and made use of the fan-shaped auditorium, first employed by the English architect Edward Shepherd in 1733, with rising rows of seats all facing the stage directly. The orchestra and the conductor were out of sight in a sunk pit, and the whole attention of the audience was thus concentrated on the stage. Most of these features were planned by Wagner himself. Alterations have been made in recent years, but the main design remains the same. The Festspielhaus opened in Aug. 1876 with a complete production, on four evenings, of 'Der Ring des Nibelungen'. Up to 1944 the six later operas and the Ring cycle were performed at varying intervals—39 festivals in 69 years. After Wagner's death in 1883, control of the festivals passed to his widow, and, from 1908 to 1930, to his son Siegfried. During this period there was a somewhat rigid adherence to the rules laid down by Wagner himself. From 1931 to 1944, Siegfried's widow, Winifred, a Yorkshirewoman, was in charge. In 1945 the U.S. army captured Bayreuth, and used the Festspielhaus for entertainments for their troops. On 29 July 1951 Wagner's grandsons, Wieland and Wolfgang, reopened the theatre for its original purpose, and there is now an annual festival which fills the theatre to capacity. There have been a number of innovations in scenery, lighting, and production, and in 1961 the score of an opera—'Tannhäuser'—was 'edited' for the first time. Also during that season the first coloured singer was heard at Bayreuth.

The Royal Opera House at Bayreuth was built by the Bibienas in 1748 and has so far escaped damage. It is a perfect example of eighteenth-century rococo theatre architecture, and occasional concerts given there display its exquisite acoustics to perfection.

BEAUMARCHAIS, PIERRE-AUGUSTIN CARON DE (1732–99), French dramatist, who wrote his first play, *Eugénie*, in 1764 after a visit to Madrid to extricate his sister from an unhappy love-affair. It had a cool reception when first produced at the Comédie-Française in 1767, but after rewriting was a moderate success, as was *Les Deux Amis* (1770). The turmoil of Beaumarchais's private life was reflected in the opposition which greeted his first great play, *Le Barbier de Séville*. Originally intended as a play with music, and later used as the basis of an opera by Rossini, it was refused by the Comédie-Italienne (q.v.), who thought its hero a caricature of their leading actor, formerly a barber. It was accepted by the Comédie-Française soon after its completion in 1772, but constantly delayed and not acted until 1775, before an audience which still felt secure from the Revolution which it presaged. Nine years later, after an even harder struggle with the censorship, *Le Mariage de Figaro* (1784)—used by Mozart for his famous opera—was finally seen by a public which was beginning to realize the dangers that lay before it, and Figaro, older and wiser, criticizes not an individual man, as in the earlier play, but society as a whole.

These two plays sum up Beaumarchais's whole life and character. He is himself the precocious page, the handsome Almaviva—he was three times married—and above all Figaro, the jack-of-all-trades. His later dramatic works are less interesting. More important was the part he played in breaking the stranglehold of the actors on their authors, and in instituting, through the Société des Auteurs, of which he was the founder, the system of payment for plays by means of a fixed percentage on takings (see ROYALTY).

BEAUMONT, SIR FRANCIS (1584–1616), English dramatist, whose name is so associated with that of Fletcher (q.v.) that they are usually spoken of in one breath, and scholars are still disentangling their separate contributions from the bulk of work that passes under their joint names. Their collaboration began in about 1610 and covered, according to some authorities, not more than six or seven plays, though in collections published in 1647 and 1679 fifty-three are assigned to them. Later investigations have attributed large parts of these to Jonson, Massinger, Middleton, Rowley, Shirley, and Tourneur (qq.v.). Beaumont, who may have been sole author of the well-known *The Knight of the Burning Pestle* (1607), which makes fun of the audiences that flocked to see the romantic historical plays popular at the time, ceased to write for the stage on his marriage in 1613, although his work was once or twice seen at Court entertainments (for further details see FLETCHER).

BEAUMONT, MURIEL (1881–1957), see DU MAURIER, SIR GERALD.

BEAUVAL [really JEAN PITEL] (c. 1635–1709), French actor, who in 1661 was in the provincial troupe of Filandre (q.v.), where he met and married in about 1665 the actress JEANNE OLIVIER DE BOURGUIGNON (c. 1648–1720). After their marriage they left Filandre to join another troupe, and from there went to Molière's company in 1670. Beauval, though a mediocre actor, was apparently good as Thomas Diafoirus in Molière's *Le Malade imaginaire* (1673), in which his wife played Toinette and his daughter, LOUISE (c. 1665–1740), the child Louison. Mme Beauval was an excellent comic actress, given to irresistible fits of laughter, a trait which Molière incorporated into her part of Nicole in his play *Le Bourgeois Gentilhomme* (1671). She also played Zerbinette in Molière's *Les Fourberies de Scapin* (also 1671). After Molière's death the Beauvals went to the Hôtel de Bourgogne, and became members of the Comédie-Française (q.v.) on its foundation in 1680, the elder Beauvals retiring in 1704. Louise, whose third husband Beaubour was also a member of the company, retired with him in 1718.

BEAZLEY, SAMUEL (1786–1851), English theatre architect, designer of the Lyceum, the St. James's, the City of London, that part of the Adelphi fronting on the Strand, and the colonnade of Drury Lane. His buildings, though plain and somewhat uninteresting, were good and well adapted for their purpose. A prolific dramatist, mainly of ephemeral farces and short comedies, Beazley was also responsible for poor translations of several operatic libretti.

BECHER, LADY, see O'NEILL, ELIZA.

BECK, HEINRICH (1760–1803), German actor, who made his first appearance at Gotha, his birthplace, in 1777, under Ekhof (q.v.). He was a friend and contemporary of Iffland (q.v.), with whom, after Ekhof's death in 1778, he went to Mannheim, where he created the part of Ferdinand in Schiller's *Kabale und Liebe* (1784), in which his wife, Karoline Ziegler, played Louise.

BECK, JULIAN (1925–85), see LIVING THEATRE.

BECKETT, SAMUEL (1906–), an Irishman resident in Paris since 1938, who has written mainly in French. In 1969 he was awarded the Nobel Prize for Literature. He was already well known as a novelist when his first play, *En attendant Godot*, was produced by Roger Blin in 1953. Two years later it was seen in London, in the author's own translation, as *Waiting for Godot*. In it Beckett abandoned conventional structure and development both in plot and language, to create a situation in which two tramps, indecisive and incapable of action, suffer and wait hopefully for help which never comes. The play is considered one of the masterpieces of the Theatre of the Absurd (q.v.). In 1957 came *Fin de partie*, which had its first performance in London on the same night as a wordless pantomime, *Acte sans paroles*. An English version of the former, as *Endgame*, was produced in London in 1958, accompanied by *Krapp's Last Tape*, a monologue originally written in English, and produced in Paris in 1960 as *La Dernière Bande. Oh! les beaux jours* (*Happy Days*), which is virtually a monologue for an actress progressively buried in the earth until only her head remains visible, had its first production in New York in 1961. In 1962 it was seen in translation in London, where it was also played in French by Madeleine Renaud in 1965. *Comédie* (*Play*), first produced in Germany in 1963, and in London and Paris in 1964, had three characters, again only heads protruding from urns, and their short dialogue was repeated *da capo*. In this, and in all his later plays, which include *Va et Vient* (1966) and *Silence* (1970), Beckett has undoubtedly moved further and further away from theatrical convention, perhaps in an effort to drive home the lesson of *Waiting for Godot*—man's lack of viable communication with other men, and his unawareness of his failure to control his destiny. This was also the theme of a performance in Paris in 1970 by Jack MacGowran, *Beginning to End*, based on all Beckett's works, not only the plays, in which the only character represents Lucky, from *Waiting for Godot*. In 1969 a Samuel Beckett Theatre, designed by Buckminster Fuller, was planned for St. Peter's College, Oxford, the building to be under one of the quadrangles. It was hoped that this would be ready to open in 1972 with a complete cycle of Beckett's plays, and would then be used for the production of subsidized experimental works in the fields of art, music, and theatre. In March 1970 a gala performance at the Oxford Playhouse in support of the scheme, which was devised by one of St. Peter's dons, Francis Warner, included five performances of Beckett's latest work, *Breath*, which lasts about 30 seconds and encompasses human life between the cry of a newborn child and the last gasp of a dying man.

BECQUE, HENRY [also **HENRI**] **FRANÇOIS** (1837–99), French dramatist, an outstanding exponent of naturalistic drama in the style of Zola (q.v.). His first important play was *Michel Pauper* (1870), which was underrated on its first production and only appreciated in a revival of 1886. Meanwhile Becque had written the two plays with which his name is usually associated, *Les Corbeaux* (1882) and *La Parisienne* (1885), both naturalistic dramas of great force and uncompromising honesty, which present rapacious or amoral characters who seem unaware of their own degradation. These *comédies rosses*, as they were called, were not wholly successful until Antoine's Théâtre Libre (q.v.) provided a stage suitable for them.

Beekman Street Theatre, NEW YORK, see CHAPEL STREET THEATRE.

BEERBOHM, SIR MAX [really **HENRY MAXIMILIAN**] (1872–1956), English author and critic, half-brother of the actor-manager Tree (q.v.). He was dramatic critic of the *Saturday Review* from 1898 to 1910. In 1908 he reviewed a production of Ibsen's *Rosmersholm* at Terry's Theatre in London in which an American actress, FLORENCE KAHN (1877–1951), played Rebecca West. She had been leading lady to Mansfield (q.v.) in America, and was already well known as an interpreter of Ibsen's heroines. She retired from the stage on her marriage to Beerbohm shortly afterwards, making a few reappearances in later years, notably as Åse in the Old Vic production of Ibsen's *Peer Gynt* in 1935. Beerbohm was the author of a one-act play, *A Social Success*, in which George Alexander (q.v.) made his first appearance on the music-halls in 1913, and also based on one of his own short stories a one-act play entitled *The Happy Hypocrite*, produced at the Royalty Theatre in 1900 by Mrs. Patrick Campbell (q.v.). A three-act version by Clemence Dane, with incidental music by Richard Addinsell, was produced at His Majesty's

in 1936, with Ivor Novello (q.v.) in the title-role.

BEESTON, CHRISTOPHER (?1570–1638), an important figure of the Jacobean and Caroline stage. He began his career as an actor with Strange's Men (q.v.), and in 1602 was with Worcester's Men at the Rose Theatre, remaining with them when they became Queen Anne's Men (q.v.) on the accession of James I in 1603. In 1616, he acquired and adapted the Cockpit (q.v.) in Drury Lane, later known as the Phoenix, which he leased to various companies. In 1625 he formed a new company, known as Queen Henrietta's Men (q.v.), and when it disbanded in 1636, he collected and trained a group called Beeston's Boys, some of whom later made their name in the Restoration theatre. On his death, control of the company passed to his son William (q.v.).

BEESTON, WILLIAM (c. 1601–82), English theatre manager, son of Christopher Beeston (q.v.), under whom he acted as a young man. On his father's death he took over control of the company known as Beeston's Boys and appeared with them at the Cockpit, his father's old theatre. After the closing of the theatres in 1642, he acquired Salisbury Court (q.v.), which was wrecked by Commonwealth soldiers in 1649 after unauthorized productions. Beeston, who was himself imprisoned, is suspected of being the 'ill Beest' who in 1652 betrayed to the authorities the actors who were appearing secretly at the Vere Street Theatre (q.v.). When the theatres reopened in 1660, he refurbished Salisbury Court, and ran it with a company which he trained himself, probably passing on to them some of the traditions of Elizabethan stage business which he had learned from his father.

BEHAN, BRENDAN (1923–64), Irish dramatist, whose early experiences of prison life gave him the material for his first play, *The Quare Fellow*, produced in Dublin in 1954 and in London, by Joan Littlewood (q.v.), two years later. It was followed in 1958 by *The Hostage*, first written and produced in Gaelic. This tragi-comic account of Irish Republican Army activities in a seedy brothel ends with the shooting of an English soldier, the hostage of the title, almost by accident. In its construction, with interspersed songs and dances and direct addresses to the

audience, it showed the influence of
Brecht (q.v.), an influence which can be
seen even more clearly in Behan's last
play, *Richard's Cork Leg*, which he left
unfinished at his death.

BEHN, MRS. APHRA (1640–89), playwright and novelist and the first Englishwoman to earn a living by her pen.
Brought up in the West Indies, the scene
of her novel *Oroonoko* (dramatized in
1695 by Southerne), she returned to
England in 1658 and married a merchant
of Dutch extraction. Her first play, *The
Forced Marriage; or, the Jealous Bridegroom* (1670), was a tragi-comedy given
at Lincoln's Inn Fields Theatre with
Betterton (q.v.) and his wife in the leading
parts. It was, however, in comedies of
intrigue that she did her best work, and
her first substantial success came with
The Rover; or, the Banished Cavalier
(1677). It was followed by several other
comedies, of which *The Feign'd Curtizans;
or, a Night's Intrigue* (1678), *The Round-
heads; or, the Good Old Cause* (1681), and
*The City-Heiress; or, Sir Timothy Treat-
All* (1682) owed their success to their
topicality. Her later plays were less
successful, though *The Emperor of the
Moon* (1687), a pantomime-farce based on
a *commedia dell'arte* scenario recently
played in Paris, is historically interesting.
Anthony Leigh played Scaramouche and
Thomas Jevon Harlequin; the play was
frequently revived and was the forerunner of the many harlequinades which
later led to the English pantomime (q.v.).

BEHRMAN, SAMUEL NATHANIEL (1893–
1973), American dramatist, whose most
successful plays were adaptations intended
to display the histrionic talents of Lynn
Fontanne and her husband (see LUNT).
The first of these was Jean Giraudoux's
Amphitryon 38 (1937), followed by *The
Pirate* (1942), based on a play by Ludwig
Fulda, and the chronicle of a long
marriage, *I Know my Love* (1949), based
on *Auprès de ma Blonde*, by Marcel
Achard. Other successful dramatizations were *Serena Blandish* (1929), on a
novel by Enid Bagnold (q.v.), *Jacobowsky
and the Colonel* (1944), on a play by Werfel,
Fanny (1945), the book for a successful
musical comedy based on Pagnol, and
Jane (1952), on a story by Somerset
Maugham (first seen in London in 1947).
Behrman's own dilemma, that of an
author whose desire to write serious plays

was defeated by his gift for light, sparkling comedy, was the subject of an amusing trifle, *No Time for Comedy* (1939).
Another comedy, *The Cold Wind and the
Warm* (1958), based on his own autobiography, was less successful, as was his last
play, *But for Whom Charlie* (1964) (see
WASHINGTON SQUARE THEATRE).

BÉJART, a family of actors intimately
connected with Molière (q.v.). The eldest
daughter, MADELEINE (1618–72), was
already well known as an actress when
Molière met her and joined the company
of which she was a member. After touring
the provinces for some years, she returned
with him to Paris in 1658, as did her elder
brother, JOSEPH (1616–59), her sister
GENEVIÈVE (1624–75), of whom little is
known, and her younger brother, LOUIS
(1630–78), known as L'Éguisé on account
of his sharp tongue. He was slightly lame,
a trait which Molière incorporated into
his part of La Flêche in *L'Avare* (1668),
where it has remained traditional. Joseph,
in spite of a slight stutter, was a useful
member of the company, and his death
so soon after settling in Paris was a great
blow. He was taken ill during a performance of Molière's *L'Étourdi*.

The youngest and most important
member of the family was ARMANDE-
GRÉSINDE-CLAIRE-ELISABETH (1642–1700),
whom Molière married in 1662. She made
her first appearance on the stage as Élise
in his *Critique de L'École des femmes*
(1663), and after 1664 played most of
Molière's heroines, which he wrote
specially for her. She was an excellent
actress, who owed all her training to her
husband, but in private their marriage was
not a success. After Molière's death she
kept the company together until 1680,
when it was merged in the newly founded
Comédie-Française (q.v.), and married
as her second husband the actor Guérin
d'Étriché.

Bel Savage Inn, LONDON, see INNS USED
AS THEATRES.

BELASCO [originally VALASCO], DAVID
(1853–1931), American actor-manager and
playwright, and for many years one of the
outstanding personalities of the American
stage. On the stage as a child, he later led
the usual life of an itinerant actor, travelling the Pacific coast, dramatizing novels,
adapting old plays, and devising spectacular melodramas, with battles, fires, and a

Passion Play with real sheep. In 1882 Daniel Frohman summoned him to become stage manager of the Madison Square Theatre (q.v.), where he had first appeared unsuccessfully in 1879. In 1885, after his first visit to London, he became Steele Mackaye's stage manager at the Lyceum (q.v.), where he remained until 1890, continuing to turn out a number of plays, mainly in collaboration. Success came with *The Girl I Left Behind Me* (1893), *The Heart of Maryland* (1895), with Maurice Barrymore (q.v.) as the hero, *Zaza* (1899), starring Mrs. Leslie Carter (q.v.), and finally *Madame Butterfly* (1900), with Blanche Bates (q.v.). This dramatization of a story by John Luther Long was used by Puccini as the basis of an opera, as was *The Girl of the Golden West* (1905). Meanwhile Belasco had begun his association with the actor David Warfield (q.v.) in Klein's *The Auctioneer* (1901), and in the following year opened the first Belasco Theatre (see REPUBLIC). Its success enabled Belasco to build a new theatre, known first as the Stuyvesant, under which name it opened in 1907, becoming the Belasco (see below) in 1910. Here Belasco remained until his death, his last production being *Mima* (1928), adapted from Molnár's *The Red Mill*. He thus ended his career as he began it, by adapting the work of another. He contributed little that was original to the American stage, and in no way encouraged national American drama, but belongs to the great age of American stagecraft, and his great contribution to the American scene lay in his elaborate décors and the passion for realism which led him, in his melodrama *The Governor's Lady* (1912), to place an exact replica of a Child's restaurant on the stage. He should be judged on what he did and not on what he failed to do. He made good use of the mechanical inventions of his time, as well as interesting and far-reaching experiments in the use of light. Nor should his long fight against the stranglehold of the Theatrical Syndicate (q.v.), and his ultimate triumph, be forgotten, since it involved the whole question of the freedom of the American theatre, and the independence of the artist in the theatre. His large collection of theatrical material is now housed in the New York Public Library.

Belasco Theatre, NEW YORK. (1) The first theatre of this name, on West 42nd Street between 7th and 8th Avenues, opened as the Republic (q.v.) on 27 Sept. 1900 with Herne's *Sag Harbor*. Two years later it was renamed by Belasco (q.v.), who opened it on 19 Sept. It reverted to its old name in 1910, and in 1942 became a cinema.

(2) The second Belasco, on West 44th Street, between Broadway and 6th Avenue, opened as the Stuyvesant on 16 Oct. 1907 with Belasco's *A Grand Army Man*, and was renamed the Belasco in 1910, opening on 3 Sept. with *The Lily*, an adaptation by Belasco of Leroux's *Le Lys* (1908). It was at one time leased by Katharine Cornell (q.v.), who produced there a translation of Obey's *Le Viol de Lucrèce* (1931), as *Lucrece* (1932), and Sidney Howard's *Alien Corn* (1933). Two of the plays of Elmer Rice (q.v.) were produced at the Belasco in 1934, *Judgement Day* and *Between Two Worlds*, and from 1935 to 1941 the Group Theatre (q.v.) had their headquarters there, producing among other things two plays by Clifford Odets (q.v.). From 1949 to 1953 the theatre was used for broadcasting, but then housed a successful run of Teichmann and Kaufman's *The Solid Gold Cadillac*, and in 1960 of Tad Mosel's *All the Way Home*, adapted from James Agee's novel, *A Death in the Family*. In 1964 the National Repertory Theatre, with Eva Le Gallienne, played a season at the Belasco, which is no longer controlled by the Belasco estate.

Belfast Arts Theatre, an organization which corresponds to the Dublin Gate Theatre (see DUBLIN). Founded (as the Mask Theatre) in 1944 by Hubert and Dorothy Wilmot, it opened in a converted loft with Charles Morgan's *The Flashing Stream*. Three years later, with many successful productions of European classics behind it, it assumed its present name. Two important American plays, Kingsley's *Darkness at Noon* and Van Druten's *I Am a Camera*, had their European premières there, and Anouilh's *Waltz of the Toreadors* its first production in English. In 1961 the Wilmots, who were eventually forced to lower their standards somewhat by the demands of their audiences for comedies and thrillers, moved to a new playhouse in Botanic Avenue, which opened on 19 Apr. with Tennessee Williams's *Orpheus Descending*. The comfortable auditorium seats 500 and there are good front-of-house and backstage facilities.

Belgrade Theatre, COVENTRY, the first civic theatre to be built in England, and the first new professional theatre since the Oxford Playhouse of 1938. It was named in recognition of a gift of timber from the city of Belgrade. Designed by the city architects, it seats 899 and has a conventional proscenium stage with a forestage over the orchestra pit. It is run by an independent Trust largely composed of City Councillors. Under its first director, Bryan Bailey (q v.), it opened on 27 Mar. 1958 with *Half in Earnest*, a musical version by Vivian Ellis of Wilde's *The Importance of Being Earnest*. The present director is Warren Jenkins. Among the many new plays presented since 1958 have been several by Arnold Wesker (q.v.). Besides encouraging new playwrights, the theatre has made serious efforts to attract a large young audience through its Young Stagers' Club, and a programme of theatre appreciation run for local schools. The building, which has excellent foyer accommodation, a restaurant, and a bar, is also used for concerts, and displays the work of local artists.

Belgravia Theatre, LONDON, see ROYAL COURT THEATRE (1).

BELL, JOHN (1745–1831), pioneer English publisher and bookseller, who was responsible for *Bell's British Theatre*, a comprehensive selection of plays, each prefaced by an interesting character portrait. His 1773 acting edition of Shakespeare, edited by Francis Gentleman (q.v.), was based on the prompt-books of the Theatres Royal, and is interesting as showing what was actually performed on the stage at the time.

BELL, MARIE (1900–), French actress and theatre manager, who has appeared at the Comédie-Française in a number of tragic roles, including Racine's Phèdre, Bérénice, and Agrippine (in *Britannicus*). She has also been seen at other theatres in Paris in several modern plays, including the first production by Barrault (q.v.) of Paul Claudel's *Le Soulier de satin* (1943), in which she played Prouhèze. She was also in the first productions of Marceau's *La Bonne Soupe* (1959) and Genet's *Le Balcon* (1960), and in the 1930s had a distinguished career in films.

Bell Inn, LONDON, see INNS USED AS THEATRES.

BELLAMY, GEORGE ANNE (*c.* 1727–88), English actress, who received her first names from a mishearing of Georgiana at her christening. She is believed to have made her first appearance on the stage at Covent Garden in 1744 in Otway's *The Orphan*, but may have been seen there two years earlier as Miss Prue in Congreve's *Love for Love*. She was at her best in romantic and tragic parts, being an admirable Juliet to the Romeo of Garrick (q.v.), who admired her sufficiently to make her one of his leading ladies at Drury Lane. But she had very little professional integrity and much of her success was due to her youth and beauty. Arrogant and extravagant, she was twice married, once bigamously, and because of the scandals in which she was involved, and the loss of her looks through dissipation, managers became chary of engaging her. However, though held in very little esteem by the public or her fellow-actors, she continued to appear intermittently until her retirement in 1785, in which year an *Apology* for her life was published. Edited by another hand, this was a sensational affair, in six volumes, readable rather than reliable.

BELLEROCHE, see POISSON.

BELLEVILLE, see TURLUPIN.

BELLWOOD [really MAHONEY], BESSIE (1847–96), a music-hall performer, best remembered for her singing of 'What Cheer, Riah!' She was for some time a rabbit-skinner in the New Cut, near the Old Vic. After a riotous first appearance at the Star, Bermondsey, she was given an audition at the Holborn, and turned down as being 'too quiet', but went on to achieve an enviable success, and many racy stories, some probably apocryphal, are associated with her name. She had a happy knack of indulging in repartee with members of the audience, who invariably got as good as they gave. In private life she was a warm-hearted, generous woman and a fervent Catholic.

Belmont Theatre, NEW YORK, a small playhouse on West 48th Street which opened on 18 Jan. 1918 as the Norworth. It was named after the comedian Jack Norworth (q.v.), but changed its name three months later. In 1923 it housed a year's run of *You and I*, the first play of Philip Barry (q.v.). A later success was

Van Druten's *Young Woodley* (1925), after which the fortunes of the house declined. It became a cinema in 1927 and was finally demolished.

Below, see STAGE DIRECTIONS.

Beltrame, see BARBIERI, NICCOLÒ.

BENAVENTE Y MARTÍNEZ, JACINTO (1866–1954), the most successful Spanish playwright of his day, awarded the Nobel Prize for Literature in 1922. He was the author of over 150 plays, including translations of Shakespeare and Molière. The best-known of his works outside Spain were *Los intereses creados* (1907), which, as *The Bonds of Interest*, was the first play presented in New York by the Theatre Guild (q.v.) in 1919—it was seen in London a year later; and *La malquerida* (1913), which, as *The Passion Flower*, was produced in New York in 1920 and in London in 1926. Among his other plays the most important are *Gente conocida* (1896), *El marido de la Téllez* (1897), *La noche del sábado* (1903), *Los malhechores del bien* (1905), and *Más fuerte que el amor* (1906). Although his reputation has declined since his death, he was in the 1920s highly thought of in England, where four volumes of his plays in translation, by J. G. Underhill, were published between 1917 and 1924, as well as a full-length study of his work (also 1924) by Walter Starkie.

BENCHLEY, ROBERT CHARLES (1889–1945), American man of letters and well-known humorist, who in 1920 became dramatic critic of *Life*, and in 1929 of *The New Yorker*, proving himself a good judge of actors and plays. He retired in 1939 to devote all his time to acting in films. There is no collected volume of his theatrical criticisms, but many of them can be found scattered through his books which include *The Early Worm* (1927), *My Ten Years in a Quandary* (1936), and *After 1903—What?* (1938).

Benefit, a special performance, common in the eighteenth and early nineteenth centuries, of which the financial proceeds, after deduction of expenses, were given to a member of the company, who was allowed to choose the play for the evening. Before the introduction of the royalty system (q.v.), a performance was sometimes given for the benefit of an author,

or it could be for a player who was ill and in need of money, or for his widow or other needy dependents. According to Colley Cibber (q.v.) in his *Apology* (1740), the first benefit performance in England was given in about 1686 for Mrs. Elizabeth Barry (q.v.), but it did not become common practice until much later. There is an interesting account of the way it worked in Dickens's *Nicholas Nickleby* (1838), and the abuses of the system in the early American theatre can be studied in Odell's *Annals of the New York Stage* (1925–49). It was an unsatisfactory arrangement, which exposed the actor to petty humiliations and kept him in a constant state of financial uncertainty, and it gradually died out between 1840 and 1870. A comprehensive account of the whole matter can be found in Sir St. Vincent Troubridge's *The Benefit System in the British Theatre* (1967). A slightly more dignified method of making money was the BESPEAK PERFORMANCE, whereby a wealthy patron or local authority would buy most of the tickets for one evening and sell or give them away, choosing the play to be performed from the company's current repertory. But in that case the proceeds were divided among the members of the company and not given to an individual.

BENELLI, SEM (1875–1949), Italian dramatist, considered in some ways a successor to D'Annunzio (q.v.), though with less poetry. Among his plays, which were first produced by the Compagnia Stabile Argentina, founded in 1906, the most successful was *La cena delle beffe* (1909), a Renaissance melodrama which, as *The Jest*, was played in New York in 1919 by the Barrymore brothers (q.v.). It was in blank verse, as were Benelli's other successful plays, *La maschera di Bruto* (1908) and *L'Amore dei tre re* (1910).

BENFIELD, ROBERT (?–1649), English actor, who joined the King's Men (see CHAMBERLAIN'S MEN) in 1615, replacing Ostler (q.v.), in whose part of Antonio in Webster's *The Duchess of Malfi* he appeared in 1619. His name appears in the list of actors in Shakespeare's plays, and in those of Beaumont and Fletcher. He also played the part of Junius Rusticus in *The Roman Actor* (1626) and of Ladislaus, King of Hungary, in *The Picture* (1629), both by Massinger.

BENGER, SIR THOMAS, see MASTER OF THE REVELS.

BENNETT, ALAN (1934–), English actor and dramatist, who in 1960 appeared at the Edinburgh Festival in the epoch-making revue, *Beyond the Fringe*, of which he was part-author. This subsequently had a long run in London and in New York, and was given several awards for excellence, including a special citation in 1963 by the New York Drama Critics' Circle. In 1968 Bennett's first play, a musical entitled *Forty Years On* in which he himself appeared, had a successful run, with John Gielgud (q.v.) (followed by Emlyn Williams, q.v.) as the retiring headmaster of a minor public school in whose honour the boys enact a savagely satiric pageant of recent British history.

BENNETT, (ENOCH) ARNOLD (1867–1931), English novelist and dramatist, whose plays enjoyed considerable success in the theatre. His plots were ingeniously constructed, and his character-drawing had vitality and was mellowed by a homely humour. His most successful plays were *Milestones* (1912), which was written in collaboration with Edward Knoblock (q.v.), as was his last play, *London Life* (1924); and *The Great Adventure* (1913), which owed much to the acting of Henry Ainley (q.v.). *Milestones*, which has been revived several times, was seen at the Yvonne Arnaud Theatre (q.v.) in 1965.

BENOIS, ALEXANDRE (1870–1960), theatre artist, great-uncle of the English actor and dramatist, Peter Ustinov (q.v.). Born in St. Petersburg, he belonged to a family which had long been associated with the theatre, his great-grandfather having been director of the Fenice Theatre in Venice and his grandfather architect of the Bolshoi Theatre in Moscow. His finest work was done for Diaghilev's Ballets Russes, including 'Petrushka', 'Les Sylphides', 'Giselle', and many others. In 1957, at the age of 87, he did a superb set of designs, both costume and scenery, for a revival, in London and Milan, of 'The Nutcracker'. His work had a great influence in the theatre, and he helped immeasurably to raise the prestige of the scene designer. He was also the author of two admirable books of autobiography.

BENSON, SIR FRANK ROBERT (1858–1939), English actor-manager, best remembered for the Shakespearian company with which he visited Stratford-upon-Avon (q.v.) annually from 1886 to 1916, appearing in a repertory of seven or eight plays during the summer festival there, and at other times travelling all over the provinces, thus keeping the plays of Shakespeare always before the public and providing a good training-school for a number of young players. While at Oxford he had been a prominent member of the O.U.D.S. (see OXFORD), and he made his first appearance on the professional stage in 1882, at the Lyceum under Irving (q.v.), playing Paris in *Romeo and Juliet*. It was in the following year that he formed his own company, and in due course he directed it in all Shakespeare's plays with the exception of *Titus Andronicus* and *Troilus and Cressida*. In 1916, on the occasion of the Shakespeare Tercentenary celebrations at Drury Lane, he was knighted by George V for his services to the theatre, being the only actor so far to be knighted actually in a theatre. He married in 1886 a member of his company, CONSTANCE FEATHERSTONHAUGH [really GERTRUDE CONSTANCE SAMWELL] (1860–1946), who continued to play leading parts with him for many years.

BEOLCO, ANGELO (c. 1501/2–?42), one of the earliest Italian actors and dramatists connected with the origins of Italian comedy and of the *commedia dell'arte* (q.v.). He was an educated amateur who acted in Venice, in Ferrara, and in Padua in his own plays, during the carnival season, under the name of Ruzzante, 'the gossip', a shrewd peasant who indulges in long and amusing soliloquies. His plays, which are fully written out and not scenarios for improvisation, are in the dialect of Padua, his birthplace. They were edited by Lovarini, and translated into French by Ruzzante's biographer, A. Mortier, in 1925–6.

BÉRAIN, JEAN (1637–1711), French theatrical designer, who replaced Vigarani (q.v.) at the Salle des Machines and also as scenic designer to the Paris Opéra. In 1674 he succeeded Gissey as designer to the King, and the costumes and decorations which he prepared for Court spectacles had a great influence on all forms of contemporary art, not only in France but all over Europe. Their most striking characteristic is the complete synthesis of fantasy and contemporary taste. There was no attempt at realism or archaeological reconstruction, and even in costumes for Romans, Turks, or mythological characters, the exotic elements were absorbed with an intensely personal style which left its impress on contemporaries and successors alike. Many of Bérain's designs can be seen in Paris—in the Louvre and the Musée de l'Opéra—in the Library at Versailles, and in London at the Victoria and Albert Museum. They were preserved, sometimes in copies or tracings, by the pious hand of his son JEAN (1678–1726), who succeeded him in his official functions, but, though industrious and inventive, lacked his originality and skill.

BÉRARD, CHRISTIAN (1902–49), French artist and theatre designer whose work, which was characterized by a wonderful feeling for the visual aspects of the theatre and great skill in the use of colour, had a great influence on European stage design. After designing for most of the great choreographers of his time, he began in 1934 a fruitful collaboration with Jouvet (q.v.), starting with Cocteau's *La Machine infernale*, and continuing through such important and diverse productions as Beaumarchais's *La Folle Journée*, Giraudoux's *La Folle de Chaillot* (1945), Genet's *Les Bonnes*, and Molière's *Don Juan* (both 1947). He also designed a number of productions for other theatres, including the Comédie-Française, and, for the Renaud–Barrault company, Molière's *Amphitryon* (1946) and *Les Fourberies de Scapin* (1949). He died while supervising the lighting of this last play on the night before its production.

BERGERAC, (SAVINIEN) CYRANO DE (1619–55), French author, who was in the Compagnie des Gardes under M. de Carbon de Casteljaloux. His friendship with Molière and Scarron (qq.v.) turned his thoughts to the stage, and he wrote several plays, from one of which, *Le Pedant joué* (written between 1643 and 1649), Molière took a scene for *Les Fourberies de Scapin* (1671). Cyrano's Gareau, a dialect-speaking peasant, may also have been the model for several of Molière's Lubins and Pierrots, and Scarron may have been indebted to Cyrano for some of his *Dom Japhet* (1652). Cyrano disliked the actor Montfleury (q.v.), and once forbade him to appear on the stage for a month. When Montfleury disobeyed, Cyrano went to the theatre

and enforced obedience at the point of the sword. He was killed by a wooden beam which fell on his head. Both these incidents, and also Cyrano's immense nose, which led him to fight many duels with those who remarked on it, were used by Edmond Rostand (q.v.) in his play, *Cyrano de Bergerac* (1898), in which Coquelin *aîné* (q.v.) played the title-role.

BERGMAN, HJALMAR FREDERIK (1883–1931), Swedish dramatist and novelist, whose early 'marionette' plays, *Dödens Arlekin* (1917) and *Herr Sleeman kommer* (1918), were written under the influence of Maeterlinck (q.v.). The most successful of his later plays, in which comedy has replaced the tragic mood of his earlier work, were *Swedenhielms* (1925), which portrays the eccentric family of a Nobel prizewinner and as *The Family First* was produced at the Birmingham Repertory Theatre in 1960, and *Patrasket* (1928), a folk comedy with a Jewish setting.

BERGSTRØM, HJALMAR (1868–1914), Danish dramatist, one of the best-known of his period outside his own country. In his plays he deals, under the influence of Ibsen (q.v.), with such social problems as the struggle between the classes—as in *Lynggaard & Co.* (1905)—and feminine emancipation—as in *Karen Bornemann* (1907).

BERINGER, ESMÉ (1875–1972) and VERA (1879–1964), English actresses who were on the stage as children, often appearing in the same play, as they sometimes did when adult. Vera, who created the title-role in the English production of Mrs. Hodgson Burnett's *Little Lord Fauntleroy* (1888) and the dual title-roles in Mark Twain's *The Prince and the Pauper* (1890), was seen in 1896 as Juliet to her sister's Romeo. During her long and successful career she wrote or adapted a number of plays, among them a version of Molière's *Les Précieuses ridicules* as *The Blue Stockings* (1913). She retired in 1938, after playing the Queen to the Hamlet of her sister Esmé, who was then sixty-two, and had made an outstanding reputation as a Shakespearian actress. In 1937 Esmé also made a great success as Gran in Mazo de la Roche's *Whiteoaks*. She continued to act until her retirement in 1954.

Berlin. There was no very strong theatre tradition in Berlin until in 1786 Döbbelin took over the theatre there from a French company and with the help of Fleck (q.v.) ran it successfully until his death in 1793. Three years later Iffland (q.v.) inaugurated what was to prove the first successful German National Theatre, training a company in the naturalistic style of acting he had learned in Mannheim, and making the Berlin theatre the equal of those in Hamburg and Vienna. On his death in 1814 he was succeeded by Brühl, who brought with him the great actor Ludwig Devrient (q.v.). Between them they made the theatre notable for its productions of Goethe, Shakespeare, and Calderón. Devrient died in 1832, and the theatre, which had been destroyed by fire in 1817 and rebuilt in a neo-classical style, entered on a period of decadence and triviality which was to last for another fifty years.

A new phase in the theatrical life of Berlin began in the 1880s, with the founding in 1883 of the Deutsches Theater under Adolf L'Arronge (q.v.), and in 1889 of the Freie Bühne under Otto Brahm (q.v.), who in 1894, after L'Arronge's retirement, was appointed director of the Deutsches Theater. Following the precedent set by the Freie Bühne with its production of such plays as Ibsen's Ghosts and Hauptmann's Vor Sonnenaufgang, this became the home of naturalistic drama. In 1907 Reinhardt (q.v.), who in 1901 had founded what later became known as the Little Theatre on Unter den Linden, took over the Deutsches Theater, where he had played as a young man, and inaugurated a series of productions which made Berlin one of the outstanding theatrical centres in Europe. Much of his best work was done there, including a production of Sophocles' Oedipus Rex in the Zirkus Schumann in 1910, and of Aeschylus' Oresteia in the Grosses Schauspielhaus in 1919, on an open stage with every possible contemporary mechanical device.

Between the two world wars Piscator (q.v.) was in Berlin as director of the Zentral Theater from 1923 to 1924, the Volksbühne (where Reinhardt had worked from 1915 to 1918) from 1924 to 1927, and finally of his own Piscator Theater from 1927 to 1929. After he and Reinhardt left Germany, Berlin sank to a low level artistically, but rose again in the years after the Second World War, particularly with the rebuilding in 1951 of the Schiller Theater, whose company was seen in London in 1964. A strong impetus to theatrical life was also given by the return

from exile in 1949 of Brecht (q.v.), who remained in Berlin until his death in 1956.

Berliner Ensemble, see BRECHT, BERTOLT.

Bernadon, a Viennese comic character created by Kurz (q.v.), a restless and impetuous youth whose adventures lead him into the world of the supernatural, where his comic genius ranges itself on the side of white, as opposed to black, magic. The best of these adventures are found in Kurz's Die 33 Schelmereien des Bernadon.

BERNARD, JEAN-JACQUES (1888–1972), French dramatist, son of Tristan Bernard (q.v.), but a writer in quite a different style, since his work deals with the tragedy of unrequited or unacknowledged love, and derives from the école intimiste (see THEATRE OF SILENCE) founded by Maeterlinck (q.v.). Several of his plays were seen in London in translation, among them The Sulky Fire (Le Feu qui reprend mal, 1921) in 1926, The Unquiet Spirit (L'Âme en peine, 1926) in 1928, Martine (1922) in 1929, The Springtime of Others (Le Printemps des autres, 1924) in 1934, and Invitation to a Voyage (L'Invitation au voyage, 1924) in 1937. They were all several times revived, at the Gate or the Arts Theatre, up to 1949, but the only one to be seen in New York appears to have been Martine, in 1928.

BERNARD, TRISTAN (1866–1947), French dramatist, author of a number of light comedies which have little literary value but are deftly constructed, with the chief character entangled in petty intrigues from which the author extricates him with great ingenuity. Several of them have been translated into English, and Triplepatte (1905), adapted by Clyde Fitch (q.v.) as Toddles, was popular both in London and New York.

BERNHARDT [really BERNARD], SARAH HENRIETTE ROSINE (1845–1923), French actress, world-famous for her acting and her eccentricities, with a voice which has been likened to a 'golden bell', or the 'silver sound of running water'. It constituted one of her main charms, and outlasted her physical beauty and slim figure. In 1862 she made her first appearance at the Comédie-Française, where she had a brief and stormy career. She left it for good in 1880, having first established herself as a leading actress by her Cordelia (in *King Lear*) and Queen (in Hugo's *Ruy Blas*) in 1872. These were followed by outstanding performances as Racine's Phèdre and as Doña Sol in Hugo's *Hernani*, her greatest part, as it was that of Rachel (q.v.). She then set out on her travels, making her first appearance in London in 1879 and in New York in 1880, and scoring an immediate triumph in both capitals. She returned to them many times in later years, always with success, her last appearance in London being in *Daniel* in 1921, not long before her death. In Paris she managed several theatres, including the Ambigu-Comique in 1882, before opening the old Théâtre des Nations as the Théâtre Sarah Bernhardt on 1 Jan. 1899. Among the plays in which she scored her greatest successes, apart from *Phèdre*, were the younger Dumas's *La Dame aux camélias*, Sardou's *Fédora*, *Théodora*, and *La Tosca*, the plays of Edmond Rostand, particularly *L'Aiglon*, with which her name was always associated, and *Hamlet*. She was an accomplished painter and sculptress, wrote poetry and plays, and a volume of reminiscences published in 1907 and translated into English the same year as *My Double Life* (the American edition, also 1907, and reprinted in 1968, was entitled *Memories of My Life*).

BERNINI, GIOVANNI LORENZO (1598–1680), Italian scene and machine designer, some of whose effects were seen in Rome by Richard Lascelles, contemporary of Inigo Jones (q.v.), and described by him in his *Italian Voyage* (1670). He was responsible for the décor of the theatre built by the Barberini family, and for some of the stage sets. He excelled in such effects as floods, sunsets, sunrises, flying machines, articulated monsters, collapsing buildings, and transformation scenes of all kinds

BERNSTEIN [*née* FRANKAU], ALINE (1881–1955), American scene designer, and founder in 1937, with Irene Lewisohn, of the Museum of Costume Art in Rockefeller Center, New York. Her first work for the stage was done in 1924, with designs for *The Little Clay Cart* in a production given by the Neighborhood Playhouse (q.v.). She was then responsible for the décor of a number of important productions, including Philip Moeller's *Caprice* (1928) and Sherwood's *Reunion in Vienna* (1931) for the Theatre

Guild (q.v.); Chekhov's *The Cherry Orchard* (1928) and *The Seagull* (1929) and Molnár's *Liliom* (1932) for the Civic Repertory Theatre under Eva Le Gallienne (q.v.); and, for other managements, Barry's *The Animal Kingdom* and Emlyn Williams's *The Late Christopher Bean* (both 1932); the dramatization of Christopher Morley's *Thunder on the Left* (1933); Elmer Rice's *Judgement Day* (1934); and two plays by Lillian Hellman, *The Children's Hour* (1934) and *The Little Foxes* (1939). Her designs for the American production of Cocteau's *The Eagle Has Two Heads* (1949) were also much admired.

BERTINAZZI, CARLO (1713–83), the last of the great Arlequins of the Comédie-Italienne, which he joined in 1741. Known as Carlin, he was much admired by Garrick, who said his back wore the expression his face would have shown had the mask not covered it.

Bespeak Performance, see BENEFIT.

BETTERTON, THOMAS (?1635–1710), English actor, and the greatest figure of the Restoration stage. He was in the company with which John Rhodes reopened the Cockpit (q.v.) in 1660, and soon after joined Davenant's company at Lincoln's Inn Fields Theatre (q.v.). After Davenant's death in 1671, the company, led by Betterton, moved to a new theatre in Dorset Garden (q.v.), and remained there until it was amalgamated with the company at the Theatre Royal in 1682. In 1695 Betterton broke with the management of the Theatre Royal and reopened the theatre in Lincoln's Inn Fields most successfully with the first performance of Congreve's *Love for Love*, moving ten years later to Vanbrugh's new theatre in the Hay (see HER MAJESTY'S THEATRE). He was a good manager and an excellent actor, both in comedy and tragedy, his Hamlet and Sir Toby Belch (in *Twelfth Night*) being equally admired. He adapted a number of Shakespeare's plays to suit the taste of the time, and in 1690 turned Fletcher's *The Prophetess* (1622) into an opera with music by Purcell. This ended with an elaborate masque whose stage directions show to what a pitch stage mechanism had been brought by this time, influenced no doubt by the machinery of opera, and by Betterton's own study in Paris of French theatrical effects. Betterton's wife was MARY SANDERSON (?-1712), one of the first English actresses, whom Pepys in his Diary always refers to as Ianthe, from her excellent playing of that part in Davenant's *The Siege of Rhodes*.

BETTI, UGO (1892-1953), Italian playwright, much of whose work shows the influence of Pirandello (q.v.). A lawyer by profession, he gave many of his plays a legal setting, as in his most important play, *Corruzione al Palazzo di Giustizia* (1949), which, as *Corruption in the Palace of Justice*, was seen in New York in 1963. Betti's other plays include two light comedies, *Una bella domenica di settembre* (1937) and *Il paese delle vacanze* (1942), and the more serious works *Frana allo scalo Nord* (1936), *Ispezione* (1947), *Lotta fino all'alba* (1949), and *La regina e gli insorti* (1951). His last plays, *L'aiuola bruciata* and *La fuggitiva*, were produced posthumously in 1953. Three of Betti's plays were seen in London in 1955 in English translations by Henry Reed—*L'aiuola bruciata*, as *The Burnt Flower Bed*, at the Arts Theatre in Sept., *La regina e gli insorti*, as *The Queen and the Rebels*, at the Haymarket in Oct., and *Il paese delle vacanze*, as *Summertime*, at the Apollo in Nov. *Ispezione*, as *Island Investigations*, was given an amateur production in 1956 by the University of Bristol Dramatic Society, and in 1957 *Delitto all'isola delle capre* (1948), as *Crime on Goat Island*, was produced at the Oxford Playhouse. In 1952 *Il Giocatore* (1951), as *The Gambler*, was produced in New York in an adaptation by Alfred Drake, who also played the leading role.

BETTY, WILLIAM HENRY WEST (1791-1874), a child prodigy, known as the Young Roscius, who from 1804 to 1805 took London by storm. He was first seen at Covent Garden on 1 Dec. 1804 as Achmet in John Brown's tragedy *Barbarossa*, and subsequently at Drury Lane in such parts as Hamlet, Romeo, Richard III, Osman in Voltaire's *Zara*, Rolla in Sheridan's *Pizarro*, Frederick in Mrs. Inchbald's *Lovers' Vows*, and Young Norval in Home's *Douglas*, in which character he was painted by Northcott and Opie. After a brief and hectic success, interspersed by strenuous summer tours, opinion turned against him, and he was hissed off the stage when he attempted Richard III. He went as an undergraduate

to Cambridge in 1808, and three years later again appeared on the stage, without success. He was ignored, his father squandered his money, and the rest of his long life—he was well over eighty when he died—was passed in complete obscurity. An account of his career—*The Prodigy, a Study of the Strange Life of Master Betty*, by Giles Playfair—was published in 1967.

BEVERLEY, WILLIAM ROXBY (c. 1814-89), English scene painter, who first worked for the Theatre Royal, Manchester, under his father, WILLIAM ROXBY (1765-1842). Some years later he did good work for the Vestris-Mathews management at the London Lyceum (see LYCEUM (1)), achieving his greatest success in Planché's extravaganza, *The Island of Jewels* (1849). Beverley's long and fruitful association with Drury Lane, where his best work was done for the annual pantomime, began in 1854 and lasted through successive managements until 1885. He worked intermittently also elsewhere, and for Charles Kean (q.v.) at the Princess's designed the sets for *King John*, *Henry IV, Part I*, and *Macbeth*, and for an elaborate production of Milton's *Comus*. Next to Stanfield (q.v.), Beverley, who was a one-surface painter firmly opposed to the innovation of 'built stuff' (q.v.), was perhaps the most distinguished scene painter of the nineteenth century in England, and much assisted the development of the art of scene painting by his original methods and use of new inventions.

BIANCOLELLI, GIUSEPPE DOMENICO (c. 1637-88), an actor and playwright of the *commedia dell'arte* (q.v.), who became famous as Dominique, playing the part of Arlequin. He was the son and grandson of actors, and in 1654 was invited by Mazarin to join the Italian company in Paris. At that time the Italian actors played only in their own language, and it was Dominique who obtained permission from Louis XIV, who much admired his acting, for them to play in French, in spite of the determined opposition of the Comédie-Française. Dominique later became a naturalized Frenchman and married an actress. Two of his daughters were on the stage, one marrying an actor at the Comédie-Française (see LA THORILLIÈRE). His youngest son, PIETRO FRANCESCO (1680-1734), acted in Paris both as

Arlequin and as Pierrot, until the Italian players were banished in 1697. As Dominique le Jeune, he was a member of the company which Lélio (see RICCOBONI) took back to Paris in 1716, and remained with it until his death, playing in the first productions of some of the plays of Marivaux (q.v.).

BIBBIENA, BERNARDO DOVIZI DA (1470–1520), an Italian cardinal, author in his youth of a comedy, the *Calandria* (freely adapted from the *Menaechmi* of Plautus), first performed at Urbino during the carnival of 1506. A year later it was seen in Rome, and then at most of the princely Courts of Italy, with much success, according to the contemporary descriptions of its production which survive.

BIBIENA (also BIBBIENA, DA BIBBIENA). A family of scenic artists and architects, originally of Florence, whose work, in pure baroque style, is found all over Europe, though Parma and Vienna probably saw their greatest achievements. The family name was Galli, and Bibiena (or Bibbiena) was added later, from the birthplace of GIOVAN MARIA GALLI (1625–65), father of FERDINANDO (1657–1743) and FRANCESCO (1659–1739), who together founded the family fortunes and renown. While still a young man, Ferdinando worked in the beautiful Teatro Farnese built by Aleotti, which he left to go to Vienna. There, with the help of his brother and his sons, he was responsible for the decorations of many Court fêtes and theatrical performances. His eldest son, ALESSANDRO (1686–1748), became an architect, but the three younger ones, GIUSEPPE (1695–1756), ANTONIO (1697–c. 1774), and GIOVANNI MARIA (1700–c. 1777), worked in the theatre. Giuseppe's son CARLO (1721–87), one of whose stage settings is preserved at Drottningholm (q.v.), was associated with his father in the building and decoration of the fine opera-house at Bayreuth (q.v.). The family made its home in Bologna, but its members can be traced all over Europe. They worked so much in collaboration that it is sometimes impossible to apportion their work individually. They introduced many innovations into scenic design, particularly with their development of the perspective scene, or *scena d'angolo*, which inaugurated a new era in stage setting, and worked not only for royal patrons, but for productions in

Jesuit colleges, in churches where the tradition of religious plays was continued, and for the rich municipalities of Italy.

Bible-History, a name given by modern scholarship to the medieval play based on Scripture and formerly known as the Mystery Play (q.v.).

BICKERSTAFFE, ISAAC (1735–1812), English dramatist, considered in his day the equal of John Gay (q.v.) as a writer of ballad operas. The first of these, *Thomas and Sally; or, the Sailor's Return,* was given at Covent Garden in 1760. It was followed by *Love in a Village* (1762), based on *The Village Opera* (1728) of Charles Johnson. It has been frequently revived down to the present day. Another piece of the same nature, *The Maid of the Mill* (1765), held the stage for many years, and is found in the repertory of the Toy Theatre (q.v.). Among Bickerstaffe's later productions the best was *Lionel and Clarissa* (1768), which was revived at the Lyric, Hammersmith, in 1925, under Nigel Playfair (q.v.).

BIDERMANN, JAKOB (1578–1639), a Jesuit priest, and an outstanding writer of plays for presentation in Jesuit colleges (see JESUIT DRAMA). The best of those which have survived is *Cenodoxus,* the story of a pious hypocrite in Paris whose soul, after death, is tried and cast into Hell. The play ends with the founding by St. Bruno, who has witnessed the condemnation, of the religious order of Carthusians. *Cenodoxus* was first performed on 2 July 1602 in Augsburg, and again in Munich in 1609. In 1958 it was produced at the Residenztheater in Munich as part of the city's celebration of its 800th anniversary, in an abridged German text based on a translation from the original Latin published in 1635.

Bijou Theatre. (1) LONDON. A small theatre of this name, formerly a concert hall attached to Her Majesty's Theatre (q.v.), was used for minstrel shows, light entertainment, and by amateurs. It was destroyed when the main theatre was burnt down on 6 Dec. 1867.

(2) LONDON. A small theatre in Bayswater, also used by amateurs. In 1905 Oscar Wilde's *Salome* had its first London production there. In 1925 Lena Ashwell (q.v.) took it over and renamed it the Century. It was later called the Twentieth Century.

(3) New York, a small playhouse devoted to light entertainment. Situated at 1239 Broadway, it opened as the Brighton in 1878. It then became Wood's Broadway Theatre, and the Broadway Opera House. On 7 July 1883 it was pulled down and a larger theatre of the same name was built on the site, opening on 1 Dec. with Offenbach. It was at this theatre that Julia Marlowe (q.v.) made her début as an adult actress. It continued in use, mainly as a home of musical and light entertainment, until 1911.

(4) New York, on West 45th Street. This was opened by the Shuberts on 12 Apr. 1917. Among the plays produced there were revivals of Barrie's *What Every Woman Knows* in 1926, with Helen Hayes (q.v.), and of Ibsen's *The Lady from the Sea* in 1929, with Blanche Yurka (q.v.). The last successful production, in 1931, was Benn Levy's *Springtime for Henry*. In 1938 the Bijou became a cinema, the Toho, showing Japanese films, but it reopened as a theatre again in 1945, when *Life with Father* (1939), by Howard Lindsay and Russel Crouse, moved there from the Empire and stayed until 1947. Ten years later Graham Greene's *The Potting Shed* had a long run.

BILL-BELOTSERKOVSKY, Vladimir Naumovich (1884–1970), Soviet dramatist, who added Bill, his nickname in the U.S.A., where he worked from 1911 to 1917, to his family name. His first play, *Echo* (1924), depicts United States dockers refusing to load arms for anti-Soviet use. *Hurricane* (or *Storm*), produced in 1925 at the Mossoviet Theatre, a fine stirring piece of propaganda about the struggles of a Revolutionary leader in a small village during the Civil War, was a landmark in Soviet theatre history, being the first realistic play about the new Soviet state. It has been produced all over Eastern Europe, either in its original form, or in a new version prepared by the author in 1951 which was staged by Yuri Zavadsky (q.v.), also at the Mossoviet. Of Bill-Belotserkovsky's later plays, one, produced in 1934, was published in 1938 in an English translation by Anthony Wixley as *Life is Calling* (it is also known as *Life Goes Forward*). The plot is somewhat conventional, but the tension is heightened by the conflict, not only between the characters' emotions, but between social duty and personal happiness. A later play on the same theme, produced in 1936, shows the adjustment of an old Russian intellectual to the new social order. None of Bill-Belotserkovsky's later plays achieved the success of his early work.

Billy Rose Theatre, see NATIONAL THEATRE, NEW YORK (2) and ZIEGFELD THEATRE.

Biltmore Theatre, New York, on 47th Street between Broadway and 8th Avenue. Built by the Chanins, it opened on 7 Dec. 1925 and had an undistinguished career until 1928, when it found itself in trouble over *Pleasure Man*, by Mae West (q.v.), which was closed by the police after three performances. In 1936 the Federal Theatre Project presented with some success its experimental Living Newspaper, *Triple-A Plowed Under*, by Arthur Arent. In the same year Warner Brothers bought the theatre, and George Abbott (q.v.) staged for them a number of successful shows, including Monks and Finklehoff's *Brother Rat* (1936) and Sidney Blow's *All That Glitters* (1938). Later productions at this theatre included *My Sister Eileen* (1940), based on stories by Ruth McKenny, F. Hugh Herbert's *Kiss and Tell* (1943), and Phoebe and Henry Ephron's *Take Her, She's Mine* (1961), the last two being also directed by Abbott. In 1963 Neil Simon's *Barefoot in the Park* began a long run, and in 1968 came the epoch-making *Hair*, a musical by Gerome Ragni and James Rado.

Bio-Mechanics, the name given to a method of production evolved by Meyerhold (q.v.). Reducing the actor to the status of puppet, to be manipulated at the whim of the director, it calls for the complete elimination of the player's personality and the subjugation of his mind and body to a series of acrobatic turns. It further demands the stripping of the stage to the bare bones, the elimination of 'detail' scenery, and the willing co-operation of the audience in building up an imaginary stage-picture. Meyerhold himself admitted that his method was in a large measure based on Pavlov's theory of association. It has also, because of its insistence on conventional and stylized gesture, been compared to the Japanese *kabuki* (q.v.). A cerebral rather than an emotional theatre, it served its purpose in the early days of the Russian Revolution by clearing away the inessentials of production which cluttered up the old theatres; but it was fated to be outstripped by the forces it had liberated, and finally became outmoded.

BIRD, ROBERT MONTGOMERY (1806–54), American playwright, who first came into prominence when in 1831 Edwin Forrest (q.v.) appeared as Spartacus in his romantic tragedy, *The Gladiator*. It was an immediate success, and Forrest selected it for his first appearance at Drury Lane in 1836, continuing to act in it until his retirement in 1872. John McCullough also played the part, in which he made his last appearance in 1884. It was seen on the stage as late as 1892. Bird wrote two more plays for Forrest, *Oralloossa* (1832) and *The Broker of Bogotá* (1834), and revised for him *Metamora*, by Stone (q.v.). All three were popular and frequently revived, but owing to the chaotic state of the copyright laws at that time, Bird made no money from them. He therefore withdrew from the theatre and sought a livelihood elsewhere.

BIRD, THEOPHILUS (1608–64), English actor, who bridges the gap between the Caroline and Restoration theatres. He was the son of an actor, WILLIAM (?–1624), who appears frequently in Henslowe's diary as a member of the Admiral's Men (q.v.). Theophilus is first found playing female parts with Queen Henrietta's Men (q.v.). By 1635 he had graduated to male parts, and played Massinissa in Thomas Nabbe's *Hannibal and Scipio*. Shortly afterwards he married Anne, eldest daughter of Christopher Beeston (q.v.). In 1637 he joined the King's Men (see CHAMBERLAIN'S MEN) at Blackfriars, remaining with them until the closing of the theatres in 1642. He is named first in Downes's list of actors who appeared immediately on the reopening of the theatres in 1660, and Pepys notes a rumour that he had broken his leg while fencing in a revival of Suckling's *Aglaura* in 1662.

Birmingham. Best known as the home of a famous repertory theatre, Birmingham has a long theatre history, typical in its early days of many English provincial towns. Two theatrical booths existed before 1730, but the first permanent building was erected in Moor Street about 1740. A theatre in King Street opened in 1751, another in New Street in 1774. This last was twice rebuilt after fires, in 1792 and 1820. The father of Macready (q.v.) became its manager in 1795.

Touring companies were first introduced in 1849, but the resident stock company lingered on until 1878. The theatre closed in 1901, was rebuilt and reopened in 1904, and finally demolished in 1957. Another theatre, the Prince of Wales's, was destroyed by enemy action during the Second World War.

The Birmingham Repertory Theatre, one of the most significant enterprises launched in the English theatre during the first half of the twentieth century, began with private theatricals in the home of Barry Jackson (q.v.). From these emerged in 1907 the Pilgrim Players, an amateur company which put on at local halls, up to 1913, twenty-eight productions, mainly of plays unlikely to be seen in the commercial theatre. Inspired by the founding of the Manchester and Liverpool Repertory Theatres (qq.v.), Jackson, who was a wealthy man, built and equipped a theatre in Station Street to house a professional company, which opened on 15 Feb. 1913 in *Twelfth Night*. During the next ten years a wide variety of uncommercial plays was produced, including Drinkwater's *Abraham Lincoln* (1918) and the first English performance of Shaw's *Back to Methuselah* (1923), one of many Shaw plays produced by Jackson. In 1924, disheartened by lack of civic support, Jackson threatened to close the theatre, but the Birmingham Civic Society guaranteed a sufficient number of season-ticket holders to keep it open. The situation was further ameliorated by the subsequent success of such plays as Phillpott's *The Farmer's Wife* (1924) and Besier's *The Barretts of Wimpole Street* (1930), both of which were transferred to London, together with controversial modern-dress productions of *Hamlet* (1925) and *Macbeth* (1928). From 1929 to 1938 the Birmingham Repertory also provided the nucleus of the company which appeared at the Malvern Festival (q.v.). In 1935 Jackson transferred the Birmingham theatre to a Board of Trustees, which still controls it, but remained its director until his death in 1961. Two years later the company celebrated its golden jubilee, and made plans to move to a new theatre in 1971.

BISHOP, GEORGE WALTER (1886–1965), English dramatic critic, who was editor of *The Era* from 1928 until 1932, when he became theatre correspondent of the *Daily Telegraph*, and book editor from

1937, remaining there until his death. His enthusiasm for the theatre and his retentive memory made him an admirable correspondent. He was also an excellent organizer, and revived the tradition whereby the *Daily Telegraph* made itself responsible for special stage celebrations, including Marie Tempest's jubilee (1935) and Irving's centenary (1938). In 1957 Bishop published his autobiography as *My Betters*. He was also the author of *Barry Jackson and the London Stage* (1933).

BJØRNSON, BJØRNSTJERNE (1832–1910), Norwegian novelist, poet, and dramatist, whose work, though perhaps less powerful than that of his contemporary Henrik Ibsen (q.v.), was in its day more popular, partly because of his reputation as a novelist and song-writer, and because of his influence in contemporary politics. His plays may be roughly grouped in three periods—the first mainly historical and patriotic: *Kong Sverre* (1861); *Maria Stuart i Skotland* (1864); the second, realistic social dramas which often treat of matters which Ibsen was to write about a few years later, culminating in *En Handske* (1883); and the third marking the increasing interest in spiritual rather than social problems characteristic of his last years: *Over Ævne I* (1883), probably Bjørnson's greatest play, seen in London in 1901 as *Beyond Human Power*; *Over Ævne II* (1895); and, his last play, *Naar den ny Vin blomstrer* (1905). Bjørnson was awarded the Nobel Prize for Literature in 1903, the first Scandinavian writer to receive it. In 1858 he had married the actress, Karoline Reimers, and their son, BJÖRN (1859–1942), was a well-known actor and theatre manager who joined the Meininger Company (q.v.) in 1880. In 1885 he became a director of the Christiania [Oslo] theatre, which his father had managed in the 1850s, and in 1899 took over the newly established Nationalteater there. During the next forty years he served the Norwegian theatre in many different capacities.

BLACK, GEORGE (1890–1945), a Northern music-hall manager who went to London in 1928, and next to C. B. Cochran (q.v.) was the outstanding figure in the music-hall world between the two world wars. His Crazy Gang shows (q.v.) at the Palladium, with Flanagan and Allen and Nervo and Knox, caused a minor revolu-

tion in the profession, bringing back some of the atmosphere of the old 'halls'. Black was also responsible for a number of shows at the Hippodrome, notably *The Fleet's Lit Up* (1938), *Black Velvet* (1939), and *Black Vanities* (1941). He was excellent at spotting nascent talent, but in later life he became somewhat intolerant of criticism, and after the poor notices given to Ronald Gow's musical play, *Jenny Jones* (1944), he refrained from inviting the critics to his next production.

Blackfriars Theatre, LONDON. There were two Blackfriars theatres, one succeeding the other, both built within the boundaries of the old Blackfriars monastery, the site of which is now covered by the offices of *The Times* and Playhouse Yard. The first, probably fitted up in one of the smaller halls, was used by the Children of the Chapel Royal and of Windsor Chapel under their Master, Richard Farrant, from 1576 until his death in 1580. From 1583 to 1584 it was used by a company of children from Oxford's company, Paul's, and the Chapel (see BOY COMPANIES). It then lapsed and was let out as lodgings. In 1596 James Burbage (q.v.) adapted another hall for use by his company from the Theatre (q.v.). He died before its completion, and in 1600 his sons leased it to the Children of the Chapel, who played there until 1608, when the Burbages' company, now known as the King's Men (see CHAMBERLAIN'S MEN), appeared there, remaining in possession until the closing of the theatres in 1642. The building was finally demolished in 1655. It was probably at the second Blackfriars that scenery was first used (apart from Masques, q.v.), as it is referred to in Suckling's *Aglaura* (1637) and in Habington's *Queen of Aragon* (1640), both performed there.

BLAGROVE, THOMAS, see MASTER OF THE REVELS.

BLANCHAR, PIERRE (1896–1963), French actor of striking presence and impressive delivery, who was at the Odéon from 1919 to 1923. After distinguishing himself in such plays as Pagnol's *Jazz* (1925), Achard's *Domino* (1931), and Salacrou's *L'Inconnue d'Arras* (1935), he joined the Comédie-Française in 1939. Leaving there in 1946, he continued to appear both on the stage and in films. Among the new plays in which he was seen to advantage were Montherlant's *Malatesta* (1950) and

Camus's dramatization of Dostoievsky's *The Possessed* (1958).

BLANCHARD, EDWARD LEMAN (1820–89), younger son of the heavy-comedy actor WILLIAM BLANCHARD (1769–1835). He became famous in his own day as a writer of pantomime, producing at least one annually from 1844 until his death, generally under the pseudonym of Francisco Frost. Most of them were given at Drury Lane. He was also responsible for a number of farces, some burlesques, including one of Dickens, *The Cricket on Our Own Hearth* (1846), and a comedy, *The Road of Life*, produced at the Olympic in 1843. He edited the plays of Shakespeare, and was for many years (from 1863) dramatic critic of the *Daily Telegraph*. From 1850 to 1879 he wrote dramatic criticism for the *Era*. None of his work, which was mainly topical and spectacular, has survived on the stage.

Two actors, father and son, both named THOMAS BLANCHARD, of whom the first died in 1797 and the second in 1859, do not appear to have been related to the above.

BLANCHARD, KITTY (1847–1911), see RANKIN, ARTHUR.

Blanchard's Amphitheatre, NEW YORK, see CHATHAM THEATRE (1).

BLAND, GEORGE (?–1807), see JORDAN, D.

BLONDEL, see MINSTREL.

Blood-tub, see GAFF.

Blues, see BORDER.

BOADEN, JAMES (1762–1839), English playwright, critic, and journalist, editor of the *Oracle*. He was a keen Shakespearian and took part in the controversy over the forgeries of Ireland (q.v.). In 1837 he published a pamphlet, identifying the 'Mr. W. H.' of the sonnets as William Herbert, Earl of Pembroke. He was the author of several forgotten plays and of *The Life of Kemble* (1825), *The Life of Mrs. Siddons* (1827), and *The Life of Mrs. Jordan* (1831).

Boar's Head Inn, LONDON, see INNS USED AS THEATRES.

Board Alley Theatre, see BOSTON.

Boards, the component parts of the stage floor, which run up- and down-stage supported on joists running crossways; used also as a phrase indicating the acting profession, to be 'on the boards' or to 'tread the boards' signifying 'to be an actor'. In modern theatres the boards form an unbroken expanse, but in earlier times they were removable, to facilitate the working of traps and machinery (qq.v.). This meant that each joist had to be supported separately by its own system of vertical posts rising from the floor of the cellar under the stage. With a raked stage a certain stress was exerted which tended to make the stage slide in the direction of the slope, and since the working of the traps and the bridges made it impossible to counteract this by permanent cross-bracing, there can be found, beneath old raked stages, a system of metal strap-hooks, linking one row of uprights with the next behind, and so knitting the whole together. These tie-bars could be unhooked when necessary to allow the passage of a piece of scenery.

Boat Truck, a platform, running on castors, on which scenes, or sections of scenes, can be moved on and off stage. Two such trucks, pivoted each at the down-stage and off-stage corners, so as to swing in and out over the acting area, are known as a SCISSOR STAGE. A further variant is the WAGGON STAGE, run on a system of rails and lifts. As many as five Waggon Stages can be found in some large theatres, each capable of moving aside from the acting area, or of rising and sinking in the cellar, with a full load of scenery.

BOBÈCHE [really ANTOINE MANDELOT] (1791–*c.* 1840), a farce-player of the Paris boulevards, who, with red jacket and grey tricorne hat with butterfly antennae, amused the holiday crowds with his *parades* (q.v.) in company with GALIMAFRÉ [really AUGUSTE GUÉRIN] (1790–1870). Both became extremely popular, and were invited to private houses to entertain the guests, but the topical jokes of Bobèche offended Napoleon and he was banished. He returned under the Restoration, and was again successful, but later went into management in the provinces and is not heard of again. Galimafré, who refused to act after 1814, joined the stage staff of the Gaîté and later of the Opéra-Comique, and died in retirement. A play based on the lives of these two comedians, by the brothers Cogniard, was produced at the Palais-Royal in 1837.

Bobo, see GRACIOSO.

BODEL, JEAN (*c.* 1165–1210), a minstrel of Arras, and with his fellow-citizen Adam de la Halle (q.v.) the founder of French secular drama. His *Jeu de Saint Nicolas*, which tells the story of a miracle worked by an image of the saint during the Crusades, contains many contemporary allusions which seem to indicate that Bodel had himself been on a Crusade. Though not, from a literary point of view, as good as Adam de la Halle's work, it is more dramatic, and was probably better in performance. In about 1202 Bodel contracted leprosy and retired to a lazarhouse.

BOECK, JOHANN MICHAEL (1743–93), German actor, who was the first to play Karl Moor in Schiller's *Die Räuber* when it was put on under Dalberg at Mannheim in 1782, with Iffland (q.v.), whom Boeck greatly helped and supported in his work, as Franz Moor. He was not a particularly intelligent actor, but he had a fine presence and a passionate style which made him acceptable to the audience. His wife, SOPHIA SCHULZE, who had received her early training under Schönemann (q.v.), was also a very popular member of the Mannheim company, and in her youth was excellent in breeches parts.

BOGUSŁAWSKI, WOJCIECH (1757–1829), Polish actor and director, who was virtually the founder of the Polish theatre. In 1778 he joined the company of the Teatr Narodowy (National Theatre) in Warsaw, founded in 1765, and became its director in 1783. During the next thirty years he was actively engaged in the financing and building of theatres throughout the country (Vilna in 1785, Lwów in 1794), often engaging and directing the companies himself. He encouraged new Polish playwrights, among them FRANCISZEK ZABŁOCKI (1754–1821) and JULIAN NIEMCEWICZ (1757–1841), and also wrote a number of plays, of which *Cracovians and Mountaineers* (1749) was the most popular. He was the first Polish actor to play Hamlet, appearing in 1797 in a translation prepared by himself from the German version of F. L. Schröder (q.v.). A theatre named after him opened in Warsaw in 1901.

BOILEAU-DESPRÉAUX, NICOLAS (1636–1711), a French critic whose writings brought a new and invigorating atmosphere into the literary debates of Paris and exercised a great influence on French literature and drama. He was not a poet, but a writer of verse, and a good one. With no imagination or warmth, he had plenty of common sense and an uncanny flair for the best in art. He was the friend of many great writers of his time, particularly of Racine (q.v.)—whom he taught to write verse—and of Molière (q.v.). It was at the height of his friendship with Boileau that Molière wrote his greatest plays, *Tartuffe*, *Le Misanthrope*, and *Don Juan*.

BOITO, ARRIGO (1842–1918), Italian poet and composer, and the first to realize that the libretto of an opera should have some literary value. His own opera, 'Mefistofele' (1868), based on Goethe's *Faust*, was not a great success, and it is as the librettist of Verdi's 'Otello' (1887) and 'Falstaff' (1893) that he is chiefly remembered. His handling of the themes is excellent, and his translations keep closely to the Shakespearian originals without sacrificing the sense to the music.

BOKER, GEORGE HENRY (1823–90), American dramatist, chiefly remembered as one of the few successful writers in modern times of poetic tragedy, being in this respect the American counterpart of the later English writer, Stephen Phillips (q.v.). Boker wrote a number of plays, of which the most popular was *Francesca da Rimini*, first produced in New York in 1855. In 1883 it was revived by Lawrence Barrett (q.v.) with himself as Lanciotto, Francesca's husband, who in Boker's version becomes the chief character in the play. It remained in Barrett's repertory for many years and was again revived in 1901 by Otis Skinner (q.v.). The play was never acted from the printed version, as Boker himself altered it considerably for production and it was heavily revised by William Winter (q.v.) for Barrett's revival.

BOLT, ROBERT OXTON (1924–), English dramatist, whose first play, *The Critic and the Heart*, was staged at the Oxford Playhouse in 1957. He first came into prominence when *Flowering Cherry*, with Ralph Richardson (q.v.) in the leading part, was seen at the Haymarket in London later the same year. This moving study of a man foredoomed to failure was seen in New York in 1959. It was followed in

1960 by *The Tiger and the Horse*, in which Michael Redgrave (q.v.) appeared with his daughter Vanessa, and by *A Man for All Seasons*, an outstanding portrait of Sir Thomas More, played by Paul Scofield (q.v.). This had a long run in New York also, and was then filmed. Bolt's next play, *Gentle Jack* (1963), in which Edith Evans (q.v.) appeared, was not a success, and had only a short run in London, but in 1970, after the production of a play for children, *The Thwarting of Baron Bolligrew* (1965), and *Brother and Sister* (1967), seen only in the provinces, Bolt returned to his former excellence with *Vivat! Vivat Regina!*, which takes as its theme the relationship between Elizabeth Tudor and Mary Queen of Scots. First seen at Chichester (q.v.) in 1970, this was successfully transferred to London.

BONARELLI DELLA ROVERE, GUIDOBALDO (1563–1608), Italian dramatist, author of the best-known pastoral of the seventeenth century, the *Filli di Sciro*, produced at Ferrara in 1607. This, as *Scyros*, was given at Cambridge in a Latin translation by Samuel Brooke before Charles, Prince of Wales, on 2 or 3 Mar. 1613, and in an English translation about twenty years later before the Court in London. A second English translation, by Gilbert Talbot, was played in London in 1657. The first was printed in 1655, the second remains in manuscript.

BOND, EDWARD (1935–), English dramatist, whose plays have from the beginning aroused fierce controversy. The first, *The Pope's Wedding*, was produced at the Royal Court (q.v.) in 1962 as a Sunday-night production without décor; but it was with *Saved* (1965), also at the Royal Court, that Bond first came into prominence, mainly because of the scene in which a baby is stoned to death in its pram. This and the two following plays, *Early Morning* and *Narrow Road to the Deep North* (both 1968), were all revived in 1969 in an 'Edward Bond season' by the Royal Court, an indication of the importance attributed to this dramatist by those who first promoted his work. *Saved* was also chosen as the English entry for the 1969 Belgrade Festival during a European tour. Though it is as yet too soon to evaluate Bond's importance in the development of modern English drama, he has undoubtedly added some impressive works to the con-

temporary repertoire, among them a short anti-apartheid play entitled *Black Mass*, first seen at Sheffield in 1970.

Booked Flat, see FLAT.

BOOTE, ROSIE (1878–1958), a celebrated Gaiety Girl, who in 1901 married the fourth Marquess of Headfort and retired from the stage, though she continued to attend almost all first nights in London practically up to the time of her death. After being trained as a dancer, she joined the chorus at George Edwardes's Gaiety Theatre during the run of *The Shop Girl* in 1895. In 1898 she played the small part of Marietta, the flower girl, in *The Runaway Girl*, and two years later made a great success as Isabel Blyth in *The Messenger Boy*, singing Monckton's 'Maisie'. She was much regretted on her retirement, as a great future in musical comedy had been predicted for her.

BOOTH, BARTON (1681–1733), English actor, who showed great aptitude for the stage in a performance of Terence's *Andria* while still at Westminster School. In 1700, after gaining experience in Dublin and in the provinces, he was engaged by Betterton (q.v.) for Lincoln's Inn Fields Theatre. Though a good tragic actor, he was slow to establish himself, due possibly to the jealousy of Wilks (q.v.). He was, however, successful as Pyrrhus in Philips's *The Distrest Mother* in 1712, and as Addison's Cato, his greatest part, in the following year. He was manager of Drury Lane with Cibber and Wilks after Doggett's retirement. The most striking feature of his acting was his adoption of 'attitudes'— the pose, for instance, in which, as Othello, he listened, with appropriate gestures, to Emilia's address to the dying Desdemona. In these he was unexcelled, and even those who were jealous of his popularity conceded his effectiveness at such points.

BOOTH, EDWIN THOMAS (1833–93), an outstanding tragedian, and the first American actor to achieve a European reputation. Son of the English actor Junius Brutus Booth senior (q.v.), he made his first appearance at sixteen in his father's company, and soon established an enviable reputation. Although at his best in tragedy he was, like his father, much admired as Sir Giles Overreach in Massinger's *A New Way to Pay Old Debts*, which he played on his first visit to London in 1861, together with Shylock in *The Merchant of Venice* and the title-role in Bulwer-Lytton's *Richelieu*. From 1863 to 1867 he was manager of the Winter Garden (see METROPOLITAN THEATRE), where in 1864 he played a record hundred performances of *Hamlet*. After the destruction by fire of the Winter Garden in 1867 he built his own theatre (see BOOTH'S). In London again in 1881, he appeared at the Lyceum by invitation of Henry Irving (q.v.), alternating with him the roles of Othello and Iago. In 1888 he presented his house in Gramercy Park to the newly founded Players' Club (which still occupies it), living there till his death. He was an unhappy man, and his habitual melancholia was aggravated by the shock consequent on the assassination of Lincoln by his youngest brother John Wilkes Booth (q.v.).

BOOTH, JOHN WILKES (1839–65), American actor, who assassinated Lincoln, then President of the United States, during a performance at Ford's Theatre, Washington, of Tom Taylor's *Our American Cousin*, on 14 Apr. 1865 at 10.22 p.m. There are two conflicting theories current about this unfortunate act. One presents Booth as a wild, undisciplined, and embittered madman, jealous of the success of his elder brother, Edwin (q.v.), and seeking notoriety through crime, the other as an excellent actor, though eccentric, whose action was due to motives of mistaken patriotism. For a systematic survey of the whole question, see *The Mad Booths of Maryland* (1940), by Stanley Kimmel.

BOOTH, JUNIUS BRUTUS, senior (1796–1852), an English tragic actor who spent the latter part of his life in America. He was on the stage at seventeen, and after touring the provinces for some years appeared as Richard III at Covent Garden, where he proved a serious rival to Edmund Kean (q.v.). Among his most successful parts were Sir Giles Overreach in Massinger's *A New Way to Pay Old Debts*, Posthumus Leonatus in *Cymbeline*, and, in 1818, Shylock in *The Merchant of Venice*. In 1820 he went to Drury Lane, playing Iago to Kean's Othello, Edgar to his Lear, and Pierre (in Otway's *Venice Preserv'd*) to his Jaffier. In 1821 he went to America, where he may be said to have founded the tradition of tragic acting. He made his first appearance in New York

in 1821 in his favourite part, Richard III. He appears to have been an actor in the grand style, rough and unpolished but full of fire and eloquence, with a resonant voice and ample gestures. There was, however, a streak of insanity in him, aggravated by habitual intemperance, which he passed on to his actor sons, Edwin, John Wilkes, the assassin of Lincoln, and Junius Brutus junior (qq.v.).

BOOTH, JUNIUS BRUTUS, junior (1821–83), American actor, brother of Edwin and John Wilkes Booth (qq.v.). He made his first appearance on the stage on tour with his father Junius Brutus Booth senior (q.v.), and was for many years a useful member of the stock company at the Bowery Theatre, New York. One of his best parts was Dan Lowrie in Frances Hodgson Burnett's *That Lass o' Lowrie's* (1878), which he also played on tour. He was three times married, and had two sons on the stage. The elder shot himself and his wife in a London hotel; the younger, SYDNEY BARTON BOOTH (1873–1937), who made his début at Wallack's in 1892, became a successful actor and also spent two seasons in vaudeville.

Booth Theatre, NEW YORK, on West 45th Street. Built by Winthrop Ames, this opened on 16 Oct. 1913 with *The Great Adventure*, based by Arnold Bennett on his novel *Buried Alive*. A minor part was played by Guthrie McClintic (q.v.). The Booth is still in use, and has had a number of successes, including Kaufman and Hart's *You Can't Take It With You* (1936), which ran for two years. In 1925 there was a production of *Hamlet* in modern dress with Basil Sidney, and in 1946 a fantastic production of Molière's *Le Bourgeois gentilhomme* as *The Would-Be Gentleman*, with the comedian Bobby Clark as M. Jourdain. Later productions included Inge's *Come Back, Little Sheba* (1950), with Shirley Booth, and the two-character play, Gibson's *Two for the Seesaw* (1958).

Booth's Theatre, NEW YORK, on the south-west corner of 6th Avenue and 23rd Street. Built for Edwin Booth (q.v.), this opened on 3 Feb. 1869 with Booth and Mary McVicker, later his second wife, as Romeo and Juliet. The stage, which was not raked (the wings were supported by braces), had a tall stage house, probably the first in New York, and large hydraulic-ally-powered elevator traps for lowering three-dimensional scenery into the basement. Booth had hoped to establish his theatre as a national home of poetic drama, but in spite of excellent performances by himself and a succession of visiting stars, the venture failed, and in 1873 Booth went bankrupt. The theatre passed under the control of Jarrett and Palmer on 30 May 1874, and was used for productions of plays by Boucicault (q.v.), who in 1879 became its lessee. It was later sold, and after a final production of *Romeo and Juliet* by Maurice Barrymore and Modjeska (qq.v.) it closed on 30 Apr. 1883. It was demolished and a department store built on the site.

BOQUET, LOUIS-RENÉ, see COSTUME.

Border, a narrow strip of painted cloth, battened at the top edge only, used to hide the top of the stage from the audience. If the lower edge is cut to shape, it is known as a Cloud or Tree Border. The use of clouds for masking the top of almost any scene was formerly common (see CLOUDINGS). In Victorian times plain sky borders were sometimes known as Blues. Tails, or Legs, on a border are long vertically-hanging extensions at each end, forming with the border an arch over the scene.

Border Light, see BATTEN.

Boston, a town important in the history of the American theatre, though the early companies had much opposition to contend with, and as late as 1792 plays given in the rooms later known as the Board Alley Theatre still had to be billed as 'Moral Lectures'. In 1794 the Federal Street Theatre was built, rebuilt after a fire four years later, and finally destroyed, after a long and chequered career, in 1852. Two years later the present Boston Theatre was built. The Haymarket, built in 1796, was pulled down in 1803. The Tremont Theatre, which opened in 1827 and was destroyed by fire in 1852, was for a time the successful rival of the Federal, but was itself outshone by the Boston Museum, which opened in 1841. Other Boston theatres were the Howard Athenaeum, opened by J. H. Hackett (q.v.) in 1846, and the National, which opened in 1832 as the American Amphitheatre, later became the Warren, and was destroyed by fire in 1852. The Boston Museum, which had a long and glorious history, reached the height of its popularity in 1873–83, with a fine stock company and good visiting stars. It finally closed in 1893.

BOTTOMLEY, GORDON (1874–1948), English poet, and one of the few to bring verse-plays successfully into the professional theatre. His *King Lear's Wife* (1915), *Britain's Daughters* (1922), *Gruach* (1923), and *Laodice and Danae* (1930), in which the influence of Shakespeare is counterbalanced by that of the Japanese Nō play (q.v.), were all seen in London, though they have not been revived. Their themes are taken from Celtic and Northern legend and early history, and Bottomley introduced to England, as Yeats did to Ireland, the Celtic and Northern twilight, the old world of fear and evil. He wrote also a number of one-act plays, and the Exeter Cathedral Festival play for 1933, *The Acts of St. Peter*.

BOUCHER, FRANÇOIS (1703–70), famous French artist, who in 1734 designed a series of theatrical costumes to illustrate a new edition of Molière. This may have led to his being engaged, some time before 1737, to design costumes for the Paris Opéra, where in 1744 he succeeded Servandony (q.v.) as official decorator. A rapid increase in his work outside the theatre caused him to resign his post in 1748, when he was succeeded by J. B. Martin.

BOUCICAULT, DIONYSIUS GEORGE (1859–1929), English actor and dramatist, known as 'Dot'. The elder son of Dionysius Boucicault and his wife Agnes Robertson (qq.v.), he made his first appearance in his father's company in New York in 1879, and then appeared in London and toured Australia with Robert Brough. From 1901 to 1915 he directed the plays given at the Duke of York's Theatre, London, under the management of Charles Frohman (q.v.). He was an excellent actor, particularly in later life, two of his outstanding parts being Sir William Gower in Pinero's *Trelawny of the 'Wells'* (1898) and Carraway Pim in A. A. Milne's *Mr. Pim Passes By* (1920). He married in 1901 the English actress Irene Vanbrugh (q.v.), who appeared in many of his productions.

BOUCICAULT [also BOURCICAULT, and BOURSIQUOT], DIONYSIUS LARDNER (1822–

90), known as 'Dion', actor and dramatist, whose life and works were divided between England and the U.S.A. A prolific author, credited with as many as 150 plays, he had his first success as a dramatist with *London Assurance*, a comedy of contemporary life produced at Covent Garden on 4 Mar. 1841, with Charles Mathews the younger (q.v.) as Dazzle. It was frequently revived up to the time of the author's death, and in 1970 was seen at the Aldwych in a production by the Royal Shakespeare Company. Boucicault, who was a skilled adapter of other men's work, prepared successful versions of two French plays as *The Corsican Brothers* (1852) and *Louis XI* (1855) for the Princess's (q.v.), and made a dramatization of Dickens's *The Cricket on the Hearth* as *Dot* (1859), in which the great American actor Joseph Jefferson (q.v.) played his first serious part, Caleb Plummer. Among Boucicault's Irish plays the most successful were *The Colleen Bawn* (1860) and *The Shaughraun* (1874). He was the first dramatist to treat the American Negro seriously on the stage, in *The Octoroon; or, Life in Louisiana* (1859), and may have been the first in England to receive a royalty (q.v.) on his plays instead of a lump sum. In New York he participated actively in the passing of an amendment to the existing Act on dramatic copyright, which became law in 1856. Boucicault was three times married, his second wife being Agnes Robertson (q.v.), and his third an American actress, Louise Thorndike.

BOUCICAULT, NINA (1867–1950), English actress, daughter of the elder Boucicault and his wife Agnes Robertson (qq.v.). Born in London, she made her first appearance with her father in New York in 1883, playing Eily O'Connor in a revival of his *The Colleen Bawn*. She was first seen in London in 1892, her second appearance there being as Kitty Verdun in the original production of Brandon Thomas's *Charley's Aunt*. She had a long and successful career on the London stage, making her last appearance in 1936 as the Countess Mortimer in the first public performance of Granville-Barker's *Waste*. It is, however, as the first actress to play Peter in Barrie's *Peter Pan* (1904) that she is chiefly remembered.

Boulevard du Temple, a fairground in Paris which became a centre of entertainment, with circuses, booths (in which

Bobèche (q.v.) and Galimafré revived memories of the earlier *parades* (q.v.)), children's theatres, and puppet-shows. During the Revolution, a number of small permanent theatres were built there (see AMBIGU-COMIQUE and GAÎTÉ) in which actors like Deburau and Frédérick (qq.v.) appeared in plays, often by Dumas *père* (q.v.) and later by the prolific writer of melodramas, Pixérécourt (q.v.). From the latter's works it got its nickname of 'the Boulevard of Crime'. The whole picturesque scene, with its sideshows, waxworks, fireworks, museums, cafés, concerts, and perambulating ballad-singers, was swept away in Haussmann's rebuilding of Paris in 1862, and the Boulevard Voltaire now occupies most of the site.

BOURCHIER, ARTHUR (1863–1927), English actor, husband of Violet Vanbrugh (q.v.), whom he married in 1894. He was one of the founders of the Oxford University Dramatic Society (see OXFORD), and on leaving the university made his first professional appearance as Jaques in *As You Like It* at Wolverhampton. After his marriage he toured with his wife, who played the leading part in many of his productions, and from 1900 to 1906 was in management at the Garrick Theatre, London. In 1910 he joined Beerbohm Tree at His Majesty's Theatre, where he was seen in a number of Shakespearian parts, being particularly admired as Henry VIII. He later appeared at the Oxford Music-Hall as Old Bill in a sketch based on Bairnsfather's *The Better 'Ole*. He was at his best in truculent or hearty parts, but had little subtlety and hotly resented criticism. In 1918 he married as his second wife an actress, Violet Marion Kyrle Bellew.

Bouschet, JAN, see ENGLISH COMEDIANS.

Bowery Theatre, NEW YORK. (1) The first Bowery Theatre, under Gilfert and George H. Barrett, opened on 23 Oct. 1826 with Holcroft's *The Road to Ruin*. The theatre was lit by gas; not with naked jets, as previously at the Chatham (q.v.), but with the flames enclosed in glass shades. Edwin Forrest (q.v.) made many of his early successes at the Bowery, first appearing there as Othello. On 26 May 1828 the theatre was burnt down, and the actors had to migrate to the Sans Souci (see NIBLO'S GARDEN). A second Bowery opened on 20 Aug. of the same year, again with Forrest as its star, and a year later Hamblin (q.v.) entered on twenty years of management. Under him the Bowery was the first theatre in New York to have continuous runs, in opposition to the constant changes of bill as still practised at the old-fashioned Park Theatre (q.v.). The Bowery saw, in the season of 1835–6, the last appearance in New York of the great actor Cooper (q.v.) and the first of Charlotte Cushman (q.v.), as Lady Macbeth. In Sept. 1836 the theatre was once again burnt down, but a third Bowery was ready by 1 Jan. 1837. It was destined to have a short and uninteresting history, as it was destroyed by fire on 18 Feb. 1838 and not reopened until 6 May 1839, once more under the management of Hamblin. A series of unsuccessful plays had brought the fortunes of the theatre to a very low ebb when on 25 Apr. 1845, for the fourth time in less than seventeen years, it was destroyed by fire. It was again rebuilt, opening on 4 Aug. 1845.

In 1851 an actor who was to be the idol of the Bowery audiences, Edward Eddy (q.v.), made his appearance in a series of strong parts. He took over in 1857, but he was unable to restore prosperity to the old theatre and closed it after one season. On 7 Aug. 1858 it reopened under George L. Fox (q.v.) and James W. Lingard with plays and pantomimes. When they left, the old Bowery, by now the oldest playhouse in New York, was once again subjected to a series of incompetent managers. During the Civil War it was occupied by the military, and then became a circus. After thorough renovation, Fox reopened it and put on a succession of novelties, including a pantomime based on the tale of Old Dame Trot and her Wonderful Cat. Long after old-fashioned farce had vanished from New York's new playhouses it continued to flourish at the old Bowery, but melodrama was always its staple fare. The theatre then fell a victim to the prevalent craze for burlesque, and finally closed in 1878, having spanned more than fifty years of the young American theatre. A year later it reopened as the Thalia for plays in German, and it was finally destroyed by fire in 1929.

(2) THE NEW BOWERY opened on 5 Sept. 1859, under Fox and Lingard, with a good company, some filched from the old Bowery, where the managers had been in office the previous year. It had a short and undistinguished career, enlivened only by visits from guest stars and the inevitable *Uncle Tom's Cabin* in Aiken's adaptation. The season of 1866–7 was well under way, mainly with melodrama and pantomime, when on 18 Dec. 1866 the theatre was destroyed by fire. It was never rebuilt.

Box-Set, a scene representing the three walls and ceiling of a room, not by means of perspective painting on wings, backcloth, and borders, as in early scenery, but by an arrangement of flats (see FLAT) which form continuous walls, with practicable doors and windows, completely covered in by a Ceiling-cloth. The flats are lined-and-cleated together, edge to edge, on any desired ground plan (or, particularly if they are to be used on revolving stages, joined by hinges), with Reveals, or false thickness-pieces, to give solidity to the openings and Returns, or setbacks, in the walls. The bottoms of openings in a door or arch flat are strengthened by flat metal strips called Sill-irons. The box-set was first used in Mme Vestris's production of W. B. Bernard's *The Conquering Game* at the Olympic on 28 Nov. 1832, and brought to perfection in her production of Boucicault's *London Assurance* at Covent Garden in 1841. It became general, except for opera and ballet, but is now being superseded by the open-stage set.

Boy Bishop, see FEAST OF FOOLS.

Boy Companies. During the sixteenth century the boys who formed part of the Royal choirs often acted plays at Court, and in 1576 the Children of the Chapel made their first public appearance at Blackfriars (q.v.), which was for some time after used exclusively by them and the Children of Paul's. Their popularity is attested by Hamlet's reference to the 'little eyases'. They achieved a quasi-professional status, and gave first performances of many important plays, including *Cynthia's Revels* (1600) and *The Poetaster* (1601) by Ben Jonson (q.v.), and almost all the plays of Lyly (q.v.).

BOYLE, ROGER, see ORRERY, LORD.

BOYLE, WILLIAM (1853–1923), Irish dramatist, whose first play, *The Building Fund* (1905), was produced at the newly established Abbey Theatre (q.v.). With this, and with his later plays, *The Eloquent Dempsey* and *The Mineral Workers* (both 1906), Boyle helped to establish a new type of 'realistic' Irish play which materially altered the character of the Abbey Theatre as Yeats and Lady Gregory (qq.v.) had originally envisaged it.

BRACCO, ROBERTO (1862–1943), Italian playwright, whose works, neglected under the Fascist regime, are only now becoming known. His most accomplished play, and the most significant historically, is *Il piccolo santo* (1909), remarkable for having anticipated the Theatre of Silence (q.v.). He showed himself a brilliant writer of comedy in *Uno degli onesti* (1900), and again in *Il perfetto amore* (1910), a highly sophisticated vehicle for a virtuoso actor and actress. *Don Pietro Caruso* (1895) and *Sperduti nel buio* (1901) are naturalistic studies of Neapolitan lower life, ironic and pathetic and uncompromisingly theatrical. Bracco resembles Giacosa (q.v.) in manifesting in his plays influences from Dumas *fils* (*Una donna*, 1892, and *Maschere*, 1893) to Ibsen (*Il trionfo*, 1895, and *I fantasmi*, 1906), but, unlike Giacosa, he established a personal identity and added to the techniques of serious drama.

Brace, see FLAT.

BRACEGIRDLE, ANNE (c. 1673/4–1748), one of the first English actresses, protégée and pupil of Betterton (q.v.). She is mentioned in Downes's *Roscius Anglicanus* (1708) as playing young women's parts at the Theatre Royal in 1688. She made her greatest successes as the heroines of Congreve (q.v.), whose mistress she was for some years, and was particularly applauded as Millamant in his *The Way of the World* (1700). She retired in 1707 to make way for the rising young actress Anne Oldfield (q.v.).

BRADY, WILLIAM ALOYSIUS (1863–1950), American actor and theatre manager, who made his first appearance on the stage in San Francisco in 1882 and toured successfully for a long time as Svengali in du Maurier's *Trilby*. From 1896 until its demolition in 1909 he managed the Manhattan Theatre in New York (see STANDARD THEATRE (2)), and he also built and managed the Forty-Eighth Street Theatre and the Playhouse (qq.v.). Many of his productions starred his second wife, Grace George (q.v.). By his first wife Brady was the father of the actress ALICE BRADY (1892–1939), who first appeared on the stage in 1909, but, like her father, was connected with the early days of the film industry, in which much of her later career was passed.

BRAHM [really ABRAHAMSOHN], OTTO (1856–1912), a German literary critic whose interest in contemporary drama, and particularly in the work of Antoine (q.v.) at the Théâtre Libre, led him to found in 1899 the Freie Bühne (q.v.). He had already been responsible for the appearance of a journal under the same name, later changed to *Die neue deutsche Rundschau*, and the main purpose of his new venture was to encourage the work of naturalistic playwrights by bringing together a group of actors who could adequately interpret their work. For four years Brahm directed his company, led by Emanuel Reicher, in a programme of new plays, both German and foreign. He did good work in clearing the German stage of many outmoded traditions and bringing it into the mainstream of European drama, but his methods, based on those of Stanislavsky (q.v.), though admirable when applied to the social dramas of Ibsen or Hauptmann (qq.v.), were less successful with comedy or with the classics. In 1894 Brahm's company was merged in that of the Deutsches Theater (q.v.), where he continued to direct plays in the new naturalistic style.

BRAITHWAITE, DAME LILIAN (1873–1948), English actress, who in 1943 was created D.B.E. for her services to the theatre. She had already had some amateur experience when in 1892 she played leading parts in South Africa with the Shakespeare company of her husband Gerald Lawrence (q.v.). She later toured in England with Frank Benson (q.v.), again in Shakespeare, and was with George Alexander (q.v.) at the St. James's Theatre in London for several seasons. Among her outstanding parts were Florence Lancaster in Noël Coward's *The Vortex* (1924), in which she was also seen in New York a year later; Elizabeth I in the English version of André Josset's *Elisabeth, la femme sans homme*; and Abby Brewster in the London production of Joseph Kesselring's *Arsenic and Old Lace* (1942), which ran for over three years.

BRANDES, JOHANN CHRISTIAN (1735–99), a German actor and playwright, whose reminiscences, *Meine Lebensgeschichte* (1800), give an excellent account of a touring company during the eighteenth century. In 1757 he joined Schönemann's company, of which Ekhof (q.v.) was a member, but this was not a success, and he did better in the company of an old harlequin-player, Schuch, who was a good friend to him. As he confesses in his memoirs, Brandes was a poor actor, but he prided himself on his plays, now forgotten, and on his monodramas (q.v.) (a genre of his own invention), of which the most successful was *Ariadne auf Naxos*. His wife, ESTHER CHARLOTTE HENRIETTA KOCH (1746–84), was a good actress, particularly in tragedy, and his eldest daughter MINNA (1765–88), the godchild of Lessing (q.v.), was also on the stage. After she died, Brandes retired to Berlin, where he appeared occasionally at the National Theatre under Iffland (q.v.).

BRANSBY WILLIAMS, see WILLIAMS, BRANSBY.

BRAYTON, LILY (1876–1953), see ASCHE, OSCAR.

Bread and Puppet Theatre, see ROYAL COURT THEATRE (2).

BRECHT, (EUGEN) BERTOLT FRIEDRICH (1898–1956), German dramatist and poet. He was studying medicine in Munich when an interest in the theatre led him first to dramatic criticism in the *Augsburger Volkswille* and then to the writing of plays. The first to be performed was *Trommeln in der Nacht*, by the Munich Kammerspiele in 1922; it was awarded the Kleist prize. The sober and somewhat cynical tone of this study of a soldier returning from the war marks the beginning of a reaction against Expressionism (q.v.), under whose influence Brecht had previously written *Baal* and *In the Jungle of Cities*, not performed until 1923.

In 1924 Brecht settled in Berlin, and while working as assistant to Max Reinhardt (q.v.) at the Deutsches Theater, wrote a number of plays which show him attempting to find and develop his own style, and putting into practice, long before he formulated it in writing, his theory of 'alienation' (q.v.), which sought to detach the subject-matter of the drama by destroying the illusion, interrupting the course of the action, and lowering the tension so that the audience could remain emotionally disengaged during the performance and capable of taking an intelligent view of what it was offered.

Brecht's first real success with the theatre-going public came with the production at the Theater am Schiffbauerdamm in 1928 of *Die Dreigroschenoper*, an adaptation of John Gay's *The Beggar's Opera* with music by Kurt Weill, who also collaborated with Brecht in the operas 'Happy End' (1929), and 'Aufstieg und Fall der Stadt Mahagonny' and 'Der Jasager' (both 1930). Like all Brecht's adaptations, which include *Pauken und Trompeten*, based on Farquhar's *The Recruiting Officer*, *Koriolan*, based on Shakespeare's *Coriolanus*, and *Edward II*, based on Marlowe, it was so different from the original as to constitute virtually a new work. The Marxism which was to become an all-determining force in Brecht's work did not appear strongly until the early 1930s, when he wrote a number of short didactic plays, the best of which are probably *Die Massnahme* and *Die Ausnahme und die Regel*, as well as *Die Heilige Johanna der Schlachthöfe*—the most ambitious of Brecht's plays up to that time, which was begun in 1930 but not produced until 1959. With the advent of Hitler to power in 1933, Brecht left Germany with his second wife, HELENE WEIGEL (1900–71), and two children— 'Changing countries more often than his shoes', as he says in one of his poems—for Switzerland, Denmark, Finland, and finally, in 1941, California.

It was during these years in exile that Brecht wrote what are generally considered to be his best plays—*Mutter Courage und ihre Kinder*, *Das Leben des Galilei*, *Der gute Mensch von Sezuan*, and *Der kaukäsische Kreidekreis*—which combine a maturity of vision and depth of expression with a wider sympathy for the human predicament than is found in any of his earlier works. In 1947 Brecht received an invitation from the East German government to take charge of a subsidized theatre in East Berlin, and there, back in the Theater am Schiffbauerdamm, he established his Berliner Ensemble and produced the plays written in exile. Most popular of all was the production of *Mutter Courage* with Helene Weigel, at the peak of her career, playing the title-role. The high standard of acting and production, as well as the plays themselves, made the company famous far beyond their own country. Their visit to Paris in 1955 was received with enthusiasm, and they were rehearsing for a visit to London when Brecht died suddenly in Aug. 1956.

It is still too early to assess Brecht's place in the history of the theatre; but his influence has been extensive both in England and in America, disseminated by critics and writers, and by productions of his plays in the original and in translation. On their first visit to London in 1956 (they have not yet (1970) appeared in New York), the Berliner Ensemble under Brecht's widow were seen at the Palace Theatre in *Mutter Courage und ihre Kinder, Pauken und Trompeten*, and *Der kaukasische Kreidekreis*. On a second visit, in 1965, they played at the National Theatre (Old Vic) in *Die Dreigroschenoper, Koriolan, Die Tage der Commune*, and *Der aufhaltsame Aufstieg des Arturo Ui*. In translation, the first play to be seen in London was probably *Señora Carrar's Rifles*, directed by John Fernald in 1938 for Unity (see UNITY THEATRE (1)). Other productions at this theatre were *Mother Courage, Simone Machard*, and *The Exception and the Rule*. *Mother Courage* was also done by Theatre Workshop in 1955 with Joan Littlewood in the title-role, and at the National Theatre in 1965 with Madge Ryan. In 1956 *The Good Woman of Setzuan*, with Peggy Ashcroft in the dual role of the prostitute Shen-Te and her male cousin, was seen at the Royal Court Theatre, where an adaptation of *The Threepenny Opera* by Marc Blitzstein (see THEATRE DE LYS) had been seen earlier in the year, and where 'Happy End' was to have its London première in 1965. *The Life of Galileo*, first seen at Birmingham University, and in New York in 1947, was produced at the Mermaid Theatre in 1963, as was *Schweik in the Second World War*. The Royal Shakespeare Company at the Aldwych did *The Caucasian Chalk Circle* in 1962, and in 1965 *Puntila* (which, as *Herr Puntila und sein Knecht*, was written in 1940 while Brecht was in Finland, but not produced until 1948, at Zürich). In 1963 Peter O'Toole was seen in *Baal* at the Phoenix, and the opera 'Aufstieg und Fall der Stadt Mahagonny' was produced at Sadler's Wells. In 1964 *Saint Joan of the Stockyards* was seen at the Queen's, London, after an initial production at the Dublin Festival in 1961, and in 1968 Brecht's adaptation of Marlowe's *Edward II* was put on by the National Theatre company. *Pauken und Trompeten*, put back into English as *Trumpets and Drums*, was seen at the Royal Lyceum, Edinburgh, in 1969, and an early one-act play, *Lux in Tenebris*, was presented by the Quipu

Basement Theatre in London in 1970. Later the same year Brecht's last play, *Turandot*, a Marxist variant on Gozzi's original work, was produced by the Oxford Experimental Theatre Club, as *Turandot, or The Whitewashers' Congress*, while it was still in rehearsal by the Berliner Ensemble. This play, which Brecht left unfinished at his death, was begun in 1930 but not completed in draft until 1954. It was published in 1967. In New York a programme, *Brecht on Brecht*, an anthology compiled from his works by George Tabori, had a long run at the Theatre de Lys in 1962, and was seen at the Royal Court in London in 1971. Other plays seen in New York in translation include *The Good Woman of Setzuan* in 1956, *Mother Courage and her Children* in 1963, *Arturo Ui* in 1964, and *The Caucasian Chalk Circle* in 1965.

Breeches Parts, the name given to roles written for handsome young heroes in romantic comedy and played by personable young women; not to be confused with the temporary assumption of male attire for the purpose of disguise by such heroines as Rosalind in *As You Like It* or Viola in *Twelfth Night*, nor with the serious undertaking of such parts as Hamlet, Romeo, or Richard III by intrepid actresses (see BERINGER and CUSHMAN). The classic example of a breeches part is Sir Harry Wildair in Farquhar's *The Constant Couple* (1699), as played by Peg Woffington and later by Mrs. Jordan (qq.v.). Others who wore the breeches with success were Nell Gwynn, Mrs. Bracegirdle, and Mrs. Mountfort (qq.v.), the last being considered outstanding as Lothario in Rowe's *The Fair Penitent* and Macheath in Gay's *The Beggar's Opera*. This fashion for playing *en travesti* formed an essential part of Regency spectacle and Victorian extravaganza, the great exponent in the latter style being Madame Vestris (q.v.), and was one of the formative elements in the development of the Principal Boy (played by a young woman) in pantomime (q.v.). In more recent times Sarah Bernhardt (q.v.), who also played Hamlet, made a great success in a serious 'breeches' part, the young Duc de Reichstadt in Rostand's *L'Aiglon* (1900).

Bridge, a mechanical device for raising heavy pieces of scenery from below up to stage level. The joists and floor-boards are cut and framed, usually with sliders, to allow a large platform, framed and tied, to rise in corner-grooves with the aid of counterweights and a winch. Great variety is found in the design of bridges, and today the electrically-controlled bridges of a large theatre may reach a high degree of engineering complexity.

BRIDGES, DR. JOHN, see STEVENSON, WILLIAM.

BRIDGES-ADAMS, WILLIAM (1889–1965), English theatre director, who gained his experience of the stage in several provincial repertory companies, including Bristol and Birmingham. In 1919 he was appointed director of the Shakespeare Memorial Theatre (q.v.) in succession to Frank Benson. He remained there until 1934, directing twenty-nine plays by Shakespeare and keeping the company together after the destruction of the theatre by fire in 1926 until it moved into the new theatre in 1932. He also took the company several times on tour to Canada and the U.S.A. After leaving Stratford he worked with the British Council (q.v.), where he initiated the policy of sending theatrical companies abroad, mostly across Europe. He was the author of several books on the theatre, including *The British Theatre* (1944), *Looking at a Play* (1947), and *The Irresistible Theatre, Vol I: From the Conquest to the Commonwealth* (1957), of which no more appeared. In 1960 he was appointed C.B.E. for services to the theatre.

BRIDIE, JAMES [really DR. OSBORNE HENRY MAVOR] (1888–1951), a Scottish doctor who continued in active practice until 1938 and was also an outstanding playwright and part-founder of the Citizens' Theatre (see GLASGOW). His best-known plays, most of which were seen in London, are *The Anatomist* and *Tobias and the Angel* (both 1930), *Jonah and the Whale* (1932), *A Sleeping Clergyman* (1933), *Colonel Wotherspoon* (1934), *The Black Eye* (1935), *Storm in a Teacup* (1936) (an adaptation of Bruno Frank's *Sturm in Wasserglas*, with a Scots setting), and *Mr. Bolfry* (1943). In 1949 his *Daphne Laureola*, with Edith Evans (q.v.) in the title-role, had a great success, and in the following year he wrote, for the Edinburgh Festival, *The Queen's Comedy*, which many consider his best work. Bridie's last plays were produced posthumously by the Glasgow Citizens'

Theatre, *The Baikie Charivari* in 1952, *Meeting at Night* in 1954. The latter was revived at Leeds in 1964, and was seen on tour towards the end of 1970. Bridie was appointed C.B.E. for services to the stage in 1946.

BRIEUX, EUGÈNE (1858–1932), French dramatist, whose plays are naturalistic dramas in the tradition of Zola and Henry Becque (qq.v.). In him, however, bitterness and misery were tempered by a deep pity for humanity, and he railed not so much at the sins of the flesh as at the social conditions which produced them. His best-known plays are *Les Trois Filles de M. Dupont* (1898), which portrays the dangers of a marriage of convenience; *La Robe rouge* (1900), which exposes the abuses of the judiciary system; *Les Avariés* (1902), a study of venereal disease, which, as *Damaged Goods*, created a sensation in England and America; and *Maternité* (1903), which deals with birth-control.

Brighella, one of the *zanni* or servant roles of the *commedia dell'arte* (q.v.). Originally a thief and a bully, with much in him of the Neapolitan street-corner boy, he later became a lackey, though retaining his love of intrigue and lying. Through the establishment of an Italian company in Paris (see COMÉDIE-ITALIENNE), he may have influenced the development of the French valets of Marivaux (q.v.), and through them the Figaro of Beaumarchais (q.v.).

BRIGHOUSE, HAROLD (1882–1958), English dramatist, usually referred to as one of the so-called 'Manchester School', as his early realistic comedies of North-country life were produced at the Gaiety Theatre there under Miss Horniman (q.v.). The only one of his works to survive on the stage, *Hobson's Choice*, was first seen in London in 1916, at the Apollo Theatre, where it scored an instant success. It has been revived many times, notably at the National Theatre (Old Vic) in 1965.

Brighton, a coastal town in the south of England which is an important stopping-place for plays on their way into or out of London, had its first permanent theatre in 1774. In 1790, the lessee, Fox, built a new theatre in Duke Street at the cost of £500. This was later remodelled in horseshoe form, and a royal box added. It closed in 1806, when a theatre in New Road was built. This opened in 1807 under Brunton. In 1854 Nye Chart took it over, and in

1866, having bought the old theatre, demolished it and built the present Theatre Royal on the same site. His management lasted until his death in 1876, when he was succeeded by his widow. It was while playing at this theatre in Oct. 1891 that Fred Terry and Julia Neilson (qq.v.) were married. Touring companies started to visit the theatre in 1868, but the stock company existed up to 1873. There was in Hove an adapted church hall, known as the Little Theatre, which opened in 1901 and closed in 1928.

Brighton Theatre, NEW YORK, see BIJOU THEATRE (3).

Bristle Trap, see TRAP.

Bristol, home of the Bristol Old Vic and of the first university in England to have a drama department (see UNIVERSITY DEPARTMENTS OF DRAMA), had its first theatre in 1729, built by John Hippisley at Jacob's Wells. In 1766, a new theatre in King Street was erected at a cost of £5,000. The architect was John Paty, who obtained plans from Saunders, a carpenter at Drury Lane, several of whose features were incorporated into the new playhouse. A royal patent, which gave the building the right to call itself the Theatre Royal, was obtained in 1778. The stock company remained in residence until 1878, and the theatre then became the home of variety and pantomime until in 1943 it reopened as the BRISTOL OLD VIC (with a drama school attached) with the help of the Council for the Encouragement of Music and the Arts (see ARTS COUNCIL). It was thus the first theatre in England to be state-aided. In 1962 the Arts Council relinquished its lease of the theatre, which was taken over by the City Council to be run by a Theatre Trust. In recent years some dozen new productions at the Bristol Old Vic, mostly directed by the resident director, Val May, have been transferred to London, among them Frank Marcus's *The Killing of Sister George* (1965), Priestley's adaptation of Iris Murdoch's *A Severed Head* (1963), William Francis's documentary, *Portrait of a Queen* (1965), *Fiorello!* (1962), an American musical which unfortunately failed to repeat its Bristol success, Barry England's *Conduct Unbecoming* (1969), and Fairchild's *Poor Horace* (1970). In 1970 the Bristol Old Vic closed for repair and redevelopment, and the company went on tour, returning to play at the Little Theatre, Bristol, pending the reopening of their own theatre early in 1972.

Britannia Theatre, LONDON, in High Street, Hoxton, on the site of an Elizabethan tavern called the Pimlico, to which Shakespeare is said to have resorted. It was originally attached to the Britannia Saloon, which SAM LANE (1804–71) built and opened as a place of entertainment on Easter Monday 1841. The abolition of the old Patents in 1843 enabled him to stage complete plays, and the Brit, as it was called, prospered. In 1850 Lane enlarged and improved it, and in 1858 built on the site a theatre which held nearly 4,000 people (reduced in 1866 to 3,000). After his death his widow, SARA LANE (1823–99), an excellent actress, related by marriage to the Lupinos (qq.v.), who played Principal Boy in pantomime till she was in her seventies, continued in management, and ran the theatre successfully until her death over a quarter of a century later. No London theatre was ever for so long under one management, and it became famous for its melodramatic spectacles and Christmas pantomimes. It was first used for the showing of films in 1913, and from 1923 until its destruction by bombing in 1940 was used exclusively as a cinema.

British Actors' Equity Association, see EQUITY.

British Council, an organization founded in 1934 for the purpose of promoting cultural relations between the United Kingdom and the rest of the world. A Drama Department was established in 1937. This was amalgamated with the Music Department in 1961. Its main activities are sponsoring overseas tours by British players, distributing copies of British plays with a view to their performance overseas, providing information on theatrical matters, and sponsoring visits to Britain (sometimes by the award of scholarships) by foreign theatrical personalities for the purpose of observing the British theatre. Publications by the Council include *Drama since 1939, The British Theatre,* three annual surveys of *The Year's Work in the Theatre* for the years 1948 to 1951, *Drama 1945–50,* and *The British Theatre since 1950.*

British Drama League (B.D.L.), an organization founded in 1919 by Geoffrey Whitworth to assist and encourage all those interested in the art of the theatre. It now has over 5,000 affiliated members, including some professional companies, though its work lies mainly among amateurs. It maintains a library, from which books and sets of plays for reading can be obtained by post; a Reference Library; an Information and Advisory Service; a Training Department for amateur producers and actors; a Theatregoers' Club in London; a Junior League, with lectures and special courses for young people; and an Overseas Department which deals specifically with visitors and foreign students anxious to learn something of the British theatre. The League also organizes an annual Festival of Community Drama, holds an annual Conference on Theatre in different parts of the country, and publishes a critical quarterly, *Drama*. Much the same sort of work is done for Scotland by the Scottish Community Drama Association (S.C.D.A.), founded in 1926.

British Theatre Museum Association. This was founded in Oct. 1957 on the initiative of the Society for Theatre Research (q.v.), which had convened a meeting of interested parties in 1955. Its objects are to preserve theatrical material in Great Britain, and to make it available to the public by the establishment of a Theatre Museum. Trustees were appointed to hold gifts and bequests, and Laurence Irving, grandson of Henry Irving (q.v.), became the first Chairman of the Association. A large amount of material has already been donated, among which may be mentioned the Henry Irving archives containing some 4,000 items, the Murray Carrington and Ernest Short collections, and the archives of the English Stage Company (see ROYAL COURT THEATRE (2)). In 1962 premises were found at Leighton House, Kensington. Sir Hugh Casson devised a scheme of decoration, and the Museum was opened to the public on 18 June 1963. It has since staged a number of exhibitions with material drawn from its own collection.

BRITTON, HUTIN (1876–1965), see LANG, MATHESON.

BRIZARD [really BRITARD], JEAN-BAPTISTE (1721–91), French actor, who joined the company of the Comédie-Française in 1757, after a long apprenticeship in the provinces. He was much admired as Henry of Navarre in Collé's *La Partie de chasse d'Henri IV* when in 1774 it was finally passed by the censor. Brizard was the first French actor to play Shakespeare's King Lear, in the adaptation by Ducis, in 1782.

BROADHURST, GEORGE HOWELLS (1866–1952), American dramatist, whose work marks the transition at the end of the nineteenth century from the old melodrama to modern comedy. His early plays were farces like *What Happened to Jones* (1897) and *Why Smith Left Home* (1899), but a more serious note was struck later, notably in *The Man of the Hour* (1906), probably his best play. He returned, however, to his earlier style in 1911 with *Bought and Paid For*, and with *The Crimson Alibi*, produced at his own theatre (see below) in 1919.

Broadhurst Theatre, NEW YORK, at 235 West 44th Street. Named after the dramatist George Broadhurst (see above), this opened on 27 Sept. 1917 with the first production in New York of Shaw's *Misalliance*. In 1931 *Hamlet* was seen in a vast setting designed by Norman Bel Geddes (q.v.), but was less successful than the musical comedies which followed it. In 1933 the Pulitzer Prize-winner, *Men in White*, by Sidney Kingsley, was seen at this theatre, as was Housman's *Victoria Regina* (1935), in which Helen Hayes (q.v.) was outstanding as the Queen. In 1959 *Fiorello!*, a musical based on the life of New York's Mayor La Guardia, started a successful run, and in 1964 came *Oh, What a Lovely War!*, played by the Theatre Workshop company from London in a production by Joan Littlewood (q.v.).

Broadway, NEW YORK, the symbol for the commercial theatre in the United States, as the West End or Shaftesbury Avenue in London is for England (see also New York theatres under their own names).

Broadway Music-Hall, NEW YORK, see BROADWAY THEATRE (2).

Broadway Opera House, NEW YORK, see BIJOU THEATRE (3).

Broadway Theatre, NEW YORK. (1) The first Broadway theatre, built by Trimble, opened on 27 Sept. 1847 with Sheridan's *The School for Scandal*. It had been intended as a stock house but, after the final destruction by fire of the old Park Theatre (q.v.), took its place as the home of visiting stars. Forrest was there when the Astor Place riot took place (see

ASTOR PLACE OPERA HOUSE). Charlotte Cushman reappeared there in 1849 after four years in England, and it was there that *Francesca da Rimini*, by Boker (q.v.), was first seen in 1855. Soon afterwards, the walls of the theatre collapsed and had to be rebuilt. From 1857 onwards its reputation declined, and it finally closed on 2 Apr. 1859.

(2) On 2 Sept. 1861 Wallack's old theatre (SEE STAR THEATRE) opened as the Broadway Music-Hall. It had a chequered career, under a variety of names, and saw one of the few appearances in New York of the assassin of Lincoln, John Wilkes Booth (q.v.), as Richard III. It was for some time known as the Olympic, but finally, renovated and redecorated, it opened as the Broadway Theatre under George Wood. It had a short life, as in 1868 the site of the theatre was required for shops, and it closed on 28 Apr. 1869, being subsequently demolished.

(3) A hall on West 41st Street, originally known as the Metropolitan Casino, which opened on 27 May 1880, reopened as the Broadway on 3 Mar. 1888 with Sardou's *La Tosca*. Among the European actors who visited this theatre were Modjeska and Salvini (qq.v.). Early in 1913 it became a cinema. Closed in 1928, it was pulled down a year later.

(4) On Broadway at 53rd Street. This was originally a cinema which opened in 1924, but from 1930 to 1933 it was used for revue and for *Earl Carroll's Vanities*. After a further session as a cinema, it again became a theatre and housed a number of productions, including the Negro version of 'Carmen', *Carmen Jones* (1943), and *Gypsy* (1959), a musical based on the life of Gypsy Rose Lee, with Ethel Merman starring as Gypsy's mother.

Daly's Theatre (q.v.), originally Banvard's Museum, was also known as the Broadway for the season of 1877-8, as was the Euterpean Hall for a few unsuccessful weeks.

BROCHET, HENRI (1898-1952), see GHÉON, HENRI.

BROCKMANN, JOHANN FRANZ HIERONYMUS (1745-1812), German actor, the friend and pupil of Schröder (q.v.), to whose company he belonged in Hamburg. He played Hamlet in the first production there of a German version of the play in 1776, with Schröder as the Ghost. He later went to the Burgtheater in Vienna,

where he was highly thought of and remained until his death.

BROOK, PETER STEPHEN PAUL (1925-), English director of plays and operas, whose early work aroused much controversy but produced interesting results. He was in his late teens when he directed Marlowe's *Dr. Faustus* and Cocteau's *The Infernal Machine* on the minute stages of the Torch and Chanticleer theatres in London. In 1945 he was at the Birmingham Repertory Theatre, and in 1946 at Stratford-upon-Avon, where he directed an enchanting *Love's Labour's Lost*, costumed *à la Watteau*, and in 1947 was responsible for a *Romeo and Juliet* which unleashed the fury of the critics, mainly on account of the clumsy cutting and handling of the verse. A production of Strauss's 'Salome' at Covent Garden in 1949, with designs by Salvador Dali, again aroused criticism. Brook then vindicated himself triumphantly with productions of Anouilh's *Ring Round the Moon* and Shakespeare's *Measure for Measure* (both 1950), followed by an excellent revival in 1953 of Otway's *Venice Preserv'd* at the Lyric, Hammersmith. His later productions included Fry's *The Dark is Light Enough* (1954) and Anouilh's *The Lark* and Shakespeare's *Titus Andronicus* (both 1955). Also in 1955 he directed Scofield (q.v.) in *Hamlet*, the company later going to Moscow—the first English company to appear there since 1917. In 1962 he was appointed co-director, with Peter Hall and Michel Saint-Denis, of the Royal Shakespeare Company (q.v.), directing at Stratford-upon-Avon *King Lear* (1962), again with Scofield, and, at the Aldwych, the company's London home, in the same year, *The Persecution and Assassination of Marat as performed by the Inmates of the Asylum of Charenton under the direction of the Marquis de Sade* (usually known as the *Marat/Sade*) by the German dramatist, Peter Weiss (q.v.), written and directed under the influence of the Theatre of Cruelty of Artaud (q.v.). This was followed by an experimental documentary, *US* (1966), which dramatized the intervention of American troops in Vietnam. In 1968 he set out his ideas on the modern theatre in *The Empty Space*, and two years later, under the influence of Grotowski (q.v.), opened an International Centre for Theatre Research in a disused tapestry factory in Paris, where, with his assistants Geoffrey Reeves and Andrei

Sherban, he will direct an international group of actors in experimental work. Brook was appointed C.B.E. in 1965 for services to the theatre.

BROOKE, GUSTAVUS VAUGHAN (1818–66), an actor of Irish extraction, who first appeared in Dublin and then toured England and Scotland as the Dublin (or Hibernian) Roscius. In spite of a good presence and a fine voice, he failed to fulfil the promise of his early years, mainly owing to habits of intemperance. After a chequered career, during which he alternately triumphed and failed in such parts as Othello, Richard III, Hamlet, and Shylock in London, the United States, and Australia, he found himself in Warwick jail. Once released, he determined to rehabilitate himself, set sail again for Australia, and was drowned when his ship sank in the Bay of Biscay. His second wife, whom he married in 1863, was the American actress AVONIA JONES (1839–67), whose death was hastened by grief at his loss. Brooke's life was written by W. J. Lawrence (1892).

BROOKFIELD, CHARLES (1857–1913), see REVUE.

Brooklyn Theatre, NEW YORK, the second playhouse to be built in this district (for the first, see PARK THEATRE (3)). It opened on 2 Oct. 1871 under F. B. Conway (q.v.), whose widow took over when he died and remained there until her death in 1875. Her daughter Minnie then took over, but was unsuccessful, and left after a few months. On 20 Sept. 1875 the theatre reopened under Palmer for a brief but exciting season, and on 5 Dec. 1876 it was burnt down during a performance of Oxenford's *The Two Orphans* (see FIRES IN THEATRES).

Brooks Atkinson Theatre, NEW YORK, on 47th Street between Broadway and 8th Avenue. As the Mansfield, this opened on 15 Feb. 1926, the first important event in its history being a visit from the Moscow Habimah Players in Ansky's *The Dybbuk* in December. Some successful musical comedies followed, and in 1930 Marc Connelly's *The Green Pastures*, with Richard B. Harrison (q.v.) as 'de Lawd' and décor by Robert Edmond Jones (q.v.), had a long run. Among later productions were Gordon Sherry's *Black Limelight* (1936) and Robert Ardrey's *Thunder Rock* (1939), both of which were less successful

than in London, and Ruth Gordon's nostalgic evocation of the past, *Years Ago* (1946). The theatre was then used for radio and television shows, but reopened on 12 Sept. 1960 under its present name, given it in honour of the American drama critic Brooks Atkinson (q.v.), who had just retired. In 1961 Neil Simon's *Come Blow Your Horn* started a long run, and in 1964 came Rolf Hochhuth's *The Deputy*, followed in the same year by Tennessee Williams's *The Milk Train Doesn't Stop Here Anymore*.

BROUGH, FANNY WHITESIDE (1854–1914), English actress, daughter of the dramatist ROBERT BARNABAS BROUGH (1828–60) and niece of Lionel Brough (q.v.). She made her first appearance in Manchester in 1869 in a pantomime written by her uncle, WILLIAM BROUGH (1826–70), and a year later was seen in London under Mrs. John Wood (q.v.). Although she sometimes appeared in Shakespearian parts in her early years, she was at her best in modern comedy, and during her long career on the London stage appeared in many successful productions, playing Clara in a revival of LYTTON's *Money* in 1872, and creating the part Mary Melrose in H. J. Byron's *Our Boys* (1875). In 1888 she made an outstanding success as Mary O'Brien in Mrs. Hodgson Burnett's *The Real Little Lord Fauntleroy*, and in 1895 she created the part of Lady Markby in Wilde's *An Ideal Husband*. In 1901 she appeared with Charles Hawtrey (q.v.) in Anstey's *The Man from Blankley's*, and in 1909 made a great success as the Hon. Mrs. Beamish in the sporting melodrama, *The Whip*, at Drury Lane.

BROUGH, LIONEL (1836–1900), English actor, father of Mary and uncle of Fanny Brough (qq.v.). He made his first appearance in an extravaganza by his brother WILLIAM BROUGH (1826–70), who like their eldest brother, ROBERT BARNABAS BROUGH (1828–60), was a prolific playwright. By 1873 Lionel, who was not a character actor but a clown in the best sense, was principal low comedian at the Gaiety Theatre (q.v.) under Hollingshead, where his gift for improvisation and his rich sense of humour found full scope in burlesque. But he was also excellent as Tony Lumpkin in Goldsmith's *She Stoops to Conquer* and as Bob Acres in Sheridan's *The Rivals*, and he played some of Shakespeare's clowns at Her Majesty's under Tree (q.v.).

BROUGH, MARY (1863–1934), English actress, daughter of Lionel Brough (q.v.). She first appeared on the stage at Brighton in 1881 and later the same year was seen in London. Like her cousin Fanny Brough (q.v.), she was at her best in comedy, and had already had a long and successful career when in 1925 she joined the Aldwych Theatre company to play Mrs. Spoker in *A Cuckoo in the Nest*, by Ben Travers (q.v.). She remained there to appear in all his subsequent productions up to *Dirty Work* in 1932. Her brother SYDNEY BROUGH (1868–1911) was also on the stage, playing mainly in comedy from 1885 to his death.

BROUGHAM, JOHN (1810–80), American actor and dramatist, who made his first appearance in London in July 1830 in Egan's *Tom and Jerry*. He later became manager of the Lyceum, and in 1842 went to America, making his début at the Park Theatre. On 23 Dec. 1850 he opened his own theatre on Broadway, Brougham's Lyceum, which, under such an experienced manager and such a jovial, popular personality, ought to have succeeded. Unfortunately, Brougham put his trust in short burlesques and farces, which had once been popular but were now outmoded, and in less than two years his theatre had passed into the control of the elder James Wallack (q.v.), who started it on a glorious career on 25 Jan. 1852. Brougham, who had meanwhile continued to act, opened his second playhouse, on the site of the present Madison Square Theatre (q.v.), on 25 Jan. 1869. This again was not a success. He retired from management and returned to the stage, making his last appearance on 25 Oct. 1879 at Booth's. He was essentially a comedian and did his best work in such traditional stage-Irishman roles as Sir Lucius O'Trigger in Sheridan's *The Rivals*, and as Micawber in Dickens's *David Copperfield* and Dazzle in Boucicault's *London Assurance*.

BROWN, IVOR JOHN CARNEGIE (1891–1974), English author and dramatic critic, who joined the *Manchester Guardian* in 1913. In 1928 he became dramatic critic of the *Observer*. He also wrote for the *Saturday Review*, *Illustrated London News*, and the *Sketch*. In 1942 he was appointed editor of the *Observer*, but continued as its dramatic critic, retiring in 1954. He was succeeded by Kenneth Tynan (q.v.), and later, for a year, by Bamber Gas-

coigne. His writings on the theatre include *Masques and Phases* (1926), *First Player* (1927), *Parties of the Play* (1928), and (with George Fearon) *Amazing Monument, A Short History of the Shakespeare Industry* (1939). An excellent life of Shakespeare was published in 1949, *Shakespeare in his Time* in 1960, *How Shakespeare Spent the Day* in 1963, and *Shaw in his Time* in 1965.

BROWN, JOHN MASON (1900–), American dramatic critic, who in 1924 became associated with the monthly *Theatre Arts* (q.v.). In 1929 he was appointed dramatic critic of the *New York Evening Post*, and in 1939 went to the *World-Telegram*. After service in the U.S. Navy during the Second World War he became dramatic critic of the weekly *Saturday Review of Literature*. He also lectured extensively on the theatre. The best of his work was collected in *Two on the Aisle* (1938), while *Upstage: The American Theatre in Performance* (1930) gives a good picture of the American stage in the 1920s. Among his other books are *The Modern Theatre in Revolt* (1929), *Letters from Greenroom Ghosts* (1934), *The Art of Playgoing* (1936), *Seeing Things* (1946), *Seeing More Things* (1948), and *Still Seeing Things* (1950).

BROWNE, E(LLIOTT) MARTIN (1900–80), English actor and director closely associated with the revival of poetic, and particularly religious, drama in England. In 1935 he was responsible for the production of *Murder in the Cathedral* by T. S. Eliot (q.v.), in which he played the Fourth Tempter and Knight. It was first seen in the Chapter House at Canterbury Cathedral, and then in London and on tour. In 1938 it was seen in New York, and in 1970 was produced in Canterbury Cathedral to celebrate the 800th anniversary of Becket's martyrdom. Browne was the director of all T. S. Eliot's dramatic works, about which he has many interesting things to say in *The Making of T. S. Eliot's Plays*, published in 1969. He was also responsible for a series of plays by poets at the Mercury Theatre, including Ronald Duncan's *This Way to the Tomb!* (1945) and Fry's *A Phoenix Too Frequent* (1946). In 1951 Browne, who had directed the Pilgrim Players on tour in a repertory of religious plays, revived in its native city for the first time since 1572 the York cycle of Mystery Plays, producing it there again in 1954, 1957, and 1966. From 1948 to 1957 he was head of the British Drama League (q.v.), and then went to inaugurate a Program in Religious Drama at the Union Theological Seminary, New York, where, with his wife, HENZIE RAEBURN (1900–), as lecturer, he was visiting professor until 1962. On returning to England he became Honorary Drama Adviser to the rebuilt Coventry Cathedral, and was also President of Radius (formerly the Religious Drama Society of Great Britain). He was created C.B.E. in 1952.

BROWNE, MAURICE (1881–1955), dramatist, manager, and actor. Born and educated in England, he first made his name in the United States, where he is credited with the founding of the Little Theatre movement by his establishment in 1912 of the Chicago Little Theatre, which he directed for several years. He appeared in London in 1927, and in 1929 presented, at the Savoy Theatre, *Journey's End* by R. C. Sherriff (q.v.). First seen at the end of 1928 in a production by the Stage Society, this play about the First World War had an unexpected success, which encouraged Browne to remain in management. In 1930 he produced *Othello* with Paul Robeson (q.v.) in the title-role, himself playing Iago, and before his retirement in 1939 he was responsible for a number of other interesting productions. His autobiography, *Too Late to Lament*, which betrays a certain bitterness and dissatisfaction with his chosen career, was published soon after his death.

BROWNE, ROBERT (*fl.* 1583–?1620/40), an Elizabethan actor well known on the Continent between 1590 and 1620. He is first mentioned as one of the Earl of Worcester's players in 1583. In 1592 he took a company of English actors to Holland and Germany with a repertory of jigs, biblical plays, early English comedies, and plays by Marlowe. In Aug. 1592 he made the first of many visits to Frankfurt Fair and in 1595 he and his companions were appointed players and musicians in the service of Maurice, Landgrave of Hesse-Kassel. Browne was intermittently in London at the beginning of the seventeenth century, but he continued to visit Frankfurt and other German towns, and spent the winter of 1619 at the Court of Bohemia in Prague. The last mention of him is at the Easter Fair in Frankfurt in 1620. He may have returned to England then, and be identical with a Robert Browne who toured the English provinces with a puppet-show during 1638 and 1639. His work on the Continent was continued

by his friend and pupil John Green (see ENGLISH COMEDIANS).

BROWNE, W. GRAHAM (1870–1937), see TEMPEST, MARIE.

BROWNING, ROBERT (1812–89), English poet, three of whose verse plays were produced in the theatre: *Strafford*, written for Macready (q.v.), in 1837, *A Blot in the 'Scutcheon* in 1843, and *Colombe's Birthday*, published in 1844 and seen briefly at the Haymarket in 1853. In all of them Helen Faucit (q.v.) appeared. None of them was particularly successful, and they serve only to mark the great cleavage between poetry and the stage in the nineteenth century. In 1925 Browning's dramatic poem *Pippa Passes*, which had been seen at the Neighborhood Playhouse (q.v.) in New York in 1917, was successfully staged for the first time in England by Nugent Monck at the Maddermarket (q.v.). It was revived at the Oxford Playhouse in 1968.

BRUCKNER, FERDINAND [really THEODOR TAGGER] (1891–1958), an Austrian dramatist whose first play, *Krankheit der Jugend* (1926), caused something of a sensation: it dealt with a group of medical students preoccupied with the idea of suicide, death being the one certain alternative to disillusionment. Several of his later plays are apparently historical but deal with modern problems, as in *Die Verbrecher* (1928), which is ostensibly about Elizabeth I of England, while *Napoleon der Erste* (1937) and *Heroische Komödie* (1942) are concerned with Hitler's rise to power. Bruckner, who left Germany in 1933, returned in 1951, and apart from Brecht and Zuckmayer (qq.v.), was the only refugee German playwright to re-establish himself in the German theatre after the Second World War. His later plays include *Der Tod einer Puppe* (1956) and *Der Kampf mit dem Engel* (1957).

BRUEYS, DAVID-AUGUSTIN DE (1640–1723), French dramatist, who collaborated with JEAN DE BIGOT PALAPRAT (1650–1721) in several plays for the Comédie-Française, among them *Le Grondeur* and *Le Muet* (both 1691). Brueys also wrote a number of plays on his own, including a new and most successful version of the farce of *Maistre Pierre Pathelin*, which, as *L'Avocat Pathelin* (1706), remained in the repertory of the Comédie-Française for many years.

BRUNELLESCHI, FILIPPO (1377–1440), see PARADISO.

BRUNO, GIORDANO (1548–1600), Italian philosopher, author of one play, *Il Candelaio* (*c.* 1582), a brilliant satire which castigated the corrupt customs of the time with unabated candour and for that reason was banned. During his travels, Bruno went to England and visited Oxford at the invitation of Sir Philip Sidney. Among the contemporary English authors who met him may have been Thomas Carew, whose masque *Coelum Britannicum*, performed at Whitehall in 1634, shows traces of his influence. Some scholars have found a like influence in Shakespeare, particularly in *Hamlet*, while others see something more akin to Bruno's work in that of Ben Jonson (q.v.). Bruno was burnt at the stake by order of the Inquisition in 1600. In 1965, *Il Candelaio*, in a cut and modernized version, had what was probably its first professional performance. A play by Morris West, *The Heretic*, based on Bruno's life, had a brief run in London in 1970.

Brunswick Theatre, LONDON, see ROYALTY THEATRE (1).

BRUNTON, LOUISA (1779–1860), English actress, sister of Mrs. Merry (q.v.). She made her first appearance at Covent Garden in 1803, where her father, JOHN BRUNTON (1741–1822), was a member of the company, and soon proved herself an excellent actress, particularly in light comedy. Among her best parts were Beatrice in *Much Ado About Nothing* and Dorinda in Farquhar's *The Beaux' Stratagem*. She retired from the stage in 1807, on her marriage to the Earl of Craven. Her brother JOHN (1775–1849), who was also an actor, was the father of Elizabeth, who married Frederick Yates (q.v.).

BRUSCAMBILLE [really JEAN DESLAURIERS] (*fl.* 1610–34), a mountebank at the Paris fairs in the early seventeenth century who went to the Hôtel de Bourgogne (q.v.) to play in farce. He won fame as a speaker of witty prologues which he composed himself, summing up the life of the contemporary actor in the oftquoted epigram, 'une vie sans soucis et quelquefois sans six sous'.

BÜCHNER, GEORG (1813–37), a German dramatist, whose best and strongest play, *Dantons Tod* (first produced in 1902), retains its vitality, as was proved by revivals in Berlin in 1927, in New York in 1938, and in London in 1971. It depicts Danton as a disillusioned man sickened by the bloodshed which he has helped to start, and is amazingly objective for a young revolutionary. Little else remains of Büchner's work, except the dramatic fragments of *Woyzeck* on which Alban Berg later based his opera 'Wozzeck' (1925), and the 'political fairytale' *Leonce und Lena*, published in 1850.

BUCK, SIR GEORGE, see MASTER OF THE REVELS.

BUCKINGHAM, GEORGE VILLIERS, second Duke of (1628–87), English nobleman, the original of Zimri in Dryden's poem *Absalom and Achitophel* (1681). Keenly interested in contemporary drama, he satirized Dryden and the heroic verse play in *The Rehearsal* (1671), which provided a model for many later burlesques of which the best was Sheridan's *The Critic; or, a Tragedy Rehearsed* (1779). In 1666 Pepys noted in his diary that he had seen and enjoyed at Drury Lane a new version by Buckingham of *The Chances*, a comedy based by Fletcher (q.v.) on a story by Cervantes, first acted in 1623.

BUCKSTONE, JOHN BALDWIN (1802–79), English actor and dramatist, who made his first appearance in the famous melodrama, *The Dog of Montargis*, in a barn in Peckham. In 1827 he appeared at the Adelphi in one of his own plays, *Luke the Labourer*, and later became manager of the Haymarket (q.v.). For many years he was a prolific playwright, chiefly of melodramas and farces, the best-known being *Married Life* (1834), *Single Life* (1839), *The Green Bushes; or, a Hundred Years Ago* (1845), and *The Flowers of the Forest* (1847). He was a most popular comedian, of great breadth and humour, and the mere sound of his voice, a mixture of chuckle and drawl, heard off-stage was enough to set the audience laughing.

Buen Retiro, MADRID, see CALDERÓN DE LA BARCA, P.

Built Stuff, a scenic term for all specially carpentered, three-dimensional objects. The most common is perhaps the rostrum (q.v.), which may vary in size from a small throne-dais to an 8-ft.-high platform, approached by steps or a ramp; but it includes also such things as columns, banks, trees, porches, and mantelpieces, constructed mainly of reinforced chicken-wire, glued and shaped canvas, and papiermâché.

BULGAKOV, MIKHAEL AFANASEYEV (1891–1940), Soviet dramatist, who turned his own novel, *The White Guard*, dealing with the Civil War in the Ukraine, into a play. As *The Days of the Turbins* (or *The Last of the Turbins*), this was produced by the Moscow Art Theatre under Stanislavsky (q.v.) in 1926. As *The White Guard* it was produced in London in 1938 in an adaptation by Rodney Ackland. In 1928 Bulgakov, who had joined the staff of the Moscow Art Theatre (q.v.), prepared for the company there an excellent dramatization of Gogol's *Dead Souls*, and in 1936 wrote a play based on the life of Molière. In 1941 his last play, based on *Don Quixote*, was produced posthumously at the Vakhtangov (q.v.).

Bull Inn, LONDON, see INNS USED AS THEATRES.

BULWER-LYTTON, EDWARD, see LYTTON.

BUONTALENTI, BERNARDO (1536–1608), an Italian machinist and scene designer, architect of a theatre in Florence which opened in 1585, who entered the service of the Medici in 1547 and worked for them for the rest of his life. Among his many duties were the organization of firework displays (hence his nickname 'delle Girandole') and the construction of theatrical machinery and scenery for Grand Ducal festivities. Drawings and engravings of his work for the Florentine *Intermezzi* of 1589, in honour of the marriage of Ferdinand I of Tuscany, have been preserved and are among the most important early documents of scenic history.

BURBAGE [also BURBADGE and BURBEGE], JAMES (*c.* 1530–97), the builder of the first permanent playhouse in London. Known simply as the Theatre (q.v.), this opened in 1576, and was used by the Earl of Leicester's players, whom Burbage, a carpenter by trade, had joined in about 1572. In 1596 Burbage took over and adapted part of Blackfriars (q.v.) as an indoor theatre, but he died before obtaining permission to use it. Three years later his son CUTHBERT (*c.* 1566–1636)

dismantled the Theatre and used the timber to build the first Globe (q.v.) on Bankside, the scene of his brother Richard's (q.v.) greatest triumphs.

BURBAGE, RICHARD (*c.* 1567–1619), the first great English actor. Son of James Burbage (q.v.), he began his acting career early, probably in 1584 with the Admiral's Men, becoming leading man of the Chamberlain's Men (q.v.) in 1594. At the Globe (q.v.), under the management of his elder brother Cuthbert, he created a number of Shakespeare's heroes, including Hamlet, Lear, Othello, and Richard III. He also appeared in the first productions of plays by Jonson, Kyd, and Webster (qq.v.). He had a high reputation and his name long remained synonymous with all that was best in acting.

Burgtheater, see VIENNA.

BURKE, BILLIE (1884–1970), see ZIEGFELD, FLORENZ.

BURKE, CHARLES (1822–54), American actor, the son of the actress CORNELIA FRANCES THOMÁS (1796–1849) by her first husband, and thus the elder half-brother of the famous Joseph Jefferson (q.v.). In 1850 he made a dramatization of Washington Irving's *Rip Van Winkle* in which Jefferson, who was later to be identified with the leading character, played the small part of the innkeeper.

Burla (pl. *burle*), the longer comic interlude of the *commedia dell'arte* (q.v.), usually involving a practical joke, perhaps the tripping up of one character by another, or a certain amount of horseplay. The slighter decoration of a comic touch was known as a *lazzo* (q.v.).

Burlesque. (1) In the seventeenth- and eighteenth-century English theatre, a satire based on a popular play or dramatic fashion which offered elements suitable for parody. The first was Buckingham's *The Rehearsal* (1671), which made fun of Dryden and heroic drama (q.v.). The genre continued through John Gay's *The Beggar's Opera* (1728), Henry Fielding's *Tom Thumb* (1730), and Henry Carey's *The Tragedy of Chrononhotonthologus* (1734), to culminate in Sheridan's *The Critic* (1779), which satirizes the sentimentality of his own day. In the nineteenth century the burlesque, though still based on a popular contemporary play, lost the original element of implied criticism and became a vehicle for high spirits and execrable puns, as in *The Corsican 'Bothers'; or, the Troublesome Twins* (1869) and *Robert MacMaire; or, the Roadside Inn Turned Inside Out* (1870), both by H. J. Byron (q.v.), the best writer of such burlesques. They were finally killed by the new style of playwriting initiated by T. W. Robertson (q.v.). A survival of the genre lingered on in the late nineteenth century in the work of the famous quartet at the Gaiety Theatre headed by Nellie Farren (q.v.), and in the twentieth century reappeared in short scenes burlesquing current Shakespearian productions or long-running successes in such works as *The Gate Revue* (1938), *The Little Revue* (1939), and *Sweet and Low* (1943).

(2) EXTRAVAGANZA. It is almost impossible to disentangle the extravaganza, which has now entirely disappeared, from the burlesque, but the main difference seems to be that the former, based on a well-known story from mythology or folk-tale, had no particular satiric target in mind and was intended for amusement only. The best writer of extravaganzas was J. R. Planché (q.v.).

(3) BURLETTA. This began in the mid-eighteenth century with the efforts made by the smaller theatres to evade the Licensing Laws. Legally any piece in three acts with at least five songs was a burletta and so could be performed at an unlicensed theatre. This accounts for some of the incongruous interpolations found in nineteenth-century adaptations of plays by Shakespeare.

(4) In the U.S.A., American burlesque, a native sex and comedy entertainment originally intended for men only, was devised by MICHAEL BENNETT LEAVITT (1843–1935) in about 1868 and known popularly as 'burleycue' or 'leg show'. The performance was divided into three parts. The first combined chorus numbers and monologues with comedy sketches known as 'bits'; the second, known as the 'olio', was made up of variety acts: acrobats, instrumentalists, magicians, freak entertainers, and sentimental-song singers; the third also had chorus numbers, 'bits', and an occasional travesty on politics or current plays, the only claim which the show had to be called a burlesque. The final number was called the 'Extra Added Attraction', and was usually a 'hootchy-kootchy' or *danse du ventre*. In about 1920 the strip-tease, an innovation of uncertain origin, was introduced to counteract the competition of the films. Ostensibly simple, this had an involved routine which ended with the girl exposing herself for one moment completely nude except for a G-string. The most famous strip-tease artiste was GYPSY ROSE LEE [really ROSE LOUISE HOVICH] (1914–70), who succeeded in establishing her act as a conventional Broadway revue speciality.

With the enforcement of Prohibition, burlesque lost its hold over the public and was finally barred from New York in Apr. 1942.

Burletta, see BURLESQUE (3).

BURNABY, DAVE (1881–1949), see PIERROT.

BURNACINI, GIOVANNI (?–1656), architect of a theatre in Vienna which opened in 1652, for which he also designed the scenery. His son, LODOVICO OTTAVIO (1636–1707), was also a scenic designer, and a representative of stage baroque at its richest and most typical. Some of his best work was done in Vienna, where he worked for Leopold I.

Burnt-cork Minstrels, see MINSTREL SHOW.

BURTON [really JENKINS], RICHARD WALTER (1925–84), stage and film actor, son of a Welsh miner, who took his stage name from that of his benefactor, Philip Burton. He made his first appearance in Emlyn Williams's *The Druid's Rest* (1944), and then appeared in three plays by Christopher Fry—*The Lady's Not For Burning* (1949) (in which he made his New York début in 1950), and *The Boy with a Cart* and *A Phoenix Too Frequent* (both 1950). In 1953–4 he was at the Old Vic, playing, among other parts, Hamlet, the Bastard in *King John*, Toby Belch in *Twelfth Night*, Caliban in *The Tempest*, and Othello and Iago alternately with John Neville (q.v.). He also played Hamlet in New York in 1964, having previously appeared there in the musical *Camelot* (1960). His later career was mainly in films. He married as his second wife the film star Elizabeth Taylor and appeared with her at Oxford (q.v.) in 1966 in a stage production of Marlowe's *Dr. Faustus*, directed by his former tutor, Nevil Coghill (q.v.), for the O.U.D.S., which resulted in a profit of £9,000, to be used for the benefit of playgoing in Oxford. In 1970 a further gift from Burton of £50,000 enabled the Trustees of the Oxford Playhouse to plan extensions and improvements to the theatre.

BURTON, WILLIAM EVANS (1804–60), actor-manager and dramatist, who first appeared on the stage in London in 1831, and three years later went to the United States. After some years on the stage there, he took over Palmo's Opera House in Chambers Street, New York, redecorated it, and opened it on 10 July 1848 as Burton's. He remained there until 1856, and under him it became one of the most important theatres of its day.

Buskin, the English name for the *cothurnus* (q.v.), a long boot worn by Greek actors. It is sometimes taken to refer to tragedy only, in opposition to the sock (q.v.), a flat shoe worn by the comic actor. The itinerant actors of the English town and countryside were often called buskers, from buskin, but the word is now confined to those who entertain theatre queues.

BUTLER, SAMUEL (?–1812) and SAMUEL S. W. (1797–1845), see RICHMOND THEATRE (2).

BUTT, SIR ALFRED (1878–1962), see REVUE.

BYRON, GEORGE GORDON, LORD (1788–1824), English poet, and author of several plays in verse of which only one was staged during his lifetime. This was *Marino Faliero* (1821), which was seen at Drury Lane. *Werner* was not seen until 1830, when Macready (q.v.) played in it, also at Drury Lane; Phelps revived it in 1844 at Sadler's Wells, Irving at the Lyceum in 1887. *Sardanapalus* was produced by Macready in 1834. *Manfred* and *The Two Foscari* were given at Covent Garden in 1834 and 1838 respectively. *Cain*, written in 1821, does not appear to have been produced in England. It has been six times translated into German, in which language it was produced at Frankfurt-on-Main in 1958 and at Lucerne in 1960. Byron joined the Committee of Drury Lane in 1815, and his letters are full of references to theatrical matters of the day.

BYRON, HENRY JAMES (1834–84), English actor and dramatist, best-known for a series of burlesques staged at the smaller London theatres, of which the first was seen in 1857, the last in about 1881. Byron, who first acted in London in one of his own comedies in 1869, was seen almost entirely in his own plays. In 1865 he contributed a burlesque of Bellini's opera 'La Sonnambula' to the Bancrofts' opening programme at the Prince of Wales's Theatre (see SCALA), and two of his comedies, *War to the Knife* (1865) and *A Hundred Thousand Pounds* (1866), were given there, as well as several burlesques and extravaganzas. On 16 Jan. 1875 at the Vaudeville Theatre, under the management of David James and Thomas Thorne, he produced his best-known play, *Our Boys*. He wrote about 150 plays on themes from mythology, nursery tale, opera, legend, and topical events; his style, though ingenious, was heavily overloaded with wearisome puns, and in his more serious plays he tended to rely on stock types. At his best he reflected the prevailing taste of the day, against which T. W. Robertson (q.v.) rebelled, and that, and his own charming personality, accounted for much of his ephemeral success.

C

CAECILIUS STATIUS (*c.* 219–*c.* 166 B.C.), Roman dramatist, who, between the death of Plautus and the advent of Terence (qq.v.), translated Greek comedies, mainly by Menander (q.v.), for the Roman stage. Some forty titles and about three hundred lines have survived. Caecilius allowed himself considerable freedom in expression and style, as Plautus had done, and many of his 'translations' differ widely from the original, no doubt in an effort to pander to popular Roman taste. His plays, which were not at first well received, finally succeeded because of the steady support given them by the famous actor-producer Ambivius Turpio.

Café La Mama, see MERCURY THEATRE and ROYAL COURT THEATRE (2).

CAIN [also CANE], ANDREW (*fl.* 1620–44), English actor, who became a player in 1622 and is often referred to as 'Cane the Clown' and 'Cane of the Fortune'. He was one of the actors who continued playing surreptitiously at the Red Bull (q.v.) after the closing of the theatres in 1642. Thirty years later he was still remembered for his jigs.

CALDERÓN DE LA BARCA, PEDRO (1600–81), Spanish dramatist, successor to Lope de Vega (q.v.). He wrote about two hundred plays, the best of his secular comedies dating from the years 1625 to 1640, during which time he also prepared a number of elaborate spectacles for the Court theatre in Philip IV's newly built palace of Buen Retiro. In 1651 he was ordained priest, and from then on until his death wrote only Court plays and *autos sacramentales* (q.v.). The best-known of his religious plays are *La cena de Baltasar* (*c.* 1634), and *El gran teatro del mundo* (*c.* 1641) on which Hofmannsthal (q.v.) based his *Grosse Weltheater* (1922) for Reinhardt's Salzburg Festival. Of his secular comedies, the best-known are *La vida es sueño* (*c.* 1638) and *El alcalde de Zalamea* (*c.* 1640). Edward FitzGerald published very full adaptations of both these plays, of which the first, as *Life's a Dream*, was produced at the Royal Court Theatre on 7 June 1926. Calderón had a considerable influence on European drama. A number of his plays became known to English Restoration dramatists through contemporary French translations, the best-known English adaptations of the time being Tuke's *Adventures of Five Hours* (1663) and Wycherley's *The Gentleman Dancing-Master* (1673). Part of Calderón's play on the life of St. Cyprian, *El magico prodigioso* (1637), was translated by Shelley. Among his purely romantic comedies for Buen Retiro the best are *Casa con dos puertos mal es de guarda* and *La dama duende* (both *c.* 1629).

Caledonian Theatre, see GLASGOW.

Call Board, see STAGE DOOR.

Call Doors, see PROSCENIUM DOORS.

CALMO, ANDREA (1509/10–*c.* 1561), an early Italian dramatist and amateur actor, younger contemporary and rival of Ruzzante (see BEOLCO), who seems to have exercised considerable influence on the early development of the *commedia dell'arte* (q.v.). His plays were edited by Rossi in 1888. As an actor he specialized in old men, and may have played a part comparable to Pantalone (see PANTALOON), though the name was not yet in use.

CALVERT, LOUIS (1859–1923), English actor, son of the Manchester theatre manager CHARLES CALVERT (1828–79) and his wife ADELAIDE HELEN BIDDLES (or BEDELLS) (1837–1921), an actress who appeared successfully under her husband's management and was also the author of *Trotty Veck* (1872), based on Dickens's *The Chimes*. Louis was one of eight children, all on the stage, and the only one to achieve success. He appeared with most of the leading actor-managers of his day, and was a member of the Vedrenne-Barker company at the Royal Court Theatre (q.v.), where he created the part of Broadbent in Shaw's *John Bull's Other Island* (1904). In 1912 he played Creon to the Oedipus of Martin-Harvey (q.v.) in Reinhardt's production of Sophocles' *Oedipus the King* at Covent Garden. He several times formed and managed his own company, in London or on tour in England and America. At his best in dramatic parts which gave full scope to his fine voice and robust personality, he could also play comedy with polished technique. He was the author of a most useful handbook on acting, *Problems of an Actor* (1918).

Cambridge. Religious plays were probably given in Cambridge churches as early as elsewhere (see LITURGICAL DRAMA), but the first reference dates from 1350, in connection with the staging of *The Children of Israel*. By the sixteenth century the acting of plays in Latin and English as part of the students' curriculum was evidently firmly established, as Kirchmayer's *Pammachius* was produced at Christ's College in 1546 and Queen Elizabeth I, in 1564, saw a performance of Plautus' *Aulularia* in the chapel of King's College, which in 1605 was also the setting for the first performance of a Latin translation of Guarini's famous pastoral, *Il Pastor Fido* (1598). In 1613 Trinity men entertained Prince Charles (later Charles I) with a performance of a Latin translation of Bonarelli's *Filli di Sciro* (1706) (as *Scyros*), and two years later James I insisted on a repeat performance of Ruggles's *Ignoramus*, based on *La Trappolaria* by Della Porta (q.v.). But although the Chamberlain's Men (q.v.) are believed to have played *Hamlet* in Cambridge in 1603, non-academic acting was not encouraged, and performances at nearby Stourbridge Fair usually led to trouble. As the Commonwealth approached, even college plays grew fewer, and the last recorded play to be performed, at Trinity before the future Charles II, was *The Guardian*, by Abraham Cowley (q.v.). Although in the eighteenth century the town was regularly visited by a professional company on the Norwich circuit, and there was a theatre at Barnwell which later became the Festival Theatre (see GRAY), there was no revival of the old traditions of college acting until the founding in 1855 of the Amateur Dramatic Club (A.D.C.) by F. C. Burnand, later editor of *Punch* and a prolific writer of light plays. This society, which has produced a number of excellent professional actors, among them Michael Redgrave (q.v.), Robert Eddison, and Peter Woodthorpe, and celebrated its centenary on 12 June 1955, is still active. Another

important society, the Footlights, was founded in 1883, and has also produced a number of good actors, among them Jack and Claude Hulbert, Jimmy Edwards, and, more recently, Jonathan Miller (q.v.), part-author of *Beyond the Fringe* (1960). The annual Footlights revue has become an important feature of Cambridge theatrical life and is often seen in London for a short season. In 1907 the Marlowe Dramatic Society was founded with Rupert Brooke as its first President. It maintains a tradition of anonymity, and one excellent feature of its work, mainly in Shakespeare, has been the fine speaking of verse (see RYLANDS). Among the professionals to emerge from the Marlowe Society were some outstanding directors, including Peter Hall and John Barton (qq.v.). The Arts Theatre, which since 1926 has housed the Footlights, was built and presented to Cambridge by John Maynard Keynes and his wife, the former ballet dancer Lydia Lopokova. Under George Rylands it continues to do good work. Productions of Greek plays in the original began in 1882 with Sophocles' *Ajax*. A year later came Aristophanes' *Birds*, with music by Parry, and then a production triennially. The future Provost of Kings, J. T. Sheppard, was responsible for ten of these, beginning with Aeschylus' *Oresteia* and ending with Sophocles' *Oedipus Coloneus*. For each of these a modern English composer was commissioned to write or arrange the music, an excellent precedent which is still followed.

Cambridge Theatre, LONDON, in Seven Dials, built for Bertie A. Meyer and opened by him on 4 Sept. 1930 with Beatrice Lillie (q.v.) in *Charlot's Masquerade*. A year later the Chauve-Souris played a season there, and *Elizabeth of England*, adapted by Ashley Dukes from a play by Bruckner, had a successful run. On the whole, however, the theatre was used for transfers and revivals until in 1946 Jay Pomeroy took it over for artistically successful but financially unrewarding seasons of opera. Menotti's 'The Consul' was first heard there in 1951. In 1960 *Billy Liar*, by Keith Waterhouse and Willis Hall, began a long run, and in 1963 came *Half-a-Sixpence*, a musical based on Wells's novel *Kipps*, with Tommy Steele in the title-role. In 1968 John Hanson appeared successfully in revivals of the musical comedies *The Desert Song* and *The Student Prince*, and in 1969

Pinero's *The Magistrate*, with Alastair Sim, was transferred from the Chichester Festival Theatre for a long run. In 1970 the National Theatre company appeared at the Cambridge in a season of plays from their current repertory.

Cameri Theatre (formerly KAMERI—The Chamber—THEATRE), ISRAEL. Founded by Joseph Millo, this opened on 10 Oct. 1945 with a Hebrew translation of Goldoni's *The Servant of Two Masters*, followed by classic and contemporary plays from a wide range of European drama. Original Israeli plays were added to the repertory in 1948, the first being Moshe Shamir's *He Walked Through the Fields*. This was revived in 1956 for the company's first appearance at the Théâtre des Nations (q.v.), when they were also seen in Brecht's *The Good Woman of Setzuan*. On a later visit, in 1965, they achieved a great success with a musical adaptation of Sammy Gronemann's *The King and the Cobbler*, which they played also in London during the World Theatre season of 1967. In 1969, under the English director Frith Banbury (q.v.), they added Peter Nichols's *A Day in the Death of Joe Egg* to their repertory, which already included such modern plays as Pinter's *The Homecoming* and Arthur Miller's *The Price*. The Cameri, which since 1967 has been the official municipal theatre of Tel Aviv, sends touring companies all over Israel in a varied programme of plays.

CAMERON, BEATRICE (1868–1940), American actress, wife of Richard Mansfield (q.v.), whom she married in 1892. She appeared with him in the first American productions of Shaw's *Arms and the Man* (1894), playing Raina, and *The Devil's Disciple* (1897), playing Judith Anderson. She also played Nora in Ibsen's *A Doll's House* the first time it was given in English in New York under that title. She retired in 1898.

CAMPBELL, BARTLEY (1843–88), one of the first American dramatists to make playwriting his only profession. He wrote a number of melodramas, of which the first was *Through Fire* (1871) and the most successful *My Partner* (1879), a drama of the American frontier based on the stories of Bret Harte. Among his later plays were *The Galley Slave* (1879) and *The White Slave* (1882), emotional melodramas which he directed and financed

himself, thus losing the fortune which *My Partner* had brought him. He died insane. His plays have no literary quality, but are important in the history of the late nineteenth-century American stage.

CAMPBELL [really STORY], HERBERT EDWARD (1844–1904), a music-hall performer, who was on the halls as a solo turn and appeared regularly in Drury Lane pantomimes from Boxing Night, 1882, until the year of his death. With his large fat figure and jolly red face he proved a wonderful foil to diminutive Dan Leno (q.v.) during the many years they played together in pantomime.

CAMPBELL, MRS. PATRICK [*née* BEATRICE STELLA TANNER] (1865–1940), English actress, who through her devastating wit and marked eccentricities became a legend in her lifetime. She was already well known when she created Paula in *The Second Mrs. Tanqueray* (1893) and Agnes in *The Notorious Mrs. Ebbsmith* (1895), both by Pinero (q.v.). She also played in Shakespeare and Ibsen, the title-roles in Sudermann's *Magda* and Sardou's *Fédora*, and Mélisande in Maeterlinck's *Pelléas et Mélisande* in English and in French—the latter to the Pelléas of Sarah Bernhardt (q.v.) in 1904. One of the best of her later creations was Anastasia Rakonitz in G. B. Stern's *The Matriarch* (1929). Shaw (q.v.), who called her 'perilously bewitching', wrote for her the part of Eliza Doolittle in *Pygmalion* (1914), and exchanged letters with her over a long period. This correspondence was published after his death, and on it an American actor, Jerome Kilty, based a dramatic dialogue, *Dear Liar* (1960), in which he himself played Shaw.

CAMPEN, JACOB VAN (c. 1595–1657), Dutch architect, the designer of the first theatre in Amsterdam, the Schouwburg, which opened on 3 Jan. 1638 with an historical tragedy, *Gijsbrecht van Amstel*, by Joost van den Vondel (q.v.). Modelled on Palladio's Teatro Olimpico in Vicenza, it had an elaborate *scena stabile*, or permanent setting, with a balcony on each side and no proscenium arch, one ceiling covering both auditorium and stage, and a central arch reminiscent of the earlier open-air stages of the Rederijkers (q.v.). In 1665 van Campen's theatre was rebuilt by JAN VOS (1615–67) with a contemporary-style Italian proscenium arch flanked by pillars, an orchestra pit in front of the stage, and painted canvas scenery. This was burnt down in 1772.

CAMPIAN [also CAMPION], THOMAS (1567–1620), English poet and composer of more than a hundred songs to the lute, a friend of Philip Rosseter (q.v.), Master of the Queen's Revels, through whom he may have had some contact with the public stage. His own dramatic works, however, were performed only at Court, and consisted of masques for official festivities for which, unlike Ben Jonson (q.v.), he wrote both the words and the music. The texts were printed in the 1909 edition of Campian's works edited by Percival Vivian. They embody notes on costume and scenery which add considerably to our information about the staging of the masque (q.v.) in the Jacobean period.

CAMUS, ALBERT (1913–60), French dramatist and novelist, who from 1936 to 1939 gained experience of the theatre with a left-wing group in Algiers, the Théâtre du Travail (later de l'Équipe), for which he directed and acted in a wide variety of plays. While editing a clandestine newspaper during the German occupation of France, he wrote two important plays, *Le Malentendu* (1944) and *Caligula* (1945). In the latter the young actor Gérard Philipe (q.v.) made a great success. Both plays stress the absurdity of the human condition, a theme which is taken further in *L'État de siège* (1948) (based on his own novel, *La Peste*, by Camus and Jean-Louis Barrault, q.v.), in which the plague is symbolic of the evil that thwarts mankind in its quest for freedom. Among Camus's later plays were *Les Justes* (1949) and adaptations of Calderón, Faulkner (again with Barrault), Lope de Vega, and Dostoievsky (*Les Possédés*, 1959), which show him experimenting in an effort to achieve a wider and freer theatrical technique. This interesting development was brought to a tragic close by his death in a car crash. He had been awarded the Nobel Prize for Literature in 1957.

Cancan, see MOULIN ROUGE.

Candler Theatre, NEW YORK, see SAM H. HARRIS THEATRE.

CANE, ANDREW, see CAIN.

Canterbury Music-Hall, LONDON, in Lambeth. In 1848 Charles Morton (q.v.)

took over the Canterbury Arms and ran weekly concerts there. These proved so popular that three years later he was able to build a hall on the site of the tavern's old skittle-alley. Most of the famous stars of the early music-hall appeared at the Canterbury Hall, as it was called, and by the time Morton gave up, in 1867, the earlier classical music and ballad-singing had been discarded in favour of comedy. Later, ballets were added, one of the most successful being the spectacular 'Trafalgar'. Among the royal visitors to the Canterbury in its heyday were the Prince of Wales (later Edward VII), the Duke of Cambridge, and the Duke and Duchess of Teck, and for many years the bar was a favourite rendezvous of the members of the music-hall profession. The building, which was reconstructed in 1876 and first officially called a music-hall in 1887, was destroyed in 1942.

Capa y Espada, COMEDIAS DE, see CLOAK-AND-SWORD PLAYS.

ČAPEK, JOSEF (1887–1945) and KAREL (1890–1938), Czech journalists and playwrights, Josef being also an artist. They worked and lived together in Prague all their lives, Karel dying two months before Josef was arrested by the Germans and taken to Belsen, where he died of typhus. After the success of Karel's play, *R.U.R.* (*Rossum's Universal Robots*) (1920), seen in London in 1923, the brothers collaborated in their best-known work, *The Insect Play* (1921), also staged as *The World We Live In* and *And So Ad Infinitum*. This was produced in London in 1923 by Nigel Playfair (q.v.) and in New York, as *The Insect Comedy*, in 1948. Both this and *R.U.R.* were satires, depicting the horrors of regimentation. Karel then wrote *The Makropulos Secret* (1922), which deals with the desirability or otherwise of long life and was seen in London in 1930, and together the brothers wrote their last play in collaboration, *Adam the Creator* (1927), which shows man trying to rebuild the world destroyed by the robots in *R.U.R.* Karel's last plays were the anti-fascist *Power and Glory* (1937), seen in London in 1938, and *The Mother* (1938). He was also the author of an amusing monograph, *How a Play is Produced*.

Capitano, IL, the braggart soldier of the *commedia dell'arte*, vainglorious and cowardly, usually a Spaniard. Andreini (q.v.) was one of the first to play him, as Capitan Spavento, while Silvio Fiorillo (q.v.) renamed him Matamoros (death to the Moors, anglicized as Captain Matamore). He may derive from Plautus' *Miles gloriosus*, and perhaps contributed something to Shakespeare's Armado in *Love's Labour's Lost* and Pistol, the associate of Falstaff in *Henry IV, Part 2* and *The Merry Wives of Windsor*.

CAPON, WILLIAM (1757–1827), English architect and painter, who in 1791 was appointed scenic director of the new Drury Lane Theatre by John Philip Kemble (q.v.). Of a plodding, pedestrian temperament, he was a painstaking antiquarian, which accorded well with Kemble's plans for scenic reform, and he designed a number of approximately correct scenes, including streets of ancient houses copied from actual remains of the period, which did away with the old system of flats and wings in favour of built stuff (q.v.). One drawback to Capon's work was, incidentally, the difficulty of shifting such heavy and cumbersome pieces. He continued to work at Drury Lane after Kemble's departure in 1802, until in 1809 the theatre was burnt down. He then worked for Kemble again at the new Covent Garden Theatre (q.v.) where many of his sets remained in use for years, serving as stock pieces until the arrival of Macready (q.v.). The precursor of Charles Kean (q.v.) in the application of archaeological studies to the stage, Capon had also something of Kean's pedantic inaccuracy, and delighted the public with his Anglo-Norman hall for *Hamlet*, which was made up of fragments from the periods of Edward the Confessor, William Rufus, and Henry I.

CAREW, JAMES (1876–1938), see TERRY, DAME ELLEN.

CAREY, JOYCE LILIAN (1898–), see LAWRENCE, GERALD.

CARL, KARL [really KARL ANDREAS VON BERNBRUNN] (1789–1854), Austrian actor, playwright, and theatre manager, who introduced the comic Viennese character Staberl (see BÄUERLE) to Munich, depriving the part of its specifically Viennese characteristics, but making it, in his 'Staberliaden', popular throughout Germany. In 1826 Carl became director of the Theater in der Josefstadt in Vienna, and began a long and successful association with the actor-playwright Nestroy (q.v.). From 1827 to 1845 he managed the Theater an der Wien, and in 1847 built a new theatre on the site of the old Leopoldstädter Theater. He was a ruthless business man, knew exactly how to give the public what it wanted, particularly in regard to local farce (*Posse*), and died a millionaire.

CARLIN, see BERTINAZZI, CARLO.

Carlton Theatre, LONDON. (1) Greenwich, built by Sefton Parry in 1864 to replace the derelict Theatre Royal, Deptford. After an undistinguished career, it fell into disuse when the Broadway Theatre, Deptford, was built in 1897.

(2) Haymarket, opened on 27 Apr. 1927 with a musical play, *Lady Luck*. It had a short theatrical history and became a cinema in 1929.

CARNEY, KATE (1868–1950), a much-loved star of the music-halls, who made her début on 10 Feb. 1890 at the Albert as a singer of Irish melodies. These, however, quickly gave way to Cockney songs, which she sang dressed in a coster suit of 'pearlies' and a vast hat with towering feathers—the feminine equivalent of Albert Chevalier's (q.v.) costermonger. Her most popular ditties were 'Liza Johnson' and 'Three Pots a Shilling'. In 1935 she appeared at the Royal Variety Performance and sang two of her old songs, the audience joining heartily in the chorus.

Carnival Play, see FASTNACHTSSPIEL.

CARON, LESLIE (1931–), see HALL, PETER.

Carpenter's Scene, an insertion into a pantomime or big spectacular musical show, played in front of a backcloth while elaborate scenery is set up behind out of sight of the audience. In Victorian times it was used also in serious plays, but was no longer needed when the practice of dropping the front curtain between scene-changes became general.

Carpet Cut, a long narrow stage-opening behind the front curtain, stretching nearly the whole width of the proscenium opening. It serves to trap the edge of a carpet or stagecloth, so that the actor cannot be tripped up by it.

Carriage-and-Frame (or CHARIOT-AND-POLE), a device for changing the scenery wings, common on the Continent and sometimes used in England. Each wing-piece is suspended just clear of the stage floor on a frame (or mast) which projects downwards through a long slit in the stage and is borne on a wheeled carriage. This arrangement exists in duplicate at every wing-position, and the two carriages at each position are connected by ropes, working in opposite directions, to a common shaft serving the whole series, in such a way that one carriage of each pair moves off as its neighbour moves on. The withdrawn wing may then be replaced by the wing for the next scene and the process repeated when required. This system was devised by Torelli (q.v.) and can still be seen in operation at Drottningholm (q.v.).

CARROLL, EARL (1893–1948), American theatre manager and producer, who settled in New York in 1912, and in 1922 built the first Earl Carroll Theatre there. From 1923 until 1936 he produced fifteen 'editions' of *Earl Carroll's Vanities*, a series of revues modelled on the *Follies* of Ziegfeld (q.v.), featuring comedians alternating with lines of chorus girls. He also presented two *Sketch Book* revues and about sixty legitimate plays, of which the most famous was Leon Gordon's *White Cargo* (1923). In 1931 he opened a second Earl Carroll Theatre on the same site and in 1938 moved to Hollywood, where he opened a third theatre and was active in management until his death in an air accident.

CARROLL, PAUL VINCENT (1900–68), Irish dramatist, who from 1921 to 1937 was a schoolmaster in Glasgow (q.v.), where he helped to found the Curtain Theatre and later, with James Bridie (q.v.), the Citizens'. His early plays were performed in Dublin at the Abbey Theatre (q.v.), where *Things That Are Caesar's* (1932) won first prize for a new play. It was seen in London and New York in 1933, and was followed by *The Wise Have Not Spoken* (1933; London, 1946; New York, 1954). Carroll's next play, and probably his best, was *Shadow and Substance* (1934; London, 1943), which was produced in New York in 1938 and received an award as the best foreign play of the year, as did *The White Steed* in the following year. This was seen in London in 1947. The best of Carroll's later plays are probably *Green Cars Go East*, a sympathetic picture of life in the Glasgow slums, seen at the Glasgow

Citizens' Theatre in 1940, and *The Strings, My Lord, Are False*, seen in Dublin and New York in 1942.

CARROLL, SYDNEY W. [really GEORGE FREDERICK CARL WHITEMAN] (1877–1958), actor, dramatic critic, and theatre manager. Born in Melbourne, he settled in London and was drama critic of the *Sunday Times* from 1918 to 1923. From 1928 to 1939 he was mainly responsible for the *Daily Telegraph*'s weekly theatre page. He also founded, in 1933, the Open Air Theatre in Regent's Park. Carroll was successively manager of a number of London theatres, among them the Ambassadors, the Criterion, His Majesty's, the New, and the Shaftesbury (qq.v.). He was part-author of several plays, published a volume of dramatic criticism, and wrote a book on acting.

CARTER, MRS. LESLIE [*née* CAROLINE LOUISE DUDLEY] (1862–1937), American actress, chiefly remembered for her appearance in productions by Belasco (q.v.), who trained and launched her. Her first outstanding success was as the heroine of his melodrama, *The Heart of Maryland* (1895), in which she also appeared in London in 1898. She was seen there again in 1900 in his *Zaza*, in which she had appeared in New York the year before. She made her last appearance under Belasco's management in 1901, and then toured under her own and other managements with some success.

CARTON [really CRITCHETT], RICHARD CLAUDE (1856–1928), an English dramatist whose early plays were much influenced by Dickens, the best being *Liberty Hall* (1892). In 1898 he scored a success with a farcical comedy, *Lord and Lady Algy*, which poked discreet fun at the aristocracy and was much enjoyed by the elegant audiences of the time. He continued to write successfully in the same vein, his plays providing excellent starring vehicles for his wife, KATHERINE MACKENZIE COMPTON (1853–1928), daughter of Henry Compton (q.v.), who made her first appearance in London in 1877 as Julia in Sheridan's *The Rivals*, was for some years at the St. James's Theatre, and from 1885 onwards appeared almost exclusively in her husband's plays.

CARTWRIGHT, WILLIAM. There were two early English actors of this name.

probably father and son. The elder appears in Henslowe's diary as a member of the Admiral's Men (q.v.). He is thought to have died in 1650. The younger was born c. 1606, and may have acted as a boy, but his first recorded appearance is in 1634. He was at Salisbury Court (q.v.) when the theatres closed in 1642, and was one of the actors who later played surreptitiously at the Cockpit (q.v.). He was still alive in his eightieth year, and the date of his death is unknown. A WILLIAM CARTWRIGHT (1611–43) who was a Proctor at Oxford University was the author of four plays written as academic exercises for the students there, and probably performed at Christ Church between 1635 and 1638.

Casino Theatre, NEW YORK, on the southeast corner of Broadway and 39th Street, for almost fifty years the leading musical-comedy house of New York. Built in massively Moorish style, it held 1,300 people. It opened on 21 Oct. 1883, and among the musical plays produced there were *Florodora* (1900), *A Chinese Honeymoon* (1902), *Wildflower* (1923), and *The Vagabond King* (1925). The house's last hit was *The Desert Song* (1926). It was pulled down in 1930.

(For Metropolitan Casino, New York, see BROADWAY THEATRE (3); for the London Casino, see PRINCE EDWARD THEATRE.)

CASSON, SIR LEWIS THOMAS (1875–1969), English actor who after some amateur experience made his first professional appearances on the stage at the Court Theatre under the Vedrenne-Barker management from 1904 to 1907, playing mainly in Shakespeare and Shaw. In 1908 he became a member of the repertory company at the Gaiety Theatre, Manchester, under Miss Horniman (q.v.), which he directed from 1911 to 1914. It was there that he met and married Sybil Thorndike (q.v.), with whom he produced a season of Greek plays at the Holborn Empire in 1922. They also appeared together at the Little Theatre between 1920 and 1922 in seasons of Grand Guignol. Casson then devoted most of his time to direction, though continuing to act from time to time, notably as Stogumber in Shaw's *St. Joan* (1924) and Buckingham in *Henry VIII* (1926), and in leading roles with the Old Vic in the 1927–28 season. With his wife he made many overseas tours in the 1920s and 1930s, and

in 1940 accompanied her on a tour of the Welsh coalfields in *Macbeth*. He was knighted in 1945 for services to the theatre. After the Second World War he again toured extensively with Dame Sybil in dramatic recitals, and gave some excellent performances in such parts as Professor Linden in Priestley's *The Linden Tree* (1947), Sir Horace Darke in Clemence Dane's *Eighty in the Shade* (1959), and Telyegin in Chekhov's *Uncle Vanya* at the Chichester Festival in 1962. He made his last appearance (at the age of ninety) in a revival of Kesselring's *Arsenic and Old Lace* (1966). In 1970 a Studio Theatre in Cardiff, named after him, became the home of the Welsh Theatre Company.

CASTRO Y BELLVÍS, GUILLÉN DE (1569–1631), a Spanish dramatist whose main claim to fame rests on his dramatization of the ballads celebrating Spain's national hero, *Las mocedades del Cid*, from which Corneille (q.v.) took the main outline of his *Le Cid* (1636). Its sequel, *Las hazañas del Cid*, was also successful, as were a number of other intensely national dramas, in all of which Castro followed in the steps of his friend and contemporary, Lope de Vega (q.v.), though with less charm and vitality.

Catherine Street Theatre, LONDON, see ROYAL PANTHEON.

CATHERINE THE GREAT, EMPRESS OF RUSSIA (1729–96), see SHAKESPEARE IN TRANSLATION and SHUSHERIN, Y. E.

Catwalk, a narrow bridge slung on iron stirrups from the grid above the stage, running from one fly-floor to another to enable the fly-men to reach and adjust any portion of the hung scenery (see FLIES).

Cauldron Trap, see TRAP.

CAVE, JOE [JOSEPH] ARNOLD (1823–1912), an early music-hall performer in blackface, singer and violinist who later became a prominent music-hall proprietor and manager, running, among other places, the Old Vic, The Elephant and Castle, and the Marylebone (later West London Theatre).

CAWARDEN, SIR THOMAS, see MASTER OF THE REVELS.

CECCHINI, PIER MARIA (1575–1645), an actor and author of the *commedia* *dell'arte* (q.v.), whose stage name was Fritellino. He joined a professional company in about 1591 and, after touring Italy, appeared in Paris, returning there later as leader of the Accesi (q.v.). In the company was his wife, ORSOLA, whom he married in 1594. She was probably the daughter of Flaminio Scala, her stage name being Flaminia, and with her husband she was also associated with the Fedeli (q.v.).

Ceiling-Cloth, see CLOTH.

CÉLESTE, MME CÉLINE (1814–82), a famous French dancer and pantomimist, who appeared with much success on the Parisian stage as a child. In 1827 she went with a troupe of dancers to New York, where she was much admired for her exquisite dancing and expressive gesture, and in 1830 she was seen in London. She relied almost entirely on dumb show, and did not attempt a speaking part in English until 1838. She created a number of parts in new plays, including Madame Defarge in a dramatization of Dickens's *A Tale of Two Cities* (1860), and scored a triumph in Haines's *The French Spy* (1837). She was manager of the Adelphi Theatre in London for a short time in association with the elder Ben Webster (q.v.). She made her last appearance in New York in 1865, and in London in 1874, reappearing for one performance in a revival of Buckstone's *The Green Bushes* as Miami, one of her best parts, at Drury Lane in 1878. From her photographs she appears to have been an extremely plain woman, but highly intelligent, and contemporary accounts leave no doubt of the beauty and expressiveness of her dancing and miming.

Cellar, the space under the stage which houses the machinery for traps, scene-changing, and special effects. In England the system by which tall framed pieces of scenery slid in grooves (q.v.) on the stage meant that the cellar could be shallower than on the Continent, where framed backgrounds (as opposed to hanging drops) had to be lowered beneath the stage. The average English cellar, therefore, usually consisted of a mezzanine floor below the stage floor, with a well in the central part, whereas the Continental cellar (the *dessous*) was often four or five storeys deep.

Celle, a castle between Hanover and Hamburg which contains the oldest existing playhouse in Germany. Designed by Arighini in baroque style, it has a horseshoe-shaped auditorium seating 330. It was first used in 1674, mainly for intimate opera. When the castle became the summer residence of the Hanoverian Court, plays and balls were given there until in 1705 the Elector became George I of England. The theatre was then abandoned and not used again until 1772, when the exiled Queen Caroline Matilde of Denmark arranged for three seasons of plays there. During the nineteenth century it was seldom used, but was kept in good condition until in 1935 it was restored and redecorated. The stage was enlarged and a fly-door was added to permit the use of elaborate scenery. It reopened on 13 May 1935. During the Second World War it escaped damage, and in 1950 a permanent repertory company was installed there.

C.E.M.A. (COUNCIL FOR THE ENCOURAGE-MENT OF MUSIC AND THE ARTS), see ARTS COUNCIL.

Censorship, see DRAMATIC CENSORSHIP.

Center Theatre, NEW YORK, in Rockefeller Center, on the corner of 49th St. and 6th Avenue (Avenue of the Americas). This held 3,700 people and opened on 29 Dec. 1932 as a cinema, but with a stage-show between films. In 1934 the stage was rebuilt, and as the Center Theatre the building reopened with a musical, *The Great Waltz*, on 22 Sept. It was then used for spectacular shows, including ballet, operas, and pageants. In 1940 came the first ice-show, which was successful enough to warrant an annual revival. The theatre was demolished in 1954.

CENTLIVRE, MRS. SUSANNAH (1667–1723), English actress and dramatist, who married as her third husband in 1706 Joseph Centlivre, cook to Queen Anne. Among her many comedies of intrigue, in which she rivalled the verve and ingenuity of Aphra Behn (q.v.), the best are *The Busybody* (1709), *The Wonder, a Woman Keeps a Secret* (1714), and *A Bold Stroke for a Wife* (1718). All three were frequently revived, and the second, whose initial success was largely due to the acting of Anne Oldfield (q.v.) as Violante, later provided a vehicle for Garrick (q.v.) in the part of Don Felix. Mrs. Centlivre was also the author of a sentimental drama, *The*

Gamester (1705), based to some extent on a French play, *Le Joueur* (1696), by Regnier, but with the moral tone of Cibber and Steele (qq.v.).

Central Theatre, NEW YORK, on the west side of Broadway near 47th Street. This opened on 9 Sept. 1918 with Owen Davis's *Forever After*. Under the management of Weber and Fields (q.v.) it had some success, but was then used for transfers of successful plays rather than new productions, and in 1928 it became a cinema. In 1956, as the Holiday, it reverted to use as a theatre, but three years later again became a cinema.

Central Theatre of the Soviet Army, MOSCOW. This was founded in 1919, as the Red Army Theatre, the original company being drawn from small groups of soldiers who had been giving performances for army audiences since 1917. Its first director was Zavadsky (q.v.), but it was Popov (q.v.), its director from 1937 until his death in 1961, who made it one of the outstanding theatres of the Soviet Union. One of his first productions, of *The Taming of the Shrew* (1938), was unforgettable and made theatre history. But new Soviet plays were not neglected and included Chepurin's *People of Stalingrad* (1944), Vinnikov's *The Broad Steppe* (1949), an excellent evocation of the war years, Vishnevsky's *The Unforgettable 1919th* (1952), *Virgin Soil Upturned*, based on Sholokhov's novel, Pogodin's *It Will Never Tarnish* (1961), and Shteyn's *A Game Without Rules* (1962). Since 1958 the theatre has also included in its repertory a number of foreign plays, among them Shaw's *Mrs. Warren's Profession*.

Centre 42, see ROUNDHOUSE.

Centres Dramatiques, theatrical enterprises established in different districts of France with the object of fostering drama in the provinces. Supported by the State and the municipality, they are usually based on a university town, from which a professional company, formed sometimes from a local successful amateur group, sets out to tour the surrounding district carrying its own scenery, costumes, and props. The repertory consists normally of French and other classics—preferably comedies—and translations of modern foreign plays. New French plays are rarely performed, since most authors still prefer

Paris for a first production. The first centres, which opened in 1947, were based on Strasbourg and St.-Etienne, the former occupying a building specially designed by the theatre architect Pierre Sonrel. Others include the Grenier de Toulouse, which in 1969 celebrated its 20th anniversary by taking over a theatre specially built for it by the municipality and named in memory of Daniel Sorano (q.v.), and the Théâtre de la Cité, based on Villeurbanne (Rhône), founded in 1957 by Roger Planchon (q.v.).

Century Grove, see CENTURY THEATRE (1).

Century Theatre, NEW YORK. (1) Originally the New Theatre, on Central Park West at 62nd Street, this opened on 6 Nov. 1909 with Julia Marlowe and E. H. Sothern (qq.v.) in *Antony and Cleopatra*. It was not a success, so the theatre closed, and reopened as the Century on 15 Sept. 1911. Its main successes were musical shows, but in 1916 the Shakespeare Tercentenary was celebrated with a fine production of *The Tempest*, while in 1921 Martin-Harvey (q.v.) in *Hamlet*, and in 1924 Reinhardt's production of the spectacle-play, *The Miracle*, with fine scenery by Norman Bel Geddes (q.v.), were both successful. The theatre closed in 1929 and was pulled down a year later. There was a small theatre on the roof of the Century, known as the Cocoanut Grove or the Century Grove, which staged intimate revue and plays for children.

(2) On 7th Avenue below Central Park South, a big theatre which was opened by the Shuberts as the Jolson on 6 Oct. 1921. In 1923 there was an epoch-making visit by the company of the Moscow Art Theatre under Stanislavsky (q.v.). These fine actors, of whom three—Varvara Bulgakova, Maria Ouspenskaya, and Akim Tamiroff—remained in the U.S.A. and contributed largely to its theatrical life, were seen in Tolstoy, Gorky, Chekhov, and Turgenev, and the influence of their productions could long be traced on the American stage. The following year saw the arrival of another great foreign actor, Firmin Gémier (q.v.), from the Odéon in Paris, and a long run of the famous musical *The Student Prince*. In 1932 a company called the Shakespeare Theatre occupied the Century, giving fifteen of Shakespeare's plays at low prices to an audience composed mainly of students. The theatre, which from 1934 to 1937 was known as the Venice, has also housed a Negro operetta,

an Italian company, the Federal Theatre Project (q.v.), Maurice Schwartz (q.v.) with his Yiddish Players, and, in 1946, the Old Vic company from London, headed by Laurence Olivier and Ralph Richardson (qq.v.). It was pulled down in 1961.

(For the Century Theatre, London, see ADELPHI THEATRE (1) and BIJOU THEATRE (2).)

CERVANTES SAAVEDRA, MIGUEL DE (1547–1616), Spanish novelist and dramatist, who in 1615 published a volume containing eight comedies and eight *entremeses* or comic interludes. The best of the comedies are *Pedro de Urdemalas*, translated by Walter Starkie in 1964 as *Pedro, the Artful Dodger*, and *El rufián dichoso*, which gives an excellent picture of contemporary Spanish life. Of the *entremeses*, which constitute Cervantes' main contribution to Spanish dramatic literature, the best are *El viejo celoso* and *El retablo de las maravillas*. All eight were published in 1948 in an English translation by S. Griswold Morley. Cervantes himself said that he wrote more than thirty plays, but only two versions survive, both written and possibly staged between 1580 and 1590—*El cerco de Numancia*, a tragedy, and *Los tratos de Argel*, based on his experiences while the captive of Algerian pirates. It is, however, as the author of the satirical romance *Don Quixote de la Mancha* (Part I, 1605; Part II, 1615) that Cervantes is chiefly remembered, and there have been innumerable dramatizations of it in many languages. In English the first version was by Durfey. This was performed in 1694 with incidental music by Purcell. In 1895 Irving (q.v.) played Don Quixote in a version by W. G. Wills. In 1965 an American musical, *Man of La Mancha*, began a three-year run in New York and was seen in London in 1968. In Dec. 1969 *The Travails of Sancho Panza*, by James Saunders (q.v.), was performed as a Christmas entertainment by the National Theatre at the Old Vic. In France, one of the most successful productions of Gaston Baty (q.v.) was his own *Dulcinée* (1938), based on an episode from *Don Quixote*.

Český Krumlov, CZECHOSLOVAKIA, a castle about a hundred miles from Prague which contains a small theatre built in 1766—the same year as that at Drottningholm (q.v.). It has a small, horseshoe-shaped auditorium and a magnificent baroque proscenium. The theatre's most exciting

asset, however, is ten sets of contemporary scenery, which are probably the oldest surviving in Europe. Painted by two artists from Vienna, Jan Wetschela and Leo Merkla, these are invaluable in showing how the sumptuous perspective scenes of such artists as the Bibienas (q.v.) were translated into wood and canvas. The sets, one of which is normally displayed on the stage, while others are set up in the adjacent riding-school, are for the usual scenes—palace, wood, harbour, and so on—and one, for a street, has for back-drop one of the angled views leading down two asymmetrical perspectives for which the Bibienas were famous. The stage machinery consists of axles, ropes, and winches for instantaneous changes of scenery, as at Drottningholm, and there are four traps in the stage floor. Performances are occasionally given, but the precious and indeed unique scenery is considered too fragile to be used very often.

Chamberlain's Men, the Elizabethan company of actors with which Shakespeare was mainly connected, and for which he wrote the bulk of his plays (for the chronology of these, see SHAKESPEARE). It was founded in 1594 and occupied the Theatre, built by James Burbage (q.v.), in plays by Shakespeare and others, including Jonson (q.v.). In 1599 the company left the Theatre and went to the Globe (q.v.). In 1601 the actors got into trouble for performing Shakespeare's *Richard II*, which, taken in conjunction with the Earl of Essex's unsuccessful rebellion, smacked of treason; but they got off lightly, though they may have had to go on tour for a while. They were playing at Court not long before Elizabeth I's death in 1603, and shortly afterwards came under the direct patronage of James I. As the King's Men they outshone all other Jacobean and Caroline companies, not excepting Alleyn's (see ADMIRAL'S MEN). They continued to act Shakespeare's plays as they were written, but as he withdrew more and more from the theatre, his place was taken by Beaumont and Fletcher (qq.v.), whose earliest play for the King's Men, *Philaster*, dates from 1610. Two years earlier the company had taken over the second Blackfriars (q.v.) for use in the winter, but continued to use the Globe, which was burnt down after a performance of *Henry VIII*, Shakespeare's last play, in 1613. Rebuilt in the following year, it saw the first production of Webster's *The Duchess of Malfi*.

The death of Shakespeare in 1616 and of Burbage three years later caused an upheaval, and a number of actors migrated to other companies. Joseph Taylor (q.v.) took Burbage's place, and Heminge and Condell (qq.v.), who had been business managers for so long, were replaced by Taylor and John Lowin (q.v.). A great event in the company's history was the publication in 1623 of the First Folio of Shakespeare's plays, the largest collection of contemporary plays yet to appear in print. The following year saw the production of *A Game at Chess* by Middleton (q.v.), at which the Spanish Ambassador took umbrage. The players were admonished and fined, and the play shelved. On the death of James I, the company came under the patronage of his son. During the new reign they had trouble over the lease of the Globe, which was finally extended to 1644, and with the Puritan inhabitants of Blackfriars, who tried to get the theatre there closed. That this was not done was probably due to the interest which the king, and particularly his queen, took in the players. They were constantly commanded to Court, appearing often in the Cockpit at Whitehall, which had been refashioned as an indoor theatre. Massinger (q.v.) was their main dramatist, and was succeeded on his death by James Shirley (q.v.). Evil times, however, were coming, and in 1642 the theatres were shut, the players disbanded, and organized theatrical activity ceased until 1660.

CHAMBERS, MARY (c. 1780–1849), see KEAN, EDMUND.

Chambers Street Theatre, NEW YORK, so called by Eddy (q.v.) when in 1856 he took it over from Burton (q.v.) for a season of farce and melodrama. Previously Palmo's Opera House, it was renamed the American Theatre during the tenancy of E. L. Davenport, father of Fanny (q.v.), who opened it on 13 Feb. 1857. It finally closed on 30 March in the same year.

Champagne Charlie, see LEYBOURNE, GEORGE.

CHAMPION, HARRY (1866–1942), a music-hall comedian who first appeared about 1888 in black-face as Will Conray. Under his own name he later became famous for such comic songs as 'Ginger, Ye're Barmy', 'Any Old Iron', and 'Boiled Beef and Carrots', delivered at terrific speed, with great zest and vitality, and accompanied by a jigging dance.

CHAMPMESLÉ, MLLE [really MARIE DESMARES] (1642–98), one of the earliest French tragic actresses, and the creator of many famous roles, including the heroines of *Bérénice* (1670) and *Phèdre* (1677), by Racine (q.v.), whose mistress she was. Mlle Champmeslé began her career at the Marais (q.v.), and in 1665 married the actor CHARLES CHEVILLET CHAMPMESLÉ (1642–1701), author of a number of light comedies, of which the best-known were *Crispin chevalier* (1682) and *Le Florentin* (1685). Both he and his wife became members of the Comédie-Française (q.v.) on its foundation in 1680, but the husband, who had been considered a good tragic actor in his youth, was soon overshadowed by the success of his wife, who played opposite Baron (q.v.) until her death.

Champs-Elysées, THÉÂTRE DES, PARIS, see FOLIES-MARIGNY.

CHANCEREL, LÉON (1886–1965), French dramatist and director, a pupil of Jacques Copeau (q.v.). He was also with Jouvet (q.v.) at the Champs-Élysées in 1926, and from 1929 to 1939 directed the Comédiens Routiers, a touring company which played to young audiences. In 1935 he founded in Paris a company of young actors to play to children. Known as Le Théâtre de L'Oncle Sebastien, its plays were improvised, in deliberate imitation of the *commedia dell'arte* (q v.). Chancerel, who succeeded Jouvet as President of the Société d'Histoire du Théâtre, was head of the Centre Dramatique in Paris. After his death a prize was established in his name to be awarded every two years to the writer of the best new play for children.

CHANFRAU, FRANK S. [really FRANCIS] (1824–84), American actor, best remembered for his playing of Mose, the New York fireman, in *A Glance at New York* (1848) and other plays in the same style by Benjamin Baker (q.v.), and later by Chanfrau himself, who became identified with the part. He was for a time the lessee of the Chatham Theatre (q.v.), which he renamed the National, and where, later in 1848, he continued Mose's adventures in *The Mysteries and Miseries of New York* and other plays. Among his other parts the best-known was the pioneer Kit

Redding in Spencer and Tayleure's *Kit the Arkansas Traveller* (1870), which he played until 1882, his son HENRY, also an actor, continuing to play it until 1890. In 1858 the elder Chanfrau married an actress, HENRIETTA BAKER [really JEANNETTE DAVIS] (1837–1909), who played Portia in the production of *Julius Caesar* in 1864 which brought together for the only time on the stage Edwin Booth (q.v.) and his two brothers.

Chanin's Theatre, NEW YORK, see FORTY-SIXTH STREET THEATRE.

CHANTILLY, MLLE (1727–72), see FAVART, CHARLES-SIMON.

Chapel Street Theatre, NEW YORK. This was opened by David Douglass (q.v.) in 1761, in what was later Beekman Street, by which name the theatre is often called. It was here that the first known performance of *Hamlet* in New York was given, on 26 Nov., with the younger Hallam (q.v.) as Hamlet. After the departure of Douglass's company in May 1762, the theatre was used occasionally by amateurs, and by officers of the British garrison. In May 1766 a professional company was appearing in Dodsley's *The King and the Miller of Mansfield* when the Sons of Liberty, an unruly band of anti-Britishers to whom all players were suspect, broke up the performance and greatly damaged the building, which was not used again.

CHAPMAN, GEORGE (*c.* 1560–1634), English poet and dramatist, author of the translation of Homer which inspired Keats's sonnet. He may have served as the original of Shakespeare's Holofernes in *Love's Labour's Lost* and Thersites in *Troilus and Cressida*, but this lacks proof. Most of his early plays are lost, but of the tragedies that have survived the most important is *Bussy d'Ambois*, acted in about 1604 by the Children of Paul's, who also appeared in *Eastward Ho!* (1605), a comedy written by Chapman in collaboration with Jonson and Marston (qq.v.). This gave offence to James I and caused the imprisonment of the authors. Chapman narrowly escaped prison again in 1608, when a play in two parts, *The Conspiracy and Tragedy of Charles, Duke of Byron*, upset the French ambassador. Chapman's best comedies are *May Day*

(1602), and *All Fools* (*c.* 1604), both produced at Blackfriars and based on Terence (q.v.).

CHAPMAN, WILLIAM (1764–1839), one of the earliest and possibly the first of the American showboat managers. He made his début on the London stage in 1803, and in 1827 appeared in New York at the Bowery Theatre (q.v.). With his wife and numerous children he went on tour, and in Pittsburgh had built for him by a Captain Brown a 'floating theatre' on which he played up and down the Ohio and the Mississippi (see SHOWBOAT). He died on board, and his widow continued to run the business for some years, finally selling it in about 1847 to Sol Smith (q.v.).

CHAPPUZEAU, SAMUEL (1625–1701), a French man of letters, author of *Le Théâtre françois* (1674), which consists of three parts: (1) *De l'usage de la comédie*, a defence of the theatre; (2) *Des auteurs qui soutiennent le théâtre*, a dictionary of dramatists; and (3) *De la conduite des comédiens*, an apology for players, with lives of many of the best-known up to the date of publication. This third part contains a long chapter on Molière, who had just died. Though somewhat inaccurate, the work as a whole is an important source-book of the seventeenth-century French theatre. An early farce by Chappuzeau, published in Lyons in 1656, may have been acted by Molière's company in the provinces, or alternatively Molière may have seen or read it, since it seems to have had some influence on his own play, *Les Précieuses ridicules* (1658).

Charing Cross Theatre, LONDON, see TOOLE'S THEATRE.

Chariot-and-Pole, see CARRIAGE-AND-FRAME.

CHARKE, CHARLOTTE (1713–*c.* 1760), see CIBBER, THEOPHILUS.

Charles Hopkins Theatre, NEW YORK, see PUNCH AND JUDY THEATRE.

Charleston, a town important in the early history of American drama. Otway's *The Orphan* was produced there in 1735, and Farquhar's *The Recruiting Officer* a year later, in a theatre in Dock Street which remained in use until 1763, when Douglass (q.v.) built a new theatre to house the American Company. After the War of Independence Charleston was one of the first towns to be visited by a theatrical company.

CHARLOT, ANDRÉ (1882–1956), see REVUE.

Chatham Theatre, NEW YORK. (1) This theatre, built by Barrière in 1824 in a pleasure-resort named Chatham Gardens, soon proved a serious rival to the old-established Park Theatre (q.v.). Originally known as the Pavilion, it seated 1,300 and was the first theatre in New York to be lit by gas-jets. Its architect and scenic designer was Hugh Reinagle, its machinist George Conklin. After the death of Barrière on 18 Feb. 1826, Henry Wallack (q.v.) took over, later renaming it the American Opera House, and in 1830 Blanchard ran it as the Amphitheatre with a mixture of equestrian and straight drama. It finally closed in 1832, under Hamblin, and became a Presbyterian chapel.

(2) On the south-east side of Chatham Street. The New Chatham Theatre, as it was called, opened on 11 Sept. 1839 under James Anderson from the Bowery. He was succeeded by the elder Thorne, who retired in 1843. In 1848 the great American comedian Frank Chanfrau (q.v.) took it over and renamed it Chanfrau's New National Theatre. It was henceforth known as the National, and Purdy, its next manager, kept the name. It was at this theatre that Edwin Booth (q.v.) made his first appearance in New York on 27 Sept. 1850. One of the greatest successes here, in 1853, was Aiken's dramatization of Harriet Beecher Stowe's anti-slavery novel, *Uncle Tom's Cabin*. During Purdy's last season in 1859 Adah Isaacs Menken (q.v.) made her first appearance in New York as a young and untried actress. On 9 July 1860 fire damaged much of the building, but it continued in use, as the Union Theatre, the National Concert Hall, and once again the Chatham. It finally became the National Music Hall, and in Oct. 1862 it was pulled down.

Chauve-Souris, see BALIEFF, NIKITA.

CHAYEFSKY, PADDY [really SIDNEY] (1923–81), American dramatist, whose best-known play, *The Tenth Man* (1959), was seen in London in 1961. *The Latent Heterosexual*, first produced in Dallas in 1968, was also seen in London in the same year, with Roy Dotrice (q.v.) as John Morley, the leading character. Chayefsky's other plays, which have not yet been seen

in London, include *Middle of the Night* (1956), *Gideon* (1961), and *The Passion of Josef P.* (1964). He also wrote a number of film scripts, as well as plays for radio and television.

CHEKHOV, ANTON PAVLOVICH (1860–1904), Russian dramatist, possibly the one best known outside Russia, whose plays are in the repertory of every country. He came of humble parentage, but graduated as a doctor from Moscow University in 1884, and always thought of himself as more of a doctor than a writer. Well known for his short stories even during his student days, he was early attracted by the theatre, and his first plays were one-act comedies—*The Bear* (1888), *The Proposal* (1889), *The Wedding* (1890)—for which he always retained an amused affection. His first full-length plays, *Ivanov* (1887) and *The Wood-Demon* (1889), were unsuccessful, as was *The Seagull* (1896) when performed at the old-fashioned Alexandrinsky Theatre (q.v.) in St. Petersburg, the reason being that it had nothing in common with the plays currently popular and was incomprehensible to actors trained in the old traditions. Chekhov might have given up the theatre entirely had not Nemirovich-Danchenko persuaded him to let the newly founded Moscow Art Theatre (q.v.) revive *The Seagull*. The production was a success, and was followed by *Uncle Vanya* (1899) (a recast version of *The Wood-Demon*), *Three Sisters* (1901), and *The Cherry Orchard* (1904), in all of which Chekhov's wife Olga Knipper-Chekhova (q.v.) played leading parts. Chekhov died shortly afterwards, at the height of his powers. His plays portray the constant attrition of daily life, and the waste, under the social conditions of Old Russia, of youthful energy and talent. At the same time they contain a note of hope for the future which is heavily stressed in modern Russian productions. This hopefulness seems to accord with Chekhov's own view of his plays, but not with Stanislavsky's, who wrote that he wept when he first read *The Cherry Orchard*, and who conveyed to its first audience his own impressions of regret and impermanence. But however one interprets the plays, they demand a subtlety of ensemble playing which was not available in Russia until the founding of the Moscow Art Theatre. Chekhov may still, particularly in translation, be falsified, but gradually the truth of his work, both for his own time and for ever, is imposing itself on his interpreters. The forces at work, however obscurely, in Chekhov's dramas are those which produced the Russian Revolution, and the great speech by the student Trofimov at the end of Act II of *The Cherry Orchard*—the celebrated 'All Russia is our garden'—is not only a concise review of then recent Russian history, but an astonishingly accurate prediction of the Revolution itself.

As far as can be ascertained, the first of Chekhov's plays to be acted in English was *The Seagull* (Glasgow Repertory Theatre, 1909, and London Little Theatre, 1912). Shaw persuaded the Stage Society to produce *The Cherry Orchard* in 1911 and *Uncle Vanya* in 1914. These early productions failed, but helped to make Chekhov's work known to actors and critics alike. *Three Sisters* was produced in London for the first time in 1920, but the first production to be commercially successful was *The Cherry Orchard*, brought to London in 1925 by Fagan (q.v.) from the Oxford Playhouse. Even more successful was a series of productions by Komisarjevsky at the Barnes Theatre under Philip Ridgeway (*Ivanov*, 1925; *Uncle Vanya, Three Sisters, The Cherry Orchard*, 1926), which finally naturalized Chekhov in England. It would be impossible to list all the subsequent London, provincial, repertory, and amateur productions of Chekhov, but it is worth noting that his early, unfinished play, *Platonov*, first produced in Russia in the 1920s, was seen in London in 1960, after a preliminary production at the Nottingham Playhouse. The Moscow Art Theatre, on a visit to London, played *The Cherry Orchard* in Russian in 1928 at the Garrick Theatre and in 1958 at Sadler's Wells, together with *Uncle Vanya* and *Three Sisters. The Cherry Orchard* was seen again in 1964. America's introduction to Chekhov was in Russian, when Paul Orlenev and Alla Nazimova (q.v.) appeared in *The Seagull* in 1905. In an English translation, this was produced by the Washington Square Players (q.v.) in 1916, but American interest in Chekhov dates from the visits of the Moscow Art Theatre in 1923 and 1924, and subsequent American productions have been strongly influenced by Stanislavsky.

There have been a number of translations of Chekhov's plays into English. The standard acting versions for many years were those of Constance Garnett (1923), which have frequently been used as the basis of new adaptations. The Penguin Classics published versions of *The Cherry Orchard, Three Sisters*, and *Ivanov* by Elisaveta Fen. All Chekhov's plays are contained in the first three volumes of The Oxford Chekhov, in translations by Ronald Hingley based on the definitive Moscow edition of 1944–51.

Chelsea Theatre, LONDON, see ROYAL COURT THEATRE (1).

CHÉNIER, MARIE-JOSEPH (1764–1811), French dramatist (younger brother of the poet André Chénier, who was guillotined in 1794), and one of the few important literary figures of the French Revolution. He had already produced some unsuccessful plays when, after a battle with the censor lasting two years, his *Charles IX* was performed in 1789. It was enthusiastically received, mainly owing to the magnificent acting of Talma (q.v.), who later opened the Théâtre de la République with Chénier's *Henri VIII* (1791), following it in the same year with his *Jean Calas*, and in 1792 with *Caius Gracchus*, another revolutionary play well suited to the temper of the time. Chénier was now at the height of his popularity. He was also active in politics and, as a member of the Convention, he voted for the death of Louis XVI. His political career came to an end in 1802, when he opposed the rising star of Napoleon. He continued to write, but without success, and his *Timoléon*, first performed in 1792, was proscribed and burnt by order of the censor. Only one copy, saved by an actress who much admired him (see VESTRIS, FRANÇOISE), escaped destruction.

Cherokee Kid, see ROGERS, WILL.

Chester Cycle, see MYSTERY PLAY.

Chestnut Street Theatre, PHILADELPHIA, between 6th and 7th Streets, built in 1793 for the company brought from England by Thomas Wignell (q.v.). A copy of the Theatre Royal at Bath, holding about 2,000 people, it opened on 17 Feb. 1794. Known as 'Old Drury', it was one of the first theatres in the United States to be lit by gas (25 Nov. 1816). Wignell remained there until his death, being succeeded jointly by William Warren and William Wood (qq.v.). Under them the theatre had practically a monopoly of acting in Philadelphia until the opening in 1811 of the Walnut Street Theatre (q.v.). In 1828 Wood's retirement and competition from the Walnut Street and from Mrs. John Drew (q.v.) at the Arch Street Theatre caused the company to go bankrupt. The theatre was then used for visiting stars and touring companies. It was damaged by fire in 1820, and completely destroyed in 1856. A new theatre opened in 1863 and closed in 1910. It was finally demolished in 1917.

CHETTLE, HENRY (*c.* 1560–1607), a prolific Elizabethan playwright, credited by Henslowe (q.v.) in his diary with a long list of plays, mostly written in collaboration and now lost. Of those that survive, the only one he appears to have produced unaided was *Hoffman*, known also as *Revenge for a Father* (*c.* 1602), which follows the pattern of the 'revenge tragedy' set by Kyd (q.v.). Chettle was also a printer, in which capacity he published the pamphlets of Nashe (q.v.), and *A Groatsworth of Wit* (1592), which contains the attack made on Shakespeare by Robert Greene (q.v.).

CHEVALIER, ALBERT (1861–1923), a music-hall performer best remembered for his Cockney songs like 'Knocked 'em in the Old Kent Road' and 'My Old Dutch'. Originally an actor, he was persuaded to appear on the halls by Charlie Coborn (q.v.), making an immediate success at the Pavilion in 1891 singing his own composition 'The Coster's Serenade'. He was also the author of many sentimental sketches and ballads, an unsuccessful play, *The Land of Nod*, and a volume of memoirs entitled *Before I Forget*.

CHEVALIER, MAURICE (1888–1972), French actor and music-hall artist, equally popular in Paris, London, and New York. He was with Mistinguett (q.v.) at the Folies-Bergère from 1909 to 1913, and in 1919 made his first appearance in London in the revue *Hullo, America!* In 1929 he sang songs from his repertoire at the New Amsterdam Roof Garden in Ziegfeld's Theatre in New York, and embarked on a long and consistently successful career, which he recounted in part in his memoirs, *The Man in the Straw Hat*, published in 1949. This straw hat was, indeed, his trademark, and its debonair flourish, combined with a slightly raffish appearance, a quizzical smile, and a seductive voice

with a charming broken-English accent, helped to make him a popular idol.

CHIARELLI, LUIGI (1884–1947), Italian dramatist, regarded as the chief exponent of the *teatro grottesco*. The literary quality of his work is slight, but he is an excellent craftsman. His best-known play is *La maschera e il volto* (1916), which, as *The Mask and the Face*, was seen in London in 1924, and later the same year in New York, in an adaptation by C. B. Fernald. Chiarelli's other plays, which include *Fuochi d'artificio* (1923) and two light comedies, *Una più due* (1935) and *Il cerchio magico* (1937), have not yet been seen in translation.

Chichester Festival Theatre. The enterprise shown in the founding of the Shakespeare Festival Theatre in Stratford, Ontario (see STRATFORD (2)) inspired an amateur actor, Leslie Evershed-Martin, to plan a somewhat similar theatre for Chichester. It opened on 3 July 1962 under Sir Laurence Olivier (q.v.) for a season of ten weeks, during which Chekhov's *Uncle Vanya* (with Olivier and a strong supporting cast) proved the most successful play in the repertoire. In later seasons new plays were produced, among them Arden's *The Workhouse Donkey* and *Armstrong's Last Goodnight*, Shaffer's *Royal Hunt of the Sun* and *Black Comedy*, Ustinov's *The Unknown Soldier and his Wife*, and Bolt's *Vivat! Vivat Regina!*, as well as classics such as *Othello*, *The Tempest*, Wycherley's *The Country Wife*, and Ibsen's *Peer Gynt*, light comedies like Pinero's *Trelawny of the 'Wells'* and *The Magistrate*, and foreign plays, among them Brecht's *The Caucasian Chalk Circle* with the Israeli actor Topol. At the end of the 1965 season Olivier resigned and was replaced by John Clements (q.v.). The theatre is set on the edge of the town among trees, has a large open stage with the audience on three sides, a semi-permanent balcony, a catwalk all round the interior wall, and access to the stage from numerous entrances in the stage wall and also from two auditorium staircases. Lighting is from lamps suspended from the spider's-web structure of the tent-like roof. There are bars in the large foyer, and a detached restaurant in the grounds. In addition to the summer season of plays by a professional company, the theatre is used for Sunday concerts and poetry readings, and during the winter for performances by local amateur and visiting companies.

Children of the Chapel, of Paul's, see BOY COMPANIES.

CHIRGWIN, GEORGE H. (1854–1922), a popular English entertainer, who was first with a Minstrel Show (q.v.) and then went to the music-halls, where from 1877 he was billed as the White-Eyed Kaffir because of the white lozenge-shaped patch round his right eye. He celebrated his jubilee at the Oxford in 1911. His best-known stage songs were 'The Blind Boy' and 'My Fiddle is My Sweetheart', which he sang in a high-pitched, piping voice, accompanying himself on the banjo.

Chocolate-Coloured Coon, see ELLIOTT, G. H.

CHODOROV, JEROME (1911–   ), see FIELDS, JOSEPH.

Choregus. In Athens certain specific financial burdens or liturgies were imposed in rotation on citizens whose wealth exceeded a certain sum. One of these was the equipping and paying of a chorus for a tragic, comic, or dithyrambic contest. It was important to the poet that his *choregus* should be of a generous nature, since the presentation of the play depended on the amount of money he was prepared to spend. *Choregi* therefore were assigned by lot.

Chorus, in Greek drama a group of actors who stood aside from the main action of the play and commented on it, as in Aeschylus and Sophocles (qq.v.). In this sense, the word has been revived in some modern verse plays, notably *Murder in the Cathedral* (1935) by T. S. Eliot (q.v.). On the Elizabethan stage the chorus was the speaker of an introductory prologue, a legacy from Euripides via Seneca (qq.v.). In the late nineteenth century the word meant the chorus of a musical comedy, usually consisting of handsome but static young men, and beautiful young women in lovely clothes who sang and danced gracefully in unison. By the 1920s they wore fewer clothes and reached a very high standard of precision dancing. The men were often dispensed with. Under the influence of the American musical the chorus now has a larger share in the plot, and is expected to excel in all forms of dance.

CHRISTIE [*née* MILLER], DAME AGATHA MARY CLARISSA (1890–1976), who writes under her first husband's name, her present name being Mallowan. Although chiefly renowned for her detective novels, she has a place in theatrical history as the author of *The Mousetrap*, which opened on 25 Nov. 1952 and has been running ever since. This was originally a play for radio, which she herself adapted for the theatre. It was produced in New York in 1960. She also dramatized several of her own novels, among them *Ten Little Niggers* (1943), seen in New York in 1944 as *Ten Little Indians* and filmed as *And Then There Were None*; *Appointment with Death* (1945); *Death on the Nile* (1946); *The Hollow* (1951); and *Witness for the Prosecution* (1953), which was still on when *Spider's Web* (1954) was presented, thus giving her, with *The Mousetrap*, three plays running concurrently in the West End. She then wrote *Verdict* and *The Unexpected Guest* (both 1958) and adapted *Go Back for Murder* (1960) from her novel *Five Little Pigs*. Among adaptations of her novels by other hands, the most successful was *Love from a Stranger* (1936), based by Frank Vosper on *Philomel Cottage*. She was appointed C.B.E. in 1956 and D.B.E. in 1970, on the occasion of her eightieth birthday, when she published her eightieth book.

CHRONEGK, LUDWIG (1837–91), see MEININGER COMPANY.

CIBBER, COLLEY (1671–1757), English actor, manager, and playwright, author of an *Apology for the Life of Mr. Colley Cibber, Comedian*, published in 1740, which contains some admirable descriptions of Restoration acting. He was himself a good actor in such parts as Lord Foppington in *The Relapse; or, Virtue in Danger* by Vanbrugh (q.v.), and in his own comedies, which form a link between the bawdy humour of Restoration comedy of manners, and the sentimental comedy of Steele (q.v.). The first of them, produced in 1696 at Drury Lane, where Cibber was later joint manager, was *Love's Last Shift; or, the Fool in Fashion*. Among his later works the most successful were *She Would and She Would Not; or, the Kind Impostor* (1702), which was revived by Daly (q.v.) in New York as late as 1886, and *The Careless Husband* (1704), in which Anne Oldfield (q.v.) played Lady Betty Modish. Cibber's tragedies were mostly failures, but he achieved success in 1700 with an adaptation of Shakespeare's *Richard III* which remained the standard text for nearly two hundred years, and in 1717 with *The Non-Juror*, an adaptation of Molière's *Tartuffe*. In 1730 he was appointed Poet Laureate, a post previously held by other versifiers, including Shadwell, Tate, and Rowe. In spite of his many good qualities, he was highly unpopular, mainly because of his self-satisfied air and boundless conceit, and was satirized by Pope in *The Dunciad*, by Dr. Johnson, and by Fielding in several plays and in the novel *Joseph Andrews*. Cibber had a certain facility in doctoring other men's work, as can be seen from his completion of Vanbrugh's unfinished play, *The Journey to London*, produced at Drury Lane in 1728 as *The Provoked Husband*, with Anne Oldfield as Lady Townly.

CIBBER, THEOPHILUS (1703–58), English actor, son of Colley Cibber (q.v.). He made his first appearance on the stage at the age of sixteen, and appeared to have the makings of a good actor in eccentric roles and Irish comedy. But the scandals caused by his disorderly life drove him from London, and he was drowned on his way to appear at the Smock Alley Theatre, Dublin. He married as his second wife SUSANNA MARIA ARNE (1714–66), sister of the celebrated composer, who became an excellent actress, and was for many years with Garrick (q.v.) at Drury Lane. Although at her best in tragedy, she was also good in comedy, and made her last appearance as Lady Bute in Vanbrugh's *The Provoked Wife*. Theophilus's sister CHARLOTTE (1713–*c*. 1760), who made a few brief appearances on the stage, was as eccentric and unpredictable as her brother, and led a nomadic and eventful life which she described in *A Narrative of the Life of Mrs. Charlotte Charke* (her married name), published in 1755.

CICOGNINI, GIACINTO ANDREA (1606–60), a prolific and popular Italian dramatist, much influenced by the Spanish theatre, which had come into Italy by way of Naples, where, under a Spanish viceroy, the plays of Lope de Vega and Calderón (qq.v.) were frequently performed by visiting Spanish companies. He was probably the first Italian dramatist to handle the legend of Don Juan.

CINTHIO, IL, see GIRALDI.

CINTIO, see COSTANTINI, ANGELO.

Circle-in-the-Square, NEW YORK, at 5 Sheridan Square, a playhouse designed specifically for arena productions by the Loft Players under José Quintero (q.v.). Among the plays produced there (mainly revivals) were Richardson and Berney's *Dark of the Moon* (the opening production, on 15 Feb. 1951), Tennessee Williams's *Summer and Smoke* (1952), Truman Capote's *The Grass Harp* (1953), and Arthur Hayes's *The Girl on the Via Flaminia* (1954). In 1954 the theatre was closed as a fire hazard, but after adequate safety measures had been taken it re-opened, to become one of off-Broadway's most popular playhouses. In 1956, under the direction of Quintero, it gave a production of O'Neill's *The Iceman Cometh* which in the opinion of some critics was superior to that of the original production by the Theatre Guild (q.v.) in 1946. In 1959 the demolition of the building forced the company to move to new premises at 159 Bleecker Street (a remodelled music-hall), where they opened on 3 Mar. 1960 with Genet's *The Balcony*, and continued their former policy, achieving success with productions of Dylan Thomas's *Under Milk Wood* (1961), Thornton Wilder's *Three Plays for Bleecker Street* (1962), revivals of O'Neill, and, in 1970, Athol Fugard's *Boesman and Lena*.

Circus, in Roman times an arena for chariot-racing and gladiatorial combats. In modern times, an entertainment usually given in a tent (the Big Top), with performing horses, lions, sea-lions, and other animals, acrobats, wire-walkers, trapeze-artists, and clowns (q.v.). In the early nineteenth century the fashion for spectacular shows led to equestrian drama and the use of live horses in such plays as *Mazeppa* and even in *Richard III*, where the King's horse White Surrey had an important part. From the circuses of Paris came the vogue for aquatic drama, when the stage was flooded for representations of the battle of Trafalgar and other sea-fights. And from France also came dog drama, whose masterpiece was *Le Chien de Montargis; ou, le Forêt de Bondy* (1814) by Pixérécourt (q.v.)

Cité, Théâtre de la, PARIS, a large playhouse which opened as the Palais-Variétés on 20 Oct. 1792, mainly for broad farce and pantomime. It took the name Cité in 1793, became a circus, reopened as a theatre in 1800 under Saint-Aubin, and passed from hand to hand with constant changes of name until it closed in 1807. As the Prado, it was later a well-known dance hall.

Citizens' Theatre, GLASGOW, see GLASGOW.

City of London Theatre. This stood in Norton Folgate, adjoining Bishopsgate. It was designed by Samuel Beazley (q.v.) and opened on 27 Mar. 1837. Its most successful years were from 1848 to 1866 under the management of Nelson Lee, a playwright and producer of pantomimes, who gave his audiences good value for their money—3d. in the gallery, 6d. in the pit. In 1868 the stage area was taken for an extension of the railway. The auditorium became a soup kitchen and later a Temperance Hall, and was destroyed by fire in 1871.

City Pantheon, LONDON, see CITY THEATRE (2).

City Theatre. (1) NEW YORK, a small playhouse at 15 Warren Street, which opened on 2 July 1822 with a company of English actors who had recently been at the Park (q.v.). An outbreak of yellow fever brought their first season to a premature end, and the theatre closed in 1823.

(2) LONDON, a disused chapel in Grub Street, E.C. (later Milton Street), which in 1829 was converted into a theatre. Its name was afterwards changed to the City Pantheon. Edmund Kean played there in 1831, and later a company played at both the City and the Coburg (see OLD VIC), being taken to and fro in hackney coaches. In the following year Harriet Smithson (q.v.), who married the composer Berlioz, appeared there. It was last used as a theatre in 1836, and then became a warehouse.

(3) NEW YORK, in the upper part of the City Saloon on Broadway. It opened on 13 July 1837 with Joe Cowell (q.v.) as Crack in Thomas Knight's *The Turnpike Gate,* but in spite of his popularity the venture soon failed.

Civic Repertory Company, NEW YORK, see LE GALLIENNE, EVA.

Civic Theatre, a term applied originally in Great Britain to a theatre which, as distinct from a municipal theatre run commercially in a holiday resort, would be provided by the local authority as a cultural amenity supported from public funds and managed by a local Trust (as a charitable institution), an Artistic Director being appointed by the Trust to be responsible for programme planning and the daily running of the theatre. It was expected that Clause 132 of the Local Government Act 1948, which empowered local authorities to spend the proceeds of not more than a sixpenny rate on the provision of entertainment 'of any nature', would help towards the establishment of civic theatres, but, in the event, music has so far been the major recipient of such funds. Support of the theatre by the local authorities is now increasing, but not necessarily in the form of civic theatres as originally conceived. Non-profit-distributing repertory companies (as, for example, the Colchester Repertory Company) may be housed in municipally-owned buildings, or receive a subsidy from the local authority while retaining complete artistic freedom (the Theatre Royal, Lincoln, or the Theatre Royal, Windsor, house such companies). A local authority may lend money to a Trust for the building of a theatre, as was the case for the Playhouse, Nottingham, or the Belgrade Theatre, Coventry (q.v.), or may acquire a theatre building to save it from demolition, and either run it itself, as with the Sunderland Empire, or through a Trust, as with the Connaught, Worthing, or the Bristol Old Vic. Or it may itself build a new theatre, as, for example, the one in the Basildon Arts Centre. The two main types of theatre now emerging in which local authorities are interested are first, those whose programmes are controlled by the local authority's own Entertainments Officer (the Ashcroft, Croydon, or the Congress, Eastbourne); and secondly, those built and run by a Trust with varying degrees of local authority support, and housing a resident company (the Thorndike Theatre, Leatherhead, the Octagon, Bolton, or the Greenwich Theatre, London). (See also EDINBURGH.)

CLAIRON, CLAIRE-JOSÈPHE-HIPPOLYTE LÉRIS (Leyris) DE LA TUDE (1723–1803), outstanding French actress, who was first a singer at the Comédie-Italienne and later at the Paris Opéra. But her real talent was for acting, and she was transferred to the Comédie-Française, where she chose to make her début in the title-role of Racine's *Phèdre.* Her performance on 19 Sept. 1743 was hailed with acclamation, particularly by Voltaire (q.v.), in many of whose plays she was to appear. With her fellow-actor Lekain (q.v.), also a protégé of Voltaire, she initiated reforms in stage costume and also, in about 1753, abandoned her declamatory style of speech for a freer and more natural delivery. She was later imprisoned for refusing to play with an actor who had brought disgrace on the company and did not return to the theatre. In 1773 she was invited to the Court of the Margrave of Anspach, and there wrote her *Mémoires et réflexions sur l'art dramatique*, published in 1799. She died in Paris in poverty, her actor's pension having ceased with the outbreak of the Revolution.

Clarence Theatre, LONDON, see PAN-HARMONIUM.

CLARKE, JOHN SLEEPER (1833–99), American actor and theatre manager, who made his début in 1851 in Boston, and later became joint lessee of the Arch Street Theatre, Philadelphia. He married a sister of the American actor Edwin Booth (q.v.), and with him managed several American theatres. He was first seen in London in Oct. 1867, and in 1872 became manager of Toole's Theatre (q.v.). He later took over the Haymarket and the Strand (qq.v.), appearing at all three theatres under his own management.

CLAUDEL, PAUL (1868–1955), French poet, dramatist, and diplomat, who was successively Ambassador in Tokyo, Washington, and Brussels. His early works were published anonymously for fear their ardent Catholicism should harm his career, and all his plays must be considered as statements of his belief in Christianity, depicting the unending struggle between good and evil and the redemption of mankind through sacrifice. Although he began writing plays in 1889, he envisaged for their performance a form of total theatre which had not yet arrived. The first to be staged were *L'Annonce faite à Marie* (1912) and *L'Échange* (1914). Both were seen in London in productions by the Pioneer Players under Edith Craig (q.v.), the first as *The Tidings Brought to Mary* in 1915, the second as *The Exchange* in 1916. In 1919 Sybil Thorndike (q.v.) gave an outstanding performance as Synge de Coûfontaine in *The Hostage*, a translation of *L'Ôtage*, first produced in Paris in 1914. Most of

Claudel's plays were given their first performance outside France—*Le Pain dur* (1926) in Oldenburg, *Le Père humilié* (1928) in Dresden, *Le Repos du septième jour* (also 1928) in Warsaw, *Protée* (1929) in Groningen, *Christophe Colomb* (1930) in Berlin, *La Ville* (1931) in Brussels, *Jeanne d'Arc au bûcher* (1938) in Basle. In Germany, and in America, where *The Tidings Brought to Mary* was seen in 1923, they aroused great interest among reformers of theatrical presentation, since their complex structure offered infinite scope for experimental staging. But it was Jean-Louis Barrault (q.v.), working closely in collaboration with Claudel, who first brought his work to the notice of the general public with a production at the Comédie-Française on 27 Nov. 1943 of what many regard as Claudel's greatest play, *Le Soulier de satin*. Further interest was aroused by Barrault's productions, with his own company at the Théâtre Marigny, of *Partage de Midi* (first seen in 1916) in 1948, and of *Christophe Colomb* in 1953. All three were seen in London in French during visits from the Renaud-Barrault company, *Partage de Midi* in 1951, *Christophe Colomb* in 1956 (and in New York in 1957), and *Le Soulier de satin* in 1965. Of Claudel's other plays, *Le Pain dur* and *Le Père humilié* were translated in 1946 by John Heard, who also provided a new translation of *L'Ôtage*. *Jeanne d'Arc au bûcher*, with music by Honegger (who also wrote the incidental music for *Le Soulier de satin*), was first performed in London in 1954. Claudel's last play, *L'Histoire de Tobie et de Sara*, had its first production at the Avignon Festival in Sept. 1947 under Vilar (q.v.). Most of Claudel's works were revised and rewritten several times, and two or more versions exist of all his major plays.

CLAXTON, KATE (1848–1924), American actress, who from 1870 to 1873 was a member of the company established by Daly (q.v.) at the Fifth Avenue Theatre. In 1874 she scored an outstanding success as Louise, the blind girl in Oxenford's *The Two Orphans*, a melodrama adapted from the French, and for the rest of her life was identified with this part, which she acted all over the United States. She was appearing in it at the Brooklyn Theatre in 1876 when fire destroyed the building, with the loss of two hundred lives.

CLAYTON, JOHN ALFRED (1842–88), see ROBERTSON, AGNES.

CLEMENTS, SIR JOHN SELBY (1910–89), English actor-manager, who in 1935, after five years' experience on the stage, founded the Intimate Theatre in Palmer's Green, a suburb of London, where he directed a weekly repertory of plays old and new, in many of which he appeared himself. The theatre was the first in London to reopen after the outbreak of war in Sept. 1939. Clements later directed a number of plays for E.N.S.A. (q.v.) and in the West End, and in 1946 appeared under his own management at the St. James's Theatre with his second wife, KAY HAMMOND [DOROTHY KATHERINE STANDING] (1909–80), already well known for her playing of such parts as Diana Lake in Rattigan's *French Without Tears* (1936) and Elvira in Coward's *Blithe Spirit* (1941). She later appeared with her husband in many of his productions, notably as Mrs. Sullen in Farquhar's *The Beaux' Stratagem* (1949), in which he played Archer. This had a record run at the Phoenix, under Clements's own management. When in 1951 he directed Shaw's *Man and Superman*, with himself and his wife as John Tanner and Ann Whitefield, he included in it a number of performances of the 'Don Juan in Hell' scene, which is usually omitted, with himself as Don Juan. He later appeared as Professor Higgins in Shaw's *Pygmalion*, with Kay Hammond as Eliza Doolittle, and from 1955 to 1957 was in management at the Saville, again presenting some excellent revivals of classic plays, among them Sheridan's *The Rivals* and Congreve's *The Way of the World*. Among the plays with which he was later associated were Benn W. Levy's *The Rape of the Belt* (1957), which he directed, playing Heracles to his wife's Hippolyte, and two plays by Ronald Millar based on novels by C. P. Snow, *The Affair* (1961) and *The Masters* (1963). In 1965 he was appointed director of the Chichester Festival Theatre (q.v.), where he directed revivals of Phillpotts's *The Farmer's Wife* and Pinero's *The Magistrate* and appeared as Captain Shotover (in Shaw's *Heartbreak House*) and as Macbeth, Prospero (in *The Tempest*), and Antony (in *Antony and Cleopatra*). He was knighted in 1968 for services to the theatre.

CLIVE, KITTY [really CATHERINE RAFTOR] (1711–85), English actress, who achieved a great reputation in the playing of farce, burlesque, and low comedy, her first outstanding success being as Phillida in *Love in a Riddle* (1729), by Colley Cibber (q.v.). Most of her career was spent at Drury Lane, where she and Garrick (q.v.) were constantly at loggerheads, partly because of his determination to prevent her appearing in tragedy and high comedy roles, for which she was quite unsuited. As Portia in *The Merchant of Venice* she burlesqued the Trial Scene by mimicking famous lawyers of the day. On her retirement in 1769 Horace Walpole, who admired her greatly, presented her with a small house—'Clive's-Den'—on Strawberry Hill, where her company and conversation were much relished by his friends, particularly Dr. Johnson. She was frequently painted, notably by Hogarth, and was the author of several short farces.

Cloak-and-sword plays (*Comedias de capa y espada*), a name often taken to mean any romantic costume play with a strong love interest and some duelling. It was formerly applied to any play which depended less on spectacle than on intrigue for its appeal, and in seventeenth-century Spain such plays formed a sub-division of the *comedias de ingenio* (comedies of wit). The characters disguised themselves with their cloaks, and so introduced the necessary complications into the plot, and with their swords they fought the duels which inevitably resulted.

Closet Drama, the term used for plays intended for reading only and not for production on a stage. Among the most important were those of Seneca (q.v.). Many plays in verse by established poets, particularly in the nineteenth century, were intended mainly for reading, though some have proved successful in production (see TENNYSON). Closet drama also includes translations of foreign plays not necessarily intended for the stage.

Cloth, the name given to a large unframed expanse of canvas used for scenery, usually attached at top and bottom to a sandwich batten. A CUT-CLOTH is one with openings which, if elaborately fretted, may need the reinforcement of a piece of netting, glued on behind. A GAUZE-CLOTH consists of an unbroken stretch of fine net which appears opaque when lit from the front, but transparent, almost to vanishing point, when lit from behind. Such a cloth can be painted in dye to appear as a normal cloth. The STAGE-CLOTH, which is an expanse of painted canvas, is laid on the stage as a floor covering. It is painted in a plain colour, or patterned to suit a scene, and further and self-describing varieties of it are known, such as SAND-CLOTH, for desert and other scenes. The CEILING-CLOTH is a canvas stretch battened out and suspended flat over the top of a Box-Set (q.v.).

Cloud Border, see BORDER.

Cloudings, a term formerly applied to permanent cloud borders used to mask the top of a scene. They could be drawn off sideways by hooked poles, and are mentioned as late as 1743. The detail of their arrangement is not clear, but they recall the form of border used by Inigo Jones (q.v.) in his last masque, *Salmacida Spolia* (1640), which had also 'side-clouds'. These could presumably be drawn off to reveal another set behind, thus changing a stormy sky into a calm one, or vice versa.

Clown, a composite comic character, who may be a simpleton, a knave, or a Court jester. Shakespeare provides examples of all three with Costard in *Love's Labour's Lost*, Autolycus in *A Winter's Tale*, and Touchstone in *As You Like It*. One of the formative elements of the Elizabethan clown was the Old Vice of the medieval liturgical play, who tripped up the Devil and played tricks on the serious characters. The best-known players of clowns in Shakespeare's time were Tarleton and Kempe (qq.v.). The *commedia dell'arte* Arlecchino first came into England as a clown, but ended up as the young lover Harlequin (q.v.) in the pantomime, where the part of the Clown, a purely English importation, was immortalized by Grimaldi (q.v.), known as Joey, a name applied to many clowns since. Today clowns are found only in circuses (where they have evolved a special type known as Auguste) or seasonally in pantomime (q.v.). In the heyday of the music-hall the image of the clown as a dolt was perpetuated by the 'red-nosed' comedian, his more polished counterpart by such accomplished players as Grock (q.v.).

CLUNES, ALEC [really ALEXANDER] S. DE MORO (1912–70), English actor,

director, and theatre manager. Both his parents were on the stage, and he himself made his professional début, after considerable experience as an amateur, in 1934, when he joined Ben Greet's company on tour. He was for several seasons at the Old Vic, and also appeared at the Malvern Festival and at Stratford-upon-Avon. In May 1942 he took over the Arts Theatre (q.v.), where he remained until 1953, producing about a hundred and thirty plays, ranging from his initial production, a revival of Odets's *Awake and Sing*, to English classics and new plays, including Fry's *The Lady's Not for Burning* (1948), in which he created the part of Thomas Mendip, subsequently played by Gielgud at the Globe. After leaving the Arts he was seen in a series of parts, including Claudius to the Hamlet of Paul Scofield (1955), Caliban in *The Tempest* at Stratford-upon-Avon (1957), and, his last part, the Bishop of Chichester in Hochhuth's *Soldiers* (1968). He was also a collector of prints and drawings and a dealer in theatre books, and the author of an illustrated history of the London stage, *The British Theatre* (1964).

CLURMAN, HAROLD EDGAR (1901–80), American actor, theatre director, and critic. He made his first appearance on the stage in 1924 at the Greenwich Village Theatre, and in the following year joined the Theatre Guild (q.v.), appearing in its productions of Shaw's *Caesar and Cleopatra* in 1925 and Werfel's *Goat Song* in 1926. He was later instrumental in the founding of the Group Theatre (q.v.), for which he directed his first play on Broadway, Odets's *Awake and Sing*, in 1935, following which he had a long list of important productions to his credit, including Carson McCullers's *The Member of the Wedding* (1950), Inge's *Bus Stop* (1955), Anouilh's *The Waltz of the Toreadors* (1957), O'Neill's *A Touch of the Poet* (1958), and Shaw's *Heartbreak House* (1959). In 1955 he was responsible for the London production of Giraudoux's *Tiger at the Gates*, starring Michael Redgrave, which was subsequently seen in New York. In addition, he became dramatic critic of the *Nation* in 1953, and from 1959 to 1963 was the New York theatre critic of the London *Observer*. He lectured and wrote extensively on the theatre, being the author of *The Fervent Years: the Story of the Group Theatre* (1945) and *Lies Like Truth: Theatre*

Reviews and Essays (1958), and a frequent contributor to *Theatre Arts*. In 1963 he became executive consultant to the Vivian Beaumont repertory company (see LINCOLN CENTER).

COATES, ROBERT (1772–1848), a wealthy and eccentric gentleman from the West Indies, who in 1810 rented the Theatre Royal, Bath, in order to display himself as Romeo; hence his nickname, 'Romeo' Coates. Taking the hilarity of the audience as a tribute to his genius, he finally appeared at the Haymarket in London, again as Romeo, wearing a sky-blue spangled cloak, tight red pantaloons, a muslin vest, a full-bottomed wig, and a tall hat. He had a brief blaze of notoriety, but the public soon tired of his absurdities and he relapsed into obscurity.

COBORN, CHARLIE [really COLIN WHITTON McCALLUM] (1852–1945), English music-hall star, who first called himself Charles Lawrie but later took his name from Coborn Street, Poplar. His most famous songs were 'Two Lovely Black Eyes' (1886) and 'The Man Who Broke the Bank at Monte Carlo' (1890). During the Second World War he was indefatigable in entertaining the troops, singing almost to the day of his death with surprising vigour.

Coburg Theatre, LONDON, see OLD VIC.

COBURN, CHARLES DOUVILLE (1877–1961), American actor and manager, who in 1901 made his first appearance in New York, subsequently touring the United States in Hall Caine's *The Manxman*. With his wife, IVAH WILLS (1882–1937), he organized in 1906 the Coburn Shakespearean Players, in which both played leading parts for many years. Coburn was outstanding as Falstaff, and as James Telfer in a New York production of Pinero's *Trelawny of the 'Wells'*. One of his greatest successes was as Wu Hoo Git in *The Yellow Jacket*, a play in the Chinese manner by George Hazelton and J. H. Benrimo which he frequently revived on tour. In 1934 the Coburns inaugurated the Mohawk Dramatic Summer Festival at Union College, Schenectady, which became an annual event. Coburn retired from the stage on his wife's death, but returned briefly in 1946 to play Falstaff in *The Merry Wives of Windsor* for the Theatre Guild (q.v.) on tour.

COCHRAN, SIR CHARLES BLAKE (1872–1951), one of the master showmen of his day. After experience in practically every branch of popular entertainment, he went into management, his first venture, in New York in 1897, being a production of Ibsen's *John Gabriel Borkman*. In London in 1911 he promoted and managed the production of *The Miracle* at Olympia by Reinhardt (q.v.), which he revived at the Lyceum in 1932. In 1914 he entered the field of revue, his most memorable productions being those at the London Pavilion between 1918 and 1931. Three of these were by Noël Coward (q.v.), several of whose plays he later promoted, including *Bitter Sweet* (1929) and *Cavalcade* (1931). He was responsible for the first appearance in London of Sacha Guitry (q.v.) in 1920 and for the first London productions of *Anna Christie* (1923), by O'Neill (q.v.), of *The Road to Rome* (1928), by Sherwood (q.v.), of the Heywards' Negro play *Porgy* (1929), on which Gershwin later based his opera 'Porgy and Bess', and of *The Silver Tassie* (also 1929), by O'Casey (q.v.). Cochran, who was knighted in 1948 for services to the theatre, wrote three volumes of reminiscences—*Secrets of a Showman* (1925), *I Had Almost Forgotten* (1932), and *Cock-a-Doodle-Do* (1941), the last title being taken from his nickname in the theatre, 'Cocky'.

Cockpit, LONDON (later the Phoenix), a public theatre in Drury Lane, where for many years its name was perpetuated in Pitt Place. It should not be confused with the Cockpit at Whitehall, which was used for the private presentation of plays before the Court. The Drury Lane Cockpit, built for cock-fights by John Best in 1609, was converted into a roofed or 'private' theatre in 1616 by Christopher Beeston (q.v.). It was about the same size as and very similar to the Blackfriars (q.v.). On Shrove Tuesday 1617 the London apprentices, in the course of their usual rowdy merrymaking on that day, sacked and set fire to it. It was quickly rebuilt and renamed the Phoenix, though the old name continued in use. From 1636/7 Beeston used it for a company of young boys, which was run after his death by his son William.

It was closed with all the other theatres in 1642, but illicit performances must have been given there, as it was raided by Parliamentary soldiers in 1649. Two of

Davenant's 'plays with music' (or early operas) were performed at the Cockpit, *The Cruelty of the Spaniards in Peru* (1658) and *Sir Francis Drake* (1659).

When the theatres reopened Rhodes, formerly prompter at the Blackfriars theatre, played at the Cockpit with a troupe of youngsters, many of whom, like Betterton (q.v.), became famous. The theatre fell out of use after the opening of Drury Lane (q.v.).

Cocoanut Grove, see CENTURY THEATRE (1).

COCTEAU, (CLEMENT EUGÈNE) JEAN MAURICE (1889–1963), an important figure in French intellectual life as poet, novelist, critic, artist, and film director. It would be impossible to detail here all the facets of his many-sided activity, which involved most of the outstanding artists and musicians of his day, including Christian Bérard (q.v.), Stravinsky, with whom he collaborated on 'Oedipus Rex' (1927), Honegger, and Satie. As a dramatist he first came into prominence with a new version of Sophocles' *Antigone* (1922), directed by Dullin (q.v.) in a setting by Picasso. This was followed by *Orphée* (1924), directed by Pitoëff (q.v.). In 1934 Jouvet (q.v.) was responsible for the production of another excursion into Greek mythology with *La Machine infernale*, based on the story of Oedipus. Cocteau's versatility is shown by the variety of his dramatic works, which include, in addition to the plays mentioned above, modern problem plays—*Les Mariés de la Tour Eiffel* (1921), a 'spectacle play with music' first performed at the Comédie-Française by Berthe Bovy; *Les Parents terribles* (1938); *Les Monstres sacrés* (1940); *La Machine à écrire* (1941); two one-act monologues for an actress— *La Voix humaine* (1930) and *Le Bel Indifférent* (1941), written for Piaf; an excursion into Arthurian legend, *Les Chevaliers de la Table Ronde* (1937); a tragic love-story in verse, *Renaud et Armide* (1943), produced at the Comédie-Française with Marie Bell and Maurice Escande in the title-roles; and a romantic costume play, *L'Aigle à deux têtes* (1946). Although several of Cocteau's plays (*Orphée*, 1927; *The Human Voice*, 1938; *The Infernal Machine*, 1940; *Intimate Relations*, 1951; and *The Holy Terrors*, 1952) have been translated into English and performed in London, mainly at club theatres like the Arts and the Gate (qq.v.), the only one to achieve a com-

mercial success was *The Eagle Has Two Heads*, which had a long run in 1946 with Eileen Herlie as the Queen, the part originally played by Edwige Feuillère (q.v.). It was also seen briefly a year later in New York, where *Intimate Relations* had been produced in 1932 and *The Infernal Machine* was to come in 1958; but on the whole Cocteau's plays have had less influence outside France than his films and ballets. A biography of him, entitled *Jean Cocteau, The Man and the Mirror*, by Elizabeth Sprigge and Jean-Jacques Kihm, was published in 1968.

COFFEY, CHARLES (?–1745), see BALLAD OPERA.

COGHILL, NEVILL HENRY KENDAL AYLMER (1899–1980), an Oxford tutor who, like Rylands (q.v.) at Cambridge, was closely connected with the theatre, both professional and University. From 1925 to 1957 he was English Tutor at Exeter College, and from 1957 to 1966, when he retired, Merton Professor of English Literature. In 1940 he founded the Friends of the O.U.D.S. (see OXFORD), which he directed for many years, and in 1945 was a member of the Oxford University Drama Commission, which toured the United States seeking the basis for the establishment of a University Theatre. This was eventually achieved with the taking over of the Playhouse by the University, Coghill remaining Chairman of the Governing Board until his retirement. He produced many Shakespearian and modern plays in Oxford, both with the O.U.D.S. and with the O.U. Experimental Club. In 1945 he directed *A Midsummer Night's Dream* at the Haymarket in London, with John Gielgud and Peggy Ashcroft (qq.v.) as Oberon and Titania, and in 1968, with Martin Starkie, prepared a dramatization of some of Chaucer's *Canterbury Tales* which had a long run in London. He had previously published a version of the complete work in modern English which was much admired, and was also the author of *Shakespeare's Professional Skills* (1964).

COGHLAN, ROSE (1851–1932), a distinguished actress who was on the stage as a child, and in 1869 made her adult début under Hollingshead at the old Gaiety Theatre, London. Two years later she went to New York with her brother CHARLES (1842–99), who appeared with her at Wallack's, where she played leading parts for many years. One of her most successful roles was Lady Teazle in Sheridan's *The School for Scandal*. She also appeared in such modern plays as Jones and Herman's *The Silver King*, Tom Taylor's *Masks and Faces*, Sardou's *Diplomacy*, and Wilde's *A Woman of No Importance*. In 1902 she became an American citizen. Her fine voice, distinguished presence, and technical ability kept her in demand, and in 1916 she celebrated her stage jubilee. She was frequently seen in vaudeville, and in 1920 made her last appearance in Belasco's production of *Deburau*, by Sacha Guitry, translated by Granville-Barker.

COHAN, GEORGE MICHAEL (1878–1942), American actor, dramatist, and manager, and the only one, apart from Edwin Booth (q.v.), to be commemorated by a statue in New York. Unveiled on 11 Sept. 1959, this stands in Duffy Square. Cohan appeared as a child in a vaudeville act with his parents, and began writing skits and songs in his teens. He was twenty-three when his first play was produced on Broadway, and among his later works the most successful were *Forty-Five Minutes from Broadway* (1905), *Seven Keys to Baldpate* (1913), based on Earl Biggars's novel, and *The Song and Dance Man* (1923), in which he played a second-rate variety performer who thinks himself perfect—a curious anticipation of Archie Rice in Osborne's *The Entertainer* (1957). Cohan also appeared with success in such plays as O'Neill's *Ah, Wilderness!* (1933) and Kaufmann's *I'd Rather Be Right* (1937) and in 1925 published a volume of autobiography. In 1968 a musical, *George M.*, based on his career, was produced on Broadway with Joel Grey in the title-role. (See also GEORGE M. COHAN THEATRE.)

Cohan and Harris Theatre, NEW YORK, see SAM H. HARRIS THEATRE.

COHEN, GUSTAVE (1879–1958), French scholar, whose researches on the medieval theatre of France have materially added to our knowledge of liturgical drama (q.v.). His *Histoire de la mise en scène dans le théâtre religieux français au moyen âge*, first published in 1906, was re-edited and brought up to date in 1926, after the discovery of the documents relating to the Mystery of the Passion given at Mons in 1501. In the 1930s Cohen adapted a number of medieval religious plays for performance by a group of students, known as Les Théophiliens from the title of their first production, *Le Mystère de Théophile*, by Rutebeuf (q.v.). From 1939 to 1945 he lived and worked in the United States and Canada, continuing his researches into medieval texts and also publishing books on the theatre of the Renaissance and seventeenth century.

COLERIDGE, SAMUEL TAYLOR (1772–1834), English poet, critic, and philosopher, author of several plays in verse, of which one, *Remorse*, written in 1797 as *Osorio*, was produced at Drury Lane in 1813 with moderate success. The others, which include several translations from the German, remained unacted, except for a Christmas entertainment which, with alterations by Dibdin, was produced at the Surrey Theatre in 1818. Coleridge's chief importance in theatre history lies in his critical and editorial work on Shakespeare, though he was handicapped by ignorance of Elizabethan stage conditions, which Malone was only just bringing to light.

Coliseum, LONDON, a variety theatre in St. Martin's Lane which was opened by Stoll (q.v.) on 24 Dec. 1904. It was the first London theatre to have a revolving stage. In 1931 it deserted variety for musical comedy with a successful production of *White Horse Inn* and the equally successful *Casanova* (1932) with music by Johann Strauss. Revues, straight plays, and ice-shows followed. From 1936 onwards an annual pantomime was staged. After the Second World War the theatre housed a succession of American musicals, which included *Annie Get Your Gun* (1947), *Kiss Me, Kate* (1949), and *Guys and Dolls* (1953). In 1961, after the run of *The Most Happy Fella*, the theatre closed and re-opened as a cinema. In 1968 it became the home of the Sadler's Wells Opera Company.

COLLIER, CONSTANCE (1878–1955), English actress, on the stage as a child, who became one of the famous Gaiety Girls in 1893, but left to play serious parts, scoring a success as Chiara the Gypsy in Esmond's *One Summer's Day* (1897) and as Lady Castlemaine in Kester's *Sweet Nell of Old Drury* (1900). She then went to Her Majesty's under Tree (q.v.) and appeared in all his major productions from 1901 to 1908. In 1908 she made her first appearance in New York, and then divided her time between London and the United States, playing Gertrude in London to the Hamlet of John Barrymore (q.v.) in 1925. Among the parts she created, she was outstanding as Nancy in Comyns Carr's version of Dickens's *Oliver Twist* (1915), the Duchess of Towers in the stage version of du Maurier's *Peter Ibbetson* (1915), and the Duchesse de Surennes in Somerset Maugham's *Our Betters* (1923). She also played Anastasia in the New York production of G. B. Stern's *The Matriarch* (1930), the part played in London by Mrs. Patrick Campbell (q.v.) the year before. She was part-author with Ivor Novello of *The Rat* (1924) and *Down Hill* (1926), both of which she directed in London. In 1929 she published a volume of reminiscences entitled *Harlequinade*.

COLLIER, JEREMY (1656–1726), a non-juror and pamphleteer, best known for his attack on the theatre in his *Short View of the Immorality and Profaneness of the English Stage*, published in 1697–8. He had many sensible and courageous things to say, but his work was marred by excessive pedantry and ignorance of the history and technique of the theatre, and he laid himself open to ridicule by his lack of proportion and literary ability. Nevertheless, his work had a salutary effect, reflecting and perhaps assisting a reform which was overdue.

COLLIER, JOHN PAYNE (1789–1883), English dramatic and literary historian, who ruined what would have been valuable research work on Shakespeare and his contemporaries by his habit of forging entries in Elizabethan documents, many of which still persist in spite of rectification by later scholars. It is impossible to say how far his forgeries extend. They have been traced in State Papers and in private collections to which he was given access, and it was his manuscript additions to a second folio of Shakespeare which first aroused suspicion. Proof of his guilt, which he never admitted, was found in his papers after his death.

COLLINS, LOTTIE (1866–1910), a music-hall performer who achieved fame with a single song—'Ta-Ra-Ra-Boom-De-Ay', written by Harry Sayers (1857–1934)—which she introduced into the pantomime of *Dick Whittington* at the Grand, Islington, in 1891. It was so successful that George Edwardes (q.v.) engaged the singer to perform it at the Gaiety Theatre in the burlesque *Cinder-Ellen-Up-Too-Late* while the pantomime was still running. Lottie Collins would rush from one theatre to another, start her song on a low note, then place her hands on her hips and whirl into a swift, high-kicking dance. She repeated her performance for many years in English music-halls, and was paid £200 a week for doing it in America, where the song had originally failed. Her daughter JOSÉ (1887–1958) was a fine singer, who appeared with great success in many musical comedies, the best-known being Lonsdale's *The Maid of the Mountains* (1917), under which title she wrote her reminiscences in 1932.

COLLINS, SAM [really SAMUEL VAGG] (1826–65), a chimney-sweep who became the original music-hall Irish Comedian, first singing 'Paddy's Wedding' and 'The Limerick Races' at Evans's Song-and-Supper Rooms, and then starring at all the London halls. In 1863 he took over the Lansdowne Arms at Islington Green, opening it as Collins's on 4 Nov., and ran it till his death. It was later used as a repertory theatre, but has now been pulled down. On Collins's grave in Kensal Green cemetery are carved pictures of the hat, the shillelagh, and the shamrock, with which he always appeared.

COLLINS, (WILLIAM) WILKIE (1824–89), see DICKENS, CHARLES.

COLMAN, GEORGE the elder (1732–94), English dramatist, who was drawn to the theatre by his friendship with Garrick (q.v.), to whom his first play, *Polly Honeycombe*, a farce acted at Drury Lane in 1760, was attributed. It was not acknowledged by its author until after the success of *The Jealous Wife* (1761), which, with *The Clandestine Marriage* (1766), represents Colman's best work. The latter was frequently revived, the part of Lord Ogleby (which Garrick refused, leaving it to King, q.v.) being a favourite with many leading character actors. Colman was manager of Covent Garden when the plays of Goldsmith (q.v.) were first produced there, and in 1776 took over the Haymarket (q.v.). Among the plays which he produced there were several by his son, George (q.v.).

COLMAN, GEORGE the younger (1762–1836), son of the above, who in 1794 succeeded his father as manager of Covent Garden and remained there till 1803. Reckless and extravagant, he was constantly involved in lawsuits and also hampered by a secret marriage contracted in 1784 with a young actress, Clara Morris. From 1824 until his death he was Examiner of Plays, in which capacity he showed an unexpected prudery. He had none of the rectitude and stability of his father, but he was a good dramatist, excelling in the delineation of comic characters, many of which long remained in favour—among them Dr. Pangloss in *The Heir-at-Law* (1797) and Dennis Brulgruddery in *John Bull; or, The Englishman's Fireside* (1803). Sir Edward Mortimer (in *The Iron Chest*, 1796, based on Godwin's novel, *Caleb Williams*) provided an excellent tragic part for Edmund Kean (q.v.), who revived it in 1816. For the elder Mathews (q.v.) Colman wrote *The Actor of all Work; or, First and Second Floor* (1817), in which two rooms were shown on stage simultaneously, something of an innovation at the time. One of his most successful plays was *Inkle and Yarico*, a comic opera with music by Samuel Arnold which the elder Colman produced at the Haymarket in 1787.

Colonial Theatre, NEW YORK, see HAMP-DEN, WALTER.

COLUM, PADRAIC (1881–1972), Irish writer who contributed three plays to the Irish Dramatic Movement which had a strong influence upon the realistic development that followed. The first, *Broken Soil*, was produced by the Fays (q.v.) in 1903, and at the Abbey Theatre (q.v.) in 1905. Revised and retitled *The Fiddler's House*, it was revived at the Abbey in 1909. *The Land* (1905) and *Thomas Muskerry* (1910) were also seen at the Abbey. Colum's work gave a strong impetus to the second phase of the movement, and when he abandoned the theatre for other forms of literature one of the leaders of the realistic drama was lost to the Irish theatre.

Columbine, the young girl of the English Harlequinade (q.v.), the daughter, ward, or wife of the old man Pantaloon, in love with Harlequin, with whom she eventually elopes. She evolved from one of the maid-servants in the *commedia dell'arte* (q.v.), whose name, Colombina, was used by several actresses of the Italian comedy in Paris in the late seventeenth century, and came into England in the eighteenth century with the growing popularity of pantomime (q.v.).

Columbus Circle Theatre, NEW YORK, see MAJESTIC THEATRE (1).

Comedia a fantasía, a noticia, see TORRES NAHARRO.

Comedias de capa y espada, see CLOAK-AND-SWORD PLAYS.

Comédie-Canadienne, THÉÂTRE DE LA, see GÉLINAS, GRATIEN.

Comédie-Française, the national theatre of France, which was officially founded in 1680 by Louis XIV, who ordered the actors at the Hôtel de Bourgogne (q.v.) to join the troupe formed on Molière's death in 1673 by the amalgamation of his actors with those at the Marais (q.v.). The new company was installed in the theatre built for Lully in the rue Guénégaud, and was known as the Comédie-Française to distinguish it from the Italian company which took over the Hôtel de Bourgogne (see COMÉDIE-ITALIENNE). In honour of France's great actor-dramatist the theatre is also known as La Maison de Molière. Its other name is the Théâtre Français. In 1689 the company moved from the old theatre in the rue Guénégaud to a new one in St. Germain-des-Prés, built by François d'Orbay, where they remained until 1770. After some years in the Salle des Machines at the Tuileries the company again moved to a new theatre on the present site of the Odéon. The Revolution caused a split, some actors under Talma (q.v.) going to the Palais-Royal, renamed the Théâtre de la République, the rest under Molé (q.v.) remaining where they were as the Théâtre de la Nation. For the next few years the history of the theatre in Paris is confused, but in 1803 the company of the Comédie-Française was reconstituted in the theatre occupied by Talma and has since remained stable, though in the up-heaval it lost the monopoly which it had enjoyed for so long.

The organization of the Comédie-Française is interesting, as it resembles that of the original medieval Confrérie de la Passion (q.v.), and also in some respects that of the Elizabethan company at the Globe (q.v.). Its constitution as originally laid down by Louis XIV was redrafted by Napoleon on his way to Moscow and amended in 1959. Admission to the company depends on merit. The actor is allowed to choose his own parts in tragedy and comedy for his first appearances. If successful, he becomes a *pensionnaire*, drawing a fixed salary, and later a full member, or *sociétaire*, holding a share or part share in the company and replacing a member who has retired or died. On retirement, which is not usually permitted under twenty years' service, though many great actors have left in a fury before then, the *sociétaire* is entitled to a pension for the rest of his life. The oldest actor, in years of service not in age, is the head of the company, and is known as the *doyen*. The green-room is a meeting-place for actors and distinguished visitors, where each member of the company in turn performs the duties of host. The library and archives of the Comédie-Française house a rich collection of theatre material.

Comédie-Italienne, the name given in 1680, on the formation of the Comédie-Française (q.v.), to the Italian actors in Paris (see COMMEDIA DELL'ARTE) who settled themselves in the theatre of the Hôtel de Bourgogne (q.v.). They had already begun to use French for some scenes in their improvised plays, and under Dominique (see BIANCOLELLI) they received permission from Louis XIV to act entirely in that language. A number of French dramatists, including Dufresny and Regnard (qq.v.), wrote plays for them, but in 1697 they were banished from France for a fancied slight to Mme de Maintenon in their production of *La Fausse Prude*. On the death of Louis XIV in 1715 they returned under Lélio (see RICCOBONI), but completely revolutionized their repertory and style of acting, appearing with great success in the plays of Marivaux (q.v.). The company was soon Italian only in name, the last Italian actor being Carlin (see BERTINAZZI). In 1752 they ventured to play the newly fashionable genre, *opera buffa*, with such success that they devoted themselves entirely to music, leaving the Hôtel de Bourgogne in 1783 for a new theatre on the Boulevard des Italiens, named after them. During the Revolution this was known as the Théâtre Favart, and its success was menaced by the rivalry of the Théâtre Feydeau (formerly the Théâtre de Monsieur). In 1801 the two companies amalgamated as the Opéra-Comique, a name which was retained for the present theatre, built after the destruction by fire in 1835 of the old one.

Comedy, a term which in its modern use covers a wide variety of plays. These differ from tragedy in that they have a happy ending, and from farce in that they contain some subtlety and character-drawing. The word, meaning 'a revel-song', from the Greek *comos* and *ode*, was applied to the satiric plays of Aristophanes and to the works of Terence and Plautus (qq.v.; see also FABULA). In medieval times it meant any story with a happy ending. The Renaissance brought the term back to the theatre, but without its former satiric connotation; it also lost in course of time its connection with 'comic' and 'comedian', terms now reserved for low humour, though on the Continent the latter term in the generic sense of actor was used later than in England, where in the eighteenth century it was applied to players of farcical parts and in the late nineteenth century to music-hall acts.

Comedy is, by its nature, difficult to translate, as its appeal depends on local and topical interest. Because of this, innumerable comedies enormously successful in their own day were soon forgotten. This handicap is, however, subject to the overriding force of genius, and the comedies of Aristophanes, Shakespeare, and Molière (qq.v.) can still be enjoyed by most audiences, even in translation.

English comedies have been classified under various headings—Comedy of Humours, as written by Ben Jonson (q.v.) under classical influence; of Manners, as written by Restoration dramatists like Congreve (q.v.) under the influence of Molière; of Intrigue (from Spain via France), as written by Mrs. Aphra Behn (q.v.); and Sentimental Comedy, as written by Steele (q.v.) in reaction from Restoration Comedy. But all these types merge and overlap, and in the theatre today it is impossible to assign any given play to a specific genre.

In France the fusion of tragedy and comedy into pathos produced the tearful comedies (*comédie larmoyante*) of Nivelle de la Chaussée (q.v.), a genre which never became acclimatized in England, though it is akin to Sentimental Comedy. It had an immense vogue on the Continent, however, and La Chaussée's plays were translated and imitated in Italy, Holland, and particularly in Germany, where their influence can be seen in the early works of

Lessing (q.v.), notably in *Miss Sara Sampson* (1755). (See also OLD COMEDY.)

Comedy Theatre. (1) LONDON, in Panton Street, off the Haymarket. It opened successfully on 15 Oct. 1881, and three years later was taken over by Violet Melnotte (q.v.), who ran it until in 1887 Tree (q.v.) ventured into management for the first time with W. Outram Tristan's *The Red Lamp*, one of his most successful productions. He was succeeded by Hawtrey (q.v.) and Comyns Carr, under whom Cyril Maude and his wife Winifred Emery (qq.v.) appeared in several long-running plays. But the theatre was in low water when on 28 Oct. 1902 Lewis Waller (q.v.) produced there Booth Tarkington's *Monsieur Beaucaire*, which had an unexpected success. For many years the theatre was run by Arthur Chudleigh, under whom Gerald du Maurier (q.v.) appeared in *Raffles* (1906), based on a story by E. W. Hornung, and on 10 Oct. 1914 Alfred Butt presented the American actress Laurette Taylor (q.v.) in her husband's play, *Peg o' My Heart*. From 1915 to 1918, the theatre, which had been redecorated in 1911, housed revue. In 1933 and again in 1954 extensive alterations were made to the building, which was one of the last in London to keep its old-time green baize act-drop. In 1936 it once more had a great success with *Busman's Honeymoon*, by Dorothy Sayers and M. St. C. Byrne. It was slightly damaged during the Second World War, but continued in constant use, and in Oct. 1956 became the headquarters of the New Watergate Theatre Club, formed to present plays banned by the Lord Chamberlain. Club productions included Arthur Miller's *A View from the Bridge* (1956), Robert Anderson's *Tea and Sympathy* (1957), and Tennessee Williams's *Cat on a Hot Tin Roof* (1958). In 1959 Peter Shaffer's first play, *Five Finger Exercise*, was seen at the Comedy and among later productions there have been Marceau's *La Bonne Soupe* (1961), *An Evening of British Rubbish* (1963), and Spike Milligan in *Son of Oblomov* (1964), based on Goncharov's novel. In 1967 Peter Nichols's *Day in the Death of Joe Egg* was successful, but in 1969 an American musical, *Your Own Thing*, based on *Twelfth Night*, failed to appeal to English audiences.

(2) NEW YORK, on 41st Street between Broadway and 6th Avenue. Built by the Shuberts as a small, intimate playhouse, this theatre, which opened on 9 Sept. 1909 with Zangwill's *The Melting Pot*, saw the first production in New York of *Fanny's First Play* (1912) by Shaw (q.v.), and some early appearances of the Washington Square Players (q.v.) and of Ruth Draper (q.v.), who in 1928–9 created a record with five months' solo playing. In 1937–8, renamed the Mercury, the theatre housed a stimulating season by Orson Welles (q.v.) which included *Julius Caesar* in modern dress and a revival of Dekker's Elizabethan comedy, *The Shoemaker's Holiday*. In 1939 the Artef Players appeared in Gutzkow's *Uriel Acosta* and other Yiddish plays, and in 1942 the building was demolished.

COMELLA, LUCIANO FRANCISCO (1751–1812), see FERNÁNDEZ DE MORATÍN, LEANDRO.

Commedia dell'arte, the name usually given to the Italian popular improvised comedy which flourished from the sixteenth to the early eighteenth centuries. Other names for it are *a soggetto*, because it was acted in accordance with a scenario or pre-arranged synopsis; *all'improvviso*, because the actors made up their speeches as they went along; *dei zanni* (see ZANY), from the comic servants who provided most of the humour; *dei maschere*, because most of the actors wore masks; and *all'italiana*, because its home was Italy. *Dell'arte*, the only phrase to survive in general use, is hard to translate exactly, but means roughly 'of the profession', because the actors were trained professionals. The written drama of this period in Italy was known as the *commedia erudita* (q.v.), to distinguish it from the *commedia dell'arte*.

The history of the *commedia dell'arte* is obscure and has had to be pieced together from fragments. It has something in common with the Atellan farce (q.v.), or even with the earlier Greek comedies (see ARISTOPHANES and MENANDER), but there is as yet no proof of a direct link between them. It seems to have had its origin in the sixteenth-century rustic farces of southern Italy, played at Carnival time by amateur groups headed by such men as Ruzzante (see BEOLCO) or Calmo (q.v.). But their plays were written out and have survived. The professional groups which were soon to be found all over Europe worked from a synopsis, not a complete text, improvising dialogue and situations.

Some of them became famous (see ACCESI, CONFIDENTI, FEDELI, GELOSI) and acted at the Courts of Spain and France. Some even penetrated to England and to Russia. Each member of the company had his or her own character or 'mask' and played nothing else—the old man (Pantalone, from which we get Pantaloon (q.v.)), the learned pedant (Il Dottore), the swashbuckling soldier (Il Capitano (q.v.), derived perhaps from Plautus' *Miles gloriosus*), the serving maids, and the comic servants. It was from among these last that the best-known survivals of the *commedia dell'arte* came, though very different from their originals. The Harlequin and Columbine of the English Harlequinade (q.v.) derive from Arlecchino, via the French Arlequin, and Colombina; Punch, of the English Punch and Judy (q.v.), from Pulcinella (q.v.) via the French Polichinelle and the early English Punchinello; Pierrot (q.v.) from Pedrolino; and the French comic characters Mezzetin, Scapin, and Scaramouche (who never became acclimatized in England) from Mezzetino, Scapino, and Scaramuccia (qq.v.).

The *commedia dell'arte*, which flourished during the sixteenth and seventeenth centuries, was in decline by the eighteenth. Goldoni (q.v.) tried to revive it by substituting written texts for the skeleton plays used hitherto, Gozzi (q.v.) by incorporating the main ingredients of the actors' art in fairytale fantasies which allowed room for farcical improvisation. Neither was successful, nor were later nineteenth-century attempts at revival. Although we have many scenarii, we do not know how to use them. The tradition is lost. But in dying, the *commedia dell'arte* left a great legacy to the European theatre, not only in the characters mentioned above but in the English pantomime (q.v.) and above all in the French literary theatre, where a mingling of Italian improvisation and French premeditation combined to produce the plays of Marivaux (q.v.). The first *commedia dell'arte* company is mentioned in Paris in 1570, and later companies, including the Gelosi, are found at the Hôtel de Bourgogne and the Petit-Bourbon. They made a long stay under Louis XIII, and in 1658 Molière (q.v.) shared the Petit-Bourbon with them. On the founding of the Comédie-Française (q.v.) in 1680 they became known as the Comédie-Italienne (q.v.), to distinguish them from their rivals.

Commedia erudita, the learned counterpart in the early sixteenth-century Italian theatre of the popular *commedia dell'arte* (q.v.). The eminent Italian scholar, K. M. Lea, says of it, 'the proper preparation for the *commedia erudita* . . . is to acquire a taste for Plautus and Terence, a good working knowledge of the *Decamerone* and other *novelle*, a relish for realism in the close representation of men and manners, and a callous, quick enjoyment of human folly'. The masterpieces of the *commedia erudita* are the early plays of Aretino and Ariosto (qq.v.), *La Calandria* (1506) of Bibbiena (q.v.), and *La Mandragola* (1520) of Machiavelli (q.v.).

Commonwealth Company, U.S.A., see LUDLOW, NOAH and SMITH, SOL.

Commonwealth Theatre, NEW YORK, see ANTHONY STREET THEATRE.

Compagnie des Quinze, see COPEAU, JACQUES and SAINT-DENIS, MICHEL.

Compagnons de Jeux, de Notre-Dame, see GHÉON, HENRI.

COMPTON, EDWARD (1854–1918), English actor-manager, son of Henry Compton (q.v.) and founder of the COMPTON COMEDY COMPANY, which from 1881 to 1918 toured the English provinces in a repertory of plays by Shakespeare, Sheridan, Goldsmith, and other classic authors. An excellent actor, perhaps insufficiently appreciated, Edward appeared several times in London with his wife, VIRGINIA FRANCES BATEMAN (1853–1940), daughter of the American impresario H. L. Bateman (q.v.), whom he married in 1882. Of their five children four went on the stage, the best-known being Fay (q.v.). The fifth, Montague Compton Mackenzie, who reverted to the family name, is a distinguished novelist.

COMPTON, FAY [really VIRGINIA LILLIAN EMMELINE] (1894–1978), English actress, daughter of Edward Compton (q.v.). She has had a long and distinguished career in the theatre, making her début in the 'Follies' of her first husband, H. G. Pélissier (q.v.), and being the first to play the title-role in Barrie's *Mary Rose* (1920) and Phoebe Throssel in his *Quality Street* (1921). She also appeared with her third husband, Leon Quartermaine (q.v.), in Ashley Dukes's *The Man with a Load of Mischief* (1925). Among her later successes were Fanny

Grey in *Autumn Crocus* (1931) and Dorothy Hilton in *Call It a Day* (1935), both by Dodie Smith, and Martha Dacre in Esther McCracken's *No Medals* (1944). At the first Chichester Festival (q.v.) in 1962 she played Maman in Chekhov's *Uncle Vanya*. In the course of her career she played Ophelia to the Hamlets of John Barrymore (1925) and of John Gielgud (1939), and was seen in a number of Shakespearian parts at the Open-Air Theatre, Regent's Park. She also appeared in pantomime and variety. In 1926 she published a volume of reminiscences entitled *Rosemary*.

COMPTON, HENRY [really CHARLES MACKENZIE] (1805–77), actor and theatre manager, a collateral descendant of the Scottish actor-manager DAVID ROSS (1728–90). He took his grandmother's maiden name when he went on the stage, married an actress, EMMELINE MONTAGUE (?–1910), and had nine children, all connected with the theatre, his eldest daughter Katherine marrying the dramatist R. C. Carton (q v.). His very interesting memoirs were published in 1879 by his son Edward (q.v.).

Concert Theatre, NEW YORK, see JOHN GOLDEN THEATRE (I).

CONDELL, HENRY (?–1627), Elizabethan actor, first mentioned in 1598 as playing in Jonson's *Every Man in His Humour*. His only other known role was the Cardinal in Webster's *The Duchess of Malfi* (1614), but he is believed to have played Horatio in *Hamlet* (c. 1599). He was one of the sharers in the Blackfriars and Globe Theatres (qq.v.), and to him and his fellow-actor Heminge (q.v.) we owe the printing of Shakespeare's complete works, thirty-six plays in one volume, known as the First Folio. Published in 1623, this cost twenty shillings. Although there is no record of how many copies were first printed, a second edition was not needed until 1636.

Confidenti, a company of the *commedia dell'arte* (q.v.), first mentioned in 1574, which toured Italy, France, and Spain, and by 1580 was under the control of GIOVANNI PELLESINI (c. 1526–1612), who played Pedrolino (see PIERROT). Some of the Gelosi may have joined it after the death of Isabella Andreini (q.v.) in 1604, but its history remains obscure until it re-emerges in about 1610, under the patronage of Giovanni dei Medici, with FLAMINIO SCALA (*fl.* 1600–21), known as Flavio, as its leader. The collection of *scenarii* which he published in 1611 was probably compiled for this company, which toured mainly in Italy and was disbanded in 1621, some of the actors joining the Fedeli (q.v.) in Paris.

Confrérie de la Passion, an association of the burghers of Paris, formed in 1402 for the performance of religious plays. Their first permanent theatre was in the disused hall of the Guest-House of the Trinity outside the walls of Paris, in the direction of the Porte Saint-Denis. In 1518 they were given a monopoly of acting in Paris which later proved a serious hindrance to the establishment of a permanent professional theatre. When the Confraternity left their first home, they built themselves a theatre in the ruins of the palace of the Dukes of Burgundy, ornamenting its doors with the emblems of the Passion (see HÔTEL DE BOURGOGNE). No sooner was it ready for their occupation in 1548 than they were forbidden to act religious plays. From about 1570 onwards they leased the theatre to touring and foreign actors, but always tried to prevent any company from settling permanently. This soon became impossible, but they still insisted on the payment of a levy for every performance from the established company, and their monopoly lingered on until 1675, after the death of Molière and only a few years before the foundation in 1680 of the present Comédie-Française (q.v.).

CONGREVE, WILLIAM (1670–1729), the greatest English writer of Restoration comedy of manners. His first play, *The Old Bachelor*, was produced at Drury Lane in Mar. 1693 with a fine cast headed by Betterton and Mrs. Bracegirdle (qq.v.). It was followed by *The Double Dealer*, given in 1694 by the same company. The following year saw Betterton's secession from Drury Lane and his reopening of the old theatre in Lincoln's Inn Fields (q.v.) with Congreve's *Love for Love*, with himself as Valentine and Mrs. Bracegirdle as Angelica. This was followed by Congreve's only tragedy, *The Mourning Bride* (1697), in which the part of Almeria, first played by Mrs. Bracegirdle, was for long a favourite with tragedy queens. It has not been seen in London, except for a brief appearance at the Scala in 1925, since 1804. Some caprice on the part of the public caused Congreve's last and best play, *The Way of the World* (1700), to be coldly received. Pique, laziness, and ill-health then drove him from the theatre, but his comedies continued to hold the stage. Recent revivals include *The Way of the World* in 1924, when Edith Evans (q.v.) made one of her earliest successes as Millamant; in 1953, with Gielgud (q.v.) as Mirabell and Margaret Rutherford (q.v.) as a superb Lady Wishfort; in 1956 with John Clements (q.v.) and his wife Kay Hammond; and in 1969 by the National Theatre company with Geraldine McEwan (q.v.). *Love for Love* was also revived by Gielgud in 1943 and by the National Theatre in 1965; *The Double Dealer* was seen at the Old Vic in 1959 and at the Royal Court in 1969.

Connaught Theatre, LONDON. This opened as the Royal Amphitheatre, Holborn, in 1867, and became a playhouse in 1873 under John Hollingshead, who staged there burlesque runs from the Gaiety (q.v.), pantomimes and straight plays. It was at one time known as the Alcazar, and closed in 1886.

CONNELLY, MARC(US) COOK (1890–1980), SEE KAUFMAN, GEORGE.

CONQUEST, GEORGE AUGUSTUS (1837–1901), English dramatist, acrobat, and pantomimist, son of BENJAMIN [really OLIVER] (1805–72), who adopted the name of Conquest when he went on the stage and was for many years manager of the Grecian (q.v.), for which George, alone or in collaboration, wrote over one hundred melodramas, many of them adapted from the French. In collaboration with Henry Spry he also wrote and produced nearly fifty pantomimes, celebrated for their brilliant flying ballets and acrobatic effects—on one occasion no less than thirty traps were used. He took over the Grecian on his father's death and remained there until 1879, when he left for a tour of America. He returned shortly afterwards, permanently crippled by a serious accident on stage, and in 1881 took over the Surrey Theatre (q.v.), making it famous for its melodramas and pantomimes. It passed on his death to his eldest son GEORGE (1858–1926), an excellent comedian and pantomime Dame, who sold it in 1904. George's younger brothers, FRED (1871–1941) and ARTHUR (1875–1945), were both comedians and animal

impersonators, the former being well known for his pantomime Goose, the latter for his music-hall act, 'Daphne, the chimpanzee'.

CONTAT, LOUISE (1760–1813), French actress, who made her first appearance at the Comédie-Française in 1776. She excelled in high comedy, and was particularly admired in the plays of Marivaux (q.v.) when they were eventually admitted to the repertory. In 1784 she created the part of Suzanne in *Le Mariage de Figaro,* by Beaumarchais (q.v.), her younger sister, aged thirteen, appearing with her as Franchette.

CONTI, ITALIA (1874–1946), English actress who first appeared at the Lyceum in 1891, and then toured extensively in England and Australia. In 1911 she was engaged by Charles Hawtrey (q.v.) to train the children who were to appear in the fairy play *Where the Rainbow Ends,* by Clifford Mills and John Ramsey (music by Roger Quilter), and this led her to found the school for the theatrical training of children which still bears her name. She devoted the rest of her life to it, among her outstanding pupils being Gertrude Lawrence (q.v.). From 1929 to 1938 she appeared annually at the Holborn Empire in the Christmas production of *Where the Rainbow Ends* as Mrs. Carey. The Italia Conti School celebrated its jubilee in 1961.

CONWAY [really RUGG], WILLIAM AUGUSTUS (1789–1828), Irish actor, first seen on the stage in Dublin in 1812, and later in England. In 1824 he went to New York and appeared at the Park Theatre (q.v.) as Hamlet, Coriolanus, Romeo, and Othello, with great success. An actor in the style of Kemble, Conway seemed on the threshold of a brilliant career; but he was morbidly sensitive to criticism and, his morbidity increasing with age, he threw himself overboard while on the way to Charleston and was drowned. His son, FREDERICK BARTLETT (1819–74), with his wife SARAH CROCKER (1834–75), opened the first theatre in Brooklyn (see PARK THEATRE (3)) in 1863, and the Brooklyn Theatre (q.v.) in 1871. Their daughter, MINNIE [really MARIANNE] LEVY (1854–96), married the actor Osmond Tearle (q.v.).

COOK, EDWARD DUTTON (1829–83), English dramatic critic, who was on the

Pall Mall Gazette from 1867 to 1875 and the *World* from 1875 to 1883. His writings on the theatre include *A Book of the Play* (1876), *Hours with the Players* (2 vols., 1881), *Nights at the Play*, which contains many of Cook's notices of the early London appearances of Irving and Ellen Terry, and *On the Stage* (both 2 vols., 1883). He also contributed articles on actors and dramatists to the *Dictionary of National Biography*, and with Leopold Lewis was the author of a play entitled *The Dove and the Serpent*, which was produced at the City of London Theatre in 1859.

COOKE, GEORGE FREDERICK (1756–1812), an eccentric and unstable English actor who made his first appearance in Lincoln in 1773 and spent twenty years in the provinces. He had already contracted the habit of intemperance which was to be his ruin when, on 31 Oct. 1800, he appeared as Richard III at Covent Garden. He was immediately successful and remained there for ten years, constantly in trouble with the management, undisciplined, dissipated, usually in debt, and often in prison. He seemed to play better when drunk, and was probably somewhat insane with constant inebriation. In 1810 he went to New York, appearing at the Park Theatre (q.v.) before an enthusiastic audience who, however, fell away during his second season when he proved himself as undependable as in England. With Dunlap (q.v.) as his manager he toured America, but was already dying, and but for his good constitution would not have lasted so long. He was buried in New York, where Edmund Kean (q.v.) erected a monument to his memory. He was a powerful actor, unequalled at expressing the worst passions of mankind. Careless in studying his parts, he picked them up quickly and played them intuitively. He had great gifts, and an earlier success in London might have helped him to conquer his drunkenness and develop his genius to the full.

COOKE, THOMAS POTTER (known as TIPPY) (1786–1864), English actor who forsook the Navy in 1804 to appear at several minor theatres in London. In 1820 he made his first success as Ruthven in *The Vampire; or, the Bride of the Isles* by Planché (q.v.), following it with the Monster in *Presumption; or, the Fate of*

Frankenstein (1823), based on Mary Shelley's novel. But it was as William in Jerrold's nautical melodrama *Black-Eyed Susan* (1829) and Harry Halyard in Blanchard's *Poll and My Partner Joe* that he was best remembered. He retired in 1860.

COOKMAN, ANTHONY VICTOR (1894–1962), English dramatic critic who was on the staff of the *Manchester Guardian* under C. P. Scott and in 1925 went to the London *Times*, where he succeeded Charles Morgan (q.v.) in 1939. From 1945 until his death he was also dramatic critic of the *Tatler*.

COOPER, DAME GLADYS (1888–1971), distinguished English actress, who in 1967 was created D.B.E. in recognition of her services to the theatre. She made her first appearance in London in 1906 in *The Belle of Mayfair*, and was subsequently seen with great success both in musical comedy and in straight plays. In 1917, with Frank Curzon (up to 1927), she took over the management of the Playhouse (q.v.), remaining there until 1933, presenting, and often appearing in, a varied programme of old and new plays. She was particularly admired in revivals of Pinero's *The Second Mrs. Tanqueray* in 1922 and Sudermann's *Magda* in 1923 and in the first productions of Frederick Lonsdale's *The Last of Mrs. Cheyney* (1925) and Somerset Maugham's *The Sacred Flame* (1929). In 1934 she made the first of many appearances in New York, where in 1955 she made a great success as Mrs. St. Maugham in the American production of Enid Bagnold's *The Chalk Garden*, a part she also played briefly in London in 1956 and again shortly before her death. She was the author of two volumes of autobiography, *Gladys Cooper* (1931) and *Without Veils* (1953).

COOPER, THOMAS ABTHORPE (1776–1849), English-born American actor who, after appearing at Covent Garden with some success, went with Wignell (q.v.) in 1796 to Philadelphia, and spent the rest of his life in the United States, except for visits to Drury Lane in 1803 and 1827. He joined Dunlap's American Company (q.v.) and in 1806 became lessee of the Park Theatre (q.v.), where he appeared in most of the great tragic roles of Shakespeare, his best part being Macbeth. He was also outstanding as Jaffier in Otway's

Venice Preserv'd, but continued to act too long, and towards the end of his life his popularity declined. He is important in the early history of the American theatre, and was one of the first English actors to become an American citizen.

Co-Optimists, see PIERROT.

COOTE, BERT (1868–1938), see VICTORIA PALACE, LONDON.

COPEAU, JACQUES (1879–1949), French actor and director, whose work had an immense influence on the theatre in Europe and America. Although interested in the innovations of Antoine (q.v.), he disliked the realistic theatre and in 1913 founded the Théâtre du Vieux-Colombier in an effort to bring back, as he said, 'true beauty and poetry' to the French stage. His repertory was based mainly on Molière and Shakespeare, and he had one of his earliest successes in 1914 with *Twelfth Night*, translated by Théodore Lascaris as *Nuit des rois*. In 1921, in collaboration with Suzanne Bing, he produced *A Winter's Tale* as *Conte d'hiver*, and later published French versions of Shakespeare's major tragedies. At the Atelier in 1937 he staged, as *Rosalinde*, his own free adaptation of *As You Like It*. He also published an annotated edition of Molière and was the author of several books on the theatre. He trained his actors himself, and in his original company were Charles Dullin and Louis Jouvet (qq.v.), who later founded their own theatres. During the First World War Copeau spent two years at the Garrick Theatre (1917–19) in New York, and returned to France convinced that the training of young actors was an essential part of the reforms he envisaged in the theatre. So in 1924 he withdrew to his native Burgundy with a group of youngsters, later known as 'les Copiaus', with whom he worked on various facets of technical training, giving performances at irregular intervals in the surrounding villages. Several of his actors later joined the Compagnie des Quinze, directed by his nephew and collaborator Michel Saint-Denis (q.v.). By 1936 the importance of Copeau's work had been recognized and he became one of the directors of the Comédie-Française, retiring in 1941.

Copyright in a Dramatic Work. In England, by the beginning of the nineteenth century, the right of the dramatist (as of other writers) to prevent the making of copies of his work by unauthorized persons, for a limited period of time, had been established by various Acts of Parliament. There was as yet, however, no statutory protection for stage productions. It was the Dramatic Copyright Act of 1833, commonly known as Bulwer-Lytton's (q.v.) Act, which finally gave to the author of 'any tragedy, comedy, play, opera, farce, or other dramatic entertainment', again for only a limited period, the sole right to perform it, or authorize its performance. In 1842 the Literary Copyright Act consolidated the law relating to the protection of dramatic, as well as literary and musical property, and brought within the terms of a single statute the two rights so far recognized, 'copyright' or the right of 'multiplying' copies, and 'performing right' or the right of representation. However, performances of dramatizations of non-dramatic works were not covered by the Act, and the only way in which a novelist, for instance, could protect himself from unauthorized stage productions of his works was by dramatizing those works himself and so acquiring the right of representation in them as 'dramatic pieces'. Another institution brought into being by the ambiguous phrasing of the Act was the 'copyright performance'. It was generally believed, though with no clear legal support, that if a play was published before being performed, the 'performing right' was lost. This led to the practice, much indulged in by Shaw (q.v.), for instance, of hiring actors to give a public reading of a manuscript play in a hall, or other 'place of public entertainment', usually without costumes or scenery. These 'copyright performances' have often led to considerable confusion in the dating of first performances of well-known plays. Meanwhile the Berne Convention of 1886, which had established the International Copyright Union, having been amended in 1896 and in 1908, it was essential that Great Britain should keep abreast of international developments, particularly those covered by the 1908 revisions. A committee was therefore appointed, many of whose recommendations were incorporated in the Copyright Act of 1911, which for the first time merged the right of multiplying copies and the right of representation in the general term 'copyright'. And for the first time no formalities were necessary to obtain copyright. This Act remained in force until the Copyright Act of 1956, which was made necessary by the introduction of films, records, radio, and television, and by the provisions of the 1948 Brussels Convention and the Universal Copyright Convention signed at Geneva in 1952. The 1956 Act covered the reproduction of any original dramatic work in any form in public. The words 'original' and 'in public' were not precisely defined in the Act and their definition has therefore been a matter for the courts on various occasions. The normal period of copyright is now fifty years from the death of the author, or, in the case of joint authorship, of the last surviving author. American copyright derived initially from a British Act of 1710. The first comprehensive American Act was passed in 1790. During the nineteenth century various amendments were made to the Act, but by the early years of the twentieth century the mass of piecemeal copyright legislation and case law had reached very much the same confused state as that obtaining in Great Britain at the end of the nineteenth, and a report on the position, made by the first Recorder of Copyrights in 1903, prepared the way for the passing of the Copyright Act of 1909, which, with certain amendments, remains in force today. The original clause requiring that all material seeking copyright protection in the United States should have been manufactured there has now been removed in the case of new works by British authors. All that is necessary for British authors is to comply with the provisions of the Universal Copyright Convention to which both the United Kingdom and United States had become parties by 1957. Plays, published or unpublished, by British authors should, however, still be registered at the Library of Congress, Washington, D.C., as proceedings for infringement of the copyright in a play cannot be instituted in the United States if the play has not been so registered. All the European countries, their colonies and mandated territories, as well as the United Kingdom and the British Commonwealth, are members of the International Copyright Union, whose basic principles, as set out at the 1886 Berne Convention, were revised at Stockholm in 1967. The International Copyright Union protection is more comprehensive than the Universal Copyright Convention protection. The United States is not a member of the International Copyright Convention. Absentees from both organizations are the U.S.S.R. and China.

COQUELIN, CONSTANT-BENOÎT (1841–1909), French actor, known as Coquelin *aîné* to distinguish him from his younger brother, ERNEST-ALEXANDRE-HONORÉ (1848–1909), also an actor, known as Coquelin *cadet*. They were both at the Comédie-Française, but Coquelin *aîné*, after a long absence on tour in Europe and America, finally left in 1892. Six years later he appeared at the Porte-Saint-Martin in the part always associated with him, Cyrano de Bergerac in the play of that name by Rostand (q.v.), in which his son JEAN (1865–1944) played Ragueneau, the pastry cook. Coquelin was rehearsing the leading part in another play by Rostand, *Chantecler*, when he died suddenly. A big man, with a fine voice and presence, he was outstanding in the great comic roles of Molière and in romantic and flamboyant modern parts. He was the author of two books, *L'Art et le comédien* (1880) and *Les Comédiens par un comédien* (1882).

CORCORAN, KATHARINE (1857–1943), see HERNE, JAMES A.

CORNEILLE, PIERRE (1606–84), France's first great tragic dramatist, born in Rouen. His first plays were comedies, produced in Paris between 1629 and 1633, and it was not until 1635 that he wrote his first tragedy, *Médée*. This was well but not enthusiastically received, and after a quarrel with Richelieu (q.v.) Corneille returned to Rouen. Here, in renewing his acquaintance with Spanish literature, he came across *Las mocedades del Cid*, a tale of Spain's national hero by Guillén de Castro y Bellvís (q.v.), on which he based his tragi-comedy *Le Cid*, now regarded as the first important landmark in French dramatic literature. It was produced early in 1637 at the Théâtre du Marais (q.v.) with Montdory (q.v.) in the name-part. It was an immediate success, and an English translation by Joseph Rutter was acted in London later the same year.

The success of *Le Cid* was followed by that of *Horace* (1640), *Cinna* (1641), *Polyeucte* (1642), and *La Mort de Pompée* (1643), also at the Marais but, owing to Montdory's retirement in 1637, with Floridor (q.v.) in the name-parts. Floridor also played the leading part, Dorante, in Corneille's finest comedy, *Le Menteur*, based on *La verdad sospechosa* by Alarcón (q.v.). It had a great success, which unfortunately was not repeated in 1638 with its sequel, *La Suite du menteur*.

With *Rodogune*, *Théodore* (both 1645), and *Héraclius* (1646), Corneille was established as France's major dramatist, and in 1647 was elected a member of the French Academy. A disappointing play, *Don Sanche d'Aragon* (1649), and a spectacle-play, *Andromède* (1650), written to show off Torelli's machinery at the Petit-Bourbon, were followed by one of Corneille's best and most popular plays, *Nicomède* (1651) (see MOLIÈRE), and by a disastrous failure, *Pertharite* (1652), after which Corneille abandoned the theatre until 1659, when Floridor appeared at the Hôtel de Bourgogne (q.v.) in *Oedipe*. This enjoyed a moderate success and was followed by another spectacle-play, *La Toison d'or* (1660), written for the marriage of Louis XIV. But Corneille's powers were failing; *Sertorius* (1661), *Sophonisbe* (1663), *Othon* (1664), and *Agésilas* (1666) had little success, while *Attila* (1667) and *Tite et Bérénice* (1670), both produced by Molière, who had a great admiration for Corneille, were overshadowed by the rising popularity of Racine (q.v.). After collaborating with Molière in a charming *tragédie-ballet*, *Psyché* (1671), Corneille wrote only two more plays, *Pulchérie* (1672) and *Suréna* (1674).

Corneille's reputation, which during his lifetime earned him the title of 'le grand', was a little eclipsed in the eighteenth century, but the nineteenth restored him to his true place. His work is unequal, perhaps because the form of French tragedy which he adopted and did so much to further was not really suited to his genius. But he rightly ranks first among French tragic dramatists, and the best of his plays still hold the stage.

CORNEILLE, THOMAS (1625–1709), French dramatist, known as M. Corneille de l'Isle, to distinguish him from his more famous brother Pierre Corneille (q.v.). Thomas was the author of more than forty plays, all successful in their day and all forgotten, of which the best are usually thought to be *Ariane* (1672) and *Le Comte d'Essex* (1678), the latter a rewriting of a play by La Calprenède (q.v.) on the same subject.

CORNELL, KATHARINE (1898–1974), an outstanding American actress, who made a great success in London in 1919 as Jo in a dramatization of Louisa M. Alcott's *Little Women*, and first came into prominence in New York when she appeared in Clemence Dane's *A Bill of Divorcement* (1921) and *Will Shakespeare* (1923). In 1931 she appeared under her own management as Elizabeth Moulton-Barrett in Besier's *The Barretts of Wimpole Street*, a part which she played many times and with which her name is always associated. It was directed by her husband, Guthrie McClintic (q.v.), who was responsible for many other productions in which she appeared, notably Sidney Howard's *Alien Corn* (1933), *Romeo and Juliet* (1934), Shaw's *Candida* (1937) and *The Doctor's Dilemma* (1941), *Antony and Cleopatra* (1947), Christopher Fry's *The Dark is Light Enough* (1955), and Jerome Kilty's *Dear Liar* (1960), in which she played Mrs. Patrick Campbell (q.v.). She was the author of two books of reminiscences, *I Wanted to be an Actress* (1939) and *Curtain Going Up* (1943).

Cornish Rounds. There are in Cornwall, particularly in the west of the county, remains of circular earthworks which are believed to have been open-air theatres used for annual performances of medieval Mystery Plays. These could accommodate a large number of spectators grouped round a central area or 'playing-place' (*plen an gwary*). Some of them were still in use in the seventeenth century. The surviving plans for two plays given in such a theatre show that Heaven was at the eastern end, with Hell on the north. There must also have been stages of varying levels on the central area. In 1968 students from Bristol University Drama Department presented the cycle of Cornish Mystery Plays, using the original method of staging, on the Piran Round at Perranporth.

Coronet Theatre, NEW YORK, see EUGENE O'NEILL THEATRE.

Corsican Trap, see TRAP.

Cort Theatre, NEW YORK, on West 48th Street between 6th and 7th Avenues. This opened on 20 Dec. 1912 with Laurette Taylor (q.v.) in her husband's immensely successful comedy, *Peg o' My Heart*. In 1916 Charles Coburn (q.v.) and his wife appeared in a revival of Hazelton and Benrimo's *The Yellow Jacket*, and in 1919 came the successful production of

Drinkwater's *Abraham Lincoln*; 1930 saw a magnificent revival of Chekhov's *Uncle Vanya*. *The Green Bay Tree*, by Mordaunt Shairp, with Laurence Olivier (q.v.) and his first wife Jill Esmond in an elegant setting by Robert Edmond Jones (q.v.), had a good run in 1933. Also successful were the fine war play, *A Bell for Adano* (1944), based on a novel by John Hersey; a translation of Anouilh's Resistance play, *Antigone* (1946), with Katharine Cornell (q.v.); Joseph Kramm's *The Shrike* (1952); *The Diary of Anne Frank* (1955), dramatized from the original diary; Dore Schary's *Sunrise at Campobello* (1958), with Ralph Bellamy as Franklin D. Roosevelt; and *Purlie Victorious* (1961), by Ossie Davis, which had a long run before transferring to the Broadway Theatre and then to Anta.

Cosmopolitan Theatre, NEW YORK, see MAJESTIC THEATRE (1).

COSSA, PIETRO (1830–81), Italian playwright, who created a new form of tragedy in verse by applying the formulae of bourgeois realism to plots taken from Roman and Italian history. His best play, *Nerone* (1871), was translated into English by Frances E. Trollope shortly after its publication. Other important plays are the anti-clerical *Cola di Rienzo* (1874), *Messalina* (1875), which like *Nerone* is remarkable for the vitality of its central character, and *Giuliano l'apostata* (1877).

COSTANTINI, ANGELO (*c.* 1655–1729), Italian actor of the *commedia dell'arte* (q.v.), who first appeared with the troupe of the Duke of Modena. In 1683 he joined the Italian Company in Paris, ostensibly to share the role of Arlequin with Biancolelli (q.v.), but played it so seldom that he finally adopted and enlarged that of Mezzetino (q.v.). In the company with him was the famous Scaramouche, Tiberio Fiorillo (q.v.), whose life he wrote, rather inaccurately. It was published in 1695 (reprinted 1876). When the Italians were banished from Paris in 1697 (see COMÉDIE-ITALIENNE), Costantini went to Brunswick, where he had the misfortune to be the successful rival in love of the Elector of Saxony, which cost him twenty years in prison. His brother, GIOVAN BATTISTA (?–1720), was also an actor, who as Cintio played young lovers in the Paris troupe in succession to Marc'Antonio Romagnesi.

COSTELLO, TOM (1863–1945), a music-hall performer who went to London from Birmingham in 1886. He made his name on the halls with a song entitled 'Comrades', but is probably better remembered as the hen-pecked husband singing 'At Trinity Church I met me Doom'. He was also a fine singer of stirring patriotic ballads, often in naval officer's uniform. He retired from the halls at the time of the First World War, but returned with the Veterans of Variety in the 1920s.

Costume, THEATRICAL. From earliest times costuming has been an essential part of the theatre. In Greek tragedy the actors wore masks (q.v.) and long robes with sleeves, quite unlike the dress of the day. In the Old Comedy of Aristophanes (q.v.) the chorus wore symbolic details like horses' heads and tails, or feathered wings, while the chief characters wore loose tunics, grotesquely padded, and a large red leather phallus. This was later abandoned, and in the New Comedy of Menander (q.v.) actors wore the ordinary clothes of the time. When the Romans took over Greek tragedy and comedy they adopted the existing costumes, with the addition of the *toga* and *stola* and also, for tragedy, the high boot (*cothurnus*) and the exaggeratedly high peak (*onkos*) over the forehead. By the time of the Caesars, stage costumes, except for the popular pantomimes, which were played almost in the nude, and the patchwork rags of the Atellan farce (q.v.), had become very elaborate and colourful. This trend continued as the Empire moved towards its dissolution, and in the sixth century actresses incurred the disapproval of the Church for wearing sumptuous dresses of cloth of gold enriched with pearls.

When the theatre, which had disappeared with the collapse of the civilized world, was reborn in the liturgical drama (q.v.), the priests and choirboys who acted the first short Easter and Nativity plays wore their usual robes, with some simple additions, such as veils for the women characters, crowns for the Three Kings, or a rough cloak for a shepherd. But once the plays were moved from the church to the market-place and acted by laymen, costuming again became important, and sometimes the Mystery Play (q.v.) of the later Middle Ages was most expensively dressed, with golden robes for God and His angels, and fantastic leather garments for the Devil and his attendant imps. Although no attempt at historical accuracy was made, a slight oriental touch seems to have crept into the costumes of the Magi, according to some costume designs which have survived. In the Morality Play (q.v.) the allegorical figures which represented the virtues and vices wore richly fantasticated versions of contemporary dress, except for the Devil, who kept the costume he had worn in the Miracle play. His attendant, 'the Old Vice', a new character, was usually dressed as a fool or jester, with a long-eared cap decorated with bells, a cockscomb, and a parti-coloured close-fitting tunic and leggings, reminiscent of the costumes of the Roman farce-players. Much the same type of costume was worn by the masked actors of the *commedia dell'arte* (q.v.), though, except for the lovers, who wore contemporary dress, each character was recognizably from a different part of Italy: Pulcinella from Naples, Arlecchino from Bergamo, Pantalone from Venice, while the Capitano was a Spaniard, Spain at this time still holding considerable tracts of territory in Italy. The gaudy rags of Arlecchino soon became stylized into the diamonds of brightly contrasted silk worn by Harlequin (q.v.) today, the white belted and bloused suit of Pulcinella was stereotyped by Watteau into the familiar garb of Pierrot (q.v.), but otherwise the characters retained their individuality, cropping up in unexpected places but having little influence on the evolution of theatrical costume in general. The main line of development was through the academic theatre of Renaissance Italy and the Court play. The Italian *intermezzi*, triumphs and pageants, the French *ballets de cour*, the English masques, gave immense scope for fantastic mythological costumes, often, for the men, based on the 'Roman' pattern, with a plumed headdress, a breastplate moulded to the body, and some variation of the Roman kilt, a fashion which also invaded the public stage and continued to be used for the tragic hero for over two hundred years. The women's costumes, as always, followed contemporary fashions, with no attempt at historical accuracy. In the Court entertainment and in the public theatre, however, traces of medieval costuming can be found in the grotesque elements—the Wild Men in the masque, the Old Vice, referred to by Shakespeare—together with some borrowings from the *commedia*

dell'arte. Many of the designs for costumes worn during the extravagant entertainments devised on the Continent, particularly in France to enhance the prestige of Louis XIV, still survive. Some of the earliest were by the great Italian stage designer Torelli (q.v.), but French designers soon took over, the most influential being Jean Bérain (q.v.), whose work, not only for the theatre but over the whole field of decorative art, synthesizes all the tendencies of the time, as did that of his contemporary Burnacini (q.v.) in Vienna. But after the death of Louis XIV the elegant balance of *le style Bérain* declined into the fantasies of rococo, best studied in the work of the artists Gillot and Watteau, in the costume designs of Boucher (q.v.), and in the shepherds and shepherdesses of J. B. Martin. It achieved its finest development on stage in the designs of LOUIS-RENÉ BOQUET, who from 1760 to 1782 worked both for the Paris Opéra and for the Court. Like Bérain, he was content to work mainly in a contemporary style, suggesting character or period by some small decorative detail. His designs have great charm, and his costumes, both male and female, are characterized by his use of wide paniers, forming a kind of ballet skirt covered with rococo detail. This panier-skirt reached as far as England, where Quin (q.v.) wore it for Thomson's Coriolanus. Among the reforms of Garrick (q.v.) was the abolition of such garments in favour of contemporary styles, Macbeth, for instance, being acted in the scarlet of the King's livery; and in 1758, when playing the part of an ancient Greek, Garrick insisted on wearing the costume of a Venetian gondolier on the grounds that the majority of Venetian gondoliers were of Greek origin! His leading actresses in tragedy also wore contemporary costume, including the high head-dresses of the 1770s with a crown or flowing veil, or, for Eastern potentates, a turban with a waving plume. Twenty years earlier Voltaire (q.v.), helped by the actor Lekain (q.v.), had begun a campaign for correct costuming, at least in classical plays. In his *Orphelin de la Chine* (1755), Lekain as the hero wore an embroidered robe in place of the usual panier-skirt, and the heroine, played by Mlle Clairon (q.v.), a simple sleeveless dress which, though not noticeably Chinese, was less incongruous than the exaggerated skirt of the time, held out by hip-pads; and when playing Roxane in a revival of Racine's *Bajazet*, she appeared in fairly close approximation to Turkish costume. A great advance towards accuracy was made by the actor Talma (q.v.) when in 1789 he appeared as Brutus, in Voltaire's play of that name, with bare legs and arms. The reaction of the public was unfavourable, but by the end of the century the Revolutionary passion for anything remotely connected with antiquity had made classical costumes acceptable on the stage. During the early nineteenth century the popularity of Scott's novels, many of which were dramatized, led to a growth of interest in 'historical' costumes, which meant in practice the addition of Elizabethan, Stuart, and other details to contemporary dress. The resulting mixture is not without charm, but bears very little relation to historical accuracy. The first step towards 'antiquarian' detail in dress was made by Planché (q.v.) with his costume designs for Charles Kemble's production of *King John* at Covent Garden in 1823. His example was followed by Charles Kean (q.v.), who strove for accuracy in his productions of Shakespeare at the Princess's in the 1850s, though as Hermione in *The Winter's Tale* Mrs. Kean wore a perfectly correct Grecian costume, but over a crinoline. And Mrs. Bancroft (q.v.), playing Peg Woffington in what she fondly imagined was eighteenth-century dress, now looks, in the photographs that survive, purely contemporary. However, towards the end of the nineteenth century the triumph of realism in the theatre meant on the one hand an almost pedantic accuracy in dress which was sometimes very untheatrical, and on the other an increase in the number of modern plays in which the characters wore the dress of the day. Consequently the designer, excluded from the 'legitimate' stage, let his fancy run riot in lighter musical productions, and in opera. In ballet the tyranny of the *tutu*, first worn by Taglioni in 'La Sylphide' in 1832, defeated the efforts even of such a fine designer as Paul Lormier at the Paris Opéra to dress the ballerina in historical costume. It was Diaghilev (q.v.) who effected this change, mainly through the exotic designs of LÉON BAKST (1866–1924), who brought to western Europe a riot of oriental colour which first dazzled and then delighted audiences in London and Paris. Every department of theatrical design was influenced by his stylized treatment of unhistorical costume. Diaghilev's employment of Bakst, and later of such great names in art as Braque, Picasso, Marie Laurencin, and de Chirico, was symptomatic of the way in which the theatre was once again making use for its own purposes of outstanding artists in their own right, a practice which had lapsed somewhat during the nineteenth century with designers like Comelli and Wilhelm, who devoted all their time to the theatre. All over Europe in the first half of the twentieth century artists were once again called on to design costumes for the stage which, though more or less accurate, nevertheless contained some elements of fantastication or formalization, particularly for the plays of Shakespeare. This was true also of the United States, where stage design, once liberated from an outdated European tradition, had gone ahead with such artists as Norman Bel Geddes and Robert Edmond Jones (qq.v.). In New York too, as in Europe, the musicals and revues provided the designer with opportunities which could not be found elsewhere, as did the non-realistic drama which flowered briefly after the Second World War with such plays as Fry's *The Lady's Not For Burning* (1948). Now, when realistic drama is again in the ascendant, the many talented designers of Europe and the U.S.A. find their chief outlet, apart from ballet and opera, in revivals of classical plays, particularly Shakespeare, and in such historical 'pageants' as Peter Shaffer's *The Royal Hunt of the Sun* (1964).

Cothurnus (*Kothornos*), the Greek word for a woman's boot. In the *Frogs* of Aristophanes (q.v.) the effeminate Dionysus wears *cothurni*, which were loose-fitting and came high up the calf. The word is sometimes taken to refer specifically to the actors' footwear in tragedy (see BUSKIN), and so is used to describe an elevated, high-flown, artificial style of tragic acting, but there is no evidence in antiquity for this. Nor is there any evidence that the tragic actor's boot had thick soles; these were a device of the late Hellenistic and Roman period, when tragic acting had become very stiff and artificial.

Council for the Encouragement of Music and the Arts, see ARTS COUNCIL.

COUNSELL, JOHN (1905–87), English actor and theatre manager, who in 1938 took over the Theatre Royal, Windsor, where he had appeared in 1933 and ran it for several decades. He intended to make it a weekly repertory theatre, but being so near London, and in an area which supplies a good local audience with a wide range of preferences, he found he could safely vary his programme and also engage particular actors for one production only. The theatre therefore has no resident company. Each play is separately cast and runs for two weeks. Counsell, who was a member of the O.U.D.S. while at Oxford and later director of the repertory company there, made his first appearance on the stage in A. A. Milne's *Mr. Pim Passes By* in 1928, and had had wide experience in acting and directing before going to Windsor. With his wife, MARY KERRIDGE (1914–), an accomplished actress who often appeared under his direction, he built up a strong and independent organization, and was responsible for a number of interesting productions, some of which transferred to the West End.

Counterweight House, the name given to a theatre where the scenery is worked by a modern system of endless lines and counterweights, as opposed to the traditional system of lines from a fly-floor used in a Rope (or Hand-worked) House (q.v.). Since in this system no great lengths of spare rope have to be accommodated, the counterweight house need not have a fly-floor.

Court Theatre, LONDON, see ROYAL COURT THEATRE.

COURTELINE [really MOINEAUX], GEORGES-VICTOR-MARCEL (1858–1929), French dramatist, author of a number of amusing farces, some of which were produced by Antoine (q.v.) before finding their way eventually into the repertory of the Comédie-Française. They deal with the humours of military life, as in *Lidoire* (1891) and *Les Gaîtés de l'escadron* (1895), and of the law, as in *L'Article 330* (1901); or, as in what is perhaps his best play, *Boubouroche* (1893), with episodes in the life of ordinary people, salted with much wit and a certain gross brutality which recalls the farces of the early French theatre.

COURTNEIDGE, DAME (ESMERALDA) CICELY (1893–1980), English actress, who made her first appearance on the stage in Manchester at the age of eight, playing Peasblossom in *A Midsummer Night's Dream*. She was first seen in London in 1907 when she embarked on an outstanding career in musical comedy, variety, and revue, usually in partnership with her husband, JACK HULBERT (1892–1978). In later years she was also seen in farces by Ronald Millar (q.v.) and in 1971 appeared in *Move Over, Mrs. Markham,* by Ray Cooney and John Chapman. She was appointed D.B.E. in 1972 for services to the theatre.

Covent Garden Theatre, LONDON. There has been a theatre on the site of the present Royal Opera House, Covent Garden, since 1732, when John Rich (q.v.) built a Theatre Royal there, on land which had formerly been part of a convent garden (hence the name), and opened it on 7 Dec. 1732 with a revival of Congreve's *The Way of the World.* The early years were uneventful, but on 20 Nov. 1740 Peg Woffington (q.v.) electrified the town with her famous 'breeches part', Sir Harry Wildair in Farquhar's *The Constant Couple.* It was here also that she made her last appearance, in 1757. Among other famous actors seen under Rich, who performed only in his own pantomimes, were George Anne Bellamy, Spranger Barry, and, for a short time, Garrick (qq.v.). Rich was succeeded on his death by his son-in-law, John Beard, who in 1767 disposed of the Patent to George Colman the elder (q.v.) and three partners, one of whom, Harris, became sole manager in 1774. In the previous year Goldsmith's *She Stoops to Conquer* had been produced (15 Mar.), and Macklin (q.v.) had appeared as Macbeth (23 Oct.) dressed in roughly realistic Scottish garb, though not actually in a kilt. He was to be seen again, when a very old man, in his own play, *The Man of the World,* in 1781, and he made his last appearance at this theatre, as Shylock, in 1789. In 1792 the theatre, which had been much altered in 1784, was virtually rebuilt. Frederick Cooke (q.v.) made his London début there in 1800 as Richard III, and in 1803 John Philip Kemble (q.v.) appeared under his own management with his sister, Sarah Siddons (q.v.). One of his first importations was the child prodigy, Master Betty (q.v.).

On 20 Aug. 1808 the theatre was burnt down, twenty-three firemen losing their lives. In this fire perished Handel's organ and the manuscript scores of some of his operas. A new theatre, designed by Robert Smirke and modelled on the Temple of Minerva on the Acropolis, arose on the site, and opened on 18 Sept. 1809 with *Macbeth*. An increase in the price of seats caused the famous O.P. (Old Prices) Riots. After continual disturbances every night for about two months, Kemble was forced to apologize and return to the old prices.

Between 1809 and 1821 many famous actors and singers appeared at Covent Garden, as did pantomimists like Byrne, Farley, Bologna, Ellar, and Grimaldi (q.v.). On 29 June 1812 Mrs. Siddons made her farewell appearance, and on 16 Sept. 1816 Macready (q.v.) his first. Kemble retired on 23 June 1817 (in which year the theatre was first lit by gas), and his brother Charles took over. It was under Charles's management in 1823 that a production of *King John* took place, with 'historically accurate' costumes and scenery designed by Planché (q.v.). This was probably the most important innovation in costuming since Macklin's *Macbeth*. The theatre prospered when Charles Kemble's daughter Fanny (q.v.) played leading parts there, with immense success.

Macready, who first introduced limelight at Covent Garden, many years before it was in regular use, was in management from 1837 to 1839, and was succeeded by Mme Vestris (q.v.), with her husband Charles Mathews. Her greatest success was Boucicault's *London Assurance* in 1841. After she left in 1842 the theatre fell on hard times and was finally closed, to reopen on 6 Apr. 1847 as the Royal Italian Opera House. From this time onwards the story of Covent Garden is the story of opera in London, and it ceased to be a home of 'legitimate' drama. On 5 Mar. 1856, after a Bal Masqué, it was again burnt down, and the present theatre, designed by Sir Edward M. Barry, opened on 15 May 1858. The only further theatrical entertainments were a handful of pantomimes, some revues, and in 1912 Reinhardt's production of Sophocles' *Oedipus Rex*, starring Martin-Harvey (q.v.).

(For a theatre in New York nicknamed Covent Garden, see NATIONAL THEATRE, NEW YORK (1).)

Coventry Cycle, see MYSTERY PLAY.

Coventry Hocktide Play, see HOCKTIDE PLAY.

COWARD, SIR NOËL PIERCE (1899–1973), English actor, director, and composer, and a prolific dramatist, who was on the stage from childhood, making his first appearance on 27 Jan. 1911 in *The Goldfish*, a fairy play. His early plays, which include *The Young Idea* (1923), *The Vortex* (1924), and *Fallen Angels* (1925), aroused a great deal of controversy, as did *Hay Fever* (also 1925). Coward then wrote several revues for Cochran, including *On With the Dance* (also 1925) and *This Year of Grace* (1928). The inevitable reaction to his success came with a riot on the first night of *Sirocco* (1927), but he was again successful in 1929 with the sentimental romance *Bitter Sweet*, in 1930 with *Private Lives*, and in 1931 with the patriotic *Cavalcade*. These were followed by *Design for Living* (1932), the nine one-act plays of *To-Night at 8.30* (1935), *Blithe Spirit* (1941), which was made into a musical as *High Spirits* (1964), *Present Laughter* (1942), *Peace in Our Time* (1947), *Nude With Violin* (1956), *Waiting in the Wings* (1960), and *Sail Away* (1962). He also adapted the farce, *Occupe-toi d'Amélie*, by Feydeau (q.v.), as *Look After Lulu* (1959). In 1966 a triple bill, 'Suite in Three Keys', consisting of *A Song at Twilight*, *Shadows of the Evening*, and *Come Into the Garden, Maud*, was seen in London. Coward, who had also a successful career in films, appeared in the first productions of many of his own plays, some of which have recently been revived, among them *Hay Fever*, *Blithe Spirit*, *Private Lives*, and *Fallen Angels*. He was the author of two volumes of autobiography, *Present Indicative* (1937) and *Future Indefinite* (1954). In Dec. 1969 a midnight matinée in honour of his seventieth birthday was given in London under the title of *A Talent to Amuse*, and on 1 Jan. 1970 he was knighted for services to the theatre.

COWELL [really WHITSHED], JOE [really JOSEPH] LEATHLEY (1792–1863), a comic actor well known in England and America, particularly for his playing of Crack in Knight's 'musical entertainment', *The Turnpike Gate* (first produced in 1799), which he revived many times, making his last appearance in it in New York in 1850. He was related by marriage to the Siddonses and Batemans (qq.v.), and in 1844 published his autobiography.

COWELL, SAM(UEL) HOUGHTON (1820–64), second son of the comedian Joe

Cowell (q.v.), and one of the earliest stars of the English music-halls. As a child he toured the U.S.A. billed as the Young American Roscius, and later in London became known as a singer of comic songs, appearing at the Canterbury and Grecian (qq.v.), where his most popular songs were 'Villikins and his Dinah' (first sung by Frederick Robson, q.v.) and 'The Rat-catcher's Daughter'. Of his nine children, SYDNEY (1846–1925) and FLORENCE [Mrs. A. B. Tapping] (1852–1926) were well-known actresses, as was Florence's daughter, known as SYDNEY FAIRBROTHER (1872–1941), who in her later years was outstanding in comic character parts and in the music-hall sketch *A Sister to Assist 'Er*.

COWL, JANE (1884–1950), American actress and playwright, who made her first appearance on the stage under Belasco (q.v.) in his *Sweet Kitty Bellairs* (1903). She subsequently played a number of parts in his productions, including Trinidad in *The Rose of the Rancho* (1906) and Mrs. Pettinger in *A Grand Army Man* (1907), and soon established a reputation as one of the leading actresses of the day. Her finest part was probably Juliet, which she played in 1923 to the Romeo of Rollo Peters, but she was also seen in other Shakespearian plays, including *Antony and Cleopatra* in 1924 and *Twelfth Night*, playing Viola, in 1930, and was much admired in revivals of the younger Dumas's *Camille* in 1931 and Shaw's *Captain Brassbound's Conversion* in 1940 and *Candida* in 1942. Among the new plays in which she appeared were Coward's *Easy Virtue* (1925), in which she made her first appearance in London a year later, Robert Sherwood's *The Road to Rome* (1927), Edward Sheldon's *Jenny* (1929), Thornton Wilder's *The Merchant of Yonkers* (1938), and Van Druten's *Old Acquaintance* (1940). She appeared also in her own plays, *Lilac Time* (1917), written in collaboration with Jane Murfin, *Information, Please* (1918), and *Smilin' Through* (1919). *Hervey House*, written in collaboration with Reginald Lawrence, was seen in London in 1935, directed by Tyrone Guthrie.

COWLEY, ABRAHAM (1618–67), English poet, whose comedy of manners, *The Guardian*, which satirized Puritans and Royalists alike, was played before Prince Charles (later Charles II) at Cambridge in 1642. As *Cutter of Coleman Street*, this was staged in Dec. 1661 at the Duke's House (see LINCOLN'S INN FIELDS THEATRE), where Pepys (q.v.) saw and enjoyed it.

COWLEY [*née* PARKHOUSE], **HANNAH** (1743–1809), one of the first English women playwrights, whose work marks the transition from Restoration to eighteenth-century comedy of manners. The most successful of her plays, which include *The Runaway* (1776), to which Garrick is said to have made some improvements, and *A Bold Stroke for a Husband* (1783), was *The Belle's Stratagem*, based on *La Fausse Agnès* by Destouches (q.v.). First produced at Covent Garden in 1780 with Mrs. Jordan (q.v.) as Letitia, it was many times revived, notably by Irving (q.v.) in 1881, with himself as Doricourt (a part he played several times) and Ellen Terry (q.v.) as Letitia. The play was last seen in London in 1913, and was one of the first plays to be given in the New World, being in the repertory of the Hallams and Hodgkinson (qq.v.) in New York in 1794. It was frequently revived there also, Ada Rehan (q.v.) playing Letitia in 1893 to the Doricourt of Bourchier (q.v.).

COWLEY, RICHARD (?–1619), an Elizabethan actor who was the first man to play Verges in *Much Ado About Nothing* (*c.* 1598), probably to the Dogberry of Kempe (q.v.). He was one of Lord Strange's Men in 1593, and joined the Chamberlain's Men (q.v.) on their formation in the following year.

COX, ROBERT (?–1655), an English actor who was on the stage before 1639. After the closing of the playhouses in 1642 he evaded the ban on acting by appearing in short farcical pieces (see DROLL), interspersed with rope-dancing and conjuring, at country fairs and in London. He was arrested while acting at the Red Bull playhouse in 1653, and imprisoned. The chief items in his repertory were published in 1662 by Francis Kirkman as *The Wits; or, Sport upon Sport*. The frontispiece of the second edition (1672) has the earliest known illustration of footlights on the English stage.

CRABTREE, CHARLOTTE (1847–1924), an American actress, known as Lotta. An attractive red-headed child, she toured the mining-camps of California from the ages of eight to eighteen, and then went to New York, where she made her first success in 1867 in Brougham's dramatization of Dickens's *The Old Curiosity Shop*, in which she played Little Nell and the Marchioness. She was outstanding in burlesque and extravaganza, and in slight plays specially written for her, like Fred Marsden's *Musette*, in which she toured indefatigably. She retired in 1891, having amassed a large fortune which she left to charity.

CRAIG, EDITH GERALDINE AILSA (1869–1947), daughter of Ellen Terry and E. W. Godwin (qq.v.), who was on the stage as a child and a young woman, playing with her mother and Irving (q.v.) at the Lyceum. During Ellen Terry's tour of America in 1907 she acted as stage-manager, and then studied music. From 1911 she directed the Pioneer Players in London, for whom she also designed costumes and scenery. In 1929, on the first anniversary of Ellen Terry's death, she inaugurated an annual Shakespeare matinée in the converted barn adjacent to the house at Small Hythe where Ellen Terry spent her last years and which has now become the Ellen Terry Museum.

CRAIG, (EDWARD HENRY) GORDON (1872–1966), the son of Ellen Terry and E. W. Godwin (qq.v.), who was on the stage as a child and a young man, but later turned to scene design. In 1903 he prepared some interesting sets for Fred Terry's production of Calvert's *For Sword or Song* and for his mother's production of Ibsen's *The Vikings*. He was also responsible for the designs for Otway's *Venice Preserv'd* in Berlin in 1905, Ibsen's *Rosmersholm* (for Duse, q.v.) in Florence in 1906, and *Hamlet* at the Moscow Art Theatre (q.v.) in 1912. In 1908 he settled in Florence, founded and edited *The Mask*, a journal devoted to the art of the theatre, and ran a school of acting in the Arena Goldoni. His work had an immense influence on production methods in Europe and America, more by his originality and prodigality of ideas than by his actual achievements. His theories can be studied in his books, *The Art of the Theatre* (1905); *On the Art of the Theatre* (1911), incorporating the previous book and frequently translated; *Towards a New Theatre* (1913), which contains forty plates of scenic designs; *The Marionette* (1918); *The Theatre Advancing* (1921);

Books and Theatres (1925). He also wrote books on Irving and Ellen Terry, and in 1926 he designed the costumes and scenery for Ibsen's *The Pretenders* at Copenhagen, his designs for the production being subsequently published in portfolio. In 1957 he published a volume of autobiography, *Index to the Story of My Days, 1872–1907*. Shortly before his death his vast theatrical library was bought by the French Government for the Rondel Collection.

Craig Theatre, NEW YORK, see ADELPHI THEATRE (2).

CRANE, RALPH (c. 1550/60–after 1624), an underwriter in the Privy Seal Office who added to his income by copying plays for authors and actors. His copy of *Sir John van Olden Barnavelt* (attributed to Fletcher and Massinger), made for the King's Men (see CHAMBERLAIN'S MEN) in 1619, was used as a prompt copy, and copies by him of Middleton's *A Game at Chess* (1624) are in the Bodleian and the British Museum respectively. He also made the copy of Middleton's *The Witch* (1615) which is in the Bodleian. An immense amount of similar copying must have been done for the playhouses, and it is curious that so little is known about it. It was probably poorly paid, and done by hacks and hangers-on of the literary profession.

CRANE, WILLIAM HENRY (1845–1928), an American actor who intended to become an opera singer, but proved so good in comedy that he finally devoted himself to straight acting in comic parts. In 1877 he joined forces with Stuart Robson (q.v.), and they appeared as the two Dromios in *The Comedy of Errors*. Among the other plays in which they were seen together the most successful was *The Henrietta* (1887), specially written for them by Bronson Howard (q.v.). After parting amicably from his companion in 1889 Crane continued to appear successfully, notably as Falstaff in *The Merry Wives of Windsor* and Sir Toby Belch in *Twelfth Night* and in such modern plays as Grundy's *Business is Business* (1904) (an adaptation of Mirbeau's *Les Affaires sont les affaires*, 1903), until his retirement in 1916.

CRATES, Greek dramatist of Athens, one of the masters of Old Comedy, who won his first prize in 450 B.C. He was a contemporary of Aristophanes (q.v.), who praised him in the *Knights* for his wit and graceful style.

CRATINUS (*c.* 520–*c.* 423 B.C.), Greek dramatist of Athens. In the *Knights* Aristophanes (q.v.) makes fun of him as a worn-out drunkard; in the following year (424 B.C.) Cratinus had his revenge by defeating Aristophanes' *Clouds* with his own *Wine-Flask*, probably his last play.

CRAVEN, LADY ELIZABETH [later the MARGRAVINE OF ANSPACH] (1750–1828), see PRIVATE THEATRES IN ENGLAND.

CRAVEN, HAWES [really HENRY HAWES CRAVEN GREEN] (1837–1910), English scene painter, who served his apprenticeship at the Britannia, Hoxton. His first outstanding work was done for Wilkie Collins's *The Lighthouse*, produced at the Olympic in 1857. He also worked at Covent Garden and Drury Lane, but his finest work was done for Irving (q.v.) at the Lyceum, where he was considered the equal of Stanfield and Beverley (qq.v.) in craftsmanship, and their superior in his grasp of theatrical essentials. As an innovator in stage decoration he ranks with de Loutherbourg (q.v.), and was a pioneer in the skilful use of the new electric lighting.

CRAWFORD, CHERYL (1902–86), American actress and theatre director, who made her first appearance on the stage in 1923 for the Theatre Guild (q.v.), with which she was associated for a long time, appearing in many of its productions and acting as its casting manager from 1928 to 1930. She was also active in the foundation and running of the Group Theatre (q.v.) in 1930, of the American Repertory Theatre, in association with Eva Le Gallienne and Margaret Webster (qq.v.), in 1946, and of the Actors' Studio (see METHOD), of which she long remained an executive producer, in 1947. In 1950 she became one of the directors of the Anta play series produced annually by the American National Theatre and Academy (q.v.). Among her other activities, she presented, often in association with other producers, a number of plays, including Tennessee Williams's *The Rose Tattoo* (1951), *Camino Real* (1953), and *Sweet Bird of Youth* (1959), Frisch's *Andorra* and Brecht's *Mother Courage and her Children* (both 1963).

Crazy Gang, an association of seven English comedians, consisting of the three double-act teams, Flanagan and Allen (qq.v.), Nervo and Knox, Naughton and Gold, together with 'Monsewer' Eddie Gray. They were brought together by George Black (q.v.) to appear in a series of revues at the London Palladium which began with *Life Begins at Oxford Circus* (1935) and ended with *These Foolish Things* (1938). From 1947 to 1961 the Gang, without Chesney, who had retired owing to ill-health, was seen at the Victoria Palace in another series of 'crazy' revues, from *Together Again* (1947) to *The Young in Heart* (1960).

CRÉBILLON [really DE CRAIS-BILLON], PROSPER JOLYOT DE (1674–1762), French dramatist, author of a number of tragedies of which the best is probably *Rhadamiste et Zénobie* (1711). In his own day he was considered the successor of Racine (q.v.), but his plays are travesties, melodramas rather than true tragedies. His audiences put up with them for the sake of the romantic element and the atmosphere of terror which he succeeded so well in imparting, and they remained popular until ousted by the even more melodramatic works of the elder Dumas (q.v.). Crébillon used his position as dramatic censor to oppose Voltaire (q.v.), who in revenge took as the subjects of five of his plays situations already treated by Crébillon and handled them more successfully.

Crepidata, see FABULA (1).

Crispin, a character of French comedy who derives from the *commedia dell'arte* mask of the *zanni* Scaramuccia (q.v.), gallicized as Scaramouche. As originally played in Paris by Raymond Poisson (q.v.), he had in him also something of the braggart soldier (see CAPITANO), but successive generations of Poissons, playing the part until 1735, made it more that of a quick-witted unscrupulous valet. The name was introduced into theatrical literature by Scarron (q.v.), and is found in such later titles as *Crispin rival de son maître*, *Crispin musicien*, and *Crispin gentilhomme*.

Criterion Theatre. (1) LONDON, in Piccadilly Circus, an underground theatre which opened on 21 Mar. 1874. Success came in 1877 with *Pink Dominoes*, adapted by James Albery from a French farce. In the cast was Charles Wyndham (q.v.), who in 1879 took over the theatre, remaining its lessee until his death in 1919, when it passed to his widow, who continued to appear there. The theatre was reconstructed in 1883–4, when electricity was installed. It was at the Criterion that many of the plays of Henry Arthur Jones (q.v.) were first produced. The theatre was again remodelled in 1902, and five years later Wyndham returned to score a success in Hubert H. Davies's *The Mollusc* (1907). One of the greatest successes of the First World War, Walter Ellis's *A Little Bit of Fluff*, began its long run here in 1915, and later successes included Sydney Blow's *Lord Richard in the Pantry* (1919), Hackett's *Ambrose Applejohn's Adventure* (1921), *Musical Chairs* (1932), by Ronald Mackenzie, who was killed in a car accident in the same year, Rattigan's *French Without Tears* (1936), and *Tony Draws a Horse* (1939), by Lesley Storm. During the Second World War the theatre became a B.B.C. studio, but reverted to use as a theatre in Sept. 1945 with a revival of Sheridan's *The Rivals* in which Edith Evans (q.v.) played Mrs. Malaprop. Among later successes have been Macrae's *Traveller's Joy* (1948) with Yvonne Arnaud, Beckett's *Waiting for Godot* (1955), transferred from the Arts (q.v.), Anouilh's *Waltz of the Toreadors* (1956), and *A Severed Head* (1963), dramatized from Iris Murdoch's novel by J. B. Priestley, which ran until March 1966. It was followed by an American two-character play, *The Owl and the Pussycat*, by Bill Manhoff. In 1969 Roy Dotrice (q.v.) appeared in *Brief Lives*, a solo performance based on John Aubrey's writings (previously seen at the Hampstead Theatre Club in 1967), and later that year Leonard Webb's *So What About Love?* began a successful run.

(2) NEW YORK. This opened as the Lyric in 1895. In 1899, having been sold at auction, it reopened as the Criterion under Charles Frohman. Among its early productions were Julia Marlowe in *Barbara Frietchie* (1899) and John Hare and Irene Vanbrugh in Pinero's *The Gay Lord Quex* (1900). The last production, before the house became a cinema, was a version of Brieux's *La Robe rouge* as *The Letter of the Law*, with Lionel Barrymore. The building was demolished in 1935, together with the old Olympic Music-Hall (see NEW YORK THEATRE (2)).

The Herald Square Theatre, New York, originally the Colosseum, was named the Criterion from 1882 to 1885.

CROFT, MICHAEL, see NATIONAL YOUTH THEATRE.

CROMMELYNCK, FERNAND (1888–1970), French-language Belgian playwright, who was for some time an actor. His early plays, which included *Le Sculpteur des masques* and *Le Marchand des regrets*, written before the First World War, though praised for their originality, had little success, but with *Le Cocu magnifique*, a study of jealousy, first seen in Paris in 1921, he scored an immediate triumph and left the stage to devote all his time to playwriting. *Le Cocu magnifique* was translated into several languages, and under its original title, but in an English version by Ivor Montagu, was staged in London in 1932 with Peggy Ashcroft (q.v.) as Stella. Crommelynck's later plays, which include *Tripes d'or*, a satire on snobbery, and *Chaud et froid*, which in 1958 was broadcast on the Third Programme in English, failed to achieve a comparable success, and he is remembered mainly for *Le Cocu magnifique*.

Cross Keys Inn, LONDON, see INNS USED AS THEATRES.

CROTHERS, RACHEL (1878–1958), American actress and dramatist, whose plays, which she directed herself, include *A Man's World* (1910), an attack on the 'double standard of morality' which has been regarded as one of the most significant plays of its time; *He and She* (also known as *The Herfords*) (1911); *Nice People* (1921), a study of post-war youth; *As Husbands Go* (1931), which contrasts the English and the American conception of marriage; and, her most important work, a deft study of feminine psychology, *Susan and God* (1937).

CROUSE, RUSSELL (1893–1966), see LINDSAY, HOWARD.

Crow Street Theatre, see DUBLIN.

CROWNE, JOHN (?1640–1703 or 1714), a Restoration dramatist, creator of Sir Courtly Nice in his play of that name (1685) based on Moreto (q.v.)—a favourite part with many actors. He also wrote a heroic drama, *The Destruction of*

Jerusalem (1677), produced at the Theatre Royal with elaborate scenery. Like many of Crowne's forgotten plays, this seems to have owed its initial success to its settings, painted by Aggas and Towers, who later sued the theatre for payment.

Cruelty, THEATRE OF, see THEATRE OF CRUELTY.

Cruger's Wharf Theatre, NEW YORK, built in 1758 by David Douglass (q.v.) for a company which included the widow of Lewis Hallam (q.v.) and her three children. They opened in Rowe's *Jane Shore*, and after a season of two months ended with *Richard III*, after which 'the Theatre on Mr. Cruger's Wharff' was used no more. It was sometimes referred to as the Wharf Theatre.

CRUZ CANO Y OLMEDILLA, RAMÓN FRANCISCO DE LA (1731–94), a Spanish writer of lively one-act *sainetes* (q.v.), vivid farces or satirical sketches which owe nothing to the prevailing neo-classical literary fashion of his time but are the descendants of the *pasos* and *entremeses* of the sixteenth and seventeenth centuries and forerunners of the nineteenth-century sketches of daily life and realistic drama. Ramón de la Cruz also wrote libretti for *zarzuelas* (q.v.) depicting the customs of the lower classes of Madrid, an innovation in a genre which had hitherto concerned itself largely with the more complicated love intrigues of classical gods and goddesses.

CUEVA, JUAN DE LA (*c.* 1550–*c.* 1610), Spanish dramatist whose most important plays were produced in Seville between 1578 and 1581. Writing in the period when classical influence was still paramount, Cueva owes a considerable debt to Seneca (q.v.), but he was also the first writer of plays based on Spanish history. His dramas on Bernardo el Carpio and King Sancho, and the tragedy of the *Siete infantes de Lara* paved the way for the great Spanish dramas of Lope de Vega (q.v.) and his contemporaries. Cueva was also an innovator in the Spanish comedy of manners with his *Comedia del viejo enamorado* and *El infamador*.

CUMBERLAND, RICHARD (1732–1811), English dramatist, with Hugh Kelly (q.v.) the most typical exponent of the eighteenth-century style which received its death-blow at the hands of Goldsmith and Sheridan (qq.v.). He wrote a number of poor tragedies, and his most characteristic work is found in his sentimental domestic comedies. He first achieved recognition with *The Brothers* (1769), but his best-known play is *The West Indian* (1771), produced with great success by Garrick. *The Jew* (1794), one of the first plays to plead the cause of Jewry, was frequently revived and translated into several languages, providing a fine part for outstanding actors of the day. Cumberland was extremely sensitive to criticism, and figures in Sheridan's *The Critic* (1779) as Sir Fretful Plagiary.

Cup-and-Saucer Drama, see ROBERTSON, T. W.

Curtain. In a theatre which has a proscenium arch (see PROSCENIUM) it is usual—though not today essential—to have a FRONT or HOUSE CURTAIN, which opens and closes at the beginning and end of each act. In the English Restoration theatre it rose after the prologue and fell after the epilogue. It was not until the mid-eighteenth century or later that it fell during the performance, and even then it was sometimes replaced by the act-drop (q.v.). The Front Curtain can rise vertically into the flies, with or without festoons; be divided centrally and taken sideways on the traverse principle; or be bunched up sideways to the outer top corners. It is then called a Tableau Curtain or Tabs (q.v.), a name often applied to any front curtain, or even to a curtain setting on the stage itself. Also in the proscenium opening is the Safety Curtain (q.v.). (See also ADVERTISEMENT CURTAIN.)

Curtain-Music, Curtain-Tune, see ACT-TUNES.

Curtain-Raiser, a one-act play, usually farcical, which in the nineteenth century served to whet the appetite of the audience before the main five-act drama of the evening, the last relic of the days when a full evening's entertainment included several plays to which latecomers were admitted on payment of a reduced fee. Like the After-piece (q.v.), it has disappeared in the twentieth century with the professional theatre's adherence to the single bill, but there are signs that it may return under another name.

Curtain Set, the simplest method of dressing the stage for a performance, with one or more side curtains, a back curtain, borders (q.v.) and perhaps a traverse curtain, centrally divided and running off to the sides of the stage on a wire or railway. It is a favourite stand-by of amateurs and Little Theatres and can be used with remarkable ingenuity. It has, strictly speaking, no scenic function, but achieves one if, for the playing of a scene, a small set-piece is placed before the back curtain. (For the varieties of front curtain, see CURTAIN.)

Curtain Theatre, LONDON. This opened in 1577, the year after the Theatre (q.v.). It took its name from the land on which it stood, Curtain Close in Finsbury Fields. In shape, form, and design it resembled the Theatre, but theatrically it had a much more distinguished record. The Chamberlain's Men (q.v.) appeared there under Burbage, and flourished in spite of threats to close the theatre and the rivalry of the Fortune (q.v.). Jonson's *Every Man in His Humour* was probably first performed at the Curtain in 1598 with Shakespeare as Knowell, and some scholars believe that Shakespeare's *Romeo and Juliet* (c. 1595) was first acted there, and also *Henry V* in 1599, the Curtain being 'the wooden O' referred to by the Chorus (but see GLOBE (1)). Robert Armin (q.v.) was a member of the company, describing himself in 1600 as 'Clonnico del Curtaino Snuffe'. The last recorded use of it as a theatre is in 1622, by Prince Charles's Men (q.v.), and the last reference to the building dates from 1627. It was still standing in 1642 and perhaps as late as 1660.

CUSHMAN, CHARLOTTE SAUNDERS (1816–76), American actress, good in such parts as Lady Macbeth, which she played in New York, and later in London, with Macready (q.v.), Mrs. Haller in Kotzebue's *The Stranger*, and above all Meg Merrilies in a dramatization of Scott's *Guy Mannering*. She also played Lady Gay Spanker in the first American production of Boucicault's *London Assurance* in 1841. In 1845 she was seen in London at the Princess's in the above parts, as well as Rosalind in *As You Like It*, Beatrice in *Much Ado About Nothing*, and Portia in *The Merchant of Venice*. Being of a somewhat masculine cast of countenance, she also played a number of male roles, including Hamlet, Romeo to the Juliet of her younger sister SUSAN (1822–59), Oberon in *A Midsummer Night's Dream*, and Claude Melnotte in Bulwer-Lytton's *The Lady of Lyons*. During the last years of her life she gave a great many Shakespeare readings, which proved very successful. In 1907 a Charlotte Cushman Club, which still flourishes, was established in Philadelphia. Its clubroom contains many interesting theatrical relics, paintings, and material contemporary with her career.

Cut-Cloth, see CLOTH.

Cyclorama, a curved plaster or canvas wall, built round the greater part of the stage and used to give an illusion of space and distance, and for sky and cloud effects, obtained by the diffusion of light reflected from it on to the acting area. The two essentials are complete rigidity and an absolutely unbroken surface. This means that, as a permanent feature of the stage, the cyclorama becomes a hindrance when not in use. It can substantially reduce the amount of scenery needed to mask the stage, but only in plays where its special qualities are called for. Otherwise it interferes with the suspension of hanging cloths and reduces the width of the openings giving access at each side. Because of this it is often replaced by a partial, or shallow, cyclorama, or even by a plain canvas or flat distempered wall. Moveable cycloramas have been evolved, but not widely adopted, partly because of the difficulty of keeping them absolutely rigid. The cyclorama is known in Germany, where it was first used, as a *Rundhorizont* (for *Kuppelhorizont*, see FORTUNY).

D

Dadaism, an anti-social philosophy of the 1920s which, though it created only a passing sensation at the time, was later to have a vital influence on European drama. Irrational, nihilistic, and destructive, it attacked the foundations of so-called 'society' and set out to arouse in its audiences the sense of anger and outrage later evoked by Artaud's Theatre of Cruelty (q.v.), and also exploited the sense of futility and non-comprehension which gave rise to the Theatre of the Absurd (q.v.).

DALBERG, BARON WOLFGANG HERIBERT VON (1750–1806), a wealthy aristocrat whose interest in the theatre led to his appointment in 1778 as honorary director of the newly opened National Theatre at Mannheim (q.v.). After the death of Ekhof (q.v.) later the same year Dalberg arranged for the actors in his company to be transferred to Mannheim, and with them and Iffland (q.v.), whose first plays were produced there, the theatre flourished, Dalberg preparing for it the first German version of Shakespeare's *Julius Caesar*. But Dalberg's most memorable achievement was the production in 1782 of *Die Räuber*, by Schiller (q.v.), then young and unknown, who was appointed theatre poet from 1783 to 1784, during which time his *Fiesco* and *Kabale und Liebe* also appeared. The National Theatre continued to prosper until the rigours of war reached Mannheim in 1796, when the company was disbanded and Iffland left to go to Berlin.

DALIN, OLOF (1708–63), Swedish historian, critic, and playwright, and the tutor of King Gustav III (1746–92), who under his influence took a great interest in the theatre, writing or collaborating in plays for performance at Court, encouraging new playwrights, supporting the National Theatre in Stockholm in the 1730s, and being instrumental in founding and financing the Royal Swedish Dramatic Theatre in 1788 Dalin himself was responsible for the introduction on to the Swedish stage of French classical tragedy with his *Brynhilda*. This was produced in 1738, in the same year as his comedy, *Den*

afundsjuke, which shows the influence both of Molière and of Holberg (qq.v.).

DALSKY, MAMONT (1865–1918), see ALEXANDRINSKY THEATRE.

DALY, (JOHN) AUGUSTIN (1839–99), American manager, dramatic critic, and dramatist, who wrote and adapted a number of plays, among them *Leah the Forsaken* (1862) (from Mosenthal's *Deborah*) and a melodrama, *Under the Gaslight; or, Life and Love in These Times* (1867). In 1869 he took over the management of the Fifth Avenue Theatre, New York (q.v.), which was burnt down in 1873. Daly then opened another theatre, also on Fifth Avenue, which he left in 1879 to found his own theatre (see DALY'S) with a fine company headed by John Drew and Ada Rehan, which in 1884 played at Toole's Theatre (q.v.) in London with such success that, after further visits between 1886 and 1890, Daly decided to have his own theatre there. Both in New York and in London Daly's first nights were important events, and he set a high standard, in spite of his tendency to tamper with the text of established classics.

DALY, (PETER CHRISTOPHER) ARNOLD (1875–1927), American actor, who in 1903 played Marchbanks in the first public performance in New York of Shaw's *Candida*. Being intensely interested in Shaw's work, he presented *The Man of Destiny* the following year in a double bill with *How He Lied to Her Husband*, specially written for him, and in 1905 gave the first public performances of *Mrs. Warren's Profession* and *You Never Can Tell*. He also revived *Arms and the Man*, in which Mansfield (q.v.) had appeared in 1894. The opposition to the new 'theatre of ideas', however, became too much for him, and he went back to the usual run-of-the-mill life of the contemporary theatre, dying in a fire in his early fifties.

Daly's Theatre. (1) NEW YORK, originally Banvard's, and later Wood's, Museum. It opened in 1867 and changed its name a year later. Although the repertory was mainly burlesque, variety, and melodrama, straight plays were occasionally performed after 1872, the year in which Laura Keene (q.v.) made her last appearance there. After several seasons as the Broadway and the New Broadway, the theatre was remodelled and redecorated, opening on 17 Sept. 1879 as Daly's. It became one of the leading playhouses of New York, particularly after the loss of the second Park Theatre (q.v.) in 1882 and the Union Square Theatre (q.v.) in 1888. One of its most successful productions was a revival of *The Taming of the Shrew*, which opened on 17 Jan. 1887, starring Ada Rehan (q.v.), who had first been seen at this theatre as far back as 1875 in Lumley's *The Thoroughbred*. Daly continued to manage the theatre until his death in 1899, and it retained his name until it was demolished in 1920, having been a cinema since 1915. (See also FIFTH AVENUE THEATRE.)

(2) LONDON, in Cranbourn Street, Leicester Square, built for Daly by George Edwardes (q.v.). The foundation stone was laid on 30 Oct. 1891 by Ada Rehan, who appeared as Katharina in the opening production, *The Taming of the Shrew*, on 27 June 1893. Subsequently Daly gave Sheridan Knowles's *The Hunchback* its last production in London to date, and Tennyson's *The Foresters* its only one. The latter failed, but was notable as the first play in this theatre to be lighted entirely by electricity. In 1895 Daly, who had not had the success he hoped for, withdrew and the theatre eventually passed under the control of George Edwardes, who made it a home of musical comedy with successive productions of *An Artist's Model* (1895), *The Geisha* (1896), *San Toy* (1899), *A Country Girl* (1902), *The Merry Widow* (1907) with Lily Elsie and Joseph Coynes, and *The Dollar Princess* (1909). Edwardes's last production at Daly's was *The Marriage Market* (1913). He died two years later. In 1917 Oscar Asche produced there *The Maid of the Mountains* with José Collins, followed in 1920 by *A Southern Maid*, in 1922 by *The Lady of the Rose* with Harry Welchman and Phyllis Dare, and in 1923 by *Madame Pompadour* with Evelyn Laye and Derek Oldham. In Nov. 1927 the first production of *Sirocco*, by Noël Coward, caused a riot, and the theatre returned to musical comedy. In spite of revivals of many former successes, its fortunes declined, and on 25 Sept. 1937 it closed. It was then pulled down and a cinema erected on the site.

(3) NEW YORK, on West 63rd Street. This was built as the Davenport in 1909, and in 1919 became a cinema for children. In 1922 it was renamed Daly's. Its first important production was a revival of Congreve's *Love for Love* in 1925. It was known successively as the Recital, the Park Lane, and (in 1934) Gilmore's. It was leased in 1936 by the Federal Theatre Project (q.v.), who gave there the first New York production of Shaw's *On the Rocks* in 1938. It stood empty for some years, being used by the Shuberts for storage before being demolished in 1957.

Dame, a female character in the English pantomime (q.v.) which is traditionally played by an actor. Among the familiar Dame parts are Aladdin's mother, Widow Twankey (a name taken by H. J. Byron (q.v.) from a Chinese tea-exporting port), Idle Jack's mother (in *Jack and the Beanstalk*), known as Dame Durden or Dame Trot, and usually Cinderella's ugly sisters, who go under many pairs of names. If they are played by women, then their mother, the Baroness, is played by a male comedian. Other Dame parts are the Cook in *Dick Whittington*, the Queen of Hearts, Mother Goose, and Mrs. Crusoe. Among famous players of Dame parts have been Dan Leno, George Robey, Will Fyffe, Barry Lupino, Shaun Glenville, and Clarkson Rose.

D'AMICO, SILVIO (1887–1955), Italian theatre scholar, professor of the History of the Theatre at the St. Cecilia Academy in Rome, who inaugurated and, until his death, edited the monumental *Enciclopedia dello Spettacolo*. He was dramatic critic of several Italian papers, founding and editing the theatre review *Scenario* in 1932 and the *Rivista italiana del dramma* in 1937. He also founded in 1935 the Academy of Dramatic Art named after him. He wrote many books on the theatre, of which the most important was his *Storia del teatro drammatico* (1939–40; 3rd edition in 4 vols., 1953).

DANCE, SIR GEORGE (1858–1932), English theatrical manager, author, and songwriter, whose song, 'Girls are the Ruin of Men', was sung by Vesta Tilley (q.v.). He also wrote the libretti of several musical plays, among them *The Nautch Girl* (1891) and *A Chinese Honeymoon* (1899). Dance, who became one of the most successful and powerful theatre managers in the United Kingdom, often with as many as twenty-four companies on tour at once, was knighted in 1932 in recognition of his services to the theatre, which included a gift of £30,000 for the reconstruction of the Old Vic. His son, ERIC, who died in a prison camp during the Second World War, was responsible for the building of the Oxford Playhouse (see OXFORD) which opened in 1938.

DANCER, ANN (1734–1801), see BARRY, SPRANGER.

DANCHENKO, VLADIMIR NEMIROVICH-, see NEMIROVICH-DANCHENKO.

DANCOURT, FLORENT CARTON (1661–1725), French dramatist and actor, husband of the actress MARIE-THÉRÈSE LENOIR (1663–1725), daughter of La Thorillière and god-daughter of Molière (qq.v.). After some years in the provinces Dancourt, with his wife, joined the Comédie-Française and remained there until 1718. During this time he wrote more than fifty plays which, though never approaching the true comedy of Molière, show wit and observation and much skill in etching the contemporary scene. The best are *Le Chevalier à la mode* (1687), written in collaboration with Saint-Yon, an excellent portrait of contemporary life with much satire at the expense of *parvenu* financiers; *La Maison de campagne* (1688); and the one-act *Les Vendanges de Suresnes* (1695), the most frequently revived of all his works. In *La Foire de Bezons* (also 1695) Dancourt's two daughters, MARIE-ANNE-ARMANDE (1684–1745), known as Manon, and MARIE-ANNE-MICHELLE (1685–1780), known as Mimi, made their first appearance on the stage. They became members of the Comédie-Française in 1701. Manon retired a year later on her marriage, but Mimi remained for many years, and was still drawing her pension at the age of 95.

DANE, CLEMENCE [really WINIFRED ASH-TON] (1888–1965), English playwright and novelist, who took her pseudonym from the church of St. Clement Danes in the Strand. Her first play, *A Bill of Divorcement* (1921), which deals sympathetically with the problem of divorce on the grounds of insanity, brought Katharine Cornell (q.v.) before the public when produced in New York. Among her later plays were *Will Shakespeare* (also 1921), *Naboth's Vineyard* and *Granite* (both 1926), *Wild Decembers* (1932), a play on the Brontës, and *Eighty in the Shade* (1958), written for Sybil Thorndike and Lewis Casson (qq.v.). Her knowledge of the theatre was shown also in her novels, *Broome Stages* and *The Flower Girls*. She was appointed C.B.E. in the Coronation Honours List of 1953 for her services to the theatrical profession. She was also an excellent sculptor, and her bust of Ivor Novello stands in the foyer of Drury Lane Theatre.

DANGEVILLE, MLLE [really MARIE-ANNE BOTOT] (1714–96), French actress, member of a family who served the Comédie-Française for three generations. She was at her best in comedy and some of her greatest triumphs were made in the plays of Marivaux (q.v.). Her retirement in 1763 was much regretted by the public and by her fellow actors, who often arranged surprise visits to her house in Vaugirard. It was there that some of the actors of the Comédie-Française first performed Collé's *Partie de chasse d'Henri IV*, which Louis XV had banned from the public stage.

D'ANNUNZIO [really RAPAGNETTA], GABRIELE (1863–1938), Italian poet, novelist, and dramatist, who came into prominence politically when in 1919 he captured the port of Fiume for Italy, relinquishing his authority a year later. His plays, which are simple in structure but rich in poetry and sensuality, aroused much controversy. None reflects a mature mind, none—except perhaps *La figlia di Jorio* (1904)—is truly dramatic. His stage directions reveal the extent and accuracy of his archaeological knowledge, but his people are puppets driven by elemental passions, and his plays live mainly by their poetry. Among the best known are *La città morta* (1898) and *La Gioconda* (1899) in which Eleonora Duse (q.v.) was outstanding, *Francesca da Rimini* (1902), and *La Piave* (1918). None of them remains in the repertory, but his religious play in French, *Le Martyre de Saint-Sebastien* (1911), is sometimes revived in a cut version for the sake of the incidental music by Debussy.

DARLINGTON, WILLIAM AUBREY (1890–1979), English dramatic critic and dramatist, author of the successful farce, *Alf's*

Button (1924), which he based on one of his own novels. Appointed dramatic critic of the *Daily Telegraph* in 1920, he held that position until 1968, continuing to write feature articles on the theatre after his retirement. He was also drama correspondent of the *New York Times* from 1939 to 1960. His later plays included *Carpet Slippers* (1930), *A Knight Passed By* (1931), and *Marcia Gets Her Own Back* (1938). He was also the author of several books on the theatre—*Through the Fourth Wall* (1922), *Literature in the Theatre* (1925), *The Actor and His Audience* (1949), *Six Thousand and One Nights* (1960)—and of short lives of Sheridan and Barrie (qq.v.). In 1941 he published a volume of reminiscences, *I Do What I Like*. He was created C.B.E. in 1967 for services to literature and the theatre.

DAUBENY, PETER LAUDERDALE (1921–75), English impresario and theatre manager, who started his career as an actor under William Armstrong at the Liverpool Repertory Theatre. He was responsible for a long series of London productions, some of the most successful being Werfel's *Jacobowsky and the Colonel* (1945), Hugh Mills's *The House by the Lake* (1956), Michael Redgrave's version of Henry James's *The Aspern Papers* (1959), and Billetdoux's *Chin-Chin* (1960). He also arranged the importation, often under great difficulties, of many outstanding foreign theatrical groups, notably the Berliner Ensemble in 1956, a visit which had immense repercussions in the English theatre as a whole. Although not all his importations met with general approval—as witness the uproar which greeted Jack Gelber's *The Connection* in 1961—he certainly helped to widen the horizon of the London playgoer, and with his annual World Theatre season from 1964 to 1973 played, without official support, the role undertaken in Paris by the Government-subsidized Théâtre des Nations (q.v.). During these seasons, which took place at the Aldwych Theatre (q.v.) while the resident company was on tour, many different foreign companies appeared, as may easily be seen by a random selection—the Comédie-Française in Molière and Feydeau, the Schiller Theater in Goethe and Max Frisch, the Abbey Theatre in Boucicault and O'Casey, the Moscow Art Theatre in Chekhov and Gogol, the

Japanese *nō* theatre. In 1973 Daubeny was knighted for services to the theatre.

DAVENANT, SIR WILLIAM (1606–68), English dramatist and theatre manager, reputed to be the natural son of Shakespeare (q.v.) by the hostess of the Crown Inn, Cornmarket, Oxford. There is no proof of this, though Shakespeare may have been his godfather. Before the closing of the playhouses in 1642 Davenant had written a number of plays and Court masques in the style of Ben Jonson (q.v.), whom he succeeded as Poet Laureate in 1638. During the Civil War he fought on the King's side, and was knighted by Charles I in 1643. Towards the end of the Commonwealth he managed to evade the ban on stage plays and by announcing them as 'music and instruction' got permission to put on *The Siege of Rhodes* (1656), considered by some the first English opera, *The Spaniards in Peru* (1658), and *Sir Francis Drake* (1659). On the Restoration in 1660 he obtained from Charles II a patent (see also KILLIGREW) under which he opened Lincoln's Inn Fields Theatre (q.v.) as the Duke's House, with a company led by Thomas Betterton (q.v.). Later he built a new theatre in Dorset Garden (q.v.), but died before it opened. Davenant, who was responsible for several adaptations of Shakespeare to suit the tastes of the time, was also one of the first to encourage the vogue for machinery, dancing, and music which came in with the proscenium theatre and elaborate scenery, and his work, though not always to the taste of later critics, gave a great impetus to the development of the English theatre. He was originally the person aimed at in the character of Bayes in Buckingham's *The Rehearsal* (1671), which was altered after his death so as to satirize Dryden (q.v.) instead.

DAVENPORT, FANNY LILY GIPSY (1850–98), American actress, daughter of the American actor EDWARD LOOMIS DAVENPORT (1815–77) and the English actress FANNY ELIZABETH VINING (1829–91). She was on the stage as a child with her parents, making her adult début in 1865 as Mrs. Mildmay in *Still Waters Run Deep*, by Tom Taylor (q.v.). She was leading lady for Augustin Daly (q.v.) in New York from 1869 to 1877, and then formed her own company, starring with it in the principal theatres of the United States.

Her range of parts was wide, including Shakespeare's heroines and such contemporary women as Polly Eccles in Robertson's *Caste* and Lady Gay Spanker in Boucicault's *London Assurance*. Between 1883 and 1895 she also appeared in four plays by Sardou (q.v.)—*Fedora, Tosca, Cleopatra*, and *Gismonda*. One of her sisters, Blanche, was an opera singer, another, MAY (1856–1927), an actress, who was on the stage as a child and later joined Daly's company. She retired on her marriage to William Seymour (q.v.). Fanny's brothers, EDGAR LONGFELLOW (1862–1918) and HARRY GEORGE BRYANT (1866–1949), were both well-known actors, the latter marrying the actress Phyllis Rankin, with whom he appeared for many years in vaudeville. He was one of the first actors to appear in films (in 1912) and his later career was mainly in Hollywood.

DAVENPORT, JEAN (1829–1903) and THOMAS (1792–1851), see LANDER; LIZZIE (?–1899), see MATHEWS, C. J.; LOUISE, see SHERIDAN, W. E.

Davenport Theatre, New York, see DALY'S THEATRE (3).

DAVIS, FAY (1872–1945), see LAWRENCE, GERALD.

DAVIS, HALLIE FLANAGAN, see FLANAGAN.

DAVIS, OWEN (1874–1956), American dramatist who, finding no market for his tragedies in verse, wrote over a hundred ephemeral but remunerative melodramas. In 1921, however, he returned to his earlier ideals with a sincere and moving play, *The Detour*, which was recognized as one of the best productions of the year, in spite of its lack of financial success when compared with his earlier works. It was followed by *Icebound*, a study of New England farming folk which was awarded the Pulitzer Prize for 1923. Unfortunately his later work failed to maintain the promise of these two plays, though in 1936 he made, with his son, a good dramatization of Edith Wharton's novel, *Ethan Frome*. In 1931 he published his autobiography, *I'd Like To Do It Again.*

Davis's Amphitheatre, LONDON, see ASTLEY'S AMPHITHEATRE.

DAY, JOHN (c. 1574–c. 1640), English dramatist who, in collaboration with Chettle (q.v.), wrote the first part of The

Blind Beggar of Bethnal Green, also known as *Thomas Strowd* (1600). In 1601, possibly with a different collaborator, he added two further parts. Day's later plays include *The Travels of Three English Brothers* (1607), *The Parliament of Bees* (1608), and the ill-fated *Isle of Gulls*, given in 1606 by the Children at Blackfriars, which because of its satire on English and Scottish relations caused the imprisonment of those connected with its production.

DE BERGERAC, CYRANO, see BERGERAC.

DE BRIE, MLLE [really CATHERINE LECLERC DU ROZET] (c. 1630–1706), a French actress, who as Mlle de Rose joined the company of Molière (q.v.) in 1650. A year later she married a member of the company, EDMÉ VILLEQUIN DE BRIE (1607–76), who had been with Molière in the provinces and played small parts like the fencing master in *Le Bourgeois gentilhomme* (1671). A fine actress in comedy, she created many of Molière's best women's parts, including Cathos in *Les Précieuses ridicules* (1658) and Agnès in *L'École des femmes* (1662). She was one of the original members of the Comédie-Française and retired on pension in 1685.

DE COURVILLE, ALBERT (1887–1960), see REVUE.

DE FILIPPO, EDUARDO (1900–84), Italian actor and dramatist, son of an actor, Eduardo Scarpetta. With his brother Peppino (q.v.) and his sister TITINA [ANASTASIA] (1898–1963), he was on the stage from his earliest years, and in 1931 opened a theatre in Naples which soon achieved a high reputation in a series of productions based on the methods of the *commedia dell'arte* (q.v.). In 1945 the two brothers separated to form independent companies, Titina going with Eduardo and remaining with him until her death, appearing in many of his plays. Among the most important of these are *Napoli milionaria* (1945), *Questi fantasmi* and *Filomena Marturano* (both 1946), *Le voci di dentro* (1948), *La grande magia* (1949), *La paura numero uno* (1950), *Bene mio e core mio* (1955), and *Il figlio di Pulcinella* (1959). De Filippo, who was sometimes referred to as the Pirandello (q.v.) of the Italian dialect play, had great skill in play construction, fostered by his training as a farce-player. In English translations, two of his plays— *Saturday, Sunday, Monday* (1973) and

Filumena (1977)—were successfully produced in London and New York.

DE FILIPPO, PEPPINO (1903–80), Italian actor and playwright, who with his brother Eduardo (q.v.) founded a theatre in Naples in 1931 for the production of pantomimes and farces in the style of the *commedia dell'arte* (q.v.). He remained there until 1945, when he left to head a separate company, with which he appeared in London in 1964 during the World Theatre season (see ALDWYCH) in his own play, *Metamorphoses of a Wandering Minstrel*.

DE LOUTHERBOURG, PHILIP JAMES, see LOUTHERBOURG.

DE VILLIERS, C. D., see VILLIERS.

DEAN, BASIL (1888–1978), English actor, dramatist, and theatre director, who was for four years a member of the repertory company at the Gaiety, Manchester (see HORNIMAN), and in 1911 became first director of the Liverpool Repertory Theatre (q.v.). From there he went to Birmingham under Barry Jackson (q.v.), and was later active in the London theatre, both as manager (with Alec Rea as ReandeaN from 1919 to 1926) and as director, being responsible, among other productions, for Clemence Dane's *A Bill of Divorcement* (1921), Margaret Kennedy's *The Constant Nymph* (1926), Van Druten's *Young Woodley* (1928), Dodie Smith's *Autumn Crocus* (1931), and Priestley's *Johnson Over Jordan* (1939). He was a pioneer of stage lighting, importing much new equipment from America and Germany and devising some of his own. During both world wars he organized entertainments for the troops, and in 1939 became director of the Entertainments National Service Association (E.N.S.A.), an assignment he later described in his book *The Theatre at War* (1955). He returned to the West End theatre after the war with Priestley's *An Inspector Calls* (1946), and also organized the first British Repertory Theatre Festival in 1948. In 1947 he was awarded the C.B.E. for his services to the theatre. His son Winton is a noted music critic and an authority on Handel.

DEAN, JULIA (1830–68), American actress, grand-daughter of the English actor Samuel Drake (q.v.) who went to the United States in 1810 and became a pioneer theatre manager in Kentucky. She appeared as a child under the management of Ludlow and Smith (qq.v.) and in 1846 made her adult début in New York as Julia in Sheridan Knowles's *The Hunchback*. At her best in roles of tenderness and pathos, such as Scribe's Adrienne Lecouvreur or Mrs. Haller in Kotzebue's *The Stranger*, she had a few years of immense popularity, but after an unhappy marriage which ended in divorce, her fortunes declined. It was with Julia Dean that Belasco (q.v.), as a small boy, made his first appearance on the stage in 1856 when he was carried on as the child in Kotzebue's *Pizarro*. He also played Willie in her production of Mrs. Henry Wood's *East Lynne*.

DEBURAU, JEAN-GASPARD (1796–1846), famous French pantomimist, creator of the pale, lovesick Pierrot (q.v.) who has since remained a popular figure in the public imagination. In 1820 he was engaged for the Funambules on the Boulevard du Temple (q.v.), where he remained until his death. He was at first an inconspicuous member of the company, but as he developed, with great subtlety and many delicate touches, his concept of Pierrot as the ever-hopeful and disappointed lover, as the child, the prince, the poet, and the eternal seeker, Paris flocked to see him and his praises were sung by all the critics, particularly by Jules Janin, who devoted a whole volume to his work. His son CHARLES (1829–73) carried on the Pierrot tradition after his creator's death, without his father's genius but with a vast store of goodwill and popularity, and remained at the Funambules until it was destroyed in 1862.

DÉJAZET, PAULINE-VIRGINIE (1798–1875), French actress, who was already well known as a vaudeville player of male roles at the Variétés and the Gymnase when in 1831 she went to the newly opened Palais Royal (q.v.), where she stayed for thirteen years, becoming one of the most popular actresses in Paris. Leaving after an argument over her salary, she continued her triumphant career at the Variétés and the Gaîté, still playing masculine roles as well as great ladies and pretty peasant girls. Some idea of her versatility is given by the fact that her parts included Voltaire, Rousseau, Napoleon, Henri IV, and Ninon de Lenclos. In 1859 she took over the Folies-

Nouvelles (q.v.), renamed it the Théâtre Déjazet, and appeared there in a number of new plays under the management of her son Eugène. At the age of sixty-two she made a great hit in a male part in Sardou's *Monsieur Garat*. She made her last appearance in Paris in 1870, and in the same year was seen in London at the Opéra Comique in a season of French plays. Her last years were unhappy and, harassed by financial difficulties, she was forced to play continuously in the provinces to support her children and grandchildren.

DEKKER, THOMAS (*c.* 1572–*c.* 1632), English dramatist, who worked mainly in collaboration and had a hand in more than forty plays, of which about fifteen survive, several having been destroyed in manuscript by Warburton's cook (q.v.). The most important is his own comedy, *The Shoemaker's Holiday* (1599), which tells how Simon Eyre, a master shoemaker, became Lord Mayor of London. Robust and full-blooded, it shows a promise which was not fulfilled in his later works. These include *Satiromastix* (1601), written in collaboration with Marston (q.v.); *The Honest Whore* (1604) and *The Roaring Girl* (1610), in which he collaborated with Middleton (q.v.); and, in collaboration with Massinger (q.v.), a tragedy, *The Virgin Martyr*, given at the Red Bull playhouse in 1620 but probably dating in a different version from some ten years earlier. Dekker is also believed to have had a hand in *The Witch of Edmonton* (1621). In his later years he wrote a number of pamphlets in imitation of Nashe (q.v.), including *The Gull's Handbook* (1609), a satiric account of the fops and gallants of the day which gives some interesting information about the contemporary theatre.

DELAUNAY, LOUIS-ARSÈNE (1826–1903), French actor, who first appeared at the Comédie-Française on 25 Apr. 1848 and had a long and brilliant career, playing young lovers till he was nearly sixty, seldom knowing failure, and becoming the idol of the public. His first outstanding success was made in a one-act play by A. Barthet, *Le Moineau de Lesbie* (1849), in which he appeared with Rachel (q.v.). He was the original Fortunio in Alfred de Musset's *Le Chandelier* (1848), and was so much admired as Cœlio in the same author's *Les Caprices de Marianne* (1851)

that after his retirement in 1886 it went out of the repertory for many years. In the course of his long career Delaunay appeared in a number of new plays, and also in revivals of the plays of Marivaux and Regnard, and was in *Hernani*, by Victor Hugo (q.v.) when it was first produced at the Comédie-Française.

DELLA PORTA, GIAMBATTISTA (1538–1613), an author of the Italian *commedia erudita* (q.v.), fourteen of whose plays have survived out of a possible thirty-three. They are in prose, on subjects taken mainly from Boccaccio and Plautus, though *Il due fratelli rivali* is based on the story by Bandello which also supplied Shakespeare with the plot of *Much Ado About Nothing*. Two of Della Porta's plays, *La Fantesca* and *La Cintia*, were translated by Walter Hawkesworth and performed at Trinity College, Cambridge, as *Leander* (in 1598) and *Labyrinthus* (in 1603) respectively, and *La Trappolaria* was used by George Ruggle (q.v.) as the basis of his *Ignoramus*, which James I much enjoyed when he visited Cambridge in 1615.

DELYSIA [really LAPIZE], ALICE (1889–1979), French actress and singer, who made her first appearance in 1903 at the Moulin Rouge and was later seen at the Variétés and the Folies-Bergère. In 1905 she made her first appearance in the United States at Daly's. In 1914 Cochran (q.v.) engaged her for London, where she made a great success in the revue *Odds and Ends*. She continued to appear under Cochran's management for many years, and in his memoirs he constantly pays tribute to her loyalty and good nature.

DENCH, JUDI (1934–), English actress, who made her first appearance at the Old Vic as Ophelia in *Hamlet* in 1957, and played a wide variety of Shakespearian parts over the next four years, including Juliet (to the Romeo of John Stride (q.v.), produced by Zeffirelli) which she also played with the Royal Shakespeare Company in 1962. She was seen in her first modern part, Dorcas Bellboys in a revival of John Whiting's *A Penny for a Song*, in the same year, and was then at the Oxford Playhouse, where she appeared in Arbuzov's *The Twelfth Hour* (1964) and *The Promise* (1967), the latter subsequently being seen in London. In 1965 she appeared in a revival of Coward's *Private Lives*, and in 1968 made a great success as

Sally Bowles in *Cabaret*, a musical version of Van Druten's *I Am a Camera* (1954), based on stories by Isherwood. In 1969 she rejoined the Royal Shakespeare Company to play the dual role of Hermione and Perdita in *The Winter's Tale* and Viola in *Twelfth Night*, and in 1970 was seen as Shaw's Major Barbara, and as Grace Harkaway in a revival of Boucicault's *London Assurance* at the Aldwych in London.

DENNY, FRANCES ANN (1798–1875), see DRAKE, SAMUEL.

DERWENT, CLARENCE (1884–1959), actor, playwright, and director, who was for five years in the company of Frank Benson, subsequently spent two years at the Gaiety, Manchester, and appeared in London in 1910 under Tree. In 1915 he went to America, where he had a long and distinguished career on Broadway, making his last appearance in Giraudoux's *The Madwoman of Chaillot* (1948). In 1945 he instituted the Clarence Derwent awards, given annually in New York (and in London since 1948) for the two best performances by players in supporting roles, and in 1946 he was elected President of the Actors' Equity Association of America.

Deschamps, see PICARD, L.-B.

DESEINE, MLLE (?–1759), see DUFRESNE.

DESJARDINS, MARIE-CATHERINE-HORTENSE (1632–83), one of the first women playwrights of France. She left home after an unhappy love-affair and may have become an actress, possibly in the provincial company run by Molière (q.v.). She was later taken under the protection of the Duchesse de Rohan, and wrote poetry, novels, and plays, of which *Manlius*, a classical tragedy, was successfully produced at the Hôtel de Bourgogne in 1662, remaining in the repertory of the Comédie-Française until the end of the eighteenth century. She was also the author of a comedy, *Le Favory* (1665), produced by Molière at the Palais-Royal.

DESMARETZ DE SAINT-SORLIN, JEAN (1595–1676), French novelist, poet, and dramatist, one of the original members of the French Academy, who helped Richelieu (q.v.) in his extensive systems of literary reform. He is best remembered for his comedy, *Les Visionnaires* (1637), probably the most important in French dramatic literature before Corneille's *Le Menteur* (1643). A witty comment on the foibles of fashionable society, it was produced at the Marais with Montdory (q.v.) as the hallucinated old-fashioned poet who believes himself to be a great modernist. It had some influence on Molière, who revived it twice at the Palais-Royal. Desmaretz wrote several other plays, including the greater part of *Mirame* (1641), the first production to be staged in Richelieu's private theatre.

DESŒILLETS, MLLE [really ALIX FAVIOT] (1621–70), French actress, who was appearing at the Marais (q.v.) when Corneille saw and admired her as Viriate in his *Sertorius* in 1662. Later in the same year she joined the company at the Hôtel de Bourgogne, and proved herself an excellent actress in tragedy, creating a number of important roles, among them the title-role in Corneille's *Sophonisbe* (1663) and Hermione in Racine's *Andromaque* (1667). During an illness she was replaced in the latter part by the young Mlle Champmeslé (q.v.), who was so good that the elder actress retired from the theatre in tears, and never acted again.

DESTOUCHES [really PHILIPPE NÉRICAULT] (1680–1754), French dramatist, and an important link in the development of eighteenth-century *drame* from seventeenth-century comedy. He was an imitator of Molière, but spoilt his early plays—*L'Ingrat*, *L'Irresolu*, *Le Médisant*—by emphasizing the moral, which Molière had allowed to emerge naturally in the course of the action. In 1716 he was at the French Embassy in London, where he contracted a secret marriage with an Englishwoman which later supplied material for one of his best plays, *Le Philosophe marié* (1727). His most important play, however, is *Le Glorieux* (1732), which was translated into English in 1791. It pictures the struggle between the old nobility and the newly rich who are rising to power, and some traits of the central character are said to have been taken from the actor Dufresne (q.v.), who played the part. Destouches left several plays in manuscript, of which one, *La Fausse Agnès*, was produced posthumously with some success. (See also COWLEY, HANNAH.)

Detail Scenery, the name given to small, changeable pieces of scenery used for a particular scene in or before a formalized setting.

Deus ex Machina (the god from the machine), the name given to a device in the Greek classical theatre by which at the end of the play a god descended from Olympus to sort out the complications of the plot. The 'machine' (*mechane*) was the crane which could raise or lower an actor, and its use was parodied by Aristophanes (q.v.).

Deuteragonist, see PROTAGONIST.

Deutsches Theater, a private play-producing society founded in Berlin in 1883 for the purpose of staging good plays in repertory, as a protest against the deadening effect of long runs and outmoded theatrical tradition. Under Adolf L'Arronge (q.v.) and Ludwig Barnay a group of actors led by Josef Kainz and Agnes Sorma (qq.v.) presented classical historical plays in the style of the Meininger Company (q.v.). In 1894 the enterprise was given a new direction by its affiliation with the Freie Bühne (q.v.). The Deutsches Theater had another period of fame under Max Reinhardt (q.v.), who went there in 1905 from the Neues Theater with a band of young actors trained in his own methods. Here he was able to realize some of his ambitious schemes of production, in which music, scenery, ballet, and mime all played their parts. In the crisis following on the First World War the company collapsed, but was later revived under Heinz Hilpert.

DEVINE, GEORGE ALEXANDER CASSADY (1910–65), English actor and theatre director. While at Oxford he was a prominent member of the O.U.D.S., and in 1932 made his début on the professional stage in *The Merchant of Venice*. He was then at the Old Vic for a season, and in 1937 joined John Gielgud's company at the Queen's. From 1936 to its closure in 1939 he was on the staff of the London Theatre Studio, founded by Michel Saint-Denis (q.v.). After six years in the army he again joined Saint-Denis, who was directing the Old Vic School, and was responsible for the short-lived Young Vic (q.v.). In 1954 he gave an outstanding performance as Tesman to the Hedda Gabler of Peggy Ashcroft (q.v.). Two years later he was appointed director of the English Stage Company, which he had helped to found, at the Royal Court Theatre (q.v.), and remained with it until

shortly before his death. Apart from directing plays for the company, he also gave some excellent performances, notably as Mr. Shu Fu in Brecht's *The Good Woman of Setzuan* (1956), Mr. Pinchwife in Wycherley's *The Country Wife*, and the Old Man in Ionesco's *The Chairs* (both 1957). He was appointed C.B.E. in 1957 for his services to the theatre. In 1966 a George Devine Award was instituted, from the proceeds of a gala matinée at the Old Vic, to provide financial encouragement to young workers in the theatre. Among the recipients so far have been Edward Bond (q.v.) and Donald Howarth.

DEVRIENT, (PHILIPP) EDUARD (1801–77), an outstanding member of an important family of German actors, nephew of LUDWIG DEVRIENT (1784–1832) who was renowned for his playing of Falstaff. In 1852 Eduard became director of the Court Theatre in Karlsruhe, where he brought the company to a high pitch of excellence. He also induced his audience to accept an unusual number of German classics in the repertory, and his versions of Shakespeare (pub. 1869–71 as *Deutscher Bühnen- und Familien-Shakespeare*), though somewhat bowdlerized, were more suitable for the stage than A. W. von Schlegel's literary translations. He was the first to write a detailed account of the theatre in Germany in his *Geschichte der deutschen Schauspielkunst* (1848). His brothers KARL AUGUST (1797–1872) and (GUSTAV) EMIL (1803–72) were both outstanding actors, the first in strong character parts—Schiller's Wallenstein, Goethe's Faust, Shakespeare's Lear and Shylock—the second in such heroic parts as Shakespeare's Hamlet and Goethe's Tasso and Egmont. Emil was for forty years at the Dresden Court Theatre. Eduard's son OTTO (1838–94) was also a good actor and an excellent director. Karl's son MAX (1857–1929) spent many years at the Vienna Burgtheater, where he excelled in the plays of Goethe and Schiller, and was much admired as Petruchio in *The Taming of the Shrew*.

DIAGHILEV, SERGE (1872–1929), Russian impresario, founder and director till his death of the Ballets Russes company which through its dancing and choreography revolutionized the art of ballet in western Europe, and through the décors and costumes designed for it by such artists as Bakst, Benois, Derain, Goncharova, and Picasso influenced the development of art everywhere, providing in the theatre a glorious finale to the history of scene-painting and of elaborate symbolic costume. Diaghilev's great achievement was that he raised ballet from a diverting entertainment to a serious theatrical art, which absorbed the creative energies of the greatest artists and musicians of his time. His company was first seen in Paris in 1911, in London in 1913, and in New York in 1916. Thereafter, though based on Monte Carlo, it toured extensively, but never returned to Russia, cut off by war and revolution. There was, however, no lack of Russian-trained dancers, choreographers, and designers to maintain the standards set by Diaghilev until enough recruits from other countries had been trained to carry on. The impetus given to dancing and décor by Diaghilev's work lasted far beyond his death, and was ultimately responsible for the emergence of national ballet companies in England and the United States.

DIBDIN, CHARLES (1745–1814), English dramatist, actor, and composer of many ballads, among them 'Tom Bowling' and 'The Lass that Loved a Sailor', and of a number of ballad operas, of which *The Waterman* (1774) long remained a favourite and passed into the repertory of the Toy Theatre (q.v.). He was a good actor, and made a great success as Mungo in Bickerstaffe's *The Padlock* (1768), for which he wrote the music. From 1788 to 1805 he gave one-man entertainments at the Sans Souci Theatre (q.v.). He was extremely quarrelsome, and his troubles with other managers, particularly Garrick (q.v.), are related at length in his autobiography, *The Professional Life of Mr. Dibdin*. Two of his sons by the actress Harriet Pitt were on the stage, Thomas (q.v.), who took his father's name, and CHARLES ISAAC MUNGO PITT (1768–1833), a successful writer of plays and pantomimes, whose memoirs were published by the Society for Theatre Research in 1956.

DIBDIN, THOMAS JOHN PITT (1771–1841), English actor and playwright, son of Charles Dibdin (q.v.) and the actress Harriet Pitt. Under his mother's name he first appeared on the stage at the age of four as Cupid to the Venus of Sarah Siddons (q.v.). He was later apprenticed to an upholsterer, but ran away to become an actor, scene painter, and dramatist, taking the name of Dibdin in 1800 in order to annoy his father, whom he accused of neglecting him and his brothers. He was the composer of about 2,000 songs in the style of the elder Dibdin, to whom they are often attributed, and his most successful pantomime was *Harlequin and Mother Goose* (1806), in which Grimaldi (q.v.) first played Clown. Dibdin's theatrical glorifications of the Navy, as in *The Mouth of the Nile* (1798) and *Nelson's Glory* (1805), were also extremely popular. He was the author of one of the many translations of Caigniez's *La Pie voleuse*, as *The Magpie; or, the Maid of Palaiseau* (1815). He married an actress named Nancy Hilliar and had four children who, under their grandmother's name of Pitt, were all connected with the stage. Some of their children went to the United States, where there are still several Pitts in theatre management.

DICKENS, CHARLES JOHN HUFFAM (1812–70), the great English novelist, was all his life intimately connected with the stage and had an immense influence on it through the numerous dramatizations of his books. Although there is no proof that he was ever an actor, both *Nicholas Nickleby* and *Great Expectations* show an intimate knowledge of theatrical life between 1837 and 1844, and those who saw him in his many amateur appearances, and in his famous readings from his own works, considered that he would have made an excellent comedian. He had a small theatre, where with his friends and family he gave private performances before a distinguished audience. Two plays by the novelist and dramatist (WILLIAM) WILKIE COLLINS (1824–89)—*The Frozen Deep* and *The Lighthouse* (both 1857)—were given there before their professional productions at the Olympic, and Dickens also collaborated with Collins in *No Thoroughfare*, which was produced in 1867 with Fechter and Ben Webster in the cast.

It would be impossible to catalogue here the plays based on Dickens's novels, many of which were done before the books had finished appearing in fortnightly parts. The most persistent adapters were W. T. Moncrieff (q.v.) and Edward Stirling, husband of Fanny Stirling (q.v.), but Albert Smith (q.v.) made the first adaptations of the Christmas Books and W. S. Gilbert (q.v.) of *Great Expectations*. Owing to the absence of copyright laws, Dickens's novels were pirated for the American stage, and he received nothing from the numerous adaptations in common use. Dickens's characters are so vivid, his plots so dramatic, that it is not surprising they dramatized well. At Christmas 1845 different versions of *The Cricket on the Hearth* were being given at twelve London theatres, all of which were later surpassed by Boucicault's adaptation entitled *Dot* (New York, 1859; London, 1862). Among the actors who appeared as Dickens's characters were Toole (q.v.) as the Artful Dodger (from *Oliver Twist*) and Bob Cratchit (from *A Christmas Carol*); Mrs. Robert Keeley (q.v.) as Oliver Twist, Smike (from *Nicholas Nickleby*), Little Nell (from *The Old Curiosity Shop*), and Dot (from *The Cricket on the Hearth*); Joseph Jefferson (q.v.) as Newman Noggs (from *Nicholas Nickleby*) and Caleb Plummer (from *The Cricket on the Hearth*); George Fawcett Rowe and John Brougham (qq.v.) as Micawber (from *David Copperfield*, the latter in his own version of the book; Lotta (see CRABTREE) as Little Nell and the Marchioness (from *The Old Curiosity Shop*); Mme Céleste (q.v.) as Mme Defarge (from *A Tale of Two Cities*); Irving (q.v.) as Jingle (from *The Pickwick Papers*); Tree (q.v.) as Fagin (from *Oliver Twist*); Seymour Hicks (q.v.) as Scrooge (from *A Christmas Carol*) in a music-hall sketch based on the book; and, most famous of all, Sir John Martin-Harvey (q.v.) as Sidney Carton in *The Only Way*, a dramatization of *A Tale of Two Cities*. Bransby Williams (q.v.) had a whole gallery of Dickens characters, while Betsey Prig and Sairey Gamp (from *Martin Chuzzlewit*) were for a long time acted by men, the most popular exponent of the latter being John S. Clarke (q.v.). In the 1960s a new turn was given to adaptations of Dickens's novels (many of which have been serialized as radio and television plays) by the conversion of *Oliver Twist* and *The Pickwick Papers* into musicals, as *Oliver!* and *Pickwick*, and in 1969 there was a musical version of *A Tale of Two Cities* as *Two Cities*. In 1951 Emlyn Williams (q.v.) successfully re-created Dickens reading from his own novels, a solo performance which he repeated many times in Europe, America and South Africa.

DIDEROT, DENIS (1713–84), French man of letters, first editor of *L'Encyclopédie* (1751–77). His plays—*Le fils naturel* (pub. in 1757, perf. 1771) and *Le Père de famille* (pub. in 1758, perf. 1761)—form only a minor part of his literary work. Yet they are important, as is his *Paradoxe sur le comédien*, for they helped to spread new ideas and, through Lessing (q.v.), had a great influence on European drama of the nineteenth century. Diderot was an exponent of bourgeois drama, that offshoot of *comédie larmoyante* whose mixed sentiment, virtue, and sheer priggishness appealed so strongly to the middle-class audiences of the eighteenth century, and even during his lifetime his plays were translated into German, English, Dutch, and Italian. But the best of Diderot's work for the theatre must be looked for elsewhere: in his *Observations sur Garrick*, his *Dissertation sur le poème dramatique*, and his *Entretien avec Dorval*, in which he envisaged the actor as a member of a united company rather than a self-sufficient 'star', and was well in advance of his time in pleading for much closer collaboration between actor and dramatist.

Digby Cycle, see MYSTERY PLAY.

DIGGES, DUDLEY (1879–1947), Irish-American actor, who first appeared with the Irish National Players in 1901–3, and after the Abbey Players' second visit to London accepted an invitation to go to America, where he spent the rest of his life, becoming one of the outstanding actors of New York and a potent force in the theatre there. He began his American career in 1905 in the first production in New York of Shaw's *John Bull's Other Island*, and was later with Mrs. Fiske and George Arliss, acting as the latter's stage manager for seven years. He joined the company of the Theatre Guild (q.v.) in 1919, and remained with it until 1930, playing a wide variety of parts and directing some of the plays, notably Shaw's *Pygmalion* and *The Doctor's Dilemma*. He later produced an all-star revival of *Becky Sharp*, based on Thackeray's *Vanity Fair*, and in 1937 was seen as Franz Joseph in Maxwell Anderson's *The Masque of Kings*. His last part, and one of his finest, was Harry Hope in O'Neill's *The Iceman Cometh* (1946).

DIGGES, (JOHN) DUDLEY WEST (1720–86), English actor, who served his apprenticeship in Edinburgh, where he was the first to play Young Norval in Home's *Douglas* (1756). By a curious coincidence he played Old Norval in the same play in 1780 at the Haymarket, where he appeared between 1777 and 1781 as Macbeth, Lear, Shylock (in *The Merchant of Venice*), Wolsey (in *Henry VIII*), and Addison's Cato. He then went to Dublin and acted there till incapacitated by paralysis in 1784. In his prime he had a noble presence and a fine resonant voice.

DIONYSUS, a Greek nature-god associated with wine (Bacchus being the roughly equivalent Latin name), whose worship took many forms, the most remarkable being the revels in which his votaries, women in particular, withdrew for a time into the wild and experienced a mystical communion with nature (see Euripides' *Bacchae*). As a vegetation-spirit, who died and was reborn each year, he was associated both with rites designed to promote fertility and with mystery-religions which based their teaching on the problems of death, purgation, and rebirth.

In so dynamic a worship there are obvious contacts with every form of drama, and in fact Greek drama, whether tragic, satyric, or comic, was always strictly associated with the festivals of Dionysus. In Old Comedy (see ARISTOPHANES) the phallus (as a symbol of fertility) and the Dionysiac *comos* or revel (whence 'comedy', q.v.) are constant features. In satyr-drama (q.v.) direct Dionysiac influence is obvious, the satyrs (part human, part goat or horse) being attendants on Dionysus.

With tragedy (q.v.) the connection is less obvious. Dionysiac subjects are common, which is understandable in view of the dramatic nature of the Dionysus legend, but in no case is tragedy Dionysiac in spirit or content. The question remains obscure, but it is certain that the worship of Dionysus stimulated the lively dramatic sense of the Greeks and his festivals provided a congenial atmosphere in which diverse forms of drama could grow to maturity.

Director (on the Continent, *le régisseur*), the person responsible for the artistic interpretation of a play, and for rehearsals. He has no jurisdiction over the financial side, which is in the hands of the producer (q.v.), or manager. The director, who now seldom appears in the play which he is directing, has in the present century achieved a predominant position in the theatre, discharging on his own a function formerly assumed by the author, the chief actor, or the stage manager, who was often also the prompter. The first director in the modern sense was George Duke of Saxe-Meiningen (see MEININGER COMPANY). The first to advance to the position from that of stage manager was the American, David Belasco (q.v.). Many directors have achieved international fame (Stanislavsky, Reinhardt, Komisarjevsky, Guthrie, Brook, Zeffirelli (qq.v.)), many more are famous in their own countries. It has been said that the ideal director must be an actor, artist, architect, electrician, and an expert in geography, history, costume, accessories, and scenery, and have a wide knowledge and understanding of human nature—the last trait being the most essential.

Disguising, the word used in fifteenth- and early sixteenth-century England to designate any entertainment which involved play-acting or the wearing of masks. In about 1512 it was replaced by mask or masque (q.v.), and it was obsolete by 1544.

Dithyramb, a hymn in honour of Dionysus (q.v.), performed by a chorus of fifty and relating an incident in his life. The leader of the chorus later became a soloist (see PROTAGONIST), and in the ensuing dialogue between him and the rest of the chorus is believed to lie the origin of tragedy (q.v.).

DMITREVSKY, IVAN AFANASYEVICH (1733–1821), one of the first outstanding actors in Russia. He first appeared with Volkov (q.v.), and later joined the professional company founded by Sumarokov (q.v.). Between 1765 and 1768 he was twice sent abroad to complete his theatrical education, and spent most of the time in Paris with the leading French actors of the day. He was extremely gifted, and appeared with equal success in tragic and comic parts. His best performances were considered to be the title-roles in Molière's *Le Misanthrope* and Sumarokov's *Dmitri the Impostor*, and Starodum in *The Minor*, by Fonvizin. Among his pupils was Alexei Yakovlev (q.v.).

DMITRI OF ROSTOV, SAINT [really DANIEL TUPTALO] (1651–1709), Russian bishop, author of several religious plays in rhyming syllabic verse based on the medieval Mystery play (q.v.). They include *The Nativity Play*, *The Penitent Sinner*,

Esther and Ahasuerus, and *The Resurrection of Christ*. Biblical characters appear in them side by side with such allegorical figures as Jealousy, Hope, Despair, and Death, while humorous peasants, like Mak the sheep-stealer in *The Second Shepherd's Play* in the English Wakefield cycle, comment irreverently on the sacred action. It was in Dmitri's *Esther and Ahasuerus* that the great Russian actor Dmitrevsky (q.v.) made his first appearance before the Court in 1752.

DMITRIEV, VLADIMIR VLADIMIROVICH (1900–48), Soviet stage designer whose early death was much regretted, as he had prepared some superb designs for a production of Smetana's opera, 'The Bartered Bride', which he did not live to see. Only the year before, in 1947, he had designed a most evocative setting for Virta's *Our Daily Bread* at the Moscow Art Theatre, in which a quiet autumnal landscape formed a poignant contrast to the feverish activity within the house, seen through its lighted windows. Other important plays for which he designed the décor were Ostrovsky's *The Last Sacrifice* when it was revived at the Moscow Art Theatre in 1944, and Gorky's last plays, *Yegor Bulichev and Others* and *Dostigayev and Others*, produced at the Vakhtangov in 1932 and 1933.

DOBUJINSKY, MSTISLAV (1875–1957), Russian artist and stage designer, a member, with Benois and Bakst, of the group *Mir Iskusstva* (The World of Art), whose ideas were introduced to western Europe by Diaghilev (q.v.). Before leaving Russia he worked with Stanislavsky (q.v.) at the Moscow Art Theatre, and also with Meyerhold (q.v.), but his finest work, which showed an unusual combination of accuracy of atmosphere with profound imagination, was done for the ballet, and particularly for productions of 'Petrushka', 'Coppelia', 'The Nutcracker', and 'Swan Lake'.

Dock Street Theatre, see CHARLESTON.

Documentary Drama, see LIVING NEWSPAPER and THEATRE OF FACT.

DODD, JAMES WILLIAM (1734–96), English comedian, the last of the fops who began with Colley Cibber (q.v.). After playing in the provinces, he went to Drury Lane in 1765, and in 1777 created the parts of Lord Foppington and Sir Benjamin

Backbite in Sheridan's *A Trip to Scarborough* and *The School for Scandal* respectively. He was also the first to play Dangle in Sheridan's *The Critic* (1779). One of his finest parts was Aguecheek in *Twelfth Night*, in which Charles Lamb saw and admired him, but he was also good as Bob Acres (when Drury Lane revived Sheridan's *The Rivals*, first seen at Covent Garden), and as Tattle in Congreve's *Love for Love*.

DODSLEY, ROBERT (1703–64), an interesting figure in the literary world of eighteenth-century London. Having run away from home, he was working as a footman in London when his literary gifts attracted the attention of Pope and Defoe. Helped by them, and by the success of his first play, *The Toy Shop* (1735), he established himself as a bookseller and publisher at the sign of Tully's Head in Pall Mall, where he issued works by such authors as Pope and Dr. Johnson, and also published a *Select Collection of Old Plays*, later revised and edited by Hazlitt. His best-known play was *The King and the Miller of Mansfield* (1737), which, with its sequel, *Sir John Cockle at Court* (1738), was first given at Drury Lane and frequently revived. It provided the basis for Collé's *Partie de chasse d'Henri IV*, and is still obtainable in the repertory of the nineteenth-century Toy Theatre (q.v.). Dodsley's last play, *Cleone* (1758), was a tragedy which owed much of its success to the acting of George Anne Bellamy (q.v.) and was revived by Mrs. Siddons (q.v.) in 1786. He also wrote the libretto of a ballad opera, *The Blind Beggar of Bethnal Green* (1741).

Dog Drama, see CIRCUS.

DOGGETT, THOMAS (c. 1670–1721), English actor, a fine low comedian for whom Congreve (q.v.) wrote the parts of Fondlewife in *The Old Bachelor* (1693) and Ben in *Love for Love* (1695). In 1711 he became joint manager of Drury Lane with Colley Cibber (q.v.), who in his *Apology* has left an excellent pen-portrait of him, and Wilks (q.v.), retiring in disgust when Barton Booth (q.v.), whose politics Doggett disapproved of, was given a share in the patent. In 1714, in honour of the accession of George I, Doggett instituted the Doggett Coat and Badge for Thames watermen, a trophy which is still rowed for annually on 1 Aug. and plays an important part in the plot of *The Waterman* (1774), a ballad opera by Charles Dibdin (q.v.).

DOLCE, LODOVICO (1508–68), Italian dramatist who, like Macbeth, 'supped full with horrors'. One of the most successful of his tragedies was *Marianna* (1565), a retelling of the story of Herod and Mariamne which is, for its period, unusually subtle. His *Giocasta*, based on Euripides' *Phoenician Women*, was performed at Gray's Inn in 1566 as *Jocasta*, in an English translation by George Gascoigne (q.v.).

Dominion Theatre, LONDON, a large playhouse on the site of a famous brewery at the junction of Tottenham Court Road and Oxford Street. It opened on 3 Oct. 1929 with an American musical comedy, *Follow Through*, followed by another musical, *Silver Wings* (1930), based on a comedy of 1922 called *The Broken Wing*, by Paul Dickey and Charles Goddard. Other stage productions were a Christmas pantomime, *Aladdin* (1930), and a revival of Léhar's operetta, *The Land of Smiles* (1932), but films had already been shown in the intervals, and at the end of 1932 the building became a cinema.

DOMINIQUE, see BIANCOLELLI, G. D.

DON JUAN, a character derived from an old Spanish legend, who first took the stage in *El burlador de Sevilla y Convidado de piedra* (before 1630) by Tirso de Molina (q.v.) and has since become a constantly recurring figure in European literature. Tirso's play is in two parts: the first depicts Don Juan's character and activities, the second shows the result of his encounter with the marble statue, who by supernatural means punishes the villain for his many crimes. Don Juan is not portrayed merely as a sensual man but is the embodiment of self-will, unable to curb his desires although he knows they are evil. There is no lack of Catholic belief in him, as there is in the character portrayed by Molière (q.v.) in *Le Festin de pierre* (1665). He does not doubt that retribution will come, but he continually puts off repentance, hoping through God's mercy and long-suffering to remain immune as long as possible.

Among many other works on the same theme are Mozart's opera 'Don Giovanni', Byron's poem *Don Juan*, Goldoni's *El dissoluto*, a Russian version by Pushkin,

several works in Spanish, the best being *Don Juan Tenorio* by Zorrilla (q.v.), Rostand's *La dernière nuit de Don Juan*, *Don Juan, oder Die Liebe zur Geometrie* (1953), by Frisch (q.v.), and Ronald Duncan's *Don Juan* and *The Death of Satan* (both 1956). Don Juan also appears in the third act of *Man and Superman* (1905), by Bernard Shaw (q.v.), and in *Camino Real* (1953), by Tennessee Williams (q.v.).

DONAT, ROBERT (1905–58), English actor, who was with Benson (q.v.) for some time, and later played leading parts at the Festival Theatre, Cambridge, under Terence Gray (q.v.). Among his successes were Charles Cameron in Bridie's *A Sleeping Clergyman* (1933) and Captain Shotover in Shaw's *Heartbreak House* (1943). He was with the Old Vic in 1939, and again in 1953, when he played Becket in T. S. Eliot's *Murder in the Cathedral*, making his last appearance on the stage before the ill-health from which he had suffered for many years forced him to retire. His life was written in 1968 by J. C. Trewin.

DOONE, RUPERT (1904–66), see GROUP THEATRE (2).

Doors of Entrance, see PROSCENIUM DOORS.

DORIMOND [really NICHOLAS DROUIN] (*c.* 1628–*c.* 1670), a French provincial actor-manager, whose early career bears some resemblance to that of Molière (q.v.), though he never succeeded in establishing himself in Paris. With his wife, who after his death appeared at the Marais, he directed the Troupe of Mademoiselle, in which the son of Floridor (q.v.) also played for a short time. Dorimond was the author of nine plays, including one on the subject of Don Juan (q.v.), which were given by the above company, probably between 1657 and 1660, and his farces may have been seen by, and had some influence on, Molière, who no doubt encountered Dorimond's company on his wanderings.

Dorset Garden Theatre, LONDON (the second Duke's House). This playhouse, designed by Wren, was intended for Davenant (q.v.), who died before it was completed. It was then run by his widow, and later by his sons. It stood by the Thames, south of Salisbury Court, and had a flight of steps, known as Dorset

Stairs, down to the water for the benefit of those arriving by boat. On the front of the building was the coat of arms of the Duke of York, patron of the players, who were known as the Duke's Men. The interior was magnificently decorated, with a striking proscenium arch, shown in the illustrations to Settle's *Empress of Morocco*, which was acted there in 1673. The theatre opened on 9 Nov. 1671 with a revival of Dryden's *Sir Martin Mar-All*, and later gave the first performances of his *Mr. Limberham; or, the Kind Keeper* (1678) and *The Spanish Friar; or, the Double Discovery* (1680). Other authors whose plays were first produced at Dorset Garden were Mrs. Aphra Behn, D'Urfey, Etherege, and Ravenscroft (qq.v.), whose adaptation of Molière's *Le Bourgeois gentilhomme* as *Mamamouchi; or, the Citizen turned Gentleman* (1672) was one of the first new plays to be seen there. Opera, for which the theatre later became famous, began with Davenant's musical version of *Macbeth* (1673) and Shadwell's *The Tempest; or, the Enchanted Island* (1674). The latter's *Psyche* (1675), with music by Matthew Locke, was also very successful. Under the skilful direction of Betterton (q.v.), who lived in an apartment over the theatre and with Harris (q.v.) was the company's leading man, Dorset Garden flourished, and from 1672, when Drury Lane was burnt down, to 1674, when it reopened, was the only theatre in London. In 1682, owing to financial losses at both theatres, the companies amalgamated, making Drury Lane their headquarters, but still with Betterton, displacing Charles Hart and Michael Mohun (qq.v.) of the Drury Lane company, as their leading man. After the union Dorset Garden was used mainly for opera. In 1689 it was renamed the Queen's Theatre, as a compliment to Queen Mary II, but it gradually declined, being used finally for acrobatic and wild beast shows. The last mention of it dates from 1706.

DORVAL (*née* DELAUNAY), MARIE-THOMASE-AMÉLIE (1798–1849), French actress, who made her first success as Amélie in the melodrama *Trente Ans, ou la Vie d'un joueur* (1827), playing opposite Frédérick (q.v.). On 21 Apr. 1835 she made her first appearance at the Comédie-Française, giving a performance as Kitty Bell in Alfred de Vigny's *Chatterton* which long remained in the memory of those who saw it. She later appeared in Hugo's *Angélo* (1835), and might have remained at the Comédie-Française until her retirement, but she found the restrictions irksome and the jealousy of Mlle Mars (q.v.) insupportable. She therefore returned to the popular theatres, where she again appeared with Frédérick. In 1842 she played Racine's Phèdre at the Odéon with marked success, but her health failed after a gruelling provincial tour and she returned to Paris to die in poverty.

DORVIGNY [really LOUIS-FRANÇOIS ARCHAMBAULT] (1742–1812), French actor and dramatist, a reputed son of Louis XV, whom he certainly resembled in looks. Though idle and dissipated, he wrote with immense facility, and turned out some three hundred light comedies and farces, many of them never printed. Most of them were produced at the Foire Saint-Laurent (see FAIRS) in the 1770s, and Dorvigny's comic characters, Janot and Jocrisse, delighted uncritical audiences for years. The Comédie-Française, hoping to profit by his success, finally staged two of his plays but the academic atmosphere stifled them and they failed. The life of Dorvigny, a bohemian and a wit, usually penniless and often inebriated, was written by Charles Monselet.

DOSTOIEVSKY, FEODOR MIKHAILOVICH (1821–81), distinguished Russian novelist, several of whose novels have been dramatized, notably *The Idiot* and *The Brothers Karamazov*. These were produced in Russia before 1917 and have been revived since. *The Insulted and Injured* (also known in English as *The Despised and Rejected*) was adapted for the Moscow Art Theatre by V. A. Solovyov, and in 1946 an adaptation of *Crime and Punishment*, by Rodney Ackland, was given with some success in London, John Gielgud (q.v.) playing Raskolnikoff. *The Idiot*, in an adaptation by Simon Gray, was seen at the Old Vic in 1970 in a production by the National Theatre company directed by Anthony Quayle.

DOTRICE, ROY (1923–   ), English actor, who became interested in the theatre while a prisoner of war in Germany in the Second World War. He made his first appearance in 1945 in revue, and then spent some twelve years in repertory companies, laying the foundations of a career which flowered during his years with the Royal Shakespeare Company, where he played, among other parts, Father Ambrose in Whiting's *The Devils* (1961), Simon Chachava in Brecht's *The Caucasian Chalk Circle* (1962), Caliban in *The Tempest* (1963), and Shallow in *Henry IV, Part 2* (1964). He also played the title-role in Brecht's *Puntila* (1965) and John Morley in Paddy Chayefsky's *The Latent Heterosexual* (1968). In 1969 he created something of a sensation with his solo performance as John Aubrey in *Brief Lives*. First seen for a short run in 1967 at the Hampstead Theatre Club and then on Broadway, this was an admirable re-creation of the malicious seventeenth-century diarist and his age, drawn from his own writings and played throughout in an evocative set—a dim, cluttered room which gave point and poignancy to the old man's rambling reminiscences. In 1970 Dotrice was seen at Chichester as Ibsen's Peer Gynt.

Double Masque, see MASQUE.

DOUGLASS, DAVID (?–1786), the first American actor-manager, who in 1758 met and married the widow of the elder Hallam (q.v.) in Jamaica. Amalgamating her actors and his own, he named them the American Company and took them back to New York, where he built a theatre on Cruger's Wharf (q.v.), another in Beekman Street (see CHAPEL STREET THEATRE), and a third in John Street (q.v.). He was also responsible for the erection of the first permanent theatre in the United States, the Southwark (q.v.) in Phila-delphia, which opened in 1766, in spite of opposition from the Puritan element in the town. It was under Douglass's manage-ment that the American Company did Godfrey's *The Prince of Parthia* (1767), the first American tragedy to be profes-sionally produced, and that John Henry (q.v.) later to succeed Douglass as mana-ger, first joined the company in New York.

DOWNES, JOHN (*fl.* 1662–1710), author of *Roscius Anglicanus* (1708), a volume of scattered theatrical notes which is one of the rare sources of information on the early Restoration theatre. Downes wanted to be an actor, but his first appearance in Davenant's *The Siege of Rhodes* in 1661 was such a fiasco that he gave up, and worked back-stage as prompter and book-keeper, in which capacity he took charge of the playscripts, copied the actors' parts, and

attended all rehearsals and performances. *Roscius Anglicanus* was reprinted in 1886 in an edition by Joseph Knight, and in 1930 in a new edition by Montague Summers.

Down Stage (the acting area nearest the audience), see STAGE DIRECTIONS.

DOWTON, WILLIAM (1764–1851), Eng-lish actor, who in 1791 joined the travel-ling company of Sarah Baker (q.v.) and soon became her leading man, marrying her daughter SALLY (1768–1817) in 1794. Two years later he was seen by Sheridan and engaged for Drury Lane, where he was soon recognized as an outstanding player of such elderly characters as Sir Anthony Absolute in Sheridan's *The Rivals*, Old Hardcastle in Goldsmith's *She Stoops to Conquer*, and Old Dornton in Holcroft's *The Road to Ruin*. He was also much admired as Falstaff. He had two sons who went on the stage—HENRY (?–1827) and WILLIAM PATON (1797–1883). The latter took over the management of Mrs. Baker's company from his father and in 1832 joined him at Drury Lane.

D'OYLY CARTE, RICHARD (1844–1901), theatrical impresario, who encouraged the early collaboration of Gilbert and Sullivan and with the proceeds built the Savoy Theatre (q.v.), the first in London to be lighted by electricity. It opened with *Patience*, transferred from the Opera Comique (q.v.). D'Oyly Carte also built the Royal English Opera House, Cam-bridge Circus (now the Palace Theatre, q.v.), in an endeavour to encourage the writing and production of English light opera. He did much to raise the musical taste of his generation, gave employment to young singers, and founded the com-pany for the production of the works of Gilbert and Sullivan which still bears his name.

Drag, the English term for Female Impersonation (q.v.) (see also LA RUE, DANNY).

DRAKE, SAMUEL (1772–1847), English actor, who in 1810 went to America to become a pioneer of the theatre there. In 1815, with a company composed of his family and a few outsiders, including Noah Miller Ludlow (q.v.), he set out from Albany, N.Y., for Pittsburgh, acting wherever he could find a suitable building and an audience. He then undertook a hazardous journey into Kentucky, where he established the theatre on a firm basis, with centres in Frankfort, Lexington, and Louisville. He also visited Missouri in 1820, and Cincinnati, where in 1826 his son Alex and daughter-in-law, the former FRANCES ANN DENNY (1798–1875), later the undisputed tragedy queen of the West, took over until Alex's death in 1830. Sam's grand-daughter, Julia Dean (q.v.), was also on the stage.

Drama. (1) A term applied loosely to the whole body of work written for the theatre, as English drama, French drama, or to a group of plays related by their style or content, as Restoration drama, realistic drama. (2) A term applicable to any situation in which there is conflict and, for theatrical purposes, resolution of that conflict with the assumption of character. This implies the co-operation of at least two actors, or, as in early Greek drama, a protagonist and a chorus, and rules out narrative and monologue. The dramatic instinct is inherent in man, and the most rudimentary dialogue with song and dance may be classed as drama. In a narrower sense the word is applied to plays of high emotional content, which at their best may be literary masterpieces and at their worst degenerate into melodrama. The term dramatist is not necessarily restricted to a writer of such dramas, but serves, like playwright, to designate anyone writing for the theatre.

Dramatic Censorship. In all countries there has from earliest times been some form of censorship of dramatic works, usually from the political angle, though many forays against theatrical performances were made in the cause of morality or public order and decency. In Great Britain the wide powers of supervision and control over the stage which were vested in the Lord Chamberlain, until they were abolished by the Theatres Act, 1968, derived originally from the function of a minor official in the Royal Household, the Master of the Revels (q.v.), first appointed in the reign of Henry VII. When the work of suppressing heresy or sedition in the drama became too heavy for him, it was taken over by his superior officer, who for over two centuries concerned himself almost exclusively with political and religious issues arising from play texts, and paid attention to the moral aspect of the theatre only to the extent of prohibiting riotous or immoral behaviour at dramatic performances. The first Act of Parliament directly concerned with control over the stage was passed under James I and reinforced by the Act of 1713 under which 'common players of Interludes' were classed as 'rogues and vagabonds' and punished as such in accordance with the provision of various earlier statutes. It was not until the passing of the Licensing Act of 1737 that the dual role played by the Lord Chamberlain in the theatre was clearly defined. He was the issuer of licences for theatres, halls, and other places of entertainment, with the exception of Covent Garden and Drury Lane (qq.v.), and also of licences permitting the performance of new plays which had been read and approved of by his official readers. His authority under both headings was consolidated by the Theatres Act of 1843. The regulations then laid down for buildings to which theatrical licences might be granted are still in force. It is only the Lord Chamberlain's right of censorship over the text of a new play which was abolished in 1968 by the Theatres Act of that year. Previously a play or other entertainment which had obtained the Lord Chamberlain's licence —many times withheld in respect of plays which are now part of our dramatic heritage—could be staged virtually without fear of prosecution. Now there is no pre-production censorship and proceedings can only be begun *after* production. Obscenity under the Theatres Act is based on the definition in the Obscene Publications Act of 1959. In the United States, where no office corresponding to that of the Lord Chamberlain and no separate legislation in regard to the theatre has ever existed, information can be (and often has been) lodged with the police after the production of a play deemed immoral or obscene, and the actors have been arrested on stage and taken into custody to be tried under the Federal and State laws dealing with literary works as a whole.

Dramatic Copyright, see COPYRIGHT IN A DRAMATIC WORK.

Drame, the name given by Diderot (q.v.) to eighteenth-century plays which dealt with the domestic problems of daily life. Early examples can be found in the *comédies larmoyantes* of Nivelle de la Chaussée (q.v.). They differed from the earlier *tragédies-bourgeoises* (which include some of Voltaire's plays) in that they were serious rather than tragic and usually ended happily, or at least peacefully, with a reconciliation after repentance for past errors. Typical of the *drame bourgeois* were the plays of Diderot himself, and those of Louis Sébastien Mercier (q.v.).

DRAPER, RUTH (1884–1956), American actress who achieved world-wide fame as a speaker of dramatic monologues which she wrote herself. She first employed her gift for mimicry in short sketches destined for performance at private parties and charity performances, and it was not until 1920, at the age of thirty-six, that she made her first professional appearance at the Aeolian Hall, London, on 29 Jan. She quickly established herself as an international figure and for the rest of her life toured continuously, elaborating and adding to her repertory but never changing the basic formula—a bare stage, a minimum of props, and herself as one person responding to invisible companions (as in 'Opening a Bazaar' or 'Showing the Garden') or as several people in succession (as in 'Three Generations', 'Mr. Clifford and Three Women', or 'An English House Party'). Her career was a long series of triumphs on the Continent, in New York, where she often remained in the same theatre for four or five months, and in England. She was seen for the last time in London at the St. James's Theatre in July 1956, and died in her sleep on 29–30 Dec. of that year, after appearing at the New York Playhouse. The basic texts of some of her best-known monologues were included in *The Art of Ruth Draper* (1960), by M. D. Zabel, but they are *aides-mémoire* only, since she varied her dialogue at every performance.

DREW, JOHN (1853–1927), American actor, son of Mrs. John Drew (q.v.), under whom he made his first appearance in Philadelphia. In 1875 he was engaged by Augustin Daly (q.v.) to play opposite Ada Rehan (q.v.). He was seen in London several times in the 1880s, being much admired for his Petruchio in *The Taming of the Shrew*. In 1892 he appeared under the management of the Frohmans in many modern comedies, often with Maude Adams (q.v.), making frequent visits to the larger cities of the United States. One of his finest performances in later life was as Major Pendennis in a dramatization of Thackeray's novel, produced in 1916, and he was last seen in a tour of Pinero's *Trelawny of the 'Wells'*. In 1903 he presented the library of the theatre historian and bibliographer Robert W. Lowe, which he had acquired, to Harvard (q.v.), thus inaugurating the fine theatre collection there. He was the author of *My Years on the Stage* (1922).

DREW, MRS. JOHN [*née* LOUISA LANE] (1820–97), American actress and theatre manager, daughter of English actors who could trace their theatrical ancestry back to Elizabethan days. She was on the stage in London as a small child, and in 1827 went with her widowed mother to New York, where she appeared as five characters in one play, in the style of Clara Fisher (q.v.), with much success and also played such juvenile parts as the Duke of York (in *Richard III*) and the son of William Tell in Sheridan Knowles's play of that name. She spent practically the whole of her long life on the stage, and from 1860 to 1892 managed the stock company at the Arch Street Theatre, Philadelphia, which flourished under her firm rule. From 1880 to 1892 she toured constantly as Mrs. Malaprop (in Sheridan's *The Rivals*), one of her best parts, with Joseph Jefferson (q.v.) as Bob Acres. A woman of strong, almost masculine, personality, she had already had two husbands before in 1850 she married JOHN DREW (1827–62), an Irish actor who in his brief career was considered an excellent portrayer of Irish and eccentric characters. Two of their children were on the stage, John (q.v.) and Georgiana, who married Maurice Barrymore (q.v.). The majestic personality of Mrs. John Drew and the eccentricities of her famous Barrymore grandchildren, as well as their unpredictable tempers, formed the subject of *The Royal Family* (1927), a play by Edna Ferber and George S. Kaufman, produced in London in 1934 as *Theatre Royal* with Marie Tempest (q.v.) as the formidable matriarch and Laurence Olivier (q.v.) as her youngest son.

DRINKWATER, JOHN (1882–1937), English poet and dramatist, who was for some years actor and general manager at the Birmingham Repertory Theatre (q.v.). The most successful of his early plays in verse was $X = O$, an episode of the Trojan War. But it was in his prose play,

Abraham Lincoln, first produced in Birmingham, that he did his finest work. Transferred to the Lyric, Hammersmith, in 1919 under the management of Nigel Playfair, it ran for a year, and has been frequently revived. It was also well received in New York. Later, but less successful, chronicle plays were *Mary Stuart* (1922), *Oliver Cromwell* and *Robert E. Lee* (both 1923). In 1927 his comedy, *Bird in Hand*, opened the season at the Birmingham Repertory Theatre and later had a long run in London.

Droll, the name given to a short comic sketch, usually a scene taken from a longer play. It originated in London during the Puritan interregnum (1642–60), when the actors, deprived of the right to act, of scenery, of costumes, and often of their playhouses, nevertheless managed to give a certain amount of entertainment. For their illicit purposes long plays were useless, so they invented the 'droll'—the term is short for Droll Humours or Drolleries—rounding it off with dancing in the manner of the Jig (q.v.). Some of the most famous drolls are taken from Shakespeare—'Bottom the Weaver' from *A Midsummer Night's Dream* and 'The Grave-makers' from *Hamlet*. Others were from biblical sources. The best-known player of drolls was Robert Cox (q.v.). Droll was also the name applied to early puppet shows, and was given to collections of humorous or satiric verse, not dramatic, as in 'Westminster Drolleries' (1672). It was sometimes used to designate actors, particularly players of humorous parts, and men of quick wit and good company. Pepys uses it in this sense of Killigrew (q.v.), and in the late nineteenth century it was applied to such comediennes as LOUIE FREEAR (1871–1939), who was equally successful in minstrel shows, music-halls, musical comedy, and Shakespeare.

Drop, originally an unframed canvas backcloth, first used about 1690, which offered a plain surface for painting, free from the central join which marked the alternative 'pair of flats'. The early method of handling it was to roll it on a bottom roller which ascended by means of lines, furling up the cloth as it rose. Records show that swords, cloaks, or dress hems frequently got caught up in the ascending roller, to the detriment of dramatic dignity. An alternative method

was by 'tumbling'. A batten was fixed across the back of the cloth, a third of the way up, and it was taken away in bights, with a loose roller, or 'tumbler', inside the bight to weight the cloth and keep the bend straight.

As it is not possible to have a door or practicable window in an unframed cloth, today such a cloth is often provided with battens at the back to which doors and windows can be fixed, thus making it, in effect, a single flat which can be flown like an ordinary cloth. The lack of height above the stage made this impracticable in the early theatre.

Drottningholm Theatre and Museum, SWEDEN, part of a royal palace on an island near Stockholm, built in 1766. Until 1771 it was used by a French company resident in Stockholm, and in the summer by courtiers for amateur productions, becoming, with the palace, State property in 1777. It had its most brilliant period during the reign of Gustaf III (1772–92), when a Frenchman, Louis-Jean Desprez, designed scenery and costumes for it. In the nineteenth century it fell into disuse, but its employment as a lumber-room saved it from demolition or modernization, and in 1921 it was restored under Dr. Agne Beijer, the only alteration being the substitution of electric light for the former wax candles. The stage is about 57 feet deep and 27 feet wide at the footlights. The eighteenth-century stage machinery on the Carriage-and-Frame system (q.v.) is still in working order, and there are more than thirty sets of usable scenery of the same period. The theatre is now used for occasional summer seasons of early opera. The museum exhibits, which include a rich deposit of seventeenth- and eighteenth-century French stage designs, are housed in the former royal apartments.

Drum-and-Shaft, an early system of moving scenery (known also as the BARREL SYSTEM) by which a rope controlling a piece of scenery was attached to a cylindrical shaft which could be turned by a lever. Alternatively, a circular drum, of a diameter greater than that of the shaft, could be built round part of it and the shaft rotated by pulling on a line wound round the drum.

Where a number of pieces have to be moved simultaneously the drum-and-shaft system has many advantages, as it can be varied by the use of drums of different diameters used on the same shaft, with separate pieces of scenery attached to the different drums. The individual pieces then move at various speeds, as in a cloud effect, where a number of clustered cloud-pieces are required to expand into a great aureole. But the system has now been abandoned, and all pieces of flown scenery are worked independently.

Druriolanus, AUGUSTUS, see HARRIS, SIR AUGUSTUS.

Drury Lane, London's most famous theatre and the oldest still in use. The first theatre on the site, built by Killigrew under a Charter granted by Charles II in 1662 (see PATENT THEATRES), opened on 7 May 1663 as the Theatre Royal, Bridges Street, with a revival of *The Humorous Lieutenant*, by Fletcher (q.v.). On the night of 25 June 1672 it was destroyed by fire, with the loss of the entire wardrobe and stock of scenery. Killigrew then took his company to the Lincoln's Inn Fields Theatre (q.v.) while the new Drury Lane, designed by Sir Christopher Wren, was being built. It opened, again with a play by Fletcher, possibly in collaboration with Middleton (q.v.), *The Beggar's Bush*, on 26 Mar. 1674. With Dryden (q.v.) as its playwright, it prospered for a while, but suffered from the popularity of Dorset Garden (q.v.) and in 1676 was forced to close. By 1682 London could support only one theatre, so a combined company under Betterton (q.v.) occupied Drury Lane until the ill-treatment of the actors by the Patent holder, Christopher Rich (q.v.), led some of them to go with Betterton to Lincoln's Inn Fields. In 1709 Rich lost his Patent, and the theatre closed (for a mock inventory of the sale that then took place, see *The Tatler*, No. 42). A triumvirate composed of Cibber, Wilks, and Doggett (qq.v.) then took over and with Anne Oldfield (q.v.) as their leading lady, inaugurated in 1711 an era of prosperity which lasted until Charles Fleetwood, a gambler who had acquired the whole of the Patent, ran the theatre into debt. A bad period followed, the one noteworthy production being a revival on 14 Feb. 1741 of *The Merchant of Venice* with the tragedian Macklin (q.v.) as Shylock, a part played for many years by the low comedian. It was under Fleetwood that a riot took place on 5 May 1737, caused by the abolition of the

custom of allowing free admission to the gallery for footmen attending their masters (see FOOTMEN'S GALLERY), and it was from the Royal Box at Drury Lane that the news of the defeat of Prince Charles Edward at Culloden on 16 Apr. 1746 was first made known to the public. On 11 May 1742 Garrick (q.v.) made his first appearance at Drury Lane, as Chaumont in Otway's *The Orphan*, and was then seen as Lear and Richard III. Five years later he took over the management, engaged a good company, instituted a number of reforms which included regular rehearsals and the removal of spectators from the stage, and for the next thirty years made the theatre prosperous. In 1775 it was extensively altered and redecorated by the Adam brothers. In 1776 Garrick retired and was succeeded by Sheridan (q.v.), whose first outstanding production was his own comedy, *The School for Scandal*, on 8 May 1777. The theatre was damaged in the Gordon Riots of 1780, and a company of Guards was thereafter posted nightly to protect it, a custom which was not abolished until 1896. On 10 Oct. 1782 Mrs. Siddons (q.v.) made a triumphant appearance in Southerne's *Isabella; or, the Fatal Marriage*, and a year later was joined by her brother, John Philip Kemble (q.v.), who played Hamlet on 30 Sept. In 1788 Sheridan, who was busy with politics, handed over the active management of the theatre to Kemble.

In 1791 the theatre closed, to be rebuilt to a design by Holland. It opened again on 12 Mar. 1794 with a concert. Plays began on 21 Apr. with Kemble and Mrs. Siddons in *Macbeth*. During the epilogue an iron safety curtain (q.v.) was lowered to prove that the theatre was protected against fire. Fifteen years later, on 24 Feb. 1809, it was burnt down. Meanwhile, there had been an attempted assassination of George III in the theatre in 1800, Sheridan had so mismanaged affairs that Kemble had left for Covent Garden in 1802, taking his sister with him, and melodrama and spectacle had brought real elephants and performing dogs on the stage.

After the fire there were no funds available for rebuilding until the brewer, Samuel Whitbread, a sharer with Sheridan in the Patent, raised £400,000. On 10 Oct. 1812 a new theatre, designed by Wyatt, open with *Hamlet*. Two years later, on 26 Jan. 1814, Edmund Kean (q.v.) made his first appearance, playing Shylock. But even his success could not keep pace with rising costs, and after a long series of disasters, and a very few successes, the unhappy story ended with the withdrawal in 1878 of the manager, F. B. Chatterton, who from sad experience laid it down that 'Shakespeare spells ruin, and Byron bankruptcy'.

The theatre remained closed until on 1 Nov. 1879 Augustus Harris (q.v.) opened it with a revival of *Henry V*, and made a success with spectacular, realistic melo-dramas and an annual pantomime of great splendour in which Dan Leno—who first appeared at the Lane in 1889—and Herbert Campbell (qq.v.) played together for many years. On the death of Harris, Arthur Collins took over. Among the highlights of his management were Irving's last London season, Ellen Terry's Jubilee (both 1905), Forbes-Robertson's farewell performance (1913), and the Shakespeare Tercentenary performance in 1916 of *Julius Caesar*, after which Frank Benson (q.v.) was knighted by George V in the Royal Box with a property sword. Collins retired in 1923. After a run of successful musical shows, including *Rose Marie* (1925) and *The Land of Smiles* (1931), came Coward's *Cavalcade* (also 1931) and the long series of musical plays by Ivor Novello (q.v.) who, understanding the needs of the great house, wrote, composed, and acted in a series of successful plays with music—*Glamorous Night* (1935), *Careless Rapture* (1936), *Crest of the Wave* (1937), and *The Dancing Years* (1939), which was still running when the theatre closed on the outbreak of war in 1939. A few days later it became the headquarters of E.N.S.A. (q.v.), and in spite of being bombed in 1940 continued to be used. After the war it again became a theatre, and housed a number of American musicals, beginning with *Oklahoma!* in 1947, followed by *Carousel* (1950), *South Pacific* (1951), *The King and I* (1953), *My Fair Lady* (1958), *The Boys from Syracuse* (1963) (first produced in New York in 1938), which had only a short run, *Camelot* (1964), *Hello Dolly!* (1965), and *The Great Waltz* (1970).

Little Drury Lane was the name given by Elliston to the Olympic Theatre (q.v.) in 1813.

DRUTEN, JOHN VAN, see VAN DRUTEN.

DRYDEN, JOHN (1631–1700), English critic, poet, and satirist, and a prolific dramatist, whose most characteristic work was done in the field of heroic drama (q.v.) with *The Indian Queen* (1664), written in collaboration with his brother-in-law, Sir Robert Howard, its sequel, *The Indian Emperor* (1665), *Tyrannic Love* (1669), and the vast two-part *Almanzor and Almahide* (1670/1), usually called, from its subtitle, *The Conquest of Granada*. This contains all the elements, good and bad, of heroic drama—rant, bombast, poetry, vigour, battles, murder, and violent action. It was satirized unmercifully by Buckingham (q.v.) in *The Rehearsal* (1671), and the genre, which was alien to the English dramatic genius, soon died a natural death. Dryden's last plays in this style were *Amboyna* (1673) and *Aureng-Zebe* (1675), and from the restraints of the rhymed couplet he then turned to blank verse for the play usually considered his masterpiece—*All for Love* (1677), which takes its plot from Shakespeare's *Antony and Cleopatra* but is otherwise all Dryden's. It contains some fine poetry and is well constructed, observing more strictly than any other English tragedy the three unities (q.v.). Critics have called it 'the happiest result of French influence on English tragedy'. It also provides excellent parts for the chief actors, and has been frequently revived. Among Dryden's other plays, the best are the tragi-comedies *The Rival Ladies* (1664), from the Spanish, and *Secret Love; or, the Maiden Queen* (1667), from the French, in which the part of Florimel was played by Nell Gwynn (q.v.), and the comedies *Sir Martin Mar-All; or, the Feigned Innocence* (1667) and *Marriage à-la-Mode* (1671). He also wrote numerous prologues and epilogues for his own and other plays, which provide a good deal of information on the theatre of his time, and made new versions of Shakespeare's *Troilus and Cressida* (1679) and Plautus' *Amphitryon* (1690).

DU CROISY [really PHILIBERT GASSOT] (1626–95), French actor, who joined the company of Molière (q.v.) at the Petit-Bourbon in 1659, and was the first to play Tartuffe, both in 1667 when the character was called Panulphe and under its present name in 1669. After Molière's death he remained with the company, retiring in 1689. He had two daughters, both actresses, of whom one married Paul Poisson (q.v.) and in her old age wrote articles on Molière and his company for the *Mercure de France* (1738).

DU MAURIER, Sir Gerald Hubert
Edward (1873–1934), English actor-
manager, who in 1895 appeared under
Tree at the Haymarket, playing a small
part in the dramatization of *Trilby*, a
novel by his father George du Maurier
(1834–96). Gerald first came into prominence at the Duke of York's Theatre
under Charles Frohman (q.v.), where he
appeared in Barrie's *The Admirable
Crichton* (1902) with Muriel Beaumont
(1881–1957), whom he married shortly
afterwards. He was also the first to play
Mr. Darling and Captain Hook in
Barrie's *Peter Pan* (1904). His greatest
success, however, came at the Comedy in
1906 with E. W. Hornung's *Raffles*,
Arsène Lupin (1909), from the French of
F. de Croisset, and *Alias Jimmie Valentine*
(1910), by Paul Armstrong. He then
joined Frank Curzon in management at
Wyndham's Theatre (q.v.), and appeared
there in a series of successful light
comedies. His range of parts was limited;
but within those limits he was seldom
excelled, and he could on occasion step
beyond them, as was proved by his portrayal of Will Dearth in Barrie's *Dear
Brutus* in 1917. A more typical part, and
one which brought him solid success, was
'Sapper's' *Bulldog Drummond* in 1921.
A year later he was knighted for his
services to the theatre. His last outstanding performances were in Lonsdale's *The
Last of Mrs. Cheyney* (1925) and Pertwee's
Interference (1927) at the St. James's
Theatre. His life, *Gerald, a Portrait* (1934),
was written by his daughter Daphne
du Maurier (1907–89), novelist and
author of the plays *Rebecca* (1940), *The
Years Between* (1945), and *September
Tide* (1949).

DU PARC, Mlle [*née* Marquise-Thérèse
de Gorla] (1633–68), French actress, wife
of the actor Gros-René [really René
Berthelot] (*c.* 1630–64). They were both
members of the company headed by
Molière (q.v.), the husband being a good
comedian overshadowed by the excellence
of his wife. A woman of great beauty and
majestic presence, she was better in
tragedy than in comedy, and probably for
this reason left Molière in 1666 to join the
company at the Hôtel de Bourgogne,
where she played the title-role in Racine's
Andromaque (1667). She died suddenly,
and Racine, whose mistress she had been,
was later accused of having poisoned her
to make way for Mlle Champmeslé (q.v.).

Dublin. The first theatre in Dublin was
built in 1635. It closed in 1642, under the
Commonwealth, and was replaced at the
Restoration by the Smock Alley, known
also as the Orange Street Theatre. This
was used mainly for plays imported from
London with guest stars, and for an
indigenous theatre Ireland had to wait
until the end of the nineteenth century and
the Irish Literary Movement. The Smock
Alley Theatre was at its best from about
1730 to 1760, particularly during the ten-
year tenancy of Thomas Sheridan, father
of the dramatist (q.v.) and himself a good
actor. It then declined and was finally
converted into a corn store. Almost its
only rival was the Crow Street Theatre,
which opened in 1758 under Spranger
Barry (q.v.) and flourished until Harris,
an actor from Covent Garden, opened
the Theatre Royal in 1819. The Crow
Street Theatre then closed and was pulled
down in the early 1830s. The Theatre
Royal perished by fire in 1880, and a
much larger theatre of the same name
replaced it. This is now a cinema. It
housed touring companies from England
in spectacular drama, as did the Queen's
Theatre in Brunswick Square, where
several Irish plays by Boucicault (q.v.)
were seen. The Gaiety, a smaller, more
intimate playhouse, was used by the Irish
Literary Theatre group from 1900 until
the opening of the Abbey Theatre (q.v.).
Intended as a theatre of poetry and symbolism, the Abbey Theatre quickly turned
to realism, and it was not until 1942, with
the founding by Austin Clarke of the
Lyric Theatre, that pure poetic drama
returned to the Dublin stage, though some
excellent poetic dramas were produced in
the intervening years at the Dublin Gate
Theatre. Founded in 1928 by Hilton
Edwards and Micheál MacLiammóir
(qq.v.), this was intended to complement
the work of the Abbey by producing
mainly plays from abroad—Goethe,
Ibsen, Chekhov, O'Neill, Elmer Rice, and
many others—though some Irish dramatists, notably Denis Johnston (q.v.), found
the atmosphere of the Gate more congenial
than that of the Abbey. The Gate Theatre's
first productions were given at the small
Peacock Theatre adjoining the Abbey, but
in 1929 the company moved to the
Rotunda (renamed The Gate) and soon
achieved a solid reputation, consolidated
by European tours. In 1936 a company
run by Lord Longford (q.v.) and his wife
Cihrstine took over the Gate for six

months in the year, alternating with the earlier company and touring during the other six months. The arrangement worked well until 1956, when the theatre, which had become a fire risk, had to be closed for reconstruction. After it reopened it was used only intermittently and had again to be closed in 1970 on account of dry rot, but it opened once more, after further repairs, in 1971.

Another Dublin theatre of some importance was the Pike, founded in the 1950s by Alan Simpson and his wife, Carolyn Swift, in a converted Georgian mews, where in 1954 Beckett's *Waiting for Godot* had its first production in English and Brendan Behan's *The Quare Fellow* its world première. In 1957, the year in which the Dublin Festival was founded, Simpson was arrested for staging the European première of Tennessee Williams's *The Rose Tattoo*. This led to the temporary abandonment of the Dublin Festival, but it was revived in 1959 and has since been held annually with great success and an increasing preponderance of good Irish plays.

Dublin Roscius, see BROOKE, G.V.

Duchess Theatre, LONDON, in Catherine Street, a small theatre which opened on 25 Nov. 1929, and later housed some early productions by the People's National Theatre company under Nancy Price (q.v.). In 1934 J. B. Priestley (q.v.), whose *Laburnum Grove* had had a successful run at the theatre the previous year, took it over and produced there his own plays, *Eden End* and *Cornelius*. In 1935 Emlyn Williams (q.v.) appeared in his own thriller, *Night Must Fall*, which ran for a year and was followed by the first West End appearance of T. S. Eliot's *Murder in the Cathedral*. Another Priestley play which had a long run was *Time and the Conways* (1937). In 1938 Emlyn Williams returned in *The Corn is Green*, which was still running when the theatre closed on the outbreak of war in Sept. 1939. It reopened shortly afterwards, but closed again until 1942, when Coward's *Blithe Spirit*, first produced at the Piccadilly (q.v.), had a long run. Successful productions since then have included Priestley's *The Linden Tree* (1947), Rattigan's *The Deep Blue Sea* (1952), and three plays transferred from other theatres, Pinter's *The Caretaker* from the Arts in 1960, Bill

Naughton's *Alfie* from the Mermaid in 1963, and Beverley Cross's *Boeing-Boeing* (based on a play by Marc Camoletti) from the Apollo in 1965.

DUCIS, JEAN-FRANÇOIS (1733–1816), French dramatist, best known as the first adapter for the French stage of the plays of Shakespeare, which he probably read in the deplorable translations of Le Tourneur and Laplace, since there is no proof that he himself knew English. His adaptations were often so drastic that nothing remained of the original but the title, but Ducis well understood the temper of the time, and knew that audiences at the Comédie-Française would accept Shakespeare only with modifications. *Hamlet* (1769), in which Molé (q.v.) appeared in the title-role, was followed by *Romeo and Juliet*, *King Lear*, *Macbeth*, *King John*, and *Othello*. This last, given in 1792, owed much of its success to the fine acting of Talma (q.v.). When we remember that none of Ducis's own plays has survived, it is interesting to note that in connection with his adaptation of *King John* a contemporary critic deplored his wasting his undoubted talents on such rubbish. Ducis became a member of the French Academy in succession to Voltaire (q.v.), and after the failure of his last play in 1801 retired to live quietly at Versailles, where he died.

DUFF, MRS. [*née* MARY ANN DYKE] (1794–1857), American actress, born in London. With her sister Elizabeth, later the wife of the Irish poet and composer Tom Moore, she appeared in Dublin, and then married William Murray of the Theatre Royal, Edinburgh, brother-in-law of Mrs. Siddons's son Henry. He died almost immediately, and she remarried, her second husband being an Irish actor, JOHN DUFF (1787–1831), with whom she went to America. She made a great reputation in Boston and Philadelphia, but was never wholly accepted by audiences in New York, where she made her first appearance in 1823 as Hermione in Philips's *The Distrest Mother* to the Orestes of the elder Booth (q.v.). She had no gift for comedy, and was at her best in tragic or pathetic parts. The early death of her second husband left her with seven small children, and in a moment of financial stress she married an American actor, CHARLES YOUNG (?–1874). The marriage was never consummated and was annulled.

In 1835 Mrs. Duff married for the fourth time, and retired after making her last appearance in New Orleans the following year.

DUFRESNE [really ABRAHAM-ALEXIS QUINAULT] (1693–1767), French actor, sometimes known as Quinault-Dufresne. With his wife, MLLE DESEINE [really CATH-ERINE-MARIE-JEANNE DUPRÉ] (?–1759), he was a member of the Comédie-Française, as were his father, his elder brother, and his three sisters. He made his debut as Oreste in Crébillon's Électre in 1712, and though at first the simplicity of his acting was against him, he came into his own after the retirement of Beaubourg in 1718. He had a fine voice and a good presence, reminding many of the great Michel Baron (q.v.), whose traditions he had inherited through the teaching of Pon-teuil. Dufresne was the first to play the name-part in Voltaire's Œdipe (1718), and Destouches (q.v.) wrote for him his best comedy, Le Glorieux (1732), in which Dufresne hardly had to act, so completely was he the person Destouches was satirizing.

DUFRESNE, CHARLES (c. 1611–c. 1684), a French actor-manager, first found in the provinces in about 1643 as leader of a company under the patronage of the Duc d'Épernon. A year or two later he was joined by the remnants of the ill-starred Illustre-Théâtre (q.v.), and soon ceded his leadership to Molière (q.v.), with whom he returned to Paris in 1658, retiring a year later. Even before Molière and the Béjarts (q.v.) joined him, his company was considered one of the best in France.

DUFRESNY, CHARLES-RIVIÈRE (1654–1724), French dramatist, reputed to be a great-grandson of Henri IV. He began by writing for the Italian actors established at the Hôtel de Bourgogne (q.v.), and after their departure from Paris in 1697 turned his undoubted talents to the service of the Comédie-Française. Of his numerous plays the best was the one-act Esprit de contradiction (1700). Others, successful when first produced, were Le Double veuvage (1702), La Coquette du village (1715), and Le Mariage fait et rompu (1721), all of which kept their place in the repertory for some time. Dufresny was very conscious of the weight of tradition in comedy and made some effort to shake it off, as may be seen from his prologue to Le Négligent (1692), in which he complains that a good comic writer is blamed for copying Molière (q.v.) and a bad one for not doing so. He was, however, too indolent to produce work of lasting value.

DUGAZON [really JEAN-BAPTISTE-HENRI GOURGAUD] (1746–1809), French actor, son of a provincial manager who made an unsuccessful attempt to join the Comédie-Française in 1739. The son was accepted into the company in 1771 and proved himself an excellent comedian, at his best in farcical roles, particularly in revivals of plays by Scarron (q.v.). In 1786 he joined the staff of the newly founded School of Declamation, which in 1793 became the Conservatoire. One of his pupils there was Talma (q.v.), whom he later supported in the upheavals of the Revolution, joining him at the Comédie-Française again when it was reconstituted under Napoleon. He was the brother of the actresses Françoise Vestris (q.v.) and MARIE-MARGUERITE GOURGAUD (1742–99), who played soubrette roles at the Comédie-Française from 1767 onwards.

Duke of York's Theatre, LONDON, in St. Martin's Lane. This opened on 10 Sept. 1892 as the Trafalgar Square Theatre, and it was there that the first performances of Ibsen's The Master Builder, with Elizabeth Robins (q.v.), were given in 1893, for matinées only. In 1895 the theatre took its present name and had its first success with The Gay Parisienne, in which that quaint droll, LOUIE FREEAR (1871–1939), who had been on the stage since early child-hood, first made a name for herself. In 1897 Charles Frohman (q.v.) took over the theatre, and began a successful tenancy, introducing many well-known American actors to London, among them Maxine Elliott (q.v.) in 1899. The younger Dion (Dot) Boucicault (q.v.) was appoin-ted resident manager in 1901, and under him several plays by Barrie (q.v.) had their first productions, including The Admir-able Crichton (1902), Peter Pan (1904), Alice Sit-By-The-Fire (1905), and What Every Woman Knows (1908). In 1910 Frohman tried to introduce the repertory system to London, but the time was not yet ripe and the venture failed. The theatre reverted to straight runs of Pinero, Barrie, Shaw, and Somerset Maugham, whose Land of Promise (1914) was the last new play put on by Frohman before he died in the Lusitania disaster in

1915. Two later successes at this theatre were Jean Webster's *Daddy Long-Legs* (1916) and Lady Lever's *Brown Sugar* (1920). In 1923 Violet Melnotte (q.v.) took control, her first success being Charlot's revue, *London Calling*, written mostly by Noël Coward, whose *Easy Virtue* was produced here three years later. In 1929 Peggy Ashcroft (q.v.) appeared in a small part in *Jew Süss*, adapted by Ashley Dukes from Feuchtwanger's novel for Matheson Lang (q.v.), who had made a success with *Such Men Are Dangerous* (1928), again adapted by Dukes from a German play by Alfred Neumann. Violet Melnotte died in 1935, and various managements came and went. As a result of enemy action the theatre closed in 1940, reopening in May 1943 with Carroll's *Shadow and Substance*. Since then it has had a fairly stable career, numbering among its productions Roland Pertwee's *Is Your Honeymoon Really Necessary?* (1944), with Ralph Lynn, *The Happy Marriage* (1952), with John Clements (who adapted it) and Kay Hammond, Hugh Mills's *House by the Lake* (1956), with Flora Robson, a translation of Anouilh's *Pauvre Bitos* (1963), with Donald Pleasence, Frank Marcus's *The Killing of Sister George* (1965), and *The Heretic* (1970), on Giordano Bruno (q.v.), by Morris West.

Duke's House, Duke's Men, LONDON, see DORSET GARDEN and LINCOLN'S INN FIELDS THEATRE.

Duke's Theatre, LONDON, see HOLBORN THEATRE.

DUKES, ASHLEY (1885–1959), English dramatist, theatre manager, and dramatic critic, who in 1933 opened the Mercury Theatre (q.v.), a small playhouse in Notting Hill Gate, for the production of new and foreign plays, particularly poetic drama. Dukes's knowledge of Continental drama was turned to good account in the adaptations of French and German plays which he did for the London stage. The best-known of these are Toller's *From Morn to Midnight* (1920), Guitry's *Mozart* (1926), Neumann's *Such Men Are Dangerous* (1928), and Feuchtwanger's *Jew Süss* (1929). He also adapted part of a fifteenth-century Spanish play, *La Celestina*, which, however, he considerably falsified. As *The Matchmaker's Arms* (1930), it provided an excellent part for Sybil Thorndike (q.v.). Another of his

adaptations was ot Machiavelli's *Mandragola* (1939). Of Dukes's own plays the most successful was *The Man with a Load of Mischief* (1924), in which Fay Compton (q.v.) scored a great success as the Lady. This was later made into a small-scale musical, with music by John Clifton, presented at the Intimate Theatre, Palmers Green, in 1968. Dukes was also the author of several books on the theatre and of an autobiography, *The Scene is Changed* (1943).

DULLIN, CHARLES (1885–1949), French actor and producer, a pupil of Gémier (q.v.), who, after some appearances in melodrama, joined Copeau (q.v.) when he first opened the Vieux-Colombier. In 1919 Dullin formed his own company and, after some preliminary training, took it on a long tour in the provinces. Back in Paris, confronted by many difficulties and always short of money, he finally succeeded in establishing himself and his actors in the Théâtre de l'Atelier, which soon gained a great reputation as one of the outstanding experimental theatres of Paris. The list of plays produced at the Atelier covers the classics of France, the comedies of Aristophanes, translations of famous foreign plays, among them Calderón's *La Vida es sueño* (1922), Shakespeare and Ben Jonson, Pirandello for the first time in France, and such new French plays as Cocteau's *Antigone* (also 1922). Himself an excellent actor, Dullin ran a school of acting connected with his theatre, and in 1936 was invited to become one of the producers at the Comédie-Française. During the occupation of France he toured the unoccupied zone with Molière's *L'Avare*, and in 1943 he was responsible for the first production of *Les Mouches*, by Sartre (q.v.).

DUMAS *père*, ALEXANDRE [really DAVY DE LA PAILLETERIE, Dumas being the name of his Haitian grandmother] (1802–70), a prolific writer, of Creole parentage, now mainly remembered for his novels, but whose dramas played an important part in the French Romantic movement. Influenced in part by the visit to Paris in 1827 of an English company under Charles Kemble (q.v.) with a repertory of plays by Shakespeare, Dumas wrote *Henri III et sa cour* (1829), the first triumph of the Romantic theatre. *Antony* (1831) was then produced at the Porte-Saint-Martin (q.v.), as was Dumas's most famous play, *La*

Tour de Nesle (1832), which for terror and rapidity of action—not to mention the number of corpses—surpassed anything seen on the French stage since the days of Alexandre Hardy (q.v.). Dumas then turned to his own novels, of which in all he wrote nearly a hundred, and made them into plays. Some of them were produced at the Théâtre Historique, which he built and financed himself, facing ruin when it failed and finally giving up the theatre entirely.

DUMAS *fils*, ALEXANDRE (1824–95), French novelist and dramatist, natural son of the above. He entered the theatre by way of a dramatization of his own novel, *La Dame aux camélias*. First acted in 1852, this became one of the outstanding theatrical successes of the second half of the nineteenth century, and is occasionally revived today. In England, America, and Italy it was originally known as *Camille*. It was destined to remain the younger Dumas's only romantic play, for he later turned to social problems and became the leading exponent of what has been called 'the useful theatre', which regards the stage as a pulpit for the expounding of moral principles. Dumas *fils* had little liking for the bohemian society in which his childhood had been passed and to which he gave a permanent label in the title of his play, *Le Demi-Monde* (1855). The bitterness of his illegitimacy found expression in *Le Fils naturel* (1858) and *Un Père prodigue* (1859), while social problems of the day were ventilated in such plays as *La Question d'argent* (1857), *L'Étrangère* (1876), and his last play, *Francillon* (1887). In his own day a popular and powerful social dramatist, he is now only remembered by his least typical work, mainly because the consumptive and pathetic figure of Marguerite Gautier offers a fine part for an ambitious and passionate actress.

Dumb Ballet, see TRAP.

DUMESNIL, MARIE-FRANÇOISE (1713–1803), French actress, who joined the company of the Comédie-Française in 1737. She was excellent in passionate roles, and Voltaire attributed to her much of the success of his *Mérope* (1743). Unlike her contemporary rival Mlle Clairon (q.v.), she had no interest in the reform of theatrical costume and always wore contemporary dress in rich materials,

loaded with jewels. She retired in 1775, but remained in full possession of her faculties until the end of her long life, and was able to pass on to younger actors many traditions temporarily lost during the upheavals of the French Revolution.

Dumfries. The first theatre, which opened in 1792 under the management of Williamson, formerly of the Haymarket, London, was based on the design of the Theatre Royal, Bristol (q.v.). The scenery was by Alexander Nasmyth, and Robert Burns was an active supporter. In 1811 it became the Theatre Royal. Its history was very much that of any provincial theatre. Its managers included Stephen Kemble and the elder Macready, and Phelps (q.v.) was a member of the stock company in the 1834–5 season. A frequenter of the theatre in the 1870s was J. M. Barrie (q.v.), then a schoolboy at Dumfries Academy. In 1909 it closed, and from 1911 to 1954 it was used as a cinema. In 1959 the Dumfries Guild of Players, a long-established amateur group, bought it, and after carrying out some internal reconstruction, reopened it as a theatre the following year. Each season they present six productions of their own interspersed with plays, concerts, and ballet by touring professional artists sponsored by the Arts Council.

DUNLAP, WILLIAM (1766–1839), the dominating force of the young American stage from 1790 to 1810. He went to England in 1784 to study art, but neglected his work for the theatre, attending plays by Shakespeare and contemporary comedies and studying the work of such actors as the Kembles and Mrs. Siddons (qq.v.). In 1787 he returned to the United States and wrote a comedy for the American Company (q.v.), which was accepted but not acted. A second comedy, *The Father; or, American Shandyism*, was produced at the John Street Theatre, New York, on 7 Sept. 1789.

Dunlap continued to write for the American Company and in 1796 became one of its managers, strengthening it by the inclusion of the first Joseph Jefferson (q.v.). Two years later, on 29 Jan. 1798, he and Hodgkinson (q.v.) opened the Park Theatre, New York, with *As You Like It*. One of the first plays to be done there was *André*, a tragedy which Dunlap based on an incident in the War of Independence, thus making it the first native tragedy on

American material. Hodgkinson played André, and the part of Bland, his friend, was taken by a young English actor, Thomas Abthorpe Cooper (q.v.), who was later to succeed Dunlap as lessee and manager of the theatre.

In 1798 Hodgkinson left the management of the Park Theatre and Dunlap continued alone, producing his own adaptations of French or German plays, particularly those by Kotzebue (q.v.), and some of his own plays, including *Leicester* and *The Italian Father*. Many of them were performed also in Boston at the Haymarket and in Philadelphia at the Chestnut Street Theatre. In Feb. 1805, harassed by temperamental actors and an epidemic of yellow fever, Dunlap went bankrupt and was forced to close the theatre. A year later he became assistant stage manager of the Park under Cooper, in which capacity he was responsible in 1809 for the engagement of Edgar Allan Poe's parents to play in Monk Lewis's *The Castle Spectre*. In 1812 he accompanied Cooke (q.v.) on his American tour, and then retired from the theatre to devote himself entirely to literature and painting. In 1832 he published an invaluable *History of the American Theatre*.

Dunlop Street Theatre, see GLASGOW.

DUNSANY, EDWARD JOHN MORETON DRAX PLUNKETT, LORD (1878–1957), a man of wide interests who in his capacity as a dramatist was connected with the early years of the Abbey Theatre (q.v.), where his first plays were produced. They were also seen in London, but most of his work was seen only in Ireland or in amateur productions, though *If* had a long run at the Ambassadors in London in 1921. A versatile writer, his plays range from one-act farces (*Cheezo*), through fantasy (*The Old King's Tale*) and satire (*The Lost Silk Hat*), to full-length tragedy (*Alexander*) and comedy (*Mr. Faithful*).

DUNVILLE [really WALLEN], T. E. (*c.* 1868–1924), an eccentric music-hall comedian who specialized in songs made up of short terse sentences delivered in an explosive manner—'Little boy, Pair of skates, Broken ice, Heaven's gates'. He was appearing as an extra turn at Bolton in 1899 when he first caught the eye of an enterprising manager and became a success overnight. For years he was top of the bill, wearing the extraordinary

make-up—long black coat, small hat, baggy trousers, big boots, and ugly face with red nose—which he often tried in vain to alter. His bills always announced him as 'Sticking Here for a Week', and showed him suspended from the wall. Depressed by the declining popularity of the music-hall after the First World War, he committed suicide by drowning himself in the Thames.

Duodrama, see MONODRAMA.

DURAS, MARGUERITE (1914–   ), French novelist and dramatist, whose plays belong basically to the Theatre of the Absurd (q.v.), but who seeks to temper the vision of life as fundamentally ridiculous by means of a surface realism. Her first play, *Le Square* (1956), dealt with the impossibility of direct communication between human beings. It was followed by *Les Viaducts de la Seine-et-Oise* (1963), in which two old people almost commit the perfect crime by throwing portions of a dismembered body into the waggons of passing goods trains. As *The Viaduct*, it was seen at the Yvonne Arnaud Theatre (q.v.) in 1968, with Sybil Thorndike and Max Adrian as the old couple. It was later revised and retitled *L'Amante Anglaise* (in English *The Lovers of Viorne*), and with Madeleine Renaud was seen in Paris and London in 1969. The original version was followed in 1965 by *Les Eaux et Forêts*, a bitter comedy on the theme of ingratitude, and by a study of divorce, *La Musica*, which, with *Le Square*, was seen briefly in London in 1966, the year in which the author's first full-length play, *Des Journées dans les arbres*, was directed by Jean-Louis Barrault at the Odéon. This study of the relationship between an ageing woman and her son, a compulsive gambler, again stresses the impossibility of communication. As *Days in the Trees*, it was produced at the Aldwych in London in June 1966, with Peggy Ashcroft as the Mother.

D'URFEY, THOMAS (1653–1723), Restoration dramatist and song-writer, author of a number of plays, mainly based on earlier English or foreign dramatists, none of which has survived on the stage. The earlier ones are purely farcical, but later ones are tinged with the sentimentality which was soon to bulk so large in English drama. D'Urfey was one of the writers most savagely attacked for indecency by

Jeremy Collier (q.v.) in his *Short View*, and in 1698 he was prosecuted for profanity.

DÜRRENMATT, FRIEDRICH (1921–), Swiss dramatist whose work shows the influence of Brecht and also of Wedekind (qq.v.) and the Expressionists, particularly in his first play, *Es steht geschrieben* (1947). His first big success in the theatre was gained with the mock-heroic *Romulus der Grosse* (1949). Of Dürrenmatt's other plays, the two produced in 1954—*Ein Engel kommt nach Babylon* and *Die Ehe des Herrn Mississippi* (produced at the Arts Theatre, London, in 1959)—are not well known outside the German-speaking world, but *Der Besuch der alten Dame* (1956) was produced in England and the United States by the Lunts (q.v.) as *The Visit*, while *Die Physiker* (1962), as *The Physicists*, was a great success at the Aldwych Theatre in 1963 in a production by the Royal Shakespeare Company. The same company produced *The Meteor* in 1966, but it had a poor press and only a short run. In 1969 a new play, based on a theme from Strindberg, was produced in Basle, and later in Düsseldorf, under the title *Play Strindberg*. Dürrenmatt is interested in exploring the possibilities of dramatic technique, and although he has said in *Theaterprobleme* (1955) that our disintegrating world is a subject for comedy and not for tragedy, fundamentally his plays are deeply pessimistic and reflect the uncertainty of the times.

DU RYER, PIERRE (*c.* 1600–58), French dramatist, whose early plays, produced in 1628–9, were spectacular tragi-comedies in the style of Hardy (q.v.), calling for elaborate staging in the old-fashioned multiple setting (q.v.), and ignoring the unities of time and place. Several comedies followed, containing good parts for the comedian Gros-Guillaume (q.v.), of which the best was *Les Vendanges de Suresne* (1633), and then, under the influence of Mairet's *Sophonisbé* (1634), Ryer turned his attention to tragedy. The most successful of his later plays was *Scévole* (1644), which remained in the repertory of the Comédie-Française for over a hundred years and was one of the plays given by the short-lived Illustre-Théâtre (q.v.). In the opinion of competent critics, Ryer

did more than anyone, except Mairet and Corneille (qq.v.), to establish French classical tragedy.

DUSE, ELEONORA (1858–1924), famous Italian actress, contemporary and rival of Sarah Bernhardt (q.v.). Coming from a family of strolling players, she was on the stage from the age of four, and at fourteen played Juliet, a performance immortalized by D'Annunzio in his novel, *Il fuoco*. In 1878 she was engaged by Ernesto Rossi (q.v.) as his leading lady, and went on tour with him, soon becoming one of the greatest actresses of the day. In 1885 she toured South America and appeared in the United States in 1893, 1903, and again just before her death. In 1881 she went to Russia, where she was much admired by Chekhov (q.v.), who may have had her in mind when he wrote the part of Mme Arkadina in *The Seagull*. In London in 1895 she and Bernhardt both appeared as Magda in Sudermann's *Heimat*, dividing the loyalties of the public and critics. Shaw (q.v.) preferred Duse and Clement Scott (q.v.) Bernhardt. A dark, slender woman, with mobile features and most expressive gestures, Duse used no make-up and was noted for her ability to blush or turn pale at will. She was at her best in strong emotional parts, particularly Sardou's Tosca, Fédora, and Théodora, and in Dumas *fils*'s *La Dame aux camélias*, though her Hostess in Goldoni's comedy, *La Locandiera*, was also much admired. She was outstanding in Ibsen, one of her finest parts being Rebecca West in a revival of *Rosmersholm* directed by Gordon Craig (q.v.) in Florence in 1906. In her late thirties she ardently championed the poetic drama of D'Annunzio (q.v.), and her acting in his *La città morta* and *La Gioconda* (both 1898) made him famous as a dramatist, though her association with him caused her much loss of money and reputation, particularly after the failure of his *Gloria* at Naples in 1899. She retired in 1913, but returned briefly to the stage a year before her death.

Dust Hole, LONDON, see SCALA THEATRE.

DYMOV, OSSIP (1878–1959), see SCHWARTZ, MAURICE.

E

Earl Carroll Theatre, NEW YORK, see CARROLL, EARL.

East London Theatre, see ROYALTY THEATRE (I).

EBERLE, OSKAR (1902–56), Swiss theatre director, who in the 1930s achieved an international reputation with his revival of the sixteenth-century Lucerne Passion Play, and of Calderón's *El gran teatro del mundo*, which he staged in the square in front of the church at Einsiedeln, one of the earliest centres of medieval liturgical drama (q.v.). He also directed the official Festival play at the Swiss national exhibition in Zürich in 1939, and was responsible for the production of Cäsar von Arx's *Bundesfeierspiel* at Schnyz in 1941. In 1955 he directed the Festival play at Vevey, where a wine festival with drama and music has been held intermittently since 1797, and for his production a vast wood and concrete open-air auditorium was specially constructed. His last production, at Altdorf in the year of his death, was a revival of the *Tellspiel*, a play based on the exploits of William Tell which was first performed at Altdorf in 1512 and has been constantly revived since, the present version by Jacob Ruf dating from 1545.

Ecclesiastical Drama, see LITURGICAL DRAMA.

ECHEGARAY, JOSÉ (1832–1916), Spanish dramatist, awarded the Nobel Prize for Literature in 1905. His plays retain the verse-form and much of the imagery of the Romantics, but deal mainly with social problems, and though enthusiastically received, caused fierce controversy. They had a great influence, not only in Spain but on the European theatre generally. The best-known are *O locura o santidad* (1877), *El loco Dios* (1900), *El hijo de Don Juan* (1892), a study of inherited disease which owes something to Ibsen's *Ghosts*, and, most important of all, *El gran Galeoto* (1881), produced in England as *Calumny* and in the United States as *The World and His Wife*. Its theme is that slanderous tongues may cause the downfall of the most virtuous, since a woman

wrongfully accused of being a poet's mistress finally becomes so, driven to it by the oppression of unfounded scandal.

EDDY, EDWARD (1822–75), American actor, long popular at the Bowery Theatre (q.v.), where he first appeared on 13 Mar. 1851 in Bulwer-Lytton's *Richelieu*. He was also seen as Othello, as Claude Melnotte in Lytton's *The Lady of Lyons*, and in the name-part of one of the many versions of *Belphegor*. He was at his best in youthful, melodramatic parts, earning for himself the sobriquet of 'robustious Eddy', and his most popular role was Edmond Dantès in Dumas *père*'s *The Count of Monte Cristo*. He was at Burton's in 1856 and also at the Metropolitan, but his style was not suited to the fashionable theatres, and he went back to triumph at the Bowery as Richard III and in similar parts until his popularity waned.

Eden Palace of Varieties, LONDON, see KINGSWAY THEATRE.

Eden Theatre, NEW YORK, see PHOENIX THEATRE (2).

EDESON, ROBERT (1868–1931), American actor, who before he went into films spent many years on the stage. He was appearing in H. J. Byron's *Our Boys* at the Boston Museum in 1892 when Charles Frohman (q.v.) engaged him for the Empire, New York, where he appeared for several seasons, making a great success as Gavin Dishart in Barrie's *The Little Minister* in 1897, playing opposite Maude Adams (q.v.). He was seen in London in 1899 as David Brandon in Zangwill's *Children of the Ghetto*, and in 1907 in his favourite part, Soangataha in de Mille's *Strongheart*. He made his last stage appearance as the Vagrant in the Čapeks' *The Insect Play* (retitled *The World We Live In*) in 1922 and then went into motion pictures.

Edinburgh. In spite of the opposition of the Church, efforts appear to have been made in the seventeenth and eighteenth centuries to establish a theatre in Edinburgh. The scanty records indicate a succession of performances there and in nearby towns between 1663 and 1689, including the first known Scottish performance of *Macbeth* in 1672, while an advertisement of 1715 reveals the existence of an established company. The best-documented of early managements is that of Tony Aston (q.v.) from 1725 to 1728. In 1736 the poet Allan Ramsay (q.v.) opened a theatre in Carrubber's Close, only to have it closed by the Licensing Act of 1737. From 1741 there were theatrical seasons every year, the law being evaded by the device of charging, not for the play, but for an introductory concert. In 1747 a concert hall in the Canongate opened as a theatre and in 1756 saw the first performance of John Home's *Douglas*. A patent was obtained for it in 1767, and it then became Edinburgh's first Theatre Royal, under the management of the well-known Scottish actor DONALD ROSS (1728–90), ancestor of Edward Compton (q.v.). Two years later a new Theatre Royal was built at the east end of Princes Street. Many distinguished players appeared there, including, in 1784 and 1785, Mrs. Siddons (q.v.), whose younger brother Stephen Kemble managed the theatre from 1791 to 1800. Her son Henry Siddons took over in 1809, but so mismanaged his financial affairs that when he died in 1815 his widow and her brother William Murray, joint managers with him, were left heavily in debt. They nevertheless managed to keep the theatre open, and up to 1851, when Murray retired, it had a period of almost unbroken success. It was pulled down in 1859, but not before it had had a further period of success from 1857 to 1859, when Henry Irving (q.v.) was a member of the resident stock company, playing a wide variety of parts under the management of R. H. WYNDHAM (1817–94), and going with him to a new Theatre Royal in June 1859. This was the Queen's, named in honour of Queen Victoria, and it stood on the site of an earlier theatre which had been known by many names before, as the Adelphi, it was destroyed by fire in 1853. It was destined to be burnt down again in 1865, 1875, and 1884, but it was always rebuilt on the same site. A later theatre, the Lyceum, which opened in 1883 with a visit from Irving and Ellen Terry, became in 1965 Scotland's first Civic Theatre, absorbing the assets of the Edinburgh Gateway Theatre, which opened in 1946 and was from 1953 till its closure in 1965 occupied for eight months of the year by an independent company whose first Chairman was Robert Kemp. The Civic Theatre, administered by a Trust, opened on 1 Oct. 1965 with a resident company under Tom Fleming in a season of international plays which included a new version of Goldoni's *Il Servitore di due Padrone* as *The Servant o'twa maisters* and Brecht's *Life of Galileo*. This theatre is used for the main drama contributions to the Edinburgh International Festival of Music and Drama, which was founded in 1947. Running for three weeks from the middle of August, this has brought to Edinburgh many famous foreign companies and a number of English companies in new plays, including those of T. S. Eliot, O'Casey (*Cock-a-Doodle Dandy*), Ionesco (*Exit the King*), and Fry (*Curtmantle*). There have also been productions of new Scottish plays, and revivals in the Assembly Hall and elsewhere of Lyndsay's *Ane Pleasant Satyre of the Thrie Estaitis*, Ramsay's *The Gentle Shepherd*, and Home's *Douglas*.

EDOUIN, WILLIE (1846–1908), see THOMPSON, LYDIA.

EDWARDES, GEORGE (1852–1915), London theatre manager, known as 'the Guv'nor', who in 1885 went into partnership with John Hollingshead at the old Gaiety (q.v.), remaining there when Hollingshead withdrew a year later and replacing the old-fashioned burlesque by the new-style musical comedy. Under him the Gaiety flourished, and its chorus of 'Gaiety girls' became famous for their beauty and technical accomplishments. His list of successes at the Apollo, Daly's (which he built for the American impresario, Augustin Daly, q.v.), the Gaiety, the Prince of Wales's, and elsewhere, was remarkable, and included most of the long-running musical comedies of the day—*The Shop Girl* (1894), *The Geisha* (1896), *The Runaway Girl* (1898), *San Toy* (1899), *A Country Girl* (1902), *The Merry Widow* (1907), and *The Quaker Girl* (1910).

EDWARDS, HILTON (1903–82), Irish actor and theatre director, who in 1928, with MacLiammóir (q.v.), founded the Gate Theatre in Dublin (q.v.). He had been from 1922 to 1924 at the Old Vic in London, where he played in a number of Shakespearian productions and also sang in opera. After a tour of South Africa in 1927, he went to Ireland, and remained there, directing and playing in a number of important productions at the Gate. With his company he then toured Europe, Northern Africa, and the United States, and appeared in London, notably in MacLiammóir's *Ill Met by Moonlight* (1947). In 1953 he directed *Hamlet* at Elsinore, playing Claudius, and later he directed MacLiammóir's solo programmes, *The Importance of Being Oscar* (1960) and *I Must Be Talking to My Friends* (1963). The former was first seen at the Dublin Festival, for which Edwards also directed and played in Paterson's *The Roses are Real* (1963) and Brian Friel's *Philadelphia, Here I Come* (1964), both of which were subsequently seen in London, and *King Herod Explains* (1969) by Conor Cruise O'Brien. In 1970, while awaiting the reopening of the Gate Theatre, which had been closed for repairs, he directed a production of Chekhov's *The Seagull* at the Abbey Theatre (q.v.).

EDWIN, JOHN (1749–90), English comedian, who on the death of his friend and benefactor Ned Shuter (q.v.) in 1776, took his place at Covent Garden, where he remained until his death, being himself succeeded by Munden (q.v.). He had already played many of Shuter's favourite parts in the provinces, and during several summer seasons appeared at the Haymarket in plays by O'Keeffe (q.v.), who wrote for him the comic songs in which he excelled. A good reliable actor, who managed to be both humorous and handsome, he played with restraint and subtlety. Among his best parts were Dogberry in *Much Ado About Nothing*, the First Grave-digger in *Hamlet*, Launcelot Gobbo in *The Merchant of Venice*, and Sir Hugh Evans in *The Merry Wives of Windsor*. He was also good as Sir Anthony Absolute in Sheridan's *The Rivals*, which Shuter had been the first to play.

Effects Man, see NOISES OFF.

EGAN, PIERCE (1772–1849), English sporting journalist whose book, *Life in London* (1821), was dramatized in a number of different versions as *Tom and Jerry; or, Life in London*. It was immensely popular in England and in the United States and may have suggested to Dickens the basic idea of *The Pickwick Papers*. Egan was also the author of *The Life of an Actor* (1824), an amusing account of the progress of

Peregrine Proteus from poverty in the provinces to a performance before royalty.

EKHOF, KONRAD (1720–78), German actor, who in 1740 joined the newly formed company of Schönemann (q.v.), where he remained for seventeen years, perfecting his art and discarding the stiff declamatory style of Carolina Neuber (q.v.) for a more natural style of acting hitherto unknown in Germany. He was at the height of his powers when in 1767 he joined Ackermann (q.v.) at Hamburg, where the latter had just opened Germany's first National Theatre. He remained there for five years, but was forced to leave because of the jealousy and arrogance of the young Schröder (q.v.). After several miserable years spent touring with Abel Seyler, Ekhof joined the company at the Court theatre in Weimar, where in later years he met and acted with Goethe (q.v.), to whom he imparted some of the theatrical reminiscences which figure in *Wilhelm Meister*. After a disastrous fire at Weimar in 1775, Ekhof became chief actor and director at Gotha, where one of his last official acts was to engage Iffland (q.v.) for the company. He made his last appearance as the Ghost in an adaptation of *Hamlet* by Schröder, now famous and at the head of his profession.

Ekkyklema, or 'wheel-out', a Greek theatrical term which has given rise to a good deal of controversy. At one time it was thought to apply to a movable platform on which a group of actors showing, for instance, Clytemnestra standing over the murdered bodies of Agamemnon and Cassandra (in Aeschylus' *Oresteia*) could be pushed on stage or brought forward on a turn-table. It is now thought to indicate nothing more than a couch on wheels, or a prearranged grouping revealed by the opening of the central double doors in the stage wall.

Electric Lighting, see LIGHTING.

ELEN, GUS [really ERNEST AUGUSTUS] (1862–1940), a music-hall performer who first appeared in the old taverns of the 1880s and became famous as the singer of London cockney ditties, especially 'Never Introduce yer Donah to a Pal' and 'You Could Almost Shut yer Eyes and 'ear 'em Grow'. Some of his characterizations had the true Dickensian touch, and "E Dunno

Where 'e Are', 'Down the Road', 'If It Wasn't For the 'ouses in Between', and 'Wait Till the Work Comes Round' are music-hall classics. In 1935 he came out of retirement to appear in a Command Performance at the London Palladium, with great success.

Elephant and Castle Theatre, LONDON, a playhouse devoted to 'transpontine melodrama' and pantomime, built in 1872 on the site of Newington Butts (q.v.). After a steady but unspectacular career, during which it catered mainly for a local audience, it closed in 1928, and four years later, after partial rebuilding, reopened as a cinema, retaining its old name and some of the original edifice.

ELIOT, THOMAS STEARNS (1888–1965), poet and dramatist, American by birth but English by adoption, who initiated an important revival of poetic drama with a play on the murder of Thomas à Becket, *Murder in the Cathedral* (1935). First acted in the Chapter House of Canterbury Cathedral, it was subsequently revived several times with great success in commercial theatres in Britain and the United States. A later play, *The Family Reunion* (1939), based on the *Oresteia* of Aeschylus, was less successful, mainly because Eliot failed to integrate the ritualism of the chorus with the realism of the setting. Of his last three plays, commissioned for performance at the Edinburgh Festival, *The Cocktail Party* (1949) and *The Confidential Clerk* (1953) were based on Euripides' *Alcestis* and *Ion* respectively; *The Elder Statesman* (1958) on Sophocles' *Oedipus at Colonus*. In them Eliot moves closer to a mannered realism, disguising his serious purpose under the form of modern drawing-room comedy, and discarding the closely-wrought poetic style of the earlier plays for a plain undecorated verse.

Elizabethan Playhouse. The structure of the public playhouses used by Shakespeare and his contemporaries had so much influence on the writing and production of their plays that it seems worth considering it in detail. Before Burbage built the Theatre (q.v.) in 1576, English actors had played on temporary stages set up in the open air, in noblemen's houses, or in innyards, both in London and in the provinces. All these influenced the final form of the permanent playhouse, as did the triumphal arches set up for royal occasions and the ceremonial stages of the Dutch Rederijkers (q.v.). But the main influence was undoubtedly the innyard, whose characteristic features of a large open unroofed space surrounded by galleries giving access to bed-chambers can be found not only in the Theatre, but in the later Curtain, the Fortune, the famous Globe, the Hope, the Rose, and the Swan (qq.v.). These were all wooden structures, roughly circular or octagonal in shape, with a large platform-stage, backing on to one wall, jutting out into the central space. Round this space, still called a 'yard', ran two or perhaps three galleries with thatched roofs. The first probably continued behind the stage, and so formed an upper room, reminiscent of the musicians' gallery in a nobleman's Great Hall. This could be used either for instrumentalists, battlements, or first-storey windows. Underneath it may have been the 'inner stage' (q.v.), a feature which has given rise to much controversy. Whether it was a separate room, or merely the corridor behind the stage-wall revealed by drawing a curtain, some form of 'inner stage' is so often called for in Elizabethan plays that it must have existed, perhaps only in some theatres, and not in all. The fact that the Spanish stage, which, being based on the *corral* or square surrounded by houses with windows and balconies (SEE THEATRE BUILDINGS), closely resembled the Elizabethan stage in many respects, also had some form of 'inner stage', would seem to add further evidence for its existence. Other features of the Elizabethan stage were the tiring-house, or actors' dressing-room, behind the stage wall. This permanent architectural façade was pierced by doors of entrance, over which projected a roof—the Heavens, supported by pillars. Above the balcony at the back of the stage was a hut to house the machinery used for raising or lowering actors or properties on to the stage, and above this a tower from which a trumpeter announced the start of a performance and a flag flew during it. Under the stage, hidden by boarding or drapery, a cellar held the machinery for projecting ghosts and devils through the trap doors, which also served for Ophelia's grave in *Hamlet* and the witches' cauldron in *Macbeth*. The stage itself was partly railed, and privileged spectators could pay to sit on it (see AUDIENCE ON THE STAGE). The galleries were furnished with wooden stools or benches, and round three sides of the stage stood the groundlings. In all parts of the house the audience, which entered through one main door, amused itself by cracking and eating nuts and munching apples, often throwing the cores at the actors. So little direct evidence about the Elizabethan theatre is extant that much has had to be deduced from other sources, but it seems possible that the interior of the buildings was brightly painted, with pillars worked to resemble marble, and splendidly-coloured curtains. The so-called 'private theatres' (see BLACKFRIARS) were equally colourful and, of course, roofed. They approximated more to the 'tennis-court' theatres (q.v.) of Paris, and it was from them, rather than from the public theatres, that the Restoration play-houses developed after the Puritan Inter-regnum (q.v.) of 1642–60.

Elizabethan Stage Society, see POEL, WILLIAM.

Elizabethan Theatre Trust, AUSTRALIA, founded in 1954 to celebrate the visit of Queen Elizabeth II to Australia and to provide the first step in the establishment of an Australian National Theatre. Intended to assist promising playwrights and train young actors, it appointed a Board of Trustees under Hugh Hunt (q.v.), who in 1960 was succeeded by Neil Hutchinson. As a basis for its activities, which consist mainly in the provision of touring companies covering the whole country, it took over the Majestic Theatre in Sydney, built in 1917 and later a cinema. After renovations, this reopened as the Elizabethan on 27 July 1955 with a cast of guest artists from England in Rattigan's *The Sleeping Prince*. The Trust's own company, headed by Judith Anderson (q.v.), made its début in Robinson Jeffers's *Medea* at Canberra in the following September, and then em-barked on a long tour. One of the new Australian plays, first seen at Melbourne in Nov. 1955, was Ray Lawler's *The Summer of the Seventeenth Doll*, which was seen in London in 1957, as was Alan Seymour's play about Anzac Day, *The One Day of the Year*, in 1961. The Trust maintains a permanent resident company at the Elizabethan Theatre, and in addition to its touring companies sends also groups to play in schools and caters for younger playgoers with performances by pup-pets.

ELLIOTT, GEORGE HENRY (1884–1962), a music-hall comedian known as the Chocolate-Coloured Coon. Born in Eng-land, he was taken to America, where he joined a Minstrel show (q.v.), but returned to England to tour the music-halls, making his first appearance in London at Sadler's Wells in 1902. A fine singer and dancer, and an excellent pantomime performer, he continued to work until his death, being particularly admired for his soft-shoe dancing. One of his best-known songs was 'I Used to Sigh for the Silvery Moon'.

ELLIOTT, MAXINE [really JESSIE DERMOT] (1868–1940), an American actress who adopted her stage name at the suggestion of Dion Boucicault (q.v.). In 1895 she joined the company of Augustin Daly (q.v.), appearing in his productions in New York and in London, where she was first seen as Sylvia in *Two Gentlemen of Verona*. After touring Australia with her husband Nat Goodwin (q.v.), she re-turned to America and was seen with him in a number of new plays, including several by Clyde Fitch (q.v.). In 1908 she built her own theatre in New York (see MAXINE ELLIOTT's), but shortly before the First World War she retired to England, where she had many friends (including Edward VII). From 1914 to 1918 she was active in war-work in England and Bel-gium, which impoverished her to such an extent that in 1920 she returned to the stage and became once again one of the best-loved stars of the American theatre. Her sister, (MAY) GERTRUDE (1874–1950), also an actress, married in 1900 Johnston Forbes-Robertson (q.v.), being his leading lady until his retirement in 1913, after which she toured under her own manage-ment, returning to New York in 1936 to play the Queen to Leslie Howard's Hamlet.

ELLISTON, ROBERT WILLIAM (1774–1831), English actor, who toured the provinces and in 1796 made his London début at the Haymarket. Charles Dibdin (q.v.) wrote a number of entertainments for him, and he was frequently seen at Drury Lane, being one of the most popular actors of the day, second only to Garrick (q.v.) in tragedy. Eccentric and extravagant, and a heavy drinker, he had been manager of many small theatres before in 1819 he achieved his ambition of managing Drury Lane (q.v.). He engaged a good company, which included Edmund Kean (q.v.) both before and after his visit to America, but his resources could not stand up to his extravagance and his outside speculations and in 1826 he went bankrupt. He then returned to the Surrey and in 1829 made a substantial profit from the production of Jerrold's *Black-Eyed Susan*, starring T. P. Cooke (q.v.). He continued to act, appearing on the stage for the last time only a fortnight before his death.

ELTINGE, JULIAN [really WILLIAM DALTON] (1883–1941), American actor, chiefly known as a performer in 'drag' (see FEMALE IMPERSONATION). He made his first appearance in a woman's part in the musical comedy *Mr. Wix of Wickham* in 1905, and in 1911 was seen in a dual role (as Mrs. Monte and Hal Blake) in *The Fascinating Widow*, a musical specially written for him. A series of successful plays and films followed until his retirement in 1930. He was seen briefly on the stage and in night clubs in 1940 (see also ELTINGE THEATRE).

Eltinge Theatre, NEW YORK, on West 42nd Street. Named after Julian Eltinge (q.v.), this opened on 11 Sept. 1912 with a melodrama, *Within the Law*, which established Jane Cowl (q.v.) as a star. It housed a number of interesting plays before, in 1930, it became a home of burlesque, notorious for the daring and vulgarity of its strip-tease acts and its dubious jokes. It was closed in 1942 and later became a cinema.

Embassy Theatre, LONDON, at Hampstead. This opened as a try-out theatre for new plays on 11 Sept. 1928, and later sent several good plays to the West End, including Anthony Asquith's *Ten Minute Alibi* (1933) and Michael Egan's *The Dominant Sex* (1934). During the Second World War it was damaged by enemy action but, repaired and reopened in 1945, it did good work under the management of Anthony Hawtrey. After his death in 1955 it closed, and two years later was taken over by the Central School of Speech and Drama.

EMERY, JOHN (1777–1822), English actor, son of the actor MACKLE EMERY (1740–1825). In 1798 he was engaged by Covent Garden to take the place of the comedian John Quick (q.v.) and, apart from a short engagement at the Haymarket, remained there until his sudden

death. His Caliban in *The Tempest* was highly praised, and he was good as Sir Toby Belch in *Twelfth Night*, the First Grave-digger in *Hamlet*, and Dogberry in *Much Ado About Nothing*. He was also an artist, and between 1801 and 1817 exhibited frequently at the Royal Academy. His son Sam(uel) and grand-daughter Winifred (qq.v.) were also on the stage.

EMERY, SAM(UEL) ANDERSON (1817–81), English actor, son of John Emery (q.v.), much of whose talent he inherited. He was with the Keeleys (q.v.) at the Lyceum from 1844 to 1847, where he was the first to play Jonas and Will Fern in Stirling's dramatizations of Dickens's *Martin Chuzzlewit* (1844) and *The Chimes* (1845) and John Peerybingle in Albert Smith's version of *The Cricket on the Hearth* (also 1845). In 1853 he went to the Olympic, and in the following year became lessee of the Marylebone (see WEST LONDON), making his last appearance in London in 1878. His daughter, Winifred (q.v.), was also on the stage.

EMERY, (ISABEL) WINIFRED (1862–1924), English actress, daughter of Sam Emery (q.v.). She began her long and distinguished career in 1870 in Liverpool, where she appeared as the child Geraldine in Buckstone's *Green Bushes*. Four years later she was at the Princess's Theatre, London, in pantomime, and she made her début as an adult actress at the Imperial in 1879. She appeared with Wilson Barrett, Hare, and Irving—with whom she went to America—and in 1888 married Cyril Maude (q.v.), becoming his leading lady when he went into management at the Haymarket in 1896.

EMNEY, FRED (1865–1917), English actor who, after many years in light opera and musical comedy, toured the music-halls with the famous sketches *A Sister to Assist 'er*, *Getting Over a Stile*, and the riotous *Plumbers*. He also appeared as the Dame (q.v.) in many Drury Lane pantomimes, dying of injuries received on the stage in *Cinderella* when he slipped on the soap-suds in a knock-about comedy scene. His son, also FRED (1900–80), became a leading comedian on the musical comedy stage and in revue, being part-author of *Big Boy* (1945) and *Happy as a King* (1953), two musical plays in which he also appeared. In later life he gave several successful performances in straight comedy, playing Admiral Ranklin in Pinero's *The Schoolmistress* in 1950 and Ormonroyd, the photographer, in Priestley's *When We Are Married* in 1970.

Empire, a famous London music-hall in Leicester Square. Erected on a site used for entertainment since 1849, it opened unsuccessfully as the Empire Theatre on 17 Apr. 1884 and closed shortly after, to reopen on 22 Dec. 1887 as a Theatre of Varieties. Like its rival the Alhambra (q.v.), it soon became famous for its ballets; its ballet-mistress was Katti Lanner, its leading dancers Adeline Genée, Fred Farren, Lydia Kyasht, and Phyllis Bedells. One of the great features of the Empire was its promenade, which was attacked as a haunt of vice by Mrs. Ormiston Chant in her Purity Campaign in 1894. Shortly before the First World War revue became very popular, and was followed by a series of musical comedies which included *The Lilac Domino* (1918), *Irene* (1920), and *The Rebel Maid* (1921). Later successes were a spectacular production of *Henry VIII* (1925), with Sybil Thorndike (q.v.) as Queen Katharine, and the Astaires in *Lady, Be Good!* (1926). After a final performance on 22 Jan. 1927 the theatre closed. It was demolished and a cinema built on the site. (For the Empire, Islington, see GRAND THEATRE.)

Empire Theatre, NEW YORK, on the southeast corner of Broadway and 40th Street. Built for Charles Frohman (q.v.), it opened on 25 Jan. 1893 with Belasco's *The Girl I Left Behind Me*, and soon built up a reputation for consistently successful productions, mainly of sophisticated comedy. Some of the highlights of its career were Maude Adams (q.v.) in Barrie's *Peter Pan* (1905), Ellen Terry (q.v.) in Shaw's *Captain Brassbound's Conversion* (1907), Ethel Barrymore (q.v.) in Pinero's *Mid-Channel* (1910), and Jane Cowl (q.v.) in Coward's *Easy Virtue* (1925). In 1926 the theatre was temporarily closed by the authorities after the production of *The Captive*, a translation of Bourdet's controversial play, *La Prisonnière*. In 1936 *Hamlet*, with Gielgud (q.v.), ran for 132 performances, breaking the American records set up by Edwin Booth and John Barrymore (qq.v.), and on 8 Nov. 1939 came the first night of *Life With Father*, by Howard Lindsay and Russel Crouse, which occupied the theatre for six years. On its transfer to the Bijou

(q.v.), the Empire housed the Lunts (q.v.) in Rattigan's *O Mistress Mine* (1946), which they had played in London the previous year as *Love in Idleness*. The last production at this theatre was Arthur Laurents's *The Time of the Cuckoo*. It closed on 30 May 1953 and the building was demolished in the same year.

ENCINA, JUAN DEL (*c.* 1468–*c.* 1537), one of the founders, with Torres Naharro and Vicente (qq.v.), of Spanish drama, which he helped to secularize by the use in his *églogas* of rustic dialect and scenes of daily life. These dialogues between shepherds and shepherdesses, based on biblical themes, were intended for performance at Court or in the houses of the nobility, and were probably first acted by noblemen or their servants. But they were also the first serious plays to be performed by professional actors travelling the countryside.

English Aristophanes, see FOOTE, SAMUEL.

English Comedians, the name given to the troupes of English actors who toured the Continent during the sixteenth and seventeenth centuries. The first record is of a company of instrumentalists at the Danish Court in 1579–80. Six years later English actors under Kempe (q.v.) appeared at Elsinore. They were then invited to Dresden, and thereafter mention of them is found in the archives of many German towns. They probably performed jigs (q.v.) and short comic sketches whose humour was broad enough to be obvious even to a foreign audience. Though they played in English, their clown pattered in Low German. The outstanding name in connection with the English Comedians is Robert Browne (q.v.), who in 1592 took a company on an extended tour of the Continent, during which they played *Gammer Gurton's Needle*, several biblical plays, and some of Marlowe's works at Frankfurt fair. Another company, under SACKVILLE, was for some time at Wolfenbüttel (q.v.), whose ruler, Heinrich Julius of Brunswick, wrote plays in which an English influence is apparent, particularly in the character of the Fool, played by Sackville under the name of Jan Bouschet (Posset). Another princely enthusiast of the drama, Count Moritz of Hesse, built a private theatre in 1606 where Browne's company played for some time, and JOHN GREEN, Browne's successor, was in Poland as early as 1607. The next notable name to crop up in the records is that of Robert Reynolds (q.v.), who made a great reputation as a clown under the name of Pickelhering, while JOHN SPENCER (known as Stockfisch), with headquarters in Berlin, went as far afield as The Hague and Dresden.

Two collections of texts from the English Comedians' repertory were printed, one in 1620, one in 1630, the first containing plays of English origin, while the second is wholly German. They show that pirated editions and older versions of plays, heavily cut, were generally used, with the addition of horseplay for the groundlings and music and dancing for the more sophisticated among the audience. The actors who went abroad, though obviously adventurous, were perhaps not in the front rank of their profession. Their acting would therefore tend to be violent and declamatory, with much boisterous action and broad effects in comedy. From the literary point of view their influence was no doubt deplorable, but they gave the Germans their first taste of tragedy, and counteracted the native tendency to excessive discussion. In these respects they certainly revolutionized German drama in a manner long overdue. In spite of the troubles of the Thirty Years War, a number of English actors continued to play on the Continent, particularly during the Puritan interregnum of 1642–60, the last authenticated record of them dating from 1659. But such was the prestige of the *Englische Komödianten*, as they were called, that the name was used for publicity purposes as late as the eighteenth century. The constant passage of actors to and from the Continent, and the consequent interchange of ideas and subjects for drama, has produced some interesting problems of comparative literature, particularly in regard to the legend of Dr. Faustus.

English Opera House, LONDON, see LYCEUM THEATRE (I), PALACE THEATRE, and ROYALTY THEATRE (2).

English Portable Theatres. The provision of an adequate stage has always been one of the chief difficulties of theatrical touring companies. In the late sixteenth and early seventeenth centuries actors appear to have used country inns, as in London (see INNS USED AS THEATRES), and adapted barns. But as the theatres in London became more elaborate, these proved inadequate, and the creation of self-contained portable theatres or booths was a natural growth to satisfy an obvious need. The first ones, set up in fairgrounds, were probably nothing more than tents, but by the eighteenth century they had become very elaborate, and some are known by name—Lee and Harper's, Fielding's, Hippisley's, Yeates's, and Mme Violante's. At least one 'Great Theatrical Boothe' was always found at the great summer fairs in London—Bartholomew, Smithfield, Southwark, Mayfair, and Greenwich—during which the London theatres were closed, relinquishing their audiences, and sometimes their actors, to the fairground (see also FAIRS). The rest of the summer would be spent touring the country wakes, a tradition that lasted for over two hundred years. The largest portable theatre up to the middle of the nineteenth century was Richardson's, but dozens of others continued to cover the country when they gave up, among them 'Johnson's Thespian Temple', 'Baker's Pavilion', 'Douglass's Travelling Shakespearean Saloon', Holloway's, Wadbrook and Scard's, Maggie Morton's, and many others, until the spread of the cinema deprived the old 'fit-ups' of their audiences.

The fairground theatres seem in general to have conformed to a set pattern. The stage itself was solidly constructed, sometimes on the carts that carried the show round, and was furnished with a few simple backcloths and properties. The auditorium consisted of a canvas tent that could be easily rolled up and transported on the wagons. The seats were almost always plain wooden planks. There might be a built-up front of gaudily painted canvas flats, and a platform outside, upon which some of the performers would parade as an advertisement for the marvels within. This 'parade' (q.v.) was often very elaborate, and sometimes even superior to the actual performance.

The performances themselves were gone through as quickly as possible so as to clear the seats for another audience, on a busy day as often as a dozen times. The plays were, for the most part, strong drama, based on popular legends and stories from the classics, the Bible, or English history; sometimes they dramatized sensational topical murders (*Maria Marten* is the most famous example), presented pantomimes, or adapted current theatrical successes. There was hardly ever a written script. The actors were expected to improvise, and the result usually bore very little resemblance to the original. Like the puppet-show (see PUPPET), whose repertory was very similar, the fairground theatre preserved some interesting elements of Elizabethan stage tradition.

There are indications that the travelling theatre has still not exhausted its usefulness. From 1919 to 1937 the Arts League of Service (q.v.) toured the country with an easily portable entertainment of traditional English song and drama, and later several companies undertook extensive tours to theatreless provincial towns. Well-appointed provincial theatres and village halls will reduce, but never perhaps entirely destroy, the need for live portable theatres, of which at least one still flourishes in Ireland.

English Stage Company, an organization formed to present modern plays, both English and foreign, in London and to encourage young dramatists. Under the artistic direction of George Devine (q.v.), it opened on 2 Apr. 1956 at the Royal Court Theatre (q.v.), where it still remains and under which heading its subsequent history is dealt with.

E.N.S.A., see ENTERTAINMENTS NATIONAL SERVICE ASSOCIATION.

ENTERS, ANGNA (1907–89), an American solo entertainer whose programme consisted of a series of wordless mime and dance sketches. Her range was wide, and with a gesture she could evoke an Impressionist picture of a wood on a hot summer's day or the sad ennui of provincial life in France in 1910, an ageing prostitute or a Byzantine ikon. She made her first appearance in New York in 1924, and was seen in 1927 in London, where she returned many times in between extensive tours of America and other parts of the world. An accomplished painter, she also wrote a number of books, in one of which, *Artist's Life* (1958), she described her professional life in the theatre and showed how much thought and hard work had gone into the making of her apparently effortless entertainment.

Entertainments National Service Association (E.N.S.A.), an organization formed in 1938–9 to provide entertainment for the British and allied armed forces and war-workers during the Second World War. It was directed by Basil Dean (q.v.) and had its headquarters at Drury Lane Theatre, London. Working closely in collaboration with the Navy, Army, and Air Force Institute (N.A.A.F.I.), which was responsible for the financial side, it provided all types of entertainment, from full-length plays and symphony orchestras to concert parties and solo instrumentalists, in the camps, factories, and hostels of Great Britain, and on all war-fronts, from the Mediterranean to India, and from Africa to the Faroes.

ENTHOVEN [*née* ROMAINE], **GABRIELLE** (1868–1950), English theatre historian, who in 1924 presented to the Victoria and Albert Museum in London the vast collection of theatre material which bears her name. This includes innumerable playbills, engravings, prints, books, models, and newspaper cuttings, covering the history of theatrical production in London from the eighteenth century onwards, and is constantly being added to by gifts and bequests. Mrs. Enthoven was herself a good amateur actress and the author of several plays, including an English adaptation of one of D'Annunzio's French plays, *Le Chèvrefeuille* (1913), which, as *The Honeysuckle*, was produced in New York in 1921. In 1948 she became the first President of the newly founded Society for Theatre Research (q.v.).

Entremés, a Spanish term which derives originally from the French *entremets*, applied to a diversion, dramatic or nondramatic, which took place between the courses of a banquet. In Catalonia such diversions were termed *entremeses* and this name was transferred to the dramatic interludes which enlivened the Corpus Christi procession. In Castilian the term was applied in the sixteenth and seventeenth centuries to a short comic interlude, often ending in a dance, which was performed in the public theatres between the acts of a play. Most of the well-known dramatists of the period wrote *entremeses*, among them Cervantes, Lope de Vega, and Calderón (qq.v.) (see also GÉNERO CHICO and SAINETE).

Epic Theatre, a phrase taken from Aristotle (q.v.), where it implies a series of incidents presented without regard to theatrical conventions, and used in the 1920s by such pioneers as Brecht and

Piscator (qq.v.) of episodic productions designed to appeal more to the audience's reason than to its emotions, thus excluding sympathy and identification with the drama being portrayed on stage (see also ALIENATION). It employs a multi-level technique of narration, and places the main emphasis on the social and political background of the play. Typical of Epic Theatre was a production by Piscator of a dramatized version of Leo Tolstoy's vast novel *War and Peace*. This was first seen in Berlin, and in 1962 made a brief appearance at the Bristol Old Vic and in London.

Epilogue, see PROLOGUE.

Equestrian Drama, see CIRCUS.

Equity, the professional actors' association in England and America. British Actors' Equity was founded on 1 Dec. 1929 to regulate all questions relating to actors' salaries, working conditions, and terms of employment, in London and in the provinces, and to advise the Ministry of Labour on the issuing of work permits for foreign actors. Before its foundation there had been attempts to organize theatre workers in the hope of improving salaries and back-stage conditions, which by the end of the nineteenth century were often extremely bad. Irving (q.v.) was president of the first Actors' Association, formed in 1891, but this had a short life, as did the first Actors' Union, founded in 1905. Equity now looks after the interests of all those working in the theatre and films, on radio and in television. Variety artists originally had their own Federation, but this amalgamated with Equity in 1968.

Unlike British Equity, American Equity (Actors' Equity Association) deals only with performers in the legitimate theatre. It is affiliated to the American Federation of Labor, and was founded on 16 May 1913. In August 1919 it called its first strike and was successful in gaining better conditions, and also official recognition. A second strike in 1960 resulted in further improvements in members' contracts, and in 1961 a policy of racial non-segregation was set on foot.

ERCKMANN–CHATRIAN, the pseudonym of two French authors who wrote novels and plays in collaboration, ÉMILE ERCKMANN (1822–99) and LOUIS-GRATIEN-CHARLES-ALEXANDRE CHATRIAN (1826–

90). They are best remembered for their melodrama, *Le Juif polonais*, which, in an English adaptation by Leopold Lewis as *The Bells*, provided Irving (q.v.) with the fine part of Mathias, in which he made his first great success at the Lyceum in 1871. He played the part many times, and after his death it was played also by his elder son, H. B. Irving, and by Martin-Harvey (qq.v.). In 1969 *The Bells* again had a brief run in London with Marius Goring as Mathias.

Erlanger's Theatre, NEW YORK, see ST. JAMES THEATRE.

ERVINE, JOHN ST. JOHN GREER (1883–1971), Irish dramatist and critic, who later settled in England, where he was dramatic critic for a number of papers, including the *Morning Post* and the *Observer*. He also wrote *The Theatre in My Time* and *How to Write a Play*. He was for a time manager of the Abbey Theatre (q.v.) in Dublin, where his early plays, among them *Mixed Marriage* (1911) and *John Ferguson* (1915), were first produced. In 1913, at the Gaiety, Manchester, Sybil Thorndike (q.v.) gave a moving performance in his *Jane Clegg*, as did Edith Evans in London in 1937 in the best of his later serious plays, *Robert's Wife*. He was also the author of several light comedies, of which *The First Mrs. Fraser* (1929) ran for more than two years with Marie Tempest (q.v.) in the title-role.

ESMOND [really JACK], HENRY VERNON (1869–1922), English actor-manager and dramatist, who first appeared in London in 1889 and was for a time associated with E. S. Willard and Edward Terry. He then joined George Alexander (q.v.) at the St. James's, where he scored a big success as Cayley Drummle in Pinero's *The Second Mrs. Tanqueray* (1893). He was also Little Billee in the first production of du Maurier's *Trilby* (1895). While at the St. James's he began writing plays, mainly sentimental comedies of the period, which had a great vogue and in which he later toured with his wife, EVA MOORE (1870–1955). The best-known of these is *Eliza Comes to Stay* (1913). His last play, which had a considerable success, was *The Law Divine*, produced at Wyndham's in 1918. His daughter Jill, also an actress, was the first wife of Laurence Olivier (q.v.).

ESPY, L' [really FRANÇOIS BEDEAU] (*c.* 1600–64), French actor, the elder brother of the clown Jodelet (q.v.). He joined the company of Molière (q.v.) in 1659, but soon gave up acting in favour of management, and was responsible for overseeing the alterations made in Richelieu's old theatre, the Palais-Royal, before Molière took possession of it in 1661. He retired in 1664, being then well over sixty.

ESSLAIR, FERDINAND (1772–1840), German actor, who made his début at Innsbruck and for many years toured the provinces until in 1820 he was appointed leading actor and manager of the Court theatre in Munich. Here he remained for a long time, becoming one of the most popular actors in Germany. At the height of his fame he again undertook an extended tour, being everywhere fêted and applauded. He was at his best in Schiller's plays, particularly as Wilhelm Tell and Wallenstein.

ESTCOURT, DICK (1668–1712), a Restoration actor immortalized by Steele in *The Spectator*, No. 468. He does not appear to have been a particularly good actor, but he was an amazing mimic, and his natural good humour and vivacity made him a favourite in any company. Shortly before his death he became landlord of the Bumper Tavern in St. James's Street, London.

ESTÉBANEZ, JOAQUÍN, see TAMAYO Y BAUS. MANUEL.

Ethel Barrymore Theatre, NEW YORK, on 47th Street between Broadway and 8th Avenue. Built by Lee Shubert, this opened on 20 Dec. 1928 with Ethel Barrymore (q.v.), in whose honour it was named, playing Sister Gracia in *The Kingdom of God* by the Spanish dramatist Martínez Sierra (q.v.). Its history, though not sensational, has been one of almost unvaried success. Among its outstanding productions have been Coward's *Design for Living* (1933) and *Point Valaine* (1935), Elsie Schauffler's *Parnell* (also 1935), with Margaret Rawlings as Kitty O'Shea, *Night Must Fall* (1936), by Emlyn Williams, who also appeared in it, and Clare Boothe's scathing comedy, *The Women* (also 1936). In 1947 Tennessee Williams's *A Streetcar Named Desire*, with Marlon Brando and Jessica Tandy as Stanley Kowalski and Blanche du Bois, won both the Pulitzer Prize and the New York Drama Critics' Circle award, a feat repeated ten years

later by Ketti Frings's adaptation of Wolfe's novel, *Look Homeward, Angel*.

ETHEREGE, SIR GEORGE (1634–91), English Restoration dramatist, the first to attempt, in *The Comical Revenge; or, Love in a Tub* (1664), the social comedy of manners developed by Congreve (q.v.) and later perfected by Sheridan (q.v.). This, and his two later plays, *She Would if She Could* (1668) and *The Man of Mode* (1676), show the influence of Molière (q.v.). The latter, with its brilliant dialogue and character-drawing, is a typical Restoration comedy, containing the 'prince of fops', Sir Fopling Flutter, and the witty Dorimant, often considered to be a portrait of Lord Rochester, as Bellair is of Etherege himself.

Ethiopian Operas, see RICE, T. D.

EURIPIDES (484–406/7 B.C.), Athenian tragic poet, who is said to have written ninety-two plays, of which there survive seventeen tragedies, one quite entertaining satyr-play, the *Cyclops*, and a large number of fragments (an indication of his later popularity), which include substantial parts of the *Hypsipyle* (on papyrus). The extant plays are: *Cyclops*, *Alcestis* (438 B.C.), *Medea* (431), *Hippolytus* (428), *Children of Heracles* (?c. 428), *Andromache*, *Hecuba*, *Heracles Furens*, *Suppliants*, *Ion*, *Electra*, *Trojan Women* (415), *Iphigenia in Tauris* (?414), *Helen* (412), *Phoenician Women* (411), *Orestes* (408), and the *Bacchae* and *Iphigenia in Aulis*, both produced posthumously. Included with these plays in the manuscripts is a weak play, *Rhesus*, sometimes thought to be an early play by Euripides, but more probably a fourth-century work.

In his lifetime Euripides aroused great interest and great opposition by his realism, his interest in abnormal psychology, and his portraits of women in love. He was the first dramatist to deal with the individual rather than the community, with personal passions rather than broad questions of morality and religion, and with specific social problems like war. After his death his fame eclipsed that of Aeschylus and Sophocles (qq.v.), for he alone could speak directly to the new world established by Alexander's conquests. In modern times his reputation has fluctuated, and he has been both unduly disparaged and overpraised. But most critics would agree with Aristotle (q.v.)

that he was 'the most tragic of the tragic poets'.

The best-known of his tragedies are the *Medea*, *Hippolytus*, *Bacchae*, *Trojan Women*, *Hecuba*, *Electra*, and *Orestes*, the last two being powerful studies in morbidity and insanity. Of the rest, the *Alcestis*, *Ion*, and *Iphigenia in Tauris* are excellent tragi-comedies or romantic dramas, the *Helen* is delightful high comedy, and the *Phoenician Women* is a pageant-play. All these (except the last) show a skill in construction, and a delicacy and wit both in the dialogue and in the characterization, which are of the very highest order, and the comic elements, even more than in the later plays of Aristophanes (q.v.), foreshadow the New Comedy of the fourth century and of Menander (q.v.).

Euripides continued to use the three actors and chorus as finally established by Sophocles, but one of his innovations, the 'prologue' (q.v.), has been important in the history of the drama. Early Greek tragedies began with the entrance-song of the chorus; the extant plays of Sophocles begin with a histrionic scene, which was, in Greek, a 'prologos'. What Euripides did was to invent a formal 'prologue', spoken sometimes by a character in the play, sometimes by an external god, which summarized the story up to the point where the action begins. This, via Seneca (q.v.), is the origin of the 'prologue' in Elizabethan drama. Linked with this is the progressive detachment of the chorus from the action, inevitable when plays began to deal with private rather than public issues, which led to the Elizabethan idea of an extraneous person called the 'Chorus' speaking a 'prologue'.

Eugene O'Neill Theatre, NEW YORK, on West 49th Street, between Broadway and 8th Avenue. This opened as the Forrest on 24 Nov. 1925. Its history was uneventful until on 17 Sept. 1934 *Tobacco Road*, based on a novel by Erskine Caldwell, was transferred there from the John Golden Theatre (q.v.), where it had opened on 4 Dec. 1933; it ran until 31 May 1941. In 1945 the theatre closed, and after extensive alterations reopened as the Coronet, its first success being a revival of Elmer Rice's *Dream Girl*, followed by Arthur Miller's *All My Sons* (1947). The theatre received its present name in honour of America's most famous playwright in 1959, its first production being Inge's *A Loss of Roses* on 28 Nov. In 1969

it housed a new play by Neil Simon (q.v.), *Last of the Red Hot Lovers*.

Euston Palace of Varieties, LONDON, see REGENT THEATRE.

EVANS, DAME EDITH (1888–1976), English actress, created D.B.E. in 1946 for her services to the theatre. She first appeared as an amateur with the Elizabethan Stage Society, playing Cressida in a production of *Troilus and Cressida* by William Poel (q.v.) in 1912. As a professional, she first came prominently before the public in 1924 with a fine performance as Millamant in Congreve's *The Way of the World*, in which, in 1948, she was again outstanding as Lady Wishfort. She was with the Old Vic in 1925–6, and in 1936, playing a variety of Shakespearian parts as well as Lady Fidget in Wycherley's *The Country Wife*. Among her other outstanding parts were the Serpent and the She-Ancient in *Back to Methuselah* (1924) and Orinthia in *The Apple Cart* (1929), both plays by Shaw; Lady Bracknell in Wilde's *The Importance of Being Earnest* (1939); Katerina Ivanovna in a dramatization of Dostoievsky's *Crime and Punishment* (1946); Lady Pitts in Bridie's *Daphne Laureola* (1949); and the Countess Rosmarin in Fry's 'winter' play, *The Dark is Light Enough* (1954). In 1958 she appeared as Queen Katharine in *Henry VIII* at the Old Vic and on tour, and in 1959 was a member of the Royal Shakespeare Company in Stratford-upon-Avon, returning to modern plays in *Gentle Jack* (1963), by Robert Bolt, and *The Chinese Prime Minister* (1965), by Enid Bagnold, in whose *The Chalk Garden* (1956) she had previously appeared with great success.

EVANS, MAURICE HERBERT (1901–89), English actor, who made his first success as Lieutenant Raleigh in Sherriff's *Journey's End* (1928). He joined the Old Vic company in 1934 and was seen in a variety of plays, including *Hamlet* in its entirety, with great success. He first went to America in 1935, and remained there, eventually becoming an American citizen in 1941. His outstanding appearances in Shakespeare on Broadway included Romeo in 1935, to the Juliet of Katharine Cornell (q.v.), Richard II in 1937, Hamlet in 1938, Falstaff in *Henry IV, Part I* in 1939, Malvolio in *Twelfth Night* in 1940, and Macbeth in 1941, these last five productions being all directed by Margaret Webster (q.v.). During the Second World

War Evans entertained the troops with his so-called G.I. version of *Hamlet*, which he subsequently published. He also played a number of Shaw parts in New York, including John Tanner in *Man and Superman* (1947), Dick Dudgeon in *The Devil's Disciple* (1950), King Magnus in *The Apple Cart* (1956), and Captain Shotover in *Heartbreak House* (1959). In 1962–3 he appeared with Helen Hayes (q.v.) in a programme of extracts from Shakespeare.

EVANS, WILL (1873–1931), English music-hall comedian, son of a pantomime clown with whom he appeared as a child, making his first appearance at Drury Lane at Christmas, 1881. As an adult he specialized in burlesque sketches, of which the most successful were *Building a Chicken House*, *Whitewashing the Ceiling*, and *Papering a House*, and for many years he imported the same style of knockabout humour into kitchen scenes in Drury Lane pantomimes. He was part-author of the famous farce, *Tons of Money* (1922), and of *The Other Mr. Gibbs* (1924).

Everyman Theatre, LONDON, at Hampstead. Though mainly known as a cinema, from 1920 to 1926 it played an important part in theatrical history under the management of Norman MacDermott (q.v.), with seasons of Shaw and Ibsen, first performances in London of O'Neill's *Diff'rent* (1921) and *The Long Voyage Home* (1925), and first performances of foreign plays in translation, among them Benavente's *The Bonds of Interest*, Chiarelli's *The Mask and the Face* (1924), and Pirandello's *Henry IV* (1925). Among plays transferred to West End theatres from the Everyman were C. K. Munro's *At Mrs. Beam's* and Sutton Vane's *Outward Bound* (both 1923), and Noël Coward's *The Vortex* (1924). These plays were all directed by MacDermott, who also designed the costumes and scenery for most of them. His last production at the Everyman was Chesterton's *The Man Who Was Thursday*.

EVREINOV, NIKOLAI NIKOLAIVICH (1879–1953), Russian dramatist, a symbolist writer whose revolt against the naturalistic theatre led him to write *The Theatre of the Soul* (1912), a 'monodrama' in which various aspects of the same person are played by different actors. His *Revisor* (also 1912) illustrated amusingly

what such directors as Stanislavsky and Reinhardt (qq.v.) might do to Gogol's masterpiece, *The Inspector-General*, and in *The Fourth Wall* (1915) an ultra-realistic director is let loose on Goethe's *Faust*. A later play, *The Chief Thing* (1921), which deals with the power of illusion, has some affinity with the work of Pirandello (q.v.); but Evreinov's theories were soon swept aside by the new 'socialist realism' (q.v.) of the Soviet era, in which they had no place. Two of his short plays were translated by C. E. Bechhofer and published in *Five Russian Plays* (1916) as *A Merry Death* and *The Beautiful Despot*.

Exeter. The first theatre in Exeter, probably in about 1735, was a room in the Seven Stars Inn just outside the city boundary. There is, however, evidence of acting by waits, mummers, and minstrels as early as 1362, and in the fifteenth century the Skinners' Guild performed part of a religious cycle every Corpus Christi. In the early sixteenth century performances by strolling players are noted in the city accounts, as are also payments to players 'not to play', an early effect of Puritanism. The last recorded performance before the Commonwealth was in 1625. It was followed by a bad visitation of plague, which effectually put an end to playgoing in Exeter, and in spite of the Restoration it was not until the early eighteenth century that a company from Bath appeared in the city, and even, during the late 1730s, erected a small theatre. This was closed by the Theatres Act of 1737 and became a Methodist chapel. It later reverted to its original use as a station on the Bath circuit. It was managed for a year in the 1760s by Thomas Jefferson, great-grandfather of the famous American actor Joseph Jefferson (q.v.). In 1787 a new theatre was built, based on the plans of Sadler's Wells (q.v.). Among the London stars who appeared at this theatre were Stephen Kemble, Mrs. Siddons, Master Betty, and Edmund Kean (qq.v.). It was destroyed by fire on 7 Mar. 1820. The only part to survive was the colonnade. This was incorporated into a new building, which opened on 10 Jan. 1821 with *The Merchant of Venice*. Kean again played at this theatre, as did Dowton, Mme Vestris, Charles and Fanny Kemble, Macready, and Phelps (qq.v.). In 1880 the first performance of *Hearts of Oak*, by a local travelling salesman later better known as

Henry Arthur Jones (q.v.), had in its cast Jerome K. Jerome (q.v.). This theatre, known from Feb. 1828 as the Theatre Royal, was also destroyed by fire on 7 Feb. 1885. A new Theatre Royal opened on 13 Oct. 1886 and was destined to be destroyed in one of the worst fires in the history of the English theatre, when on 5 Sept. 1887, during a performance of *Romany Rye*, by G. R. Sims, the theatre was burnt down with the loss of 186 lives. It was not until 7 Oct. 1889 that a new theatre opened. It prospered for a time, and even survived the vicissitudes of the 1920s and 1930s and escaped damage by bombing during the Second World War, becoming well known after the war for its long-running annual Christmas pantomimes. It closed and was demolished in 1962. Exeter was then left without a theatre until the opening in 1967 of the Northcott (see UNIVERSITY DEPARTMENTS OF DRAMA).

Exit, 'he goes out', see STAGE DIRECTIONS.

Expressionism, a movement that began in Germany in about 1910, and is best typified by the plays of Georg Kaiser and Ernst Toller (qq.v.). The term was first used in 1901 by Auguste Hervé to describe some of his paintings conceived in reaction against Impressionism in art. It was later used of art, music, and literature, as well as plays that displayed reality as seen by the artist looking out from within, instead of, as with Impressionism, reality as it affects the artist inwardly. The Expressionist theatre was a theatre of protest, mainly against the contemporary social order and the domination of the family. Most of its dramatists were poets who used the theatre to further their ideas, and it was partly their use of poetic language that led to the collapse of the movement. It was too personal, as was the concentration of attention on the central figure, the author–hero whose reactions are 'expressed' in the play. Among the forerunners of Expressionism were Strindberg and Wedekind (qq.v.), but the first drama of the Expressionist movement is usually considered to be *Der Bettler*, by Reinhard Johannes Sorge (q.v.). Other dramatists important in the movement were WALTER HASENCLEVER (1890–1940), whose *Der Sohn* (1916) was the first Expressionist drama to be seen in the theatre; FRITZ VON UNRUH (1885–), whose plays, of which the most successful was *Ein Geschlecht* (1917), had a military background; and ERNST BARLACH (1870–1938), author of *Der arme Vetter* (1917). One of the few dramatists outside Germany who was influenced by Expressionist drama was O'Neill (q.v.), particularly in *The Emperor Jones* (1920) and *The Hairy Ape* (1922).

Extravaganza, see BURLESQUE (2).

EYSOLDT, GERTRUD (1870–1955), German actress, who made her first appearance on the stage at Meiningen in 1890. After touring in Germany and Russia she appeared in Berlin in 1899, and later played under Reinhardt (q.v.). An extremely clever and subtle actress, she was at her best in modern realistic parts, particularly in the works of Wedekind (q.v.), in which she played opposite the author. She was also good in Ibsen, in such parts as Wilde's Salome and Shakespeare's Cleopatra, and in the plays of Maeterlinck (q.v.).

F

FABBRI, DIEGO (1911–), Italian playwright, influenced both by Betti and Pirandello (qq.v.), whose most significant works are: *Inquisizione* (1950), *Il seduttore* (1951), *Processo di famiglia* (1953), *Processo a Gesù* (1955), and *La bugiarda* (1956), in which the Compagnia dei Giovani appeared at the Aldwych, London, during the World Theatre season of 1965. He has also dramatized Dostoievsky's *The Devils* and *The Brothers Karamazov*, published in 1961 in the volume *I demoni*. His plays are well known on the Continent and in South America, but though several have been translated into English they have as yet had little impact on the English theatre.

Fabula, a generic Latin name for a play, under which many different types of drama were grouped. The most important was the *fabula Atellana* (see ATELLAN FARCE). The other main groups were:

(1) PALLIATA, a play translated into Latin from Greek New Comedy (see MENANDER); from *pallium*, a Greek cloak. It may also have been called *crepidata*, from *crepida*, a Greek shoe. The chief writer of such plays was Terence (q.v.).

(2) PRAETEXTA, an original play in Latin on a theme taken from Roman legend or history; from *toga praetextata*, the purple-bordered toga worn by magistrats.

(3) TOGATA, a Roman comedy based on scenes of contemporary daily life in the town, as distinct from the country background of the Atellan farce; from *toga*, the long garment worn by the Roman citizen. The cast of a *togata* was smaller, and the plot simpler, than in the *palliata*.

FAGAN, JAMES BERNARD (1873–1933), playwright and director, born in Ulster, who began his stage career in the company of Frank Benson (q.v.) and was for a time with Tree (q.v.) at Her Majesty's. He later took over the management of the Royal Court Theatre in London, but his best work was done at Oxford (q.v.), where from 1923 to 1925 he directed a series of excellent productions with a repertory company which included at various times Flora Robson, John Gielgud, and Tyrone Guthrie (qq.v.). In 1929 he became director of the Festival Theatre, Cambridge. Among his own plays, the best-known are *And So to Bed* (1926), based on Pepys's Diary, and *The Improper Duchess* (1931), in both of which Yvonne Arnaud (q.v.) made a great success.

FAIR, WILLIAM B. (1851–1909), music-hall artist, best remembered for his performance of 'Tommy, Make Room for your Uncle', which he sang at as many as six halls a night. With the fortune it brought him he took over the Surrey Gardens Music-Hall (q.v.), but lost all his money, returned to the halls as Chairman (see HOLBORN EMPIRE), and ended as a link-man outside the Coliseum

FAIRBROTHER, SYDNEY (1872–1941), see COWELL, SAM.

Fairs. In England and Europe the big fairs, held usually in the spring and autumn, were from the beginning associated with theatrical enterprise. This was most noticeable in the case of the Parisian fairs of Saint-Germain in early spring and Saint-Laurent in August and September, and some of the best-known farce-players of seventeenth-century Paris came from the fairgrounds. But the development of the *forains*, as they were called, came at the end of the seventeenth and in the eighteenth centuries, when they replaced their temporary wooden booths by permanent playhouses in which they continued to act when the fair was over. Their popularity proved very irritating to the Comédie-Française and the Comédie-Italienne (qq.v.), until the latter made common cause with the enemy and combined with the *forains* to form the Opéra-Comique, occupying during the summer months the Théâtre de la Foire Saint-Laurent, built in 1721 and finally destroyed in the rebuilding of the Opéra-Comique in 1761. The Théâtre de la Foire Saint-Germain survived until 1756. After the French Revolution the freedom accorded to the theatres led the *forains* to settle permanently on the Boulevard du Temple (q.v.), where a number of small but important playhouses were built, including the Funambules, the Gaîeté, and the Ambigu-Comique, as well as innumerable small booths of acrobats and marionettes. The whole thing was swept away at the height of its success by Haussmann in his rebuilding scheme in 1862, thus breaking the last link between the modern theatre and the old fairground actor.

In England the fairs of Saint Bartholomew, immortalized by Ben Jonson (q.v.), Smithfield, and Southwark, as well as the smaller Greenwich and May fairs, were always connected with theatrical entertainments, particularly puppet shows, though some booths were used by live actors (see SETTLE). The theatrical development of the English fairs was, however, less noticeable than in France, perhaps because of the weather, and there is no record of any permanent playhouses being built on fairgrounds.

Of the German fairs, those of Leipzig and Frankfurt are best known in connection with theatrical matters. It was at Frankfurt fair that the English Comedians (q.v.) appeared most frequently and had, if anywhere, a permanent home, while Leipzig fair saw the reforms of Gottsched first put into action by the great actress Caroline Neuber (q.v.). Fairs also played a big part in the history of the early Russian theatre, which, however, developed somewhat differently from the rest of Europe. Little information seems to be available on the fairs of Italy and Spain, but no doubt the *commedia dell'arte* in the first, and the travelling companies of such actor-managers as Lope de Rueda (q.v.) in the second, were to be found wherever they saw the chance of a ready-made audience.

FALCKENBERG, OTTO (1873–1947), see MUNICH.

Falling Flaps, see TRANSFORMATION SCENE.

False Pros(cenium) (also known as Inner Pros(cenium), and in French as *le manteau d'Harlequin*), an arrangement of wings and top border, painted and profiled to resemble draped curtains, with folds, swags, fringes, cords, and tassels. It served to reduce the size of the proscenium opening and was suitable for any set of scenery. It could also be used with a cyclorama (q.v.) to reduce the amount of scenery needed to dress the stage. In modern proscenium theatres the wings are often replaced by a fixed pair of narrow flats covered in black velvet, known as Tormentors.

Fan Effect, see TRANSFORMATION SCENE.

Farce, an extreme form of comedy in which laughter is raised at the expense of probability, particularly by horseplay and bodily assault. It originated in the rustic merrymakings of folk-drama, of which little written record remains but which probably influenced the development of Greek comedy (see SATYR-DRAMA). Farce was popular in Rome (see ATELLAN FARCE), and formed the stock-in-trade of the *commedia dell'arte* (q.v.). It was also popular in France in late medieval times, and the old traditions, which had a great influence on Molière (q.v.), were maintained in seventeenth-century Paris by Gaultier-Garguille, Gros-Guillaume, and Turlupin (qq.v.), finally dying out with Jodelet (q.v.). Of the old farces, many of which were never written down, the best-known is *Maître Pierre Pathelin*, which has survived revision, adaptation, and even translation, without losing its robust humour. There were elements of farce in early English biblical plays, and farcical interludes were written for production in schools, but, as in Italy and Germany, the influence of the French farce was paramount, culminating in the works of John Heywood (q.v.).

In the eighteenth and nineteenth centuries short sketches, billed as farces, were popular in the English-speaking theatre as light relief after a five-act tragedy. They are mostly forgotten, though some of them achieved success through their association with a particular comedian. In modern usage the word farce is applied to a full-length play dealing with some absurd situation, generally based on extra-marital adventures—hence the term 'bedroom farce'. Owing to its robust character, farce survives translation better than comedy, as is shown by the recent success in England of the farces of Feydeau (q.v.), some of the best of their kind. An early exponent of modern farce in England was Pinero (q.v.), several of whose early farces have been successfully revived. A famous example of an early full-length farce which still holds the stage is *Charley's Aunt* (1892), by Brandon Thomas. In the 1920s and '30s there was a series of successful farces at the Aldwych Theatre (q.v.), mostly written by Ben Travers, and in the 1950s and '60s a similar series was produced by Brian Rix at the Whitehall (q.v.) (see also GARRICK THEATRE (2)).

FARJEON, HERBERT (1887–1945), English actor, playwright, and dramatic critic, author, with his sister Eleanor, of the musical plays *The Two Bouquets* (1936). *An Elephant in Arcady* (1938), and *The Glass Slipper* (1944). He was also the author and director of witty, intimate-revue sketches seen mainly at the Little Theatre, London, and elsewhere in the 1930s. A scholarly man, editor of the Nonesuch Edition of Shakespeare and of the *Shakespeare Journal* from 1922 to 1925, he had much of the charm and geniality of his grandfather, Joseph Jefferson (q.v.). A selection of his criticisms of Shakespearian productions from 1913 to 1944 was published in 1949 as *The Shakespearean Scene*. His elder brothers, Harry and Joseph Jefferson Farjeon, were well known as composer and author respectively.

FARQUHAR, GEORGE (1678–1707), a late Restoration dramatist, born in Ireland. He was for a time an actor at the Smock Alley Theatre in Dublin, but in 1697 went to London, where his first play, *Love and a Bottle*, was successfully presented at Drury Lane in 1698. It was followed by an even more successful play, *The Constant Couple; or, a Trip to the Jubilee* (1699). The hero, Sir Harry Wildair, first played by Wilks (q.v.), later provided a famous 'breeches part' for Peg Woffington (q.v.). Farquhar's last plays, *The Recruiting Officer* (1706) and *The Beaux' Stratagem* (1707), were equally successful and still hold the stage. The first, on which Brecht (q.v.) based his *Pauken und Trompetten*, was revived at the Old Vic in 1963 with Olivier (q.v.) as Brazen, the second in 1970 with Maggie Smith (q.v.) as Mrs. Sullen. It was in this part, originally played by Anne Oldfield (q.v.), that Edith Evans (q.v.) made a great success in 1927. *The Beaux' Stratagem* was also in the repertory of the Chichester Festival Theatre in 1967.

FARR, FLORENCE [MRS. EDWARD EMERY] (1860–1917), English actress and director, chiefly connected with the introduction of Ibsen, Shaw, and Yeats (qq.v.) to the English stage. In 1891 she played Rebecca West in the first production in London of Ibsen's *Rosmersholm*, and in the following year appeared as Blanche in *Widowers' Houses*, the first of Shaw's plays to be staged. Financed by Miss Horniman (q.v.), she produced at the Avenue Theatre in

1894 Shaw's *Arms and the Man*, in which she created the part of Louka, preceded by the one-act *The Land of Heart's Desire*, the first of Yeats's plays to be performed. She was later associated with Yeats in Dublin, playing Aleel the Minstrel in *The Countess Cathleen* on its first production in 1899, and with the Vedrenne-Barker management at the Court Theatre, arranging the music and training the chorus for the productions of Euripides' *Trojan Women* (1905) and *Hippolytus* (1906), in which she played the Leader of the Chorus and the Nurse respectively.

FARREN, ELIZABETH (1759–1829), English actress, child of strolling players, with whom she appeared from her earliest years. She made her first appearance in London on 9 June 1777 at the Haymarket as Kate Hardcastle in Goldsmith's *She Stoops to Conquer*, and then went to Drury Lane, where she excelled as a player of fine ladies, for which her natural elegance, tall, slim figure, and beautiful voice rendered her particularly suitable. The Earl of Derby was in love with her for many years, and married her on the death of his wife in 1797, in which year she made her last appearance on the stage, as Lady Teazle in Sheridan's *The School for Scandal*.

FARREN, NELLIE [really ELLEN] (1848–1904), English actress, descendant of a long line of actors, her great-grandfather WILLIAM (1725–95) having appeared as Careless and Leicester in the first productions of Sheridan's *The School for Scandal* (1777) and *The Critic* (1779) respectively, while his son WILLIAM (1786–1861) was unequalled in his day as Sir Peter Teazle, also in *The School for Scandal*, and in many Shakespearian roles. Nellie's father, HENRY (1826–60), was on the stage in London before going to America, where he was manager of a theatre in St. Louis at the time of his early death. She herself was a favourite at the old Gaiety Theatre (q.v.), where she was one of the famous burlesque quartet with Edward Terry, Kate Vaughan, and Edward Royce. Being small and slight, she specialized in the playing of boys' parts—Smike in Dickens's *Nicholas Nickleby*, Sam Willoughby in Tom Taylor's *Ticket-of-Leave Man*, and the cheeky Cockney lads in H. J. Byron's burlesques and extravaganzas. Her husband, ROBERT SOUTAR (1827–1908), an actor and dramatist, was for many years stage manager at the Gaiety. Her two sons were also on the stage, JOSEPH, whose career stretched over fifty years, dying in 1962 at the age of ninety-one.

Fastnachtsspiel, the German Carnival or Shrovetide play of the fifteenth century, in one act, performed mainly by students and artisans. It shows, in its somewhat crude couplets, a mingling of religious and popular elements interesting in the light of later developments in German drama and is somewhat akin to the French *sotie* (q.v.), though without its political satire. The subjects of the Carnival plays are those which would appeal to the mainly urban audiences before whom they were usually acted—the weaknesses and venial sins of lawyers and their clients, doctors and their patients, clerics and their female parishioners. In most of these farces the Narr (q.v.) or fool is the central character, sometimes with a dull-witted companion to serve as a butt for his practical jokes. At first the plays were presented in the simplest possible way, rather in the style of the English mumming play (q.v.), but later, when the town guilds took over, a raised stage and hangings, with a few properties, became general, though nothing as elaborate as the organized companies of the Parisian *enfants sans souci* ever emerged. Many of the Carnival plays were written by the Mastersingers, of whom the best-known is Hans Sachs (q.v.).

Fate Drama, the name given to a type of early nineteenth-century German play inaugurated by Werner's *Der vierundzwanzigste Februar* (1809), in which a malignant fate dogs the footsteps of the chief character, driving him, by a chain of fortuitous circumstances, to commit a horrible crime, often the unwitting murder of a son by his own father. The genre was further exploited by Adolf Müllner in *Der neunundzwanzigste Februar* (1812) and by the young Grillparzer (q.v.) in his first play, *Die Ahnfrau* (1817).

FAUCIT, HELEN [really HELENA SAVILLE] (1817–98), English actress, who was prepared for the stage by one of the Farrens, Percival, great-uncle of Nellie (q.v.). She first appeared in the provinces in 1833 and was seen in London three years later as Julia in a revival of Sheridan Knowles's *The Hunchback*. One of her best parts

was Pauline in Bulwer-Lytton's *The Lady of Lyons* (1838), in which she played opposite Macready (q.v.). She also played in Browning's poetic dramas, *Strafford* (1837), *A Blot in the 'Scutcheon* (1843), and *Colombe's Birthday* (1853), and it was said that her refusal to appear in Matthew Arnold's *Merope* led him to abandon its production. She was outstanding in Shakespeare, and out of her experiences wrote *On Some of Shakespeare's Female Characters* (1885). She married in 1851, becoming Lady Martin when her husband was knighted in 1880, and in later life acted only for charity.

FAUST, JOHANN (c. 1488–1541), a wandering conjurer and entertainer whose name became linked with a medieval legend of a man in league with the devil. The story of his adventures was published in a Frankfurt chapbook in 1587, which in an English translation provided the material for a play, *The Tragical History of Doctor Faustus* (c. 1588), by Christopher Marlowe (q.v.). The legend returned to the country of its origin via the English Comedians (q.v.), and lived on in a puppet-show until once more taken up seriously by Lessing (q.v.) in 1759. Only fragments of his work remain, but it is evident that he envisaged Faust as a scholar whose inquiring mind finds itself in conflict with the limits imposed by God on human knowledge, but whose soul is in the end to be saved by divine grace. During the period of *Sturm und Drang* (q.v.) the Faust legend made a strong appeal, being used by Müller, Klinger (in a novel), and particularly by Goethe (q.v.), whose play on the subject, in two parts, engaged his attention from 1774 to his death in 1832. In it Faust, though tempted by Mephistopheles and guilty of the death of Gretchen, defies the devil and escapes him, his soul, as in Lessing's version, being eventually borne up to heaven. Since Goethe, the subject has been treated in German by Lenau, Heine, Grabbe, and others; in French by Paul Valéry; and in English by Wills (1885), and Rawson (1924) (from Goethe), and by Stephen Phillips and Comyns Carr in collaboration. It has also supplied the libretti for operas by Boito, Busoni, Gounod, and others.

Fauteuil, see STALL.

FAVART, CHARLES-SIMON (1710–92), French dramatist, and the first man to make a solid reputation out of the writing of libretti for light opera, in which genre he was the mentor and forerunner of Marmontel and Sedaine. He had much in common with La Fontaine as regards style and easy versification and also something of his wit and good humour. His best works are written to be sung and read poorly. His one straight play was an amusing trifle entitled *L'Anglais à Bordeaux*, given at the Comédie-Française in 1763. He married MLLE CHANTILLY [really MARIE-JUSTINE-BENOISTE DURONCERAY] (1727–72), an actress at the Comédie-Italienne who was credited with the first introduction of historical and local details into her stage costumes, a practice followed soon after at the Comédie-Française by Lekain and Mlle Clairon (qq.v.).

Favart, THÉÂTRE, see COMÉDIE-ITALIENNE.

FAVERSHAM, WILLIAM (1868–1940), American actor-manager, born in London, where he made a brief appearance on the stage before going to New York in 1887. He then played small parts at the Lyceum with Daniel Frohman's company, and was for two years with Mrs. Fiske (q.v.). In 1893 he was engaged by Charles Frohman for the Empire Theatre (q.v.) and remained there for eight years, playing a wide variety of parts and starring as Romeo to the Juliet of Maude Adams (q.v.). He appeared in a number of modern plays, and in 1909 made his first independent venture with the production at the Lyric Theatre, New York, of Stephen Phillips's *Herod*, in which he played the name-part. It was, however, his production of *Julius Caesar* in 1912, in which he played Mark Antony, that set the seal on his growing reputation both as actor and director. With a fine cast, the play ran for some time in New York and then went on tour, being followed by productions of *Othello* and *Romeo and Juliet*. After a further series of new plays, Faversham toured Australia, and on his return was seen in several more plays by Shakespeare, and as Jeeter Lester in Kirkland's long-running *Tobacco Road* (1933).

FAY, FRANK J. (1870–1931) and **WILLIAM GEORGE** (1872–1947), Irish actors, who were important in the early history of the modern Irish theatrical revival, forming in 1898 the Irish National Dramatic Society (see IRISH LITERARY THEATRE). In 1902 they directed and acted in a number of plays by Yeats (q.v.), and in 1904 took over the Abbey Theatre (q.v.), where they appeared in most of the plays seen in the early years, among them Synge's *Playboy of the Western World* (1907), in which W. G. played Christy Mahon and Frank his rival, Shawn Keogh. A year later they left Dublin and went to New York, where they directed and appeared in a repertory of Irish plays under the management of Charles Frohman. Some years later, Frank returned to the Abbey to play in a revival of Yeats's *The Hour-Glass*, and finally settled in Dublin as a teacher of elocution. W. G. returned to England in 1914 and was at both the Nottingham and Birmingham repertory theatres. Among his later parts in London were the Tramp in Synge's *The Shadow of the Glen* (1930), Mr. Cassidy in Bridie's *Storm in a Teacup* (1935), and the name-part in Carroll's *Father Malachy's Miracle* (1945). In 1940 he was seen as Stephano in the Old Vic production of *The Tempest*. He was the author of *The Fays of the Abbey Theatre* (1935) and of a volume of reminiscences, *Merely Players*, and in 1932 published *A Short Glossary of Theatrical Terms*.

Feast of Fools, the generic name given to the New Year revels of the minor clergy in European cathedrals and collegiate churches. It seems to have originated in France in about the twelfth century, and may have had some connection with the festivities of the Roman Kalends. During the feast the minor clergy took over the functions of their superiors and gave free rein to their turbulence and high spirits. The entertainments from the beginning seem to have included some form of crude drama. A KING (or, in schools, a BOY BISHOP) was appointed, who headed a procession riding on the donkey which appears later in liturgical drama in the scenes of Balaam's Ass and the Flight into Egypt. The Feast of Fools, which is known to have been celebrated in England at Lincoln, Beverley, Salisbury, and St. Paul's, died out in England in the fourteenth century, and the place of the King was usurped by the ABBOT or LORD OF MISRULE or UNREASON, who during the fifteenth and early sixteenth centuries was appointed to oversee the Christmas revels at Court, at the colleges of the universities (particularly at St. John's and Merton in

Oxford, where appointments were made as late as 1577), and at the Inns of Court, where the custom lingered on intermittently until the 1660s.

FEATHERSTONHAUGH, CONSTANCE (1860–1946), see BENSON, FRANK.

FECHTER, CHARLES ALBERT (1824–79), an actor who played in French and English, both in Europe and in America, with equal success. He made his début at the Comédie-Française in 1840, but soon left to make his reputation elsewhere and became an outstanding *jeune premier*, being the first to play Armand Duval in Dumas *fils*'s *La Dame aux camélias* (1852). He had already played in English several times in London, where he was much admired in spite of a marked French accent, when in 1861 his revolutionary Hamlet brought him fame. His reading of the part brought out its subtlety and depth, and even those who clung to the old traditional style were impressed by his interpretation. His next venture, Othello, was not so successful, and in a subsequent revival he played Iago. In 1863 he took over the management of the London Lyceum (q.v.), appearing there with great success in a series of melodramas. In 1869 he went to New York, where he appeared in a number of his old successes as well as in new plays. His imperious and quarrelsome nature made him many enemies, and he left for a short visit to England, returning to New York to appear only in revivals. In 1876, after breaking his leg, he retired to a farm near Philadelphia.

Fedeli, a company of actors of the Italian *commedia dell'arte* (q.v.), formed in about 1598 by the younger Andreini (q.v.). It first came into prominence in 1603, and later took in actors from the Gelosi and Accesi. For some time the company's Arlecchino was the famous Tristano Martinelli (q.v.), who paid prolonged visits to Paris, his acting, and that of Andreini, being much admired by Louis XIII. The Fedeli also toured extensively in Italy, and seems to have continued in existence until shortly after 1644. It was officially under the protection of the Duke of Mantua in succession to the Gelosi (q.v.).

Federal Street Theatre, see BOSTON.

Federal Theatre Project, an effort by the United States government, within the framework of the Works Progress Administration (W.P.A.), to establish a nationwide network designed to give employment to needy professional theatre people in socially useful jobs. Under the direction of Hallie Flanagan (q.v.), it began work in the summer of 1935 and its charter was officially ratified on 1 Oct. It encouraged writers to do experimental work, using actors, scene designers, and musicians in the quantity required to comply with government regulations, and in its short life did much to stimulate directing, acting, and scene designing all over the country, working through regional assistants controlled from Washington. It also attracted to the theatre vast new audiences who came to see not only revivals of classic European and American plays, but also such new ventures as Sinclair Lewis's *It Can't Happen Here* (1936), produced simultaneously in twenty-one cities; regional plays like Paul Green's *The Lost Colony* (1937), on Manteo Island in North Carolina; the production by a Negro company of *The Swing Mikado* (1939); and above all the newly invented Living Newspaper (q.v.), terse presentations in cinema technique of important issues of the day, of which the best were probably *Triple-A Plowed Under* (1936) and *One-Third of a Nation* (1938), both by Arthur Arent. It was in some measure the success of the Living Newspaper, with its unbiased presentation of facts, that led to the downfall of the Federal Theatre, which was closed by the government on political grounds on 30 June 1939.

FEDOROVITCH, SOPHIE (1893–1953), stage designer, who came to England in 1924, and from 1926 onwards designed settings for most of the leading ballet companies of the time, including Sadler's Wells. The keynote of her art was simplicity, and she had a great gift for creating atmosphere by skilful lighting and an uncluttered set which left the imagination free to roam. Her last work was done for Gluck's 'Orpheus', presented at Covent Garden after her death.

FÉLIX, ÉLISA, see RACHEL.

FELLOWES, AMY (?–1898), see TERRISS, WILLIAM.

Female Impersonation. In the Greek and Elizabethan theatres female parts were always played by boys and men, as they were for centuries in China and Japan, where the actress is still a comparatively recent phenomenon. Some actors have become renowned for their excellent portrayal of women—Bathyllus in Rome, Alizon in Paris, Ned Kynaston in London, Mei Lan-Fang in China. The 'woman' in the Negro minstrel shows was always played by a man. The greatest American exponent of the art of female impersonation was probably Eltinge (q.v.). In *The Passing Show* and the *Ziegfeld Follies* in the 1920s Bert Savoy played the part of a vulgar but good-natured young 'gal about town'. The tradition is being carried on in New York by THOMAS CRAIG JONES (1920–), who differs from his predecessors in that he imitates, not womankind, but specific women. In England the Dame (q.v.) in pantomime is played by an actor, but this is less impersonation than burlesque and caricature, as is also the case in Brandon Thomas's *Charley's Aunt* (1892). Today the finest exponent of 'drag', as female impersonation is known in England, is Danny La Rue (q.v.).

FENN, EZEKIEL (1620–?), a boy actor who played Sophonisba, the chief female part in Nabbes's *Hannibal and Scipio*, in 1635. He must already have had a good deal of experience, since at about the same time he played Winifred, an even more exacting role, in a revival of Dekker and Rowley's *The Witch of Edmonton*. He was with Queen Henrietta's Men at the Cockpit (q.v.), playing his first male part in 1639, and stayed on with Beeston after their removal, possibly as one of the older members of Beeston's Boys. It is not known what happened to him when the theatres closed in 1642.

FENNELL, JAMES (1766–1816), an actor who gained his experience in the English provinces and in 1792 went to America, where he was very popular. He was a member of the American Company (q.v.), and also of Wignell's company in Philadelphia. His best part was always considered to be Othello, though he appeared in most of the tragic roles of the current repertory, including Jaffier in Otway's *Venice Preserv'd*, which he played at the Park Theatre, New York, in 1799, in company with Cooper and Mrs. Melmoth. In 1814, four years after his retirement, he published his autobiography, entitled *An Apology for the Life of James Fennell*.

FENTON [really BESWICK], LAVINIA (1708–60), English actress, and the first to play Polly Peachum in Gay's *The Beggar's Opera*. She made her first appearance on the stage at the Haymarket in 1726 as Monimia in Otway's *The Orphan*, and was an immediate success, being pretty, witty, and only eighteen. Her appearance as Polly at Lincoln's Inn Fields on 29 Jan. 1728 sealed her reputation, and she became one of the most talked-of women of the London stage. She made her last appearance on 28 June the same year and then retired to live with the Duke of Bolton, whom she married in 1751.

FERBER, EDNA (1887–1968), see KAUFMAN, GEORGE.

FERNÁNDEZ DE MORATÍN, LEANDRO (1760–1828), the most successful of the Spanish neo-classical dramatists, combining the contemporary style of France and the Venetian comedy of Goldoni (q.v.) with traditional Spanish elements. One of his early successes was *El café* or *La comedia nueva* (1792), a brilliant satire on the extravagant but popular dramas of the time as exemplified in the ephemeral works of LUCIANO COMELLA (1751–1812). His most famous play, however, is *El sí de las niñas* (1806), in which the author upholds the woman's right to marry the man she loves, a situation reminiscent of Goldoni's *I rusteghi*. Moratín was a great admirer of Molière and made excellent translations of *L'École des maris* and *Le Médecin malgré lui*. He also translated *Hamlet* into Spanish, and wrote a history of the Spanish theatre which was published two years after his death.

FERRARI, PAOLO (1822–89), one of the most popular Italian dramatists of his time, who won fame when in 1853 his play about Goldoni, *Goldoni e le sue sedici commedie*, was awarded a prize offered by a Florentine dramatic academy. It was followed by several other plays, of which *Il suicidio* (1875) held the stage for many years; but Ferrari's best-known work is undoubtedly *La satira e Parini* (1856), of which one character, the Marchese Colombi, is as familiar to Italian audiences as Mrs. Malaprop in Sheridan's *The Rivals* is to English.

FERREIRA, ANTÓNIO (1528–69), author of Portugal's finest tragedy, *Castro* (pub. 1587), on the murder in 1355 of Inés de Castro, mistress of Pedro, eldest son of Alfonso IV, which is also the first Portuguese play to combine classical models with native material. He also wrote two comedies, *Cioso* and *Bristo* (pub. 1622).

Festival Theatre, CAMBRIDGE, see GRAY, TERENCE.

FEUILLÈRE [really CUNATI], EDWIGE (1907–), French actress, who first appeared in light comedies at the Palais-Royal and Bouffes-Parisiens under the name of Cora Lynn. In 1931 she made her début at the Comédie-Française, but left to go into films, and returned to Paris in 1934 to play elsewhere. The pre-eminence of her acting was first apparent in 1937, when she appeared in Becque's *La Parisienne*, and in Dumas *fils*'s *La Dame aux camélias*, in which she was seen in London in 1955. She appeared as Lia in the first production of Giraudoux's *Sodome et Gomorrhe* (1943) and as the Queen in Cocteau's *L'Aigle à deux têtes* (1946), and a year later joined the Barrault-Renaud company to play Ysé, one of her finest parts, in *Partage de midi*, by Claudel (q.v.). She was seen in this in London in 1951 and 1968. In 1957, in which year she appeared as the Queen in a French version of *La regina e gli insorti*, by Betti (q.v.), she was again in London, appearing with her own company at the Palace Theatre in a repertory which included Racine's *Phèdre* and Becque's *La Parisienne*.

FEYDEAU, GEORGES-LÉON-JULES-MARIE (1862–1921), French dramatist, son of the novelist ERNEST-AIMÉ FEYDEAU (1821–73), and author of more than sixty farces, some written in collaboration. He had his first success with *Tailleur pour dames* (1887) and continued writing until his death, his last play, *Cent million qui tombent*, being produced posthumously. Among his plays were *Le Système Ribadier* (1892), *Le Dindon* (1896), *La Dame de Chez Maxim* (1899), seen in London in 1902 as *The Girl from Maxim's*, and some one-act farces, including *Feu la mère de Madame* (1908), seen in London during the World Theatre season of 1967; *On purge bébé* (1910); *Mais n'te promène donc pas toute nue!* (1912); and *Hortense a dit: J'm'en fous!* (1916). Regarded in his lifetime as nothing more than an adroit purveyor of light entertainment, Feydeau has in the last twenty years come to be regarded as an outstanding writer of classic farce, and his reputation has been consolidated by productions of his best plays at the Comédie-Française and elsewhere. Several of his masterpieces have been seen in London in translation, among them *L'Hôtel du Libre Échange* (1899) as *Hotel Paradiso* in 1956, in an adaptation by Peter Glenville starring Alec Guinness; *Occupe-toi d'Amélie* (1908) as *Look After Lulu* (1959), by Noël Coward, with Anthony Quayle and Vivien Leigh; *Une puce à l'oreille* (1907) as *A Flea in Her Ear* (1965), and *Un Fil à la patte* (1908) as *Cat Among the Pigeons* (1969), both adapted by John Mortimer (q.v.), the former for the National Theatre at the Old Vic, the latter for the Prince of Wales'. *Un Fil à la patte* was also seen in French during the World Theatre season of 1964. In 1967 the Tavistock Repertory Company produced a translation of *Le Ruban* (1894) as *Honours Even*, and in 1969 *Monsieur Chasse* (1892), as *The Birdwatcher*, was seen at the Yvonne Arnaud Theatre in Guildford.

Feydeau, THÉÂTRE, see COMÉDIE-ITALIENNE.

Fiabe, the name given by Carlo Gozzi (q.v.) to the 'fairytale' plays in which he tried to reanimate the moribund *commedia dell'arte* (q.v.) with a mixture of fantasy and fooling in a set text which nevertheless allowed scope for improvisation.

FIELD, NATHAN (1587–1620), English actor and playwright, who was taken from St. Paul's School in 1600 to become a boy-actor with the Children of the Chapel at Blackfriars (q.v.), where he appeared in *Cynthia's Revels* and the following year in *The Poetaster*, both by Jonson (q.v.), in whose *Epicœne; or, the Silent Woman* (1609) he also appeared in later life. He was an excellent actor, particularly admired in such parts as the title-role in Chapman's *Bussy d'Ambois* (c. 1604), and in 1615 joined the King's Men (see CHAMBERLAIN'S MEN), possibly in succession to Shakespeare. He was the author of two plays, *A Woman is a Weathercock* (1609) and *Amends for Ladies* (1611), and collaborated in several works with Massinger and Fletcher (qq.v.).

FIELDING, HENRY (1707–54), English novelist who also played an important part in the history of the London theatre, since it was mainly owing to his satirical attacks on the Government in *The Welsh Opera; or, the Grey Mare the Better Horse* (1731), *Don Quixote in England* (1734), *Pasquin* (1736), and *The Historical*

Register for the Year 1736 (1737), that the Licensing Act of 1737 was rushed through by Walpole on a flimsy pretext (see DRAMATIC CENSORSHIP and GIFFARD). This confirmed the monopoly of Drury Lane and Covent Garden which lasted until 1843, and created a censorship of plays which lasted until 1968. The closing of the Haymarket, where all the above plays were produced, the last two under his own management, hit Fielding hard, and he left the theatre for novel-writing. Of his earlier plays, mainly social satires, the only one of note is *Tom Thumb the Great; or, the Tragedy of Tragedies* (1730), which attacked the conventions of heroic drama.

FIELDING, TIMOTHY (?–1738), a small-part actor who in 1733 became landlord of the Buffalo Head Tavern in Bloomsbury. For some years he had a booth at Bartholomew Fair, and by a confusion of names it was said at one time that the booth had belonged to Henry Fielding (q.v.). Timothy acted the part of Mr. Furnish the upholsterer in Henry's play *The Miser* (1733).

FIELDS, GRACIE [really GRACE STANSFIELD] (1898–1979), a Lancashire comedienne and singer of popular ballads in the closing days of music-hall. In 1923, while touring in *Mr. Tower of London*, she married ARCHIE PITT [really SELINGER] (1885–1940), a Cockney comedian. She scored a notable success when the revue reached London and later appeared in cabaret at the Café Royal in *The Show's the Thing*, by Pitt, which ran for eighteen months, and in *One Week of Grace*. She then toured the United States and South Africa and was received everywhere with acclamation. During the Second World War she gave numerous concerts for the troops and undertook a concert tour in America which raised nearly £500,000 for the Navy League. Her second husband, Monty Banks, died in 1946, and five years later she married Boris Alperovici, with whom she settled in semi-retirement on Capri, returning to England occasionally to appear in excerpts from her repertory. In 1938 she was appointed C.B.E. for services to the stage.

FIELDS, JOSEPH (1895–1966), son of Lew Fields (see WEBER AND FIELDS), American dramatist and director, who collaborated with JEROME CHODOROV (1911–) in several plays, including the successful

My Sister Eileen (1940), *Wonderful Town* (1953), and *Anniversary Waltz* (1954), and with Anita Loos in *Gentlemen Prefer Blondes* (1949). He directed *Flower Drum Song* in New York in 1958 and in London in 1960, having also been responsible for the London production of *Anniversary Waltz* in 1955. His brother HERBERT (1897–1958) and sister DOROTHY (1905–74) were responsible for the lyrics and libretti of many shows, among them the successful musicals *Mexican Hayride* (1944) and *Annie Get Your Gun* (1946).

FIELDS, LEW (1867–1941), see WEBER AND FIELDS.

FIELDS [really DUKINFIELD], WILLIAM CLAUDE (1879–1946), American comedian, who made his first professional appearance as a 'tramp juggler' in July 1897, appeared in New York in 1898 in a slapstick comedy routine, and soon became a vaudeville star on the Keith circuit. In 1900 he appeared at the Palace Theatre, London, and thereafter toured Europe. He gradually introduced comic monologues into his act and evolved from juggler to eccentric comedian, finally abandoning vaudeville permanently to appear as a comedian in seven editions of the *Ziegfeld Follies* (1915–21) and in *George White's Scandals* (1922). In 1923 he played a strolling carnival swindler, a type of character he had been portraying in sketches for some time, in the musical *Poppy*. In 1931 he turned exclusively to film work.

Fifth Avenue Theatre, NEW YORK. (1) This was originally the Fifth Avenue Opera House on 24th Street near Broadway. On 2 Sept. 1867 it opened as a theatre, but closed abruptly after a fight in the auditorium in which a man was killed. It opened again on 25 Jan. 1869, when John Brougham (q.v.) appeared there in one of his own plays, and finally, on 16 Aug. 1869, it became Daly's Fifth Avenue Theatre, with a good company which included Mrs. Gilbert and Fanny Davenport (qq.v.). Daly's first outstanding success at this theatre was his own version of Meilhac and Halevy's *Frou-Frou*, but he was anxious to encourage American dramatists and on 21 Dec. 1870 produced *Saratoga*, by Bronson Howard (q.v.), which had a long run. In 1872 the theatre was redecorated and much improved, but on New Year's Day 1873 it was burnt down and not rebuilt. The site was later used for the Fifth Avenue Hall (see MADISON SQUARE THEATRE).

(2) On 3 Dec. 1873 Daly opened his second Fifth Avenue Theatre at Broadway and 28th Street. A production on 21 Feb. 1874 of *Love's Labour's Lost*, which had not previously been seen in New York, failed, and the financial panic of 1873–4 had a bad effect. Success came with the production on 17 Feb. 1875 of Daly's own play, *The Big Bonanza*, in which John Drew (q.v.) made his New York début as Bob Ruggles. The following season saw the New York production of the popular London success, H. J. Byron's *Our Boys*, in which Georgiana Drew, later the wife of Maurice Barrymore (q.v.), made her first appearance in New York. In 1876 Charles Coghlan appeared in *As You Like It*, playing Orlando to the Rosalind of Fanny Davenport (q.v.), and on 5 Dec. the same year he was seen in a revival of Sheridan's *The School for Scandal* whose opening-night success was marred by the disastrous Brooklyn Theatre fire (see FIRES IN THEATRES). By 1878 Daly was finding the financial loss on the theatre too great, and left to take over Banvard's Museum (see DALY'S THEATRE (1)). The Fifth Avenue then came under the management of Stephen Fiske, and Mary Anderson (q.v.), at the age of eighteen, made her début there, followed by Helena Modjeska (q.v.). After that the theatre was leased to various travelling companies and frequently housed light opera, including several of the Savoy operas under D'Oyly Carte. After many changes of name, it was pulled down in 1908.

Fifty-Eighth Street Theatre, NEW YORK, see JOHN GOLDEN THEATRE (1).

Fifty-First Street Theatre, NEW YORK, see MARK HELLINGER THEATRE.

Fifty-Fourth Street Theatre, NEW YORK, see ADELPHI THEATRE (2).

FILANDRE [really JEAN-BAPTISTE DE MOUCHAINGRE] (1616–91), a French actor-manager whose long and active life was spent entirely in the provinces, where he led a company which toured northern France, Holland, and Belgium. He is believed to have served as a model for Léandre in Scarron's novel, *Le Roman comique* (1651). Floridor (q.v.) was for a short time associated with Filandre, as were Beauval (q.v.) and his wife, who created some of Molière's most charming feminine roles.

FILIPPO, E. and P., see DE FILIPPO.

FINN, HENRY JAMES (c. 1790–1840), American actor and playwright, who deserted the law for the theatre. After working in Charleston and Boston he joined the company at the Park Theatre (q.v.). When it was burnt down in 1820 he went to the Anthony Street Theatre, playing Hamlet there, as he did at the Chatham Theatre (q.v.) in 1824. After making a success as Aguecheek in *Twelfth Night* he gave up tragedy for comedy, in which he was inimitable, and in 1825 appeared in his own play, *Montgomery; or, the Falls of Montmorency*, as Sergeant Welcome Sobersides, an amusing Yankee character who was later incorporated into *The Indian Wife* (1830) and played by James H. Hackett (q.v.).

FINNEY, ALBERT (1936–), English actor, who gained his experience at the Birmingham Repertory Theatre, where he worked from 1956 to 1958, playing among other parts Macbeth and Henry V. He then went to Stratford-upon-Avon, playing Edgar to the Lear of Charles Laughton, with whom he had previously appeared in Jane Arden's *The Party* (1958). It was, however, his appearance in London in a new musical, *The Lily-White Boys*, and his performance in Waterhouse and Hall's *Billy Liar* (both 1960), which first brought him into prominence. His reputation was further enhanced by his playing of the title-role in Osborne's *Luther* (1961) at the Royal Court, in which part he was also seen in New York in 1963. For his performance in this play during a brief visit to the Théâtre des Nations in Paris in July 1961 he was nominated 'the best actor of the season'. In 1965 he joined the National Theatre company, creating at the Chichester Festival of 1965 the role of John Armstrong in Arden's *Armstrong's Last Goodnight*, which he also played in London at the Old Vic. He had already made a great reputation in films and on television, and since founding an independent production company in 1965 he has been seen less often in the theatre.

FIORILLO, SILVIO (?–c. 1632), an actor of the *commedia dell'arte* (q.v.) who was the original Capitan Matamoros, and probably the first Pulcinella (q.v.). He had a company of his own in Naples, his birthplace, in the last years of the sixteenth century, and later appeared with other companies. He was also the author of several scenarii for *commedia dell'arte* plays. His son, GIOVAN BATTISTA (*fl.* 1614–51) played Trappolino and Scaramuccia.

FIORILLO, TIBERIO (1608–94), a *commedia dell'arte* actor who was apparently no relation to the above, though he was at one time thought to be his son. His surname is also found as Fiurelli or Fiorilli. He was already famous throughout Italy when in the 1640s he visited Paris, where he settled permanently in 1661. The company to which he belonged shared both the Petit Bourbon and the Palais-Royal with Molière (q.v.), who was always ready to admit how much he had benefited by his contact with the Italian actors. Fiorillo was the finest, if not the first, player of Scaramuccia (q.v.), who as Scaramouche became a stock character in French comedy. His biography, a somewhat inaccurate compilation entitled *La Vie de Scaramouche*, by Costantini (q.v.), was published in 1695, and reprinted with introduction and notes by Louis Moland in 1876. Fiorillo visited London several times, notably in 1673, when he became the rage, displacing French puppets and English actors in the affections of fashionable society. He was a fine dancer and acrobat and at the age of eighty was still so supple that he could tap a man's cheek with his foot.

Fires in Theatres. Fire has always been a major hazard in the theatre. Drury Lane and Covent Garden have both been burnt down twice, the first in 1672 and 1809, the second in 1808 and 1856. The first recorded theatre fire in America was that of the Federal Street Theatre in Boston in 1798, and between then and 1876, when the Brooklyn Theatre (q.v.) went up in flames during the last act of Oxenford's *The Two Orphans* with the loss of about three hundred lives, including two members of the cast, over seventy-five serious fire disasters were reported. In Richmond, Virginia, on 26 Dec. 1811, seventy persons lost their lives when the candles of a stage chandelier set fire to the scenery. But it was the introduction of gas lighting, coupled with the vogue for very large theatres, that caused the heavy death-tolls in nineteenth-century disasters: in the Lehman Theatre in St. Petersburg in 1836, 800 casualties; in Quebec in 1846, 100; in Karlsruhe a year later, 631; in Leghorn in 1857, 100. The greatest disaster of all time, however, was probably the fire in a Chinese theatre in 1845 which killed 1,670 persons. These and other tragedies caused a tightening-up of fire regulations. A theatre fire in Liverpool in 1878 led to the passing of the Act under which English provincial theatres are still licensed. This, however, did not prevent the double tragedy of the Theatre Royal, Exeter, which was burnt down in 1885, rebuilt, and burnt down again in 1887 with 186 dead. In America, where strong safety measures were taken after the Brooklyn fire, the futility of stringent regulations without equally stringent enforcement procedures was demonstrated on 30 Dec. 1903 when the supposedly fireproof Iroquois Theatre in Chicago became the scene of the worst catastrophe in the history of the American theatre. During a performance with too many people standing, a fire, though quickly controlled, led to a panic which resulted in the loss of over 600 lives. With the introduction of electric lighting, fireproofing of stage materials, and a comprehensive code of fire regulations which laid the onus for prevention of fire squarely on the theatre managers, conditions improved, and fires in theatres are now comparatively rare, though the evasion of the regulations caused nearly 500 deaths at the Cocoanut Grove in Boston on 28 Nov. 1942, and two years later, on 6 July 1944, a circus fire at Hartford, Conn., caused 168 deaths, mostly of children.

FISHER, CLARA (1811–93), a child prodigy who made her first appearance on the stage in London at the age of six, being much admired as Richard III, Shylock in *The Merchant of Venice*, and Young Norval in Home's *Douglas*, as well as in *The Actress of All Work* (1819), in which she impersonated a number of characters. At the age of sixteen she went to New York, making her début at the Park Theatre as the four Mowbrays in the farce *Old and Young*, and for the next few years toured in light opera and vaudeville. In 1834 she married a musician, James G. Maeder, but remained on the stage, though with less success than before.

She retired in 1844, but returned later to star in *opéra bouffe*, finally retiring in 1880.

First Folio (1623), the first complete edition of Shakespeare's plays (see CHAMBERLAIN'S MEN; CONDELL, HENRY; HEMINGE, JOHN; and SHAKESPEARE, WILLIAM).

FISKE, MINNIE MADDERN [really MARIE AUGUSTA DAVEY] (1865–1932), one of the outstanding women of the American stage, associated with the introduction of Ibsen (q.v.) to New York, and from 1893 a potent force in the battle for theatrical realism. The child of theatrical parents, she appeared with them on the stage at the age of three under her mother's maiden name of Maddern, and at five went to New York, where she embarked on a round of juvenile parts which included the Duke of York in *Richard III* and Prince Arthur in *King John*. At thirteen she graduated to adult parts, being seen as the Widow Melnotte in Bulwer-Lytton's *The Lady of Lyons*. One of her most successful parts was Mercy Baxter in *Caprice* (1884), which Henry P. Taylor wrote specially for her. She retired from the stage in 1890 on her marriage to HARRISON GREY FISKE (1861–1942), but three years later returned to star in her husband's play, *Hester Crewe*. It was, however, her playing of Tess in a dramatization of Hardy's novel in 1897 that finally established her reputation. She was also very much admired as Becky Sharp in Langdon Mitchell's dramatization of Thackeray's *Vanity Fair* (1899), with Maurice Barrymore (q.v.) as Rawdon Crawley and Tyrone Power (q.v.) as Steyne. Since her husband's opposition to the Theatrical Syndicate (q.v.) prevented her from appearing in their theatres, she rented the Manhattan (see STANDARD THEATRE (2)) in 1901, and for six years appeared there with an excellent company in a series of fine plays, including Ibsen's *A Doll's House* (1902) and *Hedda Gabler* (1903). She was also responsible for the first professional production of a play from Baker's 'English 47' class, *Salvation Nell* (1908), by Sheldon (q.v.), which she staged at the Hackett Theatre (see WALLACK THEATRE). After an unsuccessful appearance in films she returned to the New York stage in a series of light comedies, and then made a long tour in Sheridan's *The Rivals*, in which she proved herself the best Mrs. Malaprop since Mrs. John Drew (q.v.). In 1927 she again went on tour as Mrs. Alving in Ibsen's *Ghosts*, and one of her last productions was *Much Ado About Nothing*, in which she played Beatrice.

FITCH, (WILLIAM) CLYDE (1865–1909), one of America's best-loved and most prolific dramatists, author of about fifty plays, the first being *Beau Brummell* (1890), commissioned by Richard Mansfield (q.v.). The best of his early works were *Nathan Hale* (1898) and *Barbara Frietchie* (1899), based on American history and giving proof of qualities which might have taken Fitch far as a social historian had he not been content to dabble in light comedy and melodrama. He was at the height of his popularity in 1901 when *The Climbers* and *Lovers' Lane*, social comedies of life in New York, and *Captain Jinks of the Horse Marines*, in which Ethel Barrymore (q.v.) made a great success, were running simultaneously in New York, while Tree (q.v.) in London was appearing in *The Last of the Dandies*. Among Fitch's other plays were *The Moth and the Flame* (1898) and *The Cowboy and the Lady* (1899), both melodramas, *The Stubbornness of Geraldine* and *The Girl with the Green Eyes* (both 1902), *The Woman in the Case* (1905), and *Truth* (1907), sometimes considered to be his best work.

FITZBALL, EDWARD (1792–1873), English dramatist, author of a vast number of immensely popular melodramas now forgotten. He dramatized most of the novels of Sir Walter Scott, and helped forward the development of Nautical Drama (q.v.) with such plays as *The Pilot* (1825). His *Jonathan Bradford* (1833), based on a sensational murder case, made a fortune for the manager of the Surrey (q.v.), where it was first produced, and at Drury Lane he provided libretti for the light operas staged by Alfred Bunn. In 1859 he published his autobiography, *Thirty-Five Years of a Dramatic Author's Life*, which contains a good deal of interesting material on the theatrical life of the time. Several of his melodramas, notably *The Red Rover* (1829) and *Paul Clifford* (1835), are in the repertory of the Toy Theatre (q.v.).

Fitzroy Theatre, LONDON, see SCALA THEATRE.

FLAMINIA, see CECCHINI, P. M.

FLANAGAN, Bud [really ROBERT WIN-THROP] (1896–1968), English comedian, who with his partner Chesney Allen (q.v.) popularized a number of songs, including his own 'Underneath the Arches' and 'Run Rabbit Run'. He received the O.B.E. in 1959, and was three times King Rat of the Grand Order of Water Rats (see also CRAZY GANG).

FLANAGAN, HALLIE [née FERGUSON; later MRS. PHILIP H. DAVIS] (1890–1969), American theatre historian and organizer, author of *Shifting Scenes of the Modern European Theatre* (1928) and *Arena* (1940), an account of the Federal Theatre Project (q.v.). In 1927 she was appointed Professor of Drama and Director of the Experimental Theatre at Vassar, leaving there in 1941 to occupy the same position at Smith College, Northampton, Mass., where she remained until her retirement in 1955. She wrote the story of her experiences at Vassar in *Dynamo* (1943) and was also a prolific contributor on theatrical topics to many leading American magazines.

FLANDERS, MICHAEL HENRY (1922–75), English actor, lyric-writer, and entertainer, who made his first appearance at the Oxford Playhouse in 1941, playing Valentine in Shaw's *You Never Can Tell*. In 1943, while on active service, he contracted poliomyelitis and was thereafter confined to a wheelchair; but this in no way hindered his theatrical career, which ranged from collaboration in the writing of such revues as *Penny Plain* (1951) and *Airs on a Shoestring* (1953) to opera libretti, an English version of Stravinsky's 'The Soldier's Tale' (1956) in which he appeared at the Festival Hall, and an appearance in the London production of Brecht's *The Caucasian Chalk Circle* (1962). He was, however, probably best known for the revue *At the Drop of a Hat* (1956), a two-man entertainment in which he appeared with Donald Swann (q.v.) at the New Lindsey, Flanders providing the lyrics and dialogue and Swann the music. When transferred to the Fortune this ran for over two years. It was equally successful in New York and on tour throughout the world, as was the second version, *At the Drop of Another Hat*, first seen at the Haymarket in 1963.

Flat, an essential part of modern scenery, consisting of stretched canvas or hardboard on a wooden frame. Flats, which are normally 18 feet high by up to 6 or 8 feet wide, can be used in various combinations, and when connected by throwlines make up the three walls of a boxset (q.v.). A BOOKED FLAT consists of two flats hinged together, a FRENCH FLAT of sufficient flats battened together to form a back wall, the whole being 'flown' in one piece like a drop (q.v.). When standing separately, a flat may be edged by a cut-out FLIPPER, or hinged piece of profiling, and is supported by a STAGE BRACE, or rod, hooked to the back of the flat at one end and screwed or weighted down at the other. A FRENCH BRACE is a triangular framework of wood hinged to the back of a flat, to be opened out and weighted when necessary. A BACKING FLAT is one set outside a door or other stage opening to prevent the audience seeing back-stage.

FLAVIO, see CONFIDENTI.

FLECK, JOHANN FRIEDRICH FERDINAND (1757–1801), German actor who excelled in the heroic parts of the *Sturm und Drang* period. He was much admired by his contemporaries in the plays of Schiller (q.v.), particularly as Don Carlos and Wallenstein and as Karl Moor in *Die Räuber*. In spite of the instability of his temperament, which made his acting unpredictable, his magnetism was such that he could easily win back any audience he had alienated by his capriciousness. He was stage director of the Berlin National Theatre when Iffland (q.v.) went there in 1796, and his early death was a great loss, as his romanticism might have helped to modernize Iffland's cautious and old-fashioned repertory.

FLECKER, (HERMAN) JAMES ELROY (1884–1915), English poet, author of the poetic plays *Hassan* and *Don Juan*. The first was produced at His Majesty's in 1923, with music by Delius, and proved a success, owing as much to the splendour of its oriental costumes and scenery and the excellence of its cast as to its inherent poetic beauty. *Don Juan*, more modern and realistic in style than *Hassan*, was written in 1910–11 and had only a private production by the Three Hundred Club (see STAGE SOCIETY). Both plays have been revived, *Don Juan* unofficially at the Gateway Theatre, Edinburgh, during the 1950 Festival, and *Hassan* by Basil Dean unsuccessfully at the Cambridge Theatre, London, during the Festival of Britain in 1951.

FLEETWOOD, CHARLES (?–c. 1745), a wealthy gentleman who took an interest in the theatre and became manager of Drury Lane (q.v.), where he ruined himself and everyone who came in contact with him, selling out in 1744. It was under his management that Macklin (q.v.) played his epoch-making Shylock in *The Merchant of Venice* in 1741 and that Garrick (q.v.) came to Drury Lane from Goodman's Fields. Fleetwood also abolished in 1737 the free entry of lackeys into the Footmen's Gallery (q.v.), thus doing away with a constant source of annoyance and disorder.

FLESCHELLES, see GAULTIER-GAR-GUILLE.

FLETCHER, JOHN (1579–1625), English poet and dramatist, who spent most of his life actively writing for the stage, either alone or in collaboration. His name is so closely connected with that of Beaumont (q.v.) that more than fifty plays have been ascribed to their joint authorship, of which perhaps only some six or seven were really by them. Fletcher was already known as the author of a pastoral, *The Faithful Shepherdess* (1608), before his name is first found linked with that of Beaumont in some commendatory verses prefixed to a reprint of Jonson's *Volpone*. Their chief plays in collaboration were *Philaster* (1610), *The Maid's Tragedy* and *A King and No King* (both 1611), and *The Scornful Lady* (1613). After that Fletcher continued writing alone but is believed to have had a hand in the composition of Shakespeare's *Henry VIII* (also 1613). He is certainly noted in the Stationers' Register as having collaborated with Shakespeare in *The History of Cardenio* (1613), now lost. One play assigned to him, *The Chances* (1623), was rewritten by Buckingham (q.v.) in 1666 and acted with some success. It was revived in 1922 by the Phoenix Society (q.v.) and in 1962 at the Chichester Festival Theatre (q.v.).

FLEURY [really ABRAHAM-JOSEPH BÉNARD] (1750–1822), French actor, son of the manager of a theatre at Nancy, where he made his first appearances. Encouraged by Voltaire (q.v.), who discerned great promise in him, he appeared at the Comédie-Française in 1774, helped by Lekain (q.v.), who had known his father. After gaining further experience in the provinces he returned to the Comédie-Française in 1778, remaining there until his retirement in 1818, being its seventeenth *doyen*. After the Revolution he was one of the members of the company reconstituted in 1799. An excellent actor, he owed his position to hard work and an innate feeling for the theatre, being almost totally uneducated. He had a natural nobility of carriage and character and was a master of polished comedy, being particularly admired as Alceste in Molière's *Le Misanthrope*.

Flies, the name given to the space above the stage, hidden from the audience, where scenery can be lifted clear from the stage, or 'flown', by the manipulation of ropes. In the traditional Rope House (q.v.), the stage hands in charge of the flies were known as FLY-MEN; they worked on FLY-FLOORS, or galleries running along each side of the stage. Between the fly-floors there were formerly catwalks, or narrow communicating bridges over each set of wings, slung on iron stirrups from the grid to which the ropes, or lines, were attached. These enabled the fly-men, or lines-men, to reach any point about the stage to ensure the proper hanging of the scenery. Usually the rope-ends were tied off on the rail of the fly-floor on the prompt side. Large Continental theatres and opera houses sometimes had as many as three pairs of fly-floors, but English theatres rarely had more than one pair. (For an alternative method of handling scenery, which is now controlled electrically, see COUNTERWEIGHT HOUSE.)

Flipper, see FLAT.

FLORENCE, WILLIAM JERMYN (or JAMES) [really BERNARD CONLIN] (1831–91), American actor, who made his New York début in 1849 at Niblo's Garden in dialect impersonations. Two years later, while appearing at the Broadway Theatre, he married the actress MALVINA PRAY (1831–1906), sister of Mrs. Barney Williams (q.v.), and with her toured the United States in a repertory of Irish plays. They were first seen in London in 1856, when they appeared at Drury Lane in a farce, *The Yankee Housekeeper*, with great success. Among Florence's best parts were Captain Cuttle in Dickens's *Dombey and Son*, Bob Brierly in Tom Taylor's *The Ticket-of-Leave Man*, which he was the first to play in America, and Bardwell Slote in Woolf's *The Mighty Dollar* (1861), a play which remained in his repertory for many years. He was good in burlesque and as a comedian ranked with Joseph Jefferson (q.v.), playing Sir Lucius O'Trigger to his Bob Acres in Sheridan's *The Rivals* and Zekiel Homespun to his Dr. Pangloss in the younger Colman's *The Heir-at-Law*. Florence was responsible for the first production in New York of Robertson's *Caste*, which he had memorized in London, staging it at the Broadway Theatre on 5 Aug. 1867, only four months after its first appearance, with the realistic scenery and atmosphere of the Bancroft production. This caused a good deal of controversy, as Lester Wallack (q.v.) had bought the American rights of the play, but in the absence of copyright laws he had no redress against piracy. Probably fearing to challenge comparison with Florence's excellent production, Wallack did not himself stage the play until 1875. Florence, who was at first inclined to justify his behaviour on the score of expediency, later regretted it, but maintained that he did not know Wallack had already bought the play for New York. His feat of memory, which extended to the words and the business, recalls that of Holcroft (q.v.) memorizing for translation Beaumarchais's *Le Mariage de Figaro* nearly a hundred years before.

FLORIDOR [really JOSIAS DE SOULAS, SIEUR DE PRIMEFOSSE] (1608–72), French actor, leader of a troupe of strolling players whom he took to London in 1635, appearing before the Court and at the Cockpit in Drury Lane. Three years later he toured the French provinces with Filandre (q.v.), and then joined the company of the Théâtre du Marais (q.v.). Some of his best performances were given in the plays of Pierre Corneille (q.v.), and it may have been Floridor's move to the Hôtel de Bourgogne (q.v.) which induced Corneille to give his later plays to that theatre rather than the Marais. Floridor soon became the leader of the company, his quiet, authoritative acting being in marked contrast to the bombastic style of his colleague, Montfleury, and he was the only actor spared by Molière (q.v.) in his mockery of the rival troupe in *L'Impromptu de Versailles* (1663).

Fly-Floor, Fly-Men, see FLIES.

Flying Effects. From the earliest days of the theatre, the ingenuity of the machin-

ists has been directed to achieving the illusion of flight. In the Greek theatre the *deus ex machina* was lowered and raised by a form of crane. In medieval and Renaissance times flying effects varied from the simple rise and fall of a figure on a movable platform concealed behind a cloud border to the elaborate undulating flight of a character across the stage. The mechanism needed to produce such effects was already well known in England by the Restoration period, when references to 'flyings' are frequently found, and by the end of the eighteenth century there were in existence diagrams of the procedure to be followed for complicated flights. By the mid-nineteenth century the machines in use included a most complicated piece of apparatus for controlling the circulatory gyrations of a pair of flying figures. In the pantomimes of the early twentieth century an organization known as Kirby's Flying Ballet gave many brilliant and graceful performances. In such effects, where no cloud or chariot was used for the character being flown, a line was attached to a hook at the player's back which formed part of a harness worn under the costume. It was easily fixed or discarded, but a safety device prevented the line from leaving the hook in flight.

FOGERTY, ELSIE (1866–1945), English actress and speech specialist, who trained for the stage in London and Paris and made her first appearance in 1879. Her interest in the problems of diction led her to found the Central School of Speech Training and Dramatic Art in London, which she directed until her death. She was also the author of several manuals of speechcraft and of *The Speaking of English Verse*, and was closely concerned with the development of the British Drama League (q.v.) and of the Diploma in Dramatic Art established by the University of London in 1923. In 1936 she was appointed C.B.E. for services to the English language, many famous actors and actresses having had reason to be grateful to her for her tuition. Her biography, *Fogie*, by Marion Cole, was published in 1967.

Foire Saint-Germain, Saint-Laurent, PARIS, see FAIRS.

FOLGER, HENRY CLAY (1857–1930), American businessman, founder of the great Shakespeare Library in Washington which bears his name. Beginning with a modest set of Shakespeare's plays in thirteen volumes, he went on to acquire the finest collection of Shakespeariana in the world, which he left to the nation. Under Dr. Joseph Quincy Adams, the great Shakespearian scholar who became its first director, the collection, administered by Amherst College, increased rapidly in size and scope and now contains a series of English manuscripts from 1475 to 1640 which is exceeded in value and rarity only by those in the British Museum and the Bodleian Library.

Folies-Bergère, a famous music-hall in Paris, which opened on 1 May 1869 with a mixed bill of light opera and pantomime. It soon became the rendezvous of the young men of the town, who either watched the successive turns on the stage or loitered in the immense promenade which was one of the great attractions of the house. The Folies-Bergère caters to a large extent for visitors, whether French or foreign, and one of the main features of every programme is a bevy of beautiful young women, either stark naked or clad only in inessentials. For the rest, the turns consist of acrobats, singers, and sketches, the last extremely vulgar or surpassingly beautiful, the scenic resources of the theatre being immense though its stage is small. Many of the greatest names of the entertainment world have appeared on its bills.

(For the Folies-Bergère, New York, see HELEN HAYES THEATRE.)

Folies-Dramatiques, THÉÂTRE DES, PARIS, on the Boulevard du Temple. This was built on the site of the first Ambigu-Comique (q.v.), which was destroyed by fire in 1827. It opened with melodrama on 22 Jan. 1831 and had a successful career, catering mainly for a local audience with short runs of patriotic and melodramatic plays by the Cogniard brothers, Comberousse, de Kock, Théaulon, and others. In 1834 the great actor Frédérick (q.v.) had one of his first successes at this theatre in his own play *Robert Macaire*. When the Boulevard du Temple was demolished in 1862 a new Folies-Dramatiques was built in the rue de Bondy, which became a home of light musical shows.

(For the Folies-Dramatiques in London, see KINGSWAY THEATRE.)

Folies-Marigny, THÉÂTRE DES, PARIS, a small playhouse, originally the Salle Lacaze, used by the Bouffes-Parisiens. In 1858 the son of the great pantomimist Deburau (q.v.) opened it under his own name, but it was not a success and soon became the Théâtre des Champs-Elysées. In 1862 it was taken over by the director of one of the theatres on the Boulevard du Temple (q.v.) which had been demolished for road-widening, and renamed the Folies-Marigny. It was then used for vaudeville and was fairly successful until 1869, after which it passed from hand to hand and was finally destroyed in 1881. A circular building for a panorama was erected on the site of the theatre and is still standing. It became a music-hall in 1896, the Marigny-Théâtre in 1901, the Comédie-Marigny in 1913. In 1925 it was bought by Léon Volterra, whose widow still owns it. From 1946 to 1956 it housed the company of Jean-Louis Barrault and his wife Madeleine Renaud (qq.v.) in a repertory of distinguished plays.

Folies-Nouvelles, THÉÂTRE DES, PARIS, a small theatre which had a short but brilliant career. It opened in 1852 and under several successive names was a home of pantomime and light opera. Two years later it became the Folies-Nouvelles, with programmes like those of the old fairground theatres, simple, crude, and naïvely charming. It had a great vogue until 1859 and then became a straight theatre, being renamed Théâtre Déjazet after the actress Pauline-Virginie Déjazet (q.v.), who appeared there in plays by Sardou and others under the management of her son. It later reverted to light entertainment.

Folk Festivals. These festivals, connected with the activities of the agricultural year, must have existed from the time of the first organized communities. In Europe they survived the rise and fall of Greece and Rome and the coming of Christianity, but lost much of their significance and were often kept up merely 'for fun' or 'for luck'. The Church, considering them an undesirable pagan survival, tried either to suppress them or to graft them on to its own festivals. But they were irrepressible and constantly broke out again, often under the aegis of the parish priest. Wandering minstrels may have had some slight share in them, but they depended mainly on local talent. The main folk festivals of England and elsewhere were Plough Monday, May-day, Midsummer Day, Harvest Home, and Christmas. Of these, May-day, with a May Queen, Maypole, Morris dancers, Jack-in-the-Green or Jack-a'-Lantern, and Hobby Horse, often with the addition of Robin Hood (q.v.) and his Merry Men, was the most important. Most of the festivities were athletic rather than dramatic, but traces of a rudimentary play can be found (see MUMMING PLAY and PLOUGH MONDAY).

Folk Play. Under this heading may be grouped the rough-and-ready dramatic entertainments given at village festivals by the villagers themselves. These were derived from the dramatic tendencies inherent in primitive folk festivals (q.v.), and were given either on May-day, at Harvest Home, or at Christmas, when to the central theme of a symbolic death and resurrection, which comes from remotest antiquity, were added the names and feats of local worthies. Later, though not before 1596, these were replaced by the Seven Champions of Christendom or other heroes, probably under the influence of the village schoolmaster (cf. Holofernes in *Love's Labour's Lost*). St. George may have figured among them from the earliest times, as patron saint of England. With some dramatic action went a good deal of song and dance, of which the Sword Dance and the Morris Dance are the main survivals, except for the Mumming Play (q.v.). Practically no written records of the folk play survive and it contributed very little to the main current of modern drama; but its influence should not on that account be entirely disregarded.

Follies, see PÉLISSIER, H. G. and ZIEGFELD, F.

Folly Theatre, LONDON, see TOOLE'S THEATRE.

FOLZ, HANS (c. 1435–1513), see MASTER-SINGERS.

FONTANNE, LYNN (1887–   ), see LUNT, ALFRED.

FONVIZIN, DENIS IVANOVICH (1744–92), early Russian dramatist who forms the link between the neo-classical literary plays of Sumarokov and the social comedies of Ostrovsky (qq.v.). His first attempt at play-writing was a comedy, *The Minor*, contrasting the uneducated noblemen of the provinces with the cultured nobility of the city. He put it aside unfinished in favour of a second play, *The Brigadier-General*, which he read before the Court in 1766 with great success. It satirized the newly-rich illiterates in society and the fashion for praising everything from western Europe at the expense of everything Russian. It was not until 1781 that Fonvizin took up *The Minor* again and rewrote it, sharpening his satire on the landowners and their politics. As they were then in power, his daring was his downfall, and he was forced into premature retirement. Nevertheless, *The Minor* remains a small classic and is still in the repertory of the Soviet theatre. Although Fonvizin wrote in the comic tradition of Molière (q.v.) and the French eighteenth century, he infused into his work a native Russian element of folk comedy which was to come to fruition in his successors.

Fool, the licensed buffoon of the medieval Feast of Fools (q.v.) and later a member of the French *sociétés joyeuses*; not to be confused with the Court Fool or King's Jester, who was a permanent member of the Royal Household. The traditional costume of the fool, adopted by the Court Fool at some unknown date in imitation of his humbler rival, is a cap with horns or ass's ears, and sometimes bells, covering the head and shoulders; a parti-coloured jacket and trousers, usually tight-fitting, since the fool was also an acrobat; and occasionally a tail. He carried a *marotte*, or bauble, either a replica of a fool's head on a stick or a bladder filled with dried peas; exceptionally a wooden sword or 'dagger of lath', a relic of his predecessor the Old Vice, the Devil's attendant in the medieval Morality Play (q.v.). This costume may be a survival of the head and skin of the sacrificial animal worn by worshippers at the primitive folk festivals, while the ass's ears were taken from the ass used in the procession of the Feast of Fools. The grotesque fool of the Morris dancers and of village festivities invariably had a tail. Shakespeare's fools have nothing to do with the Feast of Fools or with the folk revellers, but derive from the Court Fool, already by his time a tradition in Europe and England (see also CLOWN). In dramatic use fools were often used as vehicles for social satire (see NARR).

Fools, FEAST OF, see FEAST OF FOOLS.

FOOTE, MARIA (c. 1797–1867), English actress, daughter of a Samuel Foote who claimed some relationship with the dramatist (see below). She played Juliet while still quite young and in 1814 was at Covent Garden, where in 1815 she played Statira to the Alexander of Master Betty (q.v.) in Lee's *Alexander the Great*. She was seen in London and on tour with moderate success until in 1831 she retired to marry the Earl of Harrington.

FOOTE, SAMUEL (1720–77), English actor and dramatist, who in 1747 took over the Haymarket Theatre, where he evaded the Licensing Act of 1737, which limited the performance of plays to Covent Garden and Drury Lane, by inviting his friends to a dish of tea or chocolate, their invitation-card giving admittance to an entertainment in which Foote mimicked his fellow-actors and other public characters. In 1749, having inherited a fortune, he went to Paris, spent it, and returned to take up a life of hard work as actor-manager and playwright, his first successful farces being *The Englishman in Paris* (1753) and its sequel, *The Englishman Returned from Paris* (1756). He then took over the Haymarket again and staged there his best play, *The Minor* (1760), a satire on Whitefield and the Methodists in which he himself played Shift, a character intended to ridicule Tate Wilkinson (q.v.). In 1766 he lost a leg through some ducal horseplay, and in compensation the then Duke of York, who was present at the accident, procured for him a Royal Patent for the Haymarket, where he was able to present summer seasons of 'legitimate' drama with leading actors. He had a bitter wit, and his plays were mainly devised with the idea of holding his enemies, particularly Garrick (q.v.), up to ridicule. He had a keen eye also for character, and wrote brilliant sketches of contemporary manners which caused him to be nicknamed the 'English Aristophanes'. Short, fat, flabby, with an ugly but intelligent face and bright eyes, he was at once feared and admired by his contemporaries. He died on the way to France after disposing of his Patent to George Colman the elder (q.v.). Portraits of him were painted by Zoffany and Reynolds.

Footlights, see LIGHTING.

Footlights Trap, see TRAP.

Footmen's Gallery. At the Restoration the usual charge for the upper gallery was a shilling, but at Dorset Garden, and later at Drury Lane, footmen waiting for their masters were admitted free at the end of the fourth act. Christopher Rich (q.v.), hoping to curry favour with the rougher element, allowed the footmen, from 1697 onwards, to occupy the Drury Lane gallery without payment from the opening of the play, which led to much noise and disorder. This abuse was finally abolished by Fleetwood (q.v.) in 1737.

FORBES-ROBERTSON, JEAN (1905–62), English actress, the second daughter of Johnston Forbes-Robertson (q.v.). She made her first appearance on the stage in South Africa in 1921, touring with her mother Gertrude, sister of Maxine Elliott (q.v.), under the name of Anne McEwen. She returned to London in 1925 and under her own name was seen as Sonya in Komisarjevsky's production of Chekhov's *Uncle Vanya* in 1926, as Juliet in *Romeo and Juliet* in 1927, and as Viola in *Twelfth Night* in 1928. For eight consecutive years, from 1927 to 1934, she played Peter Pan in Barrie's play, her slight boyish appearance being admirably suited to the part, as it was also to Puck in *A Midsummer Night's Dream* in 1937 and Jim Hawkins in R. L. Stevenson's *Treasure Island* in 1945. She was excellent in Ibsen, particularly as Rebecca West (in *Rosmersholm*) and Hedda (in *Hedda Gabler*), and in such parts as Lady Teazle in Sheridan's *The School for Scandal* and Marguerite in the younger Dumas's *The Lady of the Camellias*. She also appeared in a number of modern plays, being particularly admired as Jenny Lyndon in Rodney Ackland's *Strange Orchestra* (1932) and Kay in Priestley's *Time and the Conways* (1937).

FORBES-ROBERTSON, SIR JOHNSTON (1853–1937), English actor-manager, who made his first appearance in 1874 and from then until his retirement in 1913 had an outstandingly successful career. He scored his first important success in W. S. Gilbert's *Dan'l Druce, Blacksmith* in 1876, and after appearing with the Bancrofts (q.v.) played opposite Modjeska (q.v.) as Romeo, as Armand Duval in *Heartsease* (a version of the younger Dumas's *La dame aux camélias*), and as Maurice de Saxe in Scribe's *Adrienne Lecouvreur*. In 1882 he was at the Lyceum under Irving (q.v.) and then toured England and America with Mary Anderson (q.v.), making his first appearance in New York with her—as Orlando in *As You Like It*—in 1885. In 1895 he took over the management of the Lyceum in London, where his acting of Hamlet, combined with the nobility of his appearance and the beauty of his voice, made a deep impression, many critics acclaiming him as the best Hamlet of his day. Among his other outstanding parts were Buckingham in *Henry VIII*, Dick Helder in Kipling's *The Light That Failed* (1903), and The Stranger in Jerome K. Jerome's *The Passing of the Third Floor Back* (1908). In 1900 he married Gertrude, sister of Maxine Elliott (q.v.), their daughter Jean (q.v.) becoming an excellent actress. Forbes-Robertson was knighted for services to the stage during the last week of his farewell season at Drury Lane. His three brothers, Ian, Norman (Forbes), and Eric (John Kelt) were also on the stage, as was his nephew Frank.

FORD, JOHN (1586–1639), English dramatist, several of whose plays are lost, destroyed by Warburton's cook (q.v.), who used them to line pie-dishes. He may have been part-author with Dekker and Samuel Rowley (qq.v.) of *The Witch of Edmonton* (1621) and *The Sun's Darling* (1624). His own extant works include four romantic and somewhat effeminate dramas which contributed to the continued emasculation of the English stage before the closing of the theatres in 1642—*The Lover's Melancholy* (*c.* 1625), *Love's Sacrifice* (*c.* 1627), *The Broken Heart* (1629), which was revived at the Chichester Festival Theatre (q.v.) in 1962, and, his best-known work, *'Tis Pity She's a Whore* (*c.* 1628). This was revived in 1661 and then not seen again until it was staged by the Phoenix Society in 1923. Donald Wolfit revived it at the Strand Theatre in 1941 and it was seen at the Mermaid Theatre in 1961. In the same year Visconti (q.v.), the Italian director, was responsible for an excellent production of a French version in Paris under the title of *Dommage qu'elle soit putain*.

FORD, JOHN THOMSON (1829–94), American theatre manager, who was managing Ford's Theatre in Washington when Abraham Lincoln was assassinated on 14 Apr. 1865 by the actor John Wilkes Booth (q.v.). With his brother he was imprisoned for thirty-nine days, but was later acquitted of complicity in the crime and continued his career, managing a number of other theatres and being for some forty years an active and honourable member of the American theatrical profession.

Ford's Theatre, WASHINGTON, D.C. It was in this theatre that Abraham Lincoln was assassinated on 14 Apr. 1865 by the actor John Wilkes Booth (q.v.) during a performance by Laura Keene's company of Tom Taylor's *Our American Cousin*. It had originally been a Baptist chapel and fears that its conversion would prove disastrous had already been reinforced by a bad fire in 1863. After the assassination it was closed and taken over by the government for use as an office building. It was later used for storage and as an army medical museum On 9 June 1893, the day on which John Wilkes Booth's elder brother Edwin Booth (q.v.) died, part of the old theatre collapsed, killing and injuring a number of people. The building then remained derelict for some time but in 1932 it became a Lincoln museum, and plans were made for the restoration of the theatre in its original form, as far as possible. This was eventually achieved, and on 12 Feb. 1968 the theatre reopened with *John Brown's Body*, by Stephen Vincent Benét, performed by the Circle-in-the-Square company, which annually presents a theatrical season of some four or five plays from October to April. Although the capacity of the theatre has been reduced from nearly 2,000 to about 700, and electricity has replaced gas, many of the theatre's former features have been restored or retained, in particular the large forestage with boxes on each side typical of the late eighteenth-century playhouse. During the summer the theatre presents for visitors a *son et lumière* account of the events of 14 Apr. 1865.

FORDE, FLORRIE [really **FLORENCE FLANAGAN**] (1876–1940), music-hall singer who came from Melbourne, where she was known as the Australian Marie Lloyd. She first appeared in London on August Bank Holiday 1897 and was particularly good at putting over a chorus. On one occasion the audience made her repeat an old favourite thirty-three times. A massive woman, she was in her time a famous Principal Boy (q.v.) and a great star. Her best-known songs were 'Down at the Old Bull and Bush', 'Has Anybody Here Seen Kelly?', 'Hold Your Hand Out, Naughty Boy', and 'Oh, Oh, Antonio'.

Forestage, a term applied to the small area of the stage in front of the proscenium arch and the front curtain, the final vestige of the apron stage of the Restoration theatre, itself a modified form of the Elizabethan platform stage. Its loss proved a great handicap in staging revivals of Elizabethan and Restoration drama in modern theatres, and in some new theatre buildings, particularly those intended for experimental or academic work, forestages have been built out in front of the proscenium arch. At Stratford-upon-Avon and the Old Vic (qq.v.) they have also been added to the existing stages.

Formalism, a method of theatrical presentation popular in Russia soon after the October Revolution and put into practice by Meyerhold, Akimov in his earlier period, and, to a lesser degree, Taïrov (qq.v.). It entailed the schooling of the actor so that he became the producer's puppet, and insistence on exterior symbolism at the expense of inner truth. Although it helped to clear the stage of the old falsities and conventions of pre-Revolutionary days, when pushed too far it resulted in a complete lack of harmony between actor and audience, and in the long run intellectual isolation so cut formalist producers off from the new audiences that they had either to return to the warmth and intimacy of normal human relationships or leave the theatre.

FORMBY, GEORGE (1905–61), son of a Lancashire music-hall comedian of the same name, who went on the halls after his father's death in 1921 under the name of George Hoy. His act consisted of songs and patter to the accompaniment of the ukulele. He reverted to his own name after a year or so, but his act never varied. During the Second World War he entertained the troops all over the world, with his wife Beryl as his partner. He toured Canada in 1950, starred in the stage show *Zip Goes a Million* in London in 1951, visited South Africa and Australia in 1955, and in 1956 was seen in pantomime.

FORREST, EDWIN (1806–72), one of the finest American tragic actors of the nineteenth century. His early years were hard, overshadowed by poverty and thwarted ambition, but in the end he triumphed and became the acknowledged head of his profession for nearly thirty years. Yet even then the defects of his character made him as many enemies as friends, and no one received more abuse mingled with the praise which was his due. He had great advantages of person, expressive features, and a powerful voice, but his acting lacked delicacy and in his early years he was much criticized for 'ranting'. This he later cured to some extent, and was then outstanding as Lear, Hamlet, Othello, Macbeth, and Mark Antony in *Julius Caesar*. Among his other parts were Spartacus in *The Gladiator* (1831), by Bird (q.v.), the title-role in *Metamora*, originally written by Stone (q.v.) but revised by Bird, Jaffier in Otway's *Venice Preserv'd*, Rolla in Sheridan's *Pizarro*, and Virginius in Sheridan Knowles's play of that name. He appeared in London in 1836 with some success, but on a later visit in 1845 was received with marked hostility, which he attributed to the machinations of Macready (q.v.). Their quarrel led eventually to the fatal Astor Place riot in New York in 1849, when Macready barely escaped with his life. This caused Forrest to be ostracized by the more sober members of the community, but he became the idol of the masses, who looked on him as their champion against the tyranny of the English. In his last years Forrest knew the bitterness of failure, and died a lonely, unhappy man, making his last appearance at the Globe Theatre, Boston, on 2 Apr. 1872 in Bulwer-Lytton's *Richelieu*.

Forrest Theatre, NEW YORK, see EUGENE O'NEILL THEATRE.

FORT, PAUL (1872–1960), French director and theatre manager, who at seventeen years of age, in reaction against the realism of Antoine's Théâtre Libre (q.v), founded the Théâtre d'Art for the production of poetic plays. Unfortunately his theories of symbolic and abstract art led him to look on his actors also as abstractions, and defeated by their solid reality he gave up his theatre after only two years, being succeeded in its management by Lugné-Poë (q.v.).

Fortune Theatre, LONDON. (1) The first Fortune Theatre was built by Henslowe (q.v.) in Golden Lane, Cripplegate. It was modelled on the Globe (q.v.) and its dimensions were almost the same (the builders' contract for the theatre still exists), but it was built of plain unpainted timber. It took its name from a statue of the Goddess of Fortune over the entrance, and opened in the autumn of 1600 with a performance by the Admiral's Men (q.v.), who occupied it continuously for many years. In 1621 it was burnt down but rebuilt in brick and reopened two years later. After the closing of the theatres in 1642 the Fortune was used occasionally for surreptitious performances until in 1649 Commonwealth soldiers entered and dismantled it. It was finally pulled down in 1661.

(2) A small theatre in Russell Street, Drury Lane, built for Laurence Cowen, who opened it on 8 Nov. 1924 with his own play, *Sinners*. Externally, it was intended to resemble the old Fortune but the likeness was based upon a print of doubtful authenticity. It had few successes in its early years, except for Lonsdale's *On Approval* and a season of O'Casey plays, both in 1927. For some time it was used mainly for amateur productions and Sunday shows. In 1946 it finally achieved success with *At the Drop of a Hat*, by Flanders and Swann (qq.v.). This ran for over seven hundred performances. In 1961 the Cambridge Footlights revue, *Beyond the Fringe*, started a long and successful career. In 1967 *The Promise*, by the Russian dramatist Aleksei Arbuzov (q.v.), was seen at this theatre, transferred from the Oxford Playhouse.

FORTUNY, MARIANO (1871–1949), Italian scene designer and lighting expert, who in 1902 invented a system of lighting, called after him, which simulated diffused daylight on stage by the use of a 'sky-dome' (*Kuppelhorizont*). This reflected electric light back from bands of coloured silk on to the acting area, direct lighting still being achieved by the use of spot-lights. Fortuny's own sky-dome, a true half-dome of silk which could be closed and taken from one theatre to another, enabled him to produce some beautiful effects, particularly of space and distance, but completely blocked the side entrances to the stage and was also very expensive because of the amount of electric current it consumed. It has been largely replaced by the *Rundhorizont*, or cyclorama (q.v.).

Forty-Eighth Street Theatre, NEW YORK. Built for William A. Brady (q.v.), this

opened on 12 Aug. 1912 and housed opera and musical comedy, including Gilbert and Sullivan, as well as a number of successful straight plays. In 1922 came Kelly's delightful satire on Little Theatres, *The Torchbearers*, which ran for several months. Later successes were Jean Bart's *The Squall* (1926), with Blanche Yurka, a revival of Boucicault's *The Streets of New York* (1931), *Harvey* (1944), by Mary Chase, and *Stalag 17* (1951), by Donald Bevan and Edmund Trzcinski. Robert Anderson's *Tea and Sympathy*, which opened at the Ethel Barrymore Theatre in 1953, finished its long run here in June 1955. Two months later, when the theatre was unoccupied, a water tank fell through the roof, causing considerable damage to the auditorium, and the building was demolished later the same year. From 1937 to 1943 it was known as the Windsor Theatre.

Forty-Fourth Street Theatre, NEW YORK. This opened as a music-hall under Weber and Fields (qq.v.) on 21 Nov. 1912. It housed in its basement for some time the famous Little Club, and on its roof was a smaller theatre, later known as the Nora Bayes (see NORWORTH). This little playhouse was considered somewhat un-lucky, housing few successful productions, but Little Theatre tournaments were held there and in Dec. 1922 some of Gersh-win's first tunes were heard there in a 'musical melodrama'. In 1935 it was oc-cupied for a short time by the Yale Puppeteers, and two years later it was taken over by the Federal Theatre Project (q.v.). It was scheduled for demolition in 1945, together with its parent house.

In 1913 the Forty-Fourth Street Theatre saw a successful revival of *The Geisha* and in 1915 Robert B. Mantell appeared there in a classical repertory which showed, among other things, what the nineteenth century had demanded of an actor's memory. His parts in this season included Shakespeare's Lear, King John, Macbeth, Hamlet, Richard III, Romeo, and Shylock (in *The Merchant of Venice*), as well as Bulwer-Lytton's Richelieu and Bouci-cault's Louis XI. After Mantell left the theatre returned to light opera and musical plays. An outstanding production seen in 1930 was Gilbert Seldes's adaptation of Aristophanes' *Lysistrata*. Other plays seen at this theatre included Priestley's *The Good Companions* in 1931, a fleeting glimpse of Pierre Fresnay and Yvonne

Printemps in Coward's *Conversation Piece* in 1934, Walter Hampden in a four-week classical repertory in 1935, the short-lived but memorable *Johnny Johnson*, by Paul Green, with incidental music by Kurt Weill, in 1936, and in 1943 Moss Hart's musical documentary on aviation, *Winged Victory*. The theatre was demolished in 1945.

Forty-Ninth Street Theatre, NEW YORK, on the north side between Broadway and 8th Avenue. This opened on 26 Dec. 1921, and early in the following year Morris Gest presented the Chauve-Souris for a season which continued during the summer on the roof of the old Century Theatre. A series of successful new plays followed, though Coward's *Fallen Angels* was a failure in 1927. In 1928 came a fine revival of Ibsen's *The Wild Duck* with Blanche Yurka (q.v.), followed by *Hedda Gabler* in 1929, and a year later the public were delighted by the great Chinese actor, Mei Lan-Fang (q.v.). Among later productions were Drinkwater's *Bird in Hand* (1930), a revival of Strindberg's *The Father* (1931) with Robert Loraine (q.v.), a season of Yiddish plays with Maurice Schwartz, and three productions by the Federal Theatre Project (q.v.). The last play seen in the theatre was a modern-dress revival of Ibsen's *The Wild Duck* in Apr. 1938, after which it became a cinema.

Forty-Sixth Street Theatre, NEW YORK, west of Broadway. This opened as Chanin's on 24 Dec. 1925 and took its present name in 1932. It was intended for musical shows, and has housed such successes as *Hellzapoppin* (1938), *Du Barry Was a Lady* (1939), *Panama Hattie* (1940), *Finian's Rainbow* (1947), *Guys and Dolls* (1950), *Damn Yankees* (1955), and *How to Succeed in Business Without Really Trying* (1961). In 1958 Gielgud (q.v.) occupied the theatre with his one-man recital of passages from Shakespeare, *Ages of Man*.

FOX, G. L. [really GEORGE WASHINGTON LAFAYETTE] (1825–77), American actor and pantomimist. He was on the stage as a child, and from 1850 to 1858 was at the National Theatre (see CHATHAM THEATRE (2)), where in 1853 he persuaded the management to put on an adaptation by Aiken (q.v.) of Harriet Beecher Stowe's *Uncle Tom's Cabin*, which was an outstanding success and proved to be far the best of the many extant versions. Later Fox, with Lingard, produced plays and pantomimes at the Bowery Theatre (q.v.), and in 1867 Fox appeared as Bottom in *A Midsummer Night's Dream* (see OLYMPIC THEATRE (3)). A year later he was first seen in his famous pantomime, *Humpty-Dumpty*, and continued to appear in successive editions of it on tour until his death. Much of the pantomime 'business' in his shows was devised by his brother, CHARLES KEMBLE FOX (1833–75), who appeared on the stage as a child with his parents and brothers and sister, and played Pantaloon in his elder brother's pantomimes.

FOY, EDDIE [really EDWIN FITZGERALD] (1856–1928), American actor and vaudeville player. He was a singer and entertainer from childhood, and in 1878 toured the Western boom towns with a minstrel troupe. He was later seen in comedy and melodrama, and from 1888 to 1894 played the leading part in a long series of extravaganzas in Chicago. He was acting in the Iroquois Theatre there in 1903 when fire broke out, and did his best to calm the audience, but without success, the ensuing panic resulting in the loss of over 600 lives. Foy, who was an eccentric comedian with many mannerisms and a distinctive clown make-up, played in musical comedy until 1913 and then went into vaudeville, accompanied by his seven children, with whom he made his last appearance in 1927. He subsequently wrote his autobiography, *Clowning Through Life* (1928).

FRAGSON [really POTTS], HARRY (1869–1913), a music-hall performer, popular in Paris, where he played with a Cockney accent, and in London, where he played with a French accent. He appeared before Royalty on several occasions and was seen in pantomime at Drury Lane. When he played Dandini in *Cinderella*, the character, out of compliment to his Anglo-French reputation, was re-christened Dandigny. He was shot by his father in a fit of insanity.

FRANK, BRUNO (1887–1946), German playwright, author of a number of light, sophisticated comedies. Of these, *Sturm in Wasserglas* (1930) was successfully produced in London as *Storm in a Teacup* (1936) and in America as *Storm over Patsy* (1937). Frank also wrote some historical dramas, of which the best and most characteristic was *Zwölftausend* (1927). In an English translation as *Twelve Thousand* this was successful in New York in 1928 and was seen at the Embassy Theatre in London in 1931.

Franklin Theatre, NEW YORK, a small building at 175 Chatham Street which opened on 7 Sept. 1835 with Thomas Morton's *The School of Reform*, followed by some classic comedies. It soon degenerated into melodrama and farce, however, in spite of a visit by the older Booth (q.v.) in 1836–7; but it is memorable as being the first theatre in New York at which the famous Joseph Jefferson (q.v.) appeared in 1837, at the age of eight. It also saw the first production in New York of the anonymous *Fifteen Years of a New York Fireman's Life* (1841) and Bulwer-Lytton's *Money* (1842). It then gave up legitimate drama and under various names became the home of pantomime and minstrel shows.

FRANZ, ELLEN (1839–1923), see MEININGER COMPANY.

FRASER, CLAUDE LOVAT (1890–1921), English artist and stage designer, whose settings for *As You Like It* and Gay's *The Beggar's Opera* at the Lyric Theatre, Hammersmith, in 1920 may be said to have inaugurated a new era in stage design. He also worked extensively for ballet and opera. He took his inspiration from the eighteenth and early nineteenth centuries and his work embodied a gay, brightly-coloured romanticism. His early death was a great loss to English art and to the theatre, and his influence, when one considers how brief his career was, has been phenomenal. An account of his work can be found in the memoirs of his wife, Grace Lovat Fraser, *In the Days of My Youth*, published in 1970.

Frazee Theatre, NEW YORK, see WALLACK THEATRE.

FRÉDÉRICK [really ANTOINE-LOUIS-PROSPER LEMAÎTRE] (1800–76), French actor, who embodied in himself all the glory and excesses of the Romantic drama, many of whose heroes he created. Usually known as Frédérick (his grandfather's name, which he took when he went on the stage), he was a unique personality, his art proceeding from a judicious blending of application and

intuition. He never appeared at the Comédie-Française, but spent most of his time in the theatres of the Boulevard du Temple (q.v.), where he made his first appearance at the Variétés-Amusantes at the age of fifteen as the lion in a pantomime based on the story of Pyramus and Thisbe. He then went to the Funambules and to the Cirque-Olympique, where melodramas were played between the circus acts, and soon became one of the most popular actors in Paris. In 1823 he appeared at the Ambigu-Comique as Robert Macaire in *L'Auberge des Adrets*, a part ever after associated with him. The play had been written as a serious melodrama, but Frédérick, sensing that the public was ready for something new, made it a success by burlesquing it, and followed it with a sequel, *Robert Macaire* (1834), much of which he wrote himself and which he played in London in 1835. Like Beaumarchais's Figaro, Macaire had political repercussions, and it was said that he contributed not a little to the downfall of Louis-Philippe. Between these plays Frédérick had made a tremendous impression at the Porte-Saint-Martin in *Trente ans, ou la Vie d'un joueur* (1827), a powerful play on the evils of gambling in which he appeared in London on his first visit in 1828. Among his later successes were Othello, in Ducis's translation, and several of the leading roles in the plays of Dumas *père*, notably *Kean, ou Désordre et génie* (1836), which was specially written for him, as was Balzac's *Vautrin* (1840). When in 1838 Dumas and Hugo took over the old Théâtre Ventadour and renamed it the Théâtre de la Renaissance (q.v.), Frédérick inaugurated it as the home of Romantic drama with an electrifying performance as the hero of Hugo's *Ruy Blas*, a play which gave great offence to Queen Victoria when she saw it in London in 1852, though she had previously been one of the actor's greatest admirers. She had particularly enjoyed his Don César de Bazan in 1845 and commented favourably in her diary in 1847 on his performance in *Le Docteur noir*. Frédérick's last years were unhappy. The taste of the public had changed and he could find only trivial or unsuitable plays to appear in, though he continued to act with little diminution of his power until shortly before his death.

FREDRO, ALEKSANDER (1793–1876), Polish poet and playwright. Son of an aristocratic family, he served in Napoleon's Grand Army from 1809 to 1814 and then settled down on his estates. His comedies, which are written in strict classic form and in impeccable verse, deal with the life of the country gentleman as he knew it or had heard of it from his elders. Among them the best are *Husband and Wife* (1822), which deals boldly with the problems of marriage, *Maidens' Vows* (1833), and *Vengeance* (1834). An English version of the lively farce *Ladies and Hussars* (1825) was acted in New York in 1925. His plays are still in the Polish repertory and in 1964 his comedy, *The Life Annuity* (1835), was performed in London by a Polish company during the World Theatre season.

FREEAR, LOUIE (1871–1939), see DROLL and DUKE OF YORK'S THEATRE.

FREEDLEY, GEORGE REYNOLDS (1904–67), American theatre historian, founder and director of the Theatre Collection of the New York Public Library, now housed at Lincoln Center (q.v.). A graduate of the Baker Workshop at Yale, Freedley was for a short time an actor and stage manager on Broadway, where he first appeared in 1928, being associated a year later with the Theatre Guild (q.v.). In 1931 he joined the staff of the New York Public Library to administer the theatre section based on the recently presented David Belasco Collection. He was also one of the founders of the Theatre Library Association in 1939 and was closely associated with the running of the American National Theatre and Academy (q.v.). From 1938 until his death he was drama critic and drama feature writer of the New York *Morning Telegraph*, and lectured and wrote extensively on theatre history. He was also part-author of *Theatre Collections in Libraries and Museums* (with Rosamond Gilder) (1936), of *A History of the Theatre* (with John Reeves) (1941; rev. 1955), and of *A History of Modern Drama* (with Barrett H. Clark) (1947).

Freie Bühne (Free Stage), an organization founded in Berlin by Otto Brahm (q.v.) in 1889 on the lines of Antoine's Théâtre Libre (q.v.) in Paris, for the production of plays of the new naturalistic school of writers inspired by Ibsen (q.v.). The society had no permanent theatre and played only at matinées. Its first production was Ibsen's *Ghosts*, followed by plays by Tolstoy, Strindberg, and Zola. The first German

play to be given was *Vor Sonnenaufgang*, by Hauptmann (q.v.), but the real manifesto of the new movement was *Die Familie Selicke*, by Arno Holz (1890), a sordid picture of lower middle-class life played in a realistic manner against an equally realistic background by a specially trained company led by Emanuel Reicher. In 1894 Brahm, realizing that the work of the Freie Bühne, though successful, was insufficient for his purpose, affiliated it to the well-established Deutsches Theater (q.v.) founded in 1883. In 1890 the FREIE VOLKSBÜHNE was established in Berlin for the purpose of bringing good plays at low prices within the reach of the working-class population.

French Brace, French Flat, see FLAT.

FREYTAG, GUSTAV (1816–95), German writer. Best known as the author of sociological and historical novels, he began his literary career as a dramatist, and became the German exponent of the 'well-made' play of France. His best work was a comedy, *Die Journalisten* (1852), a good-humoured portrayal of party politics in a small town during an election. This can still be read with pleasure, but his attempts at serious problem-plays and an historical tragedy in verse are less attractive. In 1863 he published his *Technik des Dramas*, with its famous pyramid, or diagrammatic plot, of a 'well-made' play.

FRIDOLIN, see GÉLINAS, GRATIEN.

FRISCH, MAX RUDOLF (1911–   ), Swiss playwright, a disciple of Brecht (q.v.), whose influence is apparent in the early plays, *Nun singen sie wieder* (1945), *Die chinesische Mauer* (1946), *Als der Krieg zu Ende war* (1949), and *Graf Öderland* (1951). In complete contrast to these moral and episodic dramas Frisch has also written plays of a more romantic flavour, such as *Santa Cruz* (1946), a blend of dream and reality, and *Don Juan, oder Die Liebe zur Geometrie* (1953), in which he gives a new twist to the old legend, since Don Juan's only interest in life is geometry. He has no time for women, so they are attracted to him and in the end he finds that his only way of escape is marriage. (This play was performed in English by Hull University drama students in 1968.) In 1958 Frisch produced a short play, *Biedermann und die Brandstifter*, which, as *The Fire Raisers*, had a successful run at the Royal Court in London in 1961, and as *The Firebugs* was seen in New York in 1963. Frisch's next play, *Andorra* (1961), the story of a non-Jewish illegitimate child, brought up as a Jew, who is murdered by an anti-Semitic invader, had a resounding success. It was seen in New York in 1963, and was twice performed in London in 1964, in German by the Schiller Theater company at the Aldwych during the World Theatre season, and in English at the National Theatre. Together with several of Frisch's other plays, it has been published in an English translation.

FRITELLINO, see CECCHINI, P. M.

FROHMAN, CHARLES (1860–1915), American theatre manager, well known in London, which he first visited in 1880 with Haverley's Minstrels. Having laid the foundation of his future prosperity with the production of Bronson Howard's *Shenandoah* in New York in 1888, he returned to London, where he negotiated the transfer of a number of successful plays and musical comedies to New York. In 1897 he became lessee of the Duke of York's Theatre (q.v.), where he attempted to establish a true repertory system and was responsible for many notable productions, including Barrie's *Peter Pan* (1904). He had already in 1893 taken over the management of the Empire Theatre (q.v.) in New York, and at the time of his death (he was drowned in the torpedoing of the *Lusitania*) he had a controlling interest in several other theatres which passed to his brother Daniel (q.v.).

FROHMAN, DANIEL (1851–1940), American theatre manager, elder brother of the above. In 1885, with his brother GUSTAVE (1855–1930), who was associated with him in many ventures, he took over the management of the Lyceum (q.v.) in New York, which Steele Mackaye (q.v.) had just built on Fourth Avenue, and ran it with an excellent stock company until it was demolished in 1902. He then opened a new Lyceum on 45th Street, having his own fine apartments on the top floor. In 1911 he published a volume of reminiscences, *Memories of a Manager*, following it in 1935 with *Daniel Frohman Presents*.

Front Curtain, see CURTAIN.

Front of House, a term applied to those parts of a theatre which are used by the audience as distinct from the actors. These include the auditorium, passages, lobbies and foyers, the bars, cloakrooms, and refreshment-rooms, and the box-office or pay-box for the booking of seats, the whole being under the supervision of a front-of-house manager.

FRY [really HARRIS, Fry being his mother's maiden name], CHRISTOPHER (1907–), English dramatist, who first attracted notice with a one-act *jeu d'esprit*, *A Phoenix Too Frequent* (1946), which had been preceded by a religious play about St. Cuthbert, *The Boy with a Cart* (1938) and by *The Tower* (1939), written for a festival at Tewkesbury. In 1948 *Thor, With Angels* was produced at the Canterbury Festival and *The Firstborn*, on the story of Moses, at the Edinburgh Festival. It was, however, the production, first at the Arts Theatre in 1948 and then at the Globe Theatre in 1949, of *The Lady's Not For Burning* that brought him into prominence. With Gielgud (q.v.) replacing Alec Clunes as Thomas Mendip, and a distinguished cast, the play had a long run, and seemed to herald a renaissance of poetry on the English stage. Fry's next play, written for Laurence Olivier (q.v.), was *Venus Observed* (1950), and in the same year he translated Anouilh's *L'Invitation au château*, which, as *Ring Round the Moon*, with Scofield (q.v.) in the dual role of the twin hero and villain, also had a long run. In 1954 Edith Evans (q.v.) starred in *The Dark is Light Enough*. Meanwhile Fry had reverted to his earlier biblical vein with *A Sleep of Prisoners*, a play planned for performance in churches. It was first seen at St. Thomas's, Regent Street, in 1951 and frequently revived. In 1955 came two more translations, Anouilh's *L'Alouette* (on Joan of Arc) as *The Lark* and Giraudoux's *La Guerre de Troie n'aura pas lieu* as *Tiger at the Gates*. It was by now evident, however, that the trend of the time was away from rather than towards poetry, and Fry's next play, *Curtmantle* (on Henry II and Becket), had its first production in a Dutch translation at the opening on 1 Mar. 1961 of the Stadsschouwburg, Tilburg, The Netherlands. It was seen in London a year later in a production by the London company of the Royal Shakespeare Theatre but had only a moderate success. The same was true of his most recent play to date, *A Yard of Sun* (1970), first produced at the Nottingham Playhouse and brought to

London by that company for a week's run at the Old Vic.

Full Scenery, a system of setting the stage where all the parts of the stage picture belong to the current scene only and must be changed for another scene, as opposed to Detail Scenery, where some elements only are changed against a permanent background which remains in place for the whole of the performance.

FULLER, ISAAC (1606–72), English scene painter, who studied in Paris under François Perrier, probably at the new Academy there. He worked for the Restoration theatre and in 1669 painted a scene of Paradise for Dryden's *Tyrannic Love*, later suing Killigrew's company (see DRURY LANE) for payment. He was awarded £335 10s. od.—a large sum in those days—but his scene may have been utilized for other plays also.

FULLER, ROSALINDE (1892–1982), English actress, who made her first success in America, where in 1922 she played Ophelia to the Hamlet of John Barrymore (q.v.). She made her first appearance in London in 1927, among her outstanding parts being the Betrothed in Raynal's *The Unknown Warrior* and Irina in Chekhov's *Three Sisters*. She was also seen in a number of Shaw plays, and in 1940 she joined Donald Wolfit's Shakespeare company, playing Viola in *Twelfth Night*, Katharina in *The Taming of the Shrew*, Portia in *The Merchant of Venice*, Desdemona in *Othello*, and Beatrice in *Much Ado About Nothing*. In 1950 she first appeared in a solo programme entitled *Masks and Faces*, consisting of her own adaptations of a number of short sketches from such authors as Dickens, Maupassant, Henry James, and Katherine Mansfield, performed in costume but with a minimum of scenery. She subsequently toured in this, and in a similar programme entitled *Subject to Love*, under the auspices of the British Council, visiting the Middle East in 1958, South Africa in 1960 and 1961, Australia in 1962, and the Far East in 1964. She also made several tours of the United States. She was awarded the M.B.E. in 1966 for services to the theatre.

Fulton Theatre, NEW YORK, see HELEN HAYES THEATRE.

Funambules, THÉÂTRE DES, PARIS, on the old Boulevard du Temple. As its name indicates (*funambulus* being the Latin for rope-walker), it was originally a booth for acrobats. A permanent theatre was built on the site in 1816 and four years later the great pantomimist Deburau (q.v.) appeared there, as did Frédérick (q.v.) in his early days. At first the productions in which they appeared still had Harlequin as their chief character, but by degrees Deburau built up his famous characterization of Pierrot until he became the theatre's only star actor, remaining there until his death in 1846, three years after the theatre had been rebuilt and enlarged. He was succeeded as Pierrot by his son Charles until the theatre was swept away in the demolition of the Boulevard du Temple necessitated by the rebuilding of Paris in 1862.

FURTENBACH, JOSEF (1591–1667), German architect, author of several works which add to our knowledge of the stage conditions of his time. His *Architectura Civilis* (1628), which contains some valuable engravings of stage settings, also has one of the earliest references to the use of footlights (see LIGHTING), confirmed by a further description of them by Sabbattini (q.v.) ten years later. Furtenbach, who built a theatre in Ulm with scenery consisting of three-sided revolving prisms, or *telari*, also mentions a sunk strip at the back of the acting area in which lamps were placed to light the backcloth from below. In his *Mannhaffter Kunst-Spiegel* (1663) he gives a plan and description of a type of indoor stage, such as those used by the Jesuits (see JESUIT DRAMA) for afternoon performances, which had large windows lighting the acting area. Even so, torches were sometime needed for the closing scenes, and lighting effects were indicated during the play for sunshine, moonlight, or lightning.

G

GABRIEL, ANGE-JACQUES (1698–1782), see VERSAILLES.

GABRIELLI, FRANCESCO (?–1654), see SCAPINO.

Gaelic Drama. An important element in the development of the modern Irish theatre was the production of plays in Irish. Some were first seen at the Abbey Theatre (q.v.), but they were mainly produced by the Gaelic Drama League in Dublin, Galway, and the surrounding districts. Though some plays in Irish were produced by amateurs around 1900, the first to be done professionally was *Casadh an tSugáin* (*The Twisting of the Rope*) (1901), by DOUGLAS HYDE (1860–1949), founder of the Gaelic League in 1893. His dramatic works and those of his contemporaries became well known throughout Ireland, one of his successors being Micheál MacLiammóir (q.v.), author of *Diarmuid agus Gráinne* (1928), the first play performed by the newly formed Taibhdhearc na Gaillimhe (Galway Theatre), which MacLiammóir directed from its foundation until 1931. As well as plays in Irish specially written for this theatre, which is subsidized by the Government, many Gaelic translations of English and European writers were also performed. Among them were several by Bernard Shaw (q.v.), whose *Saint Joan* was translated in 1941 by the actress Siobhan McKenna, who also played the title-role. She later played the same part in English in London in 1954 and in New York in 1956. She also translated into Gaelic and played in Barrie's *Mary Rose* in 1942. Other Gaelic writers who have been active in the Galway Theatre include Liam O'Flaherty and Padraig O'Conaire.

In Dublin a number of Gaelic plays were produced at the Damer Hall with great success, among them the original version, in Irish, of Brendan Behan's *The Hostage* (*An Giall*), which in translation was successfully produced in London in 1958, in New York in 1960, and in many European cities, including Paris in 1962. To further public interest in Gaelic drama the Abbey Theatre stages one-act plays in Irish after the main production of the evening, and in 1945, with *Muireann agus an Prionnsa*, by Micheál O h-Aodha, it inaugurated a series of Gaelic pantomimes.

Gaff, a nineteenth-century term for an improvised theatre in the poorer quarters of London and other large towns, on whose stage an inadequate company dealt robustly with a repertory of melodrama. The entrance fee was a penny or twopence. The lowest type of gaff was known as a blood-tub.

Gaiety Theatre. (1) LONDON, in the Strand (in the part now Aldwych). This opened on 21 Dec. 1868 under the management of John Hollingshead (q.v.) with a mixed bill which included a burlesque of Meyerbeer's opera 'Robert le Diable' by W. S. Gilbert. With a good company which included Nellie Farren (q.v.), Madge Robertson (see KENDAL), Marie Litton, and Alfred Wigan, and scenery designed by Grieve (q.v.), the theatre prospered. In 1869 Dickens, an inveterate playgoer, saw his last play there the year before his death—H. J. Byron's *Uncle Dick's Darling* —and prophesied the future greatness of a young actor appearing in it, Henry Irving (q.v.). In Dec. 1871 came the production of the first collaboration between Gilbert and Sullivan, *Thespis; or, the Gods Grown Old*. But the great feature of the Gaiety was its burlesques, with the famous quartet Edward Terry, Kate Vaughan, E. W. Royce, and Nellie Farren, who first played together in 1876 in Byron's *Little Don Caesar de Bazan*. In 1885 Fred Leslie joined the company, proving a perfect foil to Nellie Farren, with whom he first appeared in *Little Jack Sheppard*. A year later Hollingshead retired and George Edwardes (q.v.) took over, his first production being a comic opera, 'Dorothy', in which Hayden Coffin made a success with an interpolated song, 'Queen of My Heart'. Burlesques, however, continued to occupy most of the bill, one, *Ruy Blas; or, the Blasé Roué* (1889), containing the famous *pas de quatre* with Fred Leslie, C. Danby, Ben Nathan, and Fred Storey dressed as ballet girls and made up to look like Irving, Toole, Edward Terry, and Wilson Barrett. Irving protested and the make-up was altered. In Dec. 1892 Edwardes transferred from the Prince of Wales' (q.v.) a new type of show called *In Town*, now considered the first musical comedy. It was followed by several similar shows, all with the word 'girl' in their titles and the 'Gaiety Girls', famous for their good looks, in their choruses. But the end of the theatre was approaching, as the site was needed for the Aldwych reconstruction. The last production was *The Toreador* (1901), a musical comedy which introduced a new star, Gertie Millar (q.v.), and on 4 July 1903 the theatre closed for demolition.

(2) LONDON. The new Gaiety Theatre, built by George Edwardes on the Aldwych–Strand corner, opened on 26 Oct. 1903 with a new musical comedy, *The Orchid*, again with Gertie Millar. Among its later successes were *The Girls of Gottenberg* (1907) and *Our Miss Gibbs* (1909). When Edwardes died in 1915 the fortunes of the Gaiety declined in spite of the success of a new comedian, Leslie Henson, who first appeared in *To-Night's the Night* (1915), and after a chequered career it closed on 25 Feb. 1939. It remained derelict until 1957 and was then demolished (in spite of Leslie Henson's frantic last-minute efforts to save it) and an office block built on the site.

(3) NEW YORK, on West 46th Street. This opened on 31 Aug. 1908, and a year later W. S. Gilbert's *The Fortune Hunter*, with John Barrymore (q.v.), had a good run, as did a dramatization of Jean Webster's *Daddy Long-Legs* in 1914. In 1918 *Lightnin'* brought stardom to FRANK BACON (1864–1922), its part-author. It ran for three years and proved to be his last play, as he died during the Chicago run which followed its New York success. In 1932 the Gaiety was renamed the Victoria, housing only burlesque and films.

(For the Gaiety, Manchester, see HORNIMAN, A.E.F. and REPERTORY THEATRE MOVEMENT; see also DUBLIN.)

Gaîté, THÉÂTRE DE LA, PARIS, on the Boulevard du Temple, originally Nicolet's marionette theatre. It became the Gaîté after the upheavals of the Revolution, and was notable as being the first French theatre which was not state-aided. From 1808 it flourished, its only rival in the production of popular melodrama, pantomime, and vaudeville being the Ambigu-Comique (q.v.). It was managed by Pixérécourt (q.v.) from 1825 to 1835, when it was rebuilt after a disastrous fire. When the Gaîté disappeared in the demolition of the Boulevard du Temple in 1862 the name was transferred to a new theatre which under Offenbach became a home of light operetta and spectacular musical shows.

Galanty Show, see SHADOW-SHOW.

GALDÓS, BENITO PÉREZ (1843–1920), the greatest Spanish novelist of the nineteenth century, who in the 1890s turned to the theatre, which had fascinated him in his youth. Unfortunately his plays, unlike his novels, were mostly stiff and unconvincing and he lacked a sense of the theatre. But some of them are interesting and show the influence of both Zola and Ibsen (qq.v.), particularly in *La loca de la casa* (1893), *Electra* (1901), which was considered anti-clerical and therefore highly controversial, and *El abuelo* (1904), which, like Ibsen's *Ghosts*, deals with the problems of heredity.

GALIMAFRÉ, see BOBÈCHE.

Gallery, in the nineteenth-century English theatre the highest and cheapest part of the house, where places could not be booked in advance. The seating consisted of wooden benches, usually without backs. The occupants of the gallery, from their elevated position, were, in about 1752, nicknamed the 'Gods', and often formed the most perceptive and certainly the most vociferous part of the audience (see also FOOTMEN'S GALLERY).

GALLI-BIBIENA, GALLI-BIBBIENA, GALLI DA BIBBIENA, see BIBIENA.

GALLIENNE, EVA LE, see LE GALLIENNE.

Gallo Theatre, NEW YORK, see NEW YORKER THEATRE.

GALSWORTHY, JOHN (1867–1933), English novelist and dramatist, best remembered for the series of novels which make up *The Forsyte Saga*. He was also the author of a number of plays dealing with questions of social justice in the fashion of his time. *The Silver Box* (1906), which deals with the inequality before the law of a rich thief and a poor one, and *Strife* (1909), which explores the effect of an industrial strike, were both well received and several times revived up to 1933, as was his best-known play, *Justice* (1910). This includes a scene showing the effect of solitary confinement on its leading character, Falder, and is sometimes credited with having led to a reform of prison practice in this respect. Of his later plays, in which the reformer seems to have triumphed over the dramatist, the most successful were *The Skin Game* (1920), *Loyalties* (1922), and *Old English* (1924). His last play, *The Roof* (1929), was not a success. An effort in 1968 to revive *The Foundations*, first produced in 1917, was also unsuccessful, and at present it seems unlikely that Galsworthy's plays will return to the repertory, except perhaps for *Justice*, which was seen in London in 1968. For his services to literature he was awarded the O.M. in 1929 and received the Nobel Prize for Literature in 1932.

GALVIN, SYDNEY (1892–1962), see LENO, DAN.

GANASSA, ZAN [real name probably ALBERTO NASELI] (*fl.* 1568–83), one of the first actors of the *commedia dell'arte* (q.v.) to take a company abroad. He was in Paris in 1571–2, but his most successful tours were in Spain, where frequent references to him are found in the 1570s. His influence on the development of the Spanish theatre was considerable, mainly through his contact with Lope de Rueda (q.v.). A painting in the Bayeux Museum, reproduced in Ducharte's *The Italian Comedy* (1967), is believed to represent a performance by Ganassa's troupe assisted by a group of French noblemen.

GANTILLON, SIMON (1887–1961), French dramatist, whose most important play was *Maya*, produced by Baty (q.v.) at the Théâtre Montparnasse in 1924. This had a great success at the time, and it was with an English translation of it that Peter Godfrey opened the second Gate Theatre (q.v.) in London on 22 Nov. 1927. It was revived in 1932, and produced again by Godfrey in 1944 as the opening play of his Gate Theatre in Hollywood.

GARCÍA DE LA HUERTA, VICENTE (1734–87), a Spanish dramatist who revolted against the eighteenth-century neglect of Spanish classics in favour of French translations, though in his own selection of forgotten Spanish plays, published in 1785/6, he did not always choose the best, entirely omitting Lope de Vega, Tirso de Molina, and Alarcón (qq.v.). He was much influenced by the

theory of the three unities (q.v.) imposed on Spain by Luzán's *Poética* (1737), and his own most successful play, *La Raquel* (1778), was modelled on French lines; but its inspiration was entirely Spanish and in the general poverty of eighteenth-century Spanish drama it stands out as a not unworthy successor to the plays of the Golden Age.

GARCÍA GUTIÉRREZ, ANTONIO (1813–84), Spanish dramatist of the Romantic period, whose somewhat inferior play *El trovador* (1836) achieved world-wide popularity when it was used by Verdi as the basis of his opera 'Il Trovatore' (1853). His work shows the influence of Dumas *père*, two of whose melodramas he translated into Spanish together with several plays by Scribe.

GARCÍA LORCA, FEDERICO, see LORCA.

Garden Theatre, NEW YORK, at 61 Madison Avenue. This opened on 27 Sept. 1890 and in the following year saw the reappearance in New York of Sarah Bernhardt (q.v.) in Sardou's *La Tosca*. Other interesting productions were Gilbert's *The Mountebanks* (1893) (with music by Alfred Cellier), a dramatization of Ouida's *Under Two Flags* (1901), and a translation of Hauptmann's *Die Weber* (1892) as *The Weavers* (1915). In Jan. 1910 a season of Shakespeare's plays was given by Ben Greet (q.v.) and his company. In 1919 the theatre became the Jewish (later Yiddish) Art Theatre; it was demolished in 1925.

GARNIER, ROBERT (*c.* 1535–*c.* 1600), a lawyer who prepared the way for French classical tragedy by his eight plays on Greek models, of which the best was *Les Juives* (1583). He began writing for the theatre in 1568 and made many important innovations later adopted by other dramatists. But he suffered, as did all his contemporaries, from the belief that to follow the best models was necessarily to excel, and he saw Greece only through the eyes of Rome.

GARRICK, DAVID (1717–79), one of the greatest of English actors, who was responsible for a radical change in the style of acting in his day, replacing the formal declamation of Quin (q.v.) by an easy, natural manner of speech. During his long management of Drury Lane (q.v.)

he also instituted many reforms both before and behind the curtain, the most important being the introduction of stage lighting concealed from the audience and the banishment of spectators from the stage (see also VOLTAIRE). At the age of eleven he appeared with some success as Sergeant Kite in a schoolboy production of Farquhar's *The Recruiting Officer*. Later, being sent to study under Dr. Johnson (q.v.) at Lichfield, he accompanied the latter to London and there appeared in amateur theatricals. Early in 1741 he also played small parts at Goodman's Fields under Giffard (q.v.), for whom he acted at Ipswich living the summer under the name of Lyddal. Returning to Goodman's Fields, he made his formal début as Richard III on 19 Oct. with such success that he was engaged for Drury Lane, where on 11 May 1742 he embarked on a triumphant career which suffered no serious check until his retirement in 1776. Though apparently unsuited to tragedy, being on the small side, he was unsurpassed as the tragic heroes of the contemporary theatre and in such parts as Hamlet, Macbeth, and particularly Lear—which he played in a scarlet coat. He himself said that he modelled the madness of Lear, in which he was considered outstanding, on that of an unfortunate man who had accidentally killed his two-year-old child by dropping it from a window. He was equally admired in comedy, some of his best parts being Abel Drugger in Jonson's *The Alchemist*, Benedick in *Much Ado About Nothing*, and Ranger in Hoadley's *The Suspicious Husband*. As Bayes in Buckingham's *The Rehearsal* he scored a signal triumph with his mimicry of well-known actors of the time.

His fiery temper, vanity, and snobbishness, as well as his sudden rise to fame, made him many enemies, among them Macklin and the malicious Samuel Foote (qq.v.). He had also to contend with the petulance of unacted authors and disappointed small-part actors and was not always responsible for the quarrels in which he found himself involved, notably with Dr. Johnson over the failure of *Irene* (1749) and with Colman the elder (q.v.), whom he offended by refusing to play the part of Lord Ogleby in *The Clandestine Marriage* (1766), a comedy on which they had collaborated. Garrick was a vivacious and competent dramatist, at his best about equal to Colley Cibber

(q.v.), but much of his work was mere hack-writing and adapting of old plays. His rewriting of Wycherley's *The Country Wife* as *The Country Girl* (1766) held the stage for many years, as did his adaptations of *The Taming of the Shrew* and *The Winter's Tale* as *Katherine and Petruchio* and *Florizel and Perdita* (both 1756). Of his own plays, the farce *Miss in her Teens* (1747), in which he played Fribble, and *Bon Ton; or, High Life Above Stairs* (1775) were the most successful. He was also a prolific writer of epilogues and prologues, published with his other works in a three-volume edition in 1785. One of his most publicized achievements was his Shakespeare Jubilee at Stratford-upon-Avon (q.v.) in 1769, which was remarkable for a number of odes, songs, speeches, and other effusions by David Garrick, of which the manuscript has been lost, and for the complete absence of anything by Shakespeare.

It was in 1747 that Garrick first took over the management of Drury Lane, where the major part of his career was spent. He gathered round him a good company, his leading ladies being Mrs. Abington, Mrs. Bellamy, Mrs. Cibber, who was said to resemble him like a sister, and Peg Woffington (qq.v.). Among the men were Spranger Barry, Tom King, and Richard Yates (qq.v.). Garrick's management was marred by two riots, the first in 1755, occasioned by the appearance of French dancers in Noverre's ballet, *The Chinese Festival*, just as war between England and France was about to break out, the second in 1762, when the concession of 'half-price after the third act' was abolished but had to be restored. This led Garrick to retire for a time, and from 1763 to 1765 he travelled on the Continent with his wife, EVA MARIA VIOLETTI [really VEIGEL] (1724–1822), a dancer whom he had married in 1749. He was well received everywhere, particularly in France, and returned, greatly refreshed, to a public surfeited with musical spectacle which was glad to see him in a succession of his greatest parts. He made his farewell appearance on 10 June 1776 as Felix in Mrs. Centlivre's *The Wonder, a Woman Keeps a Secret*, and retired to Hampton, where he died, eliciting from Dr. Johnson the memorable epitaph: 'I am disappointed by that stroke of death which has eclipsed the gaiety of nations and impoverished the public stock of harmless pleasure.' He was buried in Westminster Abbey. His brother GEORGE (1722–79), who had been his right-hand man for many years, died a few days later because, said the wits of the time, 'Davy wanted him'.

Garrick was several times painted by Sir Joshua Reynolds, one of whose portraits of him hangs in the Garrick Club (q.v.), named in honour of the great actor, as was the Garrick Theatre, London (q.v.). A fine portrait by Gainsborough, done in 1766 and said by Mrs. Garrick to be the best ever painted, was lost when the Stratford-upon-Avon Town Hall was destroyed by fire in 1946.

Garrick Club, LONDON, founded by the Duke of Sussex and named in honour of David Garrick (q.v.). It opened in Nov. 1831, though its premises (Probatt's Family Hotel, King Street) were not ready for the use of members until Feb. 1832. The present clubhouse opened on 4 July 1864 and stands on part of old Rose Street and that warren of crowded alleys which lay between King Street and St. Martin's Lane, home of Curll, the bookseller at the 'Pope's Head'—associated too with Samuel Butler and Samuel Johnson. The club, which is restricted to seven hundred members, has a fine collection of theatrical portraits of which an annotated catalogue was prepared in 1908 by Robert Walters. In 1896 the Revd. R. H. Barham, author of The Ingoldsby Legends, published a collection of short biographies of 135 of its former members (see also Percy Fitzgerald's History of the Garrick Club).

Garrick Theatre. (1) LONDON, in Leman Street, E.1. This opened in Jan. 1831 and took its name from its proximity to the old theatre in Goodman's Fields where Garrick (q.v.) made his début. In 1846 it was burned down and rebuilt, and in 1854 was renamed the Albert and Garrick Royal Amphitheatre. It held a very low position, even among East End theatres, and was practically a 'gaff' (q.v.). In 1873–4 the actor J. B. Howe, a great local favourite, took it and made a gallant bid for popularity, but went bankrupt in 1875. The theatre remained empty until in 1879 Tree (q.v.) appeared there, under the management of Miss May Bulmer, and made a great success as Bonneteau in the opéra bouffe, A Cruise to China Shortly afterwards the building was demolished and a police-station erected on the site.

(2) LONDON, in Charing Cross Road, opposite the statue of Irving. Financed by W. S. Gilbert (q.v.), this opened under Hare (q.v.) on 24 Apr. 1889 with Pinero's The Profligate. In 1890 came Grundy's A Pair of Spectacles, which had a long run. Five years later The Notorious Mrs. Ebbsmith, also by Pinero, caused a sensation with Mrs. Patrick Campbell (q.v.) in the title-role. After Hare left the theatre its standing declined until in 1900 Arthur Bourchier (q.v.) leased it and inaugurated with his wife, Violet Vanbrugh, a long and brilliant period of productions ranging from Shakespeare to farce. In 1911 Knoblock's Kismet, with Oscar Asche and Lily Brayton, was an outstanding success, as was a revival of The Merry Wives of Windsor. For many years after this the theatre had no regular policy or management, and was used for revue. Closed in 1939, it reopened in 1941, and in 1944 scored a success with Thomas Job's Uncle Harry. In 1960 Fings Ain't Wot They Used T'Be, transferred from Theatre Workshop (q.v.), started a long run, and was followed by Charles Dyer's Rattle of a Simple Man (1962). In 1965 an unexpectedly popular revival of the old Aldwych farce, Thark, was transferred to this theatre from the Yvonne Arnaud at Guildford. On 15 Mar. 1967 Brian Rix inaugurated a season of farce in repertory with Stand by Your Bedouin, by Ray Cooney and Tony Hilton.

(3) NEW YORK, on 35th Street between 5th and 6th Avenues. This opened as Harrigan's Theatre on 29 Dec. 1890. In 1895 Richard Mansfield (q.v.) took it over and renamed it the Garrick, opening on 23 Apr. with Shaw's Arms and the Man, the longest run under his management being that of William Gillette in his own play, Secret Service; Gillette also appeared as Sherlock Holmes, a part always associated with him. Among later productions were Captain Jinks of the Horse Marines (1901) with Ethel Barrymore (q.v.), The Stubbornness of Geraldine (1902), and Her Own Way (1903), all by Clyde Fitch, while 1905 saw a successful run of Shaw's You Never Can Tell. From 1917 to 1919 the theatre was occupied by a French company under Jacques Copeau (q.v.), who named it after his theatre in Paris, the Vieux-Colombier, and inaugurated his tenancy on 20 Nov. 1917 with a performance of Molière's Les Fourberies de Scapin. On 19 Apr. 1919 the Theatre Guild (q.v.) opened at the Garrick, which

then reverted to its old name, with Benavente's *The Bonds of Interest*, followed by *John Ferguson* and *Jane Clegg*, both by St. John Ervine. Among later productions were Shaw's *Heartbreak House* (1920), Milne's *Mr. Pim Passes By* and Molnár's *Liliom* (both 1921), Andreyev's *He Who Gets Slapped* and Karel Čapek's *R.U.R.* (both 1922), Ibsen's *Peer Gynt* and Rice's *The Adding Machine* (both 1923). In 1924 came the Lunts in Molnár's *The Guardsman*. In 1925 the Theatre Guild moved into its own playhouse (see ANTA THEATRE) and in 1932 the Garrick was pulled down. The Provincetown Players (q.v.) made their last appearance there in 1929.

GASCOIGNE, GEORGE (*c.* 1542–77), a scholar of Cambridge who helped to prepare the entertainments given before Elizabeth I at Kenilworth and Woodstock in 1575. He was also the author of a translation of Lodovico Dolce's *Giocasta* (based on Euripides' *Phoenician Women*) as *Jocasta*, and of Ariosto's *I Suppositi* (based on Plautus' *Captivi*) as *The Supposes*, both performed at Gray's Inn in 1566. *The Supposes*, which provided Shakespeare with the subplot of Bianca and her suitors in *The Taming of the Shrew*, was also produced at Trinity College, Oxford, in 1582.

GASKILL, WILLIAM (1930–), English theatre director who, after spending several years as actor and stage manager in various repertory companies, went to the Royal Court (q.v.), where in 1958 he directed a double bill, *A Resounding Tinkle* and *The Hole* by N. F. Simpson, whose *One-Way Pendulum* he also directed in 1959. In the meantime he had been responsible for the production of Osborne's *Epitaph for George Dillon* in London and in New York, where he also directed Dürrenmatt's *The Deadly Game* (1960). Between visits to Stratford-upon-Avon to direct *Richard III* in 1961 and *Cymbeline* in 1962, he directed for the Royal Shakespeare Company in London Brecht's *The Caucasian Chalk Circle* (also 1962), and was responsible also for Brecht's *Baal* at the Phoenix in 1963. He was then appointed an associate director of the National Theatre Company, for which he directed Farquhar's *The Recruiting Officer* and in 1965 Brecht's *Mother Courage and her Children* and Arden's *Armstrong's Last Goodnight*. He then

returned to the Royal Court, where he was responsible for the first production of several controversial new plays, including Edward Bond's *Saved* (1965) and *Early Morning* (1968), as well as revivals of *Macbeth* and Chekhov's *Three Sisters;* but he was again at the Old Vic in 1970, when he directed Farquhar's *The Beaux' Stratagem* with Maggie Smith (q.v.) as Mrs. Sullen.

Gas Lighting, see LIGHTING.

GASSMANN, VITTORIO (1912–), Italian actor-manager, who in 1950 founded the Teatro Popolare Italiano—somewhat on the lines of Vilar's Théâtre National Populaire (q.v.)—which he brought to London in 1963 in a programme which consisted of excerpts from his repertory under the general title of *The Heroes*. Among his productions, in most of which he starred himself, have been *Romeo and Juliet*, Betti's *Il Giocatore*, Dumas's *Kean*, Ibsen's *Peer Gynt*, and revivals of Aeschylus (the *Persians*), Euripides (the *Bacchae*), and Sophocles (the *Oedipus Rex*). He has also appeared as Hamlet, and in 1956 alternated the parts of Othello and Iago. One of his best parts was the title-role in Alfieri's *Oreste*, and he was also excellent as Troilus in a production of *Troilus and Cressida* in the Boboli Gardens in Florence.

GASSNER, JOHN [really JENÖ] WALDHORN (1903–67), American theatre critic, historian, and playwright, born in Hungary. He had already held a number of academic posts when in 1956 he became Professor of Dramatic Literature at Yale. In 1928 he began reading and adapting foreign plays for the Theatre Guild (q.v.), among them Emil Ludwig's *Versailles* as *Peace Palace* (1931) and Stefan Zweig's *Jeremiah* (1939), and in 1940 he dramatized Robinson Jeffers's poem, *The Tower Beyond Tragedy*, for Judith Anderson (q.v.). He also made modern acting versions of Sophocles' *Antigone* and *Oedipus Rex*, and of *Everyman* and *The Second Shepherd's Play*. He wrote several books on the theatre, among them *Masters of the Drama* (1940, rev. 1951), *The Theatre in Our Time* (1954), *Form and Idea in the Modern Theatre* (1956), and *Theatre at the Crossroads* (1960), and edited a number of play anthologies, including ten volumes of American plays and about ten of English and Continental plays. He was for many years drama critic successively of *New Theatre Magazine*, *Forum*, *Time*, *The Educational Theatre Journal*, and *Theatre Arts*. His last work, *The Reader's Encyclopedia of World Drama*, compiled in collaboration with Edward Quinn, was published shortly after his death.

Gate Theatre, DUBLIN, see DUBLIN.

Gate Theatre, LONDON, a small club theatre for the production of foreign and uncommercial plays which opened on 30 Oct. 1925 on the top floor of a warehouse in Floral Street, Covent Garden, under the management of Peter Godfrey (q.v.), with Susan Glaspell's *Bernice*. It had its first success in 1926 with *From Morn to Midnight*, by Toller (q.v.), after a long and favourable review by James Agate (q.v.). In 1927 the theatre moved to a site behind the shops in Villiers Street, off the Strand, at right angles to the arches of Hungerford Bridge, where it occupied part of the premises of the old Hungerford Music-Hall—the rest later becoming part of the Players' Theatre (q.v.). The Hungerford was opened by the Gattis as a restaurant in 1867 and by 1875 had become one of the recognized halls of London. It flourished until 1903, and was usually known as Gatti's-under-the-Arches to distinguish it from Gatti's Music-Hall (q.v.) in the Westminster Bridge Road. The new Gate Theatre opened on 22 Nov. with Gantillon's *Maya*, and continued its former policy with outstanding success until 1932. Its fortunes then began to decline, until in 1934 Norman Marshall (q.v.) took over, reopening with Toller's *Miracle in America*. Among his successful productions, some of which were transferred to West End theatres after battles with the censorship, were Laurence Housman's *Victoria Regina* (1935), Elsie Schauffler's *Parnell*, Leslie and Sewell Stokes's *Oscar Wilde*, and Lillian Hellman's *The Children's Hour* (all 1936), Josset's *Elisabeth La Femme Sans Homme* (1938), Steinbeck's *Of Mice and Men* (1939), and the witty annual Gate revues. On 16 Apr. 1941 the theatre was badly damaged by bombing and was not reopened.

In 1944 Peter Godfrey opened a short-lived Gate Theatre in Hollywood with Gantillon's *Maya*.

Gateway Theatre, EDINBURGH, see EDINBURGH.

Gatti's Music-Hall, LONDON, in the Westminster Bridge Road. This opened as a restaurant in 1862 and became a music-hall in 1865, Harry Lauder making his first London appearance there in 1900. It was sometimes known as Gatti's-in-the-Road, or over-the-Water, to distinguish it from Gatti's-under-the-Arches (see GATE THEATRE and PLAYERS' THEATRE).

GAULTIER-GARGUILLE [really HUGUES GUÉRU] (*c.* 1573–1633), French actor, and chief farce-player, with Gros-Guillaume and Turlupin (qq.v.), of the company at the Hôtel de Bourgogne, to which he may have graduated from the Paris fairs. As Fleschelles he also played serious parts, but it is as a low comedian that he is best remembered. He figures as himself, with other members of the company, in Gougenot's *La Comédie des comédiens*, produced at the Hôtel de Bourgogne in the year of his death.

GAUSSIN [really GAUSSEM], JEANNE-CATHERINE (1711–67), French actress, who in 1730 made her first appearance at the Comédie-Française where she succeeded Mlle Duclos in tragedy. She was better in roles demanding tenderness and grief than in the sterner passions, and she never lost her youthful look, still playing young girls at the age of fifty-two. She appeared in several of Voltaire's plays, notably *Zaïre* (1732), and was considered outstanding in the sentimental comedies of La Chaussée.

Gauze-Cloth, see CLOTH.

GAY, JOHN (1685–1732), English poet and satirist, and author of the famous ballad opera, *The Beggar's Opera*, first given at Lincoln's Inn Fields in 1728 under John Rich, thus, as it was said, 'making Gay rich and Rich gay'. A light-hearted mixture of political satire and burlesque of Italian opera, then a fashionable craze, it had music selected by Pepusch from well-known airs, subsequently arranged by Linley. It was constantly revived and the music rearranged, notably by Frederic Austin for a production at the Lyric, Hammersmith, in 1920, and by Benjamin Britten for Sadler's Wells in 1948. In 1929 a German adaptation was made by Brecht (q.v.) as *Die Dreigroschenoper*, with music by Kurt Weill. *Polly*, a sequel to *The Beggar's*

Opera, was not produced for many years owing to political censorship, but was finally given at the Haymarket in 1777 with alterations by the elder George Colman (q.v.). Gay was also the author of several comedies and of the libretto of Handel's 'Acis and Galatea' (1731), but his fame rests almost entirely on *The Beggar's Opera*.

GEDDES, NORMAN BEL (1893–1958), American scenic designer and a pioneer of décor in the American theatre. As early as 1915 he had the idea of a theatre without a proscenium, and in 1923 he won instant recognition with his magnificent designs for Reinhardt's American production of *The Miracle*. In 1931 he designed a complex of steps and rostrums for a production of *Hamlet* far in advance of anything that had so far been seen. Another of his successful experiments was the multiple setting for Kingsley's *Dead End* (1935). His plan for a monumental production of Dante's *Divine Comedy* at Madison Square Garden, for which he designed an immense circular stage, was unfortunately never carried out, nor was his scheme for a 'theatre-in-the-round' in 1930. But these and other seminal ideas had a great influence on the development of modern American stage design. His period of activity in the theatre was at its height during the 1930s, after which he concentrated mainly upon industrial design. His daughter BARBARA (1922–) first appeared on the stage in New York in 1941, and in 1945 made a great success in Arnaud d'Usseau and James Gow's *Deep Are the Roots*. Among her later parts were Rose Pemberton in Graham Greene's *The Living Room* (1954) and Margaret in Tennessee Williams's *Cat on a Hot Tin Roof* (1955).

GELBER, JACK ALLEN (1932–), see LIVING THEATRE.

GÉLINAS, GRATIEN (1909–), known as Fridolin, the first outstanding actor of the French-Canadian theatre. He took his stage name from the leading character in the revues, the 'Fridolinons', which he wrote for production at the Monument National, Montreal, from 1938 to 1946. Two years later his play '*Tit-Coq* (*Lil' Rooster*) broke all Canadian records with a run of more than 450 performances In 1958 Gélinas founded the Théâtre de la Comédie Canadienne, housing it in a former burlesque theatre, bought and re-

decorated with a donation from a brewery. The opening production was Anouilh's *L'Alouette*, in both its French and English versions. Gélinas's own play, the immensely successful *Bousille et les justes* (1959), was also played in both languages in Montreal and on tour, as was *Hier, les enfants dansaient* (1966). The company has also staged plays by other Canadian authors, among them Marcel Dubé and Guy DuFresne, and a number imported from abroad, including Lawler's *The Summer of the Seventeenth Doll*, done by the Crest Theatre from Toronto. In 1956 Gélinas appeared with other French-Canadian actors at the Shakespeare Festival Theatre in Stratford, Ontario (q.v.), playing Charles VI in *Henry V* and Dr. Caius in *The Merry Wives of Windsor*. He has also appeared on radio and in a number of films.

Gelosi, one of the earliest and best-known of the *commedia dell'arte* (q.v.) companies, which after an initial visit to France in 1571 was summoned to play before the French king, Henri III, at Blois in 1577, and from there went to Paris, thus inaugurating the visits of the Italian players which later had such a marked influence on the French theatre (see COMÉDIE-ITALIENNE). In the company, which was attached to the household of the Duke of Mantua, were Francesco Andreini (q.v.) and his wife Isabella. After constant travelling, the Gelosi returned to Paris in 1602. On their way back to Italy in 1604 Isabella died at Lyons and her husband disbanded the troupe.

GÉMIER, FIRMIN (1869–1933), French actor and producer, pupil of Antoine (q.v.), whom he succeeded as director of the Odéon in 1906. He was an excellent actor and a good director but it was as a teacher that his influence made itself felt in the modern French theatre. He was the first to emphasize the importance of improvisation and systematic exercises in the training of young actors, in the style of Stanislavsky (q.v.), whose contemporary and disciple he was. One of his most famous pupils was Charles Dullin (q.v.), who, after developing his methods still further, passed them on to Barrault and Vilar (qq.v.). The idea of the present Centres Dramatiques (q.v.), and of the Théâtre National Populaire (q.v.), was implicit in Gémier's early efforts, both before and after the First World War, to found such a theatre with his Théâtre National Ambulant (1911–12) and Théâtre National Populaire (1920). An excellent life of Gémier, by Paul Blanchart, was published in 1954.

Genée Theatre, a small intimate playhouse at East Grinstead in Surrey. Named after the ballerina ADELINE GENÉE (1878–1970), it opened on 29 Jan. 1967 with a gala performance of ballet. The first play to be performed there, on 1 Feb., was *Just Good Friends*, a translation of the farce *Le Plus Heureux de Trois*, by Labiche and Goudinet. A varied programme of plays followed, but by the end of the year the theatre, which cost £100,000, given by private donors, was in financial difficulties and was forced to close for six months. It reopened on 10 June 1968 with a revival of Coward's *Private Lives*, under the directorship of Allan Campbell (replacing the former director Peter Potter), and has since continued to present a varied programme of plays.

General Utility, see STOCK COMPANY.

Género Chico, or *teatro por horas*, a generic term applied in Spain to a form of light dramatic entertainment, dating from about 1868 and at the height of its popularity towards the end of the nineteenth century. It had a distinguished ancestry, since it was derived from the earlier *sainete* (q.v.), and consisted at first of one-act scenes of everyday life, usually set in Madrid and heightened to the point of caricature. As the fashion for musical accompaniment became more widespread, *género chico* became synonymous with the one-act *zarzuela* (q.v.). It has been superseded by the *astracanadas*, sketches with wildly improbable plots and a dialogue thick with untranslatable puns and plays on words.

GENET, JEAN (1909–86), French poet, novelist, and dramatist, who spent much of his early life in prison. Perhaps because of this, his plays are characterized by the frenzied rebellion of the characters against conventional morality. At first attacked as scandalous and obscene, his work is now recognized as having created in fact the 'Theatre of Cruelty' dreamed of by Artaud (q.v.). His first play, *Les Bonnes* (1947), produced by Jouvet (q.v.), was seen in London, in French, in 1952. In English, as *The Maids*, it was produced in

New York in 1955 and in London in 1956. It served to introduce Genet's basic conception of a play both as a masquerade in which the characters act out their secret desires and as a ceremony which, like the Catholic mass, unites spectators and actors in a metaphysical experience beyond the normal conceptions of good and evil. This conception was developed, strengthened by the use of brilliant language, in *Haute Surveillance* (1949) (produced in New York in 1958 and in London in 1961 as *Deathwatch*), *Le Balcon* (first produced as *The Balcony* in London in 1957 and in New York in 1960, in which year it was first seen in Paris), and *Les Nègres* (1959), which as *The Blacks* had a long run in New York in 1961 and was seen in London the same year. Genet's last play, *Les Paravents* (*The Screens*), dealing with the Algerian situation, had a stormy reception at the Odéon in 1966.

GENTLEMAN, FRANCIS (1728–84), actor, and author of *The Dramatic Censor* (2 vols., 1770), which deals judiciously though verbosely with a number of plays but is mainly valuable for its remarks on actors at the end of each article. On his way to London from Dublin, his native city, Gentleman acted with Macklin at Chester and had two tragedies presented at Bath, where from 1752 to 1755 he acted as 'Mr. Cooke'. The best of his own plays was *The Modish Wife* (1761), and he also made an adaptation of Ben Jonson's *The Alchemist* which as *The Tobacconist* (c. 1760) was successful enough to be included in the play collections of Dibdin and Oxberry.

GEORGE, GRACE (1879–1961), American actress, wife of the manager William A. Brady (q.v.). She played the lead in many of her husband's productions, and was particularly admired in such parts as Lady Teazle in Sheridan's *The School for Scandal*, Barbara Undershaft in the first American production of Shaw's *Major Barbara* (1915), and the title-role in St. John Ervine's *The First Mrs. Fraser* (1929). Her only appearance in London was at the Duke of York's in 1907 as Cyprienne in Sardou's *Divorçons*, which many considered her finest part.

GEORGE, MLLE [really MARGUERITE-JOSÉPHINE WEYMER] (1787–1867), French tragic actress, who made her début at the

Comédie-Française in 1802 as Racine's Iphigénie. Her majestic bearing and fine voice assured her instant success in tragic parts, but in 1808 she eloped with a dancer named Louis Laporte and went to Russia, where she acted with a French company for five years. Back at the Comédie-Française, she was again successful until in 1817 her fellow actors, tiring of her ungovernable temper, which made her many enemies, asked her to resign. She then went to London and on tour, and in 1822 returned to Paris to star at the Odéon. She was reputed to have been successively the mistress of Napoleon, Talleyrand, Metternich, and Ouvrard, and for many years lived with the manager Harel, following him into the provinces and to the Porte-Saint-Martin (q.v.) in Paris, where she appeared with great success in romantic drama. Increasing stoutness led her to retire and she became a teacher of elocution, but her extravagance forced her back to the stage, where she found herself outmoded and forgotten. She struggled on for some time, but finally retired to die in obscurity.

George M. Cohan Theatre, NEW YORK, on Broadway at 43rd Street. This was opened on 13 Feb. 1911 by Cohan (q.v.) who on 25 Sept. appeared there with his parents in his own play, *The Little Millionaire*, as he did again in *Broadway Jones* (1912). Among later successes at this theatre were the Jewish comedy *Potash and Perlmutter* (1913), by Charles Klein and Montague Glass, the farces *It Pays to Advertise* (1914), by Walter Hackett, *Come Out of the Kitchen* (1916), by A. E. Thomas, and several musical comedies, including *Two Little Girls in Blue* (1921). Clemence Dane's *A Bill of Divorcement* (also 1921) established Katharine Cornell (q.v.) as a star and was followed in the same year by Ed Wynn in his own musical comedy, *The Perfect Fool*, from which he took his nickname. The last years of the theatre were uneventful, the final production being a musical, *The Dubarry* (1932), with Grace Moore. A year later it became a cinema, and in 1938 it was demolished.

GEORGE II OF SAXE-MEININGEN (1823–1914), see MEININGER COMPANY.

GERMANOVA, MARIA NIKOLAEVNA (1884–1940), Russian actress, who in 1904 joined the company of the Moscow

Art Theatre (q.v.), remaining there until 1920. Her intensity and delicate appearance were eminently suited to the expressionist dramas with which Nemirovich-Danchenko endeavoured to counterbalance Stanislavsky's naturalism, and among her best roles were Agnes in Ibsen's poetic play, *Brand*, the Fairy in Maeterlinck's *The Blue Bird*, Grushenka in Dostoievsky's *The Brothers Karamazov*, and the title-role in Andreyev's *Katerina Ivanovna* (1912), which was written for her. From 1922 to 1929 she toured with the Prague Group of the Moscow Art Theatre, visiting Paris in 1926 and London in 1928, and retiring in 1930.

GHELDERODE, MICHEL DE (1898–1962), Belgian dramatist, who created in his plays a world which recalls the Flemish fairgrounds painted by Breughel and Bosch, peopled by crippled beggars, dwarfs and jesters, flagellating monks, sadistic kings, and lecherous and drunken men and women. In grotesque decaying settings they act out a burlesque of the human condition, engulfed by the obscene deformities of the flesh which end in death. Although Ghelderode's early plays, *La Mort regarde à la fenêtre* (1918) and *Le Repas des fauves* (1919), were first acted in French, as were the later *Christophe Colomb* (1927) and *Les Femmes au tombeau* (1928), several of his most important works, beginning with *Barabbas* (also 1928), were originally produced in Flemish by the Théâtre Populaire Flamand. Though highly regarded in Belgium, Ghelderode was little known outside his own country until the production of *Hop! Signor* (1935) in Paris in 1947, followed by *Escurial* (1927) in 1948 and *Mademoiselle Jaïre* (1934) and *Fastes d'enfer* (1929) in 1949. This last caused such a scandal that it was withdrawn and later productions of Ghelderode were seen only in small Left Bank theatres in Paris. His work is almost unknown in England and the United States. In addition to the plays mentioned above he wrote *La Mort du Docteur Faust* (1928), *Pantagleize* (1929), *Magie rouge* (1931), *Sir Halewyn* and *La Ballade du grande macabre* (both 1934), *La Pie sur le gibet* (1935), and *L'École des buffons* (1937).

GHÉON, HENRI (1875–1943), French dramatist, and an important figure in the modern revival of religious drama. His early plays, among them *Le Pauvre*

sous l'escalier (1913), were produced by Copeau (q.v.) at the Vieux-Colombier, but from 1920 onwards he was engaged in the writing and directing of almost a hundred plays on religious and biblical themes for colleges, schools, and parish churches. The best-known of these, combining poetry and theatricality with great simplicity and religious feeling, is *Le Noël sur la place* (1935). As *Christmas in the Market Place*, in a translation by Eric Crozier, it has had many professional and amateur productions in England. It was originally acted by the Compagnons de Jeux, a semi-amateur company organized in 1932 by HENRI BROCHET (1898–1952), himself an excellent actor and religious dramatist, to take the place of Ghéon's earlier troupe, the Compagnons de Notre-Dame.

GHERARDI, EVARISTO (1663–1700), an actor of the *commedia dell'arte* (q.v.) and a famous Harlequin, whose professional career was spent entirely in Paris, where he made his début in 1689 in a revival of Regnard's *Le Divorce*. He is chiefly remembered now for his publication of the repertory of scenarii used by the Italians in Paris.

Ghost Glide, see TRAP.

GIACOMETTI, PAOLO (1816–82), Italian dramatist, whose plays are of a homely popular type known as *teatro da arena*—a phrase which may be said to cover drama appealing to 'simple minds and honest hearts'. His reputation is widespread in his own country. His best play is probably *La morte civile* (1861), a dramatization of a social theme which has as its hero an escaped convict who, unable to return to his wife and daughter, commits suicide.

GIACOSA, GIUSEPPE (1847–1906), the librettist, with Luigi Illica, of Puccini's 'La Boheme' (1896), 'Tosca' (1900), and 'Madame Butterfly' (1904), and after Verga (q.v.) the best of Italy's realistic dramatists. Among his plays of social comment the most important are *Tristi amori* (1887), *I Diritti dell'anima* (1894), obviously influenced by Ibsen's *A Doll's House, Come le foglie* (1900), and *Il più forte* (1904), the last being somewhat akin to Shaw's *Mrs. Warren's Profession*. Giacosa also wrote some charming comedies, of which the most popular was *La zampa del gatto* (1883), and two historical plays, *Una partita a scacchi*

(1871) and *Signora di Challant* (1891), the latter providing a popular part for both Duse and Bernhardt. At his death he left four unpublished comedies which have now been added to his complete works. One of them, *L'onorevole Ercole Malladri*, first seen at the Carignano Theatre on 20 Oct. 1884, was revived by the Piccolo Teatro della Città di Torino in 1956 to mark the fiftieth anniversary of his death.

Gibbon's Tennis-Court, LONDON, see VERE STREET THEATRE.

GIBBS, WOLCOTT (1902–58), American author, who in 1939 replaced Robert Benchley (q.v.) on *The New Yorker* and soon became recognized as a valuable addition to the ranks of American dramatic critics. A shrewd and alert playgoer, he often wrote more brilliantly of bad plays than of good ones; but his irony was a tonic which Broadway badly needed, and though he wrote with humorous and sardonic detachment he never descended to 'wise-crack' reviewing. He was an excellent writer of parodies, and his book *A Season in the Sun* (1952) contains a dozen biting burlesques of contemporary novelists and playwrights.

GIDE, ANDRÉ (1869–1951), French novelist and dramatist, whose early plays, *Le Roi Candaule* and *Saül*, made little stir, but whose *Œdipe* (1932), which dramatized a situation often found in Gide's writing—the conflict between individualism and religious submission—was favourably received. It was, however, with his translations of Shakespeare that he did his best work for the theatre—*Antony and Cleopatra* and *Hamlet* in particular. The latter was in his mind for many years. He published a brilliant first act in 1928, but it was a chance meeting with Jean-Louis Barrault (q.v.) in 1942 that led him to finish the play, with which the Renaud–Barrault company opened their first season at the Théâtre Marigny on 17 Oct. 1946. Two years later Barrault was seen in this translation at the Edinburgh Festival. It was also for Barrault's company that Gide dramatized Kafka's *The Trial*, which opened on 10 Oct. 1947 and was revived by Barrault at the Odéon in 1962.

GIELGUD, SIR (ARTHUR) JOHN (1904–), English actor and director, grand-nephew of Ellen Terry (q.v.) and great-grandson of the Polish actress Madame Aszperger. He made his first appearance on the stage at the Old Vic in 1921 as the Herald in *Henry V*, returning there in 1929 and 1930 to appear in a series of leading parts, including Romeo, Richard II, Macbeth, and Hamlet, his finest part, which he played again at the Lyceum (q.v.) in 1939 before it finally closed and then at Elsinore in Denmark. On the reopening of Sadler's Wells (q.v.) in 1931 he appeared as Malvolio in *Twelfth Night*, and subsequently took Shakespeare back into the West End with revivals of *Hamlet* (1934) and *Romeo and Juliet* (1935) at the New Theatre (q.v.). From 1937 to 1938 he directed and played with his own company (see QUEEN'S THEATRE (2)) in a distinguished repertory, and from 1944 to 1945 was at the Haymarket (q.v.) in another series of fine plays. At Stratford-upon-Avon in 1950–1 he was seen as Angelo in *Measure for Measure*, Benedick in *Much Ado About Nothing*, Cassius in *Julius Caesar*, and Lear, a part in which he was also seen in London in 1955 in a Japanese setting by Isamu Noguchi. Also in 1951 he gave a very fine performance as Leontes in *The Winter's Tale*. Although he is at his best in Shakespeare, he has also appeared with success in such classic parts as Valentine and Mirabell in Congreve's *Love for Love* and *The Way of the World*, Jaffier in Otway's *Venice Preserv'd*, Joseph Surface in Sheridan's *The School for Scandal*, Vershinin, Trigorin, and Gaev in Chekhov's *Three Sisters*, *The Seagull*, and *The Cherry Orchard*, and John Worthing in Wilde's *The Importance of Being Earnest*. Among the modern plays in which he has appeared are Fry's *The Lady's Not for Burning* (1949), Coward's *Nude With Violin* (1956), Graham Greene's *The Potting Shed* (1958), Edward Albee's *Tiny Alice* (1964) in New York (where he has appeared many times since his Hamlet at the Empire in 1936), Alan Bennett's *Forty Years On* (1968), Peter Shaffer's *The Battle of Shrivings* and David Storey's *Home* (both 1970). It was in 1958 that he first appeared in *Ages of Man*, a solo recital of passages from Shakespeare arranged by George Rylands, which was an immediate success. He reopened the Queen's Theatre, London, with it in 1959 and has since toured in it all over the world. He is the author of an autobiography, *Early Stages* (1938), and of a collection of essays and speeches, *Stage Directions* (1963), and was knighted in 1953 for services to the stage.

GIFFARD, HENRY (1694/5–1772), English actor and manager, in whose company Garrick (q.v.) made his first appearances on the stage in 1741 at Goodman's Fields Theatre, which Giffard had opened in 1733 with a revival of Lillo's *George Barnwell*. He remained there with a good company, headed by Yates, until 1737, in which year he took to Walpole, who rewarded him with £1,000, the script of a scurrilous play entitled *The Golden Rump*, which was used by the Government as an excuse for passing the Licensing Bill of 1737. Since this led to the closing of all unlicensed playhouses, Giffard found himself without a theatre, but subsequently managed to reopen Goodman's Fields. When Fleetwood (q.v.) engaged Garrick for Drury Lane, he took on also Giffard and his wife, a fine actress who played Lady Macbeth and other leading parts opposite Garrick. Little more was heard of Giffard, who for a short time held part of the Patent of Drury Lane, relinquishing it because he could not stomach Fleetwood's extravagances.

GILBERT, MRS. GEORGE H. (*née* ANN HARTLEY) (1821–1904), a much-loved American actress, who in her later years was extremely popular as a player of eccentric spinsters and aristocratic dowagers. In London in 1846 she married an actor, GEORGE GILBERT (?–1866), with whom she emigrated to the United States, continuing to act after his death with Mrs. John Wood's company at the Olympic, New York. Her first important part was the Marquise de St. Maur in the pirated production of Robertson's *Caste* in 1867 (see FLORENCE). The period of her greatest fame, however, was from 1869 to 1899, when she was in Daly's company, and with Ada Rehan and John Drew (qq.v.) formed a unique combination of artistic and technical skill. When Daly died she was engaged by the Frohmans, with whom she remained until her death. During her long career she played with most of the famous actors and managements of her time.

GILBERT [really GIBBS], JOHN (1810–89), American actor, who made his début in Boston in 1828. He then toured the Mississippi river towns until 1834 and returned to the Tremont Theatre, Boston, until it closed, playing the parts of elderly men. He was particularly good as Sir Anthony Absolute and Sir Peter Teazle in

Sheridan's *The Rivals* and *The School for Scandal* respectively. In 1847 he had a successful season in London and then returned to play at the Park Theatre, New York, until it was destroyed by fire. He was with Lester Wallack's company from 1861 until it was disbanded in 1888, dying the following year while touring with Jefferson (q.v.) in *The Rivals*. He was a man of some erudition, and after his death his widow presented his fine collection of books to the Boston Public Library.

GILBERT, SIR WILLIAM SCHWENCK (1836–1911), English dramatist, whose name is always associated in the public mind with that of Sir Arthur Sullivan, who wrote the music to his libretti for the famous Savoy operas—so called because they were mainly produced at the Savoy Theatre (q.v.). Gilbert was encouraged to write for the stage by T. W. Robertson (q.v.), and his first play was a burlesque commissioned for a Christmas entertainment. He also wrote dramatic sketches for the entertainers Mr. and Mrs. German Reed. Among his early plays were *The Palace of Truth* (1870), *Pygmalion and Galatea* (1871), *Sweethearts* (1874), *Broken Hearts* (1875), *Dan'l Druce, Blacksmith* (1876), long a favourite part with character actors, and *Engaged* (1877). His collaboration with Sullivan began with *Thespis; or, the Gods Grown Old*, an operatic extravaganza produced at the Gaiety on 26 Dec. 1871. The first of the well-known light operas, however, was *Trial by Jury* (1875). The partnership continued for over twenty years and ended with *The Grand Duke* (1896), though *The Gondoliers* (1889) was the last of those which still hold the stage. The others are: *The Sorcerer* (1877), *H.M.S. Pinafore* (1878), *The Pirates of Penzance* (1880), *Patience* (1881), *Iolanthe* (1882), *Princess Ida* (1884), *The Mikado* (1885), *Ruddigore* (1887), and *The Yeoman of the Guard* (1888). *Utopia Limited* (1893) has not been revived.

Gilbert wrote libretti for other composers, but with little success, just as Sullivan wrote music for other dramatists but failed to recapture the brilliance of the Savoy operas. Their partnership was not happy, Gilbert being a man of irascible temperament and a martinet in the theatre. He used the profits from his plays to build the Garrick Theatre (q.v.), and he was knighted for services to the stage in 1907. Of all his theatrical work

only the libretti for Sullivan have survived (but see PLANCHÉ).

GILCHRIST, CONNIE (1865–1946), English actress, who made her first appearance on the stage as a child in pantomime, and in later years was at the Gaiety (q.v.) as a skipping-rope dancer. In 1880 she made a hit as Libby Ray in Woolf's *The Mighty Dollar*, but she preferred burlesque to straight comedy, and returned to it to have a brief but glorious career before she left the stage in the late 1880s to become the Countess of Orkney. Her name is best remembered in connection with the supreme example of 'judicial ignorance', when Mr. Justice Coleridge in *Scott v. Sampson* asked: 'Who is Miss Connie Gilchrist?'.

GILDER, (JANET) ROSAMOND DE KAY (1891–), American drama critic, who from 1924 to 1948 was on the staff of *Theatre Arts Monthly* (q.v.). She has been actively concerned with the foundation and work of the Federal Theatre Project, the American National Theatre and Academy, and the Institute for Advanced Studies in the Theatre Arts (qq.v.). For many years she headed the U.S. delegations to the Congresses of the International Theatre Institute (q.v), of which she was one of the founders. She was its President from 1963 to 1967, and in 1969 was nominated first President of the independent International Theatre Institute of the United States, Inc., housed in the Anta Theatre (q.v.). She is the author of *A Theatre Library* (1932), *Theatre Collections in Libraries and Museums* (with George Freedley, 1936), *John Gielgud's Hamlet* (1937), and *Enter the Actress* (1961). In 1950 she edited a *Theatre Arts Anthology* and in 1969 *Theatre I*.

GILLETTE, WILLIAM (1855–1937), American actor and dramatist, author of a number of adaptations and dramatizations of novels in most of which he appeared himself, among them Conan Doyle's *Sherlock Holmes* (1899), with which his name is always associated. He played Holmes with outstanding success both in England and America, and frequently revived it up to his retirement in 1932. Of his original plays the best were the spy stories of the Civil War, *Held by the Enemy* (1886) and *Secret Service* (1895). He also wrote a comedy,

Too Much Jonson (1894). He appeared in Barrie's *The Admirable Crichton* and *Dear Brutus*; but his best work was done in his own plays, which without him would probably not bear revival.

Gilmore's Theatre, NEW YORK, see DALY'S THEATRE (3).

GILPIN, CHARLES SIDNEY (1878–1930), American Negro actor, who spent many years as a minstrel in vaudeville. In 1916 he became manager of the first all-Negro stock company in New York, at the Lafayette Theatre, Harlem. Among his later Broadway parts were the Negro clergyman in Drinkwater's *Abraham Lincoln* (1919) and Brutus Jones in O'Neill's *The Emperor Jones* (1921). The latter provided him with a great emotional part in which he was at once powerful, terrifying, and extremely moving. He retired in 1926, but occasionally reappeared in revivals of *The Emperor Jones* until his death.

GINGOLD, HERMIONE FERDINANDA (1897–1987), English actress, who made her first appearance on the stage at the age of eleven. At seventeen she played Jessica in *The Merchant of Venice* at the Old Vic, and then appeared in a number of plays until in 1936 she was seen at the Saville in the revue *Spread It Abroad*, by Herbert Farjeon, and revealed herself as a comedienne of the first rank. Her reputation was further enhanced by her appearance in the *Gate Revue* in 1938 and *Swinging the Gate* in 1940, and in the long-running *Sweet and Low* series of revues at the Ambassadors from 1943 to 1947. She made her first appearance in the United States in revue in 1951 and remained there, touring in revue and in such plays as Noël Coward's *Fallen Angels* and Rattigan's *The Sleeping Prince*, until 1969, when she returned to London to star in *Highly Confidential*, by Robert Tanitch. Although her performance as a 1920s James Bond crossed with Mata Hari aroused enthusiasm among her faithful public, the play was not a success and she returned to New York, where she had a successful career in films and television. In 1945 she published an autobiography, *The World Is Square*, and in 1962 *Sirens Should be Seen and Not Heard*. By her first husband, the publisher Michael Joseph (her second was Eric Maschwitz),

she was the mother of the late Stephen Joseph (q.v.).

GIRALDI, GIOVANNI BATTISTA (1504–73), Italian humanist, known as 'il Cinthio'. He was the author of a number of 'horror' tragedies written under the influence of Seneca (q.v.), of which the first, *Orbecche* (1543), was performed before the Duke of Ferrara and his Court at the house of the author, with scenery and music specially commissioned for the occasion. Two of Giraldi's later plays, *L'Altile* (1543) and *Epizia* (1547), were based on stories which he later included in his *Hecatommithi* (1565), a collection of *novelle* in the style of Boccaccio's *Decameron*. *Epizia*, translated into English by George Whetstone as *Promos and Cassandra* (1578), provided Shakespeare with the plot of *Measure for Measure*, and from another play, *Disdemona and the Moor*, he took the subject of *Othello*. Greene, Shirley, and Beaumont and Fletcher (qq.v.) also used material from the *Hecatommithi*, which was one of the sources of *The Palace of Pleasure* (1566), a collection of stories translated into English by William Painter.

GIRAUDOUX, (HIPPOLYTE) JEAN (1882–1944), French novelist and dramatist, whose fruitful collaboration with the actor Louis Jouvet (q.v.) produced some of the finest plays of the period. He was forty-five and a well-known novelist before his first play, *Siegfried* (1928), was produced at the Champs-Élysées, and as a dramatist his reputation grew with each succeeding play. The best-known is probably *Amphitryon 38* (1929), which, in an English adaptation by S. N. Behrman, had a great success in England and America with the Lunts (q.v.) as Jupiter and Alcmena. After *Judith* (1931), a biblical tragedy, came the enchanting *Intermezzo* (1933), a mixture of fantasy and realism seen in London in 1956 in a production by the Renaud–Barrault company. In *La Guerre de Troie n'aura pas lieu* (1935), Giraudoux examines the causes of the Trojan War, which could, he says, have been averted but for a lie and a misunderstanding. As *Tiger at the Gates* (with Michael Redgrave (q.v.) as Hector) this play made a belated but successful appearance in London in 1955 in a translation by Christopher Fry, going on to achieve an equal success in New York.

Its poignancy was perhaps reinforced for English-speaking audiences by the intervention of the Second World War between the French- and English-language productions.

After *Supplément au Voyage de Cook* (1935), *Électre* (1937), *L'Impromptu de Paris* (1937), an attack on contemporary French dramatic critics in the style of Molière, and the one-act *Cantique des Cantiques* (1938), Giraudoux produced what many believe to be his finest work, *Ondine* (also 1938), a retelling of the legend of the water-nymph on which he brought to bear all the poetry and imagination of which he was capable and (in the second act) all the theatrical tricks which he knew Jouvet could stage for him. Produced on 3 May 1939, its run was cut short in 1940 and it was not revived until 1949. It was seen in London in 1953 (at the Lyric, Hammersmith) in a production by the Théâtre National de Belgique, and in an English translation was one of the successes of the Royal Shakespeare's London season at the Aldwych in 1961, Leslie Caron playing Ondine.

In 1942 *L'Apollon de Bellac* was produced in Rio de Janeiro by Jouvet, who directed its first production in France in 1947. In 1943 came the première in Paris of *Sodome et Gomorrhe*, in which Lia, the leading role, was played by Edwige Feuillère (q.v.). But it was with *La Folle de Chaillot*, produced posthumously on 19 Dec. 1945, that Giraudoux's magic re-established itself. The play was an instant success in Paris and, as *The Madwoman of Chaillot*, in New York in 1948 with Martita Hunt, whose performance was much admired in London also (in 1951), though the play had only a short run there. It was revived briefly in Oxford in 1967 with Elisabeth Bergner in the title-role. In 1969 an American musical version, *Dear World*, was produced in New York but was not a success. Giraudoux's last play, *Pour Lucrèce* (1953), directed by Barrault at the Marigny with Edwige Feuillère as Paola, was not as successful as had been hoped, in spite of moments of great beauty. But revivals of some of his earlier plays have shown that they have qualities which will endure in the theatre.

GITANA, GERTIE [really GERTRUDE MARY ASTBURY] (1887–1957), one of the best-loved stars of the old English music-hall. She joined a children's troupe at the age of four and was eight when she first appeared as a single turn at the Tivoli, Barrow-in-Furness. In 1904 she made her first appearance in London, at the Lyceum, which had been rebuilt as a music-hall, but it was at the Holborn Empire shortly after that she scored her first outstanding success. By the time she was sixteen she was topping the bill all over the country, and her success was enhanced when she first sang the song always connected with her name, 'Nellie Dean'. In 1928 she married DON ROSS, who in 1947 was responsible for the production of an 'old-time' music-hall bill, 'Thanks for the Memory', in which Gertie Gitana herself appeared with her close friends Nellie Wallace and Ella Shields and many other stars. A year later she was seen at a Royal Variety Performance. She took her name Gitana from the fact that the first troupe she played with wore conventional gipsy costumes.

Glasgow. Like Edinburgh (q.v.), with whom it shared theatrical managements until the early years of the nineteenth century, Glasgow had a long struggle before it achieved a permanent playhouse. The first, erected in 1753, was dismantled by the owner after Whitefield had preached against it. A fire was started in the second on the eve of the opening performance in 1764. Damage was slight, and the theatre survived until burnt down in 1780. The famous Dunlop Street Theatre was built by John Jackson and opened in 1782. It underwent an eclipse when the Queen Street Theatre Royal was built in 1805, and was sold, to become a warehouse. Part of the building was, however, used for miscellaneous entertainments and in 1824 it was all brought into use again, as the Caledonian Theatre, by John Henry Alexander, who rebuilt it twice during his long management. It became the Theatre Royal in 1829, when he acquired the Queen Street patent. In 1849 a false alarm of fire caused a disastrous panic in which at least sixty-five persons lost their lives. Burnt down in 1863, the theatre was rebuilt, but demolished in 1869. The Queen Street Theatre, which was designed by David Hamilton, with stock scenery by Alexander Nasmyth and advanced machinery, was burnt down in 1829. Here Edmund Kean and his son Charles (qq.v.) first played together to a packed house with over two hundred people on the stage. Other theatres in Glasgow were the Adelphi, which opened in 1842 and was destroyed by fire in 1848, the City, which opened and was burnt down in 1845, the Prince's, opened in 1849, and the Royalty, opened in 1879. In 1867 a music-hall was built which in 1869 became the Theatre Royal, Glasgow, and was rebuilt on the same site after its destruction by fire in 1879 and again in 1895. It is now the headquarters of Scottish Television. Surviving Glasgow theatres include the Princess's, opened as Her Majesty's in 1877, the King's (1902), and the Alhambra (1912). In 1909 the Glasgow Repertory Theatre, under the direction of Alfred Wareing, started its career with a production of Shaw's *You Never Can Tell* in the Royalty Theatre, where from 1909 to 1914 it produced plays by many English and Continental dramatists, including *The Seagull* (1909), claimed as the first British performance of a play by Chekhov. It also produced a few Scottish plays, among them John Ferguson's *Campbell of Kilmohr*. The venture closed down on the outbreak of the First World War and the remaining funds were transferred to the St. Andrew Society, which later launched the movement that produced the Scottish National Players (q.v.).

In 1943 the Glasgow Citizens' Theatre was founded by a group which included James Bridie and Paul Vincent Carroll (qq.v.). It produced, among other plays, Bridie's *Forrigan Reel* (1946) and *The Tintock Cup* (1949). Under the direction of Tyrone Guthrie (q.v.) the company also appeared at the Edinburgh Festival in 1948 in Lyndsay's *Ane Pleasant Satyre of the Thrie Estaitis*. With the establishment in 1950 of a College of Dramatic Art, the Citizens' Theatre has found it easier to form a company able to present both English and Scottish plays. Notable first productions have been of Bridie's last play, *The Baikie Charivari* (1952), and of John Arden's *Armstrong's Last Goodnight* (1964). The company celebrated its twenty-first birthday with a revival of Bridie's *A Sleeping Clergyman*. In 1965 the establishment of the Close Theatre Club, under the same roof as the Citizens' and run in association with it, provided a second theatre designed for experimental work.

GLASPELL, SUSAN (1882–1948), American novelist and dramatist, active in the formation of the Provincetown Players (q.v.), who produced several of her one-act plays and, in 1915, her first three-act

play, *Bernice*, in which she herself played the devoted servant, Abbie. Her finest work for the theatre was *Alison's House* (1930), based partly on the life of the American poet Emily Dickinson. Produced by Eva Le Gallienne at the Civic Repertory Theatre in New York, this was awarded the Pulitzer Prize for drama. It was seen in London in 1932.

GLEICH, JOSEPH ALOIS (1772–1841), a prolific Austrian playwright, author of some 220 plays and one of the founders of the Viennese popular theatre which succeeded the old improvised burlesque, a theatre compounded of magic, farce, and parody. Gleich, who was at one time official playwright to both the Leopoldstädter and the Josefstädter theatres, did his best work in the so-called '*Besserungsstück*', the moral tale which forces the sinner to recognize the error of his ways but always by way of slapstick comedy. The best example of this is *Der Eheteufel auf Reisen* (1822), in which the chief character, who blames his wife for their matrimonial difficulties, is 'magicked' into becoming a partner in five different marriages and ends by confessing that man is usually the guilty party.

GLENVILLE, PETER (1913–) and SHAUN (1884–1968), see WARD, DOROTHY.

Globe Theatre, LONDON. (1) This theatre, which is always associated with Shakespeare (q.v.), was built in 1599 on Bankside, Southwark, by Cuthbert Burbage (q v.) with timber from London's first playhouse, the Theatre (q.v.), built by his father. It was round, with a large platform-stage with a 'tiring-house' behind and a thatched roof over the stage and the three galleries. Above the stage rose a tower or penthouse from which a flag was flown when the theatre was open. A trumpet was blown from there to give warning of the play's opening. A spectator entering by the one main door who paid a penny and stood in the pit was known as a groundling; a further penny would admit him to a gallery; and for a third penny he could have a seat. Stools on the stage were for privileged people, usually young noblemen who entered through the stage door at the back. In this theatre a strong company led by Richard Burbage (q.v.) presented most of the plays of Shakespeare for the first time, as well as those of other contemporary dramatists, their only rivals being Henslowe's company at the Fortune under Alleyn (qq.v.). In 1613 the Globe was burnt down after a performance of Shakespeare's *Henry VIII*. It was rebuilt with a tiled roof in place of the thatch which had caused the fire, and reopened in 1614. It remained in use until the closing of the theatres in 1642, and in 1644 was pulled down. The site is now occupied by a brewery. A replica of the Globe, designed by the Shakespearian scholar, Dr. John Cranford Adams, was erected in 1950 at Hofstra College, Long Island.

(2) Sefton Parry, a speculator who had a hand in several London theatres, built a Globe Theatre in Newcastle Street, Strand, which opened on 28 Nov. 1868. It was not a success, and constantly changed hands until in 1884 Charles Hawtrey (q.v.) transferred his play, *The Private Secretary*, to the Globe from the Prince of Wales', where it had not done well in spite of the presence of Tree (q.v.) in the lead. With Penley (q.v.) in his place it was a success, and became one of the classic stage farces, as did Brandon Thomas's *Charley's Aunt* (1892), transferred from the Royalty (q.v.). In March 1902 the theatre closed after a revival of *Sweet Nell of Old Drury* with Fred Terry and Julia Neilson (qq.v.). It was a jerry-built place and it and the Opera Comique (q.v.), which backed on to it, were known as the Rickety Twins. Had a fire broken out it would have been a death-trap.

(3) The present Globe, in Shaftesbury Avenue, opened on 27 Dec. 1906 as the Hicks, with Seymour Hicks and his wife Ellaline Terriss (qq.v.) in *The Beauty of Bath*, transferred from the Aldwych. It was under the management of Charles Frohman (q.v.), who in 1909 renamed it the Globe and made it his London headquarters. After his death in 1915 it was acquired by Alfred Butt, who transferred there the successful comedy, *Peg o' My Heart*, by J. Hartley Manners. In the following year Gaby Deslys made her last London appearance in the musical *Suzette*, and from 1918 to 1927 the theatre was under the joint management of Marie Löhr and her husband Anthony Prinsep. Among their successful productions, in most of which Marie Löhr appeared, were Somerset Maugham's *Our Betters* (1923) and Noël Coward's *Fallen Angels* (1925). In 1930 Maurice Browne presented the German actor Moissi (q.v.) in *Hamlet* and the Pitoëffs (q.v.) in Shaw's *Saint Joan*. A year later came Fagan's *The Improper Duchess*, with Yvonne Arnaud

(q.v.), and in 1935 Dodie Smith's *Call It a Day*. In Feb. 1937 H. M. Tennent took over, opening with a revival of Shaw's *Candida*. Among the successful productions of this management were St. John Ervine's *Robert's Wife* (1937), with Owen Nares and Edith Evans, Emlyn Williams's *Morning Star* (1942), Terence Rattigan's *While the Sun Shines* (1943), Christopher Fry's *The Lady's Not for Burning* (1949), and Anouilh's *Ring Round the Moon* (1950), with Paul Scofield (q.v.). Gielgud was seen in 1956 in Noël Coward's *Nude With Violin* and in 1958 in Graham Greene's *The Potting Shed*, and Scofield again in 1960 in Robert Bolt's play about Sir Thomas More, *A Man for All Seasons*. In 1965 Flanders and Swann appeared in *At the Drop of Another Hat*, and on 15 June 1966 Terence Frisby's *There's a Girl in My Soup* began a long run.

(See also ROTUNDA; for the Globe Theatre, New York, see LUNT-FONTANNE THEATRE.)

Glove-Puppet, see PUNCH AND JUDY and PUPPET.

GODFREY, PETER (1899–1970), English actor and theatre director, who went on the stage at the age of sixteen and for ten years worked mainly in repertory theatres. In order to stage contemporary foreign plays which interested him but were not at that time commercially acceptable, he founded in 1925, with his first wife Molly Veness, the Gate Theatre (q.v.), where he directed over 350 plays by such dramatists as Toller, Gantillon, Lenormand, and O'Neill, with a number of young players who later became famous, among them Flora Robson, Beatrix Lehmann, and Eric Portman. After 1932 membership of the club declined and in spite of an experimental amalgamation with Terence Gray's Festival Theatre at Cambridge (q.v.), Godfrey was forced to close in 1934. His last productions were Pirandello's *As You Desire Me* and the younger Dumas's *The Lady of the Camellias* with Jean Forbes-Robertson (q.v.) in the leading roles. He was succeeded by Norman Marshall (q.v.). He then went to America, and in 1942 became a film director in Hollywood, where he also for a short time ran a Gate Theatre on the lines of his London venture.

GODFREY, THOMAS (1736–63), the first playwright of the United States, who in

1759 wrote a tragedy entitled *The Prince of Parthia* which he sent to Douglass (q.v.), manager of the American Company. It was received too late for production during the current season, and Godfrey died before it was either acted or printed. Douglass played it for one night at the Southwark Theatre in 1767 and it was then not acted again until its revival at the University of Pennsylvania in 1915. It was published in 1765 with other works by Godfrey, and shows plainly the influence of Shakespeare and of the plays which were in the repertory of the elder Hallam (q.v.) in about 1754.

Gods, see GALLERY.

GODWIN, EDWARD WILLIAM (1833–86), archaeologist, architect, and theatrical designer, who was living in Bristol in 1862 when he first met the 15-year-old Ellen Terry (q.v.). After the breakdown of her early marriage with G. F. Watts she lived with him from 1868 to 1875, during which time their two children, Edith and Edward, were born (see CRAIG). Later, in London, Godwin supervised the Bancrofts' production of *The Merchant of Venice* in which Ellen Terry played Portia, and from then on was much absorbed by work for the theatre. He wrote a good deal on archaeology in relation to the stage, and for the production of a Greek play designed a classical theatre which was built inside the existing structure of Hengler's Circus. In 1908 Gordon Craig reprinted in *The Mask* his father's articles on 'The Architecture and Costumes of Shakespeare's Plays', first published in *The Architect* in 1875. Godwin's life, as *The Conscious Stone* (1949), was written by Dudley Harbron.

GOETHE, JOHANN WOLFGANG VON (1749–1832), Germany's greatest man of letters, who devoted a not inconsiderable part of his time and genius to the theatre. His first play, *Götz von Berlichingen* (1771, rev. 1773), was written under the influence of Shakespeare's plays, which he first saw in Strasbourg in 1770, during a visit to the German writer and critic, Herder. With its somewhat idealized portrait of a robber baron, who is depicted as an honourable man in revolt against tyranny, it became the spearhead of the revolutionary *Sturm und Drang* movement and a pattern for other young German dramatists, including the greatest

of them all, Schiller (q.v.). The success of Goethe's short novel, *Die Leiden des jungen Werther* (1774), confirmed his position as the leader of the young Romantics, but the only important plays which he wrote at this period were the domestic dramas *Stella* and *Clavigo*. The latter, with its Spanish setting, still acts well, and was seen in London during the World Theatre season of 1964. In 1775 Goethe, at the invitation of the reigning duke, went to Weimar (q.v.), which was to be his home for the rest of his life. Among his other official duties he was responsible for ducal entertainments, which included the directing of plays with a group of young courtiers. He was himself a good actor and appeared in several of his own productions, notably as Orestes in 1779 in the first draft of his *Iphigenie auf Tauris*, based on Euripides. It was at Weimar that he first met the actor Schröder (q.v.), who taught him a great deal about the practical side of the theatre which proved of immense value when in 1791, by which time amateur dramatics were out of fashion, he became director of a professional company established in the Court theatre at Weimar. Here Goethe was responsible for the first production of most of the plays of Schiller, who was his co-director for some years, and with the help of Iffland (q.v.) established a company which became known throughout Europe for the excellence of its acting and the high standard of its repertory. Another interesting result of Goethe's friendship with Schröder was the first draft of the novel *Wilhelm Meisters Lehrjahre* (1795), which, discovered in Zürich, was published in 1910 as *Wilhelm Meisters theatralische Sendung*. This shows that the novel was originally to have been set entirely in the world of the travelling actor Serlo (based on Schröder). It was Goethe's sojourn in Italy from 1786 to 1788, and the revelation of the glories of the antique world, which led him to rewrite and enlarge the scope of his book, turning the quest for the perfect theatre into the quest for true citizenship. The influence of this visit to Italy, which may be regarded as a turning point in Goethe's career, can also be seen in his rewriting of *Iphigenie auf Tauris* (1788) and in the finished versions of two further plays, *Egmont* (1787) and *Torquato Tasso* (1789). But the crowning achievement of Goethe's career, both as playwright and poet, is his *Faust*. Begun in the early 1770s, the first draft of this was completed in about 1775 in Weimar, where it was discovered over a hundred years later and published in 1887 as the *Urfaust*. Part I of the finished version was published in 1808, Part II posthumously in 1832. Goethe worked on it continuously until his death. Its language and style vary from harsh prose and lively four-beat doggerel to radiant iambics, flamboyant alexandrines, and stately trimeters. It has scenes of undying comedy and heart-rending tragedy in Part I, of detached satire and philosophical symbolism in Part II. Although it has been staged in its entirety, it cannot really be adequately contained in the theatre in spite of the dramatic effectiveness of such episodes as the prison scene in Part I and the blinding of Faust in Part II; Gretchen, and Faust himself, are fine dramatic figures, but the vastness of the conception and strength of the execution of this panorama of man's spirit make it impossible to judge it from the point of view of an ordinary play. Producers who are drawn to it in spite of the tremendous problems involved in its production are often forced to fall back on the less complicated version of the *Urfaust*.

GOGOL, NIKOLAI VASILIEVICH (1809–52), Russian writer and dramatist, and the first great realist of the Russian theatre. Work on his first play, a satire on bureaucracy, was abandoned because he knew it would not pass the censor. Some scenes, slightly altered, were later published. The complete manuscript was destroyed by Gogol during the mental illness which overshadowed the end of his life. Two other plays, both satires, were started and left, to be finished in 1842, but Gogol's dramatic masterpiece, *The Inspector-General* (or *The Government Inspector*, also known as *Revizor*), had a curious history, since it was actually produced at the Court theatre in the presence of the Tsar in 1836. It deals with official corruption in a small town, where an impecunious impostor is mistaken for a government official and treated accordingly, and came opportunely at a moment when the authorities were engaged in re-organizing municipal affairs. But the satire proved too biting and was viciously attacked, as a result of which Gogol left Russia, not to return till 1848, already broken in health. In its unsparing realism the play had a great influence in Russia,

and has been widely translated and produced in Europe and America. It was first played in London in 1920 as *The Government Inspector*, and in New York in 1923 as *The Inspector-General*. An English translation of one of Gogol's amusing but less important comedies, *Marriage* (1842), was produced at the Mermaid Theatre in 1956 as *The Marriage Broker*.

In 1928 Gogol's novel, *Dead Souls*, dramatized by Bulgakov (q.v.), was presented by Stanislavsky at the Moscow Art Theatre. It was seen in London in Russian during the World Theatre season of 1964 at the Aldwych. In 1959 the Moscow Transport Theatre was renamed the Gogol in honour of the dramatist's 150th anniversary.

GOLDEN, JOHN (1874–1955), see JOHN GOLDEN THEATRE.

Golden Theatre, NEW YORK, see ROYALE THEATRE.

GOLDFADEN [really GOLDENFODIM], ABRAHAM (1840–1908), the first important Yiddish dramatist and the first to put women on the stage in Yiddish plays. In 1862, while a student at Zhitomir, he played the title-role in the memorable first performance of Ettinger's *Serkele*, written in about 1825. He soon became known as a writer, and a number of his folk songs and dramatic sketches were performed by the Brody Singers, who in Oct. 1876 performed in Simon Marks's Wine Cellar in Jassy a two-act musical entertainment in Yiddish which Goldfaden had prepared for them. Its success encouraged him to form a company for the production of his own plays, of which he wrote about four hundred. Among the best-known are *The Recruits* (1877), *The Witch* (1879), *The Two Kune Lemels* and *Shulamit* (both 1880), *Dr. Almosado* (1882), and *Bar Kochba* (1883). At the time of his death his last play, *Son of My People* (1908), was running at the Yiddish People's Theatre in New York, where he had settled in 1903, opening a school of drama. The great Jewish actor, MAURICE MOSKOVITCH [really MARSKOFF] (1871–1940), was one of his pupils. Goldfaden was also the author of the first Hebrew play seen in New York, *David at War* (1904).

GOLDONI, CARLO (1709–93), Italian dramatist, whose first play, *Belisario*, was acted by Imer's company in the Arena at Verona on 24 Nov 1734. Although this was a tragicomedy, in his later plays he set out to reform the now moribund *commedia dell'arte* (q.v.) by substituting written texts for the scenarii which it used as a basis for improvisation. He was bitterly opposed by Carlo Gozzi (q.v.), who was trying to reform the contemporary stage by making use of what was left of the *commedia dell'arte* and adapting it to his own ends.

Goldoni began his reforms in 1738 with *Mòmolo Cortesan*, which had one part fully written out. In 1746 he signed a five-year contract with Girolamo Medebac, whose company was playing in Venice at the Teatro Sant'Angelo, and wrote for him, among other plays, *La vedova scaltra* (1748), *La buona moglie* and *Il cavaliere e la dama* (both 1749), and *Il teatro comico* (1750), in which he sets out his plans for reform. Like Pirandello's later *Sei personaggi in cerca d'autore* (1921), this sends up its curtain on a bare working stage and has for its cast a troupe of actors about to rehearse.

The years 1748 to 1753 saw Goldoni at the height of his fame with the production of *Il bugiardo* and *La bottega del caffè* (both 1750) and his masterpiece, *La locandiera* (1751), a picture of feminine coquetry which later delighted audiences all over Europe and America, particularly when the heroine, Mirandolina, was played by Eleonora Duse (q.v.).

Goldoni then left Medebac to join Vendramin's company at the Teatro San Luca, where he almost immediately found himself in difficulties, mainly due to the size of the theatre and the hostility of a mediocre rival, Pietro Chiari. In spite of this, he wrote some of his best plays for Vendramin, among them *Gl' innamorati* (1759), *La casa nova*, *I rusteghi*, and *Le baruffe chiozzotte* (all 1760).

In April 1761 Goldoni went to Paris, where he remained until his death. Here again he found himself embroiled in the struggle with older actors who clung to improvisation and resented change. Among the plays of this period, most of which were written in French for the Comédie-Italienne (q.v.), were *Sior Tòdero Brontolon* (1762), *Il Ventaglio* (1763), and *Le Bourru bienfaisant* (1771). Goldoni's works include an autobiography, a number of comedies estimated at between 150 and 200 (some of these may be duplicates, since the same play was often given under

different titles in French and Italian), 10 tragedies, and 83 libretti for *melodrammi*.

GOLDSMITH, OLIVER (1730–74), English poet, novelist, and dramatist, whose two plays, *The Good-Natured Man* (1768) and *She Stoops to Conquer* (1773), stand, like the works of Sheridan (q.v.) his contemporary, far in advance of the drama of his time. The first, produced by Colman at Covent Garden, had a cool reception, but the second, also at Covent Garden, was an immediate success. It has little in common with the genteel comedy of the day and has been constantly revived. Goldsmith wrote nothing more for the theatre, but in 1878 his novel, *The Vicar of Wakefield*, was made into a charming play with Ellen Terry (q.v.) as the young heroine, Olivia.

Goliard, a name given to the wandering scholars and clerks of the early Middle Ages who, unamenable to discipline, joined themselves to the nomadic entertainers of the time and were often confused with them, as in an order of 1281 that 'no clerks shall be jongleurs, goliards or buffoons'. They imparted a flavour of classical learning to the often crude performances of their less erudite fellows, and even when, as happened in the fourteenth century, the word was used for 'minstrel' without any clerical association, the goliard is still shown rhyming in Latin (cf. *Piers Plowman*).

GOMBAULD, JEAN (1570–1666), one of the original members of the French Academy and a frequenter of the Hôtel de Rambouillet. He was also well received at Court, being in favour with the Queen Mother. Among his literary works was a pastoral, given in 1630; it was of little account, but helped by its example to enforce a regard for the three unities (q.v.) which Mairet (q.v.) had recently been advocating. Its success at the time of its production was probably due more to its author's reputation on other counts than to its own merits.

GONCHAROVA, NATHALIE (1881–1962), Russian scenic designer, most of whose work was done for the ballet. In 1914, with her husband, the artist Michel Larionov, she settled in Paris, where she was associated for many years with Diaghilev (q.v.), designing the décor for

Fokine's version of 'The Golden Cockerel' and Stravinsky's 'Les Noces'. She also designed 'Bolero' for Ida Rubinstein and several sets for the Chauve-Souris. In 1926 she designed the sets and costumes for the second version of 'The Firebird', the only example of her work in the current British repertory. There are, however, a large number of her ballet designs at the Victoria and Albert Museum.

GONCOURT. Two brothers, EDMOND-LOUIS-ANTOINE HUOT DE (1822–96) and JULES-ALFRED HUOT DE (1830–70), French novelists and men of letters, whose careers cannot be separated, since they lived and wrote in collaboration. The theatre held an important place in their work, although their own plays are negligible. *Henriette Maréchal* (1865) failed in an atmosphere of political recrimination and *La Patrie en danger*, written in 1873, had to wait until 1889 before it was put on at Antoine's Théâtre Libre. Several plays taken from the Goncourts' own novels fared no better, and their effect on the French theatre would have been very slight had it not been for their influence on Zola (q.v.) and the apostles of realism. They were also interested in the history of the French theatre and wrote a number of books on the actresses of the eighteenth century.

GOODMAN, CARDELL (or CARDONNEL) (c. 1649–99), an actor in Killigrew's company at Drury Lane, whose less endearing attributes were probably responsible for his nickname of 'Scum'. His manners and habits seem to have been reprehensible and he was the acknowledged pet of the notorious Duchess of Cleveland, repaying her by trying to murder two of her children. The son of a clergyman, 'Scum' turned to the stage after he had been expelled from Cambridge, and was first seen in 1677, his best parts being apparently Shakespeare's Julius Caesar and Alexander in Lee's *The Rival Queens* (1678). He later turned highwayman, was captured, and pardoned by James II; in return for this magnanimity he became implicated in a plot to kill William III and fled to Paris, where he died in obscurity.

Goodman's Fields Theatre, LONDON. There were two, or possibly three, theatres of this name. In 1729 Thomas Odell opened one in Leman Street, Whitechapel, where Fielding's *The Temple Beau* (1730) was first produced. Not having much knowledge of theatrical affairs, Odell soon retired, handing over to Giffard (q.v.), who apparently in 1733 built a new theatre in Ayliffe Street, where he had a good company which included THOMAS WALKER (1698–1744), the original Macheath of Gay's *The Beggar's Opera*, Richard Yates and Harry Woodward (qq.v.), and a low comedian named Bullock. When the passing of the Licensing Act in 1737, for which he was mainly responsible, lost Giffard his licence, he tried to evade the law by issuing tickets of admission at 1s., 2s., and 3s. for a concert 'at the late theatre in Ayliffe Street'. He then performed a play, for which there was no extra charge, between the two halves of the concert. In this way he revived in 1741 *The Winter's Tale*, which had not been seen for over a hundred years, himself playing Leontes and his wife Hermione. It was at this theatre that David Garrick (q.v.) made his professional début on 9 Oct. 1741 as Richard III. At the end of the season the theatre closed, never to reopen. Meanwhile, at Odell's theatre in Leman Street, exhibitions of rope-walking and acrobats had been given. It now tried its fortune as a theatre again, but very obscurely, and closed in 1751. It became a warehouse, and was burned down in 1802.

There would seem to have been yet another and older theatre hereabouts, for a periodical called *The Observator* stated in 1703 that 'the great playhouse has calved a young one in Goodman's Fields, in the passage by the Ship Tavern, between Prescot Street and Chambers Street'. But of this there is no other record.

GOODWIN, NAT [really NATHANIEL] CARL (1857–1919), American actor, who made his début in Boston, his birthplace, in 1874 at the Howard Athenaeum in Joseph Bradford's *Law in New York*. His career as a vaudeville comedian began at Tony Pastor's Opera House, New York, in 1875, and the following year he scored an immense success at the New York Lyceum with imitations of the popular actors of the day. Although best known as an actor of light comedy, he was also successful in such serious plays as Augustus Thomas's *In Mizzoura* (1893) and Clyde Fitch's *Nathan Hale* (1899), which was written for him and in which he played opposite his third wife, Maxine Elliott (q.v.). In 1901 he played Shylock to her Portia and in 1903 appeared as Bottom, but Shakespeare proved beyond his range and he returned to modern comedy. The trade-mark of his mature years was a drily humorous manner which made him popular as a comedian and as a vaudeville raconteur. A book of reminiscences, *Nat Goodwin's Book*, appeared in 1914.

GORCHAKOV, NICOLAI MIKHAILOVICH (1899–1958), Russian producer, who began his career as a student of Vakhtangov's (q.v.), soon after the Revolution. In 1924 he joined the company of the Moscow Art Theatre as assistant director under Stanislavsky (q.v.), being responsible for a number of productions, including Katayev's *Squaring the Circle*, Kron's *An Officer of the Fleet*, and a Russian version of Sheridan's *The School for Scandal*. From 1933 to 1938 he was director of the Moscow Theatre of Drama, and from 1941 to 1943 was artistic director of the Theatre of Satire. In 1939 he was appointed to the Chair of Theatre Production at the Lunacharsky State Institute of Theatre Art in Moscow. He wrote widely on theatrical subjects, and one of his books, based on shorthand notes taken during Stanislavsky's rehearsals, was published in an American translation as *Stanislavsky Directs* (1962). One of his last productions was Rakhmanov's *The Troubled Past*, which the Moscow Art Theatre company performed in London during their visit in May 1958.

GORDIN, JACOB (1853–1909), Jewish dramatist, born in the Ukraine, who in 1891 emigrated to New York and was drawn into the orbit of the newly founded Yiddish theatre there. The success of his first play encouraged him to continue, and he wrote about eighty plays, of which *The Jewish King Lear* (1892), *Mirele Efros* (1898), which portrays a feminine counterpart of Shakespeare's Lear, and *God, Man and Devil* (1900), based to some extent on Goethe's *Faust*, are the best-known. Like most of his contemporaries, Gordin took much of his material from non-Jewish plays, adapting and rewriting them with Jewish characters against a Jewish background, setting his face against improvisation and insisting on adherence to the written text. In its simplicity, seriousness, and characterization, his work marks a great advance on what had gone before.

GORKY, MAXIM [really ALEXEI MAXIMOVICH PESHKOV] (1868–1936), one of the greatest Russian dramatists, and the only one to belong equally to the Tsarist and Soviet epochs. Of his plays, the two most important were staged under the different régimes, *The Lower Depths* in 1902 and *Yegor Bulychov and Others* in 1932. By temperament and conviction, however, Gorky belongs whole-heartedly to Soviet Russia, and by his work helped to bring about the establishment of the new regime. In acknowledgement of this, his birthplace, Nizhny-Novgorod, has been renamed after him (see also GRAND GORKY THEATRE).

Gorky (whose pseudonym means 'bitter') had a hard life, spending many years in exile, and was self-educated, but he had some good friends, among them Chekhov (q.v.), who in 1902 persuaded the Moscow Art Theatre (q.v.) to stage his first play, *Scenes in the House of Bersemenov* (known also as *Smug Citizens*). It was given in a cut version, but even so was sufficiently outspoken to cause trouble. It was followed by Gorky's finest play, *The Lower Depths*, which depicts with horrifying realism the lives of some of the inhabitants of Moscow's underworld, huddled together in a damp cellar. Its production was one of the highlights of the Moscow Art Theatre's history. It was seen in London in 1903 in a translation by Laurence Irving and has been revived several times, the most recent production being at the Aldwych in 1972. In New York it was first produced in 1930 as *At the Bottom*, and as *The Lower Depths* was revived in 1964. It was followed by a number of lesser plays, among them *The Children of the Sun* (1905), *Enemies* (1906, but not produced in Russia till 1933), *Vassa Zheleznova* (1911), and some one-act sketches; but it was not until Gorky began his trilogy on the decay of the Russian bourgeoisie that he again attained the dramatic stature reached by *The Lower Depths*. Of this projected trilogy only two parts were staged, *Yegor Bulichev and Others* in 1932 and in 1933 *Dostigayev and Others*. The Third part, *Somov and Others*, was never finished. Several of Gorky's novels, however, among them *Foma Gordeyev* (1899) and *Mother* (1907), were successfully dramatized by other hands.

Goset, see MOSCOW STATE JEWISH THEATRE.

GÔT, EDMOND-FRANÇOIS-JULES (1822–1901), French actor, who passed the whole of his long and honourable career at the Comédie-Française, of which he was the twenty-ninth *doyen.* He made his début in comedy roles on 17 July 1844, playing Mascarille in Molière's *Les Précieuses ridicules,* and became a member of the company in 1850. He was one of the finest and most dependable actors of his day, and played innumerable new parts, as well as most of the classic repertory.

GOTTSCHED, JOHANN CHRISTOPH (1700–66), German literary critic who tried to reform the German stage on the lines of the French classical theatre. He was helped by the actress Caroline Neuber (q.v.), for whom he prepared a model repertory, later published in six volumes as the *Deutsche Schaubühne nach den Regeln der alten Griechen und Römer eingerichtet* (1740–45). This consisted of adaptations of French plays by himself, his wife, and his friends, with a few original works of which the best were those of J. E. Schlegel. Some of them were acted by Carolina Neuber's company in place of the traditional farces featuring Hanswurst (q.v.), whom she banished from the stage. She also produced Gottsched's own plays, of which *Der sterbende Cato* (1732), based on Addison's *Cato* (1713), was at first successful; but by 1740 Gottsched, who had quarrelled with Carolina Neuber, no longer had any contact with or influence on the theatre. However, his *Nöthiger Vorrath zur Geschichte der deutschen dramatischen Dichtkunst* (1757–65) is a well-documented bibliography of German drama from the sixteenth century onwards.

GOUGH, ROBERT (?–1625), English actor, brother-in-law of Augustine Phillips (q.v.), who is first heard of in about 1592, playing a woman's part. It has been conjectured, on slender evidence, that he created some of Shakespeare's female parts, including Juliet and Portia. He was a member of the King's Men (see CHAMBERLAIN'S MEN), and succeeded on Phillips's death to his share in the company. He is named in the actor-list in the First Folio. His son ALEXANDER (1614–?) was also on the stage from an early age, and later became a publisher of plays.

GOURGAUD, FRANÇOISE, see VESTRIS, F.; MARIE-MARGUÉRITE (1742–99), see DUGAZON.

GOWARD, MARY ANN (1806–99), see KEELEY, ROBERT.

GOZZI, CARLO (1720–1806), Italian dramatist, who tried to adapt the masks of the moribund *commedia dell'arte* (q.v.) to a written and literary theatre. In this he was partly inspired by his jealousy of Goldoni (q.v.), who was endeavouring to reform the Italian stage by substituting written comedy of character and intrigue for the old improvised plays. Gozzi's first play, *L'Amore delle tre melarance* (1761), partly written and partly improvised, and some of his later work was produced by Sacchi, one of the best-known actors of the day, whose leading lady was Teodora Ricci.

Gozzi's *fiabe,* or fairytale plays, of which the best was probably *L'Augellino belverde* (1764), were more successful in his lifetime in Germany and France than in Italy. It was thought at one time that they would not bear revival, but perhaps because Gozzi's vein of fantasy, in which he anticipated Pirandello (q.v.) in his use of myth and the working of the subconscious, is increasingly relevant to our age there have in this century been some notable productions of *Il Corvo, Turandot* (particularly at the Vakhtangov Theatre in Moscow in 1922), *L'Augellino belverde* and *Il Re cervo.* As *The King Stag,* this last was produced by the Young Vic in 1946, and later by several children's theatre companies. *Turandot,* first produced in 1762, provided the libretto for an opera by Puccini, and *L'Amore delle tre melarance* for one by Prokofiev.

GRABBE, CHRISTIAN DIETRICH (1801–36), German poet and dramatist, who with Büchner was the dramatic mouthpiece of the 'Young Germany' movement. His ambitious *Don Juan und Faust* (1829), which strives to emulate both Mozart and Goethe, has some striking scenes. A later play, *Napoleon, oder die hundert Tage* (1831), consists of little more than a long series of sketches, loosely strung together. Grabbe led an unhappy, harassed life and died young. He was later made the hero of a play, *Der Einsame* (1925), by Hanns Johst.

Gracioso, the comic servant in the Spanish drama of the Golden Age, corresponding to the Elizabethan fool in England. His immediate ancestor is the *bobo* of Lope de Rueda's interludes, or *pasos* (q.v.). In the plays of Lope de Vega (q.v.) the actions of the *gracioso* burlesque or parody those of his master and his language is generally lively and popular. With Calderón (q.v.) the *gracioso* is used to present yet another facet of the moral or doctrinal lesson implicit in the play, whether *comedia* or *auto sacramental*. In the comedies of Moreto (q.v.) the complicated intrigue is set on foot and maintained by the *gracioso* and his female counterpart.

Grafton Theatre, LONDON, a playhouse in Tottenham Court Road which opened in 1931 with a revival of J. Hastings Turner's *The Lilies of the Field* under Helena Pickard (Lady Hardwicke) and Beatrix Thomson. A few plays were revived and then the venture was given up. Productions were occasionally seen there in the next few years, and from 1939 to 1945 the theatre was occupied by the B.B.C. It is no longer in use.

GRAHAM, MARY ANN (1728–87), see YATES, RICHARD.

GRAMATICA, IRMA (1873–1962) and EMMA (1875–1965), children of strolling players. They were both on the stage from their earliest years, Irma as a young girl becoming well known for her skilful playing of the young heroines of contemporary French plays in translation, her finest part being Thérèse in Zola's *Thérèse Raquin*. She was also excellent as Katharina in *The Taming of the Shrew*. She made her last appearance as Lady Macbeth to the Macbeth of Ruggeri (q.v.) in 1938, after which she retired. Her sister Emma, though originally less promising as an actress, soon became an exceptionally fine portrayer of the more mature women of Ibsen, Pirandello, and particularly Shaw. She played in the Italian versions of *Mrs. Warren's Profession*, *Pygmalion*, *Saint Joan*, and *Caesar and Cleopatra*, and was also seen as Marchbanks in *Candida*. A romantic actress, less lyrical than Irma, but stronger, she was an excellent linguist and acted both in German and Spanish.

Grand Gorky Theatre, LENINGRAD, founded in 1919 by Alexander Blok. Gorky (q.v.), whose plays were first seen in Leningrad at this theatre, took a great interest in it and helped to guide it through its early troubles. Its first production was Schiller's *Don Carlos*, followed by a number of classic and a few modern plays. Then came a period of Expressionism, when Toller, Kaiser, Shaw, and O'Neill (qq.v.) were produced in the constructivist style. From 1925 onwards Soviet plays were introduced into the repertory and in 1933 Gorky's *Enemies* was given its first production at this theatre, being seen at the Moscow Art Theatre two years later. Among the theatre's scenic designers were Alexandre Benois (q.v.), who left Russia to join Diaghilev, and Akimov (q.v.), who remained and made a name for himself later as a director. During the Second World War the company was evacuated, and returned to find their building damaged. It was soon repaired and the theatre embarked on an ambitious programme, including the revival of a fine production of *King Lear* which had been cut short by the outbreak of war. The company appeared in London during the World Theatre season of 1966 in a new play, a musical entitled *Grandma, Uncle Iliko, Hilarion and I*, and in Dostoievsky's *The Idiot*, dramatized and presented by its artistic director, Tovstonogov (q.v.), with Innokenty Smoktunovsky as Prince Myshkin.

Grand Guignol, see GUIGNOL.

Grand Opera House, NEW YORK, on the north-west corner of 8th Avenue and 23rd Street. This opened on 9 Jan. 1868 as Pike's Opera House, from the name of its first owner. Its early years were uneventful and it was often closed between visits from touring companies. In Feb. 1869 it reopened as the Grand Opera House for a season of *opéra bouffe*, and from 1872 to 1874 it was managed by Daly (q.v.). Under him Mrs. John Wood (q.v.) made her last appearance in New York, playing Peachblossom in a revival of his melodrama, *Under the Gaslight; or, Life and Love in These Times*. Fechter (q.v.) was seen as the elder Dumas's Count of Monte Cristo, and Fay Templeton, later a variety star, played Puck in *A Midsummer Night's Dream*. After a visit in 1875 from E. L. Davenport the theatre closed, to reopen after redecoration as a local 'family' house, with inexpensive seats, for visits from Broadway successes on tour with a sprinkling of stars. This policy proved successful for many years, but in 1938 the theatre became a cinema and the building was demolished in 1961.

Grand Theatre, LONDON, in Upper Street, Islington, originally a music-hall called the Philharmonic which opened in 1860. At the end of 1870 it became the home of *opéra bouffe*, with Emily Soldene as its star, and West End audiences flocked to North London to see her. It was burned down in Sept. 1882. One notable event in its life had been the temporary loss of its licence through the introduction of the cancan. Rebuilt and enlarged, the theatre reopened in the autumn of 1883 as the Grand, but was burned down again in Dec. 1887. Rebuilt more elaborately still, it reopened on 1 Dec. 1888 to perish by fire once more in Feb. 1900. Again reopened, it became the Empire, Islington, in 1908 and the Islington Palace in 1912. Its pantomimes were famous, and Harry Randall (q.v.) played in them for many seasons. After becoming a music-hall, the Islington Empire, in 1918 and then a cinema, it was demolished in 1942.

GRANDVAL, FRANÇOIS-CHARLES; RACOT DE (1710–84), French actor, who made his début at the Comédie-Française at the age of nineteen as Andronic in Campistron's tragedy of that name. He became a great favourite with the public, particularly in tragedy, retiring in 1766. Financial difficulties caused him to return to the theatre, where his renewed success caused much jealousy. Howled down while appearing in a revival of Voltaire's *Alzire* by a gang of toughs believed to have been hired for the occasion by some of his fellow-actors, he again retired, this time for good. He wrote a certain amount of witty verse, and some scurrilous but amusing comedies are attributed to him.

GRANOVSKY, ALEXANDER [really ABRAHAM OZARK] (1890–1937), Jewish actor and director, who in 1919 founded in Leningrad the Jewish Theatre Studio, which later moved to Moscow and became the Moscow State Jewish Theatre (q.v.). His first production in Leningrad was Maeterlinck's *Les Aveugles*, with the text freely adapted to his own theories of dramatic effect. His opening evening in Moscow in 1921 was devoted to short sketches by Sholom Aleichem (q.v.), and he then concentrated on the production of plays by Yiddish dramatists. Granovsky's

methods were perhaps most clearly shown in his own dramatization of Peretz's poem, *Night in the Old Market* (1925). With no more than a thousand words of text to work on, he made music the basic element, while a subtle use of lighting evoked the presence of the dead who, with the market people and the *badchan*, or professional jester, made up the characters of the play. In 1928, while on a European tour, Granovsky resigned his directorship of the theatre, being succeeded by his chief actor Mikhoels (q.v.), and in 1930 produced *Uriel Acosta* for Habimah in Berlin.

GRANVILLE-BARKER, HARLEY, see BARKER.

GRASS, GÜNTER (1927–), German novelist and dramatist. He was already well known in England through translations of his best-selling novels, *The Tin Drum* and *Dog Years*, when the Royal Shakespeare Company put on at the Aldwych in 1970 a translation of *Die Plebejer proben den Aufstand* as *The Plebeians Rehearse the Uprising*. First performed at the Schiller Theater in West Berlin in 1966, it had its English première in 1968 in a production by the Oxford Experimental Theatre Club. It deals with the abortive workers' rising in East Berlin in 1953 and its intrusion into a rehearsal of a Communist version of Shakespeare's *Coriolanus* being held under a director— the Boss—whom many have seen as a portrait of Brecht (q.v.). Among Grass's other plays, all of which stem from the Theatre of the Absurd (q.v.), *Zweiunddreissig Zähne* and *Die Bösen Köche* have not yet been seen in English. A one-act play of 1960 was included in a 1968 anthology, *Postwar German Theatre*, under the title *Rocking Back and Forth*, and late in 1970 a recital programme entitled *Cross-Section of Grass*, at the Purcell Room in London, included another short play, *Only Ten Minutes to Buffalo*, as well as scenes from *Flood* and from *Onkel, Onkel*, Grass's first play, together with readings of poems and extracts from his novels.

GRASSO, GIOVANNI (1873–1930), a Sicilian actor, son and grandson of puppet-masters, who was encouraged to go on the stage by the great Italian actor Rossi (q.v.), under whom he trained. He was seen all over Europe, and was considered a fine actor of the realistic school, being at his best in the plays of Pirandello (q.v.). He was several times seen in London, where in 1910 his Othello was considered outstanding.

Grave Trap, see TRAP.

GRAY, TERENCE (1895–   ), co-founder in 1926 of the Festival Theatre, Cambridge (formerly the Barnwell), which during his brief management had an influence, particularly on the Continent, out of all proportion to the work actually done there. Like Craig (q.v.), whose theories on lighting and stagecraft were the basis of his experiments, Gray fertilized the theatre more by his ideas than by his achievements. He abolished the proscenium arch and footlights and built out a forestage connected with the auditorium by a staircase, broken by platforms on different levels which offered exceptional opportunities for significant groupings. On this, with the young Maurice Evans (q.v.) as his leading man, and with interesting experiments in lighting by Harold Ridge, who later became an authority on stage lighting, Gray produced the *Oresteia*, following it with a number of English and foreign classical and modern plays, including Shakespeare. The choreography was by Ninette de Valois, Gray's cousin, whose dancers later formed the nucleus of the Vic-Wells ballet. In 1929 Anmer Hall brought a company, headed by Flora Robson and Robert Donat to the theatre, profiting by the experience gained there to build the Westminster Theatre (q.v.) in London, and in 1932 Norman Marshall (q.v.) ran a season there. Gray returned intermittently, but finally abandoned his project in 1933, after the first performance in English of Aeschylus' *Suppliants*. The theatre was then bought by a commercial management and restored in a conventional style. It is now owned by the Trustees of the Arts Theatre (see CAMBRIDGE) and used as a workshop and costume store.

Grease-paint, see MAKE-UP.

Great Queen Street Theatre, LONDON, see KINGSWAY THEATRE.

Grecian Theatre, LONDON, in the grounds of the Eagle Saloon, in Shepherdess Walk, City Road, Shoreditch. This opened in 1832 under Thomas (nicknamed 'Brayvo') Rouse for the production of light opera.

Frederick Robson (q.v.) had his first London engagement at the Grecian in 1844, remaining there for five years, and Sims Reeves sang in its chorus. In 1851 Benjamin Conquest succeeded Rouse and obtained a theatre licence, presenting plays by Shakespeare, which lost money, and pantomimes by his son George (q.v.), which proved profitable. He rebuilt the theatre in 1858, and George, who inherited it in 1872, again rebuilt it in 1876. Three years later he sold it to Clark who, after losing a fortune on it, sold it to the Salvation Army in 1882.

GREEN, JOHN, see ENGLISH COMEDIANS.

GREEN, PAUL ELIOT (1894–1981), American dramatist, whose first plays, mainly in one act, were produced by the Carolina Playmakers. They dealt with the problems of the Negroes and poor whites in the South, as did his later full-length plays, of which *In Abraham's Bosom* (1926) was awarded the Pulitzer Prize for drama. Other full-length plays were *The Field God* (1927), a study of religious repression among the farmer folk of eastern North Carolina, *Tread the Green Grass* (1929), *The House of Connelly* (1931), and *Roll, Sweet Chariot* (1934). *Johnny Johnson* (1936), with music by Kurt Weill, was a forerunner of Green's symphonic plays with music, none of which has yet been seen in the professional theatre. His best one-act plays were *Lonesome Road* (1926) and *Hymn to the Rising Sun* (1936). In 1941 Green dramatized *Native Son*, by the Negro novelist Richard Wright.

Green Room, the name given to the room behind the stage in which the actors and actresses gathered before and after the performance to chat or entertain friends. It has almost disappeared as such from the modern English theatre, but still exists, in a modified form, at Drury Lane (q.v.). The first reference to the green room occurs in Shadwell's informative *A True Widow*, given at Dorset Garden in Dec. 1678. It seems probable that it was called the green room simply because it was hung or painted in green. It was also known as the Scene Room, a term later applied to the room where scenery was stored, and the theory has been advanced that 'green' was a corruption of 'scene'. In the larger early English theatres were sometimes several green rooms, strictly graded in use according to the salary of the player, who could be fined for presuming to use a green room above his station.

Greencoat Men, footmen in green liveries who, in the early Restoration theatre, placed or removed essential pieces of furniture in full view of the audience.

GREENE, (HENRY) GRAHAM (1904–), distinguished English novelist, who turned to the theatre as a means of giving expression to certain strongly-held opinions. A Roman Catholic, his work bears the strong impress of his faith, though his expression of it is not always acceptable to the authorities. His first contact with the theatre was through the successful dramatization of his novel *Brighton Rock* (1943). Two further adaptations, *The Heart of the Matter* (1950) and *The Power and the Glory* (1956), were not as successful as Greene's own plays, written directly for the theatre. The first was *The Living Room* (1953), in which Dorothy Tutin gave a fine performance as Rose Pemberton. This had a short run in New York a year later. It was followed by *The Potting Shed*, first seen in New York in 1957 and in London, with John Gielgud, in 1958. *The Complaisant Lover* was seen in London in 1959 with Ralph Richardson and in New York in 1961 with Michael Redgrave. *Carving a Statue* (1964), again with Ralph Richardson, has not been seen in New York. Graham Greene was appointed Companion of Honour on 1 Jan. 1966.

GREENE, ROBERT (c. 1560–92), English dramatist, who led a wild and dissipated life and shortly before his early death wrote his famous recantation, *A Groatsworth of Wit bought with a Million of Repentance*, chiefly remembered now for its malicious attack on Shakespeare—the earliest allusion to his standing as a dramatist—'an upstart crow beautified with our feathers, and in his opinion the only Shake-scene in the country'. Greene is thought to have had a hand in the *Henry VI* which Shakespeare later rewrote, as well as in Kyd's *The Spanish Tragedy* and many other plays of the time. Among those plays which can definitely be ascribed to him the most important are a romantic comedy, *James IV of Scotland* (c. 1591), and *The Honourable History of Friar Bacon and Friar Bungay*, a study of white magic probably intended

as a counterblast to the black magic of *Doctor Faustus* (c. 1589) (see MARLOWE, C.). It may have been acted a few years before its first publication in 1594 and was constantly revived up to 1630. It is occasionally acted by amateur and university societies, when it still proves popular.

Greenwich Theatre, CROOM'S HILL, LONDON, S.E.10. This opened in the 1860s as Crowden's Music-Hall, and later became Barnard's Palace and then the Hippodrome. Between the First and Second World Wars it was used as a cinema and then as a warehouse. In 1962 its present director, Ewan Hooper, began a campaign for its restoration and reopening as a community theatre for south-east London, and in Oct. 1969 opened it with a new musical, *Martin Luther King*, followed by *Spithead*, a documentary on the Royal Navy mutiny in 1797. Since then a number of new plays have been staged, including Iris Murdoch's *The Servants and the Snow* and John Mortimer's *A Voyage Round My Father* (both 1970). The theatre, in which much of the 1860 structure has been retained, has a hexagonal thrust stage protruding into a steeply-raked auditorium which seats 426 people. Among its front-of-house amenities are Barnard's restaurant, Crowden's coffee bar, and an art gallery. Attached to the theatre is the Bowsprit Company, which tours local schools and at Christmas gives matinée performances for children in the theatre.

Greenwich Village Theatre, NEW YORK, see MACGOWAN, KENNETH and PROVINCETOWN PLAYERS.

GREET, SIR BEN [really PHILIP BARLING] (1857–1936), English actor-manager, knighted in 1929 for his services to the theatre. He first appeared on the stage in 1879 and after three years in Sarah Thorne's company at Margate went to London, where he appeared with a number of outstanding actors, including Lawrence Barrett and Mary Anderson (qq.v.). It was in 1886 that he gave the first of his many open-air productions of Shakespeare's plays and formed the company with which he toured the United Kingdom and America, rivalling Benson (q.v.) as a trainer of young actors. Greet was for many years in New York but returned to London in 1914 and helped to found the Old Vic (q.v.), where between

1915 and 1918 he directed twenty-four of Shakespeare's plays, including *Hamlet* in its entirety as well as a number of other classics. In his later years he concentrated mainly on production of plays for schools and open-air performances, but was seen as the First Grave-digger in *Hamlet* at the Lyceum in 1926 and as Egeus in a charity matinée of *A Midsummer Night's Dream* in 1927. In 1929 he celebrated his stage jubilee, but continued active until his death.

GREGORY, (ISABELLA) AUGUSTA, LADY (1852–1932), Irish dramatist and theatre manager, mainly responsible, with Yeats (q.v.), for the founding of the Irish Literary Theatre (q.v.), which eventually resulted in the establishment in Dublin of the Abbey Theatre (q.v.) for the production of Irish plays. She described the early days of the Irish literary revival in *Our Irish Theatre* (1914) and also wrote a number of plays for it, mainly one-act, collaborating with Yeats in *The Pot of Broth* and *Cathleen ni Houlihan* (both 1902). Of her own plays, the best are the short comedies of peasant life, *Spreading the News* (1904), *Hyacinth Halvey* (1906), and *The Rising of the Moon* (1908). She also prepared a number of adaptations for the Abbey, of which *The Kiltartan Molière*, a version of several of Molière's plays in West of Ireland speech, is the best-known.

GREGORY, JOHANN GOTTFRIED (1631–75), German pastor, who in 1658 was appointed to the Lutheran Church in Moscow, where ten years later he founded a school. On 17 Oct. 1672 he was responsible for the first organized dramatic entertainment given before the Russian Court on the orders of Alexei, father of Peter the Great. This was *The Play of Artaxerxes*, taken from the repertory of the English Comedians (q.v.). With scenery by the Dutch painter, Peter Engles, this was acted by German students in a wooden 'House of Comedy' erected in the summer palace at Preobrazhenskoye. The performance lasted ten hours and was enlivened by songs, music, dancing, and comic interludes. Gregory later produced *The Comedy of Young Tobias* (1673) and, with Russian students he had trained acting for the first time, *The Comedy of Holofernes* (1674). Gregory is portrayed in *A Comedian of the Seventeenth Century*, by Ostrovsky (q.v.). His theatre survived until Alexei's death in Jan. 1676.

GREIN, JACK [really JACOB] THOMAS (1862–1935), a Dutchman who became a naturalized Englishman in 1895, and who, as playwright, critic, and manager, did much to further productions of the new 'theatre of ideas' in London at the turn of the century. In 1891, inspired by the example of Antoine (q.v.), he founded the Independent Theatre Club in London, which he inaugurated at the Royalty Theatre (q.v.) with an 'invitation' performance of *Ghosts* by Ibsen (q.v.), translated by William Archer. The critics, particularly Clement Scott (q.v.), damned the play, but the Independent Theatre survived, and in 1892 put on *Widowers' Houses*, the first play by Shaw (q.v.) to be seen in London. Grein's dramatic criticisms for a number of English and Continental papers were published in five volumes from 1898 to 1903, and two further collections appeared in 1921 and 1924. In 1936 his widow ('Michael Orme') published his life story as *J. T. Grein; the Story of a Pioneer*.

GRENFELL [*née* PHIPPS], JOYCE IRENE (1910–79), English diseuse, who made her first appearance on the stage in *The Little Revue* (1939) in a selection of the monologues with which she had for some time been entertaining her friends privately. She was immediately successful, proving herself an excellent mimic and an accurate though kindly satirist of contemporary manners. During the Second World War she toured the service hospitals (being awarded the O.B.E. in 1946), and returned to London in 1945 in Noël Coward's revue *Sigh No More*. She made her first appearance in New York in *Joyce Grenfell Requests the Pleasure* (1955), and was seen all over the world in her one-woman entertainment. She also appeared in a number of films.

GRESSET, JEAN-BAPTISTE-LOUIS (1709–77), French dramatist, and author of a charming poem, *Vert-Vert* (1734), dealing with the adventures of a parrot in a convent, which led to his expulsion from the Jesuit order. Thrown on his own resources, Gresset wrote several plays, of which the most successful was *Le Méchant* (1754). An earlier play, *Edouard III* (1740), though subtitled 'a tragedy', is really a sentimental bourgeois drama, and like all Gresset's other works shows the influence of the artificial cult of the day for the simple life. This is particularly noticeable in *Sidnei* (1745), a by-product of the anglomania of eighteenth-century France set in an English village, in which the hero's valet is the sole survivor of old French comedy in a morass of sentiment.

GRÉVIN, JACQUES (*c.* 1538–*c.* 1570), a doctor by profession, who was one of the precursors of French classical tragedy. His serious plays have been overshadowed by his one comedy, *Les Esbahis*, given before the Court at the Collège de Beauvais in 1560 in honour of the marriage of the young Duchess of Lorraine, who was present at the performance with her father, Henri II.

GRIBOYEDOV, ALEXANDER SERGEIVICH (1795–1829), Russian dramatist and diplomat, who was assassinated in Teheran while acting as Russian Minister to Persia. He first became interested in the theatre in 1815 while residing in St. Petersburg (Leningrad), and with one exception his comedies were translated from the French or written in collaboration with friends. The exception is the classic play, *Gore ot Ooma* or *Woe From Wit* (also known as *Wit Works Woe*, *Too Clever by Half*, *The Trouble with Reason*, and *The Disadvantages of Being Clever*, though *Woe to the Wise* would perhaps be nearer the mark, since *Ooma* means also sincerity, intelligence, and far-sighted liberalism). The play deals with the disillusionment of a young man, arriving in Moscow full of liberal and progressive ideas, when he comes up against the stupidity and trickery of a corrupt society, and was the first dramatic protest against the Tsarist regime, with its bribery, ignorance, and cupidity in high places. Human and dramatic, classic in form yet realistic and satiric in content, written with sparkling wit and sympathetic insight, it is one of the great plays of the Russian theatre and is frequently revived, the part of Chatsky being to young Russian actors what Hamlet is to English, while Famusov, the conservative father, is a favourite part with older actors. It was banned during Griboyedov's lifetime but circulated in manuscript, and a cut version was printed four years after his death. The full text was published only in 1861. The play was first performed in the cut version at the Bolshoi Theatre in St. Petersburg in 1831 and was produced by the Moscow Art Theatre in full in 1906, with Kachalov and Moskvin (qq.v.), who again played Chatsky and Famusov when it was revived in 1938.

GRIEG, (JOHAN) NORDAHL BRUN (1902–43), Norwegian poet, novelist, and playwright. His death in the Second World War while on a bombing mission over Berlin on 2 Dec. 1943 robbed Norway of a promising young dramatist whose best work was probably still to come. His two most important plays, *Vår Aere og Vår Makt* (1935), a passionate anti-war play, and *Nederlaget* (1936), a tragedy of the Paris Commune, were both well known outside Scandinavia and the latter certainly had some influence on Brecht (q.v.) when he came to treat the same subject in *Die Tage der Kommune*. Among Grieg's earlier plays were *En Ung Mands Kjærlighet* and *Barabbas* (both 1927), the latter dealing with the civil war in China, and *Atlanterhavet* (1932). Grieg, who was distantly related to the composer Edvard Grieg, had a good knowledge of English and not only wrote a volume on English poetry, *De unge døde* (1932), but during a lengthy sojourn in Russia, from 1932 to 1935, translated the novels of Jack London into Norwegian. On the outbreak of the Second World War he was instrumental in smuggling Norway's gold reserves into England.

GRIEVE, WILLIAM (1800–44), English scene designer who as a young man worked at Covent Garden, where his father, JOHN HENDERSON (1770–1845), and brother, THOMAS (1799–1882), had been employed by John Philip Kemble (q.v.) and the Vestris–Mathews management (in 1839) respectively. William, who did his best work for Drury Lane, was, after the retirement of Stanfield (q.v.), considered to be the finest scenic artist of his day and his early death was a great loss to the theatre. His moonlit scenes were particularly remarked and he was the first theatre artist to be called before the curtain by the applause of the audience. His brother Thomas's son, THOMAS WALFORD (1841–82), worked as his father's assistant, his painting being remarkable for the brilliance of its style and the artistic beauty of its composition.

GRIFFITH, HUBERT (1896–1953), English dramatic critic and dramatist, who in 1945 became dramatic critic of the *Sunday Graphic* and of the *New English Review*, remaining with them until his death. His first play, *Tunnel Trench*, which dealt with the First World War, inaugurated the Duchess Theatre (q.v.) in 1929. His later plays included *Red Sunday* (1929), on the murder of Rasputin, *Youth at the Helm* (1934), an adaptation from the German of Paul Vulpius, and *Distant Point* (1937), from the Russian of Afinogenov (q.v.). Griffith was also the author of *Iconoclastes, or the Future of Shakespeare* (1928), and of a translation of the memoirs of Mistinguett published in 1938.

GRIFFITH, LYDIA (1832–97), see SEYMOUR, WILLIAM.

GRILLPARZER, FRANZ (1791–1872), the greatest Austrian dramatist of the Romantic period, whose first play, *Die Ahnfrau* (1817), was produced by Schreyvogel (q.v.) at the Theater an der Wien. It was followed by two plays on classical themes, *Sappho* (1818) and *Das goldene Vliess* (1820), and an historical play in the style of Schiller, *König Ottokars Glück und Ende*. Written in 1823, this was banned by the censor for two years because of the resemblance between the career of its hero and that of Napoleon Bonaparte. It was then produced at the Burgtheater, but it was not until it was transferred to the more spacious stage of the Theater an der Wien that its qualities were fully realized. It is now considered one of the masterpieces of the German-speaking theatre. Of Grillparzer's other plays, which include *Ein treuer Diener seines Herrn* (1826) and *Des Meeres und der Liebe Wellen* (1829), on the story of Hero and Leander, the most important is his adaptation of *La vida es sueño*, by Calderón (q.v.), as *Der Traum ein Leben* (1834), the result of an interest in Spanish literature which manifested itself also in his choice of poetic metres. Grillparzer's only comedy, *Weh' dem, der lügt* (1838), was somewhat too sophisticated for an audience conditioned to the lighter forms of popular theatre, and failed on its first production at the Burgtheater, with the result that Grillparzer turned from the theatre and wrote only for his own amusement. His last three plays, *Ein Bruderzwist in Habsburg, Die Jüdin von Toledo*, and *Libussa*, were published posthumously. The first was produced at the Burg-

theater in the autumn of 1872; *Libussa*, which some consider Grillparzer's best work, was also seen at the Burgtheater two years later, with Charlotte Wolter in the title-role. *Die Jüdin von Toledo* had to wait till 1888 for its first production.

GRIMALDI, JOSEPH (1778–1837), pantomime clown, and the originator of the only member of the harlequinade (q.v.) who does not derive from the *commedia dell'arte* (q.v.), being purely English in origin. He was the son of GIUSEPPE GRIMALDI (1713–88), ballet-master at Drury Lane from 1758 to 1788, and first appeared on the stage at Sadler's Wells when only three years old. As a boy he played with Dubois in pantomime and in 1806 was engaged for Covent Garden, where he first appeared as Clown in the Christmas entertainment *Harlequin and Mother Goose; or, the Golden Egg*, specially written for him by Thomas Dibdin (q.v.). This gave full scope to his varied talents as a comic singer, dancer, acrobat, and pantomimist, out of which he evolved the character, half knavish, half doltish, thereafter named Joey in his honour. He was a great inventor of pantomime tricks, such as the construction, with profound thought and great labour, of a post-chaise out of a basket and some cheeses, or a hussar's uniform from a coal-scuttle, a pelisse, and a muff. In contrast to these leisurely jokes, his acrobatics were characterized by dynamic energy which finally wore him out. He left Covent Garden in 1823, his place being taken by his dissolute and drunken son JOSEPH (1802–32), and made his last appearance at Sadler's Wells on 17 Mar. 1828. He was given a benefit by Drury Lane on 27 June, at which, seated before the footlights, he sang his most famous song, 'Hot Codlins' (i.e. roasted apples). He then retired to Pentonville, where he died, and was buried in the churchyard of St. James's Chapel on Pentonville Hill, now a public garden, where his tombstone can still be seen. His memoirs, completed shortly before his death, were edited by Charles Dickens and republished in 1969 in a new edition by Richard Findlater, who in 1955 published also *Grimaldi, King of Clowns*, a survey of his life and work.

GRINGORE, PIERRE (*c.* 1475–1538), the chief fool, or *mère-sotte*, of the Parisian company, *les enfants sans souci*, for whom he wrote a number of topical and satiric farces (see SOTIE) between 1502 and 1515, playing in them himself. His best work is found in *Le Jeu du Prince des Sots*, an attack on Pope Julius II in support of the policy of Louis XII which was acted in the Halles (the main market place in Paris) on Shrove Tuesday, 1511. Under Louis XII's successor, François I, Gringore was suspected of being a political agitator and left Paris to enter the service of the Duke of Lorraine. He wrote only one more play, a *Mystère* on the life of Saint Louis (Louis IX), the first to be written on a French national theme. The spelling of his name as Gringoire, sometimes found nowadays, proceeds from an error in Victor Hugo's novel, *Notre-Dame de Paris*, published in 1831.

Gripsholm, SWEDEN, site of a small but beautiful theatre in one of the round towers of Gustavus Vasa's fortress, whose scenery and machinery still remain intact. One set of scenes reproduces exactly the pillared décor of the semicircular auditorium, and when it is in position the audience seems to be enclosed in a circular jewel-box, glowing with colour. The theatre, which opened in 1782, has been carefully restored and is used for occasional performances in the summer months.

GROCK [really ADRIEN WELLACH] (1880–1959), the supreme clown of his generation, born in Switzerland. As a boy he toured the Continent with a circus, and in 1903 joined forces with a clown named Brick, changing his own name to Grock. Later, with a different partner, he appeared on the music-hall stage in Berlin and in 1911 was engaged by Cochran (q.v.) for the Palace Theatre, London. Subsequently he played in London almost continuously up to 1924, mainly at the Coliseum. His clowning, though in dumb show, was so expressive that its meaning was instantly apparent to everyone. Although he was an accomplished performer on more than twenty musical instruments, his 'act' consisted in failing to play any of them. The chair he sat on would collapse and entangle him, the piano he wanted to play was too far away. He would exhaust himself pushing it to the piano-stool and then slide across it in an attempt to stop his bowler hat falling off and so revealing his baldness. His distress when this became apparent was a masterpiece of dumb show.

He kept his head shaved for this gag, wearing a wig in private life.

Grooves, a characteristic of English, as opposed to Continental, stage machinery, by means of which wings and flats were slid on and off stage in full view of the audience, the top and bottom of each flat (q.v.) running in a groove between two strips of timber built into the stage structure. The origin of the groove can be found in the Court Masque (q.v.), as seen in the designs of Inigo Jones. For the pastoral *Florimène* in 1635 only the back shutters ran in grooves, but by 1640, for William Davenant's *Salmacida Spolia*, there were not only long grooves at the back of the stage for the back scenes but also a series of short grooves on each side for the wings, allowing for up to four changes of scenery at each place. During the Commonwealth a simplified system of grooves, for back shutters only, was used for Davenant's *The Siege of Rhodes* (1656). Although stage directions in plays from 1660 onwards refer indirectly to the use of grooves, the first direct mention of them dates from 1743, at Covent Garden. They were also used in early theatres in America, where in 1897 they were referred to as 'old-fashioned'. During the time they remained in use, several innovations were made to enable the scenery to be changed more quickly, the most efficient being the Drum-and-Shaft (q.v.). Even so, there were many disadvantages attached to the use of grooves. As they always had to run parallel to the front of the stage because of the difficulty of placing them obliquely on a raked floor, masking was poor, and spectators in side boxes could see deeply into the wings. Also because of the rake, the wing flats became shorter as one advanced upstage, so each could be used only in one position and interchangeability was impossible. Sometimes the scenes stuck in the grooves, or moved raggedly, and when in about 1820 the bottom grooves were removed and the upper ones cut and hinged, the noise of the falling arms, and of the chains used to check their fall at an exactly correct level, became a nuisance. All these factors combined to bring about the abolition of the grooves system in favour of the Continental Carriage-and-Frame (q.v.), which was first installed at Covent Garden in 1857. The last London theatre to use grooves was the Lyceum, where they were removed in 1880 by Irving (q.v.), who also began at the same time the practice of dropping the front curtain to cover scene changes.

GROS-GUILLAUME [really ROBERT GUÉRIN] (*fl.* 1598–1634), farce-player with Turlupin and Gaultier-Garguille (qq.v.) at the Hôtel de Bourgogne, where he appeared with the company of Valleran-Lecomte (q.v.) after playing at the Paris fairs. A fat man, with black eyes and mobile features, he was also known as *le fariné*, from his habit of whitening his face with flour, a comic trick originating perhaps from his early days as a baker's apprentice. As La Fleur he played serious parts, but is best remembered as a low comedian, in which capacity he figures in Gougenot's *La comédie des comédiens* (1633).

GROS-RENÉ (*c.* 1630–64), see DU PARC, MLLE.

GROSSMITH, a family of English actors, of whom GEORGE (1847–1912) and WALTER WEEDON (1852–1919) were joint authors of the inimitable *The Diary of a Nobody* (1892), dramatized in 1954. George, who also wrote his autobiography as *A Society Clown*, was primarily an entertainer with sketches at the piano but appeared in Gilbert and Sullivan's operettas at the Savoy from 1881 to 1889. His brother was the author of several plays, of which the most successful were *The Night of the Party* (1901), in which he toured England and the United States, and *The Duffer* (1905). George's sons, GEORGE (1874–1935) and LAWRENCE (1877–1944), both had long careers on the stage, the former being well known for his impersonation of the 'dude' in musical comedy and revue. He was part-author with Fred Thompson of the revue *The Bing Boys are Here* (1916) and with P. G. Wodehouse of *The Cabaret Girl* (1922).

GROTO, LUIGI (1541–85), Italian dramatist and poet, known as *Il Cieco d'Adria*— the blind man of Adria, the town in which he lived. His play *Adriana* (1578) was probably the first dramatization of the story by Bandello on which Shakespeare based his *Romeo and Juliet* (*c.* 1595), though it is unlikely that Shakespeare knew of it. Groto also wrote a number of pastorals and comedies, and several popular horror-tragedies, of which *Dalida*

(1572) was translated into Latin by a clergyman named William Alabaster and, as *Roxana*, was produced at Trinity College, Cambridge, in about 1592.

GROTOWSKI, JERZY (1933–), Polish theatre director, whose experimental work has proved seminal in the European and American theatre. After training in Poland, he graduated from the Moscow State Institute of Theatre Arts (Gitis), and in 1959 became director of a theatre in Opole. Shortly afterwards he moved to Wrocław, where he established an experimental Laboratory Theatre which has already become well known through its many tours abroad, its three most important productions being *Akropolis*, by Wyspiański (q.v.), *El principe constante*, by Calderón, translated and adapted by Słowacki (q.v.), and *Apocalypsis cum figuris*, based on a collection of biblical texts and liturgical chants interspersed with quotations from such authors as Dostoievsky, T. S. Eliot, and Simone Weil. Trained in the theories of Stanislavsky (q.v.), Grotowski has not, as some critics think, rejected them, but has developed them in a psychophysical rather than a purely psychological direction. For him the actor is paramount, and must make use of all the physical and mental powers at his disposal—gesture, mime, grouping, intonation, association of ideas, visual metaphors—in order to achieve a close fusion of meaning and movement. Apparent spontaneity and even violence must be rigorously controlled. In reaction against the 'wealth' of the contemporary theatre, with its lighting, scenery, costumes, and music, and its all-powerful director, Grotowski envisages a 'poor' theatre, stripped of inessentials and relying entirely on the brain and body of the actor. His ideas, as well as those of critics and others who have written about his work, have been collected in a volume entitled *Towards a Poor Theatre*, published in English in 1968 by a Danish publisher with a preface by Peter Brook (q.v.), whose own recent work has been much influenced by Grotowski. The Theatre Laboratory gave its first performance outside Poland in 1966, when it toured the Scandinavian countries. It was later seen at the Théâtre des Nations in Paris. Visits to Holland, Belgium, Italy, Yugoslavia, Mexico, Iran, the Lebanon, and West Berlin have enhanced its growing reputation, which has survived the controversies aroused by its early appearances. In 1968 *Akropolis* was seen at the Edinburgh Festival and a year later the group appeared in London, Manchester, and Nottingham. It has also been seen in New York, where its influence has been apparent in the work of the choreographer Jerome Robbins.

Groundrow, originally a strip of gas lights laid flat along the stage to illuminate the foot of a back scene, and then, by transference, the low cut-out strip of scenery placed in front to mask them. It is now applied to all long, low pieces of scenery, made of canvas stretched on wood, cut, or profiled, along the upper edge to represent, for example, a hedge with a stile in it or a bank topped by low bushes.

Group Theatre. (1) NEW YORK, an organization formed by Harold Clurman, Lee Strasberg, and Cheryl Crawford (qq.v.), which evolved from the Theatre Guild (q.v.), under whose auspices it produced a Russian play in translation, *Red Rust*, by Kirchon and Ouspensky, at the Martin Beck Theatre in 1929. Two years later, after a production of Paul Green's *The House of Connelly*, it became an independent entity and was responsible, among many other plays, for the production of Maxwell Anderson's *Night Over Taos* (1932), Sidney Kingsley's *Men in White* (1933), and Robert Ardrey's *Thunder Rock* and William Saroyan's *My Heart's in the Highlands* (both 1939). The Group also sponsored the work of the young dramatist Clifford Odets (q.v.). The company was disbanded in 1941. Its history is chronicled in Clurman's *The Fervent Years* (1945).

(2) LONDON, a private play-producing society founded in 1933 at the Westminster Theatre (q.v.), where most of its productions, mainly directed by RUPERT DOONE (1904–66), took place. These included the poetic plays of Auden and Isherwood (*The Dog Beneath the Skin*, 1936; *The Ascent of F. 6*, 1937; *On the Frontier*, 1939), T. S. Eliot's *Sweeney Agonistes* (1935), Stephen Spender's *Trial of a Judge* (1938), and a revival of *Timon of Athens* in modern dress (1935). Incidental music to some of the plays was written by Benjamin Britten. During the Second World War the society lapsed, but in 1950 it was re-formed and gave its first production (a translation of Sartre's *Les Mouches*, as *The Flies*) on 2 Dec. It continued to function spasmodically

for a couple of years but finally disappeared in about 1953.

GRÜNDGENS, GUSTAF (1899–1963), German actor and director. He had already had some acting experience when in 1931 he joined the Deutsches Theater under Reinhardt (q.v.), thus laying the foundations of his future career. Tall, blond, and extremely good-looking, he made a striking Hamlet when in 1938 he appeared in the part with a German company at Elsinore. He was then General Superintendent of the Prussian State theatres but during the Second World War proved himself sufficiently anti-Nazi to warrant his release from a Soviet internment camp after a brief stay in 1946. During the next seven years he was director of the Düsseldorf Ensemble, making it one of the outstanding German companies. His last seven years were spent at Hamburg, where he produced a number of important modern plays, including Lawrence Durrell's *Sappho*, Brecht's *Saint Joan of the Stockyards*, and Shaw's *Caesar and Cleopatra*, in which he played Caesar. One of his finest achievements was the production, after a long period of neglect in the theatre, of both parts of Goethe's *Faust*, in which he played Mephistopheles with acclaim in Edinburgh, New York, Moscow, and Leningrad. He was investigating the possibilities of a tour of South America when he died suddenly in Manila.

GRUNDY, SYDNEY (1848–1914), English dramatist, author of a number of comedies and farces, many of them adapted from the French, of which the only one to survive is the farce *A Pair of Spectacles* (1890). This was immensely successful and provided John Hare (q.v.) as Benjamin Goldfinch with a part which he played to perfection and revived many times, both in London and on tour.

GRYPHIUS [really GREIF], ANDREAS (1616–64), German baroque dramatist, author of a number of tragedies written in lofty poetic prose with scenes of horror and bloodshed which violate all the canons of classical restraint. His tragic heroes ranged from Papinianus to Charles I of England, who had just (1649) been beheaded. But he could descend to more mundane levels, as, for instance, in several farcical satires and in *Cardenio und Celinde* (1647), which is the first German *tragédie-*

bourgeoise, with only one domestic murder and a final miraculous transformation of the repentant sinners.

GUAL, ADRIÁ (1872–1943), Catalan dramatist and theatre director, founder of the Theatre Intím in Barcelona, which from 1903 to 1904 presented masterpieces of world drama from Aeschylus to Ibsen, as well as the works of such Spanish dramatists as Benavente (q.v.). The technical and artistic innovations which Gual introduced, his careful training of his actors, and his experiments in scenic design had little immediate result outside Catalonia but bore fruit in the dramatic renaissance in Madrid in the 1920s and 1930s inaugurated by Martínez Sierra (q.v.). Gual, like Martínez Sierra, was much influenced in his early writings by Maeterlinck (q.v.), but none of his plays, of which the best is probably *Misteri de Dolor*, has survived on the stage.

GUARINI, GIOVANNI BATTISTA (1537–1612), Italian dramatist, author of *Il Pastor Fido*, a pastoral tragi-comedy which stands with *L'Aminta* of Tasso (q.v.) as the outstanding achievement of the Italian pastoral drama. It was begun in 1569 but not published until 1590, and was first produced at Mantua in 1598 with much splendour and success. Frequently reprinted and translated, it had a great influence on the pastoral and romantic literature of England and France in the seventeenth century. It was performed in English in 1601 and in a Latin translation at Cambridge, by King's College men, in 1605.

GUÉRIN D'ÉTRICHÉ, ISAAC FRANÇOIS (*c.* 1636–1728), French actor, one of the troupe at the Théâtre du Marais, who in 1677 married Molière's widow (see BÉJART). He became a member of the Comédie-Française on its foundation and was its third *doyen*, continuing to act until he was over eighty. He was much admired in such elderly parts as Harpagon in Molière's *L'Avare*, and was also the first to play a number of leading roles in early eighteenth-century plays.

Guignol, the name of a French puppet which originated in Lyons, probably in the last years of the eighteenth century, and may have been invented by a puppet-master named LAURENT MOURQUET (1744–1844), grafting native humour on to

Polichinelle (see PUNCH). In Paris the name attached itself to cabarets which, like the Théâtre du Grand Guignol, specialized in short plays of violence, murder, rape, ghostly apparitions, and suicide. In a modified form these made their appearance in London in 1908 and have been seen sporadically ever since, notably in the seasons of Grand Guignol at the Little Theatre in 1920, at the Granville, Walham Green, in 1945, and at the Irving in 1951. English Grand Guignol never reached the intensity of the French, however, and its true home is in the small theatres of Montmartre.

In the French theatre a 'guignol' is also a small room just beside the stage, with mirror and washbasin, used for quick changes or hasty repairs.

GUILBERT, YVETTE (1869–1944), French diseuse, who made her début at the Théâtre des Variétés in 1889 and was then heard at a number of *cafés-concerts* in songs specially written for her. Tall, thin to the point of emaciation, with a voice to match, she became the rage of Paris, and her long black gloves, originally a result of her poverty, became a mark of distinction which she retained till the end. Her art, vivacity, and charm made her a great favourite at the Empire and Coliseum in London, and she also made a long stay in America, reappearing in London in the 1920s in a series of recitals. She was the author of a volume of reminiscences entitled *The Song of My Life*.

Guild Theatre, NEW YORK, see ANTA THEATRE.

GUINNESS, SIR ALEC (1914–), English actor, knighted in 1959, who first attracted attention with his Aguecheek in *Twelfth Night* at the Old Vic in 1937. A year later he appeared as Hamlet in an uncut modern-dress production of the play by Tyrone Guthrie (q.v.), playing the part again in his own production (in Elizabethan dress) in 1951. He has appeared in a number of Shakespearian parts, including Richard III in the opening season of the Festival Theatre at Stratford, Ontario (q.v.), but has also shown his versatility in a wide range of modern parts, including Garcin in Sartre's *Huis-Clos* (as *Vicious Circle*) in 1946, Sir Henry Harcourt-Reilly in T. S. Eliot's *The Cocktail Party* (at the Edinburgh Festival in 1949 and the Chichester Festival in

1968), T. E. Lawrence in Rattigan's *Ross* in 1960, Beringer in Ionesco's *Le Roi se meurt* (as *Exit the King*) in 1963, and Mrs. Artminster (a travesty role) in Simon Gray's *Wise Child* in 1967. A protean actor, and an excellent mimic, he has also had a long and successful career in films.

Guiser, Guisard, see MASQUE.

GUITRY, SACHA (1885–1957), French actor and author, son of the actor LUCIEN-GERMAIN GUITRY (1860–1925), under whose management he made his first appearance in Paris in 1902 at the Théâtre de la Renaissance. He wrote nearly a hundred light comedies, directing and appearing in them himself. Many of them were seen in London, where he made his first appearance in 1920 in *Nono*, partnered by his second wife, Yvonne Printemps (q.v.).

GUTHRIE, SIR (WILLIAM) TYRONE (1900–71), English actor and director, knighted in 1961, who made his first appearance on the stage at Oxford in 1924. After directing several productions at the Festival Theatre, Cambridge (q.v.), from 1929 to 1930, he was responsible for Bridie's *The Anatomist*, with which the Westminster Theatre (q.v.) opened on 7 Oct. 1931. Much of his best work was done in Shakespeare, particularly at the Old Vic in 1933 and 1936. From 1939 to 1945 he was Administrator of the Old Vic and Sadler's Wells Theatres, and from 1953 to 1957 he ran the Shakespeare Festival Theatre at Stratford, Ontario, which was largely his creation. On 7 May 1963 a theatre named after him opened in Minneapolis, where he directed several productions, notably of Chekhov's *Three Sisters* and Jonson's *Volpone*, as well as *Henry V*, *Richard III*, and a *Twelfth Night* which made Feste the chief character in the play. Guthrie twice directed *Hamlet*, in 1937 with Laurence Olivier and in 1938 with Alec Guinness (qq.v.). For the Edinburgh Festival he revived in 1948 the old Scottish Morality play, *Ane Pleasant Satyre of the Thrie Estaitis*, by Lyndsay (q.v.), and in 1949 the ballad opera *The Gentle Shepherd*, by Allan Ramsay (q.v.). A creative artist who was not afraid to experiment, often with unexpected success, he was admirable in his handling of crowd scenes. He worked in many European countries, including Germany and Finland, and in Israel. In 1967 he returned to the Old Vic to direct the National Theatre company in Molière's *Tartuffe*, with John Gielgud as Orgon, and Jonson's *Volpone*. He was the author of *Theatre Prospect* (1932), *A Life in the Theatre* (1960), and *Tyrone Guthrie on Acting* (1971).

GUTZKOW, KARL FERDINAND (1811–78), German writer, mainly remembered as the author of *Uriel Acosta*, a moving and terrible picture of the struggle for intellectual freedom, written in 1847, which has become a recognized classic of world drama and is in the repertory of almost all Jewish theatres. It was first seen in England in 1905 and has been played, both in the original and in translation, in most European countries and in America.

GWYNN, NELL [really ELEANOR] (1650–87), English actress, who made her first appearance on the stage at the age of fifteen in Dryden's *The Indian Emperor*. Though greatly admired in male attire as Florimel in Dryden's *Secret Love* two years later, she was not a good actress, but her charm and vivacity brought her success and she was much in demand as a speaker of prologues and epilogues. It was while reciting the epilogue to Dryden's *Tyrannic Love* (1669) that she attracted the notice of Charles II, becoming his mistress shortly after. She made her last appearance on the stage in Dryden's *Conquest of Granada* (1670). Tradition maintains that the founding of Chelsea Hospital was due to her influence. She became the subject of a number of plays, including Paul Kester's *Sweet Nell of Old Drury* (1900), in which Julia Neilson and her husband Fred Terry (qq.v.) toured for many years.

Gymnase-Dramatique, THÉÂTRE DU, PARIS. This opened on 23 Dec. 1820 with Scribe (q.v.) as its dramatist, its company including Virginie Déjazet (q.v.) and the eleven-year-old Léontine Fay. It was at first intended as a showcase for young actors from the Conservatoire and was licensed to play classical plays condensed into one act. This soon proved impracticable and it turned to vaudeville. The Gymnase, as it was usually called, was one of the first theatres in Paris to be lit by gas. For a short time it was known as the Théâtre de Madame, but in 1830 reverted to its former name. During the next few years it saw the début of Rachel (q.v.) and of Rose Chéri, who married the director

Monsigny and remained as his leading lady for the next twenty years. Gradually the theatre turned to more serious plays, and in 1852 *La Dame aux camélias* was given there, followed by other plays by Dumas *fils*, and by Sand, Augier, and Feuillet. It then became a serious rival to the Comédie-Française (q.v.), and under successive directors has retained its position among the important theatres of Paris.

There was a small children's theatre, known as the Gymnase-Enfantin, founded by Joly in 1829, which was burnt down in 1843.

H

Habimah (from the Hebrew word for stage), a company formed in Moscow in 1917 for the production of plays in Hebrew. It soon attracted the attention of Stanislavsky (q.v.), and following its first public performance of four one-act plays it was affiliated to the Moscow Art Theatre with Vakhtangov (q.v.) as its director. His finest production for Habimah was Ansky's *The Dybbuk* in 1922; already a sick man, he died a few months later. It had always been the intention of Habimah to settle in Israel, which it did in 1931, after a preliminary visit in 1928 and a tour of Europe and America during which *Twelfth Night* and Gutzkow's *Uriel Acosta* were produced. A theatre building, with a drama school and library, was opened in 1945 in Tel Aviv and in 1953 Habimah was officially declared a National Theatre. On 2 Apr. 1970 a performance of Dekker's *The Shoemaker's Holiday* in Hebrew inaugurated a new, comfortable, and well-equipped National Theatre building.

HACKETT, JAMES HENRY (1800–71), American actor, who made his first appearance in 1826 and became famous for his portrayal of Yankee characters, particularly Nimrod Wildfire in Paulding's *The Lion of the West* (1831). He was the first American actor to appear in London as a star, playing Falstaff, one of his best parts, in 1833, and several of his Yankee characterizations, which were well received. He was manager of the Astor Place Opera House (q.v.) on the occasion of the Macready riot. A scholarly, handsome, and hard-working actor, he had a definite influence on the development of the American theatre by his encouragement of native playwrights. By a second marriage (his first wife was the actress CATHARINE LEE SUGG, 1797–1845) he was the father of the romantic actor J. K. Hackett (q.v.).

HACKETT, JAMES KETELTAS (1869–1926), American actor, son of J. H. Hackett (q.v.). He was a fine romantic actor who played leading Shakespeare and Sheridan roles under Daly in 1892 and in 1895 joined Daniel Frohman's company at the Lyceum in New York, where he appeared in Hope's *The Prisoner of Zenda* and other romantic plays. With the profits from his production of Sutro's *The Walls of Jericho* (1905) he opened his own theatre in New York (see WALLACK THEATRE), and later, with the proceeds of a legacy, put on an *Othello* with sets by Joseph Urban (q.v.) which marked an important step forward in the history of American stagecraft and scenic design.

HACKETT, WALTER (1876–1944), see WHITEHALL THEATRE.

HAFNER, PHILIPP (1735–64), Austrian playwright and theatre director, usually regarded as the originator of the *Volksstück*, the typical Viennese comedy of manners which depends more on situation than on character. As an admirer of Lessing (q.v.), he endeavoured to replace the impromptu burlesque by plays of literary content and insisted on faithfulness to the author's text. But he was also quick to defend the rights of the living theatre against the over-zealous 'improver', and his own plays, of which the most important are *Megära die förchterliche Hexe* (1755), *Der geplagte Odoardo* (1762), and *Der Furchtsame* (1764), strike a judicious balance between literary and theatrical elements, the latter owing much to his close friendship with the actor Prehauser (q.v.).

HAGGARD, STEPHEN (1911–43), see SEYLER, ATHENE.

HAINES, JOSEPH (?–1701), English actor, an excellent comedian who joined the company run by Killigrew (q.v.) at the Theatre Royal to play clowns and buffoons. He was one of the first English Harlequins, in Ravenscroft's adaptation of Molière's *Les Fourberies de Scapin*, which was ready for production in 1676 when it was forestalled by Otway's version, seen at Dorset Garden in Dec. of that year. Ravenscroft remodelled it on the lines of a *commedia dell'arte* version by Tiberio Fiorelli (q.v.) then running in Paris, and it was finally produced in May 1677, after Haines had made a special journey to Paris to study the methods and stage-machinery used there.

HALL, ANMER (1863–1953), see WESTMINSTER THEATRE.

HALL, PETER REGINALD FREDERICK (1930–), English director and theatre manager who, after directing amateur productions at Cambridge, did his first professional production in 1953 at the Theatre Royal, Windsor. Two years later he was at the Arts Theatre (q.v.), where he directed, among other new plays, Beckett's *Waiting for Godot* and Betti's *The Burnt Flower-Bed* (both 1955) and Anouilh's *The Waltz of the Toreadors* (1956). Also in 1956 he directed Colette's *Gigi* at the New Theatre with his first wife, the French dancer and actress LESLIE CARON (1931–), in the title-role, and was responsible for an enchanting *Love's Labour's Lost* at Stratford-upon-Avon, where he later produced *Cymbeline* (1957), *Twelfth Night* (1958), *A Midsummer Night's Dream* 1959), and *The Two Gentlemen of Verona* (1960), becoming director of the theatre in 1960. It was under Peter Hall that the Aldwych (q.v.) became in 1960 the London home of the Stratford company, and as the Royal Shakespeare Theatre withdrew from the organization set up to establish the National Theatre (q.v.), of which Hall was appointed director in 1973, in succession to Olivier. He was appointed C.B.E. in 1963.

Hall Keeper, see STAGE DOOR.

HALLAM, LEWIS, the elder (1714–56), an English actor closely connected with the establishment of the professional theatre in the United States. Son of the actor Adam Hallam, he had already had considerable experience on the stage in London when in 1752 he took his wife and children (but see MATTOCKS), with a company of ten actors, to Williamsburg, Virginia, where on 15 Sept. they appeared in *The Merchant of Venice* and Jonson's *The Alchemist*. A year later Hallam refurbished and reopened the Nassau Street Theatre (q.v.), where his company, in the face of some opposition, appeared in a wide variety of plays. Later, after a visit to Philadelphia and Charleston, he went to Jamaica, where he died, his widow marrying David Douglass (q.v.) shortly afterwards.

HALLAM, LEWIS, the younger (*c.* 1740–1808), son of Lewis Hallam (see above), who went with his father to Williamsburg in 1752 and in 1757 became leading man of the combined companies of his mother and stepfather, going with them to New York, where in 1758, as the American Company (q.v.), they played in a temporary theatre on Cruger's Wharf. Lewis was an excellent actor and appeared in Godfrey's *The Prince of Parthia* (1767), the first American play to be given a professional production. After the death of Douglass in 1786 he took over the American Company, first with Henry and later with Hodgkinson and Dunlap (qq.v.), until 1797, when he retired from management, though he continued to act until his death.

HALLSTRÖM, PER (1866–1960), Swedish dramatist, who between 1898 and 1918 wrote a number of plays, and also translated the works of Shakespeare into Swedish (1922–31).

Ham, a term of derision used by actors today of the old-fashioned rant and fustian which they believe to have characterized nineteenth-century acting, particularly in melodrama. The derivation of the word is uncertain, but it seems to have originated in America in about 1912 and to have found its way to England after the First World War. In essence, 'ham' acting is tragic or dramatic acting which reproduces only the external characteristics and is devoid of inner truth or feeling, covering its deficiencies with a veneer of overworked tricks of technique, empty bombast, and showy but meaningless gestures.

HAMBLIN, THOMAS SOWERBY (1800–53), actor and theatre manager, chiefly remembered for his connection with the Bowery Theatre (q.v.) in its most successful years. Born in London, he had appeared in leading parts at Drury Lane before in 1825 he went to New York and played Hamlet at the Park. He became lessee of the Bowery in 1829, rebuilt it after the disastrous fire of 1836, and only relinquished it in 1850 after further fires in 1838 and 1845. Ill luck seemed to dog him, for in 1848 he rented and redecorated the old Park Theatre and opened it on 4 Sept., only to see it destroyed by fire three months later, whereupon he retired.

Hamburg, a town important in German theatrical history, since it was there that the first National Theatre was established, with Lessing (q.v.) as its accredited dramatic critic. It opened in 1767 and closed two years later, its lack of success being due to poor plays, backstage intrigues, and public apathy. The one outstanding event was the first production of Lessing's *Minna von Barnhelm* (1767), the first masterpiece of German comedy. Later, under Schmidt, pupil of F. L. Schröder (q.v.), it revived as the Stadttheater and had some moments of splendour, particularly when in 1820 Schmidt revived *Der zerbrochene Krug* by Kleist (q.v.), a comedy first produced by Goethe (q.v.) in Weimar in 1808. A second playhouse, the Thalia Theater, opened in 1843 for the production of popular comedy, and a fresh impulse to theatrical life in Hamburg came in 1900–1 from the Deutsches Schauspielhaus, whose repertory included plays by such authors as Ibsen, Shaw, and Molnár.

HAMMERSTEIN, OSCAR (1895–1960), son and nephew of theatrical managers, and grandson of the impresario OSCAR HAMMERSTEIN (1847–1919), who built theatres in London and New York. The younger Hammerstein began his career as a stage manager on Broadway, but soon gave all his time to writing and was probably the most prolific and successful lyricwriter of his generation. He first came into prominence with *Wildflower* (1923), followed by *Rose Marie* (1924), *The Desert Song* (1926), *Show Boat* (1927) (from the book by Edna Ferber), *The Gang's All Here* (1931), and *Music in the Air* (1932). It was in 1943 that he began his collaboration with the composer Richard Rodgers which resulted in the epoch-making musical, *Oklahoma!* This was followed by *Carmen Jones* (also 1943), *Carousel* (1945), *South Pacific* (1949), *The King and I* (1951), and, his last libretto, *The Sound of Music* (1959).

Hammerstein's Theatre, NEW YORK, see MANHATTAN THEATRE.

HAMMOND, KAY (1909–   ), see CLEMENTS, SIR JOHN.

HAMMOND, PERCY (1873–1936), American dramatic critic, for fifteen years, from 1921 until his death, on the staff of the *New York Tribune* (later the *Herald-Tribune*). He had previously been drama editor of the *Chicago Evening Post*, and from 1909 was dramatic critic of the *Chicago Tribune*, where his outspoken criticisms resulted in his being barred from some theatres for two years. Always a meticulous stylist, his integrity made him many enemies, but in the end his honesty, which often showed itself in frank disapproval, won him an audience. Deploring vulgarity and bad taste, he is reported to have said that 'the human knee is a joint, not an entertainment'.

HAMPDEN [really DOUGHERTY], WALTER (1879–1956), American actor, born in New York but first seen on the stage in England, where he was for some years in the company of Frank Benson (q.v.), laying the foundation of his future excellence in New York in such parts as Hamlet, Macbeth, Romeo, and Othello. He returned to the United States in 1907 and played opposite Nazimova (q.v.) in a season of Ibsen and other modern plays. In 1923 he appeared in Rostand's *Cyrano de Bergerac*, which he revived several times. In 1925 he took over the Colonial Theatre in New York, which had opened in 1905, renamed it after himself, and remained there until 1930, starring in Shakespeare and in such old and new plays as Bulwer-Lytton's *Richelieu* and Echegaray's *The Bonds of Interest* (both 1929). From 1930 to 1939 he toured, mainly in revivals of his former successes, and then returned to New York, where in 1947 he was associated with the American Repertory Theatre, playing Cardinal Wolsey in the initial production, *Henry VIII*, in which Eva Le Gallienne (q.v.) played the Queen.

Hampstead Theatre Club, LONDON, a civic club theatre founded in 1959. At its first home, the Moreland Hall, Hampstead, it staged the first London productions of Pinter's *The Room* and *The Dumb Waiter* (both 1960) and of Ionesco's *Jacques* (1961). In April 1963 it moved to its own prefabricated premises at Swiss Cottage, which seated a hundred and fifty spectators on a single steeply-raked tier. Among many notable productions on its open-end stage were Laurie Lee's *Cider with Rosie* (1963), Donald Howarth's *A Lily in Little India* (1965), and John Bowen's *After the Rain* (1966). The club was founded by James Roose-Evans, who remained its director until his departure in 1970 to concentrate on work with its experimental offshoot, Stage Two. The parent club then moved to new premises nearby under the direction of Vivian Matalon, the opening production being John Bowen's *The Disorderly Women*.

HAMPTON, CHRISTOPHER (1946–), English dramatist, whose first play, *When Did You Last See My Mother?*, written while he was still an undergraduate, was so successful when given a Sunday night production at the Royal Court in 1966 that it was immediately transferred to the West End. Hampton then became resident dramatist at the Royal Court, where his next play, *Total Eclipse*, dealing with the relationship between Rimbaud and Verlaine, was produced in 1968. It was followed by *The Philanthropist* (1970), in which Alec McCowen (q.v.) gave an excellent performance as Philip, an amiable but dispirited don, whose good intentions are constantly defeated by stronger personalities.

Hand-Props, see PROPS.

Hand-Puppet, see PUNCH AND JUDY and PUPPET.

Hand-worked House, see ROPE HOUSE.

HANKIN, EDWARD CHARLES ST. JOHN (1869–1909), a somewhat cynical English dramatist who, in revolt against the sentimentalism of the nineteenth-century theatre, renounced all faith in human nature, attacking abuses but in no way suggesting remedies for them. Among his plays the most successful were *The Return of the Prodigal* (1905), in which the central figure, a young wastrel, is supported by his father and brother in case he should damage their reputations; *The Charity that Began at Home* (1906), a bitter attack on indiscriminate benevolence; *The Cassilis Engagement* (1907), where a misalliance is avoided when the bookmaker's daughter is invited to visit her fiancé's country-house family and breaks off her engagement because of the dullness of their lives; and *The Last of the De Mullins* (1908), which deals with the opposition of her family to the New Woman of the period who chooses to earn her own living. *The Return of the Prodigal* was revived in 1948, with Gielgud (q.v.) as the young wastrel, but proved very out of date and had only a short run; Hankin's other plays have not been revived.

HANLON-LEES, a troupe of international acrobatic actors, consisting of the six sons of Thomas Hanlon, manager of the Theatre Royal, Manchester, together with the famous acrobat, 'Professor' John Lees. Their most famous show was *Voyage en Suisse*, presented at the Théâtre des Variétés in Paris in 1879 and at the Gaiety, London, in 1880. 'It included a bus smash, a chaotic scene on board a ship in a storm, an exploding Pullman car, a banquet transformed into a wholesale juggling party after one of the Hanlons had crashed through the ceiling on to the table, and one of the cleverest drunken scenes ever presented on the stage.' An account of the performance, from which the above is quoted, is given by Dr. Thomas Walton in an article entitled 'Entortillationists' in *Life and Letters To-day* for April 1941, and an analysis of the technical trickwork of the drunken scene, by Richard Southern, was published in the September 1941 number of the same journal. In 1883 the three surviving Hanlons, GEORGE (1839–?), WILLIAM (1844–1923), and EDWARD (1854–1931), appeared at the Fifth Avenue Theatre, New York, in a show entitled *Fantasma*.

Hans Stockfisch, see ENGLISH COMEDIANS.

Hanswurst, a comic figure from Austrian folk-lore who in the early eighteenth century replaced the *zanni* of the *commedia dell'arte* (q.v.) and the Pickelherring or Jan Bouschet of the English Comedians (q.v.) in the popular Viennese comedies of the time. Originally a peasant from Salzburg, he soon lost his rustic simplicity and became a sly, astute knave with a knack of wriggling his way out of awkward situations. His costume consisted of a loose red jacket with an enormous blue heart on the chest bearing the letters H.W. and round yellow buttons; yellow pantaloons, red braces, a fool's ruff, and a topknot tied with a bow; a green pointed hat; a thick, short beard and heavy eyebrows; and a wooden lath stuck in a broad leather belt. The character was evolved and developed by the actor-manager Stranitzky (q.v.) and in the hands of his successor, the Viennese actor Prehauser (q.v.), became more sophisticated and less coarse in his verbal and visual clowning. As the age of improvised fooling drew to an end, the popularity of Hanswurst, who had infiltrated himself into every form of dramatic entertainment, was challenged by that of Kasperle and Thaddädl (qq.v.).

HARDWICKE, SIR CEDRIC WEBSTER
(1893–1964), English actor, knighted in
1934 for services to the stage. He had had
some pre-war acting experience when in
1922 he returned from war service and
joined the Birmingham Repertory Theatre
(q.v.), where his most successful parts
were Churdles Ash in Phillpotts's *The
Farmer's Wife* and Caesar in Shaw's
Caesar and Cleopatra, in which he was
subsequently seen in London. At the
Malvern Festival (q.v.) he created the parts
of Magnus and the Burglar in Shaw's
The Apple Cart (1929) and *Too True to be
Good* (1932) and Edward Moulton-
Barrett in Besier's *The Barretts of Wimpole
Street* (1930), which also had a long run
in London and on tour. He first went to
the United States in 1936 and returned
there in 1937 to play the title-role
in Barré Lyndon's *The Amazing Dr.
Clitterhouse*. After a season at the Old Vic
in 1948 during which he played Sir Toby
Belch in *Twelfth Night*, the title-role in
Marlowe's *Doctor Faustus*, and Gaev in
Chekhov's *The Cherry Orchard*, he settled
permanently in New York, where in 1959
he made a great success as Koichi Asano
in Spigelgass's *A Majority of One*. He
published two volumes of reminiscences,
Let's Pretend (1932) and *A Victorian in
Orbit* (1961). His first wife was the
English actress Helena Pickard (q.v.).

HARDY, ALEXANDRE (*c*. 1575–*c*. 1631),
the first professional French playwright,
attached to the company under Valleran-
Lecomte (q.v.) which settled at the Hôtel
de Bourgogne (q.v.), where his plays, of
which about forty survive from a possible
six or seven hundred, were given in the
old-fashioned simultaneous settings designed by Mahelot. They represent every
type of contemporary drama but are
usually classified as tragi-comedies, though
many of them verge on melodrama. With
a spark of genius Hardy might have
changed the course of French dramatic
literature, but his facility and easy success
told against him and he lived to see the
triumphs of Corneille (q.v.), who first
made contact with the theatre through his
plays, and of the unities (q.v.), which he
had disregarded.

HARE [really FAIRS], SIR JOHN (1844–
1921), English actor-manager, knighted in
1907 for services to the theatre. In 1865
he was engaged by the Bancrofts (q.v.),
appearing with them at the Prince of
Wales' Theatre in the plays of T. W.
Robertson (q.v.). He was manager of the
Royal Court (q.v.) from 1875 to 1879 and
then went into partnership with Kendal at
the St. James's (q.v.), where one of his
outstanding successes was Pinero's *The
Money Spinner* (1881). From 1889 to
1895 he was at the Garrick (q.v.), where he
first played Benjamin Goldfinch in
Grundy's *A Pair of Spectacles* (1890), a
part with which his name is always
associated. He made his first appearance
in New York on 23 Dec. 1895 in Pinero's
The Notorious Mrs. Ebbsmith and then
revived several of his former successes,
touring as Old Eccles in Robertson's
Caste, in which he had played Sam
Gerridge on its first production in 1867,
and finally retiring in 1911.

HARE, J. ROBERTSON (1891–1979), English actor, who had a long and successful career as a farce-player, particularly in the plays of Ben Travers (q.v.),
with whom he was associated, in partnership with Ralph Lynn (q.v.) at the
Aldwych from 1925 to 1933 and again in
other London theatres in the 1940s. He
made his first appearance on the stage in
1911 in Carton's *The Bear Leaders*, and
spent several years touring the provinces.
Apart from the 'Aldwych farces', he
also appeared in such plays as Vernon
Sylvaine's *Aren't Men Beasts!* (1936) and
One Wild Oat (1948) and Ronald Millar's
The Bride and the Bachelor (1956) and *The
Bride Comes Back* (1960). In 1963 he was
seen as Erronius in the American musical,
*A Funny Thing Happened on the Way to
the Forum*.

Harlequin, the young lover of Columbine
in the English harlequinade. His name,
though not his status, derives from the
zanni Arlecchino (q.v.) of the *commedia
dell'arte*, where he was one of the quick-
witted, unscrupulous serving-men; and
so he remained in Italy. But in France
Marivaux (q.v.) turned him into a pretty
simpleton, while in the English harlequinade (q.v.) he was first a romantic magician
and later a languishing, lackadaisical
lover, foppishly dressed in a close-fitting
suit of bright silk diamonds (derived from
the patches on his original rags), sometimes with lace frill and ruffles. He retained
from his origins the small black cat-faced
mask, and a lath or bat of thin wood
which acted as a magic wand (see TRANS-
FORMATION SCENE).

Harlequinade, an important element in the development of the English pantomime (q.v.). It evolved from the fusion of the dumbshow of the *commedia dell'arte* actors at the Paris fairground theatres, where dialogue was forbidden, with the convention which, in burlesques of contemporary dramas, allowed Arlequin (see ARLECCHINO) to assume diverse personalities without losing his own identity. In the 'Italian night scenes' presented in London in the late seventeenth century the actors were comic acrobatic dancers and mimeplayers who had no occasion to speak, and through a misunderstanding of the duplication of parts it became established, in such early pantomimes as Thurmond's *Harlequin Dr. Faustus* and *Harlequin Sheppard* (both 1724), that Harlequin must be someone other than himself. To achieve this, it was customary in the eighteenth century for Harlequin, in an 'opening' scene, to figure as a persecuted lover befriended by a good fairy, who gave him a magic wand and changed him and his companion into Harlequin and Columbine. The rest of the performance was devoted to the escape of the lovers from Columbine's father, Pantaloon (q.v.), and his blundering servant, usually Pierrot (q.v), with the help of the magic wand which, when slapped on a side wing or on the stage, gave the signal for a change of scene (see TRANSFORMATION SCENE). In the early nineteenth century, when Grimaldi (q.v.) made Clown the chief character of the Harlequinade, the love scenes became nothing more than an occasional *pas de deux* by Harlequin and Columbine between bouts of horseplay—shop-lifting, a buttered slide for angry shopkeepers to slip up on, a pail of paste emptied over a dandy's head, a red-hot poker frequently laid upon unsuspecting trousers, and the 'spill and pelt', when vegetables from a costermonger's overturned barrow were flung in battle. Throughout the nineteenth century the 'opening scene' increased in length, and when fairytales became popular for this purpose the Harlequinade dwindled into a plotless epilogue. Harlequin was not even allowed to be the hero in the fairytale (see PRINCIPAL BOY), though for some years there was a pretence of changing one character into the other at the last minute by means of traps, which lowered the hero out of sight and set Harlequin on the stage at the same instant. But it was not long before the Harlequinade, placed after the grand finale, lost all meaning, and it finally disappeared during the Second World War.

HARLEVILLE, (JEAN-FRANÇOIS) COLLIN D' (1755–1806), French dramatist, whose first play, *L'Inconstant* (1786), was performed at Versailles, and later at the Comédie-Française. It was followed by *L'Optimiste* (1788), in which d'Harleville criticizes Rousseau's *homme sensible,* showing that such a man can be happy only if he closes his eyes to facts. His best-known play is *Les Châteaux en Espagne* (1789), an amusing study of a man who, like Voltaire's Candide, thinks everything is for the best in the best of all possible worlds. Its success nearly cost d'Harleville his head, for it aroused the jealousy of Fabre d'Églantine, who had him arrested as an enemy of the new Republic. But he escaped the guillotine and lived to write several more plays, the best being *Le Vieux célibataire* (1792).

HARPER, ELIZABETH (1757–1849), see BANNISTER, JOHN.

HARRIGAN, NED [really EDWARD] (1845–1911), American actor, manager, and dramatist, whose partnership with the female impersonator TONY HART [really ANTHONY CANNON] (1855–91) first brought him into prominence in New York in 1872. As 'Harrigan and Hart' they produced many successful shows, including *The Mulligan Guards,* a series in which Harrigan played Dan Mulligan and Hart his wife Cordelia. They parted company after a fire in 1884 had destroyed the theatre in which they were appearing, but Harrigan continued to act, appearing in revivals of some of his own plays, among them *Old Lavender* (first produced in 1877) and *The Major* (first produced in 1881). In 1890 he opened a theatre under his own name (see GARRICK THEATRE (3)), where he remained for five years. He composed a number of songs and over eighty vaudeville sketches, his characters being recognizable types of old New York, chiefly Irish- and German-Americans and Negroes.

HARRINGTON, COUNTESS OF, see FOOTE, MARIA.

HARRIS, AUGUSTUS GLOSSOP (1825–73), English actor and theatre manager, son of Joseph Glossop, first manager of the

Royal Coburg Theatre (see OLD VIC), and an opera singer named Mme Féron. Why Harris assumed the name by which he is known is uncertain. He was first seen on the stage in America at the age of eight, and later went to London, where he appeared at the Princess's Theatre, taking over the management when Charles Kean (q.v.) retired in 1859. It was under him that Fechter (q.v.) made his first appearance in London. But it is as the manager responsible for opera and ballet at Covent Garden for twenty-seven years that he is chiefly remembered. He also directed opera in Madrid, Paris, Berlin, and St. Petersburg (Leningrad), proving himself an excellent stage manager, with a good eye for grouping and colour. He was the father of the theatre manager Sir Augustus Harris (q.v.).

HARRIS, SIR AUGUSTUS HENRY GLOSSOP (1852–96), son of Augustus Harris (q.v.), manager for many years of Covent Garden. The son took over Drury Lane in 1879 and remained there until his death, his devotion to his theatre earning him the nickname of 'Augustus Druriolanus'. He made a speciality of spectacular melodramas and elaborate Christmas shows, and although some critics held him responsible for the vulgarization of the pantomime (q.v.) by the introduction of music-hall turns, particularly knockabout comedians, he had a feeling for the old harlequinade (q.v.), providing for it lavish scenery and machinery and engaging excellent clowns and acrobats. He was knighted in 1891, not for his undoubted services to the theatre but because he happened to be Sheriff of the City of London when the German Emperor paid a visit there.

HARRIS, HENRY (c. 1634–1704), English actor of the Restoration period, who in 1661 joined the company of Davenant (q.v.) at the Duke's House (see LINCOLN'S INN FIELDS THEATRE), where he played the title-roles in *Henry V* (1664) and *Mustapha, Son of Solyman the Magnificent* (1665), both by Orrery. He was also seen in several Shakespearian parts; a pastel drawing by Greenhill showing him as Wolsey in *Henry VIII* now hangs in Magdalen College, Oxford. In 1668, on the death of Davenant, he became joint manager of the theatre with Betterton (q.v.), and was also a shareholder in the new Duke's House (see DORSET GARDEN

THEATRE). He made his last appearance in 1681 as the Cardinal in Crowne's *Henry VI*.

Harris Theatre, NEW YORK, see WALLACK THEATRE.

HARRISON, RICHARD BERRY (1864–1935), an American Negro actor, son of slaves who escaped to Canada. He was working as a teacher of dramatics and elocution, and touring with a repertory of Shakespearian and other recitations, when he was persuaded to play De Lawd in Connelly's *The Green Pastures* (1930), in which he immediately made a great success, appearing in the part nearly two thousand times. He was for the greater part of his life a lecturer, teacher, and arranger of festivals for Negro schools and churches, and his one great regret was that he had never appeared in any of the plays of Shakespeare, whose works he knew so well.

HART, CHARLES (?–1683), English actor, who was in the company of Killigrew (q.v.) at the Theatre Royal. He had been on the stage as a boy, playing the important role of the Duchess in Shirley's *The Cardinal* in 1641, apparently with much success. He then became a soldier, returning to the stage at the Restoration. He was the original Celadon in Dryden's *Secret Love* (1667), in which he played opposite Nell Gwynn (q.v.) as Florimel. He was excellent in heroic parts, particularly as Alexander in Lee's *The Rival Queens* (1677), and when on the stage became so absorbed in his parts that it was almost impossible to distract his attention. He retired on pension when the Dorset Garden and Theatre Royal companies amalgamated in 1682.

HART, CHRISTINE (?–1829), see SCHRÖDER, F. L.

HART, MOSS (1904–61), American dramatist and director, whose play, *Once in a Lifetime*, after extensive rewriting by George S. Kaufman (q.v.), was produced in 1930 with marked success. This led to a long collaboration between the two men which resulted in such successes as *Merrily We Roll Along* (1934); *You Can't Take It With You* (1936), which was awarded a Pulitzer Prize; *I'd Rather Be Right* (1937); and *The Man Who Came to Dinner* (1939). Hart also wrote a number of plays on his own, including *Lady in the Dark* (1941),

Winged Victory (1943), and *Christopher Blake* (1946). He directed a number of his own plays and also, among other productions, the famous musical comedies *My Fair Lady* (1956, London 1958) and *Camelot* (1960, London 1964). In 1959 he published an outstanding autobiography entitled *Act One*, which unfortunately ended with the production of *Once in a Lifetime*. It is to be regretted that the projected second volume was never completed.

HART, TONY (1855–91), see HARRIGAN, NED.

Hart House Theatre, a small but well-equipped playhouse in the central students' building of the University of Toronto, Canada, founded in 1919 by Vincent Massey (later Canadian High Commissioner in London) and his actor-brother Raymond as an experimental art theatre intended both for the University and for the town, a function which it continued to perform until well into the 1930s under a succession of able directors. It closed on the outbreak of war in 1939, and in 1947 reopened on a new basis, relinquishing its former semi-independent status to become an integral part of the University.

HARTLEY (*née* WHITE), ELIZABETH (1751–1824), English actress of great beauty, the favourite model of Reynolds, three of whose portraits of her are in the Garrick Club (q.v.). An excellent actress, she was much admired in such parts as Rowe's Jane Shore, in which she made her first appearance at Covent Garden in 1772, remaining there until her retirement. She was also good in comedy and was the first to play Lady Touchwood in Mrs. Cowley's *The Belle's Stratagem* (1780).

Harvard University, CAMBRIDGE, MASS., the oldest institution of higher learning in the U.S.A. The first plays known to have been acted there were Addison's *Cato*, Whitehead's *The Roman Father*, and Otway's *The Orphan*, performed surreptitiously by students. Acting was later encouraged, and the Hasty Pudding Club was formed, its productions now being mainly musicals. The Harvard Dramatic Club was started in 1908 and for many years produced only plays written by students or graduates of Harvard or Radcliffe (the women's college in Cambridge). It later concentrated on foreign plays. It was at Harvard that Professor Baker (q.v.) inaugurated in 1905 his course of play-writing, 'English 47'. Harvard possesses one of the finest theatre collections in the world, begun in 1903 and now housed in the Houghton Library. A descriptive catalogue of the engraved portraits in the collection was issued in four volumes (1930–4) under the editorship of Mrs. Lillian A. Hall.

HARVEY, SIR JOHN MARTIN- (1863–1944), English actor-manager, knighted in 1921 for services to the theatre. After fourteen years with Irving (q.v.) at the Lyceum he inaugurated his own management of the theatre in 1899 with an adaptation of Dickens's *A Tale of Two Cities* entitled *The Only Way*, playing Sydney Carton, a part which started him on his career as a romantic actor. Among his later productions were *Hamlet*, in which he played for the first time in 1904 and frequently revived, *Richard III*, *The Taming of the Shrew*, and *Henry V*. He was also seen in such romantic melodramas as Rutherford's *The Breed of the Treshams* (1903), and in Maeterlinck's *The Burgomaster of Stilemonde* (1918). In 1912 he gave a magnificent performance in a production by Reinhardt (q.v.) of Sophocles' *Oedipus Rex*, and then toured all over the world in a repertory of his favourite parts. A handsome man, with clear-cut sensitive features and a distinguished presence, he was regarded by many as the lineal descendant of Irving and his death broke the last link with the Victorian stage. He might have risen to greater heights had he not become so identified with the somewhat melodramatic role of Sydney Carton, which he was constantly forced to revive in order to satisfy an adoring public. He published his autobiography in 1933. In 1889 he married ANGELITA HELENA MARGARITA DE SILVA FERRO (1869–1949), known as NINA, who was his leading lady for many years.

HARWOOD, HAROLD MARSH (1874–1959), English dramatist and theatre manager. With his wife, FRYNIWYD TENNYSON JESSE (1889–1958), a great-niece of Lord Tennyson, he wrote a number of successful plays, among them *The Mask* (1913), *Billeted* (1917), *The Pelican* (1924), and *A Pin to See the Peepshow* (1951), based on the Bywaters-Thompson murder case. He is best remembered, however, for *The Grain of Mustard Seed* (1920) and *The Man in Possession* (1930). The latter, which is a favourite with amateur and repertory companies, was first produced in a double bill with the one-act *In the Zone*, by Eugene O'Neill (q.v.). From 1919 to 1932 Harwood was lessee of the Ambassadors Theatre (q.v.).

HARWOOD, JOHN EDMUND (1771–1809), American actor, celebrated for his portrayal of Falstaff in *Henry IV*, which he first played at the Park Theatre in New York in 1806, with Cooper (q.v.) as his Hotspur. Harwood was for some years at the Chestnut Street Theatre, Philadelphia, under Wignall (q.v.), being much admired in low-comedy parts. He was engaged by Dunlap (q.v.) for the Park in 1803 and remained there until his death, making his first outstanding success as Dennis Brulgruddery in the younger Colman's *John Bull; or, the Englishman's Fireside*. He later changed his style of acting, appearing as polished gentlemen, for which his fine presence and handsome countenance made him eminently suitable. He married the grand-daughter of Benjamin Franklin.

HASENCLEVER, WALTER (1890–1940), see EXPRESSIONISM.

HASENHUT, ANTON (1766–1841), Austrian actor, creator of the comic character Thaddädl (q.v.) which, in spite of imitations, died with him, since he alone was able to give life to what, despite its roots in Viennese comic tradition, was essentially a sophisticated literary conception. Hasenhut, who was one of the most popular actors of the day, was much admired by Grillparzer (q.v.), who wrote a poem in celebration of his art.

Haupt- und Staatsaktion, the name given to the plays in the vernacular presented in Germany and Austria in the seventeenth century, first by the English Comedians (q.v.) and later by the first professional strolling players of the German-speaking lands. Their main feature was a serious plot, usually concerned with kings and conquerors, interrupted by comic interludes featuring the clown Pickelherring, later replaced by Hanswurst (q.v.). It was the inroads made by the latter which led to condemnation of the plays by the reformer Gottsched (q.v.).

HAUPTMANN, GERHART (1862–1946), German dramatist, a Silesian by birth, who often used his native dialect in his plays. Attracted by the activities of the Freie Bühne (q.v.) in Berlin, he offered them his first play, *Vor Sonnenaufgang*, a grim naturalistic drama which they produced in 1889. With all its faults, and its overtones of angry revolt, it clearly revealed that compassion for suffering humanity which pervades all his writing. It was followed by other plays in much the same style, including *Einsame Menschen* (1891), a study of marital incompatibility which arose perhaps from his own experience, since he had recently separated from his wife, whom he had married in 1885. The first period of his activity ended with *Die Weber* (1892), a drama of social comment based on the revolt of the Silesian weavers in 1844. It made a powerful impression when first produced and an even stronger impression when revived in the 1960s.

Hauptmann's next play, *Der Biberpelz* (1893), was a satiric comedy on Prussian officialdom and bigotry, but he was at heart a romantic, and the fantasy of *Hanneles Himmelfahrt* (also 1893) led to essays in the symbolic style with *Die versunkene Glocke* (1896) and other less successful plays. Also in 1896 his historical drama on the Peasants' War in the time of Luther, *Florian Geyer*, was not successful, though it has since been acclaimed for its portrait of Götz von Berlichingen, very different from the portrayal of the same man by Goethe (q.v.). Hauptmann was awarded the Nobel Prize for Literature in 1912. His last dramatic work, written under the shadow of the Second World War, was a cycle of four plays on the doom of the Atrides (see PISCATOR). Some of his plays have been translated into English. *Die versunkene Glocke*, as *The Sunken Bell*, was seen in New York in 1900 and in London in 1907; *Hanneles Himmelfahrt* as *Hannele* in New York in 1910, in London in 1924, and, as *The Assumption of Hannele*, in New York again in 1924; *Die Weber* as *The Weavers* in New York in 1915; it has not yet been acted professionally in London but was broadcast in English in 1962. Miles Malleson's adaptation of *Vor Sonnenuntergang* (1932) as *Before Sunset* was seen in London in 1933 with Werner Krauss (q.v.) as Matthew Clausen. In 1969 the Hauptmann archives, which included all his manuscript plays, diaries, and letters as well as a library of 4,000 volumes, was acquired by the West Berlin State Library, after being inaccessible for twenty years, and should prove an invaluable source of information for scholars working on the history of the German theatre in Hauptmann's day.

HAUSER, FRANK (1922–), see OXFORD.

HAUTEROCHE, NOËL-JACQUES LE BRETON DE (c. 1616–1707), a French actor and dramatist, who was at the Marais before going to the Hôtel de Bourgogne (q.v.). Though Molière (q.v.) made fun of him in *L'Impromptu de Versailles* (1663), he was a good actor and became one of the original members of the Comédie-Française on its foundation in 1680, retiring in 1684 and being later stricken with blindness. He wrote a number of comedies reminiscent of Molière, some of which were to remain in the repertory until late in the nineteenth century. Among them were *Crispin médecin* (1670) and *Crispin musicien* (1674), written for Raymond Poisson (q.v.), and *La Dame invisible* (1684), based on *La dama duende* by Calderón (q.v.). Many years later this play provided the actor Préville (q.v.) with one of his greatest successes.

HAWTREY, SIR CHARLES HENRY (1858–1923), English actor-manager and a fine light comedian, knighted in 1922 for services to the theatre. A much better actor than his popularity in the part of a typical English gentleman and man-about-town ever allowed him to appear, he had no equal in what was known as a 'Hawtrey' part. In 1883, two years after his first appearance in London, he adapted a German play by Von Moser as *The Private Secretary*. When first tried out in London in 1884 it was not a success, but Hawtrey's faith in it was justified when, transferred from the Prince's to the Globe, with W. S. Penley (q.v.) in the title-role instead of Tree (q.v.), it ran for over two years. It has frequently been revived, rivalling even *Charley's Aunt* (see THOMAS, W. B.) in popularity. Among other plays which Hawtrey produced and appeared in, the most successful were Carton's *Lord and Lady Algy* (1898), Ganthony's *A Message from Mars* (1899), Anstey's *The Man from Blankley's* (1901), George A. Birmingham's *General John Regan* (1913), and Walter Hackett's *Ambrose Applejohn's Adventure* (1921).

HAY, IAN [really JOHN HAY BEITH] (1876–1952), English playwright and novelist, who also had a distinguished military career. He was awarded the M.C. and the C.B.E. during the First World War and at the time of his death was a Major-General and Public Relations Officer at the War Office. His first plays were dramatizations of his light novels *Happy-Go-Lucky* (as *Tilly of Bloomsbury*, 1919) *A Safety Match* (1921), and *Housemaster* (1936). Much of his work was done in collaboration—*Good Luck* (1923) with Seymour Hicks, *A Damsel in Distress* (1928) and *Leave It to Psmith* (1930) with P. G. Wodehouse, *Orders are Orders* (1932) with Anthony Armstrong, *The Middle Watch* (1929) and *The Midshipmaid* (1931) with Stephen King-Hall. He also dramatized Edgar Wallace's novel, *The Frog* (1936). He never attempted to sound a serious note in his plays, which often bordered on farce, but his high spirits and good humour carried the plot along and added much to the gaiety of the London stage during the interval between the two World Wars.

HAYE, HELEN (1874–1957), a highly accomplished English actress of the old school, with superb carriage and clear, audible diction. Her career spanned well over fifty years, as she made her first appearance in Hastings in 1898, in Robertson's *School*, and her last in London in 1953, as the Dowager Empress of Russia in Guy Bolton's adaptation of Marcelle Maurette's *Anastasia*. After touring with Frank Benson (q.v.), she joined Tree (q.v.) in London, playing the Queen in *Hamlet* and Olivia in *Twelfth Night*. She excelled in such parts as Lady Sneerwell in Sheridan's *The School for Scandal*, which she played at the Old Vic in 1935, and the Dowager Lady Monchensey in T. S. Eliot's *The Family Reunion* (1939). She taught for many years at the Royal Academy of Dramatic Art, where her pupils included Flora Robson, Charles Laughton, and John Gielgud.

HAYES [really BROWN], HELEN (1900–), American actress who made her first appearance on the stage at the age of five, playing the lead in Frances Hodgson Burnett's *Little Lord Fauntleroy* at seven, the dual lead in Mark Twain's *The Prince and the Pauper* at eight, and graduating easily, by way of Eleanor Porter's Pollyanna and Margaret in Barrie's *Dear Brutus*, to adult roles from about 1920 onwards. She made a great success in Kaufman and Connelly's *To the Ladies* (1922) and appeared for the Theatre Guild (q.v.) as Cleopatra in Shaw's *Caesar and Cleopatra* in 1925. In 1933 she again had an outstanding success as Mary Queen of Scots in Maxwell Anderson's *Mary of Scotland*, and was much admired as Viola in *Twelfth Night* in 1940. Her greatest triumph, however, was the name-part in the American production of Laurence Housman's *Victoria Regina* in 1935, in which she was seen in New York and later throughout the United States. In 1948 she made her first appearance in London as the mother, Amanda, in Tennessee Williams's *The Glass Menagerie*. Back in New York she played Nora Melody in O'Neill's *A Touch of the Poet* (1958) at the Helen Hayes Theatre (q.v.), and in 1961 undertook a world tour with *The Glass Menagerie*, Wilder's *The Skin of Our Teeth*, and William Gibson's *The Miracle Worker*. In the summer of 1962 she and Maurice Evans (q.v.) appeared at the Shakespeare Festival Theatre, Stratford, Connecticut, in *Shakespeare Revisited*, a programme of scenes from the plays which they then took on a nation-wide tour. In 1968 she published her autobiography as *On Reflection*, and retired from the stage at the end of that year.

Haymarket Theatre, LONDON. In 1720 John Potter, a carpenter, built a 'Little Theatre in the Hay' on the site of the old King's Head tavern. Its early years were uneventful, the first recorded performance being given on 29 Dec. 1720 by a visiting French company. In 1726 Madame Violante, a rope-walker who discovered Peg Woffington (q.v.), was there with a troupe of acrobats, and in 1729 Samuel Johnson of Cheshire put on a wild burlesque entitled *Hurlothrumbo; or, the Supernatural*, which proved very popular and ran for thirty nights. In the 1730s the satires of Henry Fielding (q.v.), which attacked the Government and the Royal Family, brought notoriety to the theatre but also led indirectly to the passing of the Licensing Act of 1737 (see DRAMATIC CENSORSHIP), which caused it to close down. It stood empty until in 1747 Samuel Foote (q.v.) took it over, evading the law by various ingenious methods. In 1766 he finally obtained a patent, valid for the summer months only, and the Haymarket became a Theatre Royal, a title which it still retains. Foote sold out in 1776 to the elder Colman (q.v.), who made many improvements and launched the theatre on a period of prosperity, all the great actors of the day appearing there in the summer when Drury Lane and Covent Garden were closed. But on 3 Feb. 1794 (the year in which Colman was succeeded by his son) the first Royal Command Performance in the history of the theatre drew such an enormous crowd that fifteen people were trampled to death and many injured. Further trouble arose in 1805 when the tailors of London took exception to a revival of Foote's satire, *The Tailors*, starring Dowton, and rioted inside and outside the theatre until dispersed by the Life Guards. Meanwhile, a number of eminent actors had made their débuts at the Haymarket—Elliston in 1796, the elder Mathews in 1803, and Liston early in 1805. Two years later the tragedian Charles Mayne Young had a successful season at the Haymarket, and in 1810 Robert Coates, an eccentric amateur, caused great merriment by his attempted portrayal of Romeo. Unfortunately, the younger Colman proved an indifferent manager, always in financial difficulties, and in 1817 he was imprisoned for debt. His brother-in-law and partner, David Morris, carried on alone and in 1820 built the present Haymarket, a little to the south of the old building which was replaced by shops and a café. The new building, designed by Nash, opened on 4 July 1821 with Sheridan's *The Rivals* and in 1825 had a great success with Liston, always a prime favourite in comedy, in Poole's farce, *Paul Pry*. In 1833 Julia Glover, who had already played Hamlet at the Lyceum, appeared as Falstaff in *The Merry Wives of Windsor*.

In 1837 Benjamin Webster (q.v.) became manager, and under him the theatre was substantially altered, gas lighting being installed (the Haymarket was the last theatre in London to use candles) and the forestage and proscenium doors abolished. The theatre prospered, Phelps making his début there in 1837, Barry Sullivan in 1853, while between those two dates most of the great players of the day were seen. One of the good new plays, in which Webster himself appeared, was *Masks and Faces* (1852), by Tom Taylor and Charles Reade. A year later Webster was succeeded by Buckstone (q.v.), an excellent comedian whose ghost is said still to haunt the theatre. As Drury Lane at this time was little better than a showbooth and

Covent Garden was given over to opera, the Haymarket became the leading playhouse of London, Buckstone maintaining a fine company and often keeping open until 1 a.m., people flocking in after other shows to see a farce. It was under Buckstone's management that the American actor Edwin Booth (q.v.) made his first appearance in London in 1861, the year in which E. A. Sothern (q.v.) also came from the United States to appear as Lord Dundreary in Taylor's *Our American Cousin*. Sothern made a further success in 1864 in *David Garrick*, by the then unknown T. W. Robertson (q.v.). Buckstone retired in 1879 and the Bancrofts (q.v.) took possession. They remodelled the interior of the theatre, doing away with the pit, which led to a riot on the opening night, 31 Jan. 1880, when Bulwer-Lytton's *Money* was revived. They ran the theatre successfully, adding immensely to its prestige, until they retired in July 1885. In the autumn of 1887 the theatre passed into the hands of Tree (q.v.), whose greatest success at this period was du Maurier's *Trilby* (1895) with himself as Svengali and Dorothea Baird as Trilby. A year later Tree moved to his own theatre (see HER MAJESTY'S) and Cyril Maude took over the Haymarket with Frederick Harrison, opening on 17 Oct. 1896 with *Under the Red Robe* (from Stanley Weyman's novel). After a long period of success, marked by fine acting in good plays with splendid settings, Maude withdrew in 1905; but Harrison carried on until his death in 1926, being succeeded by Horace Watson, and he in turn by his son and grandson. The theatre escaped damage from enemy action during the Second World War and in 1944–5 housed a fine company in repertory under Gielgud. In 1948 the American actress, Helen Hayes, made her first appearance in London at the Haymarket in Tennessee Williams's *The Glass Menagerie*. Later successful productions included *The Heiress* (1949), a dramatization of Henry James's *Washington Square*; N. C. Hunter's *A Day by the Sea* (1953); Enid Bagnold's *The Chalk Garden* (1956); Robert Bolt's *Flowering Cherry* (1957); Rattigan's *Ross* (1960), on T. E. Lawrence; Flanders and Swann in *At the Drop of Another Hat* (1962); Graham Greene's *Carving a Statue* (1964); and Peter Luke's *Hadrian VII* (1969), transferred from the Mermaid (q.v.).

(For an American Haymarket, see BOSTON.)

HAZLITT, WILLIAM (1778–1830), English essayist and critic, and the first of the great dramatic critics, contemporary of Leigh Hunt, Coleridge, and Lamb (qq.v.). From 1813 to 1818 he reviewed plays for the *Examiner*, the *Morning Chronicle*, the *Champion*, and *The Times*, and it was his good fortune to be living in an age of great acting, displayed chiefly in revivals of Shakespeare. A selection of his criticism was published as *A View of the English Stage* (1818). He was also the author of *The Characters of Shakespeare's Plays* (1817) and *The Literature of the Age of Elizabeth* (1820). In his zeal for bygone dramatists Hazlitt was once led to say he loved the written drama more than the acted but he nevertheless took a vivid delight in acting and much enjoyed the society of actors.

Heavy Father, Woman, see STOCK COMPANY.

HEBBEL, FRIEDRICH (1813–63), German dramatist, son of a poor North German mason, whose work bears the imprint of the bitter struggles of his early years. Obsessed by the tragedy of life, he probed ceaselessly for the cause of that tragedy, finding it less in the realm of guilt and human frailty than in the very process of life and progress. His intuitive insight into feminine psychology resulted in a series of subtle portraits, as in *Judith* (1840), his first play, *Maria Magdalena* (1844), a powerful middle-class tragedy which anticipates the later naturalism of Ibsen, and *Herodes und Mariamne* (1850), a fierce tragedy of jealousy. He was also the author of *Gyges und sein Ring* (1856) and the trilogy of *Die Nibelungen* (1861), his last work. He was fortunate in finding an excellent interpreter of his heroines in his wife, Christine Enghaus (1817–1910).

HEIBERG, GUNNAR EDVARD RODE (1857–1929), Norwegian dramatist, whose work shows the influence of Ibsen (q.v.) in his later years. A writer of great skill and originality, often somewhat satiric, he was the author of several volumes of dramatic criticism and was also for a time director of the Norwegian theatre at Bergen. His first play, *Tante Ulrikke*, was produced in 1884, and the plays by which he is best known, *Balkonen* and *Kjærlighedens Tragedie*, both serious studies of contemporary social problems, in 1894 and 1904 respectively. His last play,

Paradesengen (1913)—*The Catafalque*—is a somewhat bitter satire concerning the unseemly behaviour of a great man's heirs quarrelling over their heritage.

HEIBERG, JOHAN LUDVIG (1791–1860), Danish poet, dramatist, literary critic, journalist, and theatre director, whose influence on the Danish drama to some extent counteracted that of Oehlenschlaeger (q.v.). He was strongly influenced by French and Spanish plays and transmitted much of their thought and ideas through his comedies, his vaudevilles, and his dramatic criticism. He defined the nature of the vaudeville, which he had himself fostered in Denmark, in his *Om Vaudevillen som Dramatisk Digtart* in 1826, and in 1827 founded the *Kjøbenhavns flyvende Post*, whose dramatic criticism had a stronger influence than any similar body of work before that of Georg Brandes. Characteristic of his romantic plays are *Elverhøj* (1828) and *Fata Morgana* (1838), and of his comedies and satires *En Sjæl efter Døden* (1841) and *Nøddeknækkerne* (1845). He was director from 1847 to 1854 of the Royal Theatre, Copenhagen, where his wife JOHANNE LUISE PÄTGES (1812–90), an excellent and extremely versatile actress, had made her first appearance in 1826. She appeared in many of her husband's plays and was supreme among Danish actresses in her own generation. After giving up acting in 1864 she remained active for a further ten years as a director.

HEIJERMANS, HERMAN (1864–1924), the first Dutch dramatist to become well known outside his own country. Under the influence of the new naturalism (q.v.) he explored in his numerous plays, many of them in one act, the miseries and inequalities of the contemporary social scene. Of his early plays, *Ahasverus* (1893) was produced at Antoine's Théâtre Libre soon after its production in Amsterdam; *Ghetto* (1898) was seen in London and New York the year after its original production; and *In de Jonge Jan* (1903), a one-act play written for the Dutch actor Henri de Vries, was taken by him to New York in 1906 as *A Case of Arson*. But Heijermans's best-known play is *Op Hoop van Zegen* (1900), a 'mass drama' in the style of *Die Weber* by Gerhart Hauptmann (q.v.), which deals with the life of the fisherfolk in a small port on the North Sea. In an English translation, as *The Good Hope*, this was seen in London in 1903 with Ellen Terry (q.v.) as the old mother, Kniertjie. In 1927 it was produced in New York by Eva Le Gallienne with her Civic Repertory Company.

HEINRICH JULIUS, DUKE OF BRUNSWICK (1564–1613), a noble playwright whose favourite theme was matrimonial discord, usually with the onus on the female side, unless the husband, through sheer stupidity, deserved his punishment. The Duke, who succeeded to his title in 1589, was a patron of the English Comedians (q.v.), who visited Wolfenbüttel some time early in the 1590s, and a company of English actors under Sackville was attached to the royal household from 1596 intermittently until the Duke's death. His own plays show considerable English influence. In all of them the fool is endowed with sound common sense, and in *Vincentius Ladislaus* (1594), based on a scenario of the *commedia dell'arte* (q.v.), he gets the better of the braggart soldier.

HELBURN, THERESA (1887–1959), see LANGNER, LAWRENCE.

HELD, ANNA (1873–1918), see ZIEGFELD, FLORENZ.

Helen Hayes Theatre, NEW YORK, on 46th Street between Broadway and 8th Avenue. Originally a theatre restaurant, the Folies-Bergère, which opened on 27 Apr. 1911 and closed after a few months, it was remodelled and reopened as the Fulton Theatre on 20 Oct. with a series of short-lived comedies. Its first success was *The Yellow Jacket* (1912), a play in the Chinese style by Hazelton and Benrimo. Equally successful, though in a more serious vein, was Brieux's *Les Avariés* under the title of *Damaged Goods* (1913). A revival of Oscar Wilde's *A Woman of No Importance* in 1916 had a moderate success, and in 1922 Anne Nichols's *Abie's Irish Rose* began its long run at the Fulton before moving to the Republic. Among later productions were Lonsdale's *The High Road* (1928), the Stokes's *Oscar Wilde* (1938) with Robert Morley (q.v.) in the name-part, and Kesselring's *Arsenic and Old Lace* (1941). A moving play on the Negro problem, *Deep Are the Roots* (1945), by Arnaud d'Usseau and James Gow, was seen at the Fulton, which in 1955 was given its present name in recognition of the stage jubilee of Helen Hayes (q.v.), who appeared there in 1958 as Nora in O'Neill's *A Touch of the Poet*.

In 1961 Jean Kerr's *Mary, Mary* started a three-year run and was followed by the same author's *Poor Richard* (1964).

HELLMAN, LILLIAN (1905–84), American dramatist, whose first play, *The Children's Hour* (1934; London, 1936), aroused extraordinary interest with its story of a neurotic schoolgirl's defamation of her teachers. *The Little Foxes* (1939; London, 1942), the study of a predatory family of industrial entrepreneurs, and *Watch on the Rhine* (1941; London, 1942), which dramatized the struggle of an anti-Nazi leader against his betrayer, a Roumanian aristocrat living near Washington, fulfilled the promise of her début, as did *The Searching Wind* (1944), which exposed the errors of an American career diplomat whose moral fibre was no stronger in his private life than in his public policy of appeasement. In *Another Part of the Forest* (1946) Miss Hellman returned to the antecedent history of her 'little foxes' with a Jonsonian picaresque comedy of villains out-smarting one another. *The Autumn Garden* (1951) was a powerful group study in frustration and *Toys in the Attic* (New York and London, 1960) a searing study of failure and possessiveness. She also adapted a number of novels for the stage, among them Voltaire's *Candide* (1956) and Blechman's *How Much?* as *My Mother, My Father and Me* (1963).

HELPMANN, SIR ROBERT MURRAY (1909–86), ballet dancer and choreographer who successfully achieved the transition to actor and director, bringing to both careers the same meticulous attention to detail and artistic integrity. Born in Australia, he joined the Vic-Wells Ballet in 1933 and was principal dancer of the Sadler's Wells Ballet from its inception till 1950. He became well known as a choreographer for such ballets as 'Comus', 'Hamlet', 'Miracle in the Gorbals', and 'Adam Zero', in which he also danced. In 1937 he made his first appearance as an actor with the Old Vic company, playing Oberon in *A Midsummer Night's Dream*. In 1944 he was seen as Hamlet, again with the Old Vic, and later appeared with that company in such diverse parts as Shylock in *The Merchant of Venice*, Petruchio in *The Taming of the Shrew*, Angelo in *Measure for Measure*, and Richard III. He also played Shylock, Hamlet, and King John at Stratford-upon-Avon in 1948. Among other parts in which he ap-

peared were Flamineo in Webster's *The White Devil* in 1947, the Doctor in Shaw's *The Millionairess* in 1952, Georges de Valera in Sartre's *Nekrassov* in 1957, and Sebastien in Coward's *Nude With Violin* in the same year in succession to Gielgud. He devised the choreography for a number of play productions and directed T. S. Eliot's *Murder in the Cathedral*, as well as *The Tempest*, *Antony and Cleopatra*, and *Romeo and Juliet*, for the Old Vic. At the time of his death he was director, with Peggy van Praagh, of the Australian Ballet. He was knighted in 1968 for services to the theatre.

HELTAI, JENŐ (1871–1957), Hungarian dramatist, author of a number of light comedies depicting the gayer side of life in Budapest, of which *Jó Üzlet* was translated into English as *A Good Bargain*. A more serious historical verse-play, *A Néma Levente* (1936), was translated by Humbert Wolfe and produced in London as *The Silent Knight* a year later.

HEMINGE [also HEMINGES and HEMMINGS], JOHN (1556–1630), English actor, a member of the company with which Shakespeare (q.v.) was connected and probably the first actor to play Falstaff. He held considerable shares in the Globe and Blackfriars (qq.v.). To him and Condell (q.v.) we owe the printing in 1623 of the First Folio of Shakespeare's plays, which might otherwise have been lost or survived only in mutilated fragments.

HENDERSON, ALEXANDER (1829–86), see TOOLE'S THEATRE.

HENDERSON, JOHN (1747–85), English actor, whose early passion for the stage. was fostered by Garrick (q.v.), who gave him a letter of recommendation to Palmer at Bath, where he was engaged at a guinea a week. He made his first appearance on 6 Oct. 1772 as Hamlet and was successful. Several years of hard work followed, during which he was painted by Gainsborough as Macbeth, a portrait which shows him to be a stoutly built, fair-haired man with a strong, determined face—not handsome, but commanding. In 1777 he was engaged by Colman to play Shylock in *The Merchant of Venice* at the Haymarket in London, which he did on 11 June with instantaneous success, even Macklin (q.v.), that great player of Shylock, congratulating him. He returned to

Bath, but in the following year Sheridan engaged him for Drury Lane. He went from there to Covent Garden, and never again left London except on tour. One of his greatest parts was Falstaff. He died young of overwork and early privations and was buried in Westminster Abbey near Garrick.

HENRY, JOHN (1738–94), an actor who was for many years one of the leading men of the American Company (q.v.), which he joined in 1767 at the John Street Theatre, New York, under Douglass (q.v.). He was an Irishman, and had already appeared in Dublin and London before he sailed for the New World. On the return of the American Company from the West Indies, where they had taken refuge during the War of Independence, Henry assumed the management jointly with the younger Hallam (q.v.). He accepted and played in the first play by Dunlap (q.v.), and was responsible in 1792 for the importation from England of that excellent actor John Hodgkinson (q.v.). He was twice married, his first wife, an actress named Storer, dying young. He then married a younger member of the Storer family, MARIA (c. 1760–95), who also became a member of the American Company, where her imperious temper caused much trouble.

Henry Miller's Theatre, NEW YORK, on 43rd Street east of Broadway. Built for the actor Henry Miller (q.v.), it opened on 1 Apr. 1918 with a translation of *Flor de la Vida* (1910), by the Quintero brothers (q.v.), under the title of *The Fountain of Youth*. After some moderate success, the theatre embarked on the production of the sophisticated drama with which its name is usually connected, beginning with Noël Coward's *The Vortex* (1925). In 1929 Sherriff's *Journey's End* had a long run and in 1934 the Theatre Guild (q.v.) occupied the stage with O'Neill's *Days Without End*, his last play for many years. Later successes were Thornton Wilder's *Our Town* (1938), Norman Krasna's *Dear Ruth* (1944), T. S. Eliot's *The Cocktail Party* (1950), Saul Levitt's *The Andersonville Trial* (1961), and the Royal Shakespeare Company's recital, *The Hollow Crown* (1963). The theatre became a cinema in 1969.

HENSEL [*née* SPARMANN], SOPHIE FRIEDERIKE (1738–89), a German actress in the company of Ackermann (q.v.) at the Hamburg National Theatre. Built on generous lines, with a face and figure of majestic beauty, she was admirable as the noble heroines of German classical drama. Even Lessing, who detested her, had to admit that she was a fine actress. In private life she was a malicious and intriguing character who caused trouble wherever she went. She married as her second husband the actor ABEL SEYLER (1730–1801), who remained faithful to her throughout all her intrigues and enmities, though she was a constant source of anxiety to him, and it was only after her death that he was able to retire peacefully into the country.

HENSLER, KARL FRIEDRICH (1761–1825), see RITTERDRAMA.

HENSLOWE, PHILIP (?–1616), English impresario, important in the history of the Elizabethan stage as being the owner of the Fortune, Hope, and Rose playhouses (qq.v.). His stepdaughter Joan married the actor Alleyn (q.v.), who on his father-in-law's death inherited his property and papers, the latter now being housed in Dulwich College. Among them is his diary, a basic document for the study of Elizabethan theatre organization. In it he entered accounts for his various theatres, loans made to actors, payments made to dramatists, and various private memoranda. Since some of the actors in the companies which used his theatres were contracted to Henslowe personally, and not, as was usually the case in Elizabethan companies, to their fellow actors, and as he paid the dramatists for their work, it follows that he had a large say in the choice of play and method of presentation. That his relations with his actors were not always cordial is proved by a document headed *Articles of Grievance, and Articles of Oppression, against Mr. Hinchlowe*, drawn up in 1615, in which he is accused of embezzling their money and unlawfully retaining their property. There is no note of how the controversy ended, but evidently Henslowe kept actors and dramatists in his debt in order to retain his hold over them. This arrangement was not as good, nor did it make for such stability, as that in force among the Chamberlain's Men (q.v.), where the actors, led by Burbage (q.v.), were joint owners of their own theatre, responsible only to each other.

HENSON, LESLIE (1891–1957), English actor and producer, whose career before the First World War was mainly in musical comedy, in which he appeared both in New York and in London with equal success. After war service he returned to the stage in *Kissing Time* (1919), and was later much appreciated in *Funny Face* (1928) and in Austin Melford's farces, *It's a Boy* (1930) and *It's a Girl* (1931). He was also an engagingly amusing Pepys in the musical version of Fagan's *And So to Bed* in 1951. During the Second World War he toured continuously, playing to the troops, and for nearly twenty years was President of the Royal General Theatrical Fund. In 1926 he published a volume of reminiscences as *My Laugh Story*. At the time of his death he was rehearsing as Widow Twankay for a pantomime at Windsor.

HEPBURN, KATHARINE HOUGHTON (1909–), American actress, equally well known as a film star. She made her first appearance on the stage in 1928, and in 1939, after extensive experience in New York and on tour, made a hit as Tracy Lord in Philip Barry's *The Philadelphia Story*. After many years in Hollywood, she returned to the stage in 1950 to play Rosalind in *As You Like It*, and two years later made her first appearance in London as the Lady in Shaw's *The Millionairess*. A long series of Shakespearian parts followed, both in Australia with the Old Vic company and at the American Shakespeare Festival Theatre at Stratford, Conn., and she then returned to films. In Dec. 1969 she was again seen on the stage, playing the lead in a musical, *Coco*, based on the life of the French fashion designer Chanel.

Her Majesty's Theatre, LONDON, in the Haymarket. The first theatre on this site was the Queen's, named for Queen Anne and changed on her death in 1714 to the King's. It was designed by Vanbrugh and with Congreve (q.v.) as its manager it opened on 9 Apr. 1705. In spite of the excellence of Betterton's company in Vanbrugh's own play, *The Confederacy*, the venture was not a success, as the theatre was too big for plays. It became the first English opera-house, many of Handel's operas being first produced there, from 'Rinaldo' in 1711 to 'Jupiter in Argos' in 1739. His 'Esther', the first oratorio to be heard in England, was also

given there in 1732. On 17 June 1789 the building was destroyed by fire and a new theatre was built, opening on 26 Mar. 1791, still as the King's, the name being changed to Her Majesty's on the accession of Queen Victoria in 1837. It was devoted entirely to opera and ballet, with great success, until it was again burnt down in Dec. 1867. Although it was rebuilt and reopened in 1869, it never regained its former popularity. In 1890 it finally closed and was demolished, only the Royal Opera Arcade being left standing. Some years later the site was acquired by the actor-manager Herbert Beerbohm Tree (q.v.), who built there a new theatre out of the money provided by his successful production at the Haymarket (q.v.) of George du Maurier's *Trilby*, dramatized by Paul Potter. As Her Majesty's, this opened successfully on 28 Apr. 1897 with *The Seats of the Mighty*, by Gilbert Parker, followed by a succession of excellent productions, including Shakespeare and new plays, which formed a distinguished repertory. It was at this theatre that in 1904 Tree instituted a drama school which eventually moved to other premises to become the Royal Academy of Dramatic Art. The theatre was renamed His Majesty's on the accession of Edward VII in 1901 and kept this name until the accession of Elizabeth II in 1952, when it again became Her Majesty's. After Tree's retirement in 1915 the theatre lost that eminence which he had given it, but in 1916 it saw the beginning of the phenomenal run of Oscar Asche's oriental musical fantasy *Chu-Chin-Chow*. Later successes were *Cairo* (1921), also by Asche; Flecker's *Hassan* (1923), with incidental music by Delius; Noël Coward's *Bitter Sweet* (1929), with Peggy Wood; *The Good Companions* (1931), based on Priestley's best-selling novel; *Henry IV, Part I* (1935), with George Robey (q.v.) as Falstaff; and Max Beerbohm's *The Happy Hypocrite* (1936), dramatized by Clemence Dane. Jack Hylton later took over the theatre and was responsible for a number of interesting productions there, including Philip Yordan's *Anna Lucasta* (1947). In 1954 John Patrick's *The Tea House of the August Moon* began a long run, and four years later *West Side Story*, a modern interpretation of *Romeo and Juliet* by Arthur Laurents with music by Leonard Bernstein, which began a new chapter in the history of American musicals, opened and ran until June 1961. After that a long run was achieved by a transfer from the Mermaid of *Lock Up Your Daughters* (1962), adapted by Bernard Miles from Fielding's *Rape Upon Rape*. In Feb. 1967 *Fiddler on the Roof*, an American musical based on a story by Sholom Aleichem (q.v.), began a run which lasted several years.

HERBERT, SIR HENRY (1596–1673), Master of the Revels from 1623 until his death, in which capacity he controlled the actors and licensed the theatres. He was also responsible for the censorship of plays and for collecting the fees due for each performance of licensed drama at the official playhouses. The extant passages taken from the lost manuscript of his office book, which he kept from 1622 to 1642, have been collected in Professor J. Q. Adams's *Dramatic Records of Sir Henry Herbert* (1917) and form a precious deposit of material on the stage history of the period. At the Restoration Sir Henry made strenuous efforts to revive the powers of his office but was routed by the royal monopoly granted to Killigrew and Davenant (qq.v.), the former assuming the title of Master of the Revels on Herbert's death and passing it on to his son. But the office was of no importance, and with the Licensing Act of 1737 its main function, the censorship of plays, passed to the Lord Chamberlain, where it remained until the abolition of the censorship in 1968 (see DRAMATIC CENSORSHIP).

HERMANN, DAVID (1876–1930), see VILNA TROUPE.

HERNE [really AHEARN], JAMES A. (1839–1901), American actor and dramatist, who made his first appearance on the stage in 1859. He was for some time stage manager of Maguire's New Theatre in San Francisco, where he appeared in a number of adaptations of Dickens's novels which later had a great influence on his own writing. He also worked with Belasco (q.v.), collaborating with him in a number of plays, including *Hearts of Oak*. This was pure melodrama, but Herne's later works showed more realism and sobriety, mainly under the influence of his wife, KATHARINE CORCORAN (1857–1943), a fine actress who played most of his heroines. His first important play was a sombre drama of marital infidelity, *Margaret*

Fleming (1890). It was followed by *Shore Acres* (1892), which became one of the most popular plays of the day, mainly through the character of Uncle Nat (Nathaniel Berry). *The Reverend Griffith Davenport* (1899), a tale of the Civil War of which no complete copy remains, and *Sag Harbor* (1900), a rewriting of the old *Hearts of Oak*, in which Herne was acting when he died, complete the number of his works. They have little literary value, but *Margaret Fleming* marks a great advance on the American plays of its day, which probably accounts for its lack of success when first produced.

Heroic Drama, the name given to a style of playwriting imported into England during the Restoration in imitation of French classical tragedy. Written in rhymed couplets, and observing strictly the unities of time, place, and action, it deals mainly with the Spanish theme of 'love and honour' on the lines of Corneille's *Le Cid*. Its chief exponent was Dryden (q.v.), whose *Conquest of Granada* (1670/1) best displays both its faults and virtues. Its vogue was short-lived and it was finally killed by Buckingham's satire on it in *The Rehearsal* (1671).

HERON, MATILDA AGNES (1830–77), American actress, who made her début in Philadelphia in 1851 and later achieved recognition as Marguerite Gautier in Dumas *fils*'s *The Lady of the Camellias*, which she had seen while on a visit to Paris, subsequently making a fairly accurate version of it in which she toured all over the United States. She was not, however, the first to play the part in America, Jean Davenport (see LANDER) having forestalled her with an innocuous adaptation entitled *Camille; or, the Fate of a Coquette*. Miss Heron's version was particularly successful in New York and she made a fortune out of it, most of which she spent or gave away. She later played Medea in Euripides' tragedy and Nancy in a dramatization of Dickens's *Oliver Twist*, and was seen in several of her own plays. Among the actresses she trained for the stage was her daughter by her second marriage, Hélène Stoepel, known as BIJOU HERON (1862–1937), who married Henry Miller (q.v.).

HERTZ, HENRIK (1798–1870), a Danish dramatist, of Jewish parentage, now chiefly remembered for his dramatic criticism, written in collaboration with, or in defence of, J. L. Heiberg (q.v.), and for his romantic historical dramas. The most successful of these, *Kong Renés Datter* (1843), was translated into English, as *King Rene's Daughter*, by Theodore Martin for his wife Helen Faucit (q.v.). Iolanthe, the blind heroine, was however first played in London in 1849 by Mrs. Stirling (q.v.). Helen Faucit played it in a revival in 1855 (having previously played it in the provinces) and she also chose it for her last appearance at the Lyceum in 1876, Irving (q.v.) playing Count Tristram. In 1880 Wills made a new version of the play under the title of *Iolanthe*, in which Ellen Terry (q.v.) made a great success. Hertz's most characteristic comedies are perhaps *Herr Burchardt og hans Familie* and *Flyttedager* (both 1827) and *Sparekassen* (1836). His last play, *Tre Dage i Padua* (1869), was produced not long before his death.

HERVIEU, PAUL (1857–1915), French dramatist, whose plays resemble those of Brieux (q.v.) in their preoccupation with social problems. He endeavoured to introduce into a modern setting the ancient elements of tragedy, but was concerned not so much with the fugitive inequalities of social custom as with the unchangeable vices of individuals—egotism, vanity, indifference, deceit. He was constantly preoccupied with the problems of divorce and the child, as in *Les Tenailles* (1895) and *La Loi de l'homme* (1897), usually considered his best plays, and in *Le Dédale* (1903) and *Connais-toi* (1909). One of his most interesting plays is *Les Paroles restent* (1892), which traces the destructive course of a slanderous rumour that ruins several lives, while *La Course du flambeau* (1901) is devoted to the perennial problem of maternal love and filial ingratitude.

HEVESI, DR. SÁNDOR (1873–1939), Hungarian director and theatre manager, who in 1904 founded his own company, Thalia, and produced a number of modern Hungarian plays and translations of foreign dramatists. He was much influenced by the theories of Gordon Craig (q.v.), which he endeavoured to put into effect when he was appointed director of the State Theatre in Budapest.

HEWES, HENRY (1917–), American writer, who since 1952 has been dramatic

critic of the *Saturday Review*. In 1954 his adaptation of *La Belle Aventure*, by Robert de Flers and others, as *Accounting for Love* was produced at the Saville in London, and in 1957 he was responsible for the adapting and directing of an experimental version of *Hamlet* produced at the Theatre de Lys in New York with Siobhan McKenna. He has been active in the American National Theatre and Academy (q.v.) as well as serving as executive secretary of the Board of Standards and Planning for the Living Theatre in New York since 1956. From 1958 to 1961 he edited the off-Broadway section of the *Best Plays* series, and with the edition for 1961–2 succeeded Louis Kronenberger as over-all editor of the series.

HEYWOOD, JOHN (*c.* 1497–1580), early English dramatist, author of a number of interludes which mark the transition from medieval plays to the comedy of Elizabethan times. He married Elizabeth Rastell, niece of Sir Thomas More, and probably owed much to the influence of More, who took a great interest in plays and playing. His best-known work is *The Playe called the foure P.P.; a newe and a very mery enterlude of a palmer, a pardoner, a potycary, a pedler*, each of whom tries to outdo the others in lying. The palmer wins when he says that in all his travels he never yet knew one woman out of patience. This was acted in about 1520, probably at Court, and was published some twenty years later by Heywood's brother-in-law, William Rastell, as were *The Play of the Wether* and *The Play of Love* (both 1533). *The Dialogue of Wit and Folly*, which probably dates from the same year, remained in manuscript until 1846, when it was issued by the Percy Reprint Society. Two further interludes are sometimes attributed to Heywood, *The Pardoner and the Frere* and *Johan Johan*, which were both published anonymously by Rastell in 1533, while he may be the author of *Thersites*, also attributed to Udall (q.v.).

HEYWOOD, THOMAS (*c.* 1570–1641), English actor and dramatist, who may have been connected with John Heywood (q.v.), though there is no proof of this. He worked mainly for Henslowe (q.v.), his first effort, in collaboration with Chettle and others, being the chronicle play *Edward IV* (1599). His only other historical play was a two-part survey of the early years of Elizabeth I entitled *If You Know Not Me, You Know Nobody* (1604/5). In c. 1600 he produced a somewhat absurd romantic drama, *The Four Prentices of London*, which was satirized by Beaumont (q.v.) in *The Knight of the Burning Pestle* (1607). Of his other plays, which include *The Wise Woman of Hogsdon* (1604), *The Rape of Lucrece* (1607), and *The Fair Maid of the West* (1610), the most important is the domestic tragedy *A Woman Killed With Kindness* (1604), which has been several times revived. Heywood, who was a member of the Admiral's and Queen Anne's Men (qq.v.), retired from the theatre on the death of the Queen in 1619, but returned after some years, producing a number of new plays, among them *The English Traveller* (1625), as well as revivals of his earlier works. He also wrote pageants for the Lord Mayor's Show annually for many years. In spite of his many excellences he undoubtedly contributed to the decadence of later Elizabethan drama, particularly by the almost complete separation between his main and sub-plots and by the weakness of his poetic diction. Among his non-dramatic works the most interesting was an *Apology for Actors*, published in 1612.

Hibernian Roscius, see BROOKE, G. V.

HICKS, SIR (EDWARD) SEYMOUR (1871–1949), English actor-manager and dramatist, knighted in 1935 for services to the stage. He was the author of a number of plays, among them *Bluebell in Fairyland* (1901). *The Gay Gordons* (1907), and *Sleeping Partners* (1917), in which his performance was a *tour de force* of silent acting, and part-author of others, including adaptations from French drama such as *The Man in Dress Clothes* (1922). With Charles Brookfield he produced the first revue seen in London, *Under the Clock* (1893). He published several volumes of reminiscences, and was the first actor to take a party of entertainers to France in the First World War and again in the Second. In the course of his long and varied life he topped the bill in the music-halls and appeared with equal success in musical comedy and straight plays, being particularly admired as Valentine Brown in Barrie's *Quality Street* (1902). He married Ellaline Terriss (q.v.), who appeared with him in many of his own and other authors' plays.

(For HICKS THEATRE, see GLOBE (3).)

HILL, AARON (1685–1750), English playwright, satirized by Pope in the *Dunciad* (1728), who is chiefly remembered for his adaptations of three plays by Voltaire (q.v.) (*Zaïre*, *Alzire*, and *Mérope*) and for his connection with Handel, whose first London opera, 'Rinaldo', with an English libretto by Hill, was produced at the Queen's Theatre (see HER MAJESTY'S) in 1711 during Hill's management there. Of his own plays the most successful was a farce, *The Walking Statue; or, the Devil in the Wine Cellar*, first produced in 1710 and frequently revived up to 1745. His letters and journals contain a good deal of entertaining information about the theatre of his time.

HILL, JENNY (1851–96), an early music-hall performer who first worked in a public-house, where she amused the customers by her songs and dances. She married an acrobat who deserted her, leaving her with a child to support. She went to London and, after heartbreaking delays and poverty, got an audition at the Pavilion, where she was an immediate success. Billed as 'The Vital Spark', she sang and danced and did male impersonations, eventually earning enough to buy a large estate in Streatham, where she gave extravagant parties and where she eventually retired, broken in health, to lead the life of an invalid until her death at the early age of forty-five.

Hippodrome, LONDON, in Cranbourne Street, Westminster. This opened on 15 Jan. 1900 as a circus with a large water-tank which was used for aquatic spectacles. It later became a music-hall and in 1909 was reconstructed internally, the circus arena being covered by stalls. Ballet and variety were seen there, and from 1912 to 1925 Albert de Courville staged a number of successful revues. These were followed by an equally successful series of musical comedies, among them *Sunny* (1926), *Hit the Deck* (1927), *Mr. Cinders* (1929), and *Please, Teacher* (1935). Among later productions were the revue *The Fleet's Lit Up* (1938), Ivor Novello's musical comedy *Perchance to Dream* (1945), and Herman Wouk's play *The Caine Mutiny Court-Martial* (1956). In 1958, after complete reconstruction of the interior, the building opened as a combined restaurant and cabaret, the Talk of the Town, and was no longer used as a theatre.

Hippodrome Theatre, NEW YORK. This theatre, the largest in America, seating 6,600 people, was situated on 6th Avenue between 43rd and 44th Streets. It opened on 12 Apr. 1905 with a lavish spectacle entitled *A Yankee Circus on Mars*, and a year later was taken over by the Shuberts, who were succeeded by Dillingham. Every kind of entertainment was given, including grand opera. In 1923, as B. F. Keith's Hippodrome, it became a vaudeville house, and in 1928, as the R.K.O. Hippodrome, a cinema. Closed in 1932, it reopened in 1933 as the New York Hippodrome, and in 1935 was taken over by Billy Rose, whose spectacular *Jumbo* marked the end of the Hippodrome as a theatre. It was finally demolished in Aug. 1939.

HIRSCHBEIN, PERETZ (1880–1949), Jewish actor and dramatist, and founder of the first Yiddish Art Theatre in Odessa. Although his first play, *Miriam* (pub. 1905), was written in Hebrew, he founded his company in 1908 for the production of plays in Yiddish, in which language he wrote his later works, translating them into Hebrew himself. Among the most important are *The Blacksmith's Daughters* (1915) and *Green Fields* (1919), both idylls of Jewish country life, the latter being considered one of the finest works of Yiddish dramatic literature. It was translated into English by Joseph C. Landis and published in 1966 in *The Dybbuk and Other Great Yiddish Plays*.

HOADLY, BENJAMIN (1706–57), a well-known English physician, son of a bishop, who in 1747 offered Garrick (q.v.) a comedy entitled *The Suspicious Husband*. Though it reads poorly, with Garrick in the part of Ranger—in which he was much admired—it made an unexpected success and was often revived. It was Hoadly's only important contribution to the theatre, though he is believed to have written another comedy, now lost.

Hobby-Horse, a character common in folk festivals throughout Europe, and probably a survival of the primitive worshipper clad in the skin of a sacrificial animal. The portrayer of the hobby-horse rode on a wooden or wicker framework shaped like a horse, usually with a green saddle-cloth. In England he accompanied the Morris dancers and sometimes the Mummers. By

Elizabethan times he was already beginning to be 'forgot', as Shakespeare and Ben Jonson bear witness (for his survival in the company of the Christmas mummers, see MUMMING PLAY). Hobby-horses were also used to represent horsemen, as in the Hocktide Play (q.v.) in Coventry.

HOBSON, HAROLD (1904–), English dramatic critic, who throughout his career, which began in 1931 as dramatic critic to the *Christian Science Monitor*, has championed the cause of the *avant-garde* and experimental theatre. He has also been passionately devoted to the modern French theatre, on which he wrote an interesting work, *The French Theatre of Today* (1953). In recognition of his services to French dramatic literature he was appointed Chevalier of the Legion of Honour in 1960. In 1944 he joined the *Sunday Times* as assistant dramatic critic, becoming chief critic (a position he still holds) in 1947. Among his books are *Theatre* (1948) and *Theatre II* (1950), which contain selections from his published criticisms, *Verdict at Midnight* (1952), a selection of dramatic criticism from 1880 to 1949, and *The Theatre Now* (1953).

HOCHHUTH, ROLF (1931–), German dramatist, whose first play, *Der Stellvertreter*, was a very long documentary denouncing the Pope, Pius XII, for not intervening on behalf of the Jews during the Second World War. In an abridged version, it was first produced by Piscator (q.v.) in Berlin in 1963 and caused international controversy. As *The Representative*, it was seen in London in 1963, and as *The Deputy*, in New York a year later. In his next play, *Soldaten: Nekrolog auf Genf*, which again had to be heavily cut before its first production in Berlin by Utzerath, Piscator's successor, in 1967, Hochhuth attacked Churchill, accusing him of instigating the bombing of Dresden and other civilian targets and of being implicated in the death of the Polish general Sikorski, who was killed while flying in an R.A.F. plane. In spite of favourable representations by their literary adviser, Kenneth Tynan (q.v.), and others, the governors of the National Theatre in London refused to allow the play to be put on at the Old Vic, and as *Soldiers* it had its first production in English in Toronto in Feb. 1968, with the Canadian actor John Colicos as Churchill. It was then seen briefly on Broadway, and opened at the New Theatre, London, in December of that year, where it ran for about four months. Its production in England was only made possible by the ending of the censorship. In 1970 a new play by Hochhuth, *Guerillas*, set in modern America, was produced in Germany.

Hocktide Play, a ritual game originally played in Coventry on Hock Tuesday (the third Tuesday after Easter Sunday) and revived as a pleasant antiquity during the Kenilworth Revels prepared for the visit of Queen Elizabeth I in July 1575. It began with a Captain Cox leading in a band of English knights (on hobbyhorses) to fight against the Danes and ended with the leading away of the Danish prisoners by the English women. It was intended to represent the massacre of the Danes by Ethelred in 1002, but this is probably a late literary assimilation of an earlier folk-festival custom, traceable in other places (Worcester, Shrewsbury, Hungerford), by which the women 'hocked' or caught the men and exacted a forfeit from them on one day, the men's turn coming the following day. The practice was forbidden at Worcester in 1450. This ceremony may in its turn be a survival of the symbolic capture of a victim for human sacrifice.

HOCHWÄLDER, FRITZ (1911–), modern dramatist, born in Vienna, but resident since 1938 in Switzerland, where he had his first success in the theatre with *Das heilige Experiment* (1943). In a translation by Eva Le Gallienne (q.v.) as *The Strong are Lonely*, this was seen in New York in 1953 and in London in 1956. It deals with the destruction of the Jesuits in Paraguay in the eighteenth century, and displays considerable theatrical skill in making a dramatic situation out of a moral issue. Although Hochwälder has not written any conventional historical plays, he again used an historical setting to reinforce his arguments in *Der öffentliche Ankläger* (1947), seen in London in 1957 as *The Public Prosecutor*, with Alan Badel (q.v.) as Fouquier-Tinville, and in *Donadieu* (1953). All his plays, which include also *Der Flüchtling* (1945), *Die Herberge* (1956), and *Der Unschuldige* (1958), are concerned with a conflict of ideas emphasized, not by the use of modern stage techniques but rather by a strict adherence to the classical unities.

HODGE, WILLIAM THOMAS (1874–1932), American actor and playwright, who after some years on tour appeared in New York in 1898 and had his first success in a revival of Herne's *Sag Harbor* in 1900. In 1908 he made a great success as the Indiana lawyer, Pike, in Booth Tarkington's *The Man from Home* and based all his future parts on this character, incorporating it into pleasant homely tales of American life in which he figured as the slow but shrewd countryman. Though these proved too unsophisticated for Broadway they found faithful audiences elsewhere, and Hodge continued to appear in them on tour until his retirement in 1931.

HODGKINSON [really MEADOWCROFT], JOHN (1767–1805), an English actor who had had some experience in the English provinces when in 1792 he accepted an offer from John Henry to join the American Company (q.v.), and spent the rest of his life in America. He soon became extremely popular, ousting Henry from management as well as from public favour, and becoming joint manager with Hallam and Dunlap of the Park Theatre (q.v.) when it first opened. A handsome man, with a good memory and a fine stage presence, Hodgkinson excelled both in tragedy and comedy. Among his best parts were André in Dunlap's tragedy of that name and Rolla in an adaptation of Kotzebue's *Pizarro*, also made by Dunlap (q.v.). His early death from yellow fever was a great loss to the American stage.

HODSON, HENRIETTA (1841–1910), English actress, who made her first appearances on the stage in the same provincial companies as the young Henry Irving (q.v.). Later she was in Bath and Bristol, where she appeared with Madge Robertson, later Mrs. Kendal (q.v.), and Kate and Ellen Terry (qq.v.). She retired from the stage on marriage but, being soon widowed, returned and in 1866 was seen in London in extravaganza. She then went to the Queen's Theatre (q.v.) and in 1868 married Henry Labouchère, one of the proprietors. She continued to act under her maiden name and later became manageress of the Royalty Theatre (q.v.). An actress of highly individual style and technical accomplishment, she was at her best in demure humour or the farcical characters of burlesque, pathos and deep sentiment lying outside her range. She retired in 1878 and three years later was instrumental in introducing Mrs. Langtry (q.v.) to the stage.

HOFMANNSTHAL, HUGO VON (1874–1929), Austrian poet and playwright, who as a young man was in the forefront of the reaction against naturalism. The verse plays of this period, such as *Gestern* (1891); *Der Tod des Tizian* (1892); *Der Tor und der Tod* (1893); *Das kleine Welttheater*, *Der weisse Fächer*, and *Der Kaiser und die Hexe* (all 1897); and *Das Bergwerk zu Falun* (1899), reveal Hofmannsthal's delight in beauty and in poetic and mystical intuitions but also show him to be a critic of aestheticism from the inside. His exquisite poetry is diluted in the later plays by his efforts to enhance the dramatic content of his dialogue, and at the turn of the century he began to experiment with subjects which were more obviously theatrical. Plays like *Der Abenteurer und die Sängerin* (1898), *Die Hochzeit der Sobeïde* (1899), *Elektra* (1903), *Das gerettete Venedig* (1904) (based on Otway's *Venice Preserv'd*), and *Ödipus und die Sphinx* (1905) indicate a wide range of interests from pagan mysteries and Dionysian experience to moral themes of love and loyalty. Hofmannsthal's plays have not yet been seen in England, where he is best known as the librettist of Richard Strauss. Their collaboration began in 1909 with 'Elektra', followed by 'Ariadne auf Naxos' (1912), 'Die Frau ohne Schatten' (1919), and 'Die ägyptische Helena' (1928), in which Hofmannsthal used subjects from myth and fairytale. The earlier 'Der Rosenkavalier' (1911), and 'Arabella' (1933), Hofmannsthal's last collaboration with Strauss, were closer to his earlier comedies. His affection for Austrian comedy, particularly that of Raimund and Nestroy (qq.v.), and his love of Molière and Calderón (qq.v.) led to translations and adaptations, some of which, for example his rewriting of Molière's *Les Fâcheux* as *Die Lästigen* (1915), can be regarded as completely new plays. Among his other comedies—*Cristinas Heimreise* (1909), *Der Schwierige* (1918), and *Der Unbestechliche* (1922)—*Der Schwierige* stands out as a masterpiece, combining high comedy of subtle human relationships with irony and social satire. *Jedermann* (1911), a rehandling of the old play of *Everyman* incorporating some elements from Hans Sachs (q.v.), was written for the Salzburg Festival which

Hofmannsthal founded in partnership with Max Reinhardt (q.v.), and was produced annually in front of the cathedral there. It was also for this festival that *Das Salzburger grosse Welttheater* (1922) was written, based on Calderón's *El gran teatro del mundo*. It prepared the way for Hofmannsthal's last drama, *Der Turm* (1925), based on Calderón's *La vida es sueño*. Its setting is seventeenth-century Poland but the complex realistic and symbolic action is legendary rather than historical. Here Hofmannsthal took up the theme of the conflict between material power and spiritual integrity, ending the first version of 1925 with a Utopian picture of a new and purified world; but a revised version of 1927 closes in tragedy, showing the spirit as indestructible but powerless and isolated in a tyrannical world.

HOLBERG, LUDVIG (1684–1754), historian, philosopher, and man of letters, who, though born in Norway, spent most of his working life in Denmark, being for many years Professor of Metaphysics at Copenhagen University. As a young man he travelled widely throughout Europe and when in 1721 he was appointed director of the Danish Theatre in Copenhagen he brought to his task a knowledge of and love for the drama unusual in Denmark at that time, his favourite playwrights being Plautus and Molière (qq.v.). There were, in fact, no contemporary Danish plays, the company at the theatre playing only in French and German. To remedy this, during the six years of his directorship Holberg wrote and produced a number of plays in Danish, bringing on to the stage Danish and Norwegian characters and situations not seen there before and creating in the vernacular a tradition of comedy which was upheld by his successors. His first production, a translation of Molière's *L'Avare* produced on 23 Sept. 1722, was followed a week later by his first original play, *Den politske Kandestøber*. He wrote in all thirty-three plays, all popular in their day and many of them known in translation in Germany, Holland, and France. He has not made much impact in England, but in 1957 one of his best plays, *Jeppe paa Bjerget, eller den forvandlede Bonde*, under its sub-title of *The Transformed Peasant*, was published in an English translation by Reginald Spink, together with two one-act plays, *The Arabian Powder* (*Det arabiske Pulver*,

1724), and *The Healing Spring* (*Kilderejsen*, 1725), preceded by an admirable introduction; under the title of *Jeppe of the Mountains*, in a translation by Michael Meyer, this play was seen at the Pitlochry Festival Theatre in 1966.

Holborn Empire, LONDON, in High Holborn. This opened as Weston's Music-Hall on 16 Nov. 1857 and had a consistently successful career, being rebuilt in 1887 and renamed the Royal Music-Hall, its chairman then being W. B. Fair (q.v.), singer of the popular 'Tommy, Make Room for Your Uncle'. Many famous stars appeared there, but round about 1900 its popularity began to decline and it closed in June 1905. Completely rebuilt, it opened on 29 Jan. 1906 as the Holborn Empire and then had a successful career. It was occasionally used as a theatre. In 1920 Sybil Thorndike (q.v.) appeared there as Hecuba in Euripides' *Trojan Women*, in the title-role of his *Medea*, and as Candida in Shaw's play of that name. From 1922 to 1938 the children's play, *Where the Rainbow Ends*, was revived annually at Christmas. On the night of 11–12 May 1941 the building was badly damaged by bombs and remained derelict until it was demolished in 1961.

Holborn Theatre, LONDON, (1) in High Holborn. Built by Sefton Parry, this theatre opened on 6 Oct. 1866 with Boucicault's *The Flying Scud*, which was a success. Subsequent productions and several managements failed and in 1875 Horace Wigan assumed control, reopening the theatre on 24 Apr. as the Mirror. In October of the same year John Clayton scored a success with a long run of *All For Her*, the first dramatization of Dickens's *A Tale of Two Cities*. On 8 Jan. 1876 the theatre, renamed the Duke's by its new manager, F. C. Burnand, reopened with his burlesque of Jerrold's *Black-Eyed Susan*, transferred from the Opera Comique. After a further undistinguished period a modern drama by Paul Merritt, *The New Babylon* (1879), proved acceptable, and had just returned to the theatre after a provincial tour when the building was destroyed by fire on 4 June 1880.

(2) In 1884 another theatre in High Holborn, which opened on 25 May 1867 as the New Royal Amphitheatre and subsequently was known by many names, was renamed the Holborn. It had an undistinguished career and closed as a theatre

in about 1887, later becoming the Holborn Stadium.

HOLCROFT, THOMAS (1744–1809), English dramatist, who is usually credited with the introduction of melodrama (q.v.) on the London stage with his *A Tale of Mystery* (1802), an adaptation of *Coelina, ou l'Enfant de mystère* (1800), by Pixérécourt (q.v.), which was several times revived. His best-known play, however, is *The Road to Ruin* (1792), with its excellent roles of Goldfinch and Old Dornton, the latter a favourite part with many elderly character actors both in London and in America, where the play was frequently revived. It was last seen in London in 1937. Holcroft, who was entirely self-educated, was a very good French scholar and had a phenomenal memory, a combination which enabled him while in Paris to learn by heart Beaumarchais's *Le Mariage de Figaro*, and to put it on the London stage in 1784 as *The Follies of a Day*. He also translated Destouches's *Les Glorieux* (1732) as *The School for Arrogance* (1791). Among his other comedies the most successful was *Love's Frailties* (1794), based on a German original, *Der deutsche Hausvater*, by Gemminger. Holcroft, who was a friend of Charles Lamb (q.v.), was editor of the *Theatrical Recorder*, which appeared monthly from 1805 to 1806 and contained plays translated from the French and Spanish. His *Memoirs*, edited by Hazlitt, were published posthumously in 1816.

Holiday Theatre, NEW YORK, see CENTRAL THEATRE.

HOLLAND, GEORGE (1791–1870), an English actor, who after appearing on the London stage went to the United States and founded a family of American actors. He made his first appearance in New York in 1827, travelled extensively, and was well known in the South, where he was for some years in management with Ludlow and Sol Smith (qq.v.). He also spent six years at Mitchell's famous Olympic (q.v.) in burlesque. From 1855 to 1867 he played character parts in Wallack's company, being outstanding as Tony Lumpkin in Goldsmith's *She Stoops to Conquer*, which he was still playing at the age of seventy-five. It was in connection with his funeral that the famous New York 'Little Church Around the Corner' first received its name, since Jefferson (q.v.) was directed to it under that name by a clergyman who refused to bury an actor in his own church-yard. Two of Holland's sons, EDMUND MILTON (1848–1913) and JOSEPH JEFFERSON (1860–1926), were on the stage, the former appearing with Jefferson in the first New York production of *Rip Van Winkle*. As E. Milton he acted at Wallack's for thirteen years and had just joined Belasco's company when he died. His brother, named after his famous godfather, was in Daly's company from 1886 to 1889 and toured with many famous actors. A versatile light comedian, he became paralysed in 1904 but remained in close touch with the stage, being responsible for the direction of several amateur societies.

HOLLINGSHEAD, JOHN (1827–1904), English theatre manager, whose name is chiefly associated with the Gaiety Theatre (q.v.). He opened it on 21 Dec. 1868 and remained there for eighteen years, being succeeded by George Edwardes (q.v.), who was to make it the home of musical comedy. Under Hollingshead it had been used mainly for burlesque. Hollingshead is credited with the introduction of matinées and with being the first manager to use electric light outside the theatre (in 1886). In 1880 he staged a translation by William Archer (q.v.) of *Samfundets Støtter* as *Quicksands; or, the Pillars of Society*, the first play by Ibsen to be seen in London.

Hollywood Theatre, NEW YORK, see MARK HELLINGER THEATRE.

HOLT, HELEN (1863–1937), see TREE, SIR HERBERT.

HOLZ, ARNO (1863–1929), German novelist and dramatist, whose *Die Familie Selicke* (1890), written in collaboration with Johannes Schlaf, became the manifesto of the new school of naturalistic drama. Produced by the recently founded Freie Bühne (q.v.), this dreary catalogue of misery, rape, disease, and death, set against a sordidly realistic background and devoid of all theatrical tricks, proved a rallying point for the younger dramatists, among them Gerhart Hauptmann (q.v.). Holz wrote a number of other plays but, lacking the collaboration of Schlaf, without success.

HOME, THE REV. JOHN (1722–1808), a Scottish minister, author of the tragedy *Douglas*, first seen in Edinburgh in 1756 with Dudley West Digges (q.v.) as Young Norval. It caused much controversy, many members of the Church of Scotland being against the theatre and horrified that one of their clergy should write for it, but it was a triumph with the audience, a voice from the pit crying out on the first night: 'Whaur's yer Wully Shakespeare noo?' In 1757 it was seen at Covent Garden with Spranger Barry (q.v.) playing Young Norval to the Lady Randolph of Peg Woffington (q.v.). The play was constantly revived, Lady Randolph being a favourite part with Sarah Siddons (q.v.), while many young actors in England and America, including Master Betty and Howard Payne (qq.v.), delighted in Young Norval. It is in the repertory of the Toy Theatre (q.v.) and can still be performed on a Toy Theatre stage. It was revived at the Edinburgh Festival in 1950 with Sybil Thorndike (q.v.) as Lady Randolph and her son-in-law Douglas Campbell as Young Norval. Its author wrote other tragedies, but they were not successful, and *Douglas* remains his one claim to fame.

HOME, WILLIAM DOUGLAS (1912–), English dramatist, who was for a time on the stage, making his first appearance in London in 1937 in Dodie Smith's *Bonnet Over the Windmill*. After the Second World War, in which he took part from 1940 to 1944, he devoted his energies to playwriting and acted only occasionally in his own plays. He first achieved success with two political comedies, *The Chiltern Hundreds* (1947) and its sequel *The Manor of Northstead* (1954), in both of which A. E. Matthews (q.v.) appeared in the leading roles, and with a social comedy, *The Reluctant Debutante* (1955). Among his other plays are *Now Barabbas . . .* (1947), *Ambassador Extraordinary* (1948), *The Bad Samaritan* (1953), *Aunt Edwina* (1959), and *A Friend Indeed* (1966). None of these was as well received as his earlier plays, but he was again successful with *The Secretary Bird* (1968), starring Kenneth More as the husband who keeps his wife by apparently agreeing to let her go with her lover, and with *The Jockey Club Stakes* (1970), a comedy about racing, starring Alastair Sim.

Hope Theatre, LONDON. This began as the Bear Garden for bull- and bear-baiting, and in about 1613 was adapted by Henslowe (q.v.) to house plays as well. In shape and size it resembled the Swan (q.v.), but the stage could be removed for the baitings and there were stables for six bulls and three horses. Henslowe and his leading actor, Alleyn (q.v.), probably hoped to capture the audience of the Globe (q.v.), which had just been burnt down, and engaged the Lady Elizabeth's Men headed by Nathan Field (q.v.), who spent the season of 1614–15 at the Hope, as it was now called. One of the new plays in which they appeared was Jonson's *Bartholomew Fair* (1614). Henslowe died in Jan. 1616 and a new agreement was made between Edward Alleyn and the actors, now known as Prince Charles's Men. But constant quarrels and litigation went on for a couple of years, during which time the Globe was rebuilt. The Hope reverted entirely to baiting and was dismantled in 1656, though the building was apparently still standing in 1682–3.

Hopkins Theatre, NEW YORK, see PUNCH AND JUDY THEATRE.

HOPPER, DE WOLF [really WILLIAM DE WOLF HOPPER] (1858–1935), an American actor who played in light opera for some years, establishing a reputation as an eccentric comedian with a fine bass voice. In 1891 he directed and appeared in a musical comedy, being responsible five years later for Sousa's *El Capitán*, in which he also appeared in London in 1899. He then returned to light opera and was excellent in Gilbert and Sullivan, where his clear diction proved invaluable in such parts as the Lord Chancellor in *Iolanthe*, with its 'Nightmare' patter song. His favourite part, however, was Jack Point in *The Yeomen of the Guard*. From 1918 onwards, the vogue for light opera having waned, he mainly toured in revivals. In 1927 he published his memoirs, *Once a Clown, Always a Clown*.

HORNIMAN, ANNIE ELIZABETH FREDERICKA (1860–1937), theatre manager and patron, one of the seminal influences in the Irish and English theatres at the beginning of the twentieth century. Realizing from travels abroad the important part played in the cultural life of various countries, particularly Germany, by a subsidized repertory theatre, she made funds available in 1894 for a season at the Avenue Theatre (see PLAYHOUSE) which included *Arms and the Man*, the first play by Shaw (q.v.) to be seen publicly, and *The Land of Heart's Desire*, by Yeats (q.v.). This not only marked the beginning of what may be called the 'modern theatre' movement of

the time but also aroused Miss Horniman's interest in the new Irish Theatre Movement, and led her to build the Abbey Theatre (q.v.) in Dublin. She also bought and refurbished the Gaiety Theatre, Manchester, where from 1908 to 1917 she maintained an excellent repertory company and put on more than two hundred plays, old and new, among them the works of the so-called Manchester School (see MANCHESTER) and *Jane Clegg* (1913), an early play by St. John Ervine (q.v.). They were mainly directed by Lewis Casson, who married a member of the company, Sybil Thorndike (q.v.), thus inaugurating one of the most famous stage partnerships of the English theatre. By its example the Gaiety venture assisted the establishment of repertory theatres in other English provincial towns, though it was not itself a success financially. In 1917 the company was disbanded and in 1921 the building which had housed it became a cinema. But Miss Horniman lived long enough to see her pioneer work bear fruit (see REPERTORY THEATRE MOVEMENT) and players who had served their apprenticeship under her at the head of their profession in London. On her death she left her extensive library of plays to the British Drama League (q.v.).

Hôtel d'Argent, THÉÂTRE DE L', PARIS. In 1598 an actor-manager from the French provinces, Pierre Venier, brought a company to the Foire Saint-Germain and then took it to an improvised theatre in the Hôtel d'Argent in the rue de la Verrerie. He was allowed to remain there for a short time on payment of a tax to the Confrérie de la Passion (q.v.), which at that time held the monopoly of acting in Paris. This theatre must have remained in use intermittently for many years, for in 1607 Venier was there again with his daughter Marie Venier (q.v.) and her husband, who had temporarily left the company at the Hôtel de Bourgogne (q.v.), to which they both belonged. The assassination of Henri IV in 1610 caused both troupes to leave Paris, and on their return they all went together to the Hôtel de Bourgogne, while a new troupe under Montdory (q.v.) leased the Hôtel d'Argent.

Hôtel de Bourgogne, THÉÂTRE DE L', the first and most important theatre of Paris and one of the components of the later Comédie-Française (q.v.). It was built by the Confrérie de la Passion (q.v.) in the ruins of the palace of the Dukes of Burgundy, and was ready for occupation in 1548; but in the same year the company was forbidden to act religious plays. Deprived of the greater part of their repertory, they did what they could with farces and secular romances but gradually lost their audiences and were glad to hire out the hall to travelling companies from the French provinces. The first more or less permanent company to occupy the theatre was that of the provincial actor-manager Valleran-Lecomte (q.v.), usually known as the King's Players. The hall was sometimes let to rival French or visiting Italian companies, but the King's Players gradually asserted their pre-eminence until in 1634 Montdory (q.v.) established a rival theatre in the Marais (q.v.). His early retirement again left the Hôtel de Bourgogne, under Floridor and Mont-fleury (qq.v.), in an unchallenged position until the arrival of Molière (q.v.) in 1658. Many of the outstanding plays of the seventeenth century, with the exception of Corneille's Le Cid, were first seen at the Hôtel de Bourgogne, until in 1680 the company was finally merged with other actors to form the Comédie-Française, which moved to a theatre in the rue Guénégaud, while the stage of the Hôtel de Bourgogne was occupied intermittently by the Italian actors until 1783 (see COMÉDIE-ITALIENNE).

HOUDAR DE LA MOTTE, ANTOINE (1672–1731), French dramatist, who almost gave up writing for the theatre after the failure of his first play, Les Originaux (1693), but returned to write opera libretti and lyrics for ballets, some of them the best since Quinault (q.v.). His verses, though lacking in vigour, are graceful and charming. His one important dramatic work is a tragedy, Inès de Castro, which was performed with great success at the Comédie-Française in 1723, but his comedies, which include La Matrone d'Éphèse (1702), were well enough known to be parodied at the unlicensed theatres of the Parisian fairs.

HOUGHTON, (WILLIAM) STANLEY (1881–1913), English playwright, and the best of the so-called Manchester School (see MANCHESTER). His plays, which deal with the revolt against parental authority and the struggle between the generations, were first seen at the Gaiety, Manchester, except for Hindle Wakes, usually considered his masterpiece, which was produced at the

Aldwych, London, in 1912. In it Fanny Hawthorn, a working girl, refuses to marry the cowardly, vacillating, rich man's son who has seduced her, a reversal of things which took contemporary play-goers by surprise. Like Houghton's other plays, particularly The Dear Departed (1908) and The Younger Generation (1910), it has proved popular with amateur and repertory companies.

House Curtain, see CURTAIN.

House of Ostrovsky, see MALY THEATRE, MOSCOW.

HOUSEMAN, JOHN (1902–), see WELLES, ORSON.

HOUSMAN, LAURENCE (1865–1959), English author and playwright, whose first play, Bethlehem, was directed by Gordon Craig (q.v.) in 1902. Two years later, with Granville-Barker, he wrote Prunella, a delicate fantasy with music by Joseph Moorat which was first seen at the Royal Court and several times revived. His one-act plays on Queen Victoria were banned by the censor, and a selection of them, as Victoria Regina, was seen privately at the Gate Theatre in 1935 with Pamela Stanley in the title-role. It was not until Edward VIII intervened in 1936 that they were licensed for public performance, and a year later they were seen at the Lyric, again with Pamela Stanley as the Queen. Further one-act plays in a series entitled Little Plays of St. Francis have often been performed by amateurs, though never professionally. In 1937 Housman published a volume of reminiscences, The Unexpected Years.

HOWARD, BRONSON (1842–1908), American playwright, important in the development of the theatre in the United States, since he was one of the first to make use of native material with any skill and assiduity, and also the first to make his living solely by playwriting, since his predecessors, like Bird and Boker (qq.v.), had other sources of income. Success came to him in 1870 with Saratoga, a farcical comedy produced by Daly. As Brighton (1874), it was adapted for the London stage, Wyndham (q.v.) playing the hero, Bob Sackett. Howard wrote several other comedies, including The Banker's Daughter (1878), which had previously been seen in 1871 as Lilian's Last Love and, as The Old Love and the New, was successful in London in 1879. But his most important play was probably Young Mrs. Winthrop

(1882), which marks a great advance in his development as well as in that of the American stage, and was the first of Howard's plays to be produced in London (in 1884) without alteration or adaptation. The most successful of his later plays were *The Henrietta* (1887), a satire on financial life, and *Shenandoah* (1888), a drama of the War between the States. Howard worked hard to improve the lot of the American playwright and in 1891 founded the American Dramatists' Club, now the Dramatists' Guild, Inc.

HOWARD, SIDNEY COE (1891–1939), American playwright, who studied under G. P. Baker (q.v.) at Harvard, and had adapted several plays, including Vildrac's *S.S. Tenacity* (1922) and an episode from *Don Quixote* entitled *Sancho Panza* (1923), before his *They Knew What They Wanted* (1924), set in the California grape-growers' country, brought him the Pulitzer Prize and a great popular success, which was repeated with *The Silver Cord* (1926), a study of maternal possessiveness. Among his later plays *Alien Corn* (1933), a study of small-town life, owed much of its success to the acting of Katharine Cornell (q.v.) as Elsa Brandt. It was followed by two adaptations, *The Late Christopher Bean* (1932), based on Fauchois's *Prenez garde à la peinture*, and *Dodsworth* (1934), based on Sinclair Lewis's novel of that name. *Yellow Jack* (also 1934) was a very successful dramatization of the fight against yellow fever, and *The Ghost of Yankee Doodle* (1937) showed how, in all classes of society, economic considerations override the normal aversion to war. Howard had just finished the first draft of *Madam, Will You Walk?* when he was killed in an accident. It was produced on tour, and again in New York in 1953, but lacking revision by the author, was not a success.

Howard Athenaeum, see BOSTON.

HOYT, CHARLES HALE (1860–1900), American dramatist, whose numerous and forgotten plays were mainly farcical comedies depicting characters of the cities and small towns of the day. They have little literary quality and their wit evaporates in print, but in their day they gave pleasure to thousands, and were an important part of New York's entertainment in the last twenty years of the nineteenth century. Among the most popular were *The Texas Steer; or, Money Makes*

the Mare Go (1890), first given in 1882 as *A Case of Wine*; *A Trip to Chinatown* (1891), whose long run set up a record for the day; and *A Day and a Night in New York* (1898).

HROSWITHA (also HROTSVITHA and ROSWITHA), a Benedictine abbess of Gandersheim in Saxony, who in the tenth century wrote six plays modelled on Terence (q.v.), at that time much esteemed as a scholastic author, but dealing with subjects drawn from Christian history and morality—*Paphnutius, Dulcitius, Gallicanus, Callimachus, Abraham,* and *Sapientia.* They were intended for reading rather than production, but the use of miracles and abstract characters links them with the later Mystery and Morality Plays (qq.v.). The Latin is poor but the dialogue is vivacious and elements of farce are not lacking. The plays were published in 1923 in an English translation by H. J. W. Tillyard, and *Paphnutius,* which deals with the conversion of Thaïs, was produced in London in 1914 by Edith Craig (q.v.) in a translation by Christopher St. John.

HUBERT, ANDRÉ (*c.* 1634–1700), French actor, who left the Théâtre du Marais in 1664 to join the company run by Molière (q.v.). In the tradition of the time, he played old women, and created the part of Mme Jourdain in *Le Bourgeois gentilhomme* (1671). In Molière's last play, *Le Malade imaginaire* (1673), he played M. Diafoirus. He was a dependable though not outstanding actor, and after Molière's death became responsible with La Grange (q.v.) for the finance and administration of the company, retiring in 1685. His wife also worked in the theatre in a minor capacity backstage.

Hudson Theatre, NEW YORK, on West 44th Street. This handsome and elegant playhouse opened on 19 Oct. 1903 with Ethel Barrymore (q.v.) in H. H. Davies's *Cousin Kate.* Among its early successes were the first production in New York of Shaw's *Man and Superman* (1905), omitting Act III, 'Don Juan in Hell', the world première of Henry Arthur Jones's *The Hypocrites* (1906), and Somerset Maugham's *Lady Frederick* (1908). In 1910 Belasco (q.v.) filled the house with *Nobody's Widow.* Later productions included the sharply contrasted *Pollyanna* (1916), from Eleanor Porter's children's book, and Maugham's *Our Betters* (1917).

In 1919 Booth Tarkington's delightful comedy, *Clarence*, scored a success with Helen Hayes and Alfred Lunt (qq.v.) in the cast. The first performance in New York of O'Casey's *The Plough and the Stars* was seen in 1927; Cedric Hardwicke (q.v.) made a success in Barré Lyndon's *The Amazing Dr. Clitterhouse* (1937); and Ethel Barrymore returned in a dramatization of Mazo de la Roche's *Whiteoaks* (1938). In 1940 there was a revival of Congreve's *Love for Love*, and in 1945 came the Pulitzer Prize-winner, *The State of the Union*, by Howard Lindsay and Russel Crouse. In 1949 the theatre became a broadcasting studio, but reverted to live theatre and in 1960 housed Lillian Hellman's *Toys in the Attic*. In 1963 the Actors' Studio Theatre presented their initial production, a revival of O'Neill's *Strange Interlude*. In 1967 a musical, *How To Be a Jewish Mother*, had a successful run, after which the theatre became a cinema.

HUGO, VICTOR-MARIE (1802–85), one of France's greatest poets, and the leader of the French Romantic movement. He was also a dramatist, whose plays mark the entry of melodrama into the serious theatre. All alike suffer from overwhelming rhetoric, too much erudition, and not enough emotion. Yet by their vigour and their disregard of outworn conventions they operated a revolution in French theatre history. The best of them is *Ruy Blas* (1838), which has two excellent acts, the second and the fourth, and a superb ending. When played with sincerity and force, allied with impeccable technique, it still retains the power to move an audience by the passion of its lyric poetry. Yet it remains unconvincing, since Ruy Blas kills himself because he is 'only a lackey', yet has nothing of the lackey in his composition, which is that of the normal well-born romantic hero. Of Hugo's other plays, *Cromwell* (published in 1827) was not intended for the stage and would take six hours to act. It was a battle-cry, and its preface became the manifesto of the new Romantic movement. *Marion Delorme* was forbidden by the censor on political grounds and not acted until 1831, a year after *Hernani*, whose first night led to a riot at the Comédie-Française. *Lucrèce Borgia, Marie Tudor* (both 1833), and *Angelo, Tyran de Padoue* (1835), are prose melodramas, of which the second was revived with Maria Casarès as Mary in 1954 at the Théâtre

National Populaire. *Le Roi s'amuse* (1832), forbidden by the censor after one performance, was used for the libretto of Verdi's opera 'Rigoletto' (1851). The Romantic theatre carried in itself the germ of its decay and its vogue was bound to be short-lived. The failure of Hugo's last play, *Les Burgraves*, in 1843 showed that the tide had turned in favour of prose and common sense, and he withdrew from the stage.

HUNEKER, JAMES GIBBONS (1860–1921), American dramatic critic, who in 1890 became music and drama critic of the *Morning Advertiser* and the *New York Recorder*. In 1902 he joined the staff of the *Sun* and in 1912 left it for *The New York Times*. He battled in print with William Winter (q.v.) over Ibsen and Shaw, edited a two-volume edition of Shaw's dramatic criticisms from the *Saturday Review*, and through his contacts with Europe introduced and explained foreign dramatic literature to his compatriots, particularly in his studies of Becque, Hauptmann, D'Annunzio (qq.v.) and others. He collected his dramatic criticisms into several volumes, and in 1920 published an autobiography, *Steeplejack*.

Hungerford Music-Hall, LONDON, see GATE THEATRE and PLAYERS' THEATRE.

HUNT, HUGH SYDNEY (1911–), English theatre director, who in 1961 became the first Professor of Drama at Manchester University. He had already had some varied experience in play-production when in 1935 he became director of the Abbey Theatre (q.v.), where his first play, *The Invincibles*, written in collaboration with Frank O'Connor, was produced in 1938 and revived thirty years later. He is also part-author of *Moses' Rock* (1938) and *In the Train* (1958). After serving throughout the Second World War, he returned to the theatre in 1945 to become the first director of the Bristol Old Vic (see BRISTOL), where he remained until 1948, leaving to go to the Old Vic in London. In 1955 he was again involved in pioneer work in the theatre when he was appointed Director of the Elizabethan Theatre Trust (q.v.) in Australia, where he remained for five years. He then went to Manchester, and in 1969 was again appointed Artistic Director of the Abbey Theatre, a position he holds in addition to his Manchester professorship. He is the author of several books on the theatre, including *The Director in the Theatre* and *Old Vic Prefaces*: *Shakespeare and the Producer* (both 1954), *The Making of Australian Theatre* (1960), and *The Live Theatre* (1962).

HUNT, (JAMES HENRY) LEIGH (1784–1859), English poet, essayist, and critic, and one of the pioneers of modern dramatic criticism. He probably had a keener appreciation of acting than any of his contemporaries, and today his criticisms re-create the art of the great players who brought distinction to the theatre of his day. He was also the first regular critic of quality who made it his business to report upon all the principal theatrical events of his time. He was critic of the *News* from 1805 to 1807 and of his own paper, the *Examiner*, from 1808 to 1821. His play, *A Legend of Florence*, was produced at Covent Garden Theatre in 1840. In the same year he edited the dramatic works of Sheridan, and those of Wycherley, Congreve, Vanbrugh, and Farquhar, with biographical notes which inspired Macaulay to publish in *The Edinburgh Review* his famous essay on 'The Comic Dramatists of the Restoration'. The best of Leigh Hunt's theatre criticism is contained in *Dramatic Essays* (1894), which has a valuable introduction by its editor, William Archer.

HUNT, MARTITA (1900–69), English actress, who first came into prominence as the eccentric German governess in Komisarjevsky's production of Chekhov's *The Cherry Orchard* in London in 1926. Three years later she played leading Shakespearian roles at the Old Vic with Gielgud (q.v.), being more successful in such parts as Lady Macbeth and Gertrude (in *Hamlet*) than in the lighter roles of Helena (in *A Midsummer Night's Dream*) and Rosalind (in *As You Like It*). Among her later roles were the Princess in Richard Pryce's *Frolic Wind* (1935) and Miss Havisham in Dickens's *Great Expectations* (1939). Her greatest success, however, was scored in New York as Countess Aurelia in

Giraudoux's *The Madwoman of Chaillot* (1948), which unfortunately failed to repeat its success in London. She made her last appearance in *Hotel Paradiso* (1956), an adaptation by Peter Glenville of Feydeau's *L'Hôtel du Libre Échange* (1899).

HUNTER, NORMAN CHARLES (1908–71), English dramatist, who in 1951 achieved an outstanding success with *Waters of the Moon* at the Haymarket, starring Sybil Thorndike and Edith Evans (qq.v.). He had previously written a number of light comedies, of which *All Rights Reserved* (1935) and *A Party for Christmas* (1938) were seen in the West End, and in 1953 he again had a long run at the Haymarket with *A Day by the Sea*, starring Sybil Thorndike, John Gielgud, and Ralph Richardson (qq.v.). In his next play, *A Touch of the Sun* (1958), Michael Redgrave and his daughter Vanessa (qq.v.) appeared together for the first time. Of Hunter's later plays, the only one to have been seen in London is *The Tulip Tree* (1962). In 1970 a new play, *One Fair Daughter*, opened at the Perth Theatre.

HURRY, LESLIE (1909–78), English stage designer, much of whose best work was done for ballet and opera. But he was also responsible for the décor of many of Shakespeare's plays at the Old Vic and the Royal Shakespeare Theatre in Stratford-upon-Avon, and also for productions of Marlowe's *Tamburlaine the Great* (1951), Graham Greene's *The Living Room* and Otway's *Venice Preserv'd* (both 1953), Tennessee Williams's *Cat on a Hot Tin Roof* (1958), and Webster's *The Duchess of Malfi* (1960). His work is characterized by a sombre magnificence which imparts a brooding air of tragedy to his settings, shot through with sudden gleams of gold and red. He was at his best in plays which called for the conjuring-up of mystery and a sense of space, together with poetic imagery.

HYDE, DOUGLAS (1860–1949), see GAELIC DRAMA.

I

I.A.S.T.A., see INSTITUTE FOR ADVANCED STUDIES IN THE THEATRE ARTS.

IBSEN, HENRIK JOHAN (1828–1906), Norwegian dramatist, and the most important theatrical figure of his generation, whose plays completely changed the main current of European dramatic literature. At one time regarded purely as a depicter of small-town provincial life, he is now recognized as a universal genius who infused even his prose works with a profoundly passionate and tragic poetic spirit. His early years were unhappy, his first plays, *Catilina* (1850) and *Fru Inger til Østraat* (*Lady Inger of Østraat*) (1854), unsuccessful. *Gildet paa Solhaug* (*The Feast at Solhaug*) (1855) was the first to achieve recognition; *Hærmændene paa Helgeland* (*The Warriors*—or *Vikings*—*at Helgeland*) (1857), set in the heroic age of the sagas, shows what remarkable progress Ibsen had made during the time he had spent working at the theatre in Bergen, as assistant to Ole Bull. All these early plays were historical. After this Ibsen used the past as a setting for his plays only twice more—in *Kongsemnerne* (*The Pretenders*) (1864) and *Kejser og Galilæer* (*Emperor and Galilean*), a complex study of the struggle between paganism and Christianity under the Emperor Julian which was begun in 1869 but not completed until 1873.

In 1862 the theatre in Bergen went bankrupt and Ibsen moved to Christiania (Oslo), where his first play on contemporary life, a satire in verse entitled *Kjærlighedens Komedie* (*Love's Comedy*), was produced with some success. A year later he received a travelling fellowship which enabled him to visit Italy and Germany, and in 1864 he settled in Rome, where he wrote his great poetic drama *Brand*. This, published in 1865, established his reputation throughout Europe and earned him a state pension which relieved him of all financial worries. It was followed by his last play in verse, *Peer Gynt*. This, written in 1867, was produced at Christiania Theatre on 24 Feb. 1876 in a revised stage version, with incidental music by Grieg.

The four plays that followed are realistic portrayals of ageless and universal parochialism set in the small-town life of Ibsen's own day, *Samfundets Støtter* (*Pillars of Society*) (1877) is a study of public life based on a lie; *Et Dukkehjem* (*A Doll's House*) (1879) of the insidious destruction of domestic life by another lie; *Gengangere* (*Ghosts*) (1881) of the lingering poison in a marriage based on a lie; *En Folkefiende* (*An Enemy of the People*) (1882) of a man of truth in conflict with the falsity of society. All have the structural economy and simplicity that is attained only by a skilled writer at the height of his powers, and all, in thought and technique, exercised an immense influence on the contemporary theatre. Ibsen's last plays, in which symbolism plays an increasingly large part and the interest shifts gradually from the individual in society to the individual, isolated and alone, exploring strange areas of experience, include *Vildanden* (*The Wild Duck*) (1884), *Rosmersholm* (1886), *Fruen fra Havet* (*The Lady from the Sea*) (1888), *Hedda Gabler* (1890), a subtle study of feminine psychology, *Bygmester Solness* (*The Master Builder*) (1892), which is concerned with the dual nature of the man and the artist, *Lille Eyolf* (*Little Eyolf*) (1894), a study of marital relations, *John Gabriel Borkman* (1896), a study of unfulfilled genius in relation to society, and *Naar vi Døde Vaagner* (*When We Dead Awaken*) (1899), Ibsen's last pronouncement on the artist's relation to life and truth.

The impact of Ibsen on the English and American theatres was so decisive that some account of the first productions of his plays in translation seems essential. Most of them have been revived many times. The first to be produced in London was *Samfundets Støtter* in a translation by William Archer entitled *Quicksands; or The Pillars of Society* (Gaiety, 15 Dec. 1880). It was revived under its better-known sub-title with Elizabeth Robins (q.v.) as Martha in 1889. In 1884 an unsuccessful version of *Et Dukkehjem*, as *Breaking a Butterfly*, was seen at the Prince of Wales' with Tree (q.v.). The first production as *A Doll's House* was in 1889, with Janet Achurch (q.v.) as Nora. *Rosmersholm* was first seen in Feb. 1891, and a month later came the first private production of *Ghosts*, by the Independent

Theatre (see GREIN), which aroused a storm of abuse, particularly from Clement Scott (q.v.). The first public performance was not given until 14 July 1914. *Hedda Gabler* and *The Lady from the Sea* both had their first productions in 1891, and two years later came *The Master Builder*, and *An Enemy of the People* with Tree as Dr. Stockman. *The Wild Duck* followed in 1894, *Little Eyolf* in 1896, and *John Gabriel Borkman* in 1897. One of the lesser-known plays, *De Unges Forband* (*The League of Youth*), had its only English production in 1900, and in 1903, in which year *When We Dead Awaken* was first seen, Ellen Terry (q.v.) appeared in *The Vikings of Helgeland*, staged by her son, Gordon Craig (q.v.). This play has only once been revived, at the Old Vic in 1928. Later first productions were *Lady Inger of Østraat* (1906), *Olaf Liljekrans* (1911), *Brand* and *Kæmpehøien* (as *The Hero's Mound*) (both 1912), the former being seen again in 1959, *The Pretenders* (1913), with incidental music by Norman O'Neill), *Sancthansnatten* (as *St. John's Night*) (1921), and *Catilina* (1936). *Peer Gynt*, which was given privately in 1911, had its first public performance at the Old Vic in 1922, with Russell Thorndike (q.v.) as Peer. In 1909 *Love's Comedy* was given its only performance in England at the Gaiety, Manchester.

Archer was the first translator of most of Ibsen's plays, but with the lapse of time his versions have been found somewhat inadequate. In 1950 three translations by Una Ellis-Fermor were published in the Penguin Classics series—*The Pillars of the Community*, *The Wild Duck*, and *Hedda Gabler*; but these, though scholarly, were not theatrical. Good acting versions were however produced by Michael Meyer with *Brand* (1959), *An Enemy of the People* (1962), and *The Pretenders* (1963), and by Ann Jellicoe with *Rosmersholm* (1959), in which Peggy Ashcroft (q.v.) played Rebecca West, and *The Lady from the Sea* (1961). A new translation of all the plays has been undertaken by J. W. McFarlane, with introductions, commentaries, and notes on earlier drafts, where they exist. Most of the plays are also published separately in acting versions, without the scholarly apparatus.

In the United States the large number of Scandinavian immigrants and the lack of an effective censorship meant that there was less opposition to Ibsen than in England. The first of his plays to be produced there was *Et Dukkehjem*, as *The Child Wife*, in 1882. The adapter, William Laurence, transferred the scene to England, added a comic Irish maid, and used Ibsen's alternative happy ending. Helena Modjeska (q.v.) appeared in another version, entitled *Thora*, also with a happy ending, in 1883, and in 1899 the play was first given as *A Doll's House*. *Ghosts*, which in 1882 was performed in Norwegian, was first seen in English in New York in 1894, and the enthusiasm for Ibsen's work which it aroused (in spite of William Winter (q.v.), who was as abusive as Clement Scott had been) was increased by the productions of *John Gabriel Borkman* in 1897 and *Hedda Gabler* in 1898. In 1900 came *The Master Builder*, in 1904 *Rosmersholm* and *Pillars of Society*, and in 1905 *When We Dead Awake*. In 1910, in which year *Brand* was first seen, Nazimova (q.v.) gave the first performance of *Little Eyolf*, playing Rita, and in 1918 she was seen in *The Wild Duck*. In 1906 Richard Mansfield (q.v.) showed a new aspect of Ibsen's work to the American public by his production of *Peer Gynt*, the first performance of the play in translation, antedating the London production by five years. In 1911 *The Lady from the Sea* was first seen, and in 1924 Walter Hampden (q.v.) scored a success as Dr. Stockman in the first American production of *An Enemy of the People*. *The Vikings at Helgeland* was first seen in New York in 1930, and *The Pretenders* in 1960.

IFFLAND, AUGUST WILHELM (1759–1814), German actor and playwright, who virtually controlled the National Theatre at Mannheim (q.v.) from its foundation in 1778 until 1796, playing Franz Moor in the first production of Schiller's *Die Räuber* (1781) and appearing in many of his own plays. Though now forgotten, these were very successful in their own day and several them his best-known work, *Die Jäger* (1785), as *The Foresters* in 1799. Iffland catered for a popular audience, for whom he turned domestic tragedies into sentimental family dramas with happy endings. As an actor he had a fine technique but no depth, and he was at his best in elderly witty roles in dignified comedy. In 1796 he left Mannheim for Berlin, where he remained until his death, training a number of young actors, including Ludwig Devrient, not in his own virtuosity but in the serious, sober style of Schröder (q.v.). In 1798 he published his autobiography as *Meine theatralische Laufbahn*.

Illustre-Théâtre, the name taken by the company with which Molière (q.v.) made his first appearance on the professional stage. The contract drawn up between the first members, among whom were three of the Béjart family (q.v.), is dated 30 June 1643 and was modelled upon that of the Confrérie de la Passion (q.v.). In essentials it provided the basic constitution of the Comédie-Française (q.v.) on its foundation in 1680, still in force today. On 1 Jan. 1644 the new company, whose members were all young and inexperienced, opened in Paris, but with little success, and by Aug. 1645 it had come to an ignominious end. Its repertory, which was mainly tragic, with very little comedy, is known to have included plays by Corneille, du Ryer, and Tristan l'Hermite, as well as some specially written for it by Nicholas Desfontaines, a member of the company, all of which had the word *illustre* in the title.

Imperial Theatre. (1) LONDON, in Tothill Street, Westminster, originally the Aquarium Theatre, part of the Royal Aquarium Summer and Winter Garden. It opened on 15 Apr. 1876, and it was there that Phelps (q.v.) made his last appearance in 1878. On 21 Apr. 1879, under the management of Marie Litton (Mrs. Wybrow Robertson), the name was changed to the Imperial. It closed in 1899, and Lily Langtry (q.v.) then took over, virtually rebuilt it and reopened it on 22 Apr. 1901 with Berton's *A Royal Necklace*. In spite of good reviews of her acting in the dual roles of Marie Antoinette and Mlle Olivia, and of the sumptuous costumes and scenery (the latter by Telbin, q.v.), the play was not a success, and in 1903 Mrs. Langtry withdrew. Ellen Terry (q.v.) then presented Ibsen's *The Vikings at Helgeland*, designed and directed by her son Gordon Craig (q.v.), and appeared herself as Beatrice in *Much Ado About Nothing*. Lewis Waller (q.v.) was at the Imperial for three years, presenting a series of romantic plays of which the most successful, apart from the perennial *Monsieur Beaucaire* by Booth Tarkington, was Conan Doyle's *Brigadier Gerard*. The last play seen at this theatre was Dix and Sutherland's *Boy O'Carrol* (1906), with Martin Harvey (q.v.). The theatre was then dismantled and taken to Canning Town, where it was re-erected as the Imperial Palace, later a cinema which was destroyed by fire in 1931.

(2) NEW YORK, on 45th Street between Broadway and 8th Avenue, one of the most successful theatres in the city. It opened on 24 Dec. 1923, mainly for musical shows, though in 1936 Leslie Howard appeared there in *Hamlet*. It then reverted to musicals and in 1946 housed *Annie Get Your Gun* with Ethel Merman, who also starred in *Call Me Madam* (1950). Later successful musicals were *The Most Happy Fella* (1956), *Carnival!* (1961), *Oliver!* (1963), *Fiddler on the Roof* (1964), and *Zorba* (1968).

INCHBALD [*née* SIMPSON], ELIZABETH (1753–1821), English actress and dramatist who appeared with her husband in the provinces and went to Covent Garden after his death in 1779. Ten years later she gave up acting in order to devote herself entirely to playwriting. She was a capable purveyor of sentimental comedy, and though her plays, which were mainly adaptations from the French or German, have not been revived, they were successful in their own day. The best were probably *I'll Tell You What* (1785), *Wives as They Were, and Maids as They Are* (1797), and her last comedy, *To Marry or Not to Marry* (1805). She also edited several important collections of English tragedies and comedies. An account of her life and times was written by S. R. Littlewood in 1921.

Incidental Music, the term used for music written expressly for a dramatic performance, and which seldom survives the play for which it was intended. Mendelssohn's Overture to *A Midsummer Night's Dream*, written in 1826, was not incidental music but a symphonic poem for concert performance based on the subject of Shakespeare's play. The music Mendelssohn wrote for a production of the play in 1843 *was* incidental music, properly speaking, and the overture became part of it.

Plays with incidental music are in no sense primarily musical works except, precisely, 'incidentally'. Thus the origin of incidental music must not be looked for in the stage entertainments of Renaissance Italy nor in those which plainly derived from them in England (see MASQUE). Traces of it can be seen, however, in Elizabethan drama and also in classical

Spanish drama. It is clear that Shakespeare's plays demanded a good deal of music, not only for interpolated songs, for sennets (a word probably derived from *sonata*), and for tuckets (from *toccata*), but also for interludes and dances. It is evident that there must have been music at the opening of *Twelfth Night* and in the last acts of *A Midsummer Night's Dream* and *Much Ado About Nothing*. In Spain, the plays of Calderón, Lope de Vega (qq.v.), and many other playwrights continually call for music of various sorts; yet they have too much action and spoken dialogue to be classed as operas. Their music is not casual but it is clearly incidental. In English Restoration plays it has been said to be casual, but this is to ignore the important contributions made by Purcell to the production of plays by such dramatists as Beaumont and Fletcher, Congreve, Dryden, and Shakespeare (qq.v.). His music for plays must indeed be called incidental, and marks an important historical advance in the use of music in the theatre. Nowhere else in Europe in the seventeenth century did incidental music result in anything as fine as the stage works of Purcell. The reason for this is twofold—the flourishing condition of the spoken drama in England and the failure of opera to thrive there as it did on the Continent, except in Spain, where the spoken drama, as well as opera, was in decline.

There was not much call for incidental music anywhere during the eighteenth century, mainly owing to the popularity of various types of light operatic forms of entertainment in which the music, though often trivial, was nevertheless essential and not incidental. But it did at least prepare the way for developments in the nineteenth century by enlarging and improving the orchestral resources of the theatre. The opera orchestras in London and Paris were the best of their time, while in Italy, except at one or two ducal courts, they were the only ones. In Germany conditions were much more favourable to the development of incidental music. Although the German Court theatres vied with each other in lavish productions of opera, the majority of them were situated in small provincial towns—Bonn, Brunswick, Karlsruhe, Kassel, Mannheim, Weimar—and depended for their audiences on the Court's household and, in some places, the university. Drama provided a change of bill but, except in a few towns like

Vienna, had to be given in the same theatre. The necessity for keeping an orchestra in readiness for operatic performances led to an increase in the amount of music used in plays, primarily in order to provide employment for the musicians, and it was not long before playwrights made the most of the musical facilities available by inserting into their new plays not only songs and dances and processions to music, but scenes of excitement or pathos in which the spoken words were accompanied by an orchestral undercurrent. The melodrama popular in England later in the century, in which murder, robberies, suicides, and furtive escapes took place to appropriate music, was nothing more than a debased form of this earlier practice.

By the second half of the nineteenth century incidental music was established as a separate category of some importance with such works as Bizet's music for Daudet's *L'Arlésienne* (1872) and Grieg's for Ibsen's *Peer Gynt* (1876). Everywhere poetic drama, in particular, was provided with some form of music, often by famous composers. Both Fauré in 1898 and Sibelius in 1905 wrote incidental music for Maeterlinck's *Pelléas et Mélisande*, a play which has now been superseded by the music-drama based on it by Debussy. In Russia, Balakirev wrote music for *King Lear* (1861) and Tchaikovsky for *Hamlet* (1891). In England, incidental music was rarely taken seriously until the twentieth century, and nothing much of importance emerged in the nineteenth, though something in the nature of a false start was made towards its close with music commissioned from Sullivan for productions of Shakespeare between 1862 and 1888, as well as for Tennyson's *The Foresters* in 1892 and Comyns Carr's *King Arthur* in 1895. All this has now gone to waste, though a revival of *The Tempest* in London in 1921 in which some of Sullivan's music was used, together with some new and very striking music by Bliss, showed how good Sullivan could be at theatre music of this kind. He was certainly superior to Edward German, the favourite composer of many actor-managers who admired his talent for simple melodies and agreeably picturesque, if distant, period imitation. Of German's scores for plays, nothing remains but his dances for Shakespeare's *Henry VIII* (1892) and for Anthony Hope's *English Nell* (1900). Little produced before 1900 was of much more value than the music provided by Jimmie Glover to accompany the villain's misdeeds in Drury Lane melodramas. There were some exceptions, but they were mainly for academic performances—Stanford's music for Aeschylus' *Eumenides* (1885) and Sophocles' *Oedipus Tyrannus* (1887) in Cambridge; Parry's for productions of Aristophanes in Oxford between 1883 and 1914; and Vaughan Williams's for Aristophanes' *Wasps* (1909), also in Cambridge. Stanford too provided good incidental music for two London plays, Tennyson's *Queen Mary* (1876) and *Becket* (1893), in which Henry Irving (q.v.) appeared at the Lyceum.

With the turn of the century things began to improve. The incidental music by Norman O'Neill for plays at the Haymarket, where he was musical director for many years, was slight, but combined a special aptitude for the requirements of the stage with graceful, sometimes fanciful invention, particularly in the scores for Maeterlinck's *The Blue Bird* (1909), Barrie's *Mary Rose* (1920), and Ashley Dukes's *The Man With a Load of Mischief* (1925). A more eminent composer, Elgar, wrote music for Yeats's *Grania and Diarmid* (1902) and for *The Starlight Express* (1915), a play by Violet Pearn based on Algernon Blackwood's novel, *A Prisoner in Fairyland*. Other outstanding composers of incidental music at this time were Armstrong Gibbs—for Maeterlinck's *The Betrothal* (1921); Eugene Goossens—for Maugham's *East of Suez* (1922), Margaret Kennedy's *The Constant Nymph* (1926), and Dodie Smith's *Autumn Crocus* (1931); Frederic Austin—for the Čapeks' *The Insect Play* (1923) and Congreve's *The Way of the World* (1924); and, most important of all, Delius—for J. E. Flecker's *Hassan* (1923). Much of the best incidental music in recent years has been composed for productions of Shakespeare's plays, particularly at Stratford-upon-Avon under the musical directorship of Raymond Leppard; but no less a composer than Benjamin Britten wrote the music for the London productions of Priestley's *Johnson Over Jordan* (1939), Ronald Duncan's *This Way to the Tomb* and Webster's *The Duchess of Malfi* (both 1945). Yet most modern incidental music, unlike Mendelssohn's for *A Midsummer Night's Dream* and Grieg's for *Peer Gynt*, which is still heard in the concert hall, has not outlived the productions it was written for. Some of it has not even been published.

Even more ephemeral are the tape-recorded scores, which are not so much incidental music as 'sound effects'. The new mediums of *musique concrète* and electronic music, though they have proved very effective in creating atmosphere, as in Peter Brook's spine-chilling accompaniment to his production of *Titus Andronicus* at Stratford-upon-Avon in 1957, or Raymond Leppard's 'enchanted' music for *The Tempest*, also at Stratford in 1963, have not survived in performance. Today's incidental music is, more truly than ever before, entirely 'incidental'.

Incorporated Stage Society, see STAGE SOCIETY.

Independent Theatre, LONDON, see GREIN, J. T.; **Theatre Club,** see KINGSWAY THEATRE.

INGE, WILLIAM (1913–73), American dramatist, who in 1953 was awarded a Pulitzer Prize for *Picnic*. He had previously scored a success with *Come Back, Little Sheba* (1950), with Shirley Booth in the lead, and then wrote *Bus Stop* (1955), *The Dark at the Top of the Stairs* (1957), and *A Loss of Roses* (1959). This last play, which was Inge's first failure on Broadway, was seen in England—at the Pembroke Theatre, Croydon—in 1962 in a production by Peter Cotes, who also produced *Come Back, Little Sheba* at the Golders Green Hippodrome in 1952.

INGEGNERI, ANGELO (c. 1550–c. 1631), see LIGHTING.

Inner Stage, a presumed feature of the Elizabethan theatre which has aroused a great deal of controversy. It was formerly thought to be either a large curtained recess behind the back wall or a structure projecting on to the stage from the back wall (see TERENCE–STAGE). Some form of concealment must have existed, as stage directions in a number of Elizabethan plays demand 'a discovery' by the drawing of a curtain (for example, Ferdinand and Miranda playing chess in *The Tempest*). But it is now thought that the 'inner stage' was nothing more than part of a narrow corridor behind the stage-wall which could be made visible through an opening usually closed by a door or a curtain. As it would not have been possible for many people in the audience to see a scene played inside this recess under the canopy, it seems probable that actors so 'discovered' came forward on to the main stage to join in the action of the play as Ferdinand and Miranda evidently do when they see Alonso and Prospero shortly afterwards. There may also have been small structures—caves, tents, monuments, even simple rooms—either standing free on the stage, as they did in the masque (q.v.), or abutting on the back wall. Some such arrangement would have been necessary for the monument scene in *Antony and Cleopatra*. Stage directions prove the existence of a similar 'inner stage' in the Spanish theatre (see AUTO), where a curtain might be drawn back to reveal a crib, or a statue of the Virgin, or the empty tomb of the Resurrection. Because of the uncertainty over its size and position, the term 'inner stage' is now being abandoned in favour of the expression 'discovery space', which allows for a wide variety of interpretations.

Inns Used as Theatres, LONDON. These may have been converted, or merely equipped with a trestle stage at one end of the yard. The best-known were the BEL SAVAGE on Ludgate Hill in the City of London, where plays were performed from 1579 to 1588 and occasionally thereafter; the BELL in Gracious (now Gracechurch) Street in the City of London, which was used for plays in 1576 and 1583; the BOAR'S HEAD in Aldgate, where a 'lewd' play called *A Sack Full of News* was suppressed in 1557, the players being kept under arrest for twenty-four hours; another BOAR'S HEAD somewhere in Middlesex, which was in use between 1602 and 1608; the BULL in Bishopsgate Street in the City of London, which was used for plays before 1575 and until some time after 1594; the CROSS KEYS, also in Gracious Street, where plays were performed before 1579 and up to about 1596; and the RED LION in Stepney, where a play called *Samson* was performed in 1567.

Institute for Advanced Studies in the Theatre Arts (I.A.S.T.A.), NEW YORK, an educational venture founded in 1958 to provide opportunities for professional theatre workers to study the style and technique of foreign theatres by working under a director from abroad and attending courses on subjects relating to the play which was being produced. The first visitor was Willi Schmidt, from Berlin, who directed a new English version of Schiller's *Kabale und Liebe*. Subsequent productions included Molière's *Le Misanthrope* under Jacques Charon, Congreve's *The Way of the World*, under George Devine, and Sophocles' *Electra*, under Dimitrios Rondiris, as well as *kabuki* and *nō* plays directed by leading actors from Japan, *commedia dell'arte* scenarii, and Indian dance-dramas.

Interlude, the early English name for a short dramatic sketch, from the late Latin *interludium*. It is often taken as the starting-point of English drama, and seems to have some affinity with the Italian *tramesso*, signifying an entertainment given during a banquet. By extension it passed to short pieces played between the acts of a long play, for which Renaissance Italy adopted the term *intermedi* or *intermezzi* (q.v.). The former gave rise to the French *intermède* and the Spanish *entremés* (q.v.). The first writer to make the English interlude a complete and independent dramatic form was John Heywood (q.v.). The Players of the King's Interludes (*Lusores Regis*) are first recorded under Henry VII in 1493 and in 1503 went to Scotland to take part in the wedding festivities of the King's daughter Margaret and James IV. They also played in private houses, and may be the company referred to in *Sir Thomas More* (1595). They disappeared under Elizabeth I, the last survivor dying in 1580. During their last years they were sometimes referred to as the Queen's Players, but should not be confused with Queen Elizabeth's Men (q.v.), the best-known London company of the 1580s, founded in 1583.

Intermezzi (INTERMEDII), interpolations of a light, often comic, character performed between the acts of serious drama or opera in Italy in the late fifteenth and early sixteenth centuries. They usually dealt with mythological subjects, and could be given as independent entertainments for guests at royal or noble festivals, on the lines of the English 'disguising' and dumbshow, the French *momeries* and *entremets*, or the Spanish *entremeses*.

International Federation for Theatre Research. A meeting of delegates from over twenty countries, held in London in July 1955 at the invitation of the Society for Theatre Research (q.v.), resulted in the formation of an international body devoted to the collection, preservation, and dissemination of theatrical material throughout the world. The Federation, which publishes a bilingual journal, *Theatre Research/Recherches Théâtrales*, admits to full membership institutions engaged wholly in theatre research (those only partly so engaged can become associate members) and has also a category of individual members. Committee meetings are held annually and are accompanied by a symposium at which experts are invited to speak on a subject chosen by the host country. A world conference, open to the public, of which the first took place in Venice in 1957, is held every four years, the proceedings being later published in volume form. The Federation has established an international centre for theatre research in the Casa Goldoni, Venice, where work on the cataloguing of theatre material in libraries, museums, and collections is being carried on, and where international summer courses are held.

International Theatre Institute (I.T.I.). This body, which exists to promote international co-operation and exchange of ideas among all workers in the theatre, was founded as a branch of Unesco in Prague in July 1948, after discussions in Paris a year earlier. It works through fifty national centres, with headquarters in Paris, and publishes a quarterly illustrated journal, *World Theatre*. A world congress is held every two years, together with conferences and colloquiums on such specific problems as the training of the actor or theatre architecture. The British Centre, which was one of the first to be founded, helps those who come from abroad to study the English theatre, and those going from Great Britain to study the theatre abroad. It also serves as a central information bureau for all workers in the theatre at home and abroad. The American Centre, now an independent body housed in the Anta Theatre (q.v.), covers much the same ground as that outlined above, as do all the other centres, some of which are extremely active.

IONESCO, EUGÈNE (1912–), French playwright of Roumanian origin, exponent and virtual founder of the Theatre of the Absurd (q.v.). Under the influence of Artaud (q.v.), he rejected both the realistic and the psychological theatre, seeking a return to that primitive form of drama which, in the savage poetic imagination of Genet (q.v.), was to result

in the establishment of the Theatre of Cruelty (q.v.). Ionesco's plays, which are mainly in one act, stress the impotence of language as a means of communication. They include *La Cantatrice chauve* (1950), *La Leçon* (1951), and *Les Chaises* (1952) (seen in London as *The Bald Prima Donna* (1956), *The Lesson* (1955), and *The Chairs* (1957) respectively), *Victimes du devoir* and *La Jeune Fille à marier* (both 1953), *Jacques, ou la soumission* (1955, but written in 1950), *L'Impromptu de l'Alma* (1956), *L'Avenir est dans les œufs* (1958), and *Le Nouveau Locataire* (1967, but written in 1955 and first performed in Finland in that year; as *The New Tenant* it was seen in London in 1956). Ionesco's first full-length play, *Amédée, ou Comment s'en débarrasser* (1954), seen in London in French in 1963, together with *L'Avenir est dans les œufs*, was only partially successful. He endeavoured to rectify this by introducing into his next full-length play, *Tueur sans gages* (1959), seen in London as *The Killer* in 1968, a more conventionally sympathetic hero—the Berenger who reappears in *Rhinocéros* (1960), *Le Roi se meurt* (1962), and *Le Piéton de l'air* (1963). The first two, as *Rhinoceros* (1960) and *Exit the King* (1963), were both successful when produced at the Royal Court Theatre in London with Laurence Olivier (in *Rhinoceros*) and Alec Guinness (in *Exit the King*). In 1966 a new play, *La Soif et la faim*, was produced at the Comédie-Française; in 1968 *Délire à deux*, which had previously been seen at the Manchester Library Theatre in 1965 as *Bedlam Galore for Two or More*, was again produced, in a different translation, at the Yvonne Arnaud Theatre in Guildford.

IRELAND, WILLIAM HENRY (1775–1835), a brilliant but eccentric Englishman, who at the age of nineteen forged a number of legal and personal papers purporting to relate to Shakespeare which for a time deceived even the experts. He also persuaded Sheridan (q.v.) to put on at Drury Lane, on 2 Apr. 1796, a forged play, *Vortigern and Rowena*. Although John Philip Kemble and Mrs. Jordan (qq.v.) played the title-roles, this failed, thus preventing Ireland from bringing forward further forgeries, of which *Henry II* was already written and *William the Conqueror* nearly completed. All Ireland's forgeries were published by his father, a dealer in prints and rare books who never ceased to believe in them, saying his son was too stupid to have composed them. They were exposed by Malone (q.v.) and Ireland was forced to confess. The story has been well told in John Mair's *The Fourth Forger* (1938).

Irish Literary Theatre. Founded by Lady Gregory, Edward Martyn, George Moore, and Yeats (qq.v.), this was the first manifestation in drama of the Irish literary revival. From 1899 to 1901 a short season took place annually at which new Irish plays, including Yeats's *The Countess Cathleen*, were performed by English actors, and the first modern Gaelic play, Hyde's *Casadh an tSugain*, was given by Gaelic-speaking amateurs. The enterprise was then taken over by the Irish National Dramatic Society, a professional company run by W. G. and Frank Fay (qq.v.). Among their productions were several plays by Yeats and Lady Gregory and the first plays of Synge (q.v.). It was probably the appearance of this company in London on 2 May 1903 which led Miss Horniman to build the Abbey Theatre (q.v.).

IRON, see SAFETY CURTAIN.

IRVING, SIR HENRY [really JOHN HENRY BRODRIBB] (1838–1905), English actor-manager who, in partnership with Ellen Terry (q.v.), dominated the London stage during the last thirty years of Queen Victoria's reign and was the first actor to be knighted—in 1895—for services to the theatre. After some amateur experience, he made his first professional appearance at the Lyceum, Sunderland, on 29 Sept. 1856. An unsuccessful appearance in London at the Princess's in 1859 drove him back to the provinces, where he remained until 1866. He then returned to appear at the St. James's, where on 6 Oct. his success as Doricourt in Mrs. Cowley's *The Belle's Stratagem* led to his remaining in the company. A year later he went to the Queen's, Long Acre, where on 26 Dec. he first played with Ellen Terry in *Katherine and Petruchio*, an adaptation by Garrick (q.v.) of *The Taming of the Shrew*. In 1869 he made a hit with Toole (q.v.) at the Gaiety as Mr. Reginald Chevenix in *Uncle Dick's Darling*, by H. J. Byron, and at the Vaudeville in 1870 he was equally successful as Digby Grant in Albery's *Two Roses*.

It was on 11 Sept. 1871 that he appeared for the first time at the Lyceum Theatre (q.v.), with which he was for so long associated. It had always been an unlucky house and Irving's Jingle, in Albery's adaptation of Dickens's *The Pickwick Papers*, did nothing to restore its fortunes. Bateman (q.v.), the manager, was in despair and reluctantly agreed that on 25 Nov. Irving should appear in *The Bells*, an adaptation by Leopold Lewis of Erckmann-Chatrian's *Le Juif polonais*. It was an immediate success, and Irving completed his conquest of London audiences in Wills's *Charles I* (1872) and *Eugene Aram* (1873) and in a revival of Bulwer-Lytton's *Richelieu* (also 1873). In 1874 he played Hamlet, the part in which, on 30 Dec. 1878, he inaugurated his management of the Lyceum. Under him the chief productions were Shakespeare's *The Merchant of Venice* (1879), *Romeo and Juliet* and *Much Ado About Nothing* (both 1882), *Twelfth Night* (1884), *Henry VIII* and *King Lear* (both 1892), and *Cymbeline* (1896). Plays by other authors included Bulwer-Lytton's *The Lady of Lyons* (1879), Boucicault's *The Corsican Brothers* (1880), Tennyson's *The Cup* and Albery's *Two Roses* (both 1881), Tennyson's *Becket* (1893), Comyns Carr's *King Arthur*, Conan Doyle's *A Story of Waterloo*, and Wills's *Don Quixote* (all 1895), Comyns Carr's *Madame Sans-Gêne* (1897), and Laurence Irving's *Peter the Great* (1898). In 1899 Irving nominally gave up the Lyceum and for the first time since 1878 appeared under another management. His tenancy expired in 1901, in which year he appeared as Coriolanus, and in 1902 he made his last appearance at the Lyceum as Shylock in *The Merchant of Venice*. In 1903 he was at Drury Lane, where he gave his last London season in 1905, making his final appearance in London on 15 June, at Her Majesty's Theatre in Lionel Brough's Testimonial Matinée, as Corporal Gregory Brewster in *A Story of Waterloo*. He died at Bradford on the night of 13 Oct. 1905, during a provincial tour, after playing in Tennyson's *Becket*.

Irving made several Canadian and American tours—in 1883, 1887, 1893, 1899, 1901, and 1903. His first appearance in New York was at the Star Theatre on 29 Oct. 1883 in *The Bells*, and his last at the Harlem Opera House on 25 Mar. 1904 in Boucicault's *Louis XI*.

Irving made an unhappy marriage, soon separating from his wife, by whom he had two sons, Henry and Laurence (qq.v.).

IRVING, HENRY BRODRIBB (1870–1919), English actor-manager, elder son of Henry Irving, brother of the elder Laurence Irving, and father of the younger (qq.v.). He made his first appearance on the stage under Hare (q.v.) in 1891, playing Lord Beaufoy in Robertson's *School*, and was for a time with Ben Greet and George Alexander (qq.v.). He also ran his own company, which toured the provinces, and was manager of several London theatres. In the course of his long career he revived many of his father's famous parts both in England and in America, and in 1902 he created the title-role in Barrie's *The Admirable Crichton*. He married in 1896 the actress Dorothea Baird (q.v.), who was for some years his leading lady.

IRVING, LAURENCE HENRY FORSTER (1897–1988), English stage designer and theatre historian, son of H. B. Irving (q.v.), who in 1951 published the definitive biography of his grandfather Henry Irving (q.v.), *Henry Irving: The Actor and his World*, and continued the story of the Irving family in *Successors* (1967). As artist and scenic designer he was responsible for the décor of many London productions, including T. S. Eliot's *Murder in the Cathedral* (1935); he was also the first chairman of the British Theatre Museum Association (q.v.).

IRVING, LAURENCE SIDNEY (1871–1914), English actor and playwright, younger son of Henry Irving (q.v.). He made his first appearance in 1891 in Frank Benson's company, and in 1898 and 1899 was seen at the Lyceum with his father. He was the author of a number of plays, of which the most successful was *The Unwritten Law* (1910). He also translated for Henry Irving Sardou's *Robespierre* (1899) and *Dante* (1903), and wrote for him the tragedy *Peter the Great*. With his wife Mabel Hackney, he was drowned when the *Empress of Ireland* sank after a collision in the St. Lawrence.

IRVING, WASHINGTON (1783–1859), the first American author to gain recognition abroad. In 1802–3 he published, in the *New York Morning Chronicle*, a series of essays entitled 'The Letters of Jonathan Oldstyle', several of which give vivid pictures of the contemporary New York stage. He later collaborated with John Howard Payne (q.v.) in *Charles II; or, the Merry Monarch* (1824) and *Richelieu*

(1826)—also known as *The French Libertine*—both adapted from French originals. Irving's short story *Rip Van Winkle* (first published in 1819) was adapted for the stage by James H. Hackett (q.v.) in 1825. Other adaptations followed, the most successful being that of Joseph Jefferson and Dion Boucicault (qq.v.), in which Jefferson scored his greatest success, playing the title-role regularly from its first production in 1865 until his retirement in 1904.

Irving Place Theatre, NEW YORK, see SCHWARTZ, MAURICE.

ISAACS [*née* RICH], EDITH JULIET (1878–1956), American theatre critic and historian who, as editor of *Theatre Arts* (q.v.) from 1919 to 1945, exercised a unique and beneficial influence on the American theatre as a whole. Among the activities in which she played a leading part were the National Theatre Conference, which functioned from 1930 to 1937; the campaign for better theatre buildings in New York, particularly backstage; the establishment of the Federal Theatre Project (q.v.); and the founding of the American National Theatre and Academy (q.v.). Apart from her articles in *Theatre Arts*, she was the author or editor of *Theatre* (1927), *Architecture for the New Theatre* (1935), and *The Negro in the American Theatre* (1947).

Islington Empire, Palace, see GRAND THEATRE.

Italian Opera House, NEW YORK, see NATIONAL THEATRE, NEW YORK (1).

IVANOV, VSEVOLOD VYACHESLAVOVICH (1895–1963), Soviet dramatist, whose first play, *Armoured Train 14–69* (1927), is a landmark in the history of the modern Russian theatre, since it was the first Soviet play to be successfully produced by the Moscow Art Theatre (q.v.). It deals with the capture of a train-load of ammunition during the Civil War, and is a melodramatic but effective piece of propaganda which perhaps suffered a little from the determined naturalism of the Moscow Art Theatre production. It has since been revived and retains its place in the repertory. Ivanov's later plays were less interesting, though *The Doves See the Cruisers Departing* (1938), about events in the Far East, had some success, as did *Lomonosov* (1953), based on the life of the virtual founder of Russian science.

J

Jack-in-the-Green, see FOLK FESTIVALS and
ROBIN HOOD.

JACKSON, ANNE (1782–1869), see
MATHEWS, CHARLES.

JACKSON, SIR BARRY VINCENT (1879–
1961), a wealthy amateur of the theatre,
who in 1913 built a repertory theatre in
Birmingham (q.v.), and maintained it
for twenty-two years as a creative force
in the face of local indifference. Among
the many plays which he directed were
several of his own, including *The Christmas
Party* (1913, and often revived), a real
pantomime for children. He also presented
his own versions of Ghéon's *The Marvel-
lous History of St. Bernard* (1925),
Beaumarchais's *The Marriage of Figaro*
and Andreyev's *He Who Gets Slapped*
(both 1926), adapted Wyss's *The Swiss
Family Robinson* (1938), dramatized
Dickens's *The Cricket on the Hearth* (1941)
and Fielding's *Jonathan Wild* (1942), and
contributed revue sketches to the Birmingham Repertory Theatre's Christmas entertainments. Always regarding the theatre
as a workshop for artistic experiment
rather than as a museum for the preservation of tradition, he produced Shakespeare
in modern dress in a sincere and on the
whole successful attempt to break free
from convention. He also helped to
establish the reputation of Bernard Shaw
(q.v.) by his production of *Back to
Methuselah* in Birmingham in 1923, and
by founding the Malvern Festival (q.v.)
for the production of Shaw's plays. From
1945 to 1948 Jackson was director of the
Memorial Theatre at Stratford-upon-
Avon (q.v.). He was knighted in 1925 for
his services to the theatre.

JAMES, DAVID (1839–93), English actor,
uncle of the American manager David
Belasco (q.v.). His success in contemporary burlesques—he was much admired as
Mercury in Burnand's *Ixion; or, The Man
at the Wheel* (1863)—led him to participate
in the building of the Vaudeville Theatre
(q.v.) in the hope of establishing a home of
burlesque. The first productions having
proved unsuccessful, the management put
on Albery's *Two Roses* (1870), which
helped to launch Henry Irving (q.v.), who
played Digby Grant, on his successful

career. The theatre also had an immense
success with H. J. Byron's *Our Boys*
(1875). James later returned to burlesque
in *Little Jack Sheppard* (1886) at the
Gaiety, but was also good in such straight
parts as Eccles (in Robertson's *Caste*) and
Stout (in Bulwer-Lytton's *Money*).

JAMES, HENRY (1843–1916), American
novelist, who in 1915 became a British
subject. He had a great love for the
theatre but his early plays were unsuccessful and, after the hostile reception
accorded to *Guy Domville* (1895) on its
production by Alexander (q.v.) at the St.
James's Theatre, he devoted himself
chiefly to novel-writing. The success he
had longed for came after his death, with
dramatizations of his novels by other
writers produced both in London and New
York—notably *Berkeley Square* (1928;
New York 1929), based on the unfinished
The Sense of the Past; *The Heiress* (1947),
based on *Washington Square*; *The Innocents* (1950), based on *The Turn of the
Screw* (which also provided the libretto for
an opera by Benjamin Britten in 1954);
The Aspern Papers (1959), adapted by
Michael Redgrave (q.v.), who also played
in London the chief part played in New
York in 1962 by Maurice Evans (q.v.);
The Wings of the Dove (1963); *A Boston
Story*, based on James's first published
novel, *Watch and Ward*, and *The Spoils*,
based on *The Spoils of Poynton* (both
1968). Another version of this last novel
had been seen briefly at the May Fair
Theatre, London, in 1969. In 1948 James's
own plays were published in one volume,
and in 1949 his scattered writings on the
theatre were collected in *The Scenic
Art: Notes on Acting and the Drama
1872–1901*. Of his own plays, *The High Bid*,
first produced in London in 1909, was successfully revived at the Mermaid in 1967
and *The Outcry* (1911) at the Arts Theatre
a year later. In 1969 *The Other House*,
written in 1893 but not performed, was
produced at the Mermaid.

JAMES, LOUIS (1842–1910), American
actor, who made his début in 1863 and
was for some years with Mrs. John Drew
(q.v.) at the Arch Street Theatre, Philadelphia. In 1871 he joined Daly (q.v.) at
the Fifth Avenue Theatre, and from 1880

to 1885 was leading man with Lawrence Barrett (q.v.), with whom he first appeared in London in 1884 as Heywood in W. D. Howells's *Yorick's Love*. With MARIE WAINWRIGHT (1853–1923) as his leading lady he toured extensively in a repertory of Shakespearian and other classics, and remained on the stage until his death, which occurred while he was dressing to play Wolsey in *Henry VIII*.

James Street Theatre, LONDON. This small eighteenth-century theatre or amusement hall stood between the Haymarket and Whitcomb Street. It was used mostly for variety, but pantomimes were given there, and occasionally plays, its seats being priced at 3*d.*, 4*d.*, 6*d.*, and 1*s.*

Jan Bouschet, see ENGLISH COMEDIANS.

JANAUSCHEK, FRANCESCA ROMANA MADDALENA (1830–1904), Czech actress, who made her début in Prague in 1846 and two years later became leading lady of the Frankfurt Stadttheater. She remained there for some years and then went to Dresden, building up a great reputation as an interpreter of tragic drama in such parts as Schiller's Maria Stuart and Shakespeare's Lady Macbeth. She toured extensively in Europe and in the United States, where she was highly thought of. In 1873 she undertook to play in English, appearing in a number of Shakespearian and other roles. Her later years were spent mainly in America, where she died four years after suffering a stroke which paralysed her. She was one of the last of the great international actresses in the grand tragic style.

JANIN, JULES-GABRIEL (1804–74), French journalist and dramatic critic, most of whose best work was done for the *Journal des Débats*. For forty years he wrote a weekly article on the theatre, his outspokenness frequently landing him in lawsuits and quarrels. But his enthusiasm for good acting made him a powerful advocate, and it was he who first drew the attention of the Parisian public to Rachel and Deburau (qq.v.). A prolific writer, he published lives of both these players, and also a history of French dramatic literature, as well as innumerable works of criticism and several novels. Celebrated and feared during his lifetime, he was soon forgotten, but his books are useful sources for contemporary theatrical and social history.

JANIS, ELSIE (1889–1956), see REVUE.

JARRY, ALFRED (1873–1907), French poet and playwright, whose *Ubu Roi* is today looked on as the founder-play of the modern *avant-garde* theatre and as a seminal influence on the French surrealist movement. Written when Jarry was fifteen years old, this savage attack on society and the conventions of the naturalistic theatre was first performed in 1888 as a marionette play. In 1896 Firmin Gémier (q.v.) gave it its first live stage production. The history of Père Ubu, the cowardly, coarse, pompously cruel and unashamedly amoral bourgeois who, in a parody of Sophocles' *Oedipus Rex*, makes himself King, scandalized the audiences of the time and still has considerable impact, as was shown by a successful revival in 1958 at the Théâtre National Populaire directed by Jean Vilar (q.v.). An English adaptation was produced at the Royal Court in 1966. Many of the marionette elements expressly demanded by Jarry in his stage directions—masks, slapstick, placards, unrealistic props, stylized speech, and crude pantomime—can be found again in the work of such writers and directors as Genet and Planchon (qq.v.). Jarry continued the story of Ubu in *Ubu enchaîné* (1899) and *Ubu sur la butte* (1901), but with less success. In his novel, *Gestes et opinions du Docteur Faustroll* (1911), he elaborated the theory of 'pataphysics', which has been defined as 'the science of impossible solutions' and is at the root of the Theatre of the Absurd (q.v.).

Java, see SHADOW-SHOW.

Jeannetta Cochrane Theatre, LONDON, in Southampton Row. This is a proscenium-stage theatre seating about three hundred people. It serves as a workshop theatre for the Central School of Arts and Design, which it adjoins. Since it opened in 1965 it has, however, also been available for outside lettings, and has been used for Christmas shows, for the annual summer seasons of the National Youth Theatre (q.v.), as a central London showcase for the Ballet Rambert, and, from 1966 to 1967, as a home for the London Traverse Company under the direction of Jim Haynes.

JEFFERSON, JOSEPH (1829–1905), one of the outstanding personalities of the American stage and the third actor of his name, the earlier ones being his father (1804–42) and his grandfather (1774–1832). His great-grandfather, THOMAS (1732–1807), was at Drury Lane under Garrick. The first Joseph emigrated to America in 1795 and appeared successfully in New York, Boston, and Philadelphia; the second was an artist as well as an actor and did a good deal of scene painting. The third made his first appearance on the stage at the age of four and lived the hard life of a strolling player, finally achieving recognition in his twenties, when he joined the company of Laura Keene (q.v.), making a great success as Dr. Pangloss in the younger Colman's *The Heir-at-Law* and as Asa Trenchard in the first production of Tom Taylor's *Our American Cousin* (1858). At the Winter Garden in 1859 he played Caleb Plummer in *Dot*, an adaptation of Dickens's *The Cricket on the Hearth*, and Salem Scudder in *The Octoroon*, both by Boucicault (q.v.), who in 1864 made for Jefferson the new dramatization of Washington Irving's *Rip Van Winkle* in which he was to star for the rest of his life. There had been earlier versions of the story, and Jefferson himself had played Rip Van Winkle as early as 1859, but it was in Boucicault's version, which he so altered and adapted over the years that it became virtually his own, that he made his greatest success, appearing in it in London at the Adelphi in 1865 and in New York a year later. For fifteen years he appeared in little else, and his presentation of Rip was everywhere acclaimed as a masterpiece. Then, in 1880, he revived Sheridan's *The Rivals*, playing Bob Acres to the Mrs. Malaprop of Mrs. John Drew (q.v.). In this too he toured successfully for many years, but it was as Caleb Plummer that he made his last appearance, on 7 May 1904, after seventy-one years on the stage. He had succeeded Edwin Booth (q.v.) in 1893 as president of the Players' Club, and in 1890 published an excellent autobiography (reissued in 1949). By the marriage of his daugher to the novelist B. L. Farjeon he was the grandfather of Herbert Farjeon (q.v.).

JENNER, CARYL [really PAMELA PENELOPE RIPMAN] (1917–73), English director and theatre manager, who was in the forefront of the movement to establish a professional theatre for children in England. She made her first appearance on the stage in 1935, at the Gate Theatre, but almost immediately gave up acting in favour of stage management, and in Dec. 1938, at the age of twenty-one, became resident producer at the Amersham Repertory Theatre, where she remained for ten years. She then formed and managed several touring companies which, under the generic title of English Theatre for Children, visited remote villages and schools in England and Northern Ireland. She gave her first London production in 1959, and for several years presented plays for children at the Arts Theatre, where in 1962 she established the headquarters of the Unicorn Theatre for Young People, with one resident company and three on tour. The shortage of good plays for children was a constant anxiety, and of those she presented the best were probably *The Tingalary Bird* (1964), by Mary Melwood, *The Wappy Water Bus* (1965), by Marged Smith, and John Arden's *The Royal Pardon, or the Soldier who Became an Actor* (1967). It was always her ambition to open an independent theatre for children with a strong team of writers to provide new plays for it, but she died before achieving it.

JEROME, JEROME KLAPKA (1859–1927), English humorist, novelist, playwright, and actor, author of *On the Stage and Off* (1888) and *Stageland: Curious Habits and Customs of its Inhabitants* (1889). He also wrote several plays, but the only one now remembered is *The Passing of the Third Floor Back* (1908), in which Forbes-Robertson (q.v.) scored a signal triumph as the mysterious and Christ-like stranger whose sojourn in a Bloomsbury lodging-house changes the lives of all its inhabitants.

JERROLD, DOUGLAS WILLIAM (1803–57), English playwright and journalist, who was associated from its foundation in 1841 until his death with the humorous journal *Punch*. As a playwright he had a good deal of contemporary success, though none of his plays has survived on the stage. Among them were the farce *Paul Pry* (1827), the melodrama *Fifteen Years of a Drunkard's Life* (1828), both produced at the Coburg (see OLD VIC), and the nautical drama *Black-Eyed Susan; or, All in the Downs* (1829), in which T. P. Cooke (q.v.) made a great success. Jerrold's son, WILLIAM BLANCHARD (1826–84), was also a prolific playwright, one of his farces, *Cool as a Cucumber* (1851), providing the younger Charles Mathews (q.v.) with one of his best parts.

JESSE, FRYNIWYD TENNYSON (1889–1958), see HARWOOD, H. M.

JESSNER, LEOPOLD (1878–1945), German director and theatre manager, who abandoned the use of scenery in his productions in favour of different levels connected by stairways (*Jessnertreppe* or *Spieltreppe*). During his years as director of the National Theatre in Berlin, from 1919 to 1925, he was considered one of the most advanced exponents of Expressionism (q.v.). Among his notable productions were Shakespeare's *Richard III*, Schiller's *Wilhelm Tell*, and Wedekind's *Der Marquis von Keith*.

Jessop's Saloon, LONDON, see ROYAL PANTHEON THEATRE.

Jester, see CLOWN and FOOL.

Jesuit Drama, a term which covers a wide variety of plays, mainly in Latin, written to be acted by pupils in Jesuit colleges. Originally, as in other educational institutions (see SCHOOL DRAMA), these were simple scholastic exercises, but over the years, particularly in Vienna under the influence of opera and ballet, they became full-scale productions involving elaborate scenery, machinery, costumes, music, and dancing, as well as an almost professional technique in acting and diction. The earliest mention of a play produced in a Jesuit college dates from 1551, when an unspecified tragedy was performed at the Collegio Mamertino in Messina, founded as the first Jesuit school three years earlier. In 1555 the first Jesuit play was seen in Vienna. This was followed by a production at Córdoba in 1556, at Ingoldstadt in 1558, and in Munich in 1560. There were already thirty-three Jesuit colleges in Europe when Ignatius de Loyola, the founder of the Order, died in 1556. By 1587 there were a hundred and fifty, and by the early seventeenth century the figure had reached something like three hundred. And for over two centuries at least one play a year, and often more than one, was performed in each college. The total of plays specially written for these performances was enormous. Only the best were published, but recent researches in the libraries of many European countries have brought to light a great many manuscripts, most of which still await adequate investigation. The early plays were based mainly on classical or biblical subjects—Theseus, Hercules, David, Saul, Absalom—but later, stories of saints and martyrs—Theodoric, Hermenegildus—were used, as well as personifications of abstract characters—Fides, Pax, Ecclesia. The popularity of plays based on the stories of women—Judith, Esther, St. Catharine, St. Elizabeth of Hungary—led to the early abolition of the rule concerning the portrayal on stage by the boy pupils of female personages. The use of Latin was less easily disregarded, bound up as it was with its use in class and in daily conversation between masters and pupils. It seems to have been used in conjunction with the vernacular first in Spain, but the *Christus Judex* (1569) of Stefano Tuccio (q.v.) was translated into Italian in 1584 and into German in 1603. During the seventeenth century many plays appeared in French or in Italian, and by the beginning of the eighteenth century most Jesuit plays were written in the language of the country in which they were to be produced. Parallel with the increased use of the vernacular went the introduction of operatic arias, interludes, and ballets. Of all the splendid productions given in Vienna the most memorable appears to have been the *Pietas Victrix* (1659) of Nicolaus Avancinus (q.v.), which had forty-six speaking characters as well as crowds of senators, soldiers, sailors, citizens, naiads, Tritons, and angels. The technical development reached by Jesuit stagecraft can be studied in the illustrations to the published text of the play, which was acted on a large stage equipped with seven transformation scenes. Lighting effects were increasingly elaborate, and though the plays often began in daylight, which came through large windows on each side of the stage, they usually ended by torchlight, while in the course of the action sun, moon, and stars, comets, fireworks, and conflagrations were regularly required. All this, added to the splendour of the costumes and the large choruses and orchestras—often employing as many as forty singers and thirty-two instrumentalists—made the Jesuit play a serious rival to the public theatres. In Paris in the seventeenth century the three theatres in the Lycée Louis-le-Grand, where Louis XIV and his Court often watched the productions, were better equipped than the Comédie-Française and almost on a par with the

Paris Opéra. Jesuit drama continued to flourish in such conditions all over Europe (except, for religious reasons, in England) until the Order was suppressed in 1773. But it left its mark on the developing theatres wherever it was played, notably through the works of such authors as Avancinus, Bidermann (q.v.), and many others, and through its influence on pupils who were to become playwrights, among them Calderón, Corneille, Goldoni, Le Sage, Molière, and Voltaire (qq.v.).

JEVON, THOMAS (?–1688), one of the first English actors to play Harlequin, in Aphra Behn's *The Emperor of the Moon* (1687). He also wrote a farce, *The Devil of a Wife; or, a Comical Transformation* (1686), which in 1731 was adapted by Charles Coffey as a three-act play with music entitled *The Devil to Pay.* Cut to one act, this later became a popular ballad opera (q.v.).

Jewish Drama Ensemble, see MOSCOW STATE JEWISH THEATRE.

Jig, an Elizabethan after-piece, given in the public theatres only, consisting of a rhymed farce sung and danced by three or four characters. The songs were sung to existing popular tunes, and the subject-matter was often libellous or lewd. The best-known exponents of the jig were Tarleton and Kempe (qq.v.). It disappeared from the legitimate theatre with the closing of the theatres in 1642 but remained in the repertory of strolling players and actors in fair-booths, while it became increasingly popular in Germany from the late sixteenth century onwards, being taken there by the English Comedians (q.v.). It may have exercised a formative influence on the development of the German *Singspiel* as well as on that of the English ballad opera.

Jim Crow, see RICE, T. D.

JODELET [really JULIEN BEDEAU] (*c.* 1600–60), a French comedian, who in the 1650s appeared at the Marais (q.v.) in a series of farces written specially for him, mostly with his name in the title—*Jodelet, ou le maître-valet, Jodelet duelliste, Jodelet astrologue.* He was extremely popular and had only to show his flour-whitened face to raise a laugh, while he frequently added gags of his own to the author's lines. When Molière (q.v.) first

established himself in Paris in 1658 he persuaded Jodelet to join his company, thus securing the co-operation of the one comedian whose rivalry he had reason to fear. He wrote for him the part of the valet in *Les Précieuses ridicules* (1659) and may also have intended him to play the title-role in *Sganarelle* (1660); but unfortunately the comedian died just before its production and Molière played the part himself.

JODELLE, ÉTIENNE (1532–73), French Renaissance writer whose *Cléopâtre captive* was the first French tragedy to be constructed on classical lines. Together with a comedy, also on a classical model, it was performed before Henri II and his Court in 1552, with Jodelle, not yet twenty-one, as Cleopatra. It was a great success, and was subsequently given by a professional company at the Hôtel de Bourgogne, as were some of Jodelle's later plays, of which only *Didon* (1558) is now remembered.

Jodrell Theatre, LONDON, see KINGSWAY THEATRE.

John Golden Theatre, NEW YORK. (1) At 202 West 58th Street, between Broadway and 7th Avenue. Named after the actor, song-writer, and theatre director JOHN GOLDEN (1874–1955), for whom it was built, this opened on 1 Nov. 1926 and was almost immediately taken over by the Theatre Guild (q.v.), who staged there before the end of the year two plays by Sidney Howard (q.v.)—*Ned McCobb's Daughter* and *The Silver Cord.* In 1928 the Theatre Guild again occupied the theatre with O'Neill's *Strange Interlude.* After a short period as the Fifty-Eighth Street Theatre in 1935–6, the building, as the Film-Arte, became the home of foreign films, making a brief return to live entertainment, as the Concert Theatre, in 1942, with intimate revue. It is now used for radio and television shows.

(2) On 25th Street, between Broadway and 8th Avenue. This opened as the Masque Theatre on 24 Feb. 1927 with *Puppets of Passion,* a translation of *Marionette, che passione!* by the Italian dramatist Pier Maria de San Secondo, and on 4 Dec. 1933 saw the first night in New York of Kirkland's long-running *Tobacco Road.* In 1937 John Golden took over, renaming the building after himself. His first successful production was Paul Vincent Carroll's *Shadow and Substance*

(1938). Later the theatre housed a series of late revues which included *At the Drop of a Hat* (1959) and *Beyond the Fringe* (1962), both imported from London.

John Street Theatre, the first permanent playhouse in New York. It opened in Dec. 1767 with Farquhar's *The Beaux' Stratagem,* and is described by Dunlap (q.v.), whose first play was produced there in 1789, in his *History of the American Stage.* There is also a reference to it in *The Contrast,* by Royall Tyler (q.v.), performed at the theatre in 1787, where Jonathan the country bumpkin describes his first visit to a theatre. But a print of the interior, dated 1791, is now known to be a forgery. Over the years the American Company (q.v.) gave regular seasons there, except during the War of Independence, when it was renamed the Theatre Royal and used by officers of the British garrison. Many plays by Shakespeare and English Restoration dramatists had their American premières at this theatre, including *Hamlet* in a version by Garrick (q.v.) which omitted the grave-diggers and Osric. George Washington, who was fond of the theatre, visited John Street three times in 1789, the year of his inauguration as President. On 6 May he saw Sheridan's *The School for Scandal;* on 5 June Colman and Garrick's *The Clandestine Marriage;* and on 24 Nov. he heard himself alluded to on the stage in Dunlap's *Darby's Return.* The theatre was used for the last time on 13 Jan. 1798 and was later sold for £115.

JOHNSON, ELIZABETH (*fl.* 1790–1810), American actress, who made her first appearance in Boston in 1795 with the American Company (q.v.) and went with them to the John Street Theatre, New York, the following year. She played Rosalind in *As You Like It* on the opening night of the Park Theatre (q.v.) in 1798, and was later seen as Juliet (in *Romeo and Juliet*) and Imogen (in *Cymbeline*) to the Romeo and Iachimo of Cooper (q.v.). She was one of the first actresses in New York to play male parts seriously, appearing in 1804 as Young Norval in Home's *Douglas.* Her husband, John, a good utility actor, was for a short time manager of the Park, where his daughter, Ellen, later Mrs. Hilson, made her first appearance on the stage at the age of five.

JOHNSON, DR. SAMUEL (1709–84), the great English lexicographer, was the author of a five-act tragedy, *Irene,* which his friend and fellow townsman David Garrick (q.v.) produced at Drury Lane in 1749 with little success. Johnson's edition of Shakespeare is valuable for the light it throws on the editor rather than on the author, since he had little knowledge of Elizabethan drama or stage conditions, and was not temperamentally a research worker. He should not be confused with SAMUEL JOHNSON of Cheshire, author of *Hurlothrumbo* (1729) and other burlesques.

JOHNSTON, (WILLIAM) DENIS (1901–84), Irish dramatist, several of whose plays were produced at the Gate Theatre in Dublin (q.v.), of which he was joint manager. The early ones—*The Old Lady Says No!* (1929), *The Moon in the Yellow River* (1931), and *A Bride for the Unicorn* (1933), a symbolist drama akin to Strindberg's *A Dream Play*—contain some of his best work. The later plays, with their uneasy mixture of symbolism and reality, were not so successful, except for *The Dreaming Dust* (1940), based on the life of Jonathan Swift. Johnston also translated Toller's *Die blinde Göttin* (1934) as *Blind Man's Buff* (1936), and in 1956 scored an unexpected success with *Strange Occurrence on Ireland's Eye.*

JOHNSTON, HENRY ERSKINE (1777–1845), Scottish actor, who made his first appearance on the stage at the Theatre Royal, Edinburgh, playing Hamlet with no experience or training. He then created a sensation as Young Norval in a revival of Home's *Douglas* and was nicknamed the Scottish Roscius. Too much undeserved adulation went to his head and prevented him from taking his work seriously, but his youth and handsome presence took him to Covent Garden in 1797, where he created the parts of Henry in Morton's *Speed the Plough* (1800) and Ronaldi in Holcroft's *A Tale of Mystery* (1802), after which he lapsed into obscurity.

JOLLY, GEORGE (*fl.* 1640–73), English actor, leader of the last known company of the English Comedians (q.v.) who exerted so great an influence on the German theatre. He may have been at the Fortune Theatre in London in 1640, and is first found in Germany in 1648. He was particularly active in Frankfurt, where Prince Charles (later Charles II) may have seen him act. It is interesting to note that he already had women in his company in 1654, whereas they were not seen on the stage in London until after 1660. Jolly returned to England at the Restoration and appeared at the Cockpit (q.v.), where the French theatre historian Chappuzeau saw him in 1665. But Davenant and Killigrew (qq.v.) appealed against his infringement of their Patents, and he had to give up acting, contenting himself with running a school for the training of young actors.

Jolson Theatre, NEW YORK, see CENTURY THEATRE (2).

JONES, AVONIA (1839–67), see BROOKE, G. V.

JONES, HENRY ARTHUR (1851–1929), English playwright, whose first play, the one-act *It's Only Round the Corner*, was performed in Exeter in 1878. A year later *A Clerical Error* was put on in London by Wilson Barrett (q.v.), who afterwards made a great success as Wilfred Denver in *The Silver King* (1882), a melodrama by Jones and Henry Herman which established Jones's reputation. Although his contemporaries regarded him as one of the new school of dramatists whose aims and ambitions he described in *The Renaissance of the English Drama* (1895), *Foundations of a National Drama* (1913), and *The Theatre of Ideas* (1915), it was the melodramatic element rather than the social criticism which drew the public to such plays as *Saints and Sinners* (1884), *The Dancing Girl* (1891), *The Case of Rebellious Susan* (1894), *The Triumph of the Philistines* (1895), and particularly *Michael and his Lost Angel* (1896), a controversial play which was withdrawn after ten performances, mainly on account of the scene before the altar where the priest publicly confesses his adultery, after having some years before exacted a similar penance from a young woman in his congregation. This melodramatic strain was also responsible for the success of *The Liars* (1897) and *Mrs. Dane's Defence* (1900), whose third act is still considered a masterpiece of dramatic tension and naturalistic dialogue. Although Jones was writing at the time of Ibsen's introduction to English playgoers, he was very little influenced by him. Shaw (q.v.) praised Jones at the expense of his contemporary Pinero (q.v.), whose work he disliked, but posterity has reversed this judgement, and the best of Pinero's work survives, whereas Jones is forgotten, perhaps because his social and moral criticisms lacked a firm philosophical basis and the redeeming gift of humour.

JONES, INIGO (1573–1652), English architect and artist, and the first to be associated with scenic decoration in England. Having studied in Italy and worked in Denmark, he was in 1604–5 attached to the household of Prince Henry and, in addition to his work as an architect, took entire control of the masques (see MASQUE) given at Court. Of the thirteen seen there between 1605 and 1613, nine were certainly of his devising, the others probably, the first being *The Mask of Blackness* by Jonson (q.v.), who later fell out with Jones and satirized him in several of his plays. Jones was also in charge of the plays given at Oxford in Christ Church Hall in Aug. 1605, where he first used revolving screens in the Italian manner. He later used as many as five changes of scenery, with backcloths, shutters, or flats painted and arranged in perspective. These ran in grooves (q.v.) and were supplemented by a turn-table (*machina versatilis*) which presented to the audience different facets of a solid structure. Jones also introduced into England the picture-stage framed in the proscenium arch. Many of his designs have been preserved in the library of the Duke of Devonshire at Chatsworth.

JONES, JOSEPH STEVEN (1809–77), American actor and author, creator of a number of Yankee characters, of whom Solon Shingle in *The People's Lawyer* (1839) was the most popular, John E. Owens (q.v.) making his final appearance in the part in New York in 1884. The Honorable Jefferson S. Batkins, another Yankee character in *The Silver Spoon* (1852), was first played by the younger William Warren (q.v.) at the Boston Museum, and the play survived on the stage until well into the twentieth century.

JONES, MARGO (1913–55), American producer and theatre director, who in 1943 was responsible for the staging of an early play by Tennessee Williams (q.v.) at the Cleveland Playhouse, and in 1945 founded an experimental theatre in Dallas where she did nine productions each year of old and new plays, described in her book *Theatre-in-the-Round* (1951). Her work was first seen on Broadway in 1945 when, with Eddie Dowling, she again directed a play by Tennessee Williams, *The Glass Menagerie*, starring Laurette Taylor (q.v.). In 1948 she also directed Williams's *Summer and Smoke*, which she had staged at Dallas the previous year. Among her other productions were Maxwell Anderson's *Joan of Lorraine* (1946), with Ingrid Bergman, and Owen Crump's *Southern Exposure* (1950). After her death the theatre she had founded continued to function under different directors until the end of 1959, the last production being *Othello*.

JONES, ROBERT EDMOND (1887–1954), American writer, lecturer, director, and above all scene designer, whose first designs (for Ashley Dukes's *The Man Who Married a Dumb Wife* in 1915) began a revolution in American scene design. His ability to integrate his designs with all the aspects of the play made his work memorable, particularly when he also directed the actors, as he did in *The Great God Brown* (1926) by O'Neill (q.v.), with all of whose early plays he was connected through his association with the Provincetown Players (q.v.). He was also responsible for the décor of a number of Shakespearian productions, his *Othello* in 1937 being much admired, and of such modern plays as Carson and Parker's *The Jest* (1919), Marc Connelly's *The Green Pastures* (1930), Maxwell Anderson's *Night over Taos* (1932), and Sidney Howard's adaptation of a Chinese play, *Lute Song* (1946). He was also part-author, with Kenneth Macgowan (q.v.), of *Continental Stagecraft* (1922).

JONSON, BEN(JAMIN) (1572–1637), English dramatist, friend and contemporary of Shakespeare (q.v.), who played Kno'well in Jonson's first play, *Every Man in His Humour* (1598). This was followed by *Every Man Out of His Humour* and *The Case is Altered* (both 1599) and by *Cynthia's Revels* (1600), performed at Blackfriars by the Children of the Chapel. The Chapel Children also appeared in *The Poetaster* (1601), in which Jonson, a quarrelsome man, vented his spleen on some of his contemporaries, including Dekker and Marston (qq.v.), who immediately replied in *Satiromastix*, ridiculing Jonson. But the quarrel was patched up in time for Marston to collaborate with Jonson and Chapman (q.v.) in *Eastwood Ho!* (1605). This, because of its satirical reflection on James I's Scottish policy, landed the authors in prison, where Jonson had already found himself earlier for his part in the lost play *The Isle of Dogs* (1597). He had also been in trouble over his first tragedy, *Sejanus* (1603), which the authorities considered seditious. The troubles of his early life are reflected in the plays he wrote then, and his best work was undoubtedly done in the more peaceful period which extends from the production of *Volpone; or, the Fox* in 1606 to that of *The Devil is an Ass* in 1616. The intervening years saw the production of *Epicœne; or, the Silent Woman* (1609), *The Alchemist* (1610), a second tragedy entitled *Catiline* (1611), and the farcical *Bartholomew Fair* (1614), whose slight plot serves to link together a number of short scenes portraying a typical London holiday crowd. Some of the above plays have been revived, *Volpone* in particular providing Donald Wolfit (q.v.) with one of his best parts. It was first seen in New York in 1928, in a production by the Theatre Guild, and in Paris, under Dullin, in 1931. A musical version entitled *Foxy*, with Bert Lahr (q.v.), had a short run on Broadway in 1964. *The Alchemist* (which provided Garrick (q.v.) with one of his best comic parts in Abel Drugger) was revived by the Old Vic in 1947 (with Alec Guinness as Drugger) and 1962, and at the Chichester Festival in 1970; it was seen in New York in 1948. *Bartholomew Fair* has not been produced professionally in New York, but was seen in London in 1950 (Old Vic) and 1969 (Royal Shakespeare Company). *Epicœne*, on which Richard Strauss based the libretto of his opera 'Die Schweigsame Frau' (1935), has not been seen in London since the Phoenix Society revival of 1924. Jonson's last plays, written between 1625 and 1633, were less successful in their own day and have not been revived. Between 1605 and 1612, with Inigo Jones (q.v.), who was responsible for the costumes and scenery, Jonson presented at Court eight masques, in one of which—*Oberon, the Fairy Prince* —the young Prince Henry, eldest son of James I, appeared shortly before his death in 1611.

JORDAN, DOROTHY [really DOROTHEA] (1761–1816), English actress who excelled as high-spirited hoydens and in breeches parts. She was the illegitimate daughter of a man named Francis Bland, but unlike her brother, the actor GEORGE BLAND (?–1807), she did not use her father's surname, but went on the stage as Miss Francis. She made her first appearance in Dublin in 1779 and in 1782 was in England, where she was befriended by Tate Wilkinson (q.v.). As Mrs. Jordan, a name suggested by Wilkinson, though she was never married, she made her first appearance with his provincial company as Calista in Rowe's *The Fair Penitent*, and remained with him until engaged by Sheridan (q.v.) for Drury Lane, making her first appearance there with great success on 15 Oct. 1785 as Peggy in Garrick's *The Country Girl*. She later proved equally successful as Priscilla Tomboy in a musical farce, *The Romp* (based on Bickerstaffe's *Love in the City*), in which part she was painted by Romney, as Miss Hoyden in Sheridan's *A Trip to Scarborough*, as Lady Teazle in the same author's *The School for Scandal*, as Miss Prue in Congreve's *Love for Love*, and as Sir Harry Wildair in Farquhar's *The Constant Couple*, in which part she was painted by Chalmers. She was also the model for Hoppner's Comic Muse. In 1796 she appeared as Rowena in *Vortigern and Rowena*, a Shakespeare forgery by Ireland (q.v.). From 1791 to 1811 she was the mistress of the Duke of Clarence (later William IV), by whom she had ten children. Her last years were unhappy. She made her final appearance on the stage in 1814 and retired to die in Paris.

Jornada, the name given in Spain to each division of a play, corresponding to the English 'act'. It probably comes from the Italian *giornata*, found occasionally in a *sacra rappresentazione* (q.v.). The word in its present form was first used by Torres Naharro (q.v.).

Josefstädter Theater, see VIENNA.

JOSEPH, STEPHEN (1921–67), English actor and director, son of Hermione Gingold (q.v.). He began his theatrical career as a director at the Lowestoft Repertory Theatre and then went to America, where he graduated in drama at the State University of Iowa. On his return to England in 1955 he formed a Sunday society for the express purpose of presenting plays 'in the round', which was henceforward to be his main preoccupation. Basing his company first on Scarborough and later on Stoke-on-Trent, where the former Victoria Theatre was adapted for arena performances, he worked enthusiastically to convert audiences and actors to his way of thinking, touring theatreless towns in his neighbourhood and occasionally bringing his company to the Mahatma Gandhi Hall in London. In 1962 he was appointed to a Fellowship in the newly founded Department of Drama at Manchester University, being the first holder of the post, which involved both teaching and research. An enthusiastic innovator, his early death was a great loss to the theatre. He was the author of several books on technical aspects of the theatre, including *Theatre-in-the-Round* (1955), *Scene-painting and Design* and *Actor and Architect* (both 1964), and *New Theatre Forms* (1968), which deals with the end stage (as at the Mermaid, q.v.) and the three-sided stage (as at Chichester, q.v.) as well as his own arena stage. In 1962 he edited *Adaptable Theatres*, a report on the London Congress of the International Association of Theatre Technicians. After his death his work at Stoke-on-Trent was carried on by Peter Cheeseman.

JOUVET, LOUIS (1887–1951), French actor and director, who in 1913 joined Copeau (q.v.) at the Théâtre du Vieux-Colombier, where he first attracted attention by his performances as Aguecheek in *Twelfth Night* and Autolycus in *The Winter's Tale*. He was with Copeau in America from 1917 to 1919, but returned to Paris in 1922 to open his own theatre, where one of his first successes was *Knock, ou le Triomphe de la médecine* (1923), by Jules Romains (q.v.), in which he played the title-role. Later, at the Comédie des Champs-Élysées and at the Athénée, where he settled in 1934, he directed and played in many first performances of the works of Jean Giraudoux (q.v.). Some of Jouvet's finest work was done in the plays of Molière, for whom he had an intense admiration. Among his greatest successes were the title-role in *Tartuffe* and Géronte in *Les Fourberies de Scapin*. He became a professor at the Conservatoire in 1935, and in 1936 was a member, together with Baty, Dullin, and Pitoëff (qq.v.), of the cartel of directors appointed by the State to run the Comédie-Française.

JUVARRA, FILIPPO (1676–1736), an Italian architect who in 1708, while working in Rome, designed and built a small theatre (probably for rod-puppets) for Cardinal Pietro Ottoboni, a great lover of plays and operas. It was demolished on Ottoboni's death and no trace of it remains, but some of Juvarra's scene designs for it, made between 1708 and 1714, still exist, among them an album now at the Victoria and Albert Museum in London.

Juvenile Drama, see TOY THEATRE.

Juvenile Lead, see STOCK COMPANY.

K

Kabuki, the popular theatre of Japan, as opposed to the aristocratic *nō* play (q.v.). As its name implies—*ka* = singing, *bu* = dancing, *ki* = acting—it combines the three main theatrical arts, allied to an astonishing virtuosity, particularly in the playing of female parts, by highly trained actors. In its present form *kabuki* dates from about the middle of the seventeenth century, though some of its elements go back a thousand years. Since 1945 the many small *kabuki* troupes which used to tour the countryside have been disbanded and performances are given only in the larger cities. The plays are performed on a wide, shallow platform which since *c.* 1760 has incorporated a revolving stage, later adopted by the Western theatre also. Another characteristic of the *kabuki* theatre, taken from the *nō* play, is the *hana-michi*, or 'flower way', running along the left-hand wall of the auditorium to the stage at the level of the spectators' heads. Along this the actors make their entrances and exits, or withdraw for an aside. They wear rich brocaded costumes for historical parts, plain dress for scenes from daily life and, unlike the *nō* actors, are not masked. Music is provided by a small group of instrumentalists placed inconspicuously behind a lattice on the right of the stage. There are also two stage hands, the *kurogo* and the *kōken*, one hooded, the other not, who are by tradition invisible. They date from the time when each of the chief actors had a 'shadow' who crouched beside him holding a light on the end of a bamboo pole to illuminate the play of his features. The *kabuki* plays, which have no particular literary value, being frameworks for the display of technical accomplishments by the actors, take their subjects from many sources—history, myth, daily life, even from the *nō* plays, or from the puppet-theatre or *bunraku*. For a performance based on a puppet-play a singer, or *jōruri*, seated on the stage, recites the story which the actors are miming; for a *nō* play, the *samisen* players are joined by a group of *nō* musicians. In the old days performances by *kabuki* actors could extend over several days, and they still last from midday to midnight, the audience, in family groups, coming and going from the boxes in the audi-torium, eating and talking during the less exacting parts of the performance and giving all their attention to the great set speeches and dance-dramas which, together with comic episodes and historical set-pieces, make up the programme. A number of *kabuki* plays have been translated into English, two important volumes being Ernst's *Three Japanese Plays from the Traditional Theatre* (1959) and Richie and Watanabe's *Six Kabuki Plays* (1963).

KACHALOV [really SHVERUBOVICH], VASILI IVANOVICH (1875–1948), Russian actor, who in 1900 joined the company of the Moscow Art Theatre (q.v.). He appeared in a number of outstanding productions, including *Julius Caesar*, *Hamlet*, and Ibsen's *Brand*, and created the roles of Ivan Karamazov in Dostoievsky's *The Brothers Karamazov*, Vershinin in Ivanov's *Armoured Train 14–69*, and the Reader in Tolstoy's *Resurrection*, one of his best parts. Possessed of a fine voice and an excellent presence, Kachalov was one of the actors whose careers marked the transition from Imperialist to Soviet Russia. For the revival of Griboyedev's *Woe from Wit* by the Moscow Art Theatre in 1938 he again played the hero, Chatsky, the part he had played in the original production in 1906.

KAHN, FLORENCE (1877–1951), see BEER-BOHM, MAX.

KAINZ, JOSEF (1858–1910), German actor, famed for the richness and beauty of his voice and the purity of his diction. He made his first appearance on the stage in 1874 in Vienna, where in 1899 he returned to end his days as a leading member of the Imperial Theatre. He was for some time in Munich, where he was the friend and favourite actor of King Ludwig II of Bavaria, and in 1883 played opposite Agnes Sorma (q.v.) in the newly founded Deutsches Theater in Berlin. He also toured extensively in America, where he appeared in many of his best parts, which included Romeo, Hamlet, and the heroes of Grillparzer. He was also good in Molière's *Tartuffe*, Rostand's *Cyrano de Bergerac*, and as Oswald in Ibsen's *Ghosts*.

KAISER, GEORG (1878–1945), German dramatist, leader of the so-called Expressionist school of drama. His early plays, of which *Die jüdische Witwe* (1911) is typical, were satirical comedies directed against Romanticism. The First World War led him, however, to question the ethical foundations of a society blindly rushing to destruction, and his *Von morgens bis mitternachts* (1916) satirizes both the futility of modern civilization and the robot-like men who are caught in its meshes. This sombre history of a bank clerk whose bid for freedom leads to suicide was seen in London in 1920 and in New York in 1922 as *From Morn to Midnight*. It was followed by the powerful trilogy, *Die Koralle* and *Gas, Parts I and II* (1917–20), a symbolic picture of industrialism crashing to destruction and taking with it the civilization it has ruined. Kaiser, whose other plays include the historical drama *Die Bürger von Calais* (1914) and the melodramatic *Der Brand im Opernhaus* (1919), had a great influence on the European theatre in the 1920s and 1930s.

KÁLIDÁSA (?373–?415), an early and important writer of Sanskrit drama. Three of his plays have survived, and it was the translation of one of them, *Śakuntalā*, known also as *The Recovered Ring*, by Sir William Jones, published in Calcutta in 1790, that first drew the attention of Western authors, particularly Goethe (q.v.), to the beauties of Sanskrit literature. *Śakuntalā* was seen for the first time in English at an open-air performance in Regent's Park by the Elizabethan Stage Society on 3 July 1899.

Kameri Theatre, ISRAEL, see CAMERI THEATRE.

Kamerny Theatre, MOSCOW. This theatre, whose name means Chamber, or Intimate, Theatre, was founded in 1914 by Alexander Taïrov (q.v.) as an experimental theatre for those to whom the naturalistic methods of the Moscow Art Theatre (q.v.) no longer appealed. Here he sought to work out his theory of 'synthetic theatre', which, unlike the 'conditioned theatre' of Meyerhold (q.v.), made the actor the centre of attention, combining in his person acrobat, singer, dancer, pantomimist, comedian, and tragedian. Taïrov's first successful production was Vishnevsky's *The Optimistic Tragedy* (1934), in which his wife, Alice Koonen, played the heroine. The theatre then became important for its produc-

tions of non-Russian plays, providing a link with Western drama at a time when it was badly needed. Taïrov even made the interesting if not entirely successful experiment of linking a version of Shaw's *Caesar and Cleopatra* with Shakespeare's *Antony and Cleopatra* in a single evening, with a fragment of Pushkin thrown in for good measure. After his death in 1950 the theatre was reorganized and its identity lost, many of the company joining the newly opened Pushkin Theatre (q.v.).

KARATYGIN, VASILY ANDREYEVICH (1802–53), famous Russian tragedian, son of an actor, who made his first appearance on the stage in 1820. He was remarkable for the care with which he studied his roles, returning where possible to the original sources and labouring for historical accuracy in costume and décor, though he was opposed to the realistic style of acting and the innovations of Shchepkin (q.v.). In contrast to his contemporary Mochalov (q.v.), he developed a subtle and calculated technique which enabled him to play the most varied roles, though his preference was always for classical tragedy. He was also much admired in the patriotic drama of the day, and his influence on the style of Russian acting was apparent until well into the present century.

Kasperle, originally a German puppet, somewhat akin to the English Punch (q.v.). Imported into the live theatre, he took on many of the characteristics of Hanswurst (q.v.), and in the hands of Laroche (q.v.) developed into an important element in Viennese popular comedy.

KATAYEV, VALENTIN PETROVICH (1897–), Soviet dramatist, whose most successful play, which has been produced in many countries, was *Squaring the Circle* (1928), an amusing comedy about two ill-assorted couples who, owing to the housing shortage, are compelled to live in one room and finally change partners. First produced at the Moscow Art Theatre, it was seen in New York in 1935 and in London three years later. Katayev is also the author of a number of other comedies, including *The Primrose Path* (1934), which the Federal Theatre Project produced in New York in 1939, and an amusing trifle called *The Blue Scarf* (1943), in which a soldier at the front receives a scarf in a bundle of comforts, and is all prepared to fall in love with the youthful donor, only to find it is a schoolboy. Among his more serious plays are *Lone White Sail* (1937), which, in a revised version, had a successful run in 1951, *I, Son of the Working People* (1938), and a play for children, *Son of the Regiment* (1946).

KAUFMAN, GEORGE SIMON (1889–1961), American journalist and dramatist, whose first plays were written in collaboration with MARC(US) COOK CONNELLY (1890–1980), the most successful being *Dulcy* (1921) and *Beggar on Horseback* (1924). Their collaboration then ended, Kaufman alone producing an amusing farce, *The Butter and Egg Man* (1925), and Connelly the fine Negro play, *The Green Pastures* (1930). Kaufman then collaborated with Moss Hart (q.v.) in such plays as *Once in a Lifetime* (1930), *Merrily We Roll Along* (1934), *You Can't Take It With You* (1936), *I'd Rather Be Right* (1937), and *The Man Who Came to Dinner* (1939). Kaufman, who was known as 'the Great Collaborator', also wrote several plays with EDNA FERBER (1887–1968), among them *The Royal Family* (1927), based on the lives of the Drews and the Barrymores (qq.v.) and produced in London in 1934 as *Theatre Royal*.

KAYE, DANNY [really DAVID DANIEL KOMINSKI] (1913–), American actor and entertainer, who first appeared on the stage in 1928. He made his first appearance on Broadway in 1939 in *The Straw Hat Review* and in 1941 made a hit as Russell Paxton in Moss Hart's *Lady in the Dark*. He had appeared in London in 1938, but it was not until he returned to star at the Palladium in 1948 that he achieved complete recognition there. He has since been outstandingly successful in films, and is also highly thought of for his untiring work on behalf of the United Nations International Children's Emergency Fund.

KAZAN, ELIA (1909–), American actor and director, who made his first stage appearances for the Group Theatre (q.v.), playing Agate Keller in *Waiting for Lefty* (1935) and Eddie Fuselli in *Golden Boy* (1937), both by Clifford Odets (q.v.). In 1940 he played Ficzur (the Sparrow) in a revival of Molnár's *Liliom*. Kazan, who has also had a distinguished career in films, has directed a number of plays, including Wilder's *The*

Skin of Our Teeth (1942), Tennessee Williams's *A Streetcar Named Desire* (1947) and *Cat on a Hot Tin Roof* (1955), Arthur Miller's *Death of a Salesman* (1949), and Archibald MacLeish's *J.B.* (1958). In 1947 he helped to found the Actors' Studio (see METHOD), a workshop where professional actors could experiment and study their art, and worked closely with it until 1962, when he was appointed co-director of the Lincoln Center Repertory Theater, a position he resigned in 1965 (see LINCOLN CENTER).

KEAN, CHARLES JOHN (1811–68), English actor-manager, son of the tragedian Edmund Kean (q.v.). He was a serious, hard-working man, with none of the genius of his father but a good deal more application and common sense, and with his wife ELLEN TREE (1806–80), a good actress who played opposite him in many leading roles, he controlled an excellent company. His tenancy of the Princess's Theatre (q.v.) from 1850 to 1859 was particularly memorable. His plays, carefully chosen and well rehearsed, were set and costumed lavishly but with some attempt at historical accuracy, and his productions had a great influence on George II, Duke of Saxe-Meiningen (see MEININGER COMPANY), who was a frequent visitor to the theatre in London with his first wife, a niece of Queen Victoria.

KEAN, EDMUND (1787/90–1833), English tragic actor, a foundling who was on the stage as a child and later led the hard life of a strolling player until on 26 Jan. 1814 he appeared at Drury Lane as Shylock in *The Merchant of Venice*, discarding the traditional comedian's red beard and wig which even Macklin (q.v.) had not dared to tamper with, and playing the character for the first time as a swarthy fiend with a butcher's knife in his grasp and blood-lust in his eyes. The audience acclaimed him, and he continued to delight them in villainous parts—Macbeth, Iago, and Richard III in Shakespeare's plays, Sir Giles Overreach in Massinger's *A New Way to Pay Old Debts*, and Barabas in Marlowe's *The Jew of Malta*. Without nobility or tenderness, he failed in such parts as Hamlet or Romeo, even as Othello, and he had no aptitude for comedy. But in the delineation of outright wickedness he was unsurpassed. Unfortunately the privations of his early years, and some untameable wildness in his character, led to heavy drinking and scandalous behaviour, and the audiences who were won over by his superb acting were alienated by his unreliability, both in London and in the United States, where he made his first appearance in 1820. By his wife MARY CHAMBERS (c. 1780–1849), an actress whom he married in 1808 while they were both in a provincial company, he was the father of Charles Kean (q.v.). He made his last appearance on the stage as Othello to the Iago of his son on 25 Mar. 1833, collapsed during the performance, and died a few weeks later.

KEAN, THOMAS (fl. mid-eighteenth century), manager, with WALTER MURRAY, of a company of actors of whom little is at present known. They may have been amateurs, but if not, they were the first professional players to appear in the New World. In 1749 they acted Addison's *Cato* and other plays in a converted warehouse in Philadelphia, and in 1750 appeared in a theatre in Nassau Street, New York, in a repertory which included Shakespeare's *Richard III* as altered by Colley Cibber (q.v.), Congreve's *Love for Love*, Otway's *The Orphan*, and Lillo's *George Barnwell*. Later they visited, among other places, Williamsburg in Virginia and Annapolis in Maryland. Nothing is known of them after 1753.

KEANE, DORIS (1881–1945), see SHELDON, EDWARD.

KEDROV, MIKHAIL NIKOLAYEVICH (1893–1972), Russian actor and director, a pupil of Stanislavsky (q.v.), some of whose works he edited. He joined the company at the Moscow Art Theatre (q.v.) in 1924, and remained there until his death. He directed the production of Chekhov's *Uncle Vanya* in which the company was seen at Sadler's Wells in London in 1958, and also appeared at the Aldwych in the 1970 World Theatre season. Among his many productions one of the most acclaimed was a version of *The Winter's Tale* which was three years in rehearsal.

KEELEY, ROBERT (1793–1869), English actor, who ran away from his apprenticeship to join a strolling company. In 1821 he made a great success at the Olympic as Jemmy Green in Moncrieff's *Tom and Jerry*, and in the following year he played Jerry in the sequel, *Life in London*, at Sadler's Wells. A fine low comedian, his stolid look and slow, jerky speech added much to the humour of his acting. Among his most famous parts were Dogberry in

Much Ado About Nothing, Jacob Earwig in Selby's farce, *The Boots at the Swan* (1842), and Mrs. Sairey Gamp in a dramatization of Dickens's *Martin Chuzzlewit*. His wife, MARY ANN GOWARD (1806–99), was an excellent actress, at her best in pathetic parts like Smike in Stirling's *The Fortunes of Smike; or, a Sequel to Nicholas Nickleby* (1840). But her greatest triumph was the title-role in Buckstone's version of *Jack Sheppard* (1839), in which the highwayman was portrayed as a wild youngster, defrauded of his heritage and driven to bad ways by the animosity of Jonathan Wild the thief-taker.

KEENE, LAURA [really MARY MOSS or FOSS] (c. 1830–73), American actress and theatre manager, who after some stage experience in England and Australia, settled in 1855 in the United States, where she was the first woman to become a theatre manager. On 18 Nov. 1856 she opened her own playhouse (see OLYMPIC THEATRE (3)) with *As You Like It*, in which she played Rosalind, and remained there until 1863. In her company were Joseph Jefferson and E. A. Sothern (qq.v.). The latter was responsible for the success in 1858 of Tom Taylor's *Our American Cousin*, which the company was playing at Ford's Theatre, Washington, on 14 Apr. 1865, when Abraham Lincoln was assassinated. After a somewhat difficult period, Laura Keene returned to New York in 1871, reopened the Fourteenth Street Theatre under her own name, and made her last appearance on the stage in a melodrama, *The Sea of Ice*, at Wood's Museum (see DALY'S THEATRE) on 27 Apr. 1872.

KEITH, BENJAMIN FRANKLIN (1846–1914), see VAUDEVILLE.

KELLY, CHARLES (1839–85), see TERRY, DAME ELLEN.

KELLY, FANNY [really FRANCES MARIA] (1790–1882), English actress, the subject of the essay 'Barbara S—' by Charles Lamb (q.v.). She was on the stage as a child, and as an adult actress was associated for over thirty years with Drury Lane, where she revived some of the parts previously played by Mrs. Jordan (q.v.). On her retirement in 1840 she opened a training school for young actresses (see ROYALTY THEATRE (2)), but it was not a success, and she was forced to give it up, confining her activities to Shakespeare readings and private teaching.

KELLY, GEORGE EDWARD (1887–1974), American dramatist, whose first full-length play, *The Torchbearers* (1922), was a satire on the pretentiousness of amateur theatricals. He expanded a vaudeville skit, *Poor Aubrey*, into a hilarious satire entitled *The Show-Off* (1924), and was awarded the Pulitzer Prize for *Craig's Wife* (1925), a relentless exposé of feminine possessiveness and lovelessness. Among his later plays, none of which was quite so successful, were *Daisy Mayme* (1926), *Behold the Bridegroom* (1927), and *Maggie the Magnificent* (1929). After the failure of *Philip Goes Forth* (1931), Kelly withdrew from the theatre for some years, returning unsuccessfully in 1936 with a comedy, *Reflected Glory*. It was not until 1945 that his work was seen on stage again with *The Deep Mrs. Sykes*, a satire on feminine intuition which was followed in 1946 by his last play, *The Fatal Weakness*, a study in feminine romanticism.

KELLY, HUGH (1739–77), English playwright, whose sentimental comedy, *False Delicacy*, was produced at Drury Lane by Garrick (q.v.) in 1768 to offset the success of Goldsmith's *The Good-Natured Man* at Covent Garden. It eclipsed its rival for a short time but is now forgotten, though it was played in the provinces, several times revived in London, and translated into French and German. Kelly wrote several other plays, of which *The School for Wives* (1773) was the least sentimental and almost approached the true spirit of the comedy of manners.

KEMBLE, FANNY [really FRANCES ANNE] (1809–93), English actress, daughter of Charles Kemble (see KEMBLE, J. P.) and his wife MARIA THERESA DE CAMP (1773–1838), also an actress. In 1829 Fanny saved her father from bankruptcy by appearing at Covent Garden, which he was then managing, as Juliet in *Romeo and Juliet*. She was an immediate success and for three seasons brought prosperity to the theatre, appearing as Portia in *The Merchant of Venice*, Beatrice in *Much Ado About Nothing*, Lady Teazle in Sheridan's *The School for Scandal*, and reviving a number of tragic parts formerly associated with her aunt, Mrs. Siddons (q.v.), among them Isabella in Southerne's *The Fatal Marriage*, Euphrasia in Murphy's *The Grecian Daughter*, Calista in Rowe's *The Fair Penitent*, and Belvidera in Otway's

Venice Preserv'd. She also created the part of Julia in Sheridan Knowles's *The Hunchback* (1832). Unlike most of the family, Fanny seems to have been good both in comedy and tragedy. She married an American in 1834 and left the stage, but divorced him in 1845 and returned to give readings in England and the United States, finally settling in 1868 in London, where she died.

KEMBLE, JOHN PHILIP (1757–1823), English actor, brother of Mrs. Siddons (q.v.). He appeared on the stage as a child with his parents, and after being educated abroad returned to become a stately, formal actor, at his best in heavy dramatic parts. He made his London début at Drury Lane in 1783 as Hamlet, in which character he was painted by Lawrence, and played all the great tragic parts of the current repertory—Wolsey in *Henry VIII*, Brutus in *Julius Caesar*, the Stranger in Thompson's adaptation of Kotzebue's *Menschenhass und Reue*, Rolla in Sheridan's *Pizarro*, Addison's Cato, and above all Shakespeare's Coriolanus, in which he made his farewell appearance on 23 June 1817. His stiffness of gesture and somewhat pedantic manner rendered him unfit for comedy, nor was he good in romantic parts, in spite of his handsome presence. Even in tragedy he eschewed sudden bursts of pathos or passion, achieving his effects by a steady and studied intensity of feeling. More respected than loved, he was nevertheless much admired, and his influence on the London theatre of his time was salutary. He was successively manager of Drury Lane and Covent Garden, and introduced a number of reforms at both theatres in the administration and in the provision of costume and scenery. His younger brothers were also on the stage, STEPHEN (1758–1822), a poor actor, becoming in later life so fat that he could play Falstaff without padding, and CHARLES (1775–1854), who was the father of Fanny Kemble (q.v.), playing mainly romantic lovers or fine gentlemen, Romeo being considered his best part.

KEMBLE, ROGER (1722–1802), English actor, who toured the provinces with his wife SARAH WARD (?–1807) and numerous children, of whom the eldest became the great Sarah Siddons (q.v.). Her brothers John Philip (q.v.), Stephen, Charles, and Henry were also on the stage. Of her four younger sisters, all actresses, ELIZABETH

(1761–1836) became well known on the American stage as Mrs. Whitlock.

KEMP, THOMAS CHARLES (1891–1955), dramatic critic, who from 1935 until his death was on the *Birmingham Post*. Born in Birmingham, he became an important figure in theatrical life there, being for some time chairman of the Crescent Theatre, for which he wrote several plays. He also lectured on Shakespeare both in Birmingham and at Stratford-upon-Avon. He was a great admirer of Sir Barry Jackson (q.v.), and was the author of *The Birmingham Repertory Theatre: The Playhouse and the Man* (1944). He also collaborated with J. C. Trewin (q.v.) in a history of the Shakespeare Memorial Theatre, *The Stratford Festival* (1953).

KEMPE, WILLIAM (?–1603), a famous Elizabethan clown, the original Dogberry in *Much Ado About Nothing* (c. 1598) and a great player of jigs. He was a member of the company which went with the Earl of Leicester to Holland in 1585–6, and was at the Danish Court in Elsinore in the latter year. He became one of the Chamberlain's Men (q.v.) on the formation of the company in 1594, remaining with them until 1600, in which year he danced his famous morris from London to Norwich.

KEMPSON, RACHEL (1910–), see REDGRAVE, MICHAEL.

KENDAL [really GRIMSTON], **WILLIAM HUNTER** (1843–1917), English actor-manager, who in 1874 married the actress MADGE [really MARGARET] ROBERTSON (1848–1935), sister of T. W. Robertson (q.v.). Together they ran an excellent company and formed an exemplary partnership, both on and off stage, which did much to raise the status of their profession. They were with the Bancrofts (q.v.) at the Prince of Wales's, where they appeared in the first production of Clement Scott's translation of Sardou's *Dora* (as *Diplomacy*) in 1878, and then went into partnership with Hare (q.v.) at the St. James's, playing leading parts in many notable productions. Kendal was somewhat overshadowed by the brilliance of his wife, but was nevertheless a good, reliable actor and an excellent business man. He retired in 1908, at the same time as his wife, who in 1926, in recognition of her work for the English theatre, was appointed D.B.E.

KERR, WALTER F. (1913–), American dramatic critic, who from 1945 to 1949 was Associate Professor of Drama at the Catholic University. He was then appointed dramatic critic of the Catholic weekly, *The Commonweal*, a position which he held until 1951, when he became dramatic critic of the New York *Herald Tribune*. He is the author of several books on the theatre, including *How Not to Write a Play* (1955) and *Criticism and Censorship* (1957), and has collected many of his critical essays, notably in *Pieces at Eight* (1957). In 1963 his *Theatre in Spite of Itself* was awarded the George Jean Nathan Prize for dramatic criticism. With his wife, the playwright JEAN KERR (*née* BRIDGET JEAN COLLINS) (1923–), whose play *Mary, Mary* (1961) had a successful run in London in 1963, he wrote the revue *Touch and Go* (1949), also seen in London (in 1950), and the book for the musical *Goldilocks* (1958).

KERRIDGE, MARY (1914–), see COUNSELL, JOHN.

KESTER, PAUL (1870–1933), American dramatist, who adapted a number of foreign plays for the American stage, usually with a particular player in mind. Two of his most successful adaptations were of novels by Charles Major, *When Knighthood was in Flower* (1901) and *Dorothy Vernon of Haddon Hall* (1903). As *Dorothy o' the Hall*, the latter was played in London in 1906 by Fred Terry and his wife Julia Neilson (qq.v.). They had already had a great success in 1900 as Charles II and Nell Gwynn in Kester's *Sweet Nell of Old Drury*, which remained in their repertory for over thirty years. When it was first produced in the United States a few months after the London production, the part of Nell Gwynn was played by Ada Rehan (q.v.).

KILLIGREW, THOMAS (1612–83), English dramatist and theatre manager, founder of Drury Lane Theatre (q.v.) under a Charter granted by Charles II. With Davenant (q.v.), he held the monopoly of acting in Restoration London, and on the death of Sir Henry Herbert (q.v.) in 1673 became Master of the King's Revels. He also established a school for young actors in the Barbican. Before the closing of the theatres in 1642 he had had several plays produced, including *The Parson's Wedding* (1640), based on Calderón, which when it was revived in 1664, with a cast of women only, made even Pepys blush.

KILTY, JEROME (1922–), see SHAW, G.B.

KING, TOM (1730–1804), English actor, who was at Drury Lane under Garrick (q.v.), first appearing there in Oct. 1748. At his best in comedy, he was much admired as Touchstone (in *As You Like It*) and Malvolio (in *Twelfth Night*). He also created the character of Lord Ogleby in the elder Colman's *The Clandestine Marriage* (1766) after Garrick had refused it, and was the first to play Sir Peter Teazle and Puff in Sheridan's *The School for Scandal* (1777) and *The Critic* (1779). He also appeared as Sir Anthony Absolute, first played at Covent Garden by Shuter (q.v.) in 1775, when Sheridan's *The Rivals* was revived at Drury Lane in 1777. He made his last appearance on the stage, as Sir Peter, in 1802.

(See also SADLER'S WELLS.)

King of Misrule, see FEAST OF FOOLS.

King's Concert Rooms, LONDON, see SCALA THEATRE.

King's Jester, see LENO, DAN.

King's Men, see CHAMBERLAIN'S MEN.

King's Theatre, LONDON, see HER MAJESTY'S and PANTHEON.

KINGSLEY, SIDNEY (1906–), American dramatist, whose first play, *Men in White* (1933), a vivid picture of hospital life, won the Pulitzer Prize. It was seen in London in 1934. Since then he has written *Dead End* (1935), a study of crime-breeding slum conditions; *Ten Million Ghosts* (1936), an indictment of profiteering in munitions in the First World War; *The Patriots* (1943), a play based on early American history which won the New York Drama Critics' Award; *Detective Story* (1949); *Lunatics and Lovers* (1954); and *Night Life* (1962). He also dramatized *The World We Make* (1939), a novel by Millen Brand, and Arthur Koestler's anti-Communist novel, *Darkness at Noon* (1951).

KINGSTON [really SILVER, *née* KONSTAM], GERTRUDE (1866–1937), English actress and theatre manager, for whom Bernard Shaw wrote the part of the Empress Catherine II in *Great Catherine* (1913). She made her first appearance in London in 1888 and after a long and successful career in the commercial theatre opened the Little Theatre (q.v.) in John Street, London, intending to make it a home of repertory. The venture was not a success, but her efforts, like those of Lena Ashwell at the Kingsway (qq.v.), later bore fruit in the establishment of the repertory system, mainly outside London.

Kingsway Theatre, LONDON, in Great Queen Street, Holborn. This opened as the Novelty Theatre on 9 Dec. 1882 and had a chequered career with frequent changes of name, being known as the Folies-Dramatiques in 1883, the Jodrell (after its manageress) in 1888, the New Queen's in 1890, and the Eden Palace of Varieties in 1894, reverting at intervals to its original name. It was at this theatre, on 7 June 1889, that the first performance in English of Ibsen's *A Doll's House* was given, in William Archer's translation, Janet Achurch (q.v.) playing Nora. In 1898 the theatre closed for two years, and was then bought by W. S. Penley (q.v.) with the money he had made out of Hawtrey's *The Private Secretary*. He reconstructed it and opened it as the Great Queen Street Theatre on 24 Mar. 1900 but retired after eighteen months, having lost most of his fortune. On 10 Mar. 1902 the theatre was the scene of one of the few London productions by Gordon Craig (q.v.), who put on for the Purcell Society, with Martin Shaw as musical director, Handel's 'Acis and Galatea' and Purcell's 'Masque of Love'. Later events at this theatre were visits from a German company, productions of old English plays by the Mermaid Society under Philip Carr, and the first London visit, in 1907, of the company from the Abbey Theatre (q.v.) in Dublin, during which they appeared in Synge's *The Playboy of the Western World*. Lena Ashwell (q.v.) then took over, reconstructed and redecorated the interior of the building, and opened it as the Kingsway on 9 Oct. 1907 with Wharton's *Irene Wycherley*. Outstanding events of the next few years were Granville-Barker's tenancy, during which the most successful production was Arnold Bennett's *The Great Adventure* (1913), with Henry Ainley (q.v.), and the visit in 1925 of Barry Jackson's company from the Birmingham Repertory Theatre (q.v.), which was seen in a number of plays, including the first 'modern-dress' *Hamlet*. The theatre then continued its erratic course and from 1932 to 1933 was the home of the Independent Theatre Club, formed to stage plays banned by the censor. These included Ludwig's *Versailles*, and Schnitzler's *Fraulein Elsa* with Peggy Ashcroft (q.v.). On 11 May 1940 the theatre suffered considerable damage from bombing and was forced to close. In 1954 an effort by the English Stage Company to reopen it came to nothing. They went to the Royal Court (q.v.), and the Kingsway remained derelict until it was pulled down in 1956.

Kirby's Flying Ballet, see FLYING EFFECTS.

KIRCHMAYER, THOMAS (1511–63), German Protestant humanist, and author, under the pseudonym Naogeorg, of several anti-Catholic plays, of which the most important was *Pammachius* (1538). Written in Latin, in which language it was first performed, it was translated into German for a production at Zwickau, and some time between 1538 and 1548 an English version in four parts, now lost, was prepared by John Bale of Ossory. A performance in the original Latin was seen at Cambridge in 1545.

KIRSHON, VLADIMIR MIKHAILOVICH (1902–38), Soviet dramatist, and author, with Ouspensky, of a play dealing with the problems of Russian youth at odds with the new regime. This was produced at the Mossoviet Theatre in 1926. As *Red Rust*, in a translation by V. and F. Vernon which was published in 1930, it was seen in London in Feb. 1929 with Gielgud (q.v.) in the part of Fedor, and in New York later the same year. Though discursive and somewhat melodramatic, it is an interesting study of a transitional epoch. It was, however, too superficial to be of lasting value, a criticism which seems to apply to all Kirshon's later works.

KISFALUDY, KÁROLY (1788–1830), Hungarian writer and dramatist, author of several historical tragedies and of a number of successful comedies in which he first introduced to the Hungarian stage the peasant types which afterwards became so popular. The Kisfaludy Society, named after him, is Hungary's most important literary society, and was responsible for the translation and editing of a complete edition of Shakespeare's plays published in 1864. The translations were made by outstanding poets and writers and are still in general use on the Hungarian stage.

Klaw Theatre, NEW YORK, on 45th Street between Broadway and 8th Avenue. It opened on 2 Mar. 1921 with Tallulah Bankhead, Katharine Cornell, and a fine supporting cast in Rachel Crothers's *Nice People*. This was followed by W. J. Hurlbut's *The Lilies of the Field* (also 1921) and *Meet the Wife* (1923), by Lynn Starling. Henry Hatcher's *Hell-Bent for Heaven* (also 1923), a mountaineering drama which won the Pulitzer Prize, was first seen at the Klaw for four matinées. In 1925–6 the Theatre Guild (q.v.) occupied the theatre with its Shavian double bill, *Androcles and the Lion* and *The Man of Destiny*. The theatre was re-named the Avon in 1929, and on 15 Nov. 1931 Cornelia Otis Skinner (q.v.) appeared there in her monodrama, *The Wives of Henry VIII*, followed by Constance Collier (q.v.) and a fine cast in a revival of Coward's *Hay Fever*. The last legitimate production at this theatre was *Tight Britches* (1934), by John Taintor Foote and Hubert Hales, after which it became a broadcasting studio. In Jan. 1954 it was pulled down.

KLEIN, CHARLES (1867–1915), American dramatist whose first successful play was *Heartsease* (1897) (not to be confused with Mortimer's version of the younger Dumas's *La Dame aux camélias*, prepared for Modjeska in 1880 under the same title). Two later plays which had an enormous success were *The Auctioneer* (1901) and *The Music Master* (1904), both written for and produced by Belasco (q.v.). They were quite trivial and unoriginal, and owed their success to the acting of David Warfield (q.v.), for whom they were designed. In 1913 Klein was responsible, with Montague Glass, for a dramatization of some Jewish short stories which, as *Potash and Perlmutter*, had a great success in New York and London. Klein was play-reader for Charles Frohman (q.v.), and was drowned with him in the sinking of the *Lusitania*.

KLEIST, (BERND WILHELM) HEINRICH VON (1777–1811), German dramatist, whose one-act play, *Der zerbrochene Krug* (1808), is considered one of the finest comedies in the German language. In it a village magistrate with Falstaffian virtuosity in lying tries a case in which he is himself the culprit. It was first produced by Goethe (q.v.) at Weimar, and has been translated into English, in a cut version, as *The Broken Pitcher*, and into Scots as *The Chippit Chantie*. Kleist's other plays include a tragedy based on the story of the Amazon queen, *Penthesilea* (also 1808), *Die Hermannsschlacht* (1809), and *Das Käthchen von Heilbronn* (1810), a study of Griselda-like devotion first seen at the Vienna Burgtheater. The best-known, however, is *Prinz Friedrich von Homburg* (also 1810), which in 1951, in a French translation, with Gérard Philipe (q.v.) in the title-role, was one of the outstanding successes of the Avignon Festival (q.v.). It has also been used as the libretto of an opera by Hans Werner Henze, first performed in 1960. Kleist, whose genius was unrecognized during his lifetime, committed suicide.

KNEPP [also KNIPP], MARY (?-1677), one of the first English actresses, who was in Killigrew's company with Nell Gwynn (q.v.). She was a friend of Pepys, in whose diary she often appears, usually as a source of back-stage gossip. A merry, lively woman, at her best in comedy, she was much in demand for the speaking of the witty prologues and epilogues that were in fashion at the time.

Knickerbocker Theatre, NEW YORK, a large playhouse on the north-east corner of 38th Street and Broadway. As Abbey's (named after its first manager, H. E. Abbey, q.v.), it opened on 8 Nov. 1893 with Irving (q.v.) in Tennyson's *Becket*. Many visiting stars, among them Mounet-Sully (in Victor Hugo's *Hernani*), Réjane (in Sardou's *Madame Sans-Gêne*), and John Hare (in Pinero's *The Notorious Mrs. Ebbsmith*), made their first appearances in New York at this theatre. On 14 Sept. 1896 it was renamed the Knickerbocker. Among the outstanding productions then seen there were Kester's *Sweet Nell of Old Drury* (1900) with Ada Rehan (q.v.), and Barrie's *Quality Street* (1901) with Maude Adams (q.v.). In 1911 Knoblock's *Kismet*, with Otis Skinner (q.v.) as Hajj, was an instantaneous success and had a long run. The theatre then became famous for its musicals, though the last production to be seen there, in 1929, was a play, Philip Dunning's *Sweet Land of Liberty*, which had only eight perform-

ances. The theatre then closed, and was demolished in 1930.

The Bowery Amphitheatre in New York was called the Knickerbocker when for a short time in 1844 it was run as a theatre.

KNIPPER-CHEKHOVA, OLGA LEON-ARDOVNA (1870-1959), Russian actress, who joined the Moscow Art Theatre on its foundation and appeared in all the plays of Chekhov (q.v.), whom she married in 1901. After his death she remained with the company as one of its leading actresses, and in 1943, at the three-hundredth performance of *The Cherry Orchard*, she was still playing the part of Madame Ranevskaya which she had created in 1904. She was one of the outstanding figures of the Soviet stage and an important link with pre-Revolutionary days.

KNOBLOCK [really KNOBLAUCH], EDWARD (1874-1945), a dramatist who, though born and educated in the United States, spent much of his life in England and on the Continent. His detailed knowledge of the stage—he was for a time an actor—made him an admirable and reliable 'play carpenter' rather than an original dramatist. Of his own plays the most successful were *Kismet* (1911), an Arabian Nights fantasy done by Oscar Asche in England and Otis Skinner in New York and frequently revived, and *Marie-Odile* (1915), a tale of the Franco-Prussian War beautifully produced by David Belasco. Much of Knoblock's best work was, however, done in collaboration. With Arnold Bennett he wrote *Milestones* (1912), with Seymour Hicks *England Expects* (1914), with J. B. Priestley *The Good Companions* (1931), and with Beverley Nichols *Evensong* (1932), the last two from their respective novels. Knoblock also dramatized J. E. Goodman's *Simon Called Peter* (1924), Vicki Baum's *Grand Hotel* (1931), and A. J. Cronin's *Hatter's Castle* (1932), translated a number of French plays, and in 1938 supervised the Irving Centenary Matinée at the Lyceum.

KNOWLES, JAMES SHERIDAN (1784-1862), cousin of R. B. Sheridan (q.v.) and a friend of Hazlitt, Coleridge, and Lamb. His first play, a tragedy entitled *Virginius* (1820), was written for Edmund Kean (q.v.), who refused it, thus allowing Macready (q.v.) to triumph in the part. A prolific dramatist, Knowles was much admired, but nothing of his work has survived in performance, and the only play by him to be remembered is *The Hunchback* (1832), whose heroine, Julia, first played by Fanny Kemble (q.v.), was a favourite part with many young and lovely actresses.

KNOWLES, RICHARD GEORGE (1858–1919), an outstanding figure of the old music-halls, who billed himself as the 'very peculiar American comedian' (he was born in Canada). He started his career in a variety theatre in Leadville, Colorado, in about 1875, and in 1891 went to London, where he remained a firm favourite until his death. He had a curiously quiet style, always wore a black frock coat, opera hat, and white duck trousers, and walked up and down across the stage. His best-remembered songs are 'Girlie, Girlie' and 'Brighton'.

KOCH, ESTHER (1746–84), see BRANDES.

KOMISARJEVSKAYA, VERA FEDOROVNA (1864–1910), Russian actress and theatre manager, sister of Theodore Komisarjevsky (q.v.). She made her first appearance on the stage in 1891 as Betsy in Tolstoy's *The Fruits of Enlightenment*, and in 1896 went to the Alexandrinsky (q.v.) where she played Nina in the first ill-fated production of Chekhov's *The Seagull*. She later founded her own theatre, where amid the upheavals of 1905–6 she produced plays by Gorky, Chekhov, and Ibsen. She also invited Meyerhold (q.v.) to work for her but, disagreeing with his treatment of the actor as a puppet, soon broke with him. Finding herself heavily in debt, she decided to give up her theatre and become a teacher of dramatic art, but died of smallpox during a farewell tour. She was never seen in England, but in 1908 played a season at Daly's in New York which, though artistically a success, was financially unrewarding. A woman of great charm, with a magnetic personality, she was at her best in such parts as Ibsen's Nora (in *A Doll's House*) and Hedda Gabler.

KOMISARJEVSKY, THEODORE [FEDOR] (1882–1954), brother of Vera Komisarjevskaya (q.v.) and an outstanding personality in the European theatre of his time. From 1907 to 1919 he produced a number of plays and operas in Russia. He then went to England, where he first worked as a designer, attracting attention by his association with the Russian plays produced at the little Barnes Theatre in the 1920s. Although his best work was done in productions of and designs for Russian plays, particularly Chekhov, he was also responsible for a number of controversial productions of Shakespeare at Stratford-upon-Avon, including *The Merchant of Venice* (1932), *Macbeth* (1933) with aluminium scenery and vaguely modern uniforms, *The Merry Wives of Windsor* (1935) in the style of a Viennese operetta, *King Lear* (1936), which contained some of his finest work and finally won over his critics, *The Comedy of Errors* (1938), and *The Taming of the Shrew* (1939). In London he produced a wide variety of plays, the last being Barrie's *The Boy David* (1936), with Elisabeth Bergner. Disappointed at its poor reception, he went to America, where he remained until his death. He was the author of numerous books on the theatre, including one on theatrical costume and one on Stanislavsky, whom he revered but refused to follow slavishly. He was for a time the husband of the English actress Peggy Ashcroft (q.v.).

KOONEN, ALICE (1889–1974), see TAÏROV, A. Y.

KOPIT, ARTHUR (1938–), American dramatist, whose first plays were produced at Harvard University while he was a student there. These included *On the Runway of Life You Never Know What's Coming Off Next* (1957), *Across the River and into the Jungle* (1958), *Sing to Me Through Open Windows* (1959), and *Oh Dad, Poor Dad, Mamma's Hung You in the Closet and I'm Feelin' So Sad* (1960), which finally achieved an international reputation. Seen briefly in London at the Lyric, Hammersmith, in 1961, this was revived at the Piccadilly in 1965 with Hermione Gingold (q.v.) as the possessive mother, Madame Rosepettle. It was also seen in New York in 1962, where it had a long run at the Phoenix Theatre, and in Paris in 1963 with Edwige Feuillère (q.v.) as the mother. In 1968 Kopit's next play, *Indians*, set in the Wild West with Buffalo Bill (Colonel W. F. Cody) as its central character, had its world première in London as part of an American season of new plays staged by the Royal Shakespeare Company (q.v.) at the Aldwych.

KORNEICHUK, ALEXANDER EVDOKIM-
OVICH (1905–72), Ukrainian dramatist,
whose first successful play, *The Wreck of
the Squadron* (1934), dealt with the sinking
of their fleet by Red sailors to prevent
its capture by White Russians. It was
followed by *Platon Krechet* (1935), the
story of a young Soviet surgeon, and by
Truth (1937), which shows a Ukrainian
peasant led by his search for truth to
Petrograd and Lenin at the moment of the
October Revolution. Even more successful
than these, however, was an historical
play, *Bogdan Hmelnitsky* (1939), dealing
with a Ukrainian hero who in 1648 led an
insurrection against the Poles. Another
play about Korneichuk's own country
was *In the Steppes of the Ukraine* (1940),
to which he later wrote a war-time sequel,
Partisans in the Steppes of the Ukraine
(1942). A war-play which proved very
popular was *The Front* (1943), while a
satirical comedy, *Mr. Perkins's Mission
to the Land of the Bolsheviks*, in which an
American millionaire visits Russia to discover for himself the truth about the Soviet
regime, was produced in 1944 by the
Moscow Theatre of Satire. Later plays
include *Come to Zvonkovo* (1946), *Makar
Dobrava* (1948), an inimitable portrait
of an old Donetz miner, *The Hawthorn
Grove* (1950), *Wings* (1954), *Why the Stars
Smiled* (1958), and *On the Dnieper* (1961).

KOTT, JAN (1914–   ), Polish critic and
literary historian, who since 1946 has been
Professor of Drama at Warsaw University. Like his compatriot of an earlier
generation, Wyspiański (q.v.), he has a
sound knowledge of Shakespeare's plays,
and has over the years developed his own
somewhat unusual view of some of them.
These were set down in a volume of essays
translated into English in 1964 as *Shakespeare Our Contemporary*, in which he
argues that we, like the Elizabethans, live
in an age of transition, and that in any
such era the fool holds the stage. He
illustrates his thesis by an interesting
comparison between *King Lear* and the
Endgame (1957) of Samuel Beckett (q.v.).
His ideas on *Lear*, and even more on the
sexual aspect of *A Midsummer Night's
Dream*, appear to have influenced recent
productions of these plays by Peter
Brook (q.v.), who wrote the introduction
to the English version of Kott's book.

KOTZEBUE, AUGUST FRIEDRICH FERDI-
NAND VON (1761–1819), German dramatist, who, though now forgotten, was in
his day more popular than Schiller (q.v.).
He knew exactly what the new audiences
of the revolutionary period wanted, and
his vogue, not only in Germany but all
over Europe, was immense. He wrote
over two hundred melodramas, the most
successful being *Menschenhass und Reue*
(1789), in which an erring wife obtains
forgiveness from her husband by a life
of atonement. As *The Stranger*, in an
adaptation by Benjamin Thompson, it
was produced at Drury Lane in 1798, the
heroine, Mrs. Haller, providing an excellent part for Mrs. Siddons, playing opposite her brother, John Philip Kemble
(qq.v.). It was frequently revived up to the
end of the nineteenth century. Equally
successful in the following year, with the
same leading players, was *Pizarro*, an
adaptation by R. B. Sheridan (q.v.) of
Die Spanier in Peru. In America Kotzebue's plays, in adaptations by Dunlap
(q.v.), led to a vogue for melodrama which
tended to eclipse more serious works and
pandered to a continual craving for sensationalism at the expense of truth and
probability.

KOUN, KAROLOS (1908–87), Greek
theatre director, who from 1935 was in
charge of the Art Theatre in Athens,
where he was responsible for a number of
productions of Greek and foreign plays,
including Ibsen's *The Wild Duck* (1942),
Tennessee Williams's *A Streetcar Named
Desire* (1949), Miller's *Death of a Salesman* (1950), Brecht's *The Caucasian Chalk
Circle* (1957) and *Arturo Ui* (1962), and
Ionesco's *Rhinoceros* (1963). He also directed, for the Greek National Theatre,
Pirandello's *Henry IV* and Chekhov's
Three Sisters. In 1962 he took the company from the Art Theatre to the Théâtre
des Nations in Paris, where their performance of Aristophanes' *Birds* was much
admired. This was seen in London during
the World Theatre season of 1964, and, in
conjunction with Aeschylus' *Persians*,
which was seen in London in 1965, was
taken on tour in Russia.

Krasnya Presnya Theatre, MOSCOW, see
REALISTIC THEATRE.

KRAUSS, WERNER (1884–1959), Austrian
actor, who made his first appearance on
the stage in 1904 and was soon playing
leading roles in Berlin and Vienna. In
the course of his career he became well

known for his interpretation of classical roles, particularly in Shakespeare—Macbeth, Richard III, and King Lear. Among the modern parts in which he appeared were the Crippled Piper in Reinhardt's production of *The Miracle* in New York in 1924, Napoleon in Fritz von Unruh's *Bonaparte* in 1927, and King Magnus in the German version of Shaw's *The Apple Cart* in 1934. He was first seen in London in 1933 as Matthew Clausen in Miles Malleson's adaptation of Hauptmann's *Vor Sonnenuntergang*. He also had a notable career in films.

KROG, HELGE (1889–1962), Norwegian dramatist, whose early plays, *Det store Vi* (1919) and *Jarlshus* (1923), were problem plays in the style of Ibsen (q.v.). An acute and subtle observer of the undertones of human relationships, he drew in his later plays some excellent portraits of contemporary women—Sonja in *Konkylien* (1929), Cecilie in *Underveis* (1931), and Vibeke in *Oppbrudd* (1936). In these and other plays he both portrayed and advanced the cause of women's emancipation. He was also a literary critic and a prose stylist somewhat in the style of Bernard Shaw (q.v.), his outspoken opinions leading to his becoming a political refugee in Sweden during the Second World War.

KRUTCH, JOSEPH WOOD (1893–1970), American writer and journalist, who was dramatic critic of *The Nation* from 1924 to 1959. He was also Brander Matthews Professor of Dramatic Literature at Columbia University from 1943 to 1952, and edited the plays of Congreve (1927) and O'Neill (1932). His *American Drama since 1918* (1939, rev. 1957) is a useful guide to the American stage between the two World Wars.

Kuppelhorizont, see FORTUNY, MARIANO.

KURZ, JOSEPH FELIX VON (1715–84), Austrian actor, who developed the typical Viennese peasant-clown Hanswurst

into a personal type to which he gave the name Bernadon (q.v.). He was the staunch champion of the old improvised comedy in its battle against the newly imported regular classic drama, and when the latter proved victorious in Vienna he and his wife took a company to Germany, where they were joined by the young F. L. Schröder (q.v.). Kurz later separated from his wife, who continued to lead the company while he returned to the Burgtheater in Vienna. The time for his 'Bernadoniades' was, however, over, and the new drama had obtained so strong a hold that he was forced to retire before it.

KWANAMI (1333–84), see NŌ PLAY.

KYD, THOMAS (1558–94), English dramatist, author of *The Spanish Tragedy* (c. 1585–9), one of the most popular plays of its day and the prototype of many succeeding 'revenge' tragedies (q.v.). It was constantly revived and revised, in one instance by Ben Jonson (q.v.), and survived into Restoration days, being seen by Pepys in 1668. Some scholars have noted in it a strong relation to the later tragedy of *Hamlet*; it has also been suggested that Kyd was the author of an earlier *Hamlet*, now lost, which Shakespeare used as the basis of the play which he wrote for the Chamberlain's Men (q.v.). Kyd is also one of the contemporary authors credited with *The Taming of a Shrew* (1589), again a lost play believed to have been used by Shakespeare. *The First Part of Ieronimo* (printed in 1605), whose action precedes that of *The Spanish Tragedy*, is now thought not to be by Kyd, and *Soliman and Perseda* (c. 1590), formerly attributed to him, is probably by Peele (q.v.). Some critics have detected traces of Kyd's work in *Titus Andronicus* and *Arden of Feversham*. He was an intimate friend of Marlowe (q.v.), with whom he was implicated in accusations of atheism, extricating himself in a not altogether creditable manner.

Kyōgen, see NŌ PLAY.

L

LA CALPRENÈDE, GAUTIER DE COSTES DE (1614–63), a French nobleman who was also a novelist and dramatist. His tragedies, of which the first, *La Mort de Mithridate* (1635), was produced at the Hôtel de Bourgogne (q.v.), were contemporary with the early plays of Corneille (q.v.) and contributed to the development of the classical tradition in France. Three of his subjects were taken from English history, the most interesting being *Le Comte d'Essex* (1637), in which he introduces the episode of the ring given by Elizabeth to Essex, based on current tradition. This was very successful, and in 1678 was rewritten by Corneille's younger brother Thomas (q.v.), with equal success.

LA CHAPELLE, JEAN DE (1655–1723), a French nobleman who as a young man wrote four tragedies, much influenced by Racine (q.v.). These were performed by the newly founded company of the Comédie-Française, with Baron and Mlle Champmeslé (qq.v.) in the leading roles. The most successful was *Cléopâtre* (1681), in which Baron was outstanding as Antony. The play, which was sufficiently well known to be parodied soon after its production, remained in the repertory until 1727.

LA CHAUSSÉE, (PIERRE-CLAUDE) NIVELLE DE (1692–1754), French dramatist, and the chief exponent of eighteenth-century *comédie larmoyante*. His first plays, *La Fausse Antipathie* (1733) and *Le Préjugé à la mode* (1735), were both well received, since their depiction of moral virtue and of the trials of domestic life exactly suited the new middle-class audience, with its preponderance of women and its disposition to indulge freely in sentimental tears. Having proved that he could give his audiences what they wanted, La Chaussée, whose own tastes were frankly licentious, produced forty plays in the same vein, of which the most successful were *Mélanide* (1741), perhaps the most typical *comédie larmoyante*, *L'École des mères* (1744), and *La Gouvernante* (1747), a foretaste of *East Lynne*. Although forgotten now, La Chaussée was immensely popular in his own time,

and in the wave of sentimentality which was then sweeping across Europe his plays were translated into Dutch, Italian, and English.

LA FLEUR, the name under which the great French farce-player Gros-Guillaume (q.v.) played serious parts at the Hôtel de Bourgogne from 1621 to 1624. His wife and daughter were both actresses, and the latter, who married an actor, was the mother of La Tuillerie (q.v.).

LA FOSSE, ANTOINE D'AUBIGNY DE (1653–1708), French dramatist who was over forty when his first play, *Polixène* (1696), was produced. A second play, *Manlius Capitolinus* (1698), was most successful and remained in the repertory of the Comédie-Française until 1849. Talma (q.v.), in particular, was later very good in the name-part. It was a frank imitation of Corneille and Racine, and under the guise of Roman names treated of contemporary history, being an account of the conspiracy of the Spaniards against Venice, a subject used some years earlier by Otway (q.v.) in *Venice Preserv'd* (1682).

LA GRANGE [really CHARLES VARLET] (1639–92), a French actor who joined the company of Molière in 1659, playing young lovers. He also appeared in the title-role of Racine's *Alexandre* (1665). A methodical man, he kept a register of all the plays presented by Molière at the Palais-Royal and the receipts from each, interspersed with notes on the internal affairs of the company which have proved invaluable to later students of the period. In 1664 he took over Molière's function as orator to the troupe, and was active in forwarding its affairs after Molière's death. As an act of piety in memory of his friend he edited and wrote a preface to the first collected edition of Molière's plays, published in 1682. His wife, MARIE (1639–1737), also an actress, known as Marotte from the part she played in *Les Précieuses ridicules*, was the daughter of the pastry-cook Cyprien Ragueneau, immortalized by Rostand (q.v.) in his play *Cyrano de Bergerac* (1897). She created the title-role in Molière's *La Comtesse d'Escarbagnas* (1671), and was one of the original members of the Comédie-Française, retiring on the death of her husband.

LA GRANGE-CHANCEL, FRANÇOIS-JOSEPH DE (1677–1758), French dramatist, whose first play was written when he was about thirteen. With the help of Racine (q.v.) it was put on in 1694, but was not a success. It was followed by several more tragedies, in which La Grange-Chancel again had the help and advice of Racine, but they show the continual decline of the classical ideal and the tendency, which later becomes more marked, to make sensationalism and not emotion the mainspring of the plot. The most successful were *Amasis* (1701) and *Ino et Mélicerte* (1713).

LA HARPE, JEAN-FRANÇOIS DE (1739–1802), French dramatist, whose plays, modelled on those of Voltaire (q.v.), show the continued decline of classical tragedy during the eighteenth century. The first, *Le Comte de Warwick* (1763), is usually accounted the best, though *Philoctète* (1783) and *Coriolan* (1784) were well received. It is, however, as a critic that La Harpe is best remembered. His *Cours de littérature ancienne et moderne*, based on lectures given in 1786, was for long a standard work, but he was at his best when dealing with the French seventeenth century and wrote excellent commentaries on the plays of Racine.

LA NOUE, JEAN SAUVE DE (1701–61), a French provincial actor who in 1739 had a play, *Mahomet II*, performed at the Comédie-Française. Voltaire, who was indebted to it for some of his own *Mahomet, ou le fanatisme* (1742), acknowledged his debt by allowing La Noue to perform the latter at Lille before it was given at the Comédie-Française, and by insisting that, subject to his making a satisfactory début, La Noue should play the title-role at the Comédie-Française. This he did, and then remained at the theatre until he retired in 1757 to become director of Court theatricals, a post he held till his death. In 1756 he wrote a comedy, *La Coquette corrigée*, produced at the Comédie-Italienne, which showed plainly the influence of Marivaux (q.v.). Some critics indeed rank it above Marivaux's work, mainly on account of its greater realism.

LA RUE, DANNY [really DANIEL PATRICK CARROLL] (1928–), an Irish-born female impersonator, who gained his experience in English provincial pantomime, cabaret, and nightclubs, playing in drag (see FEMALE IMPERSONATION). On 31 May 1966 he made his first appearance in a straight play in the West End, playing Danny Rhodes in Bryan Blackburn's *Come Spy With Me*. This ran for well over a year, and he then appeared in the 1967 Christmas pantomime, *The Sleeping Beauty*, at Golders Green. A further appearance in the West End in 1968, as Queen Passionella in another version of *The Sleeping Beauty*, so enhanced his growing reputation that on 9 April 1970 he appeared in his own show, *Danny La Rue at the Palace*, which had a long run.

LA THORILLIÈRE, FRANÇOIS LENOIR DE (1626–80), French actor, who was in the company at the Marais in about 1658 and later joined Molière (q.v.) at the Palais-Royal, where he played leading parts in a number of new comedies and also wrote a tragedy on the subject of Cleopatra which was performed by Molière's troupe. After Molière died La Thorillière joined the actors at the Hôtel de Bourgogne, and it was his death that precipitated the amalgamation of the companies to form the Comédie-Française (q.v.), a course to which he had been opposed. One of his daughters, Charlotte, married Baron (q.v.) in 1675, and another, Marie-Thérèse, became the wife of Dancourt (q.v.). His son PIERRE (1659–1731) was a good comic actor who joined the Comédie-Française in 1684, and married the daughter of the Italian actor Dominique (see BIANCOLELLI). Their son ANNE-MAURICE (*c.* 1697–1759) made his début at the Comédie-Française in 1722, being its *doyen* at the time of his death. He first played in tragedy, but later made an excellent reputation in romantic and serious comedy.

LA TUILLERIE [really JEAN-FRANÇOIS JUVENON] (1650–88), French actor and dramatist, grandson of the farce-player Gros-Guillaume (q.v.). He was acting at the Hôtel de Bourgogne in 1672, the year in which he married LOUISE CATHERINE (*c.* 1657–1706), daughter of the comedian Raymond Poisson (q.v.). A tall, stately man, he was at his best in tragedy, and often appeared in his own adaptations of earlier dramas. Two of his farces, *Crispin précepteur* (1680) and *Crispin bel esprit* (1681), featured the *commedia dell'arte* character (see CRISPIN) developed and played by his father-in-law. He was one of the original members of the Comédie-Française, and remained with it until his death.

LABICHE, EUGÈNE (1815–88), French dramatist, who between 1838 and 1877 wrote, alone or in collaboration, more than 150 light comedies, of which the most successful were *Un Chapeau de paille d'Italie* (1851), *Le Voyage de Monsieur Perrichon* (1860), *La Poudre aux yeux* (1861), and *La Cagnotte* (1864). These four, and some one-act farces, have been translated into English. W. S. Gilbert (q.v.) made two translations of *Un Chapeau de paille d'Italie*. The first, as *The Wedding March*, was produced at the Royal Court in 1873; the second, as *Haste to the Wedding*, with music by George Grossmith, at the Criterion in 1892. A new version, *An Italian Straw Hat*, by Thomas Walton, was seen in London in 1945 (at the Arts Theatre), in 1952 (at the Old Vic), and in 1955 (at Theatre Workshop). This version was also seen in 1957 in New York, where the play had previously been produced in 1936 as *Horse Eats Hat*. Some of Labiche's success with his contemporaries may have been due to a revolt against the serious problem-plays of such authors as the younger Dumas (q.v.). With his broad humour and predictable but well-presented situations, he gave new life and gaiety to the vaudeville inherited from Scribe (q.v.), and raised French farce to a height which it has since attained only with Feydeau (q.v.).

LABOUCHÈRE, MRS. HENRY, see HODSON, HENRIETTA.

LACKAYE, WILTON (1862–1932), American actor, who was intended for the Church, but adopted the stage after a chance visit to the Madison Square Theatre on his way to Rome. He was appearing with an amateur company when Lawrence Barrett (q.v.) gave him a part in his revival of Boker's *Francesca da Rimini* at the Star Theatre, New York, on 27 Aug. 1883. He later appeared many times with Fanny Davenport (q.v.), and in 1887 made a success in a dramatization of Rider Haggard's novel, *She*. He was

thereafter constantly in demand, appearing in a number of Shakespeare plays and in many new productions. He also played Jean Valjean in his own dramatization of Hugo's *Les Misérables*. But his greatest part was undoubtedly Svengali in du Maurier's *Trilby* (1895), which he played consecutively for two years and then in many revivals. He retired in 1927.

LACY, JOHN (?–1681), English actor, originally a dancing-master, who took to the stage when the theatres reopened in 1660 and became a great favourite with Charles II. A painting by Michael Wright which still hangs in Hampton Court shows him in three different parts—as Teague (in which he was much admired by Pepys) in Howard's *The Committee* (1662), as Mr. Scruple in John Wilson's *The Cheats* (1663), and as Monsieur Galliard in a 1662 revival of Cavendish's *The Variety* (1639). He was the first to play Bayes in Buckingham's *The Rehearsal* (1671), and was judged to have hit Dryden off to the life. His Falstaff was also much admired. He was the author of four plays, of which *Sauny the Scot* (1667) was based on *The Taming of the Shrew* and *The Dumb Lady; or, the Farrier made Physician* (1669) on Molière's *Le Médecin malgré lui*.

Lady Elizabeth's Men, a company of players formed in 1611, which appeared at Court in 1612 and in the following year amalgamated with the Revels Company (see ROSSETER). In 1614 their leading actor was Nathan Field (q.v.), but he had already left them before Henslowe's death in 1616 led several of the company to join Prince Charles's Men, a company newly formed by Alleyn (q.v.). The rest of the Lady Elizabeth's Men took to the provinces. Some time in 1622 a new London company, organized by Beeston (q.v.), appeared under the old name at the Phoenix (see COCKPIT), where they did well, producing a number of new plays. They finally disintegrated after the great plague of 1625, their place being taken by Queen Henrietta's Men (q.v.).

Lafayette Theatre, NEW YORK, on the west side of Broadway. This was a circus before it opened in 1826 as a regular playhouse, with newly installed gas-lighting. It had a good company, and during the summer Mrs. Duff (q.v.) appeared there in *Romeo* *and Juliet* and as Mrs. Haller in Kotzebue's *The Stranger*. But the theatre could not stand up to the competition of the Chatham and the Park (qq.v.) and soon closed. It reopened in Sept. 1827 under Henry Wallack, but without success, and on 11 Apr. 1829 it was totally destroyed by fire.

LAGERKVIST, PÄR FABIAN (1891–1974), Swedish poet and dramatist, who in 1951 was awarded the Nobel Prize for literature. His work shows the influence of Strindberg (q.v.), whom he much admired, particularly in his last phase. But Lagerkvist's later works, though still essentially tragic, moved towards rather than away from realism, and admitted at least an indication of a balancing redemptive element. The elliptical, suggestive form of his dialogue links him with the French exponents of the Theatre of Silence, particularly J.-J. Bernard (q.v.).

LAHR, BERT [really IRVING LAHRHEIM] (1895–1967), American comedian, who made his reputation in revue, and in 1946 scored an immense success as Skid in *Burlesque*, by Arthur Hopkins and D. G. M. Walters. He was also admirable as Gogo in Beckett's *Waiting for Godot* (1956) and as Boniface in *Hotel Paradiso* (1957), based on *L'Hôtel du Libre Échange*, a farce by Feydeau. In 1960 he toured with the American Shakespeare Festival Company as Bottom (in *A Midsummer Night's Dream*) and Autolycus (in *The Winter's Tale*). He also appeared in 1964 as Foxy in a musical version of Jonson's *Volpone*.

LAMB, CHARLES (1775–1834), English critic and essayist, who loved the theatre and wrote about it with a warm affection which throws as much light on the character of the man himself as on his subject. He wrote four plays, two of which (*The Wife's Trial; or, the Intruding Widow* and *The Pawnbroker's Daughter*) were published in *Blackwood's Magazine* in 1828 and 1830 respectively but never acted; nor was *John Woodvil*, a tragedy in the Elizabethan manner. *Mr. H—*, a farce produced at Drury Lane in 1806 with Elliston (q.v.) in the lead, was soundly hissed and not revived until 1822. It was last seen in 1885. Lamb's love for the theatre, and his knowledge of it, are best shown in his books, particularly in *Specimens of English Dramatic Poets Contempor-*

ary with Shakespeare (1808), an anthology of extracts from old plays which revealed to his contemporaries the little-known beauties of such dramatists as Marlowe, Webster, and Ford (qq.v.). Although in his essay *On the Tragedies of Shakespeare* (1811) he made out a case for reading the plays in preference to seeing them, the *Essays of Elia* (1823; 1833) contain many references to the pleasures of playgoing and affectionate recollections of such players as Munden and Fanny Kelly (qq.v.). In collaboration with his sister Mary he published in 1807 a volume of *Tales from Shakespeare* which, though now considered out of date, served as an introduction to the plays for generations of schoolchildren.

Lambs, THE, a London supper-club, consisting of twenty-four members under a 'Shepherd', which met for many years at the Gaiety Restaurant and subsequently at the Albemarle Hotel. Founded in the 1860s by a group of actors which included Irving, Bancroft, and the American actor Harry Montague (qq.v.), it survived until the 1890s. In 1875 Montague, who had returned to New York, founded a similar club there which still survives, being roughly the equivalent now of the London Savage, as the Players (q.v.) is of the Garrick (q.v.). Since 1885, when regular premises were first acquired, the American club has moved several times, but since 1904 has been ensconced at 128 West 44th Street.

LANDER [*née* DAVENPORT], JEAN MARGARET (1829–1903), American actress, daughter of the English actor-manager, THOMAS DONALD DAVENPORT (1792–1851), on whom Dickens is believed to have based Vincent Crummles in *Nicholas Nickleby*—in which case Jean, who at the age of eight was playing such unsuitable parts as Richard III and Shylock, would be the original Infant Phenomenon. She went with her parents to America in 1838 and was exploited as a child prodigy for several years, making her adult début in 1844 as Juliet. She was the first actress to play the title-roles in English versions of Scribe and Legouvé's *Adrienne Lecouvreur* and the younger Dumas's *La Dame aux Camélias* in America, the latter with Edwin Booth (q.v.) as Armand. She toured for many years in a repertory which included *The Wife*, *The Hunchback*, and *Love*, all by Sheridan Knowles,

Mrs. Lovell's *Ingomar*, Bulwer-Lytton's *The Lady of Lyons*, and Charles Reade's *Peg Woffington*. She retired from the stage on her marriage in 1860 to General Lander, but on his death in the War between the States two years later returned, being first billed as Mrs. Lander at Niblo's Garden in 1865. She made her last appearance on the stage in Boston on 1 Jan. 1877 as Hester in her own dramatization of Hawthorne's *The Scarlet Letter*.

LANE, LUPINO (1892–1959), see LUPINO.

LANE, SAM (1804–71) and SARA (1823–99), see BRITANNIA THEATRE.

LANG, (ALEXANDER) MATHESON (1879–1948), English actor-manager, who first appeared on the stage at Wolverhampton in 1897 and then joined the company of Frank Benson (q.v.), appearing in London in 1900 and subsequently touring the West Indies. On his return in 1904 he joined Granville-Barker's company at the Royal Court, but made his first outstanding success in a revival of Hall Caine's *The Christian* at the Lyceum in 1907. He then took a company to South Africa, Australia, and India, playing Shakespeare and modern romantic drama with much success. In 1913 he first appeared in Manchester as Wu Li Chang in *Mr. Wu*, an improbable Anglo-Chinese melodrama by Harry Vernon and Harold Owen. This ran for a year in London, was subsequently toured all over the world by Lang, and gave its title to his autobiography, *Mr. Wu Looks Back* (1940). With his wife, HUTIN [really NELLIE] BRITTON (1876–1965), as his leading lady, he inaugurated the Shakespeare productions at the Old Vic (q.v.) in 1914 with *The Taming of the Shrew*, *Hamlet*, and *The Merchant of Venice*. Among his later productions the most successful were *The Wandering Jew* (1920), by E. Temple Thurston, *The Chinese Bungalow* (1925), based on a novel by Marion Osmond, and adaptations by Ashley Dukes (q.v.) of *Such Men are Dangerous* (1928), based on Neumann's *Der Patriot*, and *Jew Süss* (1929), based on Feuchtwanger's novel of that name.

LANGNER, LAWRENCE (1890–1962), a potent force in the American theatre. Born in Wales, he emigrated to the U.S.A. in 1911 and became an American citizen.

In 1914 he helped to organize the Washington Square Players (q.v.), and after the First World War was instrumental in helping the group to re-form as the Theatre Guild (q.v.), of which he became a director and for which, with the playwright and producer THERESA HELBURN (1887–1959), he supervised the production of over two hundred plays. He was the founder and first president of the American Shakespeare Festival Theatre (see STRATFORD (3)), and author of a number of plays, some written or translated in collaboration with his wife, Armina Marshall. His autobiography, *The Magic Curtain*, was published in 1951, and a book on the theatre, *The Play's the Thing*, in 1960.

LANGTRY [*née* LE BRETON], LILLIE [really EMILIE CHARLOTTE] (1853–1929), English actress, known as the Jersey Lily (she was born in Jersey). In 1875 she married Edward Langtry, a wealthy Irishman, and became prominent in London society, being an intimate friend of Edward VII, then Prince of Wales. She was one of the first English society women to go on the stage, making her début under the Bancrofts (q.v.) at the Haymarket as Kate Hardcastle in Goldsmith's *She Stoops to Conquer* on 15 Dec. 1881. She later organized her own company and with it played at the Imperial (q.v.) and other London theatres, and also toured the provinces and the United States. Although never a great actress, she was a pleasing one, particularly in such parts as Rosalind in *As You Like It*.

LAPORTE (*fl.* 1584–c. 1621), see VENIER, MARIE.

LARIVEY, PIERRE DE (c. 1540–c. 1612), an early French dramatist, mainly remembered for the use made by Molière of his comedies, which were adapted from Italian originals but contained much new material. Nine of these survive, six printed in 1579, three in 1611. There may have been others, but if so, they are lost. They were acted extensively in the provinces, where Molière may have seen them, and also in Paris.

LAROCHE, JOHANN (1745–1806), Austrian actor, the creator of the comic character Kasperle (q.v.), which he first played in Graz in 1764. Five years later he went to Vienna, where he remained until his death, becoming principal comedian of the Leopoldstädter Theater under Marinelli (q.v.). In peasant costume, with a short thick beard inherited from Hanswurst (q.v.), he excelled in improvisation in broad Viennese dialect, the sound of his offstage lament, '*Anwedl, anwedl!*', evoking laughter from the audience even before he showed himself on stage.

LARRA, MARIANO JOSÉ DE (1809–37), Spanish journalist and satirist, adapter of a number of contemporary French plays for the Spanish stage, and author of one outstandingly original play, *Macías* (1834), which reflects the literary preoccupations of his time. While still neo-classical in form, the emotions exhibited in it are clearly Romantic; passion overrides the bounds of honour and even of religion. Larra's theatrical criticism is of great interest, reflecting not only his own personal preoccupations and the despair which was to end finally in suicide, but also the contemporary association of literature with political and social progress, the key to this most interesting period in Spanish theatrical history.

L'ARRONGE, ADOLF (1838–1908), German dramatist and theatre director, who from 1873 to 1878 was in charge of the Breslau Lobetheater. During this time he wrote and staged a number of successful plays, including *Mein Leopold* (1873), *Hasemanns Töchter* (1877), and *Doktor Klaus* (1878). In 1883 he founded the Deutsches Theater (q.v.), destined to become one of the leading theatres in Germany. Though L'Arronge was not wholly in sympathy with the new naturalistic drama, he nevertheless helped to prepare the way for it by gathering together a group of highly trained actors able to interpret its subtleties, and for many years he made Berlin a flourishing theatrical centre.

Late Joys, SEE PLAYERS' THEATRE.

LAUBE, HEINRICH (1806–84), German theatre manager, who became director of the Vienna Burgtheater in 1849. He brought to his task a profound knowledge of the contemporary European stage, and was insistent on good acting, careful rehearsal, and strict adherence to the author's text. His own plays, though now forgotten, were effective in production.

Laube was a friend of Wagner (q.v.), who in 1843 wrote for a journal which Laube was then editing, the *Zeitung für die elegante Welt*, the autobiographical sketch which is reprinted in vol. I of his collected works.

LAUDER, SIR HARRY [really HUGH MACLENNAN] (1870–1950), one of the most famous stars of the music-hall stage. He first appeared at the Argyle, Birkenhead, as an Irish comedian, and was immediately successful. When, in response to the demand for encores, he ran out of Irish songs, he scored an even greater success with Scots ones and thereafter remained faithful to them. Among the best known were 'I love a lassie', 'Roamin' in the Gloamin'', 'A wee Deoch-and-Doris', 'It's nice to get up in the morning', and 'Stop yer tickling, Jock'. He invariably wore a kilt and glengarry and carried a crooked stick. He also appeared in revue and in at least one straight play, Graham Moffat's *A Scrape o' the Pen* (1909). He made his first appearance in London in 1900, made numerous tours of the United States, South Africa, and Australia, and wrote several volumes of reminiscences. He was knighted in 1919 for his indefatigable entertaining of the troops on the French front during the First World War.

Laura Keene's Theatre, NEW YORK, see KEENE, LAURA and OLYMPIC THEATRE (3).

LAVEDAN, HENRI (1859–1940), French dramatist, whose plays dealt with social problems and contemporary manners, somewhat in the style of Becque (q.v.) and the naturalistic writers, but in a less downright and drastic manner. The most successful was *Le Prince d'Aurec* (1894), in which a decadent young nobleman is saved from the consequences of his folly by the sacrifices of his bourgeois mother. It was followed by a sequel, *Les Deux Noblesses* (1897), in which the hero restores the family fortunes by going into trade. Among Lavedan's other plays the comedies of manners, *Le Nouveau Jeu* (1905) and *Le Goût du vice* (1911), now forgotten, had a breezy vitality which made them popular with the audiences of his day.

LAVER, JAMES (1899–1975), English theatre historian, lecturer, dramatist, and novelist, appointed C.B.E. in 1951.

In 1922 he joined the staff of the Victoria and Albert Museum, and from 1939 to 1959 was in charge of the theatre collections there as part of his duties as Keeper of the Department of Prints and Engravings. During this time he produced a number of illustrated volumes on costume, one of his main interests, and on stage design. He also wrote a number of plays, among them *The Circle of Chalk* (1928), an adaptation of a Chinese drama (based on a German version by Klabund, *Der Kreidekreis*), and a study of Shelley, *The Heart Was Not Burned* (1938), produced at the Gate Theatre by Norman Marshall. In 1933 one of his novels, *Nymph Errant*, was successfully dramatized by Romney Brent, with music by Cole Porter. Laver's wife, VERONICA TURLEIGH (1903–71), was a distinguished actress who made her first appearance on the stage in Fagan's company at the Oxford Playhouse in 1924, playing Salome in Pinero's *Dandy Dick*. She was later seen at the Old Vic and Stratford-upon-Avon as well as in a number of London productions.

LAWLER, RAY (1921–   ), Australian actor and playwright, who had already written several light comedies, much influenced by English plays of the 1930s, when in 1949 his *Cradle of Thunder* was awarded first prize in a national competition. He then wrote several children's plays, and was directing a repertory company in Melbourne when in 1956 the newly founded Elizabethan Theatre Trust (q.v.) put on his *Summer of the Seventeenth Doll* with himself as the leading character, Barney Ibbot. This was also successfully produced in London in 1957 and in New York a year later. Lawler's next play, *The Unshaven Cheek*, was performed at the Lyceum, Edinburgh, in 1963, and was followed by *Piccadilly Bushman*, which was seen in Liverpool and at the Watford Civic Theatre in 1965 as part of the first Commonwealth Arts Festival. Neither of these has yet been seen in London. In 1970 *A Breach in the Wall*, dealing with the supposed discovery of Thomas à Becket's tomb, was performed at the Marlowe Theatre, Canterbury, to mark the opening of the Festival there.

LAWRENCE, DAVID HERBERT (1885–1930), English novelist, poet, and playwright, son of a Nottinghamshire miner, who was for a short time a teacher before devoting himself wholly to writing. His novels, considered shocking and highly controversial when first published, had already made him famous during his lifetime, but it was not until after his death that he was recognized as an outstanding poet. His plays had to wait even longer for public acclaim. One, *The Widowing of Mrs. Holroyd*, written in about 1914, was given a Sunday-night production in 1928 by the Stage Society, but the other seven, which include a biblical drama on David, remained unproduced until in 1965 *A Collier's Friday Night* (written in about 1906) was seen at the Royal Court in a 'production without décor', and in 1967 *The Daughter-in-Law* (written during, and based on, the coal strike of 1912) was given a public showing, also at the Royal Court. It was named as one of the best new plays of the year, and led to a D. H. Lawrence season at the Royal Court in 1968, when the three plays, done in repertory to emphasize their common theme of family life set in a mining background, revealed Lawrence as a starkly realistic playwright of great subtlety and vigour, exploiting the various facets of human relationships in a closed community at the beginning of the twentieth century.

LAWRENCE, GERALD (1873–1957), English actor, who served his apprenticeship with Benson (q.v.) and later joined Henry Irving (q.v.) at the Lyceum. He was playing Henry II the night Irving made his last appearance as Becket (in Tennyson's play) in 1905. He then went to America, and on his return in 1909 directed a number of Shakespeare's plays at the Royal Court Theatre, London, and the Kroll Theatre, Berlin. He also continued to act, mainly in Shakespeare, though in 1912 he gave an outstanding performance as Captain Brassbound in a revival of Shaw's *Captain Brassbound's Conversion*. After serving in the Royal Navy during the First World War, he returned to the stage in 1919, playing de Guiche to the Cyrano of Robert Loraine (q.v.) in Rostand's *Cyrano de Bergerac*. He also directed and played in Louis N. Parker's *Mr. Garrick* (1922), and in 1923 toured the provinces in a revival of Booth Tarkington's *Monsieur Beaucaire*. He made his last appearance on the stage in Oct. 1938, but continued to take an interest in theatrical affairs, presenting annually at the Royal Academy of Dramatic Art a prize for which he himself acted as judge. By his first wife, Lilian Braithwaite (q.v.), he was the father of the distinguished actress JOYCE LILIAN CAREY (1898–). His second wife, who appeared with him in many of his later productions, was FAY DAVIS (1872–1945), an American actress who came to London in 1895 and made a great success as Flavia in Anthony Hope's *The Prisoner of Zenda*.

LAWRENCE [really KLASEN], GERTRUDE (1898–1952), English actress, who studied under Italia Conti and made her first appearance in pantomime at the age of twelve. She continued her career uninterruptedly, mainly as a dancer and later as a leading lady in revue, appearing in several editions of *Charlot's Revue* both in London and in America in 1924–6. She had, however, been seen in several straight parts before making an outstanding success as Amanda Prynne in Noël Coward's *Private Lives* (1930). She was again associated with Coward (q.v.) in his nine one-act plays, *To-Night at 8.30* (1935–6), in *Fallen Angels* (1942), and in *Blithe Spirit* (1945). She spent her last years in America, where she married the theatre manager Richard Aldrich, and died at the height of her powers. In 1945 she published a volume of reminiscences entitled *A Star Danced*, which gave an excellent description of her humble beginnings and the hard work which raised her to her final eminence.

LAWRENCE, SLINGSBY, see LEWES, G. H.

LAWTON, FRANK (1904–69), English actor, who in 1928 made an immense success in the title-role of *Young Woodley* (by John Van Druten), which to some extent hindered his later career in that everything he played, however well performed, was always compared unfavourably to that part. This, coupled with his youthful appearance and quicksilver charm, prevented his being cast in the heavier roles he aspired to. Among the light comedies in which he appeared in London were Milne's *Michael and Mary* (1930) and Esther McCracken's *Quiet Wedding* (1938), and in New York, Merton Hodge's *The Wind and the Rain* (1934) and Rattigan's *French Without Tears* (1937). After war service from 1939 to 1945 he reappeared with his wife, Evelyn Laye (q.v.), in an Oscar Straus musical, *Three Waltzes* (1945), and in Daphne du

Maurier's *September Tide* (1950), and also played opposite her in London in Michael Hutton's *Silver Wedding* (1957). He made his last appearance in 1965 in a revival of Somerset Maugham's *The Circle*.

LAYE, EVELYN (1900–), English actress, who made her first appearance on the stage in 1915 and from 1923 to 1927 was seen at Daly's (q.v.) in musical comedy, creating the title-roles in *Madame Pompadour* and *The Dollar Princess* and Lili in *Lilac Time*. She made her first appearance in New York in 1929 as Sari Linden in Noël Coward's *Bitter Sweet*, which she also played in London a year later. She was later seen in variety and pantomime, playing the Principal Boy in *The Sleeping Beauty* (1938) and *Cinderella* (1943 and 1948), and after the Second World War toured extensively in a number of plays with her second husband, Frank Lawton (q.v.) (she had previously been married to the actor Sonnie Hale), with whom she also appeared in London in *Silver Wedding* (1957). In 1959 she gave an excellent performance as Lady Fitzadam in Anthony Kimmins's *The Amorous Prawn*, and in 1969 appeared in a new musical, *Phil the Fluter*.

Lazzo (pl. *lazzi*), a word used for the by-play of the comic masks of the *commedia dell'arte* (q.v.). It consisted in small items of comic decoration on the main plot, and there is no satisfactory etymology or translation of the word, which can be rendered as antics, tricks, or comic turns, according to the context (see also BURLA).

LE GALLIENNE, EVA (1899–), American actress and director, daughter of the poet Richard Le Gallienne. Born in London, she had appeared there in several small parts before going in 1915 to New York, where she has since remained. She made a great success as Julie in the first American production of Molnár's *Liliom* in 1921, and in 1926 founded the Civic Repertory Company, which opened on 26 Oct. with a production of *Saturday Night*, by the Spanish playwright Jacinto Benavente. She then appeared with her company in a programme of American and foreign plays, and did much to popularize Ibsen (q.v.) in the United States, touring in 1933–4 in her own versions of *A Doll's House*, *Hedda Gabler*, and *The Master Builder*. Shortly afterwards financial difficulties led to the disbanding of the company. With Cheryl Crawford and Margaret Webster (qq.v.), Eva Le Gallienne was one of the founders of the American Repertory Theatre, which was active from 1946 to 1948. She played Queen Katherine in the initial production, *Henry VIII*, and Ella Rentheim in Ibsen's *John Gabriel Borkman* (both 1946). She has also directed and played in many of Chekhov's plays, from *Three Sisters* (in which she played Masha) in 1926 to *The Seagull* (in which she played Madame Arkadina) in 1964. She is the author of two volumes of autobiography, *At 33* (1934) and *With a Quiet Heart* (1953), and among her work for the stage was an excellent adaptation of Lewis Carroll's *Alice in Wonderland* (1932), in which she herself played the White Queen.

LE SAGE, ALAIN-RENÉ (1668–1747), French writer, best remembered for his novels, *Le Diable boiteux* (1707) and *Gil Blas de Santillane* (1715–35). His early plays were adaptations of Lope de Vega and Rojas (qq.v.), his first original comedy being *Crispin rival de son maître* (also (1707). This was followed in 1709 by *Turcaret*, his masterpiece and one of the best comedies in the history of French drama. It satirizes the gross, purse-proud parvenu whose star was in the ascendant at the time, and reflects that bitterness against taxation which came to a head under Louis XVI. It met with a good deal of opposition but was eventually played with immense success. Unfortunately, a difference of opinion with the actors of the Comédie-Française over his next play, *Tontine*, led Le Sage to break off his association with the official theatre and write only for the playhouses of the Paris fairs, for which he produced, alone or in collaboration, over a hundred sketches of ephemeral interest. Two of Le Sage's sons went on the stage against the wish of their father, who had a low opinion of actors, but he became reconciled with the elder, RENÉ-ANDRÉ (1695–1743), known as Montménil, after seeing him give a fine performance at the Comédie-Française as Turcaret.

Leap, see TRAP.

LEAVITT, M. B. (1843–1935), see BURLESQUE (4).

LEBLANC, GEORGETTE (1876–1941), see MAETERLINCK, MAURICE.

LECOUVREUR, ADRIENNE (1692–1730), French actress, who made her début at the Comédie-Française in 1717. She was immediately successful, which caused her to suffer greatly from the jealousy of her fellow-actresses. She is said to have been better in tragedy than in comedy, but it is difficult to assess her art, for her charm and beauty were such that even her faults were forgiven her, and the public looked with an indulgent eye on her love-affairs. She was for some time the mistress of Marshal Saxe, whose desertion of her is said to have hastened her death, which was sudden and unexpected. As an actress, she was refused Christian burial, being interred secretly at night in a marshy corner of the Rue de Bourgogne. Voltaire (q.v.), in some of whose plays she appeared, was with her when she died and wrote a bitter poem on the attitude of the Church in France, which seemed to him even more monstrous when compared with the funeral of Anne Oldfield (q.v.) in Westminster Abbey in the same year. In 1849 Scribe and Legouvé (qq.v.) wrote a play on the life of Adrienne Lecouvreur which, though inaccurate, supplied Rachel and later Sarah Bernhardt (qq.v.) with an excellent part.

LEE, CANADA [really LEONARD LIONEL CORNELIUS CANEGATA] (1907–52), American Negro actor, who received his stage training with the Negro Unit of the Federal Theatre Project (q.v.), making his first appearance in its production of *The Haitian Macbeth* in 1936. In 1939 he played with Ethel Waters in Dorothy Heyward's *Mamba's Daughters*, and was also in the outstanding tragedy of Negro life, *Native Son* (1941), based on the novel by Richard Wright. Among other productions in which he appeared were the musical *South Pacific* (1943), Philip Yordan's *Anna Lucasta* (1944), first produced by the American Negro Theatre (q.v.), Maxine Wood's *On Whitman Avenue* (1946), and Dorothy Heyward's *Set My People Free* (1948). In 1945 he appeared as Caliban in *The Tempest*, directed by Margaret Webster, and in 1946 played Bosola, in a white make-up, in Webster's *The Duchess of Malfi*, directed by George Rylands.

LEE, NATHANIEL (c. 1653–92), English dramatist, author of a number of tragedies on subjects taken from ancient history, of which the best and most successful was *The Rival Queens; or, the Death of Alexander*, dealing with the jealousy between Alexander's wives, Roxana and Statira. This was first produced in 1677 with Betterton (q.v.), to whose acting it owed much of its success, as Alexander. Lee, who twice collaborated with Dryden (q.v.), was one of the most popular writers of his day, and his plays were frequently revived and printed. Their ranting verse, and plots which left the stage encumbered with corpses or lunatics, betrayed, however, a streak of insanity which later led to his being confined in Bedlam, where he died.

LEE, GYPSY ROSE (1914–70), see BURLESQUE (4).

LEE SUGG, CATHARINE (1798–1845), see HACKETT, J. H.

LEESON, HENRIETTA (1751–1826), see LEWIS, WILLIAM.

Legitimate Drama, sometimes abbreviated to 'legit.', a term which arose in the eighteenth century during the struggle of the Patent Theatres—Covent Garden and Drury Lane (qq.v.)—against the upstart and illegitimate playhouses springing up all over London. It covered in general those five-act plays (including Shakespeare's) which had little or no singing, dancing, and spectacle, and depended entirely on acting. In the nineteenth century the term was widespread and was used by actors of the old school as a defence against the encroachments of farce, musical comedy, and revue.

LEGOUVÉ, ERNEST-GABRIEL-JEAN-BAPTISTE (1807–1903), French writer, author of a number of charming one-act comedies which held the stage for many years. He is, however, best remembered for his collaboration with Scribe (q.v.) in a play based on the life of Adrienne Lecouvreur (q.v.), which was produced in 1849 with Rachel (q.v.) in the title-role, and later provided a spectacular part for Sarah Bernhardt (q.v.). A tragedy on Medea, which Legouvé also intended for Rachel, was refused by her, but, in an Italian translation, was successfully played by Ristori (q.v.).

LEGRAND, MARC-ANTOINE (1673–1728), French actor and dramatist, traditionally said to have been born the day Molière died. In 1702, after some experience with a French company in Warsaw, he joined the Comédie-Française to play comic and rustic parts. He occasionally insisted on appearing in tragedy, for which he was quite unsuited, being short and ugly. But his good humour and wit made him popular with everyone. Of his many plays the most successful was *Cartouche*, based on the career of a notorious footpad, Louis-Dominique Bourguignon, the Robin Hood of France. Hurriedly written after the man's arrest, it was first performed on 21 Sept. 1721 and repeated thirteen times, its last appearance being on the night before the real Cartouche was guillotined. Legrand was the tutor of Adrienne Lecouvreur (q.v.), and his son and daughter were both members of the Comédie-Française.

Legs, see BORDER.

Leicester's Men, the earliest organized company of Elizabethan actors, first mentioned in 1559. They formed part of the household of the Earl of Leicester, and among them were James Burbage and later William Kempe (qq.v.). This company, which first acted in London before the Queen in 1560, continued in great favour at Court until the formation in 1583 of Queen Elizabeth's Men (q.v.), which incorporated several of Leicester's best actors. But the rest continued to act under the patronage of Leicester until his death in 1588, when they were amalgamated with the Earl of Derby's Men (see STRANGE'S MEN).

LEICHNER, LUDWIG (1836–?), see MAKE-UP.

LEIGH, ANTHONY (?–1692), an actor in Davenant's company at Dorset Garden (q.v.) who was much admired by Charles II. He created the part of Father Dominic in Dryden's *The Spanish Friar* and took over the part of Teague in Howard's *The Committee*, originally created by Lacy (q.v.). He was an excellent foil to the comedian Nokes (q.v.), with whom he often played.

LEIGH, VIVIEN [really VIVIAN MARY HARTLEY] (1913–67), English actress, second wife of Sir Laurence Olivier (q.v.), whom she married (as her second husband) in 1937 and divorced in 1960.

She first came into prominence as Henriette in *The Mask of Virtue* (1935), an adaptation by Ashley Dukes (q.v.) of Carl Sternheim's *Die Marquise von Arcis*, and as Jenny Meere in Clemence Dane's dramatization of Max Beerbohm's story *The Happy Hypocrite* (1936). In 1937 she played Ophelia to Olivier's Hamlet at Elsinore. She later played a number of Shakespearian parts at the Old Vic and was also outstanding as Sabina in Wilder's *The Skin of Our Teeth* (1945). It was, however, with her Blanche du Bois in Tennessee Williams's *A Streetcar Named Desire* (1949) that she gave proof of greater powers as an actress than she had hitherto shown (her work in films, which cannot be considered here, was already outstanding), and she became one of London's leading actresses. During the Festival of Britain in 1951 she appeared with Olivier in Shaw's *Caesar and Cleopatra* and Shakespeare's *Antony and Cleopatra*, and in 1955 was at Stratford-upon-Avon, appearing as Lady Macbeth, Viola in *Twelfth Night*, and Lavinia to the Titus Andronicus of Olivier, both their performances in this little-known play being accounted memorable. She had a further success in Giraudoux's *Duel of Angels* (1957), and in 1961 undertook an extensive tour for the Old Vic with a repertory which included a new version of the younger Dumas's *The Lady of the Camellias*. She appeared in New York in 1963 as Tatiana in a musical version of Sherwood's *Tovarich*, and in England two years later toured as the Contessa Sanziani in *La Contessa*, based on a novel by Maurice Druon.

LEIGHTON, MARGARET (1922–76), English actress, who first appeared on the stage at the Birmingham Repertory Theatre in 1938. She later joined the Old Vic company, and made her first appearance in London in Aug. 1944 as the Troll King's Daughter in Ibsen's *Peer Gynt*. During the next few years she played a wide range of parts, and in 1950 emerged as a leading West End actress with her Celia Coplestone in Eliot's *The Cocktail Party*. A season at Stratford-upon-Avon was followed by an excellent performance in 1953 as Orinthia in a revival of Shaw's *The Apple Cart* (to Coward's King Magnus), and she was also much admired in Rattigan's *Separate Tables* (1954) and *Variation on a Theme* (1958) and in John Mortimer's *The Wrong Side of the Park* (1960). In 1961, in New York, where she subsequently remained for some years, she played Hannah Jelkes in Tennessee Williams's *The Night of the Iguana*, and in 1964 was in Enid Bagnold's *The Chinese Prime Minister*. In 1967 she played in the three short plays which make up Noël Coward's *Suite in Three Keys*. During a short visit to England in 1969 she appeared as Cleopatra at the Chichester Festival Theatre.

LEKAIN [really CAÏN], HENRI-LOUIS (1729–78), famous French actor who was encouraged in his career by Voltaire (q.v.), in whose *Brutus* he made his début at the Comédie-Française in 1750, playing Titus. Though small, with a harsh voice, Lekain, like Kean and Rachel (qq.v.), had that essential spark of genius that triumphs over disabilities and in spite of his faults became one of the leading actors of the day. He worked feverishly at his parts and wore himself out playing them. (There is a good description of his acting in *Mémoires et réflexions sur l'art dramatique*, by Clairon (q.v.), who was his leading lady for many years.) Ill-health caused him to retire for a time, and on his reappearance he seemed to act better than ever, as though the enforced leisure had led to a deepening of his talents. Voltaire, whose memories of French acting went back to Baron (q.v.), called him the only truly tragic actor, and he was frequently compared to Garrick (q.v.). He was responsible for many reforms in the theatre, notably for the introduction of some attempt at accuracy in historical costumes, and on 20 Aug. 1755, with Clairon, he introduced touches of *chinoiserie* into Voltaire's *L'Orphelin de la Chine*. Like Macready (q.v.), he suffered much from the ignominious status accorded to actors of his day, thought often of retiring, but loved his work too much. His death was tragic. After giving a magnificent performance as Vendôme in Voltaire's *Adélaïde du Guesclin*, he went out into the chill night air, took cold, and died just as his great benefactor and admirer was returning to Paris after thirty years of exile. The news of his funeral was the first thing Voltaire heard on his arrival.

LELIO, see ANDREINI and RICCOBONI.

LEMAÎTRE, A.-L.-P. see FRÉDÉRICK.

LEMAÎTRE, JULES-FRANÇOIS-ÉLIE (1854–1914), French author and dramatic critic, who was for many years attached to the *Journal des Débats* and *Le Temps*. One of his early works was a book on Molière. As a critic he was capable of both extreme kindness and great cruelty; but his opinions were usually sound, and taken as a whole his work was beneficial to the theatre. His articles were published in a series of volumes entitled *Impressions de théâtre*, from which a few extracts, selected and translated by Frederic Whyte, were published in London in 1924 as *Theatrical Impressions*. Lemaître was also the author of several unsuccessful plays, but his reputation rests mainly on his critical works.

LEMERCIER, (LOUIS-JEAN) NÉPOMUCÈNE (1771–1840), French dramatist, who at one time seemed destined to be the great literary figure of the Napoleonic era. Godson of the Princesse de Lamballe, he was befriended in his youth by Marie-Antoinette and was later the protégé of Napoleon and Josephine. He had great gifts, and his first play was produced when he was only sixteen. His work bridges the gap between the eighteenth and nineteenth centuries, for his *Agamemnon* (1795) was the last French tragedy on a classical theme, while *Pinto* (1800), with its lackey who liberates Portugal, seems to anticipate Hugo's *Ruy Blas*. *Christophe Colomb* (1809), inspired by readings of Shakespeare, also seems, by its flagrant disregard of the unities (q.v.), to belong to the Romantic school. But Lemercier lacked the force and vitality which might have given life to his work and is now totally forgotten.

LEMON, MARK (1809–70), English man of letters, best remembered as the first editor of *Punch*, which he established financially in its difficult early years on the money he received for his numerous and now forgotten plays, mainly farces and melodramas. Lemon was a good amateur actor, and made his first appearance at Miss Kelly's theatre in Soho (see ROYALTY THEATRE (2)), later playing in Dickens's private theatricals at Tavistock House and giving public dramatic readings.

LENNOX, COSMO GORDON- (1869–1921), see TEMPEST, MARIE.

LENO, DAN [really GEORGE GALVIN] (1860–1904), one of the best-loved and most famous stars of the English music-hall, who first appeared on the stage at the age of four. At twenty he became a champion clog-dancer, and in 1886 was engaged by Conquest (q.v.), together with his wife, a music-hall artiste named LYDIA REYNOLDS, for pantomime at the Surrey. At Christmas 1888 he appeared at Drury Lane in *The Babes in the Wood*, and for the next fifteen years was seen annually in pantomime, playing Sister Anne, the Widow Twankey, Cinderella's stepmother, the Baroness, and other parts. His last appearance, at Christmas 1903, was in *Humpty Dumpty*. Between whiles he continued to appear on the halls, mostly at the London Pavilion, where he told, in quick, staccato style, long rambling anecdotes of incidents involving himself or some other member of his family, with frequent mutterings and asides, but always with an eager, startled look and a wide smile. For his success when commanded by King Edward VII to Sandringham in 1901 he was called 'the King's Jester', and a comic paper was named after him. In the same year he wrote a burlesque autobiography called *Dan Leno—His Book*. Towards the end of his life he broke down from overwork and became insane. His son, SYDNEY PAUL GALVIN (1892–1962), who looked very like him, was also a dancer and comedian, but was best known as a writer of pantomimes.

LENOBLE, EUSTACHE (1643–1711), a French lawyer who was imprisoned for forgery, and later became a literary hack. Among his miscellaneous works were some unsuccessful plays, including three produced at the Hôtel de Bourgogne (q.v.) by the Italian actors there. One of them, *La Fausse Prude*, was taken as a reflection on Mme de Maintenon and was used by the authorities as an excuse for the banishment of the Italian troupe from Paris in 1697.

LENOIR, MARIE-THÉRÈSE (1663–1725), see DANCOURT, F. C.

LENORMAND, HENRI-RENÉ (1882–1951), French dramatist, who in reaction against realism exploited in his plays Freud's theory of the unconscious. In some of them he achieved an interesting effect by the use of short scenes played in a spotlight, the rest of the stage being blacked out. His first play, *Le Temps est un songe* (1919), was originally produced in Geneva by Pitoëff (q.v.), who then took it to Paris. As *Time Is a Dream*, it was seen in New York in 1924 and in London in 1950. Pitoëff also produced *Les Ratés* (1920) and *Le Mangeur de rêves* (1922), which as *The Eater of Dreams* was seen in London at the Gate Theatre in 1929. *Simoun*, staged by Baty (q.v.) at the Théâtre Montparnasse in 1920, was seen in London in 1927.

LENSKY, ALEXANDER PAVLOVICH (1847–1908), Russian actor, who in 1876 joined the company at the Maly Theatre (q.v.) in Moscow, and eventually became its director, in which capacity he was responsible for introducing the plays of Ibsen (q.v.) to Russian audiences. A many-sided man, being both actor and artist, he was also an inspired teacher and trained many actors for the Maly. During the difficult days after the abortive rising of 1905 he supported Yermolova (q.v.) in her efforts to revive the classical repertory, but was enlightened enough, under the influence of the Moscow Art Theatre (q.v.), to further many reforms in methods of production and rehearsal and in the replacement of old-fashioned declamation by a more natural style of acting.

LEONOV, LEONID MAXIMOVICH (1899–), one of the outstanding Soviet dramatists of his day. His *Untilovsk* (1928) was the first Soviet play to be produced by the Moscow Art Theatre. It was not a success, but the later *Skutarevski* (1934), which dealt with the problems of an old scientist torn between his work and his family and between the old and new regimes, was warmly received when it was produced at the Maly. Other interesting plays on contemporary themes are *The Orchards of the Polovtsi* (1938), played in 1948 by the Bristol Old Vic company as *The Apple Orchards*, and *The Wolf* (1939), which deals with the impact of the Soviet regime on personal problems; but the play which set the seal on Leonov's growing reputation was *Invasion* (1942), which tells with great force and pathos the story of a Soviet village under Nazi rule, the reactions of the villagers, and their contribution to freedom and final victory. This play, which has been pub-lished in an English adaptation, was one of the most successful of the Soviet war plays. Leonov seems to have written little since, but in 1957 his *Gardener in the Shade* was produced at the Mayakovsky Theatre by Okhlopkov, and a revised version of an earlier play, *Golden Chariot*, was seen at the Moscow Art Theatre.

Leopoldstädter Theater, see MARINELLI, KARL and VIENNA.

LÉOTARD, JULES (1830–70), a French wire-walker and trapeze-artist, who made his début in Paris in 1859 and had a triumphant career in Europe. His success in London, where he appeared at the Alhambra in 1861, led to the writing of the popular song 'The Daring Young Man on the Flying Trapeze'. In spite of the risks he took he never had an accident, but died of tuberculosis at the age of forty. Unlike the other trapeze-artists of the day, in their gaudily spangled costumes, he wore a sober one-piece garment, and his name has been given to the similar costume worn as a practice dress by ballet dancers. Shortly before his death he published his memoirs.

LERMONTOV, MIKHAIL YUREVICH (1814–41), famous Russian lyric poet, who also wrote three plays before dying young as the result of a duel. The first, entitled *The Spaniards* (1830), dealt ostensibly with the Inquisition in Castille but in reality with the political situation in Tsarist Russia, and was suppressed. It was first acted in 1917, after the Revolution. To the second, Lermontov, who much admired Schiller (q.v.) and the writers of the *Sturm und Drang*, gave a German title, *Menschen und Leidenschaften* (1832). In spite of later rewriting, it was not a success, and Lermontov's fame as a play-wright rests entirely on his *Maskerad*, written in 1835. Influenced by Shake-speare (q.v.), whom he called 'that immeasurable genius', with overtones of Byron, the darling of the age, he produced a tragedy of jealousy in which the hero, like Othello, murders his innocent wife. In deference to the censor he later pro-vided an alternative happy ending, but even so the play was not produced until 1852, when it was given in a mutilated text. The full version was first seen in 1864 at the Alexandrinsky (q.v.), but its history in the theatre may be said to have begun only in 1917 with a production by Meyerhold (q.v.), again at the Alexandrinsky, on 26 Feb., the night the Tsarist regime was finally overthrown. Meyerhold later produced the play at his own theatre, and in 1938 at the Alexandrinsky again, and it has since found its way into the repertory of most of the Soviet theatres. It has not yet been seen in England or the United States.

LESSING, GOTTHOLD EPHRAIM (1729–81), German playwright and dramatic critic, the opponent of the reforms of Gottsched (q.v.), which he attacked in his *Briefe, die neuste Litteratur betreffend* (1759). He later expanded his ideas on aesthetics in *Laokoon* (1766), of which only Part I was completed, and in 1767–8, as official critic to the short-lived Hamburg theatre (see ACKERMANN and HAMBURG), published a series of papers entitled the *Hamburgische Dramaturgie*. In these he again sought to replace the convention of French classical drama by a freer approach which paid lip-service to Shakespeare, whom he had not, however, fully understood, though he admired his supreme craftsmanship, his truth to nature in character-drawing, and his unerring sense of the theatre. Lessing was more at home with such writers as Dryden, whose *Essay of Dramatick Poesie* he translated into German, and Richardson, whose influence is clearly discernible in his first major work as a dramatist, *Miss Sara Sampson* (1755), in which a young girl, betrayed by her lover, is poisoned by his mistress, whereupon he commits suicide. Lessing as a young man studied the theatre at first hand behind the scenes with the company run by Carolina Neuber (q.v.), who produced his early plays. These were light comedies written in the prevailing French fashion, but he was also the author of an admirable prose comedy, *Minna von Barnhelm* (1767), and of a second tragedy, *Emilia Galotti* (1772), in which a young girl, abducted by a licentious prince, prefers death at the hand of her own father to dishonour. Towards the end of his life Lessing engaged in a prolonged struggle against narrow-minded orthodoxy, which finds expression in his final work, *Nathan der Weise*, a noble plea for religious tolerance, written in blank verse. First produced two years after his death, its merits were not recognized until Goethe (q.v.) revived it at Weimar in

1801. Translated into many languages, it was given its first professional production in English in 1967 at the Mermaid Theatre (q.v.).

LEVICK, HALPER [really LEIVICK HALPERN] (1888–1962), Jewish dramatist, considered by many critics the outstanding Yiddish writer of his time in the United States. His most important play, *The Golem*, produced by the Habimah Players in Moscow in Hebrew in 1925, was later acted in Yiddish, Polish, and English. He also wrote a number of social dramas—*Rags* (1921), *Shop* (1926), and *Chains* (1930)—and in 1945 produced *The Miracle of the Warsaw Ghetto*, which dealt with the struggle of the Polish Jews against the Nazis.

LEWES, GEORGE HENRY (1817–78), English philosopher, dramatist, and dramatic critic, grandson of the actor (CHARLES) LEE LEWES (1740–1803), who created the parts of Young Marlow in Goldsmith's *She Stoops to Conquer* (1773) and Fag in Sheridan's *The Rivals* (1775). The younger Lewes was one of a group of amateur actors formed by Dickens, and in 1849 appeared in Manchester as Shylock in *The Merchant of Venice*, anticipating Irving's conception of the part as that of 'a noble nature driven to outlawry by man'. He also played the chief part in his own tragedy, *The Noble Heart*, in the provinces in the same year, but does not appear to have acted in it in London. Under the pseudonyms of Slingsby Lawrence and Frank Churchill, Lewes wrote about a dozen other plays, most of them adapted from the French. *The Game of Speculation*, based on Balzac's *Mercadet*, was seen in London in 1851. *A Chain of Events* (1852) and *A Strange History in Nine Chapters* (1853) were written for and in collaboration with C. J. Mathews (q.v.) and produced at the Lyceum, as were Lewes's other plays, except for *Buckstone's Adventure with a Polish Princess* (1855), which was seen at the Haymarket, and *Stay at Home* (1856), seen at the Olympic.

Lewes was one of the founders of *The Leader*, for which he wrote leading articles and, as 'Vivian' from 1850 to 1854, dramatic and music criticism. In the former capacity he sometimes reviewed his own plays. In 1854, when he began his lifelong liaison with the novelist George Eliot, he left London and was succeeded on *The Leader* as dramatic critic by E. F. S. Piggott ('Chat-Huant'). In 1875 he published a collection of his critical articles under the generic title *On Actors and the Art of Acting*, and a further selection was published by William Archer and Robert W. Lowe in Vol. III of their *Dramatic Essays* (1896). Lewes, who was one of the first to appreciate the genius of Irving (q.v.), had a particular dislike of Charles Kean (q.v.), whom he harried whenever possible.

LEWIS, MABEL GWYNEDD TERRY- (1872–1957), English actress, daughter of Kate Terry (q.v.), who made her first appearance on 17 Jan. 1895 with John Hare in Grundy's *A Pair of Spectacles*. She retired on her marriage in 1904, but after the death of her husband during the First World War returned to the theatre in 1920 in Harwood's *The Grain of Mustard Seed*. She then embarked on a long and successful career, appearing in a number of revivals and creating about thirty characters, mainly elegant, aristocratic women, in plays now forgotten. She was extremely popular in New York, where she first appeared in 1923. Apart from Lady Bracknell in Wilde's *The Importance of Being Earnest*, which she played in 1930, her best parts were probably Doña Filomena in *A Hundred Years Old* (1928), by the Quintero brothers, and Lady Damaris in Pryce's *Frolic Wind* (1935).

LEWIS, MATTHEW GREGORY (1775–1818), English novelist and dramatist, usually known as 'Monk' Lewis from the title of his most famous novel, *Ambrosio; or, the Monk* (1795). This provided material for a number of sensational plays, which, together with *The Castle Spectre* (1797) and *Timour the Tartar* (1811), found their way into the repertory of the nineteenth-century Toy Theatre (q.v.). Lewis's work, which was deliberately concocted to appeal to the prevailing taste for melodrama and spectacle, was somewhat crude but offered great scope for effective acting and lavish scenery enhanced by incidental music. He was very much influenced by Kotzebue (q.v.), two of whose plays he translated. Most of his work is now forgotten.

LEWIS, WILLIAM THOMAS (1749–1811), English actor whose elegance and affability earned him the sobriquet of 'Gentleman' Lewis. He joined the company at Covent Garden in 1773 and with his wife, HENRIETTA AMELIA LEESON (1751–1826), who first appeared two years later, remained there until his retirement in 1809, when John Philip Kemble (q.v.) bought from him his one-sixth share in the Patent. For twenty-one years he was a hard-working and conscientious acting-manager, very popular with the company and one of the airiest and most mercurial of actors, succeeding the famous Harlequin Henry Woodward (q.v.) in comedy parts. In his early years he sometimes played tragedy but was totally unsuited to it, and later confined himself to the rattling, hare-brained, and impossibly lively heroes of Reynolds and O'Keeffe. He also created the part of Jeremy Diddler in Kenney's *Raising the Wind* (1803).

LEWISOHN, ALICE and IRENE, see NEIGHBORHOOD PLAYHOUSE, NEW YORK.

LEY, MARIE [really MARIA CZADA), see PISCATOR, ERWIN.

LEYBOURNE, GEORGE [really JOE SAUNDERS] (1842–84), a music-hall performer and the original 'lion comique'. He first sang in East End tavern 'free-and-easys' and was then engaged by Morton for the Canterbury. He appeared always immaculately dressed as a man-about-town with monocle, whiskers, and fur collar, singing the delights of dissipation, an art which unfortunately he did not fail to practise in his spare time. His last years were a constant struggle with disillusionment and ill health, and he made his last appearance at the Queen's, Poplar. He was popularly known as Champagne Charlie, from his singing of the song of that name.

Liberty Theatre, NEW YORK, on the south side of 42nd Street, between 7th and 8th Avenues. This theatre was for a long time famous for its spectacular farces. It opened on 4 Oct. 1904, and among its early productions was the great horse-racing drama *Wildfire* (1908), written by George Broadhurst and George Hobart for Lillian Russell. The season of 1909–10 included two important productions, Tarkington's *Springtime* and the famous musical comedy, *The Arcadians*, seen in London the previous year. A further successful importation from England was *Milestones* (1912), by Arnold Bennett and Ernest Knoblock. The great Negro musical, *Blackbirds of 1928*, had part of its long run at this theatre, and the last legitimate production was given there on 18 Mar. 1933, after which the building became a cinema.

Libretto (*pl.* libretti or librettos), 'little book', from the Italian, used mainly to denote the words, as distinct from the music, of an opera or musical play. Though often the work of second-rate writers, with little to recommend them but their adaptability to the needs of the composer, some operatic libretti have been written by fine poets and dramatists, among them Apostolo Zeno (q.v.) and the great Metastasio (q.v.), whose thirty-odd texts were set more than a thousand times by many different composers. In France the dramatists Quinault and Favart (qq.v.) were excellent librettists, while the popular and prolific Scribe (q.v.), like many of his contemporaries, added the writing of operatic texts to his other activities. Since opera never became acclimatized in England, no great names are connected with it, except that of Gay (q.v.) in ballad opera. But England can boast of the perfect collaboration of Gilbert (q.v.) and Sullivan in light opera. Dramatists in their own right whose plays have served as opera texts are Hugo von Hofmannsthal, Maurice Maeterlinck, and Oscar Wilde (qq.v.). Wagner (q.v.) avoided the dangers of collaboration by writing his own texts. Verdi was fortunate in having Boito (q.v.) as librettist for his 'Otello' and 'Falstaff'.

Even greater than the difficulty of writing a good libretto is the difficulty of translating one. In England, where poor translations for long did great disservice to the cause of opera in English, efforts were made by two distinguished music critics, Ernest Newman and E. J. Dent, to raise the standard, and they were responsible for new versions of operas by Wagner and Mozart respectively.

Licensing Act, 1737, see DRAMATIC CENSORSHIP.

Light Batten, see BATTEN.

Lighting, STAGE. The open-air performances in Greece, Rome, medieval Europe, and Elizabethan England—also in Spain's Golden Age—took place by daylight, with torches used for the final scenes. It was only in the enclosed playhouses, which began in Renaissance Italy and gradually spread across Europe, that artificial lighting was needed, and even there, according to Furtenbach (q.v.), large windows could throw light on to the stage for afternoon performances. However, the value of artificial light in the theatre was soon apparent, particularly as an additional element in the stage picture, and as early as 1545 Serlio (q.v.) advised placing candles or lamps behind coloured glass in windows, or behind bottles filled with coloured liquid to give a jewel-like effect. He also advocated the use of barbers' basins behind the lamps to act as reflectors. The auditorium was at first brightly lit by lamps or candelabra, and it was Leone di Somi (q.v.), who also used mirror reflectors behind lamps fixed to the backs of the side wings, who in 1566 first suggested reducing the amount of light in the auditorium in order to intensify the effect of the stage lighting. He also arranged for many of the stage lamps to be extinguished at the first tragic moment in a play, which apparently had a profound effect upon the spectators and put them in the right state of mind for the horrors which ensued. A later writer on the theatre, ANGELO INGEGNERI (*c.* 1550–*c.* 1613), went even further and wanted to darken the auditorium entirely, but this was not achieved for a very long time, possibly because a fashionable audience wanted to be seen as well as to see. The theatres of the seventeenth and eighteenth centuries continued to use candelabra hung over the stage and auditorium, with concealed lamps behind the wings and below the backcloth, and also FOOTLIGHTS, which, as can be inferred by a reference to them in the *Architectura Civilis* of Furtenbach, were in use by 1628, a practice further confirmed by Sabbattini (q.v.) in 1638. They are first shown in use in an English theatre in the frontispiece to Kirkman's *The Wits*, published in 1672. The unconcealed chandeliers over the stage threw a painful glare into the eyes of the spectators in the gallery, as Pepys recorded as early as 1669, and it was Garrick at Drury Lane (q.v.) in 1765 who, in imitation of the French theatre, first removed them entirely, relying on extra lamps concealed behind the wings, in addition to the footlights, to give a sufficiently strong light on stage. The same improvement was made at Covent Garden (q.v.), but with rather smelly oil-lamps instead of wax candles. Thus matters remained until the introduction of GAS, which was first used to light the stage at the Lyceum (q.v.) on 6 Aug. 1817 (it had been used for the Grand Hall and Staircase of Covent Garden in 1815). The Olympic (q.v.) was possibly the first theatre to use gas inside the playhouse, on 30 Oct. 1815, but the first London theatre to be entirely given over to gas-lighting was Drury Lane, on 6 Sept. 1817. Covent Garden followed two days later. The new lighting was considered a great improvement, and in the next ten years practically all the more important theatres in London and the provinces were converted to gas-lighting, the Haymarket being one of the last (1843). Some play-goers regretted the loss of wavering candle-light, just as some later audiences preferred the soft glow of gas to the hard brilliance of electricity. Candles, oil, and gas were all equally lethal (see FIRES IN THEATRES), but at least gas could be more easily controlled at the source, thus allowing the creation of beautiful effects of sunrise, twilight, and moonshine. Yet there were complaints that in general gas-lighting was too bright, the steady glare being fatal to the stage illusion. This was partly offset by sinking the footlights below the stage level, as planned by Fechter (q.v.) in 1863, and by the reforms of Irving (q.v.) at the Lyceum. Among other innovations, he arranged for all the lights to be regulated from the prompt corner and for the first time darkened the auditorium throughout the performance, as Ingegneri had suggested nearly three hundred years earlier. Associated with the use of gas-lighting is LIMELIGHT, which lived on into the age of electricity. The lime, or calcium flare, which was first used in 1816, gave a brilliant white light which was much used for 'realistic' beams of sun, moon, or lamp light through doors or windows. But its main use was to spotlight the chief actor and follow him about on stage, whence the expression 'to be in the limelight'. The first use of ELECTRICITY in the theatre was also for spotlighting, at the Paris Opéra in 1846, and again in 1860. But it was noisy and apt to flicker, and lime-lighting continued in use in many theatres until the invention of the incandescent bulb, which replaced the original arc-lights, as used at the Paris Hippodrome in 1878. The first American theatre to be lit in this way was the California in San Francisco on 21 Feb. 1879, and the first

English theatre was the Savoy (q.v.) on 11 Oct. 1881. Although the Paris Opéra was not completely lighted by incandescent bulbs until 1886, in general electricity was installed in most theatres in Europe and America by that time. Since then lighting has become of paramount importance. There has been a great deal of theoretical examination of the principles which should govern the art of stage lighting, based on the ideas of Appia and Craig (qq.v.), and much technical work which has evolved and perfected the complicated apparatus designed to carry out the new ideas. Interesting contributions were made in the latter field by the Italian scenic designer, Mariano Fortuny (q.v.), with his reflecting sky-dome in pleated silk, which later gave place to the cyclorama (q.v.). With the advent of such things as the Schwabe-Haseit system, the Lunnebach projector, the G.K.P. (Gayling, Kann, and Planer of Vienna) projecting process, the pure-colour media of Munroe R. Pevear, the Strand Lighting Console, the Strand System CD, and the complicated spotlights and dimmers of the American stage, lighting has moved into a realm of scientific discovery and mechanical invention, and become one of the most sensitive and essential tools of the director seeking to interpret and illuminate the text he is working on.

LILLIE, BEATRICE GLADYS [LADY ROBERT PEEL] (1898–1989), actress and entertainer, born in Canada, but equally well known and admired in England and the United States. She made her first appearance on the stage in 1914 in England, at the Chatham Music Hall, and was seen shortly afterwards in London, where for several years she played in revue, including *The Nine O'Clock Revue* (1922) which ran for a year. She then alternated between London and New York in Charlot's revues, and in 1928 was seen in New York in Noël Coward's revue, *This Year of Grace*, after which she was seen in cabaret. In 1932 she made her first appearance in a straight part, playing the Nurse in the New York première of Shaw's *Too True to be Good* under the auspices of the Theatre Guild, but returned to cabaret and revue, and during the Second World War toured for E.N.S.A. in revue sketches and one-act plays, including Coward's *Tonight at 8.30*. She returned to New York in 1944 in the revue *Seven Lively Arts*, and subsequently toured the world in several editions of a solo performance, *An Evening with Beatrice Lillie*. In 1958 she gave a delicious performance in London as Patrick Dennis's Auntie Mame, a part which she had already played in New York in succession to Greer Garson. She then reverted to her former programme, except for a time in 1964, when she played Mme Arcati—played in London in the same year by Cicely Courtneidge (q.v.)—in the New York production of *High Spirits*, a musical version of Coward's *Blithe Spirit*.

LILLO, GEORGE (1693–1739), English dramatist, best remembered for his play *The Merchant*, usually known as *The London Merchant; or, the History of George Barnwell*, which was produced at Drury Lane in 1731. Based on an old ballad, it shows how a good young man's passion for a bad woman leads him to murder his old uncle for money, the murderer and his accomplice being subsequently hanged. It was immensely successful, being known well enough to be the butt of several burlesques. It was also the play performed by the Crummles family in *When Crummles Played* (1927), based by Nigel Playfair on Dickens's *Nicholas Nickleby*. It had a great vogue on the Continent and influenced the development of domestic tragedy, particularly in Germany, through Lessing (q.v.). Lillo wrote several other plays and ballad operas, of which the most important is *The Fatal Curiosity* (1736), again based on an old ballad about a murder done in Cornwall. It was first produced at the Haymarket by Fielding (q.v.), and was chosen by Mrs. Siddons (q.v.) for her benefit in 1797, her brothers John Philip and Charles Kemble (qq.v.) appearing with her. This also had a great influence abroad, particularly on the so-called German Fate Drama (q.v.).

Limelight, see LIGHTING.

LIMERICK, MONA [really MARY CHARLOTTE LOUISE GADNEY], see PAYNE, BEN IDEN.

Lincoln, which now has a repertory company housed in a nineteenth-century theatre saved from demolition by the formation of the Lincoln Theatre Association, was the headquarters of the Lincoln circuit, which took in Grantham, Boston, Spalding, Peterborough, Huntingdon, Wisbech, and Newark-on-Trent.

From 1802 to 1847 this was controlled by the Robertson family, to which T. W. Robertson and Dame Madge Kendal (qq.v.) belonged. The first permanent theatre in Lincoln was built in about 1731 by Erasmus Audley in Drury Lane (so called after a local business man and not after the London theatre). In 1764 a new theatre was formed by the adaptation of some buildings in King's Arms Yard, nearer the centre of the city. This was managed up to about 1783 by William Herbert, who had also been manager since 1750 of the Drury Lane theatre. Lincoln Public Library, which has a large collection of playbills, has among them many announcing performances by 'Mr. Herbert's Company of Comedians'. A new theatre was built in King's Arms Yard in 1806. It was burned down in 1892 and a new one, substantially the same as the present building, arose on the same site, opening on 18 Dec. 1893 with Brandon Thomas's *Charley's Aunt*.

Lincoln Center for the Performing Arts, a cultural complex of buildings planned for New York City on a 14-acre site bounded by West 62nd and 65th Streets and Columbus and Amsterdam Avenues. Work began in 1959 and the first building to be completed was the Philharmonic Hall, which opened on 23 Sept. 1962. It was followed by the New York State Theatre for ballet and operetta on 23 Apr. 1964, and in the autumn of the same year the Library-Museum of the Performing Arts, which houses the theatre, dance, and music sections of the New York Public Library, was opened. On 21 Oct. 1965 the Vivian Beaumont Theatre, designed by Eero Saarinen with the collaboration of the stage designer Jo Mielziner (q.v.), opened with the Lincoln Center repertory company, formerly at the Washington Square Theatre (q.v.), in Büchner's *Danton's Death*, followed by Sartre's *Altona*, Brecht's *The Caucasian Chalk Circle*, and Wycherley's *The Country Wife*.

Lincoln Cycle, see MYSTERY PLAY.

Lincoln's Inn Fields Theatre, LONDON, in Portugal Street, a playhouse known also as Lisle's Tennis-Court and the Duke's House which figures prominently in the history of the seventeenth-century London theatre. Originally a tennis court built in 1656, it was converted into a theatre by Davenant (q.v.) in 1661, and was the first public theatre in England to have a proscenium arch behind the apron stage and to employ scenery which was set and struck. It opened in June 1661 (probably on the 28th) with a revival of the first part of Davenant's *The Siege of Rhodes*. The second part was given on the following day, and on 28 Aug. there was the first scenic production of *Hamlet*, with Betterton (q.v.) in the title-role. There was also a revival of *Romeo and Juliet* with the original ending one day and an alternative happy ending, by James Howard, the next. Among the outstanding new plays seen at this theatre were Tuke's *The Adventures of Five Hours* (1663), based on Calderón, and Dryden's *Sir Martin Mar-All; or, the Feigned Innocence* (1667), in which the comedian Nokes (q.v.) scored a great success. After Davenant's death in 1668 his widow, assisted by Betterton, kept the theatre going until Dorset Garden (q.v.), the new playhouse begun by Davenant, opened in 1671. Lincoln's Inn Fields then reverted to its former status as a tennis court except for an interval in 1672–4 when Killigrew's company played there after the destruction by fire of their theatre in Bridges Street (see DRURY LANE). In 1695 Betterton returned to Lincoln's Inn Fields and began a ten-year tenancy with Congreve's *Love for Love*. After a further period of disuse the theatre was reopened on 18 Dec. 1714 by John Rich (q.v.) with Farquhar's *The Recruiting Officer*. It was then a handsome house, the interior having mirrors along each side; the stage was excellent and the scenery new. The greatest event of Rich's career at Lincoln's Inn Fields was the production of Gay's *The Beggar's Opera* (1727–8), which took the town by storm.

In 1733 Rich moved to his new theatre in Bow Street (see COVENT GARDEN), and that was virtually the end of Lincoln's Inn Fields as a regular playhouse. It was let occasionally for balls, concerts, and operas, and from time to time an actor would try his luck there, as Giffard (q.v.) did when his theatre in Goodman's Fields was closed. It then became a barracks, an auction room, and a china warehouse, and was pulled down in 1848.

Lincoln's Men, a small company of Elizabethan actors, led by Laurence Dutton, who were in the service of the first Earl of Lincoln and of his son Lord Clinton, whose name they sometimes took. They appeared at Court before Queen Elizabeth I several times between 1572 and 1575 and were active in the provinces up to 1577, as was a later company of the same name from 1599 to 1610.

LINDBERG, AUGUST (1846–1916), Swedish actor-manager who toured widely in Scandinavia and did much to establish the reputation of Ibsen (q.v.). He was the first to play Oswald in *Ghosts* (1881), and among his other parts were the title-roles in *Brand*, *Peer Gynt*, and *John Gabriel Borkman*, and Solness in *The Master Builder*. He also appeared in Shakespeare's *King Lear* and *Hamlet*.

LINDSAY, HOWARD (1889–1968), American actor, dramatist, and director, who already had a long list of successes to his credit when he collaborated with RUSSEL CROUSE (1893–1966) in a dramatization of Clarence Day's *Life with Father* (1939), which, with Lindsay as Father, ran for seven years. They continued their collaboration with a dramatization of Day's *Life with Mother* (1948), and with the Pulitzer Prize-winning *State of the Union* (1945).

LINLEY, ELIZABETH ANN (1754–92), see SHERIDAN, R. B.

Lion Comique, see LEYBOURNE, GEORGE and VANCE.

Lisle's Tennis-Court, see LINCOLN'S INN FIELDS THEATRE.

LISTON, JOHN (1776–1846), English comedian, who in spite of a nervous and melancholic turn of mind in private life had only to appear on the stage to set the audience laughing. After extensive experience in the provinces he was seen at the Haymarket in 1805, playing Sheepface in *The Village Lawyer*, an adaptation of the old French farce of *Maître Pierre Pathelin*. For the next thirty years he was one of the leading players of London, where he made a fortune for several managers and authors—Pocock, Dibdin, Hook— and was the first comic actor to command a salary greater than that of a tragedian. He occasionally aspired to play tragedy himself, but without success. His Paul Pry in Poole's comedy of that name, first produced at the Haymarket in 1826, was so successful that it was imitated, dress and all, by such later players of the part as Wright in 1854 and Toole in 1866.

LISTON, VICTOR (1838–1913), a popular comedian in the early London music-halls.

He began his career at the Old Bower Saloon in Stangate Street. For some time he worked the small halls and supper-rooms such as the Cyder Cellars and the Coal Hole, until one night, at the Philharmonic, Islington, his song 'Shabby Genteel' made such a sensation that he stayed for seven months, going afterwards to the Metropolitan, Collins's, and Evans's Supper Rooms, where the Prince of Wales (later Edward VII) brought the Duke and Duchess of Sutherland specially to hear him. Later in life he became a music-hall proprietor.

Little Catherine Street Theatre, LONDON, see ROYAL PANTHEON.

Little Club, NEW YORK, see FORTY-FOURTH STREET THEATRE.

Little Drury Lane Theatre, LONDON, see OLYMPIC THEATRE (I).

Little Theatre, a term applied in Great Britain to a movement which began in the 1920s and led to the establishment of some excellent amateur theatre groups, among them the Maddermarket, the Mountview, the Questors, the Tavistock, and the Village Players, Great Hucklow (qq.v.). These companies, and a number of others, are affiliated to the Little Theatre Guild of Great Britain, which was founded in 1946 with a membership of nine, now increased to over thirty. These companies lease or own their own theatre buildings and present from four to eight productions a year. Several of them also run training courses for actors and directors and provide lectures, conferences, and visits to professional theatres for their members. The Guild itself acts as a clearing house for information and mutual assistance and publishes a useful annual report. Its oldest member is the Stockport Garrick Society, founded in 1901.

Little Theatre. (1) LONDON, in John Street, Adelphi. This small theatre, holding only 350, opened on 11 Oct. 1910 with Laurence Housman's adaptation of Aristophanes' *Lysistrata*, under the management of Gertrude Kingston (q.v.), who played the title-role. On 27 Jan. 1911 Noël Coward (q.v.) made his first appearance on the stage as Prince Mussel in a fairy play called *The Goldfish*, by a Miss Lila Field and on 19 April Shaw's *Fanny's First Play*, directed by himself, was performed anonymously. In 1913

G. K. Chesterton's *Magic* had a long run. The theatre was damaged by bombing on 4 Sept. 1917, but was repaired in 1919 and reopened a year later, when there was a season of Grand Guignol with Sybil Thorndike (q.v.), followed by *The Nine O'Clock Revue* (1922) and Farjeon's *The Little Revue Starts at Nine* (1923). Two 'horror' plays were produced here, both based on novels, Bram Stoker's *Dracula* (1927) and Mary Shelley's *Frankenstein* (1930). In 1932 Nancy Price (q.v.) made the theatre the headquarters of her People's National Theatre, the most successful productions being *Lady Precious Stream* (1934) (a traditional Chinese play translated and adapted by S. I. Hsiung) and Mazo de la Roche's *Whiteoaks* (1936). Herbert Farjeon's *Nine Sharp* (1938) and *Little Revue* (1939) were both successful, the latter being adapted to war conditions by running, from September 1939 onwards, in the afternoon. The theatre was destroyed by enemy action on 16 Apr. 1941, and demolished in 1949.

(2) NEW YORK, on 44th Street between Broadway and 8th Avenue. This opened on 12 Mar. 1912 but was not very successful. It was enlarged and redecorated by the Shuberts and in 1935 became a broadcasting studio. *The New York Times* bought it in 1941 and used it for lectures, recitals, and television. On 2 Nov. 1963 it again became a theatre, reopening with Langston Hughes's adaptation of his own novel, *Tambourines to Glory*. In 1964, when Inge's *The Subject Was Roses* was transferred there from the Royale Theatre (q.v.), its name was changed to the Winthrop Ames Theatre, in honour of its founder. It became a television studio in 1965.

Little Theatre in the Hay, LONDON, see HAYMARKET THEATRE.

Little Theatre Movement, ENGLAND, see LITTLE THEATRE; UNITED STATES OF AMERICA, see TRIBUTARY THEATRE.

LITTLE TICH [really HARRY RELPH] (1868–1928), music-hall comedian, so named as a baby from his supposed likeness to the claimant in the famous Tichborne Case. He first appeared as a child at Rosherville, near Gravesend, one of the last of London's pleasure grounds, and later toured as a black-face comedian. After a visit to America he returned to England to play in pantomime at Drury Lane and in music-halls, where his impersonations proved immensely popular. They ranged from grocers, blacksmiths, and sailors on leave, to fairy queens and Spanish dancers, and usually ended, at least until his last years, with a dance in which he balanced on the tips of his preposterous boots, which were as long as he was high.

LITTLEWOOD, (MAUDIE) JOAN (1914–), English director, founder and manager until 1961 of Theatre Workshop (q.v.). After training at the Royal Academy of Dramatic Art she turned her back on the success which might have attended her in the commercial theatre and went to Manchester, where she founded with her husband EWAN McCOLL [really JIMMY MILLER], whom she married in 1935, an amateur group, Theatre Union, which soon made a name for itself with unconventional productions of experimental plays. The group dispersed on the outbreak of war in 1939. It came together again in 1945, and in 1953 took over the lease of the Theatre Royal at Stratford, London, where Joan Littlewood, working on a system entirely her own, though it may derive from Stanislavsky and Brecht (qq.v.), was responsible for the success of a series of productions which were subsequently transferred to the West End and also made the company famous on the Continent, where Paris was the first to acclaim its brilliance. The consequent drain on her resources, and a morbid dread of the ensuing publicity, drove her in 1961 to leave Theatre Workshop to work elsewhere, but she returned in 1963 to undertake the successful production of *Oh, What a Lovely War!* In 1967 she again staged for Theatre Workshop *Macbird*, Barbara Garson's political skit on *Macbeth*, first seen off-Broadway, and *The Marie Lloyd Story*, as well as a successful pastiche of Vanbrugh's *The Provoked Wife* as *Intrigues and Amours*. In 1970 she returned again to direct *Forward, Up Your End.*

Liturgical Drama (from liturgy, the service of Holy Communion, Mass, or Eucharist, in the Christian Church), the name given to the vast cycles of biblical plays which were acted all over Europe in the Middle Ages. From the trope, or chanted text, for the Easter Celebration which begins '*Quem quaeritis?*' (Whom seek ye?) and

follows closely the Gospel account of the meeting between the angel at the tomb and the three Marys on Easter Sunday morning, a short play was evolved which was performed before Matins, with four choir-boys singing the different parts. It cannot be said with any certainty when this custom started but by the beginning of the twelfth century it was well established, taking place in front of a temporary or permanent structure representing the sepulchre, in which a cross was laid on Good Friday and removed early on Sunday morning. To the scene in which the angel announced the Resurrection to the women and they to the congregation were added further scenes showing the apostles John and Peter going into the tomb and Christ's meeting in the garden with Mary Magdalene. An important step in the evolution of liturgical drama was the interpolation, probably in the thirteenth or fourteenth century, of a scene with no Scriptural basis. This showed the three Marys stopping on their way to the tomb to buy spices for the embalming of Christ's body. The Spice Seller, who was the first comic character in the liturgical play, appeared originally in Germany, perhaps under the influence of secular drama in the vernacular, which had by that time emerged as a separate entity.

The liturgical play is found all over Europe. It seems to have been most common in Germany and France, developing somewhat differently in Italy and Spain. Even in the early days some attempt to provide costumes and properties seems to have been made, with a robe, wings, and a palm for the angel, and a spice box for the Marys. But for a long time it remained part of a church service, with choristers, priests, and nuns as the only actors. It was followed immediately by the *Te Deum* and so merged into Matins. It was not until it moved out of the church and was taken over by the secular powers that lay actors were employed and the liturgical Easter play was merged in the Mystery Play (q.v.).

Another Easter play, called the *Peregrinus* and modelled perhaps on the above, showed the Risen Christ with the disciples at Emmaus, with the addition sometimes of the three Marys and Doubting Thomas. This was originally performed at Vespers, but gradually it was amalgamated with the earlier play and lengthened by the addition of the lamentations of those stationed by the Cross on Good Friday. This led to a play on the Passion of Christ, as distinct from the Resurrection, which began with the preparations for the Last Supper, continued through the betrayal, arrest, and trial of Christ, the denial by St. Peter, the stations of the Cross, and the Crucifixion, and ended with the taking of the body of Christ from the Cross and its placing in the tomb. It was given only in a rudimentary form inside the church, mostly in mime with readings in Latin from the Bible, and did not evolve fully until it moved from the church to become the Passion Play (see MYSTERIENSPIEL), performed either alone or as part of a Mystery play (q.v.).

The Christmas services gave rise to a play on the Nativity, centred on the crib which has always been displayed at Christmas in Continental churches and has recently returned to favour in England, together with Mary, Joseph, the ox and ass, the shepherds, and the angels. But this does not seem ever to have been as important as the Easter play and, together with a scene dealing with Rachel and the massacre of the Innocents, was soon absorbed into an Epiphany play, whose focal point was the arrival of the Wise Men with their gifts. This play began with the journey of the Magi, showed their visit to Jerusalem and interview with King Herod, their meeting with the shepherds and the presentation of their gifts at the manger, their return home by a different route after being warned by an angel, Herod's anger at being outwitted, and the massacre of the Innocents, ending with the flight of Mary and Joseph with the Christ Child into Egypt. Occasionally a final scene was added showing the death of Herod and the return of the Holy Family to Nazareth. Herod, so important in later secular plays on religious subjects, was from the first a noisy, blustering fellow, whence Hamlet's phrase: 'to out-Herod Herod'. He was probably played by the 'king' chosen from among the minor clergy to preside over the Feast of Fools (q.v.).

Another Christmas play, more important for the future development of drama, was known as the Prophet Play. This was based on a narrative sermon attributed to St. Augustine, and consisted of extracts from the Old Testament prophesying the coming of the Messiah. At some time it was rewritten as a metrical dramatic dialogue incorporating the stories of the Three Children in the Fiery Furnace and Balaam and his Ass. The ass was probably another importation from the Feast of Fools.

Apart from these Christmas and Easter plays, which evolved within the framework of normal church services, others exist, written by a single author for performance in church. The manuscript works of a wandering scholar, Hilarius, a pupil of Abelard, contain three plays of this kind, a *Miracle of St. Nicholas*, *The Raising of Lazarus*, and a two-part play on Daniel probably detached from the Prophet play. There are in addition a number of anonymous plays on these subjects, those dealing with St. Nicholas being particularly connected with performances by school- or choir-boys under a Boy Bishop. There are also traces of other subjects—John the Baptist, Isaac and Rebecca, the Conversion of St. Paul—and a French play on the Wise and Foolish Virgins. Some of these plays are complicated enough to indicate the presence of professionals, the lineal descendants of the classical actors whom the Church had tried to suppress. Certainly the wandering scholars like Hilarius knew something about acting, and having written their plays, may have called in some travelling tumblers to eke out the shortcomings of the local clergy. The players in local folk-plays too may have been pressed into service. But all this is conjecture. All that can be said with certainty is that liturgical drama, which evolved from the simple chants of Easter or Christmas, had completed its evolution by the end of the thirteenth century, and that in its later development it ceased to be liturgical. Plays were still given in churches, mostly in the vernacular, in the fifteenth century, and in isolated cases even later, but they were intermixed with, and influenced by, the secular plays of the market-place to such an extent that they can no longer be considered a product of the Christian liturgy. Having given back the drama to Europe, the Church again withdrew and prepared to do battle with the theatre it had engendered.

The very successful revival, in a production by E. Martin Browne, of the twelfth-century music-drama, *The Play of Daniel*, in 1960 raised the question of the musical accompaniment to the liturgical play. Was the singing mainly unaccompanied, and if not, how many and what kind of instruments were used? Noah Greenberg, director of the New York Pro Musica Antiqua, which presented the play in New York and in a number of cathedrals in England and on the Continent, provided his company with an assortment of period instruments such as hurdy-gurdys, portable organs, cymbals, and recorders. Dr. René Clemencic, for a Viennese production of the same play, was far more liberal, and made provision for a string group, a wind group, and a percussion group, in addition to a portative organ. This led Dr. W. L. Smoldon, the foremost British authority on liturgical drama, to protest against over-elaboration, since he believes that for plays sung in Latin in the church—as opposed to the spoken vernacular plays given outside—the only accompaniment was provided by organ and chime-bells, both used sparingly.

Since musicians have only recently begun to study the surviving texts, which give only a simple line of melody for the singers, the question is not likely to be solved immediately. But at present there seems to be, in Dr. Smoldon's view, no certain evidence for the use of harmony and only the scantiest for any instrumental accompaniment, whereas Dr. Clemencic argues that all the instruments he used were represented in the painting and sculpture of the period, in the hands of saints or angels, and were therefore permissible, and that constant edicts by ecclesiastical authorities against the use of instruments in church proves how widespread the practice was. It does not, however, solve the problem of how many of the existing instruments were used at the same time. Dr. Inglis Gundry, musical director of the Sacred Music Drama Society (founded 1961), which has given presentations of six liturgical dramas in seven different churches, has some interesting things to say based on practical experience. Since actors must move during the play and scenes be done in different parts of the building, and since singers are no longer trained in the medieval tradition of unaccompanied chant nor are modern audiences conditioned to listening to it, it seems reasonable to use whatever is easiest for actors and audience, as long as it is in accordance with the style of the period and used with restraint. As Dr. Gundry wisely says: 'Actual performances in the Middle Ages may have been different in various churches, at different

periods, or on different occasions, some partially accompanied, some elaborately, some not at all.' And, he inquires, 'may not this be the reason why the accompaniment was . . . never written down?'

Liturgy, in Athens, a public service required of wealthy citizens. One such duty was the staging of a play (see CHOREGUS). In Europe the liturgy, or form of worship, of the early Christian Church gave rise to the performance of plays in Latin (see LITURGICAL DRAMA).

Liverpool, which has the oldest surviving repertory theatre in England, saw its first theatrical performances—in cockpits —in the early part of the eighteenth century. In the 1740s the Old Ropery Theatre, a converted room, was used by visiting companies, and in 1749–50 a theatre without boxes was built in Drury Lane and used by actors from London during the summer. Boxes were added in 1759, and a green-room and dressing-rooms provided in 1767. In 1772 a new theatre was built, and among its lessees was George Mattocks, whose father-in-law (see HALLAM) took the first theatrical company to the New World. In 1803 the theatre was rebuilt in horseshoe shape. It was adapted as a circus and later became a cold-storage depot. In its heyday Liverpool had a theatre season which lasted practically all the year and was independent of a circuit. It now has two theatres as well as the repertory theatre. In 1958 the New Shakespeare Theatre, formerly a music-hall, the Pigalle, was opened as a Theatre Club under the direction of Sam Wanamaker, but the venture failed after a year and the building was subsequently destroyed by fire.

The Liverpool Repertory Theatre, now known as the Playhouse, was the third to be opened in Great Britain (the earlier ones were the Abbey, Dublin (q.v.), and the Gaiety, Manchester (see HORNIMAN and REPERTORY THEATRE MOVEMENT IN GREAT BRITAIN)). Originally the Star Theatre in Williamson Square, it opened on 11 Nov. 1911, since when it has closed only for short summer vacations and for reconstruction in 1968, when it reopened with a revival of one of Irving's greatest successes, *The Lyons Mail*, by Charles Reade. Though almost entirely dependent on box-office receipts, the Playhouse does not cater for any definite class of audience or for any one type of playgoer, and its productions range from the lightest of light comedies to such serious plays as Raynal's *The Unknown Warrior* or Susan Glaspell's *The Inheritors*. The encouragement given to new and young authors has been one of the theatre's special activities and it was also one of the first repertory theatres to return to the staging of one-act plays. Every Christmas it produces a new play specially written for children. 'The Playhouse Circle', which met on alternate Sunday evenings, was for many years a valuable adjunct to the theatre's work. It had a membership of over nine hundred and many notabilities spoke at its meetings. Another collateral activity which owes its existence indirectly to the theatre is the Shute Lectureship in the Art of the Theatre at the University of Liverpool, founded in 1923 by Colonel Sir John Shute, then chairman of the Playhouse directors.

The Playhouse has been a notable school of acting. Much of its success up to the outbreak of the Second World War, at which time it had just begun to triumph over its initial difficulties and even to show a profit, was due to the work and enthusiasm of William Armstrong (q.v.), its director and resident producer from 1922 to 1944.

Living Newspaper, a stage production conceived in terms of the cinema, showing in short, swift-moving scenes problems of modern social life and the methods of dealing with them. First evolved by the Federal Theatre (q.v.) in the United States, this technique was successfully used in England for adult education and propaganda in the armed forces during the Second World War.

Living Theatre, NEW YORK, one of the most radical and influential *avant-garde* troupes, which began as an off-Broadway repertory company formed in 1947 by JULIAN BECK (1925–85) and his actress-wife JUDITH MALINA (1926–) to present new and experimental plays. They began their original and highly iconoclastic career at the Cherry Lane Theatre, where one of their first major productions was Gertrude Stein's *Dr. Faustus Lights the Lights* (1951). In the same year they moved to their own theatre at 530 Avenue of the Americas, where their most widely publicized production was Jack Gelber's *The Connection*

(1959), which they later took to Europe. In 1962 they again toured Europe with Brecht's *In the Jungle of Cities* (1960) and Gelber's *The Apple* (1961). On their return home they opened their new season with an adaptation of Brecht's *Man is Man* (1962). Their theatre closed in 1963, and in 1965 was operating in West Berlin. A return to New York in 1968 was followed by a performance of a 'collective creation' entitled *Paradise Now*. An appearance at Yale University, followed by a scantily-dressed parade through the streets, led to the arrest of Beck and his wife on charges of indecent exposure. In 1969 the company appeared in London at the Roundhouse (q.v.) in a repertory (including *Paradise Now*, *Mysteries*, the first piece created in exile, *Frankenstein*, and *Antigone*) to which, on the whole, the critics were not kind.

LLOYD, MARIE [really MATILDA ALICE VICTORIA WOOD] (1870–1922), the idol of the English music-hall audiences for many years. She made her first appearance at the Grecian (then the Royal Eagle) in 1885 as an extra turn, billed as Bella Delmere, though she soon discarded this for the name under which she became famous. She first made a hit at the 'Old Mo' (see MIDDLESEX MUSIC-HALL), singing Nellie Power's song 'The Boy I Love Sits up in the Gallery', and was then engaged for the Oxford (q.v.), where she remained for a year. From 1891 to 1893 she played 'Principal Girl' in the Drury Lane pantomimes, but the halls were her true home and she appeared in practically all the leading ones of the day. In her work she was wittily improper but never coarse or vulgar, and her humour lay less in her material than in her use of it. Among her best-known songs were 'Oh, Mr. Porter!', 'My Old Man Said Follow the Van', 'I'm One of the Ruins that Cromwell Knocked Abaht a Bit', and 'The Lambeth Walk', not to be confused with the song of that name featured in *Me and My Girl* (1937). In 1967 a musical based on her life, *The Marie Lloyd Story*, was produced by Joan Littlewood (q.v.) for Theatre Workshop, and in 1971 another, entitled *Sing a Rude Song*, was seen at the Garrick, but neither was successful, possibly owing to the difficulty of reproducing Marie Lloyd's unique personality.

Loa, the name given to the prologue, or compliment to the audience, which preceded the early Spanish theatrical performance. It ranged from a short introductory monologue to a miniature drama having some bearing on the play which was to follow. Agustín de Rojas, in his *El viaje entretenido* (1603), says that a strolling company generally had a variety of *loas* which could be fitted to any play. In the seventeenth century the *loa* appears to have been retained in the public theatres for the first performance only of a new company, although allegorical *loas sacramentales* were written for performance on Corpus Christi as an introduction to an *auto*, and continued to be an integral feature of Court performances.

London Casino, see PRINCE EDWARD THEATRE.

London Coliseum, see COLISEUM.

London Hippodrome, see HIPPODROME.

London Opera House, see STOLL THEATRE.

London Palladium. This famous music-hall opened on 26 Dec. 1910 on a site previously occupied by Hengler's circus and soon became a popular home of variety. Later it was used for revues, particularly those of de Courville (beginning with *The Whirl of the World*, 1924), and in the 1930s it housed the Crazy Gang shows which ended in 1938 with *These Foolish Things*. During these years Barrie's *Peter Pan* was seen annually until 1938. It is now used for variety, spectacular revues, and a pantomime at Christmas.

London Pavilion. (1) In Tichborne Street, Westminster. This famous music-hall, attached to the Black Dog public-house, opened on 23 Feb. 1861 and was demolished on 26 March 1885.

(2) On 30 Nov. 1885 a new Pavilion, whose façade is still standing, opened in Piccadilly with the separate tables characteristic of the old music-halls. These were abolished a year later, when tip-up seats were installed. The interior was rebuilt in 1900 but the building continued to operate as a music-hall, often with as many as twenty 'turns' on the bill, until 1918, when, under Charles Cochran (q.v.), it became a theatre housing revue and musical comedy. In 1934 it was converted into a cinema.

London Theatre Studio, see SAINT-DENIS, M.

LONG, JOHN LUTHER (1861–1927), American novelist, playwright, and librettist, whose short story, *Madame Butterfly* (1898), was dramatized by Belasco (q.v.). It was produced with great success at the Herald Square Theatre in 1900 and used by Puccini for his opera, first performed in 1904. Long later collaborated with Belasco on *The Darling of the Gods* (1902), a romantic melodrama set in ancient Japan which was produced by Tree (q.v.) in London, at His Majesty's, in 1903, and on *Adrea* (1905), a tragedy in which Mrs. Leslie Carter (q.v.) successfully played the title-role.

Longacre Theatre, NEW YORK, on 48th Street between Broadway and 8th Avenue. This opened on 1 May 1913, mainly for farces and musical comedy, and in 1925 Kaufman's *The Butter and Egg Man* had a long run there. Later the theatre housed short runs of several notable plays, among them G. B. Stern's *The Matriarch* (1930), and Obey's *Noah* (1935) with Pierre Fresnay in the title-role. Several plays by Odets (q.v.) were produced at this theatre under the auspices of the Group Theatre, and in 1944 it was taken over for broadcasting. It returned to use as a theatre in 1953 and two years later Lillian Hellman's adaptation of Anouilh's *The Lark* was produced with Julie Harris as Joan of Arc. Emlyn Williams was seen as Dylan Thomas in *A Boy Growing Up* in 1957, and in 1961 Zero Mostel starred in Ionesco's *Rhinoceros. My Sweet Charlie*, by David Westheimer, opened in 1966.

LONGFORD, EDWARD ARTHUR HENRY PAKENHAM, 6th Earl of (1902–61), Irish playwright and theatre director, chairman till his death of the Dublin Gate Theatre (see DUBLIN). The best of his own plays was probably *Yahoo* (1933), which, with Hilton Edwards as Jonathan Swift, was successful both in Dublin and in London. With his wife, CHRISTINE PATTI TREW, he translated several plays, notably the *Oresteia* of Aeschylus, the *Oedipus* of Sophocles, and the *Bacchae* of Euripides; also Molière's *Tartuffe* and *Le Bourgeois gentilhomme* and Beaumarchais's *Le Barbier de Séville*. Lady Longford, who wrote *Mr. Jiggins of Jigginstown* (1933), *Anything But the Truth* (1937), and *Sea Change* (1940), was also responsible for dramatizations of Jane Austen's *Pride and Prejudice*, Maria Edgeworth's *The*

Absentee, and Sheridan Le Fanu's *The Watcher* and *The Avenger*.

LONSDALE [really LEONARD], FREDERICK (1881–1954), English dramatist, author of a number of farcical comedies of contemporary life somewhat in the style of Somerset Maugham (q.v.), of which the most successful were *The Last of Mrs. Cheyney* and *Spring Cleaning* (both 1925), *On Approval* and *The High Road* (both 1927), and *Canaries Sometimes Sing* (1929), in which Yvonne Arnaud (q.v.) made a great success. Lonsdale, many of whose other plays were written in collaboration, was also the librettist of the musical plays *The Maid of the Mountains* (1917), *Monsieur Beaucaire* (1919), based on Booth Tarkington's novel with music by André Messager, and *Madame Pompadour* (1923), written in collaboration with Harry Graham, music by Leo Fall, in which Evelyn Laye (q.v.) played the title-role.

LOPE DE VEGA, see VEGA CARPIO.

LÓPEZ DE AYALA, ADELARDO (1829–79), Spanish dramatist and with Tamayo (q.v.) the chief representative of the transition from romanticism to realism. His early plays, among them *Un hombre de estado* (1851), are still basically romantic, but his later comedies, particularly *El tanto por ciento* (1861) and *Consuelo* (1878), are bitter attacks on the materialistic tendencies of his time.

LORAINE, ROBERT (1876–1935), English actor-manager, who made his first appearance on the stage in 1889 and subsequently made a hit as D'Artagnan in a dramatization of the elder Dumas's *The Three Musketeers* (1899). In 1911, after a visit to America, he took over the Criterion Theatre (q.v.) in London, opening with a revival of *Man and Superman* by G. B. Shaw (q.v.), whose Don Juan he had played in the first production of *Don Juan in Hell* (1907). During the First World War he made a great reputation as an aviator and was awarded the M.C. and the D.S.O. for gallantry in action. Essentially a romantic actor, he returned to the stage in 1919 in the title-role of Rostand's *Cyrano de Bergerac*, which had a long run. Among his later parts were Deburau in Sacha Guitry's play of that

name in 1921, the dual role of Rassendyl and Prince Rudolf in a revival of Hope's *The Prisoner of Zenda* in 1923, the Nobleman in the New York production of Ashley Dukes's *The Man with a Load of Mischief* in 1925, Adolf in Strindberg's *The Father* in 1927 in a double bill with Barrie's *Barbara's Wedding* in which he played the Colonel, and a number of Shakespearian parts, including Petruchio in *The Taming of the Shrew* and Mercutio in *Romeo and Juliet*, both in 1926.

LORCA, FEDERICO GARCÍA (1898–1936), Spanish poet and dramatist, assassinated during the first days of the Spanish Civil War. His influence on the reviving Spanish stage was most important, both through his own plays and through the medium of La Barraca, an itinerant amateur company which he directed. Several of his plays have been translated into English but no one has yet succeeded in conveying the haunting poetic intensity of the originals. Lorca's first play, *El maleficio de la mariposa*, was produced in 1920 by Martínez Sierra (q.v.) during his management of the Teatro Eslava, and was followed by *Mariana Pineda* (1927) and *Amor de Don Perlimplín con Belisa en su jardín* (1931). His fame rests, however, mainly upon his three great tragedies: *Bodas de sangre* (1933), seen in New York in 1935 as *Bitter Oleander*, in London in 1939 as *The Marriage of Blood*, and in London and New York in 1947 and 1949 respectively as *Blood Wedding* in a translation by the poet Roy Campbell; *Yerma* (1934), seen in London in 1957; and his last play, *La Casa de Bernarda Alba* (1936), a study of female frustration in a household of daughters ruled by a tyrannical mother. This, which many consider Lorca's best play, full of hopes for the future which were destined to remain unfulfilled, was seen in New York in 1951 as *The House of Bernarda Alba*, but has not yet been produced professionally in London, though it has had several amateur and student productions.

Lord Admiral's Men, see ADMIRAL'S MEN.

Lord Chamberlain, see DRAMATIC CENSORSHIP.

Lord Chamberlain's Men, see CHAMBERLAIN'S MEN.

Lord Howard's Men, see ADMIRAL'S MEN.

Lord of Misrule, of Unreason, see FEAST OF FOOLS.

Lord Strange's Men, see STRANGE'S MEN.

LORNE, MARION (1888–1968), see WHITE-HALL THEATRE.

LOTTA, see CRABTREE, CHARLOTTE.

LOUTHERBOURG, PHILIP JAMES DE (1740–1812), scenic director at Drury Lane (q.v.) from 1773 to 1781, a position he held under Garrick and Sheridan (qq.v.). He introduced a number of new devices, including a series of head-lights or border battens behind the proscenium which at once discouraged actors from stepping too much outside the picture and increased the importance of the scenery by the flood of illumination. He was particularly successful in producing the illusion of fire, volcanoes, sun, moonlight, and cloud-effects, and invented strikingly effective devices for thunder, guns, wind, the lapping of waves, and the patter of hail and rain. He was the first to bring a breath of naturalism into the artificial scenic conventions of the time, and paved the way for the realistic detail and local colour of Charles Kemble (q.v.). He is referred to by Mr. Puff in Sheridan's *The Critic* (1779), for which he had executed a striking design of Tilbury Fort, and was responsible in Nov. of the same year for some excellent new transparencies used in a revival of *The Winter's Tale*. A visit to the Peak district earlier in 1779 had resulted in an act-drop depicting a romantic landscape which remained in use until Drury Lane was destroyed by fire in 1809. W. J. Lawrence cites this as the earliest example of a scenic curtain in Western Europe. In 1781 Loutherbourg withdrew from the theatre, but his influence can be traced as late as 1820, in Edmund Kean's *King Lear*. He was probably the first designer in England to break up the scene by the use of perspective, and the first to make use of set scenes with raking pieces (q.v.). But the time was not yet ripe for much practicable scenery and he was for the most part sparing in his resort to built stuff (q.v.). It is mainly as Garrick's scene designer that he is remembered, and his fine work gave momentary popularity to many an otherwise unremarkable play.

Low Comedian, see STOCK COMPANY.

LOWIN, JOHN (1576–1653), English actor, and an important link between the Elizabethan and Restoration stages. He is first mentioned in 1602 and a year later was one of the King's Men (see CHAMBER-LAIN'S MEN), with whom he remained until the closing of the theatres in 1642. He was often referred to as a big man, and played the parts of bluff soldiers and gruff villains. His Falstaff was much admired, as was his Volpone in Ben Jonson's play, and his Melantius in Beaumont and Fletcher's *The Maid's Tragedy* (1611). He was probably Bosola in the first production of Webster's *The Duchess of Malfi* (1614), and played in several of Massinger's plays. He was one of the actors caught playing in the Cockpit (q.v.) during the Puritan interregnum, and Betterton (q.v.) is believed to have been coached in his part of Shakespeare's Henry VIII by Davenant on instructions from Lowin, 'who', says Downes in *Roscius Anglicanus*, 'had his Instructions from Mr. Shakespeare himself'.

Lucille La Verne Theatre, NEW YORK, see PRINCESS THEATRE.

Lucy Rushton's Theatre, NEW YORK, see NEW YORK THEATRE (1).

LUDLOW, NOAH MILLER (1795–1886), one of the pioneer actor-managers of the American theatre, who in 1817 was responsible for the first English plays to be produced in New Orleans. He travelled extensively with his own or other companies, being often the first actor to penetrate to some of the more remote regions in the South and West. From 1835 to 1853 he was in partnership with Sol Smith (q.v.) in the American Theatrical Commonwealth Company and ran several theatres simultaneously in St. Louis, New Orleans, Mobile, and other cities, often engaging outstanding stars. He was himself an excellent actor, particularly in comedy, and the author of an entertaining volume of reminiscences, *Dramatic Life as I Found It*.

LUDWIG, OTTO (1813–65), German novelist and dramatist, contemporary of Hebbel (q.v.). His best play is *Der Erbförster* (1850), a study of bourgeois life, while an apocryphal drama, *Die*

Makkabäer (1852), is written in a more romantic style. Ludwig, who studied music under Mendelssohn, was an ardent admirer of Shakespeare, on whom he published a volume of essays in 1869.

LUGNÉ-POË, AURÉLIEN-FRANÇOIS (1869–1940), French actor, director, and theatre manager, who in 1893 took over the Théâtre d'Art from Paul Fort (q.v.), renaming it the Théâtre de l'Œuvre and remaining there until 1929. In his early years he continued Fort's reaction against the realism of Antoine's Théâtre Libre by staging poetic and symbolist plays with transparent curtains against a painted backcloth, abolishing the footlights and the box set, and replacing realistic speech by formal intoning. His first production was *Pelléas et Mélisande* (1893) by Maeterlinck (q.v.), whose later plays were also first seen at the Théâtre de l'Œuvre—*L'Intruse* in 1893, *Intérieur* in 1894, *Monna Vanna* in 1902. Among the foreign authors introduced to Paris by Lugné-Poë were Ibsen, Bjørnson, Strindberg, Hauptmann, D'Annunzio, and Echegaray (qq.v.). In 1895 he directed Wilde's *Salome*, and first brought Claudel before the public with *L'Annonce faite à Marie* in 1912 and *L'Ôtage* in 1914. After leaving the Théâtre de l'Œuvre he continued to direct, being responsible in 1932 for the first production of *L'Hermine* by Anouilh (q.v.) and in 1935 of *L'Inconnue d'Arras* by Salacrou (q.v.), whose *Tour à Terre* he had presented as early as 1925. Himself an excellent actor, Lugné-Poë appeared in many of his own early productions, and in 1908 was seen in London in Jules Renard's *Poil de Carotte*.

LUN, see RICH, JOHN.

LUNACHARSKY, ANATOLI VASILEVICH (1875–1933), first Commissar for Education in Soviet Russia, an able, cultured man, to whom the U.S.S.R. owes the preservation and renewed vigour of those Imperial theatrical institutions, notably the Moscow Art Theatre (q.v.), which survived the Revolution. He was also responsible for the organization of the new Soviet theatres which sprang up in vast numbers. He realized that the new audiences, many of whom had never been in a theatre before, would eventually demand new methods and new plays, but that the old plays, both Russian and European, were part of the heritage of the new world and that it would be wrong to falsify or misinterpret them. This led to his exposition of the principles of Socialist Realism (q.v.), which inaugurated a series of fresh, vivid, and important revivals (as well as productions of new plays) of which Popov's *The Taming of the Shrew* in 1937 is the best example. Lunacharsky wrote a number of articles on the theatre which were published in two volumes (in 1924 and 1926), in which his theories, and the attempts made to put them into practice, can be further studied. A third volume was published in 1936. He was also the author of several plays. In 1934 the State Institute of Theatre Arts in Moscow was named after him.

Lunch-Time Theatres, a phenomenon of London theatrical life which began in the late 1960s and provides opportunities for the production by professional actors of new, experimental plays of under one hour in duration, given before a small audience in unorthodox surroundings, often a basement or a room in a public-house, during the week-day lunch break. They all alike suffer from problems of finding and keeping suitable central premises, and of finance, but they offer an important outlet for actors and directors, and in recognition of their work several of them have received Arts Council grants. Although they are of no benefit to a dramatist wishing to try out a full-length play, they do bring before a discerning public a number of short plays, thus helping to reinforce the welcome revival of the serious one-acter. Among the first lunch-time groups were the Ambiance, run by Ed Berman, first in Queensway, later 'in exile' at various addresses, which in 1970 produced, among other plays, Stoppard's *After Magritte* and N. F. Simpson's *Gladly Otherwise*; the Basement Theatre in Greek Street; the Lamb and Flag in Rose Street; the flourishing Quipu, which was seen at the Arts Theatre and in temporary association with the Basement Theatre and also put on full-length productions in the evening; the Soho Theatre in King Street; and the King's Head, in Upper Street, Islington.

LUNDEQUIST, GERDA (1871–1959), Swedish actress, nicknamed 'the Swedish Bernhardt' because of her beautiful voice and powerfully dramatic acting. She had a long and distinguished career on the Swedish stage, being outstanding in such parts as Lady Macbeth and Antigone.

LUNT, ALFRED DAVIS (1892–1977), American actor, who made his début in 1912, and in 1919 made a great success as Clarence in Booth Tarkington's play of that name. With his wife, LYNN [really LILLIE LOUISE] FONTANNE (1887–1983), whom he married in 1922, he built up a big reputation in London and New York in the playing of intimate modern comedy. Miss Fontanne, who made her first appearance in London in 1905, had already had a distinguished career before, with her husband, she joined the company of the Theatre Guild (q.v.) in 1924. During the next five years they appeared together in a succession of plays which included Shaw's *Arms and the Man* and *Pygmalion*, Molnár's *The Guardsman*, and Werfel's *Goat Song*. They were first seen together in London in 1929 in G. Sil-Vara's *Caprice*, adapted by Philip Moeller. Later successes were Robert Sherwood's *Reunion in Vienna* (New York, 1931; London, 1934); Coward's *Design for Living* (New York, 1933; London, 1939); Giraudoux's *Amphitryon 38*, adapted by S. N. Behrman (New York, 1937; London, 1938); and Rattigan's *Love in Idleness* (1944), seen in New York in 1946 as *O Mistress Mine*. In 1958 they appeared at the Globe Theatre, New York, renamed the Lunt–Fontanne Theatre (q.v.) in their honour, in Dürrenmatt's *The Visit*, with which they had previously toured in England under the title of *Time and Again*. Under its new name it was the first production seen at the opening of the new Royalty Theatre in London (see ROYALTY (3)) in 1960.

Lunt–Fontanne Theatre, NEW YORK, an attractive playhouse on Broadway north of 46th Street, which opened as the Globe on 10 Jan. 1910, mainly for musical shows, though at the end of the year it housed the company of Sarah Bernhardt (q.v.) in a repertory of French plays. The *Ziegfeld Follies* were there in 1921, and *George White's Scandals* in 1922 and 1923. In 1932 the theatre closed and became a cinema, but in 1958, completely remodelled and redecorated, it opened as the Lunt–Fontanne with Alfred Lunt and Lynn Fontanne (see LUNT) in Dürrenmatt's *The Visit*. In 1963 it saw a brilliant but short-lived performance of Brecht's *Arturo Ui* and from 9 Apr. to 8 Aug. 1964 Richard Burton (q.v.) appeared in *Hamlet*, setting up a new record for the run of the play in New York. A later Hamlet was Nicol Williamson in 1969, for a limited run only.

LUPINO, a vast family of English dancers, acrobats, pantomimists, and actors, descended from an Italian puppeteer who came to England in the time of James I. His seventh descendant in direct succession had sixteen children, of whom two married into the family of Sara Lane (q.v.), one having children and grandchildren on the stage. The eldest son, GEORGE (1853–1932), was the father of BARRY (1882–1962), who made his first appearance on the stage as a baby, was for some years stock comedian at the Britannia, toured extensively, and was seen in pantomime and musical comedy. He was one of the finest exponents of the Dame (q.v.) in pantomime and wrote the librettos of about fifty pantomimes himself. His two children were also on the stage. His brother STANLEY (1893–1942), also on the stage as a child, was in variety with an acrobat troupe and in pantomime for many years at Drury Lane. He was also seen in revue and musical comedy, was the author of several plays and novels, and of a volume of reminiscences, *From the Stocks to the Stars* (1934), from which many of the above details are taken. His nephew, HENRY GEORGE (1892–1959), took his great-aunt Sara's name and was known as LUPINO LANE. As Nipper Lane, he made his first appearance on the stage at the age of four, and as an adult toured extensively in variety. He was also seen in musical comedy and in pantomime, and made a great hit as Bill Snibson in the musical comedy *Me and My Girl* (1937), in which he created the well-known dance 'The Lambeth Walk'. He also had a son on the stage; some younger members of this illustrious family have made their name in films.

LUZZATO, MOSES HAYIM (1707–47), an Italian Jew, resident in Amsterdam, author of a number of plays in Hebrew, of which the earliest, written when he was only seventeen, dealt with Samson among the Philistines. For his uncle's wedding in 1727 he wrote *Migdal Oz*, a pastoral modelled on the *Pastor Fido* of Guarini (q.v.) which contains many passages of great lyric beauty. Among his later plays the most important, written for a pupil's wedding and published in 1743, was *Tehilla Layesharim*. Luzzato was also one of the first Hebrew dramatists to attempt dramatic criticism, one section of a grammar for which he was responsible containing an attempted definition of drama.

Lyceum Theatre. (1) LONDON, in Wellington Street, just off the Strand. The name of this theatre is indissolubly linked with that of Irving (q.v.), even though the actual building was largely rebuilt after his departure. There was a place of entertainment on the site as early as 1765, but it was not until 1809, when the Drury Lane company moved there after the destruction by fire of their own theatre, that it was licensed for plays. When the new Drury Lane opened in 1812 the Lyceum was rebuilt to designs by Beazley (q.v.) and licensed for the summer only, being used for mixed entertainments of opera and plays. On 16 Feb. 1830 it was burnt down, and on 12 July 1834 a new building, whose frontage still stands on Wellington Street, opened as the Royal Lyceum and English Opera House. This too was designed by Beazley and was the building in which Irving made his name. It started well, but had a chequered career until the passing of the Licensing Act of 1843 enabled it to go over to legitimate drama. Robert Keeley (q.v.) ran it from 1844 to 1847; among his successes was *Mrs. Caudle's Curtain Lectures* (1845), by Stirling. After Keeley left, Mme Vestris and the younger Mathews (qq.v.) took over, and a series of brilliant productions followed, mostly of extravaganzas by Planché (q.v.), whose melodrama *The Vampire; or, the Bride of the Isles*, which first introduced the 'vampire' trap (q.v.), had been produced in the old theatre in 1820. Unfortunately Mme Vestris and Mathews were extravagant and unbusinesslike. They went bankrupt, and the theatre was then occupied by the company from Covent Garden, which had been burnt down in 1856, but little of note happened, under constant changes of management, until in 1871 the American impresario Bateman (q.v.) took the theatre in order to present his three daughters, Kate, Virginia, and Isabel, in a London season, engaging as his leading man the young Henry Irving. Seven years later Irving took control, and with Ellen Terry (q.v.) as his leading lady inaugurated a series of fine productions which made the Lyceum the most notable theatre in London. They made their last appearance there together (though both continued

separately to appear elsewhere) on 19 July 1902 in *The Merchant of Venice*, and after their departure the fortunes of the theatre declined. It was partly demolished and rebuilt as a music-hall which opened on 31 Dec. 1904, but under the Melvilles (qq.v.) from 1910 to 1938 it became famous as the home of melodrama and pantomime. In 1939 the theatre was scheduled for demolition and six farewell performances of *Hamlet*, with John Gielgud (q.v.), took place, ending on 1 July. The outbreak of the Second World War two months later led to the abandonment of the demolition scheme and the theatre stood empty until 1945, when it became a dance hall. (See also EDINBURGH.)

(2) NEW YORK, on 4th Avenue, a small theatre built by Steele Mackaye (q.v.) which opened on 6 Apr. 1885 with his *Dakolar*. This was not a success, and he withdrew from management. It was then taken over by Daniel Frohman (q.v.), who had many successes there, and in 1902 it was pulled down.

(3) NEW YORK, on 45th Street east of Broadway, one of the city's most glamorous playhouses. Built by Daniel Frohman, it opened on 2 Nov. 1903. The first new play produced there was Barrie's *The Admirable Crichton*, and later Charles Wyndham (q.v.) brought his London company for an eight-week season. From 1916 a number of productions by Belasco (q.v.), Frohman's first stage manager at the Lyceum, preceded a fine performance by David Warfield (q.v.) as Shylock in *The Merchant of Venice* (1922). In 1929 *Berkeley Square*, by John Balderston and J. C. Squire, repeated its London success, and further successes were achieved in 1940 by Kaufman and Hart's *George Washington Slept Here*, in 1941 by Fields and Chodorov's *Junior Miss* (in which year Saroyan's *The Beautiful People* had an artistic though not commercial success), and in 1946 by Garson Kanin's *Born Yesterday*. Later productions included Odets's *The Country Girl* (1950) and three plays imported from London—Osborne's *Look Back in Anger* (1957), Shelagh Delaney's *A Taste of Honey* (1960), and Pinter's *The Caretaker* (1961). (See also BROUGHAM and the elder JAMES WALLACK.)

LYLY, JOHN (*c.* 1554–1606), English novelist and dramatist, author of *Euphues: The Anatomy of Wit* (1579) and *Euphues* *and his England* (1580), whose peculiarly involved and allusive style gave rise to the expression 'euphuism'. By his contemporaries he was regarded as an outstanding dramatist and his elegant writing had a salutary effect on some of the more full-blooded dramatists of the day. He wrote almost exclusively for a courtly audience, who delighted in the grace and artificiality of his style and in the many sly allusions to contemporary scandals with which his plays were seasoned. His first two plays, *Campaspe* and *Sapho and Phao*, were given by the Children of Paul's and of the Chapel in 1584 at Court and at Blackfriars (q.v.). His most important play, *Endimion, the Man in the Moon*, first published in 1591, may have been acted in 1588 before the Court. Of his other plays, several were pastoral comedies on mythological subjects, of ephemeral interest. Two comedies, *Midas* and *Mother Bombie*—the latter in the style of Terence—were given by the Children of Paul's, of whom Lyly was vice-master in about 1590, and a further comedy, *The Woman in the Moon*, may not have been acted. Lyly is also believed to have had a hand in numerous other plays of the time, but nothing can be ascribed to him with any certainty.

LYNDSAY, SIR DAVID (1490–c. 1554), Scottish poet, and the author of the only surviving example of a Scottish medieval Morality Play (q.v.), *Ane Pleasant Satyre of the Thrie Estaitis*. First performed at Cupar in 1552 in the presence of James V, this is a serious attack on the established Church and the authority of the Pope, interspersed with comic episodes highlighting clerical follies and abuses of the time. The complete play, which was added to and revised in 1554, is very long, but an abbreviated and modernized version was successfully produced at the Edinburgh Festival in 1948 under the direction of Tyrone Guthrie (q.v.).

LYNN, RALPH (1882–1962), English actor, best known for his appearances with Robertson Hare and Tom Walls (qq.v.) in Ben Travers's farces at the Aldwych Theatre in the 1920s. He made his first appearance on the stage in 1900 and after appearing in New York in 1913 was seen in London a year later. His first outstanding success was made as Aubrey Henry Maitland Allington in the farce *Tons of Money* (1922), by Will Evans. This was transferred to the Aldwych in 1923, and after *It Pays to Advertise*, a farce by Walter Hackett, came the first of the 'Aldwych farces', *A Cuckoo in the Nest* (1925), in which Lynn played Peter Wykeham. After appearing in the last of the series, *A Bit of a Test* (1933), he continued his career elsewhere, making a great success in the long-running farcical comedy *Is Your Honeymoon Really Necessary?* (1944), by E. Vivian Tidmarsh, which he also directed. This ran for over two years and among the plays which followed it were two more by Ben Travers, *Outrageous Fortune* (1947) and *Wild Horses* (1952), in which Lynn again teamed up with Robertson Hare.

Lyric Players, BELFAST, an important amateur group founded in 1951 by Mrs. Mary O'Malley for the performance of poetic drama. Its first productions, mainly of short plays by Yeats and other Irish writers, were given in the O'Malleys' drawing-room, but in 1952 a small theatre was built in some disused stables, and there nearly 200 plays, covering the whole range of poetic drama from the Greeks to modern times, were performed on a stage 8 feet by 10 feet. In 1956 the theatre was enlarged to accommodate a drama school and reopened with Chekhov's *The Seagull*, and in 1968, with donations headed by a £20,000 grant from the Arts Council for Northern Ireland, a new theatre was built for the company, now run as a non-profit-making association by the Lyric Players Theatre Trust. (See also BELFAST ARTS THEATRE and ULSTER GROUP THEATRE.)

Lyric Theatre. (1) LONDON, in Shaftesbury Avenue. This opened on 17 Dec. 1888, and had its first outstanding success in Jan. 1896 when Wilson Barrett (q.v.) appeared as Marcus Superbus in his own play, *The Sign of the Cross*. Seasons of French plays were given in 1897 by Réjane and in 1898 by Bernhardt (qq.v.), and in 1902 Forbes-Robertson (q.v.) appeared in *Hamlet* and *Othello*. Successful musical comedies seen at this theatre were *Florodora* (1899), *The Duchess of Dantzig* (1903), and *The Chocolate Soldier* (1910), the last based by Oscar Straus on Shaw's *Arms and the Man*. During the First World War Sheldon's *Romance*, with Owen Nares and Doris Keane, was transferred here from the

Duke of York's Theatre, and enjoyed a long run. Later productions were *Lilac Time* (1922) with Schubert's music, Dodie Smith's *Autumn Crocus* (1931), Priestley's *Dangerous Corner* (1932), Robert Sherwood's *Reunion in Vienna* (1934), Housman's *Victoria Regina* (1936) on its first public showing, Giraudoux's *Amphitryon 38* with the Lunts (q.v.) and Charles Morgan's *The Flashing Stream* (both 1938), Margery Sharp's *The Nutmeg Tree* (1941), Rattigan's *The Winslow Boy* (1946), Roussin's *The Little Hut* (1954), the long-running musical *Irma la Douce* (1958), and Peter Shaffer's *The Battle of Shrivings* (1970) with John Gielgud (q.v.).

(2) LONDON, in Hammersmith. This opened as the Lyric Hall on 17 Nov. 1888, became a theatre in 1890, and after housing a series of melodramas was extensively rebuilt and reopened on 20 July 1895. It continued to draw a good local audience until the opening of the King's, Hammersmith, in 1902, when it gradually lost its popularity. In 1918 Nigel Playfair (q.v.) took it over and made it prosperous and fashionable with productions of Drinkwater's *Abraham Lincoln* (1919), a new version of Gay's *The Beggar's Opera* (1920) with an epoch-making décor by Lovat Fraser (q.v.), revivals of Congreve's *The Way of the World* (1924) and Farquhar's *The Beaux' Stratagem* (1927) in which Edith Evans (q.v.) made a striking success, Wilde's *The Importance of Being Earnest* (1930) in black and white, and a number of new light operas and revues, of which the most successful was *Riverside Nights* (1926) by A. P. Herbert and Thomas Dunhill. It was at this theatre that Ellen Terry (q.v.) made her last appearance on the stage, as the ghost of Miss Susan Wildersham in De la Mare's *Crossings*, on 19 Nov. 1925. Playfair left in 1933. Although a number of interesting productions have since been staged there, including Gielgud in Otway's *Venice Preserv'd* (1953) and Wolfit in Montherlant's *The Master of Santiago* and *Malatesta* (1957), the theatre never regained the position it held under Playfair. It closed finally in 1966, and has now been demolished.

(3) In NEW YORK, on 42nd Street. This opened on 12 Oct. 1903, one of its earliest successes being *The Taming of the Shrew*, with Ada Rehan and Otis Skinner (qq.v.). Oscar Straus's musical comedy *The Chocolate Soldier* opened in 1909 and enjoyed a successful run. In 1911 came the first production in the United States of Ibsen's *The Lady from the Sea*, and a year later William Faversham was seen in *Julius Caesar*. Ziegfeld filled the theatre for many years with a series of musical comedies, and the last production there in 1933, before the building became a cinema, was a Negro drama with music, Hall Jonson's *Run, Little Chillun*.

(See also CRITERION THEATRE (2) and DUBLIN.)

LYTTON, EDWARD GEORGE EARLE LYTTON BULWER-LYTTON, LORD (1803–73), English novelist and dramatist, two of whose plays, first produced by Macready (q.v.), were successful enough to be parodied and constantly revived, notably by Irving (q.v.) at the Lyceum in the 1870s. These were *The Lady of Lyons; or, Love and Pride* (1838) and *Richelieu; or, the Conspiracy* (1839). A third play, *Money* (1840), a modern comedy also first produced by Macready, was almost as successful and was last seen at a Command Performance at Drury Lane in 1911 with an all-star cast. Bulwer-Lytton's other plays, some half-dozen in all, are now forgotten.

M

MacCARTHY, Sir Desmond (1877–1952), English dramatic critic, knighted in 1951 in recognition of his services to literature and the drama. He was first on the staff of *The Speaker*, during which time he published *The Court Theatre 1904-7*, a survey of the work done there under Granville-Barker (q.v.), and in 1913 moved to the *New Statesman*. He was for some years editor of *Life and Letters*. Among his collected essays the volume entitled *Drama* (1940) amounted in its representative selection to a review of the London theatre over the previous twenty-five years.

McCARTHY, Lillah (1875–1960), English actress, first wife of Granville-Barker, with whom she appeared at the Royal Court Theatre (q.v.). She created the leading roles in several plays by Shaw (q.v.), including Ann Whitefield in *Man and Superman* (1905), Jennifer Dubedat in *The Doctor's Dilemma* (1906), Margaret Knox in *Fanny's First Play* (1911), and Lavinia in *Androcles and the Lion* (1913). She also appeared as Nora, Gloria, and Raina in revivals of *John Bull's Other Island*, *You Never Can Tell*, and *Arms and the Man*. Among her other parts were Mercia in *The Sign of the Cross*, with Wilson Barrett, Dionysus in Euripides' *Bacchae*, Iphigenia in his *Iphigenia in Tauris*, and Jocasta in Sophocles' *Oedipus Rex*, with Martin-Harvey. In 1911 she took over the management of the Little Theatre (q.v.), where she first appeared in Ibsen, playing Hilda Wangel in *The Master Builder*. She was later associated with her husband in the management of the Savoy, where she appeared as Hermione in *The Winter's Tale* and Viola in *Twelfth Night*. After divorcing Barker in 1918 she continued to act for a while, but a second marriage (to Sir Frederick Keeble) took her to Oxford, and she retired from the theatre. She was the author of two volumes of reminiscences, *My Life* (1930) and *Myself and My Friends* (1933).

McCLINTIC, Guthrie (1893–1961), American actor, producer, and director, who was for a time a member of Jessie Bonstelle's stock company in Buffalo and later became assistant stage director to Winthrop Ames at the Little Theatre, New York (q.v.). He then went into management on his own account, and from 1921, in which year he married the actress Katharine Cornell (q.v.), until his death he was active in the New York theatre. He directed many of the plays in which his wife starred, notably Michael Arlen's *The Green Hat* (1925), which first brought him into prominence, Rudolf Besier's *The Barretts of Wimpole Street* (1931), *Romeo and Juliet* (1934), and Shaw's *Candida* (1937). In 1936 he directed *Hamlet* on Broadway with John Gielgud (q.v.). He was also instrumental in presenting to New York in 1952 the company of the Greek National Theatre in a season of classical plays.

McCOLL, Ewan, see LITTLEWOOD, JOAN.

McCOWEN, Alec [really Alexander] Duncan (1925–), English actor, who in 1968 made an international reputation with his performance in the title-role of Peter Luke's *Hadrian VII*, which he played in London and later in New York. A sensitive and versatile actor, he gained his experience in repertory, and first appeared in London in 1950, coming into prominence with his Daventry in Roger Macdougall's *Escapade* (1953). In 1958 he gave an excellent performance as Claverton-Ferry in T. S. Eliot's *The Elder Statesman*, and from 1959 to 1961 was with the Old Vic, where he showed his versatility by playing Richard II, Touchstone in *As You Like It*, and Malvolio in *Twelfth Night*. He was also seen as the Fool in *King Lear* at Stratford-upon-Avon in 1962. He returned to modern drama with his Father Riccardo Fontana in Hochhuth's *The Representative* (1963), the Author in Anouilh's *The Cavern* (1965), and Arthur Henderson in John Bowen's *After the Rain* (1967). He followed his Hadrian VII with an outstanding performance as Hamlet at the Birmingham Repertory Theatre in 1969 and a year later was seen again in London at the Royal Court in Christopher Hampton's *The Philanthropist*.

MACDERMOTT, Norman Alexander (1890–1977), English theatre director, who, after some experience in the provinces, took over the Everyman Theatre (q.v.), which he ran from 1920 to 1926, opening on 15 Sept. with *The Bonds of Interest*, a translation of *Los intereses creados* by Benavente (q.v.). Several of his later productions were transferred to the West End, including Munro's *At Mrs. Beam's* and Sutton Vane's *Outward Bound* (both 1923) and Chiarelli's *The Mask and the Face* and Coward's *The Vortex* (both 1924). Macdermott also revived eight of Shaw's plays. After leaving the Everyman, he continued to direct plays in London until 1936, his last important venture being O'Casey's *Within the Gates* at the Royalty in 1934.

McEWAN [really McKEOWN], GERALD-INE (1932–), English actress, who gained her experience with the repertory company at Windsor, where she was born and educated. From 1951 to 1956 she appeared in and around London in a number of light comedies, and in 1957 was seen at the Royal Court as Frankie in Carson McCullers's *The Member of the Wedding*. A year later she was seen at Stratford-upon-Avon as Olivia in *Twelfth Night*, Marina in *Pericles*, and Hero in *Much Ado About Nothing*, and went with the company on tour to Russia, a country she visited again in 1965, after joining the National Theatre company to play A Lady in Arden's *Armstrong's Last Goodnight* and Angelica in Congreve's *Love for Love*. She remained at the Old Vic for some years, appearing in Feydeau's *A Flea in Her Ear* (1966), Strindberg's *Dance of Death* (1967), Maugham's *Home and Beauty* (1968), Congreve's *The Way of the World* and Webster's *The White Devil* (both 1969). To all her parts she brings a lucid intelligence, clear speech, and the impact of an unusual personality.

MACGOWAN, KENNETH (1888–1963), American theatre director, who was for some years a dramatic critic and also worked for *Theatre Arts* (q.v.) from 1919 to 1925. From 1923 to 1926 he was associated with the Provincetown Playhouse and the Greenwich Village Theatre, producing new and unusual plays, among them a number by O'Neill (q.v.). In 1927 he briefly directed the Actors' Theatre, and later produced plays on Broadway. He was the author of several books on the theatre, including *The Theatre of To-morrow* (1922) and *Footlights across*

America (1929). He also collaborated with Robert Edmond Jones in *Continental Stagecraft* (1922) and with William Melnitz in *The Living Theatre* (1955).

MACKAY, CHARLES (c.1785–1857), Scottish actor, who first attracted attention in 1819 when he played Bailie Nicol Jarvie in Pocock's version of Scott's *Rob Roy* at the Theatre Royal, Edinburgh. His performance created a sensation and he was hailed as a star. Thenceforth he specialized, and had his greatest successes, in Scots character parts, many of them in further adaptations of Scott's novels.

MACKAYE, (JAMES MORRISON) STEELE (1842–94), American theatre designer, innovator and pioneer, who, after studying in Paris and London and gaining some experience on the professional stage, took over the old Fifth Avenue Theatre in New York and adapted it for use as a repertory theatre on Continental lines (SEE MADISON SQUARE THEATRE). Although the venture failed, it was at this theatre in 1880 that Mackaye's own play, *Hazel Kirke*, was produced for a long run. It was several times revived and in 1886 was seen in London. After leaving the Madison Square Theatre, Mackaye built his own theatre (see LYCEUM THEATRE (2)), where he established the first school of acting in New York. A dynamic personality, he had a great influence on the American theatre of his time though, being unbusinesslike, he failed to profit from his achievements. Shortly before his death from overwork and worry he had planned a vast playhouse for the Chicago World's Fair, incorporating all the most modern Continental stage equipment. Though it was never built, later architects were indebted to its plans for the introduction of new ideas and methods. Mackaye's life-story is told in *Epoch* (1927) by his son, PERCY WALLACE (1875–1956), actor and playwright, much of whose work was connected with modern masques and spectacles. He was also the author of several books on the theatre and operatic libretti.

MACKINLAY, JEAN STERLING (1882–1958), see WILLIAMS, HARCOURT.

MACKLIN [really M'LAUGHLIN], CHARLES (c. 1700–97), Irish actor, best remembered for having rescued Shylock in *The Merchant of Venice* from the clutches of the low comedian, to whom the part had been assigned since Restoration days, and making him a dignified and tragic figure. Macklin had been on the stage, mainly in the provinces, since 1716 when in 1732 he was engaged for Drury Lane. There he played secondary and comic parts such as Touchstone in *As You Like It*, Scrub in Farquhar's *The Beaux' Stratagem*, and Peachum in Gay's *The Beggar's Opera*, until he persuaded Fleetwood, then manager of Drury Lane, to revive *The Merchant of Venice*, in which he appeared on 14 Feb. 1741 and became famous overnight. He might then have risen to even greater heights, but with advancing years he became extremely quarrelsome, constantly engaging in litigation and causing trouble backstage by his jealousy of other actors. Apart from Shylock, and his Iago to the Othello of Garrick and Spranger Barry (qq.v.), his most memorable part was Macbeth, which he first played at Covent Garden on 23 Oct. 1773 in something approximating to the dress of a Highland chieftain in place of the red military coat favoured by Garrick. Macklin was also the author of a number of plays, of which two survived well into the nineteenth century—*Love à la Mode* (1759), in which he himself played the leading role, Sir Archy McSarcasm, and *The Man of the World* (1781), in which, in spite of his great age, he again played the lead, Sir Pertinax McSycophant. He made his last appearance on the stage on 7 May 1789, when he essayed Shylock but was unable to finish it.

MacLEISH, ARCHIBALD (1892–1982), American poet and dramatist, who continued the attempts made by Maxwell Anderson (q.v.) to write plays in poetry adapted to the rhythms of everyday American speech. He has had a distinguished career as a poet and lecturer on poetry, but is best known in the theatre for his play *J.B.*, a retelling of the story of Job in modern terms which was first presented at the Yale School of Drama. It was seen on Broadway in 1958 and in London three years later, since when it has been performed in many European countries. Though not wholly successful in portraying living people in terms of a cosmic myth, it nevertheless has moments of authentic tragedy; it was awarded the Pulitzer Prize for drama (MacLeish has twice been awarded the Pulitzer Prize for poetry). An earlier play, *Panic*, was seen on Broadway in 1935.

MacLIAMMÓIR, MICHEÁL (1899–1978), Irish actor, director, designer, and a playwright in both Gaelic and English. As Alfred Willmore, he was on the London stage as a child, and then studied art, travelled widely in Europe, and finally returned to Dublin. In 1928, with Hilton Edwards (q.v.), he founded the Dublin Gate Theatre (see DUBLIN), and from 1928 to 1931 directed the Galway Theatre (see GAELIC DRAMA), where he was responsible for the production of a number of new Irish plays and foreign classics in Irish, making translations of Chekhov, Shaw, and other dramatists himself. Among his own plays, the best-known are *Diarmuid and Grainne* (1928), *Ill Met by Moonlight* and *Where Stars Walk* (both 1947), and *Home for Christmas* (1950). He was the author of two volumes of reminiscences, *All for Hecuba* (1946) and *Put Money in Thy Purse* (1954), and of a theatre diary, *Each Actor on His Ass* (1962). He appeared in Dublin and London, and on tour in three one-man virtuoso performances, *The Importance of Being Oscar* (1960), based on the works of Oscar Wilde, *I Must be Talking to My Friends* (1963), and *Talking About Yeats* (1965). In 1969 a new play by MacLiammóir, *The Liar*, was seen at the Dublin Festival.

McMASTER, ANEW (1894–1962), Irish actor, founder in 1925 of a company which presented Shakespeare's plays on tour in the English provinces. He directed and acted in the productions himself, being outstanding as Shylock in *The Merchant of Venice*, Richard III, Coriolanus, Lear, and Othello. In 1933 he also played Hamlet at Stratford-upon-Avon, and later took his company to the Near East. After the Second World War he was active in Ireland, and at the time of his death was preparing to play Othello at the Dublin Festival to the Iago of MacLiammóir (q.v.). In 1968 Harold Pinter (q.v.), who toured in Ireland with McMaster in the early 1950s, published an appreciation of his life and work entitled *Mac*.

MACNAMARA, BRINSLEY [really JOHN WELDON] (1890–1963), Irish actor and dramatist, a member of the company at the Abbey Theatre (q.v.), where his first play, *The Rebellion at Ballycullen*, was staged in 1917. A series of successful plays followed, including *The Master* (1928) and *Margaret Gillan* (1933). He became a director of the Abbey, but resigned after a disagreement over Sean O'Casey's *The Silver Tassie* (written in 1928, but finally produced by the theatre against his wishes in 1935). He was for a time dramatic critic of the *Irish Times* and compiled a useful index of plays staged at the Abbey.

MACOWAN, MICHAEL (1906–80), English actor and producer, son of the actor-dramatist NORMAN MACOWAN (1877–1961) and from 1954 to 1966 head of the London Academy of Music and Dramatic Art (Lamda), for which he built in 1963 an excellent adaptable and experimental theatre. Having made his first appearance as an actor in 1925, he was on the stage until 1931 and then devoted himself entirely to production in London, particularly at the Old Vic (q.v.), where he was associated with the short-lived Old Vic Theatre School, and in Stratford-upon-Avon.

MACQUEEN-POPE, WALTER JAMES (1888–1960), English actor, manager, and theatre historian, who traced his ancestry back to the eighteenth-century actress Jane Pope (q.v.) of Drury Lane, and even further back, to Thomas Pope (q.v.) of the Globe, friend and associate of Shakespeare, and Morgan Pope of the Bear Garden. Though these claims were never fully substantiated, they gave him much pleasure and were seldom challenged. Certainly he merited a distinguished theatrical pedigree, for his devotion to the London theatre (he ignored all others) was wholehearted and he spent his life in its service. He was at some time in his career business or front-of-house manager of almost every theatre in London, and for twenty-one years was in charge of publicity at Drury Lane. After the Second World War he became well known as a lecturer and broadcaster on theatrical topics and as the author of several volumes of theatrical reminiscences. A stimulating companion, 'Popie', as he was called, excelled in communicating the glamour and excitement of Edwardian theatre-going, and his occasional inaccuracies were forgiven for the sake of the brilliant light he threw on personalities and events in the theatre of his lifetime. After his death a plaque to his memory was unveiled by Sir Donald Wolfit (q.v.) in St. Paul's Church, Covent Garden.

MACRAE, DUNCAN (1905–67), Scottish actor, associated mainly with the Edinburgh Festival (see EDINBURGH) and the Glasgow Citizens' Theatre (q.v.). For the first he played, among other parts, Flatterie in Lyndsay's *Ane Pleasant Satyre of the Thrie Estaitis* in 1948, and for the latter Mr. Oliphant in *Let Wives Tak Tent* (1949), a free adaptation by Robert Kemp of Molière's *L'École des femmes*. Although Macrae was better known in Scotland than in England, he appeared several times in London, notably in 1956 as Mr. McCrimmon in a revival of Bridie's *Mr. Bolfry*, in 1960 as John in Ionesco's *Rhinoceros*, and in 1966 in a double bill at the Mermaid made up of shortened versions of Molière's *The Miser* and *The Imaginary Invalid*. After his death an appeal was made for funds to establish as his memorial a touring company to visit Scottish towns, schools, and factories, catering especially for youth.

MACREADY, WILLIAM CHARLES (1793–1873), English actor, son of a provincial actor-manager, a fine tragedian and the only rival in his day of Edmund Kean (q.v.). He made his first appearance on the stage in 1810, and by 1819 was in demand at both Covent Garden and Drury Lane, where his Lear, Hamlet, and Macbeth were universally acclaimed. He also appeared in a number of new plays, with Helen Faucit (q.v.) as his leading lady, among them Browning's *Strafford* (1837), Bulwer-Lytton's *The Lady of Lyons* (1838) and *Richelieu* (1839), and Byron's *The Two Foscari* (1838). He was at various times manager of both patent theatres, where he introduced a number of reforms, insisting on full rehearsals, particularly of supers and crowd-scenes, and rescuing some of Shakespeare's texts from their Restoration trappings. Unfortunately his dislike of the theatre, which he had only entered because of his father's financial embarrassments, and his ungovernable temper made him many enemies, and his rivalry with the American actor, Edwin Forrest (q.v.), led to the Astor Place riot in New York in 1849, in which 22 people were killed. After this Macready was not seen again in New York, where he had first appeared in 1826, and in 1851 he retired, after playing Macbeth at Drury Lane on 26 Feb. His diary, which gives a lively picture of contemporary life as well as of the man himself, was published in 1875. A biography by the English critic J. C. Trewin was published in 1955, and another, entitled *The

Eminent Tragedian, by the American scholar Alan Downer in 1967.

MacSWINEY, OWEN, see SWINEY.

MACHIAVELLI, NICCOLÒ DI BERNARDO DEI (1469–1527), Florentine statesman and political philosopher, whose most famous work is *Il Principe* (1513). He also wrote some comedies, of which the best-known and the only one to survive on the modern stage is *La Mandragola* (1520), a pungent criticism of Florentine society which portrays the betrayal of the heroine by her credulous husband, her ardent but unscrupulous lover, and her scheming mother, aided by the corrupt priest Fra Timoteo. In a translation by Ashley Dukes it was successfuly produced at the Mercury Theatre in London during 1940. It was also published in New York in 1927 in a translation by Stark Young. In 1965, in a modernized Italian version by Carlo Terron, it was successfully revived in Milan by Peppino de Filippo (q.v.), who played Fra Timoteo.

Machine Play, the name given to a particular type of seventeenth-century French spectacle which made excessive use of the mechanical contrivances and scene-changes developed in connection with the evolution of opera, particularly by Torelli (q.v.). The first was Corneille's *Andromède* (1650), and the genre reached its peak with Molière's *Amphitryon* (1668) and *Psyché* (1671).

Machinery in the modern theatre is mainly confined to the changing of scenery (SEE BOAT TRUCKS, SCENERY) or the manipulation of light (see LIGHTING). In earlier times it played a much larger part in the production of theatrical illusions, and some of its most interesting devices are still used today in ballet, opera, and pantomime. The first machines of which we have any knowledge—and that very scanty—are the crane (*mechane*) used by early Greek dramatists to lower the god who was to unravel the complications of the plot (the *deus ex machina*, q.v.) from the top of the stage-building to the stage, and the *ekkyklema* (q.v.), a platform or couch on which a prearranged group could be shown, either by wheeling it on or by opening double doors to display it. To these devices the Hellenistic and Roman theatres added the *periaktoi* (q.v.) for scene changes and possibly the *bronteion*

or thunder sheet (see NOISES OFF). Medieval liturgical drama (q.v.) made extensive use of machinery, particularly for supernatural appearances. The early machines were simple, but by the fifteenth century had become extremely elaborate (see PARADISO). The Renaissance not only brought back an improved version of the *periaktoi* but also provided opportunities for spectacular effects connected with storms, floods, sea fights, waterfalls, avalanches, the appearance and disappearance of houses, temples, gardens, and woods, the natural phenomena of rain, snow, wind, thunder, and lightning, and the creation and manipulation of legendary beasts and exotic monsters. The development of machinery, which owed much to the popularity of opera, reached its highest point in the work of the seventeenth-century Giacomo Torelli (q.v.), many of whose inventions remained in use in the European theatre for over two hundred years. Much of his work was destroyed by his contemporary and rival Vigarani (q.v.), but the tradition of elaborate machines continued into the eighteenth century with Servandony (q.v.). Starting in Italy, the craze for machinery, and therefore spectacle, spread to Spain and France and eventually to England, where the pantomime players became famous for their use of mechanical devices. The last refuge of mechanical devices, most of which were killed by the advent of the box-set (q.v.) and by the popularity of realistic drama, followed by the adoption of the open stage and theatre-in-the-round, was melodrama (q.v.), which demanded a constant supply of snowstorms, thunderstorms, and supernatural appearances (see TRAPS).

MADÁCH, IMRE (1823–64), Hungarian dramatist, whose best play, twice translated into English as *The Tragedy of Man*, was *Az ember tragédiája* (pub. 1862). Conceived on a vast scale, somewhat on the lines of Goethe's *Faust*, this deals with the struggle between the Devil and Adam for the possession of man's soul. It was first produced at the Hungarian National Theatre in 1883 by the theatre manager Ede Paulay, and has since won international recognition.

Maddermarket, NORWICH, a theatre intended to reproduce Elizabethan stage conditions, which seats about three hundred people. It was built inside a dilapidated hall in 1921 by Nugent Monck (q.v.) to house the Norwich Players, an amateur group which he had founded in 1911. He directed and played with the company from 1921 to 1952. The theatre was altered and enlarged in 1953 and again in 1966. It is now directed by Ian Emmerson. The company, still amateur, presents a play each month for nine performances; it has produced all the thirty-seven plays associated with Shakespeare as well as foreign plays, Greek tragedies, and the works of Shaw and other modern writers.

MADDERN, MINNIE, see FISKE, M. M.

MADDOX, MICHAEL, see MEDDOKS.

Madison Square Theatre, NEW YORK, originally the Fifth Avenue Hall, built on the site of Daly's first Fifth Avenue Theatre (q.v.). This was adapted by Steele Mackaye (q.v.) for use as a repertory theatre on Continental lines, with a company made up of students whom he had trained himself. It opened on 23 Apr. 1879, but soon failed and was taken over by Daniel Frohman (q.v.), who reopened it on 4 Feb. 1880 with Mackaye's *Hazel Kirke*, a domestic drama which ran for nearly two years. In 1882 Bronson Howard's *Young Mrs. Winthrop*, one of the first good American plays, was seen at this theatre, and in 1889–90 Richard Mansfield appeared in a series of revivals and new plays, including the first straightforward translation of *A Doll's House* which, with Beatrice Cameron (q.v.) as Nora, first brought Ibsen to the attention of the general public. In 1891 the theatre was taken over by Hoyt, who later gave it his name on 1 Feb. 1905, and finally closed in March 1908.

Madrid. The first theatres in Madrid were courtyards used by travelling companies, like the ones used by early English actors, and they developed in very much the same way (see THEATRE BUILDINGS) under the aegis of two charitable brotherhoods, the Cofradía de la Pasión and the Cofradía de la Soledad, which, like the Confraternité de la Passion (q.v.) in Paris, held the monopoly of acting in the city. They were responsible for the erection of the first permanent theatre in the Corral de la Cruz in 1579, and of a second one in the Corral del Príncipe in 1582. These retained their pre-eminence until the 1640s, when a Court Theatre was built in

the palace of Buen Retiro, later opened to the public also. This, however, did not infringe the monopoly still held by the brotherhoods. It was not seriously challenged until early in the eighteenth century, when a company of Italian actors established themselves in a temporary building near the Caños del Peral. In 1719 an opera house was built on the site, replaced in 1818 by the Teatro Real. Built over a natural spring, this latter was always in trouble and was abandoned some time before the announcement in 1963 of its impending demolition. The middle years of the eighteenth century saw also the rebuilding of the two original theatres, the one in the Corral de la Cruz being renamed the Coliseo. In 1806 the Príncipe was replaced by the Teatro Espagnol, and soon after Madrid boasted more than a dozen theatres, including one devoted to the *zarzuela* (q.v.). The Eslava, which dates from this period, came into prominence in the twentieth century under the management of Martínez Sierra (q.v.), who between 1917 and 1925 introduced to the Madrid public the technical innovations of contemporary European stagecraft. In the 1930s, up to the outbreak of the civil war, two itinerant companies based on Madrid, García Lorca's La Barraca and Alejandro Casona's El Teatro del Pueblo, took drama to the people. But in spite of the continued efforts of these and of many Little Theatres (*teatros de camara*), the ravages of war virtually destroyed the indigenous Spanish theatre, and only recently has work of any world-wide significance again emerged.

MAETERLINCK, MAURICE (1862–1949), Belgian symbolist poet and dramatist, awarded the Nobel Prize for Literature in 1911. His best-known work is *Pelléas et Mélisande*, first produced in Paris in 1893 by Lugné-Poë. With incidental music by Fauré, it was seen in an English translation in London in 1898 and in New York in 1902. Mrs. Patrick Campbell (q.v.), who played Mélisande in both versions, also played the part in French in London in 1904 to the Pelléas of Sarah Bernhardt (q.v.). Several of Maeterlinck's other plays, notably *Monna Vanna* (1902), *L'Oiseau bleu* (1909) as *The Blue Bird* and its sequel *Les Fiançailles* (1917) as *The Betrothal*, were seen in English soon after their first productions. *Le Bourgmestre de Stilmonde*, considered by some critics Maeterlinck's best play, was first produced in 1919 and seen in London the same year with Martin-Harvey (q.v.) in the title-role. As *A Burgomaster of Belgium*, it was seen later in the year, less successfully, in New York, where the Washington Square Players had already produced *The Temptation of Saint Anthony* and *Interior* in 1915. In 1922 Eva Le Gallienne appeared in *Aglavaine and Selysette* (1896), playing Aglavaine, the part originally written for the actress and singer GEORGETTE LEBLANC (1876–1941), who played most of Maeterlinck's heroines from 1896 to 1910. Two of Maeterlinck's plays were used as opera libretti—*Pelléas et Mélisande* by Debussy in 1902 and *Ariane et Barbe-Bleu* (1901) by Dukas in 1907, with Georgette Leblanc, who had also appeared in the play, as Ariane.

MAFFEI, (FRANCESCO) SCIPIONE (1675–1755), Italian dramatist, author of a number of tragedies of which *Merope* (1713) was the most successful. It was seen at the Comédie-Italienne in Paris in 1713, and was published a year later, being much admired by Voltaire (q.v.), who dedicated to Maffei his own *Mérope* (1743). An English translation by William Ayre was published in 1740, though not, apparently, ever acted.

MAINTENON, MADAME DE [*née* FRANÇOISE D'AUBIGNÉ] (1635–1719), the second wife of Louis XIV, whom she married secretly in about 1684 after the death of the Queen, Marie-Thérèse. Her first husband was the novelist and dramatist Scarron (q.v.). It was for Mme de Maintenon's academy for impoverished young ladies at Saint-Cyr that Racine (q.v.), after twelve years' abstention from the theatre, wrote the poetic dramas *Esther* (1689) and *Athalie* (1691). The Italian actors in Paris (see COMÉDIE-ITALIENNE) were banished in 1697 by Louis XIV for having put on *La Fausse Prude*, by Etienne Lenoble, which offended her.

MAIRET, JEAN (1604–86), one of the most important of early French dramatists, whose *Sophonisbe* (1634), the first French tragedy to be written in accordance with the unities (q.v.), was a complete contrast to the tragicomedies and pastorals which had preceded it, and a forerunner of French classical tragedy. Unfortunately Mairet attacked Pierre Corneille (q.v.) in the quarrel over *Le Cid*, and the opprobrium this has brought him from later generations has tended to obscure his importance as a dramatist. In his own day he was as successful as Corneille himself, and even more highly thought of. He was attached as dramatist to the troupe of Montdory (q.v.) at the Marais for some years, but in 1640 gave up writing for the stage and entered the diplomatic service.

Maison de Molière, see COMÉDIE-FRANÇAISE.

Majestic Theatre, NEW YORK. (1) This theatre, on Columbus Circle, opened on 21 Jan. 1903 with a musical version of the famous children's book, *The Wizard of Oz*. This had a long run and was followed by the equally successful *Babes in Toyland*. In 1911 the theatre was renamed the Park, reopening on 23 Oct. with *The Quaker Girl*. Three years later Mrs. Patrick Campbell (q.v.) appeared there in Shaw's *Pygmalion*, and a notable revival of *The Merry Wives of Windsor* was given in 1917 with Constance Collier and Herbert Tree (qq.v.) as Mistress Ford and Falstaff. In 1923 the building became a cinema, but reverted to plays, as the Columbus Circle Theatre, with a production in 1945 of Maurice Evans's *G.I. Hamlet*. It was demolished in June 1954.

(2) A second Majestic, on 44th Street between Broadway and 8th Avenue, opened on 28 Mar. 1927. John Gielgud (q.v.) made his first appearance in New York here in 1928 in a minor part in *The Patriot* by Alfred Neumann (later seen in England in an adaptation by Ashley Dukes as *Such Men are Dangerous*), but it had only eight performances. After several more failures, the theatre reverted to musical comedy, for which it was eminently suitable, and in 1945 the Theatre Guild presented a musical version of Molnár's *Liliom*, as *Carousel*, which had a long run. Other musicals which have been successful here include *South Pacific* (1949), by Rogers and Hammerstein, and *The Music Man* (1957), by Meredith Wilson. In 1963 Gielgud's production of Sheridan's *The School for Scandal*, in which he played Joseph Surface, met with acclaim, and a year later came the long-running musical, *Fiddler on the Roof*.

(For the Majestic Theatre in Sydney, Australia, see ELIZABETHAN THEATRE TRUST.)

Make-up. The use of make-up in the theatre dates from earliest times, and was used by all actors not wearing masks. Its main purpose in the beginning was to disguise, to alter the actor's face so as to make him appear older, or more ferocious, or less human, or more godlike, the two extremes of the use of make-up in this way being the gilding of God's face in liturgical drama (q.v.) and the elaborate painting of the Japanese actors' faces in the *kabuki* plays (q.v.). The use of everyday cosmetics to enhance personal beauty was probably brought into the theatre by actresses, who sometimes applied them with a too-lavish hand, particularly after the introduction of gas-lighting at the beginning of the nineteenth century. The use of make-up in the European theatre in the sixteenth century is attested by a passage in Leone di Somi's *Dialogues on Stage Affairs* (1565). He was writing of actors in a torch- or candle-lit theatre, but even in the open-air Elizabethan theatre there is evidence of some form of character make-up—black for Negroes, umber for sunburnt peasants, red noses for drunkards, chalk-white for ghosts. In the Restoration theatre the grotesque make-up of such a character as Lady Wishfort in Congreve's *The Way of the World* (1700) was probably nothing more than a caricature of that of the contemporary lady of fashion. According to Riccoboni in his *Historical Account of the Theatres in Europe* (1738), the English actor James Spiller added forty years to his appearance by the drawing of lines on his face and the painting of his eyebrows and eyelids. But the general standard of make-up in London theatres appears to have been somewhat low, and one of the excellencies attributed to Garrick (q.v.) was his skill in making up his face to suit the age and character of his part, particularly when he played old men. Before the introduction of modern grease-paints, all make-up, whether compounded with a greasy substance or with some liquid medium, was basically a powder make-up, which was often harmful to the skin and sometimes extremely dangerous, particularly if white lead was used in its composition. Powder make-up also had the disadvantages of drying up and so hindering the mobility of the actor's features, or of melting and streaking in the heat. From the first comprehensive account of make-up in the English theatre, in Leman Thomas Rede's *The Road to the Stage* (1827), it is evident that the introduction of gas-lighting had recently led to changes in the art of making-up, and although the

paints used were still powder-based, some form of grease—usually pomatum, though butter and lard are also mentioned—was used as a foundation. Also, grease or oil was used to remove the paint after the performance. Not everyone, however, approved of the use of greasy substances. T. H. Lacy, in *The Art of Acting* (1863), says make-up should be put only on a dry non-greasy surface, a practice also recommended in the anonymous *How to 'Make-Up'* . . . by 'Haresfoot and Rouge' (1877), though the use of cold cream after the performance seems to have been generally adopted by about 1866. A revolution in make-up was achieved in the second half of the nineteenth century by the introduction of grease-paint, invented in about 1865 by LUDWIG LEICHNER (1836–?), a Wagnerian opera-singer. He opened his first factory in 1873, and his round sticks, numbered and labelled from 1, light flesh colour, to 8, a reddish brown for Indians (later increased to 20, and by 1938 to 54), were soon to be found in practically every actor's dressing-room. The first sticks were imported into London between 1877 and 1881, and a London branch of L. Leichner Ltd. opened in 1928. As well as the thick sticks of grease-paint which the actor was instructed to use over a slight coating of cocoa butter, which was also used to clean the face afterwards, there were thin sticks, or liners, in black, brown, blue, and white, used for painting in fine lines. The use of grease-paint seems to have been pretty general by 1890, and even those actors who still used powder mixed it with a harmless cold cream in place of the pearl powder (subchloride of bismuth) or hydrated oxide of bismuth which were apt to turn grey or black when exposed to fog or the fumes given off by coal fires. The introduction of electric light again caused fundamental changes in theatrical make-up, which has also more recently been influenced by the techniques of film and television make-up. Grease-paint is available now in tubes and tins as well as sticks, and has in some cases been superseded by liquid make-up applied with a sponge, or by a 'water-moist' make-up, greaseless and packed in tubes or, in the case of Max Factor's 'Pancake' make-up, in cake form, packed in plastic containers. In the modern theatre, where the make-up that embellishes and the make-up that disguises are of equal importance, the art of making-up has reached a high standard, and covers more than the simple painting and lining of the face. To age an actor or actress from twenty to sixty in one evening is now a commonplace, though in many cases such a transformation is achieved not by the player but by a make-up expert. This is perhaps truer of films and television than of the theatre, where the individual actor usually still attends to his own make-up, inventing and discarding his own methods within the limits of the materials available.

MALINA, JUDITH (1926–), see LIVING THEATRE.

MALLESON, (WILLIAM) MILES (1888–1969), English actor, who in his later years excelled in the portrayal of testy and eccentric old gentlemen. Some of his best work was done in his own very free adaptations of Molière (q.v.), which began in 1950 with *The Miser* (*L'Avare*) and included *Tartuffe, Sganarelle, The Slave of Truth* (*Le Misanthrope*), *The Imaginary Invalid* (*Le Malade imaginaire*), and *The Prodigious Snob* (*Le Bourgeois gentilhomme*). These had the merit of bringing Molière on to the English stage in versions which appealed to the average playgoer, and proved invaluable to repertory and provincial theatres, where they are frequently revived. Malleson, who made his first appearance at the Liverpool Repertory Theatre in 1911, was known in his earlier years as an excellent actor in Shakespeare—Sir Andrew Aguecheek in *Twelfth Night*, Peter Quince in *A Midsummer Night's Dream*, Launcelot Gobbo in *The Merchant of Venice*—and in Restoration comedy—Scrub in Farquhar's *The Beaux' Stratagem*, Wittol in Congreve's *The Old Bachelor*. He also played Filch in a long run of Gay's *The Beggar's Opera*, and later made a success as Foresight in Congreve's *Love for Love* and Sir Fretful Plagiary in Sheridan's *The Critic*. In more serious vein he was excellent as Old Ekdal in Ibsen's *The Wild Duck*, and made one of his few appearances in a modern play as Mr. Butterfly in Ionesco's *Rhinoceros* (1960). He was the author of a number of plays, of which the best was probably *The Fanatics* (1927).

MALONE, EDMOND (1741–1812), English man of letters, and one of the first scholars to study and annotate the works of Shakespeare. He was also the first to perceive and denounce the Shakespeare forgeries of young Ireland (q.v.). In spite of the many new facts which have been brought to light by later research, and an entirely new orientation in the study of Shakespeare as a dramatist, Malone's works, which include a biography, a chronology of the plays, and a history of the Elizabethan stage, are still valuable. The Malone Society, formed in 1907 to further the study of early English drama by reprinting texts and documents, was named after him in recognition of his eminence in the world of theatrical scholarship.

Malvern Festival. This was founded in 1929 by Barry Jackson (q.v.), whose long association with Bernard Shaw (q.v.) led him to devote the first year's programme entirely to his plays, with the first English production of *The Apple Cart* and revivals of *Back to Methuselah, Caesar and Cleopatra,* and *Heartbreak House.* Shaw became the patron-in-chief of the festival, and more than twenty of his plays were produced there, *Geneva* and *In Good King Charles's Golden Days* having their first productions in 1938 and 1939 respectively, while *Too True to be Good* (1932), *The Simpleton of the Unexpected Isles* (1935), and *Buoyant Billions* (1949) had their first English productions. Apart from Shaw, the festival ranged over four centuries of English drama, from the religious *Hickscorner* (c. 1513) and the early comedies *Ralph Roister Doister* and *Gammer Gurton's Needle,* through Heywood, Ben Jonson, Etherege, Dryden, Sheridan, Bulwer-Lytton, Henry Arthur Jones, and Pinero, to new plays by Drinkwater, Bridie, Priestley, and others. At the end of the 1937 season Sir Barry withdrew and the festival was then run by Roy Limbert, manager of the Malvern Theatre. During the Second World War Limbert maintained a skeleton organization at Malvern, but attempts to revive the festival since have met with little success.

Maly Theatre, MOSCOW. This theatre, whose name means 'small' (as opposed to *bolshoi*—big), opened on 14 Oct. 1824 with a company which had been in existence since 1806. It is the oldest theatre in the city, and the only one to keep its old-fashioned drop-curtain. With its unbroken history it has played an important part in the development of Russian drama, particularly in the 1840s, when Shchepkin (q.v.) was appearing in such plays as Gogol's *The Government Inspector* and

Griboyedov's *Woe from Wit*, and Mochalov (q.v.) in translations of Shakespeare's tragedies made directly from the original and not, as hitherto, from the French. In 1854 the Maly first produced a play by Ostrovsky (q.v.), and so began a brilliant partnership which lasted until 1885. Nowhere else, even now, can such fine productions of Ostrovsky be seen, and for many years the theatre was known as the House of Ostrovsky. The actor who first played many of the leading roles, and so helped to promote appreciation of the writer's genius, was Prov Sadovsky (q.v.), whose son and grandson continued the connection with the theatre. Other great names connected with the Maly are Alexander Lensky and Maria Yermolova (qq.v.). Having survived the Russian revolution, the theatre took its rightful place in the theatrical life of Soviet Russia with the production of Trenev's *Lyubov Yarovaya* in 1926. It has since given the first performances of many new Soviet plays, but has not neglected the classics, one of the outstanding postwar productions having been *Othello* with the veteran actor ALEXANDER OSTUSHEV (1874–1953) in the title-role. From 1950 to 1970 the theatre was directed by MIKHAIL IVANOVICH TSARYOV (1903–), who joined the company as an actor in 1937. He was succeeded by Boris Ravenskykh.

MAMOULIAN, ROUBEN (1898–1987), American theatre director, born in Georgia, U.S.S.R., who worked at the Vakhtangov (q.v.) in Moscow before going to New York, where between 1923 and 1927 he directed a number of operettas and musicals. He then directed, for the Theatre Guild (q.v.), a production of DuBose and Dorothy Heyward's Negro play *Porgy* (1927), which was seen in London in 1929, and also directed Gershwin's opera, 'Porgy and Bess' (1935), based on the play. Among his other productions for the Guild were O'Neill's *Marco Millions* (1928) and his own adaptation of Turgenev's *A Month in the Country* (1930), and for other managements he directed *Wings Over Europe* (1928), by Maurice Browne and Robert Nichols, and *R.U.R.* (1930), by Karel Čapek. It was, however, his connection with two famous musicals that made him best known everywhere. In 1943 he directed *Oklahoma!* in New York, and was then responsible for its production in

London in 1947, in Berlin in 1951, and in Paris and several Italian towns in 1955. *Carousel* he directed in New York in 1945, in London in 1950, and in California in 1954. He also had a distinguished career as a film director, introducing colour to the screen with his *Becky Sharp* (1936), based on Thackeray's *Vanity Fair*.

Manager, see PRODUCER.

Manchester. This town, which is important in English theatre history for the establishment there of the first modern repertory company (see HORNIMAN), had its first theatre in Marsden Street. An all-purpose building, it was used for plays only between 1758 and 1775. It was demolished in 1869. A company under the well-known provincial manager JAMES AUGUSTUS WHITLEY (c. 1724–81) visited it regularly from 1760 until it closed, taking in Manchester on the way from Leeds to Worcester. The first Theatre Royal, at the junction of York Street and Spring Gardens, not far from Marsden Street, opened in Oct. 1775 under Joseph Younger and George Mattocks (see MATTOCKS, MRS.). It was burned down in 1789. Rebuilt, it reopened in 1790, but it soon proved too small, and in 1807 it closed, being replaced by a vast structure in Fountain Street which ruined its first manager, father of the great tragic actor Macready (q.v.).

It was in 1907 that Miss Horniman, who had already established a repertory theatre in Dublin—the Abbey (q.v.)—took over the old Gaiety in Manchester, now a cinema, and there established the first repertory theatre in England (see REPERTORY THEATRE), with which was connected the so-called 'Manchester School of Drama', comprising the realistic playwrights Harold Brighouse, Allan Monkhouse, and Stanley Houghton. The theatre opened on 7 Sept. 1908, and fifty years later a commemorative festival was held, marked by a revival of Houghton's *Hindle Wakes* by the Library Theatre, a repertory company which was founded by the local authority in 1953 and is housed in a corporation-owned theatre. Manchester also has two large commercial theatres used by touring companies—the Opera House and the Palace.

Manet, 'he remains', see STAGE DIRECTIONS.

Manhattan Theatre, NEW YORK, on the west side of Broadway between 53rd and 54th Streets. As Hammerstein's, this opened on 30 Nov. 1927 and was used almost entirely for musical shows. In 1931 it was given its present name, but adhered to its musical policy until in 1934, after a long period of idleness, it became a music-hall. This was not successful, and the theatre then remained empty until in 1936 the Federal Theatre Project (q.v.) took it over, opening on 21 Feb. with *American Holiday* by E. L. and A. Barker. On 20 March there was a limited run of T. S. Eliot's *Murder in the Cathedral*, and in September of the same year the theatre was taken over for broadcasting.

(See also STANDARD THEATRE (2).)

MANNERS, JOHN HARTLEY (1870–1928), actor and dramatist, who after several years on the London stage went to the United States with Lily Langtry (q.v.), for whom he wrote his first play. In 1908 he settled permanently in America and from then until his death contributed more than thirty plays to the New York stage. The only one now remembered is the light comedy *Peg o' My Heart* (1912), in which his wife, Laurette Taylor (q.v.), played the title-role. It was produced in London in 1914 and several times revived, particularly on tour, as well as being translated into a number of European languages. Its success overshadowed all the author's other works and prevented his being taken seriously as a modern dramatist.

Mannheim, a city important in the history of the German stage. In 1720, when the town became a seat of government, a Court theatre was established in the castle, and between 1737 and 1741 Alessandro Galli da Bibiena built a baroque theatre there, also designing the scenery for it. A garden theatre was built at Schwetzingen in 1752, and also a small open-air theatre. In 1778 Dalberg (q.v.) became director of the newly established National Theatre in Mannheim, which under him became one of the foremost theatres in the country, particularly when, after Ekhof's death in Gotha later the same year, Dalberg engaged his troupe with Iffland (q.v.) at its head. But Dalberg's greatest service to the German theatre was undoubtedly his support of the young Schiller (q.v.), whose *Die Räuber* had its first production at Mannheim in 1782, followed by *Fiesco* and *Kabale und Liebe*.

In 1796, partly owing to the rigours of war, the fortunes of the Mannheim theatre declined and the company was disbanded. Little was done until in 1884 J. Werther reopened the old National Theatre. A sudden upsurge in theatrical activity consequent upon this led to the building in 1898 of a small theatre, called the Colosseum, intended for farce and popular drama. Three years later a larger theatre opened under the name of the Modern Theatre. The National Theatre was completely destroyed in 1943, but reopened in a temporary structure in 1945, moving to a new theatre in 1957, where the post-war repertory has included a wide selection of new European plays as well as German classics.

Manoel Theatre, MALTA, an eighteenth-century playhouse built by the Grand Master Antonio de Vilhena in 1731. It opened a year later with a performance of Maffei's *Merope*, and flourished for a century or more with a nine-month season of mixed opera and plays. Renamed the Royal Theatre by the British occupying powers, it continued pre-eminent until the building of the much larger Opera House, after which it sank into disrepair. In the 1950s steps were taken to restore it. It was bought by the Maltese Government, and in 1957 a committee was set up to rebuild and modernize it backstage while retaining the historic auditorium and façade. On 27 Dec. 1960 it reopened as the National Theatre of Malta with a season by the Ballet Rambert. It is still used for occasional summer seasons and gala performances.

MANSFIELD, RICHARD (1854–1907), American actor, who first appeared on the stage in London and in 1882 went to New York, making a success a year later as Baron Chevrial in Feuillet's *A Parisian Romance*. Among his outstanding parts were the dual roles of Dr. Jekyll and Mr. Hyde in a dramatization of Stevenson's novel, Beau Brummel in a play of that name specially written for him by Clyde Fitch (q.v.), Cyrano de Bergerac in Rostand's verse-play, and Monsieur Beaucaire in Booth Tarkington's romance. During a visit to London in 1889 he first played Richard III, and among his other Shakespearian parts were Shylock in *The Merchant of Venice*, Brutus in *Julius Caesar*, and Henry V. Mansfield was essentially a romantic actor at a time when the problem play was becoming popular, but though he had little sympathy with the new drama as a whole, he much admired Ibsen (q.v.), and in his last season of 1906–7 gave the first production in English of *Peer Gynt* with himself in the title-role. He also introduced Shaw to America, appearing as Bluntschli in *Arms and the Man* in 1894 and Dick Dudgeon in *The Devil's Disciple* in 1897, together with his wife Beatrice Cameron (q.v.).

Mansfield Theatre, NEW YORK, see BROOKS ATKINSON THEATRE.

MANTELL, ROBERT BRUCE (1854–1928), American actor, who was first on the stage in Belfast and London and visited the United States with Modjeska (q.v.) in 1878. He then returned to England, but after several years of hard work with little recognition he went back to the States for good, and in 1886 took his own company on tour. As a young man he was at his best in such romantic melodramas as Boucicault's *The Corsican Brothers*, Charles Selby's *The Marble Heart*, and Bulwer-Lytton's *The Lady of Lyons*. Later on he became somewhat heavy and uninspired, but remained popular outside New York, where his careful studies of the leading Shakespearian roles won him respectful admiration. He was four times married, usually to actresses who were his leading ladies.

MANTLE, (ROBERT) BURNS (1873–1948), American dramatic critic, who in 1898 became dramatic editor of the *Denver Times*. Later he worked as Sunday editor of the *Chicago Tribune*, and from 1922 until his retirement in 1943 he was dramatic critic of the *New York Daily News*. He inaugurated and edited annually until his death a series of play anthologies which began in 1920 with *The Best Plays of 1919–1920*. Each volume contained résumés of ten of the season's productions together with an annotated index of every play produced in New York during the year. The useful history of the modern American theatre was supplemented by two more volumes covering the years from 1899 to 1919. Mantle was also the author of *American Playwrights of Today* (1938), and with John Gassner (q.v.) edited *A Treasury of the Theatre* (1935).

Marais, THÉÂTRE DU, PARIS. Recent research places the opening of this theatre, one of the forerunners of the Comédie-Française, on 31 Dec. 1634 in a converted tennis court in the rue Vieille-du-Temple, with a company under Montdory (q.v.) which had previously appeared in *Mélite*, the first play by Corneille (q.v.), whose *Le Cid* they produced in 1636–7. Among other notable productions was Tristan's *La Mariane* (also 1636), in which Montdory was playing Herod when his health broke down and he was forced to retire. Without him the Marais went through bad times. Its best actors joined the rival company at the Hôtel de Bourgogne (q.v.), to which Corneille also gave his new plays, and those who remained reverted to the playing of old-fashioned crude popular farces. The one good thing was the arrival of Jodelet (q.v.), for whom Scarron, d'Ouville, and the younger Corneille wrote excellent farces. At a later date the Marais, which was a big theatre, specialized in spectacular performances which made use of the newly imported Italian machinery. But it never regained the place in public esteem which it had held under Montdory, and in 1673 its actors were amalgamated with those of Molière, who had just died. The combined company, which by its later fusion with the actors of the Hôtel de Bourgogne became the Comédie-Française, acted at the theatre in the rue Guénégaud which had been built for Lully's opera company, and the old Marais stage was abandoned.

MARBLE, DAN(FORTH) (1810–49), American actor, famous for his Yankee characters. He made his first appearance on the stage in 1831 and in 1836 made a great success as Sam Patch in an anonymous play of that title which he may have written or arranged himself. He followed it with two other plays on the same theme, *Sam Patch, The Itinerant Yankee* (1838) and *Sam Patch in France* (1848). In 1844 he toured England and also visited Glasgow and Dublin, where he was received with enthusiasm in a repertory of farces which gave full scope for his inimitable assumption of Yankee characteristics and Yankee dialect. He married the daughter of the elder William Warren (q.v.) of Philadelphia, and died young at the height of his popularity.

MARCEAU, MARCEL (1923–), French actor, the finest modern exponent of mime or, as he prefers to call it, mimodrama. He joined the company of Jean-Louis Barrault (q.v.) in 1945, but a year later abandoned conventional acting to study mime, basing his work on the character of the nineteenth-century French Pierrot and evolving his own Bip, a white-faced clown with sailor trousers and striped jacket. In this part, which he first played at the tiny Théâtre de Poche in Paris in 1946, he has toured all over the world, accompanied by supporting players whom he has trained himself. He has also evolved short pieces of concerted mime, including one based on Gogol's *The Overcoat*, and longer symbolic dramas like his own *The Mask-Maker*, and with the aid of a screen has contrived to appear almost simultaneously as two sharply contrasted characters—David and Goliath, or the Hunter and the Hunted. His work has given immense impetus to the study of mime by young actors, who have also benefited by the many demonstrations of his technique which he has given to students.

MARCUS, FRANK (1928–), English dramatist and dramatic critic, of German extraction though educated in England, who came into prominence in 1965 with the success of his play, *The Killing of Sister George*. This was first produced at the Bristol Old Vic and then transferred to London, where it ran for a year at the Duke of York's; it was later seen in New York. Marcus, who had previously written *Minuet for Stuffed Birds* (1950), which he directed himself at the Torch Theatre, and *The Formation Dancers* (1964), has since had another play transferred from Bristol, again to the Duke of York's: *Mrs. Mouse, Are You Within?* (1968), which did not, however, repeat the success of the previous one. He is also the author of *Cleo* (1965), *Studies in the Nude* (1967), seen at the Hampstead Theatre Club, and *The Window* (1969), a one-act incursion into *voyeurism* produced at the Ambiance lunch-time theatre. Since 1968 Marcus has been dramatic critic of the *Sunday Telegraph* and he writes also for the monthly *Plays and Players*.

MARINELLI, KARL (1744–1803), Austrian actor, dramatist, and impresario, who in his play *Der Ungar in Wien* (1773) first introduced the figure of the light-hearted romantic Magyar, later a stereotype of Viennese folk-comedy and operetta which survived long enough to be ridiculed by Shaw (q.v.) in *Arms and the Man* (1894). When Joseph II, as part of his rationalist reforms, banished the old impromptu burlesque from the Burgtheater, Marinelli provided a new home for it at the Leopold-städter Theater, which opened in 1781. Here the great comedian Johann Laroche (q.v.), who was the chief actor of the troupe until his death in 1806, established the comic character of Kasperle (q.v.), inheritor both of Hanswurst and of the puppet Punch.

Marionette, a full-length rounded puppet controlled from above the stage, originally by a rod or wire fixed to the centre of the head. Other wires were later attached to the hands and legs, giving crude but effective movements particularly suitable for scenes of violence and fighting. Early marionettes in this folk-tradition can still be seen in Sicily in plays based on episodes from the Crusades and the wars against the Turks. A great technical advance was made when the rods or stiff wires were discarded and the marionettes were manipulated by strings. This may have been done by the English puppeteer Thomas Holden in the 1870s, or even a hundred years earlier for the intricate Italian Fantoccini who appeared with such success in London, where Italian marion-ettes were first seen at the Restoration, and where the famous Puppet Theatre under the Piazza in Covent Garden, run by the dwarf puppeteer MARTIN POWELL between 1710 and 1713, was one of the most fashionable entertainments of its day. Marionettes were also used for satiric purposes by Samuel Foote (q.v.) in 1733, and by Charles Dibdin (q.v.), who erected a puppet theatre at Exeter 'Change in 1775. The fortunes of the marionette then waned, but there was a revival of interest in the early twentieth cen-tury, fostered by Gordon Craig (q.v.) with his emphasis on the actor's role as an '*über-marionette*'. This led to an artistic flowering of talent which has borne fruit in the work of the Hogarth Puppets and John Wright's Marionettes, which operate at the Angel Theatre, Islington. But the finest marionette theatre is probably that in Salzburg, which specializes in short operettas performed with Mozartian delicacy. There was also the famous Teatro dei Piccoli of Vittorio Podrecca which visited London in the 1920s. The marionettes in these theatres are usually intricately strung, with up to as many as thirty threads, which allow for a great variety of movement. But the standard marionette, which is usually made of papier-mâché, has nine threads, one to each arm and leg, two to the head, one to each shoulder, and one to the back. These are gathered on a 'crutch', or control, held in one hand by the manipulator, while with the other he plucks at the strings. (See also PUPPET.)

MARIVAUX, PIERRE CARLET DE CHAMBLAIN DE (1688–1763), French dramatist, whose highly personal and precious style of writing was nicknamed *marivaudage*, first in derision, later in admiration of its unique quality. He wrote chiefly for the Comédie-Italienne, with *La Surprise de l'amour* (1722), *La Double Inconstance* (1723), *Le Jeu de l'amour et du hasard* (1730), *Les Fausses Confidences* (1737), and *L'Épreuve* (1740). The only plays to succeed at the Comédie-Française were *La Seconde Surprise de l'amour* (1727) and a one-act play, *Le Legs* (1736), which was revived in the 1780s by Molé (q.v.). In his own day Marivaux had none of the pre-eminence accorded to him at present, contemporary audiences preferring the tearful comedies of La Chaussée (q.v.). His work appealed only to a minority and was forgotten in the upheavals of the Revolution. It came back into favour in the mid-nineteenth century, and his best plays can still be seen in France whenever there is available an actress, like Madeleine Renaud (q.v.) for instance, who can interpret his heroines. But owing to the difficulties of translation, his work has made very little impact in the English-speaking theatre.

Mark Hellinger Theatre, NEW YORK, on West 51st Street. Originally a cinema, this opened as the Hollywood in April 1930. It then ventured into legitimate drama as the 51st Street Theatre and in 1936 housed *Sweet River*, a new version of *Uncle Tom's Cabin* by George Abbott (q.v.) with fine settings by Donald Oenslager (q.v.). This was taken off after five performances and the theatre reverted to films under its old name except for a short run of *Romeo and Juliet* in 1940, with Laurence Olivier and Vivien Leigh (qq.v.). In 1949 the theatre was renamed the Mark Hellinger, and from 1956 to 1962 was occupied by the musical *My Fair Lady*, based on Shaw's *Pygmalion*. In 1969 a musical, *Coco*, based on the life

of Chanel, began its run at this theatre with Katharine Hepburn (q.v.) in the leading role.

MARLOWE, CHRISTOPHER (1564–93), a playwright of the English Renaissance and an important figure in the development of the Elizabethan stage. His first play, *Tamburlaine the Great, Part 1*, was produced in about 1587 by the Admiral's Men with Edward Alleyn (q.v.) in the title-role. *Part 2* was seen in the following year. Written in flamboyant blank verse of great poetic beauty, these plays had a great influence on Shakespeare (q.v.), who no doubt saw them on his arrival in London a few years later, since they continued to hold the stage up to the closing of the theatres in 1642. (The First Part was successfully revived at the Old Vic in 1951 with Donald Wolfit (q.v.) as Tamburlaine.) They were followed by *The Tragical History of Doctor Faustus*, based on a German medieval legend (see FAUST). Though written and probably produced in 1589, it was not printed until 1604 and has survived only in a fragmentary and much-mutilated condition, with comic scenes, featuring the Devil, interpolated by a later hand. As originally planned, it had much in common with the earlier Morality play (q.v.), and even in its mangled condition continued to be popular. It was one of the plays revived by William Poel (q.v.), in 1896, and was last seen in London at the Old Vic in 1961. Marlowe's last plays were *The Jew of Malta* (c. 1590) and *Edward II* (c. 1591–2). The hero of the former, Barabas, may have contributed something to Shakespeare's Shylock in *The Merchant of Venice*, and in 1965 the two plays were acted in repertory at the Royal Shakespeare Theatre at Stratford-upon-Avon. *Edward II*, which has affinities with Shakespeare's *Richard II*, was several times revived in the 1950s and in 1969 the title-roles in both plays were played on alternate nights at the Mermaid Theatre (q.v.) by Ian McKellen. Marlowe, who was often in danger of arrest because of his atheistical and outspoken opinions, died young in a tavern brawl, probably assassinated because of his secret-service activities. His quatercentenary in 1964 was overshadowed by that of Shakespeare, ironically enough, since there is a theory current that Marlowe was not murdered but concealed for a time, returning to write plays under Shakespeare's name.

MARLOWE, JULIA [really SARAH FRAN-
CES FROST] (1866–1950), American actress,
who was on the stage as a child and made
her adult début in New York in 1887, as
Parthenia in G. W. Lovell's *Ingomar*. She
was immediately successful and began a
long career as a leading actress, being at
her best as Shakespeare's heroines. But
she was also good in standard comedy,
playing Lydia Languish in Sheridan's *The
Rivals* with Jefferson and Mrs. John Drew
(qq.v.), Julia in Sheridan Knowles's *The
Hunchback*, and Pauline in Bulwer-
Lytton's *The Lady of Lyons*. She married
as her second husband E. H. Sothern
(q.v.), playing Juliet to his Romeo in 1904.
Three years later she made her first
appearance in London, being well received
in Shakespearian and other parts. She
retired for a time in 1915, but returned to
play mainly in Shakespeare until her final
retirement in 1924.

Marlowe Society, see CAMBRIDGE and
RYLANDS, GEORGE.

MARMONTEL, JEAN-FRANÇOIS (1723–
99), French man of letters, whose first
play, *Denys le Tyran*, was produced in
1748. Owing to the lack of good contemporary plays this pale reflection of
classical French tragedy was well received
mainly because of the acting of Mlle
Clairon (q.v.), who later became Marmontel's mistress and was persuaded by him
in about 1753 to discard her declamatory
style for a more natural style of acting, to
the ultimate benefit of the French stage.
Marmontel continued to write plays until
1753, but none of them has been revived,
and it is mainly as a critic that he is now
remembered. Indeed, he may be regarded
as the founder of French journalistic
dramatic criticism. He also wrote a number of libretti for light operas.

MAROWITZ, CHARLES (1934–   ),
American-born theatre director, who since
1956 has worked in England, having been
connected with Peter Brook (q.v.) in his
productions of *King Lear* (1962) and a
programme entitled *Theatre of Cruelty*
(1964) which set out to demonstrate the
theories propounded by Artaud (q.v.).
Marowitz has also been connected with
the Traverse Company in Edinburgh and
London, and in 1968 he opened his own
theatre, the Open Space, a small adaptable
playhouse in the Tottenham Court Road,
where he has introduced several new

American writers to English audiences
and also staged his own widely-toured
'collage' versions of *Hamlet* (first seen in
1965) and *Macbeth* (first seen in 1970).
Among his other activities he was for a
time joint editor of the short-lived *avant-
garde* theatre magazine *Encore*.

MARRIOTT, ALICE (1824–1900), see
WALLACE, EDGAR.

MARS, MLLE [really ANNE-FRANÇOISE-
HIPPOLYTE BOUTET] (1779–1847), French
actress, younger daughter of an actor-
dramatist known as MONVEL (1745–1812).
She appeared on the stage as a child and
in 1795 made her first appearance at the
Comédie-Française, where she had a long
and successful career. She was at her best
in the comedies of Molière, but was also
good in such dramas as Dumas's *Henri III
et sa Cour* (1829) and created the part of
Doña Sol in Hugo's *Hernani* (1830). She
retired in 1841, making her last appearance on 31 March as Elmire in Molière's
Tartuffe and Silvia in Marivaux's *Le Jeu
de l'amour et du hasard*, in which she was
still able to give the illusion of youthful
beauty, though well over sixty.

MARSHALL, NORMAN (1901–80), English director and theatre manager, who in
1926, after some experience on tour, was
appointed one of the directors of the
Cambridge Festival Theatre under Terence Gray (q.v.), where he was responsible
for some interesting productions. He took
over the theatre himself in 1932, directing
among other plays O'Neill's *Marco
Millions* on its first production in England.
In 1934 he took over the private Gate
Theatre (q.v.) in London, where he
presented an annual Gate revue and a
varied programme of uncommercial plays,
including several by J.-J. Bernard (q.v.),
and new plays which were subsequently
transferred to the West End. Among them
were Elsie T. Schauffler's *Parnell* (1936),
Housman's *Victoria Regina* (1937), and
Steinbeck's *Of Mice and Men* (1939).
After war service he returned to the theatre
and formed his own company, with which
he toured in an extensive repertory in
addition to directing many successful plays
in London. He also toured Europe and
India under the auspices of the British
Council with abridged versions of a
dozen Shakespeare plays, and in 1952
directed Jonson's *Volpone* at the Cameri
Theatre in Israel. In 1955 he was appoin-

ted Head of Drama for Associated Redif-fusion. He is the author of *The Other Theatre* (1947), an account of the work done in the non-commercial theatre between the two world wars.

MARSTON, JOHN (*c.* 1575–1634), English dramatist, satirized by Jonson (q.v.) as Crispinus in *The Poetaster* (1601). His first plays, *Antonio and Mellida* and *Antonio's Revenge*, were played by the Children of Paul's in 1599. Of his later plays the best were *The Malcontent* (1603) and *The Dutch Courtesan* (1604). A droll extracted from the latter, *The Cheater Cheated*, was published in Kirkman's *The Wits* (1662) and was later adapted by Aphra Behn (q.v.) as *The Revenge; or, a Match in Newgate* (1680). Marston was implicated in the trouble over *Eastward Ho!* (1605) and narrowly escaped imprisonment with Jonson and Chapman. A few years later he gave up the theatre and took holy orders. He is thought to have had a hand in the writing of Shakespeare's *Troilus and Cressida* (see *Englische Studien*, vol. xxx, 1901, article by R. Boyle).

Martin Beck Theatre, NEW YORK, on 45th Street between 8th and 9th Avenues. This opened on 11 Nov. 1924 with Leo Fall's musical play *Madame Pompadour*, and has since housed many successful musicals. It was also used by the Theatre Guild (q.v.) for *Wings Over Europe* (1928), by Maurice Browne and Robert Nichols, finely directed by Reuben Mamoulian (q.v.); for the first New York production of Shaw's *The Apple Cart* (1930); for Barry's *Hotel Universe* (also 1930); and by the Group Theatre (q.v.) for its initial productions, Green's *The House of Connelly* and Sherwood's highly successful *Reunion in Vienna* (both 1931). A visit from the Abbey Players, followed by the D'Oyly Carte company on its first appearance in New York for forty years, preceded the appearance of Katharine Cornell (q.v.) in 1934–5 in a repertory which included *Romeo and Juliet*, Besier's *The Barretts of Wimpole Street*, and Buckstone's *The Flowers of the Forest*. The first plays to be awarded the New York Drama Critics' Circle prize, *Winterset* (1935) and *High Tor* (1937), both by Maxwell Anderson (q.v.), were seen at the Martin Beck, as was Lillian Hellman's *Watch on the Rhine* (1941), which gained the same award, and O'Neill's *The Iceman Cometh* (1946). Subsequent productions

included John Patrick's *The Teahouse of the August Moon* (1953) and Leonard Bernstein's musical version of Voltaire's *Candide* (1956) (book by Lillian Hellman). This, though highly praised, had only a short run, as did Brecht's *Mother Courage and her Children* (1963), which was fol-lowed by *The Ballad of the Sad Café*, adapted by Albee (q.v.) from Carson McCullers's *novella* of the same title. In March 1968 the successful musical *Man of La Mancha*, based on *Don Quixote*, moved to this theatre from the Washington Square Theatre (q.v.) for a further long run.

MARTIN-HARVEY, SIR JOHN, see HAR-VEY

MARTINELLI, TRISTANO (*c.* 1557–1630), an actor of the *commedia dell'arte* (q.v.) who was probably the first to play Arlecchino. He was originally a member of the Confidenti under Pellesini, but appears to have been of a roving and somewhat quarrelsome disposition and is found with many different companies. He was very popular in Paris, where he appeared on several occasions, and specimens of his extempore wit were preserved in a publication entitled *Compositions de rhétorique de M. Don Arlequin* (1600). His brother DRUSIANO (?–1606/8) was probably a member of the first Italian *commedia dell'arte* company to appear in England, in 1577–8.

MARTÍNEZ DE LA ROSA, FRANCISCO (1787–1862), Spanish dramatist, and the first to import into his plays, particularly *Aben-Humeya* (1830) and *La conjuración de Venecia* (1834), the local colour and mingled tragedy and comedy of the Romantic era, though in his true comedies, of which the best is *La niña en la casa y la madre en la máscara* (1821), he followed the tradition of Fernandez de Moratín (q.v.). After the death of Ferdinand VII, Martínez de la Rosa, who had spent some years in exile in Paris, played an important part in the political life of Spain.

MARTÍNEZ SIERRA, GREGORIO (1881–1948), Spanish dramatist, author of a number of charming but rather senti-mental comedies, several of which were seen in translation in London and New York in the 1920s and 1930s—among them *Wife to a Famous Man, The Romantic Young Lady, Take Two From One, The*

Kingdom of God, Madame Pepita, and *The Two Shepherds.* The best-known, however, is *The Cradle Song* which, as *Cancion de cuna,* was first seen in Spain in 1910. In a translation by John Garrett Underhill it was produced in New York in 1921 and several times revived, notably by the Civic Repertory Theatre between 1927 and 1932. It was first seen in London in 1926 and, less successfully, in 1944, and was popular with amateur and student groups. Martínez Sierra was perhaps more important as a theatre director than as a dramatist. During his management of the Teatro Eslava—from 1917 to 1925—he introduced the Madrid public to a number of contemporary dramatists in translation and to the new techniques introduced by the Catalan director Adrià Gual (q.v.). He also staged some plays by little-known Spanish dramatists, including the first play of Federico García Lorca (q.v.).

MARTYN, EDWARD (1859–1924), one of the founders of the Irish Literary Theatre (q.v.), which as its second production, on 9 May 1899, performed *The Heather Field,* a play which reveals him as a disciple of Ibsen and Strindberg (qq.v.). It was followed in 1900 by *Maeve,* a psychological drama on the clash between England and Ireland. Martyn, who was a wealthy man, was a generous benefactor to the Irish Literary Theatre during its short life, and in 1914 helped to establish the Irish Theatre in Hawkwicke Street, Dublin.

Marylebone Music-Hall, LONDON, in Marylebone High Street. This was attached to the Rose of Normandy Tavern which stood originally in the centre of a vanished pleasure-garden known as Marylebone Gardens. Sam Collins (q.v.) converted it into a music-hall in 1858, but it was not a success and he gave up in 1861. His successor, R. F. Botting, ran it more successfully until 1890, and it finally closed in 1900.

Marylebone Theatre, LONDON, see WEST LONDON THEATRE.

MASEFIELD, JOHN (1878–1967), O.M., English poet, novelist, and dramatist, who became poet laureate in succession to Robert Bridges and was himself succeeded by Cecil Day-Lewis. His plays, which contain some of his best work, combine the traditions of classical Greek tragedy

with those of the Japanese nō play (q.v.), but though some of them have been successfully staged, they are more poetic than theatrical. Among them are *The Campden Wonder* (1907), on an unsolved murder; *The Tragedy of Nan* (1908); *The Witch* (1910), adapted from a Norwegian tragedy and several times revived; *Melloney Holtspur* (1923); and, on biblical themes, *Good Friday* (1917); *The Trial of Jesus* (1926); and *A King's Daughter* (Jezebel) (1928). Masefield was also the author of a short but stimulating book entitled *A Macbeth Production* (1945), which contains excellent advice given to a group of ex-servicemen about to produce the play and incidentally ranges over a wide field of historical and literary criticism.

Mask, a covering for the face, with openings for the eyes and mouth. It was originally made of carved wood or painted linen, later of painted cork or canvas, and later still of papier-mâché. The wearing of masks in the theatre derives from the use of animal skins and heads in primitive religious rituals. In the Greek theatre, masks served, in an all-male company, to distinguish between the male and female characters and to show the age and chief characteristic of each—hate, anger, fear, cunning, stupidity. The argument that the opening for the mouth served as an amplifier for the voice is no longer tenable. In any case the excellent acoustics of the open-air Greek theatre would have made this unnecessary. In tragedy the mask gave dignity and a certain remoteness to demi-gods and heroes, and also enabled one actor to play several parts by changing his mask. In comedy the mask helped to unify the chorus (which, as can be seen in the plays of Aristophanes (q.v.), wore identical masks of such creatures as frogs, birds, horses, etc.) and served as an additional source of humour, particularly with the comic masks of slaves. The Roman theatre took over the use of masks from the Greeks, adopting for tragedy the later exaggerated form with a high peak (*onkos*) over the forehead. Many fine copies of classical masks, in marble, still survive and can be seen in museums. They are also shown in several wall-paintings and bas-reliefs. The golden masks worn by God and the archangels in some versions of the medieval Mystery Play (q.v.) may have been a survival of the Greek tragic mask or an independent discovery of the new European theatre, but the devils' masks, though often comic in intention, seem by their horrific animal forms to be linked to early primitive religious usage. They were usually made of painted leather, and many excellent specimens can be seen in European museums, particularly in Germany. The comic actors of the later *commedia dell'arte* (q.v.) always wore masks, usually the small black 'cat-mask' which left the lower part of the face bare. Otherwise masks, which continued to be an essential factor in the Japanese *nō* play (q.v.) and other Far Eastern theatres, were discarded in Europe, and they are seldom seen on stage, though they are sometimes used for special effects by such writers as Yeats (q.v.) (*At the Hawk's Well*, 1917; *The Only Jealousy of Emer* and *The Dreaming of the Bones*, both 1919); O'Neill (q.v.) (*The Great God Brown*, 1926; *Lazarus Laughs*, 1928); and more recently by John Arden (q.v.) in *The Happy Haven* (1960). Apart from such isolated examples, the main use of masks at present is in the training of drama students, on whom they seem to have a liberating effect, particularly in improvisation. The making of masks has also provided a useful subject for handicraft in schools and elsewhere. The old English name for the black mask used by the early Tudor 'guiser' (see MASQUE) was visor.

The Latin word *persona*, meaning mask, was used by Terence (q.v.) in the sense of character, whence our expression *dramatis personae*, 'the characters in the play'. In the *commedia dell'arte* the word was used of the mask and of the person wearing it.

Mask Theatre, BELFAST, see BELFAST ARTS THEATRE.

Masking, a term used to indicate the blocking out of one actor from the sight of the audience by another, which when done unintentionally indicates poor production. It is also used of devices such as borders, wings, etc., designed to hide back-stage elements from the audience.

Masque, originally Mask, the French spelling being used first by Ben Jonson (q.v.). This spectacular entertainment, which combined music and poetry with scenery and elaborate costumes, reached its height at the English Court between 1600 and 1640, but derived originally from a primitive folk ritual featuring the arrival of guests, usually in disguise, bearing gifts to a king or nobleman, who

with his household then joined the visitors in a ceremonial dance. The presentation of the gifts soon became an excuse for flowery, flattering speeches, while the wearing of outlandish or beautiful costumes and masks, or visors, led to miming and dancing as a prelude to the final dance. Thus a dramatic formula was evolved which in Elizabethan times proved useful for the entertainment of the Queen, either in her own palace or during her 'progresses' throughout the land. In its early form the masque, known as a Disguising (q.v.) and performed by Guisers, or Guisards, was relatively simple, particularly outside London, its speeches being written by local scholars or poets, its performers recruited from local families or schools. Shakespeare makes fun of such a country masque in *Love's Labour's Lost*, and uses the form seriously in *Timon of Athens* for a typical wordless early Disguising, and in *The Tempest*. This latter already shows some of the elaboration reached by the Court masque under James I and Charles I, with the collaboration of Ben Jonson, who in 1603 succeeded Samuel Daniel as Court Poet, and the scenic designer Inigo Jones (q.v.). Their first joint work was the Twelfth Night masque of 1605, their best probably *Oberon, the Fairy Prince* (1611). One of Jonson's innovations was the anti-masque, also known as the ante-masque because it preceded the main entertainment, or the antic masque because it employed earlier elements of antic or grotesque dancing. First introduced in 1609, the anti-masque provided a violent contrast to the main theme, as hell before heaven, war before peace, a storm before a calm. The simplicity of the early masque, in which the performers appeared in one guise only—as blackamoors, wild men, shepherds—later gave way to the double masque, with two groups of characters—fishermen and market-women, sailors and milkmaids. As the spectacular side of the masque became more important, particularly the dancing, in which Charles I and Henrietta Maria became performers rather than spectators, after the fashion of the French Court, Jonson, after altercations with Jones, withdrew, his last masque being performed in 1634. He was succeeded by James Shirley, who found himself called on to provide nothing more than a scenario suitable for elaborate effects, and a few dull speeches. The Civil War put an end to the masque, which was never revived. But it had a great influence on the development of opera and ballet and provided the means of introducing the new Italian scenery to the English stage, which took over many of its spectacular effects at the Restoration. The decorative frame set up for the masque in a ballroom became the proscenium arch behind which Inigo Jones's movable shutters, or wings, trebled or quadrupled, ran in grooves (q.v.) to open or close in front of a painted backcloth or, less often, what Jones called a 'sceane of releeve' consisting of cut-out pieces on various planes. As this had to be prepared in advance and shown to the audience by drawing back the shutters, it was termed a Set Scene, whence the modern use of the word 'set' for the scenic components of a play.

It should be noted that Milton's *Comus*, though called a masque, is really a pastoral, written for a private performance, and was probably so called to distinguish it from the plays given in the public theatres.

MASSINGER, PHILIP (1583–1640), English dramatist, author of some forty plays of which half are lost; the manuscripts of at least eight were destroyed by Warburton's cook (q.v.), who used them to line pie-dishes. Of those that survive the most important is *A New Way to Pay Old Debts*, a satiric comedy which was first produced in about 1625. Allowed to lapse during the Restoration, it returned to the stage in the eighteenth century and has been constantly revived up to the present day. Sir Giles Overreach has been a favourite part with many great actors, particularly Kean (q.v.), who first played it in 1816. In 1950 and 1953 it was played by Wolfit (q.v.). Among Massinger's other plays are the romantic dramas *The Duke of Milan* (1620), *The Great Duke of Florence* (1627), and *The Roman Actor* (1626), the last also revived by Kean; the comedies *The City Madam* (1632) and *The Guardian* (1633); and the tragi-comedies *The Bondman* (1623) and *The Renegado* (1624). *The Fatal Dowry* (1619) and *The Virgin Martyr* (1620) were written in collaboration, the first with Field, the second with Dekker (qq.v.), while Massinger had a hand in several of the plays ascribed to Beaumont and Fletcher (qq.v.), and may have worked with the latter on Shakespeare's *Henry VIII* and possibly *The Two Noble Kinsmen*.

Master of the Revels, an officer first appointed in 1494 to serve under the Lord Chamberlain in connection with entertainments at Court. SIR THOMAS CAWARDEN, who supervised the revels for the coronation of Elizabeth I, was appointed Master for life in 1545, and was succeeded on his death in 1559 by SIR THOMAS BENGER, whose powers, however, were much curtailed, finance and production being controlled by other departments of the Royal Household. After the death of Benger in 1572 no new appointment was made, and work continued smoothly under the permanent under-official THOMAS BLAGROVE, who served the Revels Office faithfully for fifty-seven years. He had hoped to be given the Mastership, but in 1579 this went, through Court influence, to SIR EDMUND TILNEY, who retained it until his death in 1610. He seems to have done little active work, though he continued to act as censor of plays, as established by decrees of 1581 and 1603, and to draw acting fees for all plays publicly performed. He was succeeded by his nephew SIR GEORGE BUCK, on whose death in 1622 the office passed to its most famous holder, Sir Henry Herbert (q.v.). By the Licensing Act of 1737 the censorship of plays (abolished in 1968) became the direct responsibility of the Lord Chamberlain (see DRAMATIC CENSORSHIP), and the old office of Master of the Revels, dating from early Tudor times, became extinct. For a detailed account of the Revels office in its heyday, see Chambers, *Elizabethan Stage*, vol. i, ch. 3.

Mastersingers, members of the musical and literary guilds which flourished in the larger towns of southern Germany, particularly in Nuremberg, in the fifteenth and sixteenth centuries. The activities of such a guild are portrayed in Wagner's opera 'Die Meistersinger von Nürnberg' (1868), one of the main characters being the musician and dramatist Hans Sachs (q.v.). Other Mastersingers who are known to have written plays—mainly short farces—are HANS ROSENBLÜT (*fl.* fifteenth century) and HANS FOLZ (*c.* 1450–1515). The Mastersingers were the lineal descendants of the medieval Minnesingers, of whom the best-known was NEIDHART VON REUENTAL (*fl.* thirteenth century), author of a pastoral with farcical interludes which contains some charming melodies with all the characteristics of folksong.

MATHEWS, CHARLES (1776–1835), English actor, or rather entertainer, since the best part of his work lay in his imitations and assumptions of different characters, particularly in his *At Homes*—a form peculiar to himself which has been described as 'a whole play in the person of one man'. Mathews had from early childhood a most retentive memory and amazing powers of mimicry, coupled with an intense desire to go on the stage. This he eventually achieved, making his first appearances in Dublin in 1794. He appeared in London at the Haymarket in 1803 and soon made a reputation as an eccentric comedian. Among his successes were Sir Fretful Plagiary in Sheridan's *The Critic*, always one of his best parts, and Risk in the younger Colman's *Love Laughs at Locksmiths* (1803). In addition to many new parts which he created, he was seen as Falstaff, Sir Archy MacSarcasm in Macklin's *Love à la Mode*, and Sir Peter Teazle in Sheridan's *The School for Scandal*. It was in 1808 that he first conceived the idea of the one-man entertainments with which his name is principally connected. During the years he performed them they gradually grew to be short plays on the lines of *The Actor of All Work* (1817), which the younger Colman (q.v.) wrote specially for him. This represents a country manager interviewing applicants for a place in his company and gave Mathews an opportunity of portraying a bewildering series of totally dissimilar characters. Among the most successful of the sketches which Mathews arranged himself were *The Trip to Paris*, *Mr. Mathews and his Youthful Days*, and *The Trip to America*. By his second wife, the actress ANNE JACKSON (1782–1869), who later edited his memoirs, he was the father of Charles James Mathews (q.v.).

MATHEWS, CHARLES JAMES (1803–78), son of the above, who on the death of his father in 1835 replaced him in the management of the Adelphi Theatre. He then went to the Olympic, making his first professional appearance on the stage on 7 Dec. 1835 in his own play, *The Humpbacked Lover*. Three years later he married Mme Vestris (q.v.), and on his return to London from an unsuccessful trip to New York took over the management of Covent Garden, where he staged some fine productions, including Boucicault's *London Assurance* (1841), in which he played Dazzle, always one of his best parts.

Financially the season was a failure, as was a further venture at the Lyceum, and in the midst of their bankruptcy Mme Vestris died. Shortly after, Mathews returned to New York, where he married an actress named LIZZIE DAVENPORT (?–1899). With her help he extricated himself from his difficulties and again embarked on a successful career which lasted until his death, remaining to the end an elegant, light-hearted, and improvident creature. Tragedy and pathos were outside his range, but he was inimitable in such parts as Affable Hawk in Lewes's *The Game of Speculation*, Plumper in Jerrold's *Cool as a Cucumber*, Puff in Sheridan's *The Critic*, Sir Fopling Flutter in Etherege's *The Man of Mode*, and Young Wilding in Foote's *The Liar*. Like his father he was a good mimic and one of his most popular pieces was *Patter v. Clatter* (1838), which he wrote himself and in which he played five parts. He also appeared with his second wife in an entertainment, reminiscent of that of his father, called *Mr. and Mrs. Mathews at Home*. He had not the solid gifts of the elder Mathews, but much charm and delicacy tempered his high spirits and made him, within certain limits, one of the best light comedians of the English stage. His reminiscences were edited with biographical notes by the younger Charles Dickens.

MATTHEWS, ALBERT EDWARD (1869–1960), English actor, son of a Christy Minstrel and grand-nephew of a clown, Tom Matthews, who was a pupil of Grimaldi (q.v.). He had a long and successful career on the stage, beginning as a call-boy at the Princess's Theatre in 1886 and continuing to act almost up to his death. He never appeared in Shakespeare or classical plays, which he rightly considered outside his range, but in his own line he was inimitable. He excelled in farce, from such early examples as Pinero's *The Magistrate* and *Dandy Dick*, in which he toured when a young man, through revivals of such hardy perennials as Hawtrey's *The Private Secretary*, Brandon Thomas's *Charley's Aunt*, and Wilde's *The Importance of Being Earnest*, up to his last creation, the Earl of Lister in *The Chiltern Hundreds* (1947) and *The Manor of Northstead* (1954), both by William Douglas Home (q.v.). In private life he was an eccentric of dry humour refusing to take his success seriously and posing as the bluff country gentleman. In 1951 he was awarded the O.B.E., and in 1953 published his autobiography, *Matty*, by which name he was universally known and loved.

MATTHEWS, (JAMES) BRANDER (1852–1929), American theatre historian, playwright, and the first man to be appointed a professor of dramatic literature in the United States (at Columbia, from 1900 to 1924). By his writings and lectures he had a great influence on the professional theatre, on the practice of dramatic criticism, and on the attitude of the general theatrical public in America. He had a wide knowledge of European drama and a keen feeling for all that was best in the dramatic literature of his own and other countries. Among his own writings, which included an autobiography, *These Many Years* (1917), the most important were *The Development of the Drama* (1903), *Molière* (1910), *Shakespeare as a Playwright* (1913), and *Principles of Playmaking* (1919). With Laurence Hutton he also edited the five-volume *Actors and Actresses of Great Britain and the United States* (1886).

MATTOCKS (*née* HALLAM), MRS. ISABELLA (1746–1826), English actress, the youngest daughter of the elder Lewis Hallam (q.v.). Left behind in England when the rest of the family went to the New World, she was brought up by an aunt who was an actress, and is believed to have been on the stage from the age of five, playing small parts at Covent Garden. She made her adult début as Juliet in 1761, and a few years later married GEORGE MATTOCKS (?–1804), a provincial actor-manager with whom she toured in the summer, spending the winter seasons at Covent Garden. She had no aptitude for tragedy and no singing voice, but was excellent in comedy, particularly as a pert chambermaid. She made her last appearance on 7 June 1808 as Flora in Mrs. Centlivre's *The Wonder, a Woman Keeps a Secret*, with George Frederick Cooke (q.v.) as Don Felix.

MAUDE, CHARLES (1882–1943), see PRICE, NANCY.

MAUDE, CYRIL FRANCIS (1862–1951), English actor-manager, who was visiting the United States when he made his first appearance on the stage. This was in Denver, Colorado, in 1884 in a dramatization of Mrs. Henry Wood's *East Lynne*. A year later he was back in London, where in 1893 he made a great success as Cayley Drummle in Pinero's *The Second Mrs. Tanqueray*. Three years later, with Frederick Harrison, he took over the Haymarket (q.v.), and remained there until 1905, being responsible for a number of excellent productions with a distinguished company headed by his wife Winifred Emery (q.v.). Among his own successful appearances at this time were his Gavin Dishart in Barrie's *The Little Minister* (1897) and Eccles in a revival of Robertson's *Caste* (1902). He was also outstanding in the comedies of Sheridan and Goldsmith and made a great success as Lord Ogleby in Colman's *The Clandestine Marriage*. From 1905 to 1915 he was manager of the Avenue Theatre (see PLAYHOUSE), where he appeared in Clyde Fitch's *Toddles* (1907) and Austin Strong's version of *Rip Van Winkle* (1911). Between 1913 and 1919 he made several tours of Canada and the United States, where his greatest success (in 1913), repeated a year later in London, was as Andrew Bullivant in Hodges's *Grumpy*. Maude, who was for many years President of the Royal Academy of Dramatic Art, left the stage in 1933 and with his second wife spent a long and happy retirement in Devon, returning briefly to the Haymarket on his eightieth birthday to play Sir Peter Teazle in a scene from Sheridan's *The School for Scandal* in aid of the R.A.F. Benevolent Fund.

MAUGHAM, (WILLIAM) SOMERSET (1874–1965), English novelist and dramatist, whose first play, *A Man of Honour*, was produced in 1904. In 1908 he set up something of a record by having four plays running in London simultaneously —*Lady Frederick, Jack Straw, Mrs. Dot*, and *The Explorer*. From then until 1933, when he ceased to write for the theatre after the comparative failure of *Sheppey*, he was prolific, fashionable, and popular both in London and in New York, where all the above plays were produced soon after their London premières. Among his plays the best is probably *The Circle* (1921), which has been called an almost perfect 'serious' comedy. First seen at the Haymarket, it has been several times revived, notably by Gielgud in his season at the same theatre in 1944. Other successes were *Caroline* (1916), *Caesar's Wife* and *Home and Beauty* (both 1919), *East of Suez* (1922), *Our Betters* (1923; first seen in New York in 1917), *The Constant Wife* (1927; first seen in New York in 1926), *The Sacred Flame* (1928), *The Breadwinner* (1930), and *For Services Rendered* (1932). Maugham, who successfully continued his literary career after abandoning the theatre, was made a Companion of Honour in 1954. There are some interesting details of his theatrical career in *The Summing-Up* (1938) and *A Writer's Notebooks* (1949). Several of his short stories were adapted for the stage by other hands, notably *Miss Thompson* as *Rain* by John Colton and Clemence Randolph in 1922, and *Jane* by S. N. Behrman in 1947.

MAX, (ALEXANDRE) ÉDOUARD DE (1869–1925), French actor, a pupil of Worms (q.v.) at the Paris Conservatoire, where he took first prizes for comedy and tragedy in 1891. He made his début at the Odéon, and was already considered one of the foremost actors of his day when in 1915 he first appeared at the Comédie-Française, playing Néron in Racine's *Britannicus*. He had a short but glorious career there, dying ten years later of heart failure after playing Oreste in Racine's *Andromaque*.

Maxine Elliott's Theatre, NEW YORK, on 39th Street between Broadway and 6th Avenue. This was built for Maxine Elliott (q.v.), and opened on 30 Dec. 1908. The first outstanding success, in the following April, was Jerome K. Jerome's *The Passing of the Third Floor Back*. Synge's *The Playboy of the Western World*, played by the company from the Abbey Theatre (q.v.) in Dublin on their first American tour, caused a riot in 1911. In 1913 Doris Keane was seen in Sheldon's *Romance*, which later had a long run in London. In 1922 a dramatization of Maugham's short story *Miss Thompson* as *Rain*, by John Colton and Clemence Randolph, had a long run, and another Maugham success at this theatre was *The Constant Wife* (1926), with Ethel Barrymore (q.v.). Later productions were *Twelfth Night* (1930), with Jane Cowl (q.v.) as Viola and Pirandello's *As You Desire Me* (1931). Lillian Hellman's *The Children's Hour* was seen in 1934, and two years later the theatre was taken over by the Federal Theatre Project (q.v.) with *Horse Eats Hat* (a translation of Labiche's *Un Chapeau de paille d'Italie*) and Marlowe's *Doctor Faustus*, both directed by Orson Welles (q.v.), who also played Faustus. From 1941 the theatre was used only for

broadcasting, and it was demolished late in 1959.

May-Day, Maying, see FOLK FESTIVALS and ROBIN HOOD.

May Fair Theatre, LONDON, in Stratton Street, a small theatre in the May Fair Hotel which opened in 1963. Seating about three hundred people in a single raked tier, it is an intimate playhouse with a flexible and roomy proscenium stage which has proved particularly suitable for such plays as Pirandello's *Six Characters in Search of an Author*, the opening production, and for such later successes as Christopher Hampton's *The Philanthropist* (1970). In 1964 the revue *Beyond the Fringe* transferred to the May Fair from the Fortune for the latter part of its long run.

MAYAKOVSKY, VLADIMIR VLADIMIROVICH (1894–1930), Soviet poet and dramatist, who was helped and encouraged in his writing by Gorky (q.v.). In 1918 his *Mystery-Bouffe*, which shows the Communist revolution spreading over the whole world and is considered the first Soviet play, was produced in Moscow. In 1929 came *The Bed-Bug*, a satire portraying a Soviet world in which a pre-Revolutionary bourgeois and a bed-bug, sole survivors from the past, struggle to acclimatize themselves. This and *The Bath-House* (1930), also a satire on bourgeois elements in Soviet life, were produced by Meyerhold (q.v.) and, with their symbolic settings, robots, mechanics, and angularities, typify the drama of the period. Both plays have been several times revived. *The Bed-Bug* was first produced in English by a London University student group, and on 14 Feb. 1962 had its first professional production at the Mermaid (q.v.) in a translation by Dmitri Makaroff. Much of Mayakovsky's poetry is semi-dramatic in form and intended for declamation. Official disapproval of his work drove him to suicide but his memory is now revered and in 1954 a theatre in Moscow was called after him (see MAYAKOVSKY THEATRE).

Mayakovsky Theatre, MOSCOW, founded in 1922 as the Theatre of the Revolution for the production of propaganda plays. Its first outstanding director was Popov (q.v.), who raised its standards considerably, introducing new and worthwhile Soviet plays, like Pogodin's *Poem About an Axe* (1931), as well as excellent productions of the classics. His *Romeo and Juliet*

(1936) remained in the repertory for many years. His policy was continued by Okhlopkov (q.v.), under whom in 1954 the theatre was renamed in honour of Mayakovsky (q.v.). Okhlopkov directed it from 1943 until his death in 1967 and was responsible for such successful new plays as Virta's epic of Stalingrad, *Great Days* (1947), and also for controversial productions of *Hamlet* (1954) and Brecht's *Mother Courage* (1960).

MAYNE, RUTHERFORD [really SAMUEL WADDELL] (1878–1967), Irish dramatist, chiefly associated with the Ulster Literary Theatre (see ULSTER GROUP THEATRE), which he began to write for soon after its foundation in 1904, remaining till his death its strong supporter and leading playwright, though *Red Turf* (1911), probably his best play, and one or two of his later plays, notably *Peter* (1930) and *Bridgehead* (1934), were first seen in Dublin at the Abbey Theatre (q.v.). Like most Ulster dramatists he was mainly concerned with what is individual and characteristic in the life of Northern Ireland, but on occasion his work transcends local conditions and achieves a broad-based view of the forces which bring about tragedies in the rural communities of all countries. This universal appeal no doubt accounts for the fact that several of his plays have been translated and performed in Sweden, Norway, and the Netherlands.

MEDDOKS, MIKHAIL EGOROVICH [really MICHAEL MADDOX] (1747–1825). The researches of the Russian theatre historian Eugene Ilyin have established that in 1767 a young Englishman named Michael Maddox was in St. Petersburg with an exhibition of mechanical dolls. Ten years later he was in Moscow where he was befriended by Prince Ourusov, who held a patent from the Tsar for the building of a theatre and a monopoly of dramatic performances for ten years. This, after the destruction of his own private theatre by fire in 1780, he ceded to Maddox, who built a theatre on Petrovsky Square (where the Bolshoi Theatre now stands), and opened it with a good company mainly drawn from the private theatres of the nobility. It continued to flourish until its destruction by fire twenty-five years later. One unexpected result of Maddox's work was the adoption of the name Vauxhall, which he gave to the amusement park he opened in Moscow, as the Russian word

for a railway station. His own name, first transmuted to Meddoks, later became Medok, and it was the death of one of his direct male descendants, bearing that name, on the Russian front in the Second World War, that led to the researches indicated above.

MEDICI. All the members of this famous Italian family were patrons of the arts, and extended their interest and protection to the theatre. Two of them were dramatists—LORENZO (*c.* 1449–92), known as the Magnificent, author of a *sacra rappresentazione* produced in 1489, and LORENZINO DI PIER FRANCESCO (*fl.* early sixteenth century), one of the first Florentine writers of comedy, whose *Aridosia*, based on Plautus and Terence, was performed in 1536 with fine settings by San Gallo (q.v.). Larivey (q.v.) later based his comedy *Les Esprits* (1579) on this play.

MEDWALL, HENRY (*fl.* 1490–1514), an early English dramatist whose work was practically unknown until in 1919 the manuscript of his *Fulgens and Lucrece* came to light in a London saleroom. An Interlude performed in two parts as an entertainment at a banquet, it was probably acted in 1497, and as an example of secular drama is much earlier than anything hitherto known. With its story of the wooing of Lucretia and comic sub-plot of the wooing of her maid, it foreshadows the mingling of romantic and comic elements which was to be a feature of later Elizabethan drama.

MEGGS, MRS. MARY (?–1691), known as Orange Moll, a widow living in the parish of St. Paul's, Covent Garden, who on 10 Feb. 1662/3 was granted a licence for thirty-nine years to hawk oranges and other eatables in the newly opened theatre in Drury Lane (q.v.). A contemporary description of the fire which destroyed the theatre in 1672 says it started under the stairs 'where Orange Moll keeps her fruit'. Perhaps one of the orange-girls, of whom Nell Gwynn (q.v.) was one, went searching for fresh supplies with a naked flame. Pepys in his diary refers to Orange Moll several times, and gleaned many items of theatrical scandal from her. In 1682, when the companies of Drury Lane and Dorset Garden were amalgamated, the management engaged a new orange-woman. This led to endless disputes, and the matter was still unsettled when Orange Moll died.

MEI LAN-FANG (1894–1961), famous

Chinese actor, son and grandson of actors, known for the excellence of his playing of female roles in Peking Opera (q.v.). He was trained for the stage from the age of nine and at fourteen made his first appearance in public. Between 1919 and 1935 he visited Japan, the United States, Europe, and Russia, where he enjoyed the friendship of Stanislavsky and Nemirovich-Danchenko (qq.v.). He was the first to combine the dramatic techniques of the five roles in Peking opera into which the *tan* or female character is divided, and with his rise to fame in his early twenties the *tan* roles for the first time ousted the *loashêng*, or righteous elderly bearded male role, from its former pre-eminent place. During the Chinese civil war Mei Lan-Fang refused to appear on the stage, signifying his resolution by allowing his beard and moustaches to grow. In 1949 he returned to Peking and was appointed President of the Research Institute of Chinese Drama. He then returned to the stage and in 1958 celebrated his jubilee, retiring a year later.

Meininger Company. GEORGE II, DUKE OF SAXE-MEININGEN (1826–1914) and his morganatic wife ELLEN FRANZ (1839–1923), formerly an actress, established a resident group of actors attached to the Court theatre. The Duke, who directed the plays himself, and also designed the costumes and scenery, was ably assisted by the actor LUDWIG CHRONEGK (1837–91), who joined him in 1866 and was responsible for the controlling and disciplining of the company, and for the actual carrying-out of the Duke's intentions. The innovations for which the Meiningers became famous derived in part from the contemporary English stage. The Duke, whose first wife was a niece of Queen Victoria, often visited London, and was familiar with the methods of Charles Kean (q.v.). He followed his example in dividing his supers into small groups, each with a competent actor at its head. These latter remained in charge, and so gave coherence and continuity to the crowd scenes even when, on tour, the rest of the supers were recruited locally. The Duke also worked out the relationship of the various groups to one another and to the set, and insisted that all gestures should be within the period of the play and related to the style of the time. By the use of steps and rostrums he kept the action moving on different levels, and insisted that his star actors should from time to time play minor roles. Realizing the inadequacy of the conventional set, and again drawing his inspiration from England, he used the realistic box-set (q.v.), and so moved from two-dimensional to three-dimensional scenery. It was unfortunate that he never sought to abolish stage waits and so give Shakespeare's plays in one continuous, rapid flow, but otherwise his reforms were excellent. In 1874 his company appeared for the first time outside its own town when it visited Berlin. In 1881 it came to London, appearing at Drury Lane in *Julius Caesar*, *Twelfth Night*, and *The Winter's Tale* (in German), as well as in a number of German and other classics. Critical reaction was on the whole favourable and the *Athenaeum* went so far as to say 'so picturesque and so faultless' a performance of *Twelfth Night* had not been seen upon the modern stage. In the following years the company visited thirty-eight cities, including Brussels, where it was seen by Antoine (q.v.). Stanislavsky (q.v.) saw the Meiningers in Moscow on their second visit there in 1890 (their first was in 1885). Thus the two men who were to become the greatest exponents of stage realism, at the Théâtre-Libre and the Moscow Art Theatre (qq.v.), both came under the Meininger influence, which through them spread far into the twentieth century.

MEISL, KARL (1775–1853), Austrian playwright, who with Gleich and Bäuerle (qq.v.) represents the popular escapist theatre of Vienna during the troublesome times of the post-Napoleonic era. His numerous plays, though successful in their day, make arid reading. They depended very much on the skill with which they were produced and the accessories of costume, music, and magic. Meisl was at his best in parody, of which *Der lustige Fritz* (1818) was a good example.

MELLON, MRS. ALFRED [*née* SARAH JANE WOOLGAR] (1824–1909), English actress, who was on the stage as a child and made her adult début in London on 9 Oct. 1843 at the Adelphi under Ben Webster (q.v.), with whom she remained for many years. She appeared in a number of plays based on Dickens's novels, being seen at different times as Dot, Tilly, and Bertha in *The Cricket on the Hearth*, Mercy in *Martin Chuzzlewit*, and Mrs. Cratchit, one of her best parts, in *A*

Christmas Carol. Although she lacked the elegance needed for Old Comedy, she had plenty of high spirits and piquancy. She played opposite T. P. Cooke (q.v.) in his last appearance in Jerrold's *Black-Eyed Susan*, and was Anne Chute in the first production of Boucicault's *The Colleen Bawn* (1860). She retired in 1883.

MELLON, HARRIOT (1777–1837), English actress, who was with a strolling company at Stafford in 1795 when Sheridan (q.v.) saw her and engaged her for Drury Lane, where she remained until her retirement in 1815 on her marriage to the banker Mr. Coutts. She was at her best as the light impertinent chambermaids of comedy, in which parts Leigh Hunt (q.v.) much admired her. After her first husband's death she married the Duke of St. Albans, leaving the vast Coutts fortune to the daughter of Sir Francis Burdett, later the Baroness Burdett-Coutts, friend and patroness of Sir Henry Irving (q.v.).

MELMOTH, MRS. CHARLOTTE (1749–1823), a fine tragic actress, important in the annals of the early American stage. Born in England (her maiden name is unknown), she ran away from school with an actor named COURTNEY MELMOTH [really SAMUEL JACKSON PRATT] (1749–1814), and appeared with him in the provinces. They soon separated, but she continued to act under her married name, and was seen both at Covent Garden and Drury Lane before leaving for New York in 1793, where she made her début as Euphrasia in Murphy's *The Grecian Daughter.* The excellence of her acting, particularly as Lady Macbeth, made her a universal favourite, and caused many more tragedies to be added to the current repertoire. She was one of the leading actresses at the Park Theatre, New York (q.v.), when it first opened in 1798, and was later at the Chestnut Street Theatre (q.v.) in Philadelphia. She retired in 1812, and became a teacher of elocution in New York until her death.

MELNOTTE, VIOLET (1852–1935), English actress and theatre manageress, who took her stage name from the surname of the hero in Bulwer-Lytton's *The Lady of Lyons* (1838), her real name being unknown. After some years on the provincial stage she made her first appearance in London in 1880 with Charles Wyndham (q.v.), and in 1885 ventured into manage-

ment at the Avenue (see PLAYHOUSE) and Comedy theatres. Wishing to have her own theatre, she built the Trafalgar Square Theatre in 1892 in association with her husband FRANK WYATT (1852–1926), the original Duke of Plaza-Toro in Gilbert and Sullivan's *The Gondoliers*. This made a slow start, but as the Duke of York's (q.v.) it flourished under Charles Frohman, and eventually under Miss Melnotte herself.

Melodrama, a word of several meanings, but usually applied to plays popular all over Europe in the nineteenth century, whose elements were highly coloured and larger than life—the noble outlaw, the wronged maiden, the cold-blooded villain, working out their destinies against a background of ruined castles, haunted houses, and spectacular mountain scenery. Melodrama stems from the early works of Goethe (*Götz von Berlichingen*, 1773) and Schiller (*Die Räuber*, 1782), and its most important authors on the Continent were Kotzebue and Pixérécourt (qq.v.). It was first introduced into England through translations of their plays, particularly those made by Thomas Holcroft (q.v.), whose *A Tale of Mystery* (1802), based on Pixérécourt's *Coelina, ou l'Enfant de mystère* (1800), was the first work in England to be labelled a melodrama. It was mainly the use of music, first to separate the various incidents and later to underline them, that gave its name to this popular type of play, as *mélodrame* in its original use meant in Germany dialogue spoken to a musical accompaniment, and in France music accompanying a dumb show. But the new meaning soon took precedence over the older ones, and melodrama indicated everything that fed the popular appetite for horror and mystery, violence and double-dealing, but always with virtue triumphant. Gradually the music became less important and the setting of the play less Gothic. Planché's *The Brigand* (1829) was one of the last of the old-fashioned melodramas; the setting of Jerrold's *Fifteen Years of a Drunkard's Life* (1828) heralded an era of domestic melodrama, which ran concurrently with a vogue for plays based on real-life crimes —the anonymous *Maria Marten; or, the Murder in the Red Barn*, which became a classic of melodrama in the 1830s, or Fitz-ball's *Jonathan Bradford; or, the Murder at the Roadside Inn* (1823). The growth of a middle-class audience produced a new type of melodrama, notably at the Adelphi under Buckstone (q.v.). While the rougher element on the Surrey side enjoyed the horrors of real life borrowed from *Les Bohémiens de Paris* (1843), with its glimpses of the Paris (or London) underworld in slums and sewers, the prosperous merchant families enjoyed the equally spectacular but less violent domestic tragedies of the elder Dumas, among them *Pauline* (1840), seen by Queen Victoria at the Princess's Theatre in 1851, and *The Corsican Brothers* (1852), the latter adapted by Boucicault (q.v.). Among his other adaptations was one of *Les Pauvres de Paris*, which he economically retitled *The Poor of New York* (1851) or *The Poor of Liverpool* (1864), according to the town in which it was being acted. For London it became *The Poor of the London Streets* (1866). A new phenomenon at this time was the sudden success of the numerous dramatizations of popular novels by women writers—Harriet Beecher Stowe's *Uncle Tom's Cabin* (1852), Mrs. Henry Wood's *East Lynne* (1861), and Miss Braddon's *Lady Audley's Secret* (1862). These rivalled in popularity such plays as Tom Taylor's *The Ticket-of-Leave Man* (1863), based, like so many melodramas, on a French original, *Le Retour de Melun*, by Brisbarre and Nus. Few of the prolific dramatists of the time bothered to concoct their own plots, and all the melodramas staged by Irving (q.v.) at the Lyceum, from Leopold Lewis's *The Bells* in 1871 to Boucicault's *The Corsican Brothers* in 1880, originated on the Continent. Other actor-managers had their greatest successes with dramatizations of novels—Tree (q.v.) with du Maurier's *Trilby* (1895), Alexander (q.v.) with Anthony Hope's *The Prisoner of Zenda* (1896), Martin-Harvey (q.v.) with Dickens's *A Tale of Two Cities*, retitled *The Only Way* (1899), and Fred Terry (q.v.) with Baroness Orczy's *The Scarlet Pimpernel* (1903). Some exceptions over the years were *The Silver King* (1882), by H. A. Jones (q.v.) and H. Herman, *The Sign of the Cross* (1895), by Wilson Barrett (q.v.), and the melodramas popularized by William Terriss (q.v.) at the Adelphi. The turn of the century saw the spectacular melodramas staged at Drury Lane, with shipwrecks, railway accidents, earthquakes, and horse-racing, and the joint productions of the Melville brothers with *The Worst Woman in London* (1899) and *The Bad Girl of the*

Family (1909). Melodrama had come a long way from its original simplicity, which equated poverty with virtue and wealth with villainy. The day of true melodrama was over, though melodramatic elements continued to flourish in the theatre as they had done long before Kotzebue and Pixérécourt made them fashionable—even as far back as the plays of Euripides (q.v.).

Melodramma, a play with music, each element being equally important, which evolved in eighteenth-century Italy from the earlier pastoral (q.v.). The chief writers connected with it are Apostolo Zeno and Metastasio (qq.v.), whose libretti have since been used by innumerable operatic composers.

Melpomene, the Muse of Tragedy.

Melucha Theatre, see MOSCOW STATE JEWISH THEATRE.

MELVILLE, WALTER (1875–1937) and FREDERICK (1879–1938), two brothers who for twenty-five years were joint proprietors of the Lyceum (q.v.) in London, where they produced annually a spectacular pantomime, usually written by Fred. Elaborately produced, these filled the theatre to capacity for several months. The Melvilles, who jointly built the Prince's Theatre (see SHAFTESBURY THEATRE (2)), were also successful writers of highly coloured melodramas, simple, direct stories with virtue triumphant, much to the taste of their time. Walter was responsible for such masterpieces as *The Worst Woman in London* (1899) and *The Girl Who Took the Wrong Turning* (1906), and Fred for *Her Forbidden Marriage, The Ugliest Woman on Earth* (both 1904), and *The Bad Girl of the Family* (1909), all equally lurid, and equally successful in their day.

MENANDER (*c.* 342–292 B.C.), Greek dramatist, and the leading writer of the so-called New Comedy, as opposed to the Old Comedy of Aristophanes (q.v.). His plays were highly esteemed in his own day, and closely imitated by Plautus and Terence (qq.v.). For hundreds of years he was known to the modern world only indirectly through fragments of his works quoted by later writers, but in 1905 a papyrus, now in Cairo, was discovered, containing considerable portions of four plays—the *Heros*, the *Samia*, the *Epitrepontes*, and the *Perikeiromene*. The last was translated in 1941 with conjectural restorations by Gilbert Murray (q.v.) as *The Rape of the Locks*. In 1945 he made a similar reconstruction of the *Epitrepontes* as *The Arbitration*. In 1957 a fifth play, the *Dyskolos*, was found in a papyrus codex of the third century by Professor Martin of Geneva, who judged it to be a youthful work, written probably in 317 B.C. An English translation by Philip Vellacott, as *The Misanthrope*, was broadcast in 1959. Part of a sixth play by Menander, *The Man from Sicyon*, was discovered in 1963, and in 1965 further new fragments of *Misoumenos (The Man She Hated)* enabled experts to reconstitute the skeleton of the play.

From what is now known of Menander's work it is evident that the political, moral, and social climate of Athens had undergone great changes in the hundred years that had elapsed since Aristophanes. The exuberant fancy, burlesque, and lampooning of Old Comedy have vanished, and Menander, who is more romantic than comic, is closer in style to the later nontragic dramas of Euripides (q.v.). His plays are delicate, neatly-drawn comments on bourgeois city life, concerned chiefly with the ill-used maiden or the slavefoundling who turns out to be well born and therefore deserving of love and marriage. The use made by later dramatists of Menander's plots and personages led to the development of some of the stock characters of later comedy—the angry old man, the good-hearted rake, the officious slave—all of which he portrayed with great liveliness and charm. But as his plays dealt almost exclusively with the fortunes of individuals, they no longer provided scope for the chorus (q.v.), so important in the earlier Greek theatre, and it became nothing more than a group of singers and dancers, often tipsy revellers interrupting the continuity of the plot. Whereas the early Greek choruses were provided with lyrics of great poetic beauty, the texts of Menander's plays merely indicate 'something for the chorus'.

MENKEN, ADAH ISAACS [really DOLORES ADIOS FUERTES] (1835–68), American actress, whose theatrical reputation seems to rest entirely on her playing of Mazeppa, in a dramatization of Byron's poem, 'in a state of virtual nudity when bound to the back of the wild horse'. This equestrian drama was first given at the Coburg (see OLD VIC) in London in 1823, and continued to be popular during the next fifty years, though it was not until 1859 in New York that a woman, Charlotte Crampton, essayed the part of the hero. Menken first played it in 1863 in California, then in New York, and in 1864 at Astley's in London. In 1856 she had married John Isaacs Menken and kept his name through subsequent matrimonial and other adventures. She appears to have exercised a fatal fascination over 'literary gentlemen', including Swinburne, Dickens, and the elder Dumas.

MERCER, DAVID (1928–80), English dramatist, who was already well known for his television plays when in 1965 the Royal Shakespeare Company at the Aldwych staged his one-act political play, *The Governor's Lady*. In the same year Peter O'Toole appeared as the anti-hero of *Ride a Cock Horse*. These two plays won for their author the *Evening Standard* Award for the most promising dramatist of the year. In 1966 and 1970 the Royal Shakespeare produced *Belcher's Luck* and *After Haggerty*, and also in 1970 Michael Hordern appeared at the Criterion in *Flint*, playing the lecherous and agnostic clergyman who elopes with a pregnant Irish girl.

MERCIER, LOUIS-SÉBASTIEN (1740–1814), French dramatist, and an exponent of the *drame bourgeois* initiated by Diderot (q.v.). His plays were more successful abroad than in his own country, and were immensely popular in Germany on account of their unimpeachable morality and declamatory style. The most characteristic is *La Brouette du vinaigrier* (1784), the story of a marriage between a wealthy girl and the son of a working-class man which brought tears to the eyes of its audiences, as did the earlier *Jenneval* (1768)—an adaptation of Lillo's *The London Merchant* in which the hero escapes punishment by a last-minute conversion. Mercier, who admired Shakespeare with reservations, gave his translation of *Romeo and Juliet* a happy ending and reduced *King Lear* to a tale of a bourgeois household quarrelling over the misdeeds of the servants. Having taken refuge in Switzerland on account of his political views, Mercier returned to Paris on the outbreak of the Revolution and as a deputy he voted against the execution of

Louix XVI and in favour of a life sentence. He was later imprisoned, but was saved from the guillotine by the fall of Robespierre in 1794.

Mercury Theatre, LONDON, at Notting Hill Gate, a small but well-equipped playhouse in a former chapel, opened in 1933 by Ashley Dukes (q.v.) for the production of new and uncommercial plays and to serve as a centre for his wife's Ballet Rambert. The first production, on 19 Oct., was an adaptation of Molière's *Amphitryon*. The success of the following year was a new Russian play by Kataev, performed in translation as *Squaring the Circle*. The most important event of the theatre's early years, however, was the first London production on 1 Nov. 1935 of T. S. Eliot's *Murder in the Cathedral*, transferred from the Chapter House at Canterbury Cathedral. Two years later Auden and Isherwood's poetic play, *The Ascent of F.6*, was first seen in London, and in 1943 O'Neill's *Days Without End*. In 1945 and 1946 the Mercury became the home of poetic drama with Norman Nicholson's *The Old Man of the Mountains*, Ronald Duncan's *This Way to the Tomb!*, with music by Benjamin Britten, Anne Ridler's *The Shadow Factory*, and Christopher Fry's *A Phoenix Too Frequent*, all directed by E. Martin Browne (q.v.). In 1947 Saroyan's *The Beautiful People* and O'Neill's *S.S. Glencairn* both had their London premières at the Mercury, and in 1952 there was a performance in French of Genet's *Les Bonnes*. After the production of two of Nicholas Stuart Gray's children's plays, *Beauty and the Beast* in Dec. 1952 and *The Princess and the Swineherd* in Jan. 1953, there were no further productions for some time, and the theatre was used only by the Ballet Rambert until in 1966 the International Theatre Club presented a season of new plays, beginning with Obaldia's *Jenusia* on 7 July. The theatre was then used intermittently by visiting companies. In 1967 the Café La Mama troupe from New York was seen in *Futz*, by Rochelle Owens, and *Times Square*, by Leonard Melfi, and in 1968 Arrabal's *The Labyrinth* had a short run. In 1970 the Other Company, directed by Naftali Yavin, was seen in two experimental impromptu plays, *The Journey* and *The Pit*, involving audience participation.

(For the Mercury Theatre, New York, see COMEDY THEATRE (2).)

Mermaid Society, a small play-producing society founded by Philip Carr which in the 1900s staged a number of little-known Elizabethan works by Marlowe, Jonson, Webster, Ford, and others. It was also responsible for a production of Milton's *Comus* in the Botanical Gardens at Oxford in 1903 and of Jonson's masque, *A Hue and Cry after Cupid*, at Stratford-upon-Avon in 1904. Unfortunately information about the society is difficult to obtain and research into its work and influence is badly needed.

Mermaid Theatre, LONDON, originally a private theatre designed on Elizabethan lines by Michael Stringer and C. Walter Hodges for Bernard Miles (q.v.), and erected in a hall attached to Miles's house in St. John's Wood. It opened on 9 Sept. 1951 with a performance of Purcell's 'Dido and Aeneas', followed a week later by *The Tempest* and in 1952 by Middleton's *A Trick to Catch the Old One*. In 1953, to celebrate the coronation of Elizabeth II, the Mermaid was re-erected in the City of London for performances of *As You Like It*, *Macbeth*, and Jonson's *Eastward Ho!* On 17 Oct. 1956 the foundations of a permanent theatre, designed by Elidir Davies, were laid at Puddle Dock, near Blackfriars Bridge, on a site where Philip Rosseter (q.v.) had tried to build a theatre in 1615. The new Mermaid, built inside a bombed warehouse, opened on 28 May 1959 with a musical version of Fielding's *Rape Upon Rape* entitled *Lock Up Your Daughters*, which was an immediate success and has been several times revived. Since then there have been many interesting productions, mostly for short runs, in accordance with Miles's declared policy. These have included a number of plays for children, Brecht's *The Life of Galileo* (1960), parts of the Wakefield Mystery cycle (1961), Mayakovsky's *The Bed-Bug* (1962), the Living Theatre company from New York in Kenneth H. Brown's *The Brig* (1964), *Left-Handed Liberty*, by John Arden, written to commemorate the 750th anniversary of the sealing of Magna Carta, and Peter Luke's *Hadrian VII* (1968). This last, based on the works of Frederick Rolfe (Baron Corvo) and first seen at the Birmingham Repertory Theatre in 1967, had an unexpected and spectacular success, mainly due to the fine acting of Alec McCowen (q.v.), and was given an unusually long run at the Mermaid before being transferred to the

Haymarket. In 1970 performances of *Henry IV, Parts 1 and 2*, ostensibly being acted in a barn by an eighteenth-century band of strolling players, starred Bernard Miles as Falstaff.

MERRY, MRS. [*née* ANNE BRUNTON] (1769–1808), an actress well known in America, though born and educated in England. Sister of Louisa Brunton (q.v.), she made her first appearance on the stage at Bath, at the age of fifteen, and a year later was seen at Covent Garden, where her father, JOHN BRUNTON (1741–1822), was already established. She retired in 1792 on her marriage to ROBERT MERRY (1755–98), but when a few years later he lost all his money she accepted an offer from Wignell (q.v.) to join his company in Philadelphia. She made her first appearance there on 5 Dec. 1796 as Shakespeare's Juliet, and was soon accepted as the leading American actress of her day. Widowed in 1798, she married Wignell in 1803 but he died soon after, and in 1806 she married William Warren (q.v.). She then made several successful appearances at the Park Theatre in New York under Dunlap (q.v.), who had watched her début at Covent Garden and recommended her to Wignell, and was at the height of her success when she died suddenly in childbirth.

MERSON, BILLY [really WILLIAM HENRY THOMPSON] (1881–1947), a music-hall performer whose best-known songs were 'The Spaniard that Blighted my Life' and 'The Good Ship Yakihickidula'. He went into pantomime and revue, and in 1925 starred at Drury Lane as Hard-Boiled Herman in the musical comedy *Rose Marie*. At the Shaftesbury (q.v.) in 1926 he presented and played in a musical comedy called *My Son John*, and he also appeared in Edgar Wallace's play *The Lad* (1928).

MESSEL, OLIVER (1905–78), English artist and stage designer, who in 1958 was appointed C.B.E. in recognition of his services to the art of the theatre. He first attracted attention with masks and costumes designed for revues staged by Cochran (q.v.) in the late 1920s, and in 1932 was given the task of converting the stage and auditorium of the Lyceum (q.v.) into a cathedral for a revival of *The Miracle* directed by Reinhardt (q.v.). He has since worked in every form of theatrical art—opera, ballet, film, and straight

play—one of his most memorable settings being that for Anouilh's *Ring Round the Moon* (1950) translated by Christopher Fry (q.v.). He also designed the settings for two of Fry's own plays, *The Lady's Not For Burning* (1949) and *The Dark is Light Enough* (1954). He was responsible for the interior decoration of Miki Sekers's private theatre in Whitehaven, and is the author of *Stage Designs and Costumes* (1934).

METASTASIO [really PIETRO ANTONIO DOMENICO BONAVENTURA TRAPASSI] (1698–1782), Italian dramatist, poet, and musician. A precocious child, he wrote his first play, a tragedy entitled *Il Giustino*, at the age of fourteen, and in 1729 succeeded Apostolo Zeno (q.v.) as Court poet in Vienna, a post which he retained under Charles VI and Maria Theresa. He is now best remembered for his opera libretti, amounting to about thirty in all, which between 1724 and 1840 were set more than one thousand times, attracting successive generations of composers, among them Gluck and Handel, by their symmetrical elegance and fluent versification. Although Metastasio's masterpiece is probably *Attilio Regolo* (written in 1740, but not performed, in a setting by Hasse, until 1750), the best-known, because of its association with Mozart, who set it in 1791, is *La Clemenza di Tito* (1732).

Method, THE, the name given to an introspective approach to acting based on the system evolved by Stanislavsky (q.v.) for the actors at the Moscow Art Theatre, and set out by him in such books as *An Actor Prepares* (1926). The Method first came into prominence in the United States during the 1930s, when it was adopted by the Group Theatre (q.v.) in its reaction against what were considered the externalizing, stereotyped techniques current on the New York and London stages. Its present notoriety rests mainly on its adoption by the Actors' Studio, founded in 1947 by Elia Kazan (q.v.) and others, joined later by Lee Strasberg (q.v.), its present head. Strong feelings have been aroused by the Method, its upholders maintaining that it enables the actor to give a true interpretation of any part, based on personal experience; in fact to 're-act' and not to 'act', to 'be' and not to 'do'. Its opponents, on the other hand, point out that it intensifies the actors' self-absorption to the exclusion of the audience, and is suitable only for the type of play Stanislavsky was dealing with, notably Chekhov, and not even for Chekhov in translation, nor for Elizabethan or Restoration drama. Its greatest successes so far have been in modern American plays, particularly those of Tennessee Williams (q.v.). It is, in the long run, only one of many valid methods of approaching a part, all of which are simply convenient ways of making actors work hard and concentrate on their job. The Method has suffered most from bad actors who blame it, rather than their own inadequacy, for their failure to use it properly. In the hands of a teacher like Stanislavsky it may give excellent results. But once codified, it is open to partial, or even complete, misunderstanding, and may do more harm than good. The Method was introduced into England in 1956 but with little result, perhaps because good English actors, like good actors everywhere, are already Method actors without realizing it, since Stanislavsky's only aim was to provide material in the way of exercises, improvisation, introspection, and discussion, which would enable an actor to develop his latent possibilities and from there go on to build up his technique. But many who enjoyed the preliminary stages baulked at the subsequent need for hard work, and so brought discredit on the system. From the audience's point of view the niceties of Method or non-Method acting are unimportant, and they are content to leave the means of production to the actor and director provided the end-product is satisfactory.

Metropolitan Music-Hall, LONDON, in the Edgware Road, a music-hall which stood on the site of an old inn, the White Lion, and retained part of the earlier building in its façade until 1905. As Turnham's, a 'new-style' music-hall named after its proprietor, it opened on 8 Dec. 1862, and was renamed the Metropolitan in 1864. It prospered in spite of constant changes of management, and was rebuilt in 1897, but eventually became a television studio and closed on 6 Dec. 1962, being finally demolished in 1963.

Metropolitan Casino, NEW YORK, see BROADWAY THEATRE (3).

Metropolitan Theatre, NEW YORK, built on the site of Tripler Hall, which was burnt down on 7 Jan. 1854. The theatre opened unsuccessfully on 18 Sept. and soon became a circus. It was occasionally used for plays, and in Sept. 1855 Rachel (q.v.), with a French company, appeared there in Racine's *Phèdre* and Scribe and Legouvé's *Adrienne Lecouvreur*. In the following December Laura Keene (q.v.) took over and in spite of prejudice against a woman manager was doing well when she lost her lease on a technicality. She was succeeded by Burton (q.v.), and in 1859 by Boucicault (q.v.), who reopened the theatre as the Winter Garden on 14 Sept. with *Dot*, his own dramatization of Dickens's *The Cricket on the Hearth.* It was at this theatre, on 25 Nov. 1864, that Edwin Booth (q.v.) appeared as Brutus in *Julius Caesar* with his father as Cassius and his brother John as Antony. This was the second and final appearance on the New York stage of Lincoln's assassin. It was here also that Edwin Booth appeared in public for the first time after Lincoln's murder, to be greeted by an enthusiastic audience, who remembered his record run of a hundred performances in *Hamlet* in 1864–5. The audience was again assembling to see Booth as Romeo when, on 23 Mar. 1867, this historic theatre was burnt down and not rebuilt.

MEYERHOLD, VSEVOLOD EMILIEVICH (1874–1940), Russian actor and director, who joined the Moscow Art Theatre (q.v.) on its foundation in 1898. From 1902 to 1905 he toured the provinces with the Society of New Drama, which he founded, and in 1905 was invited by Stanislavsky (q.v.) to take charge of productions at a newly organized studio which, however, soon closed. From 1906 to 1907 he worked with Vera Komisarjevskaya (q.v.), and was able to put into practice the symbolic or stylized method, based on the idea of the actor as a super-marionette entirely subordinated to the director as envisaged by Gordon Craig (q.v.), which he had hoped to develop at the Moscow Art Theatre studio. This led to a break with Komisarjevskaya, and Meyerhold then staged some brilliant productions at the Imperial Theatres in Petrograd—the Marinsky and the Alexandrinsky (qq.v.)—and at the same time continued experimental work in his own studio under the influence of the stylized traditions of the *commedia dell'arte* (q.v.). On the outbreak of the Revolution Meyerhold was the first theatre director to offer his services to the new government, and in 1920 he was appointed head of the Theatre Section of the People's Commissariat for Education, where he began a campaign to reorganize the theatre on Revolutionary lines. His views did not entirely coincide with those of the Soviet government, as represented by Lunacharsky (q.v.), since he was all for the immediate revolutionizing of such theatres as remained, whereas Lunacharsky preferred to absorb them gradually, strengthening what was healthy and rejecting what was decadent, a process which twenty years later left Meyerhold high and dry. Yet nothing can detract from the enthusiasm, sincerity, and originality of his early work at the time when he developed his famous system of 'biomechanics' (q.v.). He was the first director to stage a Soviet play, *Mystery-Bouffe* (1918) by Mayakovsky (q.v.), whose *The Bed-Bug* (1929) and *The Bath House* (1930) he also directed. In 1936, with the triumph of Socialist Realism (q.v.), he incurred the displeasure of the authorities and was charged with having a pernicious 'foreign' influence on the Soviet theatre. His theatre was closed in 1938, and he and his wife, Zinaida Raikh, later disappeared. He is presumed to have died in prison. In recent years his reputation as an innovator and vital force in the emergence of the Soviet theatre has grown considerably, and the articles, notes for production, and other writings which he left behind show him to have been not only a great actor and producer but a keen scholar with an original and creative mind. Two volumes of his writing are being prepared for publication, and it is hoped that a full biography will appear shortly.

Mezzetino, a *zanni* or servant of the *commedia dell'arte*, with many of the characteristics of Brighella or Scapino (q.v.), though more polished. Towards the end of the seventeenth century (c. 1682) the role was altered and elaborated by Angelo Costantini (q.v.), who adopted red and white as the distinguishing colours of his costume as opposed to the green and white stripes of Scapino. A later French Mezzetin was the actor Préville (q.v.), of the Comédie-Française, who was painted by Van Loo in the part.

MICKIEWICZ, ADAM (1798–1855), the outstanding poet of Poland, whose great romantic poem, *Forefathers' Eve*, is the most important work of the Polish poetic theatre. It was composed in a fragmentary manner during his long exile in Paris, Parts II and IV being published in 1823, Part III in 1832, and the unfinished Part I after his death. It was first co-ordinated and staged by Wyspiański (q.v.) in 1901.

Middle Comedy, a term applied to the last two plays of Aristophanes (q.v.), the *Ecclesiazusae* and the *Plutus*, and those of his immediate successors, in which much of the spirit of revelry has evaporated. The plot becomes more important, the chorus less so, and the situation in general is social rather than political, with a background of private life.

Middlesex Music-Hall, LONDON, a famous hall which stood in Drury Lane. Originally attached to a public-house called the Great Mogul, it opened as the Mogul Saloon on 27 Dec. 1847 and was nicknamed the 'Old Mo', a sobriquet which it retained even when it was renamed the Middlesex Music-Hall in 1851. In 1872 it was rebuilt and subsequently enlarged, and many famous music-hall stars made their début there. In 1911 it was rebuilt as the New Middlesex Theatre of Varieties, and in 1919 it was converted into a theatre, opening as the Winter Garden on 20 May. One of its outstanding successes was *The Vagabond King* (1927), based on Justin McCarthy's *If I Were King*, with music by Friml. In 1946 Joan Temple's *No Room at the Inn*, which dealt with the evacuation of children during the Second World War, began a long run. The last important production at this theatre, which closed in 1959 and was demolished in 1965, was *Hotel Paradiso* (1956), a farce based on Feydeau's *L'Hôtel du Libre Échange*. In 1973 the New London Theatre opened on the site.

MIDDLETON, THOMAS (c. 1570–1627), English dramatist, who collaborated with Dekker (q.v.) in *The Honest Whore* (1604) and *The Roaring Girl* (1610), and alone wrote a number of plays of which the best was *A Trick to Catch the Old One* (1604–5), to which Massinger (q.v.) may be indebted for the idea of his *A New Way to Pay Old Debts* (c. 1623). Among Middleton's other works the most important are *A Chaste Maid in Cheapside* (1611) and *Women Beware Women* (1621). The latter was revived by the Royal Shakespeare

Company at the Arts Theatre, London, in the summer of 1962, and shows the mingling of fine poetry, melodramatic traits, and feminine psychology which characterizes the best of Middleton's work. He was also the author of a notorious political satire, *A Game at Chess* (1624). This dealt with the fruitless attempts which were being made to unite the royal houses of England and Spain, and at the demand of the Spanish Ambassador Middleton was severely admonished and perhaps imprisoned. The play was not revived, but it had proved immensely popular and its resounding success was not soon forgotten. Middleton, who collaborated with Rowley (q.v.) in *The Changeling* (1622), was also responsible for a number of masques and pageants now lost. He has been credited by some critics with *The Revenger's Tragedy* (1606), usually attributed to Tourneur (q.v.).

MIELZINER, Jo (1901–76), an outstanding American scene designer, who was for a short time an actor. His first stage designs were done for the Lunts (q.v.) in Molnár's *The Guardsman* (1924), since when he has been responsible for the décor of a wide variety of plays, among them *Romeo and Juliet* (1934) for Katharine Cornell (q.v.) and *Hamlet* (1936) for John Gielgud (q.v.); *Winterset* (1935), *The Wingless Victory* (1936), and *High Tor* (1937), by Maxwell Anderson (q.v.); *The Glass Menagerie* (1945), *A Streetcar Named Desire* (1947), *Summer and Smoke* (1948), and *Cat on a Hot Tin Roof* (1955), by Tennessee Williams (q.v.); *Death of a Salesman* (1949), by Arthur Miller (q.v.); and a number of musicals, including *The Boys From Syracuse* (1938), *Finian's Rainbow* (1947), *Mister Roberts* (1948), *Guys and Dolls* (1950), and *The King and I* (1951). He was also responsible for the design of the Washington Square Theatre (q.v.) and for the décor of its productions of Miller's *After the Fall* and Behrman's *But for Whom Charlie* (both 1964), and, with the Finnish architect, Eero Saarinen, he designed the Vivian Beaumont Repertory Theatre (see LINCOLN CENTER).

MIKHOELS, SALOMON [really SALOMON MIKHAILOVICH VOVSKY] (1890–1948), Jewish actor and producer, and from 1928 until his death head of the Moscow State Jewish Theatre (q.v.). He was one of the original members of the Jewish Theatre Studio formed in Leningrad by Granovsky (q.v.) in 1919, and came into prominence two years later with a performance in Sholom Aleichem's *Agents*. He soon became the company's leading actor and in 1928 took over the directorship from Granovsky. One of his finest performances was given as King Lear in Radlov's production of the play in 1935.

MILES, SIR BERNARD (1907–), English actor and director, founder of the Mermaid Theatre (q.v.), who made his first appearance on the stage in 1930. He spent many years as a general utility man in repertory companies and was so for a time with the Late Joys at the Players (q.v.). At the first Mermaid he appeared as Caliban in *The Tempest* and as Macbeth, and at the second produced and acted in *As You Like It*, *Macbeth* again, and Jonson's *Eastward Ho!* Since the opening of the third Mermaid Theatre in May 1959 he has devoted his whole time to it, and has also been seen, among other parts, as Long John Silver in a dramatization of Stevenson's *Treasure Island* and in the title-role of Brecht's *The Life of Galileo*. In 1969 he was knighted for services to the theatre. In all his efforts to provide London with a new and experimental playhouse he has been ably assisted by his actress-wife JOSEPHINE WILSON, who has appeared in a number of his productions, notably as Lady Macbeth.

Miles's Musick House, LONDON, see SADLER'S WELLS THEATRE.

MILLAR, GERTIE (1879–1952), one of the most beautiful and well-known of the famous Gaiety Girls (see GAIETY), who in 1924, after the death of her first husband, the composer Lionel Monckton, married the Earl of Dudley. The daughter of a Bradford mill-worker, she first appeared on the stage at the age of thirteen in pantomime. In 1901 she made her first appearance at the Gaiety in *The Toreador*, and was first seen in New York in 1908 in *The Girls of Gottenberg*. Among her best-remembered roles were Prudence in *The Quaker Girl* (1910) and Lady Babbie in *Gipsy Love* (1912). She retired in 1918, making her last appearance at the Prince of Wales' in the title-role of *Flora*.

MILLAR, RONALD (1919–), English actor and dramatist, who made his first appearance on the stage in the revue

Swinging the Gate (1940), and subsequently was seen in a number of productions in London before in 1946 he gave up acting to devote himself entirely to playwriting. Among his early plays, of which the first was a thriller, *Murder from Memory* (1942), the most successful were *Frieda* (1946) and *Waiting for Gillian* (1954), but it was with a farce, *The Bride and the Bachelor* (1956), and its sequel, *The Bride Comes Back* (1960), in both of which Cicely Courtneidge and Robertson Hare appeared, that he first came into prominence. He had already, in 1946, successfully dramatized a novel by Storm Jameson, *The Other Side*, and in 1961 he applied the same technique to three novels by C. P. Snow, making eminently successful stage versions of *The Affair* (1961), *The New Men* (1962), and *The Masters* (1963). These scenes from academic life in Cambridge, Millar's own university, were followed by *Robert and Elizabeth* (1964), a musical on the Brownings, and an incursion into politics with *Number Ten* (1967), the dramatization of a book about the inner workings of Downing Street with Alastair Sim as the Prime Minister, and by a farcical comedy, *They Don't Grow on Trees* (1968), in which Dora Bryan appeared in eight different roles. In 1970 *Abelard and Heloise*, based partly on Helen Waddell's life of Abelard, caused some comment because of its nude love-scene between Diana Rigg and Keith Michell and a somewhat realistic portrayal of Abelard's castration, but had a long run, in spite of a mixed reception from the critics.

MILLER, ARTHUR (1915–), American dramatist, whose first successful play, after some ten years of playwriting, was *All My Sons* (1947; London, 1948), an exposure of war profiteering. This gained the New York Drama Critics' Circle award, as did Miller's next play, *Death of a Salesman* (1949), which also received the Pulitzer Prize for Drama. It was followed by *The Crucible* (1953) and by a double bill of two one-act plays, *A View from the Bridge* and *A Memory of Two Mondays* (1955). Rewritten in three acts, *A View from the Bridge* was seen in London in 1956, as was *The Crucible*, directed by George Devine at the Royal Court. It was widely believed, though Miller denied it, that his marriage to the film-star Marilyn Monroe, which ended in divorce, had provided the background to his next

play, *After the Fall* (1964). It was with this play that the Vivian Beaumont Repertory Company opened its first season at the Washington Square Theatre (q.v.) in New York. (It was seen at the Belgrade, Coventry, in 1967.) Later in 1964 the company appeared in Miller's *Incident at Vichy*, based on an incident of the Second World War, which was seen in London in 1966. Neither of these plays pleased the critics, and in 1968 Miller returned to the scene of his early successful plays—American family life—with *The Price*, which, after its production in New York, was seen at the Dublin Festival and in London in 1969.

MILLER, HENRY (1860–1926), American actor-manager, who after touring in Canada and the United States became leading man at the Empire Theatre (q.v.) in New York. He first went into management in 1906, producing and playing in the epoch-making play, *The Great Divide*, by William Vaughn Moody (q.v.) at the Princess Theatre in New York. He also appeared in it at the Adelphi in London in 1909. In 1918 he opened his own theatre in New York (see HENRY MILLER'S THEATRE). He died suddenly during rehearsals for Dodd's *A Stranger in the House*. By his wife Bijou (see HERON) he was the father of GILBERT HERON MILLER (1884–1967), who became a well-known theatre manager in London and New York, being lessee of the St. James's Theatre (q.v.) in London from 1918 until its demolition in 1958.

MILLER, JONATHAN WOLFE (1934–), English actor and director, who qualified as a doctor at Cambridge, where he also acted in several Footlights Revues. After the unexpected success at the Edinburgh Festival of the 1960 revue, *Beyond the Fringe*, of which he was co-author with Alan Bennett, Peter Cook, and Dudley Moore, he deserted medicine for the stage and appeared in *Beyond the Fringe* in London and in New York, where it had a long run. He also directed his first play, John Osborne's *Under Plain Cover*, for the Royal Court in 1962. Since 1964 he has devoted most of his time to directing rather than acting, having been responsible for the production of Robert Lowell's triple bill, *The Old Glory*, off-Broadway in 1964, and of Minoff and Price's *Come Live With Me* on Broadway in 1967, in which year he also directed Lowell's adaptation of Aeschylus' *Prometheus Bound* at the Yale Drama School and of Herman Melville's *Benito Cereno* at the Mermaid in London. In 1968 he directed Sheridan's *The School for Scandal* for the Nottingham Playhouse. Since then he has concentrated on Shakespeare, directing *King Lear* for Nottingham in 1970, and in the same year *The Merchant of Venice*, with Olivier as Shylock, for the National Theatre at the Old Vic, *The Tempest* for the Mermaid, and *Twelfth Night*, with a mixed group from Oxford and Cambridge, for a production in the Middle Temple Hall.

Mime, from the Greek word for 'imitation', used to describe two different though related forms of dramatic entertainment and also the actors who appeared in them. The first form was that of a crudely realistic sketch, with dialogue, which appeared early in Greek dramatic history and had some influence on the Old Comedy of Aristophanes (q.v.). It flourished among the Doric peoples of Greece and later in southern Italy, influencing the development of Roman comedy, particularly that of Plautus (q.v.), and reaching in Imperial times almost incredible depths of indecency. The secondary meaning of mime was used for a play without words in which dialogue was replaced by the actor's gestures, movements, and facial expression. It is in this sense that the word is used today, both for the conveyance of meaning without words in ballet and for the work of such modern mimes as Jean-Louis Barrault and Marcel Marceau (qq.v.), who continue the nineteenth-century traditions of Deburau (q.v.) and of such silent dramas as the three-act *L'Enfant prodigue*, which in turn derived from the practices of the *commedia dell'arte* (q.v.). Modern mimes are usually accompanied by music, and properties may be used but are more often left to the imagination of the audience stimulated by the actor's art. A practical knowledge of mime is essential to every professional actor and has also proved useful in the development of amateurs, who often find it easier initially to express emotion in action rather than in dialogue. The educational aspect of mime has led to its adoption in schools and drama courses, and taken it far from its crude and boisterous beginnings.

Minnesingers, see MASTERSINGERS.

Minnesota Theatre Company, see GUTHRIE, SIR TYRONE.

MINOTIS, ALEXIS (1906–), Greek actor and director, who from 1931 to 1970 was associated with the Greek National Theatre, together with his wife, Katina Paxinou (q.v.). He made his first appearance on the stage in 1925, and in 1930 made his New York début as Orestes in a Greek production of Euripides' *Electra*. Returning to Greece, he played a wide range of ancient and modern parts for the National Theatre, directing many of the plays in which he appeared. He was first seen in London in 1939, when he played Hamlet. Among his other Shakespeare parts are Shylock, Lear, and Richard III. Since 1955 he has been responsible for the production of many classical tragedies in the open-air theatre at Epidaurus. Among the modern plays with which he has been connected are Fry's *The Dark is Light Enough* in 1958, and Dürrenmatt's *The Visit* in 1961 and *The Physicists* in 1963. In 1966 he appeared in London during the World Theatre season, playing Oedipus to his wife's Jocasta in Sophocles' *Oedipus Rex*, Talthybius to her Hecuba in Euripides' play of that name, and Oedipus again in Sophocles' *Oedipus at Colonus*. He then formed his own company, which presents mainly modern European plays.

Minstrel, the generic name for the professional entertainer of the Middle Ages, who flourished from the eleventh to the fifteenth centuries. Dressed in bright clothes, with flat-heeled shoes, clean-shaven face, and short hair, like the pantomime players of Imperial Rome, he tramped across Europe with his instrument on his back, harassed by the hostility of the Church and the restrictions of petty officialdom. Equally welcome in the marketplace or the nobleman's hall, he played his part in religious festivities and probably influenced the development of liturgical drama (q.v.); he also enlivened the tedium of pilgrimages—it was the lack of a minstrel that made Chaucer's pilgrims embark on the telling of tales—and he kept alive many theatrical traditions handed down from Greece and Rome. Even before the formation of guilds (in France in 1321; in England in 1469) there were different grades of minstrels. At the top of the profession were the poets and musicians like Blondel and Rahere (q.v.), attached to the households of kings and noblemen, whose usefulness ended when printing was invented. Next came the itinerant but respectable groups whose repertory included some rudimentary plays, farces, or dialogues suited to middle-class audiences. Lastly came the vast anonymous horde of little people—travelling singly or in pairs—rope-walkers, fire-eaters, acrobats, conjurors, tumblers, jugglers, puppet-masters, and bear-leaders, who appealed chiefly to the un-learned. They survived the Renaissance, and their lineal descendants provided the circus and music-hall artistes of a later day.

Minstrel Show, an entertainment which originated in the Negro patter songs of Jim Crow (see T. D. RICE), and from his burlesques of Shakespeare and opera, to which Negro songs were added. From 1840 to 1880 the minstrel show was the most popular form of amusement in the United States, whence it spread to England. Unlike the music-hall (q.v.), which was intended for adults only, it was essentially a family entertainment, in a hall and not in a theatre. The performers were at first white men with blacked faces (whence the name Burnt-cork Minstrels), but later true Negroes. Sitting in a semi-circle with their primitive instruments, banjos, tambourines, one-stringed fiddles, bones, etc., they sang plaintive coon songs and sentimental ballads interspersed with soft-shoe dances and outbursts of back-chat between the Interlocutor and Bones, the 'end-men'. Their humour was simple and repetitive, and after a great burst of popularity the Minstrels gradually faded away, some to the music-halls (see CHIRGWIN and STRATTON), some to stroll along the beach at seaside resorts in the summer in traditional minstrel costume—tight striped trousers and waistcoat and tall white hat or straw boater—singing and playing their banjos. Among the most famous troupes were the Christy Minstrels, the Burgess and Moore, and the Mohawks. The original formula of the Burnt-cork Minstrels was successfully revived by B.B.C. Television in the late 1940s with the Kentucky Minstrels and in the 1960s with the Black and White Minstrels, who as a live show had a long run at the Victoria Palace in London from 1962 onwards.

Miracle Play, see MYSTERY PLAY.

MIRBEAU, OCTAVE (1848–1917), French dramatist, whose realistic plays deal with contemporary problems in the style of Henri Becque (q.v.). Among them are *Les Mauvais Bergers* (1897), a study of the struggle between labour and capital, and his best play, *Les Affaires sont les affaires* (1903), a mordant satire on the big-business man who is a slave to his wealth. As *Business is Business*, this was seen in New York in 1904 and in London a year later.

Mirror Theatre, LONDON, see HOLBORN THEATRE.

Misrule, ABBOT or LORD of, see FEAST OF FOOLS.

Miss Kelly's Theatre, LONDON, see ROYALTY THEATRE (2).

MISTINGUETT [really JEANNE-MARIE BOURGEOIS] (1875–1956), French actress and dancer, the possessor of the most beautiful, and most highly insured, legs in the entertainment world. She made her first appearances in music-hall, and in 1907 was seen in straight comedy, leaving it to go to the Moulin Rouge, of which she was for some years part-proprietor. With Maurice Chevalier (q.v.) as her partner, she appeared in some sensational dances at the Folies-Bergère and was also seen at the Casino de Paris. She made her only appearance in London in Dec. 1947 at the Casino Theatre. In her early days she was an eccentric comedienne of great original-ity, specializing in the portrayal of low-class Parisian women, but later she became a queen of revue, her fabulous hats and dresses attracting as much attention as her songs and sketches. She wrote a volume of reminiscences of which an English translation by Hubert Griffith was published in 1938.

MITCHELL, MAGGIE [really MARGARET] JULIA (1832–1918), American actress, who first appeared on the stage at thirteen, playing children's parts at the Bowery Theatre (q.v.) and being particularly admired as Dickens's Oliver Twist. After some years on tour she became leading lady of Burton's company in 1857 and three years later played the part with which she is mainly associated—Fanchon in an adaptation of George Sand's novel *La Petite Fadette*. Although she was good in other parts, notably as Charlotte

Brontë's *Jane Eyre* and as Pauline in Bulwer-Lytton's *The Lady of Lyons*, she was constantly forced by an admiring public to return to Fanchon, which she played for over twenty years, remaining to the end a small, winsome, sprite-like figure, overflowing with vitality.

MITCHELL, WILLIAM (1798–1856), American manager, who worked in the English theatre for many years before emigrating to New York in 1836. There, in 1839, he took over the Olympic Theatre, opened it with Townley's *High Life Below Stairs*, and embarked on a long series of triumphs which brought the theatre fame and prosperity. He was himself an excellent actor, being particularly admired as Vincent Crummles in a dramatization of Dickens's *Nicholas Nickleby*, and he was also good in burlesque. He retired in 1850. (See also OLYMPIC THEATRE (2).)

MOCHALOV, PAVEL STEPANOVICH (1800–48), a famous Russian tragedian, and the leading exponent in Moscow of the 'intuitive' school of acting. He made his first appearance in 1817 with great success, his finest roles being Shakespeare's Hamlet (of which Belinsky has left a detailed description), Lear, and the heroes of Schiller's *Die Räuber* and *Kabale und Liebe*. With great gifts of temperament and passion, Mochalov was antipathetic to any rational methods and relied entirely on the inspiration of the moment. He was consequently extremely uneven in his acting, and this, combined with heavy drinking, weakened his hold upon his audience, though his influence persisted for some time.

MODJESKA [really MODRZEJEWSKA] (*née* OPID), HELENA (1840–1909), Polish actress, who in 1860, with her first husband, Gustave Zimajer, joined a provincial company under an assumed name which she retained for the whole of her subsequent career. She went to Warsaw in 1868, where she proved equally good in tragedy and comedy. In 1876, with her second husband, Charles Chłapowski, she emigrated to California, where she met with many setbacks. She returned to the stage, playing at the California Theatre, San Francisco, in 1877, and in spite of her poor command of the English language scored an immense success. She then toured extensively and was considered one of the leading actresses of her generation, at her best in tragedy or strong emotional parts. Her ambition was always to act Shakespeare in English in a London theatre, which she did in 1881, playing Juliet to the Romeo of Johnston Forbes-Robertson (q.v.) at the Royal Court. There were fourteen Shakespearian parts in her repertory, and she did much to extend the knowledge of Shakespeare's plays in Poland and in the United States. One of her finest moments was as Lady Macbeth in the sleep-walking scene. She retired from the stage in 1905 after a farewell performance at the Metropolitan Opera House, New York.

Mogul Saloon, LONDON, see MIDDLESEX MUSIC-HALL.

MOHUN, MICHAEL (*c.* 1620–84), English actor, and with Charles Hart (q.v.) the leading man of Killigrew's company in 1662. He had been a boy-actor under Beeston (q.v.), and was already playing adult parts before the closing of the theatres. He joined the Royalist army, became an officer, and then returned to the stage. His Iago in *Othello* was much admired, and he created many Restoration roles in tragedy and comedy, including Abdelmelech in Dryden's *The Conquest of Granada* (1670) and the title-role in Lee's *Mithridates, King of Pontus* (1678).

MOISEIWITSCH, TANYA (1914–   ), English stage designer, daughter of the pianist Benno Moiseiwitsch and his first wife, the violinist Daisy Kennedy. She began her career at the Abbey Theatre (q.v.) in Dublin, where between 1935 and 1939 she was responsible for the settings of more than fifty productions. After working as resident designer for the Oxford Playhouse from 1941 to 1944, she joined the Old Vic (q.v.) and designed sets and costumes for a number of plays produced on tour and at the New Theatre. Her first design for the Memorial Theatre at Stratford (q.v.) was a permanent set with no front curtain, used for *Henry VIII* in 1949. She also designed the setting for a cycle of history plays chosen for the Festival of Britain in 1951—*Richard II, Henry IV, Henry V*—and since 1953 onwards has divided her time between Stratford and the Shakespeare Festival Theatre in Ontario, Canada (see STRAT-

FORD (2)), where, with Tyrone Guthrie as director, she designed the first tent-like theatre for productions in the round and also did the designs for the first productions, *Richard III* and *All's Well That Ends Well*. After working for the theatre in its subsequent seasons, she was responsible in 1957, again with Guthrie, for the new theatre and for the designs for its second production, *Twelfth Night*. With Brian Jackson, she also redesigned the stage in 1962. She has continued to work in London and elsewhere, notably in Tel Aviv (*The Merchant of Venice*, 1958), and since its opening in 1963 she has been principal designer for the Tyrone Guthrie Theatre in Minneapolis, Minnesota (see GUTHRIE).

MOISSI, ALEXANDER (1880–1935), German actor of Italian origin, who played his first speaking part in German at Prague in 1902. He remained there for three years and then went to Berlin, where his fine presence and above all his rich resonant voice soon brought him into prominence. At the Deutsches Theater under Reinhardt (q.v.) he played Romeo, Hamlet, the Fool in *King Lear*, Oberon in *A Midsummer Night's Dream*, and Touchstone in *As You Like It*; also Faust and Mephistopheles in Goethe's *Faust*, Posa in Schiller's *Don Carlos*, Oswald in Ibsen's *Ghosts*, and Louis Dubedat and Marchbanks in Shaw's *The Doctor's Dilemma* and *Candida*. His Oedipus and Orestes in Reinhardt's productions of Sophocles' plays in the Zirkus Schumann in Vienna were outstanding. He was in London in 1930, playing *Hamlet* at the Globe (in W. V. Schlegel's translation) while next door, at the Queen's, Gielgud (q.v.) was playing in the uncut version, transferred from the Old Vic.

MOLÉ [really MOLET], FRANÇOIS-RENÉ (1734–1802), French actor, who joined the Comédie-Française in 1760. Though he excelled in comedy, he was the first actor to play Hamlet in French in 1769, in the adaptation made by Ducis. This was nothing like the original, but the French public liked it and Molé was considered good in the part. During the Revolution, which he welcomed, he escaped imprisonment and acted in revolutionary plays at the theatre of Mlle Montansier (q.v.), returning with his wife to the Comédie-Française when it reopened and remaining there until his death.

MOLIÈRE [really JEAN-BAPTISTE POQUELIN] (1622–73), the greatest actor and dramatist of France, author of some of the finest comedies in the history of the theatre, who in 1643 abandoned his study of the law to join a small theatrical enterprise known as the Illustre-Théâtre. The reason for this may have been his love for the leading lady, Madeleine Béjart (q.v.), as his family appears to have had no previous connection with the stage and his own experience of acting was probably confined to appearances in school productions at the Jesuit College of Clermont, where he was educated. No reason has been found for his adoption of the name of Molière, though it was no doubt used in order to spare the susceptibilities of his father, a prosperous upholsterer of Paris attached to the service of the Court. The Illustre-Théâtre soon failed, and Molière, with the Béjart family and their friends, went into the provinces, remaining there from 1645 to 1658. These were the formative years in Molière's career, during which he learnt his job as an actor and as a playwright, supplying the itinerant company, of which he soon became the leader, with a number of partly improvised farces, now lost, in the style of the *commedia dell'arte* (q.v.).

On 24 Oct. 1658 Molière's company returned to Paris and played at the Louvre before the young King, Louis XIV. *Nicomède*, by Corneille (q.v.), was coldly received, but Molière's own farce, *Le Docteur amoureux*, was an immediate success, and before long the actors were installed in the Court theatre, the Petit-Bourbon (q.v.), sharing it with an Italian company under Scaramouche (see FIORILLO, TIBERIO). With the success of *Les Précieuses ridicules* at the end of the year, Molière's position was assured, and the rest of his life is bound up with that of his theatre. After the production of *Sganarelle, ou le cocu imaginaire* (1660), the company moved to the Palais-Royal (q.v.), which became their permanent home. Here were first produced some of Molière's masterpieces—*L'École des maris* (1661), *L'École des femmes* (1662), *Le Misanthrope* and *Le Médecin malgré lui* (both 1666), *L'Avare* (1668), *Les Femmes savantes* (1672), and *Le Malade imaginaire* (1673), in which he made his last appearance on 17 Feb., dying a few hours later.

A great deal of Molière's time was spent in the preparation of plays and entertainments for the Court of Louis

XIV, for which Lully provided the music. The first was *Les Fâcheux* in 1661, but the most important—and probably the best-known of all Molière's plays—was *Le Bourgeois gentilhomme* (1670), which was first produced at Chambord and later in Paris. It was at Versailles, however, that Molière's most controversial play, *Le Tartuffe*, was first produced in 1664. This attack on pious hypocrites so offended some of Molière's most powerful enemies that it was banned from the public stage until 1667, when it was retitled *L'Imposteur*. It was given again under its original name in 1669.

In 1662 Molière married his leading lady, the youngest sister of Madeleine, Armande Béjart (q.v.), who was believed by many people to be Madeleine's daughter, even, by his most malicious enemies, Madeleine's daughter by Molière. Of the three children of the marriage the two sons, born in 1664 and 1672, lived only a few weeks; the daughter, Esprit Magdeleine, born in 1665, died in 1723. It was an unhappy marriage between a spoilt young woman and a much older man, badly overworked and already showing signs of the tuberculosis which was to cause his death at the age of fifty-one. Nevertheless it was important in Molière's development as a dramatist, since it was for Armande that he wrote some of his best women's parts. Among the other outstanding players in his company were Baron, La Grange, Mlle de Brie, and Mlle du Parc (qq.v.).

Although Molière's plays are not easy for English audiences in the original, and are extremely difficult to translate, he has always been popular in England. The Restoration dramatists borrowed from him very freely, often without acknowledgement. In the eighteenth century Cibber (q.v.) based his successful *The Non-Juror* (1717) on *Le Tartuffe*, and Fielding (q.v.) in 1732 translated both *L'Avare* and *Le Médecin malgré lui*. During the nineteenth century several new translations were published, but they were for reading rather than acting. A fresh impetus to stage presentation was given by the very free versions of Miles Malleson (q.v.). French companies visiting London usually include at least one Molière play in their repertory, a tradition which began in the season of 1718–19 with *Le Tartuffe*, *L'Étourdi*, and *George Dandin*.

MOLINA, TIRSO DE, see TIRSO

MOLNÁR [really NEUMANN], FERENČ (1878–1952), Hungarian dramatist, and one of the best-known outside his own country. He became an American citizen in 1940. His first plays were light-hearted farces of Hungarian city life, but it was with *The Devil*, a modern version of the Faust (q.v.) legend, that he first attracted attention outside Hungary. In New York, where it was already being played in German and Yiddish, it opened at two theatres—the Belasco and the Garden (qq.v.)—on the same night, 18 Aug. 1908. It was seen in London in 1909, and also in Germany and France. Molnár's best-known play, however, is *Liliom* (1909), a mixture of realism and fantasy which was produced in New York in 1921 and in London five years later, and was used by Rodgers and Hammerstein as the basis of their successful musical, *Carousel* (New York, 1945; London, 1950). Of Molnár's other plays, the best-known in translation is *The Guardsman* (1924), which provided a perfect vehicle for the Lunts (q.v.). There have also been productions in English of *The Swan*, *The Glass Slipper*, *Olympe*, and *The Red Mill* (known in America as *Mima*).

Momus, the Greek god of ridicule, and by extension of clowns. The name was frequently used to denote a clown, as in Grimaldi's (q.v.) reference to himself as 'the once Merry Momus', and became attached to one of the figures in the harlequinade (q.v.).

MONCK, NUGENT (1877–1958), English actor and director, a disciple of William Poel (q.v.) and founder in 1911 of the Norwich Players, for whom he built the Maddermarket (q.v.), where he himself produced most of the plays from 1921 to 1952 and also appeared in some of them. He also did a certain amount of theatrical work elsewhere, and was responsible for a number of pageants in and around Norwich. In 1958 he was made a C.B.E. in recognition of his work for the theatre. He was also a Fellow of the Royal Academy of Music from 1935 until his death.

MONCRIEFF, WILLIAM GEORGE THOMAS (1794–1857), English dramatist and theatre manager, author of about two hundred plays, mainly burlesques and melodramas written for the minor theatres. The most successful was *Tom and Jerry; or, Life in*

London (1821), the best of many adaptations of the book by Pierce Egan (q.v.). In 1823 Moncrieff's *The Cataract of the Ganges* was produced at Drury Lane with the added attraction of real water. He adapted Dickens's *Pickwick Papers* for the stage as *Sam Weller; or, the Pickwickians* (1837) almost before the last instalment had appeared, which aroused the anger of the author, who satirized him as 'the literary gentleman' in *Nicholas Nickleby* (1838).

MONKHOUSE, ALLAN NOBLE (1858–1936), dramatic critic and dramatist, who was on the staff of the *Manchester Guardian* when Miss Horniman (q.v.) opened her repertory theatre at the Gaiety, Manchester. He supported her enterprise in his column and wrote for her his first play, *Reaping the Whirlwind* (1908). This was followed by *Mary Broome* (1911) and *Nothing Like Leather* (1913), a satire on the Gaiety company in which Miss Horniman appeared fleetingly as herself. Monkhouse's best play, however, was produced in London after the Gaiety company had been disbanded. This was *The Conquering Hero* (1924), the story of a soldier who goes unwillingly to war, finds humiliation in battle, and returns to the irony of a triumphal welcome. Nicholas Hannen gave a moving performance as the hero, Christopher Rokeby, in a play which anticipated Sherriff's *Journey's End* (1928).

Monodrama (sometimes called Melodramma, on account of its musical accompaniment), a short solo piece for one actor or actress supported by silent figures or by choruses. It was popularized in Germany between 1775 and 1780 by the actor Brandes (q.v.). The Duodrama, a similar compilation, had two speaking characters. Both types of entertainment, which were useful in filling out the triple bill then in vogue, frequently consisted of scenes extracted and adapted from longer dramas.

MONTAGUE [really MANN], HENRY JAMES (1844–78), American actor, who was acting in London in the 1860s, and in 1870 opened the Vaudeville Theatre (q.v.) in partnership with David James (q.v.) and Thomas Thorne. In 1874 he returned to New York and for the rest of his short life was associated with Lester Wallack (q.v.). At his best in contemporary comedies—Sardou's *Diplomacy*, Robertson's *Caste*—

he owed much of his success to his youthful charm and personal magnetism.

MONTALAND, CÉLINE (1843–91), French actress, who at the age of seven appeared at the Comédie-Française in children's parts and was much admired. Going from there to the Palais-Royal (q.v.), she continued to attract the public in childish parts specially written for her and in 1860 made her adult début in the famous fairytale, *Pied de mouton*, at the Porte-Saint-Martin. She was also seen at the Gymnase, where one of her finest parts was the mother in a dramatization of Daudet's *Jack*. In 1888 she returned to the Comédie-Française, remaining there until her death.

MONTANSIER, MLLE [really MARGUERITE BRUNET] (1730–1820), French actress and theatre manager, who took her stage name from that of an aunt who brought her up. Having fallen in love with a young actor, HONORÉ BOURDON DE NEUVILLE (1736–1812), she decided to go into theatre management, and helped by powerful friends took over the theatre at Rouen. She was soon directing several other provincial theatres with equal success, Neuville acting as her business manager. While in charge of the theatre at Versailles, Mlle Montansier was presented to Marie Antoinette, who, attracted by her gaiety and wit, invited her to play at Court, which she did successfully. In 1777 she built a theatre at Versailles, demolished in 1886, which was used to try out aspirants to the Comédie-Française. On the outbreak of the Revolution she went to Paris, and it was in her house that Napoleon first met Talma (q.v.). Accused of royalist sympathies, owing to her friendship with Marie Antoinette, she was arrested but was saved from the guillotine by the fall of Robespierre. She immediately married her faithful Neuville and took over the management of a theatre at the Palais-Royal, opposite the Bibliothèque Nationale, giving it her own name. It closed in 1806 and became a café, where its previous owner was a constant visitor.

MONTCHRÉTIEN, ANTOINE DE (c. 1575–1621), early French Renaissance dramatist, who by 1600 had written several plays on classical themes which were produced at the Hôtel de Bourgogne (q.v.). In 1605, at the height of his success, he had the misfortune to kill a man in a duel, and fled to England. James I, to whom he had dedicated his play on Mary Queen of Scots, *L'Écossaise* (1603), one of the first French plays to deal with modern history, secured a pardon for him and he returned to France in 1611. In 1621 he joined the Huguenots and was killed by royalist soldiers while taking refuge in an inn. His plays are technically weak but contain passages of great lyric beauty, and his choruses, like those of Garnier (q.v.), are particularly fine, while the note of heroism which he so often sounded is similar to that of Corneille (q.v.).

MONTDORY [really GUILLAUME DES-GILBERTS] (1594–1651), French actor, the friend and interpreter of Corneille (q.v.), whose Rodrigue in *Le Cid* (1636) he was the first to play. A good business man, he built up a fine company at the Marais (q.v.) in the face of much hostility, training and directing his actors well. Among them were the parents of Michel Baron (q.v.), first leading man of the Comédie-Française. Montdory, who was an excellent actor in the old declamatory style, seldom appeared in comedy and never in farce. He was at his best in tragedy, one of his finest roles being Herod in Tristan's *La Mariane* (1636). He was appearing before Richelieu in this play when he was stricken with paralysis and forced to retire from the stage.

MONTFLEURY [really ZACHARIE JACOB] (c. 1600–67), French actor, who joined the company at the Hôtel de Bourgogne, where in 1647 he played the lead in his own play, *La Mort d'Asdrubal*. By his contemporaries he was considered a fine tragic actor, but Cyrano de Bergerac (q.v.) much disliked him and is said to have ordered him off the stage, an incident used by Rostand (q.v.) in his play on Cyrano. An enormously fat man, with a loud voice and a pompous delivery, Montfleury was satirized by Molière (q.v.) in *L'Impromptu de Versailles* (1663). There was no love lost between them, since it was Montfleury who accused Molière before Louis XIV of marrying his own daughter by Madeleine Béjart (q.v.), but the accusation was not taken seriously, and to refute it the King stood godfather to Molière's first child. Montfleury married an actress, his son Antoine (q.v.) and his daughters, FRAN-ÇOISE (c. 1640–1708), known as Mlle d'Ennebault, and LOUISE (1649–1709), being also on the stage.

MONTFLEURY, ANTOINE (1639–85),

French actor and dramatist, son of Mont-fleury (q.v.). He first came to the fore with *L'Impromptu de l'Hôtel de Condé* (1663), intended as a reply to *L'Impromptu de Versailles*, in which Molière (q.v.), earlier in the same year, had ridiculed the company to which he and his father belonged. Most of his later comedies were imitations of Molière, and though written with great vivacity and showing much wit and observation, they were soon forgotten. His one serious play, *Trasibule* (1663), resembles *Hamlet*, but he is unlikely to have been acquainted with Shakespeare's work and probably took the story from a French work based on Saxo Grammaticus, the latter being also one of Shakespeare's sources.

MONTHERLANT, HENRI DE (1896–1972), French writer, known chiefly for his novels until in 1942 the success of his first play, *La Reine morte* (based on the story of Inés de Castro), at the Comédie-Française turned his thoughts seriously to the theatre. Three more plays were produced at the Comédie-Française—*Port Royal* (1954), *Brocéliande* (1956), and *Le Cardinal d'Espagne* (1960). Of his other plays, which include *Fils de personne* (1943), *Le Maître de Santiago* (1948), *Demain il fera jour* (1949), *Celles qu'on prend dans ses bras* and *Malatesta* (both 1950), *Don Juan* (1958), and *La Guerre civile* (1965), the most interesting, *La Ville dont le prince est un enfant*, was written in 1951, but not performed until 1967. It deals with a platonic friendship between two boys which is vilified and broken by a priest not, as he thinks, out of kindness but out of jealousy. This portrayal of spiritual agony, of the conflict between love and religion, is typical of Montherlant's plays, which contain very little external action and are written in a sonorous prose that makes few concessions to realism. Yet, though they have a religious context, Montherlant, unlike Claudel (q.v.), did not consider himself a 'Catholic' writer, preferring to describe himself as a 'psychological' dramatist. Perhaps for this reason he made very little impact on the English theatre, though several of his plays were seen in translation. The first was *La Reine morte*, as *Queen After Death* (Dundee Repertory Theatre, 1952). In 1957 Donald Wolfit (q.v.) appeared at the Lyric, Hammersmith, in *The Master of Santiago* and *Malatesta*, and in 1969 Max Adrian was seen in the title-role of *The Cardinal of Spain* at the Yvonne Arnaud Theatre, Guildford. None of these plays appears to have been produced as yet in New York.

MONTMÉNIL (1695–1743), see LE SAGE, A.-R.

MONVEL (1745–1812), see MARS, MLLE.

MOODY, WILLIAM VAUGHN (1869–1910), American dramatist, whose work is important in the development of indigenous drama in the United States. The first of his plays to be staged, by Henry Miller (q.v.), was *The Great Divide* (1906), originally known as *The Sabine Woman*. It was successfully produced in London in 1909, the year in which another of Moody's plays, *The Faith Healer*, was seen in New York. Both these plays are written in a dignified, poetic style, and mark the arrival on the American scene of the serious social dramatist, still somewhat melodramatic but moving away from French farce and adaptations of sentimental novelettes. Moody's early death was a great loss to the theatre, and it was unfortunate that none of his long poetic plays was produced in his lifetime.

MOORE, EDWARD (1712–57), English dramatist, author of the fashionably sentimental plays *The Foundling* (1747) and *The Gamester* (1753). The latter, partly rewritten by Garrick (q.v.), who staged it at Drury Lane, is a domestic tragedy in the style of Lillo (q.v.). It was translated into French and had a marked influence on the development of the *tragédie bourgeoise*.

MOORE, EVA (1870–1955), see ESMOND, H. V.

MOORE, GEORGE (1852–1933), Irish novelist and one of the original founders of the Irish Literary Theatre (q.v.), helping to recruit the actors and direct the rehearsals for its first two plays, Yeats's *The Countess Cathleen* and Martyn's *The Heather Field*, produced in Dublin in 1899. A year later his own play, *The Bending of the Bough*, was performed by the same organization, and Moore then collaborated with Yeats in *Diarmuid and Grania*, which was produced in 1901—the first play of the new movement to be taken directly from Irish legend. A distinguished cast, headed by Frank Benson (q.v.), was imported to act in it, and Elgar wrote the incidental music. The notices were unfavourable, and with the winding-up of

the Irish Literary Theatre and the arrival of the Fays (q.v.) with a permanent company of Irish actors, Moore withdrew to concentrate on novel-writing.

MOORE, MARY (1862–1931), English actress and theatre manageress, who made her first appearance on the stage at the Gaiety Theatre under Hollingshead but gave up acting on her marriage to the playwright JAMES ALBERY (1838–89), whose best-known play, *Two Roses* (1870), gave Irving (q.v.), as Digby Grant, one of his earliest successes in London. In 1885 she returned to the theatre (billed as Miss Mortimer) and appeared with Charles Wyndham (q.v.), whom she eventually married. She was for many years his leading lady, being outstanding as Ada Ingot in a revival of Robertson's *David Garrick* in 1886. Her performance in Hubert Davies's *The Mollusc* (1907), in which she scarcely stirred from the settee, was also accounted a *tour de force*. After Wyndham's death she continued in the management of his theatres, assisted by her son BRONSON ALBERY (1881–1971), knighted in 1949 for services to the theatre, and Wyndham's son HOWARD (1865–1947), both extremely influential in the London theatre, Sir Bronson's work being carried on by his son Donald.

Moral Interlude, a short pedagogic drama of the sixteenth century which has much in common with the Morality Play (q.v.) but is more humorous. Outstanding English examples are *Hickscorner*, produced anonymously in about 1513, and R. Wever's *Lusty Juventus* (c. 1550).

Morality Play, a late medieval form of drama which aimed at instruction and moral teaching. Its characters are abstractions of vice and virtue, and the only trace of humour is provided by the Devil and the Old Vice, or buffoon. The only Morality play to survive in performance is *Everyman*, originally written in Dutch in about 1495. This has been successfully produced in English on the modern stage and in German as part of the Salzburg Festival in an open-air production by Reinhardt (q.v.). Historically the Morality play is important and marks a big step forward in the secularization of the vernacular drama all over Europe. One of the best English examples is Skelton's *Magnyfycence* (c. 1515), the only play by this great satirist which has survived.

MORATÍN, see FERNÁNDEZ DE MORATÍN.

MORDVINOV, NIKOLAI DMITRIEVICH (1901–66), Soviet actor, who from 1936 to 1940 was at the Gorky State Theatre in Rostov. Here his outstanding role was Petruchio in *The Taming of the Shrew*. In 1940 he went with a group of leading actors to the Mossoviet (q.v.), where he greatly influenced the acting, especially of heroic roles. Among the parts he played were Ognev in Korneichuk's *Front*, Petrov in Sofronov's *In One Town*, Arbenin in Lermontov's *Masquerade*, Othello, and in 1958 Lear. He also gave an outstandingly comic performance as the Cavaliere di Ripafratta in Goldoni's *La Locandiera*.

MOREHOUSE, WARD (1898–1966), American drama critic, who from 1942 to 1950 was on the staff of the *New York Sun*. He then wrote for the Newhouse syndicate, and his first-night reviews appeared in papers throughout the United States. His love of the theatre was revealed in 1939 in his semi-autobiographical volume, *Forty-Five Minutes Past Eight*, and he later published a biography of George M. Cohan (q.v.) subtitled *Prince of the American Theatre* (1943), *Matinée Tomorrow: 50 Years of Our Theatre* (1949), and a second volume of reminiscences, *Just the Other Day* (1953). He was the author of two plays—*Gentlemen of the Press* (1928) and *Miss Quis* (1937).

MORETO Y CABAÑA, AGUSTÍN (1618–69), Spanish dramatist, whose best plays are *El lindo Don Diego* and *El desdén con el desdén* (adapted by Molière (q.v.) as *La Princesse d'Élide*). A number of Moreto's plays were really rewritings of older themes from Lope de Vega, Tirso de Molina (qq.v.), and others, but they are none the less excellent, and in most cases exceed their originals in dramatic force and clarity. He excelled in the *comedia de figurón*, in which the chief character is a caricature of a particular trait in human nature rather than a portrait, while his inventive and engaging *gracioso* (q.v.) is particularly noteworthy.

MORGAN, CHARLES LANGBRIDGE (1894–1958), English novelist and essayist, who succeeded A. B. Walkley (q.v.) as dramatic critic of *The Times* in 1926, a position he held until 1939, when he was succeeded by A. V. Cookman (q.v.). He was also the author of three plays—*The Flashing Stream* (1938), *The River Line* (1952), and *The Burning Glass* (1954)—written with the fastidious care and nervous vitality that distinguished all his work.

MORLEY, ROBERT (1908–), English actor, who first came into prominence in London when he played Oscar Wilde at the Gate Theatre (q.v.) in 1936. A burly, bald-headed man, he is physically limited in range but has achieved wide popularity in such parts as Sheridan Whiteside in Kaufman and Hart's *The Man Who Came to Dinner* (1941), the Prince Regent in Norman Ginsbury's *The First Gentleman* (1945), Philip in Roussin's *The Little Hut* (1950), Arnold Holt and Hippo in his own plays (written in collaboration), *Edward My Son* (1947) and *Hippo Dancing* (1954), Koichi Asano in Spigelgass's *A Majority of One* (1960), and General Sir Mallalieu Fitzbuttress in Ustinov's *Halfway Up the Tree* (1967). He has also had a successful film career and in 1957 was created C.B.E. for services to the theatre.

Mormon Theatre. From the early days of the Mormons, music and acting formed part of their leisure activities, particularly after they left New York to settle in Illinois. The first productions, given in a 'Fun House' in Nauvoo, were entirely amateur, but in 1844 a professional actor, Thomas A. Lyne, who had been converted by his brother-in-law, a Mormon missionary named George Adams, produced in the Masonic Hall in Nauvoo a number of plays, including *Pizarro*, Sheridan's version of Kotzebue's *Die Spanier in Peru*, in which Brigham Young played the High Priest. In the same year the Mormons began their trek to Salt Lake City, where in 1848 they erected the first Bowery, a temporary shelter intended for religious services and entertainments, including plays. It was replaced in 1850 by a second, permanent Bowery where plays were given during the winter, among them Kotzebue's *The Stranger*. On New Year's Day 1853 an all-purpose Social Hall, designed by Brigham Young, opened with a service of dedication, giving its first theatrical performance on 17 Jan. with *Don Caesar de Bazan*, based on a French play, and Buckstone's one-act farce, *The Irish Lion*. On 19 Jan. Bulwer-Lytton's *The Lady of Lyons* was given, and on 21 Jan. *Pizarro* again. Performances were still purely amateur, husbands and wives being encouraged to appear together, and parents in the audience to bring their children. In the autumn of 1859 Henry Bowring built the Bowring Theatre, the first playhouse in the Salt Lake territory to be called a theatre. The success of this enterprise, where the newly organized Mechanics' Dramatic Association put on such plays as *Othello*, Buckstone's *Luke the Labourer*, John Tobin's *The Honeymoon*, Edward Moore's *The Gamester*, and farces like Morton's *Betsy Baker; or, Too Attentive by Half*, led to the building of the Salt Lake Theatre, which opened on 6 Mar. 1862. It was partly copied from Drury Lane, and over the entrance was placed a large bust of Shakespeare which had accompanied the Mormons on all their travels. It was in this beautiful theatre, demolished in 1928, that Brigham Young's daughters acted. A replica of it which is used by local and visiting companies has been erected on the campus of the University of Utah.

Morosco Theatre, NEW YORK, on 45th Street west of Broadway. Built by the Shuberts (q.v.), it opened on 5 Feb. 1917, and was named after Oliver Morosco, author with Elmer Harris of *Canary Cottage*, which, with music by Earl Carroll, was the first play to be given here. An interesting production in 1920 was *Beyond the Horizon*, by O'Neill (q.v.), while in the same year the success of *The Bat*, by Mary Roberts Rinehart and Avery Hopwood, started a fashion for mystery thrillers. In 1924 Joseph Schildkraut scored a personal triumph in Edwin Meyer's *The Firebrand*, and a year later the Pulitzer prize-winner, *Craig's Wife*, by George Kelly (q.v.), was first seen here. Other productions at this theatre which were awarded Pulitzer prizes were *Death of a Salesman* (1949), by Arthur Miller (q.v.), and *Cat on a Hot Tin Roof* (1955), by Tennessee Williams (q.v.). Also successful was Gore Vidal's comedy on American political life, *The Best Man* (1960). Arthur Kopit's *Oh Dad, Poor Dad, Mamma's Hung You in the Closet and I'm Feelin' So Sad* was transferred here from the Phoenix in 1963, in which year Peter Shaffer's double bill, *The Private Ear* and *The Public Eye*, was also seen. In 1970 David Storey's *Home*, which had already had a successful run in London with John Gielgud and Ralph Richardson in the leading roles, repeated its success here with the same actors.

MOROZOV, MIKHAIL MIKHAILOVICH (1897–1952), Russian Shakespearian scholar, who encouraged the production of Shakespeare's plays all over the U.S.S.R., and early in his career translated *All's Well That Ends Well* and *The Merry Wives of Windsor* (with Samuel Marshak). He also wrote (in English) a short book entitled *Shakespeare on the Soviet Stage*, with an introduction by Dover Wilson, and was a contributor to several volumes of *Shakespeare Survey*.

MORRIS, MRS. (1753–1826), American actress, whose maiden name is unknown. She was the second wife of the comedian OWEN MORRIS (?–c. 1810), and with him was a member of the American Company (q.v.). They both appeared in several first productions of Shakespearian plays in New York, including *Much Ado About Nothing*, and Mrs. Morris, who was one of the outstanding actresses of the day, played Charlotte in *The Contrast*, by Royall Tyler (q.v.), America's first indigenous comedy. In 1793 she went to Philadelphia with her husband to join Wignell's new company at the Chestnut Street Theatre (q.v.), but found herself eclipsed by Mrs. Merry (q.v.), and though she remained in Philadelphia till 1810, she never attained the position she had held in New York. Little is known of her later career, though Odell (*Annals of the New York Stage*) thinks she may have appeared at the Commonwealth Theatre, New York, as late as 1815.

MORRIS [really MORRISON], CLARA (1846–1925), American actress, on the stage as a child, who in 1872 made a great impression when she appeared at Daly's first Fifth Avenue Theatre as Cora the Creole in his play *Article 47*, based on a play by the French dramatist Belot. She was then seen in a large range of parts, and in spite of a strong accent and an extravagant, unrestrained manner was popular both in New York and on tour. Though not a good actress, she had an extraordinary power of moving an audience and could always be relied on to fill any theatre in which she appeared. Her emotional range was best seen in such parts as the heroine of the younger Dumas's *La Dame aux Camélias*, which she played as *Camille*, but she also essayed Lady Macbeth, Julia in Sheridan Knowles's *The Hunchback*, and a number of modern dramatic heroines. In 1885 she left the stage for a time owing to ill health, but in 1890 and 1892 was seen in California. She appeared in New York in 1904 in an all-star revival of Oxenford's *The Two Orphans*, and then went into vaudeville.

MORTIMER, JOHN CLIFFORD (1923–), English dramatist, by profession a barrister, whose one-act *The Dock Brief* and *What Shall We Tell Caroline?* were produced together in a double bill in 1958, the first having been originally written for television. He then contributed another one-act play, *Lunch Hour* (1961), to a triple bill at the Arts Theatre, and had his first full-length play, *The Wrong Side of the Park* (1960), produced at the Cambridge. It was followed by *Two Stars for Comfort* (1962) and *The Judge* (1967), and in 1965 Mortimer prepared an English version of Feydeau's farce, *Une Puce à l'oreille*, which as *A Flea in her Ear* was produced by the National Theatre company at the Old Vic. He then returned to the one-act form, which seems to suit him best, with four playlets set in Mill Hill, Bermondsey, Gloucester Road, and Marble Arch under the overall title of *Come As You Are* (1970), which shows different groups of middle-aged people imprisoned in sexual fantasies. A second translation of Feydeau, *Cat among the Pigeons*, from *Un Fil à la patte*, was seen in 1969, and in 1970 *A Voyage Round My Father*, already seen on television, was successfully produced at Greenwich and later in the West End.

MORTON, CHARLES (1819–1904), an early and extremely able music-hall manager, who from his association with the pioneering days was known as 'the father of the halls'. He was the first owner of both the Canterbury and the Oxford (qq.v.), and was called in to revive the failing fortunes of, among others, the London Pavilion and the Tivoli (qq.v.), which he did most successfully, mainly because he set a high standard, was good at choosing his performers, and though appreciating vulgarity, was opposed to innuendo and salacity.

MORTON, THOMAS (c. 1764–1838), English dramatist, best remembered for having created the character of Mrs. Grundy, who does not appear, but is frequently alluded to in his sentimental comedy *Speed the Plough* (1800) as the embodiment of British respectability. He wrote a number of other plays in the same style,

but his best work was probably *The School of Reform* (1805), which was frequently revived. His son, JOHN MADDISON (1811–91), was a prolific writer of one-act farces. His *Box and Cox* (1847), first produced in 1843 as *The Double-Bedded Room*, provided the libretto (by Burnand) for Sir Arthur Sullivan's first operetta, *Cox and Box* (1867).

Moscow Art Theatre. This famous theatre, now dedicated to Maxim Gorky (q.v.), is the best-known of all Russian theatrical organizations outside the U.S.S.R. Founded by Stanislavsky and Nemirovich-Danchenko (qq.v.), its early history is closely bound up with that of Chekhov (q.v.). It opened in 1898 with A. K. Tolstoy's *Tsar Feodor Ivanovich* and shortly after gave a successful performance of *The Seagull*, which had recently failed at the Alexandrinsky (q.v.). This was followed by *Uncle Vanya* (1899), *Three Sisters* (1901), and *The Cherry Orchard* (1904). The ferment which produced the abortive revolution of 1905 was reflected in the production of *The Lower Depths* (1902), by Gorky, whose *Children of the Sun* (1905) was based on an incident in that uprising. The repertory of pre-Revolutionary plays also included a number of European classics, but the only Shakespearian play to be performed at this time was *Julius Caesar*. During the upheavals of the Soviet Revolution the theatre was saved from dissolution by the intervention of Lenin and the efforts of Lunacharsky (q.v.), and after a long tour of Europe and America in 1922 and 1923 the company returned to Moscow. After several tentative productions of new plays, the theatre finally found its feet in the new world in 1927 with Ivanov's *Armoured Train 14–69*. A further landmark in its history was the production in 1932 of the first part of Gorky's proposed trilogy, *Yegor Bulychov and Others*. The theatre was now firmly established, many players who had appeared in its first productions—notably Kachalov, Moskvin, and Chekhov's widow, Olga Knipper-Chekhova (qq.v.)—spending the rest of their lives with the company and being succeeded by actors trained in the theatre's own dramatic school, from which also several important individual groups developed (see REALISTIC and VAKHTANGOV THEATRES). The Moscow Art Theatre remains the leading theatre of Russia, and in 1958, 1963, and 1970 visited

London, where its performances of Chekhov's *The Cherry Orchard, Uncle Vanya, Three Sisters*, and *The Seagull* were immensely successful. In 1968 the company moved into a new theatre, built on the site of the old one but much larger, and having in addition to the main auditorium, holding 1,800 people, a smaller one for rehearsals, two for recordings, and a drama museum.

Moscow State Jewish Theatre, known in Yiddish as Melucha and in Russian as Goset. This was founded in Leningrad, in 1919 by Granovsky (q.v.) for the production of plays in Yiddish. It later moved to Moscow, opening at the small Chagall Hall in a programme of short comedy sketches by Sholom Aleichem (q.v.), and finally achieving its own theatre seating 766. Granovsky was succeeded in 1928, during a European tour, by his assistant Mikhoels (q.v.), who in 1935 gave a fine performance as Lear in a production by Radlov (q.v.) with scenery by Tishler. After the death of Mikhoels in 1948 the company was disbanded, but was re-formed in 1962 under Vladimir Shvartser as the Jewish Drama Ensemble and toured extensively in a production of Aleichem's *Tevye the Milkman* (known in English as *Fiddler on the Roof*). Among its later productions were revivals of Aleichem's *Two Hundred Thousand*, Gordin's *Over the Ocean*, and Goldfaden's *The Witch*.

Moscow Transport Theatre, see GOGOL, N. V. and SUDAKOV, I. Y.

MOSKOVITCH, MAURICE (1871–1940), see GOLDFADEN, ABRAHAM.

MOSKVIN, IVAN MIKHAILOVICH (1874–1946), an outstanding Russian actor, who joined the Moscow Art Theatre (q.v.) on its foundation in 1898, playing the lead in its initial production of Tolstoy's *Tsar Feodor Ivanovich* and Epihodov and Lvov in Chekhov's *The Cherry Orchard* and *Ivanov*. Among his later roles were Luka in Gorky's *The Lower Depths*, Nozdrev in Gogol's *Dead Souls*, the merchant Pribitkov in Ostrovsky's *The Last Sacrifice*, and Belobrov in Kron's *Officer of the Fleet*. In 1942 he played a leading part in Pogodin's play about Lenin, *Kremlin Chimes* (see also GRIBOYEDOV).

Mossoviet Theatre, MOSCOW, founded in 1923 as the Moscow Trades Unions'

Theatre with the object of encouraging young playwrights to tackle Soviet and political themes. Its earliest and best dramatist was Bill-Belotserkovsky (q.v.), whose *Storm* (or *Hurricane*) was produced there in 1926. In 1940 the theatre came under the direction of Zavadsky (q.v.), and has since produced a number of good new Soviet plays, including Surov's *The Insult* and Shteyn's *Law of Honour* (both 1948) and Surov's *Dawn over Moscow* (1949). A revised version of *Storm*, directed by Zavadsky in 1951, was a landmark in the theatre's history, as was his production of *The Merry Wives of Windsor* in 1957. This was awarded a Lenin Prize, as was Zavadsky's revival of Lermontov's *Masquerade* in 1965, with Khatchaturian's music and décor and costumes by Boris Volkov. An excellent production of *King Lear* in 1958, with Mordvinov (q.v.) in the title-role, further enhanced the reputation of the theatre, which continued also to produce new Soviet plays, among them Solovyev's *The Dangerous Profession* (1960), Virta's *In Summer the Sky is High* (1961), Stock's *Leningrad Prospect* (1962), as well as plays by such European dramatists as Shaw, Lorca, and Heinrich Böll.

MOSTEL, ZERO [really SAMUEL JOEL] (1915–77), American actor, who gained his theatrical experience in Greenwich Village night clubs before appearing in vaudeville on Broadway in 1942. In 1946 he was seen as Hamilton Peachum in *Beggar's Holiday*, an adaptation of Gay's *The Beggar's Opera* with music by Duke Ellington, and in 1952 played Argan in *The Imaginary Invalid*, his own adaptation of Molière's *Le Malade imaginaire*. Among his later parts were Shu Fu in Brecht's *The Good Woman of Setzuan* in 1956, Leopold Bloom in Marjorie Barkentin's dramatization of part of Joyce's *Ulysses* as *Ulysses in Nighttown* in 1958, John in Ionesco's *Rhinoceros* in 1961, and Prologus in the highly successful musical *A Funny Thing Happened on the Way to the Forum* in 1962. In 1964 he again scored a great success in the musical *Fiddler on the Roof*, based on a short story by Sholom Aleichem (q.v.).

Motion, a name given in the sixteenth and seventeenth centuries to the puppet-plays of the itinerant showmen. The earliest dealt with biblical subjects, and Shakespeare refers in *The Winter's Tale* to 'a motion of the Prodigal Son'. Later the range of subjects was extended, and episodes were used from medieval romance, mythology, and contemporary history.

Moulin Rouge, PARIS, a well-known dance-hall which opened on 5 Oct. 1889. A constant feature of its programmes has been a cabaret show, in which the cancan made its first appearance, the dancers in 1893 being Grille d'Égout, la Goulue, la Môme Fromage, and Nini-patte-en-l'air. Mistinguett (q.v.) was for some years part-proprietor of the Moulin Rouge and frequently appeared there, as did most of the stars of variety and music-hall.

(For the Moulin Rouge, New York, see NEW YORK THEATRE (2).)

MOUNET-SULLY [really JEAN SULLY MOUNET] (1841–1916), a famous French actor who made his début at the Comédie-Française in 1872 as Oreste in Racine's *Andromaque*. His fine physique, beautifully modulated voice, and sombre, penetrating gaze, added to fiery, impetuous acting and great originality, soon brought him into prominence. His career was one of unclouded success and he appeared in all the great tragic roles of the French classical repertory. He was also outstanding in the plays of Victor Hugo when they were finally given at the Comédie-Française. His younger brother, PAUL (1847–1922), was also an actor, deserting the study of medicine for the stage. He first appeared at the Odéon, mainly in tragic roles, and went to the Comédie-Française in 1889, where, though not as great an actor as his brother, he was an important member of the company.

MOUNTFORT, WILLIAM (1664–92), English actor, and the author of several comedies, including a harlequinade in the Italian manner, *The Life and Death of Dr. Faustus*. He specialized in 'fine gentleman' parts, being excellent as Sparkish in Wycherley's *The Country Wife* and creating the part of Sir Courtly Nice in Crowne's play of that name. He was brutally murdered at the instigation of a certain Captain Hill, who suspected him of being a successful rival in the affections of Mrs. Bracegirdle (q.v.). His early death was a great loss to the stage. Six years previously he had married a young actress, SUSANNA PERCIVAL (1667–1703), whose playing of Melantha in Dryden's *Marriage à la Mode*, as described by

Colley Cibber (q.v.), must have been superb. She was a natural mimic, and sufficiently free from vanity to don grotesque clothes or make-up when the part called for it. In her twenties she was much admired in male attire, playing Bayes in Buckingham's *The Rehearsal* to perfection. She married as her second husband the actor JOHN BAPTISTA VERBRUGGEN (?–1708).

Mountview Theatre, 104 CROUCH HILL, LONDON, an amateur theatre group founded in 1947 by Peter Coxhead and Ralph Nossek, who had while serving in the Navy run an amateur group in Ceylon. The first production, Wilde's *The Importance of Being Earnest*, was staged in Nov. 1947 in a converted hall, held on lease after five months' preliminary work on the derelict building, which in 1949 was purchased outright. Up to 1949 one play a month was presented by the company, but from 1950 to 1975 a production was mounted every three and later every two weeks. In 1963 much of the Club's premises was destroyed by fire, and major alterations were made during rebuilding. In 1975 the company disbanded after staging approximately 1,000 plays. During its lifetime there had been attached to it a drama school offering full-time professional courses, teenage theatre groups and children's theatre. This side of the work continues to grow. In 1971 a second theatre, the Judi DENCH, opened, and in addition there are ten working studios for acting students and three for technical students, with a wardrobe of 14,000 costumes. The Theatre School is now officially recognized as one of the major theatre training establishments in England. In 1976 a second school was purchased in the vicinity to allow for expansion, and a new site for redevelopment has recently been donated to allow for two new theatres, studios, etc.

MOURQUET, LAURENT (1744–1844), see GUIGNOL.

MOWATT [*née* OGDEN], ANNA CORA (1819–70), American author and actress, mainly remembered for her social comedy, *Fashion* (1845), considered to be one of the best of the early satiric portrayals of American life. It was first produced at the Park Theatre (q.v.), so successfully that Mrs. Mowatt was encouraged to go on the stage herself, making her début as Pauline in Bulwer-Lytton's *The Lady of Lyons* in 1845. She then formed her own company, with which she visited London in 1848–50. In 1854 she published her *Autobiography*, and then retired to live quietly in London, where she died.

Multiple Setting, a term applied to the stage décor of the medieval play (known in France as *décor simultané* and in Germany as *Standort-* or *Simultanbühne*), inherited from the liturgical drama (q.v.) with its 'mansions' or 'houses' disposed about the church. When biblical dramas were first performed out of doors, the 'mansions' were disposed on three sides of an unlocalized *platea* or acting space, but by the sixteenth century, at any rate in France, they were set in a straight line or on a very slight curve. In England the different scenes of a Mystery Play (q.v.) were on perambulating pageants, and the multiple setting was not needed. It continued in France, and possibly in Germany, for a long time, and was still in use at the Hôtel de Bourgogne (q.v.) in Paris in the early seventeenth century. It is even possible that Corneille's early plays, produced at the Marais (q.v.), were staged in a multiple setting, which was finally ousted by the development of the single set used for classical tragedy, as in the plays of Racine (q.v.), and the successive scenes of the spectacular 'machine' play. The set scenes of the Renaissance stage in Italy (see TERENCE-STAGE) were single composite backgrounds and not multiple settings in the original sense, though the unlocalized acting space in front of the tragic or comic houses corresponded to the medieval *platea*. The Elizabethan public stages such as the Globe (q.v.) did not employ multiple settings, though something of the kind may have been used in the early days of the private roofed playhouse (see BLACKFRIARS), and was certainly a feature of the elaborate Court masque (q.v.).

Mumming Play. This play, which is still performed at Christmas in a few villages in England and Northern Ireland, is a rudimentary representation of the death and resurrection of a folk-hero, usually St. George (in Scotland, where the mumming play seems to have died out, he was known as Galatian or Golashans). The other characters are the Turkish Knight who kills St. George in single combat, and the Doctor who brings him back to life.

Subsidiary characters are Beelzebub, a Fool in cap and bells, Father Christmas, and Jack Finney (or Johnny Jack) the Sweeper, who acts as prologue and epilogue, clearing a space for the actors with his broom and collecting their reward, in money or in kind, at the end. The play seems to have evolved from a ritual ceremony connected with an early spring festival, but as the first references to it date from the end of the eighteenth century, nothing can be said with certainty about its origins. During the nineteenth century it was performed in villages all over the country by local men (never women), their faces blacked with soot, who rehearsed in secret and often handed their parts on by word of mouth from father to son. A large number of texts were collected and annotated by Chambers in his *The English Folk-Play* (1933), but in spite of local variants, the surprising uniformity of the plot and dialogue points to a common original, now lost. It can hardly have evolved earlier than the beginning of the seventeenth century, since the legend on which it is based was first popularized in England by Richard Johnson's *Famous History of the Seven Champions of Christendom*, published in 1596, which served as the starting-point for a number of ballads, chap-books, drolls, and puppet-plays. In these the Devil, or the Dragon, engages in single combat with each of the Seven Champions and is finally worsted. But there is no suggestion of the resurrection of a defeated warrior. The most probable explanation of the mumming plays is that village folk, introduced to the Seven Champions by travelling actors and puppet-masters in the late seventeenth and early eighteenth centuries, grafted them on to their own earlier portrayal of the winter death and spring resurrection of their crops, personified in a human being. Yet the existence of almost identical plays in such widely separated areas of England, Scotland, and Ireland is still a puzzle. Either there was an original text which enjoyed widespread popularity, or the mumming play is a remarkable product of mass telepathy.

MUNDAY, ANTHONY (*c.* 1553–1633), English pamphleteer, ballad-maker, translator, and dramatist. He is known to have collaborated in several plays, now lost, on Robin Hood and Sir John Oldcastle, and worked mainly for Henslowe (q.v.). His first extant play, *Fedele and Fortunio* (1584), may have been used by Shakespeare for *Much Ado About Nothing* (1598), while parts of *John a Kent and John a Cumber* (c. 1594) probably suggested the Bottom scenes in *A Midsummer Night's Dream* (1595). He certainly had a hand in *Sir Thomas More*, since most of the manuscript is in his writing.

MUNDEN, JOSEPH SHEPHERD (1758–1832), English comedian, who in 1790 joined the company at Covent Garden to replace Edwin (q.v.). His first outstanding success was as Old Dornton in the initial production of Holcroft's *The Road to Ruin* (1792). He was the favourite actor of Charles Lamb (q.v.), who has left an admirable description of him, and seems to have been particularly admired in drunken scenes, for which he invented new 'business' at every performance. The breadth of his acting would scarcely be conceivable today and even in his own time he was censured for caricature. But he made the fortune of many a poor play. He remained at Covent Garden for over twenty years, and then went to Drury Lane, retiring in 1824.

Munich. From the sixteenth century onwards there was a rich and varied cultural and artistic life in Munich, which was encouraged by the Bavarian Court. The Jesuits (see JESUIT DRAMA) were responsible for the first theatrical performances, which began in 1560. In 1651 the Komödienhaus on the Salvatorplatz, which survived until 1802, was constructed, and in 1662 it was the scene of a magnificent baroque festival held to celebrate the birth of an heir to the electoral throne. In 1671 a company of French actors took up their permanent residence in the theatre, remaining there until the close of the eighteenth century saw the waning of French influence. In 1753 the Residenztheater opened, and in 1812 the Theater am Isartor. In 1865 the Theater am Gärtnerplatz was founded and soon became famous for its dialect plays. In 1895 Messthaler founded the Modernes Theater, where he tried to combat the inertia of the Court theatre by producing works by modern dramatists. The Künstlertheater, founded in 1908, included in its repertory a wide variety of classical plays. Under the direction of OTTO FALCKENBERG (1873–1947) the Kammerspiele (founded in 1911) flourished as a

theatre of modern drama and saw the first production of a play by Brecht (q.v.), (*Trommeln in der Nacht*, 1922). It even succeeded in preserving a certain amount of independence during the Nazi regime. After the First World War the Hoftheater became the Bayrisches Staatstheater, and in 1923, under the direction of KARL ZEISS, gave the first performance of Brecht's *Im Dickicht der Städte*. Die Arbeitsbühne, founded in 1919 by EUGEN FELBER, had a brief but glorious existence, closing its doors in 1921 for lack of funds. In 1943-4 the Residenztheater was destroyed by bombing, but was eventually rebuilt. It reopened in 1951, and by 1963 Munich was once more in the forefront of German theatrical life.

MUNK [really PETERSEN], KAJ HARALD LEININGER (1898–1944), Danish priest and playwright, author of a number of historical plays of which *Cant* (1931) deals with Henry VIII and Anne Boleyn. *Ordet* (*The Word*) (1932), on a religious theme, is usually considered his best play, but the best-known is *Niels Ebbesen* (1943), a stirring patriotic play published during the Nazi occupation of Denmark. Munk, who had earlier attacked the Axis powers in *Sejren* (*The Victory*) (1936), dealing with Italian aggression in Abyssinia, and *Han sidder ved smeltediglen* (*He Sits by the Melting-pot*) (1938), on anti-Semitism in Germany, was shot by the Nazis on 4 Jan. 1944.

MURDOCH, JAMES EDWARD (1811–93), American actor, considered by many of his contemporaries the finest light comedian of his day. He was especially noted for his clear diction. He began his career at the Chestnut Street Theatre (q.v.) in Philadelphia and remained on the stage until 1858, appearing in England in 1856 in several of his best-known parts in which he was well received. Joseph Jefferson (q.v.), who played Moses to his Charles Surface in Sheridan's *The School for Scandal* in 1853, admired his acting immensely. Among his other parts were Benedick in *Much Ado About Nothing*, Orlando in *As You Like It*, Mercutio in *Romeo and Juliet*, Mirabell in Congreve's *The Way of the World*, and the Rover in Mrs. Aphra Behn's play of that name.

MURPHY, ARTHUR (1727–1805), English actor and dramatist, who gave up acting to devote all his energies to playwriting. He adapted Voltaire's *L'Orphelin de la Chine* (1755) for the English stage in 1759, and based some of his best comedies on Molière and other French writers, among them *The Way to Keep Him* (1760), *All in the Wrong* (1761), *The School for Guardians* (1767), and *Know Your Own Mind* (1777). His most successful tragedy, which later gave Mrs. Siddons one of her favourite parts as Euphrasia, was *The Grecian Daughter* (1772). Murphy had little originality but was adept at choosing and combining the best elements from the work of others, and had his place in the revival of the comedy of manners which produced Sheridan's *The School for Scandal* (1777).

MURRAY, ALMA (1854–1945), English actress, outstanding in poetic drama and tragedy. She was much admired by Browning when she appeared in revivals of his plays—*In a Balcony* in 1884, *Colombe's Birthday* in 1885, and *A Blot in the 'Scutcheon* in 1888. It was, however, as Beatrice in the single private performance of Shelley's *The Cenci* on 7 May 1888 that she scored her greatest triumph, and it was much regretted that the censor would not allow the play to be given a normal run. The other outstanding part which she created was Raina in Shaw's *Arms and the Man* (1894). She continued to play leading parts in many West End productions, and retired in 1915 after playing Mrs. Maylie in a dramatization of Dickens's *Oliver Twist*.

MURRAY, SIR (GEORGE) GILBERT AIMÉ (1866–1957), English classical scholar, poet, humanist, and philosopher, whose verse translations of Greek plays held the stage for many years. Though they have now been superseded, they were in their time infinitely superior to anything heard previously. Among his translations of Euripides, the *Hippolytus*, the *Trojan Women*, the *Electra*, and the *Bacchae* were first produced at the Court Theatre in London between 1904 and 1908 with Lillah McCarthy (q.v.) in the leading parts. The *Medea* was first seen at the Savoy in 1907, the *Iphigenia in Tauris* at the Kingsway in 1912. The *Alcestis* and the *Rhesus* have had only amateur performances. Murray also translated Sophocles' *Oedipus Rex*, *Antigone*, and *Oedipus at Colonus*, and Aeschylus' *Oresteia*, the *Suppliant Woman*, the

Prometheus Bound, the *Persians*, and the *Seven Against Thebes*. He was equally successful with Greek comedy, and his versions of Aristophanes' *Birds*, *Frogs*, and *Knights* were eminently actable, as were his reconstructions of Menander's *Perikeiromenê* as *The Rape of the Locks* (1941) and *Epitrepontes* as *The Arbitration* (1945).

MURRAY, THOMAS CORNELIUS (1873–1959), Irish dramatist, important in the history of the Abbey Theatre (q.v.), where his first play, *Birthright*, was produced in 1910. As in all his plays, the subject is taken from the peasant and farming life of his native county of Cork. It was followed by *Maurice Harte* (1912), a remarkable play which portrays the conflict between spiritual honesty and family affection in the mind of a young peasant; *Spring* (1918), a one-act study of poverty and the greed engendered by it; *Aftermath* (1922), a full-length tragedy on the theme of an arranged marriage; and *Autumn Fire* (1924), another tragedy of mismating, which is probably the author's best work in the three-act form.

MURRAY, WALTER, see KEAN, THOMAS.

Muse of Comedy, Thalia; of Dancing, Terpsichore; of Tragedy, Melpomene.

Museums and Collections, THEATRICAL. These fall roughly into four categories: (1) those of general national and international interest; (2) those attached to or dealing with a particular theatre; (3) those devoted to a particular player or playwright; and (4) those devoted to a particular subject. Among the first are the Bakhrushin Museum in Moscow, founded in 1894, and the Clara Ziegler Foundation in Munich (1910); the Bucardo Museum in Rome (1931); the Oslo Theatre Museum (1939); and the Toneel Museum in Amsterdam (1960). In England a modest beginning has been made with the British Theatre Museum (q.v.). In the second category the most important collection is probably that at Drottningholm (q.v.). A smaller museum in the same genre is that attached to the former Court theatre in Copenhagen. There is also one in Meiningen which is devoted to the work of the Meininger company (q.v.). Of museums attached to theatres which still function, the most important are those at La Scala, Milan, and the Paris Opéra, which cover all aspects of opera and ballet. In Russia most of the well-known theatres have their own museums, including the Moscow Art and the Vakhtangov Theatres (qq.v.). In England, Covent Garden has made an effort to collate and classify its own archives but most of the material dealing with the theatre in London is deposited in the Enthoven Collection at the Victoria and Albert Museum, which also houses the Stone Collection of Toy Theatre material and the Guy Little Collection of theatrical photographs. There is also a good deal of theatrical material scattered throughout the various departments of the British Museum and, for the French theatre, in the Bibliothèque Nationale in Paris. In New York the dance, music, and drama collections of the Public Library have been brought together at Lincoln Center (q.v.), and in Vienna the National Library has a separate theatre section. Valuable private collections have been brought together in the Bibliothèque de l'Arsenal in Paris, which houses the Rondel, Soleinne, and Gordon Craig Collections. The Bodleian Library at Oxford has the Douce Collection; in Stockholm there is the Hamilton Collection of English plays. American universities have vast theatrical deposits which are continually being added to, particularly at Harvard and Yale. Pride of place among the museums in the third category must go to the Folger Shakespeare Library in Washington. Stratford-upon-Avon and Birmingham also have libraries devoted to Shakespeare, and interesting material relating to individuals can be found in such collections as the Victor Hugo Museum in Paris, the Casa Goldoni in Venice, and the former homes of Stanislavsky and Chekhov in Russia, Lessing in Germany, Pixérécourt in France, Edwin Booth in New York. In England the only collection of this kind is that devoted to Ellen Terry in her former home at Smallhythe in Kent. In the fourth category, Leningrad has a museum devoted to the circus, and in Moscow and Munich there are specialized puppet museums.

Among the collections of theatre material in private hands, some of which are little known, the most important is probably that at Chatsworth, the home of the Duke of Devonshire, which contains a large number of drawings by Inigo Jones. This is accessible to serious students on application, as is the Mander and Mitchenson Collection in south London,

which is rich in illustrations relating to the English theatre in the nineteenth and twentieth centuries and is destined eventually for the National Theatre. There are also the Richard Southern Collection at Bristol University, Henslowe's material at Dulwich College (see ALLEYN), and the Herbert Hinkin Collection of Toy Theatre material (in Oxford).

Most art galleries contain theatrical paintings and portraits, not catalogued separately, however. The Garrick Club in London and the Players' Club in New York own fine collections. There are also a number in the drama department of Harvard University of which a catalogue in four volumes, by Lillian A. Hall, was published in 1930–2. In 1959 the Society for Theatre Research issued a catalogue of theatrical portraits in the public collections of London.

Music Box, NEW YORK, on 45th Street between Broadway and 8th Avenue. This opened on 22 Sept. 1921 with a revue which ran into several editions. Several other revues followed, as did Kaufman and Hart's *Once in a Lifetime* (1930), one of the best farces yet written about Hollywood, and *Of Thee I Sing* (1931), a collaboration between Kaufman and Morrie Ryskind which was the first musical to win the Pulitzer Prize for Drama. Later successes have been Kaufman and Ferber's *Dinner at Eight* (1932), with Constance Collier (q.v.) as the late Maxine Elliott (q.v.), Steinbeck's *Of Mice and Men* (1937), winner of the Critics' Prize, *The Man Who Came to Dinner* (1939), based by Kaufman and Hart on the antics of the late Alexander Woollcott (q.v.), and the charming *I Remember Mama* (1944), by John Van Druten. In 1949 came a musical play, Maxwell Anderson's *Lost in the Stars* (music by Kurt Weill), but recently the theatre has been used for straight plays, Anthony Shaffer's *Sleuth* being seen there in 1970.

Music-Hall, a type of variety entertainment which flourished in England during the second half of the nineteenth century. It evolved from the 'sing-songs' held in taverns, and was later housed in a hall or annexe adjoining some popular public-house, where the customers sat at small tables to eat and drink while enjoying the comic turns, ballad-singers, acrobats, and jugglers, all controlled by a chairman.

As music-hall became even more popular, special theatres or 'palaces of variety' were built to accommodate it. The first music-hall was the Canterbury (q.v.), built by Charles Morton, known as 'the father of the halls'. Later outstanding ones in London were the Alhambra and the Empire (qq.v.), famous also for their ballets, the Holborn Empire, the London Pavilion, the Metropolitan, the Middlesex or 'Old Mo', the Oxford, and the Tivoli (qq.v.). At one time every town and suburb had its Empire or Hippodrome, and music-hall 'performers', who formed a class apart in the entertainment world, travelled ceaselessly from one to another. Many of them had their individual make-up, which was their trade-mark—George Robey his eyebrows, Harry Tate his moustache, Mark Sheridan his frock coat and bell-bottomed trousers tied round the knee, Eugene Stratton his black face, George Lashwood his faultless tailoring and air of Beau Brummel. Gus Elen, Alex Hurley, and Albert Chevalier shared the 'coster' roles; George Formby exploited the Lancashire accent; R. G. Knowles never appeared without his opera hat, frock-coat, and white duck trousers. Wilkie Bard had his high Shakespearian forehead (whence his nickname of 'Bard'); Kate Carney her 'Arriet's feathers; Grock his fiddle; Harry Lauder his kilts and curly stick; Happy Fanny Fields her Dutch costume; and Vesta Tilly her faultless male attire. Dan Leno and Herbert Campbell, much-loved figures in pantomime also, Marie Lloyd, the epitome of Cockney humour, Little Tich with his enormously elongated boots, varied their attire but remained essentially themselves. Chirgwin was the unalterable 'white-ey'd Kaffir' and relied almost wholly upon two songs, 'My Fiddle is My Sweetheart' and 'The Blind Boy', asking the audience in his queer falsetto voice: 'Which will you have, ladies and gempmuns, the Fiddler or the Blind 'Un?' They always wanted both. Harry Champion specialized in songs about food—'Boiled Beef and Carrots'—delivered at terrific speed, and ending with a 'break-down' which was his own particular property. They even had their own posters, which were as individual as themselves, and T. E. Dunville, in his tight-fitting black suit, would advise the patrons of, say, the Hackney Empire that 'I'm Sticking Here for a Week'.

In its heyday the music-hall represented the sort of entertainment most loved by the 'ordinary' people—the 'masses'. It was gay, raffish, and carefree, vulgar but not suggestive, dealing with the raw material of their own emotions, their own troubles, their own rough humour. Sophistication and subtlety was its undoing. The first break with the earlier tradition came with the importation of scenes of 'straight' drama performed by 'legitimate' actors and the migration of music-hall acts into pantomime (q.v.) and musical comedy. Films, particularly the 'talkies', deprived it of part of its audience. It was later submerged by radio and television; and yet, paradoxically, the latter has led to a revival of the earlier form of music-hall, which also seems to be returning as informal entertainment to the place where it originated, the local public-house.

Music in the Theatre, see INCIDENTAL MUSIC.

Musical Comedy, a popular type of light entertainment which derives from a fusion of burlesque and light opera. The first English musical comedy was *In Town* (1892), staged at the Prince of Wales's by George Edwardes. Transferred to the Gaiety, it was followed there by *The Shop-Girl* (1894), the first of the many successful productions associated with Edwardes's name. From America came the tuneful *The Belle of New York* (1898); England sent back to America such productions as *Florodora* (1899) and the English versions of Lehár's *The Merry Widow* (1907) and Oscar Straus's *The Chocolate Soldier* (1910). In both countries the talents of composers, librettists, comedians, and beautiful chorus-girls were poured out on a host of light-hearted frolics whose tunes are still sung.

The First World War brought about many changes, but the essentials of musical comedy remained. The chief difference lay in the importation of large spectacular effects and the increased efficiency of the chorus. Among the highlights of the American scene were *Lady*, *Be Good!* (1924) and *Oh, Kay!* (1926), with music by George Gershwin; *No, No, Nanette!* (1925) and *Hit the Deck* (1927), with music by Youmans; and *Showboat* (1927), with music by Jerome Kern. These were all seen in London shortly after their New York premières. In England musical comedy had suffered something of a set-back, attention being concentrated on spectacular or intimate revue, or on the big musical plays of Ivor Novello and Noël Coward (qq.v.). In America it continued to flourish with such song-and-dance satires as Gershwin's *Of Thee I Sing* (1931), and later with the musical metamorphosis of such plays as Lynn Riggs's *Green Grow the Lilacs* and Molnár's *Liliom* into *Oklahoma!* (1943) and *Carousel* (1945). Such amalgams of a strong plot, good music, and highly accomplished choreography are now known simply as 'musicals', and represent the biggest money-makers in theatrical enterprise, with spectacular runs in London and New York. Successful composer-and-librettist teams are Rodgers and Hart (*The Boys From Syracuse*, 1938, *Pal Joey*, 1940); Rodgers and Hammerstein (*Oklahoma!*, 1943, *Carousel*, 1945, *South Pacific*, 1949, *The King and I*, 1951, *Flower Drum Song*, 1958, *The Sound of Music*, 1959); Lerner and Loewe (*Brigadoon*, 1947, *My Fair Lady*, 1956, *Camelot*, 1960). Other important composers are Cole Porter (*Anything Goes*, 1934, *Kiss Me, Kate!*, 1948); Kurt Weill (*Lady in the Dark*, 1941); Leonard Bernstein (*On the Town*, 1944, *Wonderful Town*, 1953, *West Side Story*, 1957); and Irving Berlin (*Annie Get Your Gun*, 1946, *Call Me Madam*, 1950).

The success of Sandy Wilson's *The Boy Friend* (1953) and of Julian Slade's *Salad Days* (1954) re-established British musicals as an important part of the London (and subsequently New York) scene; they were followed by Lionel Bart's *Fings Ain't Wot They Used T'Be* (1959), a Theatre Workshop production, *Oliver!* (1960), based on Dickens's *Oliver Twist*, and *Blitz!* (1962), a panorama of London in the Second World War. Among other successful English musicals of the 1960s were *Stop the World, I Want To Get Off* (1961), by Anthony Newley and Leslie Bricusse; *Oh, What a Lovely War!* (1963), a lighthearted though critical evaluation of the First World War hand-tailored for Theatre Workshop (q.v.) by Joan Littlewood and Charles Chilton; *Pickwick* (also 1963), based on Dickens and starring Harry Secombe, who also appeared in *The Four Musketeers* (1967), based on Dumas, but a long way from the original; and the long-running *Charlie Girl* (1966), starring Anna Neagle and Hy Hazell. Two American hits of 1964, which were equally popular in London in 1965 and 1967 respectively, were *Hello, Dolly!*, whose

pedigree goes back via Thornton Wilder and Johann Nestroy (qq.v.) to the English playwright John Oxenford, and *Fiddler on the Roof*, based on Sholom Aleichem's *Tevye the Milkman*. In 1966 came three musicals, which, though well received in London, were less successful than in New York—*Cabaret*, based on the Van Druten-Isherwood play *I am a Camera*, *Sweet Charity*, based on the Italian film 'Nights of Cabiria', and *Mame*, based on Patrick Dennis's novel *Auntie Mame*.

MUSSET, (LOUIS-CHARLES) ALFRED DE (1810–57), French Romantic poet, dramatist, and novelist. The failure of his first play, *La Nuit vénitienne* (1830), turned him against the theatre, and his later plays were published for readers, as *Comédies et proverbes*, between 1833 and 1837. It was not until 1847 that one of them, *Un Caprice*, was tried out at the Comédie-Française with such success that it was quickly followed by *Il faut qu'une porte soit ouverte ou fermée* and *Il·ne faut jurer de rien*. To a theatre under the influence of Balzac and Scribe (q.v.), these trifles brought back the poetry and fantasy which it was in danger of losing. Other excellent examples of Musset's skill in the fusion of classical and romantic elements are his *Caprices de Marianne*, first seen in 1851, and *On ne badine pas avec l'amour*, produced posthumously in 1861. *Fantasio* also was not seen until after the author's death, in 1866. The best of the plays, however, is undoubtedly *Lorenzaccio*, written in Venice in 1834 after Musset's tragic liaison with Georges Sand. It provided Sarah Bernhardt (q.v.) with one of her favourite *travesti* roles, in which she first appeared at the Théâtre de la Renaissance in 1896 and again at the Adelphi in London in 1897; as *Night's Candles*, it was produced in 1933 at the Queen's in London by Ernest Milton, who played Lorenzaccio. Most of Musset's plays have been translated, but they are not well known in England.

Mystère, the French equivalent of the English Mystery Play (q.v.). Its early development followed that of liturgical drama (q.v.) in general, but when the play left the church its production was taken over not, as in England, by the guilds, but by specially constituted bodies of which the most important was the Confrérie de la Passion (q.v.). Also, the plays were not performed on pageants (q.v.) but on static stages, with the various localities needed for the development of the action placed between Heaven on the actor's right and Hell-Mouth on his left. The booths which represented the localities—Nazareth, Bethlehem, Jerusalem, and so on—were usually ranged in a straight line behind the *platea*, or playing-place, as they are shown in a stage-plan for the Valenciennes Mystery Play of 1547. But an equally well-known illustration to a play on the martyrdom of Saint Apolline (1460) shows them set in a semi-circle enclosing the *platea*. Both forms were probably used for the *mystères*, as well as an arrangement of houses facing each other—though this was more often found in Germany—or in a circle, as in Cornwall. The staging of a complete cycle, which in theory could run from the Creation and the story of Adam and Eve to the Last Judgement and the disappearance of the damned into Hell assisted by attendant devils, must have been a formidable undertaking. It called for the co-operation of a large cast of amateur actors, there being as yet no professionals, the building of a stage with its booths or 'houses', perhaps the provision of seating for the audience, and certainly a vast quantity of elaborate costumes and properties. Even in the larger towns, productions were given only at intervals of several years, and usually certain scenes, perhaps the most popular or the easiest to stage, were selected for presentation, and recur most frequently in the extant manuscripts. Although as late as 1540 there was a performance in Paris of a cycle based only on the Old Testament, its stories, and that of the Nativity, seem to have been more popular in England than in France, where concentration on the events of Good Friday and Easter Sunday produced the Passion Play, which, however, reached its highest point of development in the German-speaking countries (see MYSTERIENSPIEL). The introduction of comic and extraneous material, which had begun as far back as the eleventh century with the spice-sellers, and culminated in the unrestrained antics of the devils from Hell-Mouth, finally brought the Mystery Play into disrepute. The new men of the Renaissance thought it fit only for the ignorant, the pious condemned it as irreverent. It was forbidden in Paris by an edict of 1548 and gradually disappeared throughout France.

Mysterienspiel, the German equivalent of the English Mystery Play (q.v.). Its development followed that of the liturgical drama (q.v.) all over Europe, but certain elements, particularly the comic by-play of the horrific devils from Hell-Mouth, were stressed, and the museums of Germany contain many fine specimens of medieval devil-costumes and horned head-dresses. Attention was also concentrated more on the events of Good Friday and Easter Day than on other aspects of the Bible story, and gave rise to the Passion Play. This was performed at stated intervals in many towns and villages on an open-air stage, and although a number of old-established performances lapsed during the fifteenth century, the Catholic revival of the sixteenth had the effect of bringing some of them back into production in certain parts of Switzerland, Austria, and Germany. They may still appear intermittently in a few remote villages in Germany, but the only one to have become famous is that given decennially (from 1634 with some intermissions) at Oberammergau, in Bavaria. A fusion of two Augsburg cycles, this was first performed during a visitation of plague and remains entirely amateur, the villagers dividing the parts among themselves and being responsible also for the production and scenery.

Mystery Play, the name given in England to the medieval religious drama which derives from the liturgical play (q.v.), but differs from it in being spoken instead of sung, in being wholly or partly in the vernacular and not in Latin, and in being performed out of doors and not in church. The term is partly synonymous with Miracle Play, which, however, also included plays based on the lives of the Saints and on the Acts of the Apostles, and a more satisfactory name would be Bible-History, since each play was really a cycle of plays based on stories from the Old and New Testaments. Similar plays are found all over Europe (Sp. *auto sacramental*, Fr. *mystère*, Ger. *Mysterienspiel*, It. *sacra rappresentazione*). In England a different craft-guild was responsible for the production of each self-contained section of the whole cycle—the carpenters for Noah's Ark, for instance, and the fishmongers for Jonah and the Whale. Although the static stage of the French *mystère* (q.v.) is sometimes found, each scene was usually mounted on a waggon-stage or perambulating pageant (q.v.), which progressed from one station to another, wherever an audience could be assembled to watch it. The lower half of the waggon served as a dressing-room, the play being given on the upper half, with the actors descending also to play in the *platea*, or open space in front of the pageant, which served as an unlocalized playing-place and gave rise to the similar neutral area of the Elizabethan platform stage. With these perambulating pageants, an audience might see six or eight short plays during the day, with pauses for refreshment in between. Performances were usually given at Whitsun or on the feast of Corpus Christi (the Thursday after Trinity Sunday), when good weather might reasonably be expected. In Cornwall (see CORNISH ROUNDS) there is evidence that Mystery Plays were performed in circular enclosures with the various settings indicated by booths set on the flat central area, the action moving from one to another as required by the text. The surviving English mystery play cycles are known by the names of the towns where they are believed to have been performed —the Chester, probably written by Ralph Higden; the Coventry, now believed to be the lost Lincoln cycle, which contains the carol 'Lullay thou littel tiny child'; the Wakefield (or Townley), rougher in humour and containing the farcical *Second Shepherd's Play*, with Mak the sheep-stealer; and the York. The Digby cycle contains the only surviving English play based on the life of a saint (St. Mary Magdalene). Because of the number of actors and the hard work involved, pro-

ductions of Mystery Plays took place usually at intervals of several years. The actors, all amateurs and usually all male, except when a late introduction of realism called for a nude Eve or Bathsheba, wore costumes which were often elaborate but with no attempt at historical realism. God and the archangels usually had golden masks, and the devils who shovelled the lost souls into Hell after the Last Judgement wore close-fitting leather suits with tails and animal masks. They provided the comic relief for an audience which was prepared to sit or stand for hours while the great drama unrolled before them; so did such unbiblical characters as Noah's shrewish wife and daughters-in-law. But usually the play kept closely to stories taken from the Old and New Testaments, though, judging from the extant manuscripts, English audiences seemed particularly fond of the Old Testament scenes and of the scene of the Nativity. A new interest in early English vernacular drama has led to revivals of part of the York cycle at York in a modern version by Canon Purvis, first in 1951 and triennially since; of the Chester cycle in the Church of St. Peter-upon-Cornhill, London, also in 1951, and in 1967 at Chester itself; of some of the Wakefield cycle, in an adaptation by Martial Rose, at Bretton Hall, Wakefield, at the Mermaid Theatre in London in 1961, at the Derby Playhouse in 1968, and at the Young Vic in 1970; and of the Coventry (or Lincoln) cycle at Coventry in 1962, in Winchester Cathedral in 1965, at Grantham a year later, and at Lincoln itself in 1969.

N

NAHARRO, BARTOLOMÉ DE TORRES, see TORRES NAHARRO.

NAOGEORG, see KIRCHMAYER, THOMAS.

NARES, OWEN (1888–1943), English actor, grandson of the famous scene-painter Beverley (q.v.). His charm and good looks quickly made him a reputation in light romantic parts, and he was for many years a popular 'matinée idol' in London and on tour in such plays as Edward Sheldon's *Romance* (1915) and Hutchinson's *If Winter Comes* (1923). In later life he gave signs of greater depths than he had formerly been credited with, particularly in St. John Ervine's *Robert's Wife* (1937), in which he played opposite Edith Evans (q.v.), and Daphne du Maurier's *Rebecca* (1940), but he died suddenly before he had had time to develop his new-found powers.

Narr, the Fool (q.v.) of the sixteenth-century German Carnival play. Though not originally a comic character (the fools in Sebastian Brant's narrative *Narrenschiff* or *Ship of Fools* (1494) are those who live foolishly), he is made to appear so in the plays, of which he is usually the central character. He may also be a comic peasant, like the Clown (q.v.) in Shakespeare's plays, as opposed to the more sophisticated Court jester.

NASHE, THOMAS (1567–1601), English pamphleteer and playwright, who in the late 1580s collaborated with Christopher Marlowe (q.v.) in a tragedy, *Dido, Queen of Carthage*, and in 1597 was implicated, with Ben Jonson (q.v.) and others, in the trouble over a 'seditious comedy', *The Isle of Dogs*, which landed several people in prison. The text of this play is lost, and Nashe's only extant dramatic work is *Summer's Last Will and Testament* (1592–3), designed for performance in the house of a nobleman, probably Archbishop Whitgift at Croydon. It was used by the composer Constant Lambert as the basis of a masque for orchestra, chorus, and baritone solo, first heard in 1936.

Nassau Street Theatre. A large room in Nassau Street was probably the first place to be used by professional actors in New York, when in 1750 Walter Murray and Thomas Kean (q.v.) brought a company there from Philadelphia to appear in a repertory of tragedies and farces which included Colley Cibber's version of Shakespeare's *Richard III*. In 1751 an actor from London named Robert Upton appeared unsuccessfully in *Othello* and other plays and two years later the elder Lewis Hallam (q.v.) and his company dismantled, enlarged, and refurbished the old theatre, opening their season there in the autumn with Steele's *The Conscious Lovers* and ending it in March 1754 with Moore's *The Gamester*, after which the theatre seems to have been abandoned.

NATHAN, GEORGE JEAN (1882–1958), American dramatic critic, who in 1905 joined the staff of the *New York Herald* and began his fight for the drama of ideas, denouncing the works of such contemporary American playwrights as David Belasco and Augustus Thomas (qq.v.) and introducing to playgoers the modern plays of Europe—Ibsen, Shaw, Hauptmann, and Strindberg (qq.v.). His most important discovery, however, was Eugene O'Neill (q.v.), whose early work he published in *The Smart Set*. Later Nathan championed Sean O'Casey (q.v.), being largely responsible for the New York production of *Within the Gates* (1934), and William Saroyan (q.v.), whose first play, *My Heart's in the Highlands* (1939), he praised enthusiastically. For many years he produced an annual volume on each New York theatre season, and also wrote over thirty books on the theatre, of which *The Intimate Notebooks of George Jean Nathan* is especially interesting for its portraits of O'Neill, Dreiser, Sinclair Lewis, and others.

Nation, THÉÂTRE DE LA, see COMÉDIE-FRANÇAISE.

National Operatic and Dramatic Association (N.O.D.A.), an English organization formed in 1899 by a group of amateur societies which felt the need for a combined pooling of interests and activities. Its membership has grown to well over a thousand groups, as well as a large number of individuals. Unlike the British Drama League (q.v.), it is concerned entirely with amateurs, and most of its member groups concentrate on the production of light opera, particularly Gilbert and Sullivan, and musical comedy. It publishes a bulletin three times a year, and a Year Book annually. It has a library which is particularly rich in musical and operatic items but also contains plays and sets of reading scripts which members can borrow by post.

National Theatre, LONDON. The establishment of a permanent state-supported theatre in London on the lines of the Comédie-Française (q.v.) was first suggested by David Garrick (q.v.) in the eighteenth century, and in the nineteenth Bulwer-Lytton and Irving (qq.v.) were enthusiastic supporters of the idea. But it was not until 1908 that a committee was set up to investigate the possibility of founding a National Theatre in 1916 as a tribute to England's national dramatist, Shakespeare (q.v.), on the three-hundredth anniversary of his death. Two years later the publication of a volume entitled *The National Theatre: A Scheme and Estimates*, by William Archer and Harley Granville-Barker, stimulated further interest in the project, and a large sum of money was eventually subscribed, headed by a donation of £70,000 from Sir Carl Meyer. On the outbreak of the First World War in 1914 the work of the committee was suspended, but from 1919 onwards efforts were made to interest successive governments in the idea of a National Theatre. The money in hand amounting in 1938 to £150,000, a site in South Kensington, facing the Victoria and Albert Museum, was bought, and plans by Lutyens and Cecil Masey were completed. The outbreak of the Second World War again destroyed all hopes of an immediate start on the building and after the war a more ambitious project was launched. The site at South Kensington was exchanged for one on the South Bank and it was agreed that the Old Vic (q.v.) was eventually to provide the nucleus of a National Theatre company. On Friday, 13 June 1951, Queen Elizabeth, deputizing for her husband King George VI, laid the foundation stone of the projected theatre (this was the third ceremony of its kind—the first was in Gower Street, the second, by Shaw (q.v.), in South Kensington).

The stone has since been moved and the new site for the theatre is further downstream beyond Waterloo Bridge. In August 1962 a National Theatre Board under Lord Chandos (which in Nov. 1967 became the South Bank Theatre Board under Lord Cottesloe) was set up to create and run a National Theatre company under Sir Laurence Olivier (q.v.) which, pending the erection of a theatre, was temporarily housed in the Old Vic (q.v.). Meanwhile a building designed by Denys Lasdun was approved. A model, exhibited publicly in Nov. 1967, showed two auditoria, the main one, seating 1,165, fan-shaped with an open stage, suitable for Greek and Elizabethan and many modern plays, the smaller, seating 895, rectangular with a proscenium arch. There was also a third separate experimental theatre seating 200. Work began on the site in Nov. 1969. On 16 Mar. 1976 the first theatre, the Lyttelton, opened, followed on 25 Oct. 1976 by the Olivier, and on 4 Nov. 1977 by the Cottesloe.

(For a theatre in London called the National, see QUEEN'S THEATRE (1); for the People's National Theatre, see PRICE, NANCY.)

National Theatre, NEW YORK. (1) Originally the Italian Opera House, this opened as a theatre in 1836, and under the management of the elder J. W. Wallack (q.v.) became a serious rival to the Park (q.v.). In opposition to the latter's nickname of 'Old Drury' it was often referred to as 'Covent Garden', and most of the outstanding players of the day appeared there. It was burnt down on 23 Sept. 1839. Rebuilt, it was again destroyed on 29 May 1841, and not rebuilt.

(2) On 41st Street between 7th and 8th Avenues. This opened on 1 Sept. 1921 with Sidney Howard's *Swords*. Its first success was *The Cat and the Canary* (1922), a thriller by John Willard which ran for nearly a year. Later successes were Clemence Dane's *Will Shakespeare* with Katharine Cornell and Cornelia Otis Skinner, Walter Hampden in a revival of Rostand's *Cyrano de Bergerac* (both 1923), Veiller's *The Trial of Mary Dugan* (1927), Knoblock's *Grand Hotel* (1930), O'Casey's *Within the Gates* (1934), a dramatization of Edith Wharton's *Ethan Frome* and Noël Coward's *To-night at 8.30* (both 1936), Lillian Hellman's *The Little Foxes* (1939),

and Emlyn Williams's *The Corn is Green* (1940), in which Ethel Barrymore (q.v.) gave a fine performance as the elderly school-teacher. After structural alterations the theatre reopened on 11 Nov. 1941 with Maurice Evans in *Macbeth*, and in 1959 it was bought and redecorated by BILLY ROSE (1899–   ), who named it after himself, reopening it with a revival of Shaw's *Heartbreak House*. In 1962 came Albee's controversial play, *Who's Afraid of Virginia Woolf?*, and in 1964 his *Tiny Alice*, with John Gielgud and Irene Worth. *The Right Honourable Gentleman*, by Bradley-Dyne, based on the career of Sir Charles Dilke, opened in 1965, and a revival of Noël Coward's *Private Lives* began a long run in 1969.

(For the New National Theatre, New York, see CHATHAM THEATRE (2); see also BOSTON.)

National Youth Theatre, an organization founded in 1956 by MICHAEL CROFT, a master at Alleyn's School, Dulwich, who had formerly been an actor. The first production, *Henry V*, was given at Toynbee Hall with a cast of senior boys from Alleyn's and Dulwich College. Later the scope of the company was extended to cover schools throughout London and sometimes far beyond. Girls were admitted to play women's parts, and former members were allowed to continue acting until the age of twenty-one. In spite of constant financial anxiety and the lack of central premises, the company flourished, giving excellent performances in a number of Shakespeare's plays, notably *Hamlet*, which in 1962 toured provincial schools, under the auspices of Centre 42 (see WESKER). In 1967 the Youth Theatre, as it was then called, attracted universal attention by its production of *Zigger-Zagger*, a play by Peter Terson (q.v.) dealing with football. This inaugurated a new era, during which the company, moving from its original ambiance of educational Shakespeare, concentrated on new plays, particularly those specially written for it by Terson. In 1970 it became fully professional, taking over the Shaw Theatre in Camden for its main company and at the same time sending three amateur companies to tour the Continent.

Naturalism, a movement in the theatre of the late nineteenth century which carried a step further the revolt against the artificiality of contemporary forms of playwriting and acting initiated by the selective realism of Ibsen (q.v.). *Thérèse Raquin* (1873), dramatized by Zola (q.v.) from his own novel, was the first consciously conceived naturalistic drama, Strindberg's *Miss Julie* (1888) its first masterpiece. But it was Antoine (q.v.) who established it in the theatre. The influence of his Théâtre-Libre led to the foundation of the Freie Bühne (q.v.) in Germany and the Independent Theatre (see GREIN) in London, and the movement finally attained world recognition in the work of Stanislavsky (q.v.), particularly with his production of Gorky's *The Lower Depths* (1902). In Spain naturalism is represented by Benavente's *La Malquerida* (1913) and in the United States by the early works of O'Neill and the dramatized novels of Steinbeck (qq.v.).

Naumachia, in Rome, a mimic sea-fight staged in an arena flooded for the purpose—also the name given to an amphitheatre specially built for this purpose by Augustus on the right bank of the Tiber. Naumachiae, or water-pageants, were given in Italy at the time of the Renaissance.

(For English nineteenth-century aquatic spectacles see CIRCUS.)

Nautical Drama, a type of romantic melodrama popular in England in the late eighteenth and early nineteenth centuries. An early example was Smollett's *The Reprisal; or, the Tars of Old England*, seen at Drury Lane in 1757. The 'Jack Tar' was further popularized by Charles Dibdin, by Fitzball, and by Jerrold (qq.v.) with such dramas as *Black-Eyed Susan; or, All in the Downs* (1829). It was burlesqued in Dickens's novel *Nicholas Nickleby* (1838) and later in Gilbert and Sullivan's operetta *H.M.S. Pinafore* (1878). Nautical Drama should not be confused with Aquatic Drama (see CIRCUS).

NAZIMOVA, ALLA (1879–1945), Russian actress, who in 1904 was leading lady of a St. Petersburg theatre. She then toured Europe and America, and in 1906, having learnt English in less than six months, made her first appearance in an English-speaking part—the title-role in Ibsen's *Hedda Gabler*—at the Princess Theatre, New York. She remained in America, where she was considered an outstanding exponent of Ibsen's heroines, and in 1910 appeared at the Nazimova Theatre (see

THIRTY-NINTH STREET THEATRE), built and named for her by the Shuberts, opening there with Ibsen's *Little Eyolf*. After some years in films she returned to the stage, playing with the Civic Repertory Company and the Theatre Guild in Ibsen, Chekhov, Turgenev, and O'Neill.

NEAGLE, DAME ANNA [really FLORENCE MARJORIE ROBERTSON] (1904–   ), English actress, who made her first appearance on the stage as a child in 1917 but was not seen again until 1925, when she made her adult début as a chorus-girl in a revival of Charlot's revue *Bubbly*. She remained in revue for several years, making her first appearance in New York in *Wake Up and Dream* in 1929 on its transfer there from the London Pavilion. In 1934 she made her first appearance as a Shakespearian actress, playing Rosalind in *As You Like It* at the Open Air Theatre, and in 1937 was seen as Barrie's Peter Pan. She had already had a distinguished career in films when in 1943 she married the film director Herbert Wilcox, with whom she has since been associated in a number of productions. In 1945 she played Emma in a dramatization of Jane Austen's novel and in 1953 played several parts, including Nell Gwynn and Queen Victoria, in the musical *The Glorious Days*. In 1965 she appeared as Lady Hadwell in the musical *Charlie Girl*, which ran for five years. She was appointed C.B.E. in 1952 and D.B.E. in 1969 for services to the theatre.

Neighborhood Playhouse, NEW YORK, at 466 Grand Street, on the Lower East Side, built and endowed by ALICE and IRENE LEWISOHN, who designed, choreographed, and directed most of the productions seen there. The theatre opened on 12 Feb. 1915 with a dance-drama entitled *Jephthah's Daughter*, and before it closed in 1927 with the fifth annual edition of a review entitled *Grand Street Follies* it had been responsible for a long list of productions, including short plays by Dunsany, Chekhov, Sholem Asch, Yeats, and Shaw, and the first dramatic rendering of Browning's *Pippa Passes* (1917). Later productions included a number of new dance-dramas and ballets and such varied plays as *Fortunato* by the Quintero brothers, Galsworthy's *The Mob*, Granville-Barker's *The Madras House*, O'Neill's *The First Man*, Sheridan's *The Critic*, the Hindu drama *The Little Clay Cart*, and

Ansky's *The Dybbuk*. In 1959 Alice Lewisohn (Mrs. Crawley) (Irene having died in 1944) published an account of the theatre's activities entitled *The Neighborhood Playhouse*. After the closing of the theatre, a school of acting under the same name opened at 340 East 54th Street.

NEILSON, (LILIAN) ADELAIDE [really ELIZABETH ANN BROWN] (1846–80), English actress, who in 1865 made her first appearance on the stage as Julia in Sheridan Knowles's *The Hunchback*, always one of her best and favourite parts. She was also much admired as Viola (in *Twelfth Night*) and as Juliet (in *Romeo and Juliet*), and appeared in a number of dramatizations of Scott's novels. She made her first visit to the United States in 1872 and had just returned to England from a second extended tour of that country when she died.

NEILSON, JULIA EMILIE (1868–1957), English actress, wife and partner for many years of Fred Terry (q.v.), with whom she toured indefatigably in romantic costume plays. She had first been seen on the stage in 1888 in Gilbert's *Pygmalion and Galatea*, with Mary Anderson (q.v.), and after touring with Tree (q.v.) she went with him to the Haymarket, where she remained for five years, making an outstanding success as Drusilla Ives in Henry Arthur Jones's *The Dancing Girl* (1891). She also created the parts of Hester Worsley in *A Woman of No Importance* (1893) and Lady Chiltern in *An Ideal Husband* (1895), both by Oscar Wilde. She made her first appearance in New York in 1895 in Pinero's *The Notorious Mrs. Ebbsmith*, and soon after her return to England joined her husband at the Haymarket, playing the title-role in Kester's *Sweet Nell of Old Drury* (1900). From then until Terry's retirement in 1929 she played only with him, but after his death she was seen with Seymour Hicks in his play *Vintage Wine* (1934), and in 1938 she celebrated her stage jubilee. After some years in retirement she returned to the stage to make her last appearance as Lady Ruthven in *The Widow of Forty* (1944), by Heron Carvic, second husband of her daughter Phyllis.

NEMIROVICH-DANCHENKO, VLADIMIR IVANOVICH (1859–1943), an outstanding personality of the Russian stage, both Imperial and Soviet. He had already had a number of light comedies produced at the Maly Theatre (q.v.), and was in charge of the Drama Course of the Moscow Philharmonic Society, numbering Moskvin, Olga Knipper, and Meyerhold (qq.v.) among his pupils, when in 1897 meetings and discussions with Stanislavsky (q.v.) resulted in the founding of the Moscow Art Theatre. Nemirovich-Danchenko was responsible for the literary quality of the theatre's repertory, and it was he who persuaded Chekhov (q.v.) to allow the Moscow Art Theatre to revive *The Seagull* after its failure at the Alexandrinsky (q.v.). He wrote an account of the founding of the Moscow Art Theatre, and also expounded his own philosophy of the drama, in a volume entitled *My Life in the Russian Theatre* (1937).

NERO, Roman Emperor from A.D. 54 to 68. He was devoted to the theatre and appeared frequently on stage, not only as a dancer in pantomime but as an actor in such parts as the Mad Hercules, the Blind Oedipus, the Matricide Orestes, even Canace in Travail. These were evidently tragic scenes intended to be 'sung' by a single performer. On such occasions he wore a mask to indicate his role; but the features were modelled on his own, or on those of his mistress for the time being. From his famous theatrical tour of Greece (A.D. 66–7) he returned with 1,808 triumphal crowns. Even his worst crimes do not seem to have shocked conservative opinion in Rome as much as these antics—a fact which illustrates the low status of professional entertainers under the Empire.

NERONI, BARTOLOMEO (c. 1500–71/3), Italian architect, who in 1560 erected a theatre with a proscenium arch in a great hall behind the Palace of the Senate in Siena and furnished the stage behind it with scenery modelled on the designs of Serlio (q.v.). An engraving of this has fortunately been preserved and provides valuable information on the Renaissance theatre.

NESTROY, JOHANN NEPOMUK (1801–62), Austrian actor and dramatist, who in his satiric comedies reflects the rising tide of liberalism and social discontent which was to result in the Revolution of 1848.

The foundations of his success were laid in Vienna (q.v.), his birthplace, where he first appeared in 1829. His gift for improvisation and his immense facility (he wrote at least eighty-three plays) soon made him a popular figure, though his destructive criticism often brought him into conflict with the authorities. He excelled in parody, his main target being Wagner (q.v.). He was the last outstanding exponent of Viennese popular theatre, which after him declined into operetta. His first successful play was *Der böse Geist Lumpazivagabundus* (1833), in which two young women in male attire disport themselves in local taverns. Less farcical and of more lasting value, however, are such plays of social comment and political satire as *Zu ebener Erde und im ersten Stock* (1835) and *Freiheit in Krähwinkel* (1848). In 1842 Nestroy adapted John Oxenford's farce, *A Day Well Spent; or, Three Adventures*, as *Einen Jux will er sich machen*, later used by Thornton Wilder (q.v.) as the basis for his play *The Merchant of Yonkers* (1938).

NETHERSOLE, OLGA ISABEL (1863–1951), English actress and theatre manager, who first appeared in London in 1887 and two years later was seen at the Garrick, where her portrayal of the betrayed girl, Janet Preece, in Pinero's *The Profligate* brought her immediate recognition as an actress of unusual emotional power. In 1893 she scored a further triumph with her Countess Zicka in Sardou's *Diplomacy*. She then took over the (first) Royal Court Theatre (q.v.), inaugurating her management with A. W. Gattie's *The Transgressor* (1894), in which she played Sylvia Woodville. She made her New York début later the same year in this part, at Palmer's Theatre, and undertook several tours of the United States, where she became as popular as she was in London. Although she shocked older playgoers by her realistic portrayal of fallen women in such plays as the younger Dumas's *Camille*, Sudermann's *Magda*, Pinero's *The Second Mrs. Tanqueray* and *The Notorious Mrs. Ebbsmith*, and Maeterlinck's *Mary Magdalene*, the younger generations saw her as a symbol of the revolt against prudery. In 1900 she was arrested by the New York police for alleged indecency while appearing as Fanny Legrand in Clyde Fitch's *Sapho*, but was acquitted. She retired from the stage in 1914 and devoted herself to social work, for which she was awarded the C.B.E. in 1936.

NEUBER (*née* WEISSENBORN), (FREDERIKA) CAROLINA (1697–1760), one of the earliest and best-known of German actress-managers. After an unhappy childhood she eloped with a young clerk, JOHANN NEUBER (1697–1759), and with him joined a theatrical company. Ten years later they formed a company of their own. 'Die Neuberin', as she was called, was at this time at the height of her powers and had already attracted the notice of Gottsched (q.v.), who enlisted her help in his projected reform of the German stage, persuading her in 1727 to stage French classical plays in the place of the old improvised comedies, farces, and harlequinades. High-spirited and intolerant of restraint, however, she soon found herself in conflict with his rigid principles and they parted in 1739, after which the fortunes of her company declined. Even the collaboration of the young Lessing (q.v.) was of no avail, and after struggling along until the outbreak of the Seven Years War, which reduced them to poverty, husband and wife died within a year of each other. But in spite of its unfortunate conclusion, Carolina Neuber's association with Gottsched is generally regarded as the starting-point of the modern German theatre. She did a great deal for her profession, ruling her company with a firm hand, and insisting on regularity and order. Her style of acting, in its day, was a vast improvement on the old clowning and farcical horse-play and prepared the way for the subtle and more natural methods of Ekhof and Schröder (qq.v.).

NEUVILLE, HONORÉ BOURDON DE (1736–1812), see MO NTANSIER, MLLE.

NEVILLE, JOHN (1925–   ), English actor and theatre manager, who gained his experience in repertory, and from 1950 to 1953 with the Bristol Old Vic. He then rejoined the Old Vic company in London, with which he had first appeared in 1947 as a super in *Richard II*, and remained with it until 1959, playing a wide variety of parts and in 1956 alternating Othello and Iago with Richard Burton (q.v.). After leaving the company, with which he had made two tours of the United States, he was seen briefly in a couple of modern plays, and in 1961 went to the Nottingham Playhouse, where he remained until July

1968. He became associate producer in 1961 and artistic director of the theatre in 1963, when he opened the new Playhouse building with a production of *Coriolanus*, playing the title-role himself. During his time at Nottingham, which under him achieved an excellent reputation, he appeared in a number of parts—Richard II, Mosca in Jonson's *Volpone*, Willy Loman in Miller's *Death of a Salesman*—in plays which he also directed, and was seen at the first Chichester Festival in 1962 and at the Mermaid in London in the title-role of Naughton's *Alfie* in 1963. He was awarded the O.B.E. in 1965 for services to the theatre. Two years later a production of Arout's *Beware of the Dog*, based on short stories by Chekhov, was successfully transferred from Nottingham for a three-month run in London. In 1968 Neville returned to the London theatre, directing Livings's *Honour and Offer* in 1969 and appearing as King Magnus in Shaw's *The Apple Cart* in 1970 at the Mermaid. Since 1972 he has worked mainly in Canada, where he ran an art centre in Edmonton, and then in Halifax.

New Amsterdam Theatre, NEW YORK, on West 42nd Street between 7th and 8th Avenues, renowned as the home of the *Ziegfeld Follies*. It opened on 26 Oct. 1903 with *A Midsummer Night's Dream*, followed by *Mother Goose*, a pantomime from London's Drury Lane which ran for three months. The *Ziegfeld Follies* were first seen in 1913 and returned annually until 1925. The theatre was thereafter occupied mainly by musical comedy and revue, though the last production before it became a cinema was *Othello* (1937), with Walter Huston in the title-role and sets by Robert Edmond Jones.

New Bowery Theatre, NEW YORK, see BOWERY THEATRE (2).

New Broadway Theatre, NEW YORK, see DALY'S THEATRE (1).

New Chatham Theatre, NEW YORK, see CHATHAM THEATRE (2).

New Chelsea Theatre, LONDON, see ROYAL COURT THEATRE (1).

New English Opera House, LONDON, see ROYALTY THEATRE (2).

New Lyceum Theatre, LONDON, see PANHARMONIUM.

New Royalty Theatre, LONDON, see ROYALTY THEATRE (2).

New Strand Theatre, LONDON, see STRAND THEATRE (1).

New Theatre, LONDON, in St. Martin's Lane, built for Charles Wyndham (q.v.), who opened it on 12 Mar. 1903 with a revival of Parker and Carson's *Rosemary*, after which it settled down to a consistently successful career. From 1905 to 1913 Fred Terry and Julia Neilson (qq.v.) occupied it for a six-month annual season, and many of their most successful plays were seen there, including Baroness Orczy's *The Scarlet Pimpernel* in 1905. The theatre also housed an annual revival of Barrie's *Peter Pan* for several years. Among outstanding productions have been a dramatization of Louisa M. Alcott's *Little Women* (1919), in which Katharine Cornell (q.v.) made her only London appearance, A. A. Milne's *Mr. Pim Passes By* (1920), and, in 1924, Shaw's *St. Joan* with Sybil Thorndike (q.v.). A year later came the long run of Margaret Kennedy's *The Constant Nymph*, which saw the first appearance of John Gielgud (q.v.) at a theatre which later played an important part in his career, beginning in 1933, when he appeared there in Gordon Daviot's *Richard of Bordeaux*, followed by *Hamlet* (1934), Obey's *Noah* and *Romeo and Juliet* (both 1935). Among later productions at this theatre were *The Taming of the Shrew* (1937), O'Neill's *Mourning Becomes Electra* (1938), and Priestley's *Johnson over Jordan* (1939) with Ralph Richardson (q.v.). After the bombing of the Old Vic and Sadler's Wells, the New became the London headquarters of both companies, opening on 14 Jan. 1941. Sadler's Wells withdrew in 1944 and the Old Vic in 1950, in which year T. S. Eliot's *The Cocktail Party* began a successful run. The theatre has since housed a series of excellent plays, including Dylan Thomas's *Under Milk Wood* (1956), *Summer of the Seventeenth Doll* (1957) by the Australian playwright Ray Lawler, and Wolf Mankowitz's *Make Me an Offer* from Theatre Workshop (q.v.). In 1960 Lionel Bart's *Oliver!*, a musical based on Dickens's *Oliver Twist*, began a run of several years. In 1968 Hochhuth's con-

troversial play about Churchill, *Soldiers*, had a short run, and was followed by a popular musical, *Anne of Green Gables*. On 1 Jan. 1973 the theatre changed its name to Albery (q.v.) to honour the memory of its former director.

(For the New Theatre, New York, see CENTURY THEATRE (1).)

New Victoria Palace, LONDON, see OLD VIC.

New York Shakespeare Festival, see PAPP, JOSEPH.

New York Theatre, NEW YORK. (1) At 728 Broadway. On 23 Dec. 1865 LUCY RUSHTON, an actress of little ability but great personal charm, opened this under her own name, appearing unsuccessfully in a repertory of Shakespeare and classical comedy. It then closed, to be reopened on 3 Sept. 1866 as the New York. It was to this theatre that Augustin Daly (q.v.) took his company after his first Fifth Avenue Theatre was burnt down, remaining there the whole of 1873. After his departure the theatre was known as Fox's Broadway, and eventually it became a home of variety as the Globe.

(2) On Broadway between 44th and 45th Streets. Originally the Olympia Music-Hall, which opened on 17 Dec. 1895 with Yvette Guilbert (q.v.), this theatre reopened on 24 Apr. 1899 as the New York Theatre, and among the many successes staged there were a revival of Alice Hegan Rice's *Mrs. Wiggs of the Cabbage Patch* (1906), several of George M. Cohan's plays, and the musical comedy *Naughty Marietta* (1910). The theatre was later used for vaudeville and films and was finally demolished in 1935.

New Yorker Theatre, NEW YORK, on West 54th Street between Broadway and 8th Avenue. This opened as the Gallo in 1927 with opera, followed by Margaret Anglin in Euripides' *Electra* and the Abbey Players in O'Casey's *Juno and the Paycock*. On 12 May 1930 the theatre opened under its present name with a production of Ibsen's rarely-seen *The Vikings*, with a background of colour and light in moving patterns in place of realistic scenery. In 1932 a fine Spanish company under Fernando Díaz de Mendoza and María Guerrero occupied the theatre for five weeks in an impressive repertory which ranged from Lope de Vega to the Quintero brothers. In 1933, as the Casino de Paree, it was given over to music-hall and musical comedy but on 21 March 1939, after eighteen months as the Federal Music Theatre, it reverted to its present name with a production of *The Swing Mikado*, a modernization of Gilbert and Sullivan's operetta. It is now used for radio and television shows.

NEWES, TILLY (1886–1970), see WEDE-KIND, FRANK.

Newington Butts, LONDON (now the Elephant and Castle). Although it is not known whether there was a theatre building at Newington, or whether plays were given in an inn-yard there or in an enclosure in the open air, there can be no doubt that in Elizabethan times it was a theatrical centre of some importance. This is proved by many references to it, including a list of plays performed there by the Admiral's and Chamberlain's Men in 1594, entered in the diary of Henslowe (q.v.). Newington, which was a public resort for archery and general recreation, was a good site for a theatre, being the equivalent on London's South Bank of the northern Finsbury Fields, where the first theatre buildings arose (see CURTAIN THEATRE and THEATRE, THE).

Niblo's Garden, NEW YORK, a summer resort opened by William Niblo at the corner of Broadway and Prince Street on the site of the Columbia Garden. Here, in 1828, he built a small Sans Souci Theatre which was used, in the summer only, for concerts and also for plays, particularly after the destruction by fire of the first Bowery (q.v.) in 1828 and Wallack's National Theatre (q.v.) in 1839. On 18 Sept. 1846 the Sans Souci was itself burnt down. It was not rebuilt until 1849, when on 30 July a new theatre destined to be used the whole year round made a good start. It was improved and enlarged in 1853, and two years later saw the last appearance in New York of Rachel (q.v.). On 12 Sept. 1866 came the first performance of *The Black Crook*, a fantastic mixture of drama and spectacle, with elaborate transformation scenes and a scantily-clad *corps de ballet*, which ran for 475 performances and was followed by a similar spectacle, *The White Fawn*, which was less successful. After a production on 16 Nov. 1868 of Boucicault's melodrama, *After Dark; or, London by Night*, the theatre

was given over to melodrama and spectacle and to such popular performers as Lotta (see CRABTREE) and Chanfrau (q.v.), until on 6 May 1872 it was again burnt down. Rebuilt, it opened on 30 Nov. But its great days were over, and it was too far downtown for a front-rank theatre. It served for some time as a home for visiting companies and was finally demolished in 1895.

NICHOLS, PETER (1927–), English dramatist, who had written a number of successful television plays before he had an unexpected success in the theatre with *A Day in the Death of Joe Egg* (1967), in which Joe Melia and Zena Walker played the parents of a spastic child. The play, a 'serious' comedy, was first seen at the Glasgow Citizens' Theatre, and survived the transfer to London, where it ran for several months, in spite of some revulsion from its basic situation. A later play, *The National Health* (1969), originally written for television but first produced, appropriately enough, at the National Theatre (q.v.), again made use of a potentially tragic subject—a men's ward for incurables—as the basis of a 'bitter' comedy in which death is shown as inevitable and undignified. It was voted the best play of the year by the London theatre critics, and remains in the repertory of the National Theatre.

NICKINSON, ISABELLA (1847–1906), see WALCOT, CHARLES.

NICOLET, JEAN-BAPTISTE (c. 1728–96), French acrobat and entertainer, son of a puppet-master, who played at the fairs of St.-Germain and St.-Laurent. In 1760 he had a booth on the Boulevard du Temple, which may be said to have started that thoroughfare on its career as the focal point of Paris's minor theatres. Many attained notoriety, particularly in melodrama, before Haussmann's rebuilding scheme swept them all away in 1862. Nicolet's original booth was soon replaced by a permanent building which in 1792 became the Gaîté (q.v.).

NICOLL, ALLARDYCE (1894–1976), an outstanding Scottish historian of the theatre, successively Professor of English Language and Literature in London and Birmingham Universities, and at one time head of the Department of Drama at Yale University, where he began a vast and comprehensive file of photographs of theatrical material from all over Europe which is constantly being enriched, forming a precious deposit of valuable material for the theatre research worker. Nicoll is the author of a number of useful and well-illustrated books on specialized aspects of the theatre, including *Masks, Mimes, and Miracles* and *Stuart Masques and the Renaissance Stage*, and of more popular works, such as *British Drama, The English Theatre*, and *Readings in British Drama*, intended for the use of young students and non-specialists. In 1946 he brought to a close, with the publication of his two-volume *Nineteenth Century Drama, 1850–1900*, a series of eight volumes, begun in 1923, covering the history of the English theatre from the Restoration, each period having an invaluable hand-list of plays arranged under dramatists.

Nigger Minstrels. This term, which is no longer acceptable (see MINSTREL SHOW), was originally used in Great Britain, though not in the United States, with no derogatory meaning but carrying overtones, now lost, of affection and amusement. It was applied indifferently to the Burnt-cork Minstrels (white men with blackened faces) and to the true Negro Minstrel troupes.

Nō Play, the lyrical drama of Japan, established by KWANAMI (1333–84) and his son ZEAMI (1363–1443), though the courtly language and formal style of the works attributed to them suggest an earlier derivation, as far back even as the end of the twelfth century. The *kyōgen*, or comic interludes which form part of the *nō* plays, are in the vernacular of the mid-sixteenth century, and the genre reached its point of perfection a hundred years later, since when it has changed very little. The *nō* play draws its material mainly from the Buddhist scriptures and the mythology of China and Japan, and its form from the ritual dances of the temples with accretions from folk-dances of the countryside. It is essentially a drama of soliloquy and reminiscence, and unlike Western drama has no development through conflict. Having been for a long time reserved for the amusement of the ruling class, its audiences tend still to be elderly and educated, with a sprinkling of foreign visitors. *Nō* plays are acted on a raised resonant stage of polished wood, with a temple roof over it supported on four pillars, and the audience on two sides. On the actor's left are the ten members of the chorus, behind him four musicians—a flute and three drums—and two stage hands, who by tradition are invisible. The performers enter along the *hashigakari*, a passage about forty feet long which runs at an angle backward from the right-hand edge of the stage. There is no scenery, but the costumes are sumptuous, particularly those of the First Actor (*shite*), who is introduced by the Second Actor (*waki*), and as god or hero, wearing a mask, performs the ritual dances which are the heart of the play. (See also KABUKI).

NOAH, MORDECAI MANUEL (1785–1851), early American playwright, whose first play, produced in Charleston in 1812, was a translation of *Le Pèlerin blanc* (1801), by Pixérécourt (q.v.), as *The Wandering Boys.* This was later produced at Covent Garden with alterations by John Kerr, and in its new form returned to New York, where it remained popular for many years. Noah's later plays were produced at the Park Theatre (q.v.), and it was after the third night of *The Siege of Tripoli* (now lost) on 24 May 1820 that the theatre was destroyed by fire. In a later play, *The Grecian Captive* (1822), the hero and heroine made their entrances on an elephant and a camel respectively, a spectacular device due, no doubt, to the fertile brain of the manager, Stephen Price (q.v.), who later imported real tigers on to the stage of London's Drury Lane. Noah's plays are simply written, with a good deal of action and sustained interest, and with the aid of lavish scenery, transparencies, and illuminations they held the stage for many years. The prefaces to the printed editions give an amusing account of his experiences in the theatre, and of the difficulties of the native American playwright in competition with the established English drama.

N.O.D.A., see NATIONAL OPERATIC AND DRAMATIC ASSOCIATION.

Noises off, a term covering all the sound-effects needed in a production, which for modern plays may include planes, cars, machine-guns, bombs, and all types of machinery. These are usually supplied today by a tape-recording, earlier by a gramophone record. Before that they were the responsibility of the EFFECTS MAN, who could supply not only such simple things as gunshots, glass and china breaking, doors slamming, and bells ringing, but the sound of galloping horses, usually by clattering empty coconut shells, or the fall of a body into water, sometimes accompanied by the 'splash' of a handful of rice thrown up from behind a groundrow. Snow fell in the form of white confetti or torn-up paper (usually seen through a window); rain came from an elongated pierced rose attached to a watering can. Lightning was part of stage lighting (q.v.), but thunder could be produced either by a THUNDER SHEET, a suspended sheet of iron vigorously shaken, or in the Georgian theatre by a THUNDER RUN, two long inclined wooden troughs down which heavy iron balls were rolled. Howling gales were simulated by the WIND MACHINE, in which a ribbed drum (sometimes containing dried peas to give the effect of heavy raindrops) was revolved against a sheet of silk to produce a singing note which could be varied in intensity.

NOKES, JAMES (?–1696), English actor, and a member of Davenant's company. He was a fine comedian, of whom Colley Cibber (q.v.) has left a masterly penportrait, and usually played foolish old husbands and clumsy fops, as well as a few ridiculous old ladies. His best part, among the many that he created in Restoration drama, seems to have been the title-role in Dryden's comedy *Sir Martin Mar-all* (1667).

Nora Bayes Theatre, NEW YORK, see FORTY-FOURTH STREET THEATRE.

NORTON, THOMAS (1532–84), a member of the Inner Temple who with Thomas Sackville (q.v.) wrote *Gorboduc, or Ferrex and Porrex*, the first surviving example of regular five-act Senecan tragedy in English dramatic literature. It was first acted on New Year's Day 1561/2 at an entertainment before Queen Elizabeth I in Inner Temple Hall. In theme it resembles *King Lear*, with Gorboduc, king of Britain, dividing his kingdom between his two sons, who quarrel and are both killed.

Norwich, which is best known in theatrical circles for the Maddermarket Theatre (q.v.), was the headquarters of the Norwich circuit company, which visited Ipswich, Bury, Colchester, Yarmouth, and many lesser Norfolk towns. Before

the building of the first theatre in 1758 by Thomas Ivory on Assembly Plain a number of taverns served as playingplaces, among them the White Swan, which, though it was last used for entertainment in 1771, was not finally demolished until 1961. Ivory obtained a royal patent in 1768 and was succeeded by William Wilkins, who appointed a series of managers, including Brunton, to run the circuit. A new Theatre Royal was built in 1826 at the cost of £6,000 on a site adjoining the old one. The Norwich circuit broke up about 1852, and the next ten years saw the change-over from stock to touring companies typical of the provinces at this time. The Theatre Royal, enlarged in 1913, was burnt down in 1934, but reopened in 1935. It is now used for more than six months of the year as a cinema. The Hippodrome, which closed in 1960, was the last full-time professional theatre in Norwich.

NORWID, CYPRIAN KAMIL (1821–83), Polish Romantic poet and painter. Exiled in 1842, he spent most of his life in Paris. Beginning with historical tragedies— *Wanda* and *Krakus* (both 1847)—in the manner of Słowacki, he wrote between 1862 and 1881 a number of deeply religious poetic plays. Only three of his twenty-one completed works were published during his lifetime. Rediscovered in 1904 and first acted in 1908, Norwid is now considered one of the masters of Polish drama.

NORWORTH, JACK (1879–1959), an American comedian who first appeared in 'black-face' and then went into vaudeville. With his second wife, the singer NORA BAYES (1880–1928), whom he married in 1907, he formed a double act which was successful in New York and London. He is best remembered as the singer of such tongue-twisters as 'Sister Susie' and 'Which Switch is the Switch, Miss, for Ipswich'. Among his own compositions the best loved is probably 'Shine On, Harvest Moon'. The Belmont Theatre (q.v.) was originally named after him.

NOVELLI, ERMETE (1851–1919), Italian actor, who made his first appearance on the stage at the age of eighteen, and though not at first successful soon became, by perseverance and natural genius, the outstanding Italian actor of his day. A large man, weighing some eighteen stone, he was nevertheless light on his feet and quick in action, with a fine, expressive head and mobile features. He was excellent in comedy, but it was in tragedy, as Othello, Lear, Shylock, Macbeth, and Hamlet, that he made his reputation. He toured extensively, and after appearing in several European countries visited the United States, South America, and Egypt. In 1900 he attempted to found a permanent theatre in Rome, but failed through lack of public support.

NOVELLO [really DAVIES], (DAVID) IVOR (1893–1951), actor-manager, dramatist, and composer. The son of musical parents—his mother, Clara Novello Davies (*née* Davies), a well-known choral conductor, owed her Christian names to her father's admiration for the great singer, to whom she was not related, and who was not, as is sometimes stated, her godmother—Ivor Novello, as he called himself, showed from his earliest days facility and tunefulness in the composition of light music. During the First World War he was responsible for part of the score of several successful musical comedies and also wrote 'Keep the Home Fires Burning'. He made his first appearance on the stage at the Ambassadors Theatre in London in 1921. Three years later he wrote his first play, *The Rat*, in collaboration with Constance Collier (q.v.), appearing in it himself. Among his later plays were *Symphony in Two Flats* (1929), *I Lived With You* (1932), and *We Proudly Present* (1947). He was also the author, composer, and leading man of four successive musical plays at Drury Lane—*Glamorous Night* (1935), *Careless Rapture* (1936), *Crest of the Wave* (1937), and *The Dancing Years* (1939). He was appearing in his own *King's Rhapsody* (1949) at the time of his death.

Novelty Theatre, LONDON, see KINGSWAY THEATRE.

NOVIUS (1st century B.C.), see ATELLAN FARCE.

NUNN, TREVOR (1940–), English stage director, who at the age of twenty-eight was appointed Artistic Director of the Royal Shakespeare Company (q.v.) in succession to Peter Hall. On leaving school he taught for a year and directed a Youth Drama Group in Ipswich, his birthplace, before going to Cambridge, where he studied under Dr. Leavis, whose influence on him was to a certain extent counterbalanced by that of George Rylands (q.v.). He appeared in several undergraduate productions and in 1962 went to the Belgrade Theatre, Coventry, as a trainee-director on an A.B.C. Television scholarship, later remaining there as resident director until in 1965 he joined the Royal Shakespeare Company. His first production at the Aldwych was *Henry V* (in association with John Barton). In 1966, at Stratford-upon-Avon, he directed the first revival for three hundred years of Tourneur's *The Revenger's Tragedy*, and in 1967 was responsible for an excellent revival of Vanbrugh's *The Relapse*, later seen in London, and for a production of *The Taming of the Shrew* (1968), which was also seen on tour in the United States. Among other productions for which he has received critical acclaim have been *Much Ado About Nothing* and *King Lear* (both 1968) and *Henry VIII* (1969). During his first year in charge at the Aldwych, a season of five new American plays was given, of which Albee's *A Delicate Balance* was directed by Nunn himself.

Nursery, a training school for young actors set up by Killigrew (q.v.) in Hatton Garden in about 1662, which some time in 1668 moved to the old theatre in Gibbon's Tennis-Court (see VERE STREET THEATRE). It disappeared in 1671, when the widow of William Davenant (q.v.) built a new Nursery in the Barbican. This flourished until at least 1682, being referred to in Dryden's *MacFlecknoe*, published in that year.

O

Oberammergau, see MYSTERIENSPIEL.

OBEY, ANDRÉ (1892–1975), French dramatist, whose *Noé, Le Viol de Lucrèce,* and *La Bataille de la Marne* were all produced in 1931 by the Compagnie des Quinze (see COPEAU and SAINT-DENIS). The first, which was performed in English in London in 1935 with John Gielgud (q.v.) as Noah, was remarkable for the liveliness of its beasts. The second, which made use of a modified Greek chorus, was one of the sources of the libretto of Benjamin Britten's opera 'The Rape of Lucrece' (1946).

OBRAZTSOV, SERGEI VLADIMIROVICH (1901–), the outstanding puppet-master of the Soviet Union, where he runs the State Central Puppet Theatre in Moscow. As a young man he toured England and America, returning to London in 1953 and to the United States in 1963, when two items in his repertory were particularly admired—*An Unusual* (originally *A Usual*) *Concert*, which satirizes the mannerisms and mistakes of bad concert-platform performers, and *Aladdin and His Wonderful Lamp.* Obraztsov's puppet-shows are intended mainly for adults, but appeal also to children.

O'CASEY, SEAN [really JOHN CASEY] (1880–1964), Irish dramatist, and the best-known of those who portrayed life in the slums of Dublin. He knew intimately the people of whom he wrote and the events of the troubled years in Ireland between 1915 and 1922 from which he drew the material for several of his plays. Many episodes in them stem directly from his personal experiences, as recorded in his six volumes of autobiography (1939–51; in 2 vols. 1963). The first of his plays to be produced, at the Abbey Theatre (q.v.), was *The Shadow of a Gunman* (1923; London, 1927; New York, 1932), a melo-dramatic story of the fighting in Dublin in 1920. It was followed by *Juno and the Paycock* (1924; London, 1925; New York, 1926) and *The Plough and the Stars* (Dublin and London, 1926; New York, 1927), which caused a riot in the theatre on its first night. These two plays represent the best of O'Casey's work. Both have been several times revived in London and New York. When O'Casey's next play, *The Silver Tassie* (1928), which marks a distinct change from his earlier style, was rejected by the Abbey, he left Ireland and for many years refused to allow his plays to be performed there. In *Within the Gates* (1934), set in London, and such plays as *The Star Turns Red* (1940), *Purple Dust* (written in 1940, but not seen in New York until 1956 and London in 1962), and *Oak Leaves and Lavender* (1947), O'Casey turned to the use of symbolism and ex-pressionistic devices to reinforce the Marxist ideas of his heroes. The final phase of his work, as represented by *Red Roses for Me* (1946; New York, 1955), *Cock-a-Doodle Dandy* (New York, 1958; London, 1959), and *The Bishop's Bonfire* (1961), contrasts the repressive forces of the clergy and the moneyed classes in Ire-land with the younger generation's desire for artistic, sexual, and political freedom. O'Casey's own theories on the theatre can be studied in two volumes of dramatic criticism, *The Flying Wasp* (1937) and *The Green Crow* (1957).

ODÉON, THÉÂTRE ROYAL DE L', formerly the second theatre of Paris, which ranked next to the Comédie-Française (q.v.). It was opened in 1816 by Picard, and two years later destroyed by fire. Rebuilt, it was again managed by Picard until his retirement in 1821. Its repertory consisted mainly of light opera or comedies with music. It was not until Harel took over its management in 1829 that music was left to the Opéra and the Opéra-Comique, and the Odéon built up a classical and contemporary repertory of straight plays which made it famous. In 1959 Barrault (q.v.) was appointed director of the Odéon, which was then renamed the Théâtre de France. He produced there a number of important new plays, notably *Les Para-vents* (1961) by Jean Genet (q.v.), on the war in Algeria, which caused demon-strations in the theatre. In May 1968 the Odéon became a centre of student rioting, which led to the dismissal of Barrault, and the theatre is now used by provincial and foreign companies and by the Théâtre des Nations (q.v.).

ODETS, CLIFFORD (1906–63), American dramatist, and the most gifted of those who developed a theatre of social protest in the 1930s. In 1935 he attracted attention with a long one-act play about a taxi-drivers' strike, *Waiting for Lefty*, first produced by the Group Theatre, of which he was a member, at the Civic Repertory Theatre. When this was produced on Broadway he added to it another one-acter, *Till the Day I Die*, a drama of the anti-Nazi underground in Germany seen in London in 1940. *Awake and Sing* (also 1935; London, 1938) caused him to be hailed as America's most promising young playwright, a reputation confirmed by his play about a prizefighter, *Golden Boy* (1937; London, 1938). This was, however, his last successful production, and with his later plays, which included *The Big Knife* (1949; London, 1953), a melodramatic indictment of the Hollywood film industry, and *The Country Girl* (1950) (produced in London in 1952 as *Winter Journey*), his star declined. His last play, *The Flowering Peach* (1954), was a retelling of the biblical story of Noah, which ran for some months in New York.

OEHLENSCHLAEGER, ADAM GOTTLOB (1779–1850), Danish poet and dramatist, who as a young man came into contact with the theatre in Copenhagen, first as an actor, though only for a short time, and then as a playwright. Although he was much influenced by the late eighteenth-century romanticism of German writers popular in Denmark at the time, he transmuted it into a national expression of the poetic and dramatic instincts of the Danish people, and many of his best plays—he wrote more than thirty in all—were based on the early sagas. Among his early works, the best are probably *Sanct Hans Aften-Spil* (1802) and *Hakon Jarl* (1807); among those of his later years *Hagbarth og Signe* (1815) and *Væringerne i Miklagård* (1827) are outstanding, both for dramatic depth and for the steady development of thought and character.

OENSLAGER, DONALD MITCHELL (1902–75), American scene designer, who worked under G. P. Baker (q.v.) at Harvard and later studied in Europe. With Robert Edmond Jones, Lee Simonson, and Jo Mielziner (qq.v.), he helped to create a new age of stagecraft in the United States, and made a permanent impression on the theatre there. From 1925 he designed sets for many major productions, among them Steinbeck's *Of Mice and Men* (1937), Shaw's *The Doctor's Dilemma* (1941), *Pygmalion* (1945), and *Major Barbara* (1956), Ibsen's *Peer Gynt* (1951), and Shakespeare's *Coriolanus* (1954); also for such modern plays as Leonard Spigelgass's *A Majority of One* (1959) and *The Wrong Way Light Bulb* (1969), *A Call on Kuprin*, by Jerome Lawrence and Robert E. Lee, and Henry Denker's *A Far Country* (both 1961).

Off-Broadway, a term used collectively of theatres and plays which, being mainly experimental and non-commercial, are outside the orbit of the American commercial and centralized theatre, located on Broadway (the New York equivalent of London's West End). The even more *avant-garde* productions of recent years have been further characterized as off-off-Broadway. Several off-Broadway ventures have made theatrical history (see CIRCLE-IN-THE-SQUARE, LIVING THEATRE, NEIGHBOR-HOOD PLAYHOUSE, PHOENIX THEATRE (2), PROVINCETOWN PLAYERS, THÉÂTRE DE LYS).

Ohel (the Hebrew word for tent), the theatrical company of the Israeli Jewish Labour Federation, founded in 1925. It gave its first public performance in Tel Aviv on 24 May 1926, the programme consisting of dramatizations of stories by Peretz with scenery designed by Chagall. Since then it has produced a wide variety of plays, mainly realistic comedies, staged in a portable theatre used for touring agricultural settlements and, since 1948, immigrant camps. The company toured Europe in 1934 and again in 1950, with marked success. It was disbanded in 1969.

Ohio Roscius, see ALDRICH, LOUIS.

OHNET, GEORGES (1848–1918), French novelist and dramatist, whose best-known play, *Le Maître de forges* (1883), was based on one of his own novels. As *The Ironmaster*, in an adaptation by Pinero (q.v.), it was produced in London in 1884. Ohnet wrote a number of other plays, popular in their own day but now forgotten.

O'KEEFFE, JOHN (1747–1833), Irish dramatist, who was for some years an actor in Mossop's stock company in Dublin. He went blind in his late twenties and was forced to give up acting, but continued to write plays, mainly farces and light operas. The most successful were *The Poor Soldier* (1783), with music by William Shield (seen in Dublin in 1777 as *The Shamrock; or, St. Patrick's Day*), which had a great vogue in America, and the comedy *Wild Oats; or, the Strolling Gentleman* (1791). A volume of autobiography, *Recollections of the Life of John O'Keeffe, Written by Himself*, was published in 1826.

OKHLOPKOV, NIKOLAI PAVLOVICH (1900–67), Soviet director, whose first production, in 1921, was a May-Day spectacle staged in the central square of his birthplace, Irkutsk, of which he was author, director, and chief actor. In it can be found the germ of that original style of production which he later developed more fully at the Realistic Theatre (q.v.), where he became artistic director in 1930, producing a number of new Soviet plays, among them Gorky's *Mother* and Pogodin's *Aristocrats*. For each new play he set up a different stage, or set of stages, and drew the spectators into the action. (For a detailed description of his methods, see Van Gyseghem: *Theatre in Soviet Russia*, 1943.) His work was necessarily experimental and had a somewhat limited appeal, which led to the closing of the theatre in 1938. Okhlopkov worked for a while at the Vakhtangov (q.v.), where his production of Rostand's *Cyrano de Bergerac* was notable for the originality of its interpretation, and in 1943 became director of the Theatre of the Revolution (see MAYAKOVSKY THEATRE), where his revivals of Ostrovsky's *Fear* (1953) and of *Hamlet* (1954) were much admired. He also continued his policy of producing new Soviet plays, including Arbuzov's *Endless Distance* (1958) and Pogodin's *The Little Student* (1959). (See also POPOV.)

Old Bowery Theatre, NEW YORK, see BOWERY THEATRE (1).

Old Comedy, a term which covers the early plays of Aristophanes (q.v.) and his contemporaries, as opposed to the New Comedy of Menander (q.v.). In the nineteenth century it was used in England, and also in the United States, to denote selected English comedies from Shakespeare to Sheridan.

Old Drury, see CHESTNUT STREET THEATRE,

PHILADELPHIA, DRURY LANE, LONDON, and PARK THEATRE, NEW YORK (1).

Old Man, Woman, see STOCK COMPANY.

Old Mo, see MIDDLESEX MUSIC-HALL.

Old Vic Theatre, LONDON, in the Waterloo Road, famous for its Shakespeare productions. It was originally the Royal Coburg, so named in honour of Princess Charlotte's husband, Leopold of Saxe-Coburg, who laid the foundation-stone in 1816. It opened on 11 May 1818 with a melodramatic spectacle, *Trial by Battle; or, Heaven Defend the Right*, written and produced by William Barrymore (q.v.). It soon attracted a local audience with melodramas of the most sensational kind, but its plays were apparently well-staged, and many actors enshrined in the Toy Theatre (q.v.) appeared there. The interior was handsomely decorated, one of the most interesting features being the famous curtain installed in 1820–1, which consisted of sixty-three pieces of looking-glass and reflected the whole house. Its weight put too great a strain on the roof and it had to be removed.

In 1833 the theatre, in which Edmund Kean (q.v.) had appeared two years previously, was redecorated and reopened as the Royal Victoria, being named after Princess (later Queen) Victoria. The opening production was a revival of Jerrold's *Black-Eyed Susan*. The theatre was soon nicknamed the Old Vic, and gradually sank to the level of a Blood-Tub (see GAFF). In 1871 it was sold by auction and became the New Victoria Palace. It finally closed in the early part of 1880. Emma Cons, a social reformer and the first woman member of the L.C.C., then bought the freehold and reopened the building on 27 Dec. 1880 as a temperance amusement-hall, naming it the Royal Victoria Hall and Coffee Tavern. It was intended as a cheap and decent place for family entertainment at reasonable prices, and in spite of considerable misgivings it prospered. From 1881 to 1883 William Poel (q.v.) was its manager, and the project was greatly helped by Samuel Morley, after whom Morley College, which occupied part of the building, was named. In 1900 the first opera was produced there (Balfe's 'The Bohemian Girl') and scenes from Shakespeare supplemented the usual vocal and orchestral concerts. In 1912 Emma Cons's niece, Lilian Baylis (q.v.), took over the management, and in 1914 the first regular Shakespeare season was given. Under Ben Greet, and with the devoted co-operation of such actors as Lewis Casson and Sybil Thorndike (qq.v.), the theatre survived the First World War to become the only permanent home of Shakespeare in London. In 1923 it celebrated the tercentenary of the publication of the First Folio by a performance of *Troilus and Cressida*, thus completing the cycle of all Shakespeare's plays under the management of Lilian Baylis. A succession of excellent actors and directors assured the success of the Old Vic far beyond the confines of its own territory, a success only momentarily checked by the death of Lilian Baylis in 1937. Among her outstanding contributions to the theatre of her time had been the appointment of Ninette de Valois as ballet-mistress, which resulted in the foundation of the Royal Ballet Company, and the reopening of Sadler's Wells (q.v.). The Old Vic, which had been partly demolished and reconstructed in 1927, was badly damaged by enemy action on 19 May 1941 and had to be closed, but its work continued, on tour or at the New Theatre (q.v.) in London. In 1950 it was repaired and redecorated, and it reopened on 14 Nov. 1950 with *Twelfth Night*. From 1953 to 1958 a 'five-year plan' resulted in the presentation of the thirty-six plays in the First Folio, beginning with *Hamlet* and ending with *Henry VIII*. On 15 June 1963 the Old Vic finally closed with a performance of *Measure for Measure*, and the company was disbanded. On 22 Oct. the building, which had so long served as an unofficial national theatre for the performance of Shakespeare and other classics, reopened as the temporary home of the National Theatre (q.v.) with a production of *Hamlet*. During subsequent years it housed revivals of some Shakespeare plays, and new plays, among them Shaffer's *The Royal Hunt of the Sun* (1964) and Stoppard's *Rosencrantz and Guildenstern are Dead* (1967). After the National Theatre company moved to the South Bank in 1976 the Old Vic housed several successful seasons by the Prospect Theatre Company. In 1983 it was bought by the Canadian businessman, Ed Mirvish.

OLDFIELD, ANNE [also known as NANCE] (1683–1730), English actress, successor to Mrs. Bracegirdle (q.v.). She first came into prominence when she played Lady Betty Modish in Cibber's *The Careless Husband* (1704) at Drury Lane, and was subsequently much admired as Sylvia in *The Recruiting Officer* (1706) and Mrs. Sullen in *The Beaux' Stratagem* (1707), both by Farquhar (q.v.), who had first encouraged her to go on the stage. Although she was good in tragedy, creating the part of Andromache in Philips's *The Distres't Mother* (1712) (based on Racine's *Andromaque*) and the title-role in Rowe's *Jane Shore* (1714), she much preferred comedy, one of her finest parts being Lady Townly in *The Provoked Husband* (1728), based by Cibber on an unfinished play by Sir John Vanbrugh (q.v.). She made her last appearance in Fielding's *Love in Several Masques* (also 1728). She was buried in Westminster Abbey, near Congreve, her name on her tombstone being misspelt 'Ann'. She had an exceptionally beautiful voice and clear diction, and Voltaire (q.v.) said she was the only English actress whose speech he could follow without effort.

OLDMIXON, MRS. (*née* GEORGINA SIDUS) (?–1835), English actress, daughter of an Oxford clergyman, who married a grandson of the John Oldmixon mentioned in Pope's *The Dunciad*. As Miss George, she was well known in London before leaving for Philadelphia, where in 1793 she joined the company at the Chestnut Street Theatre (q.v.). She later moved to New York, and in 1798 became a member of Dunlap's company at the newly opened Park Theatre (q.v.), playing Mrs. Candour in Sheridan's *The School for Scandal* and Ophelia in *Hamlet*. She was also seen in *Inkle and Yarico*, by George Colman the younger, in which she had appeared at the Haymarket, London, on its first production in 1787. She then retired from the stage for some years, but in 1806 reappeared, playing the Nurse in *Romeo and Juliet*, and other elderly parts, under Cooper (q.v.). After finally retiring in 1813, she opened a seminary for young ladies in New York, and appeared occasionally on the concert platform.

Olimpico. The Teatro Olimpico, in Vicenza, Italy, is an outstanding example of the academic Renaissance theatre. Built by Andrea Palladio (q.v.), it opened on 3 Mar. 1585 with an epic production of Sophocles' *Oedipus Rex*. The building, which still stands, had a superb *scaenae frons*, based on the Hellenistic and Roman theatres described by Vitruvius (q.v.).

In spite of its splendour, it had little or no influence on the development of later theatre buildings in Italy, whose opera-houses evolved from Scamozzi's theatre at Sabbionetta and Aleotti's Teatro Farnese (see THEATRE BUILDINGS).

OLIVIER, SIR LAURENCE KERR (1907–89), actor and producer, knighted in 1947 for his services to the theatre, and created a life peer in the Birthday Honours of 1970. He made his first appearance on the stage at Stratford-upon-Avon in 1922 as Katharina in a schoolboy production of *The Taming of the Shrew*. From 1926 to 1928 he was with the Birmingham Repertory company, and in 1937, after a career which ranged from modern parts to an alternation of Romeo and Mercutio with John Gielgud at the New Theatre in 1935, he joined the Old Vic (q.v.), where his reputation was chiefly made, particularly in *Hamlet*, which he played in its entirety in 1937 at the Old Vic and later at Elsinore. His versatility may be judged by his playing on one evening Hotspur and Justice Shallow in *Henry IV, Parts 1 and 2*, and on another Sophocles' Oedipus and Sheridan's Mr. Puff (in *The Critic*). In 1955 he appeared with the Royal Shakespeare Company as Titus in an outstanding revival of *Titus Andronicus*. He also proved himself a good exponent of modern drama in such parts as Archie Rice in Osborne's *The Entertainer* (1957) and Berenger in Ionesco's *Rhinoceros* (1960). In 1961 he was appointed director of the Chichester Festival Theatre (q.v.), and in the same year became the first director of the National Theatre (q.v.), producing the opening play, *Hamlet*. In 1964 he appeared for the first time as Othello. He continued to direct the Chichester Festival Theatre until 1965, when he was succeeded by John Clements. In 1961 he married, as his third wife, the actress Joan Plowright (q.v.), with whom he had appeared in several productions, notably *Rhinoceros*. He was first married to the actress Jill Esmond (daughter of H. V. Esmond and Decima Moore), by whom he had a son, and then to the actress Vivien Leigh. Both these marriages ended in divorce. He appeared in a number of films, of which the finest were his productions of *Henry V*, *Hamlet*, and *Richard III*. During the Second World War he served for a time ir the Fleet Air Arm. Among his outstanding parts in the National Theatre

repertory were Astrov in Chekhov's *Uncle Vanya* and Brazen in Farquhar's *The Recruiting Officer* (both 1963), Tattle in Congreve's *Love for Love* (1965), the Captain in Strindberg's *The Dance of Death* (1968), and Shylock in a Victorian production of *The Merchant of Venice* (1970).

Olympia Music-hall, NEW YORK, see NEW YORK THEATRE (2).

Olympic Pavilion, LONDON, see OLYMPIC THEATRE (1).

Olympic Theatre. (1) LONDON, in Wych Street, near Drury Lane (q.v.). Built by Philip Astley (q.v.), this opened as the Olympic Pavilion on 18 Sept. 1806. It was not successful, in spite of several changes of name and a varied programme, and in 1813 it was bought by Elliston (q.v.) who, after improving the interior, opened it on 19 Apr. 1813 as the Little Drury Lane Theatre. After some trouble with the Patent Theatres, it was closed on 11 May, to reopen late in Dec. as the Olympic. It prospered, and in 1818 Elliston practically rebuilt it and engaged a good company, reopening on 16 Nov. 1818 with Moncrieff's *Rochester; or, King Charles the Second's Happy Days*. When Elliston left to go to Drury Lane (q.v.), and ruined himself there, the Olympic was sold by auction to John Scott (see ADELPHI), under whom it reopened on 6 Nov. 1826, newly lit by gas, and became a home of lurid melodrama. It was not until Mme Vestris (q.v.) took over in 1830, so becoming the first woman manager in London, that the theatre became fashionable. Aided by Planché (q.v.), Vestris inaugurated a number of reforms in costume, scenery, and production, opening on 3 Jan. 1831 with a mixed bill which included Planché's extravaganza, *Olympic Revels*. He supplied her with many more spectacular successes before she gave up the theatre in 1839. It then led a precarious existence until it was burned down on 29 Mar. 1849. There was a strong suspicion of incendiarism. It was rebuilt and reopened on 26 Dec. A production of *Fashion; or, Life in New York*, by the American, Anna Cora Mowatt (q.v.), was doing well when the proprietor, Walter Watts, was arrested for fraud and the theatre closed. Reopening later in the year, it was taken over by William Farren, under whom Robson (q.v.), playing Jem Baggs in a revival of Mayhew's *The Wandering Minstrel* in 1853, first popularized 'Villikins and his Dinah'. Ten years later Taylor's famous melodrama *The Ticket-of-Leave Man* was first seen at the Olympic, its success being somewhat marred by the sudden death of Robson at the age of forty-three. Little of note happened, except for the appearances of Kate Terry (q.v.) in 1865-6, before the theatre was demolished in 1889. A new and much enlarged theatre on the site opened on 4 Dec. 1890 under Wilson Barrett (q.v.), who appeared in the opening production, *The People's Idol*, of which he was part-author. He then revived several of his old successes, and left in 1891. The theatre finally closed in 1899 and was demolished in 1905 in the reconstruction of the Aldwych area.

(2) NEW YORK, a handsome theatre at 444 Broadway, which opened on 13 Sept. 1837 with a mixed bill. It was not a success, and passed through many hands before on 9 Dec. 1839 Mitchell (q.v.) opened it as a home of light entertainment—burletta, burlesque, and extravaganza. It flourished for over ten years, surviving the depression of 1842-3 which proved fatal to so many other enterprises, and was the first theatre in New York to play a weekly matinée. Among its outstanding successes were *Hamlet Travestie* and burlesques of *Richard III* (with Mitchell as Richard, cad, and later driver, to Omnibus No. 3), of Boucicault's *London Assurance*, and of 'The Bohemian Girl' as *The Bohea-Man's Girl*. In 1848 Chanfrau (q.v.), in *A Glance at New York in 1848*, appeared as Mose, his famous fireman character. In 1849 the theatre was redecorated, but Mitchell was failing in health and took to importing stars. This policy was disastrous, and on 9 Mar. 1850 the Olympic closed abruptly. After a short spell under Burton it became a home of German drama and finally closed on 25 June 1851. A shop was later built on the site.

(3) NEW YORK. On 18 Nov. 1856 Laura Keene (q.v.) opened a theatre under her own name, and remained there with some success until 1863. The theatre then closed, to reopen on 8 Oct. 1863 as the Olympic under Mrs. John Wood (q.v.), who sponsored the first appearance in New York of Mrs. G. H. Gilbert (q.v.). Mrs. Wood's last season was memorable for the début of G. F. Rowe (q.v.), who appeared as Micawber and Silas Wegg in his own adaptations of Dickens's *David Copperfield* and *Our Mutual Friend*. In 1866 Joseph Jefferson (q.v.) appeared in Boucicault's version of *Rip Van Winkle*, which had already had some success in London. Later productions at this theatre were *A Midsummer Night's Dream* in 1867, with a panorama of London by Telbin, and Fox's famous pantomime of *Humpty-Dumpty*, which opened on 10 Mar. 1868 and ran for a year. In 1872 the theatre became a home of variety. It finally closed on 17 Apr. 1880 and was demolished, shops being built on the site.

(4) THE NEW OLYMPIC, NEW YORK, a hall built in 1856 on Broadway, which was taken over and renamed by Chanfrau, who intended to revive the mixed bills of Mitchell's Olympic. He was unsuccessful, and after a few weeks the theatre became a music-hall, as Buckley's Olympic.

The Anthony Street Theatre was known as the Olympic in 1812. There was a circus known as the Olympic Arena in 1858, a short-lived Olympic on 8th Avenue in 1860, and an Olympic Music-Hall at 600 Broadway on the site of the old Alhambra, which functioned from 1860 to 1861. Wallack's old theatre was renamed the Olympic in 1862 under Fox (see BROADWAY THEATRE (2)).

Ombres Chinoises, see SHADOW-SHOW.

O'NEILL, ELIZA (1791-1872), a delightful actress, who made her first appearance on the stage in her birthplace, Drogheda, where her father was manager of the local theatre. Going to Belfast and Dublin, she soon made a name for herself and in 1814 was engaged for Covent Garden. Her first appearance (as Juliet) in *Romeo and Juliet* was overwhelmingly successful, and for five years she had a career of unbroken triumph, being considered a worthy successor to Mrs. Siddons (q.v.), with less nobility, perhaps, but more sweetness and charm. On 13 July 1819 she made her last appearance on the stage as Mrs. Haller in Kotzebue's *The Stranger*, and then retired to marry Mr. (later Sir William) Becher.

O'NEILL, EUGENE GLADSTONE (1888-1953), American playwright, son of the well-known romantic actor JAMES O'NEILL (1847-1920). His early education was of a fragmentary nature, and after attending Princeton University for a year he signed on as a seaman on several voyages to

South America, South Africa, and elsewhere. He was working as a reporter on a newspaper when his health broke down. During six months spent in a sanatorium he began writing his first play, *The Web*. In 1914–15 he studied under Professor Baker (q.v.) at Harvard, and in 1916 was connected with the Provincetown Players (q.v.), who with the Greenwich Village Players were responsible for the production of many of his early plays. It was not until 1920 that his first full-length play was produced on Broadway. This was *Beyond the Horizon*, a starkly effective study of character laid in rural New England which was awarded the Pulitzer Prize and established him as a playwright of genuine talent and considerable skill. It was followed almost immediately by productions of four other plays—the one-act *Exorcism*; *Diff'rent*, a grim bit of dramatic irony in two acts; *The Emperor Jones*, one of his best-known and most popular plays; and *Anna Christie*, the story of a young woman who is, presumably, 'purified' by the love of a man. Its popularity was based largely on the romantic and external theatrical qualities of the acting and production. In quick succession other O'Neill plays were brought to the stage—*Gold*, *The Straw* (both 1921), and *The First Man* (1922)—each of them a failure with the public yet each revealing new facets of the author's personality. Also in 1922 came *The Hairy Ape*, a symbolic work which in many ways resembled the plays of the European Expressionists. In 1924 three new plays were produced—*Welded*, *All God's Chillun Got Wings*, and *Desire Under the Elms*, the last being the most mature work O'Neill had yet written. The short-lived *The Fountain* (1925), a romantic pseudo-historical play about Ponce de Leon, was followed by *The Great God Brown* (1926), a study of multifarious interrelationships in which extensive use was made of elaborate masks. Though it had some success in the theatre, it is more interesting as showing the development of the author's technique. Its successor, *Marco Millions* (1928), was an ironic comedy satirizing the aggressive businessman who has lost touch with beauty and the eternal verities. *Strange Interlude* (also 1928), a very long play in nine acts, is a work of extraordinary power in which, by the confusing use of asides and soliloquies, O'Neill seeks to probe deep into the hidden motives of human character.

His next play, *Lazarus Laughed*, tells the story of the resurrection of Lazarus and his ultimate triumph over death. It has not so far been professionally produced in the United States. In 1929 came *Dynamo*, an unsuccessful piece but memorable for the exciting set designed for it by Lee Simonson (q.v.). It was originally planned as the first part of a trilogy on man's efforts to find a lasting faith, but after its production O'Neill decided not to continue with the other two plays. Meantime he had been working on *Mourning Becomes Electra* (1931), a version of Aeschylus' *Oresteia* set in New England which is perhaps his most successful play. After the productions of *Ah, Wilderness!* (1933) and *Days Without End* (1934) O'Neill retired from the theatre for twelve years, refusing to allow any of his new plays to be staged. But in spite of continual ill health he went on writing, and in 1946 *The Iceman Cometh* (written in 1939) had a long run in New York. Like its companion piece, *A Moon for the Misbegotten*, which opened out of town in 1947 but was not seen on Broadway until 1957, it is partly expository drama and partly a philosophical disquisition on faith.

Several of O'Neill's plays were produced posthumously, among them *Long Day's Journey Into Night*. Written in 1941, this was first seen in Stockholm on 2 Feb. 1956 and was produced in New York in the following November. *A Touch of the Poet* (written in 1940) was produced in 1958. In Nov. 1962 *More Stately Mansions* (written in 1938) had its first performance in Stockholm in a translation which cut the playing time from ten hours to five. Most of O'Neill's plays have been produced in London: *Anna Christie* (1923), *The Emperor Jones* (1925), *Strange Interlude* and *Desire Under the Elms* (both 1931), *Mourning Becomes Electra* (1937), *Marco Millions* (1938), *Days Without End* (1943), *Long Day's Journey into Night* and *The Iceman Cometh* (both 1958), and *A Moon for the Misbegotten* (1960).

O'Neill was awarded the Nobel Prize for Literature in 1936. The Coronet Theatre in New York has now been renamed the Eugene O'Neill Theatre (q.v.) in his honour.

O'NEILL, MAIRE (1887–1952), Irish actress, sister of Sara Allgood (q.v.), and with her a member of the company at the Abbey Theatre (q.v.), where she created the part of Pegeen Mike in Synge's

The Playboy of the Western World (1907). She remained at the Abbey until 1913, playing a wide variety of parts, including the Woman in the first production of Shaw's *The Shewing-Up of Blanco Posnet* (1909), and appearing with the Abbey Players in London on several occasions. She then joined the Liverpool Repertory Company, and subsequently, during a long and distinguished career, was seen regularly in London and New York, usually in Irish plays in company with her sister and her second husband Arthur Sinclair (q.v.).

O'NEILL, NANCE (1874–1965), see RANKIN, ARTHUR.

O.P. (OPPOSITE PROMPT), see STAGE DIRECTIONS.

O.P. Riots, see COVENT GARDEN.

Open Air Theatre, REGENT'S PARK, LONDON, see CARROLL, SYDNEY and SHAKESPEARE FESTIVALS.

Open Space Theatre, LONDON, see MAROWITZ, CHARLES.

Open Stage, a raised platform built against one wall of the auditorium, with the audience on three sides. This was sometimes known in England as 'arena' theatre, a term reserved in the United States for a central playing area with the audience on all four sides (see THEATRE-IN-THE-ROUND). The open stage derives basically from the Elizabethan platform stage (see STAGE), and is in use today in a number of new theatres, including the Chichester Festival Theatre (q.v.). It was used for productions at the Assembly Hall during the Edinburgh Festival, and can be seen at the Stratford Festival Theatre (q.v.) in Stratford, Ontario. Most of the adaptable all-purpose theatres now being built make provision for open-stage productions, which, like those of theatre-in-the-round, call for an adjustment of technique by actors accustomed to the proscenium-arch theatre and a fresh approach from the audience, since they involve new problems of interpretation, staging, setting, and lighting.

Opera Comique, LONDON. This theatre, in the Strand, backed on to the Globe (q.v.). They were known as the Rickety Twins, having been hastily erected in hope of compensation—which was not forthcoming—when the area was rebuilt. Because of the long narrow entrances from three different directions the Opera Comique was also nicknamed Theatre Royal, Tunnels. Its official name was a mistake, as the public did not take kindly to a foreign title. It opened on 29 Oct. 1870 and in May 1871 actors from the Comédie-Française under Gôt, driven from home by the Franco-Prussian War, made their first appearance outside Paris. It was used mainly by visiting foreigners —including Ristori (q.v.) in 1873—with long periods of inactivity, until in Nov. 1877 D'Oyly Carte took over and produced Gilbert and Sullivan's *The Sorcerer* (1877), *H.M.S. Pinafore* (1878), *The Pirates of Penzance* (1880), and *Patience* (1881), which was transferred to the Savoy later in the year. In 1884 the theatre closed for redecoration, reopening on 6 Apr. 1885, but with little success. For some years it was used for special performances and try-outs, being partly rebuilt in 1895, and at the end of 1899 it closed for good, being demolished in 1902.

(For the Opéra-Comique in Paris, see COMÉDIE-ITALIENNE.)

Orange Moll, see MEGGS, MRS.

Orange Street Theatre, see DUBLIN.

ORLENEV, PAVEL NIKOLAYEVICH (1869–1932), Russian actor, who made his first appearance in 1886 and played mainly in St. Petersburg. In 1904 he and Alla Nazimova (q.v.) took a company of Russian actors to Europe and England and on to the United States, where they had a great artistic success. Actors and critics alike were impressed by the ensemble playing and by the actors' naturalistic style. The visit undoubtedly created an interest in Russian drama and in the stagecraft of Stanislavsky (q.v.), praised by Orlenev as his master. It was during this visit that Tolstoy's *Tsar Feodor Ivanovich* and Chekhov's *The Seagull* were first seen in America. Unfortunately the season was not a financial success, and Orlenev returned to Russia. Nervous and undisciplined in private life, he was capable of remarkable control and intense emotion in his favourite roles, among which were Raskolnikov in Dostoievsky's *Crime and Punishment*, Oswald in Ibsen's *Ghosts*, and the title-role in his *Brand*.

ORRERY, LORD (ROGER BOYLE, first Earl of Orrery) (1621–79), a Restoration nobleman and man of letters, author of some forgotten comedies, and of the successful heroic dramas *Mustapha* (1665) and *The Black Prince* (1667). These, and other plays by him, are useful in their printed versions on account of their detailed stage directions.

ORTON, JOE (1933–67), English dramatist, whose first play, *Entertaining Mr. Sloane*, was staged in 1964 and gained the *Evening Standard* Award for the best play of the year. It shocked and entertained its audience by the contrast between its prim-and-proper dialogue and the violence of its action, a contrast which was again apparent in *Loot* (1966), a satire on police corruption and the conventions of detective fiction. In 1967 an earlier radio play, *The Ruffian on the Stair*, was staged at the Royal Court as *Crimes of Passion* in a double bill with *The Erpingham Camp* (previously televised). In the same year Orton was brutally murdered by the man who shared his flat—a death as violent and bizarre as any in his plays—and the modern theatre lost one of its most articulate and promising young dramatists. His last full-length play, *What the Butler Saw*, a parody of conventional farce, was produced two years later and was well received, though it is probable that the author, had he lived longer, would have emended it considerably. A one-act play, *Funeral Games*, was produced by the Basement Theatre at the end of 1970.

OSBORNE, JOHN JAMES (1929–), English dramatist, who first came into prominence when his play *Look Back in Anger* was produced at the Royal Court Theatre by the English Stage Company. It was their first outstanding success, and the date of the first night, 8 May 1956, is considered a landmark in the modern theatre. Osborne, who was for some years an actor, making his first appearance in 1948 and remaining a member of the Royal Court company until 1957, has written a number of other plays, including *The Entertainer* (1957), in which Laurence Olivier (q.v.) gave an outstanding performance as the seedy music-hall artiste Archie Rice. *Epitaph for George Dillon* (1958), written in collaboration with Anthony Creighton, and a musical, *The World of Paul Slickey* (1959), were less successful, but *Luther* (1961), which had its first production by the English

Stage Company at the Théâtre des Nations in Paris with Albert Finney in the name-part, again created something of a stir. In 1962 Osborne was responsible for a double bill at the Royal Court, *The Blood of the Bambergs* and *Under Plain Cover* (billed as *Plays for England*), but none of these later plays reached the standard of his first two, which have been translated and acted in cities all over the world. In 1964 *Inadmissible Evidence*, in which Nicol Williamson gave a fine performance, was a success. A year later *A Patriot for Me* was refused a licence by the Lord Chamberlain and was therefore staged privately for members of the English Stage Society. The chief part was played by a famous Swiss actor, Maximilian Schell, making his first appearance in England. In 1966 Osborne 'adapted' Lope de Vega's *La fianza satisfecha* as *A Bond Honoured* for the National Theatre, where it was performed in a double bill with *Black Comedy* by Peter Shaffer (q.v.). In 1968 *Time Present* failed to enhance Osborne's reputation, and *The Hotel in Amsterdam* (also 1968), though providing an excellent part for Paul Scofield (q.v.), was otherwise negligible.

OSTLER. WILLIAM (?–1614), a boy-actor with the Children of the Chapel Royal, who appeared in Jonson's *The Poetaster* in 1601. As an adult he was taken on by the King's Men (see CHAMBERLAIN'S MEN), with whom he appeared in Jonson's *The Alchemist* (1610), and he was the original Antonio in Webster's *The Duchess of Malfi* (1614). He married the daughter of Heminge (q.v.) in 1611, and had shares in both the Globe and Blackfriars theatres (qq.v.), which Heminge tried to acquire from his widow.

OSTROVSKY, ALEXANDER NIKOLAIVICH (1823–86), Russian dramatist, whose plays, realistic studies of corruption and sharp practice, earned him the title of 'the Balzac of the Muscovite merchant'. He first came into prominence in 1848 as the author of *The Bankrupt* (later renamed *It's All in the Family*), an outspoken commentary on bogus bankruptcy which lost him his job as a Civil Servant. It was banned for thirteen years, but circulated in manuscript and became well known through private readings. He then wrote several historical plays, a fairytale play which provided the libretto for

Rimsky-Korsakov's opera, 'The Snow-Maiden' (1882), translated a number of European dramas, and embarked on the series of realistic contemporary satires for which he is best known. Some of these have been translated into English, a difficult task owing to the richness and local colouring of Ostrovsky's style. Three of the best-known, *Even a Wise Man Stumbles* (also known as *Enough Stupidity in Every Wise Man*), *Easy Money* (based on *The Taming of the Shrew*), and *Wolves and Sheep*, were published in 1944 in translations by David Magarshack, the last having a short run at the Chanticleer in London the following year. But the only play of Ostrovsky's to be well known in English is *The Storm* (written in 1859), a tragedy of intolerance which was first seen in translation in New York in 1900, and revived in 1919 and 1962. It was first seen in London in 1929, and was revived at the Old Vic by the National Theatre company in 1966.

Most of Ostrovsky's plays were produced at the Moscow Maly Theatre (q.v.), which is also known as the House of Ostrovsky. His statue stands at the entrance. In 1885, after founding the Society of Russian Playwrights, he was appointed director of the Moscow Imperial Theatres, being the first man from the theatrical world to hold this appointment, formerly a political post.

OSTUSHEV, A. (1874–1953), see MALY THEATRE, MOSCOW.

OTWAY, THOMAS (1652–85), English dramatist, who in 1670 made his first and last appearance on the stage in Aphra Behn's *The Forced Marriage*. He then turned to playwriting, and in 1675 produced *Alcibiades*, a successful tragedy which provided a fine part for Mrs. Barry (q.v.), with whom he was madly in love. It was followed by *Don Carlos* (1676), a tragedy in rhymed verse, and a comedy entitled *Friendship in Fashion* (1678), and by his two finest works, *The Orphan; or, the Unhappy Marriage* (1680) and *Venice Preserv'd; or, a Plot Discovered* (1682), tragedies in which Betterton (q.v.) and Mrs. Barry appeared together. Both plays were frequently revived during the eighteenth century. *The Orphan* was last seen in London in 1925 in a performance by the Phoenix Society, and *Venice Preserv'd*, which continued in favour during the nineteenth century, was given a splendid production at the Lyric, Hammersmith, in 1953 with Gielgud and Scofield (qq.v.) as Jaffier and Pierre. One of Otway's most successful plays in his own day was his translation of Molière's *Les Fourberies de Scapin*. As *The Cheats of Scapin*, this was produced at Dorset Garden as an after-piece to his *Titus and Berenice* (1676) (based on Racine). Another comedy, *The Soldier's Fortune*, first seen at Drury Lane in 1680, was revived at the Royal Court in 1967 with unexpected success.

O.U.D.S., see OXFORD.

OWENS, JOHN EDMOND (1823–86), London-born American actor, best known as an eccentric comedian and an outstanding interpreter of Yankee characters. His most famous part was that of Solon Shingle in Joseph S. Jones's *The People's Lawyer*, in which he toured successfully throughout the United States and also appeared in London in 1865, as noted by Dickens, who saw him. He was also good as Dr. Pangloss in the younger Colman's *The Heir-at-Law*, as Caleb Plummer in *Dot*, Dion Boucicault's dramatization of Dickens's *The Cricket on the Hearth*, in the title-role of John Poole's *Paul Pry*, and as Mr. Toodles in *The Toodles*, adapted by W. E. Burton from R. J. Raymond's *The Farmer's Daughter of the Severnside*. In 1876 he appeared in New York as Perkyn Middlewick in H. J. Byron's *Our Boys*, and later joined the stock company at Madison Square, where he played with Annie Russell (q.v.).

OXBERRY, WILLIAM (1784–1824), English actor, whose portrait hangs in the Garrick Club (q.v.). He appeared mainly in provincial and minor London theatres, and is best remembered as the author of *The Actress of All Work* (1819), a farce which depicts one actress in six different roles. It was one of the favourite vehicles of the infant prodigy Clara Fisher (q.v.). Oxberry also published a number of volumes of theatrical interest and gave his name to *Oxberry's Dramatic Biography*, published posthumously by his widow, probably with the assistance of her second husband, Leman Rede (q.v.). Oxberry's son, WILLIAM HENRY (1808–52), was also an actor and from 1843 to 1844 edited *Oxberry's Weekly Budget*, in which many melodramas otherwise unknown were first published. He adapted a number of plays from the French, of which the most successful was *Matteo Falcone; or, the Brigand and his Son* (1836).

Oxford. Although there were probably some earlier performances of religious plays in medieval Oxford, the first one to be recorded (at Magdalen) dates from about 1490. In the 1540s several colleges acted plays in Latin. There seems to have been less acting at Oxford than at Cambridge (q.v.), but in 1566 Queen Elizabeth I was present at a production in Christ Church of Edwardes's *Palaemon and Arcyte*, based on Chaucer's *The Knight's Tale*. In 1567 a comedy was produced at Merton with the intriguing title of *Wylie Beguylie*. Unfortunately, as with most other plays of the time, the manuscript is lost. A later royal visit was that of Charles I in 1636.

All the above were academic exercises, and professional companies seem to have been discouraged, though Strange's Men (q.v.) played in an inn-yard in 1590–1, the King's Men (see CHAMBERLAIN'S MEN) in a tennis-court in 1680, and a company under Betterton was in Oxford in 1703. In the eighteenth century there were some private theatricals and some quasi-official performances at Commemoration. It was not until the middle of the nineteenth century that the colleges began to form their own dramatic societies, Brasenose being first in the field. These have now become a regular feature of undergraduate life, but officially the theatre has as yet no place in the university curriculum and there is no Department of Drama as at Bristol and Manchester (see UNIVERSITY DEPARTMENTS OF DRAMA). There is, however, a University Theatre, leased by the Curators to a professional resident company, which is also used on occasion by amateur university and city societies and by visiting professional companies. Known as the Playhouse, in Beaumont Street, it was built as a non-commercial venture by Eric Dance and opened on 20 Oct. 1938 with Fagan's *And So to Bed*. It replaced an earlier and most inconvenient theatre in the Woodstock Road, a converted Big Game Museum, known also as the Red Barn, where intermittently from Oct. 1923 to Nov. 1928 J. B. Fagan (q.v.) directed a company of young actors, many of whom afterwards became famous, in a programme of English and Continental plays. The venture was ill-supported and Fagan gave up, being succeeded by

Stanford Holme and later Eric Dance. They managed to keep the theatre open, but the town preferred the touring companies which came to the commercial New Theatre in George Street.

Dance's Playhouse was the last provincial theatre to be built before the Second World War. It survived precariously until 1956, when it finally closed for financial reasons. At this point, on the initiative of Nevill Coghill (q.v.), FRANK HAUSER (1922–) was invited to bring in his Meadow Players. Opening on 1 Oct. 1956 with Giraudoux's *Electra*, he presented an impressive programme of new and classical plays. In 1961, as the result of a motion in Congregation put forward by Coghill, the University bought the remaining lease of the theatre and confirmed Hauser and his company in their tenancy. In 1963, as the result of an appeal by the Curators which raised £60,000, the theatre was redecorated and enlarged and provided with an adaptable forestage. The refurbished theatre opened on 14 Jan. 1964 with a Molière trilogy in translation (*L'École des femmes*, *La Critique de l'École des femmes*, and *L'Impromptu de Versailles*). In Feb. 1974 the Meadow Players were disbanded, and a new company under Gordon McDougall took over, opening on 15 Oct. of the same year.

Apart from college societies, the main amateur theatrical activity in Oxford was for a long time provided by the Oxford University Dramatic Society (O.U.D.S.), founded in 1885, mainly through the exertions of Arthur Bourchier (q.v.), then an undergraduate at Christ Church. The first production, given in the Town Hall, was *Henry IV, Part 1*, directed by Alan Mackinnon, who was responsible for all productions up to 1895 and also wrote a history of Oxford theatricals. By the outbreak of the First World War thirty-two productions had been given, mainly of Shakespearian comedies. During the war the society was disbanded, but it started again in 1919, the first production being Hardy's *Dynasts*. Female members of the university being barred from membership of O.U.D.S., the women's parts were always played by professional actresses of the front rank, and directors were also engaged from time to time. On the outbreak of the Second World War the society was again suspended, but a new society, known as the Friends of the O.U.D.S., was formed under Nevill Coghill, who produced six of the twelve productions from 1940 to 1947. Under him the Friends not only maintained a high standard but also succeeded in paying off outstanding debts and laying by funds for the future. Their last production was Ibsen's *The Pretenders*. Shortly afterwards the O.U.D.S. was re-formed under the presidency of Glynne Wickham, later Professor of Drama at Bristol University. A major change was that women's parts were now played by members of the women's colleges or of other amateur groups. In June 1947 the reconstituted society gave its first production, *Love's Labour's Lost*, in Merton Gardens. In May 1948 *The Masque of Hope*, written by Coghill and produced by Wickham, was acted before Princess Elizabeth (later Elizabeth II) in University College. The lack of a permanent club room since 1950 has somewhat altered the social nature of the O.U.D.S., but its level of productions remains high. Its archives, consisting of programmes, photographs, and press-cuttings, have been deposited at the Bodleian Library and an archivist is appointed annually to keep them up to date.

The Oxford Experimental Theatre Club was founded by Coghill in Feb. 1936 for the performance of neglected classics, new English or foreign plays, particularly of the *avant-garde*, and, where possible, plays by undergraduate members. The first production was Dryden's *All for Love* in 1936; other productions were Cocteau's *The Marriage on the Eiffel Tower* and *The Infernal Machine*, Pirandello's *Naked* and *Six Characters in Search of an Author*, Jonson's *Epicœne*; *or, the Silent Woman*, and the anonymous morality play, *The Castle of Perseverance*, which had not been revived since the fifteenth century.

Finally, mention should be made of the Greek plays. The first was the *Agamemnon* of Aeschylus, performed in 1880 under the patronage of the Master of Balliol, Dr. Jowett. Later productions included Euripides' *Alcestis* in 1887, Aristophanes' *Frogs* in 1892, and his *Knights* in 1897. The tradition of a play in Greek continued until the 1930s, and was revived by the O.U. Classical Society in 1967. Many college societies have also produced Greek plays in translation.

Oxford Music-Hall, LONDON, built by Charles Morton (q.v.) at the corner of Oxford Street and Tottenham Court Road. It was the first to be built specifically as a music-hall, and it opened on 26 Mar. 1861 with a mixed bill which offered good music as well as comedians and slapstick. Badly damaged by fire on 11 Feb. 1868 and 1 Nov. 1872, it was rebuilt and enlarged each time, reopening on 9 Aug. 1869 and 17 Mar. 1873 under the management of Syers. The old building, in which George Robey (q.v.) had made his first appearance on the music-hall stage in 1891, closed on 4 June 1892, and a new building opened on 31 Jan. 1893 with a strong bill, including Marie Lloyd, Bessie Bellwood, and Harry Champion (qq.v.). On the act-drop was a painting of Magdalen tower, Oxford, and the same device was emblazoned on the programmes. It was here that Harry Tate (q.v.) first appeared in London. In 1917 Cochran (q.v.) replaced the old-style music-hall bill with a play, Bairnsfather's *The Better 'Ole*, and on 17 Jan. 1921 the Oxford, converted into a theatre (though it had been called so intermittently for some time), opened with a spectacular revue called *The League of Notions*, starring the Dolly Sisters. Later Delysia (q.v.) starred in *Mayfair and Montmartre* (1922). In 1924, the year of the Wembley Exhibition, Cochran presented the Old Vic (q.v.) company for the first time in central London in a season of Shakespearian plays produced by Robert Atkins (q.v.). The theatre closed in May 1926 and the site was used for Lyons' Oxford Street Corner House.

Oxford's Men. The first mention of a company of players under this name occurs as early as 1492, and in 1547 the 'players of the Earl of Oxford', who were disbanded in 1562, caused a scandal by acting in Southwark while a dirge was being sung for Henry VIII at St. Saviour's. A new company, under the patronage of the seventeenth earl, himself something of a playwright, appeared in 1580 at the Theatre (q.v.), but got into trouble for brawling and were banished to the provinces until 1584, when they appeared at Court, John Lyly (q.v.) being with them. The company at this time included a number of boys who, with some of the Children of the Chapel and of Paul's, played at Blackfriars (q.v.). It was finally disbanded in 1602.

P

Pageant, originally the cart, or stage on wheels, on which a scene from a medieval religious play was performed (see LITURGICAL DRAMA). It consisted usually of two rooms, the lower one curtained off as a dressing-room, though it could be used to represent Hell. Later the name was transferred to the ambulating entertainments, not necessarily religious, of which the Lord Mayor's Show in London is a late survival. From this meaning of the word comes its modern connotation of 'a spectacular procession' as applied to the elaborate civic pageants so fashionable in England in the early 1900s. The first was that produced by Louis N. Parker (q.v.) at Sherborne in 1905, and it was followed by others at Warwick, Dover, York, Oxford, and many other places. During the First World War several patriotic pageants were produced at London theatres, while Drury Lane celebrated its own history in *The Pageant of Drury Lane* (1918).

A further extension of the medieval meaning of pageant is found in the Tudor and Elizabethan stationary stages set up in celebration of a royal visit or marriage, which influenced the style of the Elizabethan stage (see STAGE). On them were performed specially written allegorical interludes with songs and dances. The word was also used of the wood or canvas structures used in the Tudor masques (see MASQUE).

Palace Theatre, LONDON, in Cambridge Circus, Shaftesbury Avenue. This opened under D'Oyly Carte, as the Royal English Opera House, on 31 Jan. 1891 with Sullivan's opera 'Ivanhoe'. A year later, as the Palace Theatre of Varieties, it became a successful music-hall under Charles Morton (q.v.), who was succeeded in 1904 by Alfred Butt. It took its present name in 1911 but continued to present variety bills and revues, the first being *The Passing Show* (1914), with Elsie Janis. In 1924 the Co-Optimists were there, and in the following year the musical comedy *No, No, Nanette!* began its long run, followed by a number of other successful musicals. After some straight plays in the 1930s, the theatre reverted to revue with a series of Cochran

shows, and during the Second World War housed Cicely Courtneidge (q.v.) and Jack Hulbert in musical comedy. Among later successes were *Gay Rosalinda* (1945) and *Song of Norway* (1946); in 1949 there was a long run of Novello's *King's Rhapsody*. During the 1950s the Palace was used by a number of foreign companies—the T.N.P., the Renaud—Barrault, the Berliner Ensemble, Antonio—brought to London on the initiative of Peter Daubeny (q.v.). In 1961 the Rogers and Hammerstein musical *The Sound of Music* started a long run.

Palais-Royal, THÉÂTRE DU, PARIS. The first theatre of this name was a private playhouse in the home of Cardinal Richelieu (q.v.). Long and narrow, it was splendidly decorated, held about 600 people, and its stage was equipped with all the latest Italian machinery. It was formally inaugurated on 14 Jan. 1641 with a spectacular performance of Desmarets's *Mirame* in the presence of Louis XIII and his Court. After Richelieu's death in the following year the theatre became the property of the King and was used intermittently for Court entertainments until 1660, when it was given to Molière (q.v.) in place of the demolished Petit-Bourbon. Ten years later it was rebuilt and enlarged and equipped with the new machinery necessary for spectacular productions of opera. It reopened with Molière's *Psyché* (1671), and he continued to play there until his death in 1673. Lully, who held a monopoly of music in France, immediately claimed the Palais-Royal for his new Academy of Music, and it was so called until it was burnt down in 1763. Rebuilt, it was again destroyed by fire in 1781.

The whole area occupied by the Palais-Royal was then reconstructed as a vast pleasure-garden, and several theatres were built there, most of which at some time called themselves the Palais-Royal. One of them, which opened in 1790 as the Variétés-Amusantes, was later renamed the Théâtre de la République and housed Talma (q.v.) and his companions during the Revolution. In 1799 it became the present Comédie-Française (q.v.). Another Palais-Royal opened in 1831 and saw, among other things, the first night of Labiche's famous comedy, *Un Chapeau de paille d'Italie* (1851). In England the term 'Palais-Royal farce' was applied to the broad suggestiveness of such adaptations of French farces as *The Pink Dominos* (1877) and *The Girl from Maxim's* (1902).

Palais-Variétés, PARIS, see CITÉ, THÉÂTRE DE LA.

PALAPRAT, JEAN DE BIGOT (1650–1721), see BRUEYS, D.-A. DE.

PALLADIO [really DI PIETRO], ANDREA (1518–80), Italian architect, whose surname (from Pallas) was bestowed on him by his benefactor, J. G. Trissino, and has in turn given its name to the Palladian style of architecture, based on the principles of antiquity as Palladio interpreted them in his buildings and in his *Quattro libri dell'architettura*, published in Venice in 1570. This was translated into English by Inigo Jones (q.v.), who was a pupil and admirer of Palladio and imported his ideas into England, influencing both the theatre and public architecture there. Palladio designed the Teatro Olimpico (q.v.), which was finished after his death by his pupil Scamozzi.

Palladium Theatre, see LONDON PALLADIUM.

Palliata, see FABULA (1).

PALMER, ALBERT MARSHMAN (1838–1905), American theatre manager, who controlled successively the Union Square and Madison Square theatres, and then took over Wallack's old theatre, to which he gave his own name. He retired in 1896 and became manager for Richard Mansfield (q.v.), who had made his first appearance in New York under Palmer in 1883. Palmer, who was well educated and a man of much taste, did a great deal for the American theatre, and his influence on staging, backstage conditions, and the fostering of native talent was extremely beneficial. In his early years he produced mainly plays imported from Europe, but later turned to American dramatists, producing such new works as Clyde Fitch's *Beau Brummel* (1890) and Augustus Thomas's *Alabama* (1891).

PALMER, JOHN. There were two actors named John Palmer. The first John (1728–68), known as 'Gentleman' Palmer, was good in small comic parts, like that of Brush in Colman's *The Clandestine*

Marriage. In 1761 he married Hannah, the daughter of Mrs. Pritchard (q.v.), who was an unsuccessful actress. After Palmer's death she married a merchant named Lloyd, retired from the stage, and died in 1781. John was an extremely vain man, and would no doubt have hated to be confused, as he so often has been, with the second John (1742–98), son of Robert Palmer, pit doorkeeper at Drury Lane, where John played under Garrick from 1767 onwards, creating the part of Joseph Surface in Sheridan's *The School for Scandal* (1777). He was also good as Sir Toby Belch in *Twelfth Night*, as Falstaff, as Young Absolute in Sheridan's *The Rivals* (first played by Woodward), as Dick Amlet in Vanbrugh's *The Confederacy*, and as Young Wilding in Garrick's adaptation of Shirley's *The Gamester*. Tragedy was beyond him, and he rarely attempted it. He was a famous liar, Sheridan (q.v.) nicknaming him 'Plausible Jack'. He built the Royalty Theatre (q.v.) in Wellclose Square, but, having no licence, was forced to give it up, and rejoined the Drury Lane company. He died on the stage, while acting in Kotzebue's *The Stranger* at Liverpool.

He had two brothers, ROBERT (1754–1817), who played at Drury Lane and Covent Garden, and WILLIAM (?–1797), who was for a short time at Covent Garden, but played mainly in Dublin.

Palmo's Opera House, NEW YORK, see BURTON, W. E.

Palsgrave's Men, see ADMIRAL'S MEN.

Panharmonium, LONDON. This stood in New Road, King's Cross. It was a strange-looking building with a small portico, built originally by a teacher of singing to house concerts by his pupils. In 1832 Buckstone opened it unsuccessfully as the Clarence Theatre, its interior decorated to represent a Chinese pavilion. In 1838 it was known as the New Lyceum and sank so low that box tickets to admit four were sold for 3d. It finally became so disreputable that it was closed by order of the magistrates. In 1870 an attempt to reopen it ended in failure and it was heard of no more.

Panopticon, LONDON, see ALHAMBRA.

Pantaloon, the old man—Columbine's father, guardian, or husband—in the

English harlequinade (q.v.), where he is made the butt of Clown's jokes. As Pantalone, he was a character in the *commedia dell'arte* (q.v.), an elderly Venetian in a long black coat over a red suit, with Turkish slippers and a skullcap, by turns avaricious, suspicious, amorous, and gullible. In Elizabethan England the term Pantaloon was applicable to any old man, as in Shakespeare's reference to the sixth age of man (*As You Like It*, II. vii), 'the lean and slipper'd pantaloon, With spectacles on nose and pouch on side'.

Pantheon, LONDON, in Oxford Street, built by James Wyatt. This opened on 28 Apr. 1772, and was designed as an indoor Ranelagh or Vauxhall. It was a popular place for balls, routs, and particularly masquerades. On 17 Feb. 1791 it became an opera house, the King's, Wyatt again being responsible for the necessary alterations, and on 14 Jan. 1792 it was burnt down. Rebuilt, it opened on 9 Apr. 1795, again for masquerades and other entertainments, until after further alterations it reopened on 27 Feb. 1812 as the Pantheon Theatre. Trouble over its licence and further damage by fire kept it closed from 1814 until in 1834 it was replaced by the Pantheon Bazaar, which in 1867 became the head office of Gilbeys, the wine merchants. In 1937 it was sold to Marks & Spencer, who erected a store on the site.

Pantomime (from *pantomimus,* q.v.), a traditional Christmas entertainment in the English theatre, which derives ultimately from the *commedia dell'arte* by way of the Paris Arlequin, but with so many accretions and so much deviation as to be virtually a new genre. Although it was Weaver (q.v.) who brought the harlequinade (q.v.) to London as 'the Italian Night Scenes', it was John Rich (q.v.) who popularized it, playing Harlequin at Covent Garden. As a prelude to the harlequinade, authors first made use of classical mythology, and then, in the eighteenth century, of fairy tales and children's stories. In the nineteenth century it became inextricably mingled with burlesque (q.v.) and extravaganza (see BURLESQUE (2)), which gave rise to the tradition of a Principal Boy played by an actress and a Dame (q.v.) played by an actor, the latter being in part a survival from the time when elderly female parts,

even in a mixed cast, were played by men, young actresses being unwilling to uglify themselves. Gradually the opening scene, which had served only as an introduction to the transformation of the chief character into Harlequin, grew longer, and troupes of acrobatic dancers, like the Vokes family (q.v.), were introduced to add variety. Augustus Harris (q.v.) at Drury Lane extended this idea to include solo turns or group acts from the musichalls. While the scope of the pantomime was thus widened, its subjects were restricted to a handful of folk-tales that had proved acceptable to a young audience— *Cinderella, The Sleeping Beauty, Jack and the Beanstalk, The Babes in the Wood, Robinson Crusoe, Blue Beard,* and *Mother Goose.* The pantomime thus became a hotchpotch of incongruous elements— romance, slapstick, topical songs, male and female impersonation, acrobatics, splendid scenery and costumes, precision and ballet dancing, and specialized acts of all kinds—to such an extent that the phrase 'a proper pantomime' signifies in colloquial English 'a state of confusion'. With the continual expansion of the fairytale opening the original harlequinade was whittled away to nothing and finally disappeared. By confusion with the art of the Imperial Roman *pantomimus,* the word pantomime was also applied to eighteenth-century ballets on classical subjects, and in nineteenth-century Paris to the wordless Pierrot plays of Deburau (q.v.). The genre disappeared with the death in 1930 of Séverin, its most famous production being *L'Enfant prodigue,* widely performed during the 1890s with a girl as Pierrot. Pantomime, in the sense of expressive gestures used to convey ideas wordlessly, is an important element in acting and dancing, and the word was used also for dumb show (see MELODRAMA). Modern performers in dumb show describe their art as 'mime' (q.v.).

Pantomimus, a performer popular in Imperial Rome, who by the use of movement and gesture, often stylized, represented in turn each character in a short scene based on classical history or mythology. He wore the costume of the tragic actor, a long cloak and silken tunic, but his mask, which was often changed for each role, had no mouthpiece. He was accompanied by musicians—usually flutes, pipes, cymbals, and trumpets—and a chorus, who sang in Greek the story which the actor was performing. The most famous *pantomimi* were Pylades of Cilicia and Bathyllus of Alexandria, who played under Augustus, and Paris, put to death by Nero out of professional jealousy. The art of the *pantomimus*, though considered by St. Augustine more dangerous to morals than the circus, since it dealt exclusively with guilty passions and by its beauty and seductiveness had a disastrous effect on female spectators, was not, like its rival the Roman mime (q.v.), coarse or vulgar.

Paper Bag Players, see ROYAL COURT THEATRE (2).

PAPP [really PAPIROFSKY], JOSEPH (1921–), American theatre director, who had had over ten years' varied experience of the theatre, mainly backstage, when in 1954 he founded the New York Shakespeare Festival, whose charter dates from 19 Nov. 1954. The first productions, which included *Cymbeline* (1955), were performed in the Emanuel Presbyterian Church at 729 E. 6th Street, most of the actors giving their services. In 1958 Papp directed *Twelfth Night* at the Belvedere Lake Theatre in Central Park, where the company now has a permanent home, the Delacorte Theatre, financed by private and public donations. In spite of many financial and legal difficulties, Papp's energy and tenacity resulted in the provision for his company of an open-air auditorium with a semi-arena stage incorporating good lighting and amplification facilities, dressing-rooms, and an audience area planned for excellent sightlines and acoustics. The opening performance at the Delacorte Theatre in 1962 was *The Merchant of Venice*, followed in the same season by *The Tempest* and *King Lear*. In 1973 Papp became director of the Vivian Beaumont Theater at the Lincoln Center, where he planned to present new American plays, keeping the smaller Forum Theater for Shakespeare.

(See also SHAKESPEARE FESTIVALS.)

Parade, the short sketch acted by fairground actors outside their booth in order to induce the spectators to pay their entrance-fees to see the play given inside. A volume of plots of *parades* acted on the first-floor balcony of the Théâtre de la Foire Saint-Germain (see FAIRS), destroyed in 1756, shows the affinity of the genre with the scenarii of the Italian *commedia*

dell'arte, but there is also evidence of direct survival from French medieval farce. The *parade* died out with the disappearance of the old theatres of the fairs in the mid-eighteenth century but was revived by Bobèche (q.v.) and Galimafré on the post-Revolution Boulevard du Temple.

Paradiso, an elaborate piece of stage machinery invented by FILIPPO BRUNELLESCHI (1377–1446) for the representation of the Annunciation which took place annually in the church of San Felice in Florence. It consisted of a group of choir boys, representing cherubims, who were suspended in a copper dome from the roof of the church. This was lowered by crane to a platform, and from it then emerged the actor who was to play St. Gabriel. When he had finished his part, he re-entered the dome and returned to heaven. This device was the forerunner of many similar mobile chariots, which were improved by such additions as the clouds of cottonwool with which FRANCESCO D'ANGELO (1447–88) masked the machinery needed for Christ's Ascension. Later, painted canvas, mounted on battens, took the place of cottonwool, but the basic principle of Brunelleschi's device remained in use for the transport of any supernatural being until almost the end of the eighteenth century.

PARFAICT, FRANÇOIS (1698–1753) and CLAUDE (1701–77), brothers who collaborated in a number of works on French theatre history. Their chief publications were: *Histoire générale du théâtre français depuis son origine* (1745–9), in 15 volumes; *Mémoires pour servir à l'histoire des spectacles de la foire* (1743), in 2 volumes; *Histoire de l'ancien théâtre italien depuis son origine jusqu'à sa suppression en 1697* (1753); and *Dictionnaire des théâtres de Paris* (1756–67), in 7 volumes. Although painstaking, they were not always accurate and their judgement was sometimes at fault, but their work is valuable and full of information which cannot be found elsewhere. François also wrote plays, but none has survived on the stage.

PARIGI, GIULIO (1590–1636), a Florentine scene designer, Court architect to the Duke of Tuscany, who, with his son ALFONSO (?–1656), was one of the first designers to work for opera. His designs were comparatively simple compared with later developments, in keeping with the classical sobriety of the early Florentine scores. The work of the Parigis serves as a link between Buontalenti and Torelli (qq.v.), and had a great influence on designers who visited Florence, among them Furtenbach and Inigo Jones (qq.v.).

PARIS, a popular Roman pantomimist put to death in A.D. 67 by order of Nero (q.v.), who was jealous of his art. A second Paris was executed in A.D. 83.

Park Lane Theatre, NEW YORK, see DALY'S THEATRE (3).

Park Theatre. (1) NEW YORK, the first outstanding theatre of the United States, known as the 'Old Drury' of America. Under Hallam and Hodgkinson (qq.v.), it opened on 29 Jan. 1798 with *As You Like It*, followed on 31 Jan. by Sheridan's *The School for Scandal*. The engagement of the brilliant young actor Thomas Cooper (q.v.), who made his first appearance as Hamlet on 28 Feb., brought prosperity to the theatre, but his success was jeopardized by constant quarrels between the managers, one of whom, Dunlap (q.v.), finally took over alone. His repertory consisted mainly of contemporary successes from London and the European stage, together with some of his own plays, but older plays were sometimes staged, and on 11 June 1804 *Twelfth Night* was seen for the first time in New York. A year later Dunlap went bankrupt and was replaced by Cooper, but it was not until a business man, Stephen Price (q.v.), took control in 1808 that the theatre prospered. Under him, on 14 June 1809, the first American play on Red Indian life was produced—*The Indian Princess; or, La Belle Sauvage*, by J. N. Barker (q.v.). Price also inaugurated the policy of importing foreign stars, G. F. Cooke (q.v.) appearing under him in 1810. Ten years later, just as Edmund Kean (q.v.) was about to appear at the theatre, it was burnt down. Rebuilt, it reopened on 1 Sept. 1821 and embarked on a period of prosperity which lasted until the death of Price in 1840. It then went downhill, and when on 16 Dec. 1848 it was again destroyed by fire it was not rebuilt.

(2) NEW YORK. A second Park Theatre, on Broadway at 22nd Street, opened on 13 Apr. 1874, and had its first success on 16 Sept. 1874, when John T. Raymond (q.v.) appeared there as Colonel Sellers in a dramatization of Mark Twain's *The Gilded Age*. Henry E. Abbey (q.v.) took over the new Park late in 1876 and started it on a prosperous career which lasted until, on 30 Oct. 1882, the day on which Lily Langtry (q.v.) was to have made her New York début there, the theatre was totally destroyed by fire and never rebuilt.

(3) NEW YORK. The first professional theatre to be built in Brooklyn, after nearly forty years of unsuccessful tentatives, was also named the Park. It opened on 14 Sept. 1863 under F. B. Conway (q.v.), and soon established itself as a popular local playhouse. From 1873 onwards it housed visiting stars supported by a stock company, the last in New York. It was destroyed by fire in Nov. 1908. (For a later Park Theatre in New York, see MAJESTIC THEATRE (1).)

(4) GLASGOW. Scotland's first Little Theatre, founded in Glasgow in 1941 by John Stewart and conducted on club lines, was named the Park. A production was given monthly, each one running for a fortnight. The theatre closed in 1949 and John Stewart then founded the Pitlochry Festival (q.v.).

(For the Park Theatre, London, see ALEXANDRA THEATRE (2).)

PARKER, JOHN (1875–1952), English dramatic critic and theatrical journalist, founder and editor till his death of *Who's Who in the Theatre*. This valuable publication first appeared in 1912, in place of Parker's earlier *Green Room Book*, and has now achieved its fourteenth (jubilee) edition, edited by Freda Gaye. It contains more than 3,000 biographical entries for living actors, playwrights, directors, scene designers, etc., much useful information on performances of plays in London, cast lists for London theatres, and some special features such as the playbills of the Chichester Festival Theatre, of the Royal Shakespeare Theatre, Stratford-upon-Avon, and of Stratford, Ontario; a short history of repertory theatres in Great Britain; and a list of centres for theatre research. Interesting features of the earlier editions were the genealogical tables of theatrical families compiled by Dr. J. E. M. Bulloch, and the seating plans of London theatres.

PARKER, LOUIS NAPOLEON (1852–1944), English dramatist and pageant-master.

He was for a time music-master at Sherborne, but the success of his early plays enabled him to resign in 1892 and he then went to London to devote the rest of his long life to the theatre. Among his plays the most successful were *Rosemary* (1896), *Pomander Walk* (1910), and *Disraeli* (1911), which had a long run in America. He was also in great demand as a producer of the civic pageants so much in vogue in Edwardian England, and directed the pageants at Sherborne (1905), Warwick (1906), Dover (1908), and York (1909). During the First World War he was responsible for several patriotic pageants in London and devised *The Pageant of Drury Lane* (1918). The partitioning of his undoubted talents among his various interests was amusingly underlined by the title of his reminiscences, *Several of My Lives* (1928).

PARNELL, T. F. and VAL, see RUSSELL, FRED.

PARSONS, ALAN (1888–1933), see TREE, SIR HERBERT.

Paso, a term applied in Spain in the sixteenth century to a short comic interlude which later developed into the *entremés*. The most famous writer of *pasos* was Lope de Rueda (q.v.).

Pasquino, one of the minor *zanni* or servant roles of the *commedia dell'arte* (q.v.). The name was adopted towards the end of the sixteenth century and passed into French comedy as Pasquin, being the name of the valet in the plays of Destouches (q.v.). In the French seventeenth-century theatre the expression 'the Pasquin of the company' designated the actor who played the satiric roles in Regnard and Dufresny (qq.v.). In the eighteenth century the word 'pasquin' or 'pasquinade' was applied in England to a lampoon, squib, or satiric piece, often political. Henry Fielding (q.v.) used it as the title of a production at the Haymarket in 1736 and often signed himself Mr. Pasquin in his newspaper articles and letters.

Passion Play, see MYSTERIENSPIEL.

PASTOR, TONY [really ANTONIO] (1837–1908), American music-hall or 'vaudeville' manager, who first appeared as an infant prodigy, aged nine, under Barnum (q.v.). He later travelled with a circus,

arranging concerts in the towns he visited, and became a successful ballad-singer, being part-author of some two thousand songs. In April 1861 he made his first appearance in variety, which had sunk to a low level of obscurity and vulgarity. Determined to make it respectable, Pastor opened his own theatre in New York in June 1865. The venture was a success, and in 1881 he presented the first performance of what later came to be called vaudeville (q.v.), a word he himself never used.

Pastoral, a dramatic form which evolved in Italy from pastoral poetry, by way of the dramatic eclogue or shepherds' play. The first outstanding pastoral was Tasso's *L'Aminta* (1573), a tale of rustic love written in fine poetry with superb choruses. It was followed by Guarini's *Il Pastor Fido*, published about 1590 but probably not performed before 1596–8. Both were translated and performed in England and had a widespread influence, particularly on Lyly (q.v.) and Samuel Daniel. The first native English pastoral was *The Faithful Shepherdess* (1608) by Fletcher (q.v.), a charming play, full of poetry and invention; but the genre never became acclimatized in England, though it had some influence on the masque (q.v) and on Shakespeare. However, Dr. Greg, in *Pastoral Poetry and Pastoral Drama* (1906), claims that Milton's *Comus*, though called a masque, is essentially a pastoral, directly dependent upon previous pastoral works.

The pastoral bears no relation to real life and cannot flourish at the same time as romantic drama, which may account for its lack of success in England. It was more at home in France, where it inspired a number of authors, notably Hardy, Racan, whose *Bergeries* (pub. 1625) shows definite traces of Italian influence, and Théophile de Viau (qq.v.). It disappeared from French dramatic literature in the mid-1630s, but not before it had served as a vehicle for the introduction of the unities (q.v.) in Mairet's *Silvanire* (1630).

Pataphysics, see JARRY, ALFRED and THEATRE OF THE ABSURD.

Patent Theatres, the name given to the two chief theatres of London, Drury Lane and Covent Garden (qq.v.), which operate under Letters Patent, or charters, given by Charles II in 1662 to Thomas Killigrew (q.v.) (for Drury Lane) and Sir William Davenant (q.v.) (for Lincoln's Inn Fields, whence it descended in 1732 via Dorset Garden to Covent Garden). The charters, which in the course of the next two hundred years changed hands many times, fluctuating sharply in value, are still in existence and form an integral part of the leases of the theatres. The monopoly thus established by Charles II, and reinforced by the Theatres Act of 1737, which forbade the acting of 'legitimate' drama except at Covent Garden and Drury Lane, was finally broken in 1843. The Haymarket (q.v.) has the courtesy title of Theatre Royal by virtue of a patent obtained by Samuel Foote (q.v.) for the summer months only. During the nineteenth century a proliferation of Theatres Royal all over the country caused the term to become nothing more than a generic title for a playhouse, since these theatres were licensed by the local magistrates and not directly by the Crown.

PÄTGES, JOHANNE LUISE (1812–90), see HEIBERG, JOHAN LUDVIG.

Pavilion Music-Hall, LONDON, see LONDON PAVILION.

Pavilion Theatre, LONDON, in Whitechapel. This opened on 10 Nov. 1828, was burned down on 13 Feb. 1856, and rebuilt. Under the management of Morris Abrahams from 1871 to 1894 it catered successfully for the largely Jewish population of the neighbourhood, and many famous Jewish actors appeared at it. It was for a time a cinema, and then returned to Jewish drama. It ceased to be used for entertainment in 1934 and was demolished in 1961.

(For the Pavilion Theatre, Marylebone, see WEST LONDON THEATRE; New York, see ANTHONY STREET THEATRE and CHATHAM THEATRE (1).)

PAXINOU [née KONSTANTOPOULOU], KATINA (1900–73), outstanding Greek actress, wife of Alexis Minotis (q.v.), whom she married as her second husband in 1940. Under his direction she was seen in many of the great classical Greek tragedies, particularly in the festivals at Epidaurus. Trained as a singer, she later became an actress, and in 1932 joined the Greek National Theatre company, appearing with it in London in 1939, when she played Gertrude in *Hamlet* and Sophocles' Electra. In 1960 she went with the company to New York, where she was well known, having previously played there in 1930. For the Greek National Theatre she translated and directed many English and American plays, among them O'Neill's *Anna Christie*, and for many years she played in Ibsen's *Ghosts*, Mrs. Alving being considered one of her finest parts. She played it in English in London in 1940 and in New York in 1942, at which time she also appeared as Ibsen's Hedda Gabler. In 1966 she appeared again in London during the World Theatre season, playing Jocasta in Sophocles' *Oedipus Rex* to the Oedipus of Minotis and the title-role in Euripides' *Hecuba* to his Talthybius.

PAYNE, BEN IDEN (1881–1976), English actor and director, best remembered for his work in connection with Shakespeare. He was with Benson's company in 1899 and later helped Miss Horniman (q.v.) to establish her repertory theatre in Manchester, appearing in many of the plays himself, and acting as her general manager from 1907 to 1911. In 1913 he went to the United States, where he worked in the Philadelphia and Chicago Little Theatres, and from 1919 to 1934 was visiting Professor of Drama at the Carnegie Institute of Technology. He then returned to England to become director of the Shakespeare Theatre at Stratford-upon-Avon in succession to Bridges-Adams (q.v.). After guiding the fortunes of the theatre through the difficult first years of the Second World War, he left in 1943 to lecture in America for the Ministry of Information, and remained there to become visiting professor at several universities, finally settling at the University of Texas in 1946. By his first wife, the actress MONA LIMERICK [really MARY CHARLOTTE LOUISE GADNEY], he had a daughter, Rosalind, also an actress, who married Donald Wolfit (q.v.).

PAYNE, JOHN HOWARD (1791–1852), an American actor and dramatist, best known as the author of the lyric of 'Home, Sweet Home'. The music was by Henry Bishop, and the ballad was first sung in his opera 'Clari, the Maid of Milan' (for which Payne wrote the libretto) at Covent Garden, 8 May 1823. Payne was a precocious boy, whose first play, *Julia; or,* *the Wanderer*, was produced in New York when he was only fourteen. Three years later he went on the stage and made a great reputation, touring the larger American cities in such parts as Hamlet, Romeo, Young Norval in Home's *Douglas*, and Rolla in Kotzebue's *Pizarro*. In 1811 he appeared at the Chestnut Street Theatre, Philadelphia (q.v.), as Frederick in his own version of Kotzebue's *Das Kind der Liebe*, which, as *Lovers' Vows*, was already well known in English.

Two years later he sailed for England, and appeared at Drury Lane with great success. A visit to Paris brought him the friendship of Talma (q.v.) and the freedom of the Comédie-Française, and for many years he was engaged in the translation and adaptation of current French successes for the English and American stages. Of his own plays, the best was *Brutus; or, the Fall of Tarquin* (1818), in which Edmund Kean (q.v.) appeared at Drury Lane; of his adaptations, which included versions of several melodramas by Pixérécourt (q.v.), *Therese; or, the Orphan of Geneva* (1821) was the most successful, providing him with the money to pay off the debts incurred by his unlucky attempt to manage Sadler's Wells. With Washington Irving, a lifelong friend, he also adapted Duval's *La Jeunesse de Henry V* (1806) as *Charles II; or, the Merry Monarch* (1824). In 1842 he was appointed American Consul at Tunis, where he remained until his death.

Peacock Theatre, DUBLIN, see ABBEY THEATRE and DUBLIN.

Pedrolino, see PIERROT.

PEELE, GEORGE (c. 1558–c. 1597), English dramatist, author of *The Arraignment of Paris*, given at Court, probably in 1581; *David and Bethsabe* (c. 1587); *Edward I* (1591), which survives only in a mutilated form; and his best-known and most popular work, *The Old Wives' Tale*, written probably in 1590. This mixture of high romance and English folk-tale, which was dismissed by nineteenth-century critics as negligible and pretentious nonsense, is now considered something of a landmark in the development of English comedy. Peele, who had a fine command of language, was the author of some charming lyrics.

Peking Opera, the name given to the popular and traditional theatre of China, which was perfected in Peking in the nineteenth century, though its roots go back to about A.D. 740, when the first dramatic school, known as the Pear Garden, was founded by the T'ang Emperor Ming Huang (713–56). A flexible and harmonious combination of speech, song, orchestral music, dancing, and acrobatics, Peking Opera drew its material from well-known myths and folk-tales, and from history, and the libretto provided little more than a framework within which highly trained actors could display their skill. Over the centuries a set of conventional symbols was developed by which an oar, for instance, represented a boat, a whip indicated a horse, blue cloth stood for the sea, and waving banners for high winds. A hat wrapped in a red cloth signified a decapitated head, a woman's tiny red shoe represented needlework, a fan was a sign of frivolity. With such symbolism, allied to the equally symbolic placing of chairs, tables, and benches, the Chinese actor was able to dispense with scenery and leave a great deal to the imagination of the spectator. In the same way the costumes, sumptuous but seldom historically accurate, indicated by the predominating colour the rank and character of the wearer. Emperors wore yellow, high officials red, worthy citizens blue, rough characters black. The warrior wore a magnificent costume with tigers' heads embroidered on the wide padded shoulders, and a brilliantly coloured headdress surmounted by two pheasant plumes, often six or seven feet long, which were tossed and twirled in pride or anger. Make-up also had its significance, white indicating treachery, red courage, blue ferocity, yellow strength, gold immortality, pink and grey old age. For ceremonial occasions embroidered robes were worn with long 'rippling water' sleeves. These played an important part in the graceful, gliding ritual dances, which were accompanied by an orchestra, seated on the stage, using wooden instruments like castanets to beat the time; a small stringed instrument like a violin, which also accompanied the falsetto singing; a wind instrument resembling a clarinet; and brass percussion instruments. All the parts were played by men, and female impersonation, as in the Elizabethan theatre, reached a high point of perfection, as exemplified in the acting of Mei Lan-

Fang (q.v.), the only Chinese actor to make a reputation outside his own country. But in recent times women have appeared on the stage, and many other innovations have been introduced which may change the whole character of Peking Opera, whose fate under the present regime is uncertain.

PÉLISSIER, HARRY GABRIEL (1874–1913), English composer and entertainer, of French origin, and the first husband of Fay Compton (q.v.). He was the originator of the Pélissier Follies, who began their career on the sands and promenades of English seaside resorts and then appeared at the Apollo Theatre, London, for several seasons. They wore black-and-white pierrot costumes against a setting of black and white curtains, and were compèred by Pélissier, who wrote a good deal of their material himself. Their show was one of the best of its kind, with good music, topicality, wit, and observation, and was never equalled in spite of several efforts to use the same formula.

PELLESINI, GIOVANNI (c. 1526–1612), see CONFIDENTI and PIERROT.

Pembroke Theatre, a theatre-in-the-round, seating 440, which flourished in the London suburb of Croydon from 1959 to 1962. Though not particularly commodious or accessible, it drew audiences from London and the surrounding countryside (though not from Croydon itself, according to its founder, Clement Scott-Gilbert), who were attracted by its experimental nature—it was the only professional arena theatre near London—and by the excellence of some of its productions, several of which, including *Inherit the Wind*, by Jerome Lawrence and Robert E. Lee, were transferred to the West End. Other interesting productions were Ugo Betti's *Crime on Goat Island* (first seen at Oxford in 1957), and two plays by Inge (q.v.), *The Dark at the Top of the Stairs* and *A Loss of Roses*. The Pembroke opened at a time when Croydon had lost its last two live theatres—the Davis and the Grand—and during its short life did excellent work. In 1962 its premises were scheduled for demolition, and the company moved to a new civic theatre named in honour of Dame Peggy Ashcroft (q.v.), who was born in the borough.

Pembroke's Men, an Elizabethan theatrical company with which Shakespeare is believed to have been connected in about 1592–3. Among the plays in their repertory were Marlowe's *Edward II* and Shakespeare's *The Taming of the Shrew* and *Richard III*. These last two may have been revisions for Pembroke's Men of two other plays (anonymous) which they owned, *The Taming of a Shrew* and *The True Tragedy of Richard Duke of York*. The company's name is also on the title-page of *Titus Andronicus*, which Shakespeare had refashioned from *Titus and Vespasian* for Sussex's Men (q.v.). His connection with the company ceased in 1594, when he joined the newly formed Chamberlain's Men (q.v.). In 1597 a group of players calling themselves Pembroke's Men leased the Swan, where they got into trouble with the authorities for their production of Nashe and Jonson's *Isle of Dogs*. The theatre was closed, and some of the actors, including Jonson, were put in prison. References to Pembroke's Men are found in the provinces up to 1600, in which year they made an unsuccessful visit to the Rose in London, and are then heard of no more.

PENKETHMAN [also PINKETHMAN], **WILLIAM** (?–1725), English comedian, who had a booth at Bartholomew Fair (see FAIRS). His early years are obscure, but he is believed to have played small comic parts under Betterton (q.v.) as early as 1682. He was a member of the Drury Lane company under Cibber (q.v.), who wrote for him the parts of Don Lewis in *Love Makes a Man; or, the Fop's Fortune* (1701) and Trappanti in *She Would and She Would Not; or, the Kind Impostor* (1702). He also played Harlequin in a mask in Mrs. Behn's *The Emperor of the Moon* (1687). He continued to act until a year before his death.

PENLEY, WILLIAM SYDNEY (1852–1912), English actor-manager, who made his first appearance on the stage at the old Court Theatre in Dec. 1871 in farce, and then toured in light and comic opera. He was for some years at the Strand, playing burlesque under Mrs. Swanborough. The first outstanding success of his career came when he succeeded Tree (q.v.) in the title-role of Hawtrey's *The Private Secretary* (1884), a part with which he has become so identified that he is often believed to have been the first to play it. He was also closely connected with Brandon Thomas's *Charley's Aunt* (1892), playing Lord Fancourt Babberley during its run of 1,466 performances, a record for the period. In 1900 he opened the former Novelty Theatre as the Great Queen Street Theatre (see KINGSWAY THEATRE), and appeared there in revivals of his most successful parts, retiring a year later.

Penny Gaff, see GAFF.

Penny Plain, Twopence Coloured. For the origin of this phrase, see TOY THEATRE.

Penthouse Theatre, SEATTLE, see THEATRE-IN-THE-ROUND and UNIVERSITY DEPARTMENTS OF DRAMA.

People's National Theatre, LONDON, see PRICE, NANCY.

Pepper's Ghost, a device by which a ghost can be made to appear on stage, so called because it was perfected and patented by 'Professor' J. H. Pepper, a director of the Royal Polytechnic Institution in London. It is based, roughly speaking, on the principle that a sheet of glass can be both reflective and transparent, so that a reflection of a figure can appear side by side with an actual performer on the stage. The Ghost Illusion, as Pepper called it, was first demonstrated privately at the Polytechnic on 24 Dec. 1862, and then exhibited publicly with great success. Dickens used it in connection with his readings of *The Haunted Man.* It was first used in the theatre—though it had previously been seen in many music-halls —on 6 Apr. 1863, at the Britannia (q.v.), and several plays there were written specially to introduce it. But it was never widely adopted, probably because it was difficult to place in position, and also because the 'ghost' could not speak. This made it useless for Boucicault's *The Corsican Brothers,* for instance, where the ghost speaks in the last act. The device did, however, enjoy a semi-dramatic life in the Ghost shows, based on popular melodramas, which toured the provincial fairs until the early twentieth century, and gave rise to the expression 'It's all done with mirrors'.

PEPYS, SAMUEL (1633–1703), English diarist, who deserves mention here for the information given in his diary on the world of the theatre during the early years of the Restoration. Pepys, whose passion for the theatre was nearly as great as his love for music, kept a note of the plays he saw, recorded his impression of the actors in them, and related many stray items of backstage gossip imparted to him by one or other of his theatrical friends. To him we owe many illuminating glimpses of the green room, preserved for posterity, and of the rowdy, talkative audiences of his day.

PERCY, ESMÉ SAVILLE (1887–1957), English actor, particularly admired for his work in Shakespeare and Shaw. He studied under Bernhardt (q.v.), whom he greatly admired, and made his first appearance on the stage in Benson's company in 1904, playing leading Shakespearian parts on tour. In 1908 he was with Granville-Barker (q.v.) at the Court Theatre and then joined Miss Horniman's company in Manchester. During and after the First World War he produced over 140 plays for the troops. Back in London he joined Reandean as associate producer, and remained active in the theatre until his sudden death, which occurred shortly before the first night of Nigel Dennis's *The Making of Moo,* in which he was to have appeared. His best work was done in the plays of Shaw, on which he was a recognized authority. From 1924 to 1928, under Charles Macdona, he played a wide variety of Shaw parts—John Tanner in *Man and Superman,* Androcles in *Androcles and the Lion,* Dubedat in *The Doctor's Dilemma,* Higgins in *Pygmalion,* and King Magnus in *The Apple Cart.* He also staged the Hell scene (Act III, Sc.2)—as *Don Juan in Hell* (1928)—from *Man and Superman.* In 1949 he was appointed president of the Shaw Society. Among his later parts was Matthew Skipps in Fry's *The Lady's Not For Burning* (1949), of which he was also co-director.

PÉREZ GALDÓS, BENITO, see GALDÓS.

Periaktoi, scenic devices used in the Roman, and perhaps earlier in the Hellenistic, theatre. According to Vitruvius (q.v.), they were triangular prisms set on each side of the stage which could be revolved on their axes to indicate a change of scene, each of their three surfaces bearing an indication of a locality, as waves for the sea, ships for a harbour, trees for a wood. The publication of Vitruvius's treatise in 1511 led to the adoption and improvement of the *periak-*

toi by Renaissance theatre architects, particularly by BASTIANO DA SAN GALLO (1481-1551), who increased their size and their number, placing several one behind the other on each side of the stage, and providing removable painted canvas panels for each of the three faces of the prism, so as to make possible a greater number of variations in the scenery. These improved *periaktoi* were later known as *telari*.

PERUZZI, BALDASSARE (1481-1537), Italian scenic designer, and the first to apply the science of perspective to theatrical scenery. His flat work was as convincing as his built pieces. He was responsible for the scenery of Bibbiena's *Calandria* when it was given at Rome in 1507, the year after its first production.

Petit-Bourbon, SALLE DU, the first Court theatre of France, in the long gallery of the palace of the Dukes of Bourbon. A finely proportioned room with a stage at one end, it was used originally for balls and ballets, and the first professional company to play in it was the *commedia dell'arte* troupe, the Gelosi, in May 1577. In 1604 the famous Isabella Andreini (q.v.) played there for the last time, dying on the return journey to Italy. In 1645 Mazarin invited the great Italian scene painter and machinist Torelli (q.v.) to supervise the production of opera there, and in 1658, when the theatre was again in the possession of a *commedia dell'arte* troupe under Tiberio Fiorillo (q.v.), the famous Scaramouche, a company under Molière (q.v.), fresh from the provinces, was allowed to share it with them. They opened on 2 Nov. 1658 with five plays by Corneille (q.v.) in quick succession, and not until the end of the month did Molière put on one of his own farces, *L'Étourdi*, followed by *Le Dépit amoureux*. The Petit-Bourbon saw also the first nights of *Les Précieuses ridicules* and *Sganarelle, ou le cocu imaginaire*, before it was suddenly scheduled for demolition in October 1660. Work was begun without reference to Molière—in the full tide of his success, he found himself homeless. However, Louis XIV gave him the disused theatre in the Palais-Royal, and the Petit-Bourbon disappeared. Molière took the boxes and fittings with him, but Vigarani (q.v.), at that time Court architect and scene painter, claimed Torelli's scenery and machinery for the Salle des Machines

which he was building for the King in the Tuileries. When they had been handed over, he burnt them, hoping no doubt to destroy all traces of his admired predecessor, of whom he was extremely jealous.

Petrushka, a Russian puppet which, like the English Punch, developed from the Pulcinella (q.v.) of the *commedia dell'arte*. Usually a hand-puppet, he is the hero of many folk puppet-plays, but is best known outside Russia through Fokine's ballet 'Petrushka' (1911).

PHELPS, SAMUEL (1804-78), English actor and manager, and the first to make Sadler's Wells Theatre (q.v.) the home of Shakespeare. After touring the provinces for several years, making a solid reputation as a tragedian, he appeared in London, at the Haymarket under Webster, in 1837, playing Shylock, Hamlet, Othello, and Richard III, and then repeating his Othello to Macready's Iago at Covent Garden. After the abolition of the patent monopoly in 1843 he took over Sadler's Wells Theatre, and did much to redeem the English stage from the triviality into which it had fallen by his fine and imaginative productions of Shakespeare. Among them the most important were *Macbeth* in 1844, *Antony and Cleopatra* in 1849, and *Pericles* in 1854, the last in its original form for the first time since 1661. By the time he left Sadler's Wells in 1862 he had produced all Shakespeare's plays with the exception of *Henry VI*, *Titus Andronicus*, *Troilus and Cressida*, and *Richard II*. Lear and Othello were considered his best parts, though he was also excellent as Bottom in *A Midsummer Night's Dream*. After leaving Sadler's Wells he appeared in London and the provinces in Shakespeare and in dramatizations of Sir Walter Scott's novels, in which he was much admired. He remained on the stage until almost the end of his life, his last appearance being as Cardinal Wolsey in *Henry VIII* on 31 Mar. 1878 at the Aquarium Theatre (see IMPERIAL THEATRE). His work was continued by a number of young actors whom he had trained, and whose boast it later was that they had played Shakespeare at Sadler's Wells under Phelps.

Philadelphia, a town which from the beginning of American history has been closely connected with theatrical enterprise. A company under Kean and Murray acted Addison's *Cato* there in 1749, and it was the third town to be visited by the elder Hallam, in 1754. Douglass brought the American Company (q.v.) to Philadelphia in 1766 and built for it the first permanent theatre in the United States (see SOUTHWARK THEATRE). Later theatres in Philadelphia were the Arch Street, which became famous under the management of Mrs. John Drew (q.v.), and the Chestnut Street and the Walnut Street (qq.v.). It was not until the 1830s, when all three managers had ruined themselves by importing expensive foreign stars, that Philadelphia finally yielded its supremacy in theatrical matters to New York.

PHILEMON (*c.* 361–263 B.C.), an Athenian poet of New Comedy, who was considered the equal of Menander (q.v.). He was freely imitated by Roman writers of comedy, the *Mercator*, *Trinummus*, and *Mostellaria* of Plautus (q.v.) being adaptations of three of his plays.

Philharmonic Music-Hall, see GRAND THEATRE.

PHILIPE, GÉRARD (1922–59), French actor, whose early death deprived the European stage of one of its finest *jeunes premiers*. He studied at the Paris Conservatoire, and made his début in 1943 in Giraudoux's *Sodome et Gomorrhe*, first attracting attention in 1945 in the title-role of Camus's *Caligula*. In 1951, by which time he had made an outstanding reputation both on stage and screen, he joined the Théâtre National Populaire under Vilar (q.v.) and gave a superb performance as the hero of Corneille's *Le Cid* (he was buried in the costume he wore for this part). He continued to act for the T.N.P. until his sudden death, and his fame and popularity did much to attract a young audience. Among the plays in which he appeared in Paris, at the Avignon Festival, and on tour in Russia, the U.S.A., and Canada, were Kleist's *Prinz Friedrich von Homburg* (1951), Musset's *Lorenzaccio* (1952), Hugo's *Ruy Blas* and Shakespeare's *Richard II* (both 1954). In 1958 and 1959 he appeared in *Les Caprices de Marianne* and *On ne badine pas avec l'amour*, both by Musset. He also played Eilif in the first French production of Brecht's *Mother Courage* (1951).

PHILLIPIN, see VILLIERS, CLAUDE DE.

PHILIPS, AMBROSE (1674–1749), English dramatist, whose main claim to fame is that he wrote one of the best pseudoclassical tragedies in English, *The Distrest Mother* (1712), an adaptation of Racine's *Andromaque* (1667). It is considered second only to Addison's *Cato* (1713). Fielding parodied it, not very successfully, in *The Covent Garden Tragedy* in 1732, thus proving its continued popularity. Philips also wrote two unremarkable plays, *The Briton* (1722) and *Humphrey, Duke of Gloucester* (1723). He was nicknamed Namby-Pamby (by Swift) for his poor verses.

PHILLIPS, AUGUSTINE (?–1605), one of the actors in Shakespeare's plays, who after playing with Strange's and the Admiral's Men, joined the Chamberlain's Men (q.v.) on its formation in 1594. In his will he left 30s. to Shakespeare, Condell, and Christopher Beeston respectively. He was one of the original shareholders in the Globe Theatre (q.v.).

PHILLIPS, STEPHEN (1864–1915), English poet and dramatist, whose poetic play, *Paolo and Francesca*, when produced by Alexander (q.v.) at the St. James's Theatre on 6 Mar. 1902, was believed to have inaugurated a new era of poetry in the English theatre. Phillips, who had been for a short time an actor in the company of his cousin Frank Benson (q.v.), had already achieved some success with *Herod* (1900) and *Ulysses* (Feb. 1902), both produced by Tree (q.v.) at Her Majesty's, but a later work, *Nero* (1906), also seen at Her Majesty's, showed a considerable falling-off and, like all Phillips's work, was soon forgotten.

PHILLPOTTS, EDEN (1862–1960), English dramatist and novelist, author of a number of light comedies of English rural life, of which the most successful was *The Farmer's Wife*. First seen at the Birmingham Repertory Theatre in 1916, it was revived in 1924 with Cedric Hardwicke (q.v.) as Churdles Ash. Transferred to the Court Theatre, London, it had a long run and has been revived several times since then with success. Also produced at the Birmingham Repertory Theatre and in London were *Devonshire Cream* (1924), *Jane's Legacy* (1925), and

Yellow Sands (1926), in the last of which Phillpotts collaborated with his daughter ADELAIDE (1896–   ), also a novelist and dramatist.

Phlyax, the name given to a form of classical mime-play of the fourth century B.C. which bridges the gap between Athenian and Roman comedy. Much of it was probably improvised, and consisted of burlesques of earlier plays interspersed with scenes of daily life. Our knowledge of the *phlyakes* derives mainly from vase paintings. The form of stage depicted is important, for from it may have developed the salient forms of the Roman theatre, which differed so markedly from the Greek (see THEATRE BUILDINGS). The most primitive type consisted of posts supporting a wooden platform. Later the posts were joined by wooden panels with ornamental patterns, while still later the structure, though still not permanent, had a background for the actors which approximates to the Roman *scaenae frons*, with a practicable door and windows which were used during the play.

Phoenix Society, LONDON. This was founded in 1919 under the auspices of the Stage Society (q.v.) for the presentation of plays by early English dramatists, few of which had been seen in London since the productions of Philip Carr's Mermaid Society (q.v.) in the early 1900s. The Stage Society began the work of revival in 1915, and continued annually to produce one Restoration comedy by Farquhar, Congreve, or Vanbrugh (qq.v.) until 1919. The Phoenix was then established, and in the six years of its existence, up to 1925, was responsible for twenty-six productions, the authors including Marlowe, Ben Jonson, Beaumont and Fletcher, Heywood, Ford, Dryden, Otway, Wycherley, and Congreve. From the beginning enthusiastic support was given by established actors and actresses; two permanent and adaptable sets were designed by Norman Wilkinson (q.v.); and all but two of the productions (for which Edith Craig (q.v.) was responsible) were directed by Allan Wade. In 1923 a brilliant performance of Fletcher's pastoral (q.v.), *The Faithful Shepherdess*, was given in conjunction with Sir Thomas Beecham, who arranged and conducted the music.

There can be little doubt that the influence of these performances helped considerably to combat the indifference—in some cases the hostility—once shown to early English drama; several of the plays revived privately by the Phoenix were later frequently and successfully acted on the public stage; and a large section of English drama, undeservedly neglected, was enabled to prove in the theatre its continuing vitality.

Phoenix Theatre. (1) LONDON, on the corner of Charing Cross Road and Phoenix Street, from which it takes its name. It opened on 24 Sept. 1930 with the first production of Coward's *Private Lives*, in which he appeared with Gertrude Lawrence and Laurence Olivier (qq.v.). Later successes by Coward were *To-night at 8.30* (1936) and *Quadrille* (1952). In its early years the Phoenix had a chequered history, but it later housed a number of important plays, including Saint-Denis's production of *Twelfth Night* (1938), Gielgud's revivals of Congreve's *Love for Love* (1943) and of *The Winter's Tale* (1951) and *Much Ado About Nothing* (1952), Rattigan's *Playbill* (1948) and *The Sleeping Prince* (1953), Wilder's *The Skin of Our Teeth* (1945), Paul Scofield in *Hamlet* (1955), the long run of Lesley Storm's *Roar Like a Dove*, and in 1961 Albert Finney in Osborne's *Luther*, transferred from the Royal Court. In 1963 Brecht's *Baal*, with Peter O'Toole, had a short run, and in 1965 Gielgud (q.v.) appeared in his own version of Chekhov's *Ivanov*. In 1968 a dramatization of four of Chaucer's *Canterbury Tales* started a long run.

(For an earlier Phoenix in London, see COCKPIT.)

(2) NEW YORK. This theatre, formerly the Yiddish Art Theatre on 2nd Avenue at 12th Street, run by Maurice Schwartz (q.v.), reopened on 1 Dec. 1953 as the Phoenix with Sidney Howard's posthumous *Madam, Will You Walk?* It was intended for uncommercial plays, and the repertory was mainly European, including, between 1954 and 1956, *Coriolanus*, Chekhov's *The Seagull*, Shaw's *The Doctor's Dilemma*, Ibsen's *The Master Builder*, Strindberg's *Miss Julie*, and Turgenev's *A Month in the Country*.

(3) In 1961 the company from the Phoenix moved to a smaller theatre on East 74th Street, also named the Phoenix, which achieved critical success with Conway's *Who'll Save the Ploughboy?* and both critical and commercial success the following year with Kopit's *Oh Dad, Poor Dad, Mamma's Hung You in the*

Closet and I'm Feelin' So Sad, which had previously had a short but unsuccessful run in London. The former Phoenix, renamed the Eden, came back into theatre history in 1969 with the production of Kenneth Tynan's erotic revue, *Oh! Calcutta!*

PIAF, EDITH [really GIOVANNA EDITH GASSION] (1915–63), French singer and entertainer, daughter of an acrobat, Jean Gassion. She had a hard and unhappy childhood, and at an early age supported herself by singing in the streets. Once launched into cabaret and music-hall, she rapidly became a popular favourite and something of a cult among a group of influential critics. Among the songs which she made famous were 'Mon légionnaire', 'La vie en rose', of which she wrote both the words and the music, 'Le voyage du pauvre nègre', and 'Pour deux sous d'amour'. Her style was deceptively simple and nostalgic but technically of great expertise and always highly personal. Although she was above all a singer, either alone or with a group—she made extensive tours of Europe and America with Les Compagnons de la Chanson, for instance—she appeared in a number of films, and was also seen in the theatre in *Le Bel Indifférent* (1941), specially written for her by Cocteau (q.v.), who died on the same day as she did, and *La P'tite Lili* (1951), by Marcel Achard. In 1958 she published a volume of autobiography, *Au Bal de la Chance*, of which an English translation appeared in 1965 as *The Wheel of Fortune*.

PICARD, LOUIS-BAPTISTE (1769–1828), one of the few successful dramatists of France under Napoleon. Actor, author, and manager, he rode the storms of the Revolution, the Empire, and the Restoration with an unquenchable gaiety, flourishing under all of them. His caustic humour, which under more auspicious circumstances might have flowered into satire, took as its target the newly rich and newly risen. He excelled in depicting bourgeois or provincial interiors, and was the originator of a mingling of light satiric prose comedy with music which proved immensely popular in its day. One of his plays, *La Petite Ville* (1801), translated into German as *Die lustige Witwe*, provided Lehár with the libretto of a light opera seen in England in 1907 as

The Merry Widow. Picard's published texts give careful directions for settings and costume, in which he aimed above all at pictorial effect, and he can be credited with the creation of one new character, the valet Deschamps. Among his plays *Médiocre et rampant* (1797), whose title comes from a speech by Figaro, is perhaps the best in its picture of contemporary society, while *Le Passé, le présent et l'avenir* (1791) pays tribute to the new ideas of his time. Far more amusing, however, is the lighthearted *Le Collatéral, ou la Diligence à Joigny* (1799), which, with *La Vieille Tante* (1811) and *Les Deux Philibert* (1816), ranks among the best of his work. He was the founder and for many years the manager of the Odéon (q.v.), which stood second in importance only to the Comédie-Française. He gave up acting in 1807 in order to qualify for admission to the French Academy and for the award of the Légion d'Honneur, which even Napoleon dared not give to an actor.

Piccadilly Theatre, LONDON, in Denman Street. This opened on 27 Apr. 1928 with a musical play, *Blue Eyes*, and was then used as a cinema. It returned to live theatre in Nov. 1929, and in 1933 housed Bridie's *The Sleeping Clergyman*. It was then used for the transfer of long runs at reduced prices. After being closed for some time at the beginning of the Second World War, it reopened with Coward's *Blithe Spirit* (1941), and among later successes were Gielgud in *Macbeth* (1942) and the American musical *Panama Hattie* (1943). The building was then damaged by flying bombs, and did not reopen until 1945. Successful productions since then have included Werfel's *Jacobowsky and the Colonel* (1945), a musical version of Louisa M. Alcott's *Little Women* as *A Girl Called Jo* (1955), Ustinov's *Romanoff and Juliet* (1956), Benn Levy's *The Rape of the Belt* (1957), Lillian Hellman's *Toys in the Attic* (1960), Edward Albee's *Who's Afraid of Virginia Woolf?* (1964), and Robert Bolt's *Vivat! Vivat Regina!* (1970).

Piccolo Teatro della Città di Milano, the first post-war permanent theatre to be set up in Italy. Founded in 1947 by the actor Paolo Grassi, with a municipal grant, it later received a State subsidy, and was the model for several other similar ventures in Rome, Turin, and elsewhere; but up till now it remains supreme in its field. It opened on 14 May with Gorky's *The Lower Depths* produced by Giorgio Strehler, with Marcello Moretti, the famous Harlequin, in the cast. Since then it has built up a steadily increasing audience which includes many people who were not previously in the habit of going to the theatre, and it has toured extensively, visiting sixty-six Italian towns and twenty-six countries. Among its outstanding achievements has been its introduction of Brecht (q.v.) to Italian audiences. Apart from revivals of the classics—particularly Shakespeare and Goldoni—it has presented a number of contemporary European and American plays, and also the work of new Italian playwrights.

PICKARD, HELENA (1899–1959), English actress and theatre manager, the first wife of Cedric Hardwicke (q.v.), by whom she had one son, Edward, also an actor. They were married during the London run of Eden Phillpotts's *The Farmer's Wife*, a play with which she was closely connected, playing Sophy Smerdon on its first production in Birmingham in 1916, Sibley Sweetland in London in 1924, and Thirza Tapper in a revival of 1947. She had a consistently successful, if not spectacular, career for over forty years, appearing in a play on television a few days before her death. She made her first appearance in New York in 1936 in Wycherley's *The Country Wife*, and was subsequently seen there in Priestley's *Time and the Conways* (1938) and Rattigan's *Flare Path* (1942). She then toured Canada, lecturing and broadcasting, and returned to London to appear in a number of plays, including a revival of Pinero's *Preserving Mr. Panmure* (1950), and *The Remarkable Mr. Pennypacker* (1955), by Liam O'Brien. Known as 'Pixie' to innumerable friends, she had a charming, witty, vivacious personality which captivated on stage and off.

Pickelhering, see REYNOLDS, ROBERT.

Pierrot, a character derived from the *commedia dell'arte* (q.v.) mask, Pedrolino, a *zanni* or servant role of which GIOVANNI PELLESINI (*c.* 1526–1612) was the earliest and best-known exponent. The character had in it something of Pulcinella (q.v.), and one of its offshoots is the clown, hero of Leoncavallo's 'Pagliacci'. The transformation of Pedrolino into the earliest version of the French Pierrot is usually attributed to an Italian actor named Giuseppe Giaratone, or Giratoni, who joined the Italian company in Paris about 1665. He accentuated the character's simplicity and awkwardness, so important a feature of his later manifestations, and dressed him in the familiar costume, a loose white garment with long sleeves, ruff, and large hat whose soft brim flapped round his whitened face. This, with some slight changes, has remained his distinguishing garb ever since, but his character was fundamentally altered by Deburau (q.v.), who for twenty years, at the Funambules, played no other part. He was followed in the part by his son, and later by Paul Legrand at the Folies-Nouvelles (later the Théâtre Déjazet), but Legrand made Pierrot less amusing and more sentimental, a trait which was later developed by a host of imitators until the robust country lad of early days had become a lackadaisical, love-sick youth pining away from unrequited love, and much addicted to singing mournful ballads under a full moon.

Meanwhile, in 1890, the Pierrot of Deburau had become the hero of a wordless play, *L'Enfant prodigue*, which was seen a year later in London, where Pierrot was already well known in pantomime. His popularity led to the formation of 'pierrot-troupes' which, after an initial appearance at Henley Regatta, spread all over England, ousting the black-face minstrels (see MINSTREL SHOW) from the beaches and pier-pavilions of the seaside towns. In what became the traditional pierrot costume—short frilly white frocks for the girls, loose white (or black) suits for the men, with tall dunces' caps, the whole enlivened by coloured buttons, ruffs, and ruffles—the various members of the company sang, danced, juggled, told funny stories, or engaged in humorous backchat. The apotheosis of this form of entertainment, which was later replaced by the more sophisticated agglomeration of turns known as revue (q.v.), was reached by Pélissier (q.v.) with his Follies in the early 1900s. A successful revival of the old Pierrot show, staged by the Co-Optimists under DAVY BURNABY (1881–1949), enlivened London for several seasons in the 1920s.

Pike Theatre, DUBLIN, see DUBLIN.

Pike's Opera House, NEW YORK, see
GRAND OPERA HOUSE.

Pilgrim Players, see BIRMINGHAM; also
BROWNE, E. MARTIN.

PINERO [really PINHEIRO], SIR ARTHUR
WING (1855–1934), English dramatist,
who was an actor for ten years, making
his first appearance on the stage at the
Theatre Royal, Edinburgh, on 22 June
1874. He used his experience as an aid to
playwriting, always his main objective,
and on 6 Oct. 1877 he had his first play,
£200 a Year, produced at the Globe
Theatre. Many minor pieces followed,
including *The Money Spinner* (1881) at
the St. James's. Popularity came with
The Magistrate (1885), the first of the
Court Theatre farces which became all
the rage. It was followed by *The Schoolmistress* (1886), *Dandy Dick* (1887),
The Cabinet Minister (1890), and *The
Amazons* (1893). The first three have been
successfully revived many times and still
rank as some of the best English farces.
In 1888 a frankly sentimental play, *Sweet
Lavender*, confirmed Pinero's pre-
eminence in the contemporary theatre.
With *The Profligate* (1889) he made his
first venture into the 'theatre of ideas',
showing a new departure in his work
which was confirmed with the production
at the end of May 1893 of *The Second Mrs.
Tanqueray*, a 'problem play' in which
Mrs. Patrick Campbell (q.v.) startled
the town. In a theatre long given over to
farce, burlesque, and melodrama it
appeared revolutionary. It was a 'serious'
English play which made money. During
the next thirty years Pinero was regularly
productive. *The Notorious Mrs. Ebbsmith*
(1895) was Paula Tanqueray's successor;
Trelawny of the 'Wells' (1898) was a gay
theatrical romp which, like the farces,
has been regularly revived with success;
The Gay Lord Quex (1899) was a brilliant
piece of theatricalism, containing a third
act which is perhaps the author's masterpiece of contrivance. With the turn of the
century came a long succession of serious
plays, from *Iris* (1901) and *Letty* (1903) to
His House in Order (1906) and *Mid-
Channel* (1909). Of these *Iris* may be
reasonably considered the best. In 1909
Pinero was knighted for services to the
theatre. But he had written himself out,
and his last play, *A Cold June* (1932), was
a pathetic failure. His reputation now

rests on a handful of excellent farces and
Trelawny of the 'Wells', whose leading
role is a constant challenge to spirited
young actresses.

PINTER [really DA PINTA], HAROLD
(1930–), English actor and dramatist,
whose first play, the one-act *The Room*,
was produced by the Drama Department
of Bristol University in 1957 and was
then seen professionally in London in a
double bill with *The Dumb-Waiter* (1960).
His first full-length play, *The Birthday
Party* (1958), though well received by the
critics, had only a short run, and it was
The Caretaker (1960), with Alan Bates
(q.v.), which finally established him as
one of the outstanding younger playwrights of his day. The play, which
contains only three characters, deals with
the impossibility of communication between human beings. Though not successful in Paris, it has been seen with
acclaim all over Germany, in India, Turkey, and Yugoslavia, and in New York,
where Pinter's other plays have also been
seen. In 1962 the Royal Shakespeare
Company (q.v.) put on at the Aldwych
his one-act *The Collection*, and in 1965
a new full-length play, *The Homecoming*,
followed in 1969 by the double bill
Landscape and *Silence*. Two plays originally written for television, *Tea Party* and
The Duchess, were seen in New York and
in London in 1970, in which year Pinter
directed a production of James Joyce's
only play, *Exiles*, for the Mermaid
Theatre. Among his early works were
revue sketches and the one-act plays *A
Slight Ache* and *A Night Out* (both 1961),
The Lover and *The Dwarfs* (both 1963),
and *Night* (1969). Though Pinter's work is
basically serious, even tragic, he displays
a brisk sense of humour, the wit of his
spare, exact dialogue being particularly
lively and effective. He writes in the tradition of the Theatre of the Absurd (q.v.),
but with welcome originality.

PIRANDELLO, LUIGI (1867–1936),
Italian dramatist, awarded the Nobel
Prize for Literature in 1934. He was
already well known as a novelist and
critic before he achieved recognition as
a playwright, his early plays being one-
act adaptations of some of his own short
stories. His best-known play is *Sei personaggi in cerca d'autore* (1921), with
which he became internationally famous.
As *Six Characters in Search of an Author*,

it was produced in London and New York in 1922, and has been revived several times since. Central to an understanding of his work, it shows a group of characters in a play invading the stage during a rehearsal and insisting on becoming the arbiters of their own destiny. It forms part of a trilogy, of which the other sections, less well known in English, are *Ciascuno a suo modo* (*Each in His Own Way*) (1924) and *Questa sera si recita a soggetto* (*Tonight We Improvise*) (1929). In these, as in all his other plays, particularly in his finest tragedy, *Enrico IV* (1922), seen in London in 1925 as *Henry IV* and in 1929 as *The Mock Emperor* (and in New York as *Henry IV* in 1947), he is concerned with the futility of human endeavour and the impossibility of establishing an integrated personality for any human being. Among his plays, which have had a great influence on European drama, others which have been successfully produced in English are *Così è* (*se vi pare*) (1917) as *Right You Are, If You Think You Are*; *Lazzaro* (1929) as *Lazarus*; and *Come tu mi vuoi* (1930) as *As You Desire Me*. Of the one-act plays the best-known is perhaps *L'uomo dal fiore in bocca* (1923), which as *The Man With a Flower in his Mouth* was produced in London in 1926. Like many of Pirandello's plays, it is popular with amateur and student societies. In 1969 *Quando si è qualcuno*, written in 1933, was seen at the Theatre Royal, York, as part of the York festival, in a translation, *When One is Somebody*, by Marta Abba, who was for many years Pirandello's leading lady, and in 1970 *Liolà*, written in 1916, was produced in London during the World Theatre season by the Catania Stabile Theatre from Sicily. It also provided the libretto for Mulè's opera of the same title, first heard in 1935, a year after the first performance of Malipiero's opera based on Pirandello's *La Favola del figlio cambiato* (1933). Pirandello had an unhappy life, his wife, whom he married in 1894, becoming mentally ill in 1904. For fifteen years he cared for her at home, finding what compensation he could in his work in the theatre. He established his own theatre in Rome in 1925, where he proved himself an excellent director with an acute awareness of the technical problems of stagecraft. Under his influence the Italian straight theatre was once again able to challenge the supremacy of opera, and he himself became well known throughout Europe and in America, where he several times toured with his company, usually in his own plays.

PIRON, ALEXIS (1689–1773), French dramatist, who wrote farces for the fairground theatres and overcame the difficulty of not employing more than one speaking actor, as enacted by the law of 1718, by a series of monologues, of which the first was *Arlequin Deucalion* (1722). Encouraged by his success, he sent a comedy, *L'École des pères*, to the Comédie-Française, where it was produced in 1728. It is an interesting mingling of old and new, for it stands on the threshold of the *comédie larmoyante*, though its author still holds to the theory that comedy should seek first to amuse and only incidentally to instruct. Piron's best work, and one of the outstanding comedies of the eighteenth century, was *La Métromanie* (1738). while of his tragedies *Gustave Wasa* (1734) remained in the repertory for some time.

PISCATOR, ERWIN FRIEDRICH MAX (1893–1966), German director, a disciple of Max Reinhardt (q.v.). He evolved the first 'epic' play, so initiating the style later developed for the Berliner Ensemble by Brecht (q.v.), who worked under Piscator at the Volksbühne in Berlin from 1919 to 1930. Piscator, who ruthlessly altered the text of any play he produced to suit his own theories, was one of the first directors to use films and animated cartoons in conjunction with live actors, and his work had a great influence on contemporary play-production in Europe. In 1933 he left Germany, and in 1938 settled in New York, where a year later he founded the Dramatic Workshop at the New School for Social Research. In the 1940s the Workshop (today run on a more modest scale by Piscator's widow MARIE LEY [really MARIA CZADA]) maintained two off-Broadway theatres where a long list of productions included Piscator's own 'epic' version of Tolstoy's *War and Peace* (1942). This was seen briefly in London in 1962 in a production by the Bristol Old Vic company, so providing English audiences with their only chance of seeing Piscator's work, even at second-hand. When in 1951 Piscator returned to Germany he was responsible for a further series of interesting productions, particularly at Marburg, where he directed in 1952 Büchner's *Dantons Tod* and in 1955 Arthur Miller's *The Crucible*.

In 1961 Piscator staged Miller's *Death of a Salesman* at the Berlin Volksbühne, of which he became director a year later. His first production after his appointment was an amalgamation into a single play of four poetic plays on the House of Atreus, the last works of Gerhart Hauptmann (q.v.), in which he used, with great dramatic effect, a translucent stage lit from below, settings in the Japanese style, screens with projections from the back, and symbolic orbs of red, black, and gold.

Pit, the name given to the ground floor of the theatre auditorium, generally excavated below ground level. In the early playhouses the stage and lower boxes were approximately at ground level, and the whole space sunk between these was called the pit, from the Elizabethan cockpit, used for cock-fighting. In the early nineteenth century the lower boxes were replaced by a raised circle, with the pit extending underneath; shortly after, the old rows of pit seats near the orchestra were replaced by the higher-priced stalls, and the name 'pit' was applied only to the more distant rows. Most modern theatres have no pit.

Pitlochry, PERTHSHIRE, SCOTLAND. The Pitlochry festival owes its inception to the Shaw festival at Malvern (q.v.), as it was during a visit there that John Stewart, founder of the Park Theatre (q.v.) in Glasgow, conceived the idea of building a 'theatre in the hills' for the presentation of a festival of plays in repertory. The first season opened on 19 May 1951 in a large marquee which housed a fan-shaped auditorium and a stage with a large proscenium opening. This tent theatre was so well designed that its features were retained in the more permanent structure built in 1953. Generally speaking, Pitlochry, where Kenneth Ireland has been in charge since Stewart's death in 1957, presents six plays between April and October, including usually one Scots play, one modern work by a foreign author, a classic or near-classic, English or foreign, and a new play. The festival also features concerts, art exhibitions, and lectures.

PITOËFF, GEORGES (1885–1939), a Russian actor who settled in Paris after the First World War and founded a company which had a great influence on the French theatre of his day. He had already had some experience of the theatre, having directed an amateur company in St. Petersburg for two years before the Revolution, and after appearing in several Paris theatres he took over the Théâtre des Arts in 1924. He remained there until 1934, when he finally settled at the Mathurins, where much of his best work was done. He was an all-round man of the theatre, translating, adapting, directing, and acting in a wide variety of foreign plays. He was probably happiest when staging Shakespeare, but he also introduced Shaw and Pirandello to Parisian audiences, and among the new French dramatists whom he encouraged were Lenormand, whose *Le Mangeur de rêves* he produced in 1922, Cocteau, and Anouilh (qq.v.). He was ably assisted in his task by his wife LUDMILLA (1896–1951), an excellent actress, who after her husband's death continued to direct the company, taking it on an extended tour of America and Canada. Among the many parts which she played to perfection were Nora in Ibsen's *A Doll's House*, Marthe in Claudel's *L'Échange*, and the hostess in Goldoni's *La Locandiera*. She was also extraordinarily moving as Shaw's St. Joan, which she played in London in a French translation, together with the younger Dumas's *La Dame aux camélias*, in 1930.

PITT, ARCHIE (1885–1940), see FIELDS, GRACIE; CHARLES (1768–1833), see DIBDIN, CHARLES.

PIXÉRÉCOURT, (RENÉ-CHARLES) GUILBERT DE (1773–1844), French dramatist, mainly remembered for a succession of melodramas which over a long period provided the staple fare of the secondary theatres. The first was *Victor, ou l'enfant de la forêt* (1798), and the most successful *Coelina, ou l'Enfant de mystère* (1800), which was soon translated into German, English, and Dutch. The English version, by Holcroft (q.v.), was produced without reference to Pixérécourt at Covent Garden in 1802 as *A Tale of Mystery*, and was the first English stage production to be called a melodrama (q.v.). In spite of such plagiarisms, however, Pixérécourt made a great deal of money, most of which he lost when the Théâtre de la Gaîté, of which he was a director, was burnt down in 1835. This ended his career, and he retired to Nancy, his birthplace, to die a lingering death. He took his work seriously, and spent a long time over the production and scenery of his plays, for which he often invented new machinery and provided spectacular effects. His theories on melodrama are to be found in two published works, *Le Mélodrame* and *Dernières Réflexions sur le mélodrame*. His work shows the extent of German influence in the early nineteenth-century French theatre, and in its turn influenced the Romantic dramatists, particularly Hugo and the elder Dumas (qq.v.). He also had a great influence in England, where the main characteristics of his theatre are preserved in the drawings of the 'penny plain, twopence coloured' Toy Theatre (q.v.).

PLACIDE, HENRY (1799–1870), American actor, eldest son of ALEXANDRE PLACIDE (?–1812), rope dancer to the King of France, who emigrated to the United States in 1791, visiting England on the way and marrying an English actress. Henry was on the New York stage as a child, and in 1823 made his adult début at the Park Theatre (q.v.) in the younger Colman's *The Heir-at-Law*. He remained there for many years, except for short tours to other American towns and one appearance in London in 1841, and was later at Burton's. Like John Gilbert (q.v.), he represented the best traditions of polished acting in Old Comedy, and was excellent in the role of the high-bred English gentleman, Sir Peter Teazle in Sheridan's *The School for Scandal* being one of his best parts.

PLANCHÉ, JAMES ROBINSON (1796–1880), English dramatist, of Huguenot descent, a prolific writer of burlesques, extravaganzas, and pantomimes, of which the first was produced at Drury Lane in 1818. He was associated with Mme Vestris and Charles Mathews (qq.v.) at the Olympic and the Lyceum, and wrote for them his best work, *The Island of Jewels* (1849). His adaptation of a French melodrama as *The Vampire; or, the Bride of the Isles* (1820) first introduced to the English stage the Vamp trap (see TRAP). He was a serious student of art, and designed and supervised the costumes for the production of *King John* by Charles Kemble (q.v.) in 1823, the first to approximate to historical accuracy. An unauthorized production of one of his plays led him to press for reform in the laws governing theatrical copyright, and it was mainly his efforts that led to the passing of the Dramatic Copyright Act giving protection to dramatic authors. He also published in 1834 a *History of British Costume* which long remained a standard work. His work for the theatre, which was extremely successful in its day, seems to have had no literary merit whatever, and divorced from its music and spectacular effects is quite unreadable. It depended largely on its staging and topicality, and taken as a whole provides an excellent picture of the English stage during sixty years. According to the theatre historian Sir St. Vincent Troubridge, Gilbert's libretti for the Savoy operas were largely based on or suggested by the texts of Planché's extravaganzas (see *Notes and Queries*, vols. 180, 181).

PLANCHON, ROGER (1931–), French producer, actor, and playwright, leader of a group of amateur actors in Lyons who in 1952 turned professional and built their own hundred-seat theatre, the Théâtre de la Comédie de Lyon. By 1957 they had appeared in twenty-eight productions, including the first performances of *Le Professeur Taranne* and *Paolo Paoli* by Adamov (q.v.), and had achieved a considerable reputation as an *avant-garde* company. Planchon's productions at this time constituted, in effect, a conscious programme of investigation into stagecraft, in which he experimented with techniques borrowed from every possible source, from the Elizabethan theatre to American gangster films and silent comedies. Under the influence first of Jean Vilar and later of Brecht (qq.v.) (whose *The Good Woman of Setzuan* he produced in 1954), he brought new vigour to the presentation of classical plays. His increasing interest in epic styles led him to seek a larger theatre, and in 1957 the company moved to the 1,300-seat Théâtre de la Cité de Villeurbanne, in an industrial suburb of Lyons, where their controversial productions, which included *Henry IV, Parts 1 and 2*, attracted an entirely new and mainly working-class audience. Visiting Paris in 1960 at the invitation of Jean-Louis Barrault (q.v.), the company achieved a resounding success and was awarded a government subsidy: the Théâtre de la Cité thus became the first national theatre in the French provinces. In the same year London had the opportunity of seeing Planchon's work with the production at the Piccadilly Theatre of his own very amusing adaptation of the elder Dumas's *The Three Musketeers*, in which he played d'Artagnan. It had previously been seen at the Edinburgh Festival. Planchon's subsequent productions have included Gogol's *Dead Souls*, adapted by Adamov, Marlowe's *Edward II*, adapted by Planchon, and Brecht's *Schweik in the Second World War*. During the World Theatre season of 1969 the company of the Théâtre de la Cité was seen in London in Racine's *Bérénice*, directed by Planchon in such a way as to throw new light on this admitted masterpiece.

PLATO (427–348 B.C.), philosopher of Athens, member of a highly aristocratic family. In his youth he composed tragedies and other forms of poetry, but on coming under the influence of Socrates he burnt his plays and devoted his life to philosophy and mathematics. Much of his written work was in dialogue form—a development of the mime (q.v.)—and although in the more abstruse works, and in most of the *Republic*, the dialogue is only nominal, elsewhere it is consistently dramatic, with occasional passages of astonishing vividness and power. The character sketches of Euthyphro or Ion, or the opening scenes of the *Protagoras*, are good examples of Plato's dramatic skill; his mastery of ironic comedy is shown by his picture of the Sophists in the *Euthydemus*; of tragedy by the scene of Socrates' death in the *Phaedo*. His theories of literature and drama have had an immense influence. His 'inspirational' theory of poetry is the direct source of the idea of the *furor poeticus*, through a sixteenth-century translation of his *Ion* which greatly influenced French poets of the time. In other dialogues Plato is much less sympathetic to literature, and from the *Republic* and other works it is evident that he would admit poetry into his ideal society only under a paralysing censorship. He objects in particular to drama because it appeals especially to the ignorant, debilitates the community by appealing to its emotions and not to reason, and propagates blasphemous and impossible ideas about the deity (e.g. by repeating stories of strife between gods). These criticisms were important chiefly for the reply which they drew from Aristotle (q.v.).

Platt, the Elizabethan theatrical term for the 'plot', or prompter's outline of the action of a play, with division into acts, actors' entrances and exits, and other notes, which was written out and posted somewhere behind the scenes for help and convenience in organizing calls and properties. It should not be confused with an author's synopsis, nor with the scenarii of the *commedia dell'arte* (q.v.), which were used as a groundwork for improvisation. The 'platt' was a purely utilitarian device, of which a few stray specimens have been preserved among the papers of Henslowe (q.v.).

PLAUTUS, TITUS MACCUS [or MACCIUS] (*c.* 254–184 B.C.), Roman playwright, whose full name and dates, as given above, cannot be established with any certainty. Of the 130 plays attributed to him by the first century B.C., 20, believed to be authentic, have survived (though the *Mercator* and the *Asinaria* may not be his). They are all free renderings of Greek New Comedy, among which Plautus seems to have preferred plays with complicated plots, strongly marked characters, and scenes of love-making, revelry, trickery, and debauchery; he was himself able to supply songs, repartee, jests, puns, and topical allusions, and to dilate on congenial topics, often with small regard for what was dramatically appropriate. Although Roman dramatists were warned to abstain from political and personal satire, there seems to have been no ban on indecency, and several of Plautus' plays, among them the *Bacchides*, the *Pseudolus*, and the *Truculentus*, portray the life of the brothel, while concluding scenes of the *Casina* carry farce to outrageous lengths. But the prologue and epilogue to the *Captivi* boast of the high moral tone of that particular play, and, where the honour of a respectable woman is concerned, Plautus keeps his wit within bounds. Among the better-known plays the *Menaechmi* (source of Shakespeare's *The Comedy of Errors*) and the *Amphitruo* deal with the complications caused by mistaken identity; the *Aulularia* shows us a poor old man crazed by the discovery of a buried treasure; the *Mostellaria* or 'Ghost Story' displays the endless fertility of invention whereby the slave Tranio contrives to baffle his young master's father, unexpectedly returned from abroad; the *Rudens* tells of storm and shipwreck, a treasure recovered from the sea, and a long-lost daughter restored to her parents; in the *Captivi* the noble courage and devotion of a slave enable his master to escape from captivity. Considering the limits imposed by New Comedy, the variety of plot in Plautus' plays is considerable; and if he lacks the subtle effects of Menander and Terence (qq.v.) he offers instead a flow of wit and a vigour of language which explain his supreme popularity on the Roman stage. Within a few years of his death he had become a classic, and even when his plays had long ceased to be acted they provided a source of merriment for generations of readers. Translations of most of them have been staged by college or school dramatic societies, and the successful American musical, *A Funny Thing Happened on the Way to the Forum* (1962; London 1963) was based on material from several different ones.

Play, a generic term applied to any work written to be acted, and covering such more limiting terms as comedy, drama, farce, or tragedy. It may designate backchat between two mountebanks in the market-place or a full-length work given in a special building—a theatre—with a cast of highly trained professional actors aided by all the appurtenances of lighting, costuming, and production. The one essential is that it should be entirely or mainly spoken; if it has no dialogue it is a mime; if danced, a ballet; if entirely sung, an opera. Hybrid forms are ballad opera (q.v.), burletta (see BURLESQUE (3)), and musical comedy (q.v.). (For the use of music as an adjunct to a play, see INCIDENTAL MUSIC.)

A play can be read, but only fulfils its original intention when acted. The text may therefore be regarded as an inert body of words to which the producer, actor, and audience must contribute to bring it to life. Although the fundamental principles of drama remain constant—action, conflict, unity of purpose, resolution—the form of a play may conform to certain conventions—five-act, three-act, unity of time and place, separation (or alternatively fusion) of tragedy and comedy—which vary from age to age, and even from country to country. The form, however, comes first, the rules afterwards, even with Aristotle (q.v.). In the same way, although the art of acting is to some extent dependent on the type of play in favour at the moment, it has an independent life of its own, and at certain points in the history of the theatre there may be conflict between the text and its interpreters. A

good play may fail in its own day and only be appreciated in revival. Plays written to be read—closet drama (q.v.)—remain outside the main stream of the theatre, though this theory is refuted by the success of the plays of Alfred de Musset (q.v.) on the stage many years after they were written and by the influence on European drama of the tragedies of Seneca (q.v.), which were probably not acted but read aloud. The poetic drama of the nineteenth century, which from a purely literary point of view contains many fine things, has not proved successful on the stage. It seems likely that an inherent lack of dramatic impulse allied to too great a weight of pure poetry will always hinder its immediate effect on an audience. The author alone cannot produce a play in the full sense of the word but must have the co-operation of many other people. The earlier name for a dramatist, playwright, by its affinity with such words as wheelwright, reveals this clearly, and makes the author a fellow worker in the theatre with actor, producer, designer, stage carpenter, and so on. Some of the finest plays have been written by men experiencing all the advantages and disadvantages of actual daily participation in the work of the theatre (see, for instance, SHAKESPEARE).

Playbill, Poster, Programme, forms of publicity giving information about theatrical activities. Although posters, i.e. proclamations hung on posts, are believed to have been used in London and Paris before the middle of the seventeenth century (earlier announcements were probably written on a wall, as in Pompeii), the first known English poster, which probably served also as a playbill for distribution by hand, is in the Public Record Office and dates from 1672. On roughish paper with the Royal Arms at the top and 'Vivat Rex' at the bottom, it advertises a variety entertainment 'at the Booth at Charing-Cross'. The earliest survival for an established theatre is dated 22 Feb. 1687, and advertises a performance at Drury Lane of *A King and No King*, by Beaumont and Fletcher, who are not mentioned. In fact, it was a long time before any detailed information was given, but gradually the actors, the scenes, and even the scene designers, were listed, displacing the Royal Arms. By the end of the eighteenth century the poster, therefore, was becoming the equivalent of the modern programme. The distinction between the two arose in the nineteenth century when the poster, which still served as a playbill, was enlarged to accommodate elaborate descriptions of scenes and their painters' names, an addition necessitated by the triumphs of Telbin, Stanfield, and others. By 1850 the poster had grown to 26 in. × 17 in., and for Charles Kean at the Princess's Theatre to 20 in. × 30 in. This made it too unwieldy, even when folded in three, and in the 1850s the Olympic Theatre reverted to the small playbill for use in the theatre, supplying it free to occupants of the more expensive seats. Drury Lane adopted the new fashion soon after, and other theatres gradually followed suit.

The poster had meanwhile been developing separately, becoming larger and more elaborate, and the early wood-cuts—first used for acrobatic displays in the eighteenth century—gave way in the nineteenth to elaborate lithographs, using one colour only. The coloured poster first appeared in France in the early 1800s and was brought to perfection by Jules Chéret in the 1860s. Some of the finest posters of the 1890s were designed by Toulouse-Lautrec, but many lesser artists also produced excellent examples, including Mucha and Steinlen. The influence of the French poster spread to central Europe, where for a generation advertising art was dominated by Ludwig Hohlwein. Later the work of Reinhardt in Germany stimulated the production of fine publicity material, and the influence of Diaghilev's designers for the Ballets Russes was, as in all branches of art, of paramount importance. Many of the costume designs of Léon Bakst, with slight adaptation, made excellent posters. Most English posters of the late nineteenth century, particularly those for popular melodramas, were still illustrated by wood-cuts, but the Beggarstaff brothers (William Nicholson and James Pryde) produced some splendid theatre posters, particularly for Irving at the Lyceum, by the highly original method of building up the design in cut-out layers of different shades of brown paper. Also excellent, in the French style, were the posters designed by Aubrey Beardsley in the mid-1890s for the Avenue Theatre, later the Playhouse. The tradition of the artistic poster was carried on in the early part of the twentieth century by a number of excellent artists, including Frank Brang-

wyn and Lovat Fraser. American poster design followed that of England until the late nineteenth century, when well-known artists like Charles Dana Gibson and Norman Rockwell developed the small decorative placard. None of them, however, worked exclusively for the theatre, as many earlier poster designers had done, and with competition for their services from other advertisers, and the development of alternative sources of publicity, the poster has reverted to the form of the earlier playbill.

In the 1860s the programme, which had dwindled to a small quarto sheet, became a medium for advertisements in general, and in 1869 the St. James's Theatre in London began issuing a magazine programme in a style which has remained popular, with modifications, ever since. There was constant controversy, which continues today, as to whether theatre programmes should be charged for or not. Between the wars the charge was 6d. (except on first nights, when they were free) for a magazine issued by the refreshment contractors, which contained a good deal of light reading matter and a certain amount of information about the play and the cast, including photographs of the players. With the paper shortage in the Second World War programmes were drastically reduced in size, but came back in the 1950s at a shilling (now 10p). At the Royal Shakespeare Theatre, Stratford-upon-Avon, and at the National Theatre and the Aldwych in London, a cast-list is now provided free of charge, and only the accompanying booklet, containing interesting information on the play, its author, and previous productions in the case of revivals, is charged for. 'Gala' programmes, usually printed on silk, remained popular for over a hundred years, the earliest known example being for the New Theatre, Brighton, for 12 Oct. 1790.

Players Club, NEW YORK. This was founded in 1888 on the lines of the Garrick Club (q.v.) in London, Edwin Booth (q.v.), the first president, donating and endowing a house he had purchased for the purpose in Gramercy Park. He retained a suite of rooms in it, which are kept as he left them when he died there in 1893. The club has a large collection of theatrical relics and a fine library, which was opened to theatre research workers in 1957 as the Walter Hampden (q.v.) Memorial Library, named after the club's fourth president, who served twenty-seven years before his retirement in 1955. Ladies were formerly admitted to the premises only at an afternoon reception on Shakespeare's birthday, but since 1946 have been admitted to four annual Open Houses, featuring entertainments and refreshments. About four evenings a year (Pipe Nights) are dedicated to honouring distinguished members or guests. The club's first three presidents, Booth, Joseph Jefferson, and John Drew (qq.v.), died in office. Hampden and Howard Lindsay (q.v.), who succeeded him, both retired, Lindsay in 1965. He was succeeded by Dennis King.

Players' Theatre, LONDON, a club which in 1929 took over from Playroom Six, where in 1927 Peggy Ashcroft (q.v.) had made her London début. In 1934 it moved to premises in King Street, Covent Garden, which had formerly housed Evans's (late Joy's) Song and Supper Rooms. It soon closed, but in Dec. 1936 it was reopened by Peter Ridgeway as the New Players'. It was here, in Dec. 1937. that Harold Scott first produced the Victorian-style cabaret which later became famous as *Ridgeway's Late Joys.* After Ridgeway's death in 1938 a mixture of plays and Victorian music-hall items continued to fill the bill until 1940, when, because of the blitz, the club, directed by Leonard Sachs and known as the Players' Theatre, moved to 13 Albemarle Street. In 1945 it acquired premises under the arches of Charing Cross station in Villiers Street, off the Strand, which had originally been part of the Hungerford Music-Hall (see GATE THEATRE). The Players', whose early history is chronicled in *Late Joys at the Players' Theatre* (1943), continues to offer its old-time Victorian music-hall bill, with an annual Victorian pantomime.

PLAYFAIR, SIR NIGEL (1874–1934), English director and actor-manager, who gained his experience under Benson and Tree and in 1912 played Bottom in the Savoy production of *A Midsummer Night's Dream* by Granville-Barker (q.v.). In 1918 he took over the Lyric Theatre, Hammersmith (q.v.), where he remained until 1932, making it one of the most popular and stimulating centres of theatrical activity in London. He produced there Drinkwater's *Abraham Lincoln* (1919); a revival of Gay's *The Beggar's Opera* (1920), with settings by Claude

Lovat Fraser, which ran for nearly 1,500 performances; Congreve's *The Way of the World* (1924) and Farquhar's *The Beaux' Stratagem* (1927), both with Edith Evans; Bickerstaffe's *Lionel and Clarissa* (1925), its first revival since the original production in 1768; *Riverside Nights* (1926), an intimate revue by A. P. Herbert and others; *When Crummles Played* (1927), a burlesque of Lillo's *The London Merchant* (1731) set in the theatrical background of Dickens's *Nicholas Nickleby*; a stylized black-and-white revival of Wilde's *The Importance of Being Earnest* (1930), with John Gielgud as John Worthing; and numerous other plays old and new, in many of which he himself appeared. He was also responsible for the production of the Čapeks' *The Insect Play*, produced at the Regent Theatre in 1923, being part-author of the translation. He wrote accounts of his Hammersmith management in *The Story of the Lyric Theatre, Hammersmith* (1925) and *Hammersmith Hoy* (1930). He was knighted in 1928 for services to the British theatre.

Playhouse. (1) LONDON, in Northumberland Avenue. This opened as the Avenue Theatre on 11 Mar. 1882. The most important event of its early years was the production of Shaw's *Arms and the Man* in 1894 in a season directed by Florence Farr and financed by Miss Horniman (qq.v.). A later success was Ganthony's *A Message from Mars* (1899), which ran for about eighteen months. On 5 Dec. 1905 the roof of Charing Cross station collapsed and wrecked the theatre, which was being rebuilt by Cyril Maude (q.v.), who finally opened it on 28 Jan. 1907 with a revival of Clyde Fitch's *Toddles.* Maude was succeeded in 1917 by Gladys Cooper (q.v.), who with Frank Curzon until 1927, and then alone until 1933, staged and appeared in a long list of plays, including a distinguished revival in 1922 of Pinero's *The Second Mrs. Tanqueray*. After her departure the theatre had no settled policy, though in the 1940s several interesting plays were performed there, including Simonov's *The Russians* (1943) by the Old Vic company, and Ustinov's early play, *Blow Your Own Trumpet* (also 1943). The theatre became a B.B.C. sound studio in 1951.

(2) NEW YORK, on 48th Street between Broadway and 6th Avenue. This opened on 15 Apr. 1911 and had its first success in

Sept. with Broadhurst's *Bought and Paid For*. In 1915–16 Grace George (q.v.) appeared in a repertory which included Henry Arthur Jones's *The Liars*, the first American performance of Shaw's *Major Barbara*, and a revival of his *Captain Brassbound's Conversion*. In 1924 *The Show-Off*, by George Kelly, had a long run. The next important productions were Robert Sherwood's *The Road to Rome* (1927) and Elmer Rice's *Street Scene* (1929). The latter, which is usually considered Rice's best play, was awarded the Pulitzer Prize for Drama. After a somewhat blank period the theatre had a further success with Abbott and Holm's *Three Men on a Horse* (1935). In 1945 Tennessee Williams's *The Glass Menagerie*, in which Laurette Taylor (q.v.) made her last appearance as the mother, began a long run at this theatre, and in 1959 Gibson's *The Miracle Worker*, with Anne Bancroft, was highly successful. The building was demolished in 1968.

Plinge, WALTER, a name used on English playbills to conceal a doubling of parts, particularly in a Shakespeare play (for the American equivalent, see SPELVIN, GEORGE). There are two versions of the origin of the name, which may have been that of the landlord of a public house near the stage door of the Lyceum in about 1900 or a fictitious name for a convivial acquaintance with whom Lyceum actors (under Benson) resorted to this pub. It was first used on a playbill by Oscar Asche (q.v.). The name was never used, as Spelvin's was, for doll or animal actors, but still makes occasional appearances on London and provincial playbills.

Plough (or PLOW) **Monday,** in English folk festivals the Monday after Twelfth Night (6 Jan.). Fragmentary texts of a Plough Monday play have been recovered from the East Midlands, similar in character to the Christmas Mumming Play (q.v.), with which it was probably associated. The main differences between the two are that the characters of the Plough Monday play are farm-hands, not heroes, as in the Mumming Play, and the central incident, the death of one of the characters, is due to an accident and not to a fight. Both plays are probably survivals, later influenced by literary trends, of a primitive folk festival.

PLOWRIGHT, JOAN ANNE (1929–   ), English actress, the third wife of Laurence Olivier (q.v.), with whom she joined the National Theatre company on its inception in 1963. She had previously had several years in repertory theatres and on tour, following her first appearances at Croydon in 1951, and had been with the English Stage Company at the Royal Court for nearly a year when in Dec. 1956 she made an outstanding success as Margery Pinchwife in Wycherley's *The Country Wife*. She was also excellent as the Old Woman in Ionesco's *The Chairs* (1957), in which she made her first appearance in New York a year later; as Beatie in Wesker's *Roots* (1959), first seen at the Belgrade, Coventry; and as Daisy in Ionesco's *Rhinoceros* (1960). During the first Chichester Festival in 1962 she gave a fine performance as Sonya in Chekhov's *Uncle Vanya* which she later repeated at the Old Vic, where she has also played Hilde in Ibsen's *The Master Builder* (1964), Masha in Chekhov's *Three Sisters* (1967), Rosaline in *Love's Labour's Lost* (1968), and Portia in *The Merchant of Venice* (1970).

PLUMMER, (ARTHUR) CHRISTOPHER ORME (1929–   ), Canadian actor, and the first, with Gélinas (q.v.), to make an international reputation. He gained his early experience with the Canadian Repertory Company in Ottawa, and made his first appearance in New York in 1954. At Stratford, Conn., in 1955 he appeared as Mark Antony in *Julius Caesar* and Ferdinand in *The Tempest*, and a year later was seen at Stratford, Ontario, and at the Edinburgh Festival as Henry V, returning to Stratford in 1957 to play Hamlet and also Aguecheek in *Twelfth Night*. He has since appeared in a number of Shakespearian parts at this theatre, and at the Royal Shakespeare Theatre at Stratford-upon-Avon in 1961 was seen as Benedick in *Much Ado About Nothing* and as Richard III. Among his other parts have been Nickles in Archibald MacLeish's *J.B.* (New York, 1958), Henry II in Anouilh's *Becket* (London, 1961), the title-role in Brecht's *Arturo Ui* (New York, 1963), Pizarro in the American production of Peter Shaffer's *The Royal Hunt of the Sun* (1965), and the title-role in Rostand's *Cyrano de Bergerac* (1966) at Stratford, Ontario, with whose company he also appeared a year later as Antony in *Antony and Cleopatra* at Expo 67 in Montreal.

Plymouth Theatre, NEW YORK, on West 45th Street. This opened on 10 Oct. 1917. Among the more interesting of its early productions was Ibsen's *The Wild Duck* in 1918, this being the first time the play had been given in New York in English. Nazimova (q.v.) starred in it, and also appeared in *Hedda Gabler* and *A Doll's House*. Later in the year John Barrymore (q.v.) appeared in a dramatization of Tolstoy's *Redemption* entitled *The Living Corpse*, and in 1919 he was seen in Benelli's *The Jest* with his brother Lionel. Among later successes the most memorable was *What Price Glory?* (1924), a realistic portrayal of war by Maxwell Anderson and Laurence Stallings. In 1925 came Winthrop Ames's delightful revivals of Gilbert and Sullivan, while later successes at this theatre include *Burlesque* (1927), by Arthur Hopkins and D. G. M. Walters; Deval's *Tovarich* (1936), adapted by Robert Sherwood; Sherwood's own *Abe Lincoln in Illinois* (1938), awarded the Pulitzer Prize for Drama; *Lute Song* (1946), adapted by Sidney Howard from a Chinese play; Shaw's *Don Juan in Hell* (1952); Giraudoux's *Tiger at the Gates* (1955); Wesker's *Chips with Everything* (1963); and Alec Guinness (q.v.) as Dylan Thomas in *Dylan* (1964). Later in the 1960's Neil Simon's *The Star-Spangled Girl* (1966) and *Plaza Suite* (1969) were both successful.

POCOCK, ISAAC (1782–1835), English dramatist, a prolific writer of popular works which in a more literary age would have been relegated to the minor theatres, but which, in the general poverty of play-writing at the time, were accorded productions at Covent Garden and Drury Lane or at the least at the Haymarket. Pocock is mainly remembered today for one of his melodramas, *The Miller and His Men* (1813). This, with its romantic scenery, strong situation, and final blowing up and burning down of the mill, was one of the most popular products of the Toy Theatre (q.v.), and is occasionally revived in cardboard even now. He was also responsible for one of the many versions of the story of the thieving magpie, which as *The Magpie, or the Maid?* (1815) was another Toy Theatre favourite. Among his other plays the farce *Hit or Miss* (1810) provided the elder Mathews (q.v.) with an excellent part as Dick Cypher, and his adaptation of

Scott's *Rob Roy* (1818) first brought Macready (q.v.) into prominence.

POEL [really POLE], WILLIAM (1852–1934), English actor and director, who made his first appearance on the stage in 1876, and from 1881 to 1883 was manager of the Old Vic (q.v.) under Emma Cons. His productions for the Shakespeare Reading Society led him in 1894 to found the Elizabethan Stage Society, which was to have an enormous influence on the staging and production of Shakespeare in the first half of the twentieth century. On a stage modelled in accordance with his ideas of an Elizabethan stage, with the minimum of scenery, and with music by the Dolmetsch family, Poel produced in a variety of halls and courtyards a number of Elizabethan plays by Shakespeare, Marlowe, Jonson, Beaumont and Fletcher, Middleton, Rowley, and Ford, beginning with *Twelfth Night* in 1895. He also staged the Dutch medieval morality play, *Everyman*, for the first time for 400 years. The last production which he directed for the Elizabethan Stage Society was *Romeo and Juliet* in 1905. Financially the venture had not been a success, but artistically it had vindicated Poel's theories, and it undoubtedly stimulated other directors to experiment with simple settings and so free Shakespeare from the cumbersome trappings of the late nineteenth century. Poel continued to work in the theatre until his death, and was responsible for the revivals, under various auspices, of the old improvised *Hamlet* play of the English Comedians (q.v.), *Fratricide Punished*, given for the first time in England at the Oxford Playhouse in 1924; of the anonymous *Arden of Feversham* (1925); and of Peele's *David and Bethsabe* (1932) for the first time since 1599. He was president of the London Shakespeare League and the author of several plays and books on the theatre. An account of his life and work was written by Robert Speaight (1954).

POGODIN [really STUKALOV], NIKOLAI FEDOROVICH (1900–62), Russian dramatist, one of the outstanding figures of the Soviet stage. Originally a journalist, his first play, *Tempo* (1930), was a documentary on building produced at the Vakhtangov Theatre (q.v.), which also staged his best-known work, *Aristocrats* (1934). Both these plays were published in English translations in *Six Soviet Plays*

(1934), and *Aristocrats* was performed at Unity Theatre (q.v.) in London in 1937. Of his other plays, the most successful were *Poem About an Axe* (1931), produced by Popov (q.v.), and three plays about Lenin—*The Man With the Gun* (1937), *Kremlin Chimes* (1942), and *Lenin—The Third Pathétique* (1958). A revised version of *Kremlin Chimes* was produced in 1956 by the Moscow Art Theatre (q.v.), who in the World Theatre seasons of 1956 and 1970 were seen in London in the last two plays of the trilogy.

POISSON, a family of actors who served the French stage during three generations. The first, RAYMOND (c. 1630–90), known as Belleroche, joined the company at the Hôtel de Bourgogne in the 1650s and was an excellent comic actor, who made the character of the valet Crispin (q.v.), from Scarron's *L'Écolier de Salamanque* (1654), peculiarly his own, introducing it into several of his plays and playing the part himself. His many light comedies have been forgotten, but one is interesting—*Le Baron de la Crasse* (1663)—since it depicts a strolling company whose leader may be intended as a satirical portrait of Molière (q.v.). Two of Poisson's daughters were on the stage and married actors, but it was his son PAUL (1658–1735) who best carried on the family tradition, playing his father's old parts at the Comédie-Française from 1686 to 1724. He married an actress, and their sons PHILIPPE (1682–1743) and FRANÇOIS ARNOULD (1696–1753) were both actors.

Polish Jewish State Theatre, a flourishing organization founded in 1948 in Warsaw by Ida Kamińska, daughter of a famous actress. In 1953 it moved to Łódź, then to Wrocław, and finally returned to Warsaw, the base from which it now tours the country in a repertory of Yiddish and European classics. In 1956 it visited Belgium, Holland, and France, in 1958 Germany, France, and England, and in 1959–60 Israel. It is the last of the Yiddish Art Theatres to survive, and in assessing its future one must remember that the Jewish population of Poland has been decimated.

POLITIS, PHOTOS (1890–1934), the first director of the Greek National Theatre, founded in 1930. In the four short years before his death he established it on firm foundations, and imbued the company with his own ideas of devotion and abnegation in the service of the theatre. Although his alert and inquiring mind was open to all the influences of the contemporary experimental theatre, he was convinced that the strength of the Greek theatre lay in its past, and he always insisted on the importance of maintaining the classical repertory, a task carried on by his successors Minotis and Rondiris (qq.v.).

POLLARD, THOMAS (*fl.* first half of seventeenth century), English actor, a comedian with the King's Men (see CHAMBERLAIN'S MEN). He probably began his acting career as an apprentice in about 1610. By 1623 he had achieved some eminence as a player of comic roles, and he added considerably to his reputation in later years. With the actor Bowyer he was accused of having embezzled the wardrobe and effects of the company on the closing of the theatres in 1642, but there may be an element of exaggeration in this, since he was still *persona grata* with his old companions after this date and with them signed the dedication of the Beaumont and Fletcher folio of 1647.

POMPONIUS (1st century B.C.), see ATELLAN FARCE.

PONTE, LORENZO DA (1749–1838), see RICHMOND HILL THEATRE.

POPE, JANE (1742–1818), English actress, who was on the stage as a child, making her adult début on 27 Sept. 1759. She was immediately successful and soon succeeded Kitty Clive (q.v.), playing hoydens, chambermaids, and pert ladies. She was the original Mrs. Candour in Sheridan's *The School for Scandal* (1777) and Tilburina in his *The Critic* (1779). She is sometimes confused with a Mrs. Pope (formerly Miss Younge) who was playing Portia when Macklin (q.v.) made his last attempt at Shylock at Covent Garden in 1789. She only relinquished young characters when age and obesity forced her to, and then proved herself equally good in elderly duenna parts. She retired in May 1808.

POPE, THOMAS (?–1604), one of the actors in Shakespeare's plays, and an original shareholder in the Curtain and Globe Theatres (qq.v.). In 1586–7 he went with Kempe (q.v.) and other actors to Denmark and Germany, and joined the Chamberlain's Men (q.v.) on their formation in 1594. He is referred to as 'a clown', and may have played some of the parts created by Kempe.

POPOV, ALEXEI DMITREVICH (1892–1961), outstanding Soviet director, who was at the Moscow Art Theatre (q.v.) from 1912 to 1918. In 1923 he was at the Vakhtangov (q.v.), where his work played an important part in the development of the company, and in 1931 he was invited to direct the Theatre of the Revolution (see MAYAKOVSKY THEATRE), where he was responsible for the production of Pogodin's *Poem about an Axe* (1931) and of a *Romeo and Juliet* (1936) which remained in the repertory of the theatre for many years. He then went to the Red Army Theatre (see CENTRAL THEATRE OF THE SOVIET ARMY), where he directed an even more successful *The Taming of the Shrew* (1938) and a spectacular *A Midsummer Night's Dream* (1940). During the war, when the company was evacuated from Moscow, he produced several new Soviet plays and, back in Moscow, won acclaim for his staging of Gogol's *Revizor* (1951) and of the new version of one of Pogodin's plays about Lenin, *Kremlin Chimes* (1956). Shortly before his death he published a book on production in which he outlined his methods. Unlike Okhlopkov (q.v.), who first considered the play as a whole and then turned to the details, he began with the details, combining them into a harmonious whole.

PORTA, GIAMBATTISTA DELLA, see DELLA PORTA.

Portable Theatres, see ENGLISH PORTABLE THEATRES.

Porte-Saint-Martin, THÉÂTRE DE LA, PARIS. This arose on its present site in 1781, after the burning of the Opéra, and housed the company of the latter until 1794. It was then used for various purposes and did not open again as a theatre until 1810, after which it was used exclusively for strong drama and spectacular works. In 1822 a company of English actors tried unsuccessfully to act *Othello* there. Later the plays of Delavigne and Hugo were given, as were the spectacular fairytale shows, *La Biche au bois* and *Pied de mouton*. It was at this theatre, under the management of Harel, that Frédérick (q.v.) made his first triumphant appearance. The building was destroyed by fire

in 1871 but was rebuilt on part of the same site from the original plans.

PORTER, ERIC (1928–), English actor, who made his first appearance on the stage in 1945 at the Shakespeare Memorial Theatre. He later toured with Donald Wolfit (q.v.), and in 1952–3, was in Gielgud's repertory company at the Lyric, Hammersmith, playing Bolingbroke in *Richard II*, Fainall in Congreve's *The Way of the World*, and Reynault in Otway's *Venice Preserv'd*. He was for some years with the Old Vic company in Bristol, playing a wide range of classical parts but also appearing in such modern parts as Becket in T. S. Eliot's *Murder in the Cathedral* and Father James Browne in Graham Greene's *The Living Room*, and taking over on the death of Frederick Valk the part of Vadim Romanoff in Ustinov's *Romanoff and Juliet*. He made his first appearance in New York in 1958 with the Lunts (q.v.) in Dürrenmatt's *The Visit*, in which, under the title of *Time and Again*, he had previously toured in England. In 1959, at the Royal Court, he gave an outstanding performance as Rosmer in Ibsen's *Rosmersholm*. He then joined the Royal Shakespeare Company (q.v.), for which he has played many leading roles both in Stratford and London, including Malvolio in *Twelfth Night* (1960); the title-role in Anouilh's *Becket* (1961); Macbeth (1962); and the Pope in Hochhuth's *The Representative* (1963). In 1965 he played in the same season Shylock in *The Merchant of Venice* and Barabas in Marlowe's *The Jew of Malta*, and after making an international success as Soames in the television production of Galsworthy's *The Forsyte Saga* he returned to Stratford to play Lear in a production by Trevor Nunn (q.v.).

Porter's Hall (or PUDDLE WHARF THEATRE), LONDON, a playhouse in the precincts of Blackfriars, erected by Philip Rosseter (q.v.) in 1615. Although authorized by royal patent dated 3 June, it was objected to by the residents, and on 26 Sept. work on the building was stopped by order of the Lord Chief Justice. It must, however, have advanced sufficiently for the accommodating of plays, as the Lady Elizabeth's Men and Prince Charles's Men (qq.v.) appear to have acted there, and in Jan. 1617 another order was dispatched by the Privy Council for the suppression of 'the playhouse in the Blackfriars almost, if not fully finished'.

(For a later theatre in Blackfriars, see MERMAID.)

PORTMAN, ERIC (1903–69), English actor, who made his first appearance in 1924, playing a number of Shakespearian parts on tour with Robert Courtneidge and later at the Old Vic, where in 1928 he was much admired as Romeo to the Juliet of Jean Forbes-Robertson (q.v.). His romantic good looks and fine voice caused him to be cast mainly as the young heroes of classical comedy, but he later appeared in a number of modern plays, including Rattigan's *The Browning Version* and *Harlequinade* (1948) and both parts of *Separate Tables* (1954)—the latter for four years. In 1953 he was seen as Father James Browne in Graham Greene's *The Living Room*, and after the success in 1956 of *Separate Tables* in the United States, where he had first appeared in 1937 in a dramatization of Flaubert's *Madame Bovary*, he was seen in several important productions, including O'Neill's *A Touch of the Poet* (1958). Returning to England, he appeared in Pauline Macaulay's *The Creeper* in 1965, and made his last appearance on the stage in a revival of Galsworthy's *Justice* in 1968.

Portman Theatre, LONDON, see WEST LONDON THEATRE.

Poster, see PLAYBILL.

POWELL, MARTIN, see MARIONETTE.

POWER, TYRONE (1795–1841), Irish actor, who first appeared on the stage in 1815 but made little stir until in 1826 he took to specializing in such Irish roles as Sir Lucius O'Trigger in Sheridan's *The Rivals*. He also appeared in his own plays, among them *St. Patrick's Eve* (1832), *Paddy Cary, the Boy of Clogheen* (1833), and *O'Flannigan and the Fairies* (1836). In 1840 he left London for the United States, where he was already a firm favourite after two protracted visits, and on the return journey was drowned in the sinking of s.s. *President*. Power left a wife (*née* ANNE GILBERT) and eight children, of whom only one, MAURICE (?–1849), was on the stage; but another son, Harold, was the father of the second Tyrone, (FREDERICK) TYRONE EDMOND (1869–1931), whose stage career was mainly in

America, where he was a prominent member of Augustin Daly's company from 1890 to 1898, and in his later years appeared mainly in Shakespearian parts. His son, the third TYRONE (1914–58), later had a distinguished career in films which overshadowed his work in the theatre, but he was for some years on the American stage, being seen in *Romeo and Juliet* (1935) and Shaw's *Saint Joan* (1936) with Katharine Cornell, and as Gettner in the New York production of Christopher Fry's *The Dark is Light Enough* (1955). In 1950 he was at the Coliseum in London in *Mister Roberts*, by Thomas Heggan and Joshua Logan. Harold's niece, Norah, was the mother of the distinguished theatre director, Sir Tyrone Guthrie (q.v.).

PRADON, NICOLAS [really JACQUES] (1644–98), French dramatist remembered because his *Phèdre* was praised at the expense of Racine's when they were produced at the same time in 1677 at rival theatres in Paris. Even Pradon's first play, *Pirame et Thisbé* (1674), owed most of its success at the Hôtel de Bourgogne to the applause of the detractors of Racine (q.v.), and whatever posthumous fame he has achieved is due to the greatness of the enemies he roused against him, including the redoubtable Boileau (q.v.). So the names, at least, of his plays are remembered, though they are seldom read or acted.

Praetexta, see FABULA (2).

PRAY, MALVINA (1831–1906), see FLORENCE, W. J.; MARIA (1826–1911), see WILLIAMS, BARNEY.

PREHAUSER, GOTTFRIED (1699–1769), Austrian actor, who spent many years in a travelling company before being invited by Stranitzky (q.v.) to Vienna in 1725 to take over the part of Hanswurst (q.v.), which he had already played at Salzburg in 1720. In his hands the character, and the plays in which he appeared, underwent subtle changes, becoming noticeably more Viennese ard bourgeois in background and situation. With the decline of improvised farce in the late eighteenth century and the death of Prehauser, Hanswurst disappeared from the stage.

PRESTON, THOMAS (*fl.* 1570), the otherwise unknown author of a popular early

English tragi-comedy, *Cambyses King of Persia* (*c.* 1569), written with bombastic eloquence, thus giving rise to Falstaff's remark in Shakespeare's *Henry IV, Part I* that he must speak in passion, and would do it in 'King Cambyses' vein'. This play marks the transition from the medieval Morality Play to the Elizabethan historical drama. Its author, who may also have written *Sir Clyomon and Sir Clamydes* (*c.* 1570), was evidently not the Thomas Preston (*fl.* 1537–98) who in 1592, as Master of Trinity Hall, petitioned for the banning of plays in Cambridge (q.v.).

PRÉVILLE [really PIERRE-LOUIS DUBUS] (1721–99), French actor, who first joined a provincial company and in 1753 went to the Comédie-Française, where in roles hitherto played by F. A. Poisson (q.v.) he proved the finest comedian the company had had since J. B. Raisin (q.v.). He was excellent in the plays of Marivaux (q.v.), and was much admired for his performance of six characters in one in a revival of Boursault's *Le Mercure galant*. With his wife, also a member of the company, he retired in 1786.

PRICE, MAIRE [really MAIRE NIC SHIUBH-LAIGH, *née* MARIE WALKER] (?–1958), Irish actress, one of the founder-players in the company of the Fays' Irish National Dramatic Society, appearing as Delia Cahel in Yeats's *Cathleen ni Houlihan* on its first production in 1902, and going with the company to the Abbey Theatre (q.v.) in 1904, where she played leading parts with the sisters Sara Allgood and Maire O'Neill (qq.v.). She was at her best in tragic roles, among them Nora Burke in Synge's *The Shadow of the Glen* (1903) and Moll Woods in O'Kelly's *The Shuiler's Child* (1910). She retired in 1917, and in 1950, in collaboration with her nephew, published a book about the renaissance of the Irish theatre entitled *The Splendid Years*.

PRICE, (LILIAN) NANCY BACHE (1880–1970), English actress and theatre manager, who is best remembered as the founder and guiding spirit of the People's National Theatre in London. This venture began in 1930 with a revival at the Fortune Theatre of Anstey's *The Man from Blankley's*, and during the next few years Nancy Price was responsible for the production of over fifty plays, ranging from Euripides to Pirandello, and

including *Alison's House* (1932) by Susan Glaspell, a Chinese play by S. I. Hsiung, *Lady Precious Stream* (1934), and Mazo de la Roche's *Whiteoaks* (1936), in which she played for two years the part of old Adeline Whiteoaks. These were all produced at the Little Theatre (q.v.), which was destroyed by enemy action in 1941. Nancy Price herself made her last appearance in Eden Phillpotts's *The Orange Orchard* at the New Lindsey in 1950. In 1935 she published a volume of reminiscences, *Shadows on the Hill*. She was appointed C.B.E. in 1950 in recognition of her services to the theatre. Her husband, the actor CHARLES RAYMOND MAUDE (1882–1943), was the grandson of the singer Jenny Lind.

PRICE, STEPHEN (1783–1840), the first outstanding American theatre manager who was neither an actor nor a playwright. In 1808 he took over the management of the Park Theatre (q.v.), where he inaugurated the policy of importing famous European actors which by the time he died (still in command of the Park) had wrecked the old resident stock companies of the larger American towns. He was also noted for his love of spectacular and freakish effects—real horses and tigers on the stage, for example. It was this trait which caused many people to disapprove of his tenancy of London's Drury Lane (q.v.) from 1826 to 1830.

PRIESTLEY, JOHN BOYNTON (1894–1984), English dramatist, novelist, and critic, whose first contact with the theatre was through the dramatization of his best-selling novel *The Good Companions* (1931), which he undertook in collaboration with Edward Knoblock (q.v.). This was quickly followed by a succession of well-written and well-constructed plays —*Dangerous Corner* (1931), *Laburnum Grove* (1933), and *Eden End* (1934), and by *Time and the Conways* and *I Have Been Here Before* (both 1937), which were published that year as *Two Time Plays*. *When We Are Married* (1938), a farce with its roots set firmly in Yorkshire, was followed by a most interesting experimental play, *Johnson over Jordan* (1939), in which Ralph Richardson (q.v.) gave a fine performance as Johnson. After several less ambitious comedies Priestley returned to the style of *Dangerous Corner* with a problem play, *An Inspector Calls* (1945), followed by *The Linden Tree* (1947), *Mr. Kettle* *and Mrs. Moon* (1955), *The Glass Cage* (1957), and two plays in collaboration with his third wife Jacquetta Hawkes, a well-known archaeologist—*Dragon's Mouth* (1952) and *The White Countess* (1954). He also dramatized Iris Murdoch's novel, *A Severed Head* (1963), in collaboration with the author. His interest in international theatre led him to act as chairman of theatre conferences in Paris in 1947 and Prague in 1948 and of the British Theatre Conference in 1948, and he was the first President of the British International Theatre Institute. In 1959 he published *The Story of Theatre* for young readers, reissued in 1969 as *The Wonderful World of the Theatre*.

Prince Charles Theatre, LONDON, in Leicester Place. This opened at Christmas 1962 with the Canadian revue, *Clap Hands*, under the management of Harold Fielding. Although there were ambitious plans for round-the-clock entertainment, the theatre failed to find material suitable to its slightly old-fashioned intimacy, with the exception of a show starring Wolfit and Cicely Courtneidge (qq.v.) billed as *Fielding's Music Hall* and a transfer from the Players' Theatre (q.v.) of *Late Joys* (both 1964). It has therefore been mainly used as a cinema.

Prince Charles's Men, usually known as the Prince's Men, a theatrical company formed in 1616 on the death of Henslowe (q.v.) by his son-in-law Alleyn (q.v.). Their first settled home was the Phoenix (see COCKPIT), where they enjoyed a modicum of prosperity. In 1622 they were displaced by a new company known as the Lady Elizabeth's Men (q.v.), and went to the Curtain (q.v.). The company broke up when Charles I succeeded to the throne, and many of its important players transferred to the King's Men (see CHAMBERLAIN'S MEN). In 1631 a new company was formed under the patronage of the young Prince Charles (later Charles II), and appeared at Salisbury Court (q.v.).

Prince Edward Theatre, LONDON, in Old Compton Street, Soho. This opened on 3 Apr. 1930, but was not very successful, and its best productions were musical comedies and revues, of which *Nippy* (1930) was outstanding. In 1936, as the London Casino, it became a restaurant-cabaret, where one dined or supped and watched a spectacular stage-show. With the outbreak of war in 1939 it became the Queensberry All-Services Club but subsequently resumed operations as a theatre with variety shows, spectacle, and pantomime. In 1954 it became a cinema.

Prince Henry's Men, see ADMIRAL'S MEN.

Prince of Wales' Theatre, LONDON (the name is also found on playbills and programmes as Prince of Wales and Prince of Wales's). This opened as the Prince's Theatre in 1884 and received its present name in 1886. An adaptation of Ibsen's *A Doll's House* (as *Breaking a Butterfly*) was staged unsuccessfully at this theatre soon after it opened, and its first outstanding success was the mime-play, *L'Enfant Prodigue* (1891), which introduced Pierrot (q.v.) to London. Several musical comedies were then successful, including *A Gaiety Girl* (1893) and *Miss Hook of Holland* (1907). During the 1930s the theatre was given over to non-stop revue, and in Jan. 1937 it was closed for rebuilding. It reopened on 27 Oct., again with revue. Among plays which were later staged at this theatre were Mary Chase's *Harvey*, with Sid Field (1949), Paul Osborn's *The World of Susie Wong* (1959), and *Come Blow Your Horn* (1962), by Neil Simon (q.v.), who also wrote the books of two American musicals seen here, *Sweet Charity* (1967) and *Promises, Promises* (1969), both based on films. Also in 1969 Feydeau's *Cat Among the Pigeons* had a good run.

The Scala (q.v.), under the Bancrofts, was also known as the Prince of Wales's.

Prince's Theatre, LONDON, see ST. JAMES'S THEATRE and SHAFTESBURY THEATRE (2).

Princess Theatre, NEW YORK, at 104 West 39th Street, one of the city's smallest and most perfect playhouses. It opened on 14 Mar. 1913 with the Princess Players in four one-act plays. The first outstanding production was a translation of Brieux's *Maternité* in 1915. In 1920–1 the Provincetown Players appeared there in several of their productions, including O'Neill's *The Emperor Jones*, and in 1922 Pirandello's *Six Characters in Search of an Author* had its first New York production. In 1928 the theatre was renamed the Lucille La Verne, but after two productions reverted to its original name, only to change it to the Assembly in 1929.

It then became a cinema, except for a short interval in 1937, when it reopened as the Labour Stage with a topical revue, *Pins and Needles*, which caught the fancy of the town and ran into three editions with 1,108 performances. In 1944 it was used by Theatre Workshop, and became a cinema again in 1947. It was demolished in June 1955.

Princess's Theatre, LONDON, in Oxford Street. After the passing of the Licensing Act of 1843, the Princess's Theatre, which had opened on 30 Sept. 1840 for concerts and later been used as an opera-house, was used for plays, Charlotte Cushman (q.v.) making her London début there in *Macbeth*, with Edwin Forrest (q.v.), on 13 Feb. 1845. A number of famous actors came and went, including Macready, Fanny Kemble, and Mrs. Mowat (qq.v.), but without much success, until Charles Kean (q.v.) took over, opening on 28 Sept. 1850 with *Twelfth Night*. Kean's management was memorable, both for his productions of Shakespeare and for his success in adapting French drama to suit English audiences. Among his most popular productions in this field were Oxenford's *Pauline* (1851), Boucicault's *The Corsican Brothers* (1852) and *Louis XI* (1855), and Charles Reade's *The Courier of Lyons* (1854) (better known as *The Lyons Mail*). It was during a spectacular revival of *Henry VIII* that limelight (see LIGHTING) was used for the first time in the theatre. On 28 Apr. 1856 Ellen Terry (q.v.), then nine years old, made her first appearance on the stage as Mamillius in *The Winter's Tale*. Her elder sister, Kate, was already a member of the company. Kean left the Princess's at the end of Aug. 1859 after appearing once more as Wolsey, one of his finest parts, and Augustus Harris (q.v.) took over. Under him Henry Irving (q.v.) made his first appearance in London in Oxenford's *Ivy Hall* and then went back into the provinces. A year later Fechter (q.v.) appeared in Hugo's *Ruy Blas*, and as Hamlet, with great success. Boucicault's melodramas, including *The Streets of London* (1864), revived many times under many names, and *Arrah-na-Pogue* (1865), were followed by Charles Reade's *It's Never Too Late to Mend*, whose first night on 4 Oct. 1865 caused a riot because of the realistic flogging of a boy in the prison scene. The fortunes of the theatre then gradually declined, one of the few successes being

scored by Warner (q.v.) in Reade's *Drink* (1879), based on Zola's *L'Assommoir*. Out of the profits from this production the management decided to rebuild the theatre, which closed on 19 May 1880, and was demolished. The new Royal Princess's opened on 6 Nov. 1880 with Edwin Booth (q.v.) as Hamlet. Wilson Barrett later took over, and under him Sims's *The Lights o' London* (1881) and Jones and Herman's *The Silver King* (1882) had long runs. But there were many failures, and in Oct. 1902 the theatre closed. Three years later it became a warehouse, and in 1931 it was demolished, a Woolworths being built on the site.

Principal Boy, the chief character in the English pantomime (q.v.)—Aladdin, Dick Whittington, Robinson Crusoe, Prince Charming—traditionally played by a woman in a blond wig, short tunic, fleshings, and high heels. The character had its origin in the 'breeches parts' and in burlesque (qq.v.), but was not firmly established until the 1880s, when the chief players of the part were Harriet Vernon, Nellie Stewart, and Queenie Leighton. The tradition was carried on in the twentieth century by a number of excellent actresses, notably Dorothy Ward (q.v.), but a tendency towards realism led, as early as 1938, to the appearance of an actor in a role hitherto reserved for actresses. But this was not favourably received and such pantomimes as continue to appear still usually have a woman in the part, though less opulently curved than in the past.

PRINTEMPS, YVONNE (1895–1977), French actress and singer, who made her first appearance in Paris in revue in June 1908. She was for some time at the Folies-Bergère, and also appeared at the Palais-Royal. In 1916 she joined the company of Sacha Guitry (q.v.), whom she married in 1919, and appeared with him in a number of plays, including his own comedy, *Nono*, in which she first appeared in London in 1920. They were divorced in 1932, and she married the actor Pierre Fresnay. She played in English for the first time in Noël Coward's *Conversation Piece* (1934) and was also seen in Ben Travers's *O Mistress Mine* (1936). She made her first appearance in New York in 1926 as Mozart in Guitry's play of that name (with music by Reynaldo Hahn). In 1937 she took over the

Théâtre de la Michodière, and appeared there in a long succession of musical plays.

PRITCHARD, MRS. [*née* HANNAH VAUGHAN] (1711–68), English actress who married WILLIAM PRITCHARD (?–1763), treasurer of Drury Lane, where she was an established member of the company when Garrick (q.v.) joined it in May 1742. She remained there until her retirement a few months before her death. At first she played only in comedy, but in later years she turned to tragedy, being the first and only interpreter of Dr. Johnson's *Irene* (1749). Her finest part was Lady Macbeth, in which she made her last appearance on 25 Apr. 1768. Garrick was disconsolate, and determined never to play Macbeth again, a resolution which he broke only once, on 22 Sept., at the request of the King of Denmark, who was anxious to see him in the part. Mrs. Pritchard had a brother, HENRY VAUGHAN (?–1779), who played Falstaff at Covent Garden in 1734, and her daughter Hannah, who married the first John Palmer (q.v.), was also an actress, retiring on her marriage.

Private Theatres in England. The vogue for amateur acting in English high society, which reached its peak from 1770 to 1790, resulted in the building of several private theatres. The first was erected in 1766 for Sir Francis Delaval and the Duke of York in James Street, Westminster, but the most magnificent, which could vie with the Continental Court theatres (see CELLE, ČESKÝ KRUMLOV, DROTTNINGHOLM, GRIPSHOLM), was erected for the Earl of Barrymore at Wargrave in 1789. Rectangular in shape, it held four hundred people and contained two tiers of boxes and two stage boxes unusually placed over the orchestra well. It was provided with a series of workrooms and an adjoining salon for refreshments. After ruining its owner it was demolished in 1792. In 1793 the Margravine of Anspach [LADY ELIZABETH CRAVEN, 1750–1828] built a theatre for the production of her own plays at Brandenburgh House, Hammersmith, which remained in use until 1804. It was in castellated style and is said to have resembled the Bastille rather than a temple of the muses. An engraving of the interior shows a large central box and a parterre raised on a shallow platform after the Continental model.

A theatre in a simpler style was converted from a kitchen for Sir Watkin Williams Wynn at Wynnstay, and was used for annual performances from 1771 to 1789. Other famous theatres were those at Blenheim Palace, 1787–9, converted from a greenhouse, and the Duke of Richmond's at Richmond House, London, constructed out of two rooms by Wyatt in 1787 to hold about a hundred and fifty spectators. In an open-air theatre at Cliveden, still extant, Arne's 'Rule Britannia' was first sung in Thomson's masque, *Alfred*, in 1740.

Well-known scene painters were sometimes employed in private theatres, for instance Thomas Greenwood at Richmond and Blenheim, Inigo Richards at Wynnstay, and Malton at Brandenburgh House. The wardrobe book of Wynnstay and the sale catalogue of Wargrave are evidence of the sumptuous décor employed in the performances. Professionals frequently acted with or coached the amateurs.

The Duke of Devonshire's private theatre at Chatsworth, dating from about 1830, is the oldest still in existence. Another theatre of the period was that at Burton Constable, Yorkshire, which functioned from 1830 to 1850. Among later Victorian private theatres may be mentioned a small one attached to Campden House, Kensington, in the 1860s; Capethorne Hall, Cheshire, 1870; the artist Herkomer's at Bushey; and the singer Patti's at Craig-y-Nos, Wales, still standing. In the twentieth century Lord Bessborough gave annual productions for some years in his theatre at Stansted, and Lord Faringdon has a theatre, still in use, at Buscot Park. More recent private theatres have been used mainly for opera, the most famous being John Christie's at Glyndebourne. The latest private theatre is Nicholas Sekers's at Rosehill, Whitehaven, but both these last employ professional companies, are open to the general public, and charge for admission.

PROCTOR, FREDERICK FRANCIS (1851–1929), see VAUDEVILLE.

Producer, the American term for the man responsible for the financial side of play-production, for the buying of the play, the renting of the theatre, the engagement of actors and staff, and the handling of the receipts. In England most of these functions are assumed by the manager. Formerly the person who was responsible for the actual staging of the play was known in England as the producer, but this is now being ousted by the American 'director' (q.v.).

Programme, see PLAYBILL.

Proletcult Theatre, MOSCOW, see TRADES UNIONS THEATRE.

Prologue, an introductory poem or speech, which originally explained or commented on the action of the play which it preceded. It was first used by Euripides (q.v.) and later by the Elizabethans, who applied to it the name Chorus (q.v.). Together with the epilogue, which closed the action, the prologue was extensively used during the Restoration period, providing a good deal of incidental information on the contemporary theatre. It survived well into the eighteenth century, and disappeared with the crowded bills of the nineteenth century. It is now used only on special occasions. At their best the prologue and epilogue were witty and sometimes scurrilous commentaries on politics and social conditions, written by outstanding men of the theatre, like Dryden and Garrick (qq.v.), and spoken by the leading actor or actress.

Prompt Book, Box, Corner, Side, see STAGE DIRECTIONS.

Props, the usual term for stage properties. It covers anything essential to the action of the play which does not come under the heading of costume, scenery, or furniture. HAND-PROPS are those which an actor handles—letters, documents, revolvers, newspapers, knitting, snuff boxes, etc. These are given to him as he goes on stage and taken from him as he comes off, and are not his personal responsibility. Other props—stuffed birds, food in general, dinner plates, telephones—are placed on stage by the property man, who is responsible for all props, under the direction of the stage manager. He has for storage a property room backstage, from which he is expected to produce at a moment's notice anything that may be required. He is also charged to prevent the removal from it of oddments by members of the company.

Proscenium, in its modern meaning the permanent, or semi-permanent, wall dividing the auditorium from the stage. The opening in this wall frames the stage picture and has hanging in it the curtain (q.v.). The word is classical in origin, and in the later Greek theatre meant the area in front of the stage. In its heyday the proscenium, which has a long tradition behind it artistically, was a feature of considerable architectural complexity, forming an essential link between the auditorium and the scene. It is now more often thought of as a hindrance, particularly in the production of Shakespearian and modern epic plays, and the tendency is to abolish it where possible in favour of the open stage or theatre-in-the-round. One obstacle which confronts the experimenters in the older London theatre buildings is the presence within the proscenium arch of the Safety Curtain called for by the G.L.C. Fire Regulations.

(See also FALSE PROS.)

Proscenium Doors or DOORS OF ENTRANCE, a permanent feature of the English Restoration playhouse. Set on each side of the forestage, they had practicable knockers and bells and provided the usual means of exit and entrance for the actor. Leaving by one door and returning by another, he was presumed to be in another room even though the wings and back scene remained unchanged. The number of doors varied from four to six, not only at different theatres but in the same theatre at different periods. By the early eighteenth century they were reduced to one on each side, and by the beginning of the nineteenth they were used only by the actor 'taking a bow' after the play. They were then known as Call Doors.

Protagonist, the chief, and at first the only, actor in Greek tragedy, originally the leader of the dithyramb (q.v.): the second and third actors, introduced later, were known as the Deuteragonist and the Tritagonist. When a prize was instituted for the best actor at the festival in Athens, only the protagonist in each of the three plays was eligible for it. The limitation on the number of actors in Greek tragedy (apart from the chorus, q.v.) meant that each had to play several parts, changing his mask (q.v.) and costume for each character.

Provincetown Players, an experimental group of American actors and directors, founded in 1916 by Susan Glaspell (q.v.)

and others, who had already worked together the previous summer. Among them was Eugene O'Neill (q.v.), whose first play to be staged, *Bound East for Cardiff*, was produced at the Wharf Theatre, Provincetown, together with plays by Susan Glaspell, Edna St. Vincent Millay, and Lawrence Langner. This group later moved to New York, to the Playwrights' Theatre in Greenwich Village. In 1923 the Provincetown Playhouse opened under the management of Kenneth Macgowan, Robert Edmond Jones (qq.v.), and O'Neill, operating in conjunction with the Greenwich Village Theatre, which saw the first production of O'Neill's *Desire Under the Elms* (1924). At the Provincetown Playhouse a number of contemporary European plays were staged, of which the most interesting was Hasenclever's *Jenseits* (1920) as *Beyond* (1925), as well as revivals of several classics, including Congreve's *Love for Love*, also in 1925. In 1929, after an unsuccessful move to the Garrick Theatre (q.v.), the Provincetown Players disbanded, having fulfilled their avowed intention of giving American playwrights a chance to work out their ideas in freedom. Certainly their ardent experimentalism had given O'Neill, probably America's greatest dramatist to date, the opportunities he needed to see his work on the stage and to develop unhampered by commercial considerations.

Puddle Wharf Theatre, see PORTER'S HALL and ROSSETER, PHILIP.

Pulcinella, one of the comic servants of the *commedia dell'arte* (q.v.), a humpbacked, doltish fellow, regarded by those who look for the origin of the Italian improvised comedy in the Atellan farce (q.v.) as identical with the Maccus, or stupid servant, of Latin popular comedy. In his original Italian form he is considered typical of the Neapolitan district; as Polichinelle he stands for the quick wit of France; while as Punch (from Punchinello) he epitomizes rough English humour (see PUNCH AND JUDY). He has no part in the English harlequinade (q.v.), but some of his characteristics may have been passed on to Clown (q.v.). In the opinion of competent Italian critics the popularity of Pulcinella and the disproportionate attention paid to his buffoonery was one of the main reasons for the decline of the *commedia dell'arte*.

Pulitzer Prize for Drama, one of several literary awards established under the will of Joseph Pulitzer (1847–1911), awarded annually for the 'best original American play performed in New York'. It was first given in 1918 to Jesse Lynch Williams for *Why Marry?*, and has four times been awarded to Eugene O'Neill (q.v.)—for *Beyond the Horizon* (1920), *Anna Christie* (1922), *Strange Interlude* (1928), and (posthumously) *Long Day's Journey into Night* (1957).

Punch and Judy, an English puppet-show, once a familiar sight in the streets of large cities and still to be seen occasionally in seaside towns. In its final form the text of the play dates from about 1800, but Punch, the chief character, with his hooked nose and humped back, evolved from the Pulcinella (q.v.) of the *commedia dell'arte*, and may even go back to one of the masked mimes of the popular Greek and Roman theatre. As Polichinello, soon anglicized to Punchinello, and then shortened to Punch, he first appeared in London in 1662, as noted by Pepys (q.v.) in his diary for 9 May, and, while retaining the physical peculiarities of his Italian prototype, became the ubiquitous English buffoon of every puppet-play of the period, equally at home with Adam and Eve, Noah, or Dick Whittington, and accumulating on the way many of the characteristics of the medieval Vice (see FOOL and MYSTERY PLAY). When in the early years of the eighteenth century fashionable London grew tired of his antics, he migrated to the country fairs, took to himself a wife (first called Joan, later Judy), and adopted the familiar high-pitched voice produced by introducing a 'swazzle' or squeaker into the mouth of the showman who spoke for him. Towards the end of the century he went into eclipse and suffered a metamorphosis, emerging in the nineteenth century as a hand- or glove-puppet, instead of stringed (see PUPPET). This was a reversion to the style of the early English puppet-show which had temporarily been ousted by the Italian marionettes. It proved economically worth while, for one man could carry the portable booth on his back and present all the characters with his own two hands, with a mate (or wife) to 'bottle', or collect pennies, from the audience. In the more or less standardized version of the play, Punch, on the manipulator's right hand, remains on stage the whole time, while the left hand provides a series of characters—baby, wife, priest, doctor, policeman, hangman —for him to nag, beat, and finally kill, until he is either eaten by the crocodile, carried off by the Devil, or allowed to remain in solitary triumph, his only companion his faithful Toby—a live dog, usually a terrier, who sits, wearing a little ruff, on the ledge of the stage during the performance.

When in 1962 Punch's three hundredth anniversary was celebrated by a service in St. Paul's Church, Covent Garden, most of the Punch and Judy showmen who attended—some fifty or more—were accompanied by Toby dogs.

Punch and Judy Theatre, NEW YORK, on the north side of West 49th Street. It opened on 10 Nov. 1914 with Harold Chapin's *The Marriage of Columbine*, and one of its first successes was a dramatization of R. L. Stevenson's *Treasure Island* (1915). In 1926, renamed the Charles Hopkins, after the actor-director who built and owned it, it reopened with Karel Čapek's *The Makropulos Secret*. A record run was set up for the theatre by the 294 performances of Benn Levy's *Mrs. Moonlight* (1930), seen two years earlier in London. In 1933 the building became a cinema.

Punch's Playhouse, LONDON, see STRAND THEATRE (1).

Puppet, an inanimate figure controlled by human agency. It is found in several different forms, but the best-known in England, because of the popularity of Punch and Judy (q.v.), is the HAND- or GLOVE-PUPPET, which has a firm head and hands and a loose open costume. The operator places his hand in the costume with his first finger in the head and the second finger and thumb in the hands. He then stands behind a screen and holds the puppet above his head. The disadvantages of the hand-puppet are that gestures are limited to the movements of the three fingers, and that one performer can introduce only two characters at a time. But, in compensation, the figures are easy to make, and if papier-mâché is used for the head and hands instead of wood, they are light to manipulate and carry about. Most of the popular folk-puppets are hand-puppets, carried across Europe by wandering showmen. They all

derive from the Pulcinella (q.v.) of the *commedia dell'arte*, and, apart from the English Punch, include the French Guignol, the German Kasperle, and the Russian Petrushka (qq.v.). Even in China there are hand-puppets which are very like those found in Europe, where after the disappearance of the medieval religious drama (see MYSTERY PLAY) puppeteers continued to present stories from the Bible. These 'motions', as they were called, were very popular in England, where they could still be seen up to the beginning of the nineteenth century. Hand-puppet plays are usually based, like the Punch and Judy play, or the popular 'motion' of the Prodigal Son, on simple stories which give call for slapstick comedy, beatings, and fierce combats, but they can also be used for propaganda and educational purposes, and had a brief vogue in English schools, though they now appear to have fallen out of favour. They also provide an excellent vehicle for satire, and the witty and comic puppet-shows given in France towards the end of the nineteenth century by such puppeteers as Lemercier de Neuville and Maurice Sand made use of hand-puppets, as did the twentieth-century English puppeteer Walter Wilkinson, who wrote several books about his adventures as a travelling showman, and the Russian Nina Efimova, author of the charming *Adventures of a Russian Puppet Theatre*. The Continental-style hand-puppet theatre, where several manipulators work together, permits considerably more ambitious productions than the one-man booth used for Punch and Judy.

An extension of the hand-puppet, less well known to English audiences, is the ROD-PUPPET, a full-length rounded figure supported and controlled from below. Its movements are slow but dignified, the sweeping gestures of the arms being often very effective. The oldest and finest rod-puppets are found in Java, where they are still traditionally used in ceremonies connected with religion and magic. The only native European tradition is in the Rhineland, but the rod-puppets of Sergei Obraztsov (q.v.) are internationally famous, and striking effects with rod-puppets were achieved in Vienna by Richard Teschner, whose stage was seen through a convex lens which enlarged the figures, lending them an aura of enchantment and mystery. Rod-puppets are still used in India, where experimental work has been done with hand-puppets also, but in most cases the sophisticated marionette (q.v.) has superseded the older and cruder form of puppet. Among the puppets which do not come under any of the above headings are the intricate and almost life-size Japanese puppets, held in full view of the audience by as many as three operators and worked by wires and levers concealed in their backs. These were seen in London in 1968 when the Japanese Bunraku Theatre appeared at the Aldwych during the World Theatre season. The 'Cheeky Boys' and other dummies used by ventriloquists represent humbler examples of this type of puppet.

In America, where there is no tradition of puppetry, the art was slow to establish itself, in spite of the efforts of some small folk-puppet theatres catering for minority national groups. A few companies, among them those of Tony Sarg, Rufus Rose, and Remo Bufano, toured with some success, and at one time there was a vogue for a simplified cabaret-style puppet-show of which Bob Bromley was the outstanding exponent. There is an Association of the Puppeteers of America, and in 1952 the magnificent McPharlin collection of puppets, which now numbers over one thousand figures, together with an extensive library, was presented to the Detroit Institute of Art, where a Puppet Theatre for visiting companies has been set up. In 1930 the first international conference of puppeteers was held in Liège, and since 1957 conferences and festivals have been held every two years.

The 'Jigging Puppets', moved jerkily by a central string in time to music, which were for many centuries a popular street entertainment, the giant figures with limited movements of head and arms carried in Continental street processions, and the many different types of mechanical automata—peep-shows, water theatres, moving pictures—are all puppets, but belong rather to the non-theatrical aspect of the subject. Two other forms of puppet entertainment, using flat figures, are the Shadow-Show and the Toy Theatre (qq.v.).

Purdy's National Theatre, NEW YORK, see CHATHAM THEATRE (2).

Purim Plays, associated with the Jewish Festival of Purim on the 14th Adar (roughly early March) which commemorates the events described in the Old Testament book of Esther, appear to have developed as early as the fourteenth century under the influence of the masquerades and mumming of the Italian Carnival. Mostly in one act, traditional in style and costume, they consisted of improvised dialogue mingled with songs and dances and comic interludes. Originally restricted to the story of Esther and Haman, they later widened their scope to include other Old Testament stories, including Joseph and his brethren, David and Goliath, and even the life of Moses. Spreading to France and Germany, they eventually reached Eastern Europe, where they remained popular until the beginning of the present century. The standard plots, which show one man battling with God's help against overwhelming odds, could be adapted to local conditions within the traditional framework. The Purim plays, with their accretions of comic rabbis, apothecaries, midwives, and devils, were often in trouble with the authorities but had a considerable influence on the development of Jewish drama. The Haskala groups, which purged them of their grosser elements by relegating the comic figures to a sub-plot, introduced a serious educational element, and with the founding by Goldfaden (q.v.) of a permanent Yiddish theatre, which absorbed much of their method and material, they finally disappeared.

Puritan Interregnum. In 1642 the Puritan opposition to the theatre, which in London and elsewhere had become increasingly identified with the Stuart cause and offered excellent opportunities for subversive activities, led to the closing of all public playhouses. There is no direct evidence, however, that the Puritans as a whole were hostile to drama. Plays continued to be acted under the Commonwealth in schools—with the approbation of Cromwell himself—and possibly in private houses, and in 1656 Davenant (q.v.) was allowed to produce publicly his 'entertainment with music'—*The Siege of Rhodes*—now regarded as the first English opera. But for eighteen years, until they reopened in 1660, the theatres stood empty, some of them never to be used again, and professional actors were deprived of their means of livelihood. Some joined the army, some drifted into the provinces, some returned to earlier, half-forgotten trades. Only the boldest or most desperate, tried to evade the ban, taking refuge in the Fortune, or such small theatres as the Cockpit or the Red Bull (qq.v.). Evidence of surreptitious performances is given by records of the fining or imprisoning of the actors concerned, among them William Beeston, Robert Cox, and Timothy Reade (qq.v.).

PUSHKIN, ALEXANDER SERGEIVICH (1799–1837), Russia's first and greatest national poet, who at the age of eight wrote little plays in French which he acted with his sister. At fifteen his favourite dramatists were Molière, Racine, Voltaire, Ozerov, Fonvizin, and above all Shakespeare. It was under the influence of the last that he started work on his great drama, *Boris Godunov*. He had already realized that a truly national Russian drama could only be created by the use of Russian themes and Russian folklore, and by making Russian a language fit to rank with French or German, for which it had been so often discarded in its own country. He evidently envisaged the writing of a series of dramatic works of which *Boris Godunov* alone was completed. It is notable in being the first Russian tragedy on a political theme—the relationship between a tyrant and his people—which, though set back in time, was actually a burning contemporary problem. In other respects, too, it was revolutionary: it was broken up into scenes and episodes, it mingled poetry with prose, and made use of colloquial Russian speech. Owing to trouble with the censorship, it was not published until six years after its completion in 1825, and it was not seen on the stage for nearly fifty years, being given its first production in 1870. It was also used for the libretto of an opera by Mussorgsky first produced in 1874, in which form it is usually seen nowadays.

Just before his death in a duel, Pushkin completed a series of one-act tragedies, one dealing with Don Juan, one with the rivalry of Mozart and Salieri, the third with the character of a miser who owes something to Molière's Harpagon (in *L'Avare*) but more to Shakespeare's Shylock (in *The Merchant of Venice*). With some unfinished scenes from Russian folklore, these make up the total of Pushkin's work for the theatre. (Tchaikovsky's opera, 'Eugene Onegin', based on the poem written by Pushkin in 1831, was not produced until 1879.) Though he is not primarily remembered as a dramatist and had little direct contact with the stage, the Russian theatre owes him a great debt, since it was he who first made Russian a literary language. There are theatres bearing his name in Moscow (see below) and in Leningrad (see ALEXANDRINSKY), and his works are quoted as often by Russians as Shakespeare's are by Englishmen.

Pushkin Theatre, MOSCOW. This theatre, named after the great Russian poet Pushkin (q.v.), opened in 1951 under VASILY VASILYEVICH VANIN (1898–1951), who died shortly after. He was succeeded by Babochkin, who was responsible for most of its productions until 1954, when Tumanov (q.v.) took over. In 1961 the latter was succeeded by Boris Ravenskykh, who in 1970 went to the Maly (q.v.). Among the interesting productions seen at the Pushkin have been revivals of *Krechinsky's Wedding*, by Sukhovo-Kobylin (q.v.), staged by Vanin shortly before his death, and Ostrovsky's *At a Busy Place*, seen in 1952. In 1957 Petrov directed a successful new translation of Wilde's *The Importance of Being Earnest*, and a new play, Casona's *The Trees Die Standing*, was seen in 1958. But on the whole the theatre appears to have staged mainly revivals, including Chekhov's *Ivanov* (1960), Sholokhov's *Virgin Soil Upturned* (1963), and a dramatization by Okumchikov of Goncharov's *Oblomov* (1969).

Q

QUAGLIO, a family of scenic artists extending over several generations, of whom the first were the brothers LORENZO (1730–1804), important in the rise of neo-classicism, and GIUSEPPE (1747–1828). Of Italian origin, they worked mainly in foreign Courts and in the late eighteenth century established themselves in Munich, where their sons, grandsons, and great-grandsons were connected with the Court theatre. A Quaglio was also working at the Berlin Court Theatre as late as 1891.

QUARTERMAINE, LEON (1876–1967), English actor, who was first seen in London in 1901 with Forbes-Robertson, and was a member of Granville-Barker's company at the St. James's in 1913, where he played in Shaw, Galsworthy, and Ibsen. He was a fine Shakespearian actor, and in later years his Banquo (in *Macbeth*), John of Gaunt (in *Richard II*), Buckingham (in *Henry VIII*), and Cymbeline were memorable. He also gave a fine performance as the Man in Ashley Dukes's *The Man with a Load of Mischief* (1925), playing opposite Fay Compton (q.v.), his second wife, as the Lady. His brother CHARLES (1877–1958), husband of the actress MADGE TITHERADGE (1887–1961), was also an actor, first seen in London in 1900, who was for some years with Tree at His Majesty's. Later he appeared mainly in films.

QUAYLE, (JOHN) ANTHONY (1913–), English actor and director, who made his first appearance in London in 1931 and had already given proof of solid qualities, notably in his work during several seasons with the Old Vic, when the Second World War interrupted his career. After six years in the army he returned to the theatre with a production of Dostoievsky's *Crime and Punishment* (1946) starring John Gielgud and Edith Evans, and then went to Stratford-upon-Avon (q.v.), becoming director of the theatre there in 1948 in succession to Sir Barry Jackson (q.v.). He retired from this post in 1956, after having appeared in a wide variety of plays in addition to his other commitments, and returned to London in a succession of parts which included Eddie in Arthur

Miller's *A View from the Bridge* (1956), Aaron in *Titus Andronicus* (1957), James Tyrone in O'Neill's *Long Day's Journey into Night* (1958), Sir Charles Dilke in Bradley-Dyne's *The Right Honourable Gentleman* (1964), and Andrew Wyke in Anthony Shaffer's *Sleuth* (1970), going with this last play to New York. In 1970 he also directed a dramatization of Dostoievsky's *The Idiot* for the National Theatre in London. He has had a distinguished career in films and is the author of two novels based on his wartime experiences, *Eight Hours from England* (1945) and *On Such a Night* (1947). His first wife was the actress Hermione Hannen, his second the actress Dorothy Hyson, daughter of the musical-comedy star, Dorothy Dickson. He was appointed C.B.E. in the Birthday Honours of 1952. His daughter Jennifer (Jenny) is also on the stage.

Queen Anne's Men, a company, usually known as the Queen's Men, which was formed on the accession of James I in 1603 and included Christopher Beeston, Richard Perkins, and Thomas Heywood. It had a successful career, both in the provinces and in London, playing at the Curtain and the Red Bull (qq.v.) until 1616, when, after internal dissensions, Beeston, by then the company's manager, moved it to his new theatre, the Cockpit (q.v.). A riot by London apprentices on Shrove Tuesday 1617 proved a bad omen, and the venture failed. It was left to Prince Charles's Men (q.v.) under Taylor to make a success of the new theatre. The Queen's Men broke up on the death of their patron in 1619, Beeston remaining with the Prince's Men until 1625 (see QUEEN HENRIETTA'S MEN), the rest going back to the Red Bull or into the provinces.

Queen Elizabeth's Men, a company of players formed in 1583 which included the famous jester Tarleton (q.v.), whose *Five Plays in One* and *Three Plays in One* (later revived as *The Seven Deadly Sins*) (*c.* 1590), were played at Court in 1585. His death in 1588 was a great blow to the company, which made its last appearance at Court in 1594, and was then replaced by the Admiral's Men (q.v.).

Queen Henrietta's Men, a company of players, usually known as the Queen's Men, formed under Christopher Beeston (q.v.) some time in 1625, probably after the plague of that year had shut the theatres and disrupted the existing companies. Among the successful plays given by these actors were about twenty which their official dramatist, James Shirley (q.v.), wrote for them, alone or in collaboration, from 1625 to 1636. They also appeared at Court in Heywood's masque, *Love's Mistress* (1634), for which Inigo Jones (q.v.) designed some admirable scenery. When plague again closed the theatres in 1636, Beeston disbanded the company and formed another, Beeston's Boys, which took over the Cockpit (q.v.), while the Queen's Men were absorbed into other companies. In 1637 a new company was formed, and played at Salisbury Court until the final closing of the theatres in 1642.

Queen of Bohemia's Men, a London company formed in 1628 under the patronage of James I's daughter (see LADY ELIZABETH'S MEN). Little is known of its activities, though it is believed to have appeared at the Red Bull until 1632 and existed intermittently until 1641.

Queen Street Theatre, see GLASGOW.

Queen's Theatre, LONDON. (1) In Long Acre, originally St. Martin's Hall, which opened in 1850. It was reconstructed as a theatre under the management of Labouchère, whose future wife Henrietta Hodson (q.v.) was in the company, as were Charles Wyndham, Ellen Terry, Lionel Brough, and, for a time, Irving (qq.v.). The theatre, which had a short but lively existence, opened on 24 Oct. 1867 with Charles Reade's *The Double Marriage*. Labouchère used it mainly to display his wife's talent and lost a lot of money. The main event there was the return of Ellen Terry to the stage in 1874 to take over the part of Philippa in Reade's *Wandering Heir* from Mrs. John Wood (q.v.). In 1877 the theatre was renamed the National, opening on 27 Oct. with melodrama. But it was not successful, in spite of resuming its old name in 1878, and it closed a year later. The auditorium became a warehouse, but the façade remained standing until 1938, having been incorporated into the front of Odham's Press in 1911.

(2) In Shaftesbury Avenue, sister theatre to the Globe (q.v.), which it adjoins. It opened on 8 Oct. 1907 and was used mainly for musical plays and revivals. In 1913 it housed the fashionable tango teas, and in 1914 had its first success with *Potash and Perlmutter*. Among later productions were Fagan's *And So to Bed* (1926), with Yvonne Arnaud, the Malvern Festival production of Shaw's *The Apple Cart* (1929), with Edith Evans and Cedric Hardwicke, Gielgud's Hamlet from the Old Vic and Besier's *The Barretts of Wimpole Street* (both 1930), *Evensong* (1932), from Beverley Nichols's novel, Robert Morley's *Short Story* (1935), with Marie Tempest, and in 1937–8 Gielgud's season of *Richard II*, *The School for Scandal*, *Three Sisters*, and *The Merchant of Venice*, in all of which he appeared himself. He was also in Dodie Smith's *Dear Octopus* (1938), which was still running when the theatre closed on the outbreak of the Second World War. It had reopened, and was housing Daphne du Maurier's *Rebecca*, with Owen Nares, when on 24 Sept. 1940 it was hit by a bomb. It was derelict for nearly twenty years, but on 8 July 1959 it reopened with Gielgud in his solo recital, *Ages of Man*. Since then it has again had a successful record with such plays as *The Aspern Papers*, based by Michael Redgrave on Henry James's novel, and Bolt's *The Tiger and the Horse* (both 1960), the musical *Stop the World—I Want to Get Off* (1961), by Anthony Newley and Leslie Bricusse, Ustinov's *Halfway Up the Tree* (1967), and Barry England's *Conduct Unbecoming* (1969).

(See also HER MAJESTY'S, ROYALTY, and SCALA.)

The Trocadero Music-Hall (q.v.) was also known as the Queen's Theatre, though used only as a music-hall; so were Dorset Garden and theatres in Dublin and Edinburgh (qq.v.).

Questors Theatre, in Mattock Lane, Ealing (a suburb of London), the headquarters of an outstanding amateur group founded in 1929 by Alfred Emmet, who in 1933 turned a disused chapel into a small theatre. After the Second World War, under his enthusiasm and leadership, a large sum of money was raised for the erection of a new theatre seating three hundred and fifty people, much of the actual building work being done by the members, with professional assistance. In this adaptable theatre, which opened in 1964, plays have been staged in a proscenium-arch setting, with a variable fore-stage, on a three-sided 'thrust' stage, in the round, or in an open 'space stage'. Attached to the theatre are the Shaw Lecture Room, opened in 1958, the Stanislavsky Rehearsal Room, opened in 1960, and a number of administrative offices. The Questors, which runs a training course for amateur actors and a large number of young people's groups, has an exceptional record for the presentation of new plays, including *Next Time I'll Sing To You* (1962), by James Saunders (q.v.).

QUICK, JOHN (1748–1831), English comedian, who made his first appearance at Covent Garden in 1767 and remained there until his retirement in 1798. Unacceptable in tragedy, he had a wide range of comic parts, from Clown in pantomime to Polonius in *Hamlet*, and was the first to play Tony Lumpkin in Goldsmith's *She Stoops to Conquer* (1773) and Bob Acres in Sheridan's *The Rivals* (1775). A small, impetuous, chubby-cheeked man, he was the favourite actor of George III, and his portrait by Zoffany hangs in the Garrick Club (q.v.) in London.

QUIN, JAMES (1693–1766), English actor, the last of the declamatory school whose supremacy was challenged by Garrick (q.v.). After fourteen years at Lincoln's Inn Fields Theatre, where he first appeared as Hotspur in *Henry IV, Part 1* in 1718, later playing Othello, Lear, Falstaff, the Ghost in *Hamlet*, and Buckingham in *Richard III*, he went to Covent Garden in 1732 and then to Drury Lane. A man of great gifts but little education, and very obstinate and quarrelsome, he was a stickler for tradition, and to the end refused to alter one detail of his original costumes. A portrait of him as the hero of Thomson's *Coriolanus* (1748) shows him equipped with plumes, peruke, and full spreading short skirt in the style of the late seventeenth century. He played only in tragedy, and retired in 1751 to Bath, where he died. There is a description of his acting in Smollett's *Humphry Clinker* (1771).

QUINAULT, PHILIPPE (1635–88), French dramatist and librettist, whose first play, *Les Rivales* (1653), was put into rehearsal at the Hôtel de Bourgogne as being by Tristan l'Hermite (q.v.). When the actors discovered the truth they wanted to halve

the money that they were paying for the play, and the result of the negotiations was that the author was given a stipulated share in the receipts of each performance, and not, as hitherto, in those of the first few nights only. This has been cited as the origin of the royalty system (q.v.), but the point is disputable. By 1666 Quinault had written sixteen plays, of which *La Mère coquette* (1665) was the most successful. The last of his plays to profit from the advice of Tristan, shortly before his death, was *La Comédie sans comédie* (1655), which was a great success. Several of the characters in it bore the names of the actors playing the parts. Quinault later married a wealthy young widow, who persuaded him to give up writing for the stage, which she considered a low pastime. However, having been elected to the French Academy in 1670, Quinault felt he ought to return to literature, so collaborated with Molière (q.v.) in the lyrics for *Psyché* (1671) and 'Les Fêtes de l'Amour et de Bacchus'. This led to a meeting with the composer Lully and to a fruitful collaboration between the two. Quinault wrote a libretto for Lully every year, and his work was much admired by Louis XIV, who often, with royal condescension, suggested subjects for his pen. Such is the purifying power of music that his wife did not object to his engaging in such tasks. Quinault appeared to be at the height of his powers when he wrote what proved to be his last libretto, that for Lully's 'Armide' (1686). The death of Lully in 1687 and the influence of the religious ideas of the time then turned him finally against the stage.

There was a family of French actors named Quinault (no relation to the above), of whom the father and five children were all members of the Comédie-Française in the first half of the eighteenth century. The most famous was the second son (see DUFRESNE).

QUINTERO, JOSÉ BENJAMIN (1924–), American director, and one of the co-founders of the off-Broadway group at the Circle-in-the-Square (q.v.), for which he has directed a number of plays since 1950, including an excellent revival of O'Neill's *The Iceman Cometh* in 1956. In the same year he was responsible for the production of O'Neill's *Long Day's Journey into Night* at the Helen Hayes Theatre on Broadway. In 1958 he directed O'Neill's *A Moon for the Misbegotten* for the Festival of Two Worlds at Spoleto in Italy. Among his later productions at the Circle-in-the-Square were Brendan Behan's *The Hostage* (1958) and several revivals of plays by O'Neill, whose *Marco Millions* he directed in 1964 for the Lincoln Center Repertory Company.

QUINTERO, SERAFÍN ALVAREZ (1871–1938) and JOAQUÍN ALVAREZ (1873–1944), Spanish dramatists, brothers and collaborators in about a hundred and fifty light comedies, amusing, conventional, suffused with kindly tolerance and gentle good humour. Eight of them were translated into English by Helen and Harley Granville-Barker, of which *Fortunato* and *The Lady from Alfaqueque* (New York, 1929) were produced in London in 1928 with John Gielgud in the leading roles. *A Hundred Years Old* (New York, 1939) was also seen in London in 1928, followed in 1934 by *The Women Have Their Way* (New York, 1930) and *Doña Clarines. Don Abel Writes a Tragedy* was seen in London in 1944. *Love Passes By* and *Peace and Quiet* have not yet been professionally produced.

R

RACAN, HONORAT DE BUEIL, MARQUIS DE (1589–1670), French dramatist, whose pastoral, *Les Bergeries*, published in 1625, was first acted in 1619 as *Arthénice*. Written under the influence of Tasso's *L'Aminta* and Guarini's *Il Pastor Fido* (see PASTORAL), it contains some fine lyric passages, but is weak in construction and lacking in dramatic emphasis.

RACHEL [really ÉLISA FÉLIX] (1820–58), child of a poor Jewish family, and one of the greatest tragediennes of the French stage. Befriended by the impresario Choron, who found her singing in the streets, the thirteen-year-old girl was sent to Saint-Aulaire's drama school in the old Théâtre Molière. Further study at the Conservatoire was cut short by her father, who was anxious to make money out of her, and in 1837 she was taken into the company of the Gymnase-Dramatique (q.v.), where she attracted the attention of Jules Janin (q.v.), critic of the *Journal des Débats*. Encouraged by him, and coached by Samson (q.v.), she entered the Comédie-Française in 1838, appearing as Camille in Corneille's *Horace* with some success. Again encouraged by Janin, she appeared in other plays by Corneille (q.v.) which had been almost entirely neglected since the death of Talma (q.v.), and in the works of Racine (q.v.), whose *Phèdre* was destined to provide her with her greatest part. She also appeared in some modern plays, including a revival of *Marie Stuart*, by Lebrun, and the first production of *Adrienne Lecouvreur* (1849), by Scribe and Legouvé. But it was in the great classical roles that she appeared mainly on tour, either in the French provinces, in Europe, going as far as Russia, in London, where she first appeared in 1841 with outstanding success, or in America, where, on her one visit in 1855, she finally aggravated her tubercular condition, the result of early hardships and later overwork combined with a feverish succession of amorous intrigues. In spite of superb acting her visit to the United States was a failure financially, mainly on account of the language barrier. An account of her last tragic journey, written by a member of her company, Léon Beauvallet, was later published, and in 1968 was issued in an English translation by Collin Clair. She died at the early age of thirty-eight, leaving a great memory and a tradition of tragic acting which has never been surpassed. Rachel's four sisters, Sophie (later known as SARAH) (1819–77), Adelaide (known as LIA) (1828–72), Rachel (known as REBECCA) (1829–54), and Mélanie Émilie (known as DINAH) (1836–1909), were all on the stage, as was also her brother RAPHAËL (1825–72).

RACINE, JEAN BAPTISTE (1639–99), French playwright and poet, with Corneille (q.v.) the greatest dramatist of the seventeenth century. His first play, *La Thébaïde, ou les frères ennemis* (1664), was produced by Molière (q.v.) at the Palais-Royal. Its success led Molière to produce a second play, *Alexandre le Grand*, the following year. With rank ingratitude Racine allowed the rival company at the Hôtel de Bourgogne (q.v.) to produce the play a fortnight later, thus materially diminishing Molière's audience. As Molière's best actress, Mlle du Parc (q.v.), then left his company in order to play the lead in Racine's *Andromaque* (1667) at the rival theatre, the two men became completely estranged. With the production of *Andromaque* Racine was finally recognized as a great dramatist. It was followed by his only comedy, *Les Plaideurs* (1668), based to some extent on Aristophanes' *Wasps* and produced also at the Hôtel de Bourgogne. Frequently revived, it has been successful enough to make his admirers regret that he did not again venture into comedy. *Britannicus* (1669), which marked a return to classical tragedy, was not very successful, though it was much admired for its exquisite poetry, and the portrait of Nero is said by Boileau to have stopped Louis XIV from appearing any more in Court ballets and entertainments. With his next play Racine found himself at odds with Corneille, for either by coincidence or design they had both chosen the same subject, and the production of Racine's *Bérénice* (1670) took place a week before that of Corneille's *Tite et Bérénice*. Racine's was more generally applauded, and was followed by *Bajazet* (1672) and *Mithridate* (1673), oriental subjects treated in a completely

French and contemporary style, a reproach often levelled at Racine. They enhanced his reputation, however, and assured his position as the leading tragic dramatist of his day.

For his next play he returned to Greek tragedy, a field which was at that time being exploited by two of his rivals, Thomas Corneille and Quinault (qq.v.). His *Iphigénie* (1674) was a brilliant success, and it seemed likely that it would be followed by a succession of equally fine plays. But with *Phèdre* (1677) Racine's career as a dramatist came to an abrupt end. His many enemies, knowing the subject of his new play, persuaded Pradon (q.v.), a mediocre but fashionable writer, to compose one on the same theme. To Racine's chagrin Pradon's *Phèdre et Hippolyte* at the Palais-Royal was slightly more successful than his *Phèdre* at the Hôtel de Bourgogne. This, and perhaps even more Racine's appointment by Louis XIV as historiographer-royal, and a return to the austerity of his youth at Port-Royal, caused him to give up writing for the theatre. He retained his interest in dramatic literature, however, sufficiently to agree to the request of Mme de Maintenon (q.v.), that he should write a play for performance at her school for young ladies at Saint-Cyr. The result was the tender and poetic *Esther* (1689). It was a great success, but was not performed in public until 1721 at the Comédie-Française. By then the vogue for biblical subjects was over, and the beauty of the poetry failed to compensate for the lack of action. *Esther* was followed by *Athalie* (1691), also written for Saint-Cyr. It was produced at the Comédie-Française in 1716 and has since proved to be one of Racine's most admired works. Up to the end of the seventeenth century only two of Racine's plays had been translated into English—*Andromaque* by Crowne, and *Bérénice* by Otway. These were acted at Dorset Garden in 1674 and 1676 respectively. *Les Plaideurs* is thought to have influenced Wycherley's *The Plain Dealer* (1676). In 1707 Edmund Smith produced the first translation of *Phèdre*, which was acted at the Haymarket. Ambrose Philips's adaptation of *Andromaque* as *The Distrest Mother*, acted at Drury Lane in March 1712 and frequently revived, had an immediate success, and it is thought that this persuaded the actors to embark on Addison's *Cato*, a play which, more than any other production

of the time, shows the influence of French classical drama. Ozell, the translator of Corneille's *Le Cid*, also translated Racine, but there is no evidence that his *Britannicus*, *Alexander*, and *The Litigants* were ever acted. They were intended for a reading public, as were many later translations. Exceptions were Charles Johnson's *The Victim* (1713), based on *Iphigénie*, and *The Sultaness* (1716), based on *Bajazet*. There is no modern translation of Racine's complete works. Four of his plays were in the repertory of a French company which visited the Haymarket in Dec. 1721, and since then most visiting French companies have included at least one of his plays in their programme—but the only one which is at all familiar to London playgoers is *Phèdre*. It was in the 1721 programme, and has since been brought to London by Rachel, Ristori, Bernhardt, and Edwige Feuillère (qq.v.). On 17 Feb. 1958 Margaret Rawlings appeared at the Mahatma Gandhi Hall, London, in her own version of this play.

Radio City Music Hall, NEW YORK, the largest theatre in the world. Situated in Rockefeller Center, it opened on 29 Dec. 1932 with a galaxy of talent and a staff which included such well-known theatre personalities as Robert Edmond Jones (q.v.) and Martha Graham. It closed almost immediately, to open again with a combined cinema and stage show which has proved extremely popular. New full-length films alternate with a programme of music-hall turns which for speed and precision would be hard to beat. Owing to its enormous size and superb equipment the theatre is eminently suitable for spectacular effects, to which the well-drilled chorus, known as the Rockettes, contributes in no small degree.

Radius, see RELIGIOUS DRAMA.

RADLOV, SERGEI ERNESTOVICH (1892–1958), Soviet actor and producer, whose work was done mainly in Leningrad, where he started his theatrical career under Meyerhold (q.v.) and later opened his own theatre. Here he staged *Romeo and Juliet* and *Hamlet*, as well as Ibsen's *Ghosts*, and in 1935 a production of *Othello* which he repeated at the Moscow Maly. His outstanding achievement, however, was his production of *King Lear* for the Moscow State Jewish Theatre, with Mikhoels (q.v.) in the title-role. Although he did some good productions of Russian plays, among them Ostrovsky's *The Dowerless Bride* (1940), he was pre-eminently a producer of Shakespeare, whom he studied deeply, pondered on, and wrote about. In this he was greatly helped by his wife, who translated the plays for him.

RAEBURN, HENZIE (1900–), see BROWNE, E. MARTIN.

RAHERE (?–1144), a jester attached to the service of the English king Henry I as a permanent member of the Royal Household. He amassed a large fortune by his wit and used it to found the priory of St. Bartholomew at Smithfield, later a famous hospital. He entered the Church and in 1111 became Prebendary of St. Paul's Cathedral.

RAIMUND, FERDINAND [really JAKOB RAIMANN] (1790–1836), Austrian playwright and actor, who, though secretly preferring tragedy, was a popular farce-player at the Josefstädter and Leopoldstädter theatres in Vienna from 1813 to 1823. Although considered the greatest comic actor of his day, he decided that his unique combination of gifts needed a vehicle specially created to display them and so began to write his own plays. The first, *Der Barometermacher auf der Zauberinsel* (1823), was a great success, and was followed by *Das Mädchen aus der Feenwelt, oder der Bauer als Millionär* (1826), which preaches, with the help of magical forces and a whole host of allegorical personages, the doctrine of contentment on small means. Perhaps Raimund's greatest play is *Der Alpenkönig und der Menschenfeind* (1828), in which a kindly mountain spirit cures a misanthropist by assuming his shape and character, while the misanthrope, disguised as his own brother-in-law, has to watch the havoc caused by his suspicions and ill-will. However, all ends happily. Some of Raimund's later plays were less successful. His last years were overshadowed by the rising popularity of Nestroy (q.v.), and he finally committed suicide.

RAISIN, JEAN-BAPTISTE (1655–93), French actor who, with his sister CATHERINE (1650–1701) and brother JACQUES (1653–1702), was a member of a children's company established in Paris by his father under the patronage of the Dauphin. Among the other children were Baron (q.v.) and Jean de Villiers, who later married Catherine. As an adult actor Raisin, who was known as 'little Molière' from his excellent acting in comedy, was at the Hôtel de Bourgogne with his wife FANCHON [really FRANÇOISE PITEL DE LONGCHAMP] (1661–1721). They both became members of the Comédie-Française on its foundation in 1680. After her husband's death Fanchon became the mistress of the Dauphin, by whom she had two daughters.

Rake, the slope of the stage floor from the footlights up to the back wall, which helped to increase the illusion of scenes painted in perspective. It was limited in practice to a slope of 4°, and was often as small as $1\frac{1}{2}$°. It had serious disadvantages in the setting of scenery, as pieces set diagonally could not join neatly to squarely vertical neighbours; also the side flats of a box-set (q.v.) needed fox wedges under the base of each to compensate for the slope, or else they had to be built out of true with sloping bottom rails and ceased to be interchangeable. Moreover, any setting of pieces on a boat truck (q.v.) became dangerous, since the truck might run off on its own down the incline. Though some raked stages still remain, the modern practice is to have a flat stage floor and to rake the floor of the auditorium (q.v.).

Raking piece, a canvas-covered wooden frame with a sloping top edge, used as a small groundrow or to conceal a ramp on stage.

RAMSAY, ALLAN (1686–1758), Scottish poet, whose *Tea-Table Miscellany*, published in four volumes between 1725 and 1740, was the first considerable collection of the words of Scottish songs. He was also the author of *The Gentle Shepherd*, a pastoral published in 1725. It was not acted until 1729, when, owing to the success of Gay's *The Beggar's Opera* the year before, it was fitted out with Scottish tunes and turned into a ballad opera. In 1730, with the original dialogue turned into English by Theophilus Cibber (q.v.), it was produced at Drury Lane as *Patie and Peggy; or, the Fair Foundling*. In its original form it was revived for the Edinburgh Festival of 1949 under the direction of Tyrone Guthrie. In 1736 Ramsay, encouraged by the success of *The Gentle Shepherd*, ventured to open a theatre in Edinburgh, but it was closed under the Licensing Act introduced the following year.

RANDALL, HARRY (1860–1932), an English 'eccentric' comedian, who was on the stage as a child and later became one of the great names of music-hall. He also appeared in pantomime at the Grand, Islington, with only one break, from 1891 to 1901, playing both male and 'dame' parts. He was in the last pantomime in which Dan Leno (q.v.) appeared, *Humpty Dumpty* at Drury Lane in 1903, and proved a worthy successor to that great comedian.

RANKIN, ARTHUR MCKEE (1841–1914), American actor, who made his first appearance in 1865 at the Arch Street Theatre, Philadelphia, under Mrs. John Drew (q.v.). Four years later he married an actress, KITTY BLANCHARD (1847–1911), with whom he played at the Union Square Theatre (q.v.) and on long tours, mainly in melodrama. The best-known play in his repertory was Joaquin Miller's *The Danites*, in which he appeared in New York in 1877 and in London in 1880. He later separated from his wife, and with NANCE O'NEILL [really GERTRUDE LAMSON] (1874–1965) as his leading lady toured widely, reappearing in London in 1902. His three daughters all married well-known actors, GLADYS (1873–1914) becoming the wife of Sidney Drew, PHYLLIS (1874–1934) of Harry Davenport, and DORIS (1880–1946) of Lionel Barrymore.

RASTELL, JOHN (?–1536), brother-in-law of Sir Thomas More, and father-in-law, through the marriage of his daughter Elizabeth, of John Heywood (q.v.), some of whose interludes were printed by Rastell's son William. John Rastell is believed to have been the author of *Calisto and Meliboea*, an adaptation of part of de Rojas's *Celestina*, and of *The Dialogue of Gentleness and Nobility*, both of which were acted in his own garden at Finsbury in about 1527, and printed by him in the same year. He may also have been the author of an earlier interlude entitled *The Play of the Four Elements* (*c.* 1517).

RATTIGAN, SIR TERENCE MERVYN (1911–77), English dramatist, who first became known through his successful light comedy *French Without Tears* (1936). Later successes were *Flare Path* (1942), *While the Sun Shines* (1943), and *Love in Idleness* (1944). The last provided an excellent vehicle for the Lunts (q.v.), who played in it in London, and also in America under the title of *O Mistress Mine* (1946). A more serious play was *The Winslow Boy* (1946), the story, based on fact, of a father's fight to clear his son of a charge of theft, which won the Ellen Terry Award for the best play of the year in London and in 1947 the New York Drama Critics' Circle Award for the best foreign play on Broadway. *Playbill*, consisting of *Harlequinade* and *The Browning Version*, followed in 1948 and also received the Ellen Terry Award. *Adventure Story* (1949), with Paul Scofield as Alexander the Great, was an interesting failure, and with *Who Is Sylvia?* (1950) Rattigan appeared to return to his former vein of comedy. In 1952, however, he produced *The Deep Blue Sea*, an emotional drama which, though well written and theatrically exciting, failed to come to grips with its central problem. An excursion into Ruritanian romance, *The Sleeping Prince*, followed in 1953, in which year Rattigan published his *Collected Plays* in 2 vols., each with a long introduction by the author. It was then that he first used the term 'Aunt Edna' to indicate the ordinary unsophisticated playgoer who has no use for experimental *avant-garde* theatre. This has since proved a useful shorthand word for the dramatic critics and an 'Aunt Sally' for the progressives. Rattigan then wrote *Separate Tables* (1955), *Variations on a Theme* (1958), *Ross* (1960), with Alec Guinness (q.v.) as T. E. Lawrence, a musical version of his own *French Without Tears* (also 1960) which lasted four nights, *Man and Boy* (1963), *Bequest to the Nation* (1970), and *Cause Célèbre* which was running in London when he died in Bermuda. He was made a C.B.E. in 1958, and was knighted in 1971 for services to the theatre.

RAVENSCROFT, EDWARD (*fl.* 1671–97), English dramatist, whose career as a playwright extended from *Mamamouchi; or, the Citizen turned Gentleman*—based on Molière's *Le Bourgeois gentilhomme*—in 1672 to *The Italian Husband* in 1697; but none of his plays has survived on the stage. His best work was done in farce, and it became a tradition to give his outrageous *The London Cuckolds* (1681) at both patent theatres on Lord Mayor's Day (9 Nov.) until Garrick stopped it at Drury Lane in 1751 and Covent Garden followed suit a year later. It was revived in 1782 for the benefit of Quick (q.v.) and then disappeared for ever. Among Ravenscroft's other plays, which he took from many sources, were the comedies *The Careless Lovers* (1673) (based on Molière's *Monsieur de Pourceaugnac*), *The Wrangling Lovers* (1676), *Dame Dobson; or, the Cunning Woman* (1683), and *The Anatomist; or, the Sham Doctor* (1696). He also wrote a Harlequin play based on Molière's *Les Fourberies de Scapin* (1677) which was forestalled by Otway's (q.v.) version, an English adaptation of the Latin play *Ignoramus*, by Ruggle (q.v.), as *The English Lawyer* (also 1677), and an 'improved' version of Shakespeare's *Titus Andronicus* (1686).

RAYMOND, JOHN T. [really JOHN O'BRIEN] (1836–87), American actor, famous for his playing of Colonel Mulberry Sellers in Mark Twain's *The Gilded Age* (1874) and Ichabod Crane in *Wolfert's Roost* (1879), a dramatization of Washington Irving's *The Legend of Sleepy Hollow*. He made his first appearance in 1853, and was immediately hailed as a fine comedian. He toured and worked in stock companies for some years, and in 1861 joined Laura Keene (q.v.) in New York, taking over the part of Asa Trenchard in Tom Taylor's *Our American Cousin* from Jefferson (q.v.). He was also seen as Tony Lumpkin in Goldsmith's *She Stoops to Conquer* and as Crabtree in Sheridan's *The School for Scandal*, with great success. Raymond, who was an able and energetic man and remained on the stage until his death, had a long imperturbable face and a slow seriousness which made his comedy even more appealing. He was popular with the public and with his fellow actors, and once established as a star appeared mainly in plays by and about Americans, except for Pinero's *The Magistrate*, in which he was excellent as Posket.

READE, CHARLES (1814–84), English novelist, who was also the author of a great number of plays. Of these the best-known are *Masks and Faces* (1852), dealing with Garrick and Peg Woffington (qq.v.), which he wrote in collaboration with Tom Taylor (q.v.); *The Courier of Lyons* (1854), which became famous as *The Lyons Mail* when revived in 1877 by Henry Irving (q.v.) at the Lyceum, and *It's Never Too Late to Mend* (1864), based on his own novel. Among Reade's

later plays the best was a version of Zola's novel *L'Assommoir* as *Drink* (1879), written in collaboration with Charles Warner (q.v.). He also dramatized Tennyson's poem *Dora* in 1867. Reade was essentially a novelist, and his best work for the stage was done in collaboration with more theatrically-minded men, or based on existing foreign plays. It was Reade who persuaded Ellen Terry (q.v.) to return to the stage in 1874 after her liaison with Godwin, to take over the part of Philippa Chester in his play *The Wandering Heir*.

READE, TIMOTHY (*fl.* first half of seventeenth century), a comedian popular in London before the closing of the theatres in 1642. He probably began his career as a boy-actor in 1626, and later was at Salisbury Court with the King's Men (see CHAMBERLAIN'S MEN), joining Queen Henrietta's Men (q.v.) at a later date. From contemporary allusions it is evident that he was renowned as a dancer and a mimic. He was one of the actors who was arrested in 1647 for acting surreptitiously, perhaps at the Red Bull (q.v.).

Realism, a movement in the theatre at the end of the nineteenth century which replaced the well-made play and the declamatory acting of the period by dramas which approximated in speech and situation to the social and domestic problems of everyday life, played by actors who spoke and moved naturally against scenery which reproduced with fidelity the usual surroundings of the people they represented. The movement began with Ibsen (q.v.) and spread rapidly across Europe, upsetting the established theatre and demanding a new type of actor to interpret the new plays. This was achieved by the system of Stanislavsky (q.v.) and by the later advocates of naturalism (q.v.), which was the logical outcome of realism.

Realistic Theatre, Moscow. This small theatre, also known as the Krasnya Presnya Theatre from the district in which it was situated, opened in 1921 and was originally one of the studios attached to the Moscow Art Theatre (q.v.), on whose methods its early productions were based. A decisive change in its history came with the appointment in 1932 of Nikolai Okhlopkov (q.v.) as its artistic director. His style of production, particularly for new plays, entailed the virtual reconstruction of the acting area in the theatre, often with several stages in various parts of the auditorium used simultaneously or in quick succession, while actors and audience mingled freely, the latter sometimes being called on to take part in the action of the play. This experimental technique, while interesting and valuable, had necessarily a limited appeal, and in 1938 the theatre closed.

Recital Theatre, NEW YORK, see DALY'S THEATRE (3).

Red Army Theatre, MOSCOW, see CENTRAL THEATRE OF THE SOVIET ARMY.

Red Bull Theatre, LONDON. This was built about 1600 in Upper Street off St. John Street, Clerkenwell. It was occupied by Queen Anne's Men (q.v.) until 1616, and then by other companies. It was renovated and partly rebuilt in 1625 and may have been roofed in. It appears to have been what was later known in theatrical circles as a 'blood tub' (see GAFF), specializing in hot and strong dramas, with plenty of devils and red fire. When the theatres were closed under the Commonwealth, surreptitious shows and puppet-plays were sometimes given at the Red Bull, and at the Restoration a company under Michael Mohun acted there before moving to the renovated Cockpit. Killigrew (q.v.) was also there before he went to Vere Street, taking with him some of the best remaining actors in the Red Bull company. On 23 Mar. 1661 Pepys saw those who remained behind in a very poor production of Rowley's *All's Lost by Lust*. The theatre fell into disuse soon afterwards, but was still standing in 1663. By 1665 it had vanished.

Red Lion Inn, LONDON, see INNS USED AS THEATRES.

REDE, (THOMAS) LEMAN TERTIUS (1799-1832), English actor, who in 1824 married the widow of Oxberry (q.v.) and was responsible for many publications under the latter's name, particularly the posthumous *Oxberry's Dramatic Biography*. Rede was also the author of *The Road to the Stage* (1827), a useful manual of acting, interesting for a study of the contemporary theatre. He continued to act after his marriage and was seen at Sadler's Wells a fortnight before his death. His

younger brother, WILLIAM LEMAN (1802-47), was a prolific playwright, whose *The Old and Young Stager* (1835) was written for the début of the younger Mathews (q.v.). He also wrote *The Peregrinations of Pickwick*, based on Dickens's *Pickwick Papers*, and a burlesque of Home's *Douglas* (both 1837).

Rederijkers, the members of the Dutch Chambers of Rhetoric which in the sixteenth century were connected with manifestations of theatrical art in the main Flemish towns. The scenic backgrounds built for some of their open-air productions, in which secular and religious themes were mingled, recall the triumphal arch, and had some influence on the development of the Elizabethan playhouse (q.v.).

REDGRAVE, SIR MICHAEL SCUDAMORE (1908-85), English actor, knighted in 1959 for services to the theatre, who in 1934 joined the Liverpool Repertory Theatre (q.v.), where he remained for two years, playing a wide variety of parts and marrying a fellow member of the company, RACHEL KEMPSON (1910-), who subsequently appeared with him in many plays. They were together at the Old Vic in 1936, where Redgrave, among other parts, played Mr. Horner in a revival of Wycherley's *The Country Wife*. In this, and in his Aguecheek in *Twelfth Night* in 1938, he displayed a gift for comedy which was too rarely exploited. He also played a number of Shakespearian parts, for which he was well equipped, having a good presence and a fine speaking voice. These included Hamlet at the Old Vic, at Elsinore (1950), and in Russia (1958); Macbeth, in which he made his first appearance in New York in 1948; Richard II; Prospero in *The Tempest* (1951); Shylock in *The Merchant of Venice*, Antony in *Antony and Cleopatra*, and King Lear (1953), all at Stratford-upon-Avon. He was also seen in a number of new plays, including T.S. Eliot's *The Family Reunion* (1939), Thomas Job's *Uncle Harry* (1944), Giraudoux's *Tiger at the Gates* (1955), N. C. Hunter's *A Touch of the Sun* (1958), Robert Bolt's *The Tiger and the Horse* (1960), and his own adaptation of Henry James's *The Aspern Papers* (1959). At the first Chichester Festival in 1962 he gave an outstanding performance as Uncle Vanya in Chekhov's play, which he repeated the following year during the National Theatre's first season at the Old Vic. He was the author of three books, *The Actor's Ways and Means* (1955), *Mask or Face* (1958), and *The Mountebank's Tale* (1959). In 1965 he directed the first season at the new Yvonne Arnaud Theatre (q.v.), playing Rakitin in the opening production, Turgenev's *A Month in the Country*.

REDGRAVE, VANESSA (1937–), English actress, elder daughter of Michael Redgrave (q.v.). She appeared with her father in Hunter's *A Touch of the Sun* (1958) and Bolt's *The Tiger and the Horse* (1960), and was with the Stratford-upon-Avon company in 1959, 1961 and 1962, where among other parts her Rosalind in *As You Like It* and Imogen in *Cymbeline* were much admired. Her younger brother and sister, CORIN (1939–) and LYNN (1944–), are also on the stage, the latter having given some excellent performances with the National Theatre company. In 1970 she appeared with Richard Briers in four one-act plays by Michael Frayn under the title *The Two of Us*.

Regent Theatre, LONDON, in the Euston Road. This opened as the Euston Palace of Varieties on 26 Dec. 1900. It was used as a theatre between 1922 and 1932, and then became a cinema. Among the interesting productions there were the Čapeks' *The Insect Play* (1923), with scenery and costumes by Doris Zinkeisen, her first London assignment; Rutland Boughton's opera 'The Immortal Hour' (also 1923), with Gwen Ffrangcon-Davies; and *Romeo and Juliet* (1924), with Gwen Ffrangcon-Davies and John Gielgud (q.v.) in the chief parts, this being Gielgud's first appearance in London in a leading role.

Regency Theatre, LONDON, see SCALA THEATRE.

REGNARD, JEAN-FRANÇOIS (1655–1709), French dramatist, who wrote for the Comédie-Italienne (q.v.) from 1688 to 1696, often in collaboration with Dufresny (q.v.). From 1694 to 1708 he wrote also for the Comédie-Française, where his first successful play was *Attendez-moi sous l'orme* (1694). He followed it with several other comedies, the best being *Le Joueur* (1696) and *Le Légataire universel* (1708); the latter remained in the repertory of the theatre until the early twentieth century. He was the immediate successor of Molière (q.v.) as a writer of comedies, but suffered by comparison, his comic situations and witty dialogue being accompanied by a serious weakness in the development of character. It is, however, interesting to note in Regnard's plays the gradual emergence of the valet as the central figure, forerunner of Figaro (see BEAUMARCHAIS).

REHAN [really CREHAN], **ADA** (1860–1916), American actress, who began her career with Mrs. John Drew (q.v.) at the Arch Street Theatre, Philadelphia, where, by a printer's error, she was billed as Rehan (for Crehan), a name she retained and made famous. She was with several stock companies, playing opposite famous actors of the day, and in 1879 was engaged by Daly (q.v.) for New York, where she made her first appearance in his version of Zola's *L'Assommoir*. She became one of the most popular actresses in New York and in London, where she made her first appearance in 1884 at Toole's. She was later seen at Daly's Theatre (q.v.) in London, of which she laid the cornerstone in 1891. Her most famous part, in a repertory which covered Shakespearian and classic comedies as well as adaptations of foreign farces, was probably Katharina in *The Taming of the Shrew*. She first played this in New York in 1887, when the Induction to the play was also given there for the first time. Other parts in which she was much admired were Lady Teazle in Sheridan's *The School for Scandal* and Rosalind in *As You Like It*. She was essentially a comedienne, and that side of her art was developed by Daly to the exclusion of all others. This was unfortunate in that the plays at the turn of the century demanded a new style of acting, which made her, while still young, seem old-fashioned. After Daly's death she continued to present plays from his former repertory, but with dwindling success in spite of her attractive personality, and she made her last public appearance in May 1905. Her life had been entirely devoted to the theatre, and she never married.

Rehearsal, a session during which the director (q.v.), his cast, and his technical staff work on a play, preparing it for presentation. We know nothing of rehearsals in the classical theatre, and little of those in the medieval, though players, particularly women unable to read, must have been taught their parts orally, and great skill was obviously needed to direct the large crowds demanded by the liturgical drama (q.v.). Companies in later times were no doubt rehearsed by their leader, who was also the chief actor and often, as with Molière (q.v.), the author of the play. A glimpse of Elizabethan actors in rehearsal is given in *A Midsummer Night's Dream*. In the days of the stock company, in England and elsewhere, there were very few rehearsals. New plays were gone through to check cues and settle entrances and exits. A newcomer in an old play was left to learn his way about by trial and error, while a visiting star walked through his lines and left the company to adapt itself to his acting during the actual performance. New managements constantly began their reforms with an endeavour to institute regular rehearsals, and some degree of co-ordination was finally achieved by the stage manager, who eventually became the all-important stage director of modern times (see also AUDITION).

REINHARDT [really GOLDMANN], MAX (1873–1943), Austrian actor, manager, and outstanding director of plays. After studying drama in Vienna from 1890 to 1892, and spending a year with the resident theatre company in Salzburg, he went to the Deutsches Theater (q.v.) in Berlin, where he became noted as a masterly portrayer of old men. In 1903 he ceased to act in order to devote all his time to directing plays. A new era in theatrical presentation was at hand, heralded by the work of such men as Taïrov and Craig (qq.v.). It was to involve the use of new mechanical devices and methods of lighting, of well-schooled crowds as opposed to the star-actor system of the past, and of musicians and dancers integrated into the action of the play. Reinhardt was in the forefront of all these theatrical reforms. In order to re-create the intimate contact between actors and audience fostered by the Greek and Elizabethan theatres, he projected his stage into the arena, pushing it forward into the midst of the spectators. Scenery was replaced by highly stylized architecture, with vertical lines where the actor required to be dwarfed, horizontal where his stature was to be magnified. By the use of rhythmic mass movement—and very few producers have equalled Reinhardt in the management of crowds—he sought to sweep the spectators into the very heart of the play. No place was too vast for him. In 1910 he produced Sophocles' *Oedipus Rex* in the Zirkus Sch mann in Berlin and in 1911 was brought to London by C. B. Cochran (q.v.), first to present his wordless play *Sumurūn*, founded on *The Arabian Nights*, with his Berlin company, and then to direct *The Miracle* at Olympia. The following year saw his production of *Oedipus Rex*, with Martin-Harvey (q.v.), at Covent Garden, and among other outstanding productions must be reckoned *A Midsummer Night's Dream*—which he also produced at Oxford (on Headington Hill) in 1933, and in Hollywood in 1934— *Macbeth*, *Julius Caesar*, Aeschylus' *Agamemnon*, a season of plays in New York in 1927–8, a production in London in 1932, again under C. B. Cochran's management, of Offenbach's 'La Belle Hélène' in an English adaptation by A. P. Herbert, and numerous productions of light opera. In 1920 he founded the Salzburg Festival, where every year he staged *Everyman* in front of the Cathedral, and a number of plays, among them Goethe's *Faust*, in the theatre. It was inevitable that all this should lead to accusations of vulgarization in the theatre, but in addition to his vast spectacular shows at the Grosses Schauspielhaus in Berlin in which he appealed to the multitude, in smaller theatres such as the Kammerspiele and the Kleines Theater he staged intimate productions intended to appeal to the connoisseur, and gave to many masterpieces a subtly individualized atmosphere characterized by simple lines and subdued lighting. When Hitler came to power in 1933 Reinhardt left Germany and spent the last five years of his life in the United States.

RÉJANE [really GABRIELLE-CHARLOTTE RÉJU] (1857–1920), famous French actress, who made her first appearance in 1875 at the Vaudeville. She was soon recognized as a leading player of comedy and appeared at many Parisian theatres. She was frequently seen in London, making her first appearance there in 1894, and Shaw, in *Our Theatres in the Nineties*, while despising her choice of play, much admired her acting. Few of her parts were memorable, with the exception of the title-role in Sardou's *Madame Sans-Gêne*, in which she was seen in New York in 1895, and she never ventured on the classics. But in her own line of light comedy she was unapproachable. She opened her own theatre in Paris in 1906 and retired in 1915.

Religious Drama, in England and the United States. With the disappearance of the medieval liturgical drama (q.v.), religion as a subject for plays was, with rare exceptions, replaced on the English stage by classical history and mythology and plots drawn from contemporary life. It came back, tentatively, in the late nineteenth century, when professional writers like Henry Arthur Jones (q.v.) with *Saints and Sinners* (1884), *The Tempter* (1893), and *Michael and his Lost Angel* (1896), began to include religion and the clergy in plays of contemporary life. The best-known play of this kind is probably Jerome K. Jerome's *The Passing of the Third Floor Back* (1908). Meanwhile, the biblical 'spectacular', of which Wilson Barrett's *The Sign of the Cross* (1895) is typical, was also popular until taken over by the cinema. In all these productions it was the emotional and not the intellectual content of the religious story that was uppermost. The latter was first introduced into modern drama by G. B. Shaw (q.v.), with *Androcles and the Lion* (London, 1913; New York, 1915) and *Saint Joan* (New York, 1923; London, 1924), followed later by James Bridie (q.v.) with such plays as *Mr. Bolfry* (1943). The revival of a truly religious drama, however, came partly through the interest aroused by revivals of the old morality play *Everyman*, staged by William Poel (q.v.), and partly through the efforts of George Bell, who as Dean of Canterbury commissioned in 1928, for performance in the Cathedral, Masefield's *The Coming of Christ*. Bell became Bishop of Chichester a year later and not only appointed E. Martin Browne (q.v.) the first Director of Religious Drama for his diocese, but also became the first president of the newly founded Religious Drama Society of Great Britain (now known as RADIUS). The annual Canterbury Festival continued to call forth a notable succession of religious plays, and in 1935 T. S. Eliot's *Murder in the Cathedral*, produced by E. Martin Browne, moved to London and was an immense success in the commercial theatre also. Since then, the modern play of religion has become well established, with further plays by Eliot, Graham Greene, and Christopher Fry (qq.v.). Fry's *A Sleep of Prisoners* was specially commissioned by the Religious Drama Society for the 1951 Festival of Britain, and for the same festival the medieval York Cycle (see MYSTERY PLAY) had its first full-scale revival under E. Martin Browne. It has since been revived triennially, and other cycles—the Chester, Wakefield, and Lincoln—have also been seen in cut and modernized versions, both in their towns of origin and in the London commercial theatre. In Coventry, drama became part of the regular work of the new Cathedral on its dedication in 1962 with the appointment of a Director of Drama, the only one permanently attached to a religious foundation, though many hundreds of churches of all denominations now produce religious plays under the aegis of Radius, which acts as a consultant body, having an excellent reference and lending library, and running an annual summer school for the training of directors and actors in religious drama. It is also allied with SESAME, a movement which exploits the therapeutic aspect of drama for the physically and mentally handicapped.

In the United States, where religious plays were being written in the 1930s by Fred Eastman in Chicago, a rapid and widespread development took place in the 1950s. Under the auspices of the Rockefeller Foundation a Program in Religious Drama, with E. Martin Browne and his wife Henzie Raeburn as Visiting Professor and Lecturer, was established at the Union Theological Seminary, New York, in 1956, and in 1962 Robert E. Seaver, who had been associated with the project from its inception, took sole charge, the programme then becoming a course leading to a Master's degree in Religious Education with special emphasis on drama. Many of the most significant European religious plays have been introduced to America at the Union Seminary, whose students have disseminated its teaching throughout the United States and beyond.

Other seminaries, notably the Christian Theological Seminary at Indianapolis, have followed the example of the Union Theological Seminary, according to their resources. Touring companies have been established regionally and many parishes have begun play productions with trained directors, often touring the surrounding area. A nationwide impact is most evident when a special show is presented by Robert E. Seaver for the national conference of a denomination or other religious body. One such was the musical *For Heaven's Sake* (1961), the first of several plays which made use of the American talent for spectacle and music. The Rockefeller Foundation also made possible the first international exchanges in religious drama. At Oxford in 1955, and at Royaumont, near Paris, in 1960, delegates from twenty European countries were assembled and performances of religious plays were given in many styles and languages. Particularly interesting were the accounts of a liturgical drama movement in Sweden; of the formation of an active religious drama national society in Greece; and of the Christian use of drama stemming from native traditions in India, Japan, Thailand, and Uganda.

Renaissance, THÉÂTRE DE LA. (1) The first theatre of this name opened on 8 Nov. 1838 with a licence for plays with and without music. This aroused the jealousy of both the Comédie-Française and the Opéra, who finally caused it to close in 1841, but not before it had done some good work. The actors were headed by Frédérick and Mme Dorval (qq.v.), and the first play they appeared in was Hugo's *Ruy Blas*.

(2) The second Renaissance opened in 1873 on part of the site cleared by the burning of the Théâtre de la Porte-Saint-Martin (q.v.) in 1871. A small theatre, it unwisely endeavoured to put on strong drama. This soon gave way to light opera, the most successful being those by Lecocq. Between 1884 and 1892 the theatre was in a bad way, passing through many hands, and finally it closed. Sarah Bernhardt (q.v.), returning from a long tour abroad, took it over and made it successful, appearing there with Lucien Guitry and Coquelin *aîné*. Among her successful productions were Rostand's *La Princesse lointaine*, Sudermann's *Magda* (both 1895), Musset's *Lorenzaccio* (1896), and revivals of Racine's *Phèdre* and the younger Dumas's *La Dame aux camélias*. In 1899 Bernhardt opened her own theatre (see THÉÂTRE DES NATIONS) and the Renaissance became the Théâtre Lyrique, housing musical shows only.

RENARD, JULES (1864–1910), French novelist, whose best-known work, *Poil de Carotte*, the story of an unhappy childhood, was successfully dramatized (in one act) in 1900, and produced at the Théâtre Libre by Antoine (q.v.). The most successful of Renard's other naturalistic plays,

all in one act, was *Le Pain de ménage* (1899). In 1903 his novel *L'Écornifleur* (1892) was dramatized as *Monsieur Vernet* (in two acts).

RENAUD, MADELEINE-LUCIE (1903–), French actress, who married as her second husband Jean-Louis Barrault (q.v.), with whom she founded a company which has greatly enriched the theatrical life not only of France but of every country in which it has appeared durin₂ its tours abroad. She began her career at the Comédie-Française, where she made her mark as a player of Marivaux (q.v.), and was already an established star when Barrault joined the company. In 1943 she appeared under his direction in Claudel's *Le Soulier de satin*, and three years later became his leading lady, playing a wide range of parts from Molière, Racine, Lope de Vega, Musset, Chekhov, Giraudoux, and Fry. The beauty of her voice and person gave her an initial advantage to which years of hard work and technical mastery have added embellishments, but it is above all the fine, mature intelligence which governs all her work which has made her outstanding, and even when she does not herself appear in the company's productions one can sense her influence on them. It would be impossible to apportion between her and her husband the part of each in the company's success, since, as Barrault himself has said, their gifts are complementary, as was their training, she having proceeded by the direct classical route, he by the modern system of trial-and-error.

Repertory (Repertoire), the collection of parts played by an actor or, more usually, of plays in active production at a theatre in one season, or which can be put on at short notice, each play taking its turn in a constantly changing programme. This system, which was once followed in all theatres, has been superseded in the commercial theatres of London and New York by the run (q.v.), but is still used on the Continent. It depends on the maintenance of a reasonably large permanent company and offers the actor financial security combined with a wide range of parts. On the debit side it leads to miscasting, stagnation, complacency, and sometimes frustration for the younger actors. An effort was made in the early twentieth century to import the Continental system into England (see REPERTORY THEATRE MOVEMENT) but was not successful, and led to the present system of a weekly, fortnightly, or monthly change of bill in provincial theatres, to which the word repertory is wrongly applied. The only English theatres playing 'in repertory' at the moment are the National Theatre at the Old Vic and the Royal Shakespeare Company, the latter both at Stratford-upon-Avon and at the Aldwych Theatre in London.

Repertory Theatre Movement in Great Britain. The use of the word 'repertory' in this connection is something of a misnomer and has been further complicated by the emergence of the Civic Theatre (q.v.). The pioneers of the repertory movement, from J. T. Grein (q.v.) in 1891 to Miss Horniman (q.v.) in 1908, hoped to establish in England not only the 'new drama' of Ibsen and Shaw but also the Continental system of true 'repertory' (q.v.), whereby several plays are performed during the week with new ones in preparation. English theatre staffs and audiences had, however, become accustomed to the continuous 'run' (q.v.), and refused to co-operate. The consequence is that most so-called repertory theatres in England produce a play for a week, a fortnight, three weeks, or a month. The repertory companies thus provide an excellent training-ground for young actors, though too long a stay in one may prove exhausting. The oldest Repertory Theatre in Britain is the Liverpool (q.v.), founded in 1911. Two years later came the Birmingham (q.v.). Since then a number have been founded, of which some, like that at Windsor, established in 1938 by John Counsell (q.v.), have been successful, while others have sunk without trace.

Republic Theatre, NEW YORK, on 42nd Street west of Times Square. Built by Oscar Hammerstein (q.v.), this opened on 27 Sept. 1900 with James A. Herne in his own play, *Sag Harbor*. Two years later David Belasco (q.v.) took it over, gave it his own name, and produced there several of his own plays, including *The Darling of the Gods* (1902), *Sweet Kitty Bellairs* (1903), *Adrea* and *The Girl of the Golden West* (both 1905). He also produced Klein's *The Music Master* (1904), in which Warfield (q.v.) made a great success, and Tully's *The Rose of the Rancho* (1906), with Frances Starr. When in 1910 Belasco's second theatre, the Stuyvesant, was renamed the Belasco (q.v.), the Republic reverted to its original name. The last play seen there, before it became a burlesque house and then a cinema named the Victory, was John Huston's *Frankie and Johnny* (1930).

République, THÉÂTRE DE LA, see COMÉDIE-FRANÇAISE.

Returns, see BOX-SET.

REUENTAL, NEIDHART VON (*fl.* thirteenth century), see MASTERSINGERS.

Reveals, see BOX-SET.

Revels Office, see MASTER OF THE REVELS.

Revenge Tragedy, the name given to those Elizabethan plays of which Kyd's *The Spanish Tragedy* (c. 1585–9) was the first. Dealing with bloody deeds which demand retribution, their motto was 'an eye for an eye and a tooth for a tooth', and their sublimity could easily turn to melodrama; and indeed, in a cruder form, the revenge motif underlay many of the melodramas of the nineteenth century. In the range of Shakespeare's plays *Titus Andronicus* (c. 1592) may be considered the lowest form of the Revenge Tragedy, *Hamlet* (c. 1600–1) its finest flowering. Under the same heading come such plays as Chapman's *Bussy d'Ambois* (c. 1604), Tourneur's *The Revenger's Tragedy* (c. 1606) and *The Atheist's Tragedy* (c. 1611), John Webster's *The White Devil* (1612) and *The Duchess of Malfi* (1614), and Middleton's *The Changeling* (1622).

Revolving Stage, see KABUKI and SCENERY.

Revue, a French word used to describe a survey (or review, in which sense the word was first used in 1872 by Planché (q.v.) in his *Recollections*) of contemporary events, with songs, sketches, burlesques, monologues, and so on. No satisfactory English name has ever been found for this mixture, and the French continues in use. The first revue seen in London was *Under the Clock* (1893), by Seymour Hicks (q.v.) and CHARLES HALLAM ELTON BROOKFIELD (1857–1913). The name was later given to entertainments with spectacular costumes and effects produced mainly by ALBERT DE COURVILLE (1887–1960) at the Hippodrome (q.v.) and ANDRÉ CHARLOT (1882–1956) at the Alhambra (q.v.). In 1914 ALFRED BUTT (1878–1962) inaugurated a series of revues at the Palace (q.v.) with *The Passing Show*, which introduced the

American star, ELSIE JANIS [really BIER-BOWER] (1889–1956), to London. Many of the stars of revue, and much of its music, came from New York, where revue had been introduced in 1907 by Ziegfeld (q.v.) with his *Ziegfeld Follies*, which ran through twenty-four editions. A later producer of American revue was GEORGE WHITE (1890–1968), whose *Scandals*, beginning in 1919, became an annual feature of the New York scene. As a reaction from the spectacular show, a form of intimate revue, which relied more on wit than on dress and dancing, began with *Odds and Ends* (1914), presented by Cochran (q.v.) at the Ambassadors in London. For his later revues at the London Pavilion Cochran employed outstanding actors, dancers, designers, and writers, among them Noël Coward (q.v.), who was responsible for *This Year of Grace* (1928). The intimate revue flourished immediately before the Second World War at the Gate and the Little Theatres (qq.v.), and during and after the war at the Ambassadors with *Sweet and Low* (1943), *Sweeter and Lower* (1944), and *Sweetest and Lowest* (1946), and with such shows as *Airs on a Shoestring* (1953). Later revues in this style were *Pieces of Eight* (1959) and *One Over the Eight* (1961). A more satiric and less tuneful note was struck by the successful Cambridge Footlights production *Beyond the Fringe* (1961), with Alan Bennett, Jonathan Miller (qq.v.), Peter Cook, and Dudley Moore, which influenced such productions as *The Royal Commission Revue* (1964) at the Mermaid and had widespread repercussions both in London and New York. An offshoot of the earlier form of revue, involving a certain amount of nudity, was 'continuous revue' or 'non-stop variety' (see WINDMILL THEATRE). Somewhat apart from, but allied to, the general run of revue was the successful partnership of Michael Flanders and Donald Swann (qq.v.) in *At the Drop of a Hat* (1956). London had the opportunity of seeing recent revues from overseas with *Clap Hands* (1960) and *Les Feux-Follets* (1965) from Canada and *Wait a Minim!* (1964) from South Africa.

REYNOLDS, FREDERICK (1764–1841), English dramatist, author of over two hundred plays of which the most notorious was *The Caravan; or, the Driver and his Dog*. This saved Drury Lane from disaster when it was first produced in 1803, mainly because of the appearance on the stage of a real dog, Carlos, who dived into a tank of water to save a child from drowning. Most of Reynolds's plays were light comedies like *How to Grow Rich* (1793), melodramas, or adaptations of Shakespeare's plays as light operas. In 1827 he published a volume of reminiscences, containing many sidelights on the contemporary stage, entitled *The Life and Times of Frederick Reynolds, Written by Himself*.

REYNOLDS, LYDIA, see LENO, DAN.

REYNOLDS, ROBERT (*fl.* 1610–40), English actor, who was with Queen Anne's Men (q.v.) but in 1616 went to Germany, where he was one of the popular English Comedians (q.v.) under Robert Browne and John Green, succeeding the latter as leader of the company. As a clown, Pickelhering, he made an enviable reputation on the Continent, where records of his appearances are found up to 1640.

RHODES, JOHN (*c.* 1606–?), a London bookseller, said by Downes in *Roscius Anglicanus* to have been connected before the Commonwealth with Blackfriars Theatre (q.v.), probably as wardrobe-keeper or prompter. At the Restoration he obtained a licence to reopen the Cockpit (q.v.)—of which he had become Keeper in 1644—with a small company of players, among whom was his young apprentice Thomas Betterton (q.v.). His licence was rendered null by the patents granted to Killigrew and Davenant (qq.v.), and his actors were taken over by them, Betterton becoming leading man in Davenant's company and later the leading actor of his day. There was also a John Rhodes, presumably a different man, who was part-owner of the Fortune Playhouse in 1637.

RICCOBONI, LUIGI (*c.* 1675–1753), Italian actor of the *commedia dell'arte* (q.v.), son of the ANTONIO (*fl.* 1675–95) who played Pantalone (see PANTALOON) in London when the Italian actors paid a visit there in 1679. Luigi, who was known as Lelio, was entrusted with the task of selecting and directing the Italian company which returned to Paris in 1716, after an absence of nineteen years (see COMÉDIE-ITALIENNE). He was also the author of several books on the theatre which add materially to our knowledge of the *commedia dell'arte*. One was translated into English in 1741 as *An Historical and Critical Account of the Theatres in Europe*.

RICE [really REIZENSTEIN], ELMER LEOPOLD (1892–1967), American dramatist, whose first play, the melodramatic *On Trial* (1914), was the first American stage production to employ the flashback technique of the screen. His first major contribution to the theatre, however, was the expressionist fantasy, *The Adding Machine* (1923), which satirized the growing regimentation of man in th; machine age through the life and death of the arid book-keeper, Mr. Zero. Rice's next play, *Street Scene* (1929), later the subject of an opera by Kurt Weill, won the Pulitzer Prize for its realistic chronicle of life in the slums. *The Left Bank* (1931) described expatriation from America as an ineffectual escape from materialism, and *Counsellor-at-Law* (also 1931) drew a realistic picture of the legal profession for which Rice had been trained. The depression of the 1930s inspired *We, the People* (1933), the Reichstag trial was paralleled in *Judgment Day* (1934), and conflicting American and Soviet ideologies formed the subject of the conversation-piece *Between Two Worlds* (also 1934). When these plays failed their author retired from the theatre, but returned to Broadway in 1937 to write and direct for the Playwrights' Producing Company, which he helped to establish. Of his later plays, the most successful was the fantasy *Dream Girl* (1945), in which an over-imaginative girl encounters unexpected romance in reality. Rice's last play was *Cue for Passion* (1958), a modern psychoanalytical variation on the Hamlet theme in which Diana Wynyard (q.v.) played the Gertrude-like character, Grace Nicholson. Rice was the author of a controversial book on American drama, *The Living Theatre* (1960), and of an autobiography, *Minority Report* (1964).

RICE, JOHN (*c.* 1596–?), an Elizabethan actor who was apprenticed as a boy to Heminge (q.v.). In 1607 he recited before James I and in 1610 appeared as a nymph in a water-pageant. As an adult actor he joined the King's Men (see CHAMBERLAIN'S MEN) in 1619, probably in succession to Nathan Field (q.v.). He is in the actor-list of Shakespeare's plays, and played the Marquis of Pescara in the first production of Webster's *The Duchess of Malfi* (1614). He is presumed to have left the theatre to take Holy Orders, since Heminge, in his will of 1630, leaves 20s. to 'John Rice, Clerk, of St. Saviour's of Southwark'.

RICE, THOMAS DARTMOUTH (1808–60), an American vaudeville performer and Negro impersonator, known as Jim Crow from the refrain of his most famous song-and-dance act, which he first performed in 1828 in Kentucky. It caught the public fancy, was published in several editions, and performed all over the United States. In 1833 Rice visited Washington and there had as partner in his act the four-year-old Joseph Jefferson (q.v.), later one of America's most famous actors. Dressed as a miniature Jim Crow, with a ragged nondescript costume and a white hat, his face blacked with burnt cork, he was tumbled out of a sack at the conclusion of Rice's turn and performed the song and dance himself. In 1836 Rice appeared at the Surrey Theatre, London, and started the enormous vogue of the minstrel show (q.v.) in England. In spite of this, and of the burlesques into which he introduced old Negro songs and which formed the basis of the later minstrel show (q.v.), he never himself became part of a troupe, preferring to work alone. An eccentric man, who died in poverty, he married an Englishwoman in 1837, but she and their children predeceased him.

RICH, CHRISTOPHER (?–1714), a lawyer who in 1689 bought a share in the Drury Lane patent and by 1693 had got complete control of the theatre. He soon became known as a tyrant, a twister, and a mean man, and under his management the company went from bad to worse. Salaries were cut, expenses pared to the minimum, and he was constantly involved in lawsuits. In the end Betterton (q.v.), with some of the abler actors, broke away and formed his own company, leaving Rich to carry on with a mediocre group of players. He was finally forced out, and took over the deserted theatre in Lincoln's Inn Fields (q.v.) with the idea of refurbishing it. He died before it was ready to open, leaving it to his son John (q.v.).

RICH, JOHN (*c.* 1692–1761), English actor and theatre manager, who inherited the old theatre in Lincoln's Inn Fields from his father Christopher (q.v.), and was responsible for the production there in 1728 of Gay's *The Beggar's Opera*. With the proceeds he built the first Covent Garden Theatre (q.v.) under the patent granted by Charles II to William Davenant (q.v.), which is still in force, opening it in 1732 with a company headed by James Quin (q.v.). Though almost illiterate, John was an excellent actor in dumb-show and, developing the ideas of Weaver (q.v.), he popularized in England the Continental form of pantomime, playing Harlequin himself under the name of Lun. He produced a pantomime annually from 1717 to 1760, his own masterpiece in acting being 'Harlequin Hatched from an Egg by the Sun', which he performed in *Harlequin Sorcerer* at Tottenham Court Fair in 1741.

RICHARDSON, Sir Ralph David (1902–83), English actor, knighted in 1947 for his services to the stage. He made his first appearance in Brighton in 1921 as Lorenzo in *The Merchant of Venice*, was with the Birmingham repertory company in 1926, and later appeared in London in several plays by Priestley (q.v.), giving an exceptionally fine performance in *Johnson over Jordan* (1939). He first played at the Old Vic, where his reputation was chiefly made, in the season of 1930, and on the reopening of Sadler's Wells a year later played Sir Toby Belch in the initial production of *Twelfth Night*. During further seasons with the Old Vic he played a wide variety of parts, ranging from Petruchio in *The Taming of the Shrew* to Bottom in *A Midsummer Night's Dream*, and also appeared several times at the Malvern Festival (q.v.). After some years with the Fleet Air Arm during the Second World War, he rejoined the Old Vic company, being much admired as Ibsen's Peer Gynt and as Falstaff in *Henry IV*. In 1952 he played Macbeth, Prospero in *The Tempest*, and the title-role in Jonson's *Volpone* at Stratford-upon-Avon, and returned to the Old Vic in 1956 to give a fine performance as Timon in Shakespeare's *Timon of Athens*. Although so much of his time was spent in playing Shakespearean and other classical parts, he also appeared with success in many modern plays, apart from J.B. Priestley's. These include Barré Lyndon's *The Amazing Dr. Clitterhouse* (1936), *The Heiress* (1949), based on Henry James's *Washington Square*, Bolt's *Flowering Cherry* (1957), Graham Greene's *The Complaisant Lover* (1959), and *Carving a Statue* (1964), also by Greene. In 1970 he

appeared successfully with John Gielgud in David Storey's *Home*, both in London and New York.

RICHARDSON, Tony [really Cecil Antonio] (1928–), English stage director, who in 1955 joined the company at the Royal Court (q.v.) where, among a number of other new plays, he was responsible for the production of John Osborne's *Look Back In Anger* (1956) and *The Entertainer* (1957), both of which he subsequently directed in New York. Among other outstanding productions for the Royal Court were Ionesco's *The Chairs* and *The Lesson* in a double bill in 1958; Feydeau's *Look After Lulu* in 1959; and Osborne's *Luther* in 1961, which he also directed in New York in 1963, being subsequently responsible for the Broadway productions of Brecht's *Arturo Ui* (1963) and Tennessee Williams's *The Milk Train Doesn't Stop Here Anymore* (1964). Back in London later in 1964 he staged the first production in English of Brecht's *Saint Joan of the Stockyards*. His Shakespeare productions include, at Stratford-upon-Avon, *Pericles* in 1958 and *Othello* in 1959, and at the Royal Court *A Midsummer Night's Dream* in 1962. In 1964 he was associated with the founding of Prospect Productions, which came into prominence with linked productions of Shakespeare's *Richard II* and Marlowe's *Edward II*, both leading roles being played by the same actor, Ian McKellen.

RICHELIEU, Armand-Jean du Plessis de, Cardinal (1585–1642), a famous statesman, and for many years the virtual ruler of France. He did a great deal for the theatre and by his patronage of Montdory (q.v.) helped to establish a permanent professional theatre in Paris and to raise the status of the actor. He also wrote a number of plays in collaboration with a committee of five—Corneille, Rotrou, Boisrobert, Colletet, and Claude de l'Étoile. They were not very successful, and Corneille (q.v.) resigned after a disagreement over his share of the plot. Richelieu built a very well-equipped theatre in his palace, which later, as the Palais-Royal, became famous under Molière (q.v.). It opened on 14 Jan. 1641 in the presence of the King and Queen and a brilliant audience with a production of *Mirame*, attributed to Desmarets but partly the work of Richelieu himself. The new machinery and splendid settings, which heralded the later vogue for such accessories in opera, were received with admiration and applause, but the play had nothing like the ovation given to works by Corneille and other authors in the less splendidly equipped public theatres, and is now forgotten.

RICHEPIN, JEAN (1849–1926), French poet and dramatist, a brilliant but un-disciplined man who was for a short time an actor. He is perhaps best known for his novels and poetry, and like them his plays, of which the first was *L'Étoile* (1873), are somewhat marred by an insistent morbid-ity. They represent, nevertheless, an important part of his work, and include *Nana Sahib* (1883), *Monsieur Scapin* (1886), *Le Flibustier* (1888), *Par le glaive* (1892), *Le Chien de garde* (1898), and *Don Quichotte* (1905). They were mostly given at the Comédie-Française, though *Le Chemineau* (1897), having been accepted there subject to correction, was taken by the author to the Odéon and had an immense success.

Richmond Hill Theatre, NEW YORK. This opened on 14 Nov. 1831 with Holcroft's *The Road to Ruin*. It had a good company, led by Mrs. Duff (q.v.), who played there for two seasons, mainly in revivals. The theatre had the temerity to stage Sheridan Knowles's *The Hunchback* on the same night—18 June 1832—as the famous Park Theatre (q.v.), but was forced to close owing to an outbreak of plague which killed one of the company, an actor named Woodhill. When the theatre reopened it housed a season of Italian opera under the sponsorship of LORENZO DA PONTE (1749–1838), Mozart's librettist and Professor of Italian at Columbia University, and was later managed by Mrs. Hamblin, the famous actor James E. Murdoch (q.v.) making his first appearance in New York there. Later known as the Tivoli Gardens, it reverted to its original name, housing circus and variety shows from 1845 to 1848, and then disappeared from the records.

Richmond Theatre. (1) SURREY. The first theatre, on Richmond Hill, opened in June 1730 and closed in Oct. 1769. It was finally demolished about 1826. Practically nothing is known about it. A second theatre, the King's, on the Green, opened on 15 June 1765 and was pulled down in 1880. In 1831 it was taken over by Edmund Kean, together with the house next door, in which he died two years later. The present Richmond Theatre, also on the Green, was built in 1899 and has had a steady though not spectacular career, being used mainly for revivals and try-outs of new plays, many of which have subsequently found their way to the West End.

(2) YORKSHIRE. This is one of the only four surviving eighteenth-century play-houses in England (the others are in Bristol, Bury St. Edmunds, and Margate). It is small, with a rectangular auditorium, and is unique in having preserved its original proscenium. Built by SAMUEL BUTLER (?–1812), whose wife, FRANCES JEFFERSON, was a half-sister of the first Joseph Jefferson (q.v.), it opened in 1788 and formed part of the Richmond circuit, which included Harrogate, Beverley, Northallerton, Whitby, Kendal, and Ulverston. After Butler's death his widow ran it until 1821, when her son, SAMUEL S. W. BUTLER (1787–1845), took over. The circuit then began to break up and the Butlers' connection with the theatre ended in 1830. For a few years it was rented to visiting managers for short seasons, and in 1848 was converted into a wine cellar and auction room, the sunk pit being boarded over. In 1943 the un-restored building was used for a perform-ance in commemoration of the 850th anniversary of the enfranchisement of the borough. A Trust was formed in 1960 to restore and redecorate it, which was done at a cost of £17,000, and in 1962 it was reopened as a theatre. It is used occasion-ally for performances.

Ring, a large octagonal structure, origin-ally a chapel, which stood in Blackfriars Road, London, about 500 yards from Blackfriars Bridge. Built in 1783, it later became a well-known boxing ring, and sprang into temporary theatrical fame when Robert Atkins (q.v.) used it for some of the earliest theatre-in-the-round productions in England, producing there on 29 Nov. 1936 *Henry V* with Hubert Gregg as the King, on 17 Jan. 1937 *Much Ado About Nothing* with Jack Hawkins as Benedick, and on 14 March 1937 *The Merry Wives of Windsor* with Roy Byford as Falstaff and Irene and Violet Vanbrugh as Mistress Page and Mistress Ford. It then sank back into obscurity and was demolished some time after the Second World War. It has sometimes been con-fused with the Rotunda (q.v.), an occasional theatre and music-hall which stood near by on the corner of Stamford Street.

Rise-and-Sink, see TRANSFORMATION SCENE.

RISTORI, ADELAIDE (1822–1906), Italian actress, celebrated far beyond the confines of her native country, particularly as a player of tragic parts. The daughter of actors, she was on the stage as a child and at fourteen gave a successful interpretation of the part of Francesca da Rimini in Silvio Pellico's version of the story of Paolo and Francesca. At eighteen she played for the first time a part with which she was afterwards mainly associated—Maria Stuart in Schiller's tragedy. She retired from the stage for a short time on marriage, but returned and in 1855 went to Paris, where she soon became a serious rival to Rachel (q.v.). From Paris she went to England, Spain, and the United States, where she first appeared in 1866, touring the country with great success. In 1882 she was seen in London as Lady Macbeth and was much praised by the critics. She retired in 1885, and three years later published her memoirs, which provide an interesting account of her life and a penetrating study of her approach to her art.

Ritterdrama, an offshoot of the *Sturm und Drang* (q.v.) drama, which followed Goethe's *Götz von Berlichingen* (1773) and Klinger's *Otto* (1774). It might perhaps be translated as 'feudal' drama. In it the valour of medieval knights was shown amidst battle scenes, jousting, and pageantry, often with a marked vein of Bavarian local patriotism. Among the authors of such plays were JOSEF AUGUST VON TÖRRING (1753–1826) with *Kasper der Thorringer* (publ. 1785) and *Agnes Bernauerin* (1780), and JOSEPH MARIUS BABO (1756–1822), for some time director of the Court theatre in Munich, with *Otto von Wittelsbach* (1782). Like the *Sturm und Drang* drama, the *Ritterdrama* is written in prose, is irregular in form, and has as its theme strong passions and a contempt for convention; it did much to foster the taste for romantic and medieval settings kindled by *Götz von Berlichingen*. Reactionary influences caused the *Ritterdrama* to be banned from the Munich stage but its vogue continued elsewhere, notably in Austria, where KARL FRIEDRICH HENSLER (1761–1825) fused this type of drama with the native operatic fairytale in such plays as *Das Donauweibchen* (1797).

Ritz Theatre, NEW YORK, on 48th Street west of Broadway. This opened on 21 Mar. 1921 with Drinkwater's *Mary Stuart*, which failed, as did his *Robert E. Lee* in 1923. In 1924 came successful productions of Sutton Vane's *Outward Bound* and Galsworthy's *Old English*, with George Arliss as Sylvanus Heythorp, and in the following year Ashley Dukes's *The Man with a Load of Mischief*, with Ruth Chatterton and Robert Loraine, had a short run. A series of failures was broken in 1927 by the 27-week run of John McGowan's *Excess Baggage*, a comedy on the heartbreaks of vaudeville, while in the autumn of 1932 Ruth Draper gave a three-week season of monologues. In 1937 the theatre was taken over by the Federal Theatre Project (q.v.), which presented there Arthur Arent's Living Newspaper *Power* for over a hundred performances. A year later T. S. Eliot's *Murder in the Cathedral* had a short run, and after a Federal Theatre production of Collodi's *Pinocchio* in 1939 the theatre became a cinema. It is now used for radio and television shows.

ROBERTS, ARTHUR (1852–1933), English actor and early music-hall comedian, who in 1873 made a great success at the Middlesex (q.v.) singing 'If I Was Only Long Enough, a Soldier I Would Be'. He made his first appearance in pantomime in 1880, playing Dr. Syntax in *Mother Goose* at Drury Lane, and finally deserted the halls for the regular stage in 1883. In 1892 he played Captain Coddington in the musical farce, *In Town,* at the Prince of Wales', and afterwards specialized in the representation of immaculate guardsmen and men-about-town until 1903, when he returned to the halls in a series of short sketches. In 1924 he celebrated his stage jubilee, somewhat belatedly, with a matinée at the Alhambra, and later toured the provinces in 'The Veterans of Variety'. He was the author of a volume of reminiscences, *Fifty Years of Spoof,* published in 1927.

ROBERTSON, AGNES KELLY (1833–1916), a well-known actress, born in Scotland, where she appeared as a child, making her adult début in London in 1850 with Charles Kean (q.v.). Three years later she married the elder Dion Boucicault (q.v.) and went with him to America, playing the heroines in most of his plays. She was particularly admired in the title-role of his *Jessie Brown; or, the Relief of Lucknow* (1862) and as Jeanie Deans in *The Trial of Effie Deans* (1863), based on Scott's novel, *The Heart of Midlothian*. In 1888 her husband, anxious to marry a young actress, repudiated her, saying she was not legally married to him but only his common-law wife. Much sympathy was felt for her and for her four children, Dion junior, Nina (qq.v.), AUBREY (1869–1913), and Eva, who were thus rendered illegitimate. They were all on the stage, Eva retiring on her marriage to an actor, JOHN ALFRED CLAYTON [really CALTHROP] (1842–88), her sons and grandsons also being on the stage. Agnes herself continued to act under her married name, making her last appearance in London in 1896 as Mrs. Cregan in a revival of the elder Boucicault's *The Colleen Bawn*.

ROBERTSON, THOMAS WILLIAM (1829–71), English dramatist, eldest of the twenty-two children of an actor. Several of his brothers and sisters were on the stage, the most famous being the youngest girl, Madge (see KENDAL). Robertson himself acted as a child, and as an adult actor went to Lincoln, where the Robertson family had for many years been in control of the theatres on the Lincoln circuit. Here he made himself generally useful, painting scenery, writing songs and plays, and acting small parts. He was in fact trained in the old school which he was later to destroy, a process which can be studied, with reservations, in Pinero's *Trelawny of the 'Wells'* (1898). Of his early plays, written in the conventions of the time, the most successful was *David Garrick* (1864), based on a French play and written for E. A. Sothern (q.v.). The printed copy of this, with its elaborate directions for realistic scenery and costume, and its wealth of stage directions, is a definite pointer in the direction which Robertson was to take almost immediately with such plays as *Society* (1865), *Ours* (1866), *Caste* (1867), *Play* (1868), and *School* (1869), whose short titles came as a refreshing change after the polysyllabic nomenclature of earlier and even some contemporary works. They were all produced at the Prince of Wales' Theatre (see SCALA), where the success of *Society*

established the reputation not only of the author but of the Bancrofts (q.v.), and inaugurated what has been called 'the cup-and-saucer drama'—that is, the drama of the realistic, contemporary, domestic interior. The rooms were recognizable, the dialogue credible, the plots, though they now seem somewhat artificial, were true to the time and an immense advance on anything that had gone before. *Caste* in particular still holds the stage, and some of the others would revive well. Robertson produced his own plays and has sometimes been considered the first modern director. Years of hard work and continual rebuffs had embittered him, but with the coming of success his naturally sweet temper reasserted itself and he was able to enjoy a few years of fame before his tragically early death at the height of his career. His early efforts at realism made a deep impression on the theatre of his own day and influenced many of the dramatists who succeeded him.

ROBESON, PAUL BUSTILL (1898–1976), American Negro actor and singer, who made his first appearance on the stage in 1921. He created a sensation in 1924 when he appeared for the Provincetown Players in O'Neill's *The Emperor Jones*, playing Brutus Jones, the part in which he made his London début in 1925. He also played it in Germany in 1930. His singing of 'Ole Man River' in the London production of the musical, *Show Boat*, first revealed the haunting quality of his superb bass voice, and led him to devote much of his time to touring in recital programmes of Negro spirituals. In 1930 he was seen in London in *Othello*, which, when produced in New York in 1943, achieved the longest run to date of a Shakespeare play on Broadway. He also played the part at Stratford-upon-Avon in 1959. Among his other outstanding roles were Jim Harris in *All God's Chillun Got Wings* (1924) and 'Yank' in *The Hairy Ape* (1931), both by O'Neill. During his active career he did excellent work in furthering the interests of the Negro people, and was one of the best-known artists of his time, being highly gifted, sincere, and courageous. A biography, by his wife, was published in 1930. In 1958 he himself published *Here I Stand*, a plain statement of his beliefs which caused controversy in the United States and elsewhere, as did his visit to Russia as an avowed Communist in 1963.

ROBEY [really WADE], SIR GEORGE EDWARD (1869–1954), a popular comedian of the English music-halls, nicknamed 'the Prime Minister of Mirth'. He made his first appearance at the Oxford (q.v.) in 1891, and was then engaged for most of the leading halls of London and the provinces. Apart from popular songs, he was very successful in a series of humorous sketches, and in 1916 he appeared for the first time in revue as Lucius Bing in *The Bing Boys Are Here*, following it in 1918 with *The Bing Boys on Broadway*. Other parts which displayed his versatility were Dame Trot in *Jack and the Beanstalk* (1921), Menelaus in a new English version of Offenbach's 'La Belle Hélène' (1932), and Falstaff in *Henry IV, Part 1* (1935). He was for some years manager of the Prince's Theatre (see SHAFTESBURY THEATRE (2)), where he put on his own revue, *Bits and Pieces* (1927). His humour was robust, and he appeared to consist largely of a bowler hat and two enormous eyebrows. He was an excellent painter, a writer, a violin-maker, a cricketer, and a student of Egyptology. He was knighted shortly before his death for his services to the theatre and to charity.

Robin Hood, a legendary English hero whose name first appears in Langland's narrative poem, *Piers Plowman* (1377). He typifies the outlaw from oppression who champions the poor against the rich. Though his story may have some basis in fact, it is impossible to identify him with any historical personage, though an Elizabethan playwright, Anthony Munday (q.v.), made him the exiled Earl of Huntingdon. Since he is always dressed in green, he may be a survival of the Woodman, or Jack-in-the-Green, of the early pagan spring festivities, or he may have been imported by minstrels (q.v.) from France. By the end of the fifteenth century he and his familiar retinue of Maid Marian, Little John, Friar Tuck, and the Merry Men, with their accompanying Morris Dance, were inseparable from the village May Day revels and appeared in a number of plays which were not, however, like the Mumming and Plough Monday plays (qq.v.), true folk-plays, since they were specially written by minstrels. The May Day festivities found their way to Court, where they became mixed up with allegory and pseudo-classicism. Henry VIII in particular enjoyed many splendid Mayings, including one in which he was entertained by Robin Hood to venison in a bower. After that their popularity waned and they were finally suppressed by the Puritans. The story of Robin Hood and his Merry Men later became a favourite subject for pantomime (q.v.).

ROBINS, ELIZABETH (1862–1952), American actress, who passed the greater part of her professional life in London, where she first appeared in 1889, and was prominently identified with the introduction of Ibsen (q.v.) to the London stage, playing leading roles in the first productions of *Pillars of Society* (1889), *A Doll's House* and *Hedda Gabler* (both 1891). Two years later she appeared in *The Master Builder*, *Rosmersholm*, and *Brand*. *Little Eyolf* followed in 1896 and *John Gabriel Borkman* in 1897. She was seen also in a wide variety of other parts, notably as Mariana in Echegaray's play of that name in 1897. She then retired, apart from a brief return to the stage as Lucrezia in Stephen Phillips's *Paolo and Francesca* (1902), and devoted herself to literature, publishing a number of novels and two volumes of theatrical reminiscences.

ROBINSON, (ESMÉ STUART) LENNOX (1886–1958), Irish actor, playwright, director, and dramatic critic, whose first play, *The Clancy Name* (1908), was produced at the Dublin Abbey Theatre (q.v.), with which he remained connected until his death. It was followed by a number of poetical tragedies—*The Cross Roads* (1909), *Harvest* (1910), and *Patriots* (1912) —but it was with a comedy, *The White-Headed Boy* (1916), that he first achieved popularity outside Ireland. Later successful comedies, most of which were seen in London and New York, were *Crabbed Youth and Age* (1922), *The Far-Off Hills* (1928), *All's Over Then?* (1932), *Is Life Worth Living?* (1933)—also known as *Drama at Inish—Church Street* (1934), and *Killycreggs in Twilight* (1937). In 1939 Robinson edited *The Irish Theatre*, a collection of lectures delivered at the Abbey, and he was also the author of two volumes of reminiscences, *Curtain Up* (1941) and *A History of the Abbey Theatre* (1952).

ROBINSON, 'PERDITA' [*née* MARY DARBY] (1758–1800), English actress, who, after a short career on the stage, became the mistress of the Prince Regent, making her last appearance on 31 May 1780 as

Eliza in Lady Craven's *The Miniature Picture*. Her finest part was Perdita in *The Winter's Tale*, which she first played on 20 Nov. 1779 at Drury Lane, and it is by that name that she is best known. She was coached for her first appearance, as Juliet, by Garrick (q.v.), and appeared in the part on 10 Dec. 1776, her success already assured by her reputation for beauty and profligacy. After her short-lived affair with the Regent she would probably have returned to the theatre; but an attack of rheumatic fever left her, at twenty-four, too crippled to do so. She spent the rest of her life wandering from one spa to another and supporting herself by writing poems and novels, now forgotten.

ROBINSON, RICHARD (?-1648), English actor, who appears in the actor-list of Shakespeare's plays. He was probably a boy-actor at the Blackfriars (q.v.), and was certainly one of the King's Men (see CHAMBERLAIN'S MEN) from 1611 onwards. As a young lad he played women's parts, in which he was much admired by Ben Jonson (q.v.). He may have been apprenticed to Burbage, as he witnessed his will, and may have married his widow. He signed the dedication of the Beaumont and Fletcher folio in 1647.

ROBSON, DAME FLORA (1902–84), English actress, who made her first appearance on the stage in Clemence Dane's *Will Shakespeare* (1921), and after working with Benson and Fagan (qq.v.) reappeared in London in 1931, being particularly admired as Abbie Putnam in O'Neill's *Desire Under the Elms* and Mary Paterson in Bridie's *The Anatomist*. In 1933 she joined the Old Vic company, playing a wide variety of parts and showing a talent for high comedy as Gwendolen Fairfax in Wilde's *The Importance of Being Earnest* and Mrs. Foresight in Congreve's *Love for Love* which she was not subsequently given much opportunity to display, except in 1948, when she played Lady Cicely Waynflete in Shaw's *Captain Brassbound's Conversion*. On the whole, apart from an excellent Paulina in *The Winter's Tale* in 1951, her reputation has been made in parts requiring a high degree of controlled nervous tension in such modern plays as James Parish's *Message for Margaret* (1946), Lesley Storm's *Black Chiffon* (1949), *The Innocents* (1952), based on Henry James's *The*

Turn of the Screw, Hugh Mills's *The House by the Lake* (1956), and Michael Redgrave's adaptation of James's *The Aspern Papers* (1959). In 1962 a repertory theatre named after her opened in Newcastle-on-Tyne, and she appeared there as Miss Moffat in a revival of Emlyn Williams's *The Corn is Green*. She was created D.B.E. in 1960 for services to the theatre.

ROBSON, FREDERICK [really THOMAS ROBSON BROWNHILL] (1821–64), English actor, who made his first appearance in London in 1844 at the Grecian (q.v.), and became famous as a singer of popular ballads. After a visit to Dublin in 1850 he returned to London to become one of the mainstays of burlesque at the Olympic (q.v.), of which he later became joint manager. He was very short and ugly, and a heavy drinker, but an actor of great power, and was affectionately known as 'the great little Robson'. Among his most popular parts were Jacob Earwig in Selby's farce, *Boots at the Swan* (1842), Jim Baggs in a revival of Mayhew's farce *The Wandering Minstrel* (1853), Daddy Hardacre in Palgrave Simpson's play of that name (1857), and Sampson Burr in John Oxenford's drama *The Porter's Knot* (1858).

ROBSON, STUART [really HENRY ROBSON STUART] (1836–1903), American comedian, who first appeared on the stage as a boy of sixteen, and after ten years with leading stock companies joined the company of Laura Keene (q.v.) as principal comedian. He also spent some years with Mrs. John Drew (q.v.) at the Arch Street Theatre in Philadelphia and with Warren (q.v.) in Boston. In 1873 he was seen in London, and shortly afterwards he began a long association with W. H. Crane (q.v.), playing with him in light farce, in *The Henrietta*, which was specially written for them by Bronson Howard (q.v.), and as one of the two Dromios in *The Comedy of Errors*; he was also Falstaff to Crane's Slender in *The Merry Wives of Windsor*. In 1889 the two parted amicably, and Robson appeared in several new plays, dying suddenly while on tour shortly after celebrating his stage jubilee.

Rod-Puppet, see PUPPET.

ROGERS, WILL [really WILLIAM PENN ADAIR] (1879–1935), American comedian, who had Red Indian blood in him and spent his youth on the range, later, after a good though erratic education, becoming a cowboy. In 1902 he joined a Wild West circus in the Argentine, being billed as the Cherokee Kid. After a tour in Australia he returned to the States to appear at the St. Louis Exhibition, and in 1905 made his first appearance in New York, where he soon became very popular, joking informally with his audience. He appeared in musical comedy for the first time in 1912 and rapidly became a star on Broadway, reaching the height of success when he appeared in several editions of the *Ziegfeld Follies*. His personality was more important than his material, and his wisecracks were quoted everywhere. In the 1920s the stage lost him to Hollywood, and he also became a newspaper correspondent, a lecturer, and a radio commentator. He was killed on a flight with the aviator Wiley Post.

ROJAS ZORRILLA, FRANCISCO DE (1607–48), Spanish dramatist, author of many plays, of which the best-known is *Del rey abajo, ninguno* (otherwise known as *García del Castañar* or *El labrador más honrado*). In common with many other Golden Age dramatists, Rojas utilizes in this play three main themes: personal honour, the contrast between the peaceful countryside and the vicious Court life, and the relationships between the social classes. Rojas's comedies, in which the clown, or *gracioso* (q.v.), is often the chief personage, are distinguished by wit and neatness of versification. A typical example is *Entre bobos anda el juego*. Rojas was also the author of a number of *autos sacramentales* (q.v.).

Roll-out, see TRAP.

ROMAINS, JULES [really LOUIS-HENRI-JEAN FARIGOULE] (1885–1972), French poet and novelist, and an outstanding dramatist. His first play, *L'Armée dans la ville*, was produced by Antoine in 1911, but it was not until after the First World War that Romains began his close association with the theatre through his friendship with Cocteau and Copeau (qq.v.). He worked for a time at the Vieux-Colombier, where his *Cromedeyre-le-Vieil* was produced in 1920. But it was Jouvet (q.v.) who produced and played in his three successful farces, *M. le Trouhadec saisi par la débauche*, *Knock, ou le Triomphe de la*

Médecine (both 1923), and *Le Mariage de M. le Trouhadec* (1925). The second of these, a satire on the medical profession and the credulity of human beings, is probably Romains's best-known play. As *Dr. Knock*, it was translated by Granville-Barker and successfully produced in London in 1926 and in New York in 1928. Romains's later works include an excellent translation of Ben Jonson's *Volpone* (1928), and *Donogoo* (1931), which was successfully revived at the Comédie-Française in 1951, as was *M. le Trouhadec saisi par la débauche* in 1956. In 1955 Barrault revived *Volpone* at the Marigny, playing Mosca to Ledoux's Volpone.

ROMANI, FELICE (1788–1865), Italian poet, an author of great charm and distinction who wrote some excellent libretti for Italian operas. Two of these are from Shakespeare, whom he probably knew only through the French adaptations of Ducis—*Hamlet* for Mercadante (1822), and *Romeo and Juliet*, which was set by Vaccai in 1825 and by Bellini in 1830. Perhaps his best, and certainly his best-known, work was done for Bellini's 'La Sonnambula' (1831).

ROMASHOV, BORIS SERGEIVICH (1895–1958), Soviet dramatist, whose first play, *Meringue Pie* (1925), was a satire on bourgeois elements in Soviet society. Among his later plays, which dealt mainly with episodes of the Civil War, were *The End of Krivorilsky* (1927), *The Fiery Bridge* (1929), and *Fighters* (1934). This last, which is perhaps his most important work, dealt with the Red Army in peacetime, and the clash between private and public interests among the officers. In 1942 a play dealing with the defence of Moscow, *Shine, Stars!*, was put on at the Sverdlovsk Theatre less than a year after the events it deals with took place. Its theme was the courage of a young student galvanized by war into a man of action, and it proved immensely popular. In 1947 *A Great Force*, which depicted the conflict between conservative and progressive scientists, was seen at the Maly Theatre.

RONDIRIS, DIMITRIOS (1899–1981), Greek theatre director, who was for many years head of the Greek National Theatre. He made his first appearance on the stage in 1919, playing Florizel in *The Winter's Tale*, and during the next ten years was seen in a number of Greek theatres. He then went to Vienna, where for three years he studied the history of art and attended the Max Reinhardt seminar. On his return to Athens he was appointed a director at the National Theatre, and in 1936 staged the first Festival of Greek Tragedy, for which he directed Sophocles' *Electra* in the theatre of Herodus Atticus in Athens. This has now become an annual event, as have the productions of Greek plays at Epidaurus, which he also organized. In 1939 he directed a production of *Hamlet* which was seen in London, with Alexis Minotis (q.v.) in the title-role. He became director-general of the National Theatre in 1946, several of his subsequent productions of classical tragedies having been seen in New York, notably Sophocles' *Electra* in 1952, with Katina Paxinou (q.v.). In 1957 he founded the Piraikon Theatre in Athens, where for some years until his retirement he continued his work on the modern staging of classical tragedy, taking his company, which has now been disbanded, on tour as far afield as Russia and Israel.

ROOKE, IRENE (1878–1958), English actress, who after an orthodox career which began with Shakespeare—she played Ophelia to the Hamlet of Gordon Craig (q.v.) in 1897—and Barrie, whose Fanny Willoughby in *Quality Street* she created in 1902, became identified with the 'new movement' in English drama when she appeared as Mrs. Jones, the charwoman, in Galsworthy's *The Silver Box* (1906). She subsequently played leading parts in six of his plays—*Strife* (1909), *The Eldest Son* (1912), *The Fugitive* (1913), *The Mob* (1914), *Windows* (1922), and *Old English* (1924). She also appeared in several plays by Shaw (q.v.), and was a member of the repertory company founded in Manchester by Miss Horniman (q.v.). One of her best parts was Cromwell's mother in John Drinkwater's *Oliver Cromwell* (1923).

Rope House, a theatre which followed the traditional practice of raising scenery by hand-lines from a fly-floor, as against the modern counterweight (q.v.) system; also known as a hand-worked house.

RORKE, KATE (1866–1945), English actress, a member of an old theatrical family. She made her first appearance at the Court Theatre in 1878 as one of the school-children in Wills's *Olivia*, and in 1880 went to the Criterion (q.v.), where

she remained for a considerable time, playing in a great variety of parts. In 1885 she made a great success as Lucy Preston in Grundy's *The Silver Shield* at the Strand, and for six years from 1889 was leading lady at the Garrick with Hare (q.v.). There her greatest success was as Mrs. Goldfinch in Grundy's *A Pair of Spectacles* (1890), a part which she played again in a revival in 1917—her last appearance on the stage. In 1906 she was appointed Professor of Dramatic Art at the Guildhall School of Music, and she also had for many years her own school of acting, where she trained a number of actors who afterwards became famous.

ROSCIUS, QUINTUS (?–62 B.C.), Roman comic actor, and the most famous of his day, liked and admired by Cicero, who delivered on his behalf the speech *Pro Roscio Comoedo*. Roscius's success was the result of careful study—he thought out and practised every gesture before employing it on the stage. He was awarded a gold ring, the symbol of equestrian rank, by the dictator Sulla.

(For the African Roscius, see ALD-RIDGE, IRA; for the Dublin, or Hibernian, Roscius, see BROOKE, G. V.; for the Ohio Roscius, see ALDRICH, LOUIS; for the Scottish Roscius, see JOHNSTON, H. E.; for the Young American Roscius, see COWELL, SAM; for the Young Roscius, see BETTY, WILLIAM.)

ROSE, BILLY [really WILLIAM SAMUEL ROSENBERG] (1899–   ), see NATIONAL THEATRE (2) and ZIEGFELD THEATRE.

ROSE, CLARKSON [really ARTHUR] (1890–1968), English actor and manager. He made his first appearance on the stage in 1908, and was at the Liverpool Repertory Theatre (see LIVERPOOL) from 1911 to 1915. He then came to London to play Captain Phoenix in Pinero's *Trelawny of the 'Wells'*, was with the Birmingham (q.v.) Repertory Theatre, toured with a Shakespeare company, and was in panto-mime and revue. From 1921 onwards he devoted himself to his summer revue *Twinkle*, and every Christmas played the Dame in a provincial pantomime. He was the author of two volumes of reminiscences, *With a Twinkle in My Eye* and *Beside the Seaside*, and wrote the greater part of his own revues.

Rose Theatre, LONDON. Built for Hens-lowe (q.v.), this playhouse stood in what had been a rose garden. It opened in the autumn of 1587, but it is not known what company first played there. Strange's Men (q.v.) were there with the Admiral's Men (q.v.) in 1592, but left in 1594, the Admiral's Men remaining until they went to the Fortune (q.v.) in 1600. It was at the Rose that Alleyn (q.v.) made his reputation, and Shakespeare's *Henry VI, Part 1* probably had its first production there. From Henslowe's accounts it can be inferred that the theatre was of wood and plaster on a brick foundation, partly thatched, and octagonal in shape. The lease of the building ran out in 1605 and it was pulled down the following year.

ROSENBLÜT, HANS (*fl.* fifteenth century), see MASTERSINGERS.

ROSIMOND [really CLAUDE LA ROZE] (*c.* 1640–86), a French actor who was playing at the Marais (q.v.) when he was invited to join the company at the Palais-Royal after the death of Molière (q.v.). This he did, playing as his first part Molière's role in *Le Malade imaginaire*. He was already known as a dramatist, and it may have been his double reputation that induced La Grange and his companions to look on him as a successor to Molière. If so, he proved a disappointment, as he produced only one more play and that not a very successful one. He was an educated man, something of a scholar, and he had one of the finest libraries of plays in Paris. His comedies were often revived during his lifetime but are now forgotten. His play about Don Juan was the source of Shadwell's *The Libertine* (1675).

ROSSETER, PHILIP (*c.* 1568–1623), an English lutanist and composer who with Robert Jones and other musicians was given a patent in 1610 for a children's company, to be known as the Children of the Queen's Revels. Five years later they were given permission to erect a playhouse for the Children on the site of a house owned by Jones in Blackfriars (where the Mermaid (q.v.) now stands), to be known as Porter's Hall (q.v.) or Puddle Wharf Theatre, but the civic authorities objected and it was suppressed in 1617.

ROSSI, ERNESTO FORTUNATO GIOVANNI MARIA (1827–96), Italian actor, who in 1845 made his début in Leghorn, his birthplace. He later joined the company of Gustave Modena, and in 1852 played opposite the great Italian actress, Adelaide Ristori (q.v.), with whom he went to Paris in 1855. He quickly proved himself a fine actor in tragedy, and was the first Italian to play *Othello* (1856), at the Teatro Re in Milan in the blank-verse translation by Carcano, following it with *Hamlet* in a version by Carlo Rusconi. He was also good as Lear. He travelled widely, being much admired in Paris and Germany, and died while returning from a successful season in St. Petersburg. His method of interpreting Shakespeare was not, however, acceptable in England or America. He published two volumes of theatrical memoirs (1886 and 1888) and also translated *Julius Caesar* into Italian.

ROSTAND, EDMOND EUGÈNE ALEXIS (1868–1918), French romantic dramatist, whose colourful poetic plays were written in reaction from the drab realities of the contemporary naturalistic school of drama. The first, *Les Romanesques* (1894), a light-hearted satire on the folly of young lovers, was followed by *La Princesse lointaine* (1895), based on the legendary love of Jauffé Rudel for the Princess of Tripoli, played by Sarah Bernhardt (q.v.). A biblical play, *La Samaritaine* (1897), in which Bernhardt also appeared, was less successful, but in *Cyrano de Bergerac* (1898), written for the elder Coquelin (q.v.), Rostand achieved a fusion of romantic bravura, lyric love, and theatrical craftsmanship which has made this play a perennial favourite, both in France and in America and England, where something of its quality survives even in a pedestrian translation. A later play, *L'Aiglon* (1900), in which Bernhardt played the ill-fated son of Napoleon, had less vigour but appealed by its pathetic evocation of fallen grandeur and the frank sentimentality of its theme. Rostand's last complete play was *Chantecler* (1910), which, though not as popular as his earlier works, is by some critics accounted his best, as it is certainly his most profound. The verse is masterly, and the allegory unfolds effortlessly on two planes of consciousness, the beast's and man's. A further play, *La Dernière Nuit de Don Juan*, was left unfinished and was not performed until 1921.

Rostrum, any platform, from a small dais for a throne to a high battlement, which can be placed on the stage. It is usually made with a removable top and hinged sides, to fold flat for packing. It is reached by steps or a ramp, and quitted off-stage by 'lead-off' steps.

ROSWITHA, see HROSWITHA.

ROTROU, JEAN DE (1609–50), French dramatist, and next to Corneille (q.v.) the best and most important of his day. His first plays were produced at the Hôtel de Bourgogne, where he may have succeeded Hardy (q.v.) as official dramatist to the troupe. His popularity may be gauged from the fact that he had four plays given in Paris in 1636, the year of Corneille's *Le Cid*. More than thirty of his works survive, some of them the best examples extant of the popular tragi-comedy of the time. He was much interested in Spanish literature and translated one of Lope de Vega's plays as *La Bague de l'oubli* (1629), important as being the first extant French play to be based on one from Spain, and the first French comedy, as opposed to farce. He was also the author of one of the numerous versions of the story of Amphitryon in *Les Sosies* (1637), usually considered his best play. His *Venceslas* (1647), a tragedy based on *No hay ser padre siendo rey* by Francisco de Rojas Zorilla (q.v.), was sold to pay a gambling debt, and long remained in the repertory of the French theatre, the hero Ladislas providing an excellent part for such actors as Baron, Lekain, and Talma (qq.v.). Its first interpreter was probably Montfleury (q.v.).

Rotunda, THE, a hall in Blackfriars Road, London, at the corner of Stamford Street. It has sometimes been confused with the Ring (q.v.), which was on the opposite side of the road about five hundred yards away. Variety performances were given at the Rotunda as early as 1829, and in 1833 it opened for a few years as the Globe Theatre; but its history was undistinguished. It was later used for boxing and as a music-hall, during which time the parents of Dan Leno (q.v.) appeared there as duettists and dancers. The hall was closed after an illegal cock-fight and became an ironmongery ware-house. Traces of its theatrical past were still discernible, but it was demolished in about 1945.

(See also DUBLIN.)

Roundhouse, a large mid-nineteenth-century locomotive shed at Chalk Farm, in London, later used as a warehouse. In 1964 Arnold Wesker (q.v.) took it over to house his Centre 42, an organization founded in 1962 with the intention of interesting the trades unions in the provision of culture for their members. The first of a series of provincial festivals took place at Wellingborough with performances of *Hamlet* in schools by the National Youth Theatre (q.v.) and the production of new plays by Wesker and Bernard Kops, whose *Enter Solly Gold* was later seen at the Mermaid. In spite of grants from various bodies, this left the Centre heavily in debt. Future festivals were abandoned, and in their place the Roundhouse opened as an entertainment centre, with a theatre, cinema, and art gallery, as well as administrative offices. Since the collapse of Wesker's enterprise the theatre has housed a number of temporary and highly interesting experimental ventures, among them in 1969 Kafka's *Metamorphosis* and *In the Penal Colony* and Tony Richardson's production of *Hamlet* with Nicol Williamson. In 1970 Wesker's own play, *The Friends*, was produced there, as were Tynan's revue *Oh! Calcutta!* and a rock musical version of *Othello* entitled *Catch My Soul*, first seen in New York in 1966. The Roundhouse also provided an occasional London showcase for Theatregoround, the Royal Shakespeare Company's project for schools, which was several times seen there before moving to its own theatre, the major attraction in 1970 being John Barton's adaptation of *Henry IV* and *Henry V* as *When Thou Art King*, with Brewster Mason as Falstaff and Michael Williams as Prince Hal.

ROUSSIN, ANDRÉ JEAN-PAUL-MARIE (1911–), French dramatist, author of a number of comedies, of which *La Petite Hutte* (1947) was adapted for London by Nancy Mitford as *The Little Hut* (1950), starring Robert Morley, who made his own adaptation of *Les Œufs de l'autruche* (1948) as *Hippo Dancing* (1954). Among Roussin's other plays are *Am-Stram-Gram* (1943), *Une Grande Fille toute simple* (1944), *Bobosse* (1950), *Lorsque l'enfant paraît* (1952), *Les Glorieuses* (1960), *La Coquine* (1961), based on Fabbri's *La Bugiarda*, *L'École des autres* (1962), *Un Amour qui ne finit pas* (1963), and *On ne sait jamais* (1969).

ROWE, GEORGE FAWCETT (1834–89), American actor, who made his first appearance in New York in 1866 and for many years was a popular player of young lovers, for which his fair, handsome, boyish face and elegant figure were eminently suited. In 1872 he made a great success as Digby Grant—played in London two years previously by Irving (q.v.)—in Albery's *Two Roses*. In later years he was much admired as Micawber in *Little Em'ly* (a dramatization of Dickens's *David Copperfield*), as Waifton Stray in his own play, *Brass*, and as Hawkeye in *Leatherstocking*, his own dramatization of Fenimore Cooper's *The Last of the Mohicans*. He also translated and adapted *Sphinx* (1875), by Octave Feuillet, in which Clara Morris (q.v.) gave a powerful and horrifying performance.

ROWE, NICHOLAS (1674–1718), English dramatist of the Augustan age, and one of the few to display any real dramatic power. The best of his plays are *The Fair Penitent* (1703) (based on Massinger's *The Fatal Dowry*) and *The Tragedy of Jane Shore* (1714). Both were frequently revived, Mrs. Siddons (q.v.) being particularly admired as Calista, first played by Mrs. Barry (q.v.), and Jane Shore, first played by Anne Oldfield (q.v.). Rowe, who published an edition of Shakespeare in 1709, was also the author of *Tamerlane* (1701), in which Betterton (q.v.) was outstanding, of *The Tragedy of Lady Jane Grey* (1715), and of one unsuccessful comedy. He became Poet Laureate in 1715.

ROWLEY, SAMUEL (c. 1575–1624), English actor and dramatist, who is credited with having had a hand in a number of lost plays which preceded, and possibly provided material for, some of Shakespeare's, including *The Taming of a Shrew* (c. 1589). His only extant play, a chronicle drama on the life of Henry VIII, *When You See Me, You Know Me* (1603), was performed by the Admiral's Men (q.v.), whom he joined in 1597. They also appeared in several of his lost plays. He is believed to have altered Marlowe's *Dr. Faustus* for Henslowe (q.v.), mainly by adding some comic passages for a revival in 1602.

ROWLEY, WILLIAM (c. 1585–c. 1637), English actor and dramatist, whose best work was done in collaboration with Middleton (q.v.), notably in *The Change-*

ling (1622). Of his own plays the most important is *All's Lost by Lust* (also 1622), in which he played the clown. He had previously played the fat clown, Plumporridge, in *The Inner Temple Masque* in 1619 as a foil to John Newton's thin clown, and was the fat bishop in Middleton's *A Game at Chess* (1624).

Royal Alfred Theatre, LONDON, see WEST LONDON THEATRE.

Royal Amphitheatre, LONDON, see CONNAUGHT THEATRE.

Royal Artillery Theatre, LONDON, at Woolwich. When the old Garrison Church, which in 1863 was converted into recreation rooms for the troops stationed at Woolwich, was burnt down in 1903, a new building was erected on the site together with a small theatre. This was opened by Lord Roberts on 21 Dec. 1905, and from 1909 to 1939 was under the management of Mrs. Agnes Littler who, with her husband, was injured when a bomb dropped near the theatre in May 1918. In 1940 it was taken over by the Navy, Army, and Air Force Institute (NAAFI).

Royal Brunswick Theatre, LONDON, see ROYALTY THEATRE (1).

Royal Circus, LONDON, see SURREY THEATRE.

Royal Coburg Theatre, LONDON, see OLD VIC.

Royal Court Theatre, LONDON. (1) The first theatre of this name was on the south side of Sloane Square, and opened as the New Chelsea on 16 Apr. 1870. It was a badly transformed Nonconformist chapel, and had no success at all, in spite of changing its name to the Belgravia, until Marie Litton took it over and reopened it as the Royal Court on 25 Jan. 1871, producing several plays by W. S. Gilbert (q.v.) with some success. Later actor-managers were Hare (q.v.), from 1875 to 1879, and Wilson Barrett (q.v.), under whom Modjeska (q.v.) made her first appearance in London. Before the theatre was demolished in 1887 it housed a series of successful farces by Pinero (q.v.)—*The Magistrate* (1885), *The Schoolmistress* (1886), and *Dandy Dick* (1887). It finally closed on 22 July 1887.

(2) A new theatre on the east side of the

square opened on 24 Sept. 1888 with Grundy's *Mamma!* A new farce by Pinero, *The Cabinet Minister* (1890), provided it with its first success, and on 20 Jan. 1898 came the first night of *Trelawny of the 'Wells'*, one of his best-known plays, which has frequently been revived. A later success was Martin-Harvey's production of Charles Hannon's *A Cigarette-Maker's Romance* (1901). A brilliant period began in 1904 when J. E. Vedrenne and Granville-Barker (qq.v.) took the theatre and produced there a remarkable series of plays, both new and revivals, ranging from Shakespeare to Shaw and Galsworthy. This memorable partnership continued until 1907, and its influence on the English theatre was incalculable. Granville-Barker and Vedrenne then moved to the Savoy Theatre, and Somerset Maugham's *Lady Frederick* (also 1907) filled the Royal Court to capacity. After that its fortunes suffered a decline until J. B. Fagan (q.v.) took over and directed among other things the first production in England of Shaw's *Heartbreak House* (1921), in collaboration with the author. In 1924 Barry Jackson (q.v.) brought his company from the Birmingham Repertory Theatre to the Court, opening with the five parts of Shaw's *Back to Methuselah*, followed by Eden Phillpotts's *The Farmer's Wife*, with Cedric Hardwicke (q.v.), which ran for nearly three years. In 1928 Jackson returned with productions of *Macbeth* and *The Taming of the Shrew* in modern dress. After three seasons of Shaw plays by the Macdona Players, the theatre closed in 1932 and became a cinema. It was extensively damaged by bombs in Nov. 1940 and did not reopen until 1952. Four years later the English Stage Company under George Devine (q.v.) took over with productions of new and controversial plays which included John Osborne's *Look Back in Anger* (1956) and *The Entertainer* (1957) and Arden's *Serjeant Musgrave's Dance* (1959). These had an immense influence on the general trend of English playwriting and production, and drew a predominantly young and enthusiastic audience. When Devine died in 1965 the English Stage Company was sufficiently well established to continue its successful career, producing a great many important new plays, not only by Osborne, but by such authors as Edward Bond, Charles Wood, and David Storey (qq.v.), and by the theatre's first resident dramatist, Christopher Hampton (q.v.), who was

responsible for the new version of Chekhov's *Uncle Vanya* in which Paul Scofield appeared in 1970. It also staged some revivals, and in 1969 added to its amenities a theatre-in-the-round housed in the attic of the building and known as the Theatre Upstairs. This opened in Feb. 1969 with David Cregan's *A Comedy of the Changing Years*, followed by an American play, *La Turista*, by Sam Shepard. Later productions included Peter Gill's *Over Gardens Out* and Mike Stott's *Erogenous Zones* (both 1969), two new plays by Beckett, *Come and Go* and *Cascando*, Heathcote Williams's *AC/DC* (all 1970), and a French company under Jean Rougene in twelve short plays by Ionesco. Intended for the production of frankly experimental plays and happenings, the Theatre Upstairs has also been used by *avant-garde* companies visiting London, among them the Incubus travelling theatre in *Brain* (1970) and the Portable Theatre. Meanwhile, the Royal Court Theatre itself housed in 1967 the Paper Bag Players, an American company of four founded to introduce children to play-acting, and in 1969 the Bread and Puppet Theatre, also American but intended for adults, with such plays as *The Cry of the People for Meat*. In 1969 and 1970 came visits from the Café La Mama company, whose pioneer work in the off-Broadway theatre has had interesting repercussions in Europe. They were seen in several plays from their repertory, including a reworking of the anonymous Elizabethan tragedy, *Arden of Feversham*, and a shortened version of Jarry's *Ubu Roi*, as well as such new plays as *Rats Mass*, by Adrienne Kennedy, and *Heimskringla*, by Paul Foster. After a somewhat lean period, the English Stage Company was taken over in 1977 by the 59-year-old actor and director Stuart Burge.

Royal English Opera House, LONDON, see PALACE THEATRE.

Royal Grove LONDON, see ASTLEY'S AMPHITHEATRE,

Royal Pantheon Vheatre, LONDOM, a small nineteenth-century playhouse on the east side of Catherine Street, off the Strand, It features in Dickens's *Sketches by Boz* (1836), and was generally referred to as the Little Catherine Street Theatre. Entertainments had been given in she building, which constantly changed its name, since 1807, and on 25 Sept. 1823, lit by gas for the first time, it became the Theatre of Variety, the first time, apparently, that the name was used in London. As the (Royal) Pantheon (not to be confused with the Pantheon (q.v.) in Oxford Street), it was taken over by Smythson, from the Sans Souci (q.v.), and was used chiefly by amateurs who paid for the privilege of acting there—*Richard III*, for instance, cost £5. Female parts were played by professional actresses, usually very minor ones. After Smythson's death in 1841 the theatre changed hands several times and in 1843 was known as Jessop's Saloon, a coffee house with a dubious reputation. It later became a school of dancing, and a restaurant, and finally disappeared in 1899 in the Aldwych rebuilding scheme. It stood, roughly, in the road in front of the present Waldorf Hotel.

Royal Shakespeare Company. In 1960 the company playing at the Shakespeare Memorial Theatre (q.v.) was reorganized and given its present name. Under the directorship of Peter Hall (q.v.), later to be joined by Peter Brook and Peggy Ashcroft (qq.v.), with, from 1968, Trevor Nunn (q.v.) as Artistic Director, the company embarked on an ambitious programme which included the maintenance of a permanent base in London (see ALDWYCH THEATRE), and entailed the engagement of a large number of actors on long-term contracts, with shorter engagements of visiting stars. The permanent body was divided flexibly into several interchangeable groups so as to enable plays to be given almost continuously at Stratford, in London, and on tour. While Shakespeare remains the main preoccupation of the Stratford-based company, with selected plays being transferred to London, the London-based company is heavily orientated towards modern English and foreign experimental plays and non-Shakespearian classics. The touring companies have increased in size and scope very much since their first tentative journeys to North America and Australia before 1939, and after the war visited Moscow (in 1955) and Leningrad (in 1958). Since 1960 they have been seen all over the world, and in 1970 visited Japan—the first British theatrical company to do so—appearing with unprecedented success in *The Winter's Tale* and *The*

Merry Wives of Windsor. A further innovation, which began in Stratford but has also been seen in London, mainly at the Roundhouse (q.v.), was the establishment of a number of 'Theatregoround' productions with a more flexible staging and smaller casts than usual, so that they —and also demonstration programmes— could easily be performed in schools and youth clubs, often with the possibility of audience participation. (See also ARTS THEATRE.)

Royal Soho Theatre, LONDON, see ROYALTY THEATRE (2).

Royal Standard Music-Hall, PIMLICO, see VICTORIA PALACE.

Royal Standard Theatre, SHOREDITCH, see STANDARD THEATRE (1).

Royal Victoria Hall Theatre, LONDON, see OLD VIC.

Royale Theatre, NEW YORK, on West 45th Street between Broadway and 5th Avenue. This opened on 11 Jan. 1927 with a musical comedy, followed by further musical shows and by Winthrop Ames's productions of Gilbert and Sullivan. In 1928 came Mae West in her own play, *Diamond Lil*, which ran for nearly a year, and in 1933 Maxwell Anderson's *Both Your Houses*, a Pulitzer Prize-winner sponsored by the Theatre Guild (q.v.). The controversial *They Shall Not Die*, by John Wexley, based on the Scottsboro case, with a distinguished cast and settings by Lee Simonson (q.v.), was seen at this theatre in 1934 and in the autumn of the same year the theatre was renamed the Golden, presenting a series of moderately successful comedies. From 1936 to 1940 it was used for broadcasting, but then returned to drama under its old name. Successful productions since include Fry's *The Lady's Not for Burning* (1950), Thornton Wilder's *The Matchmaker* (1955), the revue *La Plume de ma Tante* (1958), Tennessee Williams's *The Night of the Iguana* (1961), and Elliott Baker's *The Penny Wars* (1969).

Royalty. The custom of paying a dramatist a percentage of the receipts every time his play is performed is of comparatively recent origin. In Elizabethan times plays were either bought outright, as by Henslowe (q.v.), or owned by the company to which the author-actor belonged, as with Shakespeare (q.v.). If a play was printed— a practice discouraged by the owners of the manuscript, as other companies could then act it—the author was sometimes given a small sum down. During the Restoration, when many dramatists were men of substance, the system remained much the same. It was not until the second half of the eighteenth century that a playwright could expect to get much money for his work, and that usually from a benefit (q.v.) or from the traditional 'third night' or author's night. Dr. Johnson and Oliver Goldsmith were given the proceeds of the third, sixth, and ninth nights of *Irene* (1749) and *The Good-Natured Man* (1768) respectively; but with only two or three playhouses, a small audience, and a continual change of bill, many plays failed to achieve even a third night. Towards the end of the eighteenth century—by which time Beaumarchais (q.v.) had established the royalty system in France—a return was made to the custom of buying plays outright, Morton (q.v.) receiving a thousand pounds for one of his comedies, and Mrs. Inchbald (q.v.) eight hundred for *Wives as They Were and Maids as They Are* (1797). By this time reputable publishers were also willing to pay several hundred pounds for the right to publish a play, a custom which had become almost universal, and this, in spite of piracies, added considerably to a dramatist's income.

With the nineteenth century the prestige, and consequently the money-value, of dramatic works declined sharply. Farces and musical pieces earned more than straight plays, and this led to an enormous amount of hack-work at pitiable prices, which may help to explain the constant stream of thefts, plagiarisms, and adaptations from French and German sources which flooded the English stage at its worst period.

The first movement to secure proper recognition of dramatic authorship in England was made by Planché (q.v.), and it was mainly due to his efforts, and those of Bulwer-Lytton (q.v.), that the Dramatic Copyright Act of 1833 was passed. This, however, only gave protection to plays written after 1833. It was also extremely difficult to collect acting fees from provincial managements and from America, and cases are on record of actors attending a theatre, memorizing a play, and reproducing it without payment (see FLORENCE and HOLCROFT).

Apparently the first English dramatist to receive a royalty, or at any rate a definite share in the profits, irrespective of what they might be, was the elder Boucicault (q.v.), who in 1860 suggested to Webster (q.v.), then manager of the Adelphi, that for his next play, in which he and his wife were as usual appearing in the leading parts, he should, as author, be given a fixed percentage of the takings. The play in question was either *The Colleen Bawn* or *The Octoroon*—accounts vary; but the new method netted Boucicault some £10,000, and the more astute of his fellow authors were quick to follow his example. The American critic William Winter says that the first play in America to be paid for on this system was *Valerie* (1886), by David Belasco (q.v.), but as the author received a flat rate of $250 a week, that was not a royalty in the generally accepted sense—though a great advance on the £2 or £3 a night that some authors in England were still accepting at this time. By degrees the standard rate of royalty became 5 per cent to 10 per cent, rising perhaps to 20 per cent in the case of established dramatists, while piracy was finally checked by the International Copyright Agreement of 1887 and the American Copyright Act of 1909. These made it possible for the author to enjoy the additional income derived from publication without at the same time losing his acting fees.

Royalty Theatre, LONDON. (1) On 20 June 1787 a theatre called the Royalty opened in Well Street, Wellclose Square, with *As You Like It*, but as it had no licence it was closed and the manager, John Palmer (q.v.), arrested. Several managers later tried to run it with burlesque and pantomime, including the elder Macready, and in 1813 its name was changed to the East London. It was burnt down in 1826. Rebuilt, it reopened on 25 Feb. 1828 as the Royal Brunswick, but it was so badly constructed that three days later it collapsed while the company was rehearsing *Guy Mannering*, killing fifteen people and injuring twenty.

(2) Fanny Kelly (q.v.) (Charles Lamb's 'Barbara S—') built a small theatre in Dean Street, Soho, which she used in conjunction with a school of acting. It opened on 25 May 1840 with a mixed bill, including a one-act comedy, *Summer and Winter*, in which the elder Dion Boucicault (q.v.) made his first appearance on the stage under the name of Lee Moreton; but the newly installed stage machinery,

worked by a horse, proved so noisy that it had to be removed. Miss Kelly struggled on for ten years but in the end had to give up, and a new management opened the theatre on 30 Jan. 1850 as the Royal Soho. In Nov. this was changed to the New English Opera House, perhaps the most ominous title that can be given to a London playhouse. It failed, and after a season as the Théâtre Français reopened as the New Royalty, with a company which included the young Ellen Terry (q.v.), with no better success. Among the players who made their début at the Royalty were Ada Cavendish (1863), Charles Wyndham (1864), and Adelaide Neilson (1865). Gilbert and Sullivan's *Trial by Jury* was a success in 1875, and in 1882 the theatre was closed for reconstruction, reopening on 23 Apr. 1883. Two of Ibsen's plays had their first English productions at the Royalty—*Ghosts* (1891) and *The Wild Duck* (1894), as did Shaw's *Widowers' Houses* (1892) and *You Never Can Tell* (1899), all under the auspices of the Independent Stage Society (q.v.). Brandon Thomas's farce, *Charley's Aunt*, opened there on 21 Dec. 1892, and in Nov. 1893 Poel (q.v.) staged an Elizabethan *Measure for Measure*. On 14 Sept. 1895 Bourchier reopened the theatre after installing electric light. Mrs. Patrick Campbell (q.v.) staged a series of revivals and gave the first English production of Bjørnson's *Beyond Human Power* in 1901; the Abbey Theatre Players made their first London appearance in Apr. 1904. In 1905 the theatre closed for alterations. Enlarged and redecorated, it opened again on 4 Jan. 1906, but little of importance happened until *Milestones* (1912), by Arnold Bennett and Edward Knoblock, had a long run. Further successes were Murray's *The Man from Toronto* (1918), Munro's *At Mrs. Beam's* (1923), Coward's *The Vortex* (1924), Sean O'Casey's *Juno and the Paycock* (1925), and Kimmins's *While Parents Sleep* (1932). The theatre closed on 25 Nov. 1938. It was destroyed in the blitz, and in 1953 an office block was built on the site.

(3) A small theatre formed part of the office block which arose on the site of the former Stoll Theatre (q.v.) in Kingsway. It was the first new West End theatre to be built since the Saville in 1931, and it opened on 23 June 1960 with the Lunts in Dürrenmatt's *The Visit*. Early in 1961 it became a cinema. It reopened as a theatre on 2 Apr. 1970.

RUEDA, LOPE DE (*c.* 1505–65), Spain's first actor-manager and popular dramatist, whose plays, strongly influenced by the *commedia dell'arte* (see GANASSA), were performed by his own company in squares and courtyards as well as in palaces and great houses. His dialogue, mainly written in prose, is natural, easy, and idiomatic, with a strong sense of the ridiculous and a happy satirizing of the manners of his day. His main purpose was to amuse, and in this he seems to have succeeded admirably. He was the originator of the *paso*, or comic interlude, of which the best is *Las aceitunas*. Many of his comedies are based on Italian originals, *Los engañados* being taken from the same source—the anonymous *Gl'Ingannati* (1531)—as Shakespeare's *Twelfth Night*.

RUGGERI, RUGGERO (1871–1953), Italian actor, who made his first appearance in 1888. He had a long and active career, retaining until the end his taste for strong dramatic and romantic parts. He was an excellent Iago in *Othello*, and a fine, if somewhat old-fashioned, Hamlet. In 1904 he scored a success in d'Annunzio's *La figlia di Jorio*. For some years he was a member of a company directed by Pirandello (q.v.), in whose *Enrico IV* he appeared in London shortly before his death, and he played opposite most of the famous Italian actresses of the time, among them Emma Gramatica (q.v.).

RUGGLE, GEORGE (1575–1622), a scholar of Clare Hall, Cambridge, who is believed to have written two comedies performed by his fellow students in about 1600. In 1615 his *Ignoramus*, a satire on lawyers, in Latin, with some English, was performed before James I, who was so delighted with it that he returned to Cambridge a week later to see it again. It was largely based on Della Porta's *La Trappolaria* (1596), but the chief part is a satirical portrait of the then Cambridge Recorder, Francis Brackyn. An English translation of Ruggle's play, as *Ignoramus; or, the Academical Lawyer*, by Ferdinando Parkhurst, was acted at Court in 1662 before Charles II. Ravenscroft (q.v.) also made an adaptation of it, performed at Drury Lane in 1677 as *The English Lawyer*.

Run, the total number of consecutive performances of one play, usually at one theatre. Originally all theatres worked on the repertory (q.v.) system, but with the vast increase in the number of potential theatregoers in the nineteenth century, and the improvement in transport, plays began to be given first for as long as the actor-managers were willing to appear in them, and later for as long as the audiences would come to see them. This has led to a situation in which one play—usually a lightweight comedy with low running costs, or a spectacular musical, rather than a serious or experimental play—can tie up a theatre and a number of actors over a period of years. In London the Ambassadors (q.v.) has had only one play—Agatha Christie's *The Mousetrap*—since 25 Nov. 1952, the Whitehall (q.v.) had only four plays in over twelve years, and five American musicals, from *Oklahoma!* (1947) to *My Fair Lady* (1958), accounted for over twelve years in the life of Drury Lane (q.v.). The long run is sometimes defended on the grounds that it provides financial security for the actor. But it may result in artistic stagnation, and also keeps many plays off the stage, a situation aggravated by the diminishing number of theatres.

Rundhorizont, see CYCLORAMA.

RUSHTON, LUCY (1844–?), see NEW YORK THEATRE (I).

RUSSELL, ANNA [really ANNA CLAUDIA RUSSELL-BROWN] (1911–), a solo entertainer, well known in London and the U.S.A. Trained as a singer, she uses her fine voice and wide knowledge of her art to prick the bubble of musical pretentiousness. She can hit off to a nicety the subtle differences between the folk-songs of various nations, provide words and music for a do-it-yourself Gilbert-and-Sullivan, teach, with illustrations and mime, the mastery of any instrument, and poke gentle fun at Shakespeare 'adapters' with an 'Amletto' in the style of Verdi. In 1962 she ventured to appear in a play which toured for some weeks but failed to reach London (where she was born), much to the relief of most of her admirers, who welcomed her back in her usual programme, enlivened by a Wagneresque account of her temporary aberration. She is the author of *The Power of Being a Positive Stinker* (1955) and *The Anna Russell Songbook* (1958).

RUSSELL, ANNIE (1864–1936), American actress, who was on the stage as a child, and in 1881 appeared with immense success in New York in the title-role of *Esmeralda*, written by William Gillette (q.v.) in collaboration with Frances Hodgson Burnett. At the height of her subsequent popularity she was forced to retire through illness, but in 1894 she returned, playing in a number of new plays, among them Bret Harte's *Sue*, in which she was seen in London for the first time in 1898. On a subsequent visit she appeared at the Royal Court Theatre (q.v.) under the Vedrenne–Barker management as the heroine of Shaw's *Major Barbara* on its first production in 1905. She had essayed several Shakespearian parts before she organized in 1912 an Old English Comedy company, for which she played Beatrice in *Much Ado About Nothing*, Kate Hardcastle in Goldsmith's *She Stoops to Conquer*, and Lydia Languish and Lady Teazle in Sheridan's *The Rivals* and *The School for Scandal*. She retired in 1918.

RUSSELL, FRED [really THOMAS FREDERICK PARNELL] (1862–1957), a ventriloquist, known as the 'Father of Variety' because of the part he played in the founding of the Variety Artists' Federation, of which he became President at the age of ninety. In 1906 he also founded and edited *The Performer*, the Federation's official organ, which ceased publication only a month before his death. He made his first professional appearance under Charles Morton at the Palace, changing his name because of its political associations at the time. With his doll, 'Coster Joe', he soon became 'top of the bill' in England and also undertook extensive tours of Australia, New Zealand, South Africa, America, and Ceylon. He retained his full faculties to the end of his long life, and in Jan. 1952, being nearly ninety, appeared in a music-hall programme on television. He was a member of the Grand Order of Water Rats from its foundation, and in 1903 became King Rat. He was appointed O.B.E. in 1948. Some fourteen members of his family were connected with variety, among them one of his four sons, VAL(ENTINE) CHARLES PARNELL (1894–1972), for many years associated with Moss Empires.

RUSSELL, GEORGE WILLIAM, see AE.

RUTEBEUF (*c.* 1230–*c.* 1285), a medieval minstrel who, with Adam de la Halle and Jean Bodel (qq.v.), stands at the beginning of French secular drama. His best-known play is *Le Miracle de Théophile*, which in the 1930s was revived by Gustave Cohen (q.v.) with his students at the Sorbonne, who took from it their name of 'Les Théophiliens'.

RUTHERFORD, DAME MARGARET (1892–1972), English actress, in the tradition of English eccentrics and star personalities. She made a late entry on the stage, being in her early thirties when a small legacy enabled her to give up teaching elocution and the piano. She made her first appearance in a pantomime at the Old Vic in 1925 under Robert Atkins, and subsequently played several small parts, but without much success. The turning point in her career came when in 1938 she was engaged to play the formidable and extremely eccentric Bijou Furze in *Spring Meeting*, by M. J. Farrell and John Perry. She was immediately recognized as an outstanding comedienne, and played Miss Prism in Wilde's *The Importance of Being Earnest* in the following year. Among her outstanding parts were Madame Arcati in Coward's *Blithe Spirit* (1941); Miss Whitchurch in John Dighton's farce *The Happiest Days of Your Life* (1948); Madame Desmortes (in a bath-chair) in Anouilh's *Ring Round the Moon* (1950); Lady Wishfort in Congreve's *The Way of the World* (1953), in which she gave a masterly impression of an 'old peeled wall'; Bijou again in the sequel to *Spring Meeting*, *Dazzling Prospect* (1961); and Mrs. Malaprop in Sheridan's *The Rivals* (1966). At her best in comedy, she could nevertheless play pathos and also inject a certain sinister element into some of her personifications of elderly and unpredictable old ladies. She was created D.B.E. in 1972 for services to the theatre.

RUZZANTE, see BEOLCO, ANGELO.

RYAN, LACY (1694–1760), an English actor who first appeared as Seyton to Betterton's Macbeth, in a full-bottomed wig, and played Marcus in the original production of Addison's *Cato* (1713). He had a steady, uneventful career, mostly at Covent Garden, where he played leading roles in Shakespeare in opposition to Garrick (q.v.) at Drury Lane, with little success. It is said that Garrick went to see his Richard III, intending to scoff, but was astonished by the genius and power which he saw striving to make itself felt in spite of the handicaps of insufficient training, uncouth gestures, and a slovenly presence. Ryan continued to play youthful lovers and heroes until his death, and was all his life a friend of the actor Quin (q.v.), whom he had befriended in early days.

RYLANDS, GEORGE HUMPHREY WOLFERSTAN (1902–   ), University lecturer and Fellow of King's College, Cambridge, who has been closely associated with the theatre as Chairman of the Arts Theatre, Cambridge, in succession to Maynard Keynes, and a governor of the London Old Vic. He has directed many plays in Cambridge for the A.D.C. and the Marlowe Society, being responsible, with members of the latter group, together with the assistance of professional guest artists, for the recording of all Shakespeare's plays for the British Council, for whom he also toured Australia, lecturing on Shakespeare. In London in 1944–5 he directed John Gielgud (q.v.) in *Hamlet*, and later prepared for him a one-man recital, *Ages of Man*, based on an anthology of passages from Shakespeare which he published in 1939. He was appointed C.B.E. in 1961.

S

SÁ DE MIRANDA, FRANCISCO DE (1481–1558), Portuguese dramatist, founder of the classical tradition in Portugal, in conscious opposition to the chivalresque, biblical, and folk-plays of earlier writers like Gil Vicente (q.v.). In 1526 Miranda returned from a long visit to Italy, and in two plays, *Estrangeiros* (*c.* 1528) and *Vilhalpandos* (*c.* 1538), endeavoured, without much success, to import into the Portuguese theatre the prose style and act-divisions of classical comedy and the literary correctness of the erudite Italians. Of his one verse tragedy, *Cleopatra*, no more than a dozen lines have survived. In spite of his comparative failure as a dramatist he is important in that his plays, like his poetry, helped to give Portuguese literature a solid sense of form which was lacking in the greater genius of Gil Vicente.

SAAVEDRA, ANGEL DE, DUQUE DE RIVAS (1791–1865), Spanish dramatist, whose early plays were neo-classical in form. While in exile in Paris, however, he came under the influence of the Romantic dramatists, particularly Victor Hugo (q.v.), and as a result wrote *Don Álvaro, o la fuerza de sino*. First produced in Madrid in 1835, this was acclaimed as the greatest play of Spanish Romanticism, and although this may be a little exaggerated, it undoubtedly had a great influence. Apart from its emotional range, it is noteworthy for the author's use of local colour and his detailed descriptions of the stage sets. The play later provided Piave with the libretto of Verdi's opera 'La Forza del destino' (1862). Rivas's later plays are less interesting, being costume dramas in the style of the elder Dumas (q.v.).

SABBATTINI, NICOLA (1574–1654), Italian architect, designer of the Teatro del Sole in Pesaro and author of the first treatise to be published on stage designing, *Pratica di fabricar scene e machine ne' teatri* (1638). Although some of his material was already out of date owing to the rapid technical developments in theatre machinery from 1600 onwards, he has some interesting things to say about lighting (q.v.), including a method of extinguishing all the candles on stage simultaneously by dropping on to them cylinders on wires attached to a master wire. He advocates the use of side as opposed to front or back lighting, but provides evidence for the early use in Italian theatres of concealed footlights with reflectors, with their accompanying smoke and smell.

SACHS, HANS (1494–1576), German dramatist, best known as the hero of Wagner's opera, 'Die Meistersinger von Nürnberg' (1868). He was a cobbler by trade, but from about 1518 onwards poured out a stream of plays on subjects taken from the Bible, legend, history, the classics, and popular folk-lore, all treated in a prosaic and unhistorical way and employed for the purpose of moral instruction—Sachs was one of the first writers of his day to support Luther. Most of the tragedies are travesties, but the comedies—that is, plays with happy endings but not necessarily humorous— are somewhat better. His fame rests chiefly on his Carnival plays, of which he wrote about two hundred, notable for their homespun humour and lively pictures of daily life. In them he turned the horseplay of the *Fastnachtsspiel* (q.v.) into a simple, amusing folk-play. The dialogue is natural and unforced and the rough-and-ready verse not unpleasing. Sachs trained his actors and directed his plays himself, adapting for the purpose a disused church, which thus became Germany's first theatre building.

SACKVILLE, THOMAS, first EARL OF DORSET (1536–1608), English lawyer and politician, who collaborated with a fellow student, Thomas Norton (q.v.), in the writing of the first regular Senecan English tragedy in blank verse, *Gorboduc, or Ferrex and Porrex*. This was performed before Queen Elizabeth I on New Year's Day 1562, in the hall of the Inner Temple. Sackville also contributed, to the second edition of *A Mirror for Magistrates* (1563), the 'Induction' and 'The Complaint of Buckingham', the only contributions having any literary merit.

(For the actor Sackville, see ENGLISH COMEDIANS.)

Sacra Rappresentazione, the Italian equivalent of the English Mystery Play and the French *Mystère* (qq.v.). It followed the same line of development from the liturgical drama (q.v.), and reached its highest point of excellence in the middle of the fifteenth century in Florence, where in 1454 a cycle of episodes from the Old and New Testaments called for the erection of no less than twenty-two booths or *edifizi* indicating different localities. These plays were not produced, as in England, by the guilds, or as in France by specially organized lay bodies, but by educational or religious groups of young men brought together for the purpose. As elsewhere, the over-elaboration of comic interpolations, and the gradual introduction of secular and often impious elements, led to the decline of the *sacre rappresentazioni*, which could not hold their own against the pressure of the newly discovered classical forms, and so disappeared, but not before they had had some slight influence on Renaissance drama and on the plays of the Counter-Reformation.

Sadler's Wells Theatre, LONDON. On 3 June 1683 a Mr. Sadler opened a popular pleasure-garden, which became known as Sadler's Wells, on the site of a medicinal spring in open country near London, and erected there a wooden 'Musick House' with a stage. This, later known as Miles's Musick House, was used mainly for musical interludes until in 1753 Rosoman, a local builder who had taken over the Wells in 1746, engaged a company of actors and the Musick Room became a minor theatre. *The Tempest*, probably in Dryden's version, was performed there in 1764. Early in 1765 Rosoman replaced the old wooden building by a stone one which opened with a mixed bill on 8 Apr. He continued to run the theatre successfully until his retirement in 1772, when he was succeeded by the actor Tom King (q.v.), under whom the clown Grimaldi (q.v.) appeared in 1781 as a three-year-old 'sprite', making his farewell appearance at the same theatre on 17 Mar. 1828. For several years there was a vogue for AQUATIC DRAMA, for which a large tank was installed on the stage, filled with water from the New River, in which sea fights and naval bombardments took place. The building was then known as the Aquatic Theatre. In 1844, after the breaking of the Patent Theatres' monopoly

by the Theatres Act of 1843, it was again known as Sadler's Wells and was taken over as a home for Shakespeare's plays by Phelps (q.v.), who opened it on 27 May with *Macbeth* and remained there until 1862. It then declined, and in 1878, after being used as a skating-rink and a boxing-ring, it was closed as a dangerous structure. In 1879 Mrs. Bateman (q.v.), leaving the Lyceum to the management of Henry Irving (q.v.), took over Sadler's Wells, restored and redecorated it, and opened it on 9 Oct., hoping to revive its past glories. After her death in 1881 her daughter Isabel carried on for a time, but without success, and the theatre became derelict. It closed for the last time in 1906. In 1927 Lilian Baylis (q.v.) built a new theatre on the site, hoping to make it the North London equivalent of the South London Old Vic (q.v.). It opened on 6 Jan. 1931 with *Twelfth Night* and was intended to house alternately its own productions and those from the Old Vic. This proved impracticable and in 1934 Sadler's Wells was given over entirely to ballet and opera, Shakespeare remaining at the Old Vic. It closed in 1940 and suffered minor damage from bombs. On 7 June 1945 it reopened with the world première of Benjamin Britten's first opera, 'Peter Grimes'. After the departure of the Sadler's Wells ballet company to Covent Garden in Feb. 1946, to become later the Royal Ballet, the opera company remained in sole possession until in 1968 it too moved, to the Coliseum (q.v.), and Sadler's Wells was used only by visiting companies.

SADOVSKY [really YERMILOV], PROV MIKHAILOVICH (1818–72), early Russian actor, who took his professional name from a well-known provincial actor related to him on his mother's side, who trained him for the stage. In 1839 he joined the company of the Maly Theatre (q.v.) in Moscow, and soon came to the fore in the plays of Ostrovsky (q.v.), of whose comic roles he proved to be the ideal interpreter. It was in fact mainly through Sadovsky's championship that Ostrovsky's plays were first performed and then kept in the repertory until they received due recognition from the public. Sadovsky's son and daughter-in-law were members of the Maly company, and his grandson, also named Prov, is still with the theatre, thus maintaining a family connection which dates back well over a century.

Safety Curtain, an iron or fireproof sheet which can be lowered in front of the curtain (q.v.) in a proscenium arch, designed to separate the stage and auditorium in the event of fire. By law it must be lowered once during every performance. This is usually done during an interval. The first safety curtain, nicknamed 'The Iron', was installed at Drury Lane (q.v.) in 1794.

Sainete, a name applied in Spain in the eighteenth century to the earlier *entremés* (q.v.) or comic interlude performed between the acts of a full-length play, from which it is distinguished by a new note of social criticism. The best *sainetes* were written by Ramón de la Cruz (q.v.), their racy speech and satirical view of society providing a welcome relief from the inertia of neo-classical drama or the extravagances of the popular pseudo-historical play. Modern descendants of the *sainete* are to be found in the comic playlets of the *género chico* (q.v.) and in the work of such twentieth-century dramatists as the brothers Quintero (q.v.).

SAINT-DENIS, MICHEL JACQUES (1897–1971), French actor and director, who began his career under his uncle Jacques Copeau (q.v.) at the Vieux Colombier. In 1930 he founded the Compagnie des Quinze, for which he directed *Noé, Le Viol de Lucrèce,* and *La Bataille de la Marne,* all by André Obey (q.v.), as well as a number of other plays, in all of which he appeared himself. The company achieved a great reputation, but was eventually disbanded, and Saint-Denis settled in London, directing Obey's *Noé* in translation, with John Gielgud (q.v.) as Noah, in 1935 and the Elizabethan tragicomedy *The Witch of Edmonton* at the Old Vic in 1936. He then founded the London Theatre Studio for the training of young actors. It had already made several interesting contributions to the English theatre when the outbreak of war caused it to close down. Meanwhile Saint-Denis had done several more productions in the West End, including *Macbeth* (1937), Chekhov's *Three Sisters* and Bulgakov's *The White Guard* (both 1938), and Lorca's *Marriage of Blood* (also known as *Blood Wedding*) (1939). During the Second World War he was

head of the French section of the B.B.C., as Jacques Duchesne, and for his services to the Allied cause was appointed Hon. C.B.E. He afterwards returned to the theatre, becoming head of the short-lived drama school at the Old Vic (q.v.). On its demise he returned to France to found and run the Centre Dramatique de l'Est, based on Strasbourg. In 1957 he was appointed artistic adviser to the Vivian Beaumont Repertory Theatre project in New York in connection with Lincoln Center (q.v.), and in 1962 became general artistic adviser to the Royal Shakespeare Company, for whom he directed at the Aldwych (q.v.) Brecht's *Squire Puntila and his Servant Matti* (1965). He also founded the Bilingual National Theatre School of Canada in Montreal, and was appointed its artistic director. In 1960 he published *Theatre: The Rediscovery of Style,* which contains an admirable chapter on training for the stage and another on the duties of the director and designer.

St. James Theatre, NEW YORK, on West 44th Street at 8th Avenue. This opened as Erlanger's on 26 Sept. 1927. It was intended for musical and spectacular shows and received its present name in 1932. Among its early productions were revivals of Goldsmith's *She Stoops to Conquer* and Sardou's *Diplomacy* (both 1928). In 1929 Mrs. Fiske (q.v.) made one of her last stage appearances there in Fred Ballard's *Ladies of the Jury,* followed by light opera and musical shows, returning to straight drama in 1934 with a dramatization of James Hilton's *Lost Horizon.* In 1937 critics and public alike acclaimed Margaret Webster's production of *Richard II,* with Maurice Evans (q.v.) in the name-part. The same combination was responsible for *Hamlet* in 1938 and for *Henry IV, Part 1,* with Evans as Falstaff, in 1939. The following year saw Helen Hayes and Maurice Evans in *Twelfth Night,* produced under the auspices of the Theatre Guild (q.v.), and in 1941 came *Native Son,* based by Paul Green on a novel by Richard Wright, in which the Negro actor Canada Lee (q.v.) gave a fine performance. The theatre was for a long time occupied by the Theatre Guild's production of *Oklahoma!,* a musical play based on Lynn Riggs's *Green Grow the Lilacs* (1931) which opened in 1943. Other highly successful productions have been *Where's Charley?* (1948), a musical version of Brandon Thomas's farce, *Charley's Aunt*; a spectacular musical, *The King and I* (1951), in which Gertrude Lawrence (q.v.) made her last appearance on the stage; Anouilh's *Becket* (1960); and Osborne's *Luther* (1963), in which Albert Finney (q.v.) made a successful Broadway début. This last-named moved in 1964 to the Lunt–Fontanne (q.v.) to make way for a musical, *Hello, Dolly!*, based on Thornton Wilder's *The Matchmaker*, which was still running in 1971.

St. James's Theatre, LONDON, in King Street. Designed by Samuel Beazley for John Braham, this opened on 14 Dec. 1835, but was not successful, except for a play—*The Strange Gentleman*—and a ballad opera—*The Village Coquette*—both by Dickens, staged in 1836. In 1840 a German opera company was installed by Bunn, who renamed the theatre the Prince's in honour of the Queen's consort. On 7 Feb. 1842 it reopened under its old name, and for the next twelve years, under the management of John Mitchell, housed foreign companies with guest stars, including Déjazet, Frédérick, Rachel, and Fechter (qq.v.). Mitchell, having lost a good deal of money, gave up in 1854, and managements came and went. In 1863 Louisa Herbert appeared in a dramatization of Miss Braddon's novel, *Lady Audley's Secret*. Gilbert's first play, an operatic burlesque entitled *Dulcamara; or, the Little Duck and the Great Quack*, was seen in 1866, and in the same year Irving made his first London success in Boucicault's *Hunted Down*. Mrs. John Wood (q.v.) managed the theatre from 1869 to 1876, having renovated and redecorated it, but it was not until Hare and the Kendals (qq.v.) took over, opening on 4 Oct. 1879, that it had a settled policy. Among their productions were *The Money Spinner* and *The Squire* (both 1881), by Pinero (q.v.), who was later to figure prominently in the history of the theatre. They also engaged in 1883 the young George Alexander (q.v.), who in 1891 took over the theatre himself and inaugurated the most brilliant period in its history, opening on 31 Jan. and remaining at the St. James's until his death in 1918. The last play in which he appeared was Louis N. Parker's *The Aristocrat* (1917). Gilbert Miller, the American impresario, son of Henry Miller (q.v.), then took over. Among his successful productions were Archer's *The Green Goddess* (1923), with

George Arliss; Lonsdale's *The Last of Mrs. Cheyney* (1925), with Gladys Cooper; an adaptation by Emlyn Williams of Fauchois's *Prenez-garde à la peinture* as *The Late Christopher Bean* (1933), with Cedric Hardwicke and Edith Evans; a dramatization of Jane Austen's *Pride and Prejudice* (1936), with scenery by Rex Whistler; and a fine revival of Turgenev's *A Month in the Country* (1943), with Michael Redgrave as Rakitin. The theatre suffered some damage from enemy action in Feb. 1944 but remained in use, and in 1945 saw the production by Emlyn Williams of his own play, *The Wind of Heaven*, in which he also appeared. A distinguished failure in 1949 was Rattigan's *Adventure Story*, in which Paul Scofield gave an excellent performance as Alexander the Great. In 1950 Laurence Olivier took over, appearing in Fry's *Venus Observed* and, with Vivien Leigh, in Shaw's *Caesar and Cleopatra* alternating with Shakespeare's *Antony and Cleopatra*, in celebration of the 1951 Festival of Britain. In the same year the St. James's returned to an old tradition when it housed the French company of Madeleine Renaud and Jean-Louis Barrault in a season which included Salacrou's *Les Nuits de la colère* and Edwige Feuillère in Claudel's *Partage de midi*. In 1954 Rattigan's *Separate Tables* had a successful run, but the theatre remained empty for long periods, and after some unmemorable plays, and in spite of energetic protests from the theatrical profession and the play-going public, it finally closed on 27 July 1957. It was then demolished and a block of offices was built on the site.

St. Martin's Theatre, LONDON, in West Street, St. Martin's Lane, a small theatre which opened on 23 Nov. 1916. The first public production of Brieux's *Damaged Goods*, on 17 Mar. 1917, created something of a sensation. Later in the same year Seymour Hicks (q.v.) appeared in his own play, *Sleeping Partners*, and three years later Alec L. Rea took over. The Reandean and Reandco managements, of which he was chairman, then produced a series of plays, many of them by new authors. Among them were Galsworthy's *The Skin Game* (1920) and *Loyalties* (1922); Clemence Dane's *A Bill of Divorcement* (1921), with Meggie Albanesi; Reginald Berkeley's *The White Château* (1927), considered by some critics the best play yet written about the First World War; Rodney Ackland's *Strange Orchestra* (1932), the first modern play to be directed by John Gielgud (q.v.); and Merton Hodge's *The Wind and the Rain* (1933). In 1938 Priestley's Yorkshire comedy, *When We Are Married*, had a successful run. During the Second World War, and for some years afterwards, the theatre had no settled policy, and short runs came and went, though Edward Percy's *The Shop at Sly Corner* (1945), Laurier Lister's intimate revue *Penny Plain* (1951), with Joyce Grenfell, Richard Nash's *The Rainmaker* (1956), Hugh and Margaret Williams's *The Grass is Greener* (1958), and John Chapman's *The Brides of March* (1960), did well. In 1968 Bill Naughton's successful *Spring and Port Wine*, first produced at the Mermaid in 1965, was revived for a few months, and in February 1970 Anthony Shaffer's first play, *Sleuth*, started a long run.

SAINTHILL, LOUDON (1919–69), theatre designer, born in Tasmania, who worked for some years in Australia before coming to England. In 1951 he achieved an instant success with his designs for *The Tempest* at Stratford-upon-Avon, where he was subsequently responsible for the décor for *Pericles* (1958) and *Othello* (1959). In London he worked for the Old Vic and also designed the sets for such diverse productions as Errol Johns's *Moon on a Rainbow Shawl* (1958), Tennessee Williams's *Orpheus Descending* (1959), *Half-a-Sixpence*, the musical version of Wells's *Kipps*, and Henry James's *The Wings of the Dove* (both 1963). Shortly before his death he was given a Tony award for his costume designs for a New York musical based on Chaucer's *Canterbury Tales* (1968). He also designed for the ballet, opera, and pantomime.

SALACROU, ARMAND (1899–   ), French dramatist, whose finest, but perhaps least characteristic, play is *Les Nuits de la colère*, which deals with the German occupation of France during the Second World War. Superbly acted by the Renaud–Barrault company at the Marigny in 1946, it was seen in London during their visit there in 1951, but though broadcast by the B.B.C. as *Men of Wrath*, it has not been seen on the stage in English. Unlike his younger contemporaries, Anouilh and Sartre (qq.v.),

Salacrou has made little impact upon the English or American theatre, and although performances of his plays in French have been given in London and elsewhere, mainly by student groups, the only ones to have been performed in translation appear to be *L'Inconnue d'Arras* (1935), which as *The Unknown Woman of Arras* was seen in different translations in London in 1948 and again in 1954; *Histoire de rire* (1939), produced at the Arts Theatre in 1957 as *No Laughing Matter*; *L'Archipel Lenoir* (1947), which as *The Honour of the Family* was produced at the Maddermarket Theatre in 1958 and as *Never Say Die* at the International Theatre Club in London in 1966. Salacrou's other plays include *Un Homme comme les autres* (1936), *La Terre est ronde* (1938), *Les Fiancés du Havre* (1944), *Une femme trop honnête* (1956), and *Comme les Chardons* (1964). Like *Les Fiancés du Havre*, this last was first produced at the Comédie-Française.

Salisbury Court, the last theatre to open in London before the Civil War. Built of brick, it was a 'private' roofed playhouse on the site of the present Salisbury Square, Fleet Street, and was used by the King's Men (see CHAMBERLAIN'S MEN) from its opening in 1629 till 1631. They were followed by Prince Charles's Men (q.v.)— the second company of that name—who remained in possession until 1635, and were succeeded by Queen Henrietta's Men (q.v.), who were still there when the theatres closed in 1642. During the Commonwealth surreptitious performances were given at Salisbury Court, but the interior fittings were destroyed by soldiers in Mar. 1649. William Beeston (q.v.) restored the theatre in 1660 and ran a company there from 1663 to 1664. It was burned down in the Great Fire of London in 1666.

Salle des Machines, PARIS, a small but well-equipped theatre in the Tuileries, built by Vigarani (q.v.) in 1660 to house the spectacular shows given in honour of the marriage of Louis XIV. It continued in use for many years for Court entertainments and was later under the control of the artist and scenic designer Jean Bérain. It was, however, under Servandony (q.v.) that it reached the height of its splendour, many magnificent spectacles being given there with his designs and machinery.

SALTIKOV-SHCHEDRIN, MIKHAIL EVGRAFOVICH (1826–89), one of the most brilliant satirists in Russian literature and the author of one outstanding play, *The Death of Pazukhin*, published during his lifetime but not performed until 1901. It was revived by the Moscow Art Theatre in 1914 and performed by them during a visit to New York in 1924. Another play, *Shadows*, was found among Saltikov-Shchedrin's papers and first produced in Moscow in 1914. Though his other books, including a volume of so-called 'Dramatic Essays' written in dialogue form, were not intended for the stage, several of them were subsequently dramatized.

SALVINI, TOMMASO (1829–1916), Italian actor, who as a boy appeared in the comedies of Goldoni (q.v.). At eighteen he joined the company of Adelaide Ristori (q.v.), then at the beginning of her career, and with her made his first appearances in tragedy—including *Romeo and Juliet*—at which he later excelled. He became famous all over Europe and North and South America, visiting London many times and marrying in 1875 an Englishwoman, Carlotta Sharpe. He toured the United States five times between 1873 and 1889, and in 1885 played Othello, always his finest part, to the Iago of Edwin Booth (q.v.). In 1889, his first wife having died in 1878, he married an American, Genevieve Bearman, and retired a year later. He published a volume of reminiscences, part of which appeared in an English translation in 1893.

Sam H. Harris Theatre, NEW YORK, on the south side of 42nd Street between Broadway and 8th Avenue. This opened as a cinema on 7 May 1914, but as the Candler Theatre was sometimes used for plays, Elmer Rice's *On Trial* being seen there in 1914, and Galsworthy's *Justice* in 1916. Later that year it was renamed the Cohan and Harris Theatre. It received its present name on 21 Feb. 1921, becoming a cinema again on 18 Mar. 1933. In 1922 theatrical history was made when John Barrymore (q.v.) played Hamlet 101 times, thus breaking by one performance the record previously set up by Edwin Booth (q.v.). Barrymore's record stood until 1936, when Gielgud (q.v.) played the part at the Empire for 132 consecutive performances, a record again broken in 1964 by Richard Burton (q.v.) at the Lunt-Fontanne with 138 performances.

Sam S. Shubert Theatre, NEW YORK, see SHUBERT THEATRE.

SAMSON, JOSEPH-ISIDORE (1793–1871), French actor, who was at the newly opened Odéon (q.v.) in Paris from 1819 to 1826, when he became a member of the Comédie-Française. Apart from a few years at the Palais-Royal, he remained there until he retired in 1863, becoming Doyen of the company in 1843. He was an excellent actor but it is as the teacher of Rachel (q.v.) that he is chiefly remembered. By instructing her in the classical tradition, which he had himself received from Talma (q.v.), he contributed not a little to the revival of French tragedy with which Rachel is associated. He is said to have been one of the finest teachers of acting ever known at the Conservatoire, where he remained on the staff until his death, and many of his pupils became famous. He was also the author of a number of comedies, successful in their day, but now forgotten.

SAN GALLO, BASTIANO DA (1481–1551), see PERIAKTOI.

Sand-Cloth, see CLOTH.

SANDERSON, MARY (?–1712), see BETTERTON, THOMAS.

Sanger's Grand National, LONDON, see ASTLEY'S AMPHITHEATRE.

Sans Pareil, LONDON, see ADELPHI THEATRE (1).

Sans Souci, LONDON, a small theatre built by Charles Dibdin (q.v.) at the corner of Leicester Place, Leicester Square, which opened on 8 Oct. 1796. (He had already opened one under this name in the Strand, near Southampton Street, which he ran from 31 Oct. 1791 to March 1796.) Here he appeared in his one-man 'Table Entertainments', of which he was author, composer, narrator, singer, and accompanist, until 1805, when he sold it. Edmund Kean (q.v.) as a boy gave acrobatic performances there. Although described as 'an elegant little theatre', it was too small for anything but amateur entertainments and benefits. In 1832 it was given over to vaudeville, and in 1834 a French company occupied it. After that

SARDOU 477 SARTRE

it became a warehouse and a hotel and was demolished in 1898.

(For the Sans Souci, New York, see NIBLO'S GARDEN.)

SARDOU, VICTORIEN (1831–1908), French dramatist, and one of the most successful of his day. Like Scribe (q.v.), whose successor he was, Sardou wrote copiously on a number of subjects, with expert craftsmanship and superficial brilliance. His first popular play was a comedy, *Les Pattes de mouche* (1860), produced in London as *A Scrap of Paper* (1861), but he was equally successful in historical dramas, of which the best-known is probably *Madame Sans-Gêne* (1893), in melodrama—*Fédora* (1882) and *La Tosca* (1887), the latter used by Puccini for his opera 'Tosca' (1900)—and in social dramas, of which *Dora* (1877) and *Divorçons* (1880) are typical. The former, as *Diplomacy*, in a translation by Clement Scott (q.v.), was for a long time popular with London audiences. Many of Sardou's plays were written for Sarah Bernhardt (q.v.), to whom they owed much of their success. Bernard Shaw (q.v.), who disliked everything Sardou stood for, coined the word Sardoodledom to describe his 'well-made' play; yet he had great gifts theatrically, and his characters lack only life—but it is a fatal lack.

SAROYAN, WILLIAM (1908–81), American novelist and dramatist, whose first play, the long one-act *My Heart's in the Highlands* (1939), dealt with a poet's struggle to maintain his integrity in a materialistic world. His next, *The Time of Your Life* (also 1939), was awarded the Pulitzer Prize for Drama and the Drama Critics' Award for 1940. Less successful but still interesting were *Love's Old Sweet Song* (1940) and *The Beautiful People* (1941). The lynching of an innocent tramp was the theme of the one-act play *Hello, Out There* (1942), and an irrepressible young writer's conflict with a ruthless Hollywood mogul was the subject of *Get Away, Old Man* (1943). After the comparative failure of several plays which were not seen on Broadway Saroyan again achieved success with *The Cave Dwellers* (1957). In 1960 *Sam, the Highest Jumper of Them All*, an improvisation which was good in patches, was seen in a production by Joan Littlewood (q.v.) at London's Theatre Workshop.

SARTHOU, JACQUES (1920–   ), French actor and producer, who in 1945 appeared in a production by Jean Vilar (q.v.) of T. S. Eliot's *Murder in the Cathedral* at the Vieux-Colombier. He had already written some plays, and it was as a playwright that he founded the Association des Jeunes Auteurs Dramatiques. In 1952 he formed a company to bring theatre to the working-class suburbs of Paris, based on the Théâtre de l'Île-de-France. This also performs in summer in the provinces, and has founded several conservatoires of dramatic art in such suburbs as Colombes and Noisy-le-Sec. In 1961 a festival was held in Kremlin-Bicêtre, a predominantly working-class south-eastern suburb of Paris. Among the plays performed were Giraudoux's *Supplement au voyage de Cook*, Victor Hugo's *Marie Tudor*, and a triple bill of Molière, Musset, and Marivaux, all directed by Jean Puyberneau.

SARTRE, JEAN-PAUL CHARLES AYMARD (1905–80), French writer and philosopher, and probably the best-known of the post-war French dramatists outside his own country. In the mood engendered by the disasters of the Second World War, his philosophy of existentialism—the responsibility of each man for his own acts and the consequences of them—was eagerly adopted by young people everywhere in the late 1940s and 1950s, and its principles are implicit in his dramatic works. His first play, *Les Mouches* (1942), was a modern interpretation of the Orestes story, and as *The Flies* was seen in New York in 1947 and in London in 1951. *Huis-Clos* (1944), which followed, was produced in London as *Vicious Circle* and in New York as *No Exit*, both in 1946, the year in which *Morts sans sépultures* and *La Putain respectueuse* were first seen in Paris. As *Men Without Shadows* and *The Respectable Prostitute*, these were seen in London in 1947. The English title of the latter play is a mistranslation, the title given to the American version, *The Respectful Prostitute*, in 1948 being more appropriate, since the prostitute, Lizzie, betrays her coloured lover out of a craven respect for the dictates of society. Sartre seems to suffer from alternative titles in translation, as *Morts sans sépultures* was seen in New York in 1948 as *The Victors* and *Les Mains sales* (1948) was produced in London as *Crime Passionel* and in New York as *Red Gloves*, both in the same year as the French production. The play which many French critics regarded as Sartre's best work, *Le Diable et le Bon Dieu* (1951), based on the same story as Goethe's *Götz von Berlichingen*, has not yet (1980) been seen in English, but in 1956 Unity Theatre (q.v.) gave the first English production of *Nekrassov* (1955), seen later at the Royal Court, where *Les Séquestrés d'Altona* (1959) was seen in 1961 as *Altona*. It was not seen in New York until 1965, when it was produced by the Vivian Beaumont Repertory company at Lincoln Center (q.v.) as *The Condemned of Altona*. In 1969 one of Sartre's many successful film-scripts, *L'Engrenage*, was successfully adapted for the stage, and in 1970 his adaptation of the elder Dumas's *Kean* (1836), first seen in Paris in 1953 and used as the basis for an American musical in 1961, was produced at the Oxford Playhouse with Alan Badel (q.v.), and later moved to London.

Satyr-Drama, burlesque plays which followed, and served as ribald comments on, the statutory 'tragic trilogies' in the annual dramatic contest instituted by Pisistratus in connection with the festival of Dionysus (q.v.) in Athens. In them an heroic figure, sometimes the protagonist of the preceding trilogy but very often Hercules, was shown in a farcical situation, always with a chorus of Sileni, or satyrs. These were the legendary companions of Dionysus, half-human, half-animal, with the ears and tail of a horse. The characteristics of the satyr-play, which resembled Greek tragedy in its form, were swift action, vigorous dancing, boisterous fun, and indecency in speech and gesture. Although Aristotle (q.v.) says that Greek tragedy 'developed from the satyr-play', the connection between them is not clear and must date from long before the time of the first official festival in 534 B.C. Only one satyr-play survives in its entirety, the *Cyclops* of Euripides (q.v.). There are also fragments of the *Ichneutae* by Sophocles (q.v.). The popularity of satyr-drama obviously declined during the second half of the fifth century, as in 438 B.C. Euripides' tragicomedy *Alcestis* served as the fourth play of a tetralogy which it resembled only by its general treatment and by the appearance of a 'genial' Hercules.

There is no connection between satyr-drama and satire, or between satyr-drama and any form of Greek comedy.

SAUNDERS, JAMES (1925–), English dramatist, who after writing a number of one-act plays vaguely reminiscent of Ionesco (q.v.), among them *Alas, Poor Fred* and *The Ark* (both 1959), created something of a sensation with a play based on the life and death of the Great Canfield hermit Alexander James Mason. As *Next Time I'll Sing to You* (1962), this was first presented by the Questors Theatre (q.v.) in a season of new plays, and in a revised form was successfully produced in 1963 in the West End and New York. Some more one-act plays followed, of which *Neighbours* was seen in a double bill at the Hampstead Theatre Club in 1964, a year which also saw the first production at the Questors of the controversial *A Scent of Flowers*, dealing with the time immediately after a young girl's suicide, the girl herself appearing as the chief character. This also was successfully transferred to the West End. In 1967, in collaboration with the author, Saunders dramatized Iris Murdoch's novel, *The Italian Girl*, for the Bristol Old Vic. In a production by Val May, this moved to London and ran for nearly a year at Wyndham's. It was followed by a further play for the Questors, *The Borage Pigeon Affair*, and by *The Travails of Sancho Panza* (both 1969), based on Cervantes's *Don Quixote* and specially written for production by the National Theatre company at the Old Vic.

SAURIN, BERNARD-JOSEPH (1706–81), a French lawyer who at the age of forty retired to devote his time to literature. Two of his plays were based on English works—a tragedy, *Blanche et Guiscard* (1763), on Thomson's *Tancred and Sigismunda* (1745), a *drame bourgeois*, *Beverleï* (1768), on Edward Moore's *The Gamester* (1753). The former was not as successful as the actors had hoped, according to Mlle Clairon (q.v.), who played in it, but the latter remained in the repertory for many years. Saurin probably took it from a translation by Diderot (q.v.), as there is no evidence that he knew English, but he omitted most of the melodrama and concentrated on the pathetic situation of the gambler's family, particularly Tomi, his infant son. Of Saurin's other plays, the most successful were a comedy entitled *Les Mœurs du temps* (1759) and a tragedy, *Spartacus* (1760).

Saville Theatre, LONDON, in Shaftesbury

Avenue. This opened on 8 Oct. 1931 with *For the Love of Mike*, which, billed as a 'play with tunes', inaugurated a series of successful musicals, including *He Wanted Adventure* (1933) (based on Hackett's play, *Ambrose Applejohn's Adventure*) and *Jill Darling!* (1934) with music by Vivian Ellis. In 1938 the theatre turned to straight plays with Shaw's *Geneva*, and later housed a transfer of Priestley's *Johnson over Jordan* from the New Theatre. It was damaged by enemy action in 1940 but carried on after hasty repairs, mainly with musicals and light comedy, until John Clements took over in 1955, inaugurating a fine series of revivals with Ibsen's *The Wild Duck*. He left in 1957, since when outstanding productions have included Hunter's *A Touch of the Sun*, with Michael and Vanessa Redgrave, and a musical, *Expresso Bongo*, based on a story by Wolf Mankowitz, with Paul Scofield (both 1958); Evelyn Laye in Kimmins's *The Amorous Prawn* (1959); Ustinov's *Photo Finish* (1962); Harry Secombe in *Pickwick* (1963), a musical based on Dickens's novel; and Brecht's *The Resistible Rise of Arturo Ui* (1969), from the Nottingham Playhouse. After a short run of Robin Maugham's *Enemy!*, which opened on 17 Dec. 1969, the theatre closed and was converted into two cinemas.

Savoy Theatre, LONDON, in the Strand. Built for Richard D'Oyly Carte, this opened on 10 Oct. 1881 with *Patience*, transferred from the Opera Comique (q.v.), and gave its name to the whole series of Gilbert and Sullivan collaborations, most of which were seen there, as were German's *Merrie England* (1901) and *The Princess of Kensington* (1903), which closed the long reign of light opera. In 1907 Granville-Barker and J. E. Vedrenne, fresh from their successful seasons at the Royal Court (q.v.), staged the first London production of Shaw's *Caesar and Cleopatra*. From 1912 to 1914 they were also responsible for some outstanding revivals of Shakespeare. It was at the Savoy in 1911 that the successful children's play, *Where the Rainbow Ends*, was seen for the first time. Later successes included Coward's *The Young Idea* (1923), Van Druten's *Young Woodley* (1928), and Sherriff's *Journey's End* (1929). The theatre was then closed for alterations, reopening on 21 Oct. 1929 with a revival of Gilbert and Sullivan's *The Gondoliers*. During the

next decade it was used mainly for transfers, but in 1941 *The Man Who Came to Dinner*, by Kaufman and Moss Hart, had a long run, as did two American comedies based on volumes of short stories, *My Sister Eileen* (1943) and *Life with Father* (1947). Later successes were Alec Coppel's *The Gazebo* (1960), Ronald Millar's *The Masters* (1963), based on a novel by C. P. Snow, and *The Secretary Bird* (1968), by William Douglas Home.

SCALA, FLAMINIO (*fl.* 1600–21), see CONFIDENTI.

Scala Theatre, LONDON, in Tottenham Street, Tottenham Court Road. This opened as the King's Concert Rooms in 1772, became the Tottenham Street Theatre in 1810, and in Dec. 1814 was sold to the father of the well-known scene painter William Beverley (q.v.). He renamed it the Regency Theatre, but it had little success, and in 1820 was reopened by Brunton as the West London, his daughter Elizabeth, who later married the actor Frederick Yates (q.v.), starring in many of his productions. The theatre was constantly in trouble with the Patent Theatres (q.v.) and was closed for several years, reopening in 1831 as the Queen's or alternatively the Fitzroy. It had a chequered career, sank to lurid melodrama, and was nicknamed the 'Dust Hole'. In 1865, taken over by Marie Wilton (see BANCROFT), it was completely redecorated, renamed (by royal permission) the Prince of Wales, and reopened in the presence of the future Edward VII with immediate success. It was under the management of the Bancrofts that the epoch-making plays of J. W. Robertson (q.v.) were first produced, beginning with *Society* in 1865. *Caste*, the only one to have been revived in recent times, was seen in 1867. Other important productions were *Masks and Faces* (1875), by Tom Taylor and Charles Reade, and Sardou's *Diplomacy* (1878). By 1880, when the Bancrofts left to go to the Haymarket (q.v.), the despised 'Dust Hole' had become a fashionable theatre at which such players as Ellen Terry, Robertson's sister Madge and her husband W. H. Kendal, and John Hare (qq.v.) had been glad to appear. In 1882 the theatre was condemned as structurally unsound and was closed, remaining derelict for some years and then being used as a Salvation Army hostel. In 1903 it was demolished, only the original portico remaining to serve as the stage-door entrance of a new theatre, which, as the Scala, opened on 23 Sept. 1905. It was not a success, and often stood empty or was used for films, puppet-shows, or amateur productions. Slightly damaged by enemy action in 1941, it became the headquarters of the U.S. Army Theatre Unit in 1943 and after the war was used mainly by amateurs, apart from an annual revival of Barrie's *Peter Pan* at Christmas. In 1969 it was closed, and was demolished shortly after, with a promise that a new small theatre or cinema would be incorporated in the basement of the office block to be built on its site.

Scapino, one of the *zanni* or servant roles of the *commedia dell'arte* (q.v.). Like Brighella (q.v.), Scapino was crafty and unprincipled, and when in danger lived up to his name, which means 'to run off' or 'to escape'. The first actor to play him was FRANCESCO GABRIELLI (?–1654), who was in the company which went with the younger Andreini (q.v.) to Paris in 1624. Through him and later actors of the part it passed into French comedy to end up as the quick-witted and unscrupulous valet of Molière's *Les Fourberies de Scapin* (1671).

Scaramuccia, who in France became Scaramouche, a character of the *commedia dell'arte* (q.v.) which is sometimes classed with the braggart soldier (see CAPITANO) but is perhaps more akin to the *zanni* or servant roles. The actor most closely associated with the role, though he may not have been the first to play it, was Tiberio Fiorillo (q.v.).

SCARRON, PAUL (1610–60), French playwright and novelist, who was crippled by rheumatism at the age of thirty and forced to rely on his pen for a livelihood. He wrote a number of witty though slightly scabrous farces, of which two, *Jodelet, ou le maître-valet* (1643) and *Jodelet souffleté* (1645), were acted by the comedian of that name at the Théâtre du Marais (q.v.). Several comedies followed, based on Spanish plays to which Scarron added a good deal of his own material, modernizing the originals. Of these *Don Japhet d'Arménie* (1647) was extremely successful, and was later revived by Molière, and *L'Écolier de Salamanque* (1654) is still remembered for its valet, Crispin, played for so long by the actor-

family Poisson (q.v.). Scarron may have taken from a Spanish novel, *Le viaje entretenido* (1603), by Agustin de Rojas, the idea of his own novel, *Le Roman comique* (1651), which depicts the adventures and miseries of a band of strolling players, for whose leader, Léandro, the provincial actor-manager Filandre (q.v.) is believed to have served as a model. In 1652 Scarron married a beautiful but penniless orphan, Françoise d'Aubigné, who as Mme de Maintenon (q.v.) became the second wife of Louis XIV and virtual ruler of France.

Scenario, a word now used mainly for the script of a film or for a summary of the action of a musical play. Originally it was applied to the skeleton plots of the *commedia dell'arte* (q.v.), replacing some time in the early eighteenth century the older word *soggetto*. These are not such synopses as might be drawn up by an author for his written drama, nor should they be confused with the Elizabethan 'platt' (q.v.), but theatrical documents prepared for the use of professional companies. They consist of a scene-by-scene résumé of the action of the play, together with some notes on locality and special effects. Their informal elasticity allowed the insertion of extraneous 'business' according to the discretion or ability of the actors presenting them.

Scene Room, see GREEN ROOM.

Scenery, a term which covers everything used on stage to represent the place in which an action is performed, including hangings, painted flats, cut-outs, box-sets, etc. Scenery is a comparatively recent innovation in the history of the theatre. Greek plays were acted against a stage wall which by Roman times had become a grandiose architectural façade, the *scaenae frons*. But, except for the *periaktoi* (q.v.) of Hellenistic and Roman times, the classical stage had no scenery as we know it. This is true also of the medieval period, when first the interior of the church and then its outside wall provided a permanent setting for liturgical drama (q.v.). The open-air Mystery Play (q.v.), which developed from the liturgical drama, had its special structures set up on a stage in the town square or market place, but these were in the nature of properties rather than scenery, which was first used in Renaissance Italy, where plays were given indoors with all the splendour possible. The use in the mid-fifteenth century of perspective painting to make the enclosed space seem larger was perhaps the first step in the evolution of the scenic picture, and it was Peruzzi (q.v.) who first made deliberate use of it for theatrical effects. In this he was helped by the widespread influence of the newly discovered architectural works of Vitruvius (q.v.) which culminated in the three stage-settings of Serlio (q.v.), for tragic, comic, and satyric plays. These remained for nearly three hundred years the basic elements in European scenic design. The influence of Italian scenery, as developed by Buontalenti (q.v.) and his successors in the form of a painted backcloth, first with *telari*, or three-sided prisms, in imitation of the classical *periaktoi*, and later with flat side-wings sliding in grooves, spread all over Europe and was introduced into England by Inigo Jones (q.v.). The court masques popular with the early Stuart kings from 1600 to 1640 provided him with the opportunity for designing elaborate scenic effects. These might have been adopted by the public theatres, which until then had had practically no scenery, had it not been for the outbreak of the Civil War in 1642. It was not until the Restoration in 1660 that the English theatre caught up with developments on the Continent, where Torelli (q.v.), the first professional scene painter, had taken his ideas from Venice to Paris, ousting the old-fashioned multiple setting (q.v.) still in use at the Hôtel de Bourgogne in favour of a flexible set of columns in perspective with a changeable background. Although much of the action of the Restoration play took place on the projecting apron stage which was derived from the Elizabethan platform stage, scenic artists like Aggas and Webb (qq.v.) found scope for their activities in designing sets of wings and back-cloths for Dorset Garden and Drury Lane. But it was a long time before England produced anything to rival the work of the great Continental designers like the Burnacinis (q.v.), the Mauris, the Galliaris, and above all the Bibienas (q.v.), whose work was found in almost every capital city of the time. The advent of the diagonal perspective first used by the Bibienas, and the growing popularity of landscape painting, gradually changed the whole character of theatrical decoration. Neo-classicism brought supremacy to the French designer over the Italian, and the influence of the work done by Servandony (q.v.) at the Salle des Machines in Paris was soon evident in the designs of such later Italian artists as the Quaglio brothers (q.v.). England, having escaped the influence of baroque art, was equally untouched by neo-classicism, but under the influence of Garrick's designer, Philip de Loutherbourg (q.v.), the old architectural setting was abandoned in favour of romantic landscape, with transparencies and elaborate cut-outs which did so much to enhance the attractiveness of the stage picture and were still in use a hundred years later, finding their ultimate home in pantomime (q.v.). The nineteenth century, dominated by William Grieve (q.v.) and his family, and by the histrionic talent of Clarkson Stanfield (q.v.), saw also an enthusiasm for neo-Gothic design and a growing insistence on authentic architectural detail. This new passion for accuracy began with the designs of Capon (q.v.) for John Philip Kemble's Shakespearian revivals at Drury Lane from 1794 to 1802 and at Covent Garden in the 1810s, and was continued by Charles Kean in the 1850s at the Princess's, where one of his artists was William Telbin (q.v.). So strong was the influence of the early nineteenth century on the English stage that it continued well into the 1870s with Hawes Craven (q.v.). But the day of the painted backcloth and wings was nearly over, except for opera and ballet. The growing demand for realism led to the general introduction of the box-set (q.v.), which had already been tried out in several smaller theatres, with its three solid walls and a ceiling, its real furniture and accessories, and its practicable doors and windows. The apotheosis of realism came with the founding in 1887 of Antoine's Théâtre Libre (q.v.), which limited its repertoire to the new plays of the naturalistic school. It had a great influence on Stanislavsky (q.v.), which, combined with that of the Meininger company (q.v.), led him to push naturalism to its utmost limits to such an extent that it finally transcended realism and provided the perfect instrument for the presentation of the plays of Chekhov (q.v.), in which the outward trappings of contemporary reality serve to throw into relief the underlying universality of the characters' personalities.

Meanwhile, the reaction against reality had begun in France, where the symbolists demanded simplified, often stylized, scenery, evocative rather than descriptive, with complete harmony between scenery and costume, hitherto separate and often discordant conceptions. These conditions served admirably for the plays of such authors as Maeterlinck (q.v.), and were reinforced by the publication of the works of Appia (q.v.), whose ideas on plasticity and three-dimensional scenery for a three-dimensional actor were made practicable by the adoption of electric light. Other mechanical devices which came into use at this time included the revolving stage, first used in 1896 at Munich, the sliding stage, and the waggon stage, all of which permitted quick changes of elaborate scenes already set up. But the multiplicity of machinery defeated its own ends, and once again scenic designers set out on a search for a drastic simplicity. In this the leader was Craig (q.v.), who endeavoured to build up an imaginative stage-picture, with no concessions to reality at all, by the use of large screens lit by coloured lights. This negation of scenery, by a strange irony, ran parallel with the last flare-up of the picturesque painted set, brought to perfection by the scene designers of the Russian Ballet working for Diaghilev (q.v.), who came near to realizing the ideal of the superman envisaged by Craig, combining in himself, author, producer, scene designer, and costumier. But he was working in a dying tradition. Equally versatile, but more in touch with modern tendencies, was Reinhardt (q.v.), who made use in his work of all possible styles, from the stylized scenic picture behind the proscenium arch, as in his productions of classic plays in the Hofburg in Vienna, to the open stage whose productions spilled over into the auditorium, as with *The Miracle* in London or *Jedermann* in Salzburg.

In the years immediately following the First World War, when Expressionism (q.v.), an aesthetic movement which had its roots in post-war Germany, was having a brief flowering on the European stage (though its masterpiece was a film, *The Cabinet of Dr. Caligari*), American designers began to come to the fore. Hitherto stage-sets in the United States had been based very much on the ideas prevalent earlier in Europe, with Belasco (q.v.) as the arch-apostle of realism. But with the advent of artists such as Robert Edmond Jones and Norman Bel Geddes

(qq.v.), the American theatre began to play a leading part in the development of stage designing which continues to the present day. England remained for the most part indifferent to Continental and American developments, Lovat Fraser (q.v.), the only artist who might have inaugurated a movement of far-reaching significance, dying young after producing his admirably simple semi-permanent set for a revival of Gay's *The Beggar's Opera* in 1920. In general, England remained faithful to realism and the box-set, and even the best scene designers, like Charles Ricketts, found little scope for their talents. In France the best theatre directors of the post-war age—Copeau, Jouvet, Dullin (qq.v.)—still strove to get away from the whole tradition of the painted scene. Copeau indeed dispensed with scenery entirely, and the sets of Dullin were based on Craig's idea of movable screens. In Russia the Revolution had swept away the conventional forms of theatre décor, reducing the set to bare scaffolding or the sparse clean lines of metal machinery. Décor became frankly symbolic, simplified to the point of abstraction. There could be no further progress in that direction, and the Russian stage, led by the Moscow Art Theatre (q.v.), swung back to a modified realism, and also, in the case of classical revivals, to a certain romanticism. Throughout Europe the period of fundamental innovation ended in about 1930, after which the growing threat of war inhibited the free expansion of new ideas. But it was then that England began to catch up with Continental developments, while the widespread interest taken in opera and ballet opened up new fields of which many talented designers took advantage, as did the short reign of non-realistic drama after the Second World War. This was followed by a depressing period during which décor seemed the least important element in a production, but in recent years there have been a number of interesting developments in staging which have called in question the whole concept of stage design. The enthusiasm for open stages and theatre-in-the-round seemed at one time to threaten the existence of scene painting, but designers have found inspiration in new media, and it is perhaps a measure of the vitality of the modern theatre that all styles are now possible. The only thing the director and/or designer—for often the two are combined

—has to discover is which is most in harmony with the mood and message of the play.

SCHIKANEDER, EMANUEL [really JOHANN JOSEF SCHICKENEDER] (1751–1812), Austrian dramatist, actor, and theatre director, chiefly remembered for his association with Mozart, whom he first met at Salzburg in 1780. In 1791 their collaboration produced the opera 'The Magic Flute', for which Schikaneder wrote the libretto and in which he created the part of Papageno. As well as being an excellent singer, Schikaneder, who was at the Burgtheater from 1785 to 1786, was a good actor in parts ranging from Hamlet to popular farce and *Singspiele*. A favourite of the Emperor Joseph II, he was given permission to erect a theatre in Vienna, opening the famous Theater an der Wien in 1801. This was the highlight of his career. Soon after, his fortunes declined and he died poor and insane.

SCHILLER, (JOHANN CHRISTOPH) FRIEDRICH VON (1759–1805), one of Germany's outstanding poets and dramatists. He was only twenty-two when his first play, *Die Räuber*, was accepted by Dalberg (q.v.), who produced it at Mannheim in 1782. It was an immediate success, particularly with the younger generation, and a year later Schiller was appointed official dramatist to the theatre, writing for it *Fiesco* (1783) and *Kabale und Liebe* (1784). In spite of his artistic success, Schiller, who was absent without leave from his duties as an army doctor, living under an assumed name, was heavily in debt and was befriended by Charlotte von Kalb, whose influence is apparent in his first historical tragedy, *Don Carlos* (1789). Soon after, he married, eking out a miserable existence at Jena as a teacher of history and publishing two historical works, one on the Netherlands, one on the Thirty Years War. The research undertaken for the latter provided him with the material for his great dramatic trilogy, *Wallenstein*, which was completed in 1799 and translated into English by Coleridge (q.v.). Schiller's last years, before his early death from tuberculosis, were spent in Weimar, where he enjoyed the friendship and collaboration of Goethe (q.v.), who produced some of his best works, notably the plays *Maria Stuart* (1800), *Die Jungfrau von Orleans* (1801), *Die Braut von Messina* (1803),

notable for the lyric beauty of its choruses, and his last play, *Wilhelm Tell* (1804). All Schiller's plays were translated into English, at first for reading rather than for the stage. The most influential was *Die Räuber*, which reinforced the *Sturm und Drang* movement unleashed by Goethe's *Götz von Berlichingen* (1773). As *The Red-Cross Knights*, in an adaptation by Holman, it was seen at the Haymarket in 1799 and, as *The Robbers*, at Drury Lane in 1851, a year after Planché's adaptation of *Fiesco*. *Kabale und Liebe*, as *The Harper's Daughter*, was seen at Covent Garden in 1803 and, as *Power and Principle*, at the Strand in 1850. It was seen in German in London during the World Theatre season of 1964. The only play to be seen in translation in recent years has been *Maria Stuart*, which brings together Elizabeth I and Mary Queen of Scots, who in real life never met. In a translation by Stephen Spender, this was performed by the National Theatre at the Old Vic in 1958 and 1960. Earlier translations were staged at Covent Garden in 1819 and the Court Theatre in 1880.

SCHILLER, LEON (1887–1954), Polish theatre director, who while living in Paris collaborated with Gordon Craig (q.v.) on *The Mask* (1908–9). In 1911 he organized the first exhibition of Craig's drawings in Warsaw, where he was director successively of the Teatr Polski, the Reduta Theatre, and the Bogusławski Theatre, his productions of Shakespeare at the last theatre being much admired. Like Wyspiański (q.v.), whose disciple he was, he envisaged a 'total theatre' to which everything—acting, music, scenery, lighting—should contribute, and which should be above all a theatre of ideas. His political views led to the closing of his theatre, but he continued to work elsewhere, in Łódź, Lwów, and even again in Warsaw. One of his most remarkable productions was *Roar, China!*, by Tretyakov (q.v.), but he also remained faithful to the romantic Polish repertory, producing *Forefathers' Eve* by Mickiewicz (q.v.) in several towns between 1932 and 1934, and at Sofia, in Bulgarian, in 1937. He had a great influence on the younger generation of directors and scene designers through his work at the Institute of Theatre Art, and more particularly through the theatre journal, *Pamiętnik Teatralny*, which he founded. Interned at

Auschwitz, he was released in 1941 and, since the Germans had closed all the Polish theatres, produced plays secretly. In 1944 he founded a theatre in Germany, and later took it to Łódź, where his last important production was *The Tempest* (1947). A collection of his writings on the theatre was published posthumously under the title of *Teatr Ogromny* (1961).

SCHLEGEL, AUGUST WILHELM VON (1767–1845), German dramatist and critic, nephew of the dramatist JOHANN ELIAS VON SCHLEGEL (1719–49). He was a talented translator of the plays of Shakespeare, Cervantes, and Calderón, and also wrote a number of plays himself. These, though they showed little originality, avoided the worst excesses of Romanticism. In a series of lectures given at Vienna and published there as *Über dramatische Kunst und Literatur* (1809–11), he traced for the first time the parallel development of drama in all countries.

SCHNITZLER, ARTHUR (1862–1931), Austrian dramatist, a doctor by profession, who brought to his plays something of the dispassionate attitude of the consulting-room. His first work for the theatre was *Anatol* (1893), a series of sketches centring round an unscrupulous young *galant*; this was followed by *Liebelei* (1894), in which a working-class girl kills herself on learning of the death of the young aristocrat who had been merely trifling with her affections. Among Schnitzler's later plays are *Der grüne Kakadu* (1899), a one-act play on an incident of the French Revolution in which he handles with a sure touch the change from irresponsible make-believe to grim reality; *Reigen* (1902), best remembered as the basis of the film *La Ronde*; *Der einsame Weg* (1904), a sensitive play of delicate half-lights; *Der Ruf des Lebens* (1905); and *Professor Bernhardi* (1912), his one contribution to the problem-play, in which he views from all angles the repercussions of an anti-Semitic incident in a Viennese hospital.

SCHÖNEMANN, JOHANN FRIEDRICH (1704–82), German actor, originally a harlequin in a travelling troupe. He later joined the company of Carolina Neuber (q.v.), and in 1740 formed his own company, in which were Sophia Schröder, Ekhof, and Ackermann (qq.v.), all destined to play a large part in the develop-

ment of the German theatre. Schönemann, who was good in comedy but less successful in tragedy, to which he brought the pompous declamatory style evolved by Gottsched (q.v.) and adopted by Carolina Neuber, was at first an able and astute manager, but later ruined himself by his hobby of horse-dealing, so retired, and abandoned the company to Ekhof.

School Drama, a term applied to the academic, educational plays which developed in all European countries under the influence of the humanists. Written by scholars for performance by schoolboys, they were originally in Latin, a tradition which persisted longest in the Jesuit colleges (see JESUIT DRAMA). Elsewhere they tended to slip quickly into the vernacular, and had some influence on the development of the non-academic, popular, and later professional drama. There was a great deal of dramatic activity in English schools and colleges in the first half of the sixteenth century, and the first two regular English comedies—*Ralph Roister Doister* and *Gammer Gurton's Needle*—were given at Eton (or possibly Westminster), and at Christ's College, Cambridge, respectively. The tradition of an annual school play has survived in many schools. Bradfield for many years produced a Greek play in the original in an open-air theatre annually; Harrow productions of Shakespeare in an approximation to an Elizabethan theatre made some stir under Ronald Watkins in the 1950s; Sloane School gave a long series of excellent productions under the headmastership of Guy Boas, as did Bryanston under Coade. The only surviving tradition of a Latin play in modern times is at Westminster (see WESTMINSTER PLAY); plays in Greek are occasionally given at Oxford and Cambridge (qq.v.).

(See also BOY COMPANIES.)

Schouwburg, AMSTERDAM, see CAMPEN, JACOB VAN.

SCHREYVOGEL, JOSEF (1768–1832), Austrian theatre director, who in 1814 was appointed head of the three major theatres in Vienna, the Burgtheater, the Kärntnertor, and the Theater an der Wien. Well-read and a great traveller, he endeavoured to further the literary reforms inaugurated by Sonnenfels (q.v.), and was careful to provide a balanced programme of plays, old and new, German and foreign, particularly at the Burgtheater, which under him became one of the outstanding theatres of Europe. One of his greatest achievements was the discovery and fostering of the genius of Grillparzer (q.v.).

SCHRÖDER, FRIEDRICH LUDWIG (1744–1816), a great German actor, and the first to introduce Shakespeare (q.v.) on the stage to his compatriots. The son of Sophia Schröder (q.v.), he played as a child in the travelling company of his stepfather, Ackermann (q.v.), but in 1756, on the outbreak of war, became separated from it, and for the next few years lived by his wits, becoming in the process an expert acrobat and rope-dancer. He eventually rejoined the company in Switzerland and resumed his acting career, but considered it very inferior to that of a tumbler. It was the advent of Ekhof (q.v.), then at the height of his powers, that made him realize what acting could be. During the next few years he studied and practised his art to such good effect that he gradually took over most of Ekhof's parts, leaving the older man no option but to withdraw. On Ackermann's death in 1771 the young Schröder assumed artistic leadership of the company, his mother retaining financial control, a situation which eventually caused trouble. In the meantime, however, Schröder raised the reputation of the company to an enviable height and was responsible for the production of several important new plays, including *Emilia Galotti* (1772), by Lessing (q.v.), and *Götz von Berlichingen* (1773), by Goethe (q.v.). But his chief enterprise was the introduction of Shakespeare in action to young Germans who had previously met him only on the printed page. The adaptations of Shakespeare's tragedies, in which Romeo, Juliet, Cordelia, Ophelia, and even Hamlet survived, were made by Schröder himself, and he probably knew how much of the original his audience would take. He began with *Hamlet* in 1776, in which Brockmann (q.v.) played the title-role and Schröder the Ghost (he later played Laertes, the Gravedigger, and Hamlet), and by 1780 eleven of Shakespeare's plays had been performed, of which *Othello* was a failure and *King Lear* an outstanding success. To offset all this pioneer work Schröder continued to give his audiences a more

conservative repertory of now-forgotten plays and monodramas, ballets and light musical pieces, which enhanced the prosperity and reputation of his actors. But tiring at last of the constant friction with his mother over money matters, he decided in 1782 to go with his wife CHRISTINE HART (?–1829) as guest-artist to the Burgtheater in Vienna, where he remained for four years. Though this experience added little to his own development, he exercised a salutary influence on his fellow-actors and may be said to have laid the foundations of the subtle ensemble playing which was later a distinguishing feature of that theatre's productions. He enjoyed his years in Vienna, but in 1786 had once more to take over the company which his mother, at the age of seventy-two, could no longer control. He again gave it an important position in German theatrical life, but the fire and enthusiasm of the earlier period were lacking and the energy that should have gone to the production of the last great plays of Schiller (q.v.) and Goethe was dissipated on the trivialities of Iffland and Kotzebue (qq.v.). Nevertheless, once given a free hand financially, Schröder prospered, and in 1798 he was able to buy and retire to a country estate at Holstein, where he died. His life was written by his friend, F. L. W. Meyer, and he appears in Goethe's novel *Wilhelm Meister* (1795) in the person of Serlo.

SCHRÖDER [*née* BIEREICHEL], SOPHIA CARLOTTA (1714–92), German actress, who was persuaded by the actor Ekhof (q.v.) to leave her drunken and unsatisfactory husband in order to join the company of Schönemann (q.v.). She made her début at Lüneburg as Monime in an adaptation of Racine's *Mithradate* on 15 Jan. 1740, and was immediately successful. When Ackermann (q.v.) left Schönemann to form his own company, she went with him as his leading lady, but shortly after returned to her husband. Their reconciliation resulted in the birth of one of Germany's greatest actors, Friedrich Schröder (q.v.), but the husband was unable to overcome his intemperance and Sophia returned to the stage, marrying Ackermann after her husband's death. She toured with him indefatigably, and after his death in 1771 retained a tight hold on the company, particularly as regards finance, finally driving her son, who was its leading actor and artistic manager.

to leave for Vienna. He returned in 1786, by which time she no longer had the strength to refuse his demand for a free hand, and spent the last six years of her life in unwilling retirement.

SCHWARTZ, EUGENE, see SHWARTZ.

SCHWARTZ, MAURICE (1889–1960), Jewish actor and director. Born in the Ukraine, he went to the United States as a child, and later appeared in Yiddish plays in several towns before joining the company of David Kessler in New York. In 1918 he was at the Irving Place Theatre, on the south-west corner of Irving Place and 15th Street, where in 1919 he directed a performance of *Dos Fervorfen Winkle*, by Peretz Hirschbein (q.v.). This proved a turning-point in his career; but his greatest achievement was his discovery of the work of Sholom Aleichem (q.v.), the quintessence of Jewish folk humour and characterization. Schwartz also introduced to the stage the works of a number of other Jewish writers, including OSSIP DYMOV [really PERLMANN, also known as KAIN] (1878–1959) and Halper Levick (q.v.). In 1924 he was emboldened by the success of his New York productions to undertake a tour of Europe which proved successful, and he returned to New York to open a theatre on Broadway for the production of European classics in Yiddish. This, however, failed, and in 1926 he opened a Yiddish Art Theatre on 2nd Avenue (see PHOENIX THEATRE (2)). He later toured South America and also visited Palestine (Israel), where he worked with Ohel (q.v.). His repertory was extensive, comprising some hundred and fifty roles, and under his influence a number of Yiddish Art Theatres were founded in New York; but the widespread adoption of English by Yiddish families, and a slackening of Jewish immigration to the States, caused a decline in their fortunes. In 1959 Schwartz went to Israel hoping to establish a Yiddish theatre there, but died after producing only one play, Singer's *Yoshe Kalb*.

Scissor Cross, see STAGE DIRECTIONS.

Scissor Stage, see BOAT TRUCK.

SCOFIELD, (DAVID) PAUL (1922–), English actor, who in 1945 was with the Birmingham Repertory company, where

he first came into prominence with his portrayal of the Bastard in *King John*. The following year he went to Stratford-upon-Avon under Barry Jackson (q.v.), who in 1945 had been appointed director of the theatre there, and during the next three seasons played a variety of Shakespearian parts which ranged from Don Armado in *Love's Labour's Lost* to the title-roles in *Pericles* and *Hamlet*. This last part he played again in 1955, first in London and then at the Moscow Art Theatre with the first English company to appear in Russia since the Revolution. For this, and for his other services to the theatre, he was appointed C.B.E. in 1956. In the intervening years he had been seen in a wide variety of parts, including Tegeus-Chromis in Fry's *A Phoenix Too Frequent* (1946), Alexander the Great in Rattigan's *Adventure Story* (1949), and the twin brothers, Hugo and Frederick, in Anouilh's *Ring Round the Moon* (1950). One of his few modern parts at this time was Sturgess in Charles Morgan's *The River Line* (1952), and he also played the drunken priest in Graham Greene's *The Power and the Glory* (1956). In 1953 he gave a fine performance as Pierre in Otway's *Venice Preserv'd*, and in 1960 was outstanding as Sir Thomas More in Robert Bolt's *A Man for All Seasons*. He returned to Stratford in 1962 to play Lear, giving a fine performance which was seen later in London and on tour in Europe, where it made a great impression, particularly in Russia. He followed this in 1965 with the title-role in *Timon of Athens*, and a year later was seen at the Aldwych as Khlestakov in Gogol's *The Government Inspector*. A further incursion into modern drama, as Laurie in Osborne's *The Hotel in Amsterdam* (1968), was followed by a return to the classics with a superb performance in the title-role of Chekhov's *Uncle Vanya* at the Royal Court in 1970, in which year Scofield was appointed associate director of the National Theatre (q.v.).

SCOTT, CLEMENT WILLIAM (1841–1904), English dramatic critic, who for nearly thirty years reviewed plays for the *Daily Telegraph*, putting up a determined resistance to the new drama as typified by Ibsen (q.v.). His well-known attack on *Ghosts* as 'a wretched deplorable loathsome history . . .' was the outcome of his obstinate refusal to consider anything outside his own range of conventional morality. Yet he had his good points. Shaw called him a 'dramatic reporter', and he certainly had the trick of engaging and holding the attention of the average reader by appealing to his sensibilities and not his intellect. He was for many years editor of *The Theatre*, a monthly magazine which he founded in 1877. Though too often used for the expression of Scott's own highly individual views, it is a useful source of information on the theatre of its period. In its later years it distressed its founder, who withdrew from the editorship in 1890, by supporting his rival William Archer (q.v.) in his campaign for the modern drama. It ceased publication in 1897. Scott, who published in 1897 a volume of reviews of Irving's first nights, *From 'The Bells' to 'King Arthur'*, was also the author or translator of a number of plays, usually written in collaboration. The only one to survive in performance is *Diplomacy* (1878), based by Scott and B. C. Stephenson on Sardou's *Dora* (1877). First produced by the Bancrofts (q.v.) at the Prince of Wales', it was last revived in London in 1933.

Scottish Community Drama Association (S.C.D.A.), see BRITISH DRAMA LEAGUE.

Scottish National Players. They made their first appearance under the auspices of the St. Andrew Society of Glasgow in Jan. 1921, presenting three new Scottish one-act plays. Towards the end of the year they presented two new full-length plays in the Athenaeum Theatre, Glasgow, and then ceased to be the responsibility of the St. Andrew Society, coming under a newly-formed body, the Scottish National Theatre Society. When the society was wound up in 1934 the Players continued independently, their last productions (after a war-time interruption) being in 1948. Although they had not achieved their aim of creating a Scottish pendant to the Dublin Abbey Theatre (q.v.), never acquiring a permanent home or a fully professional company, they had, between 1921 and 1931, brought into being over seventy new plays, many of them by such authors as Gordon Bottomley, James Bridie, Joe Corrie, and Robert Kemp, reflecting every aspect of Scottish life. In 1926 and 1927 their producer was Tyrone Guthrie (q.v.).

Scottish Roscius, see JOHNSTON, H. E.

SCRIBE, (AUGUSTIN) EUGÈNE (1791–1861), French dramatist, the originator and exponent of the 'well-made play'. A prolific writer, he was responsible, alone or in collaboration, for more than four hundred plays, comprising tragedies, comedies, vaudevilles, and libretti for light opera. His early plays were failures and he first came into prominence in 1815 with *Une Nuit de la Garde Nationale*. In 1820 came the first night of *Un Verre d'eau*, translated into English by Suter as *A Glass of Water; or, Great Events from Trifling Causes Spring* (1863) and by S. Grundy as *The Queen's Favourite* (1883). The most successful of Scribe's plays, and the one best remembered, was *Adrienne Lecouvreur* (1849), written in collaboration with Legouvé, who in 1874 wrote Scribe's biography. The play, though historically incorrect, provided a fine part for Rachel, and later for Sarah Bernhardt (qq.v.). In translation it was played by Ristori, Modjeska, Helena Faucit, and many others. As in all Scribe's plays, which were constructed with the utmost neatness and economy, the situations are banal, the language poor, the characters, with the exception of Adrienne herself, paste-board figures. Yet in his own day he was immensely popular. He wrote successfully for a number of theatres for more than thirty years, and his example weighed heavily on the European theatre for long after his death. Indeed, he was blamed for all the shortcomings of the dramatists who succeeded him, and in France his influence was strong on Labiche and Sardou (qq.v.)

Scruto, see TRANSFORMATION SCENE and TRAP.

SEDAINE, MICHEL-JEAN (1719–97), a French dramatist who, finding himself endowed with a facility for writing amusing lyric verse, turned out a number of excellent libretti for light operas with music by Grétry, Philidor, Monsigny, and others. One of the most successful was 'Le Roi et le Fermier', based, probably by way of Collé's *La Partie de chasse d'Henri IV*, on Dodsley's *The King and the Miller of Mansfield* (1737). Sedaine's most important work, however, and the one by which he is best remembered, is *Le Philosophe sans le savoir* (1765), a *drame bourgeois* written under the influence of Diderot (q.v.) which interprets his dramatic theories better than their originator could do in his own plays. It shows little imagination, but has a lively wit and delicately drawn characters, and is the only play of its type to have remained in the repertory. Sedaine became a member of the French Academy in 1789.

SEDLEY, SIR CHARLES (*c.* 1639–1701), Restoration dramatist, wit, and man of letters, friend of Rochester and Etherege (q.v.). He wrote several plays, of which the best are *The Mulberry-Garden* (1668), a comedy of contemporary manners which owes something to Molière's *L'École des maris* (1661) and something to Etherege's *Comical Revenge* (1664), and the lively but licentious *Bellamira; or, the Mistress* (1687), based on the *Eunuchus* of Terence.

SEDLEY-SMITH, WILLIAM HENRY (1806–72), an American actor, born in Wales, who in 1820 joined a company of strolling players, adding Smith to his real name of Sedley. He toured the English provinces for some years and in 1827 went to America, making his first appearance at the Walnut Street Theatre, Philadelphia, as Jeremy Diddler in Kenney's farce, *Raising the Wind*. From 1836 to 1860 he was manager of the Boston Museum, and also appeared in New York, being first seen there in 1840. He made his last appearance in Boston in 1869 and then went to San Francisco, where he became manager of the California Theatre until his death, and was able to be of service to the young David Belasco (q.v.). With the possible assistance of an unnamed 'gentleman', Sedley-Smith wrote *The Drunkard; or, the Fallen Saved*, a melodramatic temperance tract which achieved an astonishing success. Produced in Boston in 1844, it was revived by Barnum in New York ten years later and was the first American play to achieve almost two hundred performances. Again revived in Los Angeles in 1933, it ran for twenty-six years.

Selwyn Theatre, NEW YORK, on the north side of West 42nd Street. This opened on 2 Oct. 1918 and had a somewhat undistinguished career, its first successful run being scored in 1923 by Charles Ruggles in the English musical farce, *Mr. Battling Butler* (produced in London the previous year as *Battling Butler*). One of the most successful plays staged there was *The Royal Family* (1927), a saga based on the personalities of the Drew and Barrymore families (qq.v.) by Edna Ferber and

George S. Kaufman, which was seen in London in 1934 as *Theatre Royal*. In Dec. 1929 *Wake Up and Dream*, with music by Cole Porter, introduced the English players Jessie Matthews and Jack Buchanan to New York, in company with Tilly Losch. The last outstanding event in the history of the theatre, which then became a cinema, was a series of six matinées of Sophocles' *Electra*, produced in 1932 with Blanche Yurka and Mrs. Patrick Campbell (qq.v.).

SEMENOVA, EKATERINA SEMENOVNA (1786–1849), Russian actress, who has been compared to Mrs. Siddons (q.v.), since her main triumphs were scored in the tragedies of Shakespeare, Racine (particularly *Phèdre*), and Schiller (qq.v.). The daughter of a serf, she was sent at ten years of age to the Theatre School in St. Petersburg (Leningrad), and seven years later made her formal début, attracting attention by her acting in the somewhat frigid tragedies of Ozerov. She made a great impression on her contemporaries by her beauty and her superb contralto voice, and Pushkin (q.v.) dedicated some of his poems to her.

SENECA, LUCIUS ANNAEUS (*c.* 4 B.C.–A.D. 65), Roman dramatist, philosopher, satirist, and statesman, the tutor, and later the victim, of Nero (q.v.). Nine tragedies adapted from the Greek are attributed to him—the *Hercules Furens*, *Medea*, *Phaedra* (or *Hippolytus*), and *Troades* (all possibly based on Euripides), the *Agamemnon* (on Aeschylus), the *Oedipus*, *Phoenissae* (or *Thebais*), and *Hercules Oetaeus* (on Sophocles), and the *Thyestes* (on an unknown original). *Octavia*, based on the life of Nero's unhappy wife, is sometimes included in manuscripts with the above, but must be by a later hand. As the only extant dramas from the Roman empire, Seneca's tragedies are important historically, and their influence on the development of drama in modern times has been profound, in spite of the fact that they were written to be read aloud and not acted. In fact, there are scenes which could not be staged, nor do the actors enter and leave as in a stage-play. Characters speak, then relapse into silence, and it is not clear whether they are still present; objects which in a production would be visible to the actors are ignored; character-drawing is stereotyped—Hercules will always be heroic, Ulysses always crafty. The *recitatio*, or recited drama, aims at immediate, often verbal, effects. Plot and character are subordinated to the necessity to startle and astonish the listeners by novel excesses in emotion or expression. Yet, in spite of the fact that Seneca's alterations of his Greek models are usually for the worse, it would be unfair to deny the dramatic power of many of his scenes or the beauty of some of his choral passages, which offset the atmosphere of gloom and horror, brutality and treachery, which pervades these plays and which reflects the times in which Seneca lived. When he writes of the intrigues of countries, the instability of princes, the crimes of tyrants, the courage of men in peril of death, there is something more than mere literary artifice and imagination. He had experienced it all. Perhaps this is why, for the Renaissance, Seneca was the model writer of tragedy. His Latin was easily understood, his plays were divided into the five acts demanded by Horace, their plots, however melodramatic, were universally intelligible, even his rant and rhetoric appealed to the taste of the time. His line-by-line exchange of dialogue, his chorus, his tyrants, ghosts, and witches, his corpse-strewn stage, all reappear in Elizabethan drama, and even if such effects had already been used by pre-Shakespearian dramatists, they were reinforced by the reading, and possibly the acting, of translations of the tragedies as early as the 1550s, long before the publication of his 'Tenne Tragedies' in 1581. Their influence is already apparent in the earliest English tragedy, *Gorboduc* (1562), by Norton and Sackville, in Gascoigne's *Jocasta* (1566), and in Shakespeare's early plays, particularly *Richard III* (c. 1593) (which shows what splendid results can be achieved when Senecan material is used by a man of genius) and *Titus Andronicus* (c. 1594), and in Jonson's two tragedies, *Sejanus* (1603) and *Catiline* (1611).

SERLIO, SEBASTIANO (1475–1554), Italian painter and architect who, after working for many years on theatrical problems, published a treatise on architecture, *De architettura*, of which Part II, dealing with perspective in the theatre, appeared in 1545. An English translation, *The Second Book of Architecture*, was published in 1611. Much of it was based on the notes and drawings made by Peruzzi (q.v.), whose pupil Serlio was, during his study of the works of Vitruvius (q.v.). Serlio, who had in mind temporary theatres set up in princely or ducal banqueting-halls, described and illustrated in his book three basic permanent sets—the tragic, the comic, and the satyric—which, with their symmetrical arrangement of houses or trees in perspective on either side of a central avenue, had an immense influence on scene design everywhere. They survived the introduction of the *scena d'angolo*, or diagonal perspective, by the Bibienas (q.v.), and traces of them can still be seen in the scenery of nineteenth-century melodrama. One section of Serlio's book deals with lighting (q.v.) and with the artificial imitation of such natural phenomena as sunshine and moonlight.

SERVANDONY, JEAN-NICOLAS (1695–1766), a French scenic artist, born in Lyons, who in an effort to appear fashionably Italian changed the spelling of his name to Servandoni. After studying in Italy, he worked there and in other European countries, and was one of the first to adopt the neo-classic style in reaction against the universally popular baroque. He then settled in Paris, where he assumed control of the Salle des Machines (q.v.). The influence of the work he did there in a series of spectacular productions was soon apparent in Germany and even in Italy. Later he worked in Dresden and Vienna, and in 1749 was in London, where he married.

Sesame, see RELIGIOUS DRAMA.

Set, the surroundings, visible to an audience, in which a play develops. The word now covers everything arranged on stage, and its derivative, 'setting', has become the general term for the whole theatrical art of designing and staging the scenery of a play; but originally 'set' meant only a 'set scene'—that is, an arrangement of painted and built components prepared or 'set up' in advance and revealed by the opening of a front scene, as opposed to a 'flat scene' (see FLAT), whose parts slide on and off stage in full view of the audience. An alternation of set and flat scenes was common in the English theatre until almost the end of the nineteenth century, and with the elaboration of built stuff (q.v.) in Victorian times, a specially written front scene known as the carpenter's scene (q.v.) was often provided by the playwright to allow time for its erection. Visible scene-changing was abolished by Henry Irving (q.v.) during his management of the Lyceum from 1878 to 1899, a front curtain being lowered during the intervals behind which the scene could be changed.

SETTLE, ELKANAH (1648–1724), Restoration dramatist, whose elaborate heroic drama, *The Empress of Morocco,* was probably the first English play to be published with scenic illustrations. These depict the proscenium arch and stage sets at Dorset Garden (q.v.), where the play was first performed by Betterton and his company in 1673, though it may have been seen at Court before that. Settle, who figures as Doeg in Dryden's satire *Absalom and Achitophel,* wrote a number of other plays, but without much success. In his last years he returned to the fairs, where he had formerly worked, writing and acting in drolls at Mrs. Minn's (or Myn's) booth at Bartholomew Fair, where he is recorded as having played 'a dragon in green leather of his own invention'.

SEYLER, ABEL (1730–1801), see HENSEL, SOPHIE.

SEYLER, ATHENE (1889–   ), English actress, appointed C.B.E. in 1958 in recognition of her fifty years on the London stage. At her best in Restoration comedy, she first appeared as Melantha (in Dryden's *Marriage à la Mode*) in 1920, following it with Mrs. Frail in Congreve's *Love for Love* in 1921, and Lady Fidget in Wycherley's *The Country Wife* in 1924. She again appeared in Wycherley in 1961 at the Pembroke, Croydon, as Mrs. Caution in *The Gentleman Dancing-Master,* and in the interval played a wide variety of parts in Shakespeare, Wilde, Shaw, Chekhov, Maugham, and Rattigan, as well as in such light comedies as Van Druten's *Bell, Book and Candle* (1954) and Peter Coke's *Breath of Spring* (1958). In 1962 she played an Old Bawd in John Fletcher's *The Chances* at the first Chichester Theatre Festival with unimpaired wit and vitality. A born comedienne, she is also an inspired teacher, and *The Craft of Comedy* (1944), which she wrote in collaboration with a young actor, STEPHEN HAGGARD (1911–43), is an essential handbook for all aspiring young actors.

SEYMOUR [really CUNNINGHAM], WILLIAM GORMAN (1855–1933), son of JAMES SEYMOUR (1823–64), an actor well known in America for his playing of stage Irishmen, and his actress wife, LYDIA ELIZABETH GRIFFITH (1832–97). William was on the stage as a child, playing the Duke of York to the Richard III of Lawrence Barrett (q.v.) at the age of seven. He later played Henrick in the long run of *Rip Van Winkle* with Jefferson (q.v.), and in 1871 joined the stock company at the Globe Theatre, Boston, appearing with Edwin Forrest (q.v.) at his final performance. From 1875 until his retirement in 1927 he continued to act, and was also manager of a number of theatres, being general stage director for Charles Frohman and for the Empire Theatre, New York, from 1901 to 1919. He married an actress, MAY DAVENPORT (1856–1927), sister of Fanny Davenport (q.v.), and of their five children three went on the stage. After his death his library was presented to Princeton University to form the nucleus of a William Seymour Theatre Collection.

Shadow-Show, a form of puppetry in which flat, jointed figures are passed between a translucent screen and lighted candles or, nowadays, electric light bulbs, so that the audience, seated in front of the screen, sees only their shadows. It originated in the Far East, and in an increasingly crude form spread to Turkey and so to Greece, where it gave rise to plays centred round the comic character Karagöz (Gr. Karaghiozis) which can still be seen in a rudimentary form. As 'les Ombres Chinoises', shadow-shows were popular in Paris for about a hundred years. In 1774 Dominique Séraphin opened a theatre devoted to them in Versailles, moving in 1784 to the Palais Royal, where his nephew continued his work until 1859. It was Séraphin who first introduced to Paris the classic shadow-play, *The Broken Bridge,* in which a frustrated traveller indulges in an impassioned but silent argument with a workman on the other side of the river. This was well known in the streets of London, where, as the GALANTY SHOW, shadow-plays continued to be given up to the end of the nineteenth century, usually in Punch and Judy booths with a thin sheet stretched across the opening and candles behind. There was a literary revival of the shadow-show at the Chat

Noir in Paris in the 1880s, and in the 1930s Lotte Reiniger employed the technique of the shadow-show for her silhouette films. Her puppets were made of tin, as were those used at the Chat Noir and in the English Galanty Show, but in Java and Bali, where the shadow-play survives in its traditional form, they are cut from leather. Manipulation is by bamboo rods or concealed wires running up the centre of the figure and operated from below the screen, except in Turkey and Greece, where the rod is held at right angles to it, and fastened to the flat figure in the centre of the back.

SHADWELL, THOMAS (c. 1642–92), Restoration dramatist and Poet Laureate in succession to Dryden (q.v.). His best comedies, *Epsom Wells* (1672), *The Squire of Alsatia* (1688), and *Bury Fair* (1689), give interesting though somewhat scurrilous pictures of contemporary manners. His first play, *The Sullen Lovers; or, the Impertinents* (1668), was based on Molière's *Les Fâcheux*, but on the whole he was more indebted to Jonson. He has been much criticized for his adaptations of Shakespeare, particularly for his version of *The Tempest* as 'The Enchanted Island' (1674) in operatic form, where, following the example of Davenant and Dryden, everything was subordinated to the machinery and scenery. Shadwell, who disliked and satirized the heroic tragedy of Dryden as well as the early Restoration comedies, was a competent dramatist whose plays were most successful in his own day. The only one to have been revived is *Epsom Wells*, which had an unexpected success when produced in Nov. 1969 at the Thorndike Theatre, Leatherhead.

SHAFFER, PETER LEVIN (1926–), English dramatist, whose first play, *Five Finger Exercise*, was successfully produced in London in 1958 and in New York a year later. It was followed by a double bill, *The Private Ear* and *The Public Eye* (1962; New York, 1963), and by *The Merry Roosters Panto* (1963), written for Joan Littlewood's Theatre Workshop (q.v.). Shaffer's next play, *The Royal Hunt of the Sun*, an epic tragedy on the murder of the Aztec king Atahualpa by Pizarro, was first seen at the Chichester Festival Theatre in 1964, as was the one-act *Black Comedy* in 1965. Both were subsequently seen in London with the National Theatre company at the Old Vic, and *Black Comedy*, together with another one-act play, *The Warning Game*, was produced in New York in 1967. Another one-acter, *The White Liars* (1968), was then seen in London and was followed in 1970 by a full-length play, *The Battle of Shrivings*, which had a mixed reception, but, with Gielgud (q.v.) as an elderly pacifist intellectual reminiscent of Bertrand Russell, had a respectable run.

Shaffer's twin brother, ANTHONY (1926–), achieved a success in 1970 with his first play, *Sleuth*, starring Anthony Quayle (q.v.), which had a long run in London and was equally successful in New York.

Shaftesbury Theatre, LONDON. (1) This was the first playhouse to be built in Shaftesbury Avenue. It opened on 20 Oct. 1888 with *As You Like It*, which failed, but later E. S. Willard had some success with *The Middleman* (1889) and *Judah* (1890), both by Henry Arthur Jones (q.v.). It was not, however, until 1898 that the Shaftesbury had its first real success with *The Belle of New York*, which revolutionized musical comedy as then known and introduced Edna May to London. In 1903 another musical comedy, *In Dahomey*, with Bert Williams (q.v.) and an all-Negro cast (the first to be seen in London), was also a success, as was Lionel Monckton's *The Arcadians* (1909). In later years the theatre housed a number of successes, including the farce *Tons of Money* (1922) and three nautical comedies by Ian Hay and Stephen King-Hall, *The Middle Watch* (1929), *The Midshipmaid* (1931), and *Admirals All* (1934). On 17 Apr. 1941 it was completely demolished by enemy action and the site is now (1972) a car park.

(2) A second theatre in Shaftesbury Avenue was opened on 26 Dec. 1911 as the Prince's by the Melvilles (q.v.), who used it mainly for melodrama. Later it had no settled policy, and its productions ranged from straight plays to ballet, pantomime, and opera. There were also a number of revivals of Gilbert and Sullivan during the 1920s, and distinguished foreign visitors included Sarah Bernhardt (q.v.) in 1921, her last visit to London; Diaghilev's Ballets Russes in 1921 and 1927; and Sacha Guitry (q.v.) with Yvonne Printemps in 1922. In 1924 Darlington's *Alf's Button* had an un-

expected success, and in 1927 George Robey (q.v.) appeared in the revue *Bits and Pieces*. A year later a musical comedy, *Funny Face*, with music by George Gershwin, had a long run. From 1929 to 1946 the theatre was intermittently managed by Firth Shephard and under him two dramatizations by Ian Hay of stories by Edgar Wallace, *The Frog* (1936) and *The Gusher* (1937), had long runs, as did two musicals devised by Douglas Furber, *Wild Oats* (1938) and *Sitting Pretty* (1939). The theatre was badly blasted in 1940–1 but managed to stay open, and for a time housed the Sadler's Wells ballet and opera companies. After the war the main successes were again the Gilbert and Sullivan seasons, but there were long runs of *His Excellency* (1950), by Dorothy and Campbell Christie, and of two American musicals, *Pal Joey* (1954) and *Wonderful Town* (1955). In 1962 the theatre closed for renovation and reopened under its present name on 28 Mar. 1963 with another American musical, *How to Succeed in Business Without Really Trying*. In 1966 a farce by Philip King and Falkland Cary, *Big Bad Mouse*, had a long run, and was followed by the epoch-making American musical *Hair* (1968).

SHAKESPEARE, WILLIAM (1564–1616), English dramatist, son of John Shakespeare, a glover yeoman of Stratford-upon-Avon, and his wife Mary Arden. He was christened on 26 Apr. 1564; tradition asserts that his birthday was 23 April, St. George's Day. Presumably he attended the local grammar school. In Nov. 1582 he married Anne Hathaway of Shottery, by whom he had a son and two daughters, the son dying when eleven years old. Nothing further is heard of him until 1592, when a pamphlet written by the dying Robert Greene (q.v.) shows him well-established in London as an actor and dramatist. In 1593 and 1594 he dedicated his poems *Venus and Adonis* and *The Rape of Lucrece* to the Earl of Southampton in terms that suggest familiarity, and by the beginning of 1595 he was a 'sharer' in the Lord Chamberlain's company of actors (see CHAMBERLAIN'S MEN). Proof of his financial success in the theatre is given by his purchase of a large house, New Place, in Stratford, to which he retired in 1610, dying there on his birthday in 1616, tradition says after a too convivial evening with Jonson

(q.v.) and Drayton. He was buried in the chancel of Stratford church. In 1623 his fellow-actors Heminge and Condell (qq.v.) published a complete edition of his works (the First Folio), adding another twenty plays to the sixteen which had appeared (in quarto) during his lifetime. No indication is given of the dates of composition of the various plays, and although internal evidence has helped to establish a rough chronology, any attempt to date them exactly remains hazardous, particularly as some of the texts are obviously corrupt and others show unmistakable signs of revision. It seems likely, however, that he began by writing, unaided or in collaboration, an historical tetralogy consisting of the three parts of *Henry VI* (*Parts 2* and *3* in 1591, *Part 1* in 1592), and *Richard III* (1593), in which the Elizabethan actor Richard Burbage (q.v.) won fame. These plays were successful enough to encourage Shakespeare to write *King John* (1594). Shortly afterwards, about 1595, another historical tetralogy was started with *Richard II*, which, during the Essex conspiracy in 1601, won notoriety because of its abdication scene. The two parts of *Henry IV* (probably about 1597 or 1598) carry on the story of Henry Bolingbroke and introduce a richly contrasting comic element with the character of Falstaff (originally named Oldcastle), while the general theme is rounded off with *Henry V* (probably 1598). With this play Shakespeare closed his career as a writer of histories, save for the late *Henry VIII*, produced in the summer of 1613, in which he is believed by many scholars to have collaborated with the young John Fletcher (q.v.). Very early in his career Shakespeare tried his hand at comedy with *Love's Labour's Lost* (1592), *The Comedy of Errors* (1593), and *The Taming of the Shrew* (1593/4). In *The Two Gentlemen of Verona* (*c.* 1594) there is a definite approach towards the comedy of humour, and immediately afterwards, probably between 1595 and 1599, this finds a rich and lyrical expression in *A Midsummer Night's Dream*, *Much Ado About Nothing*, *As You Like It*, and *Twelfth Night* (prod. 1602). Shortly after the production of *Henry IV* came *The Merry Wives of Windsor*, an aberration in the series; probably tradition is right in saying it was written at the command of Queen Elizabeth, who wanted to see Falstaff in love. In *The Merchant of Venice* (1596/7) a break in the almost perfect balance observable in the other comedies is patent, and this leads to a couple of so-called 'dark comedies'—*All's Well that Ends Well* (1602) and *Measure for Measure* (prod. 1604), in which the romantic material is strained almost to breaking-point. With these may be associated the cynically bitter *Troilus and Cressida* (1602), which possibly was acted not on the public stage but privately. These plays were composed when Shakespeare was reaching towards the deepest expression of tragic concepts. At the very beginning of his career he must have had some part (but how great is questionable) in *Titus Andronicus* (c. 1592). Again, in the midst of his lyrical comedies, he made a second attempt at tragedy with *Romeo and Juliet* (about 1595). Then came the great series of tragedies and Roman plays. *Julius Caesar*, which was seen by a Swiss visitor to London in 1599, was probably the first, but *Hamlet* must have come very soon after. *Othello* may have been new when it was presented at Court in 1604. *King Lear* must have followed not many months later; it appeared at Court in 1606, and about the same time came *Macbeth*, which clearly addresses itself to a Jacobean audience. The classical subject-matter of *Julius Caesar* is paralleled in *Antony and Cleopatra*, in *Coriolanus*, and in the almost hysterical *Timon of Athens* (all probably about 1607 or 1608). *Cymbeline*, which, like *King Lear*, was based on ancient British history, was probably written about 1610. It was first acted in 1611, as was *The Winter's Tale*, similar in spirit, darker than the early comedies, including tragic incidents, yet ending with solemn happiness. *The Tempest*, gravest and serenest of all Shakespeare's dramas, was first presented at Court in 1611. To Shakespeare have been attributed, in whole or in part, several other dramas. It has now been generally accepted that he had a hand in *Pericles*, which was printed as his in 1609 and added to the Third Folio of 1664. Recent scholarship suggests that three pages of the manuscript of *Sir Thomas More*, now in the British Museum, may be in his handwriting (see also MUNDAY). Less likely, although still possible, is his participation in *Edward III* (printed in 1596) and in *The Two Noble Kinsmen*, which was printed in 1634 as by him and Fletcher.

Bare factual information, however, fades into insignificance when we consider the extraordinary range of Shakespeare's poetic achievement. He came at the right moment to make full and fresh use of an emergent drama, with a novel and flexible stage apt for his purpose, and although some of his plays were written for performance at Court, he remains primarily a 'public' dramatist, addressing himself to the demands of an audience representative of all classes, eager to listen to rich poetic utterance, keenly interested in human character, and ready to welcome both the delicacy of romantic comedy and the rigours of tragedy. Little is known for certain about the contemporary production of his plays, but sufficient to give us a general impression of the method of presentation. Since his own day methods of production have varied enormously. Although some of the plays remained in the repertory of the English theatre, from the Restoration until the end of the nineteenth century few people had an opportunity of seeing them in their original form. For this the change in theatre buildings (q.v.) and theatrical technique was partly responsible, but the blame lay chiefly with those who deliberately altered his texts to make them acceptable to the audiences of a new age. During the Commonwealth his comedies were pillaged to provide short entertainments, or drolls (q.v.). This was understandable; but there was no excuse for later remodellings except that, to a small sophisticated audience reared on French classical tragedy, Shakespeare was a barbarian whose work stood in need of purification and revision. *Macbeth* was embellished with singing and dancing. *Romeo and Juliet* was given a happy ending. Neither play was revived in its proper form until 1744. *The Tempest* and *A Midsummer Night's Dream* were turned into operas, and a new version was made of *The Taming of the Shrew*. The worst of Shakespeare's adapters was Nahum Tate (q.v.), who rewrote *King Lear*, keeping Cordelia alive in order that she might marry her lover and omitting the Fool, who was not seen again until 1838. An adaptation which survived even longer was the *Richard III* of Colley Cibber (q.v.), which contained passages from *Henry IV*, *Henry V*, *Henry VI*, and *Richard II*, as well as a good deal of Cibber's own invention. Even Garrick (q.v.), who tried to restore the original texts, and produced *Antony and Cleopatra* for the first time since 1660, still retained Cibber's *Richard III*, allowed Macbeth to die on the stage, and Juliet to wake before the death of Romeo. He himself made a short version of *The Taming of the Shrew*, as *Katherine and Petruchio* (1756), which held the stage until Ben Webster (q.v.) revived the original play at the Haymarket in 1844. Garrick's tampering with *Hamlet*, and his omission of the Grave-diggers, marks the end of this phase of Shakespearian production. The tide had already begun to turn, and in 1741 Macklin (q.v.) rescued Shylock, in the so-called *The Jew of Venice*, from the hands of the low comedian. It was a long time before actors and producers scrupulously respected the text, and John Philip Kemble (q.v.) still thought it necessary to cut, combine, and edit each play before producing it. He did, however, try to continue the reform in costume initiated by Macklin in 1773, and although his Othello was still a scarlet-coated general, his Richard III wore silk knee-breeches, and Lear defied the storm in a flowered dressing-gown, his Coriolanus combined picturesqueness with accuracy in what, in contemporary thought, approximated to Roman costume. He was helped in his endeavours by his sister, Sarah Siddons (q.v.), who was the first to discard the hoops, flounces, and enormous headgear of the tragic heroine. Their innovations bore fruit in Charles Kemble's *King John*, staged in March 1823 with historically accurate costumes designed by Planché (q.v.). With the reform in costume went a return to an accurate text. Helped by the patience and research of scholars, and by the criticisms of such men as Coleridge and Hazlitt, the plays gradually emerged from the accretions of more than a century's rewriting. On 10 Feb. 1826 Edmund Kean (q.v.) played Lear with the original ending. In 1839–40 Mme Vestris (q.v.) revived *Love's Labour's Lost* and *A Midsummer Night's Dream* with the original texts; the Theatres Act of 1843 (see DRAMATIC CENSORSHIP) enabled Phelps (q.v.) to embark on a series of productions at Sadler's Wells from 1844 to 1862, while Charles Kean (q.v.) staged his equally remarkable Shakespeare seasons at the Princess's during the 1850s. Shakespeare's text was now presented in a reasonably correct form, but his work suffered a new distortion through undue emphasis on detail, scenery, and pageantry. The archaeological correctness

of Charles Kemble heralded the magnificent spectacles of Macready (q.v.) at Covent Garden from 1837 to 1843 which, though they restored the Fool (played by a woman) to Lear and revived *The Tempest* without interpolations, helped forward the smothering process. This reached its height under Tree and Irving (qq.v.), who held up the action of the play, designed for a bare stage, by long pauses for elaborate scene-changes. It was the publication in 1888 of de Witt's drawing of the Swan Theatre (q.v.) which first turned men's minds to the possibility of restoring not only the text of Shakespeare's plays but also the physical conditions in which they were originally seen. The problem was first tackled in the early years of the twentieth century by William Poel and Nugent Monck (qq.v.), while Robert Atkins (q.v.) in the 1930s made an effort to solve the difficulties by presenting Shakespeare-in-the-round in a boxing ring. After the Second World War the stages at Stratford-upon-Avon and the Old Vic crept out beyond the proscenium arch, which was finally abolished altogether. These and other tentatives, including the Mermaid Theatre (q.v.) and the Shakespearean Festival Theatre at Stratford, Ontario (see STRATFORD (2)), showed that Shakespeare cannot adequately be presented in the proscenium-arch theatre, though even there efforts have been made to present the plays more coherently, allowing the action to flow unchecked for as long as possible. One of the landmarks in the history of Shakespearian production was undoubtedly Granville-Barker's season at the Savoy in 1912; another was the introduction in 1914 of Shakespeare at the Old Vic (q.v.) under Lilian Baylis. Experiments intended to 'bring alive' or 'modernize' the plays ranged from the modern-dress *Hamlet* (1925) of Barry Jackson (q.v.) to the fantastications of Komisarjevsky or the elaborations of Reinhardt (qq.v.). In 1948 there was a *Hamlet* set in Victorian times, in 1955 a *King Lear* with Japanese décor, and in 1960 a *Romeo and Juliet* in modern Italian style by Zeffirelli (q.v.). Since then audiences have seen *Hamlet* and *Macbeth* cut up and rearranged by Charles Marowitz (q.v.), *A Midsummer Night's Dream* produced by Peter Brook according to the ideas of Jan Kott (q.v.), and *The Merchant of Venice* with Shylock played as a nineteenth-century City merchant banker. But the main trend for many years has been the simplification of the background to permit the free flow of the verse and the unhampered action of the plot. A combination of scholarly research and theatrical experience seems the best method of dealing with the problems that inevitably arise in producing plays written in haste, printed without the author's supervision, and designed for a vanished playhouse, which have in addition suffered from the over-zealous attentions of erudite editors on the one hand and the mutilations of hack writers or 'star' actor-managers on the other.

Shakespeare Festivals. The main festivals of Shakespeare's plays by professional companies are given in the three Stratfords, in England, Canada, and the United States (see STRATFORD). Two professional open-air festivals are those in Central Park, New York City, and Regent's Park, London. The former, for which no charge is made, was founded by Joseph Papp (q.v.), whose first productions were given in 1954 in a church hall. Two years later he presented *Julius Caesar* and *The Taming of the Shrew* on a portable stage mounted on a truck, playing to capacity audiences in the East River Park amphitheatre. In 1957 the City of New York offered Papp the use of a site in Central Park, where *Romeo and Juliet*, *Macbeth*, and *The Two Gentlemen of Verona* were given to large and enthusiastic audiences. In 1962 a production of *The Merchant of Venice* opened in a new Festival Theatre on this site. It has an open-air auditorium with a semi-arena stage, good lighting and amplification facilities, dressing-rooms, and an audience-area planned for excellent sight-lines and acoustics. Plays in London's Regent's Park were given from 1900 onwards by Ben Greet (q.v.) and his Woodland Players, but it was not until 1933 that a permanent Open Air Theatre was established by Sydney Carroll (q.v.). The first production of what became an annual summer event was *Twelfth Night*, produced by Robert Atkins (q.v.), who played Sir Toby Belch and later directed and played in many of the plays given in a natural woodland setting (or in a marquee when it rained). For the 1935–6 California Pacific International Exposition an Elizabethan theatre, according to the ideas of the time, was designed by Thomas Wood Stevens and later trans-

ported to Balboa Park, San Diego, where a summer festival of plays by Shakespeare was inaugurated by B. Iden Payne in 1949. The first actors were local amateurs, but in 1954 student actors and technicians from colleges and drama schools throughout the country were enrolled. Since 1958 professional actors have been engaged to fill the major roles, while minor parts continued to be played by students. One of the oldest amateur festivals is that held during the summer vacation at Ashland, Oregon, founded in 1935. Plays were first given by college students in a roofless structure which was damaged by fire in 1940. The festival was suspended until 1947, when a new stage was built and professional actors engaged for the five or six plays given annually. An important festival, devoted entirely to *Hamlet*, played in the courtyard of Kronborg Castle at Elsinore, in Denmark, began in 1937 with a visit from Laurence Olivier (q.v.) and the Old Vic company. In 1938 there was a German company headed by Gründgens, and in 1939 another English company under John Gielgud. After the Second World War efforts were made to revive the festival. Swedish, Norwegian, Finnish, American, and Irish Hamlets were seen, and Michael Redgrave appeared with a third English company in 1950. The venture now seems to have been abandoned. Performances of *Hamlet* are also one of the highlights of the Summer Festival at Dubrovnik in Yugoslavia, and it is interesting to note that the Municipal Theatre in Istanbul begins its season each year with a performance of a play by Shakespeare. There are still a number of amateur festivals, of which the most important is probably the one held in London in the week nearest to Shakespeare's birthday (23 Apr.), when the Southwark Borough Council (a district which has close ties with Shakespeare) sponsors productions by college or other societies, one of which takes place in the yard of the George Inn, Southwark, a site which approximates as nearly as possible to the public playing-places of London actors before the building of Burbage's Theatre in 1576 (see INNS USED AS THEATRES).

Shakespeare in the United States. The first productions of Shakespeare in the New World were given by visiting English actors, whose first recorded play was *Richard III*, acted in New York City on

5 Mar. 1750 by Kean and Murray's company at their Nassau Street Theatre. This was in Colley Cibber's version. There is little information available on the texts of subsequent productions, but it is reasonable to suppose that they were substantially those current in the English theatre at the time. Although there was not, as in Europe (see SHAKESPEARE IN TRANSLATION), a language barrier or a preconceived notion of classical writing to be overcome, there were moral difficulties, and *Othello* was first introduced to Boston as 'a Moral Dialogue against the Sin of Jealousy'. Shakespeare was considered a poet to be read rather than a dramatist to be seen, and although audiences in the East could attend the plays in theatres modelled on English lines, in the West it was the lecturers, elocutionists, entertainers, and showboat companies who first popularized him, in isolated scenes and speeches. After the first fifty years it is difficult to disentangle the imported productions of Shakespeare from those of the young but vigorous American theatre. Cooper and Wallack (qq.v.), who both appeared in Shakespeare early in their careers, were typical of the new generation of actors who, though born in England, worked in the United States. The first native-born actor to play leading roles in Shakespeare was probably John Howard Payne (q.v.), the greatest undoubtedly Edwin Booth (q.v.). But the nineteenth-century personality-cult of the 'star' actor and the insistence on elaborate trappings was as prevalent in America as in England, and was reinforced by the many tours undertaken by such London companies as Charles Kean's and later Irving's.

The twentieth century saw, as in England, a gradual simplification of the setting, with the work of such designers as Robert Edmond Jones and Norman Bel Geddes (qq.v.), and a new approach to a purified text. This was reinforced by a phenomenon peculiar to the United States—the entry into the theatre of the universities, which did not take place in England until much later (see UNIVERSITY DEPARTMENTS OF DRAMA). This was not without its dangers, but it led to much scholarly work on the problems of the Elizabethan theatre and to more interest being taken in Shakespeare's plays, which have on the whole been ignored by the commercial theatre on Broadway. With no tradition of Shakespearian acting, with

the same handicap as in London of unsuitable theatres, and with no demand for them from the audience, managers have found Shakespeare's plays expensive to stage and uncertain in their box-office returns. The occasional productions have been mostly due to the efforts of an individual—John Barrymore, Eva Le Gallienne, Walter Hampden, Joseph Papp, Margaret Webster, Orson Welles (qq.v.). It may therefore be said that it was mainly the universities who kept Shakespeare alive in the United States.

Shakespeare in Translation. During the first quarter of the seventeenth century the English Comedians (q.v.), travelling on the Continent, included in their repertory cut versions of several of Shakespeare's plays. But otherwise he remained virtually unknown outside England until well into the eighteenth century, when Voltaire (q.v.) first drew attention to him in his *Lettres philosophiques* (1734). Early translations—a frigid version of *Julius Caesar* by the German Ambassador to London, Baron C. W. von Borck, in 1741; a prose summary of some of the plays in French by Antoine de La Place in 1744; bowdlerized versions in German prose by Christoph Wieland (1733-1813) published between 1762 and 1766—did little to help. The first translations to be widely read were the French prose versions by Pierre Le Tourneur (1736-88), published between 1776 and 1782. They were the only ones known in Italy too until the publication in 1819-22 of Italian versions by Michele Leoni, and, together with those of La Place, were read by the novelist Manzoni, the first Italian to be influenced by Shakespeare. They also provided Ducis (q.v.), who knew no English, with the basis of the first French stage versions used by Molé (q.v.) between 1769 and 1792. These were tailored to fit the unities (q.v.), so that Desdemona in *Othello*, for instance, was wooed, wedded, and murdered in the space of a day, while *Hamlet, Romeo and Juliet*, and *King Lear* had the happy endings given to contemporary English adaptations. In Germany it was the great actor F. L. Schröder (q.v.) who first put Shakespeare on the stage with a production of *Hamlet* at Hamburg in 1776. It gave the audience a shock, but when they had recovered from the Ghost they broke into applause. This encouraged Schröder to put on *Othello*, which was a failure, *The Merchant* *of Venice, Measure for Measure*, which had a cool reception, and finally, in 1778, *King Lear*, which was an unqualified success and was seen in Berlin, Mannheim, and elsewhere. Other translations were made by J. J. Eschenburg (the Mannheim Shakespeare, 1775–82) and by A. W. von Schlegel, the latter being completed later by Tieck and others, and republished with revisions and additions by F. Gundolf in 1908. Good acting versions of the main plays were provided between 1869 and 1871 by the actor Emil Devrient. Once introduced into Germany, Shakespeare prospered until he was finally claimed as '*unser*' (our) Shakespeare, and his genius was thought akin to that of the Teutons. In France Romanticism swept him into favour, and the visit of an English company to Paris in 1827 set the seal on his reputation. In 1839 came a new translation by Laroche with an introduction by Dumas *père* (q.v.), and from 1856 to 1867 a translation of the complete works by Jean, younger son of Victor Hugo (q.v.), whose book, *William Shakespeare* (1864), was intended to serve as a preface to his son's versions. In Italy Shakespeare established himself more slowly. Carlo Rusconi's *Hamlet* did not appear until 1839, and Giulio Carcano's standard translation in blank verse was not begun until 1843, being completed in 1882. The first Italian actor to succeed as Othello was Ernesto Rossi (q.v.) in 1856. He was also good as Hamlet, Macbeth, Lear, Coriolanus, Shylock, and Romeo, while Salvini (q.v.) triumphed as Othello and Adelaide Ristori (q.v.) as Lady Macbeth. These were all tragic roles, and although Zacconi and Ermete Novelli (qq.v.) made a success of Petruchio in *The Taming of the Shrew*, and a fine production of *A Midsummer Night's Dream* with Mendelssohn's music was given in Rome in 1910, it still seems as if the tragic aspect of Shakespeare's genius appeals more to the Latin races than his comic spirit—as was proved once more by the success of Gide's French version of *Hamlet* in 1947, ably interpreted by Barrault (q.v.). In Spain, little was heard of Shakespeare until well into the nineteenth century, nor have any of the great actors there popularized him on the stage. The first acting translations were based on Ducis. In the 1870s James (Jaime) Clark and William (Guillermo) Macpherson, Englishmen resident in Spain, undertook to make new trans-

lations from the English, but neither of them completed his task, nor did C. A. Jordana; the only complete versions so far are those of Luis Astrana Marín, in Catalan, and José Maria de Sagarra. Spanish translations are used in South America, except in Brazil, where Portuguese versions, mainly from the French, are current. In 1948 the University of Coimbra began the publication of a complete series of translations, but Shakespeare does not seem to have become popular on the Portuguese stage. The first Greek translator was Demetrios Bikelas, whose versions, made between 1876 and 1884, were acted in Athens. In 1949 a start was made on a complete edition under the auspices of the British Council in Athens. There is probably no country in the world today where some, at least, of Shakespeare's plays have not been done in translation. He has influenced the theatres not only of Europe and America, but of the Far East. The desire to read him in the original, or to translate and adapt him for their own stages, has led many people to learn English. It would be impossible to list all the translations of his plays. Many of the earliest were intended for reading only. Others were made for the stage by actors who appeared in them themselves, like the professional Peter Foersom in Denmark in the early nineteenth century, or the scholarly Dr. Tsubouchi in Japan in the 1920s. Some were adapted to local conditions, as in the early Chinese versions, or the two Zulu re-creations of *Macbeth*.

The first translations in central Europe were made from German versions. But in Hungary, as early as 1864, a complete translation of all the plays was made by a group of poets and writers under the auspices of the Kisfaludy Society. In Poland, where the great actress Modjeska (q.v.) appeared in many Shakespearian parts before playing them in English in America and England, the first direct translation was of *Hamlet* in 1840. New versions by a group of three Polish poets appeared in 1911–13. New stage versions of all the plays are to be published in the Serbo-Croat language. The first Macedonian translations appeared in 1949. The Yugoslav theatre director Branka Gavelo made some new versions which he directed and played in himself. The playwright Ivan Čankar made a number of Slovene versions, while versions in Czech were made by Vrchlický in the early years of the twentieth century; to these have been added the new acting versions of Emil Saudek. Fan Noli, a noted politician who died in 1965, translated a number of the plays into Albanian. There are excellent versions of most of the plays in Norwegian, by H. Rytter (1932). The first Swedish versions were made in 1847–51 by Carl August Hagberg, and Per Hallström's magnificent versions, on which he worked for many years, appeared in the 1920s and 1930s. In 1873 Edvard Lembcke published Danish versions of all the plays except *Titus Andronicus* and *Pericles*. In Finland Shakespeare is done in both official languages, Finnish and Swedish; he has already figured in the repertory of the Iceland National Theatre, founded in 1950. In Belgium, which also has a double-language theatre, French and Flemish versions are found, the latter by the Dutch author L. A. J. Burgersdijk, first published in 1885. In the 1940s these were revised and modernized by F. de Backer and G. A. Dudok. They are used in the Netherlands also, as are the Dutch versions of A. S. Kok. In Russia adaptations of Shakespeare in the eighteenth century bore little resemblance to the originals. Among them was a version of *The Merry Wives of Windsor* as *What It is Like to Have Linen in a Basket* (1786) by CATHERINE THE GREAT (1729–96). Later versions were usually made from the French or German—the first to be acted was *Richard III* (1833). In Soviet Russia eighteen of Shakespeare's plays, in new translations, are in the permanent repertory of the main theatres, the most popular being *Hamlet*. The plays have been translated into seventeen of the languages of the U.S.S.R., and an annual Shakespeare Conference is held at which scholars, producers, actors, and critics meet to discuss and plan productions. Shakespeare has also appeared on the Jewish stage, in Hebrew as early as 1874 (*Othello*) and in Yiddish—in Goldfaden's *The Two Kune Lemels*, a version of *Romeo and Juliet*—in 1880. None of the plays has been performed in Ladino, but two, *The Comedy of Errors* and *Romeo and Juliet*, formed the basis of novels in that language. In India, where Shakespeare is no longer performed, his plays were used for the teaching of English, and many early performances were given by students. The first versions in the vernacular may have been in Marathi in 1843. In 1850 Parsi actors performed an adaptation of *The*

Taming of the Shrew in Gujarati. There are also versions of some of the plays in Tamil, Bengali, and Kannada. In Japan in the early 1900s Oto Kawakami, the founder and leader of a new school of acting, appeared with his wife, Sada Yacco, in *Hamlet* and *Othello*, with the scene set in Japan and the actors wearing contemporary Japanese costume. Kawakami's productions were seen on tour in London and the United States where they aroused much interest. The many immigrant groups in the United States were able to attend performances of Shakespeare in their own languages given either by their own amateur groups or by visiting stars from Europe. The quatercentenary celebrations of 1964 produced a vast number of new translations. There is, for instance, to be a new Swedish translation of all the plays, and in the Daghestan Autonomous Republic plays are to be staged in the Avar, Darghen, and Lezghin languages.

Shakespeare Memorial Theatre. This famous theatre, which houses an annual festival of plays by Shakespeare (q.v.), is built on a riverside site in Stratford-upon-Avon, Shakespeare's birthplace. It was founded by Charles Edward Flower, a local brewer, whose father had been responsible for a festival in 1864 to celebrate the 300th anniversary of Shakespeare's birth. The first Shakespeare Memorial Theatre was a bright-red brick building, designed by the London architects Dodgshun and Unsworth in a pseudo-Gothic style which drew much adverse criticism, both then and later, not only because of its turreted and gabled exterior but also because of its bare interior and somewhat inadequate stage. Yet this theatre, which opened in 1879 on Shakespeare's birthday, 23 April, was destined to house many fine productions with outstanding actors, and even to win the affection of some of those who visited it until on 6 March 1926 it was burnt down. The Library and Picture Gallery, added in 1883, were spared, but the theatre was a total loss. The actors moved to a local converted cinema while plans were put in hand for a new theatre, on the same site but with an extension into the adjoining Bancroft gardens. The shell of the old theatre was converted into a Conference Hall, now used for rehearsals. The new building, which opened on 23 April 1932, was designed by Elizabeth Scott, grand-niece of the architect Sir Gilbert Scott. It was purely functional both inside and out, with high windowless blocks, a fan-shaped auditorium, and a wide stage. Again it caused considerable controversy. Just as the first theatre had been dubbed 'a wedding cake', so the second was dismissed as 'a factory' or 'a tomb'. In time it gained the affection of its audiences, but not, perhaps, of the actors, who had to suffer from the cramped conditions backstage and from the gap caused by the orchestra pit, even though the latter was put to good use for the surging movements of the crowd in, for instance, *Julius Caesar*. In 1944, under Robert Atkins (q.v.), the forestage was carried out over the orchestra pit, with a welcome gain of contact between actors and audience. But it was not until 1947, when Barry Jackson (q.v.) was in control of the theatre, that alterations were put in hand which resulted in improvements both in the auditorium and backstage, with improved audibility and the enlargement of the workshop and storage space. Further improvements were made in 1950, when the interior was reseated and the dress-circle extended across the side walls to link up with the stage. New dressing-rooms were built and an electronic switchboard set up at the back of the circle. The proscenium arch had already been abolished, and audiences for the first play of the 1951 season found the stage occupied by a permanent set designed by Tanya Moiseiwitsch (q.v.) to serve for the whole cycle of historical plays that constituted Stratford's contribution to the 1951 Festival of Britain. In 1960 the Memorial Theatre, by command of the Queen, changed its name to the Royal Shakespeare Theatre, and became the permanent Stratford home of the Royal Shakespeare Company (q.v.).

SHANK, JOHN (?–1636), English actor, who appears in the actor-list of Shakespeare's plays, and whose name is found in many different spellings. He apparently began his career with Pembroke's Men (q.v.), though no proof of this has yet been found. He is known to have been with the King's Men (see CHAMBERLAIN'S MEN), joining them either shortly before, or at the time of, the death in *c.* 1611 of Armin (q.v.), whose position as chief clown he inherited. He was a comedian, well thought of as a singer and

dancer of jigs, and appears to have been very popular with his audience, and though the written lines of his roles are often few, it seems that he was allowed considerable licence in gagging. From the number of boy-apprentices with whom his name is connected, and from the fact that so many young men are recorded in the parish burial register as having died at his house in Cripplegate, it has been inferred that he undertook the training of apprentices who lodged with him.

SHARPE, RICHARD (*c.* 1600–32), English actor, who in 1614 was one of the King's Men (see CHAMBERLAIN'S MEN), playing the title-role in Webster's *The Duchess of Malfi*. As he had probably been acting for several years before that, it is evident that he started young and gave proof of outstanding ability. From the age of about twenty-five until his early death he played romantic young heroes.

SHATTERELL. There were two English actors of this name, EDWARD and ROBERT, who may have been father and son but were more likely brothers. Edward was evidently the elder, since he is found among the actors on the Continent after the closing of the theatres, and must therefore have had some experience of acting before 1642. He was also one of those who contrived to put on surreptitious plays at the Red Bull (q.v.) in 1654. Immediately after the Restoration he is found with Mohun's company, again at the Red Bull. He then joined the first company formed by Killigrew (q.v.), but disappears from the records soon after. Robert, who was one of Beeston's Boys at the Cockpit (q.v.) before the Civil War, also joined Killigrew's company, where he remained until his death some time shortly before 1684. He was evidently a prosperous man, since in 1663 he was able to afford one of the houses built near the new Drury Lane Theatre.

SHAW, GEORGE BERNARD (1856–1950), Irish dramatist, critic, and social reformer, born in Dublin, where his mother, a singer and teacher of singing, early imbued him with a knowledge and love of music which qualified him, after migrating to London in 1876, to become music critic of the *Star* (under the pseudonym of Corno di Bassetto) from 1888 to 1890, and of the *World* from 1890 to 1894. Admirable though his music articles were, their quality was undoubtedly surpassed by that of the dramatic criticism he contributed to the *Saturday Review*— where his successor was Max Beerbohm (q.v.)—between Jan. 1895 and Dec. 1898. These articles on plays and players were later issued in book form as *Our Theatres in the Nineties*; those from the *World* were collected as *Music in London 1890–94*, and those from the *Star* as *London Music in 1888–89*.

Before writing for the *Star*, Shaw had done book-reviewing for the *Pall Mall Gazette* and art criticism for the *World*, and, subsidized by his mother, had written five unsuccessful novels which were later included in his collected works. His interest in social and political reform had also led him in 1884 to join the Fabian Society, on whose behalf he soon became a fluent and effective speaker. Though he had no particular love for the theatre of his own time, he was not slow to recognize its value as a platform which could be used to further the interests of the causes he had espoused. This, and his admiration for the 'new drama' of Ibsen (q.v.), which in translations by Shaw's friend William Archer was becoming known in London, led him to the writing of plays. The production on 9 Dec. 1892, under the auspices of the Independent Theatre Club (see GREIN), of *Widowers' Houses* (begun in 1885) inaugurated his long career as the foremost dramatist of his day. This was a private production for Club members, as were the productions in 1902 and 1905 of *Mrs. Warren's Profession* and *The Philanderer* (both written in 1893) respectively. The first of Shaw's plays to be presented publicly was *Arms and the Man*, produced at the Avenue Theatre (see PLAYHOUSE) on 21 Apr. 1894 as part of a repertory season run by Florence Farr (q.v.), who had played in the first production of *Widowers' Houses*. The others ran into trouble with the censor, and taken in conjunction with Shaw's lectures and - writings on behalf of the Fabians, caused him to be regarded in many quarters as a subversive influence. Deliberately disregarding the current conventions of the 'well-made' play, he set out to appeal to the intellect and not the emotions of his audiences, and introduced on stage subjects previously confined to the law-courts, the church pulpit, or the political platform—slum landlordism, prostitution, war, religion, family quarrels, health, economics. Thought, not action,

was the mainspring of the Shavian play. But, as audiences were eventually to realize, it was thought seasoned by wit and enlivened by eloquence, which in the long run provided more rewarding entertainment than the theatre had been able to offer for a very long time. The popularity of Shaw's plays dates from the Vedrenne–Barker seasons of 1904–7 at the Royal Court (q.v.), when ten were performed in repertory—*Candida*, *John Bull's Other Island*, *How He Lied to Her Husband*, *You Never Can Tell* (first publicly produced at the Strand in 1900), *Man and Superman* (without Act III, produced separately in 1907 as *Don Juan in Hell*), *Major Barbara*, *The Doctor's Dilemma*, *Captain Brassbound's Conversion*, with Ellen Terry (q.v.), *The Philanderer*, and the one-act *The Man of Destiny*. When at the end of 1907 Vedrenne and Barker moved to the Savoy Theatre (q.v.), they produced there *The Devil's Disciple*, first seen in New York with Richard Mansfield (q.v.) as early as 1897, and *Caesar and Cleopatra*, first performed in 1906 in German in Berlin under Max Reinhardt (q.v.) and in English in New York.

The chronology of Shaw's plays is complicated by the fact that many of them had copyright, private, amateur, or foreign professional productions before being seen in London. His most important works after *Misalliance*, which failed when presented by Frohman at the Duke of York's Theatre in London in 1910 and had an unexpected success in a New York revival in 1953, are *Fanny's First Play* (1911; New York, 1912), Shaw's first commercial success, in which he satirized the contemporary London dramatic critics William Archer (Gunn), A. B. Walkley (Trotter), and E. A. Baughan (Vaughan); *Androcles and the Lion* (1913; New York, 1915); *Pygmalion* (1914; first seen in Vienna in 1913), the source of the overwhelmingly successful American musical *My Fair Lady* (New York, 1956; London, 1958); *Heartbreak House* (New York, 1920; London, 1921), a 'fantasia' in the Russian (i.e. Chekhovian) manner first produced by the Theatre Guild (q.v.), as was the 'metabiological Pentateuch' *Back to Methuselah* (1922), considered by Shaw his masterpiece, which was first seen in London in 1924 in a production brought from Birmingham by Barry Jackson (q.v.); *Saint Joan* (New York, 1923), Shaw's finest play, in the opinion of most critics, seen in London in 1924 with Sybil Thorndike (q.v.) as an unforgettable Joan; *The Apple Cart* (1929), brought to London from the Malvern Festival (q.v.), as were *Too True to Be Good* (1932), *Geneva* (1938), and Shaw's last memorable full-length play, the delightful *In Good King Charles's Golden Days* (1939). Subtitled by Shaw 'a true history that never happened', this brings together Charles II, Isaac Newton, George Fox, Nell Gwynn, the Duchess of Cleveland, and the Duchess of Portsmouth. In addition to the plays mentioned above Shaw wrote a number of one-act pieces, often for specific occasions and seldom revived, of which the best are probably *The Dark Lady of the Sonnets* (1910), the first of Shaw's plays to be given at the Old Vic (q.v.), as a curtain-raiser to the 1930 production of *Androcles and the Lion*, and *Great Catherine* (1913), which provided the libretto for an opera by the Dutch composer Ignace Lilien, first performed at the Wiesbaden Festival in 1932.

It would be impossible to list all the revivals and translations of Shaw's major plays. Setting aside *Pygmalion*, which, like *Major Barbara* and *Caesar and Cleopatra*, has been filmed, the most popular appear to be *Saint Joan*, followed by *Candida*, *Arms and the Man*, *The Doctor's Dilemma*, and *You Never Can Tell*. *Heartbreak House* is also held in high esteem, but perhaps more by the critics than by the general public. Many of the first productions, particularly of the earlier plays, were directed by Shaw himself, who earned the respect and admiration of his actors and might, had occasion offered, have been a successful actor himself. He also supervised the printing of his plays with meticulous attention to layout and typography, and his detailed stage directions form a running commentary which helps the reader to visualize the scene. The prefaces to the published plays, which were issued separately in two volumes in 1934, enhanced his reputation as a great master of English prose, and should be read in conjunction with the plays. His other major writings relevant to the theatre are *The Quintessence of Ibsenism* (1891; rev. 1913) and *The Perfect Wagnerite* (1898; rev. 1913). Mention should also be made of the letters collected in *Ellen Terry and Bernard Shaw: a correspondence* (1931; new ed. 1949), *Florence Farr, Bernard Shaw and W. B. Yeats: Letters* (1946), and *Bernard Shaw and Mrs.*

Patrick Campbell: their correspondence (1952), on which the American actor JEROME KILTY (1922–   ) based a duologue, *Dear Liar*, performed in 1960 in New York by Katharine Cornell (q.v.) and Brian Aherne and in London by Kilty himself with his wife Cavada Humphrey. Shaw's collected letters, in four volumes, edited by Dan H. Laurence, are in course of publication (Vol. I, 1965; Vol. II, 1970). The same editor is also preparing a definitive edition of his plays, of which Vol. I was published in 1970. A collection of his autobiographical writings was also published in 1970 as *Shaw: An Autobiography 1856–1898*, edited by Stanley Weintraub. In the same year a Shaw Theatre was built in the London borough of Camden to provide the National Youth Theatre (q.v.) with a permanent home.

SHAW, GLEN(CAIRN ALEXANDER) BYAM (1904–86), English actor and director, who made his first appearance on the stage in 1923 and was seen in London two years later as Yasha in Chekhov's *The Cherry Orchard*. He gained experience in Fagan's company at the Playhouse, Oxford, and made his New York début in 1927 as Pelham Humfrey in Fagan's *And So To Bed*. He was a member of Gielgud's repertory company at the Queen's in 1937–8, and in 1939 played Horatio to Gielgud's Hamlet at the Lyceum and at Elsinore. After military service in the Second World War he returned to the theatre, but as a director, being associated with the short-lived drama school attached to the Old Vic, and producing *As You Like It* (1949) and *Henry V* (1951) for the Young Vic (q.v.). In 1953 he was appointed co-director, with Anthony Quayle, of the theatre at Stratford-upon-Avon (q.v.), becoming sole director in 1956. He was responsible for the staging of a number of plays there, in many of which his wife Angela Baddeley (q.v.) appeared. He resigned in 1960 and was succeeded by Peter Hall (q.v.). He then returned to London to direct Rattigan's *Ross* in the West End (which he also directed on Broadway a year later), and in 1962 was appointed Director of Productions (a new post) for Sadler's Wells Opera, now at the Coliseum. In 1954 he was created C.B.E. for services to the theatre.

SHCHEPKIN, MIKHAIL SEMENOVICH (1788–1863), Russian actor, son of a serf, who had already appeared in a number of productions, notably at Kursk, his birthplace, where he played in comedy from 1808 to 1816, when in 1818 his freedom was purchased by one of his admirers, Prince Repin, and he was invited to join the company at the Maly Theatre (q.v.) in Moscow. He made his début in Nov. 1822 in Zagoskin's *Gospodin Bogatonov; or, a Provincial in the Capital*. Although he was in St. Petersburg from 1825 to 1828, it was in Moscow that he did his best work, particularly during the 1840s, when he appeared in the plays of Griboyedov and Gogol (qq.v.) and as some of Shakespeare's comic characters. Encouraged by Pushkin, he published his autobiographical notebooks, which are of great artistic and theatrical interest.

SHCHUKIN, BORIS VASILIEVICH (1894–1939), Soviet actor, whose early death robbed the Russian stage of one of its outstanding figures. He was for twenty years at the Vakhtangov Theatre (q.v.), where he played leading roles. In his last years he gave some exceptionally fine performances, notably in the title-role of Gorky's *Yegor Bulichev and Others*, in Afinogenov's *Distant Point*, and as Lenin, whom he was the first actor to impersonate. After his death the street in which he lived was named after him.

SHELDON, EDWARD BREWSTER (1886–1946), American dramatist, whose first play, *Salvation Nell* (1908), was produced when he was only twenty-two and, with Mrs. Fiske (q.v.) as the heroine and her husband as director, proved a great success. Sheldon was trained in the '47 Workshop' of Professor G. P. Baker (q.v.), and was immediately hailed as the rising hope of the new American school of realistic dramatists, a position he appeared to consolidate with *The Nigger* (1909), a courageous handling of the Negro problem, and *The Boss* (1911), a study of modern industrial conditions. But all his serious work was overshadowed by the success of his popular romantic play *Romance* (1913), which, with DORIS KEANE (1881–1945) as an Italian opera singer, had a long run both in New York and London. It made an immense emotional appeal to audiences all over the world, and was translated into French and other languages. Handicapped by serious illness, Sheldon did most of his later work in collaboration, and also

translated and adapted anonymously a number of popular successes.

SHELLEY, PERCY BYSSHE (1792–1822), English Romantic poet, and author of several plays in verse, of which the best-known is *The Cenci*. Published in 1819, this was first acted by the Shelley Society in 1886, with Alma Murray (q.v.) as an outstanding Beatrice. It has been several times revived, notably in 1922 and 1926 with Sybil Thorndike, and in 1959 at the Old Vic with Barbara Jefford. Though pure poetry, it is poor drama, being confused in action and in style somewhat too reminiscent of Shakespeare, and it is unlikely to find a permanent place even in the repertory of poetic drama on the stage.

SHEPHERD, EDWARD (*c.* 1670–1747), English architect, designer of Shepherd Market, Mayfair, and of the first theatre built in Covent Garden (q.v.) in 1732.

SHERIDAN, MARK (?–1917), a music-hall comedian, whose speciality was Cockney songs with rousing choruses, often descriptive of seaside delights. One which is still sung was 'I do like to be beside the seaside'. His dress was distinctive and unvaried. He wore a top hat, a frock coat, bell-bottomed trousers fastened round the knee with a strap in imitation of the old-time navvies, big boots, and carried a cane. He reached the peak of his popularity in the 1890s, and during the First World War—whose soldiers marched to his rousing 'Here we are again'—he was beset by melancholy. While appearing in a pantomime in Glasgow he became convinced that his powers were failing, and committed suicide.

SHERIDAN, RICHARD BRINSLEY (1751–1816), English dramatist, theatre manager, and politician, whose best play, *The School for Scandal*, stands as the masterpiece of the English comedy of manners, with all the wit but none of the licentiousness of the Restoration comedy from which it derives. Sheridan, who was the son of an actor, THOMAS SHERIDAN (1721–88), and a writer, FRANCES [*née* CHAMBERLAINE] (1724–66), whose play, *The Discovery*, was produced by Garrick (q.v.) in 1763, was born in Dublin, educated at Harrow, and intended for the law. But after contracting a romantic marriage with the singer ELIZABETH ANN LINLEY

(1754–92), he settled in London and had his first play, *The Rivals*, produced at Covent Garden in 1775. This was followed later in the same year by a farce, *St. Patrick's Day; or, the Scheming Lieutenant*, and a comic opera, 'The Duenna'. In 1776 Sheridan bought Garrick's share in Drury Lane Theatre (q.v.), which he rebuilt in 1794, remaining in charge there until its destruction by fire in 1809, always in financial difficulties. His later plays, all produced at Drury Lane, include *A Trip to Scarborough*, altered from Vanbrugh's *The Relapse*, and *The School for Scandal* (both 1777); *The Critic; or, a Tragedy Rehearsed* (1779), the best of the many burlesques stemming from Buckingham's *The Rehearsal* and the only one to have been constantly revived; and in 1799, when he had practically deserted the theatre for politics, *Pizarro*, an adaptation of a popular drama by Kotzebue (q.v.). Sheridan was also part-author of several entertainments and wrote the pantomime of *Robinson Crusoe* for Drury Lane in Jan. 1781 as an after-piece to *The Winter's Tale*, as well as three new spectacular scenes for a revival of *Harlequin Fortunatus* in 1780. He is said by Oulton to have appeared as Harlequin for one night, but there is no proof of this. He certainly exploited to the full the popular taste for spectacle and pantomime, helped by the scenic artist Philip de Loutherbourg (q.v.), and all his plays were produced with remarkable scenic effects and lavish costumes. His management of Drury Lane was marked by a succession of quarrels with the managers of the smaller theatres—Astley's, Sadler's Wells, the new Royalty (qq.v.)—whose success alarmed him, and he was often instrumental in embroiling his rivals with the authorities. His last years were unhappy, and he never recovered from the destruction of Drury Lane, though he endeavoured to bear its loss with equanimity.

SHERIDAN, WILLIAM EDWARD (1840–87), American actor, with a virile and forceful personality and a fine resonant voice. He made his first successes in Philadelphia, and in the last years of his brief career was extremely popular in San Francisco, where he first appeared in 1880. Among his best parts were Louis XI in an adaptation of a French play of that title, Othello, and Shylock (in *The Merchant of Venice*), and he was

also good in Massinger's *A New Way to Pay Old Debts* and Charles Reade's *The Lyons Mail*. After serving in the Union Army during the Civil War (1861–5), he returned to the stage and appeared at Niblo's Garden as the first American Beamish McCoul in Boucicault's *Arrah-na-Pogue*. His first wife dying in 1872, he married an actress, LOUISE DAVENPORT, and with her embarked on a long tour of Australia, where he died.

SHERRIFF, ROBERT CEDRIC (1896–1975), English dramatist and novelist, who became widely known for his realistic and yet emotionally moving war play, *Journey's End* (1928), the first play dealing with the First World War to achieve success. Originally produced on a Sunday night by the Stage Society (q.v.), it was brought to the commercial theatre by Maurice Browne (q.v.), whom it established as a manager and director, and ran for two years, the all-male cast including such actors as Maurice Evans (q.v.), Colin Clive, and Robert Speaight. Dealing with the reactions of a small group of men in a dug-out just before an attack, it was subsequently translated and played all over the world. Among Sherriff's other plays are *Badger's Green* (1930); *St. Helena* (1935), written in collaboration with Jeanne de Casalis; two plays for Ralph Richardson (q.v.), *Home at Seven* (1950) and *The White Carnation* (1953); and *A Shred of Evidence* (1960). A musical, *Johnny the Priest*, based by Peter Powell on one of Sherriff's earlier plays, *The Telescope* (1957), was also seen in 1960.

SHERWOOD, ROBERT EMMET (1896–1955), American dramatist, who scored a success with his first play, *The Road to Rome* (1927), a satirical portrayal of Hannibal's march which deflated military glory. An undistinguished series of plays was followed by a further success, *Reunion in Vienna* (1931), brilliantly interpreted by the Lunts (q.v.), and by the popular but pessimistic *The Petrified Forest* (1935), which deals with the disintegration and virtual suicide of a young writer. In the same year, *Tovarich*, a light-hearted trifle which Sherwood based on a comedy by the French playwright Jacques Deval, introduced Eugénie Leontovich to London and was seen a year later in New York, where it had a long run. It was followed by a play in more sombre mood,

Idiot's Delight (1936), in which Sherwood foretold the coming of the Second World War and the further breakdown of Western civilization, and yet contrived to portray entertainingly the plight of an American show-business couple (again played by the Lunts) caught in the whirlpool of European intrigues. A chronicle play, *Abe Lincoln in Illinois* (1938), was followed by *There Shall Be No Night* (1940), a war play set in Finland, with a central character, played by Alfred Lunt, who resembled in many ways a modern patriotic and courageous Abraham Lincoln (for the London production in 1943, again with Lunt, the scene was shifted to modern Greece). This was Sherwood's last outstanding play. Actively engaged in war work, he did not return to the theatre until 1945 with *The Rugged Path*, a somewhat disappointing account of an idealistic journalist's death on a Pacific island. His last play, a mild romantic comedy about the American Revolution, *Small War on Murray Hill*, was produced posthumously in New York in 1957 but had only a short run.

SHIELS [really Morshiel], George (1886–1949), Irish playwright, who first became known for his comedies, humorous and satirical pictures of contemporary life produced at the Abbey Theatre (q.v.), Dublin, of which the most successful were *Bedmates* (1921) (in one act), *Paul Twyning* (1922), *Professor Tim* (1925), which introduced Shiels to London in 1927, and *The New Gossoon* (1930), seen in London as *The Girl on the Pillion*. Of his serious plays, which tended somewhat to melodrama, the best were *The Rugged Path* (1940), which had a long run at the Abbey, and its sequel, *The Summit* (1941).

SHIFRIN, Nisson Abramovich (1892–1959), a Soviet-Russian stage designer, whose finest settings were those which he made for a Moscow production of *The Taming of the Shrew*, directed by Popov (q.v.) in 1937. Several of these were reproduced in theatre journals at the time, and were much admired outside Russia. In 1946 one of the original drawings was shown at the Soviet Theatre Exhibition in London. The use of tapestries combined with solid furniture produced a vivid and evocative mingling of Elizabethan and Renaissance settings. Shifrin also designed some lovely settings for Popov's production of *A Midsummer Night's Dream* in 1940, and later produced a most realistic décor, from sketches made on the spot, for a documentary dealing with the siege of Stalingrad. In 1957 his designs for *The Merry Wives of Windsor*, based on the clear outlines and rich colouring of Russian folk-art, were very much admired, as was an evocation of the endless steppes, fringed by leafless branches under a clear sky, which he prepared for Sholokhov's *Virgin Soil Upturned* in the same year.

SHIRLEY, James (1596–1666), the leading dramatist of London when the Puritans shut the playhouses in 1642. He survived the Commonwealth, only to die of exposure during the Great Fire of London. He wrote about forty plays, most of which have survived in print though not on the stage. These include tragedies like *The Maid's Revenge* (1626); *The Traitor* (1631), Shirley's most powerful play, a horror-and-revenge tragedy into which he imported a masque of the Lusts and Furies; *Love's Cruelty* (1631); and *The Cardinal* (1641). His best work, however, is found in his comedies, which provide a link between those of Jonson (q.v.) and the Restoration playwrights. The most successful were *The Witty Fair One* (1628), *Hyde Park* (1632), *The Gamester* (1633), which was later adapted by Garrick, *The Lady of Pleasure* (1635), and *The Sisters* (1642). A prompt-book of this last, dating from the early years of the Restoration, supplies some interesting stage directions, and is now in the library of Sion College. Shirley was popular in the early days of the Restoration, no less than eight of his plays being revived, including *The Cardinal*, which Pepys saw in 1667.

Showboat, the name given to the floating theatres of the great North American rivers of the West, particularly the Mississippi and the Ohio, which represented an early and most successful attempt to bring drama to the pioneer settlements. It is not known who first built a showboat, or at what date. The first record of one dates from 1817, when Noah Ludlow (q.v.) took a company of players along the Cumberland River to the Mississippi. But though they moved by water, they generally acted on land, and it was William Chapman (q.v.), formerly an actor in London and

New York, who became the first manager of a showboat, described in 1831 as a flat boat with a structure on it labelled Theatre, having a ridge-roof above which projected a staff with a flag flying. The interior was long and narrow, with a shallow stage at one end and benches in front across the width of the boat, the whole lighted by candles. Here Mr. and Mrs. Chapman, with their five children, played one-night stands along the rivers wherever enough people could be found to provide an audience. The entrance fee was about 50 cents, and the staple fare strong melodrama or fairytale plays, ranging from Kotzebue's *The Stranger* to *Cinderella*. Starting in the autumn from as far up-river as possible, the showboat made its way downstream to New Orleans, where it was abandoned, the company returning to their starting-point to descend the river in a new boat. Later, steam-tugs were used to take the showboat back to its point of departure, some managers even owning their own tugs. Some years after Chapman's death his widow sold their showboat to Sol Smith (q.v.), who lost it in a collision. One of Chapman's sons may have been the actor HENRY CHAPMAN (1822–65), whose two daughters Blanche and Ella appeared in burlesque for many years on tour. Ella also visited England in 1876, and later appeared in pantomime at the Grand, Islington, and at Her Majesty's Theatre. Another showboat captain of the early days was Henry Butler, an old theatre manager who took a combined museum and playhouse up and down the Erie Canal for many years from about 1836, showing stuffed animals and waxworks by day, and at night producing nautical dramas like Jerrold's *Black-Eyed Susan*, with a sailor-actor, Jack Turner, in the hero's role. A more elaborate showboat was the Floating Circus Palace of Spaulding and Rodgers. Built in Cincinnati in 1851, it was intended for elaborate, usually equestrian, shows, and could accommodate a large audience round a central arena. In addition it had kitchens, dressing-rooms, stables, and living quarters. As well as circus, vaudeville, and minstrel acts, concerts, and a museum, the Floating Circus Palace also gave dramatic performances. Its history coincides with the heyday of the showboats, which increased in numbers and popularity until the outbreak of the Civil War in 1861 drove them off the river, never again to return in such

numbers. The spirit of showmanship survived, however, and in 1878 a Captain A. B. French (?–1902) took his *New Sensation* along the Mississippi. He had to live down a good deal of prejudice, but the high moral tone of his productions, and the good behaviour of his small company, soon made his productions popular. At one time French and his wife, the first woman to hold a pilot's licence and master's papers on the Mississippi, ran two showboats, piloting one each. A formidable rival to the Frenches was Captain E. A. Price, owner of the *Water Queen*, built in 1885. This had a stage nineteen feet across, lit by oil, a good stock of scenery, a company of about fifty, and, like all showboats, a steam calliope. It was later a floating dance-hall in Tennessee, and in 1935 was used in the filming of Edna Ferber's *Showboat*, which, successful as novel, play, and film, was the first work to popularize the story of a floating theatre. Another river-boat which figures in a film was the sidewheeler *Kate Adams*, built in 1898, which in 1926 appeared as *La Belle Revere* in *Uncle Tom's Cabin*. She was later burnt to the waterline. Another well-known manager was Captain E. E. Eisenbarth, owner of the first boat to bear the name *Cotton Blossom*. This was capable of seating a large audience, and on a stage twenty feet by eleven feet presented a three-hour entertainment of straight solid drama, usually popular melodrama. *The Cotton Blossom* was one of the first showboats to be lit by electricity. The name persisted, and a later *Cotton Blossom* was owned by a Captain Otto Hitner. In 1907 Captain Billy Bryant, author of *Children of Ol' Man River* (1936), began his career as a showboat actor when his father launched *The Princess* with a programme featuring himself and his family. By 1918 the Bryants were able to build their own boats, on which they gave successful revivals of many good old melodramas, the most popular being *Ten Nights in a Bar Room*, one of the many dramatizations of a temperance novel by William Pratt. Vaudeville, interspersed with songs and magic-lantern shows, filled up the intervals, while Captain Billy's own speeches before and after the show became famous. A typical one was printed in the *New York Times* for 12 Oct. 1930. Other well-known showboat personalities were the Menkes, four brothers who in 1917 bought French's

New Sensation from Price, who had purchased it from French's widow in 1902. They kept the old name, though the boat has been several times replaced, and in 1922–3, under Captain J. W. Menke, it made a trip lasting a year and covering 5,000 miles. Other boats owned by the Menkes were *Golden Rod*, *Hollywood*, *Wonderland*, *Sunny South*, and *Floating Hippodrome*. Their repertory was again melodrama, though in the late 1920s they made an innovation by presenting a musical comedy. In the years before the slump of 1929 a number of new managements made their appearance on the water —the *Majestic* under Nico and Reynolds, the *America*, the *River Maid*, another *Princess*, a new *Water Queen* under Captain Roy Hyatt—mostly offering melodrama and variety; but they were hard hit by the economic depression, and for some time Menke's *Golden Rod* and Bryant's *Showboat* were the only ones still functioning. Things picked up again later, however, and in 1940 Ben Lucien Burman, in his book on the Mississippi, *Big River to Cross*, was able to mention five by name as still working, as well as many other smaller and less well-known ones on distant waters. Found nowhere but in the United States, they represent a survival of the colourful pioneering days in the Golden West.

SHTEYN, ALEXANDER PETROVICH (1906–), Soviet dramatist, author of a number of successful plays, among them *The Law of Honour* (1948), dealing with Soviet scientists; *The Admiral's Flag* (1950), about the leader of the Russian fleet, Ushakov; *A Personal Affair* (1954), which shows the different ways in which people adapted themselves to the new regime; and *Prologue* (1955), which portrays the heroic days of 1905–7. In 1956 *Hotel Astoria* was produced by Okhlopkov. *The Ocean* was seen in Leningrad in 1961 and *A Game Without Rules* in Moscow in 1962.

SHUBERT, LEE (1875–1953), SAM S. (1876–1905), and JACOB J. (1880–1963), three brothers who were American theatre managers and producers and together formed the Shubert Theatre Corporation, which controlled most of the theatres in New York and the principal cities of the United States. They also established themselves in London in the 1920s, but withdrew in 1931. In 1950 the United States government brought an action

against the corporation for their monopoly of the legitimate theatre, and six years later J. J., the sole surviving brother, sold twelve of the corporation's playhouses. The Shuberts had their offices on the upper floors of the Shubert Theatre (q.v.), which was originally called the Sam S. Shubert in memory of their dead brother.

Shubert Theatre, NEW YORK, on West 44th Street. This opened on 2 Oct. 1913, under the control of Lee and J. J. Shubert (qq.v.), with Forbes-Robertson in *Hamlet*. The first American play to be seen there was *A Thousand Years Ago* (1914) by Percy Mackaye (q.v.). The theatre housed mainly musical comedy, but among its straight successes were a dramatization of Harold Frederic's novel *The Copperhead* (1918), with Lionel Barrymore (q.v.), Fagan's *And So To Bed* (1927), with Yvonne Arnaud (q.v.), and Sinclair Lewis's *Dodsworth* (1934). Elisabeth Bergner made her Broadway début there in 1935 in Margaret Kennedy's *Escape Me Never* under the auspices of the Theatre Guild (q.v.), who also sponsored the appearance of the Lunts in Sherwood's *Idiot's Delight* (1936) and Giraudoux's *Amphitryon 38* (1937) adapted by S. N. Behrman. It was at this theatre that the musical comedy *Bloomer Girl* opened on 5 Oct. 1944, running until 27 Apr. 1946. Later productions were the Lerner and Loewe musical *Paint Your Wagon* (1951); *Stop the World, I Want to Get Off* (1962), starring Anthony Newley, part-author of the show with Leslie Bricusse; the same authors' *The Roar of the Greasepaint, the Smell of the Crowd* (1965), starring Cyril Ritchard; a musical, *The Apple Tree*, based partly on stories by Mark Twain, and Albee's *Malcolm* (both 1966).

SHUSHERIN, YAKOV EMELYANOVICH (1753–1813), one of the best-known actors of the early Russian theatre, who began his career in about 1770 in the Moscow troupe of the English impresario Meddoks (q.v.). He later studied for a time under Dmitrevsky (q.v.). In 1785 he had a great success as Iarbas, the jealous rival of Aeneas in the classical tragedy, *Dido*, by Y. B. Knyazhin (1742–91), an imitator of Racine and Voltaire. He went to St. Petersburg in 1786, where he played the title-role in Sumarokov's *Dmitri the Impostor* and Count Appiani in Lessing's tragedy *Emilia Galotti*, two of his best roles. He became a favourite of the

Empress CATHERINE THE GREAT (1729–96) after appearing successfully in her comedy, *The Disconcerted Family*, and her chronicle play, *The Early Rule of Oleg*. He successfully survived the transition from the classical to the sentimental style and was especially popular in the fashionable *comédie larmoyante*, in an adaptation of *King Lear* by Gnedich, as Oedipus in Ozerov's *Oedipus in Athens*, and as Philoctetes in Sophocles' play of that name. He retired about 1811.

SHUTER, NED [really EDWARD] (1728–76), English actor, famous for his acting in comedy, who made his first appearance on the stage in 1744 and his last as Scrub in George Farquhar's *The Beaux' Stratagem* at the Haymarket on 23 Sept. 1776, five weeks before his death. In June 1746 he made his first appearance in London, playing Osric and the Third Witch to the Hamlet and Macbeth of Garrick (q.v.) at Drury Lane. He later joined the company at Covent Garden, where he created a number of parts, among them Hardcastle in Goldsmith's *She Stoops to Conquer* (1773) and Sir Anthony Absolute in Sheridan's *The Rivals* (1775). His portrait was painted by Zoffany.

SHWARTZ [also found as SCHWARTZ], EVGENYI LVOVICH (1896–1961), Soviet-Russian dramatist, who was for a time an actor, but in 1925 left the stage to devote himself entirely to writing plays for young people. Several of the most successful were based on fairytales—*The Naked King* (1934), *Red Riding Hood* (1937), *The Snow Queen* (1938)—but his best-known work, *The Dragon*, was entirely original. First produced in Moscow in 1943, it was seen in an English translation at the Royal Court Theatre (q.v.) in London in 1967, and proved to be an outspoken and hilarious debunking of political tyranny, with a daring hero, a beautiful heroine, a talking cat, villains, clowns, and a three-headed dragon. Most of Shwartz's plays were produced in Russian children's theatres, but in 1956 his last play, a satirical fairytale entitled *An Ordinary Miracle*, was directed by Akimov at the Leningrad Comedy Theatre. A study of his life and works by Tsembal was published in 1962.

SIDDONS, MRS. [*née* SARAH KEMBLE] (1755–1831), English tragic actress. She was the eldest of the twelve children of a Midland actor-manager, Roger Kemble (q.v.), and with her brothers John Philip, Charles, and Stephen, spent her childhood travelling in his company. At the age of eighteen she married WILLIAM SIDDONS (1744–1808), author and actor. Her first appearance at Drury Lane under Garrick in 1775 was a failure, and she returned to the provinces, playing at York under Tate Wilkinson (q.v.) and at Bath under John Palmer. On a second attempt in London in 1782 she was instantly acclaimed a tragic actress without equal, a position she maintained until the end of her career. She began, however, at the zenith of her powers, and unlike her eldest brother, John Philip, she did not improve with age. A superbly built and extremely dignified woman, with a rich resonant voice and great amplitude of gesture, she wisely left comedy alone, and appeared almost exclusively in tragic and heroic parts. Among her early roles were Isabella in Southerne's *The Fatal Marriage*, Belvidera in Otway's *Venice Preserv'd*, and Jane Shore in Rowe's tragedy of that name, while she was later outstanding as Constance in *King John*, Zara in Congreve's *The Mourning Bride*, and above all as Lady Macbeth, the part in which she made her farewell appearance on 29 June 1812. She returned to the stage on 9 June 1819 as Lady Randolph in Home's *Douglas* for the benefit of her younger brother Charles and his wife, but she was only a shadow of her former self. At her best there was no one to touch her, and contemporary critics were unanimous in their praise of her beauty, tenderness, and nobility. She was not much liked behind the scenes, being unapproachable and avaricious, and she had a great dislike of publicity which led her to be somewhat uncivil to her admirers. Yet her intelligence and good judgement made her the friend of such men as Dr. Johnson and Horace Walpole, while Reynolds, Lawrence, and Gainsborough delighted in painting her, the first immortalizing her beauty in 1784 in 'The Tragic Muse'. Towards the end of her career she became somewhat stout, and her acting was considered monotonous and outmoded. She was also extremely prudish, even in her youth, and jibbed at wearing man's attire when playing Rosalind in *As You Like It*, appearing in a costume which was neither that of a man nor of a woman, and extremely unbecoming. In any case she was poor in the part, and seldom played it. Her brother John Philip once referred to her as 'one of the best comic singers of the day', but as no record exists of her having appeared before the public in that role, one can only surmise that she unbent in private. She had seven children. Four died in infancy. Of the survivors, a son, HENRY (1775–1815), was for a long time connected with the Edinburgh Theatre Royal, but was accounted a poor actor. He married the sister-in-law of Sam Cowell (q.v.).

SIERRA, GREGORIO MARTÍNEZ, see MARTÍNEZ SIERRA.

Sill-Irons, see BOX-SET.

SILVA, NINA DE (1869–1949), see HARVEY, SIR JOHN MARTIN-.

SIMON, (MARVIN) NEIL (1927–), American dramatist, who began by writing sketches for revue in collaboration with his brother Daniel, with whom he also wrote his first play, *Come Blow Your Horn* (1961). He was then responsible for the book of the musical *Little Me* (1962), based on the novel by Patrick Dennis, and for the successful *Barefoot in the Park* (1963), which, like his previous plays, was seen in London shortly after its American production. Simon has since continued his successful career as a playwright with *The Odd Couple* and *The Star-Spangled Girl* (both 1966), *Plaza Suite* (1969), which was also a success in London, and with two new musicals, both based on films, *Sweet Charity* (1966) and *Promises, Promises* (1968), which had long runs in New York and later in London. A more serious note was struck in *The Last of the Red-Hot Lovers* (1969) and continued in *The Gingerbread Lady* (1970), a moving study of an ageing singer who is a compulsive alcoholic.

SIMONOV, KONSTANTIN MIKHAILOVICH (1915–79), Soviet dramatist, whose first play, *The Russian People*, dealing with the impact of war on a group of civilians and soldiers near the front line, was produced in 1942 and frequently revived. It was seen in London in 1943, as *The Russians*, in a production by the Old Vic company. It was followed by the prize-winning *A Fellow from Our Town* (also 1942) and *Wait for Me* (1943) (the title is taken from one of Simonov's own poems). This was played all over the U.S.S.R. and established the author's reputation, which continued to grow with each subsequent work from his pen. These include *The Russian Question* (1947), *Friends and Enemies* (1949), *A Foreign Shadow* (1950), the comedy *A Good Name* (1953), *The Story of a Love* (1954), produced by Akimov in Leningrad, and *The Fourth*, seen in Moscow in 1961.

SIMONOV, REUBEN NIKOLAIVICH (1899–1968), Soviet actor and director, who joined the Moscow Art Theatre's Third Studio in 1920, shortly before it became the Vakhtangov (q.v.). He was an excellent actor, one of his best parts being Cyrano de Bergerac in Rostand's play of that name, but after a brilliant performance by students whom he had trained himself in Sholokhov's *Virgin Soil Upturned* (1931), he devoted himself almost entirely to production, becoming chief director of the Vakhtangov until his death, when he was succeeded by his son E. R. Simonov. Among the elder Simonov's outstanding productions were Pogodin's *Missouri Valse* (1950), Sofronov's *In Our Time* (1952), and a revival of Gorky's *Foma Gordeyev* (1956).

SIMONSON, LEE (1888–1967), American theatrical designer, author of two books on theatre design, *The Stage Is Set* (1932) and *The Art of Scenic Design* (1950), and of a volume of memoirs, *Part of a Lifetime* (1943). His first work for the theatre was done in connection with the Washington Square Players, and he later became one of the founders and directors of the Theatre Guild (q.v.), for which much of his finest work was done, including the first productions in New York of such varied works as Masefield's *The Faithful* (1919), with a Japanese setting, Tolstoy's *The Power of Darkness* and Strindberg's *The Dance of Death* (both 1920), Molnár's *Liliom* (1921), Toller's *From Morn to Midnight* (1922), Ibsen's *Peer Gynt* and Elmer Rice's *The Adding Machine* (both 1923), O'Neill's *Marco Millions* (1928) and *Dynamo* (1929)—designing for the latter a most effective constructivist set based on the interior of a power house—Robert Sherwood's *Idiot's Delight* (1936), and Maxwell Anderson's *The Masque of Kings* (1937). He also did the settings for the Theatre Guild's world premières of Shaw's *Heartbreak House* (1920), *Back to Methuselah* (1922), and *The Simpleton* *of the Unexpected Isles* (1935). For other managements he designed mainly for new American plays, including Sherwood's *The Road to Rome* (1927), O'Neill's *Days Without End* (1934), and Maxwell Anderson's *Joan of Lorraine* (1946), and in 1947 produced some admirable settings for Wagner's Ring Cycle. He was director of the International Exhibition of Theatre Art held in New York in 1934, and was for many years a director of the American National Theatre and Academy and of the Museum of Costume Art in New York.

SIMOV, VICTOR ANDREYEVICH (1858–1935), Russian theatrical designer, who joined the Moscow Art Theatre (q.v.) on its foundation in 1898 and spent the rest of his life there, becoming, in the words of its director Stanislavsky (q.v.) 'the founding father of a new concept of stage décor'. He was responsible for the settings of Chekhov's plays on their first production—*The Seagull* (1898), *Uncle Vanya* (1899), *Three Sisters* (1901), *The Cherry Orchard* (1904)—and also for such productions as Alexei Tolstoy's *Tsar Feodor Ivanovich* (1898), Gorky's *The Lower Depths* (1902), Shakespeare's *Julius Caesar* (1903), and Leo Tolstoy's *The Living Corpse* (1911). He then left the Moscow Art Theatre for a while and designed for the Free Theatre, the Maly, and the Stanislavsky Operatic Theatre Studio. He also worked for the cinema. In 1925 he returned to the Moscow Art Theatre, and was responsible for the settings of Ivanov's *Armoured Train 14–69* (1927) and Gogol's *Dead Souls* (1932).

SIMPSON, EDMUND SHAW (1784–1848), American actor and theatre manager. Born in England, he was acting in Dublin when at the age of twenty-five he was engaged by the American manager Stephen Price (q.v.). He made his first appearance at the Park Theatre (q.v.) in New York in Oct. 1809 and remained there for nearly forty years, ceasing to act in 1833 when he was lamed in an accident, but continuing in management until 1848, when Hamblin (q.v.) took over. In his early days he played Richmond to the Richard III of Kean, Cooke, and the elder Booth (qq.v.), and was popular with his audiences in heroic and tragic parts. Appointed acting manager of the theatre in 1812, and Price's partner in 1815, he kept the theatre open in spite of the disastrous fire of 1820, mainly by importing English stars and Italian opera.

SIMPSON, NORMAN FREDERICK (1919–   ), English dramatist, whose first play, *A Resounding Tinkle*, was seen in a 'production without décor' at the Royal Court in Dec. 1957 and was revived in a double bill with another short play, *The Hole*, at the same theatre three months later. These amusingly absurd one-acters were followed in 1959 by the even more fantastic three-act *One Way Pendulum*, in which one of the characters tries to teach five hundred weighing machines to sing the Hallelujah Chorus, and by *The Cresta Run* (1965), a comedy about spying. Simpson has also contributed to a number of revues, one of his best sketches being the short *Gladly Otherwise* in *One to Another* (1959). Although considered by some critics an exponent of Ionesco's Theatre of the Absurd (q.v.), Simpson, with his play on words and his logical arguments pushed to illogical lengths, seems to follow rather the English tradition of Lewis Carroll, Tommy Handley, and the Goon Show.

SINCLAIR, ARTHUR (1883–1951), Irish actor, husband of Maire O'Neill (q.v.), who made his first appearance on the stage in 1904 in Yeats's *On Baile's Strand* with the Irish National Dramatic Society. He was at the Abbey Theatre (q.v.) in Dublin from its foundation later that year until 1916, playing in a number of important productions, including Synge's *The Playboy of the Western World* (1907) and Shaw's *The Shewing-Up of Blanco Posnet* (1909). He left after disagreements with St. John Ervine (q.v.), then manager of the theatre, and founded his own company, with which he toured Ireland and England, subsequently appearing in variety theatres in Irish sketches. Although he could act serious and even tragic parts when he wished, he preferred comedy, and built up a great reputation as an eccentric comedian. In the 1920s he appeared in the first London productions of several plays by O'Casey (q.v.), playing Boyle in *Juno and the Paycock* (1925), Fluther Good in *The Plough and the Stars* (1926), both directed by Fagan (q.v.), and Seamus Shields in *The Shadow of a Gunman* (1927), which he also directed. Among his other parts were John Duffy in Lennox Robinson's *The White-Headed Boy* (1920), in which he toured America and Australia, Mr. O'Hara in J. B. Priestley's *Spring Tide* (1936), Christopher Sly in *The Taming of the Shrew* (1937), James in *Spring Meeting* (1938), by John Perry and M. S. Farrell, and Smee in Barrie's *Peter Pan* (1944).

Singspiel, see BALLAD OPERA.

SKELTON, JOHN (*c.* 1460–1529), English poet and satirist, tutor to the son of Henry VII (later Henry VIII). He is believed to have written an interlude played before the Court at Woodstock, a comedy, and three Morality Plays, but the only one to survive is *Magnyfycence*, which was probably acted between 1515 and 1523. First printed in 1530 by John Rastell (q.v.), it was reprinted by the Early English Text Society in 1906. In this play Magnyfycence, a benevolent ruler, is corrupted by bad counsellors (Folly, Mischief, etc.), but restored by good ones (Good Hope, Perseverance, etc.).

SKINNER, OTIS (1858–1942), American actor, best remembered for his perform-ance as Hajj in Knoblock's *Kismet* (1911). He made his first appearance on the stage in Philadelphia in 1877, and in New York at Niblo's Garden in 1879. After some years with Booth and Lawrence Barrett, he joined Augustin Daly (q.v.) and with him made his first appearance in London, where he was seen as Romeo. For two years he toured with Modjeska (q.v.), playing such parts as Orlando in *As You Like It*, Benedick in *Much Ado About Nothing*, and Major Schubert in Suder-mann's *Magda*. He also played Young Absolute in Sheridan's *The Rivals* to the Sir Anthony of Joseph Jefferson (q.v.). Among his later successes were *Your Humble Servant* (1910) and *Mr. Antonio* (1916), both written for him by Booth Tarkington. In 1926 he appeared as Falstaff in *Henry IV*, *Part 1*, and two years later as the same character in *The Merry Wives of Windsor*. Among his last appearances were Shylock in *The Mer-chant of Venice* to the Portia of Maude Adams (q.v.) and Thersites in *Troilus and Cressida*. He wrote several volumes of reminiscences, including *Footlights and Spotlights* (1924) and *The Last Tragedian* (1939). His daughter, CORNELIA OTIS (1902–79), who first appeared in her father's company in 1921, was celebrated as a diseuse, and appeared in solo performances all over the United States

and in London. She was the author of a number of entertaining books, including a volume of reminiscences of Continental travel, *Our Hearts Were Young and Gay*, written in collaboration with Emily Kimbrough.

Sky-Dome, see FORTUNY, MARIANO.

Sloat, Slote, see TRAP.

SLOMAN, CHARLES (1808–70), a per-former in the early music-halls and the original of Young Nadab in Thackeray's *The Newcomes* (pub. 1853–5). He is best remembered for his doggerel verses improvised on subjects given him by members of the audience, or on the appearance and dress of those in front of him, but he was also a writer of songs, both comic and serious, for himself and other music-hall performers, including Sam Cowell (q.v.). He was at the height of his fame in the 1840s but later fell on hard times. One of his last engagements was as Chairman of the Middlesex Music-Hall—the 'Old Mo'—in Drury Lane, and he died soon after, a pauper, in the Strand Workhouse.

SŁOWACKI, JULIUSZ (1809–49), Polish poet and playwright, who was exiled in 1831 and lived thereafter in Paris. The first of his plays to be staged was *Mazeppa* (1847), in a Hungarian translation. His later plays, all produced posthumously, were performed in their original Polish and since 1918 have formed part of the national repertory. Słowacki was at first influenced mainly by the dramatic litera-ture of Germany and France, but after a visit to London in 1831, when he saw Edmund Kean (q.v.) as Richard III, his work shows clearly the influence of Shakespeare, particularly in *Balladyna* (pub. in 1839 but not staged until 1862), a play based on Polish folk-lore which contains echoes of *A Midsummer Night's Dream* and *Twelfth Night*, and in the unfinished historical drama *Horsztyński* (written in 1835), which is obviously in-debted to *Hamlet*. His finest work is usually considered to be *Kordian* (written in 1832 but not acted until 1899), which owes something to *Macbeth*. His trans-lation of Calderón's *El príncipe constante* was produced by Grotowski (q.v.) in his Laboratory Theatre, and was seen in London in 1969.

SLY, WILLIAM (?–1608), English actor, who appears in the actor-list of Shakespeare's plays. He was connected with the theatre from about 1590, when his name appears in the cast of *Seven Deadly Sins, Part II*, a lost play, probably by Tarleton (q.v.), of which the 'platt' is preserved among Henslowe's papers at Dulwich College, where there is also a portrait of Sly by an unknown artist. He joined the Chamberlain's Men (q.v.) on their formation in 1594, appearing in four plays by Ben Jonson—*Every Man in His Humour* (1598), *Every Man Out of His Humour* (1599), *Sejanus* (1603), and *Volpone* (1606). Though he was not one of the original shareholders of the Globe (q.v.), he became one at some time, since he mentions it in his will. He also had a seventh share in the Blackfriars (q.v.), later taken over by Richard Burbage (q.v.).

SMITH, ALBERT (1816–60), an interesting but forgotten figure of literary London, who dramatized several of Dickens's novels for the stage and also produced some ephemeral plays and novels of his own. His chief enterprise was a series of one-man entertainments, of which the first was *The Overland Mail* (1850). This was an amusing account of a recent trip to India, interspersed with topical songs and stories and illustrated by scenery specially painted for the occasion by the famous scene painter, William Beverley (q.v.). It proved such a success that Smith followed it with *The Ascent of Mont Blanc*, given at the Egyptian Hall, Piccadilly, again with scenery by Beverley, and then by a similar programme on China. He married Mary, the actress-daughter of Robert Keeley (q.v.), in 1859, and died at the height of his popularity. His simple entertainment, whose charm lay as much in the spontaneity and wit of its presentation as in the actual material, was frequently patronized by Queen Victoria and the royal children.

SMITH, EDWARD TYRRELL (1804–77), English theatre manager, the first to inaugurate the 'morning performance' which under Hollingshead (q.v.) became the modern afternoon matinée. He was probably the most reckless theatrical speculator of his day, having an interest in many places of entertainment, from music-halls and minor theatres like the West London and the Surrey (qq.v.) up to Drury Lane itself. He was willing to sponsor anything that he thought would make money—Rachel, Gustavus Brooke, the younger Mathews (qq.v.), Shakespeare, opera, circuses, Chinese conjurers, a Human Fly that crawled on the ceiling—and in the process he ruined himself. Yet he was in his own day a noted character and in spite of his follies made and kept friends everywhere.

SMITH, MAGGIE (1934–), English actress, who made her first appearance on the stage in Oxford, where she was educated, in 1952, playing Viola in an O.U.D.S. production of *Twelfth Night* After training at the Oxford Playhouse School she went to America to play in the revue *New Faces of '56*, and returned to London a year later to make an outstanding success in another revue, *Share My Lettuce*. She then went to the Old Vic, appearing mainly in comedy—Celia in *As You Like It*, Mistress Ford in *The Merry Wives of Windsor*—and in 1960 succeeded Joan Plowright at the Royal Court as Daisy in Ionesco's *Rhinoceros*. In this she played opposite Laurence Olivier, whose National Theatre company she joined at the end of 1963, having enhanced her growing reputation by her acting in Anouilh's *The Rehearsal* (1961), Peter Shaffer's double bill, *The Private Ear* and *The Public Eye* (1962), and Jean Kerr's *Mary, Mary* (1963). She then joined the company of the National Theatre at the Old Vic, where she was equally successful in comedy and tragedy, making her first appearance as Silvia in Farquhar's *The Recruiting Officer* (1963) and subsequently playing Desdemona in *Othello* (1964) with Laurence Olivier (q.v.). Among her later roles in comedy were Myra in a revival of Coward's *Hay Fever* (1964), Beatrice in *Much Ado About Nothing* (1965) to the Benedick of her first husband Robert Stephens (q.v.) and Mrs. Sullen in Farquhar's *The Beaux' Stratagem*. She also gave excellent performances in the title-roles of Strindberg's *Miss Julie* (1965) and Ibsen's *Hedda Gabler* (1970). In 1970 she was appointed C.B.E. in recognition of her services to the theatre. Her second husband is the dramatist Beverley Cross.

SMITH, RICHARD PENN (1799–1854), American dramatist, born in Philadelphia, and the author of some twenty plays, of which fifteen were acted. They are of all types, ranging from farce to romantic tragedy, and represent the transition in the American theatre from the play imported or inspired by Europe to the true native production of later years. Most of Smith's comedies were adaptations from the French, while his romantic plays were based mainly on incidents from American history. What is believed to have been his best work, a tragedy entitled *Caius Marius*, has not survived. It was produced in 1831 by Edwin Forrest (q.v.) with himself in the title-role, and proved extremely successful. It was possibly Forrest's aversion to the printing of plays in which he appeared that caused it to be lost. Another interesting play, also lost, was *The Actress of Padua* (1836), which was based on Victor Hugo's *Angelo*, and marks the first appearance in American theatrical history of French Romanticism. It was revived by Charlotte Cushman (q.v.) in the early 1850s, and was seen in New York as late as 1873, probably with some alterations by John Brougham (q.v.), to whom it has been attributed.

SMITH, SOL(OMON) FRANKLIN (1801–69), a pioneer of the American theatre on the frontier. After a hard childhood he ran away from home to become an actor, eventually joining a number of itinerant companies and even forming one of his own. After appearing with his wife, a singer, in St. Louis and other Mississippi towns, he went into partnership with Noah Ludlow (q.v.), and together they dominated the St. Louis stage until 1851, building there the first permanent theatre west of the Mississippi. Smith, who appeared as a star in New York at the Park Theatre (q.v.) under Simpson, and in Philadelphia under the management of Wemyss (q.v.), was at his best in low comedy, particularly in such parts as Mawworm in Bickerstaffe's *The Hypocrite*. He was a man of upright character, popular and much respected, and published three books on the theatre, the last, *Theatrical Management in the West and South* (1868), being a combination of the two earlier ones. His son, MARK [really MARCUS] (1829–74), who specialized in the playing of English gentlemen in Old Comedy, acted in America with Burton and Wallack (qq.v.), and under Mrs. John Wood (q.v.) was well received in London. He made his last appearance at the Union Square Theatre in New York in Hart

Jackson's adaptation of a French play, *One Hundred Years Old*, in 1873.

SMITH, WILLIAM (?–1696), English actor, friend of Betterton (q.v.), a tall, handsome man who created a number of roles in Restoration plays, among them Sir Fopling Flutter in Etherege's *The Man of Mode* (1676) and Chamont and Pierre in Otway's *The Orphan* (1680) and *Venice Preserv'd* (1682). Driven from the stage by the animosity of a group of young noblemen whom he was presumed to have offended, he retired to live quietly on his considerable income, but later returned to the theatre, and died while playing in *Cyrus the Great* (1696), an adaptation by Banks (q.v.) of Scudéry's *Le Grand Cyrus*.

SMITH, WILLIAM (1730–1819), English actor, known as 'Gentleman Smith' on account of his elegant figure, fine manners, and handsome face. Coached by Spranger Barry (q.v.), he made his first appearance at Covent Garden on 1 Jan. 1753. He remained there until 1774 and then went to Drury Lane, where he was the first to play Charles Surface in Sheridan's *The School for Scandal* (1777). He also played Macbeth when Mrs. Siddons (q.v.) first appeared as Lady Macbeth, and alternated Hamlet and Richard III with Garrick (q.v.), whom he greatly admired, though his own style approximated more to that of Quin (q.v.). He was playing most of the big tragic roles when John Philip Kemble (q.v.) first went to Drury Lane in 1783, and continued to appear in them until his retirement in 1788. In an age which expected its actors to turn their hands to anything from tragedy to pantomime—Garrick himself is said to have played Harlequin—Smith's proudest boast was that he had never blackened his face, never played in a farce, and never ascended through a trap-door.

SMITHSON, HARRIET [really HENRIETTA] **CONSTANCE** (1800–54), English actress, who made her first appearance at Drury Lane in 1818 in Mrs. Cowley's *The Belle's Stratagem*. She then played Lady Anne and Desdemona to the Richard III and Othello of Edmund Kean (q.v.), and was seen at Covent Garden and the Haymarket, returning to Drury Lane in 1822 to play Countess Wilhelm in John Howard Payne's *Adeline*, an adaptation of *Valentine, ou la Séduction*, by Pixérécourt. In 1827 she went with Charles Kemble (q.v.)

to Paris and was received with acclamation, returning there a year later with Macready (q.v.). Her Desdemona and Ophelia excited enormous enthusiasm, and the young Romantics of the day covered her with adulation, the critic Janin declaring that she had revealed Shakespeare to France and made his tragedies the prerogative of the actress. Her fame was short-lived, as she soon afterwards made an ill-judged and unhappy marriage with Berlioz, the French composer, and retired from the stage.

Smock Alley Theatre, see DUBLIN.

Socialist Realism, the name given to the theatrical method and approach formulated in Soviet Russia in the 1920s by Lunacharsky (q.v.). It implied a fresh approach to the plays of the past in order to bring out their relevance to the social problems of the day. By extension it became an instrument for the Communist education of the masses through the medium of the theatre and was applied to new plays also. This affected not only the director but also the playwright, since his characters were increasingly subject to the forces which led to or arose from the upheaval of 1917. Although the principles of Socialist Realism, of which Gorky (q.v.) is considered the founder and Mayakovsky (q.v.) the first director, have not altered with the passage of time, its political connotations have strengthened, and acceptance of its doctrines is taken to imply submission to the party line in the theatre as elsewhere.

Society for Theatre Research. This body was founded in 1948 after a meeting held at the Old Vic on 15 June which brought together all those interested in the problems of theatre history and the preservation of ephemeral and other material relating to the theatre. The society arranges a winter programme of lectures on specific points of theatrical history, publishes an illustrated quarterly, *Theatre Notebook*, and an annual publication, as well as occasional pamphlets, and maintains a library (housed in the Library of the Senate House of London University). It also encourages the preservation of theatres, of source material on the theatre, and of photographic records, and was instrumental in founding the British Theatre Museum (q.v.), now a separate entity. In the summer of 1955 the Society held in London the first international conference on theatre history, attended by representatives of twenty-two countries, which resulted in the formation of the International Federation for Theatre Research (q.v.). The first president of the Society was Mrs. Gabrielle Enthoven, who was succeeded on her death in 1950 by Professor Edward J. Dent. When he died in 1957 Professor Allardyce Nicoll took his place, with Dame Edith Evans (q.v.) as vice-president. The Society administers an annual prize for diction, awarded to a drama student in memory of William Poel (q.v.).

In 1956 an American Society for Theatre Research was founded by Professor A. M. Nagler and Alan Downer. Unlike most national theatre societies, it is concerned not only with American theatre but with all aspects of theatre studies which may interest its members. It holds an annual meeting in New York and publishes an occasional newsletter (three or four times a year) and an annual volume of essays, *Theatre Survey*.

Sock, from the Latin *soccus*, referring to the light, soft shoe worn by the comic actor in contrast to the heavy boot of the tragedian (see BUSKIN and COTHURNUS). By extension, the word is used to denote comedy, as in Milton's reference (in *L'Allegro*) to 'Jonson's learned sock'.

SOFRONOV, ANATOL VLADIMIROVICH (1911–), Soviet dramatist, who was born in Minsk and began his literary career while working in a factory. His plays include *In One Town* (1946) and *The Moscow Character* (1948), which were both awarded Stalin prizes, *Beketov's Career* (1949), *Impossible to Live Otherwise* (1952), and *A Man in Retirement* (1957). These all deal with topical social problems in the daily working life of the Soviet people. *Honesty* (1962), in which Vera Pashennaya gave a fine performance as the heroine Praskovya Ivanovna, deals realistically with the problems of co-operative farming.

Soggetto, an earlier name for the scenario of the *commedia dell'arte* (q.v.), which was also known as *commedia a soggetto*.

SOLDENE, EMILY (1840–1912), a musichall performer who first appeared under Morton's management at the Canterbury (q.v.), singing excerpts from opera. When he opened the Oxford (q.v.) in 1861 she appeared there also, and later became leading lady of his light opera company at the Philharmonic, Islington (see GRAND THEATRE), where the Prince of Wales (afterwards Edward VII), who had a great admiration for her, was often in the audience, as were many West End playgoers. She accompanied Morton to America when he took the company there, but retired on marriage and went to live in Australia. She published in 1897 a volume of reminiscences which contains much interesting information on the stage and music-hall of her time.

SOMI, LEONE EBREO DI (1527-92), member of a distinguished Jewish family in Mantua, the Portaleone. In 1567 he became chief arranger of theatrical entertainment to the ducal court, and at one time envisaged the opening of a permanent public playhouse in his native city. As Court poet to Cesare Gonzaga he wrote several plays, of which only one, *L'Hirifile*, is now extant, and also a series of four 'dialogues' based on his theatrical experiences. As 'The Dialogues on Stage Affairs', these were published in an English translation in Appendix B of Allardyce Nicoll's *The Development of the Theatre* (3rd ed. 1948). They provide valuable information on the state of the Italian theatre in about 1565, particularly in regard to lighting (q.v.).

SONNENFELS, JOSEF VON (1733-1817), Austrian theatre director, and a fervent advocate of the reforms of Gottsched (q.v.), which he supported in his publication *Briefe über die Wienerische Schaubühne* (1767), urging the abolition of the typical Viennese impromptu burlesque featuring Hanswurst (q.v.) in favour of serious plays of literary content modelled on classical French and German drama. In 1776 he was appointed director of the Burgtheater by Joseph II, who hoped to use drama as an educational force in his schemes for the reform of Austria. With this end in view, he banished the popular theatre to the suburbs, where it flourished, and decreed that the Burgtheater should become a national theatre for the production of serious and improving plays by dramatists like Ayrenhoff (q.v.). These had little power of survival, but the reforms begun by Sonnenfels, perhaps with too much enthusiasm, were con-

tinued in part by his successor, Schreyvogel (q.v.), who was more successful in blending the new drama with the old.

Sophocles (496-406 B.C.), Greek dramatist, who is said to have written over one hundred plays, of which seven are extant, as well as substantial portions of a satyr-drama (q.v.), the *Ichneutae* (the *Trackers*), and many fragments from the lost plays. He won eighteen victories at the Festival of Dionysus in Athens with his tragedies, the first over Aeschylus (q.v.) in 468 B.C. He is said to have won the second prize many times, and never the third. The extant plays (of uncertain date) are, roughly in chronological order, the *Ajax*, the *Antigone*, the *Trachiniae*, the *Oedipus Rex*, the *Electra*, the *Philoctetes*, and the *Oedipus Coloneus*. This last was written when he was nearly ninety and was produced posthumously in 401 B.C. by his grandson, another Sophocles.

From his earliest years Sophocles was renowned for the beauty of his voice and person, and in 480 B.C. took part in a ceremonial boys' dance to celebrate the Athenian naval victory at Salamis. If Aeschylus may be said to represent the heroic period of Athenian democracy, Sophocles typifies its triumphant maturity. The first part of his life coincided with the Age of Pericles, under whom he held high office. He lived through the greater part of the long struggle with Sparta, and died at his birthplace, Coloneus, near Athens, a few months after Euripides (q.v.) and just before the final defeat of Athens in the Peloponnesian War. All contemporary references to him show him to have been a serene, distinguished, and greatly loved figure. This serenity and charm pervade his plays. But it is a serenity that comes from triumph over suffering, not from avoidance of it. Few things in the theatre are more poignant than Sophocles' tragic climaxes. A powerful dramatist, with an amazingly supple poetic style, equalled in the subtle indication of character and emotion only by Plato (q.v.), he approached drama in a very different spirit from Aeschylus, and modified the tragic form considerably, by the introduction of a third actor. Since his main interest was in the tragic interplay of character and circumstances, he abandoned the statutory trilogy on a cosmic scale and always presented at the Festival three separate plays, whose plots are masterpieces of construction. He also reduced the role of the chorus (though increasing its number from twelve to fifteen, apparently for technical reasons) and made its functions purely lyrical—to emphasize a climax or prepare the way for a sudden change of mood. The analysis of tragedy made by Aristotle (q.v.) in his *Poetics* is based in the main on Sophoclean drama, which he regarded as the mature form of tragedy, and therefore neglected the earlier Aeschylean form.

SORANO, DANIEL (1920–62), French actor, one of the finest of his day, whose early death was a great loss to the French theatre. He began his career with the Grenier de Toulouse (see CENTRES DRAMATIQUES), which in 1965 celebrated its twentieth anniversary by taking possession of a new theatre named after him, and was seen with them on a visit to Paris, where he made a great impression as Scapin in Molière's *Les Fourberies de Scapin*. He also played Biondello in their excellent production of *The Taming of the Shrew* as *La Mégère apprivoisée*. In 1952 Sorano joined the company of the Théâtre National Populaire (q.v.), where his most notable roles, both classic and modern, were Sganarelle in *Don Juan*, Mascarille in *L'Étourdi*, and Argan in *Le Malade imaginaire*, all by Molière; Arlequin in Marivaux's *Le Triomphe de l'amour*; Figaro in Beaumarchais's *Le Mariage de Figaro*, Don César de Bazan in Victor Hugo's *Ruy Blas*, and the Chaplain in Brecht's *Mother Courage*. He was an excellent interpreter of Shakespeare and other Elizabethan dramatists, appearing in 1961 in a French version of Ford's *'Tis Pity She's a Whore* under the direction of Visconti (q.v.), and being particularly admired as Richard III and as the Porter in *Macbeth*. His last role was Shylock, with the company of J.-L. Barrault (q.v.), a powerful and sober interpretation.

SORGE, REINHARD JOHANNES (1892–1916), German poet, who began as a disciple of Nietzsche and fell, a devout Catholic, in the First World War. His most important play, *Der Bettler* (written in 1912 but not performed until 1917), was a drama of social protest, which foreshadows the revolt of the younger generation and the striving for a higher spiritual orientation, two of the most insistent themes of the Expressionist movement to which it belongs (see EXPRESSIONISM).

SORMA [really ZAREMBA], AGNES (1865–1927), German actress, who was on the stage as a child and in 1883 was engaged for the newly founded Deutsches Theater (q.v.), where she played a number of youthful parts with great success. She gave proof of deeper maturity, however, in revivals of Grillparzer (q.v.), particularly in *Weh dem, der lugt!*, in which she played opposite Joseph Kainz (q.v.). She was also seen as Juliet (in *Romeo and Juliet*), Ophelia (in *Hamlet*), and Desdemona (in *Othello*), and as Nora in Ibsen's *A Doll's House*, a part she played for many years, notably on a visit to Paris, on an extensive tour of Europe, and on her first visit to New York in 1897. She was an excellent interpreter of the heroines of Sudermann and Hauptmann (qq.v.) and, in lighter vein, of the Hostess in Goldoni's *La Locandiera*. From 1904 to 1908 she worked with Max Reinhardt (q.v.) in Berlin, and was for many years the German actress best known outside Germany.

SOTHERN, EDWARD ASKEW [really DOUGLAS STEWART], (1826–81), actor, who first appeared in the English provinces, and later went to America, where, he acted in Boston without success. Changing his name to Sothern, he joined the company of Lester Wallack (q.v.) in New York, and was later associated with Laura Keene (q.v.), with whom in 1858 he made an immense success as Lord Dundreary in her production of Tom Taylor's *Our American Cousin*, a part with which he is always associated and which he practically created. He was equally well received when in 1861 he played the part in London, where his long side-whiskers became known as 'dundrearies'. The play became almost a series of monologues by Dundreary, all the other characters being sacrificed to his popularity, and several other sketches were written to exploit the personality of Sothern's creation. Other plays in which he appeared were his own *Brother Sam* (1865), written in collaboration with Buckstone (q.v.) and Oxenford, some critics preferring his Sam to his Dundreary; T. W. Robertson's *David Garrick* (1864), where he failed in the final love scene; and *A Crushed Tragedian* (1878), a comedy by H. J. Byron which after a poor reception in London was successful in New York. Sothern was essentially an eccentric comedian, and it was in that 'line of business' that he did his best work.

SOTHERN, EDWARD HUGH (1859–1933), English actor, one of the three sons of E. A. Sothern (q.v.), whose charm and talent he inherited in full measure. After several years on the stage in England and the United States, where he toured with John McCullough, he became leading man in 1885 at the Lyceum Theatre in New York, remaining there until 1898. A light comedian and an excellent romantic hero in such popular plays as Hope's *The Prisoner of Zenda* and McCarthy's *If I Were King*, he became immensely popular with New York audiences, and in 1903 appeared in the opening production of Frohman's New Lyceum Theatre. He left there a year later and, with Julia Marlowe (q.v.), who became his second wife in 1911, headed a company formed for the production of plays by Shakespeare, opening with *Romeo and Juliet*. Also with his wife, he revisited London after an absence of twenty-five years, being seen in Shakespeare and other plays. After Julia's retirement in 1924, due to an accident, he presented, jointly with her, the scenery, costumes, and properties for ten Shakespeare plays to the Shakespeare Memorial Theatre at Stratford-upon-Avon (q.v.). He continued to act intermittently until 1927, and devoted much of his later years to public readings and lectures. In 1916 he published his reminiscences as *The Melancholy Tale of Me*. One of his best parts was Malvolio in *Twelfth Night*, and he several times revived his father's old part of Lord Dundreary in Tom Taylor's *Our American Cousin*.

Sotie, the topical and satirical play of medieval France, whose best-known author is Pierre Gringore (q.v.). The *sotie* was not a farce, though they had elements in common, and was often inspired by political or religious intrigue. It was intended for amusement only and had no moral purpose, though it often served as a prelude to a Mystery or Morality Play (qq.v.). The actors, or *sots* (fools), wore the traditional fool's costume—dunce's cap, short jacket, tights, and bells on their legs. Modern research inclines to the idea that *soties* were acted not only by amateur companies of students and law clerks but by semi-professional and more or less permanent companies, somewhat in the tradition of the *commedia dell'arte* (q.v.), each with its own repertory. The point is,

however, still obscure and needs further elucidation. There are a number of extant texts of *soties*, of which the Recueil Trepperel is the most representative.

Sound Effects, see NOISES OFF.

SOUTAR, ROBERT (1827–1908), see FARREN, NELLIE.

South London Music-Hall, one of the earliest halls in London. Built and decorated to resemble a Roman villa, it opened on 30 Dec. 1860 with E. W. Mackney in the bill. On 28 Mar. 1869 it was burnt down, but quickly rebuilt, and reopened on 19 Dec. of the same year. In 1873 it was taken over by an enterprising manager, J. J. Poole, who produced excellent spectacles and ballets there. Among his discoveries was Connie Gilchrist (q.v.). It was at this hall that Florrie Forde (q.v.) made her first appearance. It was badly damaged by enemy action in 1941 and was demolished early in 1955.

SOUTHERNE, THOMAS (1660–1746), English dramatist, friend of Dryden (q.v.) (for whose plays he wrote a number of prologues and epilogues) and of Mrs. Aphra Behn (q.v.), two of his plays, *The Fatal Marriage; or, the Innocent Adultery* (1694) and *Oroonoko* (1695), being based on her novels. These are both tragedies, as was his first play, *The Loyal Brother; or, the Persian Prince* (1682). They show a mingling of heroic and sentimental drama which had some influence on the development of eighteenth-century tragedy as typified by Nicholas Rowe (q.v.). Southerne was also the author of three comedies of manners—*Sir Antony Love; or, the Rambling Lady* (1690), *The Wives' Excuse; or, Cuckolds Make Themselves* (1691), and *The Maid's Last Prayer; or, Any, Rather than Fail* (1693)—which enjoyed a great success when they were first produced. They contain some witty scenes, but are weak in construction and overloaded with detail.

Southwark Theatre, PHILADELPHIA, the first permanent theatre in America. Built in 1766 by Douglass (q.v.), manager of the American Company, it was a rough brick and wood structure, painted red, its stage lit by oil. From its position it was sometimes called the South Street Theatre. During its first season, which opened on 12 Nov. 1766 with Vanbrugh and Cibber's

The Provoked Husband and Bickerstaffe's *Thomas and Sally; or, the Sailor's Return*, it saw the production of Godfrey's *The Prince of Parthia* (1767), the first American play to be produced professionally. During the War of Independence the theatre was closed, but after the departure of the British it reopened for a short time in the autumn of 1778. In 1784 the younger Hallam and John Henry (q.v.) returned to the Southwark before proceeding to New York, and the building continued to be used for theatrical purposes until in 1821 it was partly destroyed by fire. Rebuilt and used as a distillery, it was not finally demolished until 1912.

SOYINKA, WOLE (1934–), Nigerian playwright, who studied at the University of Ibadan, and later at Leeds University. After spending some years in London he returned in 1960 to Ibadan as Research Fellow in Drama and was then appointed Lecturer in English Literature at the University of Ife. A number of his plays have been published—*The Lion and the Jewel* and *A Dance of the Forests* in 1963, *The Road* in 1965, *Kongi's Harvest* in 1967, and a volume containing *The Swamp-Dwellers, The Trials of Brother Jero,* and *The Strong Breed* in 1969. Of these the best-known is *The Lion and the Jewel,* which had a short run at the Royal Court Theatre in London in Dec. 1966.

Spectacle Theatres, the name given to the early ornate playhouses of which only Italy has been able to preserve any sixteenth- and seventeenth-century examples. These are Palladio's Teatro Olimpico in Vicenza, Scamozzi's Court Theatre at Sabbioneta, and Aleotti's Teatro Farnese at Parma. This last was partially destroyed by bombing, but is in process of restoration. All these theatres, and many like them which no longer exist, were sumptuously decorated and had finely equipped stages, with machinery capable of dealing with the most elaborate settings.

Spectatory, see AUDITORIUM.

Spelvin, GEORGE, a fictitious stage name, the American equivalent of Walter Plinge (q.v.), used to cover doubling. It is first found in New York in 1886 in the cast-list of Charles A. Gardiner's *Karl the Peddler,* and in a comedy entitled *Hoss and Hoss* (1895), by William Collier, Sr.

and Charles Reed, is even given credit for supplying some of the gags used in the play. It is estimated that George Spelvin or his relatives (for several variations of the Christian name have been used) have figured in more than 10,000 Broadway performances since George's début. The name has also been applied, theatrically, to dead bodies, dolls substituting for babes in arms, and animal actors. The *Theatre Arts* magazine also sporadically featured a critic of critics who masqueraded under Spelvin's name.

SPENCER, GABRIEL (?–1598), an Elizabethan actor often referred to by his first name only. He was killed by Ben Jonson (q.v.) in a duel in Hoxton Fields on 22 Sept. 1598, having himself two years previously killed his opponent in a duel, and at the time of his death was a member of the Admiral's Men (q.v.).

SPENCER, JOHN, see ENGLISH COMEDIANS.

Spieltreppe, see JESSNER, L.

Spring Gardens, FOXHALL, LONDON, see VAUXHALL.

Staberl, see BÄUERLE, ADOLF and CARL, KARL.

Stage, the space in which the actors appear before the audience. In its simplest form this may be an 'open stage'—a cleared area with the audience standing or sitting all round, indoors or out, with or without a raised platform. At its most complicated—as in the proscenium-arch or picture-frame theatre (see PROSCENIUM) —it is an elaborate structure with a raked stage floor, surmounted by a fly-floor and a grid, with a cellar underneath to house the machinery needed for working traps and mechanical scene-changing. In this case the boards of the stage floor will be removable to permit the passage of actors and props from the cellar. An intermediate form of stage—the so-called 'Elizabethan stage'—is the high platform built against a permanent wall-structure with a cellar underneath. This may or may not have an enclosed space above for the provision of simple scenic effects. The spaces adjacent to the stage proper, used by actors and stage staff, form the backstage area. In the Restoration theatre that part of the stage floor which was in front of the proscenium arch was known as the forestage (q.v.), or apron stage.

The word stage is also used of the whole ensemble of acting and theatre production, as in 'the history of the English stage', excluding the texts of the plays, which belong to dramatic literature. To be 'on the stage' is to be an actor; to be 'on stage' is to appear in the scene then being played; offstage refers to a position close to the stage but invisible, though not inaudible, to the audience (see also THEATRE BUILDINGS).

Stage Brace, see FLAT.

Stage-Cloth, see CLOTH.

Stage Directions, notes added to the script of a play to convey information about its performance not already explicit in the dialogue itself. Generally speaking, they are concerned with (a) the actor's movements, (b) the scenery or stage effects.

Stage directions concerning the actor's movements are, in the English theatre, based on two important peculiarities: they are all relative to the position of an actor facing the audience—right and left are therefore reversed from the spectator's point of view—and they all date from the period when the stage was raked, or sloped upwards, towards the back. Thus, movement towards the audience is said to be DOWN STAGE, and a movement away from the audience is UP STAGE. (A derivative use of the latter word arises in stage slang when any haughty behaviour is said to be 'upstage'.) The stage is further divided into nine main zones, three upstage (at the back), Up Left, Up Centre, and Up Right; three downstage (at the front), Down Left, Down Centre, and Down Right; and three across the middle, Left, Centre, and Right. Three further terms, relating to the back wall, are Left Centre Back, Centre Back, and Right Centre Back. Further sub-divisions relating to the central area are indicated by Up Left Centre, Down Left Centre, Up Right Centre and Down Right Centre. Initials are generally used when writing all the above. Lateral movements to or from a centre line are qualified as 'off' or 'on'. 'To go off' is to leave the stage; 'to go off a little' is to withdraw to one side on stage.

Stage directions may also indicate change of position on stage, as 'cross', meaning 'go across the stage'. A SCISSOR CROSS is the crossing of two characters from opposite directions, and unless done intentionally, usually for a humorous effect, is regarded as an ugly move denoting clumsy technique. Movement round an object on stage is expressed as 'above' or 'below' that object, and not as 'in front of' or 'behind'. This dates back to the steeply raked stage of earlier times.

The simplest examples of stage directions relating to the actor's movements are such single words as 'enters' or 'turns', to which may be added the Latin word *exit* ('he goes out') inflected as a normal verb, 'you exit', 'he exits', 'they exit'. The antithesis, *manet* ('he remains'), has disappeared, but as far back as 1698 it was used to indicate that a character remained on stage at the end of a scene to take part in the next scene, even if the scenery had to be changed (which was done in full view of the audience), thus ensuring that the action of the play carried on without a break.

In printed copies of old plays, particularly melodramas, such terms as R.U.E. and L.2.E are found. These relate to the times when the side-walls of the stage were composed of separate wings, the entrance being the passage between one wing and its neighbour. Thus R.U.E. signifies Right Upper Entrance, and L.2.E. Left Second Entrance—the first entrance being that between the proscenium wing and the first wing of the scene proper. A further, and earlier, variant of this method of terminology (found as far back as 1748) was to indicate an entrance, as 'in the second (or third) grooves' (q.v.); this signified that that particular entrance took place immediately behind the wing in the second (or third) groove. Two other terms, which apply only to the English-speaking theatre, are PROMPT SIDE and OPPOSITE PROMPT, the latter usually spoken and written of as O.P. The Prompt Side is normally the stage left and O.P. the stage right, though in some theatres the PROMPT CORNER is found on the right. This Prompt Corner is a desk or table against the inner side of the proscenium wall where the prompter installs his PROMPT BOOK (a copy of the play, generally interleaved, and carrying the full directions and warnings necessary to the management of the production), and where a board of switches for signals, communicating to various parts of the theatre, is generally situated. Among the signals is the Bar Bell to warn patrons in the bars and foyers of the approaching end of an interval. On the Continent the PROMPTER'S BOX is usually sunk beneath a semi-circular hood in the centre of the footlights. When foreign opera or acting companies visit London, a central prompter's box is usually provided for them.

Stage directions covering scenery today are generally self-explanatory, but in Restoration and eighteenth-century plays the phrases 'the scene draws', 'draws off', 'draws over', or 'closes in' indicate that the two flats of the back-scene were drawn apart or drawn together to disclose or hide a scene set behind them. The simple directions 'The scene closes' and 'The scene opens' refer to the actual movement of the scenery.

In early printed plays, technical directions which have been taken over from prompters' scripts are often of great interest to students. In Theobald's *The Perfidious Brothers*, for instance, published in 1715 and acted at Lincoln's Inn Fields a year later, the initials U.D.P.S., M.D.O.P., and L.D.P.S. (indicating Upper, Middle, or Lower Doors on Prompt or Opposite Prompt Sides) show the use of six proscenium doors (q.v.) in the early eighteenth-century playhouse.

A further development in stage directions, chiefly intended to facilitate the reading of plays by the general public, came at about the end of the nineteenth century, with careful descriptions by the author of his settings and characters. These seem to have begun with Ibsen (q.v.) and were carried to great lengths by such authors as Shaw, Granville-Barker, and Barrie (qq.v.), whose stage directions refer less to the means of production than to the effect those means are intended to achieve.

Stage Door. This, situated at the back or side of the theatre, provides the usual means of access to the area back-stage for actors and stage-hands. Immediately inside it is the cubicle of the stage-door keeper (formerly known as the Hall Keeper), and in close proximity to it is the CALL BOARD, on which schedules of rehearsals, and other information needed by the actors, are posted, including the 'Notice' informing them of the end of the play's run. The stage door is never used by the audience, who enter by the main front and one or two subsidiary side entrances, but in Elizabethan times the stage- or tiring-house door was used by those members of the audience who had seats on the stage (see AUDIENCE ON THE STAGE).

Stage Lighting, see LIGHTING.

Stage Properties, see PROPS.

Stage Society, INCORPORATED, LONDON. This body was founded in 1899 for the production of plays of artistic merit which were unlikely to be acceptable to a commercial management. As it was decided to perform them with professional actors in West End theatres, they were mostly seen on Sunday nights, when the theatres were free. The Society's first production, at the Royalty on 26 Nov. 1899, was *You Never Can Tell*, by Bernard Shaw (q.v.). Subsequently a number of other plays by Shaw were first produced by the Society, including *Captain Brassbound's Conversion* (1900), *Mrs. Warren's Profession* (1902), and *Man and Superman* (1905), as well as plays by such important foreign dramatists as Afinogenov, J.-J. Bernard, Cocteau, Gogol, Gorky, Hauptmann, Kaiser, Odets, Pirandello, and Wedekind (qq.v.). In 1924 the Society amalgamated with the THREE HUNDRED CLUB, also a Sunday play-producing society founded by Phyllis Bell, wife of Geoffrey Whitworth (q.v.), which produced several interesting new plays, including J. R. Ackerley's *Prisoners of War* (1925) and Van Druten's *Young Woodley* (1928). In 1930 the Council of the Stage Society, considering that its pioneer work was no longer needed, owing to the emergence of such groups as the Gate Theatre (q.v.), suggested that it should be wound up. The proposal was rejected by an overwhelming majority and the production of plays continued until the outbreak of the Second World War, the last being Lorca's *Marriage of Blood* at the Savoy on 19 Mar. 1939.

STAGG, CHARLES (?–1735), English actor and teacher of dancing and elocution, who, with his wife Mary, figures in the earliest records of professional entertainment in the New World. Although little is known of his activities, he was in possession in 1716 of a theatre built by a merchant in Williamsburg, Virginia, U.S.A. It is possible that the Staggs may have prepared and produced the play given in 1718 in the presence of the Governor of Virginia. After Charles's death, Mary was in charge of dancing assemblies in Williamsburg, but nothing further is known about her.

Stall, the name given in the modern theatre to the individual seats between the stage front and the pit, those nearest the stage being known as Orchestra Stalls. They first appeared in the 1830s to 1840s, after the raising of the first circle had allowed the pit to extend further back. With the exception of Boxes they are the most expensive seats in the theatre. They were at one time called by their French name of *fauteuils*. In some theatres the term Balcony Stalls was applied to the front rows of the Dress Circle.

Standard Theatre. (1) LONDON, in Shoreditch. This opened in 1837 as the Royal Standard, and after some remodelling in 1845 was called the New Standard. It was up for sale in 1849 and was bought by John Douglass, who remained there until his death in 1888. Under him its pantomimes rivalled those of Drury Lane and the neighbouring Britannia (qq.v.), in Hoxton. On 21 Oct. 1866, it was burnt down and rebuilt on a larger scale, reopening in Dec. 1867 as the Standard. It had a good stock company and was the first of the north-east suburban theatres to attract visiting stars from the West End, including Henry Irving (q.v.) in 1869. The Melville family, afterwards connected for so long with the Lyceum (q.v.), ran it successfully from 1889 to 1907, but the building of other suburban theatres eventually robbed it of its audiences and in 1926 it became a cinema. It was destroyed by enemy action in 1940.

(For the Standard Music-Hall, Pimlico, London, see VICTORIA PALACE.)

(2) NEW YORK. This opened as the Eagle on 18 Oct. 1875 and had a prosperous career as a home of variety and light entertainment. Renamed the Standard, it witnessed on 15 Jan. 1879 the first production in New York of Gilbert and Sullivan's *H.M.S. Pinafore*, which had a sensational success. In 1880 the theatre had a further success with a dramatization of Bret Harte's *M'liss: An Idyll of Red Mountain*, but this was the only good play of a poor season and shortly afterwards the theatre changed hands at a very low price. Two more Gilbert and Sullivan light operas had long runs there, *Patience* in 1881 and *Iolanthe* in 1882. On 14 Dec. 1883 the theatre was destroyed by fire, but it was rebuilt and reopened on 23 Dec. 1884. In

1897, renamed the Manhattan, it opened again as a playhouse under William A. Brady (q.v.) with *What Happened to Jones*, a farce by George Broadhurst, and from 1901 to 1907 housed a company run by Mrs. Fiske (q.v.). It was demolished in 1909, a department store, Gimbel's, being built on its site.

STANFIELD, CLARKSON (1793–1867), English artist, who was for a few years a scene painter. His first work was done for the Royalty Theatre (q.v.), in Wellclose Square, London. In 1831 he was at the Theatre Royal, Edinburgh, and he then returned to London to become scenic director at the Coburg (see OLD VIC) and eventually at Drury Lane. By 1834 he had achieved sufficient recognition as an artist to give up scene painting as a profession, though occasionally he did some work for his friends, assisting Macready (q.v.) with his pantomimes in 1837 and 1842 and painting the backdrop in 1857 for the production by Dickens (q.v.) at his private theatre in Tavistock House of Wilkie Collins's *The Frozen Deep*. His last theatrical work was a drop scene for the Adelphi which he painted for Ben Webster (q.v.) in 1858.

STANISLAVSKY [really ALEXEYEV], KONSTANTIN SERGEIVICH (1863–1938), Russian actor, director, and teacher of acting. He had already had some experience of acting with amateur groups, and had directed in 1891, for the first time on the Russian stage, *The Fruits of Enlightenment*, by Leo Tolstoy (q.v.), as well as a dramatization of Dostoievsky's *Sela Stepanchikov*, when in 1898, in partnership with Nemirovich-Danchenko (q.v.), he founded the Moscow Art Theatre (q.v.), which opened a new epoch in Russian and indeed in world theatre. In its first productions (Alexei Tolstoy's *Tsar Feodor Ivanovich*, 1898; Ostrovsky's *Snow Maiden*, 1900; Leo Tolstoy's *The Power of Darkness*, 1902; Shakespeare's *Julius Caesar*, 1903) Stanislavsky put into practice the theories he had formulated under the influence of the Meininger Company (q.v.) and out of his own experience. Rejecting the current declamatory style of acting, with unrealistic costumes and scenery and stereotyped type-casting, he sought for a simplicity and truth which would give the complete illusion of reality. He trained his actors in a new way of acting, basing his methods on the psychological development of character and the drawing-out of latent powers of self-expression by precept and long practice, a process which can be studied in his published works, *My Life in Art* (1924), *An Actor Prepares* (1936), *Stanislavsky Rehearses 'Othello'* (1948), and *Building a Character* (1950). On these a whole system of actor-training has been built up, particularly by devoted Stanislavsky adherents in the United States (see THE METHOD). Among Stanislavsky's greatest achievements were his productions of the plays of Chekhov (q.v.)—*The Seagull* in 1898, *Uncle Vanya* in 1899, *Three Sisters* in 1901, and *The Cherry Orchard* in 1904—which he produced as lyric dramas, underlining the emotional elements with music and showing how Chekhov's apparently passive dialogue demands great subtlety and a psychologically-orientated internal development of the role, with great simplicity of external expression. During the years of upheaval leading to the uprising of 1905 Stanislavsky produced the plays of that 'stormy petrel of the Revolution', Maxim Gorky (q.v.), including *The Lower Depths* (1902). In the years of reaction (1905–16) he turned to the Symbolists—Maeterlinck and Andreyev (q.v.)—and aestheticized, stylized productions. Under the Soviet regime, after an initial period of adjustment, he continued his work as a fine producer of both old and new plays. He was himself a superb character actor and through long practice had evolved an astonishing technique. Among his best roles were Astrov in *Uncle Vanya*, Vershinin in *Three Sisters*, Gayev in *The Cherry Orchard*, Dr. Stockmann in Ibsen's *An Enemy of the People*, and Rakitin in Turgenev's *A Month in the Country*. In later years, owing to ill health, he gave up acting but continued to work as a producer and teacher.

STARKE, JOHANNE CHRISTIANE (1731–1809), a fine tragic and emotional German actress, who became leading lady of a company run by Koch at Leipzig. Her only rival in her own line was Sophie Hensel (q.v.), but the latter's bad temper and intriguing nature often lost her the sympathy of the audience, whereas Johanne Starke retained her friends, on stage and off. She was excellent in the title-role of Lessing's *Miss Sara Sampson* (1755), and later played older, maternal, and lachrymose roles to perfection. When her tragic style became somewhat outmoded she turned to comedy, and was a great success in the parts of comic elderly women. She played for a time under Ekhof (q.v.) at Gotha, and went with the company to Mannheim after his death.

Star Theatre, NEW YORK, the second theatre to be opened by the elder James Wallack (q.v.) under his own name, in 1861. After his death in 1864 it was managed by his son Lester Wallack (q.v.), who left it in 1881 to open his own theatre on Broadway. The old theatre then housed plays in German until on 23 Mar. 1882 it reopened as the Star, taking the place of Booth's Theatre (q.v.). It was here, on 29 Oct. 1883, that Irving, with Ellen Terry and his Lyceum company, made his first appearance in New York. He confined himself to modern plays, not wishing to challenge Edwin Booth (q.v.) in Shakespeare, and his staging, lighting, and acting proved a revelation to New York audiences. Later visitors to the Star were Booth himself, John McCullough on his farewell visit to New York in 1884, Mary Anderson in 1885, returning after two years in London, Modjeska in Barrymore's *Nadjezda* (1886), Bernhardt in her most popular parts, and Wilson Barrett (q.v.) making his American début, also in 1886. The theatre was demolished in 1901.

Star Trap, see TRAP.

STEAD, JAMES HENRY (?–1886), a music-hall performer who achieved fame in the 1870s with one song, 'The Perfect Cure', which he first sang at Weston's Music-Hall (see HOLBORN EMPIRE). Dressed in a suit with broad stripes, his pale face painted with red cheeks like a Dutch doll and adorned with a small moustache and imperial, the whole surmounted by a clown's hat, he bounded up and down all the time he was singing, his hands held tightly by his sides, and is said to have made as many as sixteen hundred leaps at each performance. When the vogue for this preposterous act waned Stead fell on hard times, and died in poverty in Seven Dials.

STEELE, SIR RICHARD (1672–1729), English dramatist, who was one of the first to temper the licentiousness of Restoration drama with sentimental moralizing. His work for the theatre falls into two periods, the first covering his three early and only moderately successful comedies, *The Funeral* (1701), *The Lying Lover* (1703), and *The Tender Husband* (1705). He then turned his energies to essay-writing for *The Tatler* and *The Spectator*, though he remained in close touch with the theatrical world, particularly Drury Lane, and in 1722 he produced his last and most important play, *The Conscious Lovers*, a sentimentalized adaptation of the *Andria* of Terence (q.v.), marked throughout by a high moral tone and produced under the supervision of Colley Cibber (q.v.) with an excellent cast which included Barton Booth, Wilks, and Mrs. Oldfield (qq.v.). It was a great success, being immediately translated into German and French, and it materially assisted the current European drift towards the *comédie larmoyante*. Steele was also the founder and editor of the first English theatrical journal, *The Theatre*, which appeared twice a week from 1719 to 1720.

STEINBECK, JOHN ERNST (1902–68), American writer, best known as a novelist, but important as a dramatist through his own dramatizations of two of his short novels, *Of Mice and Men* (pub. 1937) and *The Moon is Down* (pub. 1942), which were already dramatic both in structure and dialogue. The play *Of Mice and Men* was produced in 1937 and won the Drama Critics' Prize for its realistic picture of itinerant labour and the tragic story of a feeble-minded farm-hand. It was seen in London in 1939. *The Moon is Down* (1942; London, 1943), which was more favourably received in Europe than in New York, dramatized the occupation of a peaceful town by the Germans, and its resistance movement. Two of his novels were dramatized by other hands—*Tortilla Flat* in 1938, and *Burning Bright* in 1950. Rodgers and Hammerstein based a musical, *Pipe Dream* (1955), on Steinbeck's novel *Sweet Thursday*. In 1962 he received the Nobel Prize for Literature.

STEPHENS, ROBERT (1931–), English actor, who made his first appearance in London at the Royal Court in 1956. He remained there until 1962, playing a wide variety of parts, including the title-role in John Osborne's *Epitaph for George Dillon* (1958), in which he also made his first appearance in New York. In 1963 he joined the National Theatre company at the Old Vic, where one of his outstanding parts was Atahualpa in Peter Shaffer's

The Royal Hunt of the Sun (1964). In the previous year he had played Captain Plume in Farquhar's *The Recruiting Officer* to the Silvia of his then wife, Maggie Smith (q.v.), with whom he was also seen in *Much Ado About Nothing* (1965), Ibsen's *Hedda Gabler*, and Farquhar's *The Beaux' Stratagem* (both 1970).

STERNHEIM, CARL (1878–1942), German dramatist, whose bitter anti-bourgeois satires have caused him to be likened ot Molière and Wycherley (qq.v.). His plays deal with social climbers, newly enriched millionaires, weak-kneed would-be gallants, and financial jugglers. His biting humour, enhanced by his telegraphic style, reminiscent of the Expressionists, struck a new note in the German theatre of his time, and he ranks as one of the few modern German dramatists to succeed in comedy. Among his plays the most successful were *Die Hose* (1911), *Bürger Schippel* (1912), *Der Snob* (1913), *Tabula Rasa* (1919), *Libussa* and *Der Nebbich* (both 1922). In 1935 a translation of his *Die Marquise von Arcis* (1919, based on a story by Diderot) by Ashley Dukes, under the title of *The Mask of Virtue*, was seen in London with Vivien Leigh (q.v.) as Henriette. A revival of *Der Snob* was the first play to be produced in Berlin after the defeat of the Nazis in 1945. Sternheim's last plays were *Oscar Wilde* (1925) and *Die Schule von Usnach* (1926), which shows clearly the influence of Wedekind (q.v.). In 1962 a translation by Eric Bentley of *Die Hose* as *The Knickers* was taken to London in the repertory of the Margate Stage Company, and as *Bloomers* it was performed at the University of Sussex in 1970.

STEVENSON, WILLIAM (?–1575), a Fellow of Christ's College, Cambridge, who is believed to have been the author of *Gammer Gurton's Needle*, a play which, with *Ralph Roister Doister*, by Udall (q.v.), stands at the beginning of English comedy. No definite date can be assigned for its performance but it was probably given in Cambridge between 1552 and 1563. It was printed in 1575, the year of Stevenson's death, and may be identical with a play referred to as *Diccon the Bedlam*, the name of the chief character in *Gammer Gurton's Needle*. This play has also been attributed, with little likelihood, to DR. JOHN STILL, Bishop of Bath and Wells in 1593, and to DR. JOHN BRIDGES, who is mentioned as its author in the *Martin Marprelate* tracts. Although structurally it conforms to the classic type, its material is native English, and one of its characters, Hodge, has given his name to the conventional English farm labourer.

STEWART, DOUGLAS, see SOTHERN, E. A.

Stichomythia, a type of dialogue employed occasionally in classical Greek verse drama, in which two characters speak single lines alternately during passages of great emotional tension. The device, which has been likened to alternate strokes of hammers on the anvil, was used by Shakespeare, notably in *Richard III* (see I, ii, ll. 193–203; IV, iv, ll. 344–70). Echoes of it can be found in modern prose plays, particularly in the clipped dialogue of the 1920s, as in some of Coward's early works, and it is found in such later plays as Beckett's *Waiting for Godot* (1955), where, though outwardly comic, it engenders a mood of almost hysterical excitement. To be effective, the device must be used sparingly. It is sometimes referred to as 'cat-and-mouse', 'cut-and-parry', or 'cut-and-thrust' dialogue.

STILL, DR. JOHN, see STEVENSON, WILLIAM.

STIRLING, FANNY [*née* MARY ANNE KEHL] (1813–95), English actress, who made her first appearance in London in 1829 as Fanny Clifton. She married an actor-manager and dramatist, EDWARD STIRLING [really LAMBERT] (1809–94), most of whose plays were dramatizations of novels by Dickens. She appeared under his management at the Adelphi, and though not good in tragedy, made a success in soubrette and comedy roles, one of her best parts being Peg Woffington in Tom Taylor's *Masks and Faces* (1852). Though her acting was later considered old-fashioned, she was recognized as the last great exponent of the grand style in comedy, particularly in such parts as the Nurse in *Romeo and Juliet* and Mrs. Malaprop and Mrs. Candour in Sheridan's *The Rivals* and *The School for Scandal*. She retired from the stage in 1870, but gave recitals and taught elocution. On her husband's death she married again, becoming Lady Gregory, but died a year later.

Stock Company, the name applied in the 1850s to a permanent troupe of actors attached to one theatre or group of theatres and operating on a true repertory system with a nightly change of bill, to distinguish it from the newly emergent touring company. The system was, however, in being long before, and the term could have been applied to the companies attached to Drury Lane and Covent Garden (qq.v.) from the Restoration onwards, to the eighteenth-century circuit companies in the provinces, and to the resident theatre companies of the early nineteenth century in the larger towns of the United States. In both countries the stock company found itself threatened by the establishment of the long run (q.v.) and the touring company, which, in the 1880s, helped by cheap and easy railway transport, finally triumphed. The stock company then ceased to exist, the last in London being that of Irving (q.v.) at the Lyceum. It had been an excellent training-ground for young actors, combining a variety of stage experience with some element of security, functions now performed, with reservations, by the modern repertory theatre (q.v.). A revival of the stock company, playing in repertory in London, was successfully achieved by the Royal Shakespeare Company at the Aldwych (q.v.) in 1961 and by the National Theatre at the Old Vic (q.v.) in 1963, somewhat on the lines of the resident companies which have never ceased to occupy the subsidized theatres of Europe, such as the Comédie-Française and the Moscow Art Theatre (qq.v.). Each player in the old stock company undertook some special line of business. The TRAGEDIAN, who was also the leading man, played Hamlet and Macbeth. The OLD MAN played Sheridan's Sir Anthony Absolute (in *The Rivals*) and Sir Peter Teazle (in *The School for Scandal*). The OLD WOMAN took the Nurse (in *Romeo and Juliet*). The HEAVY FATHER was the tyrant and villain in tragedy and melodrama, while the HEAVY WOMAN played Lady Macbeth, or Emilia in *Othello*. The JUVENILE LEAD was the young lover and hero, the JUVENILE TRAGEDIAN took on Macduff (in *Macbeth*), or Laertes (in *Hamlet*), often combining such parts with light comedy roles. The LOW COMEDIAN played leading comic parts of a broad, farcical, or clownish type, and was usually given minor roles in tragedy, while the WALKING LADY or GENTLEMAN played secondary parts in comedy, such as Careless in Sheridan's *The School for Scandal*. GENERAL UTILITY played minor roles in every type of play, for a very small salary, while the SUPER, or SUPERNUMERARY, was engaged merely to walk on, had nothing to say, and was not paid at all. Among other members of a stock company were such specialists as the First Singer or Vocalist, the Principal Dancer, the Singing Chambermaid, the Countryman, and the Singing Countryman.

Stockfisch, HANS, see ENGLISH COMEDIANS.

STOLL [really GRAY], SIR OSWALD (1866–1942), English theatre manager, who took his stepfather's name, and gained his first theatrical experience at the Star Music Hall in Cardiff under his mother's management. He then joined forces with Moss, and together they built Empires for variety all over the provinces. When they finally came to London the original Empire (q.v.) in Leicester Square was not for sale, so Moss built the Hippodrome and Stoll the Coliseum (qq.v.), where he produced shows suitable for family audiences, forbidding the use by any comedian of even the mildest oath, and replacing many of the earlier vulgarities of music-hall by light music. He controlled the Stoll circuit and gave his name to the Stoll Theatre (q.v.). In 1919 he was knighted, not only for his services to the stage, but for his benevolent works and his War Seals Foundation during the First World War. He composed a number of songs, one of which was sung by Vesta Tilley (q.v.) with great success.

Stoll Theatre, LONDON, in Kingsway, near the junction with the Aldwych, built partly on the site of Gibbon's Tennis-Court (see VERE STREET THEATRE). It opened on 13 Nov. 1911 as the London Opera House, but had only a short operatic career, since it was in competition with Covent Garden (q.v.) and soon gave up the struggle. It was then used for revue and pantomime, but was often closed for long periods. It was acquired in 1916 by Sir Oswald Stoll (q.v.), who gave it his own name and turned it into a cinema with complete success. It did not return to use as a theatre until 1941, when revue and pantomime were seen there, followed by revivals of famous musical comedies. In 1947 Tom Arnold used the vast stage for Ice-Shows. In 1951 it became the headquarters of the Festival Ballet under Markova and Dolin. Gershwin's 'Porgy and Bess' had its first London production at the Stoll in 1952,

and Ingrid Bergman made her first appearance in London in Honegger's 'Joan of Arc at the Stake' in 1954. The last play seen at the theatre (on 1 July 1957) was *Titus Andronicus*, with Laurence Olivier and Vivien Leigh (qq.v.), fresh from a triumphant European tour. It closed on 4 Aug. 1957 and was demolished. An office block containing a small theatre was built on the site (see ROYALTY THEATRE (3)).

STONE, JOHN AUGUSTUS (1801–34), American dramatist, author of *Metamora, or the Last of the Wampanoags* (1829), in which Forrest (q.v.), who had awarded it first prize in a competition for a play based on American history, played the title-role. It was a great success, being revived as late as 1887. After playing in it for some years Forrest commissioned Bird (q.v.) to rewrite it, but as no complete manuscript of either version exists, it is not possible to say what alterations Bird made. Stone, who was a mediocre actor, wrote and appeared in a number of romantic historical plays which have not survived. Disappointed as actor and author, he committed suicide by drowning himself in the Schuylkill River at Phildelphia.

STOPPARD [really STRAUSSLER], TOM (1937–), English dramatist, who first came into prominence with the production at the National Theatre in 1967 of *Rosencrantz and Guildenstern Are Dead*, a play in the tradition of the Theatre of the Absurd (q.v.) in which two minor characters from *Hamlet* are shown as having no existence outside Shakespeare's play, and unable to make any independent decisions in their lives except choosing to die. This somewhat abstruse drama had an unexpected success, both in England and abroad, which led to the production in London of an earlier play, *Enter a Free Man* (1968), first seen in Hamburg in 1964, and, as *A Walk on the Water*, on television the same year. Stoppard has written a number of other television plays, and also two stage comedies, *The Real Inspector Hound* (1968) and *After Magritte* (1970). He was awarded a C.B.E. in the New Year honours of 1978.

STORER, MARIA (c. 1760–95), see HENRY, JOHN.

STOREY, DAVID MALCOLM (1933–), English novelist and playwright, who was already well-known through his books, particularly *This Sporting Life* (1960), before his first play, *The Restoration of Arnold Middleton*, was staged at the Royal Court Theatre (q.v.) in 1967. It was followed, also at the Royal Court, by *In Celebration* (1969) and the extremely successful *The Contractor* (1970), both directed by Lindsay Anderson. The second, which deals with the erection and dismantling of a marquee for a wedding reception, displayed a remarkable balance between the physical effort involved and the contacts and adjustments between the various persons. Storey's next plays were *Home* (1970), set in a mental home, in which Gielgud and Ralph Richardson (qq.v.) gave excellent performances, and *The Changing Room* (1971), which had a background of Rugby football. Both were seen also in New York, where they were chosen as the best plays of their respective seasons. They were followed by two more plays, *The Farm* and *Cromwell*.

Storm and Stress, see STURM UND DRANG.

Strand Theatre, LONDON. (1) This opened on 5 Jan. 1832 as the New Strand (Subscription) Theatre. As it had no licence, tickets were sold off the premises at 4*s.*, 3*s.*, and 2*s.* The final battle between the unlicensed houses and the patent theatres was being waged, and the opening attraction at the new theatre was a skit on the situation, called *Professionals Puzzled; or, Struggles at Starting.* It was not successful, and the theatre closed in Nov. Fanny Kelly (q.v.) reopened it in Jan. 1833 and started a dramatic school there, later transferring it to the Royalty (q.v.). Later in the year an attempt was made to evade the licensing laws by granting free admission to purchasers of an ounce of rose lozenges for 4*s.* or ½ oz. of peppermint drops for 2*s.*, but in spite of this the theatre again closed. After further struggles it managed to reopen on 25 Apr. 1836 and achieved some success with burlesques by Jerrold (q.v.), but it was not until 1848, five years after the passing of the Theatres Act, that it became a home of legitimate drama, with a succession of comedies played by William Farren, Mrs. Stirling, and Henry Compton. When they left, the theatre was renamed Punch's Playhouse, and sank into obscurity until it was taken over by the Swanboroughs and reopened on 5 Apr. 1858 as the Strand, to house a series of burlesques by H. J. Byron (q.v.) which drew large audiences, one of the earliest attractions (in Oct.) being Marie Wilton (see BANCROFT) as Pippo in a burlesque of *The Maid and the Magpie*. From 1874 to 1878 Lottie Venne (q.v.) appeared at the theatre in burlesque and light opera. Four years later, on 29 July 1882, the old theatre was condemned as a fire hazard and practically demolished. It reopened on 18 Nov. 1882, and in 1887 came under the management of the American actor, John Sleeper Clarke (q.v.). Little of note, however, occurred, except for the success of Louie Freear and Lily Elsie in Dance's *A Chinese Honeymoon* (1901), before the theatre finally closed on 13 May 1905 and was demolished to make way for the Aldwych Tube station.

(2) The present Strand Theatre, in the Aldwych, opened on 22 May 1905 as the Waldorf. After the destruction of the Avenue (see PLAYHOUSE), Cyril Maude (q.v.) made it his headquarters, remaining there until 1907, when Julia Marlowe and E. H. Sothern (qq.v.) appeared in a series of plays which included Kester's successful *When Knighthood was in Flower*. In 1909 the name of the theatre was changed to the Strand, but in 1911 it was sold to an American, F. C. Whitney, who called it after himself. He was not successful, and in 1913 it again became the Strand, Matheson Lang scoring a success there with *Mr. Wu*. In 1915 the building was slightly damaged during an air raid while occupied by Fred Terry and Julia Neilson (qq.v.) in a season of old and new plays, including Baroness Orczy's *The Scarlet Pimpernel*. Arthur Bourchier took over in 1919 and successfully produced A. E. W. Mason's *At the Villa Rose* (1920), Ian Hay's *A Safety Match* (1921), and a dramatization of Stevenson's *Treasure Island* (1922). It was at the Strand that *Anna Christie*, by Eugene O'Neill (q.v.), was first seen in London in 1923, and another successful American play was Abbott and Dunning's *Broadway* (1926). Later successes included a farce by Austin Melford, *It's a Boy* (1930), and *1066 and All That* (1935), based on the book by Sellar and Yeatman. In 1940, at the height of the blitz, Donald Wolfit (q.v.) gave midday productions of Shakespeare. During one of them, on 8 Oct., the building was badly blasted. The dressing-rooms were damaged and the actors had to scramble over debris to reach the stage, but the per-

formance continued, though costumes had to be dug out of the ruins and hastily brushed down. The theatre was soon repaired, and among later successes there have been Kesselring's *Arsenic and Old Lace* (1942); *Sailor, Beware!* (1955), a farce by Philip King and Falkland Cary which established Peggy Mount as a star; the revue *For Adults Only* (1958); two plays based by Ronald Millar on novels by C. P. Snow, *The Affair* (1961) and *The New Men* (1962); and an American musical, *A Funny Thing Happened on the Way to the Forum*, with Frankie Howerd (1963). In June 1968 *Not Now, Darling*, by Ray Cooney and John Chapman, began a long run, and a revival of Priestley's *When We Are Married* did well in 1970.

Strange's Men, an Elizabethan theatre company, presumed to be the first by which Shakespeare was employed, either as actor and playwright or as playwright only, in 1591–2. It appeared at Court in 1582, at the same time as the company of Lord Strange's father, the Earl of Derby, a duplication which has caused some confusion in the records. Strange's Men later amalgamated with the Admiral's Men (q.v.) and played at the Rose under Henslowe. Their chief actor then was Alleyn (q.v.), who retained his personal status as an Admiral's Man, though the joint company is always referred to in Court records as Strange's Men, as it is also in Henslowe's diary during a six-week season in 1592. It was at this time that Shakespeare probably wrote for the actors of this group the first part of his *Henry VI* and perhaps *The Comedy of Errors*. They also appeared in *Titus and Vespasian*, which may have been the first draft of Shakespeare's *Titus Andronicus* (1594), and in *A Jealous Comedy* (1593), a possible source of *The Merry Wives of Windsor*. The repertory of the company also included the anonymous *A Knack to Know a Knave*, Greene's *Orlando Furioso* and *Friar Bacon and Friar Bungay*, and Marlowe's *The Jew of Malta*, as well as a number of plays now lost. The company, which separated itself from the Admiral's Men early in 1594, included Kempe, Heminge (later the friend and editor of Shakespeare), Pope, and Phillips. On the death of their patron later in the year (he had succeeded his father only six months before), and on the general reshuffling of the companies which took place with the formation of the Chamberlain's Men (q.v.)

in the same year, Strange's Men went into the provinces, not to reappear at Court until 1599–1600. The last mention of them is at Islington in 1618.

STRANITZKY, JOSEPH ANTON (1676–1726), originator of the comic figure Hanswurst (q.v.). He began his theatrical career with a travelling puppet-show and in about 1705 arrived in Vienna, where he headed a company of 'German Comedians' modelled on the lines of the English Comedians (q.v.). In 1711 he took over the newly-built Kärntnertor, thus making it the first permanent home of German-language comedy. For this company Stranitzky adapted old plays and opera libretti, making Hanswurst, a role which he bequeathed to Prehauser (q.v.), the central comic character.

STRASBERG, LEE (1901–82), American theatre director, who had had some acting experience with the Theatre Guild (q.v.) when in 1931 he helped to found its offshoot, the Group Theatre (q.v.), directing with Cheryl Crawford its first production, Paul Green's *The House of Connelly*. He later directed a number of other productions, including Maxwell Anderson's *Night Over Taos* (1932), Sidney Kingsley's *Men in White* (1933), and Paul Green's *Johnny Johnson* (1936). A firm believer in the efficacy of Stanislavsky's so-called Method (q.v.) in the formation of actors, he was from 1950 director of the ACTORS' STUDIO, where its principles are applied, and he also taught acting privately. In 1965 he was responsible for the production of Chekhov's *Three Sisters* which the Studio presented during the World Theatre season in London.

Stratford. There are three towns of this name where festivals of plays by Shakespeare are held annually. One is his birthplace in the heart of England, the second is in Canada, and the third is in the United States.

(1) STRATFORD-UPON-AVON, WARWICKSHIRE. The first festival in honour of Shakespeare was organized by Garrick (q.v.) in 1769. None of his plays was acted, and little enthusiasm was aroused. Thereafter there were only sporadic productions by travelling companies, in spite of the founding of a Shakespeare Club in 1824 and the building of a theatre on part of New Place Garden in 1827. This was demolished in 1872, the last production

there being *Hamlet*, on 30 Apr. In Apr. 1864, on the initiative of the then mayor, Edward Fordham Flower, member of a local family of brewers, actors from London were invited to appear in the Grand Pavilion, built for the occasion, to celebrate the 300th anniversary of Shakespeare's birth. The plays performed were *Twelfth Night*, *The Comedy of Errors*, *Romeo and Juliet*, *As You Like It*, *Othello*, and *Much Ado About Nothing*. Some years later, Flower's son, Charles Edward Flower, gave the site for and founded a permanent theatre (see SHAKESPEARE MEMORIAL THEATRE), where on 23 Apr. 1879 the summer Shakespeare season as we now know it, though much shorter than at present, was inaugurated with Helen Faucit and Barry Sullivan (qq.v.) in *Much Ado About Nothing*, followed by *Hamlet* and *As You Like It*. Thereafter the season took place annually, with as many as ten plays by Shakespeare being given each year, and occasionally, in the early years, a play by another author, a practice which has been revived recently. From 1886 to 1916 the plays were mainly directed by Frank Benson (q.v.). In 1919 Bridges-Adams (q.v.) took over, and it was under him that in 1926 the theatre was destroyed by fire. The plays for that year were given in a hastily-adapted local cinema which continued in use until on 23 Apr. 1932 a new theatre opened with *Henry IV*, the first part being played in the afternoon, the second in the evening. Before Bridges-Adams retired in 1934, the work of three important guest-producers had been seen in Stratford—Komisarjevsky, Guthrie, and Robert Atkins (qq.v.)—and the duration of the season had been extended from three or four weeks to five months. Komisarjevsky returned under Bridges-Adams's successor, Iden Payne (q.v.), who directed the season during the first difficult years of the Second World War, being succeeded in 1943 by Milton Rosmer and in 1944 by Robert Atkins. In 1945 a new era was inaugurated with the appointment of Barry Jackson (q.v.) as director. Among the reforms which he initiated were the spacing-out of first nights over the whole season instead of crowding them all into the first fortnight—a legacy from the earlier, shorter seasons—and the appointment of a different producer for each play instead of a resident producer for the whole series. He also encouraged promising youngsters, among them the actor Paul Scofield and

the director Peter Brook (qq.v.). As a result of Jackson's work, it was a well-established theatre and company which Anthony Quayle (q.v.) took over in 1948, and a brilliant period ensued, with actors of the calibre of Gielgud, Redgrave, and Peggy Ashcroft (qq.v.) playing leading parts. In 1956 Glen Byam Shaw (q.v.), who had been co-director with Quayle for four years, during which time a second Stratford company had been formed to tour overseas, became sole director. The appointment in 1960 of Peter Hall (q.v.) as director opened a new chapter in the history of the Stratford theatre, signalized by the formation of the Royal Shakespeare Company (q.v.), under which heading its further history is dealt with.

Apart from the theatre, with its library and picture gallery, Stratford has also a library and conference centre attached to Shakespeare's birthplace, which opened in 1964, and an Institute of Shakespeare Studies, sponsored by the University of Birmingham. This grew out of the lectures and conferences arranged from 1947 to 1951 by the British Council at Mason Croft, the former home of the novelist Marie Corelli, and provides a centre for research work all the year round and a meeting-place for Shakespearian scholars from all over the world during the summer conferences. Hall Croft, the home of Shakespeare's daughter Susanna after her marriage in 1607 to Dr. John Hall, also provides a useful centre of activity during the Shakespeare season.

(2) STRATFORD, ONTARIO. On the initiative of a citizen of the town, Tom Patterson, a committee was formed which invited Tanya Moiseiwitsch and Tyrone Guthrie, both intimately connected with Stratford-upon-Avon (q.v.), to design and direct a theatre for the production of a summer festival of Shakespeare plays. The first building, a huge tent with an approximation to an Elizabethan open stage, opened on 13 July 1953 with *Richard III* and *All's Well That Ends Well*, starring Alec Guinness as Richard and Irene Worth as Helena. In 1955 Michael Langham succeeded Guthrie as director, and in 1957 the temporary tent was replaced by a permanent structure, designed by Robert Fairfield, which retained many of the features of the original. It opened on 1 July with a Canadian actor, Christopher Plummer (q.v.), as Hamlet, and has since prospered, giving annually a number of productions

which have achieved critical acclaim.

(3) STRATFORD, CONNECTICUT. The establishment of an American centre for a festival of Shakespeare's plays came about through the initiative of Lawrence Langner (q.v.), under whom the American Shakespeare Festival Theatre beside the Housatonic River, designed by Edwin Howard, opened on 12 July 1955 with *Julius Caesar*, followed in repertory by *The Tempest*. The enterprise flourished and in 1957 the festival production of *Much Ado About Nothing*, starring Katharine Hepburn (q.v.), was seen on tour in six major cities of the United States. Attached to the theatre is a school of acting, and each festival is preceded by a special programme for students only.

STRATTON, EUGENE [really EUGENE AUGUSTUS RUHLMANN] (1861–1918), an American Negro impersonator, who, like Chirgwin (q.v.), became a well-known music-hall star. At the age of seventeen, after some experience as a solo turn, he joined the Haverly Minstrels, with whom he went to London in 1880. He was then for many years with the Moore and Burgess Minstrels. When their popularity began to wane he took to the music-hall stage, making his first appearance at the Royal Holborn in 1892. As a white-faced performer he was not successful, but on resuming his Negro make-up he made an instant appeal, and became the outstanding black-face performer of the halls, particularly when he sang 'Lily of Laguna' and other coon songs by Leslie Stuart— wistful ballads to which he whistled a refrain while dancing on a darkened, spotlighted stage in soft shoes, a noiseless, moving shadow. He retired in 1914, making his last appearance at the Queen's, Poplar.

STREATER [also STREETER], ROBERT (1624–80), English painter, who was responsible for the decorations of the Sheldonian Theatre, Oxford. He was said to excel in architectural and decorative paintings on a large scale, especially those in which perspective and a knowledge of foreshortening were required. Evelyn, in his diary for 9 Feb. 1671, says he saw 'at White-hall Theatre' 'the famous play call'd *The Siege of Granada* [by Dryden] two days acted successively; there were indeed very glorious scenes and perspectives, the worke of Mr. Streater, who well understands it'.

STRINDBERG, (JOHAN) AUGUST (1849– 1912), Swedish dramatist and novelist, author of about fifty plays as well as numerous other writings of a literary and autobiographical nature, all of which reflect the conflict between his unstable temperament and the world around him, whether in his unhappy childhood, in his three tempestuous marriages (to the actress Siri von Essen, to an Austrian, Frida Uhl, and to the Swedish actress Harriet Bosse) which all ended in divorce, or in his constant struggle for recognition, and sometimes for survival, both at home and abroad. His earliest dramatic works were mainly historical and are now forgotten, except for *Lucky Peter's Journey* (1882), which, with its echoes of Ibsen's *Peer Gynt* (1867), supplied the libretto for an opera by Malcolm Williamson first performed by the Sadler's Wells Opera Company at the Coliseum in Dec. 1969. With *The Father* (1887), however, Strindberg embarked on a series of bitter realistic dramas which portrayed not so much the accidental evils of society already analysed by his Norwegian predecessors, Bjørnson and Ibsen (qq.v.), as the basic corruptions of human nature. To this period belongs one of his best-known works, *Miss Julie* (1888), as well as the short plays *The Creditors* (also 1888), *The Stronger* (1890), and two plays originally written in German, *The Bond* (1892) and *Playing with Fire* (1893). The later plays fall into two groups—on the one hand a series of powerful and original historical dramas like *Gustavus Vasa* and *Erik XIV* (both 1899), and on the other, beginning with the first two parts of a vast symbolic miracle play, *To Damascus* (1898), plays which explore in depth the inarticulate impulses of the subconscious and seem to spring from a profound and genuine mystical experience. To this group belong *Advent* (also 1898), *Easter* (1900), the two-part *The Dance of Death* (1901), and *The Dream Play* (1902). The third part of *To Damascus* dates from 1904. In 1907 came the group of so-called 'chamber plays', of which the most important, though the least characteristic, is *The Spook* (or *Ghost*) *Sonata*. The others, more realistic in style, include *The Storm* and *After the Fire*. They were produced at the Intima Teatern which Strindberg founded in Stockholm, with August Falck, to house his own plays. Here the variety and abundance of his technical invention and virtuosity had full scope, and many of the theatrical devices later fashionable in Europe and America were either anticipated by Strindberg or derive from him. Though he has never achieved in the English-speaking theatre the position accorded to Ibsen, most of his plays are available in translation and many of them have been produced, and his influence can be traced in a number of later playwrights, among them O'Neill (q.v.). The first of his plays to be seen in London was *The Father*, produced privately in 1911 and several times revived. *Advent* came in 1921, and in 1927 *Miss Julie* (which was revived for about the sixth time at the Chichester Festival Theatre in 1965) and *The Spook Sonata*. *Easter* and *The Dance of Death* followed in 1928, the latter being revived in 1967 by the National Theatre at the Old Vic with a superb performance by Olivier (q.v.) as the Captain. Other productions of Strindberg in London include *The* (as *A*) *Dream Play* (1933), *There Are Crimes and Crimes* (1946), *To Damascus* (as *The Road to Damascus*) (1937), and *The Creditors* (1952). In New York *The Father* was first seen in 1912, *The Dance of Death* in 1923; the Provincetown Players (q.v.) produced *The Creditors* in 1922, *The Spook Sonata* in 1924 (it was revived by the Living Theatre (q.v.) in 1954), and *The Dream Play* in 1926, in which year *Easter* was also seen. *Miss Julie* and *The Stronger* were played together in 1937, and *To Damascus* was seen in 1961.

Strip Light, see BATTEN.

Strip-Tease, see BURLESQUE (4).

Sturm und Drang (STORM AND STRESS), the name given to one aspect of the German Romantic movement, which took its name from the title of a characteristic play by Klinger. It dealt with violent conflicts of passion and the struggle of the individual against a hostile environment. Typical of the drama of the movement, which was very much influenced by Shakespeare, were the early plays of Goethe and Schiller (qq.v.), particularly *Götz von Berlichingen* (1773) and *Die Räuber* (1781). These, and other less important plays by H. C. Wagner, Lenz, and Klinger, had repercussions all over Europe, and their influence can be clearly seen in early nineteenth-century English melodrama (q.v.).

(See also RITTERDRAMA.)

Stuyvesant Theatre, NEW YORK, see BELASCO THEATRE.

SUDAKOV, ILYA YAKOVLEIVICH (1890–1969), Soviet actor and director, trained at the Moscow Art Theatre. In 1933 he became artistic director of the Maly Theatre (q.v.), where some of his best productions were Gutzkow's *Uriel Acosta* (1940), with sets by Rabinovich, *Invasion* (1942), by Leonov, and *Front* (1943), by Korneichuk. Among his post-war productions were revivals of Chekhov's *Uncle Vanya* (1947), Afinogenov's *Mother of Her Children* (1954), and Alexei Tolstoy's *The Road to Calvary* (1957). In 1959 he became director of the Gogol Theatre (formerly the Moscow Transport Theatre), where he remained until his death.

SUDERMANN, HERMANN (1857–1928), German novelist and dramatist, whose first play, *Die Ehre* (*Honour*), was produced with great success in 1889. He became the main exponent of the new realistic theatre in Germany, much influenced by Ibsen (q.v.), as can be seen in *Das Glück im Winkel* (1896) and *Johannsfeuer* (1900). But the play by which he is chiefly remembered is *Heimat* (1893), a work which provided a popular melodramatic vehicle for many famous actresses, including Duse and Bernhardt (qq.v.), who both played it in London at the same time in 1895. As *Magda*, in a translation by Louis N. Parker, it was first seen in English in 1896 at the Lyceum Theatre with Mrs. Patrick Campbell (q.v.) in the title-role, a part played in 1923 by Gladys Cooper (q.v.) and in 1930 by Gwen Ffrangcon-Davies. It was produced in New York in 1904 and revived in 1926.

SUETT, DICKY [really RICHARD] (1755–1805), English comedian, who made his first appearance at Drury Lane in 1780, when he was considered extremely comical, though a little too prone to gag and grimace. He was at his best in the fools of Shakespeare, which seemed to have been specially written for him. Offstage he was somewhat melancholy, a tall, thin, ungainly man much given to solemn practical jokes and outrageous puns.

SUGG, CATHARINE LEE (1797–1845), see HACKETT, J. H.

SUKHOVO-KOBYLIN, ALEXANDER VASILEIVICH (1817–1903), Russian dramatist, whose whole life was overshadowed by the death of his mistress, whom he was suspected of having murdered. He had already started to write a play, *Krechinsky's Wedding*, before this tragic event, and while in jail he finished it. It was finally staged at the Moscow Maly Theatre in 1855. Its subject, like that of his two later plays—one, *The Case*, written in 1857 and performed at the Alexandrinsky in 1881, and the other, *Tarelkin's Death*, written in 1868 and staged in a cut version in 1900 in the Theatre of the Literary Society—was the decay of the patriarchal life of old Russia, the breaking-up of the great country estates, the decadence of the nobility, and the growing power of a corrupt bureaucracy. Although Sukhovo-Kobylin truly asserted that he was not a revolutionary, he was regarded as a dangerous man and his plays were banned by the censor. He was a great friend and admirer of Gogol (q.v.), whose influence is seen in the character of Krechinsky. Sukhovo-Kobylin was also much influenced by that other great satirist of the time, Saltikov-Shchedrin (q.v.). Worn out by his struggles with the censorship, Sukhovo-Kobylin finally gave up the theatre for philosophy and retired to France, where he died.

SULLAVAN, MARGARET (1911–60), an American actress who first appeared in New York in 1931, and in 1933 took over the leading role of Paula Jordan in *Dinner at Eight*, by George S. Kaufman and Edna Ferber. After several years in films she returned to the stage to play Sally Middleton in John Van Druten's *The Voice of the Turtle* (1943), which many consider her greatest triumph, utilizing fully both her husky 'cello' voice and the candour and unaffected charm of her acting style. It was in this part that she first appeared in London in 1947. Later appearances in New York included Hester Collyer in Rattigan's *The Deep Blue Sea* (1952) and Sabrina Fairchild in Samuel Taylor's *Sabrina Fair* (1953). She died during a pre-Broadway tour of Ruth Goetz's *Sweet Love Remember'd*.

SULLIVAN, (THOMAS) BARRY (1821–91), Irish actor, who gained his experience in Ireland, Scotland (where he managed a theatre in Aberdeen for three years), and the English provinces. He made his first appearance in London in 1853 as Hamlet at the Haymarket, and then spent a season at Sadler's Wells with Phelps (q.v.). In the autumn of 1858 he went to New York and then toured the States, being well received in San Francisco, and made a long visit to Australia, returning to England to play Benedick to the Beatrice of Helen Faucit (q.v.) in the inaugural performance at the Shakespeare Memorial Theatre in Stratford-upon-Avon (q.v.) in 1879. He made his last appearance on the stage in 1887 as Richard III, in Liverpool. He was never a first-class actor, but his vigour and forcible delivery in tragedy—he was unsuited to comedy or romance, which he seldom played—made him a success with less sophisticated audiences, for whom he kept alive the old traditions of Shakespearian acting.

SUMAROKOV, ALEXEI PETROVICH (1718–77), the first Russian dramatist to write in the neo-classical style imported from Germany and France, though he took his subjects from Russian history and in his dialogue endeavoured to refine and purify the Russian language. His plays, of which the first, *Khorev*, was produced in 1749, were acted by an amateur company formed of students from the Cadet College for sons of the nobility, of which Sumarokov had been one of the first pupils on its foundation in 1732. It was mainly owing to Sumarokov's efforts that the first professional Russian company was formed, and in 1756 he was appointed head of the Russian (as distinct from the Italian and French) Theatre in St. Petersburg, remaining there until 1761, when his liberal outspokenness caused him to be dismissed from office.

SUMMERS, THE REV. (ALPHONSUS JOSEPH-MARY AUGUSTUS) MONTAGUE (1880–1946), English critic and theatre historian. He wrote widely upon Restoration drama, and in 1919 helped to found the Phoenix Society (q.v.) for the production of old plays. He also edited the plays of Congreve, Wycherley, Otway, Shadwell, and Dryden (qq.v.). His *Bibliography of Restoration Drama* is a valuable compilation, covering a period on which he was one of the foremost authorities. At the time of his death he was working on nineteenth-century melodrama, and had just completed the writing of his autobiography.

Super, Supernumerary, see STOCK COMPANY.

Surrey Gardens Music-Hall, LONDON. This opened on 15 July 1856 and was at one time owned by the music-hall artist W. B. Fair (q.v.). Burnt down in June 1861, it was rebuilt and used as a theatre from 1872 to 1877. It was finally demolished in 1878. It was often referred to as the Surrey Music-Hall and so confused with another hall of that name (see below).

Surrey Music-Hall, LONDON, a hall attached to the Grapes public-house in Southwark Bridge Road which became a music-hall in 1848. The Vokes (q.v.) appeared there, as did many other stars in their early days. In 1856 it became the Winchester, retaining that name until it was demolished in 1878.

Surrey Theatre, LONDON, in Blackfriars Road, Lambeth, originally the Royal Circus, which opened on 14 Nov. 1782. It had a troubled existence and was burnt down in 1799 and again on 12 Aug. 1805. Rebuilt the following year, it became the Surrey, a name which, after one or two changes, it kept permanently from 1819 on. Taken over in 1809 by Elliston (q.v.), who made it into a theatre, it evaded the Patent Act by incorporating a ballet into all its productions, even *Hamlet* and *Macbeth*. Elliston gave up in 1814 and the theatre continued its chequered career, sometimes as a circus, and always in low water, until Elliston came back in 1827, when he left Drury Lane. Douglas Jerrold (q.v.) then brought him *Black-Eyed Susan* (1829), which, with T. P. Cooke (q.v.) as the nautical hero, was the theatre's first outstanding success. Jerrold wrote several more plays for the Surrey, which after Elliston's death in 1831 was taken over by Osbaldiston. Among the plays the latter put on was a melodrama by Fitzball (q.v.), *Jonathan Bradford; or, the Murder at the Roadside Inn* (1833), which had a novel stage-set divided into four, with four actions going on simultaneously.

Osbaldiston was succeeded by Davidge, and then by Bunn from Drury Lane, who unsuccessfully imported opera. In 1848 'Dick' Shepherd, the originator of the rough-and-tumble melodrama usually associated with the Surrey, took over, first with Osbaldiston and then with Creswick, a fine legitimate actor. Their association was successful and lasted, with only a short break (see VEZIN), from 1848 to 1869. On 30 Jan. 1865 the theatre was burned down, but was rebuilt, reopening on 26 Dec. the same year. Nothing of importance then took place until 1881, when George Conquest (q.v.), actor, playwright, and pantomimist, took over. He ran sensational dramas, many of them written by himself, which proved very much to the taste of his patrons, and every Christmas he put on a fine pantomime. The house flourished until his death in 1901. It declined after this and became a cinema from 1920 to 1924, with a brief season of opera. Several attempts were made to reopen it, but there were too many restrictions in the lease and it became derelict. Eventually the land was purchased by the Royal Ophthalmic Hospital, and the building was pulled down in 1934.

Susie, see TOBY (2).

Sussex's Men, a company of players with whom Shakespeare (q.v.) may have been connected for a short time. They were in the service of three Earls of Sussex in succession, from 1569 to about 1618. They first appeared at Court in 1572, when their patron became Lord Chamberlain, and for a time were referred to as the Chamberlain's Men, not to be confused with the later brilliant company of the Chamberlain's Men (q.v.) which emerged in 1594. They appeared in many provincial towns and also made periodic visits to London. On one of these, in 1594, they played for six weeks under Henslowe (q.v.) at the Rose, and their one new play was *Titus Andronicus*, revised for them, from an earlier play which had belonged to Pembroke's Men (q.v.), by the hand of Shakespeare. They may have had in their repertory at this time other plays by Shakespeare, and they also appeared in Marlowe's *The Jew of Malta*, the property of Henslowe, in the anonymous *God Speed the Plough*, and in Greene's *Friar Bacon and Friar Bungay*, which had first been performed by Strange's Men (q.v.) and was published by 1594.

SVOBODA, JOSEF (1920–), Czechoslovak scene designer, whose work has been done mainly in connection with the Czech National Theatre and, more recently, the Theatre Behind the Gate (q.v.) in Prague. He has made an international reputation, and in 1966, after his work had been seen at the Edinburgh Festival and in the 1965 World Theatre season at the Aldwych, he was commissioned by the National Theatre in London to design the sets for productions at the Old Vic of Ostrovsky's *The Storm* and Chekhov's *Three Sisters*. An exhibition of his work was held in London in 1967, with working models of several designs for mobile and revolving stages. In 1970 he returned to the Old Vic to design the sets for Simon Gray's adaptation of Dostoievsky's *The Idiot*.

Swan Theatre, LONDON. Although this Elizabethan theatre did not have a very exciting history, a good deal is known about it. It stood on Bankside, in Paris (or Parish) Garden, near the popular Bear Gardens, and was built by Francis Langley. Although Langley was a respectable citizen, in favour at Court, he had difficulty in carrying out his project owing to the opposition of the Lord Mayor of London, who feared the evils which might arise from the opening of a playhouse in his domain. Langley succeeded, however, in opening the theatre, somewhere about 1594. It probably took its name from the large number of swans on the river and banks nearby. In 1596 a Dutchman, Johannes de Witt, on a visit to London, sent to a friend in Utrecht, Arend von Buchel, a drawing of the interior of the Swan which Buchel copied into his commonplace book. Although it has many puzzling features, this 'Swan drawing' is very precious, being so far the only known pictorial representation of the inside of an Elizabethan theatre. It confirms some features otherwise known only by written evidence, particularly the large open stage, the stage building with its pillars and flag, and the three galleries for spectators running round three sides of the building. There are people on and behind the stage, but controversy has arisen over whether they represent spectators and actors during a performance, or actors only during a rehearsal. De Witt estimated the theatre's capacity at three thousand persons, which was at one time considered a slip of the pen for three hundred; but later calculations incline to two thousand in the galleries alone, and the Fortune (q.v.) is thought to have been even more capacious. The building was of wood on a brick foundation with flint and mortar work between the wooden pillars, which, says de Witt, were painted to represent marble. The Swan had no permanent company, and was as much in demand for sports, fencing and so on, as for plays. There was

trouble in 1597 over the production of *The Isle of Dogs*, a seditious comedy by Nashe and Jonson (qq.v.), and in 1598 Robert Wilson challenged all comers to a contest of wit and extempore versification, a popular form of entertainment at that time, and defeated them all. In 1602 Richard Vennar announced a spectacular show called *England's Joy*, to be played at the Swan by gifted amateurs, but he was arrested before the performance could begin and the infuriated audience wrecked the interior. One of the last plays to be seen at the Swan was Middleton's *A Chaste Maid in Cheapside* (1611). With the opening by Henslowe (q.v.) of the Hope Theatre, which was modelled on the Swan, the latter was practically abandoned. It was used by actors in 1621, and the last reference to it is found in *Holland's Leaguer*, a pamphlet issued in 1632, where it is said to have 'fallen to decay, and like a dying Swanne, hanging downe her head, seemed to sing her owne dierge'.

SWANN, DONALD IBRAHIM (1923–), English composer, song-writer, and entertainer, who appeared with Michael Flanders (q.v.), his contemporary at school and at Oxford, in a two-man entertainment, *At the Drop of a Hat* (1956), for which he wrote the music and Flanders the lyrics and dialogue. This outstanding production, which ran for over two years at the Fortune Theatre in London and was then seen in New York and on extensive world tours, was followed by *At the Drop of Another Hat* (1963) at the Haymarket, in which the same formula was again successfully exploited. Although much of Swann's music was written for Flanders's lyrics, their first collaboration being in *Airs on a Shoestring* (1953), he has also set many other writers, among them Shakespeare and a number of modern Greeks (he is fluent in several languages). He has also written a quantity of modern church music, an opera, 'Perelandia', and music for radio, notably for Henry Reed's *Emily Butter*. In 1969 he toured the United States in company with three other players in a musical entertainment entitled 'Set by Swann'.

SWANSTON, ELIARD or **HILLIARD** [he himself spells it Eyllaerdt] (?–1651), a prominent actor with the King's Men (see CHAMBERLAIN'S MEN) from 1624 to the closing of the theatres in 1642. He had been an actor at least two years previous to 1624, and took a prominent part, not only in the acting but in the management of the company, being associated with Lowin and Taylor (qq.v.) in business affairs. He played a variety of roles, including the title-roles in revivals of *Othello*, *Richard III*, and Chapman's *Bussy d'Ambois*. Shadwell (q.v.) refers to him in *The Virtuoso* (1676) when Snarl says: 'I . . . have seen . . . Swanstead: Oh a brave roaring fellow! Would make the house shake again!'

SWINBOURNE, CHARLOTTE (1818–60), see VANDENHOFF, GEORGE.

SWINEY, OWEN (c. 1675–1754), Irish actor and manager, who in about 1700 was at Drury Lane, where for a time he acted as right-hand man to Christopher Rich (q.v.). In 1705 he joined with Cibber (q.v.) and others in an attempt to break Rich's stranglehold over his actors by leasing Vanbrugh's old theatre in the Haymarket, where he produced Farquhar's *The Beaux' Stratagem* with Anne Oldfield (q.v.) as Mrs. Sullen. This brought him into conflict with the licensing laws and he was forbidden to put on plays. He was for a time able to stave off ruin by pandering to the popular taste for opera, but after an unsuccessful attempt to run Drury Lane (q.v.) in partnership with Wilks, Doggett, and Cibber, he evaded his creditors by going to Venice in 1710. On his return to London in 1730 he called himself MacSwiney, by which name he is sometimes known. He became the friend and patron of Peg Woffington (q.v.), to whom he imparted the traditions of Anne Oldfield, and on his death left her all his property.

Symbolism in the Theatre. Symbols have been used on the stage since the earliest times. Much of Elizabethan 'stage furniture' was symbolic, a throne standing for a Court, a tent for a battlefield, a tree for a forest. Symbolic elements are found in Chekhov and in the later plays of Ibsen and Strindberg (qq.v.). But Symbolism as a conscious art-form, conceived as a reaction against realism, came into the theatre with Maeterlinck (q.v.), writing under the influence of Mallarmé and Verlaine. His characters have no personality of their own, but are symbols of the poet's inner life. This aspect was intensified in the early plays of Yeats (q.v.). Other dramatists to come under the influence of Symbolism include Andreyev and Evreinov in Russia, Hugo von Hofmannsthal and the later Hauptmann (with *Die versunkene Glocke*) in Germany, Synge (*The Well of the Saints*) and O'Casey (*Within the Gates*) in Ireland, and O'Neill in the United States (qq.v.).

Syndicate, see THEATRICAL SYNDICATE.

SYNGE, (EDMUND) JOHN MILLINGTON (1871–1909), Irish dramatist, and with Yeats (q.v.), who first encouraged his genius, a leading figure in the Irish dramatic revival. Although he wrote only six plays, they show unmistakable dramatic and poetic powers which might have developed further had he lived longer. They are structurally excellent, with vivid dialogue and a profound and instinctive feeling for the lives and speech patterns of the Aran peasants whom they depict. The first, *The Shadow* (or *In the Shadow*) *of the Glen* (1903), aroused some hostility when it was first produced by the Irish Literary Theatre but is now recognized as a little masterpiece. It was followed by a one-act poetic tragedy, *Riders to the Sea* (1904), which was set to music by Vaughan Williams in 1937, and by *The Well of the Saints* (1905), a comedy with underlying irony that is potentially tragic. The climax of Synge's work came with the ironic, bitter comedy of *The Playboy of the Western World* (1907), which caused a riot at the Abbey Theatre (q.v.) on its first production and again in America in 1911. Synge's only other completed play, *The Tinker's Wedding*, though written in about 1902, was not performed until 1909, after publication. On his death he left a tragedy, *Deirdre of the Sorrows*, a beautifully written version of one of the great tragic legends of Ireland, which in its unfinished state was produced at the Abbey Theatre in 1910. All Synge's plays have been performed in England and in America, and he is regarded as one of the finest playwrights to come out of Ireland.

T

TABARIN [really ANTOINE GIRARD] (?–1626), a popular figure in the streets of Paris, where in about 1618 he set up a booth on the Pont-Neuf with his brother Philippe, better known as the quack doctor Mondor. With a few companions, he would mount a trestle-platform and amuse the holiday crowd before Mondor began the serious business, selling his nostrums and boluses. Most of his material Tabarin wrote himself, or rather sketched out in the style of the *commedia dell'arte* scenarii, and from 1622 to 1632 a number of small volumes, entitled *Les Subtilités tabariniques*, were published, containing his farces, puns, jokes, and monologues. There is reason to believe that he was much influenced by the Italian actors who so often played in Paris, and from them he took the 'sack-beating' joke which Molière (q.v.) later borrowed for *Les Fourberies de Scapin* (1671). Tabarin himself never trod the boards of the legitimate theatre, but he was remembered long after his death, and his name passed into everyday speech (*faire le tabarin* = play the fool).

Tabs (short for Tableau Curtain), used originally of an act-drop which parted and rose sideways towards the outer top corners, and by extension to any front curtain or, mistakenly, to curtain settings on the stage.

TADEMA, SIR LAWRENCE ALMA- (1836–1912), English artist, of Dutch origin, who worked for Irving and Tree (qq.v.), designing for the first the costumes and scenery of *Cymbeline* (1896) and *Coriolanus* (1901), and for the second *Hypatia* (1893) (by G. Stuart Ogilvie) and *Julius Caesar* (1898).

Taganka Theatre, LENINGRAD, formerly known as the Leningrad Theatre of Comedy, see AKIMOV, N. P.

TAGORE, SIR RABINDRANATH (1861–1941), Indian poet, philosopher, and playwright, who in 1913 was awarded the Nobel Prize for Literature. In his numerous plays he successfully combined elements of Western drama, of which he had a wide knowledge, with classical Sanskrit drama and popular Bengali folk-drama. He wrote mainly in Bengali, his native language, often translating his plays into English himself. They were first performed either in Calcutta or at the school on his own estate, Santiniketan ('the house of peace'), and he frequently appeared in or directed them. The earlier ones were usually in verse, or in poetic prose, with interludes of colloquial speech, and were designed to be played on a bare stage with few, but highly symbolic, properties. The best-known among them are probably *Chitra* (1913), *The Post Office* (1914), and *Red Oleanders* (1924). In his later years he turned to dance-dramas in the Indian tradition, among them *Chitrangada* (1936), based on the earlier *Chitra*, and *Shyama* (1939), from a romantic Buddhist legend. He was knighted in 1915.

Tails, see BORDER.

TAÏROV, ALEXANDER YAKOVLEVICH (1885–1950), Soviet director, who in 1914 founded the Kamerny Theatre (q.v.). Here, with his wife ALICE KOONEN (1889–1974), who was trained under Stanislavsky at the Moscow Art Theatre (q.v.), as his leading lady, he staged a number of plays, including several by O'Neill and Shaw. Of his new Soviet productions, the most successful was probably Vishnevsky's *The Optimistic Tragedy* (1934). Although at one time Taïrov was accused of being out of touch with the new Soviet audiences, he continued to do good work in introducing Western authors to the Russian stage. In 1939 a production of Flaubert's *Madame Bovary* was much admired, as was his handling of two Russian plays in 1947, Jacobson's *Life in the Citadel* and a revival of Ostrovsky's *Guiltless, Guilty*. Though Taïrov was overshadowed by the genius of Vakhtangov (q.v.), his work was important in the development of the Soviet stage and helped in the early days to widen its horizons.

TALFOURD, SIR THOMAS NOON (1795–1854), English lawyer and man of letters, author of the tragedies *Ion* (1836), *The Athenian Captive* (1838), and *Glencoe; or, the Fate of the Macdonalds* (1840). Modelled on French tragedy, with careful observance of the unities (q.v.) and a somewhat uninspired flow of blank verse, they were produced with Macready (q.v.) in the leading roles, *Ion*, which was several times revived up to 1850, at Covent Garden, the others less successfully at the Haymarket. Talfourd wrote a good deal of dramatic criticism, and was the literary executor of Lamb (q.v.), whose works he edited after the latter's death, as he did the posthumous publications of Hazlitt (q.v.). He supported the rights of authorship in the agitation over the Copyright Act, and was an intimate friend of Dickens and Bulwer-Lytton (qq.v.), the first dedicating to him *The Pickwick Papers* (1837) and the second *The Lady of Lyons* (1838).

TALMA, FRANÇOIS-JOSEPH (1763–1826), French actor, brought up in England, where he was about to join a London company when his father sent him back to Paris. There he found his way to the newly founded École de Déclamation, and after tuition from Molé (q.v.), who became his personal friend, made his début at the Comédie-Française on 21 Nov. 1787 in Voltaire's *Mahomet*. Two years later he took over the King's part in Marie-Joseph Chénier's *Charles IX*, which the older actors had declined on political grounds, and declaimed the revolutionary speeches with such fervour that the theatre was in an uproar. Supported by the younger members of the company, he moved to the Théâtre de la République (the present Comédie-Française), where he appeared in Corneille's *Le Cid* and other classic plays as well as several adaptations of Shakespeare, including *King John*, by Ducis (q.v.). One of his greatest triumphs was scored in a revival in 1806 of *Manlius Capitolinus*, by La Fosse (q.v.). He instituted many reforms on the French stage, particularly in costuming, under the influence of the painter David, and was the first French actor to play Roman parts in a toga instead of in contemporary dress. He also reformed the theatrical speaking of verse, suppressing the exaggerations of the declamatory style and allowing the sense rather than the metre to dictate the pauses. In 1799 he was instrumental in assisting Napoleon, who admired him greatly, to draw up a new constitution for the Comédie-Française, putting it once again on a firm footing, and in 1803 he went with Napoleon to Erfurt to play before an audience which included five crowned heads. In later years he gave up comedy to concentrate entirely

on tragedy, in which he excelled. He was several times in London, where in 1817 he appeared at Covent Garden in extracts from some of his best parts, and on 23 June attended John Philip Kemble's farewell performance and banquet. He made his last appearance on 3 June 1826 in a poor play by Delaville, *Charles VI*, and died four months later. He left in manuscript some interesting reflections on the art of acting, which were published as a preface to the memoirs of Lekain (q.v.), whom he much admired. He was twice married, in 1791 to LOUISE JULIE CAREAU (1756–1805), a *demi-mondaine* and Girondist who divorced him in 1801 so that he could marry the actress CAROLINE VANHOVE (1771–1860). He was also for a time the lover of Pauline Bonaparte. Mme de Staël, who was a great admirer of his acting, included a long account of him in her book *De l'Allemagne*, published in 1810.

TAMAYO Y BAUS, MANUEL (1829–98), Spanish dramatist, with Lopez de Ayala (q.v.) the chief representative of the transition period from romanticism to realism. Under his own name, and also as JOAQUÍN ESTÉBANEZ, he wrote a number of plays, some historical, like *La locura de amor* (1855), which shows the queen Doña Juana driven mad by jealousy of her husband, others based on modern domestic and social problems, like *Lo positivo* (1862), which deals with the conflict between sentiment and interest. One of Tamayo's most interesting plays is *Un drama nuevo* (1867), in which Shakespeare appears, and in which Yorick (the 'king's jester' referred to in *Hamlet*) is the central figure, killing on the stage, during a mock fight, his supposed rival in love.

TARKINGTON, (NEWTON) BOOTH (1869–1946), American novelist, and author of a number of plays, of which the best-known is the romantic costume drama, *Monsieur Beaucaire* (1901). This was based in collaboration on his novel of the same title, but was spoilt artistically by the substitution of a conventionally happy ending for the ironic ending implicit in the book. It was nevertheless very successful in America, with Richard Mansfield (q.v.) in the name-part, and also in London, where it later provided the libretto for a musical play with a score by Messager. Among Tarkington's other plays were two for Otis Skinner (q.v.), *Your Humble*

Servant (1910) and *Mr. Antonio* (1916); a charming comedy of youth entitled *Clarence* (1919); and a social drama on the theme of snobbery, *Tweedles* (1923), which failed in production.

TARLETON, RICHARD (?-1588), the most famous of Elizabethan clowns, probably the original of Yorick, 'the king's jester', as described by Hamlet, and the 'pleasant Willy' of Spenser's *The Tears of the Muses*, 'with whom all joy and jolly merriment/Is also deaded'. He was the favourite clown of Elizabeth I until he offended her by a gibe at the expense of the Earl of Leicester. A drawing of him preserved in a manuscript in the British Museum and reproduced in *Tarleton's Jests* (a posthumous work) shows that he was short and broad, with a large, flat face, curly hair, a wavy moustache, and a small starveling beard. Tarleton himself tells us that he had a flat nose and a squint, a peculiarity well brought out in a second portrait of him discovered by W. J. Lawrence in 1920. His usual clown's dress was a russet suit and buttoned cap, with short boots strapped at the ankle, as commonly worn by rustics at this time. A leather money-bag hung from a belt at his waist, and he is depicted playing on a tabor and pipe. He was one of the Queen Elizabeth's Men (q.v.), and although it is not possible to say definitely what roles he played, a good deal of his clowning is believed to have been extempore. Marlowe and Shakespeare (qq.v.) may have had him in mind when they railed at 'clownage' —Marlowe in the Prologue to *Tamburlaine* and Shakespeare in Hamlet's advice to the players. It may have been Shakespeare's efforts to organize Tarleton's extempore gagging that led him to write such richly comic parts as Launce and Speed in *The Two Gentlemen of Verona*, Bottom in *A Midsummer Night's Dream*, Dogberry in *Much Ado About Nothing*, and the Grave-digger in *Hamlet*. There can be no doubt that the genius of Tarleton led to a persistent mingling of tragedy and farce in early Elizabethan plays; but his great *tour de force* was the Jig (q.v.). The music for some of Tarleton's jigs has been preserved, but the only libretto, *Tarltons Jigge of a horse loade of Fooles* (c. 1579), is considered by Chambers and others to be a forgery by J. P. Collier (q.v.). Tarleton is, however, known to have written a play entitled *The Seven Deadly Sins*, in two parts, of which the outline or 'platt' (q.v.)

of the second part survives only in manuscript. Several books published under Tarleton's name after his death are probably spurious, but his popularity may be judged from the number of taverns named after him, one of which, the Tabour and Pipe Man, still stood in the Borough two hundred years after his death, while the action of *Cuckqueans and Cuckolds Errant*; *or, the Bearing Down the Inn* (1601), by William Percy, takes place in the Tarlton Inn, Colchester.

TASSO, TORQUATO (1544-95), famous Italian poet, whose play *Torrismondo* (pub. 1587) shows an early mingling of tragedy and romance. Though classic in form, it deals in romantic fashion with the love of Torrismondo for Rosmonda, who turns out to be his sister. Finding himself guilty of incest in marrying her, he kills himself. Tasso was also the author of a pastoral, *L'Aminta* (1573), which with the *Pastor Fido* (1598) of Guarini (q.v.) stands at the head of a long line of similar plays, their influence spreading all over Europe. It was the source of Berowne's speech in Act IV, Scene iii of *Love's Labour's Lost*, which begins: 'From women's eyes this doctrine I derive'. Tasso's greatest work was his long epic poem *Gerusalemme liberata* (1581), which was translated into English in 1594 and again in 1600, and which may have influenced Shakespeare when writing *Cymbeline*. He is the subject of a play by Goethe (q.v.).

TATE, HARRY [really RONALD MACDONALD HUTCHISON] (1872-1940), a comedian of the music-halls, best remembered for his series of sketches on golfing, motoring, fishing, and so on. He made his first appearance at the Oxford in 1895, taking his stage name from the firm of Henry Tate & Sons, Sugar Refiners, by whom he was at one time employed. He appeared in the earliest revues at the London Hippodrome, but returned to the music-halls and in 1935 played the King in *The Sleeping Beauty*, a pantomime in which Nellie Wallace (q.v.) appeared as the Witch.

TATE, NAHUM (1652-1715), a poor poet and worse playwright, who succeeded Shadwell (q.v.) as Poet Laureate and is pilloried by Pope in *The Dunciad*. He adapted several Elizabethan plays for the Restoration stage, but is chiefly remembered for his perversions of Shakespeare's

Richard II, *King Lear*, and *Coriolanus*. His alterations to *Richard II* were intended to make Richard wholly sympathetic and blacken the character of Bolingbroke. The play was suppressed after two performances in 1680. Tate immediately rewrote it as *The Sicilian Adventurer*, which also failed. *The History of King Lear* (1681), in which the Fool is omitted and Cordelia survives to marry Edgar, remained for a hundred and fifty years the standard acting text (again adapted in 1768 by the elder Colman), and was not replaced by Shakespeare's original version until a performance by Macready (q.v.) in 1838. *Coriolanus*, as *The Ingratitude of a Commonwealth; or, the Fall of Caius Martius Coriolanus* (also 1681), was not as mangled as *King Lear*, except in the last act, which incorporates the worst features of *Titus Andronicus*, probably in a bid for popularity which failed. With Brady, Tate made a metrical version of the Psalms which remained in use for many years.

Tavistock Repertory Company, an amateur group founded in 1932, which up to the outbreak of war in 1939 was housed at the Mary Ward Settlement in Tavistock Square, Bloomsbury, under Duncan Marks. It then lapsed, but was re-formed in 1952 under F. O. M. Smith, who had been associated with it almost since its inception, and moved to Canonbury Tower, Islington, once the home of, among others, Francis Bacon and Oliver Goldsmith. The main premises were equipped as a club, while the adjacent hall was converted into a proscenium theatre seating about a hundred and sixty people in a raked auditorium. As the Tower Theatre, this opened on 15 Feb. 1953 and is now licensed for public performances. The company, which presents fifteen plays a year, has a long list of excellent productions to its credit, including the first performance in London of Tennessee Williams's *The Milk Train Doesn't Stop Here Anymore* (1968) and Arrabal's *The Cemetery* (1969).

TAYLOR, JOSEPH (c. 1585–1652), English actor, with Lowin (q.v.) the chief business manager of the King's Men (see CHAMBERLAIN'S MEN) after the death of Condell and Heminge (qq.v.). He joined the company in 1619, at which date he was already a well-known actor, and took over many of the parts played by Richard Burbage (q.v.). He also appeared as the young lovers or dashing villains in the plays of Beaumont and Fletcher (qq.v.), and was one of the actors caught playing in the Cockpit (q.v.) when it was raided by Commonwealth soldiers. Although it is unlikely that, as was once said, he was coached by Shakespeare for Hamlet, he may well have seen Burbage in the part. He is certainly said to have played it well, and also to have been good as Ferdinand in Webster's *The Duchess of Malfi*, another of Burbage's parts, as Iago in *Othello*, and as Truewit and Face in Jonson's *Epicœne* and *The Alchemist*.

TAYLOR (*née* COONEY), LAURETTE (1884–1946), American actress, who had already had a long and distinguished career, being on the stage from childhood, when in 1912 she appeared at the Cort Theatre, New York, as Peg in *Peg o' My Heart*, by her second husband, John Hartley Manners (q.v.). She also played the part in London in 1914, with immense success, and it was always thereafter associated with her. After Manners's death in 1928 she retired from the stage for a time, but returned to continue her successful career, reappearing in New York in 1938 as Mrs. Midgit in a revival of Sutton Vane's *Outward Bound*. In 1945 she gave an outstanding performance as the mother in Tennessee Williams's *The Glass Menagerie*, which ran for over a year.

TAYLOR, TOM (1817–80), English dramatist, and editor of *Punch*, whose first play, *A Trip to Kissingen*, was produced by the Keeleys (q.v.) at the Lyceum in 1844. A prolific writer, he continued his output of plays until about two years before his death. The best-known of his works are probably *To Parents and Guardians* (1846); *Masks and Faces* (1852), a comedy on the life of Peg Woffington written in collaboration with Charles Reade and frequently revived; *Still Waters Run Deep* (1855), a play based on a French novel and remarkable in its time for its frank discussion of sex; *Our American Cousin* (1858), first produced in New York and noteworthy because of the appearance in it of E. A. Sothern (q.v.) as Lord Dundreary, a part which he enlarged until it practically swamped the play; *The Overland Route* (1860); *The Ticket-of-Leave Man* (1863), a melodrama on a contemporary theme of low life which had much influence on such later works as Jones and Herman's *The Silver King*; and finally two plays written in collaboration, *New Men* *and Old Acres* (1869) and *Arkwright's Wife* (1873). Taylor was himself an enthusiastic amateur actor, playing at the private theatre of Dickens (q.v.) in Tavistock House and being one of the leading members of the Canterbury Old Stagers. There are some interesting glimpses of him in *The Story of My Life*, by Ellen Terry (q.v.). He had little originality, borrowing his material freely from many sources, but his excellent stagecraft and skilful handling of contemporary themes make him interesting as a forerunner of T. W. Robertson (q.v.).

TCHEHOV, TCHEKHOV, see CHEKHOV.

TEARLE, SIR GODFREY (1884–1953), English actor, son of Osmond Tearle (q.v.). He made his first appearance at the age of nine, and in 1899 joined his father's company on tour. He had a long and illustrious career on the London stage, and in films, one of his outstanding parts being Commander Edward Ferrers in Charles Morgan's *The Flashing Stream* (1938). He was also excellent in the title-roles of *Othello* and *Hamlet* and as Antony in *Antony and Cleopatra*. He was knighted in 1951 for services to the stage.

TEARLE, (GEORGE) OSMOND (1852–1901), English actor, who made his début in Liverpool on 26 Mar. 1869 and two years later was seen in Warrington as Hamlet, a part he subsequently played many times. After six years in the provinces he appeared in London and soon formed his own company, with which he toured. On 30 Sept. 1880 he joined the stock company at Lester Wallack's theatre in New York, making his first appearance there as Jaques in *As You Like It*, and later alternated between London and New York. In 1888 he organized a Shakespeare company which appeared with much success at Stratford-upon-Avon and proved an invaluable training-ground for young actors. He was himself a fine Shakespearian actor, combining excellent elocution with a natural elegance and dignity. He had a high reputation in the provinces, and made his last appearance on the stage at Carlisle in 1901, dying a week later. He married the actress MINNIE [really MARIANNE] LEVY CONWAY, grand-daughter of W. A. Conway (q.v.), and was the father of Sir Godfrey Tearle (q.v.).

Teatre Intim, BARCELONA, see GUAL, ADRIÁ.

Teatro Eslava, MADRID, see MARTÍNEZ SIERRA, GREGORIO.

Teatro por Horas, see GÉNERO CHICO.

Telari, see PERIAKTOI.

TELBIN, WILLIAM (1813–73), English scene painter, who worked at Drury Lane under Macready (q.v.) in 1840. He had previously been connected with several provincial theatres and was later at Covent Garden and at the Lyceum. His son, WILLIAM LEWIS TELBIN (1846–1931), was at the Manchester Theatre Royal for many years, and later in London. In 1902, after a visit to Italy, he designed the settings and costumes for Alexander's production of Stephen Phillips's *Paolo and Francesca* at the St. James's Theatre. He also worked for Irving (q.v.) at the Lyceum.

TÉLLEZ, FRAY GABRIEL, see TIRSO DE MOLINA.

TEMPEST, DAME MARIE [really MARY SUSAN ETHERINGTON] (1864–1942), English actress, created D.B.E. in 1937 for her services to the British theatre. Trained as a singer, she forsook operetta and musical comedy for straight acting in 1900, when she appeared as Nell Gwynn in Anthony Hope's *English Nell*, scoring an immediate success, as she did in two plays by her second husband, COSMO GORDON-LENNOX (1869–1921): *Becky Sharp* (1901) (based on Thackeray's *Vanity Fair*) and *The Marriage of Kitty* (1902). She subsequently revived this last play many times, both in London and New York, and toured in it and several other productions, including A. A. Milne's *Mr. Pim Passes By*, all over the world from 1914 to 1922. On her return to London she continued to appear in modern comedy and became noted for her playing of charming and elegant middle-aged women—Judith Bliss in Coward's *Hay Fever* (1924), the title-role in St. John Ervine's *The First Mrs. Fraser* (1929), and Fanny Cavendish in *Theatre Royal* (1934), the English version of *The Royal Family*, by Edna Ferber and George S. Kaufman. In 1935 she celebrated her stage jubilee with a matinée at Drury Lane in the presence of King George V and Queen Mary, the proceeds going to endow a ward for members of the theatrical profession at St. George's Hospital. She continued to act till her death, playing Georgina Leigh in Robert

Morley's *Short Story* (1935) opposite her third husband, W. GRAHAM BROWNE (1870–1937), who had appeared with her in many previous productions, some of which he directed, and Dora Randolph in Dodie Smith's *Dear Octopus* (1938), in which she made her last appearance in London.

Tennis-Court Theatres. Both in Paris and in London in the mid-seventeenth century, tennis courts were converted into theatres. Among the most famous were the Illustre-Théâtre (1644), where Molière (q.v.) first acted in Paris, and, in London, Killigrew's Vere Street Theatre (1660) and Davenant's Lincoln's Inn Fields Theatre (1661) (qq.v.). They were used only for a short time, and their conversion into theatres must have entailed no more alteration than could have been easily removed to allow them to revert to their original use. The rectangular shape of the tennis-court auditorium, which approximated more to the private than the public Elizabethan theatre auditorium, may have influenced the eventual shape of the Restoration theatre, just as the boxes round the pit may have developed partly from the 'pent-house' or covered way which ran along one side and one end of the court itself. But lacking precise contemporary details of the method and work involved in such a conversion, no definite conclusion can be arrived at.

TENNYSON, ALFRED, LORD (1809–92), great English poet, who succeeded Wordsworth as Poet Laureate. Though not very much in touch with the contemporary stage, he nevertheless contributed to the poetic drama of his day, his first plays, *Queen Mary* (1876), a frigid tragedy in blank verse on Elizabethan lines, *The Cup* (1881), and *Becket* (1893), being produced at the Lyceum by Henry Irving (q.v.), whose Becket was considered by many the finest achievement of his career. Of Tennyson's other plays in verse *The Falcon*, based on an episode in the *Decameron*, was produced at the St. James's by the Kendals in 1879; *The Promise of May* (1882), a drama of modern village life, was unsuccessful at the Globe; and *The Foresters* (1892), with music by Sullivan, was seen at the Lyceum. A play on Harold was published in Tennyson's lifetime but not performed until Apr. 1928, when it was given by the Birmingham Repertory company at the Court Theatre, London, with Laurence Olivier (q.v.) as Harold. Like many other writers of his day, Tennyson failed to amalgamate fine poetry and good theatre. None of his plays has been revived, and the success of *Becket* was mainly due to the beauty and compelling power of Irving's interpretation.

TERENCE [really PUBLIUS TERENTIUS AFER] (c. 190–159 B.C.), Roman dramatist, a freed slave, probably of African parentage. Six of his plays are extant—the *Andria* (166 B.C.), the *Hecyra* (165), the *Heauton Timorumenos* (163), the *Eunuchus* and *Phormio* (both 161), and the *Adelphi* (160). Although they are all based on Greek comedies (four on plays by Menander, q.v.), they display more originality than the comparable comedies of Plautus (q.v.) and are also less farcical, being further distinguished by their elegance and urbanity. In all the plays there are contrasts of character—in the *Adelphi*, for instance, between the strict father and the genial uncle and the two brothers, one rash, one timid; in the *Andria* there is a situation not found in Greek comedy—a young man of good family in love with a young lady of his own station, an episode which was only possible because of the greater freedom of women in Rome than in Athens. The background of all the plays is neither Greek nor Roman but somewhere independent of time and place. Perhaps because of this, Terence's works later had a universal appeal. In his own day, though he achieved some measure of success in the theatre, his audiences were only too ready to desert him in favour of rope-dancers or gladiators. Even Julius Caesar thought he lacked sufficient comic force, though many of his pithy sayings were quoted by contemporary writers. But his interest in humanity, summed up in the famous remark by a character in the *Heauton Timorumenos*: 'I am a man; and all human affairs concern me', gave his work an abiding appeal, and in the schools of the Middle Ages his plays were not only read but acted; in the tenth century the Abbess Hroswitha (q.v.) even made adaptations of them for her nuns at Gandersheim. With the coming of the Renaissance they were translated into several languages, and their influence spread to France, where it reached as far as Molière (q.v.), and to England, where it can be traced from the first English comedy, Udall's *Ralph Roister Doister* (c. 1553), through Lyly and Shakespeare (qq.v.) to Sir Richard Steele, whose *The Conscious Lovers* (1727) was an adaptation of the *Andria*. Several of the manuscripts and early printed editions of Terence have illustrations which provide useful information about the staging of Renaissance plays (see TERENCE-STAGE).

Terence-Stage, the name given to the type of stage shown in illustrations in Renaissance editions of the plays of Terence (q.v.). In the Trechsel edition of 1493 there is a woodcut which shows a two-storey structure with arches (*Fornices*) below and an auditorium (*Theatrum*) above. Three tiers of spectators are seated in front of a stage-wall (*Proscenium*) divided into sections by columns, with curtains hanging between them. There is a large forestage on which a musician is seated, providing an overture on a wind-instrument. In a box on the side wall between the spectators and the stage are two officials (*Ædiles*). The appearance of this stage is vouched for by another woodcut in the same volume, showing a scene from the *Eunuchus* with four curtained arches, each labelled with the name of a character in the play. Although this is reminiscent of the 'houses' of the liturgical drama (q.v.), the pillared façade is more like the *scaenae frons* of the late classical theatre building. There were evidently alternative forms of the *Eunuchus* stage, as a woodcut illustrating the *Heauton Timorumenos* shows the four entrances forming a three-sided structure jutting forward on to the stage, while another, for the *Adelphi*, shows five entrances, the central one also jutting forward. It is possible that some such arrangement formed the much-disputed inner stage (q.v.) of the Elizabethan theatre. Although these illustrations are of academic performances—the spectators in the *Theatrum* might equally well be expecting a lecture—this form of stage was later adapted for a less restricted audience, and resulted in the theatre built by Scamozzi at Sabbionetta in about 1588 and the Teatro Farnese built by Aleotti at Parma in about 1619. From these, based on an open loggia and a semi-circular amphitheatre, came the horseshoe-shaped auditorium and the proscenium-arch stage with its elaborate curtain, typical of later stage buildings all over the world.

Terpsichore, the Muse of Dancing.

TERRISS, ELLALINE (1871–1971), English actress, daughter of William Terriss (q.v.) and wife of the actor Seymour Hicks (q.v.). She made her first appearance under Tree at the Haymarket in 1888, and had a long and successful career, appearing with her husband in many of his own plays and productions, including *Bluebell in Fairyland*, first produced in 1901 and many times revived. One of her outstanding performances was as Phoebe Throssel in Barrie's *Quality Street* (1902). She accompanied Hicks on tour, both in straight plays and in music-hall sketches, and went with him to France in 1914 to give concerts for the troops, and in the 1920s to Australia and Canada, making her last appearance in 1935 in his *The Miracle Man*. In 1928 she published a volume of reminiscences as *Ellaline Terriss: By Herself and With Others*.

TERRISS, WILLIAM [really WILLIAM CHARLES JAMES LEWIN] (1847–97), English actor, formerly a sailor, known affectionately as Breezy Bill, or No. 1, Adelphi Terrace, as his best work was done at the Adelphi Theatre (q.v.). He first appeared on the stage unsuccessfully in 1867, and then left England with his wife, AMY FELLOWES (?–1898), for the Falkland Islands, where his daughter Ellaline (q.v.) was born. Returning to England in 1873 he again entered the theatre—as Doricourt in a revival of Mrs. Cowley's *The Belle's Stratagem*—and was successful. One of his first outstanding appearances was as Nicholas Nickleby in 1875, but he finally made his name as Squire Thornhill in *Olivia* (based by Wills on Goldsmith's *The Vicar of Wakefield*) in 1878, playing opposite Ellen Terry (q.v.). He later played Romeo to the Juliet of Adelaide Neilson (q.v.), and in 1880 joined Irving (q.v.) at the Lyceum. But he is best remembered as the hero of a series of famous melodramas at the Adelphi, among them Sims's *Harbour Lights* (1885), Belasco's *The Girl I Left Behind Me* (1895), and Seymour Hicks's *One of the Best* (also 1895), which Bernard Shaw (q.v.) reviewed as 'One of the Worst'. The success of these and many similar plays owed much to his handsome debonair presence and vigorous acting. He was one of the most popular actors of his day, and his assassination by a madman as he was entering the Adelphi Theatre on the evening of 16 Dec. 1897 was felt as a personal loss by his many admirers. A theatre at Rotherhithe, which opened on 16 Oct. 1899, was named after him. It was renamed the Rotherhithe Hippodrome in 1908.

TERRY, BENJAMIN (1818–96), English actor, son of an innkeeper at Portsmouth, who with his wife, SARAH BALLARD (1817–92), went on the stage, touring extensively in the provinces and later playing small parts with Charles Kean (q.v.) at the Princess's, where his young children were in the company and his wife helped in the wardrobe. He had eleven children in all, of whom five went on the stage—Ellen, Florence, Fred, Kate, and Marion (qq.v.) —while two other sons, GEORGE (1850–1928) and CHARLES (1857–1933), were connected with theatre management. Charles was the father of MINNIE (1882–1964) and BEATRICE (1890–   ), who were both on the stage, making their first appearances as children and continuing their careers, Minnie, who married the actor Edmund Gwenn, mainly in London, and Beatrice, in later years, in America.

TERRY, DANIEL (1789–1829), English actor, friend of Sir Walter Scott, several of whose novels he dramatized for Covent Garden. After extensive experience in the provinces, he made his first appearance in London at the Haymarket in 1812, playing Lord Ogleby in Colman's *The Clandestine Marriage*. From 1813 to 1822 he was a member of the Covent Garden company, and went to Edinburgh in 1815 to support Mrs. Siddons (q.v.) in her farewell engagement there. He was also seen at Drury Lane. In 1825, in partnership with Frederick Yates (q.v.), he took over the Adelphi, but the venture was not a success and he soon retired. He was at his best in character parts, particularly those of old men, or in strong emotional drama, but had little tenderness or subtlety and seldom attempted young lovers or the serious gentlemen of Old Comedy.

TERRY, EDWARD O'CONNOR (1844–1912), English actor and manager. In 1863 he was with the same touring company as the young Henry Irving (q.v.), and first came into prominence at Manchester, under Calvert, playing such parts as Touchstone in *As You Like It* and Dogberry in *Much Ado About Nothing*. In London in 1867 he appeared at the Surrey, and later went to the Strand (q.v.), where his acting in burlesque and light comedy brought him to the notice of Hollingshead. Engaged for the Gaiety

(q.v.), he became from 1876 a member of the famous 'Gaiety Quartet', with Nellie Farren, Kate Vaughan, and Edward Royce. In 1887 he opened a theatre in the Strand (see TERRY'S THEATRE), remaining there until 1904, in which year he married as his second wife the widow of Sir Augustus Harris (q.v.). He toured extensively in Australia, South Africa, and America, and though not an outstanding straight actor, was a good eccentric comedian and a careful and conscientious manager.

TERRY, DAME ELLEN ALICE (1847–1928), distinguished English actress, who made her first appearance on the stage at the age of nine, playing Mamillius in Charles Kean's production of *The Winter's Tale* at the Princess's. She remained with the Keans until their retirement in 1859, and in the summer of that and succeeding years toured with her sister Kate (q.v.) in *A Drawing-Room Entertainment*, in which they played together in short sketches. They were for some time with the Bristol stock company, but in 1861 Ellen returned to London to appear at the Haymarket, leaving there in January 1864 to marry the painter G. F. Watts, an ill-judged union with a man twice her age which soon came to an end. She returned to the theatre for a short time, only to leave it again to live with Edward Godwin (q.v.), by whom she had two children, Edith and Edward Gordon Craig (qq.v.). When she re-appeared in 1874 as Philippa in *The Wandering Heir*, at the insistence of the author Charles Reade (q.v.), taking over the part from Mrs. John Wood (q.v.), she was as brilliant as ever, and her long absence from the stage seemed only to have increased the excellence of her acting. This was particularly noticeable when she played Portia (in *The Merchant of Venice*) for the Bancrofts (qq.v.) at the Prince of Wales'. She remained with them for a year and then went to the Royal Court Theatre under Hare (q.v.), playing for him one of her most successful parts, the title-role in *Olivia* (1878), an adaptation by Wills of Goldsmith's novel, *The Vicar of Wakefield*. It was during the run of this play that Ellen Terry married her second husband, the actor CHARLES KELLY [really WARDELL] (1839–85). In 1878 Henry Irving (q.v.), who had recently begun his tenancy of the Lyceum, engaged Ellen Terry as his leading lady, thus inaugurating a partnership which became one of the glories of the English stage. It lasted until 1902 and ranged over a wide field, both in London and on tour, including a good deal of Shakespeare, some revivals of contemporary plays—Bulwer-Lytton's *The Lady of Lyons*, Wills's *Olivia*, Selby's *Robert Macaire*—and a few plays specially written for Irving—Wills's *Faust* (1885), Merivale's *Ravenswood* (1890), based on Scott's *The Bride of Lammermoor*, Tennyson's *Becket* (1893), and Comyns Carr's *King Arthur* (1895). After leaving the Lyceum, Ellen Terry became manager of the Imperial Theatre (q.v.), and in 1903 produced *Much Ado About Nothing* and Ibsen's *The Vikings* with scenery designed by her son Gordon Craig. She also appeared in two plays, Heijermans's *The Good Hope* (also 1903) (for the Stage Society) and Barrie's *Alice Sit-By-The-Fire* (1905), and in 1906 celebrated her stage jubilee with a mammoth matinée at Drury Lane in April at which twenty-two members of the Terry family assisted. She was at this time playing Lady Cicely Waynflete, a part specially written for her, in *Captain Brassbound's Conversion*, by Bernard Shaw (q.v.). Playing opposite her was a young American actor, JAMES CAREW [really USSELMAN] (1876–1938), whom she married as her third husband in 1907. Although the marriage lasted only two years, she seldom acted afterwards, but toured America and Australia, giving readings and lectures on Shakespeare. Four of the lectures were published in 1931, proving once again how excellent was her critical faculty and how masterly her handling of the written word. These qualities had already been apparent in her autobiography, published in 1908 (republished with notes and an additional section by Christopher St. John in 1933), and in her correspondence with Bernard Shaw, published in 1931. Throughout her career she was an inspiration to those who played with her. She was not at her best in tragedy, though some critics admired her Lady Macbeth (she was painted in the part by Sargent), and she never played Rosalind (in *As You Like It*), which seemed, above all other parts, to have been written for her. But as Shakespeare's Beatrice, Cordelia, Desdemona, Olivia, and Viola, as Goldsmith's Olivia, as Sheridan's Lady Teazle, as Lilian in Tom Taylor's *New Men and Old Acres*, and in a hundred other parts, she played with a freshness and vitality that gave life to the dullest moment. She was created D.B.E. in 1925.

TERRY, FLORENCE (1855–1896), English actress, who was on the stage as a child and later played Nerissa (in *The Merchant of Venice*) to the Portia of her elder sister, Ellen Terry (q.v.). She also played the latter's part of Olivia (in Goldsmith's *The Vicar of Wakefield*) on tour. She was a young actress of great promise, but left the stage on her marriage to William Morris in 1882.

TERRY, FRED (1864–1932), English actor-manager, who made his first appearance on the stage at the Haymarket under the Bancrofts (q.v.) in 1880, and four years later, at the Lyceum, played Sebastian (in *Twelfth Night*) to the Viola of his elder sister Ellen Terry (q.v.). A handsome, romantic actor, he is mainly remembered for his performance as Sir Percy Blakeney in Baroness Orczy's *The Scarlet Pimpernel*, which he produced under his own management in 1905 and frequently revived, in London and on tour. He was also much admired as Charles II and Sir John Manners in Kester's *Sweet Nell of Old Drury* (1900) and *Dorothy o' the Hall* (1906), and in the title-roles of *Matt o' Merrymount* (1908), by Beulah Dix and Mrs. Sutherland, and *Henry of Navarre* (1909), by William Devereux. In these and many other productions he was partnered by his wife Julia Neilson (q.v.) until his retirement in 1929. His son DENNIS NEILSON-TERRY (1895–1932), an actor of great promise, died during a tour of South Africa. By his wife, the actress MARY GLYNNE [really AITKEN] (1898–1954), he had two daughters, of whom HAZEL TERRY (1918–   ) is also on the stage. Fred's daughter PHYLLIS NEILSON-TERRY (1892–   ) first appeared under her father's management, and was much admired as Viola in *Twelfth Night*. She has played in a number of Shakespeare productions both in England and in America, toured in vaudeville, and played Principal Boy in pantomime. It was under her management that her cousin John Gielgud (q.v.) had his first professional engagement.

TERRY, KATE (1844–1924), English actress, eldest daughter of Benjamin Terry (q.v.). She was on the stage as a child, and at eight years of age played Prince Arthur in Charles Kean's production of *King John* at the Princess's, where she was also seen as Ariel in *The Tempest* (1857) and Cordelia in *King Lear* (1858). She remained with Kean until 1859, and then joined the Bristol stock company, returning to London in 1861 to play Ophelia to the Hamlet of Fechter (q.v.). She appeared in several plays by Tom Taylor (q.v.), and seemed to be heading for a brilliant career when in 1867 she left the stage on her marriage to Arthur Lewis. Of her four daughters the eldest, also Kate, became the mother of John Gielgud (q.v.), while the youngest, Mabel Terry-Lewis (q.v.), became an actress. In 1898 Kate returned briefly to the stage to play in *The Master* by G. Stuart Ogilvie, with John Hare (q.v.), but the play was not a success and she never again ventured to appear in public. She was by many critics accounted in her youth a better actress than her more famous sister Ellen (q.v.).

TERRY, MARION (1852–1930), English actress, younger sister of Ellen Terry (q.v.). She made her first appearance on the stage in 1873, and three years later scored a success as Dorothy in Gilbert's *Dan'l Druce, Blacksmith*. In 1879 she was engaged by the Bancrofts (q.v.) for the Prince of Wales', where she made her first appearance as Mabel in a new play by James Albery entitled *Duty*. An able and attractive actress, she was later with Alexander (q.v.) at the St. James's, where she created the part of Mrs. Erlynne in Wilde's *Lady Windermere's Fan* (1892); with Forbes-Robertson (q.v.) at the Lyceum, where she played Andrie Lesden in Henry Arthur Jones's *Michael and his Lost Angel* (1896); and at the Vaudeville, where she appeared as Susan Throssel in the first production of Barrie's *Quality Street* (1902). She continued to play elegant aristocratic parts until increasing arthritis forced her to retire, her last part being the Principessa della Cercola in Somerset Maugham's *Our Betters* (1923)

TERRY-LEWIS, MABEL, see LEWIS.

Terry's Theatre, LONDON, in the Strand, on the site of the Occidental Tavern, near the Coal Hole in Fountain Court, an early song-and-supper room. It was named after its manager, Edward Terry (q.v.), and opened on 17 Oct. 1887. It had a short and uneventful history, its most successful production being Pinero's *Sweet Lavender* (1888), in which Terry played the hero, Dick Phenyl. There was also a good burlesque of Gillette (q.v.) as Sherlock Holmes entitled *Sheerluck James; or, Why D'Gillette Him Off?*

(1901). Sidney Jones's musical comedy, *My Lady Mollie*, opened at Terry's in Mar. 1903 and had a long run, and the last successful production there was *Mrs. Wiggs of the Cabbage Patch* (1907), a comedy by Alice Hegan Rice and Anne Flexner. The theatre closed on 8 Oct. 1910 and became a cinema. It was demolished in 1923.

TERSON, PETER (1932–), English dramatist, whose first play to be performed, after a number had been discarded, was *A Night to Make the Angels Weep* (1964). This was produced at the Victoria Theatre, Stoke-on-Trent, by Peter Cheeseman, after extensive alterations. Terson himself has said that his plays as originally written are only starting-points for the evolution of the final script in collaboration with the director and actors. This was particularly evident in his work for the National Youth Theatre (q.v.), for which he wrote *Zigger-Zagger* (1967), *The Apprentices* (1968), *Fuzz!* (1969), and *Spring-Heeled Jack* (1970). His earlier plays, all set in the Vale of Evesham and presented at Stoke-on-Trent, where he was resident dramatist from 1963 to 1965, include *The Mighty Reservoy* (1964), *All Honour Mr. Todd* and *I'm in Charge of These Ruins* (both 1966), and *Mooney and his Caravans* (1967). This last was also seen on television, as were several other plays specially written for the medium. Among other plays for Stoke were *The Knotty* (1966), a documentary on the old North Staffordshire Railway, a dramatization of *Clayhanger* produced in 1967 in honour of Arnold Bennett's centenary, a play for children, *The Adventures of Gervaise Becket, or the Man Who Changed Places* (1969), the semi-documentary, *The 1861 Whitby Lifeboat Disaster*, and *The Affair at Bennett's Hill* (in Worcestershire) (both 1970).

Thaddädl, a comic character created by the Austrian actor Hasenhut (q.v.). Based on a German importation into the *commedia dell'arte* masks, Taddeo, Thaddädl, as developed by Hasenhut, was a clumsy youth with a falsetto voice, a perpetually infatuated, idiotically infantile booby. The best presentation of the character is found in Kringsterner's *Der Zwirnhändler* (1801).

Thalia, the Muse of Comedy.

Thalia, NEW YORK, see BOWERY THEATRE (1).

Theater an der Wien, see SCHIKANEDER, EMANUEL and VIENNA.

Theatre, THE, the first—and most appropriately named—playhouse to be erected in London. It was built by James Burbage (q.v.). Because of opposition from the Lord Mayor of London to actors appearing in inn yards (see INNS USED AS THEATRES), it had to be erected outside the City boundary, and was situated between Finsbury Fields and the public road from Bishopsgate to Shoreditch Church. Some of the money for its construction came from Burbage's father-in-law, John Braynes, probably an actor. It was a circular wooden building, without a roof, and cost between £600 and £700. The actual dimensions are not known, but the building was apparently commodious, with scaffolding for galleries and what would now be described as boxes. It opened in the autumn of 1576. Admission was one penny for standing room on the ground and a second penny for admission to the galleries; for a further penny one could obtain a stool, or what was described as a 'quiet standing'. Although the authorities disapproved, the public appear to have flocked to the new theatre, but its career, though stormy, was not very distinguished theatrically. It was used for competitions of sword-play, fencing, quarterstaff, and athletic exercises, and by a number of different companies until in 1594 the Chamberlain's Men (q.v.) took over. Plays performed there may have included the original *Hamlet*, on which Shakespeare based his play, and Marlowe's *Doctor Faustus*. Tarleton and Kempe (qq.v.) also performed 'jigges and drolls' there. In spite of good audiences, there was little profit on the Theatre and continual harassment from the authorities, so when in 1597, just after James's death, the lease ran out, his son Cuthbert pulled it down, transported the timber and other materials across the river to Bankside, and used them to build a new theatre (see GLOBE (1)).

Theatre Arts, an American magazine of international interest, which monthly surveyed the theatre all over the world in essays, reviews, and photographs. Founded in Detroit in Nov. 1916, as a quarterly under the name of *Theatre Arts Magazine*, its first editor was Sheldon Cheney. From the beginning the magazine set itself a high standard, which was consistently maintained under the subsequent editorships of Edith J. R. Isaacs and Rosamond Gilder (qq.v.). It was also responsible for the publication of a number of important theatrical books, and of portfolios of stage designs. In Feb. 1948 it was amalgamated with *The Stage*, and under a new management and editor continued to appear monthly until Jan. 1964, when it finally ceased publication.

Theatre Behind the Gate, a Czechoslovak ensemble founded in Prague in 1965 by Otomar Krejca, who had previously played leading parts with the Czech Municipal Theatre and during the 1950s was in charge of the Czech National Theatre's experimental group. The company, which shares a theatre with the Laterna Magika, produces two plays a season, each of which is rehearsed for four or five months and then taken on tour. During the World Theatre season of 1969 the Theatre Behind the Gate was seen in London in Chekhov's *Three Sisters*, Nestroy's *The Single-Ended Rope*, Schnitzler's *The Green Cockatoo*, and *An Hour of Love*, by Josef Topol, the company's resident dramatist.

Theatre Buildings. The provision of permanent roofed buildings specially erected for the performances of plays came comparatively late in theatrical history. Greek open-air theatres evolved from the ritual dithyramb (q.v.) performed round the altar of Dionysus, which took place in front of the temple, and later on a site cut out of a neighbouring hillside. This provided a natural auditorium of rising tiers of seats which extended a little more than halfway round a circular orchestra, or playing-place, backed by a low stage with a stage-wall (*skēnē*) behind. This formed one wall of the dressing-rooms and storage rooms behind and was pierced by doors through which the actors came on stage. It also housed the machinery which worked the crane by which the god (the *deus ex machina*) finally appeared from heaven to resolve the complications of the plot. All that is known of Greek theatres in the fifth century B.C., the age of the great classical tragedies and comedies, has had to be inferred from the ruins of those that still exist, many of which have been subsequently altered, rebuilt, and finally abandoned. Some, like those at Epidaurus, have been refurbished and are used for annual festivals of Greek classical plays.

The only things which seem certain about the early theatres are that the audience sat first on wooden benches and then on stone; that the chorus occupied the circular orchestra; that a raised stage was provided for the actors, of which, in classical times, there were never more than three; and that the acoustics of these early theatres were perfect, as can be verified by anyone visiting them today. The slightest whisper from the orchestra can be heard clearly by people in the topmost seats.

In the great Hellenistic theatres which replaced the simpler ones of early times, the stage was raised, often to a height of several feet, and the stage-wall became more elaborate. Columns supported a stage-roof, and the ramps which led up to the stage were built over a colonnade (the *proskênion* = proscenium, q.v.).

The Roman theatre, unlike the Greek, was built on the flat. The early ones were of wood and have disappeared. Later ones, in stone, still exist. The much diminished orchestra is little more than a semi-circle terminated by a most elaborate stage-wall (*scaenae frons*) often three storeys high, in front of which was the stage, usually about five feet above ground level. This was separated from the auditorium by a curtain which descended into a trough. The exterior of the theatre, which rose in a series of colonnades to a great height, was solidly constructed, and, in the case of amphitheatres used for chariot-races and gladiatorial combats, which had a circular arena, was also completely circular. The destruction of the Roman Empire saw the collapse of organized theatre. When it was reborn in liturgical drama (q.v.), plays were first given in churches, later in the open air, either in front of the church door, which provided an excellent stage-wall, or on raised platforms erected in the marketplace. In England biblical plays were often acted on pageants (q.v.). The Renaissance, which was in full flower in Italy while other countries still clung to their medieval traditions, brought about a great change in the design of theatres. For the first time plays were produced indoors, often on stages temporarily set up in a nobleman's hall or palace. The illustrations in late fifteenth-century editions of Terence's plays show the Renaissance stages on which they were acted. They combined elements of medieval staging with what had been learned of classical

staging from the newly discovered works of Vitruvius (q.v.), and provided models which, in various combinations, developed into the theatres which we know today (see TERENCE-STAGE). The main innovation in sixteenth-century Italy was the proscenium arch, which framed the elaborate stage-picture provided for a courtly entertainment. This is still a permanent fixture in many theatres, and it is only in recent times that theatres have been built without a proscenium wall. The rise of opera and ballet in Italy led to the evolution of the horseshoe-shaped auditorium characteristic of opera-houses all over the world and typified by the 1589 theatre at Sabbionetta and the 1619 Teatro Farnese at Parma, while the academic tradition of the classical play under the influence of Vitruvius culminated in the great Teatro Olimpico at Vicenza, with its superb *scaenae frons*, which was first used in 1585. During the sixteenth century new theatres were built all over Europe. At first each country had its own style. The early French theatres were long and narrow, with a space in front of the high stage—originally intended for the ball which followed the spectacle—rising tiers of seats, and galleries at the side. Many of the early theatres, up to the time of Molière (q.v.), were adapted tennis courts, but the Court theatres followed the Italian pattern, with a centrally-placed dais—later a Royal Box—for the accommodation of the King and Queen. In Spain the early theatres followed the pattern of the open-air stages erected in the public squares, with a stage raised on scaffolding and spectators at the windows and on the balconies of the houses all round. This was somewhat similar to the open-air Elizabethan playhouse (q.v.), which at the Restoration, and even earlier, gave way to the indoor theatre on Italian lines, though retaining in the small theatres, even in Georgian times, some purely English characteristics, with rows of boxes behind and on both sides of a central pit with benches, and a large forestage with proscenium doors on each side. But on the Continent the constant coming and going of Italian architects and stage designers led to the adoption everywhere of the operatic tradition, with baroque and rococo decorations which lingered on until the nineteenth century, when Wagner (q.v.) introduced a new concept into theatre building, doing away with ornate decorations and replacing the tiers of boxes of the older opera-houses by a single fan-shaped auditorium with a steep rake (see BAYREUTH). This, particularly in later adaptations, was not very successful, but something of its influence lingered on into the twentieth century and was apparent in the buildings which proliferated throughout the United States, particularly the Chicago Opera House, built in 1929. Many experiments in theatre design have been made since, from vast amphitheatre-type arenas for mass theatre, as in Russia, to theatres with no proscenium arch, or with a central stage, or with no stage at all. But the search for the perfect theatre building still continues, and as a theatre, once built, is difficult to get rid of, many out-of-date theatres remain which resist adaptation and are the despair of their directors.

Theatre Collections and Theatre Museums, see MUSEUMS.

Théâtre d'Art, PARIS, see LUGNÉ-POË, A.-F.; **de l'Atelier,** PARIS, see DULLIN, CHARLES; **de l'Œuvre,** PARIS, see LUGNÉ-POË.

Theatre de Lys, NEW YORK, on Christopher Street in Greenwich Village. This off-Broadway playhouse, run by Lucille Lortel, housed for seven years, from 1954 to 1961, *The Threepenny Opera*, Marc Blitzstein's English adaptation of *Die Dreigroschenoper* by Brecht (q.v.), with music by Kurt Weill, which was itself based on Gay's *The Beggar's Opera*. This was followed by George Tabori's compilation of Brecht items known as *Brecht on Brecht* (1962), which also had a long run. One of the outstanding features of the theatre was its Matinée Series, run for the American National Theatre and Academy (A.N.T.A.) by Lucille Lortel, during which established actors experimented with new forms and techniques. In Dec. 1968 a revival of the successful musical comedy, *Dames at Sea*, began another long run at this theatre.

Théâtre de Madame, PARIS, see GYMNASE-DRAMATIQUE.

Théâtre des Nations, a subsidized International Festival of Drama held annually in Paris, somewhat on the lines of the unsubsidized World Theatre season run in London by Peter Daubeny (q.v.). It began in 1954, under A. M. Julien, with an early summer season of plays by foreign companies, and was officially established in 1957, when sixteen companies acting in nine different languages appeared between March and July at the former Théâtre Sarah-Bernhardt. The organization has its own journal, *Théâtre: drame, musique, danse* (originally known as *Rendezvous des Théâtres du Monde*), which appears eleven times a year; it also arranges lectures and conferences, and was instrumental in founding an International Association of Theatre Technicians, and also of dramatic critics.

Théâtre du Vieux-Colombier, PARIS, see COPEAU, JACQUES.

Théâtre Déjazet, see DÉJAZET, PAULINE.

Théâtre-Français, PARIS, see COMÉDIE-FRANÇAISE.

Theatre Guild, NEW YORK, a society formed in 1919 for the presentation of non-commercial plays, American and foreign, under the influence of the Washington Square Players (q.v.). It has since done excellent work and, particularly in its early years, had a great influence on the development of the American theatre, many distinguished players having appeared under its aegis. Its first production, on 19 Apr. 1919, was Benavente's *The Bonds of Interest*, followed on 13 May by St. John Ervine's *John Ferguson*. On 10 Nov. 1920 it staged *Heartbreak House*, by Shaw, of whose plays the Guild was to become the prime presenter in New York. These and other early productions were performed at the Garrick Theatre (q.v.), but in 1925 the Guild built its own playhouse, now the Anta Theatre (q.v.), where productions were given up to 1943, though some plays were first seen at other theatres. After the difficult years of the late 1930s and the early 1940s, the Guild's fortunes were restored by the success of the musical *Oklahoma!*, presented under its auspices at the St. James Theatre on 31 Mar. 1943, since when the organization has continued to present a long list of notable new plays and revivals.

Théâtre Historique, PARIS, see DUMAS PÈRE.

Theatre-in-the-Round, a form of play presentation in which the audience is seated all round the acting area. It has in recent years been popular with rebels against the so-called tyranny of the proscenium (q.v.) arch. It was, however, one of the earliest forms of theatre, and was probably used for open-air performances, street theatres, and such rusti:

sports as the May-day games and the Christmas Mumming Play. Modern theatre-in-the-round first came into prominence in Russia, where in the 1930s Okhlopkov in his Realistic Theatre (q.v.) produced a number of Soviet plays on stages set up in the central area with the audience on all sides. At the same time, in England, Robert Atkins (q.v.) was producing Shakespeare in a boxing-ring at Blackfriars, an interesting experiment which seemed to have no immediate impact. It was in America, particularly in the rapidly expanding world of university drama, that theatre-in-the-round flourished and led to the erection in 1940, at the University of Washington in Seattle, of Glenn Hughes's PENTHOUSE THEATRE, which had an elliptical acting area and auditorium contained within a circular foyer, the space between them on two sides being used for prop rooms and a lighting control booth. Outside the universities the most important American exponent of theatre-in-the-round was Margo Jones (q.v.). Such theatres as the Circle-in-the-Square (q.v.) have made this type of staging familiar to off-Broadway playgoers, and in 1961 Harry Weese designed a theatre-in-the-round, known as the ARENA STAGE, for Washington, D.C., which opened with Brecht's *Caucasian Chalk Circle*. In England the main exponent of theatre-in-the-round was Stephen Joseph (q.v.), whose work, based on Scarborough, proved its value in places which might otherwise not have been able to support living theatre, and for whose company the old Victoria Theatre, Stoke-on-Trent, was reopened in 1962 as a permanent winter theatre-in-the-round. Londoners had a chance of estimating theatre-in-the-round at the short-lived but exciting Pembroke Theatre (q.v.) in Croydon. A number of new theatres, both professional and amateur, are being built with adaptable stages which can be used, among other things, for theatre-in-the-round.

Théâtre-Italien, PARIS, see COMÉDIE-ITALIENNE.

Theatre Library Association, an organization founded in 1937 by H. M. Lydenberg, then head of the New York Public Library, at the suggestion of George Freedley (q.v.), with the intention of fostering the preservation of theatrical books, pamphlets, playbills, programmes, relics, and ephemera, by the exchange of material and ideas between private and public collectors all over the world. Since May 1940 the Association has published an occasional *Broadside* on theatre work, research in progress, and the location of theatrical material, and from 1942 to 1960 it also issued a *Theatre Annual*.

Théâtre Libre, PARIS, a private theatre club founded in 1887 by André Antoine (q.v.) for the production of plays by the new naturalistic playwrights. It opened with a programme of four new one-act plays—*Jacques Damour*, by Léon Henrique, based on a story by Zola; *Mademoiselle Pomme*, by Duranty and Paul Alexis; *Le Sous-Prefet*, by Arthur Byl; and *La Cocarde*, by Jules Vidal—all directed by Antoine. It finally closed in April 1896, mainly because of financial difficulties, but during its lifetime its innovations in playwriting, direction, and acting had a great influence on the contemporary French theatre, and its settings, which were scrupulously exact reproductions of real life, helped to liberate the stage from the artificial prettiness of an earlier epoch. Its plays, which may be classified as *comédies rosses*, were usually drab representations of 'a slice of life' in which, unlike the popular melodrama of earlier times, virtue went unrewarded and vice unpunished.

Théâtre Lyrique, PARIS, see RENAISSANCE, THEATRE DE LA (2).

Theatre Music, Theatre Orchestra, see INCIDENTAL MUSIC.

Théâtre National Populaire. In 1920 the French actor-manager Firmin Gémier (q.v.) decided to found a popular theatre which should appeal to, and be supported by, the masses. After a chequered career, a Théâtre National Populaire (T.N.P.) was established in 1937 in the Palais de Chaillot, with a newly built theatre seating 2,700 spectators, a stage 70 feet deep and a proscenium opening 80 feet wide. It languished from lack of funds and audiences until in 1951 Jean Vilar (q.v.) became its director. He removed the footlights and batten lights from the stage, and extended the forestage into the audience, thus providing a flexible area for experimental productions. He also inaugurated in Nov. 1951, with the 'Weekend de Suresnes', a series of suburban performances in large halls, where, for a small inclusive fee, the public was offered two plays, a lecture or a discussion with the actors, a concert, two meals, and a dance. As well as these and other activities in Paris, the T.N.P. plays at the Avignon Festival (q.v.), founded by Vilar, and tours France and other countries. It was seen in Edinburgh in 1953 and in London in April 1956. Subsidized by the State, it was bound to give at least one hundred and fifty performances in and around Paris every year and keep its prices low. Otherwise the director was free to choose his plays and his company, which consisted of some eighteen to twenty-five actors on a yearly contract. Under Vilar's able direction the T.N.P. flourished and became the most important theatrical enterprise in France. In 1963 he resigned and was succeeded by Georges Wilson, an actor who first appeared with the T.N.P. in Alfred de Musset's *Lorenzaccio* (with Gérard Philipe, q.v.) in 1952. He later did a number of productions, and was responsible for staging *L'Illusion comique*, a little-known comedy by Corneille with which he opened his first season. In 1969 the theatre was closed after the Government had banned the production of a play criticizing General de Gaulle.

Theatre of Comedy, LENINGRAD, see AKIMOV, N. P.

Theatre of Cruelty, a term used for plays which seek to shock the spectator into an awareness of the underlying primitive ruthlessness and reality of man's precarious existence, stripped of the artificiality and restrictions of conventional behaviour. The movement stems from the works of Artaud (q.v.), particularly *Le Théâtre et son double* (1938), and was eagerly adopted by certain *avant-garde* writers and directors, especially Peter Brook (q.v.). The genre is studied in Styan's *The Dark Comedy* (1962, rev. 1968).

Theatre of Fact, a term first applied in the 1950s to documentary plays which derive in part from the technique of the American pre-war Living Newspaper (q.v.). Based entirely on the 'facts' of history, used either unadorned, as in Kipphardt's *In the Matter of J. Robert Oppenheimer* (1964) and *Die Ermittlung* (1965) by Peter Weiss (q.v.), or with some attempt at theatrical coherence and conscious arrangement, as

in *Oh, What a Lovely War!* (1963), evolved by Joan Littlewood (q.v.), the genre was typified in England by *US* (1966), directed by Peter Brook (q.v.) for the Royal Shakespeare Company at the Aldwych in London, which, on its first production, was hailed as 'the ultimate non-play so far'.

Theatre of Silence, a term used for plays which, like those of J.-J. Bernard (q.v.), are important for what they omit from their dialogue rather than for what they say—a theatre, in fact, of pregnant pauses, during which the imagination of the audience supplies the missing ingredient, which is not only unexpressed but perhaps cannot be expressed in words. Hence the French term for this type of play, *le théâtre de l'inexprimé*.

Theatre of the Absurd, the name given by Martin Esslin, in a book of that title published in 1962, to the plays of a group of dramatists, among them Beckett and Ionesco and, in England, Pinter (qq.v.), whose work has in common the basic belief that man's life is essentially without meaning or purpose and that human beings cannot communicate. This led to the abandonment of dramatic form and coherent dialogue, the futility of existence being conveyed by illogical and meaningless speeches and ultimately by complete silence. The first, and perhaps most characteristic, play in this style was Beckett's *Waiting for Godot* (1952), the last—since it has no dialogue at all—his *Breath* (1970). The movement, which liberated playwrights from many outmoded conventions, now seems to have spent itself, but not before leaving a profound and lasting impression on the theatre everywhere.

Theatre of the Baltic Fleet. In 1930 an amateur dramatic group formed of sailors from the U.S.S.R.'s Baltic Fleet, based on Leningrad, started giving concerts on board ships and in Baltic ports. Reinforced by professional actors conscripted into the Navy, it achieved professional status in 1934 under an able director, A. V. Pergament. It continued to perform during the Second World War, suffering many casualties, and was in Leningrad while it was besieged in 1942. In 1943 Vishnevsky wrote for this company *At the Walls of Leningrad* and, in collaboration with Kron and Azarov, a musical play,

Wide Spreads the Sea, dealing with the siege of Leningrad. This group is now fully professional, with a permanent base at Fleet headquarters. Most of its performances are intended for naval audiences, and plays on naval and military subjects predominate in its repertory.

Theatre of the Revolution, MOSCOW, see MAYAKOVSKY THEATRE.

Theatre Union, see LITTLEWOOD, JOAN.

Theatre Upstairs, see ROYAL COURT THEATRE (2).

Theatre Workshop, a company founded in Kendal in 1945 by a group of actors who, according to their manifesto, were 'dissatisfied with the commercial theatre on artistic, social, and political grounds'. Some of the original members had worked together in the North of England before 1939, among them Joan Littlewood (q.v.), who became the artistic director of the new group, and Gerald Raffles, who took over the administration. For seven years the company toured Great Britain and Europe, seldom remaining more than a few weeks in the same place. It had no financial backing or official support, and all income was shared equally among the members, who in 1953 took over the derelict Theatre Royal at Stratford, London (Chaucer's Stratford-atte-Bowe) —which first opened on 17 Dec. 1884— and after repairing and redecorating the interior themselves, opened in Feb. 1953 with a production of *Twelfth Night*. The company, which quickly made a name for itself, was invited to represent Great Britain at the Paris International Theatre Festivals in 1955 and 1956, playing *Arden of Feversham* and Jonson's *Volpone* on the first occasion, and *The Good Soldier Schweik* (in an English adaptation of Hasek's novel by Ewan McColl, a member of the company and Joan Littlewood's husband) on the second. On both occasions they were highly praised. They also visited Zürich, Belgrade, and Moscow, where they appeared in the Moscow Art Theatre, filling it to capacity. One of their most interesting productions was *Richard II*. Left-wing, and indeed almost communist in their ideology, they sought to revivify the English theatre by a fresh approach to established texts, or by the commissioning of working-class plays, many of which were subsequently transferred to West End theatres. The first of these was

Brendan Behan's *The Quare Fellow*, a play on prison life (1956). Others were *A Taste of Honey*, by Shelagh Delaney, *The Hostage*, by Brendan Behan (both 1958), and *Fings Ain't Wot They Used T' Be* (1959) by Frank Norman, with music by Lionel Bart. In 1961 Joan Littlewood left the company, and after a period of inactivity it started up again under Gerald Raffles. She returned in 1963 to direct *Oh, What a Lovely War!*, an improvisation by Charles Chilton and members of the company which was subsequently transferred to Wyndham's and was successful also on Broadway. In Aug. 1964 the venture again lapsed and the theatre housed a new company which made its début on 17 Sept. 1964 with a translation of Max Frisch's *Graf Öderland*. In 1974 another company, under Ken Hill and Caroline Eves, took over and opened with *The Count of Monte Cristo*.

Theatrical Syndicate, an association of American businessmen in the theatre, formed in 1896, which included the firm of Klaw and Erlanger, Charles Frohman, Al Hayman, Sam Nixon [really Samuel F. Nirdlinger], and J. Fred Zimmerman. For about sixteen years they controlled most of the theatres of New York and many of those in other big towns and gradually exerted a stranglehold over the entertainment life of the country. They were powerful enough to harm those who opposed their monopoly, forcing Mrs. Fiske (q.v.) to play in second-rate theatres on tour and Sarah Bernhardt (q.v.) to appear in a tent. Both these players, with Belasco (q.v.), helped in the end to break the syndicate.

THÉOPHILE DE VIAU (1590–1626), French poet and dramatist, author of *Pyrame et Thisbé*, a tragedy first performed at the Hôtel de Bourgogne in 1621. It was most successful, both with the public and at Court. With his contemporary the Marquis de Racan (q.v.) Théophile marks the entry into French drama of the poet and courtier, but unlike his companion he had a stormy life. As a Huguenot and a free-thinker, he was suspected of being part-author of a collection of licentious verse, *Le Parnasse satirique* (1622), and therefore exiled. Though he later became a Catholic and was allowed to return to France, he was again accused of atheism and condemned to be burnt at the stake. Escaping this fate, he was banished, and died shortly afterwards.

Theoric Fund, a grant of two obols distributed to the poorer citizens of Athens to enable them to pay for admission to the theatre during the Festivals of Dionysus. It was introduced in the time of Pericles, suppressed during the Peloponnesian War, revived in 394 B.C., when it was raised to one drachma a head, and finally abolished after the defeat of the Athenians by Philip of Macedonia at the battle of Chaeronea in 338 B.C.

THESPIS, of Icaria, in Attica, a Greek poet who is usually considered to be the founder of drama, since he was the first to use an actor in his plays in addition to the chorus and its leader. He won the prize at the first tragic contest in Athens, c. 534 B.C. Only the titles of his plays have survived and even these may not be authentic. Tradition has it that Thespis took his actors round in a cart, which formed their stage. In the nineteenth century the adjective Thespian was used of actors and acting in general, and often figured in the names of amateur companies, while 'the Thespian art' was journalese for the art of acting.

Thirty-Ninth Street Theatre, NEW YORK, a playhouse which had a short but brilliant career. It opened on 18 Apr. 1910 with Nazimova (q.v.), after whom it was then named, in Ibsen's *Little Eyolf*, which ran for six weeks. In 1911, as the Thirty-Ninth Street Theatre, it reopened on 20 Oct. with Mason's *Green Stockings*, and early in 1912 housed *A Butterfly on the Wheel*, a drama by E. G. Hemmerde and Francis Neilson which starred the English actors Charles Quartermaine and Madge Titheradge. Later in the year Annie Russell (q.v.) appeared in a season of English classics, and in 1913 John Barrymore was seen in the Harvard Prize play, *Believe Me, Xantippe!*, by Frederick Ballard. In 1919 Walter Hampden (q.v.) appeared as Hamlet. In 1925 the theatre was demolished.

THOMAS, AUGUSTUS (1857–1934), American dramatist, and one of the first to make use in his plays of American material. He succeeded Boucicault (q.v.) as adapter of foreign plays at the Madison Square Theatre under Palmer, but his first popular success, an original drama entitled *Alabama* (1891), enabled him to

resign and devote all his time to his own work. Among his later plays were several others based on a definite locality—*In Mizzoura* (1893), *Arizona* (1899), *Colorado* (1901), and *Rio Grande* (1916). His most successful play was *The Copperhead* (1918), in which Lionel Barrymore (q.v.) made a hit as Milt Shanks. An interest in hypnotism and faith-healing was shown in *The Witching Hour* (1907), *Harvest Moon* (1909), and *As a Man Thinks* (1911), but on the whole Thomas's plays were not profound, and provided entertainment of a kind acceptable to his audiences. In 1922 he published his autobiography under the title *The Print of My Remembrance*.

THOMÁS, CORNELIA FRANCES (1796–1849), see BURKE, CHARLES.

THOMAS, WALTER BRANDON (1856–1914), English actor, playwright, and song writer, best remembered for his farce *Charley's Aunt*, which has been seen in London almost every year since its first production at the Royalty on 21 Dec. 1892, when it ran for four years with W. S. Penley (q.v.) in the title-role. In later revivals Thomas played the part himself. It was filmed, has been seen as a musical, *Where's Charley?* (which was successful in New York in 1948 but not in London ten years later), and has figured in the repertory of almost every amateur and provincial theatre as well as being played all over the world in English and in innumerable translations. At one time it was running simultaneously in forty-eight theatres in twenty-two languages, among them Afrikaans, Chinese, Esperanto, Gaelic, Russian, and Zulu.

THOMPSON, JOHN (c. 1600–34), English actor, closely associated with John Shank (q.v.), to whom he may have been apprenticed. He was with the King's Men (see CHAMBERLAIN'S MEN) for some years as a boy-player, appearing as the Cardinal's Mistress in Webster's *The Duchess of Malfi* (1614). For the next ten years he played queenly or regally villainous parts, and since several of his known roles call for a song, it is reasonable to suppose that he was something of a singer. He died young, seemingly without having fulfilled his promise in adult roles.

THOMPSON, LYDIA (1836–1908), English actress, who was first a dancer at His Majesty's Theatre in 1852, and then went into burlesque, with which her name is chiefly associated. She became well known in the English provinces, and in 1868 took a troupe of golden-haired British beauties to the United States, where she remained for six years, joining forces with WILLIE EDOUIN [really WILLIAM FREDERICK BOYER] (1846–1908), an English 'eccentric' comedian who married one of her company. She returned to England in 1874, touring Australia and India on the way, and from then on alternating between London and New York. From 1886 to 1888 she was manageress of the Strand Theatre, London; she made her last appearance at the Imperial (q.v.) in 1904.

THOMSON, JAMES (1700–48), English poet, author of the long poem, *The Seasons*, and possibly of 'Rule Britannia', which first appeared in his masque of *Alfred* (1740). He was celebrated in his own day for some forgotten tragedies on classical lines: *Sophonisba* (1730); *Agamemnon* (1738), in which Cibber and Quin (qq.v.) appeared, though with little success; *Tancred and Sigismunda* (1745), possibly his best work; and *Coriolanus* (1749), given posthumously, again with Quin, and a failure. Thomson's only other play, *Edward and Eleonora*, which deals classically with the romantic theme later treated by Scott in *The Talisman*, was banned by the censor and not produced. According to Pope and others, Thomson was one of the best dramatists of his day, and the permanent eclipse of his theatrical work shows to what a low ebb the English theatre had fallen at this time in its endeavours to ape the stately measures of French classical tragedy.

THOMSON, JANE ELIZABETH (1827–1902), see VEZIN, HERMANN.

THORNDIKE, EILEEN (1891–1953), English actress, sister of Sybil Thorndike (q.v.). She made her first appearance at the Royal Court Theatre in 1909, and from 1912 to 1917 was at the Liverpool Repertory Theatre (q.v.). She retired from the stage on her marriage, and did not act again until 1930. Among her later parts were Katharine in *Henry VIII*, Viola in *Twelfth Night*, the Queen in *Hamlet*, and an outstanding Charlotte in *The Brontës of Haworth* (1932), by Elizabeth Goudge. She was also good as the Nurse in *Romeo and Juliet* and as Mrs. Hawkins in Stevenson's *Treasure Island*. She made her last appearance on the stage at the Arts

Theatre in 1950 in a revival of Fernald's *The Mask and the Face*, playing Teresa. From 1933 to 1939 she was principal of the Embassy School of Acting, and was also on the staff of the Central School of Speech Training.

THORNDIKE, (ARTHUR) RUSSELL (1885–1972), English actor, dramatist, and novelist, brother of Sybil Thorndike (q.v.). After touring extensively with Ben Greet and Matheson Lang (qq.v.), he joined Miss Horniman's company in Manchester. He was then with the Old Vic (q.v.), playing leading parts in Shakespeare, among them Hamlet, Richard II, Richard III, Lear, and Macbeth. He returned to the Old Vic many times, his best parts in later years being Touchstone in *As You Like It*, Caliban in *The Tempest*, Sly in *The Taming of the Shrew*, Pistol in *Henry IV, Part 2*, Pandarus in *Troilus and Cressida*, and Launcelot Gobbo in *The Merchant of Venice*. One of his finest performances was given in the title-role of his own play, *Dr. Syn* (1925). He was also extremely funny as Smee in revivals of Barrie's *Peter Pan* between 1950 and 1960.

THORNDIKE, DAME (AGNES) SYBIL (1882–1976), English actress, wife of Sir Lewis Casson (q.v.), whom she married in 1908. In 1931 she was created D.B.E. for her services to the English theatre, and was appointed a C.H. in 1970. She began her career under Ben Greet (q.v.), and was leading lady for several seasons at Miss Horniman's Repertory Theatre in Manchester, where she laid the foundations of her later career. From 1914 to 1918 she was at the Old Vic, where she played not only a long list of Shakespeare's heroines but also, owing to the absence of so many young actors on war service, such parts as Prince Hal in *Henry IV*, Puck in *A Midsummer Night's Dream*, Launcelot Gobbo in *The Merchant of Venice*, the Fool in *King Lear*, and Ferdinand in *The Tempest*. She returned to the Old Vic many times, and during the Second World War toured mining towns and villages with an Old Vic company, playing Lady Macbeth, Shaw's Candida, and Euripides' Medea. Among the outstanding performances of her long and distinguished career have been Hecuba in Euripides' *Trojan Women* (1920), Joan of Arc in Shaw's *Saint Joan* (1924), and the elderly schoolmistress, Miss Moffat, in *The Corn is Green* (1938), by Emlyn

Williams. To celebrate her golden wedding she appeared with her husband in *Eighty in the Shade* (1958), a play specially written for them by Clemence Dane. In 1962 they both appeared at the first Chichester Theatre Festival as the Nurse and 'Woffles' in *Uncle Vanya*, and in 1964 she was seen in a new comedy, Home's *The Reluctant Peer*. In 1968 she appeared on tour in Enid Bagnold's *Call Me Jacky*, and was later seen in a revival of Emlyn Williams's *Night Must Fall*. Her versatility was shown by her appearances in Grand Guignol, in modern comedy, in Greek tragedy, in poetic drama, and in English and foreign classics. Her biography was written in 1929 by her brother Russell (q.v.), and an illustrated account of her work appeared in 1955 as No. 4 of *World Theatre Monographs*. In 1969 a theatre named after her (see below) opened at Leatherhead.

Thorndike Theatre, LEATHERHEAD, SUR-REY. Named after the actress Sybil Thorn-dike (q.v.), this opened on 17 Sept. 1969 with *The Lion in Winter*, by James Gold-man, followed by John Graham's *There Was an Old Woman*, in which Dame Sybil herself played the leading part, a female tramp on a park bench. Further produc-tions at this theatre were a revival of Shadwell's *Epsom Wells* (first performed in 1672), and Chekhov's *The Seagull*.

THORNE, CHARLES ROBERT (1840–83), American actor, one of the five children of theatrical parents, with whom he toured from his earliest years, visiting Denver in 1859. In 1860 he was with Joseph Jefferson (q.v.) in New York, where he played in the latter's revival of Tom Taylor's *Our American Cousin*. But his career really began when in 1871 he joined the company at the Union Square Theatre (q.v.), where he was for many years immensely popular as the dashing young heroes of melodrama. A good-looking, athletic, and attractive person, not over-intelligent, he represented the ideal romantic hero of the time. In 1874 he was seen in London with some success. He made his last appearance in 1883 in Boucicault's *The Corsican Brothers*, but was forced to retire from the cast owing to illness, and died soon afterwards.

THORNE, SARAH [MRS. SARAH MAC-KNIGHT] (1837–99), English actress and theatre manageress, who ran the stock company at the Theatre Royal, Margate, where she trained a number of young players, including Violet and Irene Van-brugh (qq.v.). She came of good theatrical stock, her father being a provincial actor-manager. Her seven brothers and sisters were all on the stage, the best-known being THOMAS (1841–1918), for many years actor-manager at the Vaudeville, where with David James (q.v.) he presented and played in H. J. Byron's *Our Boys* (1875).

Three Hundred Club, LONDON, see STAGE SOCIETY.

Thunder, Thunder Run, Thunder Sheet, see NOISES OFF.

TIECK, (JOHANN) LUDWIG (1773–1853), German romantic poet and playwright, whose early plays were fairy-tales treated in a vein of Aristophanic satire. Among these were *Der gestiefelte Kater* (1796), *Ritter Blaubart* (1797), and *Die verkehrte Welt* (1798). These were followed by verse dramas—*Leben und Tod der heiligen Genoveva* (1799) and *Kaiser Oktavianus* (1804). In 1824 Tieck was appointed director of the Dresden Court theatre, where he insisted on clear diction and simplified staging. He became an influen-tial critic, and his writings on the theatre, afterwards collected as *Dramaturgische Blätter* (1826), reveal him as a man of insight and good taste. His interest in the Elizabethan theatre led him to translate several plays by Ben Jonson (q.v.), and with his daughter DOROTHEA he completed Schlegel's translations of Shakespeare, whose reputation in Germany he did much to further (see SHAKESPEARE IN TRANS-LATION).

TILLEY, VESTA [really MATILDA ALICE POWLES] (1864–1952), famous English music-hall performer, at her best in male impersonations. Her father, whose stage name was Harry Ball, was manager of Gloucester's first music-hall, the Star, and it was there that she made her first appearance on 7 Mar. 1870, billed as Little Tilley. She later appeared at Nottingham and at Birmingham, where she first put on male attire and was billed as 'The Pocket Sims Reeves'. In 1873 she first appeared in London, playing three halls a night— the Canterbury, Lusby's, and Marylebone —and added Vesta to her pet name of Tilley. From then until her retirement in 1920 she had a consistently successful career, being known as the London Idol. She played Principal Boy (q.v.) in many pantomimes, including those at Drury Lane, where she was seen for the first time in 1880, but her real home was the music-hall. Among the songs she made famous were 'Burlington Bertie', 'Jolly Good Luck to the Girl who Loves a Soldier', 'The Army of To-day's All Right', 'Six Days' Leave', 'Following in Father's Footsteps', and 'The Piccadilly Johnny with the Little Glass Eye'. In 1890 she married Walter de Frece, who was knighted in 1919 and died in 1935.

TILNEY, SIR EDMUND (?–1610), see MASTER OF THE REVELS.

Times Square Theatre, NEW YORK, on the north side of West 42nd Street. This opened on 30 Sept. 1920 with Vajda's *Fata Morgana*, translated as *The Mirage*, which ran for six months. Several musical plays were followed by Channing Pollock's *The Fool* (1922), which was more successful outside New York than on Broadway, and Maeterlinck's *Pelleas and Melisande* (1923) which, in spite of the excellent acting of Jane Cowl (q.v.), had only a short run. *Charlot's Revue of 1924*, with a large cast of London favourites, was, however, a success, as was Anita Loos's *Gentlemen Prefer Blondes* (1926), while *The Front Page* (1928), a play about journalism by Ben Hecht and Charles MacArthur, occupied the season of 1928–9. In Jan. 1931 came a long run of Coward's *Private Lives*, with the author, Gertrude Lawrence, Jill Esmond, and Laurence Olivier. The last play at this theatre, which then became a cinema, was Edward Roberts and Frank Cavett's *Forsaking All Others*, which reintroduced Tallulah Bankhead (q.v.) to Broadway in 1933.

Tireman, in the Elizabethan theatre the man in charge of the wardrobe, which was kept in the TIRING-HOUSE, or dressing-room. He also saw to the provision of stools for those members of the audience who sat on the stage, and in the private roofed theatres he looked after the lights.

TIRSO DE MOLINA [really FRAY GABRIEL TÉLLEZ] (c. 1571–1648), Spanish ecclesiastic, whose secular works include a number of plays, of which more than eighty are extant, though he claimed to have written four hundred. Their technique derives from that of his near-contemporary Lope de Vega (q.v.), whom he much admired, but was modified by his greater interest in the psychology of his characters. He was particularly good at drawing women at their wittiest and most intelligent in such comedies as *Don Gil de las calzas verdes* (c. 1611) and *El vergonzoso en palacio* (c. 1612). His historical play, *La prudencia en la mujer* (c. 1622), gives an excellent portrait of the heroic Queen María. He also wrote a number of *autos sacramentales* (q.v.) and biblical plays. His most famous work, however, is *El burlador de Sevilla y Convidado de piedra* (c. 1630), the first of many plays based on the legend of Don Juan (q.v.).

TITHERADGE, MADGE (1887–1961), see QUARTERMAINE, LEON.

Tivoli Music-Hall, one of London's most famous halls. It stood in the Strand when that thoroughfare was a great centre of amusement and night-life, and was erected on the site of a beer-hall of the same name, opening on 24 May 1890. At first it was unsuccessful, but when in 1893 Charles Morton (q.v.) was called in to run it, it picked up, and as the 'Tiv' became a popular resort. It closed on 7 Feb. 1914, and in spite of plans for its reopening was demolished and replaced by a cinema which opened in 1923. This also was demolished in 1957 and the site is now covered by a department store.

Tivoli Gardens, NEW YORK, see RICHMOND HILL THEATRE.

Toby. (1) The dog of the Punch and Judy (q.v.) show, who is a purely English character, like Clown (q.v.), having no connection with the *commedia dell'arte* or the harlequinade (qq.v.). The name seems to have come into use with the introduction of a live dog somewhere between 1820 and 1850, either because the first dog to be employed was already so called, or from association with the biblical Tobias, a favourite subject for a puppet-play, in which Tobias and the angel were accompanied by a dog. Toby is usually a small, quick-witted mongrel terrier. Wearing a ruff round his neck, he sits on the sill of the puppet-booth window and takes no part in the action, unless Punch pets him or, alternatively, urges him to bite the other characters. After the show he goes round among the audience, with whom he is a firm favourite, collecting pennies in a little bag which he holds in his mouth.

(2) A stock character in the folk theatre

of the United States, who represents the country bumpkin triumphing over the 'city slickers'. Deriving from the *commedia dell'arte*, the Shakespearian clown, the conventional stage 'silly boy', and the Yankee comedian, he has a freckled face with a blacked-out front tooth, and wears a rumpled red wig, battered hat, calico shirt, baggy jeans, and large ill-fitting boots or shoes. He first emerged in the 1900s, and Frederick R. Wilson from Horace Murphy's Comedians was the first of a long line of actors to specialize in Toby roles, which include generous use of the topical 'ad-lib', and of such theatrical gymnastics as the pratt-fall, glides, splits, and rubber-legs. It is traditional in revivals of *Uncle Tom's Cabin* for the Toby-comedian of the troupe to don black-face and a gunnysack costume to impersonate Topsy. Toby sometimes has a feminine counterpart by the name of SUSIE. Although there are still a number of small-time Toby shows in remote areas, the last of any importance closed in Wapello, Iowa, on 1 Oct. 1962, after nearly fifty years under its managers Mr. and Mrs. Neil Schaffner, who played Toby and Susie.

Togata, see FABULA (3).

TOLLER, ERNST (1893–1939), German dramatist, and one of the best and most mature writers of the Expressionist school (see EXPRESSIONISM). His first play, *Die Wandlung* (1919), written during his imprisonment as a pacifist, is a plea for tolerance and the abolition of war. Two years later came his best-known work, *Masse-Mensch* (1921), followed by *Die Maschinenstürmer* (1922), which deals with the Luddite riots of 1815 in England and was produced in London by the Stage Society as *The Machine Wreckers* in 1923, in a translation by Ashley Dukes (q.v.). It is less expressionist in technique than *Masse-Mensch*, and less pessimistic, since Toller, in the person of his hero, Jim Cobbett, foreshadows the day when the rebellious workers will be an organized and stable body of intelligent men. But Toller's later plays, of which *Hoppla, wir leben!* (1927) was staged at the Gate Theatre in London as *Hoppla!* (1929), became progressively less hopeful as he watched the domestic tragedy of Germany unfold itself, and the man who had been imprisoned for his part in the communist rising of 1919 left Germany in 1933 to become a British subject. He then went to America, lecturing and advising on drama, and committed suicide in the summer of 1939.

TOLSTOY, ALEXEI KONSTANTINOVICH (1817–75), Russian diplomat and poet, and the author of a fine historical trilogy, containing excellent crowd scenes and written with much semi-oriental imagery, in which he idealized old feudal Russia. The three plays are *The Death of Ivan the Terrible*, *Tsar Feodor Ivanovich*, and *Tsar Boris*. Written between 1866 and 1870, they were banned by the censor, who finally allowed the second to be put on as the opening production of the Moscow Art Theatre (q.v.) in 1898. Later the complete trilogy was given.

TOLSTOY, ALEXEI NIKOLAIVICH (1882–1945), one of the outstanding writers of early Soviet Russia, whose first play, written after the October Revolution, showed its influence reaching out as far as Mars. His later works included historical trilogies on Peter the Great and Ivan the Terrible. The first part of the latter, dealing with Ivan's youth and marriage, was produced at the Maly Theatre in 1943, and the second, dealing with Ivan's struggles to unite Russia, by the Moscow Art Theatre later in the same year. Among plays on modern themes the best was *The Road to Victory* (1939), dealing with an episode of the Revolution in which both Stalin and Lenin appear.

TOLSTOY, COUNT LEO NIKOLAEVICH (1828–1910), one of the great names of Russian literary and social history. His first plays, written in the 1850s under the influence of Ostrovsky and Turgenev (qq.v.), were comedies which were never finished. By the time he returned to play-writing in 1886 his whole philosophy of life had changed, and in *The Power of Darkness* he produced one of the most forceful presentations of peasant life ever written. Taken from a criminal case of the time, the sordid tale becomes, in the hands of such an artist as Tolstoy, a stark naturalistic document, revealing to what depth of degradation human beings could be reduced by the 'idiocy of village life'. Banned by the censor, it was first produced by Antoine (q.v.) at the Théâtre Libre in 1888, and in 1890 by the Freie Bühne (q.v.) in Berlin. It was not staged in Russia until 1895, when it was seen both at the

Alexandrinsky in St. Petersburg (Leningrad) and at the Moscow Maly. It was first seen in London in 1904, and in New York in 1920. Tolstoy's next play, a short comedy, *The First Distiller* (1887), attacking alcoholism, was followed by *The Fruits of Enlightenment* (or *Culture*), begun in 1886, a comedy which satirizes the parasitic life of the country gentry and their exploitation of the poverty-stricken peasants. Published in 1891, it was produced in that year by Stanislavsky (q.v.) for the Moscow Society for Art and Literature, and the following year was seen at the Moscow Maly; but the Imperial actors were ill equipped to deal with the peasant characters. Even the actors at the Moscow Art Theatre, where the play was revived some years later, could not at first tackle them successfully, and many years of experiment and experience were needed before Tolstoy's drama, which is now regarded as one of the world's classics, could be adequately portrayed. It was first seen in London in 1928. Tolstoy's last two plays, published in 1912, were left unfinished at his death. *Redemption* (or *The Living Corpse*) is an attack on the evils of contemporary Russian marriage laws. It was produced by the Moscow Art Theatre in 1911, and the hero, Fedya, later provided a fine part for Moissi (q.v.) in a German translation produced in Berlin. John Barrymore (q.v.) played the part in New York in 1918, Donald Wolfit (q.v.) in London in 1946, apparently its first production there. *The Light that Shines in Darkness*, in which the useless life of a wealthy family is contrasted with that of the poverty-stricken and overworked peasants, does not appear to have been staged; the last act exists only in outline. Three of Tolstoy's novels were, however, dramatized and produced at the Moscow Art Theatre—*Resurrection*, *Anna Karenina*, which was seen in Paris and New York in 1907 and later filmed and televised with great success, and *War and Peace*, seen in London in 1943 and 1962 and also filmed and televised.

TOOLE, JOHN LAURENCE (1830–1906), English actor and manager, who first appeared on the professional stage in Dublin in 1852, and after further experience in the English provinces established himself in London in 1856, playing Fanfaronade in Charles Webb's *Belphegor the Mountebank*, in which Marie Wilton, later Lady Bancroft (q.v.), also made her first appearance in London. Toole then played with Irving (q.v.), who remained his lifelong friend, and in 1858, on the recommendation of Dickens, another great friend, was engaged by Ben Webster (q.v.) for the Adelphi, where he remained for nine years. Among his best parts were two of Dickens's characters—Bob Cratchit in *A Christmas Carol* (1859) and Caleb Plummer in *Dot* (1862), Boucicault's title for his dramatization of *The Cricket on the Hearth*, first seen in New York in 1859. In 1869 Toole began a long association with Hollingshead (q.v.) at the Gaiety, and in 1879 he went into management at the Charing Cross Theatre (see TOOLE'S THEATRE). The most important production of his last years was a short farce entitled *Walker, London* (1892), the first theatrical work of Sir James Barrie (q.v.). Crippled by gout, Toole left the stage in 1895, when his theatre was closed, and retired to Brighton, where he died.

Toole's Theatre, LONDON, in King William Street (now William IV Street), Charing Cross. Originally a hall, this was converted into a theatre, opening as the Charing Cross on 19 June 1869. In Nov. 1872 the American actor John S. Clarke took it over, reviving Sheridan's *The Rivals* with himself as Bob Acres and Mrs. Stirling (q.v.) as Mrs. Malaprop, her first appearance in what was to become her best-known part. In 1876 Alexander Henderson took the theatre and renamed it the Folly. His wife, Lydia Thompson (q.v.), starred under him in burlesque. On 7 Nov. 1879 Toole (q.v.) started in management and on 16 Feb. 1882 reopened the theatre after a long gap, occasioned by his being on tour, under his own name, following for the first time in London a habit already established in New York, notably by Daly (q.v.), whose company made their first London appearance at Toole's in 1884. In 1892 Barrie's first play, *Walker, London*, began a successful run. Toole remained at the theatre until 1895, his last production, on 13 Feb., being Lumley's *Thoroughbred*. On 28 Sept. it closed and was demolished in the spring of 1896, the site being needed for the extension of Charing Cross Hospital.

TOOLEY [really WILKINSON], NICHOLAS (c. 1575–1623), English actor, who was with the King's Men (see CHAMBERLAIN'S MEN) from about 1605 to his death and was a friend of the Burbage family. He may indeed have been apprenticed to

Richard Burbage (q.v.), whose will he witnessed, and he was lodging in Cuthbert Burbage's house at the time of his death. It is not known with any certainty what roles he played, except for that of Forobosco in Webster's *The Duchess of Malfi* (1614), but his name appears in the actor-list of Shakespeare's plays.

TOPOL, CHAIM (1934–), Israeli actor, who had his first experience of acting while in the army, and afterwards founded a theatre of satire in Tel Aviv which achieved widespread popularity. In 1960 he went to Haifa to help with the establishment of the Municipal Theatre there, acting as assistant to the director, Joseph Millo, and appearing with the company at the Venice Biennale as Azdak in Brecht's *The Caucasian Chalk Circle*, the part in which he was seen at the Chichester Festival in 1969. He also played such parts as Petruchio in *The Taming of the Shrew*, Pat in Brendan Behan's *The Hostage*, John in Ionesco's *Rhinoceros*, and the Soldier in Frisch's *Andorra*. In 1965 he was with the Cameri Theatre (q.v.) in Tel Aviv, and he was already internationally known through his films when in 1967 he appeared in London as Tevye in the American musical *Fiddler on the Roof*, in which he scored an immense success.

TORELLI, ACHILLE (1841–1922), Italian playwright, and with Paolo Ferrari (q.v.) the first to introduce realistic social drama into the Italian theatre. His first successful play was *I mariti* (1867), a study of modern marriage as exemplified in the vicissitudes of four married couples. Of his later plays the most important are *La moglie* (1868) and *L'ultima convegno* (1898).

TORELLI, GIACOMO (1608–78), Italian architect, and a practical man of the theatre, who made many important innovations in the designing and setting of scenery, being the first inventor of a device for moving several sets of wings on and off stage simultaneously (see CARRIAGE-AND-FRAME). He was a pupil of Aleotti, the architect of the Teatro Farnese, for which Torelli may have designed the system of wings which was adopted throughout Europe and lasted, unmodified in basic essentials, until the end of the nineteenth century. In 1640 he was responsible for the building of the Teatro Novissimo in Venice, where the

magical effects of his stage mechanism earned him the nickname of '*il gran stregone*' (the great wizard, or magician). In 1645 he went to Paris, where he inaugurated the fashion for spectacle-plays, of which the finest was Corneille's *Andromède* (1650), produced at Molière's first theatre, the Petit Bourbon, which Torelli had refurbished backstage. Much of his work was destroyed by his rival Vigarani (q.v.), though the designs were preserved, and over a hundred years later the complete survey of contemporary theatre machinery given under 'Machines du Théâtre' (1772) in Diderot's *Encyclopédie* showed that it was almost all based on Torelli's ideas.

Tormentors, SEE FALSE PROS.

TORRES NAHARRO, BARTOLOMÉ DE (?–*c.* 1524), with Encina and Vicente (qq.v.) the leading Spanish dramatist of the early part of the sixteenth century. Little is known of his life, but from 1513 he was in Rome, where most of his plays appear to have been written. His collected works appeared in 1517 under the title of *Propalladia*. The important prologue distinguishes between two types of play, the *comedia a noticia* and the *comedia a fantasía*, terms which may be said to correspond to realistic and novelesque genres. Of the former type two examples have survived, the *Comedia soldadesca*, dealing with a braggart Spanish captain, and the *Comedia tinellaria*, depicting life in the servants' hall of an Italian palace. The best-known example of Torres Naharro's novelesque plays is the *Comedia Himenea*, where the relationship between master and man and the theme of the conflict of love and honour both foreshadow the plays of Lope de Vega (q.v.).

TÖRRING, JOSEF AUGUST VON (1753–1826), see RITTERDRAMA.

Tottenham Street Theatre, LONDON, see SCALA THEATRE.

TOURNEUR, CYRIL (1575–1626), English dramatist, of whose life little is known, though he was connected with the Cecils and may have been sent by them on secret missions abroad. He was in Cadiz with Sir Edward Cecil in a secretarial capacity the year before his death. He is believed to have written two plays, *The Atheist's Tragedy; or, the Honest Man's Revenge*

(c. 1611), which contains echoes of Shakespeare's *King Lear*, and *The Nobleman* (c. 1612), of which the manuscript is lost, destroyed by Warburton's cook (q.v.). An earlier play, *The Revenger's Tragedy* (1606), published anonymously, was for a long time doubtfully ascribed to him but is now thought to be by Middleton (q.v.), though it was revived under Tourneur's name at Pitlochry in 1965 and at Stratford-upon-Avon in 1966, the latter production being seen at the Aldwych (q.v.) three years later.

TOVSTONOGOV, GEORGYI ALEXANDROVICH (1915–), Soviet producer, who began his theatrical career in 1931 in the Russian theatre in Tbilisi, and in 1950 became director of the Lenkom in Leningrad. In 1956 he became chief producer at the Gorky Bolshoi Dramatic Theatre, where one of his most successful productions was *The Ocean* (1961), by Shteyn. He has a very individual style and often prefaces his productions with a prologue intended to put the audience in the right mood for what is to follow: for instance, Dostoievsky's *The Idiot*, which was seen in London during the 1966 World Theatre season with Innokenty Smoktunovsky as Prince Myshkin, was prefaced by the showing of a vast facsimile of the original title-page of the novel; Arbuzov's *It Happened in Irkutsk* opened with the hero, seated at the top of rising tiers of seats, striking chords on a piano. Tovstonogov's experiments may not always succeed, but his work is full of life and vigour and shows a fresh approach not only to new plays but also to revivals of the classics.

Tower Theatre, LONDON, see TAVISTOCK REPERTORY COMPANY.

Towneley Cycle, see MYSTERY PLAY.

TOWSE, JOHN RANKEN (1845–1927), American dramatic critic, born and educated in England, who in 1869 went to the United States and became a journalist, working for the *New York Post*. Five years later he was appointed dramatic critic of that paper, a post he held until his retirement in 1927. Imbued with the traditions of the London stage, he held newcomers like Ibsen and Shaw (qq.v.) in slight esteem, and on many matters saw eye to eye with William Winter (q.v.), denouncing the modern theatre as destitute of morality. He was the author of *Sixty Years of the Theatre*, in which he recalls the golden age of the theatre of his youth.

Toy Theatre, or JUVENILE DRAMA, names given to the collections of theatrical material, popular in the nineteenth century, which consisted of drawings of actors, scenery, and properties in a successful contemporary play, suitable for cutting out and mounting on cardboard for a performance in which they were drawn on a metal long-handled slide across a small model stage, while an unseen assistant recited an extremely condensed version of the text. The sheets which made up the complete set, usually about eight to twelve in all, could be bought for a 'penny plain, twopence coloured', the colouring being done by hand in bold, vivid hues that are as fresh today as when first applied. These sheets, which may have originated in those sold by theatrical agencies in Paris for the benefit of provincial and foreign managements, were probably first intended, in England at any rate, as theatrical souvenirs. They capture with astonishing fidelity the theatre of Grimaldi, Kean, Kemble, Liston, and Vestris (qq.v.), and the productions of Astley's, Covent Garden, Drury Lane, the Olympic, and the Surrey (qq.v.) in the early nineteenth century. The total repertory of some three hundred plays includes melodramas such as Pocock's *The Miller and His Men*, Lillo's *George Barnwell*, or Boucicault's *The Corsican Brothers*, ballad operas like Dibdin's *The Waterman*, contemporary versions of Shakespeare, and many long-forgotten pantomimes. At first considerable care was taken to reproduce the costumes, attitudes, and even the features of the actors, as well as the details of wings, backcloth, and scenic accessories. The first English Toy Theatre sheets were issued in 1811 by William West, a stationer in Exeter Street, Strand, and the production and sale of what soon became a popular children's plaything was a thriving industry between 1815 and 1835, with some fifty publishers engaged in it, among them West, Jameson, Hodgson, Skelt, Green, Park, and Webb. As the demand for sheets grew, so the quality of the drawings and reproduction fell off, but trade continued brisk until the 1850s and beyond, particularly when the sheets were given away as supplements to boys' magazines. But the old-style Juvenile Drama never quite disappeared, and as late as 1932 two shops in Hoxton, Webb and Pollock, still printed the sheets of the old plays from the original blocks. Toy-theatre material is still available from Pollock's successor at 1 Scala Street. There are good collections of Toy Theatre sheets in the Print Room of the British Museum, in the Enthoven Collection at the Victoria and Albert Museum, and at the London Museum. Its history is recorded by George Speaight in *Juvenile Drama* (1947). Similar toy theatres were popular on the Continent in the nineteenth century, particularly in Germany, Denmark, and Spain, where the characters moved in grooves rather than on slides, but the plays were usually specially written for children, and not, as in England, taken from the adult repertory.

Trades Unions Theatre, MOSCOW, originally the Proletcult, founded after the October Revolution by Sergei Eisenstein, a pupil of Meyerhold (q.v.). He turned his stage into a circus ring and staged shows of which no trace remained except in the influence they had on the audiences which came freshly to them. After Eisenstein left to devote the rest of his life to the cinema, the Proletcult Theatre passed through many vicissitudes until in 1932 it received a new name at the same time as a new director, Alexei Dikie, whose first production was Wolf's *Sailors of Cattaro*. After an initial success, the theatre gradually fell out of favour and was closed in 1936.

Trafalgar Square Theatre, LONDON, see DUKE OF YORK'S THEATRE and MELNOTTE, V.

Tragedian, see STOCK COMPANY.

Tragedy, a play dealing in an elevated, poetic style with events which depict man as the victim of destiny yet superior to it, both in grandeur and in misery. The word is of Greek origin and means 'goat-song', possibly because a goat was originally given as a prize for a play at the Festival of Dionysus. The origins of tragedy are obscure, but its earliest manifestations in the plays of Aeschylus, Euripides, and Sophocles (qq.v.) set a standard which, has never been surpassed. The form of Greek tragedy arose from the fact that it was choral in origin, consisting of a series of lyrics sung by the chorus, punctuated by histrionic interludes or 'episodes'. An ode between two episodes was known as a *stasimon*, and consisted of one or more strophes with corresponding antistrophes exactly matching in metre and therefore in melody and choreography and ending in an *epode*. The opening and closing odes were called respectively the *parodos* and the *exodos*, and the number of episodes, and therefore of *stasima* between them, varied from three to six. The most important element in Greek tragedy was the chorus, which sang, or chanted, in unison, but probably spoke through its leader. As nothing is known about the music and dancing of the chorus, and the music-rhythms of the odes cannot be translated into speech-rhythms, it is impossible to dogmatize about the original productions of the great texts which have come down to us, and all translations and revivals can only be approximations. It was the subject-matter of the plays which exercised the greatest influence on the drama of the future. Taken from the myths of gods and heroes, it retained a link with its religious origins by the beneficent intervention, usually at the end of the play, of a god who descended from above the stage by means of a crane or pulley (whence the expression *deus ex machina*, the god from the machine). The Roman theatre, which produced excellent writers of comedy in Plautus and Terence (qq.v.), had no tragic playwrights. The tragedies of Seneca (q.v.), which had an immense influence on later European drama, were closet plays, written to be read and not acted. Tragedy in Renaissance Italy, more under the direct influence of the Greeks than of Seneca, developed early, but did not produce any outstanding playwright until the eighteenth century, with Alfieri (q.v.). In France tragedy developed under the influence of Seneca, modified by the contemporary interpretation of Aristotle (q.v.) which gave rise to the theory of the unities (q.v.) of time, place, and action, though only the last was consistently observed by Greek dramatists, the unities of time and place being sometimes imposed on the play by the continuous presence of the chorus. The greatest exponents of French classical tragedy were Corneille and Racine (qq.v.), whose successors up to the end of the eighteenth century continued to employ their outward forms but without their inward excellence. In England, where the influence of Seneca was paramount, Marlowe and Shakespeare (qq.v.) evolved a form of tragedy mingled with comedy which was *sui generis*. Because of its powerful appeal to English audiences, the English theatre remained impervious to the influence of French classical tragedy, even after the Restoration, when such plays as Addison's *Cato* (1713) brought the letter but not the spirit of Corneille and Racine briefly on the English stage. Spain, too, had her native tragedy, formulated by Calderón (q.v.), and the efforts of Luzán to import French tragedy failed, as did the attempts of Gottsched and Carolina Neuber in Germany. The German theatre later produced its own writers of tragedy in Goethe and Schiller (qq.v.). But it was the melodramatic aspect of their tragedies which had the greatest appeal, and this, added to the influence of Shakespeare all over Europe at the end of the eighteenth century, produced the highly coloured melodrama (q.v.) which in the nineteenth century replaced true tragedy everywhere. Meanwhile, in the eighteenth century, in the plays of Lillo, Lessing, and Mercier (qq.v.), efforts had been made to apply the formula of classical tragedy to middle-class existence, resulting in 'domestic tragedy' or *tragédie bourgeoise*. But it was not a success. Tragedy in the narrow theatrical sense demands a cast of heroes or demi-gods, an unfamiliar background —exotic, romantic, or imaginary—and a sense of detachment heightened by the use of verse or rhetorical prose. Even the plays of Ibsen (q.v.) and his successors, though often tragic in their implications, are dramas rather than tragedies in the Greek sense. In modern times efforts have again been made to tame tragedy and bring it within the family circle. But it is interesting to note that *Murder in the Cathedral* (1935) by T. S. Eliot (q.v.), which has as protagonists a king and an archbishop, was a success, whereas his *The Family Reunion* (1939), though based on a Greek myth, was not, remaining firmly rooted in suburbia.

Tragi-comedy, a bastard form of tragedy, being a play dealing with a tragic story which ends unhappily, but which contains certain elements of comedy and the remote possibility of a happy ending. Some critics have classified *Hamlet* (*c.* 1600–1) as a tragi-comedy, but the perfect example of the type is Corneille's *Le Cid* (1637).

Tragic Carpet, a green baize cloth which in the seventeenth-century English theatre was spread on the stage before the performance of a tragedy to save the actors from dirtying their clothes when dying on the dusty boards. It continued in use into the nineteenth century and is frequently referred to in theatrical letters and memoirs.

Trampoline, the apparatus resembling a spring mattress upon which acrobats bounce. It usually has a gymnast's horizontal bar at either end. The word comes from the French *tremplin*, the name of the wedge-shaped springboard used by acrobats of many generations. In the announcements of Philip Astley (q.v.) it was anglicized as tramplin, in about 1780 became trampline, and finally took its present form.

Transformation Scene. This important element in the English pantomime (q.v.) could be achieved in several ways. An instantaneous change of part of a scene, like a shop- or house-front, was usually done by the use of FALLING FLAPS, or hinged sections of canvas, painted on both sides, turned up, and kept in position by catches. When these were released, the flaps fell by their own weight, presenting their other side to the audience. Interesting examples of this can be found in the scenic sheets of the Toy Theatre (q.v.) pantomimes. To change the whole aspect of the stage, now usually done by the flying of painted cloths and gauzes, several methods were employed. Backcloth and side wings could be drawn off simultaneously to reveal new ones behind, as in early theatres (see CARRIAGE-AND-FRAME and DRUM-AND-SHAFT), but for the swift changes needed for the pantomime in the later theatres equipped with flies (q.v.) more spectacular methods were the RISE-AND-SINK, in which the upper part of the scene was flown while the lower descended through a trap (q.v.), revealing another scene behind, and the FAN EFFECT, in which the two halves of a scene sank sideways like collapsing fans, again revealing a new scene. A quick change could also be achieved by dividing the painted back scene into vertical strips, each wound on its own roller. The rollers were then set across the stage like a row of columns, with another scene behind serving as a backcloth. When lines from the top and bottom of each column were pulled sideways the new scene was quickly drawn out, hiding the former one. The same effect could be achieved by the use of SCRUTO—thin strips of wood fastened to a canvas backing so as to form a continuous flexible sheet, like the cover of a roll-top desk. With the advent of more sophisticated lighting, however, use was made of the TRANSPARENCY, in which the back-scene was painted (except for any features intended to remain in silhouette) in transparent dye on linen or canvas. When lit from the front, this was as opaque as the previous canvas cloth, but as it was gradually lit from behind it faded or was supplemented by further painting on the back of the fabric, so that a building could, for instance, appear suddenly to be on fire, or a quiet country landscape give way to a battlefield. The further development of lighting as an element in visual scene-change gave rise to the cyclorama (q.v.), and to the use of projected scenery or coloured lights on to plain surfaces. Most of the scene-changing needed in modern plays is done during the intervals, and the old machinery and old methods have been abandoned, except in pantomime and sometimes in ballet.

Transparency, see TRANSFORMATION SCENE.

Transpontine Melodrama, a term applied, usually in genial derision, to a type of crude and extravagantly sensational play staged in the mid-nineteenth century in London's theatres 'across the bridges' (i.e. on the south side of the Thames) such as the Surrey and the Old Vic (qq.v.). By extension the term was later attached to such plays wherever performed.

Trap, a device in a stage-floor or in part of the scenery by which an actor, or a scenic detail, can be brought on stage from behind or below. It was used mainly for quick changes of scenery in pantomime, for ghostly apparitions in melodrama, or for the acrobatic foolery of the Dumb Ballet. The simplest traps, fixed into apertures cut in the stage floor and worked usually by counterweights, were the CAULDRON TRAP (for *Macbeth*), the GRAVE TRAP (for *Hamlet*), and the STAR or BRISTLE TRAP, which by means of hinged segments of thin wood or bristles attached to a circular opening allowed a body to pass through at high speed, as in the arrival of the Demon King in pantomime. The FOOTLIGHTS TRAP, a long rectangular opening in front of the curtain, was used in the nineteenth century to lower the lamps used as foot-

lights into the cellar for trimming and to darken the stage when necessary. The mechanism for this was controlled from the prompt corner.

One of the most ingenious trap mechanisms was that devised for the apparition in Boucicault's *The Corsican Brothers* (1852), which had to rise slowly and drift across the full width of the stage. The solution to this problem became known as the CORSICAN TRAP or GHOST GLIDE. A long narrow cut was made across the stage and filled in with SCRUTO, on the principle of the roll-top desk (see TRANSFORMATION SCENE), which was pulled aside by a rope drawing a small truck, with the ghost standing on it, along an inclined railway. The truck rose from a point some six feet below stage at the beginning of its travel to the level of the stage itself at the end, and was followed by another sliding floor which closed the aperture after it had passed. The effect achieved became so popular that a Corsican Trap was installed in most theatres, even, in 1858, in the little Theatre Royal at Ipswich. A variant of it was the SLOAT (or SLOTE), used to move actors or groundrows from above or below, which appears to have been standard equipment in the London theatres of the mid-nineteenth century, being first mentioned in connection with Drury Lane in 1843. In Leslie and Rowe's *The Orange Girl* (Surrey Theatre, 1864), there are elaborate directions for the use of a slote from a height downwards, and in the *Era Almanack* for 1887 Irving (q.v.) describes how in *Faust* the slote struck him on the head instead of carrying him up into the flies. Finally, there was the VAMP TRAP, said by Planché (q.v.) in his memoirs to derive its name from his melodrama *The Vampire; or, the Bride of the Isles* (1820), in which it was first used. It consisted of two spring-leaves, usually in a canvas flat, through which an actor could pass quickly as if through a solid wall. It was the use of these traps in all their variants, combined with acrobatic skill, that made English actors renowned in nineteenth-century Europe and America for their stage trickwork. In its simplest form this entailed the use of the ROLL-OUT, a flap of loose canvas left at the bottom of a hanging scene through which the actor could roll from behind and then leap to his feet as if appearing from nowhere. In combination with the Vamp Trap, this led to the supreme test of the trick player, the LEAP. In essence no more than an acrobatic jump through a concealed opening in the scenery, it could, by the skill of the actors and the clever multiplication and siting of different forms of trap, become a separate entertainment, or DUMB BALLET, of which *Fun in a Bakehouse* or *Ki Ko Kookeree* (*c.* 1871) are typical examples. There is in existence a diagrammatic plot of the latter, intended for the information of the stage-manager, showing at least eight varieties of trap. Such expertise in tumbling, which, though its development appears to have been purely English, must derive from the antics of the *commedia dell'arte* (q.v.), was already apparent in the work of Grimaldi (q.v.), and was developed by the early Lupinos and Conquests (qq.v.) until it culminated in the staggering virtuosity of the Hanlon-Lees (q.v.).

TRAVERS, BEN (1886–1980), English dramatist, and an outstanding writer of farce. He first came into prominence with the success of *A Cuckoo in the Nest* (1925), which inaugurated a series of 'Aldwych farces', so called because they were all presented at the Aldwych Theatre (q.v.) in London with casts which included Mary Brough, Robertson Hare, Ralph Lynn, and Tom Walls (qq.v.). The series continued with *Rookery Nook* (1926), *Thark* (1927), *Plunder* (1928), *A Cup of Kindness* (1929), *A Night Like This* (1930), *Turkey Time* (1931), *Dirty Work* (1932), and *A Bit of a Test* (1933). Several of these were subsequently filmed, and the first three have recently been revived in London with some success, having always been popular with repertory companies. Travers also wrote a number of plays for other theatres, including a comedy, *O Mistress Mine* (1936), starring Yvonne Printemps (q.v.), and the farces *Banana Ridge* (1939), *Spotted Dick* (1940), and *She Follows Me About* (1945), in all of which Robertson Hare again appeared, being joined in *Outrageous Fortune* (1947) and *Wild Horses* (1952) by Ralph Lynn. In the autumn of 1962 a new farce by Travers, *Coker's End*, was produced at the Yvonne Arnaud Theatre (q.v.), named after the delightful actress who had appeared in the first 'Aldwych farce', *A Cuckoo in the Nest*.

TREE, ELLEN (1806–80), see KEAN, CHARLES.

TREE, SIR HERBERT DRAPER BEERBOHM (1853–1917), English actor-manager, half-brother of Max Beerbohm (q.v.), who, after experience in amateur acting, went on the stage professionally in 1878. His chief successes in his early days were scored as the Revd. Robert Spalding in Charles Hawtrey's *The Private Secretary* and Macari in Comyns Carr's *Called Back* (both 1884). In Apr. 1887 he became manager of the Comedy Theatre (q.v.), where he produced Tristram's *The Red Lamp*, and later that year he took over the management of the Haymarket (q.v.). Among his productions there, which included Shakespeare (*The Merry Wives of Windsor*, 1889; *Hamlet*, 1892) and new plays (Henry Arthur Jones's *The Dancing Girl*, 1891; Oscar Wilde's *A Woman of No Importance*, 1893), the most successful was *Trilby* (1895), based by Paul Potter on George du Maurier's famous novel, with Dorothea Baird (q.v.) in the title-role and Tree himself as Svengali, a part which he played many times. In 1897 he opened his own theatre, Her (or His) Majesty's (q.v.), with Parker's *The Seats of the Mighty*. There he carried on the tradition, established at the Lyceum under Irving (q.v.), of lavish spectacular productions of Shakespeare, eighteen of whose plays he put on between 1888 and 1914, interspersed with such new works as Stephen Phillips's *Herod* (1900) and *Ulysses* (1902), American importations like Clyde Fitch's *The Last of the Dandies* (1901) and Belasco's *The Darling of the Gods* (1903), dramatizations of Thackeray (*Colonel Newcome*, 1906) and Dickens (*David Copperfield*, 1914), and Bernard Shaw's *Pygmalion* (also 1914) on its first production in English, with himself as Higgins and Mrs. Patrick Campbell (q.v.) as Eliza Doolittle. The play was directed by Shaw himself, but in general Tree was his own director of plays. A firm disciplinarian, founder of the Royal Academy of Dramatic Art, he was a romantic actor, delighting in grandiose effects and in the representation of eccentric characters in which his imagination had free play. A versatile man, he lectured on the theatre and was the author of three books: *An Essay on the Imaginative Faculty* (1893), *Thoughts and Afterthoughts* (1913), and *Nothing Matters* (1917). He was knighted in 1909. Leading parts in many of his productions were played by his wife HELEN MAUD (*née* HOLT) (1863–1937), whom he married in 1883. She excelled in comedy, particularly in Shakespeare, Sheridan, Shaw, and Barrie, among others, and was an active and intelligent partner in all her husband's enterprises. After his death she continued to be a familiar figure on the London stage, playing such parts as Mrs. Malaprop in Sheridan's *The Rivals* and Mistress Quickly in *Henry IV, Part 1*. Her last part was the Duchess of Stroud in Gertrude Jennings's comedy, *Our Own Lives*, at the Ambassadors in 1935. Her eldest daughter VIOLA (1884–1938) was also an actress. She married the dramatic critic ALAN PARSONS (1888–1933) in 1912.

Tree Border, see BORDER.

Tremont Theatre, see BOSTON.

TRENEV, KONSTANTIN ANDREIVICH (1884–1945), Soviet dramatist and short-story writer, whose first play, dealing with an eighteenth-century peasant insurrection, was staged by the Moscow Art Theatre in 1925. This was the theatre's first attempt at a Soviet play and was not particularly successful, but it established Trenev as a playwright. In 1926 the Maly Theatre produced the first version of his *Lyubov Yarovaya*, which, after intensive alterations, became one of the outstanding productions of the Moscow Art Theatre in 1937. The story of a school teacher in the Revolution, caught between love for her White Russian husband and loyalty to her ideals, it became popular all over the U.S.S.R. and is still acted today. Trenev's best play, however, was probably *On the Banks of the Neva*, also produced in 1937. His later plays include *Anna Luchinina* (1941), *Meeting Halfway* (1942), and *The General* (1944), in which the chief character is the famous Russian Field-Marshal Kutuzov (1745–1813).

TRETYAKOV, SERGEI MIKHAILOVICH (1892–1939), one of the earliest Soviet dramatists, whose best-known play, *Roar, China!*, was produced by Meyerhold (q.v.) in 1926. Though somewhat naïve and melodramatic, and written entirely for propaganda purposes, it is a vivid historical document, presenting with intense conviction the conflict between Chinese coolies and foreign imperialists. It was produced in New York in an English translation in 1930.

TREVELYAN [really TUCKER], HILDA (1880–1959), English actress, who as a child played in Jones and Herman's melodrama, *The Silver King*, and later toured in musical comedy. In 1904 she appeared as Wendy in the first production of Barrie's *Peter Pan*, playing the part again in many subsequent revivals. She was also in the first productions of Barrie's *Alice Sit-by-the-Fire* (1905), *What Every Woman Knows* (1908), *The Twelve-Pound Look* (1910), with which she toured the variety theatres, and *A Kiss for Cinderella* (1916), and in many revivals of other Barrie plays, including *The Little Minister*, *Quality Street*, *The Admirable Crichton*, and *Mary Rose*. She also appeared many times as Avonia Bunn in revivals of Pinero's *Trelawny of the 'Wells'*. She was in the long run of Ian Hay's *Housemaster* (1936), and retired in 1939, making her last appearance as Mrs. Wyatt in a revival of Michael Baringer's *Inquest*, a part she created in 1931. She was the wife of the dramatist Sidney Blow.

TREW, CHRISTINE PATTI, see LONGFORD, E. A. H. P.

TREWIN, JOHN COURTENAY (1908–   ), English dramatic critic, who began his career on the *Western Independent*, Plymouth, before being appointed to the staff of the *Morning Post* in London in 1934. He was for some time with the *Observer* and *Punch*, and from 1945 to 1954 was dramatic critic for *John O'London's Weekly*. He serves in the same capacity now for the *Illustrated London News*, the *Sketch*, *The Lady*, and the *Birmingham Post*. He has written a number of books on the theatre, among them *The Shakespeare Memorial Theatre* (with M. C. Day) (1932) and *The Stratford Theatre* (with T. C. Kemp) (1953); *The English Theatre* (1948); *Drama 1945–1950* and *The Theatre since 1900* (both 1951); *A Play To-night* (1952); *Dramatists of Today* (1953); *Verse Drama since 1800* (1955); *Benson and the Bensonians* and *The Turbulent Thirties* (both 1960); *The Birmingham Repertory Theatre 1913–63* (1963); *Shakespeare on the English Stage 1900–1964* (1964); *Drama in Britain 1951–64* (1965). He has also written biographies of Macready (q.v.), whose diaries he edited, and of the modern actors Alec Clunes, Edith Evans, Paul Scofield, and Sybil Thorndike (qq.v.) and since 1948 has edited the annual *Plays of the Year*.

Tributary Theatre, U.S.A., a term used by Edith J. Isaacs (q.v.) in *Theatre Arts* for the theatre outside New York, which has also been called nationwide theatre, and, on the suggestion of Kenneth Macgowan (q.v.) in *Footlights across America* (1929), local theatre. It was the equivalent of the Little Theatre (q.v.) movement in England, and under that title, soon discarded, began in the 1900s, when Little Theatres, now usually known as community theatres, were springing up everywhere. It is not always possible to distinguish the community theatre from the university theatre (see UNIVERSITY DEPARTMENTS OF DRAMA), and the two functions are often combined. Those not attached to a university should perhaps be called 'civic' theatres, though that name too is sometimes applied to a university theatre which also serves the urban area in which it is located, particularly when it houses a professional company. What is undeniable is that the resident theatre outside New York, both amateur and professional, is developing very rapidly and offers both actors and audiences the opportunity to experiment and expand indefinitely.

TRIGG, WILLIAM (*fl.* first half of seventeenth century), a boy-actor with the King's Men (see CHAMBERLAIN'S MEN), who played women's parts from about 1626 to 1632. He was probably apprenticed to John Shank (q.v.), and by 1636 he had graduated to adult parts and was a hired man. He may have joined Beeston's Boys (see BEESTON, CHRISTOPHER) at about this time, and was still with them in 1639. The date of his death is unknown, but he was still alive in 1652. He does not appear to have returned to the theatre after the Restoration.

TRISTAN L'HERMITE, FRANÇOIS (*c.* 1602–55), French dramatist, considered by his contemporaries a formidable rival to Corneille (q.v.). His first play, *La Mariane,* was produced at the Théâtre du Marais (q.v.) in 1636 with almost unprecedented success, largely due to the acting of Montdory (q.v.) as Herod, and remained in the repertory for nearly a hundred years. Encouraged by this initial success, Tristan continued to write plays, but none of them equalled his first and all are forgotten. Two were in the repertory of Molière's short-lived Illustre-Théâtre (q.v.). In his will Tristan left a large sum of money to his friend and protégé, the dramatist Quinault (q.v.).

Tritagonist, see PROTAGONIST.

Trocadero Music-Hall, LONDON, in Great Windmill Street. There was a tennis court

on this site in about 1744, which in 1820 was converted for use as a circus and theatre. In 1832 it was renamed the Albion, and in 1833 became the New Queen's Theatre, its staple fare being melodrama. After several changes of name, among them the Argyll Rooms, it became a music-hall as the Royal Trocadero Palace of Varieties, retaining the name Trocadero when in 1902 it was converted into a restaurant which became famous for its cabaret.

TROUNCER, CECIL (1898–1953), one of the finest character actors of his day. He made his first appearance on the stage in 1920 and was seen in London a year later. He had a consistently successful career, and never failed to give a good, equable performance. He worked at the Old Vic for several years, and toured in Shakespeare with Robert Atkins. He also went to South Africa with the Macdona Players in a Shaw repertory. He had a warm rich voice and a most sympathetic personality, being equally good in stylized comedy and pathos. Two of his best parts were Newton in Shaw's *In Good King Charles's Golden Days,* which he played at Malvern in 1939 and subsequently in London, and Menenius to Laurence Olivier's Coriolanus at the Old Vic the year before. Although never a 'star', he was the typical gifted, hardworking, and dedicated actor who is the backbone of the theatre, in England and elsewhere.

TSARYOV, M. I. (1903–), see MALY THEATRE, MOSCOW.

TUCCIO, STEFANO (1540–97), a Sicilian playwright important in the development of Jesuit drama (q.v.). A member of the Order, he wrote a number of plays for production by pupils of the Collegio Mamertino in Messina, of which *Juditha* (1564), based on the story of Judith and Holofernes, called for a cast of twenty-six male characters, six female, an angel, a demon, and a large chorus. His most ambitious work was a trilogy on the life of Christ—*Christus Natus,* on the Nativity, *Christus Patiens,* on the Crucifixion, and *Christus Judex,* on the Second Coming. The last of these, according to a contemporary account, moved the spectators to tears and caused sudden and miraculous conversions, not only at Messina, where it was first produced in 1569, but wherever it was subsequently acted. It was one of the first Jesuit plays to be done in the vernacular, a translation into Italian verse being seen at Bari in 1584. A second Italian translation, published in 1596, was sufficiently popular to be reprinted in Venice in 1606, and in 1752 the play was acted in Polish at Warsaw. It had already been seen in German at Olmütz in 1603. Another Italian version, heavily revised, appeared in Rome in 1698 and provided the libretto for *L'ultima scena del mondo* (1721), a 'sacred drama set to music', in three acts, with intermezzi. An Italian prose version of the original play appeared in 1727.

TUKE, Sir Samuel (?–1674), a gentleman at the Court of Charles II, who, on the suggestion of the king, wrote *The Adventures of Five Hours*, a tragi-comedy adapted from Calderón, which was produced at Lincoln's Inn Fields on 8 Jan. 1663. Although it was a great success, being highly praised by Pepys, it remained Tuke's only play, the rest of his time being spent in attendance on Charles II, for whom he performed many secret missions.

TUMANOV [really Tumanishvili], Joseph Mikhailovich (1905–), Soviet producer, born in Georgia, and from 1928 to 1932 a pupil and then a colleague of Stanislavsky (q.v.), on whom he lectured in London in 1963 on the occasion of the Stanislavsky centenary celebrations. He has been director of a number of theatres in Moscow, and is at present a professor at the Moscow Institute of Dramatic Art. During his directorship of the Pushkin Theatre (q.v.) from 1953 to 1961 he produced, among other things, a dramatization of Dickens's *Little Dorrit* (1953) and a translation of Ewan MacColl's *The Train Can Stop* (1954).

Tumbler, an acrobat; also the name given to a loose roller placed inside a rolled-up cloth (see DROP).

TURGENEV, Ivan Sergeivich (1818–83), Russian novelist and dramatist, who in 1843, while studying at Berlin University, published his first play, a romantic swashbuckling drama set in Spain. His second play, a satirical comedy in the style of Gogol (q.v.) entitled *Penniless; or, Scenes from the Life of a Young Nobleman*, was published in 1846. He later wrote

several short plays, in the style of *Comédies et Proverbes* by Musset (q.v.), among them *Where It's Thin, It Breaks*; *The Bachelor* (1849), written for Shchepkin (q.v.) and later revived with equal success by Martynov and Karatygin; and *The Boarder* (1850). In 1850 Turgenev wrote his dramatic masterpiece, *A Month in the Country*, originally entitled *The Student*. Called by the author 'a novel in dramatic form', it was heavily revised and published in 1869, but not staged until 1872. It is important as the first psychological drama in the Russian theatre, and in it Turgenev proved himself the forerunner of Chekhov (q.v.) in that he shifts the dramatic action from external to internal conflict. He might have developed this further, but his battles with the censorship, and his subsequent imprisonment and exile, led him to give up writing plays and to concentrate on short stories. He had no opinion of himself as a dramatist, and intended his plays mainly for reading. But his insight and inner realism could not fail to make them effective in performance when they were staged and interpreted as they should be—a feat which only became possible long after they were written. The only one to be well known outside Russia is *A Month in the Country*, which was first seen in London in 1926 and several times revived, notably by the Old Vic at the New Theatre in 1949, with Redgrave (q.v.) as Rakitin, a part he had previously played in 1943 in an adaptation by Emlyn Williams (q.v.), and was to play again when he opened the Yvonne Arnaud Theatre (q.v.) at Guildford in 1965. In New York the play was first produced by the Theatre Guild in 1930, and there also has been revived several times.

TURLEIGH, Veronica (1903–71), see LAVER, JAMES.

TURLUPIN [really Henri Legrand] (c. 1587–1637), a player of farcical comedy at the Hôtel de Bourgogne, where he was partnered by Gaultier-Garguille and Gros-Guillaume (qq.v.). They probably played at the Paris fairs before joining a professional company, which Turlupin did after his companions, in 1615. He excelled in broad comedy, playing roguish valets, and with the rest of the company figures as himself in *La Comédie des comédiens* (1633), by Gougenot. As Belleville he also played serious parts; but it is as a farce-player that he is best remembered.

TURNER, ANTHONY (*fl.* first half of the 17th century), English actor, who is first found at the Cockpit (q.v.) in 1622. Three years later he joined Queen Henrietta's Men (q.v.), but was evidently not one of their leading players. The parts in which he is known to have appeared include that of an old man. When the company was disbanded in 1636 Turner stayed at the Cockpit with Beeston's new company, and then seems to have become slightly more important. He was arrested in 1659 for playing illegally at the Red Bull (q.v.), and was evidently one of the more active theatrical law-breakers under the Commonwealth, in company with Edward Shatterell (q.v.).

Turnham's Music-Hall, LONDON, see METROPOLITAN MUSIC-HALL.

TWAITS, WILLIAM (?–1814), a low comedian who was appearing with some success under the elder Macready in Birmingham and Sheffield when Wood (q.v.) engaged him for his Philadelphia theatre. He played there opposite Joseph Jefferson (q.v.), and in 1805 made his first appearance in New York at a benefit night for Dunlah (q.v.), who describes him as short, with stiff carroty hair, a mobile and expressive face, and a powerful asthmatic voice which he used with great comic effect. He was at his best in farce and broad comedy, and in accordance with the tradition of the day he appeared as Polonius in *Hamlet*. He was also seen as Richard III and, somewhat incongruously, as Mercutio in *Romeo and Juliet*. More suited to his peculiar talents were the parts of the First Grave-digger in *Hamlet*, Dogberry in *Much Ado About Nothing*, Launcelot Gobbo in *The Merchant of Venice*, and Goldfinch in Holcroft's *The Road to Ruin*, all of which he played under Cooper (q.v.) at the Park Theatre, New York. He married one of the lovely Westray (q.v.) sisters, previously known on the stage as Mrs. Villiers, and shortly before his death appeared at the newly opened Anthony Street Theatre (q.v.) in New York.

Twopenny Gaff, see GAFF.

TYLER, ROYALL (1757–1826), author of the first American comedy, *The Contrast*. He was a friend of Thomas Wignell (q.v.), leading comedian of the American Company, and it was probably owing to his interest and influence that *The Contrast* was produced at the John Street Theatre on 16 Apr. 1787. In return for his help Tyler gave Wignell the copyright in his play, a light comedy in the style of Sheridan's *The School for Scandal*. It was a success, and was several times revived, though when given in Boston, Tyler's birthplace, it had, like *Othello*, to be disguised as a 'Moral Lecture in Five Parts'. It was published in 1790, George Washington heading the list of subscribers. In 1917 it was revived by Otis Skinner (q.v.). Tyler wrote several other plays, some of which are lost, but none was as successful as his first.

TYNAN, KENNETH PEACOCK (1927–80), English dramatic critic and 1963 to 1969 literary adviser to the National Theatre, in which capacity he fought, and lost, a battle for the production by that body of *Soldiers*, by ROLF HOCHHUTH. From 1951 to 1960 he was actively engaged in dramatic criticism for a number of newspapers, including the *Observer* (1954–8 and 1960–63) and the *New Yorker* (1958–60). He published three volumes of collected criticism—*He That Plays the King* (1950), *Curtains* (1961), and *Tynan Right and Left* (1968)—and a biography of Alec Guinness (q.v.). In 1969 he inaugurated, or at any rate substantially assisted, the vogue for nudity and pornography in the theatre with the production of his 'evening of elegant erotica', *Oh! Calcutta!*, first seen in New York on 17 June 1969 and in London a year later. With contributions from such well-established dramatists as Tennessee Williams, Samuel Beckett, and Jules Feiffer, the revue nevertheless failed to satisfy the critics, who found it lacking in wit and stimulation, though the public continued to patronize it for a long time.

Tyrone Guthrie Theatre, see GUTHRIE, SIR TYRONE.

U

UDALL, NICHOLAS (1505–56), English scholar, headmaster in turn of Eton and Westminster, and the author of *Ralph Roister Doister*. Written while he was at Eton for performance by the boys in place of the usual Latin comedy, it was probably performed there between 1534 and 1541, though efforts have been made to connect it with Udall's headmastership at Westminster and date it 1552. In any case, it was not printed until about 1566–7. This comedy, the first play in English to deserve that name, is much influenced by Terence and Plautus (qq.v.), and turns on the efforts of a vainglorious fool to win the heart and hand of a wealthy London widow. Although Udall is known to have written several other plays, as well as dialogues and pageants for Court festivals, where he was connected with the Revels Office under Mary Tudor, they are lost, or survive only in fragmentary form. He is sometimes credited with the authorship of *Thersites*, an interlude acted at Court in 1537 which A. W. Pollard considers to be the work of John Heywood (q.v.).

Ulster Group Theatre, BELFAST, founded in 1904 as the Ulster Literary Theatre, its first productions being *The Reformers*, by Lewis Purcell [really David Parkhill] and Bulmer Hobson's *Brian of Banba*. Although its history has run parallel with that of the Abbey Theatre (q.v.) in Dublin, dramatists like St. John Ervine, Rutherford Mayne, and George Shiels having worked for both, it nevertheless had an independent existence closely allied to local and contemporary conditions. Tours in England and the United States with new plays by such authors as Lynn Doyle and Bernard Duffy confirmed the individuality of its material and approach to theatrical problems. In 1939 the company amalgamated with other Belfast groups and took its present name. A difficult situation which developed in the 1950s due to a shortage of experienced actors and diminishing audiences was solved by the appointment of two popular local comedians, James Young and Jack Hudson, as joint managing directors. A period of prosperity followed, which provided lively regional plays, well produced and well acted, resulting in many improvements in the theatre building and a measure of security for many actors in Northern Ireland.

(See also BELFAST ARTS THEATRE and LYRIC PLAYERS, BELFAST.)

UNAMUNO, MIGUEL DE (1864–1936), Spanish philosopher, essayist, and novelist, author of a number of plays. The first, *Soledad* (1921), is concerned with loneliness and the theme of life as make-believe, a theme to which Unamuno returned in *Sombras de ensueño* (1926). *El otro* (also 1926) dramatizes the Cain-Abel relationship, and *El hermano Juan* (1929) is Unamuno's typically personal contribution to the development of the Don Juan theme, stressing the relationship between character and author in a manner reminiscent of Pirandello (q.v.). Of Unamuno's eleven plays, nine were staged, but they were not on the whole as successful in performance as an adaptation of his short story, *Nada menos que todo un hombre*, made by Julio de Hoyos.

UNDERHILL, CAVE (c. 1634–c. 1710), an actor of the Restoration period well equipped by nature for the playing of boobies and lumpish louts, such as Clodpate in Shadwell's *Epsom Wells* (1672) or Lolpoop in his *The Squire of Alsatia* (1688), Drydrubb in Southerne's *The Maid's Last Prayer; or, Any, Rather than Fail* (1692). He was also much admired as Sir Sampson Legend in Congreve's *Love for Love* (1695) and in the part of the Grave-digger in *Hamlet*, in which he made his last appearance shortly before he died, at a benefit performance given at the instigation of *The Tatler*. Colley Cibber, in his *Apology*, has left an excellent portrait of Underhill, who was esteemed one of the best comic actors of his day.

UNDERWOOD, JOHN (c. 1590–1624), a boy-actor at the Blackfriars (q.v.), where he appeared in Ben Jonson's *Cynthia's Revels* (1600) and *The Poetaster* (1601). As an adult actor he joined the King's Men (see CHAMBERLAIN'S MEN), and from 1608 to his death played with them regularly, though his only known role is that of Delio in Webster's *The Duchess of Malfi* (1614). It has been conjectured that he played juvenile leads, princes, gallants, and libertines. He owned shares in the Blackfriars, Globe, and Curtain Theatres (qq.v.).

Unicorn Theatre, ABINGDON, near Oxford, a private venture founded in 1953 with the object of converting the medieval Checker Hall (once part of Abingdon Abbey) into a miniature Elizabethan theatre. Within the framework of stone walls and timbered roof a gaily painted façade has been erected with gallery, inner stage, and apron. There is seating for just over a hundred. Productions are mainly by local amateur clubs, including college groups from Oxford, and each season the opera group sponsors a performance of an opera by Handel.

Unicorn Theatre for Young People, see JENNER, CARYL.

Union Square Theatre, NEW YORK, on the south side of Union Square. This opened as a variety hall on 11 Sept. 1871. Among the initial attractions were the Vokes family (q.v.) in their pantomime-spectacle *The Belles of the Kitchen.* On 1 June 1872 A. M. Palmer (q.v.) took over, and for ten years made the theatre one of the finest in New York. One of its greatest successes was Oxenford's *The Two Orphans* (1874), which made a fortune for Palmer and a star of Kate Claxton (q.v.). The last play done under Palmer's management was Feuillet's *A Parisian Romance* (1883), which saw the début of Richard Mansfield (q.v.) in a small part that made him famous overnight. The theatre then opened under new management, but the stock company continued until 1885, when it was disbanded. The theatre was then used by travelling stars until in Feb. 1888 it was burnt down. It was rebuilt but never regained its former brilliance, and was mostly devoted to continuous vaudeville, under various names. It later became a burlesque house and then a cinema, and in 1936 it was demolished.

Union Theatre, NEW YORK, see CHATHAM THEATRE (2).

Unities, THE THREE, of time, place, and action, elements of drama introduced into French dramatic literature by Jean

Mairet (q.v.). They demand that a play should consist of one action, represented as occurring in not more than twenty-four hours, and always in the same place. This doctrine was said to be based on the *Poetics* of Aristotle (q.v.), though in fact he insists only on the unity of action, merely mentions the unity of time, and says nothing about the unity of place, though this was to a certain extent imposed on the Greek dramatist by the presence of the chorus. The observance of the unities, defined by Boileau (q.v.) in his *Art poétique* (1674), became an essential characteristic of French classical tragedy, though both Corneille and Racine (qq.v.) ignored them when they wished, and found its way, with neo-classicism, into Spain and Italy. In England the influence of Shakespeare, who certainly had no regard for the unities of time and place, and very little for that of action, was strong enough to counteract the efforts of Restoration writers of tragedy to force English plays into French moulds.

Unity Theatre. (1) LONDON, a left-wing amateur group founded in 1936, which gave its first production on 19 Feb. in a converted Church Hall in Britannia Road, King's Cross. A year later it moved to its present premises in Goldington Street, which it purchased in 1962 and is gradually rebuilding. Unity was the first theatre to present Brecht (q.v.) in English with *Señora Carrar's Rifles* in 1938, and in the same year introduced the American Living Newspaper technique to London with a documentary on a London bus-strike. Among its interesting productions have been Clifford Odets's *Waiting for Lefty* (1936), Pogodin's *Aristocrats* and Ben Bengal's *Plant in the Sun* (in which Paul Robeson (q.v.) played the lead) (both 1937), O'Casey's *The Star Turns Red* (1940), Sartre's *Nekrassov* (1956), Adamov's *Spring '71* (1962), and Shatrov's *The Bolsheviks* (1970). The play-wright TED [really EDWARD HENRY] WILLIS [now LORD WILLIS] (1918–) was connected with Unity in the 1940s and 1950s and directed many plays there.
(2) GLASGOW, a left-wing amateur group formed in 1941, its first production being James Barke's *Major Operation.* A production of Gorky's *The Lower Depths,* brought to London in 1945, was highly praised, and a year later the company became fully professional,

achieving a notable success with Robert MacLeish's *The Gorbals Story*, a study of life in an overcrowded slum reminiscent in its mixture of broad comedy and pathos of O'Casey's early plays. Revived several times and taken on tour, it was seen briefly in London and eventually filmed. After this the company's fortunes declined and the lack of a permanent theatre led to its demise in the early 1950s.

University Departments of Drama. The first attempt to present theatre history and practice as an academic study leading to a university degree was made in the United States, where George Pierce Baker (q.v.), the first Professor of Drama at Harvard, became in 1925 the head of a post-graduate Department of Drama at Yale. Since then the number of colleges and universities which offer major or subsidiary courses in drama, including practical theatre work, has risen to over 600. Many universities also have their own theatres, a typical early one being the Playhouse, Cleveland, Ohio (1927), designed by Philip Lindsley Small under the influence of the Central European idea of a theatre centre. An early example of theatre-in-the-round (q.v.) was provided by the Penthouse Theatre, built by Glenn Hughes in 1940 for the School of Drama at the University of Washington, Seattle. Some of the university theatres function also as civic theatres, serving the surrounding districts as well as the student body, often under a professional director. In some cases professional actors have been engaged to play in a university theatre, in addition to student groups, or the university authorities have collaborated closely in the building and running of community theatres, as at the University of Minnesota, where a theatre named after Tyrone Guthrie (q.v.) opened in 1963.

In England the gradual acceptance of the theatre as a subject for academic study resulted in the establishment in 1946–7 of the first Department of Drama at Bristol University. Since then similar departments have been established at Manchester, Hull, Birmingham, and Glasgow. Most universities now have a theatre open to the public. The Nuffield, in Southampton, opened in 1964, and the Northcott, in Exeter, in 1967. The latter has a professional company and is partly a civic theatre, serving also a wide area in the south-west with touring companies

and children's theatre. The open-stage Gulbenkian Theatre at Canterbury, for the University of Kent, opened in 1968. Like the theatre attached to University College, London, which opened in the same year, this is intended mainly for students but can be leased to other amateur or professional bodies. The Gardner Centre in Brighton, for the University of Sussex, opened in 1969, and 1970 saw the opening in Cardiff of the Sherman Theatre for the University of Wales, and a theatre complex for the University of Newcastle-upon-Tyne. Edinburgh and Glasgow universities each have their own theatre, and the University of Warwick has a Workshop theatre which opened in 1970. Other universities which are planning to open theatres are Dundee, Stirling, and Ulster (at Coleraine).

Many Continental universities include some form of drama and theatre history in their syllabuses. Early in its career the International Federation for Theatre Research (q.v.) urged the founding of Chairs of Drama in all universities, with the result that these are now to be found in the universities of Amsterdam, Utrecht, Munich, Marburg, Prague, and Tokyo. It is hoped that other universities may follow suit, and especially that the first Chair of Drama will soon be established in Great Britain.

University Wits, a name given to a group of somewhat dissolute Elizabethan playwrights educated at Oxford or Cambridge and therefore contemptuous of such 'uneducated' writers as Shakespeare and Ben Jonson (qq.v.). Among them were Marlowe, Greene, Nashe, and Peele (qq.v.), the most important in the development of the English theatre being Marlowe. A lesser member of the group was THOMAS LODGE (c. 1557/8–1625), on whose pastoral romance *Rosalind* (1590) Shakespeare based his *As You Like It*.

UNRUH, FRITZ VON (1885–   ), see EXPRESSIONISM.

Up Stage, the acting area furthest from the audience (see STAGE DIRECTIONS).

URBAN, JOSEPH (1872–1933), architect and stage designer, born in Vienna, where he worked for many years before going to Boston in 1911 to design sets for the opera there. He was also in New York, where he designed settings for the *Zieg-*

feld Follies, the Metropolitan opera, and the Shakespeare productions of James H. Hackett (q.v.). He built the Ziegfeld Theatre (q.v.) in New York, with its egg-shaped interior, and introduced much of the new Continental stagecraft to American theatre audiences, making use of broad masses of colour and novel lighting effects in costume and scenery.

USTINOV, PETER ALEXANDER (1921–), English actor, dramatist, and producer, who through his mother Nadia is the grand-nephew of Alexandre Benois (q.v.). Trained under Saint-Denis (q.v.) at the London Theatre Studio, he made his first appearance in London in Aug. 1939 at the Players' Late Joys, in his own sketches, and was memorable as the ageing opera-singer, Madame Liselotte Beethoven-Finck. After some miscellaneous experiences in repertory, revue, and straight plays, in and around London, during which time his first play, a translation of Sarment's *Le Pêcheur d'ombres* as *Fishing for Shadows* (1940), was produced at the Threshold Theatre, he joined the army. He returned to the stage in June 1946 to play Petrovitch in Rodney Ackland's adaptation of Dostoievsky's *Crime and Punishment*. In 1948 he appeared in his own adaptation of Ingmar Bergman's *Hets* (*Frenzy*), and in the following year produced and acted in Linklater's *Love in Albania*. Since then he has appeared mainly in his own plays, which include *House of Regrets* (1942), *Blow Your Own Trumpet* (1943), *The Banbury Nose* (1944), *The Tragedy of Good Intentions* (1945), *The Indifferent Shepherd* (1948), *The Moment of Truth* (1951), *No Sign of the Dove* (1953), *Halfway up the Tree* (1967), and *The Unknown Soldier and His Wife* (Chichester, 1968). His first popular success in London was *The Love of Four Colonels* (1951), followed by the equally successful *Romanoff and Juliet* (1956), in both of which he gave excellent performances. In 1962 he achieved a further success with his portrayal of the eighty-year-old hero of his *Photo Finish*, which was translated into German and Dutch, and played simultaneously in four cities.

Utility, see STOCK COMPANY.

V

Vadstena, a small town in Sweden which has, in the middle of a row of early nineteenth-century houses, a small private theatre. This was built in 1826, and the last professional production was given there in 1878. Its architect and original owner are unknown. The theatre is still in working order, and is occasionally used for amateur performances.

Vakhtangov Theatre, MOSCOW, founded by and named after the Soviet actor and director EUGENE V. VAKHTANGOV (1883–1922). In 1914, while in charge of the Third Studio attached to the Moscow Art Theatre (q.v.), he directed a fine production of *Macbeth* in which he played the title-role, and six years later converted the Studio into an independent theatre. In the year of his death he directed Ansky's *The Dybbuk* for Habimah (q.v.), but the culminating point of his career was his revival of Gozzi's *Turandot* (also 1922), which he did not live to see. It remained in the repertory of his theatre, exactly as he had conceived it, for many years afterwards. Under the inspiration of his short but brilliant career, the Vakhtangov Theatre continued to do excellent work, giving the first performances of several plays by Pogodin (q.v.). In 1932 an unorthodox production of *Hamlet* by Akimov, with music by Shostakovich, roused a storm of protest. This helped to focus attention on the company, which numbered among its actors Okhlopkov and Shchukin (qq.v.). The latter made a great impression as Lenin in Pogodin's *The Man With the Gun* (1937). After the Second World War the Vakhtangov produced a number of new Soviet plays, including *City at Dawn* (1957) and *Midnight* (1960), both by Arbuzov (q.v.).

VALLERAN-LECOMTE (*fl.* 1590–c. 1613), early French actor-manager, first heard of in Bordeaux in 1592. Shortly afterwards he had his own company, with Marie Venier (q.v.) as his leading lady and Alexandre Hardy (q.v.) as his official dramatist, and early in the 1600s he established himself in Paris, at the theatre in the Hôtel de Bourgogne (q.v.), with his predecessor Agnan Sarat as his chief comedian. He remained there until

Sarat died in 1613, and retired or died himself shortly afterwards. Little is known of his acting, though he apparently appeared in serious plays as well as in the popular farces of the time.

Vamp Trap, see TRAP.

VAN CAMPEN, JACOB, see CAMPEN, JACOB VAN.

VAN DRUTEN, JOHN (1901–57), dramatist, of Dutch extraction, born in London, but later an American citizen. He first came into prominence with *Young Woodley,* a slight but charming study of adolescence which was produced in New York in 1925. Unaccountably banned by the censor in England, it was first produced privately by the Three Hundred Club (see STAGE SOCIETY) in 1928, and when the ban was removed had a successful run at the Savoy later that year. Van Druten's later plays, which are mainly light comedies, include *After All* (1929; New York 1931), a study of family relationships; *London Wall,* a comedy of office life, and *There's Always Juliet* (both 1931, the latter seen in New York in 1932); *The Distaff Side* (1933; New York, 1934), in which Sybil Thorndike (q.v.) gave a moving performance as the mother; and *Old Acquaintance* (1940; New York, 1941), a study of two women writers which was successful on both sides of the Atlantic. *The Voice of the Turtle* (1943), a war-time comedy which had a long run in New York, was coldly received in London in 1947, but Van Druten achieved a success in both capitals with *Bell, Book and Candle* (New York, 1950; London, 1954), an amusing comedy on witchcraft. In 1938 he published a volume of reminiscences, *The Way to the Present.* His adaptation of stories by Isherwood as *I am a Camera* (New York, 1951; London, 1954) was later used as the basis of a musical entitled *Cabaret* (New York, 1966; London, 1968).

VANBRUGH [really BARNES], DAME IRENE (1872–1949), younger sister of Violet Vanbrugh and wife of the younger Dion Boucicault (qq.v.). She made her first appearance on the London stage in

1888, playing the White Queen in a musical version of Lewis Carroll's *Alice in Wonderland*. At the St. James's Theatre in 1893 she played Ellean in Pinero's *The Second Mrs. Tanqueray* and in 1895 Gwendolen Fairfax in Wilde's *The Importance of Being Earnest*. She then went to the old Globe (q.v.), where she scored her first outstanding success as Sophie Fullgarney in Pinero's *The Gay Lord Quex* (1899). She became the leading interpreter of Pinero's heroines, her playing of the title-role in *Letty* in 1903 and of Nina Jesson in *His House in Order* in 1906 being memorable. She was also admirable in Barrie's plays, particularly in *The Admirable Crichton* (1902), *Alice Sit-By-The-Fire* (1905), and *Rosalind* (1912). Among her other successes were Rose in Pinero's *Trelawny of the 'Wells'* (1898) and Norah Marsh in Somerset Maugham's *The Land of Promise* (1914). In 1907 she played in the first public performance of Shaw's *The Man of Destiny*, her husband playing opposite her as Napoleon, and at Malvern in 1939 she played Queen Catherine of Braganza in *In Good King Charles's Golden Days*, also by Shaw. She celebrated her golden jubilee in 1938 with a matinée at His Majesty's Theatre, and in 1941 was created D.B.E. for services to the theatre.

VANBRUGH, SIR JOHN (1664–1726), English dramatist and architect, in which latter capacity he was responsible for the design of the first Queen's Theatre on the site of the present Her Majesty's (q.v.). This was built to house a company led by Betterton (q.v.), who appeared there in Vanbrugh's own play, *The Confederacy* (1705), based on Dancourt's *Les Bourgeoises à la mode* (1692) and often billed as *The City Wives' Confederacy*. But Vanbrugh's best plays are undoubtedly *The Relapse; or, Virtue in Danger* (1696), a sequel to and parody of *Love's Last Shift* (also 1696), by Cibber (q.v.), and *The Provoked Wife* (1697). His last play, originally called *A Journey to London*, was left unfinished at his death. It was completed and produced by Cibber in 1728 as *The Provoked Husband. The Relapse* was later rewritten for a more prudish stage by Sheridan (q.v.) as *A Trip to Scarborough* (1777), but in its original form it had a long run in London in 1947–8, and was also revived by the Royal Shakespeare Company at the Aldwych in 1967.

VANBRUGH [really BARNES], VIOLET AUGUSTA MARY (1867–1942), English actress, sister of Irene Vanbrugh and wife of Arthur Bourchier (qq.v.). She made her first appearance in London in 1886, playing in burlesque at Toole's Theatre (q.v.), and after further experience at Margate and with the Kendals was engaged in 1892 by Irving (q.v.) for the Lyceum. After her marriage in 1894 she appeared mainly in her husband's productions, both in London and on tour, but in 1910–11 joined Tree (q.v.) to give outstanding performances as Queen Katharine in *Henry VIII*—probably her finest part—and as Lady Macbeth. Among her later successful appearances was Mrs. Vexted in Robins Millar's *Thunder in the Air* (1928). She celebrated her golden jubilee in 1937, shortly after appearing as Mistress Ford in *The Merry Wives of Windsor* at the Ring, Blackfriars (q.v.), and in the Open Air Theatre, Regent's Park.

The Vanbrugh Theatre at the Royal Academy of Dramatic Art, used mainly for student shows before invited audiences, was named in honour of Violet and Irene by their brother, SIR KENNETH RALPH BARNES (1878–1957), for many years director of that institution.

VANCE, THE GREAT [really ALFRED PECK STEVENS] (1840–88), a music-hall 'lion comique', best known for his comic songs in the style of Sam Cowell (q.v.), of which the most popular was 'The Chickaleery Cove'. Inspired by the success of his friend and rival Leybourne (q.v.) with 'Champagne Charlie', he countered with the praises of Veuve Clicquot, and between them they went through the whole wine-list. Vance was also a fine singer of moral 'motto' songs, such as 'Act on the Square, Boys'. He died while appearing on Boxing Day at the Sun, Knightsbridge.

VANDENHOFF, GEORGE CHARLES (1813–85), American actor, son of the English actor JOHN VANDENHOFF (1790–1861). Born in England, George appeared first at Covent Garden in 1839, where he played Mercutio in a production of *Romeo and Juliet* with Mme Vestris (q.v.), but in 1842 he went to New York to play Hamlet at the Park Theatre (q.v.) and decided to remain in the United States. He was at one time leading man at the Chestnut Street Theatre, Philadelphia, and later at Palmo's Opera House, and also gave poetry readings and taught elocution. In 1845 he directed a production of Sophocles' *Antigone*, with music by Mendelssohn, on a stage approximating to the contemporary idea of a Greek theatre. He returned to London in 1853 and was seen as Hamlet, but had little liking for his profession and retired in 1856. He was then called to the bar, but continued to give poetry readings, and in 1860 published his reminiscences as *Leaves from an Actor's Notebook*. A tall, scholarly man of good sense and good breeding, but somewhat aloof, he made his final appearances on the stage with Geneviève Ward (q.v.) in 1878, playing Wolsey in *Henry VIII* and Gloster in Wills's *Jane Shore*. His sister, CHARLOTTE ELIZABETH [Mrs. SWINBOURNE] (1818–60), was on the London stage, and was much admired in parts requiring delicacy and pathos. She created the roles of Lydia in Sheridan Knowles's *The Love Chase* (1837) and Parthenia in Mrs. Lovell's *Ingomar* (1851).

Vanderbilt Theatre, NEW YORK, a modest but handsome playhouse on 48th Street between 6th and 7th Avenues. It opened on 7 Mar. 1918, and in 1921 had a success with the first production of O'Neill's *Anna Christie*. Later productions were less successful, except for Owen Davis's *Lazybones* (1924), with George Abbott, and Hughes's *Mulatto* (1935). The last play of any importance at this theatre, which in 1939 was taken over for broadcasting, was an all-star revival of Wilde's *The Importance of Being Earnest*. The building was demolished in 1954.

VANHOVE, CAROLINE (1771–1860), see TALMA, F.-J.

Variety, the name given in the 1880s to the entertainments offered in the newly-built Theatres of Variety which replaced the original music-halls attached to public-houses. The separate tables were abolished, and the long unbroken succession of single turns gave place to the twice-nightly bill, first organized by Maurice de Frece at the Alhambra in Liverpool, with the addition of ballet, spectacle, and short dramatic sketches. Much of the free-and-easy boisterous atmosphere of the early halls disappeared at the same time, but the old name stuck and the history of variety will be found under MUSIC-HALL (for England) and VAUDEVILLE (for the United States).

Vaudeville, a French word, possibly a corruption of Vau (or Val) de Vire, meaning 'songs from the Valley of Vire' (in Normandy), or of '*voix des villes*', songs of the city streets. It is found in its present form as early as 1674, meaning a satiric or political popular ballad. It acquired its secondary meaning of a light, satiric musical play by way of the Paris fairs, where in the unlicensed theatres *pièces en vaudevilles*, or plays in dumb-show with interpolated choruses to popular tunes, parodied the productions of the Comédie-Française. They became the staple fair of the Opéra-Comique (q.v.) on its foundation, and correspond roughly to the English ballad-opera (q.v.) or German *Singspiel*. They were written by many well-known authors, including Le Sage and Favart (qq.v.), and their popularity paved the way for the immense vogue of light opera in Paris in the nineteenth century, with libretti written by such men as Scribe (q.v.) and his numerous collaborators. When the fashion changed, the word was adopted by the new variety theatres, and with that meaning was used in the United States for the respectable family entertainment which in the 1880s, under Tony Pastor, Edward Albee (qq.v.), BENJAMIN FRANKLIN KEITH (1846–1914), and FREDERICK FRANCIS PROCTOR (1851–1929), developed out of the former variety shows of the early beer-halls, based on the English music-hall (q.v.). These variety shows had sunk to a low level of vulgarity and drunkenness, and the change was welcomed by the performers, who enjoyed working in spacious theatres provided by the new managers, while more responsive audiences encouraged the provision of better material. A new technique, employed in short comic or dramatic sketches, and many novelty acts, resulted from the improved conditions. This in turn led to the system of 'name' billing, which, though it resulted in the incongruous appearance of such actresses as Bernhardt, Lily Langtry, or Mrs. Patrick Campbell (qq.v.) on vaudeville programmes, spurred the true vaudeville artists to create new acts and new styles. Although there were many outstanding teams, like Weber and Fields (q.v.), the single artist predominated as the headliner during the halcyon period from the mid-1890s to 1925, when the popularity of films, and of the talkies which followed, led to the decline of vaudeville. The end of an era came with the closing in 1932 of Broadway's Palace Theatre as a 'two-a-day'.

Vaudeville, THÉÂTRE DU, PARIS. This was opened on 2 Jan. 1792 by the actors who were forced to leave the Comédie-Italienne when its licence was renewed for musical plays only. The company was headed by Rozières, and was frequently in trouble for the topical and political allusions found in its productions by the vigilance of the censor. It eventually fell back on the safety of semi-historical pieces, based on anecdotes of heroic figures, and in 1838 was burnt down. The company moved to the Théâtres des Nouveautés, where plays by Dumas *fils* and others were given with some success, but the theatre fell on bad times and was frequently closed. In 1868 the present building was opened under the old name, and has since had a steady, though somewhat uneventful, career.

Vaudeville Theatre, LONDON, in the Strand, built for three actor-managers, H. J. Montague, David James (qq.v.), and Thomas Thorne. It opened on 16 Apr. 1870 with Andrew Halliday's *For Love or Money*, and had its first success shortly afterwards with Albery's *Two Roses*, which introduced to London a young actor named Henry Irving (q.v.). The next outstanding success was a comedy, *Our Boys* (1875), by H. J. Byron, which ran for four years. After a further period of success with straight plays, the theatre was devoted to farces, of which one, *Confusion* (1883), by Joseph Derrick, ran for a year. Among later successes were Henry Arthur Jones's *Saints and Sinners* (1884) and a series of productions starring Cyril Maude (q.v.). In 1890 the building was closed for reconstruction, a new frontage, which still stands, being added. On 13 Jan. 1891 the theatre re-opened and later in the same year came the first performances in England of Ibsen's *Rosmersholm* (23 Feb.) and *Hedda Gabler* (20 Apr.), with Elizabeth Robins (q.v.) as Rebecca West and Hedda. From 1900 to 1906 Seymour Hicks and his wife Ellaline Terriss (qq.v.) appeared in a series of long runs under the management of Charles Frohman. Among their productions were *Bluebell in Fairyland* (1901), a Christmas entertainment which was revived in 1905 for the opening of the Aldwych (q.v.) and many times thereafter; Barrie's *Quality Street* (1902); and several musical come-dies, including *The Belle of Mayfair* (1906). In 1915 the theatre became the home of Charlot's revues, which continued until 1925, when the building was closed for reconstruction. It reopened on 23 Feb. 1926, again with revue, which continued with great success until 1937. After this the theatre went through a difficult phase, but in 1938 Robert Morley's *Goodness, How Sad!* was a success, as were Esther McCracken's *No Medals* (1944), William Douglas Home's *The Chiltern Hundreds* (1947), and the record-breaking *Salad Days* (1954), by Dorothy Reynolds and Julian Slade, which ran till 1960. Later in that year Ronald Millar's *The Bride Comes Back* was a success, and in 1968 Joyce Rayburn's *The Man Most Likely To . . .*, though unfavourably received by some critics, started a long run. In 1970 the theatre was bought by the impresario Peter Saunders from the Gatti family, who had owned it since 1892. After reconstruction and redecoration it opened with a revival of Maugham's *Lady Frederick* on 24 June, followed by William Douglas Home's new comedy, *The Jockey Club Stakes*, on 30 Sept.

VAUGHAN, HENRY (?–1779), see PRITCH-ARD, MRS.

VAUGHAN, KATE [really CATHERINE CANDELIN] (c. 1852–1903), English actress, who made her début in the music-halls in 1870 and also appeared in burlesque with her sister SUSIE VAUGHAN [really SUSAN MARY CHARLOTTE CANDELIN] (1853–1950). In 1876 Kate became a member of the famous quartet at the Gaiety (q.v.), where in 1883 she scored a success as Peggy in a revival of Garrick's *The Country Girl* (1766), based on Wycherley's *The Country Wife* (1673). This led to her appearance in a season of standard comedy at the Opera Comique in 1887, when she appeared under her own management as Lydia Languish and Lady Teazle in Sheridan's *The Rivals* and *The School for Scandal*, Kate Hardcastle in Goldsmith's *She Stoops to Conquer*, and Peg Woffington in Reade and Taylor's *Masks and Faces*, in which she later toured the provinces with H. B. Conway.

Vauxhall, a place of entertainment on the south bank of the Thames in London, originally known as Spring Gardens, Fox-hall, which opened in 1660. During the eighteenth century it was used for concerts, glee-singing, fireworks, and occasional spectacular dramatic shows. It figures in many memoirs of the period, and in Fanny Burney's novel, *Evelina* (1779). In the early nineteenth century it was known as the Royal Gardens, Vauxhall, and some of Bishop's operettas were staged there. In 1849 it was lit by gas-lamps. It was described by Dickens, and was often in trouble owing to rioting and disorders, which finally led to its being closed on 25 July 1859, the site being built over, though the name persists.

There was a Vauxhall in New York in the early part of the nineteenth century which had a small open-air theatre for summer shows. This was burnt down in 1808, but the gardens long remained a favourite resort, and several seasons of plays were given there in the 1840s. There was also one in Moscow (see MEDDOKS).

VEDRENNE, JOHN EUGENE (1867–1930), English theatre manager, best remembered for his seasons at the Royal Court Theatre from 1904 to 1907, and at the Savoy later in 1907, in association with Harley Granville-Barker (q.v.). Together they presented a number of outstanding plays, including some of Shaw's (q.v.) for the first time. Vedrenne, who was originally in commerce, became a concert agent and business manager for several theatres, and was associated with such stars as Frank Benson, Johnston Forbes-Robertson, and Lewis Waller.

VEGA CARPIO, LOPE FELIX DE (1562–1635), famous Spanish playwright, and the most prolific dramatist of all time; he himself claimed to have written 1,500 plays, though the actual number of extant texts is from 400 to 500, mostly written in neat, ingenious, and superbly lyrical verse. His first plays date from the period of the early open-air theatres of Madrid. When he began to write, the professional theatre in Spain was in its infancy, and he can rightly be considered the consolidator, if not the founder, of the commercial theatre in Spain. He played a large part in the development of the Spanish *comedia*, and the formula which he evolved for its construction in the last decade of the sixteenth century remained largely unchanged for a hundred years. His *Arte nuevo de hacer comedias* (c. 1609) is an interesting, if ironical, exposition of his views on the art of the

dramatist, written with one eye on classical precedent but based securely on practical experience. Critics have endeavoured to cope with Lope's enormous output by dividing his plays into various categories, but it is really more important to stress the unity of his dramatic production. His world is that of a Spanish Catholic of his day—he took orders in 1614. Society is viewed in an idealized light, and its multiple social distinctions are reduced to three: king, nobles, and commoners, the last usually peasants. The king, or his accredited agent, is God's vice-regent, dispensing God's justice and maintaining the natural harmony intended by the Creator. Human behaviour is governed by three things: the four 'humours' so prominent in Elizabethan drama; the systematic conceptions of Catholic moral theology (basically Thomist); and a highly stylized code of honour. It is against this background that such plays as *Peribáñez y el Comendador de Ocaña* (c. 1608), *Fuenteovejuna* (c. 1612), and *El mejor alcalde el rey* (c. 1620) should be considered. *Fuenteovejuna* deals with the rising of a village against its brutal lord; shorn of its sub-plot—the rising of that same lord against his king—the play has been interpreted in terms of the class struggle. The two plots are, however, interdependent, and both are essential to the true understanding of the play. Here and elsewhere Lope reveals himself clearly as conservative rather than revolutionary: the brutal overlord is removed because he disrupts the harmony of society, failing in his duties to the king above him as well as to the commoners beneath him. It is for this reason that he must be removed, and not merely because of his tyrannous repression of the villagers of Fuenteovejuna. This and other historical dramas of Lope have suffered from an attempt to interpret them according to the ideas of a later communist age. The plays dealing with the stylized code of honour have suffered in a similar way. Lope's handling of this theme is diverse. In the early play, *Los comendadores de Córdoba*, the outraged husband, discovering that he is openly and publicly dishonoured, takes open, public, and bloody revenge. In the mature *El castigo sin venganza*, the duke secures his public position but revenges himself privately upon the bastard son and adulterous wife who have caused the loss of his honour. His public reputation is saved, since his revenge is secret, and with it the honour of the state, but this secret revenge entails the killing of the only two persons he has loved. The subtlety of the play consists in Lope's demonstration that this state of affairs is the direct consequence of the duke's own licentiousness. The theme of honour is more than a barbaric convention.

Lope also wrote for the entertainment of the Court, usually plays with a mythological or pastoral plot which made use of the most up-to-date machinery and scenic effects. *La selva sin amor* (1629) is a particularly interesting work, being partly set to music and thus a forerunner of the later *zarzuela* (q.v.). Equally spectacular were his *autos sacramentales* (q.v.) played on three carts, the centre being the main playing-space, and the outer carts bearing complicated machinery. They have not the lyrical beauty or the subtle symbolism of those by Calderón (q.v.), but they present their theme simply, forcibly, and dramatically, and show an excellent grasp of technique.

VELTEN, JOHANNES (1640–92), German actor, who by 1669 had been a member of Carl Andreas Paulsen's troupe for some years, touring in the usual repertory, to which he added translations of some of Molière's plays and, in 1686, *Der bestrafte Brüdermord*, a version of *Hamlet* as played by the English Comedians (q.v.). In 1678, having married the daughter of an actor, he took over the company himself and managed it until his death, when it was carried on by his widow. Under different names, and with many fluctuations of fortune, this company held together until in 1771, after passing through the hands of Carolina Neuber, Schönemann, Koch, and Ackermann, it came under the leadership of Schröder (q.v.).

Venice Theatre, NEW YORK, see CENTURY THEATRE (2).

VENIER [also found as VERNIER], MARIE (*fl.* 1590–1619), the first French actress to be known by name. She was the daughter of Pierre Venier, a provincial actor-manager who was in Paris in 1600, at which time Marie, with her actor-husband LAPORTE [really MATHIEU LE FEBVRE, *fl.* 1584–*c*. 1621], was at the Hôtel de Bourgogne with Valleran-Lecomte (q.v.), with whom she had probably acted in the provinces. According

to contemporary accounts, she was a beautiful and accomplished actress, at her best in tragedy queens.

VENNE, LOTTIE (1852–1928), English actress, best known for her work in burlesque at the Strand Theatre (q.v.), where she played from 1874 to 1878. She then turned to straight comedy, though she continued intermittently to appear in musical comedy and farce. She was an excellent mimic, and in 1892 her imitations of Marion Terry, who was appearing as Mrs. Erlynne in Wilde's *Lady Windermere's Fan*, and of Lady Tree as Ophelia in the current production of *Hamlet* at Her Majesty's, ensured the success of Brookfield's burlesque, *The Poet and the Puppets*. A fine-looking woman, high-spirited and good-humoured, she was sensible enough in her later years to play elderly roles in comedy, thus retaining the affection of her public and the respect of the critics.

VERBRUGGEN, MRS. J. B. (1667–1703), see MOUNTFORT, WILLIAM.

Vere Street Theatre, LONDON, originally a tennis court built in 1634 and belonging to, or named after, a man called Gibbon; it stood in Clare Market. The out-of-work actors played there surreptitiously after the closing of the theatres, but were betrayed by someone whom a contemporary calls 'an ill Beest . . . causing the poor actors to be routed by the soldiery' (see BEESTON, WILLIAM). In 1656 Davenant gave there one of his entertainments with music and dancing. In 1660 Killigrew (q.v.) converted it into a theatre, opening with *Henry IV, Part 1* on 8 Nov., and used it while he got ready to build his new theatre (see DRURY LANE), to which he moved in 1663. Vere Street, under George Jolly, was then used as a Nursery, or training-school for young actors, by both Killigrew and his rival Davenant (q.v.) until 1671. From 1675 to 1682 it was a Nonconformist meeting-house. It was finally destroyed by fire in 1809 (see also STOLL THEATRE).

VERGA, GIOVANNI (1840–1922), Italian novelist, playwright, and short-story writer, a *verista*, or realist, whose portraits of Sicilian peasants have been compared to those of Thomas Hardy's Tess or Jude. His most successful play was his own dramatization of his short story *Cavalleria rusticana* (1884), which provided the libretto for the opera by Mascagni produced in 1890. But several others enjoyed a modified success, among them *La lupa* (1896), a study of female sexuality which was seen in London during the 1969 World Theatre season, and *La caccia al lupo* (1901), a tragedy of jealousy. The introduction to a volume of Verga's plays published in 1952 also points out the excellence of *In portineria* (1885), one of the few works set outside Sicily, and *Dal tuo al mio* (1903), a terse and evocative analysis of the clash between two classes of society. In recent years critics have become more aware of Verga's achievements in drama and of his importance as a precursor of Pirandello (q.v.).

Versailles. Although there was a good deal of theatrical entertainment at Versailles under Louis XIV (see MOLIÈRE), there was no permanent theatre there, and plays were given on temporary stages erected indoors or in the gardens. It was not until 1768 that Louis XV instructed his chief architect, ANGE-JACQUES GABRIEL (1698–1782), to build a theatre in the north wing of the château. Oval in design, and not rectangular, as earlier French theatres were, it was built of wood, much of it painted to resemble marble. The stage, almost as large as that of the Paris Opéra, was well supplied with machinery, and the floor of the auditorium could be raised to stage level to form a large room for balls and banquets. Lighting was provided by crystal chandeliers. The theatre was first used on 16 May 1770 for a banquet in honour of the marriage of the future Louis XVI to Marie-Antoinette. The first plays to be given there were Racine's *Athalie* on 23 May, with Mlle Clairon (q.v.) in the title-role, and on 20 June Voltaire's *Tancrède*. During the Revolution the theatre served as the meeting place of the Versailles branch of the Jacobins. When in 1837 Louis-Philippe made Versailles a museum of French military history, the opening ceremony was followed on 10 June by a gala performance of Molière's *Le Misanthrope*. The theatre was then used occasionally for concerts and on 18 Aug. 1855 for a banquet in honour of Queen Victoria. In 1871 it was taken over by the Assembly, who met there during the Commune. A floor was laid over the pit, and everything above it was painted

brown. This fortunately preserved the decorations below, and when in 1952 restoration began on the château, the theatre too was restored to its original colours of dark blue, pale blue, and gold. It was even found possible to replace the original material on the seats, made by the firm which had supplied it in 1768. The restoration was completed in time for an official visit by Queen Elizabeth II of England on 9 Apr. 1957, when a theatrical and musical entertainment was given. The theatre is still occasionally used for concerts, operas, and plays.

Verulamium. The Roman theatre in this second-century city (now St. Albans) was for a long time the only one known in Britain (traces of others have now been found at Canterbury and near Colchester). It was probably built between A.D. 140 and 150 and used mainly for sport, particularly cock-fighting. The orchestra, which was completely circular, with seating round two-thirds of it and a small stage-building in the remaining space, could have been used for mimes and dancing, and the stage for small-scale entertainments. In A.D. 200 the stage was enlarged, possibly to allow for the positioning of a slot for a curtain, and at the end of the third century, after a period of disuse, the theatre was rebuilt with modifications. The auditorium was extended over part of the orchestra, the floor levels were raised, and a triumphal arch was built spanning Watling Street. The building was finally abandoned at the end of the fourth century and the site used as a municipal rubbish-dump. It was rediscovered in 1847 and scientifically excavated in 1934 by Dr. Kathleen Kenyon.

VESTRIS [*née* GOURGAUD], FRANÇOISE (1743–1804), French actress, wife of the Italian ballet-dancer Angelo Vestris who settled in Paris in 1747. With her brother and sister (see DUGAZON) she was a member of the Comédie-Française, where she was the pupil of Lekain (q.v.), making her début in 1768. She created a number of tragic heroines, including the title-roles in Belloy's *Gabrielle de Vergi* (1772), Voltaire's *Irène* (1778), and Catherine de Médicis in Marie-Joseph Chénier's *Charles IX* (1789). She much admired Chénier (q.v.), and managed to secrete a copy of his *Timoléon* when he had been ordered by the censor to destroy it.

VESTRIS, MME [*née* LUCIA ELIZABETTA (or LUCY ELIZABETH) BARTOLOZZI] (1797–1856), English actress, the wife of the French ballet-dancer Armand Vestris (1788–1825), who deserted her in 1820. As Mme. Vestris, she had a distinguished career on the London stage. Although an excellent singer, she preferred to appear in light entertainment rather than grand opera, and was at her best in burlesque, or in the fashionable ladies of high comedy. She made her first success in the title-role of Moncrieff's *Giovanni in London* (1817), a burlesque of Mozart's 'Don Giovanni', and then played in Paris for several years with such success that she was able to return to London on her own terms, playing alternately at Covent Garden and Drury Lane. In 1830 she took over the Olympic Theatre (q.v.), opening with *Olympic Revels*, by Planché, who furnished her with a succession of farces and burlesques both at this theatre and later at the Lyceum (q.v.). During her tenancy of the Olympic she took into her company the younger Charles Mathews (q.v.), marrying him in 1838, and the rest of her career ran parallel to his. She was an excellent manageress, ruling her company well and effecting a number of reforms in theatre management. She also made many improvements in theatrical scenery and effects and had good taste in costume, being one of the first to use historically correct details, thus anticipating Charles Kean and the Bancrofts (qq.v.). She was responsible for the introduction of real, as opposed to fake, properties and in Nov. 1832 introduced the box-set (q.v.), complete with ceiling, on to the London stage.

VEZIN, HERMANN (1829–1910), English actor, born in the U.S.A., who came to England in 1850 and, after working for some time in the provinces, took over the Surrey Theatre (q.v.), appearing there in a fine series of classic parts. Phelps (q.v.) then engaged him for Sadler's Wells, and by 1861 he was recognized as an outstanding actor in both comedy and tragedy, being excellent as Macbeth and Othello, as Jaques in *As You Like It*, and as Sir Peter Teazle in Sheridan's *The School for Scandal*. He was also much admired as Dr. Primrose in *Olivia*, Wills's adaptation of Goldsmith's *The Vicar of Wakefield*, which he played on its first production, with Ellen Terry (q.v.) as Olivia, at the Royal Court in 1878. He

appeared as Iago to the Othello of John McCullough, and was with Irving at the Lyceum, making his last appearance under Tree on 7 Apr. 1909. A scholarly, intellectual man, of small stature, with clear-cut features, a dignified bearing, and a very lovely voice, he lacked only warmth and personal magnetism. His wife, an Australian actress, JANE ELIZABETH THOMSON (1827–1902), formerly the wife of an American actor, CHARLES YOUNG (?–1874), made her first appearance in London in 1857 and for twenty years had few rivals in Shakespeare and poetic drama.

VIAN, BORIS (1920–59), French novelist and dramatist, a disciple of Jarry (q.v.) and his theory of pataphysics. Vian's most important play is *Les Bâtisseurs d'Empire; ou, le Schmürz* (1959), a supreme example of the Theatre of the Absurd (q.v.) which in 1962 was seen in London as *The Empire Builders*. His other plays, *L'Équarrissage pour tous* (1950) and *Le Goûter des généraux*, produced posthumously in 1965 (and in London in 1967 as *The Generals' Tea-Party*), attack by implication, one in a knacker's yard, the other in a parody of a children's tea-party, the general futility of war.

VIAU, THÉOPHILE DE, see THÉOPHILE.

Vice, see COSTUME and FOOL.

VICENTE, GIL (*c.* 1465–*c.* 1537), Portuguese Court dramatist and deviser of entertainments, who may also have been a leading goldsmith of the time. Forty-four of his works survive, seventeen in Portuguese, eleven in Spanish (the language of several Portuguese queens), and sixteen using both languages, though all have Portuguese titles. His later works include a number of morality plays which had a great influence on the development of the Spanish *auto sacramental* (q.v.). The most important of them is the trilogy of the boats: *Barca do Inferno* (1517), *Barca do Purgatório* (1518), and *Barca do Glória* (1519). Of his indigenous farces, which combine knockabout humour with pungent social satire, the best is probably the *Farsa de Inês Pereira* (1523). Under the influence of Torres Naharro (q.v.), Vicente later turned to romantic comedy with the *Comédia Rubena* (1521), *Dom Duardos* (1522), and the *Comédia do Viúvo* (1524), but in the last twelve years of his life, as official

Court dramatist, he was mainly occupied with the devising of allegorical spectacles for the amusement of the Royal household, staged with great splendour and complexity and lavish expenditure on costumes and scenery.

Victoria Palace, LONDON, in Victoria Street, built on the site of Moy's Music-Hall, which opened in about 1840. In 1863 it was redecorated and reopened on 26 Dec. as the Royal Standard Music-Hall. Demolished during the rebuilding of Victoria Station and Victoria Street, it was rebuilt in 1886 and continued its successful career until 1911. It was then replaced by the present building, which opened as the Victoria Palace on 6 Nov. 1911. From 1921 to 1929 it housed an annual Christmas play, *The Windmill Man*, by Frederick Bowyer, with BERT COOTE (1868–1938) as the chief character, a mad gardener. Otherwise it continued to function as a music-hall and a home of revue until in 1934 it became a theatre with Reynolds's *Young England*, which, although meant to be a serious patriotic play, was treated with ridicule, and drew vast crowds who came to laugh, jeer, and interrupt the performance. In 1935 Seymour Hicks (q.v.) took over the Victoria Palace and produced there his own play *The Miracle Man*, following it with revivals of some of his former successes. In 1937 Lupino Lane (see LUPINO) succeeded him, and on 16 Dec. presented a musical play called *Me and My Girl* which had a long run up to the temporary closing of the theatres on the outbreak of the Second World War. It was later revived. From 1947 to 1962 the Victoria Palace was the home of the Crazy Gang (q.v.). Later it housed for many years a stage production of the B.B.C. television show, *The Black and White Minstrels*.

Victoria Theatre, LONDON, see OLD VIC; NEW YORK, see GAIETY THEATRE (3).

Vienna, as the capital of the former Austro-Hungarian empire, was for several hundred years an important theatrical centre. As early as 1497 university students were being encouraged by their humanist tutors to act plays by Terence and Plautus (q.v.) and indigenous farces which contained the germs of future developments in comedy. Under Protestant influence biblical subjects too became popular, but were soon overwhelmed by the classical splendour of Jesuit drama (q.v.), the first Jesuit production in Vienna being *Euripus sive de inanitate rerum omnium* (1555), by LEVINUS BRECHTANUS [really LEWIN BRECHT], a Franciscan from Antwerp. These Jesuit spectacles contributed not a little to the triumph in Vienna of opera and ballet from Italy, by which they were profoundly influenced and eventually eclipsed. Meanwhile the influence of the English Comedians (q.v.), who first appeared in the neighbourhood of Vienna in 1608, and the replacement of Latin by the vernacular, particularly in comedy, gave rise to the Haupt- und Staatsaktion (q.v.) with its heroic background and its all-pervading Hanswurst (q.v.), who, with his companions under Stranitzky (q.v.), occupied in 1711 the Kärntnertor, the first permanent theatre to be built in Vienna. Here Viennese popular comedy reigned supreme, moving to the Burgtheater in 1741 and remaining there until in 1776 Joseph II, continuing the cultural reforms initiated by his mother, the Empress Maria Theresa, made the Burgtheater a home of serious literary drama and banished the light-hearted comedies, enlivened by song and dance, to the remote suburbs. There, contrary to expectation, they flourished in the Leopoldstädter Theater, opened by Marinelli (q.v.) in 1781, the Josefstädter Theater, opened in 1788, and the Theater an der Wien, opened by Mozart's librettist Schikaneder (q.v.) in 1801. In these essentially Viennese theatres were developed two comic characters who typify this last phase of the old Viennese extempore farce—Kasperle and Thäddadl (qq.v.). Their brief but joyous reign gave way in the nineteenth century to a unique mixture of farce, fairytale magic, and parody, a *Volkskomödie* which culminated in the great, and practically untranslatable, plays of Raimund and Nestroy (qq.v.), and finally declined into the Viennese operetta which set out to conquer the world to the lilting rhythm of the waltz. Meanwhile the Burgtheater, having recovered from the solemn pronouncements of Joseph II, which for a time weighed heavily on its dramatists, found itself, under Schreyvogel (q.v.), staging the plays of Austria's greatest dramatist, Grillparzer (q.v.), as well as classical and romantic plays from all over Europe, which, acted by a resident company of actors drawn from every corner of the

German-speaking lands, soon made it one of the outstanding theatres of Europe, a position which, through all the fluctuations of taste and the material disasters of destruction by bombing and complete reconstruction afterwards, it still holds.

Vieux-Colombier, THÉÂTRE DU, PARIS, see COPEAU, JACQUES.

VIGARANI, GASPARE (1586–1663), Italian stage designer and machinist, inventor of many new stage effects. He was working in Modena when in 1659 he was called to Paris by Mazarin to supervise the entertainments to be given in honour of Louis XIV's approaching marriage. For these he built the Salle des Machines (q.v.) in the Tuileries, and designed its stage machinery. As the Petit Bourbon theatre was then being demolished, Vigarani claimed the scenery and machinery for use in his new theatre and burnt it all, probably in the hope of destroying the work of his rival Torelli (q.v.). After his death his son CARLO (?–c. 1693), who had been working with him, was responsible for the mechanics of Les Plaisirs de l'île enchantée (1664), an entertainment given at Versailles with the collaboration of Molière (q.v.) and Lully.

VIGNY, ALFRED VICTOR DE (1797–1863), French poet and novelist, whose interest in the theatre was first awakened by seeing an English company, headed by Charles Kemble and Harriet Smithson (qq.v.), in a season of Shakespeare plays in Paris in 1827. He then translated Romeo and Juliet, The Merchant of Venice (as Shylock), and Othello, but only the last one was performed (in 1829). Of his own plays La Maréchale d'Ancre (1831), an historical melodrama in the style of the elder Dumas (q.v.), was unsuccessful, but a one-act comedy, Quitte pour la peur (1833), was well received, mainly because of the fine acting of Marie Dorval (q.v.), for many years Vigny's mistress. She also appeared with great success in his romantic masterpiece, Chatterton (1835), playing Kitty Bell, which remained one of her finest interpretations.

VILAR, JEAN (1912–71), French actor and producer, who in 1951 was appointed head of the Théâtre National Populaire (q.v.), a position which he resigned in 1962 as a protest against the inadequate support given to it by the French government. He worked at the Atelier under Dullin (q.v.) for some years before the Second World War, and after serving in the army joined La Roulotte, a company of young touring actors. In 1943 he was seen in Paris in Synge's The Well of the Saints, and then took over the Théâtre de Poche, which seats only about a hundred persons. In 1945 he produced, first at the Vieux-Colombier and later in front of the Abbey of Bec-Hellouin, T. S. Eliot's Murder in the Cathedral, with himself as Becket. This aroused great interest, and in 1947 Vilar was asked to organize an open-air summer dramatic festival at Avignon (q.v.) which became an annual event. It was the success of this venture which led to his appointment to the T.N.P., where his productions aroused both enthusiasm and controversy. An excellent actor, as well as an inspired director, he appeared in many of his own productions, notably in the title-roles of Shakespeare's Macbeth and Richard II, Molière's Don Juan, Victor Hugo's Ruy Blas, and as the Gangster in Brecht's Arturo Ui. In 1951 he was seen as Heinrich in Sartre's Le Diable et le Bon Dieu, and played Sophocles' Oedipus with the company of Jean-Louis Barrault and Madeleine Renaud (qq.v.). A spare, ascetic-looking man, he could on stage appear amazingly handsome, and his voice had great sonority and emotional overtones. His view of the theatre as a great educational and spiritual force gave a certain gravity to all he did, and his influence on the French theatre was wholly good.

VILDRAC, CHARLES MESSAGER (1882–1971), French poet, novelist, and dramatist, whose most important play, Le Paquebot Tenacity, a study of two ex-soldiers, very dissimilar in character, waiting to emigrate to Canada, had a great success when first produced by Copeau (q.v.) at the Vieux-Colombier in 1920. As The S.S. Tenacity it was produced in London by the Stage Society at the Lyric Theatre, Hammersmith, in June 1920, and two years later was seen in New York.

Village Players, GREAT HUCKLOW, BUXTON, DERBYSHIRE, an amateur society founded in 1927 by L. du Garde Peach, who wrote and directed many of its subsequent productions. Unlike most societies it has no members and no subscriptions, the actors being chosen for a particular part and invited to play it by the director. Their names are not listed in the programme, nor are those of the devoted backstage staff. Having achieved and maintained over the years a consistently high standard in acting, direction, lighting, and costume, the theatre, in spite of its remote situation, draws its audience from far afield, even beyond the confines of its own county. In addition to plays by L. du Garde Peach and comedies specially written in the local dialect, the company, whose first production was *The Merchant of Venice*, now does two (formerly four) plays a year for three weeks each. In addition to Shakespeare, authors represented in the repertory include Sheridan, Ibsen, Shaw, Anouilh, O'Neill, Priestley, and Ustinov. At least two plays first staged at Great Hucklow—*Clive of India* (1934), by W. P. Lipscomb and R. J. Minney, and *The White Sheep of the Family* (1951), by L. du Garde Peach and Ian Hay—were subsequently produced in London. The early productions, for three nights each, were given in an adapted village hut, but in 1938 a derelict building was purchased and practically rebuilt by the players themselves as a small but well-equipped theatre.

VILLIERS, CLAUDE DESCHAMPS DE (1600–81), French actor, and author of several plays, including farces and a version of the story of Don Juan which may have influenced Molière (q.v.). He played in farce himself as Philippin, his name being often given to the character he was to portray. He was a member with Montdory of the company at the Théâtre du Marais (q.v.), where his second wife, MARGUERITE BÉGUET (?–1670), was the first to play the part of Chimène in Corneille's *Le Cid* (1636). When Montdory left the Marais in 1617, Villiers and his wife went to the Hôtel de Bourgogne (q.v.), she retiring in 1664 and he on her death six years later. Villiers is caricatured in Molière's *L'Impromptu de Versailles* (1664), together with the rest of the company at the Hôtel de Bourgogne.

VILLIERS, GEORGE, DUKE OF BUCKINGHAM, see BUCKINGHAM.

Vilna Troupe, a company founded in Vilna (Russia) in 1916 by DAVID HERMANN (1876–1930) as the Union of Yiddish Dramatic Artists (called Fado, from the initials of the original name) with the intention of continuing the reform of the Yiddish stage inaugurated by Peretz Hirschbein (q.v.). Hermann's first production was Sholom Asch's *Landsleute*, which was immediately successful, and in 1917 he moved the company to Warsaw, scoring a further success with his production, a month after the author's death, of Ansky's *The Dybbuk* in Yiddish. This was taken on tour to Berlin, London, and New York. In 1924 the company moved to Vienna, where it split up, one section going to America to join forces with Maurice Schwartz (q.v.), the other, after three years in Roumania, remaining in Warsaw until Hermann's death, after which it ceased to function. The repertory of the Vilna Troupe was at first fairly extensive and included a number of Yiddish classics, but later it became associated with and entirely dependent on *The Dybbuk*, which probably accounts for its decline.

VINCENT, MRS. J. R. [*née* MARY ANN FARLEY] (1818–87), American actress, born in England, where she joined a provincial company, married a fellow-actor, and went with him in 1846 to the National Theatre, Boston. He died shortly afterwards, but she continued to act, and in 1852 joined the company at the Boston Museum, where she remained for thirty-five years, first as leading comedienne, later playing duenna and old-lady parts. At her jubilee in 1885 she appeared in two of her finest roles, Mrs. Hardcastle in Goldsmith's *She Stoops to Conquer* and Mrs. Malaprop in Sheridan's *The Rivals*. The Vincent Memorial Hospital in Boston was founded in memory of her.

VINING, FANNY ELIZABETH (1829–91), see DAVENPORT, FANNY.

VIOLETTI, EVA MARIA (1724–1822), see GARRICK, DAVID.

VIRTA, NIKOLAI YEVGENYEVICH (1906–   ), Soviet novelist and dramatist. His early comedy, *Soldiers' Wives* (1942), was not a success, but his later plays, which include *Great Days*, based on the siege of Stalingrad, and *Our Daily Bread* (both 1947), *The Doomed Conspiracy* (1948), *The Destruction of Pompeii* (1953), *Endless Distance* (1957), and *In Summer* *the Sky is High* (1961), showed his increasing mastery of his medium, and were well received. They have been translated into many languages of the U.S.S.R. and also performed in other communist countries.

VISCONTI, Luchino (1906–76), Italian producer and scene designer, who as a young man went to Paris and became involved in film production. Although much of his early work was in films, he produced plays in Milan in 1937, and in 1945 was responsible for the introduction of plays by a number of European dramatists, particularly Cocteau (q.v.), into the repertory of the Teatro Eliseo in Rome, where in 1948 he staged Shakespeare's *As You Like It* in Italian as *Rosalinda*. In 1946, in which year he directed Beaumarchais's *Le Mariage de Figaro*, he joined the Paolo Stoppa–Rina Morelli company, for which he directed such modern works as Tennessee Williams's *The Glass Menagerie* in 1946, Anouilh's *Eurydice* in 1947, Miller's *Death of a Salesman* in 1951, and his *A View from the Bridge* in 1958. He was also responsible for productions of Chekhov's *Three Sisters* (1952) and *Uncle Vanya* (1955). In Paris in 1961 he staged a sumptuous version of Ford's *'Tis Pity She's a Whore*, as *Dommage qu'elle soit putain*. He worked with Zeffirelli on *Troilus and Cressida* in Florence, and also on Tennessee Williams's *A Streetcar Named Desire*. His later work was mainly in films and in opera.

VISHNEVSKY, Vsevolod Vitalevich (1900–51), Soviet dramatist, whose first successful play, *The Optimistic Tragedy*, was produced by Taïrov at the Kamerny Theatre (q.v.) in 1934. It dealt with the work and death in battle of a woman commissar with the Red Fleet during the early days of the Soviet regime. The part of the heroine was played by Taïrov's wife, Alice Koonen. The play was published in *Four Soviet Plays* (1937) in a translation by H. G. Scott and Robert S. Carr. In 1943, after several less successful productions, Vishnevsky collaborated with Alexander Kron, author of *Depth Prospecting*, and Alexander Azarov in a musical play, *Wide Spreads the Sea*, and also wrote *At the Walls of Leningrad*. Both these were produced at the Theatre of the Baltic Fleet (q.v.) and were well received. In 1949 his last play, *The*

Unforgettable 1919, was produced with great success. Both this and *The Optimistic Tragedy* have been retained in the repertory of the Soviet theatre.

Visor, see MASK.

VITRAC, Roger (1899–1952), French poet and playwright, one of the leaders of the French Dada movement, who in 1927 was associated with Antonin Artaud (q.v.) in the founding of the Théâtre Alfred Jarry, where his first two plays were performed under Artaud's direction: *Les Mystères de l'amour* as part of the opening programme in 1927, and *Victor, ou les Enfants au pouvoir* as its fourth and last production in 1928. *Les Mystères de l'amour*, which evokes the amorous and sadistic fantasies of a pair of lovers, is probably one of the most successful attempts to write a play on the surrealist principle of automatic writing, and foreshadows the Theatre of Cruelty (q.v.), just as *Victor, ou les Enfants au pouvoir*, which uses a parody of language and its clichés, monstrous characters (the nine-year-old child who is fully grown both mentally and physically), a farcical incident (the lady visitor who cannot stop breaking wind), and a tragi-comic dénouement (the child's choice of death as the only alternative to growing up into the adult world), foreshadows the work of Ionesco and his imitators in the Theatre of the Absurd (q.v.). It was successfully revived in Paris in 1946 and again in 1962, the latter production being directed by Anouilh (q.v.), who considers that Vitrac has had an important influence on his own work. It was seen in translation in London (at the Aldwych) in 1964. Vitrac's other plays, which include *Le Peintre* (1930), *Le Coup de Trafalgar* (1934), *Le Camelot* (1936), *Les Demoiselles du large* (1938), *Le Loup-garou* (1940), and *Le Sabre de mon père* (1951), are less well known.

VITRUVIUS POLLIO, Marcus (*fl.* 70–15 B.C.), Roman author of a treatise in ten books, *De Architectura*, of which Book V deals with theatre construction, illustrated by diagrams. Discovered in manuscript at St. Gallen in 1414, this was printed in 1484. The first edition with illustrations was published in 1511, and an Italian translation appeared in 1531. This work had a great influence on the building of Renaissance theatres, and from it the new generation of theatre designers took—though not always accurately—the idea of such devices as the *periaktoi* (q.v.), and in general the proportions and acoustic properties of the later Hellenistic and Roman theatres (see THEATRE BUILDINGS).

Vivian Beaumont Theatre, NEW YORK, see LINCOLN CENTER.

VOKES, a family of English pantomimists, consisting of FREDERICK MORTIMER (1846–88), JESSIE CATHERINE BIDDULPH (1851–84), VICTORIA (1853–94), and ROSINA (1854–94). Children of a theatrical costumier in business at 19 Henrietta Street, London, they played child parts on the legitimate stage, and first appeared as a family group at Edinburgh in 1861, being joined by an actor called WALTER FAWDON (?–1904), who also took the name of Vokes. They toured for some years, and in 1865 appeared at the Lyceum in London in *Humpty Dumpty*. From 1869 to 1879 they were the mainstay of the Drury Lane pantomimes, and were also seen at the Adelphi and elsewhere in two amusing sketches, *The Belles of the Kitchen* and *A Bunch of Berries*, making their first appearance in America in the latter in 1871. The first member of the family to break away was Rosina, who married the composer Cecil Clay and after some years in retirement went back to the stage. In 1885 she took a light comedy and burlesque company to the United States and Canada, and became a great favourite there. Her place in the family group was taken by Fred's wife Bella Moore, but the group finally broke up on the death of Jessie.

VOLKOV, FEODOR GRIGORYEVICH (1729–63), a Russian actor of great talent, and one of the founders of the Russian national theatre. He was running an amateur group in Yaroslavl when he was ordered to appear before the Court in St. Petersburg in Jan. 1752. This led to his being sent, with Dmitrevsky (q.v.) and other members of the company, to the Cadet College for the sons of the nobility, where he was trained as an actor for the Court theatre and also received a good general education. He appeared at Court again in 1755, and a year later became the leading man of what may be regarded as the first professional Russian theatrical company, organized by Sumarokov (q.v.). Attached as they were to the party responsible for the overthrow of Peter III and the accession of Catherine the Great, Volkov and his brother Grigori, who was also an actor, were rewarded with Court offices. Feodor Volkov also organized the celebrations in honour of Catherine's coronation in Moscow, and it was there, while directing a street masquerade entitled *The Triumph of Minerva*, that he caught cold and died.

VOLTAIRE [really FRANÇOIS MARIE AROUET] (1694–1778), French writer, philosopher, and historian, who took as his pseudonym an anagram of Arouet l(e) i(eune) (i.e. the younger). He holds an important place in the history of the theatre, the only aspect of his many-sided activity which need concern us here. Himself a good amateur actor, he remained passionately addicted to the theatre all his life, befriending many players, among them Lekain, La Noue, and Adrienne Lecouvreur (qq.v.), and he built several private theatres, of which the best was at Ferney, his last home. Before his visit to England in 1726—a turning-point in his life—he had written one good tragedy, *Œdipe* (1718), which was successful enough to be parodied by Dominique (see BIANCOLELLI) at the Théâtre-Italien, and two mediocre ones, *Artémire* (1720) and *Mariamne* (1724). The first-fruits of his visit to England, during which he discovered Shakespeare and appreciated him as far as was possible for a Frenchman raised in an entirely different tradition, were *Brutus* (1730), inspired by *Julius Caesar*, and the highly successful *Zaïre* (1732), which owed something to *Othello*. In the same year as his famous *Lettres philosophiques*—1734—appeared *Adélaïde du Guesclin*, which achieved only two performances. Eighteen years later, rewritten and retitled *Amélie, ou le Duc de Foix*, it had a moderate reception, while in yet another thirteen years, in its original form, under its original title, it was extremely successful. The first version was followed by *La Mort de César* (1735), *Alzire* and *L'Enfant prodigue* (both 1736)—the last pure eighteenth-century *drame*, mingling comedy and tragedy in a way which Voltaire himself later condemned—*Mahomet, ou le fanatisme* (1742), and his best play, *Mérope* (1743), which, like *Mariamne* and *Adélaïde du Guesclin*, was several times rewritten. It was followed by *Sémiramis* (1748), written to show his enemies that he could take and improve on a subject used (in 1717) by Crébillon (q.v.), who had been set up as his rival in the theatre and at Court. He proved his point with this and five other plays on subjects tackled by Crébillon, and incidentally contributed to the continued decline of French classical tragedy by the lavish use of spectacular effects. But *Sémiramis* had one important consequence. Its crowd scenes and spectacular effects led Voltaire to insist on the removal of the audience from the stage, a reform long overdue which finally took place in 1759. His next play, *Nanine* (1749), based on Richardson's *Pamela*, is again a *drame*, and well illustrates the dangers of an excess of sensibility. It was followed by *Oreste* (1749) and *Rome sauvée* (1750). Soon after, Voltaire left France for the Court of Frederick the Great, and several years elapsed before his next play was seen in Paris. This was *L'Orphelin de la Chine* (1755), based on a Chinese play. It was followed by *Tancrède* (1760), which is usually considered to be Voltaire's last good play. Six further tragedies are negligible, though *Irène* (1778) deserves a mention, since it was to attend its production at the Comédie-Française that Voltaire returned to Paris after an absence of nearly thirty years. Of four comedies written in this last period one, *L'Écossaise* (1760), owed its comparative success to its satire, while *Le Droit du seigneur* (1762) failed completely. The others were given only on the less exacting stage of Ferney.

VONDEL, JOOST VAN DEN (1587–1679), a Dutch dramatist, author of *Gijsbrecht van Amstel*, an historical tragedy performed on 3 Jan. 1638 for the opening of the Schouwburg, the first permanent theatre in Amsterdam. He was the chief dramatist of the theatre for many years, and among his later plays was one on Mary, Queen of Scots, *Maria Stuart* (1646). But he drew most of his subjects from the Old Testament, and had a great influence on the Jewish drama which developed in Amsterdam during the first half of the seventeenth century, many of the Hebrew plays written at the time being based on his work, which had much in common with the paintings of his great contemporary Rembrandt. His masterpiece, *Lucifer* (1654), may have had some influence on Milton's great poem, *Paradise Lost* (1667).

VOS, JAN (1615–67), see CAMPEN, JACOB VAN.

W

WADE, ALLAN (1881–1954), English actor, manager, and director, one of the founders of the Phoenix Society (q.v.) and director of all but two of the 26 plays produced by it. He made his first appearance on the stage in 1904, and shortly afterwards was with Frank Benson (q.v.), leaving him in 1906 to become assistant to Granville-Barker (q.v.) at the Royal Court, where he was instrumental in arranging the first visit of the company from the Abbey Theatre (q.v.), Dublin, in 1909. Most of his work was done as play-reader and producer for various managements, but he appeared in a number of plays both in London and New York, and in 1935 was appointed adjudicator in the Canadian Dominion Drama Festival. Author of a *Bibliography of W. B. Yeats* (1908), he was also responsible for translations, produced by the Stage Society, of Giraudoux's *Intermezzo* (1934) and Cocteau's *The Infernal Machine* (1935).

Waggon Stage, see BOAT TRUCK.

WAGNER, (WILHELM) RICHARD (1813–83), German poet, dramatist, and musician, the composer of many famous operas, who is important in theatre history because of his influence on theatre buildings (q.v.) and the reforms he introduced in the actual staging of his works. He was his own librettist, and designed much of the machinery and scenery used for his operas, which may be regarded as the fulfilment of the Romantic ideal—the perfect fusion of poetry, music, and the pictorial arts. In 1876 Wagner's greatest work 'Der Ring des Nibelungen' (in four parts) was produced under his own direction at the newly built theatre in Bayreuth (q.v.), where his operas are still given and where in his lifetime he controlled all the elements of what he envisaged as the *Gesamtkunstwerk*—the complete work of art embracing music, both orchestral and vocal, declamation, dancing, mime and movement, grouping, machinery, costumes, and scenery. The theories of art which he put into practice in his operas and in their production can be studied in three of his major prose works—*Die Kunst und die Revolution* (1849), *Das Kunstwerk der Zukunft* (1850), and *Oper und Drama* (1851).

WAINWRIGHT, MARIE (1853–1923), see JAMES, LOUIS.

Waits, originally night watchmen in medieval palaces, castles, and walled towns, who indicated the hour by playing upon some form of musical instrument. They later became musicians in the service of a noble person and eventually of a town, functioning as a town band. It is not always easy to distinguish the early waits from the minstrels (q.v.), but it seems likely that the former were resident, the latter itinerant; also the waits appear to have had some formal musical training. They come into the history of the theatre because from the early sixteenth century onwards they are found performing any music called for in a play. They are mentioned several times in Elizabethan plays, and in London were probably hired by the theatres from the corporation when needed, to supplement the musicians among the actors. They varied in number from four to nine, and wore the livery of the nobleman or town to which they were accredited. They were paid a nominal wage and received extra money from private individuals or theatres which hired them. They were not finally disbanded until the early nineteenth century.

Wakefield Cycle, see MYSTERY PLAY.

WAKHEVITCH, GEORGES (1907–), a stage designer, born in Odessa, whose career has been passed entirely in the French theatre. He has a wide knowledge of both the technical and theoretical aspects of design (he is himself responsible for all working plans, and oversees the construction of his sets), and does not hesitate to mingle built and painted scenery. His first work in the theatre (he began in the cinema) was for Lugné-Poë (q.v.) at the Théâtre de l'Œuvre, and he then designed for the Rideau Gris of Marseilles, where his *Macbeth* was particularly admired. He has since worked extensively for the ballet and opera in

Paris, and has been responsible for the décor of, among other plays, Anouilh's *L'Invitation au Château* (1947) at the Théâtre de l'Atelier, of the revival of Romains's *Donogoo* (1951) and Claudel's *L'Annonce faite à Marie* (1955) at the Comédie-Française, and of Claudel's *L'Échange* for the production by J.-L. Barrault (q.v.).

WALCOT, CHARLES MELTON (1816–68), American actor, born in London, who went to the United States in 1837. There he married an actress and abandoned his career as an architect to go on the stage. He made his first appearance in 1842, and was for many years connected with Mitchell's famous Olympic (q.v.), both as an eccentric comedian and as a dramatist, writing a number of topical burlesques which are now forgotten but were popular in their own day. From 1852 to 1859 he was with Wallack (q.v.). He had an alert, intelligent face with a high domed forehead, which was inherited by his son, also CHARLES MELTON (1840–1921); but whereas the father had side-whiskers and in his later years looked like a venerable clergyman, the son wore a moustache and the jovial expression of a genial British squire. In 1863 he married ISABELLA NICKINSON (1847–1906), an accomplished actress who was for many years with him at the Walnut Street Theatre, Philadelphia. They then joined Daniel Frohman (q.v.), and from 1887 onwards appeared in comic or dignified elderly parts in most of the Lyceum successes.

Waldorf Theatre, NEW YORK, on the south side of 50th Street, between 6th and 7th Avenues. This opened on 20 Oct. 1926 and had its first hit with a musical comedy in the following year. In 1929 and 1930 it was used for the Little Theatre Tournament. Also in 1930 came Leo Bulgakov's production of Gorky's *The Lower Depths* as *At the Bottom*, which had seventy-two performances and was followed by eight performances of Chekhov's *The Seagull*. A revival of Dreiser's *An American Tragedy* in 1931 ran for seventeen weeks. The last production at this theatre in 1933 was Priestley's *Dangerous Corner*, after which the building became a cinema and was demolished in 1937.

(For the Waldorf Theatre, London, see STRAND THEATRE (2).)

WALKER, THOMAS (1698–1744), see GOODMAN'S FIELDS THEATRE.

Walking Gentleman, Lady, see STOCK COMPANY.

WALKLEY, ALFRED BINGHAM (1855–1926), English dramatic critic, on *The Times* from 1900 to 1926. Previously he had written for the *Speaker*, the *National Observer*, and the *Star*. He republished a volume of his earlier criticisms as *Playhouse Impressions* (1892), and selections from his *Times* criticisms as *Drama and Life* (1907), *Pastiche and Prejudice* (1921), *More Prejudice* (1923), and *Still More Prejudice* (1925). A cultured and conscientious writer who took himself and his duties seriously, he nevertheless wrote rather as a literary than as a dramatic critic, devoting more space to the play than to the actors. Yet he wrote as well as the theatre of his time demanded; and this, in view of the productive period in which he worked, is high praise. The three lectures on dramatic criticism which he delivered to the Royal Institution in 1903, published the same year, sum up adequately his ideas on his profession.

WALLACE, (RICHARD) EDGAR HORATIO (1875–1932), English journalist, novelist, and playwright, son of a touring actor who took West End successes into the provinces, and grandson of the ALICE MARRIOTT (1824–1900) who was a well-known theatre manager and actress and a noted female Hamlet. He was the first to make a speciality of detective drama, many of his plays being based on his own books. Among the most successful were *The Ringer* (1926), *The Terror* (1927), *The Squeaker* (1928), *The Flying Squad* (1929), *On the Spot* and *Smoky Cell* (both 1930), and *The Case of the Frightened Lady* (1931), in all of which Wallace showed extraordinary perfection of detail, narrative skill, and knowledge of police methods and criminal psychology, fruits of his apprenticeship as a crime reporter.

WALLACE, NELLIE [really MRS. ELEANOR JANE LIDDY] (1870–1948), one of the great women comedians of the English music-halls. She first appeared at Birmingham in 1888 as a clog-dancer, and later toured as one of the three Sisters Wallace. Then followed a long apprenticeship of touring in various plays before she returned to the halls as a single turn. She also appeared in revue and in pantomi notably as the Wicked Witch Carabosse in *The Sleeping Beauty* at the Vaudeville in 1935. One of her most famous songs was 'I Lost Georgie in Trafalgar Square'. Nellie Wallace was a mistress of the grotesque, and one of the few successful women Dames in pantomime.

WALLACK, HENRY JOHN (1790–1870), American actor, member of a theatrical family important in the development of the theatre in New York. The son of English actors, with whom he first appeared in London, he went to the United States in 1819, and in 1824 was leading man at the Chatham Theatre (q.v.), which he took over two years later. After a visit to London, during which he was seen at Covent Garden, he returned to New York in 1837, where he worked as stage-manager for his brother James (q.v.) at the National Theatre, while continuing to act. In 1847 he made a great success as Sir Peter Teazle in Sheridan's *The School for Scandal*, and he made his last appearance on the stage, as Falstaff, in 1858.

WALLACK, JAMES WILLIAM the elder (1791–1864), an actor well known in England and America, who played juvenile leads at Drury Lane as a young man, and later divided his time between London and New York, where he first appeared in 1818, proving himself a romantic and tragic actor in the style of John Philip Kemble (q.v.). In 1837–8 he had a successful season at the National Theatre (q.v.) with his brother Henry (q.v.) as his stage-manager, and then went to Niblo's Garden and on tour. He made his last appearance in London in 1851, and a year later opened Brougham's former theatre as Wallack's. Elegantly redecorated, well equipped, and furnished with a good stock company in a repertory of Shakespeare and standard comedies, with some modern plays, it flourished for ten years, Wallack himself making his last stage appearance there in 1859. Two years later he opened a new theatre (see STAR THEATRE) on Broadway and 13th Street, but his inaugural speech marked his last public appearance, and he retired, leaving the traditions he had established to be carried on by his son Lester and his nephew, also James (qq.v.).

WALLACK, JAMES WILLIAM the younger (1818–73), American actor, son of Henry

(q.v.), under whom he served his apprenticeship to the stage. In 1837 he joined the company of his uncle James (q.v.) at the National Theatre, New York, where he quickly rose from 'walking gentleman' to juvenile lead. A man of rugged physique, he was at his best in such parts as Macbeth, Othello (and Iago), and Richard III. In a dramatization of Dickens's *Oliver Twist* staged in 1867 he was an excellent Fagin, and at Booth's Theatre in 1872–3 he also played Mathias, the part created by Irving (q.v.) in Lewis's *The Bells*, most terrifyingly. In comedy he was not so successful, except for Jaques in *As You Like It* and Mercutio in *Romeo and Juliet*. In 1865 he was a member of the stock company at Wallack's under his cousin Lester (q.v.).

WALLACK, LESTER [really JOHN JOHNSTONE] (1820–88), American actor, son of James Wallack the elder (q.v.). He first appeared on the stage in the English provinces, playing in Manchester in 1845 with Charlotte Cushman and Helen Faucit (qq.v.). He then went to New York and played a wide range of parts, comic and serious, before joining his father at the first Wallack's Theatre. He was already managing the second Wallack's (see STAR THEATRE) before his father's death in 1864, and under him, in spite of competition from Booth's and Daly's (qq.v.), it flourished until 1881. On 4 Jan. 1882 Lester opened a third Wallack's Theatre on the north-east corner of Broadway and 30th Street with a revival of Sheridan's *The School for Scandal*. Mrs. Langtry (q.v.), who was to have made her New York début on 30 Oct. that year at the second Park Theatre (q.v.) on the day it was burnt down, went to Wallack's instead. But the theatre was not a success and in 1887 Lester transferred the lease to other hands, allowing them to retain the old name. The last stock season was given under Abbey (q.v.) in 1888, in which year Lester died. His memoirs were published a year later. The theatre was then leased by Palmer (q.v.), who opened it under his own name on 8 Oct. 1888 with a French company. It reverted to its original name on 7 Dec. 1896 and finally closed in 1915 with a season of plays directed by Granville-Barker (q.v.) which included the first American production of Shaw's *Androcles and the Lion*. It was then demolished.

Wallack Theatre, NEW YORK, on West 42nd Street, between 7th and 8th Avenues. This opened as the Lew Fields Theatre (see WEBER AND FIELDS) on 5 Dec. 1904. Two years later it was taken over by James K. Hackett (q.v.), who named it after himself and appeared there with his own company in a number of successful productions. The same year saw the production of Sheldon's *Salvation Nell*, with Mrs. Fiske (q.v.). In 1911 the theatre again changed its name, this time to the Harris, and in 1921, as the Frazee, it housed a successful production of Kaufman and Connelly's *Dulcy*, with Lynn Fontanne (q.v.). In 1924 the theatre was finally named the Wallack. It became a cinema in 1931.

(For Wallack's Theatre, see WALLACK, JAMES, the elder and WALLACK, LESTER.)

WALLER, EMMA (1820–99), American actress, who made her first appearance at the Walnut Street Theatre, Philadelphia (q.v.), in Oct. 1857, as Ophelia to the Hamlet of her husband, DANIEL WILMARTH WALLER (1824–82). She was seen in New York the following year, and from then until her retirement in 1878 played leading roles there and on tour throughout the country. Among her best parts were Lady Macbeth, Queen Margaret in Cibber's version of Shakespeare's *Richard III*, which she played with Edwin Booth (q.v.), Meg Merrilies in a dramatization of Scott's *Guy Mannering*, and Julia in Sheridan Knowles's *The Hunchback*. She also, in the fashion of the time, played Hamlet and Iago. After her retirement she continued to give readings in public, and also taught elocution.

WALLER, LEWIS [really WILLIAM WALLER LEWIS] (1860–1915), English actormanager, who after some amateur experience made his first appearance as a professional at Toole's Theatre in 1883. A robust and dynamic actor, with a magnificent voice, he was at his best in costume parts and particularly in Shakespeare. His Brutus (in *Julius Caesar*), Faulconbridge (in *King John*), and above all his Henry V, were memorable. He was also much admired in the title-role of *Monsieur Beaucaire* (1902), based by Booth Tarkington on his own novel, perhaps the supreme example of Waller's particular talent. In modern-dress comedy he did not appear to such advantage, and Wilde's *An Ideal Husband*, with which he opened his management at the

Haymarket in 1895, was not a success. He married an actress, FLORENCE WEST (1862–1912), sister-in-law of the dramatic critic Clement Scott (q.v.), who appeared with her husband in many of his outstanding successes, notably as Miladi in his d'Artagnan in one of the many dramatizations of the elder Dumas's *The Three Musketeers* (1898).

WALLS, TOM (1883–1949), English actor, director, and theatre manager. He made his first appearance on the stage in Glasgow in 1905, and subsequently toured in the United States and Canada, returning to London in 1907. He had a successful career in musical comedy, and in 1922 went into management, his first venture being the immensely successful *Tons of Money*, a farce by Will Evans which, when transferred to the Aldwych (q.v.), inaugurated the long succession of 'Aldwych farces' by Ben Travers (q.v.), in all of which Tom Walls appeared, up to and including *Turkey Time* in 1931. He then went into films, but reappeared on the stage in 1938, continuing his successful career in light comedy and farce. He was for a time manager of the Fortune Theatre (q.v.), opening with Lonsdale's *On Approval* (1927), which he directed himself. He controlled a number of touring companies in the 1930s, and in 1939 took over the Alexandra in Stoke Newington, which he ran as a repertory theatre. In 1932 his horse, April the Fifth, won the Derby.

Walnut Street Theatre, PHILADELPHIA. Built as a circus in 1809, this was first used as a playhouse in 1811, when it entered into competition with the successful and well-established Chestnut Street Theatre (q.v.). It is still in use, and is the oldest playhouse in the United States. It flourished until 1829, when intense rivalry between the various managements in the city brought about the bankruptcy of them all. From then onwards it had a good stock company which supported visiting stars, but contributed little to the development of American theatrical life, whose centre moved to New York.

WALTER, EUGENE (1874–1941), American dramatist, whose early plays, though somewhat melodramatic, seemed to herald a more realistic and sober approach to social problems on the part of contemporary American playwrights. His best work was done in *Paid in Full* (1908), *The Easiest Way* (1909), and *Fine Feathers* (1913). Unfortunately, he failed to live up to his early promise and his last plays are negligible. Among them were dramatizations of two popular novels by John Fox, Jr., *The Trail of the Lonesome Pine* (1912) and *The Little Shepherd of Kingdom Come* (1916). Walter was also the author of a handbook on dramatic technique entitled *How to Write a Play* (1925).

Warburton's Cook. The well-known antiquarian and book-collector JOHN WARBURTON (1682–1759) had at one time in his possession some sixty Elizabethan and Jacobean plays in manuscript, many of them unique copies of works which had never been printed. Unfortunately, through his own carelessness and the ignorance of his servant Betsy Baker, to whom he had entrusted them, all but three were, as he himself says, 'unluckely burnd or put under Pye Bottoms'. He left a list of the titles of these lost plays, from which it appears that the chief sufferers from Betsy's depredations were Thomas Dekker, John Ford, and Philip Massinger (qq.v.). (See W. W. Greg: 'The Bakings of Betsy', in *The Library*, 1911.)

WARD, DOROTHY (1890–   ), English actress, best known for her annual appearance as Principal Boy in pantomime. She made her first appearance in 1905 in pantomime in Birmingham, and was seen in London a year later in the musical play *The Dairymaids*. Her first outstanding success was made as Louise in *The Cinema Star* (1914), by Jack Hulbert, and in New York she was acclaimed in the title-role of *Phoebe*, a musical version of Barrie's *Quality Street* (1921). She again appeared in pantomime in 1924, proving a worthy successor to such famous Principal Boys as Harriet Vernon and Queenie Leighton, her favourite parts being Jack in *Jack and the Beanstalk* and *Dick Whittington*. Her husband, SHAUN GLENVILLE [really BROWNE] (1884–1968), himself a noted comedian and music-hall artist, appeared with her in many pantomimes, notably as Dame Trot in *Jack and the Beanstalk*, Cook in *Dick Whittington*, Mrs. Crusoe, the title-role in *Mother Goose*, and the Dame in *Puss in Boots*. Their son, PETER GLENVILLE (1913–   ), is a well-known producer and director in London and New York.

WARD [really BUCHANAN], FANNIE (1872–1952), an American actress who made her first appearance on the stage at the Broadway, New York, in 1890 as Cupid in J. Cheever Goodwin's *Pippins*. In 1894 she made her first appearance in London as Eva Tudor in Lionel Monckton's *The Shop Girl* at the Gaiety. She had only one line to say—'Watch my wink!'—specially written in for her by George Edwardes (q.v.), but her beauty and charm made an instant impression and she remained in London until 1906, appearing with undiminished success in a series of light and musical comedies. On her return to New York she was seen as Rita Forrest in J. Hartley Manners's *A Marriage of Reason* (1907), and in the same year returned to London to play Nance in Channing Pollock's *In the Bishop's Carriage*, one of her most successful parts. From then onwards she pursued her career in London and New York, occasionally touring, and in 1927 and 1928 was seen in variety at the London Coliseum.

WARD, DAME (LUCY) GENEVIÈVE TERESA (1838–1922), an actress equally well-known in the United States and England, and the first to be created D.B.E. (in 1921). Originally an opera-singer (as Madame Ginevra Guerrabella), she turned to straight acting after losing her singing voice through illness and overwork, and made her début in 1873, in Manchester, as Lady Macbeth, a part which she later played in French at the Porte-Saint-Martin in Paris. She achieved success in a variety of roles, including Julia in Sheridan Knowles's *The Hunchback* and Portia in *The Merchant of Venice* (both 1874), Sophocles' Antigone, Mrs. Haller in Kotzebue's *The Stranger*, and Belvidera in Otway's *Venice Preserv'd* (all 1875). She was first seen in New York, her birthplace, in 1878, as Jane Shore in W. G. Wills's tragedy of that name, and a year later, under her own management in London, she produced *Forget-Me-Not*, by Herman Merivale and F. C. Grove, which proved such a success that she toured in it all over the world. Playing opposite her in the original production at the Lyceum was the young Johnston Forbes-Robertson (q.v.). After her last visit to America in 1891 she joined Irving (q.v.) at the Lyceum, her first appearance there being as Queen Eleanor in Tennyson's *Becket*. From 1900 she appeared rarely on the stage, but was occasionally seen with Benson (q.v.), making her last appearance with him as Queen Margaret in *Richard III* in the autumn of 1920, having appeared at the Old Vic the previous April as Volumnia in *Coriolanus*.

WARDE, FREDERICK BARKHAM (1851–1935), American actor, born in England, who in 1867 joined a small touring company, and after some years' experience in stock went to Booth's Theatre (q.v.) in New York, making an immediate success. He remained there for three years, and then went on tour until in 1881 he formed his own company, playing mainly in Shakespeare and in such old favourites as Sheridan Knowles's *Virginius*, Bird's *The Gladiator*, and Bulwer-Lytton's *The Lady of Lyons*, since he was unable to find any modern plays to his taste. He retired from the theatre in 1919, though he continued the lectures on Shakespeare and drama in general which he had begun in 1907. He was the author of *The Fools of Shakespeare* (1913) and of a volume of reminiscences, *Fifty Years of Make-Believe* (1920).

WARFIELD, DAVID (1866–1951), American actor, associated at the height of his fame with David Belasco (q.v.). In 1888 he joined a touring company, playing Melter Moss in Tom Taylor's *The Ticket-of-Leave Man*. This failed after a week and he went into variety, appearing in New York in 1890 in vaudeville and musical comedy. He was Karl in the original production of *The Belle of New York* (1897), and later spent three years in burlesque. He was adept at presenting the New York East Side Jew of his day, and had already given proof of fine qualities in his acting when in 1901 Belasco starred him in Klein's *The Auctioneer*. This was an instantaneous success and had a long run, but it was as the gentle, pathetic, self-sacrificing Anton von Barwig in *The Music Master* (1904), also by Klein, that Warfield set the seal on his growing reputation. He played nothing else, in New York and on tour, for three years. Among his later successes were Wes Bigelow in Belasco's *A Grand Army Man* (1907) and the title-roles in *The Return of Peter Grimm* (1911), also by Belasco, and Wills's *Vanderdecken* (1915), based on the story of the Flying Dutchman. He was also seen as Shylock in Belasco's production of *The Merchant of Venice* in 1922, retiring from the stage two years later.

WARNER [really LICKFOLD], CHARLES (1846–1909), English actor, who made his first appearance as a boy of fifteen with Phelps (q.v.) at Sadler's Wells, where his father, James Lickfold, was a member of the company. Forced unwillingly to study architecture, he ran away from home to return to the theatre under the assumed name of Warner, which he later retained. He first appeared in London in 1864, and in 1869 scored a hit as Steerforth in *Little Em'ly*, an adaptation by Andrew Halliday of Dickens's *David Copperfield*. He was the first Charles Middlewick in H. J. Byron's successful *Our Boys* (1875); but, though good in comedy, he was at his best in melodrama, playing at the Adelphi (q.v.) for many years. His finest part was Coupeau in *Drink* (1879), an adaptation of Zola's novel *L'Assommoir* in which he collaborated with Charles Reade (q.v.). He made his last appearance in London in 1906 in *The Winter's Tale*, playing Leontes to the Hermione of Ellen Terry (q.v.) at His Majesty's Theatre, and then went to America, where he committed suicide.

WARREN, WILLIAM (1767–1832), American actor, of English parentage, who was at one time in an English provincial company with Thomas Jefferson, great-grandfather of the famous American actor Joseph Jefferson (q.v.). In 1788 he was with Tate Wilkinson (q.v.), but his real career began when in 1796 he was invited by Wignell (q.v.) to join the company at the Chestnut Street Theatre in Philadelphia, where, except for some short visits to New York, he spent the rest of his life. He succeeded Wignell as manager of the theatre in partnership with William Wood (q.v.), and it was under them that the American actor Edwin Forrest (q.v.) made his first appearance, playing Young Norval in Home's *Douglas* in 1820. Warren, who was at his best in such parts as Falstaff, Sir Toby Belch (in *Twelfth Night*), Sir Peter Teazle and Sir Anthony Absolute (in Sheridan's *The School for Scandal* and *The Rivals* respectively), and Old Dornton (in Holcroft's *The Road to Ruin*), had a long and successful career and retired in 1829. His second wife was the famous actress Mrs. Merry (q.v.). His six children were all on the stage, the best-known being

WILLIAM (1812–88), who spent most of his life at the Boston Museum, where he first appeared in 1847, having made his first appearance on the stage at the Arch Street Theatre in Philadelphia in 1832. In 1882 he celebrated his stage jubilee, playing Dr. Pangloss in the younger Colman's *The Heir-at-Law* and Sir Peter Teazle in Sheridan's *The School for Scandal*, and retired a year later.

(For the Warren Theatre, see BOSTON.)

Washington Square Players, NEW YORK, a play-producing society founded in 1914 by a group headed by Edward Goodman which included also Lawrence Langner (q.v.). They opened in Feb. 1915 at the Bandbox Theatre, New York, in a programme of one-act plays, some of them specially written for the occasion, and in 1916 first presented full-length plays, including Chekhov's *The Seagull*, Ibsen's *Ghosts*, and Shaw's *Mrs. Warren's Profession*. In the same year they moved to the Comedy Theatre. Lee Simonson (q.v.) worked for the Washington Square Players, and Katharine Cornell (q.v.) made her first professional appearances with them. They disbanded in 1918, but it was out of their work that the Theatre Guild (q.v.) evolved. The history of the company can be found in Walter Prichard Eaton's *The Theatre Guild: The First Ten Years* (1929).

Washington Square Theatre, NEW YORK, at 40 West 4th Street, a shed-like corrugated-steel building designed by Jo Mielziner (q.v.). Built on land loaned by New York University and financed by the American National Theatre Association (q.v.), it was the temporary home of the Lincoln Center repertory company. It opened on 23 Jan. 1964 with the world première of Arthur Miller's *After the Fall*, directed by Elia Kazan (q.v.), who, with Robert Whitehead, had been appointed director of the new company. Miller's play was followed by a revival of O'Neill's *Marco Millions*, and by a new play, *But For Whom Charlie*, by S. N. Behrman. The venture was not altogether a success, and Kazan and Whitehead finally withdrew, to be succeeded by Herbert Blau and Jules Irving from the San Francisco Actors' Workshop, who in 1965 went with the company to its permanent home in the Vivian Beaumont Theatre (see LINCOLN CENTER). From Nov. 1965 to March 1968 the Washington Square Theatre was occupied by the musical, *Man of La Mancha*, based on Cervantes's *Don Quixote*.

WATERS, ETHEL (1900–77), American Negro actress and singer, who began her stage career in 1917, singing in nightclubs and vaudeville. She made her first appearance on Broadway in 1927 at Daly's Theatre in *Africana*, an all-Negro revue, and in 1933 appeared in Irving Berlin's *As Thousands Cheer*. Her first dramatic role was Hagar in the DuBose Heywards' *Mamba's Daughters* (1939), in which she proved herself an actress of the front rank. Subsequent Broadway appearances as Petunia in the musical *Cabin in the Sky* (1940) and as Berenice in Carson McCullers's *The Member of the Wedding* (1950) also enhanced her reputation. She gave many solo performances, among them *At Home with Ethel Waters* (1953), in which she sang some of the songs she had helped to make famous, including 'Dinah', 'Stormy Weather', and 'Am I Blue?'. Her autobiography, *His Eye Is on the Sparrow*, was published in 1951.

WEAVER [also WEVER], JOHN (1673–1760), a Drury Lane dancing-master who introduced to the English stage the harlequinade, from which the later pantomime (q.v.) developed, when he brought over from France 'scenical dancing' or 'Italian Night Scenes', which were stories in mime with no dialogue, based on the scenarios of the *commedia dell'arte* (q.v.). He was himself the author of several pantomime scenarios, and of a *History of Mimes and Pantomimes* published in 1728. Acting on his ideas, John Rich (q.v.) developed the specifically English form of pantomime, but to Weaver must go the credit for pioneer work in this form of entertainment.

WEBB, JOHN (1611–72), English artist. He was a pupil of Inigo Jones (q.v.), and was employed by Davenant (q.v.) to design and paint scenery for his productions, beginning with *The Siege of Rhodes* (1656). For this Webb prepared landscapes showing the general layout of the town and harbour, based probably on actual engravings of the place. In the epilogue to *The World in the Moon* (1697) the author, Settle, emphasizes the local origin of his elaborate scenery, in contrast to the French fashion of the time, with his play on the scene painter's name,

'Tis home-spun Cloth; All from an English Web'.

WEBER AND FIELDS, an American comedy team consisting of JOSEPH WEBER (1867–1942) and LEW FIELDS [really LEWIS MAURICE SHANFIELDS] (1867–1941), sons of Jewish immigrants, who at the age of nine appeared together in dime museums and beer gardens in and around New York in burnt-cork minstrelsy, followed later by a 'knockabout Dutch act' which combined slapstick clowning with comically mangled English dialogue. In their sketches Fields played Meyer—tall, thin, and tricky—and Weber appeared as Mike—short, squat, and guileless. Both wore padded suits and shallow derbies. In 1885 they established their own company, writing and acting in burlesques of the serious drama of the day (*Cyranose, Quo Vass Iss?*) which anticipated the 'revues' of the 1920s with their sketchy plots, their 'turns', and their big ensemble numbers. In 1895 they opened their own theatre, remaining there until 1904, when Fields took over the Wallack Theatre (q.v.). They were seen together in their own theatre again in 1912 (see FORTY-FOURTH STREET THEATRE). Weber retired from acting in 1918, Fields in 1929.

WEBSTER, BEN(JAMIN) (1864–1947), English actor, grandson of Benjamin Nottingham Webster (q.v.). He first appeared in the English provinces and later had a long and successful career in London, where he was first seen in 1887. He appeared with all the outstanding players of the day, not only in Shakespeare and other classics but in such new works as Shaw's *The Admirable Bashville* (1903), *The Doctor's Dilemma* (1906), *The Philanderer* (1907), and *Androcles and the Lion* (1913). In 1920 he was seen in A. A. Milne's successful comedy *Mr. Pim Passes By* and in 1932 in Gordon Daviot's *Richard of Bordeaux*. On the outbreak of war in 1939 he went to New York, where his reputation stood as high as in London, and remained there until his death, making his last appearance on Broadway in 1940 as Montague in *Romeo and Juliet*. He was the husband of the actress May Whitty (q.v.), whom he married in 1892. (For his daughter see WEBSTER, MARGARET.)

WEBSTER, BEN(JAMIN) NOTTINGHAM (1797–1882), English actor, manager, and dramatist, descended from a long line of theatrical and musical people. He had numerous brothers and half-brothers, all of whom were connected with the stage, one of them, FREDERICK (1802–78), being stage-manager at the Haymarket for many years. Frederick's grandchild, FLORENCE ANN (1860–99), who was an actress and dancer, married George Lupino (q.v.). Ben himself was first a dancer, playing Harlequin and Pantaloon in the provinces and at Drury Lane. He then took to broad comedy, proving himself a useful actor, and was with Mme Vestris (q.v.) at the Olympic. In 1837 he became lessee of the Haymarket (q.v.), which he managed for sixteen years, engaging all the best actors of the day and putting on many notable plays, in which he himself frequently appeared. In 1844 he took over the Adelphi as well, and was associated with Mme Céleste and Dion Boucicault (qq.v.), collaborating with the latter in two plays. He made an adaptation of Dickens's *The Cricket on the Hearth* in which he appeared with great success as John Peerybingle, but his finest part was Triplet in Taylor and Reade's *Masks and Faces*, which he produced both at the Haymarket and at the Adelphi in 1852. He retired in 1874. Two of his sons were actors and one a dramatist. (For his grandson see WEBSTER, BEN.)

WEBSTER, JOHN (*c.* 1580–1634), English dramatist, whose fame rests almost entirely on two plays, *The White Devil* (1612) and *The Duchess of Malfi* (1614). Both are founded on Italian *novelle* and are passionate dramas of love and political intrigue in Renaissance Italy, compounded of crude horror and sublime poetry. Indeed, in the latter respect Webster approached Shakespeare more nearly than any of his contemporaries, and both these plays have held the stage down to the present day. They provide scope for great acting and fine settings, and in the category of poetic drama remained unsurpassed by any later work, except that of Otway (q.v.), until a new conception of tragedy was imported into European literature by Ibsen (q.v.). Webster's other plays, which include *Appius and Virginia* (*c.* 1608) and *The Devil's Law Case* (1623) and some now lost, were written in collaboration and are of little importance. Practically nothing is known of his life, but he may have been an actor, perhaps the John Webster who appears among the English Comedians (q.v.) in Germany under Browne in 1596.

WEBSTER, MARGARET (1905–72), actress, director, and author, daughter of Ben Webster and his wife May Whitty (qq.v.). After appearing briefly on the stage in 1917, she made her adult début in 1924 in the chorus of Euripides' *The Trojan Women*, with Sybil Thorndike (q.v.), with whom she subsequently toured in Shaw's *Saint Joan*. On tour with Ben Greet (q.v.) in 1927 and 1928, at the Old Vic (q.v.) in 1929 and 1930, and with Gielgud in *Hamlet* (1930), she gained a knowledge of Shakespeare's plays which stood her in good stead when in 1937 she went to New York, where she made an outstanding reputation as a director of his plays. Out of her experiences she wrote *Shakespeare Without Tears* (1942), which was revised and reissued in England in 1956 as *Shakespeare Today*. Her first venture was *Richard II* with Maurice Evans (q.v.) in 1937. She directed four Shakespeare plays for the New York World's Fair in 1939, and her production of *Othello* with Paul Robeson (q.v.) in 1943, in which she herself played Emilia, broke all records for the run of a Shakespeare play on Broadway. In 1946 she was concerned with Cheryl Crawford and Eva Le Gallienne (qq.v.) in the founding and running of the American Repertory Theatre, directing the opening production, *Henry VIII*, in which she also appeared, Barrie's *What Every Woman Knows*, and Shaw's *Androcles and the Lion*, and appearing as Mrs. Borkman in Ibsen's *John Gabriel Borkman* and as the Red Queen in Eva Le Gallienne's adaptation of Lewis Carroll's *Alice in Wonderland*. She subsequently toured the United States with her own company, for which she directed a number of plays by Shakespeare. Although she later worked mainly in the United States, she did, after the Second World War, direct several plays in England, notably Hochwälder's *The Strong Are Lonely* (1955) in London, *The Merchant of Venice* (1956) at Stratford, and Sheridan's *The School for Scandal* (1959) at Birmingham. She also toured extensively in solo recitals based on the works of Shakespeare, Shaw, and the Brontë sisters, and in 1969 published a volume of reminiscences dealing mainly with her forebears, *The Same Only Different: Five Generations of a Great Theatrical Family*.

WEDEKIND, FRANK [really BENJAMIN FRANKLIN] (1864–1918), German dramatist and actor, who owed his Christian names to his father's admiration for American democracy. He first appeared in cabaret, singing his own songs, and was later an actor in Leipzig. His plays, which show the influence of Hauptmann (q.v.), nevertheless in their fantasy and symbolism point the way towards Expressionism (q.v.). In revolt against the secrecy imposed on adolescents in matters of sex he wrote *Die junge Welt* (1889, prod. 1908) and *Frühlings Erwachen* (1891, prod. 1906). In these he dealt with the problems of young love; but in *Erdgeist* (1895, prod. 1898) and its sequel *Die Büchse der Pandora* (1905), later used by Alban Berg for his unfinished opera 'Lulu' (1937), he portrays sex in its most lustful aspects. Here, and in later plays, his sex-ridden males and females, his gentlemen crooks, as in *Der Marquis von Keith* (1901), and his grotesque cranks, as in *Hidalla* (1905), typify the feverish spirit of the years before 1914. The first of Wedekind's plays to be seen in London was the one-act *Der Kammersänger* (1899), produced by the Stage Society in 1907 as *The Tenor*. In 1901 the Stage Society gave a private performance of *Spring's Awakening*, which, as *Spring Awakening*, had its first public production at the Royal Court Theatre in 1965. Subtitled 'a children's tragedy', it analyses the situation of two fourteen-year-olds who pay with their lives for the moral dishonesty of their tyrannical parents. In 1970 *Erdgeist* and *Die Büchse der Pandora* were translated and adapted by Peter Barnes as one play under the title *Lulu*. First produced at the Nottingham Playhouse, this was later transferred to the Royal Court in London, with Julia Foster as Lulu, the part first played by Wedekind's wife TILLY [really MATHILDE] NEWES (1886–1970). Wedekind's plays, which so shocked their original audiences, seem now, in an atmosphere of relaxed morals and increasing juvenile delinquency, less shocking but still valid, and several of them have been revived.

WEIGEL, HELENE (1900–71), see BRECHT, BERTOLT.

Weimar, a town in Thuringia, East Germany, associated theatrically with

Goethe (q.v.), who twice directed the Court theatre there. The first theatre in the town was built in 1696 and used by visiting professionals, including Ekhof (q.v.) in 1772. Three years later this was destroyed and replaced by a temporary theatre in the palace of the Duchess Anna Amalia, used by professionals and amateurs. It was there that from 1775 to 1783 Goethe, with a group of courtiers, produced plays for royal occasions, constantly hampered by lack of money and the irresponsibility of his amateur company. He acted himself, both in comedy and tragedy, playing Orestes to Corona Schroeter's Iphigenia in his own play, *Iphigenia auf Tauris*. But by 1781 the Court was beginning to lose interest in amateur theatricals, and three years later a new Court theatre opened with a resident professional company of which Goethe became artistic director in 1791. With the help of Schiller (q.v.), who shared his vision of a theatre which combined dramatic appeal with a high literary content, he established a repertory which included plays by himself, as well as by Schiller, his co-director from 1799 to 1805, Lessing, Shakespeare, Calderón, and Voltaire. Guest artists like Schröder and Iffland (qq.v.) were imported to strengthen the resident company, and the theatre soon became famous for its productions and particularly for Goethe's fine handling of crowd scenes. After Schiller's death in 1805 Goethe continued to direct the theatre alone until 1817, by which time it had already begun to decline in popularity. The building, which had been renovated in 1798, was burnt down in 1826 and rebuilt, but it failed to regain its audience and had a chequered career until in 1848 it came under the direction of Liszt, who remained there until 1858, producing, as well as new German plays, two operas by Wagner, 'Tannhäuser' and 'Lohengrin' (its first performance). In 1857 Dingelstedt produced a season of Shakespeare's historical plays and, in 1861, Hebbel's *Nibelungen*. After being damaged in the Second World War the theatre was rebuilt and reopened in 1948, since when it has continued to serve the town as a repertory theatre.

WEISE, CHRISTIAN (1642–1702), German dramatist, headmaster of a school at Zittau, where he wrote and produced a number of long plays which were purely academic. The chronicle plays and tragedies of his earlier days have little to recommend them, but the later comedies, in which Weise portrays the middle class on stage for the first time in the German theatre, foreshadow to some extent the work of Lessing (q.v.) a century later. His *Komödie der bösen Catherina* (1702) was based on the same plot as Shakespeare's *The Taming of the Shrew*.

WEISS, PETER (1916–   ), German dramatist, who had already directed a number of documentary and experimental films in Sweden when in 1963 his first play, *Nacht mit Gästen*, was produced at the Schillertheater Workshop in Berlin. His second play, *Die Verfolgung und Ermordung Jean Paul Marats dargestellt durch die Schauspielgruppe des Hospizes zu Charenton unter der Anleitung des Herrn de Sade*, was also produced in Berlin in 1964 and was seen in London later the same year at the Aldwych, directed by Peter Brook (q.v.) for the Royal Shakespeare Company. Its full title in English was *The Persecution and Assassination of Marat as Performed by the Inmates of the Asylum of Charenton under the Direction of the Marquis de Sade*, but it was known briefly as *Marat/Sade*. Its success led to the simultaneous production in 1965 at fourteen German theatres of Weiss's next play, *Die Ermittlung*, as well as a rehearsed reading of it, as *The Investigation*, at the Aldwych in London. Based on the transcript of the 1964 Frankfurt War Crimes Trial, it attempts to apportion the blame for the Auschwitz atrocities. This, and the previous play, have been published in English translations. They were followed in the theatre by a production in Vienna in 1967 of *Der Turm*, a stage version of a radio play first broadcast from Stockholm in Swedish. It was published in an English translation as *The Tower* in an anthology entitled *Postwar German Theatre* (1968), but neither this, nor *Die Versicherung* (*The Insurance*), a surrealist allegory in which men and beasts intermingle, first seen in Sweden in 1966 and in Germany in 1969, has yet been staged in London. Another play, which had its first production in Stockholm in 1967, was *Gesang vom Lusitanischen Popanz*, an account of the uprising in Angola and its suppression by the Portuguese. This was seen in Berlin in the same year, and in 1969 was produced in English, under the title *Song of the Lusitanian Bogey*, by the Negro Ensemble Company at the Aldwych Theatre, London, as part of the World Theatre season. A play on Vietnam followed. Its cumbersome title, *Diskurs über die Vorgeschichte und den Verlauf des lang andauernden Befreiungs-krieges in Viet Nam als Beispiel für die Notwendigkeit des bewaffneten Kampfes der Unterdrückten gegen ihre Unter-drücker sowie über die Versuche der Vereinigten Staaten von Amerika die Grundlagen der Revolution zu vernichten* (*Discourse on the pre-history and course of the long-lasting war of liberation in Vietnam as an example of the necessity for armed struggle on the part of the oppressed against their oppressors and on the attempts by the United States of America to destroy the foundations of the Revolution*), was shortened for practical purposes to *Viet Nam Diskurs* (*Vietnam Discourse*) when it was produced in Frankfurt in 1968. These documentary plays were followed in the same year by a reversion to Weiss's earlier form of popular entertainment in *Wie dem Herrn Mockinpott das Leiden ausgetrieben wird* (*How Mr. Mockinpott was Relieved of his Sufferings*), in which the chief charac-ters are two clowns, Mockinpott and Wurst. This was first seen in Hanover in 1968, and was followed at Düsseldorf in 1970 by yet another epic documentary, *Trotski im Exil* (*Trotsky in Exile*), which portrayed Trotsky not only as literally an exile from his own country but also as an exile of the mind, his vision of the future being rejected by communists and capitalists alike.

WELLES, (GEORGE) ORSON (1915–85), American actor and director, a forceful and controversial personality who had a stormy and spectacular career both in the theatre and in films. He made his first appearance in Dublin in 1931 as the Duke of Württemberg in Feucht-wänger's *Jew Süss*, and worked with the Abbey and Gate Theatres there before going back to America, where he was born. He then toured during 1933–4 with Katharine Cornell (q.v.), playing Mercutio in *Romeo and Juliet*, Marchbanks in Shaw's *Candida*, and Octavius Barrett in Besier's *The Barretts of Wimpole Street*. In 1936 he directed, for the Federal Theatre (q.v.), a Negro *Macbeth* and a new version of Labiche's *Un chapeau de paille d'Italie* as *Horse Eats Hat*, and in 1937 Marlowe's *Doctor Faustus*, playing

the title-role himself. With JOHN HOUSE-MAN [really JACQUES HAUSSMANN] (1902–), who had been associated with him in the Federal Theatre productions, he then took over the Comedy Theatre (q.v.), renamed it the Mercury, and reopened it with a controversial but successful revival of *Julius Caesar*. Even more controversial was his famous broadcast *The War of the Worlds* in 1938, which caused a panic in the United States. In 1939 he directed his own adaptation of several of Shakespeare's history plays as *Five Kings*, playing Falstaff, and in 1946 appeared in his own musical version of Jules Verne's *Around the World in Eighty Days*. He made his first appearance in London as Othello in 1951 and in 1955 was seen there again in his own version of Herman Melville's *Moby Dick*, which he played in New York in 1962. In 1960 in Dublin he again played Falstaff in *Chimes at Midnight*, based on *Henry IV* and *Henry V*, and in 1960 was responsible for the production of Ionesco's *Rhinoceros* in London, with Olivier (q.v.) in the lead.

WEMYSS, FRANCIS COURTNEY (1797–1859), English actor and manager, who spent most of his life in the United States. He was acting in London in 1821 when he was engaged for the Chestnut Street Theatre (q.v.) in Philadelphia, making his first appearance there the following year with such actors as Warren, Wood, Henry Wallack, and the elder Joseph Jefferson. He made his first appearance in New York in 1824. Though not out-standing as an actor, playing mainly small parts—he was appearing as Duncan to Macready's Macbeth on the occasion of the riot at the Astor Place Opera House (q.v.)—or as a manager, he served the American theatre well and became extremely popular, though never ceasing to be regarded as a visiting Englishman. He was the author of a most entertaining autobiography, *Twenty-Six Years of the Life of an Actor and Manager* (1847), and also edited the Philadelphia series of standard plays, published as *The Acting American Theatre*, with fine frontispieces of American actors by Neagle.

WERFEL, FRANZ (1890–1945), Austrian novelist and dramatist, whose trilogy, *Der Spiegelmensch* (1920), is an interesting resumption of the Faust–Mephistopheles theme. This symbolic drama was followed by two historical plays which had some success, *Juarez und Maximilian* (1924) and *Paulus unter den Juden* (1926). A chronicle-play dealing with the history of Jewry, *The Eternal Road* (1937), though elaborately staged and produced by Max Reinhardt in New York, was little more than a pageant. Werfel's most original contribution to the theatre, however, was his adaptation of his novel, *Bocksgesang* (1921), produced in New York in 1926 as *The Goat Song*. In this the crazy brutality of man in rebellion is symbolized by the leader, half-goat, half-man, of a peasants' revolt in the eighteenth century. He is eventually killed, but not before he has passed on his cruelty and bestiality to his child by a young nobleman's wife.

WERGELAND, HENRIK ARNOLD (1808–45), Norwegian poet and dramatist, whose best play was probably *Venetianerne* (1841), though the one which aroused the fiercest controversy was *Campbellerne* (1838). Some of his plays, notably *Sinclars Død* (1828), were written under the influence of Shakespeare.

WERNER, (FRIEDRICH LUDWIG) ZACHARIAS (1768–1823), author of the one-act tragedy *Der vierundzwanzigste Februar* (1810), which established the so-called Fate Drama (q.v.) in Germany. Werner was a poet and mystic who became a Roman Catholic priest in Vienna, where he was renowned for his preaching. His other plays, which include *Das Kreuz an der Ostsee* (1806), *Martin Luther* (1807), and *Kunigunde, die Heilige* (1815), bear a strong religious imprint, and mingle scenes of telling realism with weird fantasy. They were among the few German Romantic verse-dramas to achieve success on the contemporary stage.

WESKER, ARNOLD (1932–   ), English dramatist, whose early plays were prominent in the promotion of what was then called 'kitchen-sink' drama. His first play, *Chicken Soup with Barley*, was produced at the Belgrade Theatre (q.v.) in 1958, and subsequently transferred to the Royal Court in London. It forms the first part of a trilogy with *Roots* (1959; New York, 1960), and *I'm Talking About Jerusalem* (1960), in both of which Joan Plowright (q.v.) scored an outstanding success as Beatie. *The Kitchen*, based on Wesker's experiences as a pastry-cook,

was first seen as a 'production without décor' at the Royal Court in 1959 and, in a revised version, was produced at the Belgrade two years later. It was followed by a study of life in the R.A.F., *Chips With Everything*, which was successfully produced at the Royal Court in 1962 and in New York a year later. His next play, *Congress*, received the Marzotto Prize for the best unproduced play of 1964, and was first seen in French, in a production by the Belgian National Theatre, a year later. As *Their Very Own and Golden City* it was produced in London in 1966, but was unsuccessful, as was *The Four Seasons*, a two-character play which had been seen at the Saville Theatre in 1965—the first of Wesker's plays to be seen in London outside the Royal Court. In Jan. 1970 Wesker himself directed the première of his next play, *The Friends*, in Stockholm, and later in the same year it had a short run at the Roundhouse (q.v.), where in 1962 Wesker had tried unsuccessfully to establish a working-class theatre with the backing of the trades unions, an imaginative and worthwhile scheme which deserved more support and encouragement than it received.

WEST, FLORENCE (1862–1912), see WALLER, LEWIS.

WEST, MAE (1892–1980), American actress and entertainer, who was on the stage as a child playing Little Willie in Mrs. Henry Wood's *East Lynne*, and other juvenile parts. She withdrew from the theatre in 1903 but subsequently appeared in vaudeville, and made her adult début in 1911 in musical comedy. Two years later she was again seen in vaudeville and revue. In 1928 she played the title-role in her own production, *Diamond Lil*, probably, with its famous catch-phrase 'Come up and see me sometime', her best-known vehicle. She was seen in it again in London in 1948, having in 1933 starred in a film adaptation entitled *She Done Him Wrong*. She remained in Hollywood for the next eleven years, returning to Broadway in 1944 in her own play, *Catherine Was Great*. Apart from the above plays, she is the author of several novels, and in 1959 published her autobiography, *Goodness Had Nothing To Do With It*. A glamorous and extrovert personality, her buoyant and curvaceous appeal can be judged by the fact that the R.A.F. in 1940 named their inflatable life-jacket a 'Mae West'.

West London Theatre, in Church Street, off the Edgware Road. This opened in 1832 as the Royal Pavilion West, an unlicensed theatre for crude melodrama and comic songs. In 1835 it was renamed the Portman and two years later closed and reopened on 13 Nov. 1837 as the Royal, with much the same mixture as before. In 1842 it was largely rebuilt and given the name of the Theatre Royal, Marylebone. Under John Douglass it achieved a measure of prosperity with popular melodrama and pantomime but after his retirement managers, including E. T. Smith and the elder J. W. Wallack (qq.v.), came and went without success until in 1868 the theatre was rebuilt and enlarged and renamed the Royal Alfred, an effort being made to provide better entertainment; but in 1873 it reverted to its old name of the Marylebone, and to melodrama, which continued to fill the bill when towards the end of the nineteenth century it was renamed the West London. It became a cinema in 1932 and was damaged by enemy action in 1941. It was then used as a warehouse. While in course of demolition in 1962 it was destroyed by fire. Its history has been written in two booklets by Malcolm Morley.

(The Scala (q.v.) was known as the West London from 1820 to 1831.)

WESTERN, (Pauline) Lucille (1843–77), and **Helen** (1844–68), American actresses, daughters of a comedian and of his actress-wife who, by a second marriage after his early death, became Mrs. Jane English, the name by which she is usually known. The children toured with their mother and step-father in a mixed entertainment which gave plenty of scope for their precocious talents in acting and dancing. Helen died before she could become well known as an adult actress but Lucille was noted for her playing of strong emotional parts in such plays as Mrs. Henry Wood's *East Lynne*, the younger Dumas's *Camille* (*The Lady of the Camellias*), Taylor and Reade's *Masks and Faces*, and Kotzebue's *The Stranger*. One of her finest performances was given as Nancy in a dramatization of Dickens's *Oliver Twist*. She died at the height of her success.

Westminster Play, a production of a Latin play which is given annually by the 'Scholars in College' at Westminster School, London, interesting as being the only survival of several similar productions given at such schools as Eton, Winchester, Shrewsbury, and St. Paul's, and even earlier at the universities in the sixteenth and early seventeenth centuries (see CAMBRIDGE and OXFORD). These plays probably originated in the Christmas ceremonies connected with the election of the medieval Boy Bishop (see FEAST OF FOOLS), but the custom of acting a Latin play at Westminster was introduced during the headmastership of Dr. Alexander Nowell (1543–55). When the school was refounded by Queen Elizabeth I in 1560, the presentation of the play was confirmed in the statutes on the grounds of its educational value (see also JESUIT DRAMA and SCHOOL DRAMA). Although the plays chosen were usually by Terence or Plautus (qq.v.), in 1566 an anonymous *Sapientia Salomonis* was performed before the Queen, who had attended a production of Plautus' *Miles Gloriosus* two years earlier. From 1560 to the outbreak of the Civil War in 1642 a play was presented annually at Christmas in the College Hall. It then lapsed, and there is no further record of it until 1704, though it was probably revived at the Restoration in 1660, since Barton Booth (q.v.), who was at Westminster from 1689 to 1698, is said to have been encouraged to act by the famous Dr. Richard Busby, headmaster of the school from 1638 to 1695, who had at one time contemplated going on the stage. From 1704, when Plautus' *Amphitrion* was performed, the records are continuous up to 1938, the plays being performed from 1730 to 1938 in the New Dormitory in Little Dean's Yard, which in May 1941 was partially destroyed by an incendiary bomb. The consequent remodelling meant that it was no longer possible to perform the play there, but it has been replaced by a summer open-air performance in modern dress which seems likely to establish a new tradition.

Among the most interesting features of the Westminster Play during the eighteenth and nineteenth centuries were the Prologues and Epilogues, which date from 1704 and probably earlier. The Prologue, spoken by the Captain in front of the curtain, became in the course of time a serious review of the events of the past school year, but the Epilogue, though originally also a monologue, developed into a witty satire in Latin on contemporary events in which all the characters in the preceding play appeared in modern dress.

Westminster Theatre, LONDON, in Palace Street, near Victoria Station. This opened on 7 Oct. 1931 with Bridie's *The Anatomist*, in which Henry Ainley (q.v.) played the title-role. Until 1938 the theatre was controlled by ANMER HALL [really ALDERSON BURRELL HORNE] (1863-1953), who presented there an interesting selection of English and foreign plays, among them Pirandello's *Six Characters in Search of an Author* (1932), Granville-Barker's *Waste* (1936), O'Neill's *Mourning Becomes Electra* (1937), and Dorothy Sayers's *The Zeal of Thy House* (1938). When Hall left, the theatre was taken over by the London Mask Theatre under J. B. Priestley (q.v.), who was still in occupation when the outbreak of war on 3 Sept. 1939 caused all the London theatres to close. However, the Westminster opened again on 10 Oct. with Priestley's own play, *Music at Night*. Successful productions which followed were Afinogenov's *Distant Point* (1941), Bridie's *Mr. Bolfry* (1943), Walter Greenwood's *The Cure for Love* (1945), and James Parish's *Message for Margaret* (1946). The theatre was then bought by the Oxford Group for the production of Moral Rearmament plays and temporarily removed from public commercial use. It returned to normal use in 1949 with Lesley Storm's *Black Chiffon*, and the last successes there before the Group finally took over were Frederick Knott's *Dial M for Murder* (1952), *Carrington, V.C.* (1953), by Dorothy and Campbell Christie, and, the last production, *Any Other Business* (1958), by George Ross and Campbell Singer.

WESTON, THOMAS (1737-76), English actor, whose father was head cook to George II. He joined a strolling company and, thinking himself a tragedian, played Richard III abominably. He found his true vocation in comedy, and after playing in Shuter's and Yates's booths at Bartholomew Fair he was engaged for small parts at the Haymarket. Foote (q.v.) thought highly of his comic talent and wrote for him the part of Jerry Sneak in *The Mayor of Garret* (1763). He went also to Drury Lane and there was considered even better than Garrick (q.v.) in the part of Abel Drugger in Jonson's *The Alchemist*. The German critic Lichtenberg has left a fine description of his playing of Scrub in Farquhar's *The Beaux' Stratagem*. He was somewhat dissipated, constantly in debt, and finally died of drink.

WESTRAY, a family of actresses, of English origin, consisting of a mother, MRS. ANTHONY WESTRAY (?-1836), and three beautiful daughters. The mother married as her second husband, at Devizes in 1792, an actor named John Simpson, and four years later the whole family went to America, where the husband died in 1801. The three girls were all members of the company at the Park Theatre (q.v.) in New York, where ELLEN, who became Mrs. John Darley, remained for twenty years before joining her sister JULIANA, wife of William Burke Wood (q.v.), in Philadelphia, where she was extremely successful. The third sister, ELIZABETH, whose first husband was named Villiers, married as her second husband the comedian William Twaits (q.v.).

Wharf Theatre, NEW YORK, see CRUGER'S WHARF THEATRE.

WHEATLEY, WILLIAM (1816-76), American actor, the son of FREDERICK WHEATLEY (?-1836), an Irish actor who emigrated to the United States in 1803 and spent the rest of his life on the American stage, and his actress-wife SARAH ROSS (1790-1872). William, who made his début at the age of ten, was for several years the chief player of boys' parts at the Park Theatre (q.v.), where his parents were in the company, and after time off for his education, returned there as an adult actor in 1834. A hard worker, an excellent actor, and a good manager, he was at Niblo's Garden (q.v.) from 1862 to 1868, where his greatest achievement was the production of the spectacular ballet-extravaganza *The Black Crook* (1866). Its success netted him a fortune, on which he retired. His sister EMMA (1822-54) was also on the stage, and was a highly accomplished and popular performer.

WHELAN, ALBERT (1875-1961), a music-hall comedian who was the first to use a signature tune ('Lustige Brüder'). Born in Melbourne, he first appeared as a red-nosed comedian with a travelling company which visited mining camps, and then joined a company which was touring in *The Belle of New York*, with which he subsequently appeared in London. In 1901 he was seen at the Empire, Leicester Square, and was successful enough to be engaged for many other halls, both in London and in the provinces. A clever performer, he never altered his style. His whistled entrance tune, his immaculate evening dress, his tall hat, his stick, his white gloves, and his gold wrist-watch, were unchanged; but his songs were always new and entertaining.

WHITE, GEORGE (1890–1968), see REVUE.

White-eyed Kaffir, see CHIRGWIN, G. H.

Whitefriars Theatre, LONDON, a small private playhouse in the refectory hall of the Whitefriars monastery, situated near the present Bouverie Street. It was adapted in the style of the first Blackfriars Theatre (q.v.) by Thomas Woodford and Michael Drayton in about 1608. Among the plays produced there were Nathan Field's *A Woman is a Weathercock* (1609) and John Marston's *The Insatiate Countess* (1610). It was still in use in 1621 but its later history is obscure. Pepys, in his diary for 1660, records a visit there to see Massinger's *The Bondman*, one of his favourite plays, but he may have meant Salisbury Court (q.v.), which replaced it in 1629 and with which it is sometimes confused.

Whitehall Theatre, LONDON, a small, intimate, modern playhouse built by the playwright and manager WALTER HACKETT (1876–1944) on the site of the Old Ship Tavern. It opened on 29 Sept. 1930 with Hackett's *The Way to Treat a Woman*, transferred from the Duke of York's. With his wife MARION LORNE (1888–1968), he remained at the theatre till 1934, he writing the plays and she acting in them. Among the most successful were *The Gay Adventure* (1931), *Road House* (1932), and *Afterwards* (1933). Subsequent successes at this theatre included Norman Ginsbury's *Viceroy Sarah* and St. John Ervine's *Anthony and Anna* (both 1935), Alec Coppel's *I Killed the Count* (1937), Philip King's *Without the Prince* (1940), and Delderfield's long-running *Worm's Eye View* (1944). In 1950 the theatre was taken over by Brian Rix, who staged there a series

of farces rivalling the pre-war popularity of the old 'Aldwych farces'. These—*Reluctant Heroes* (1950), by Colin Morris, *Dry Rot* (1954) and *Simple Spymen* (1958), both by John Chapman, *One for the Pot* (1961), by Ray Cooney and Tony Hilton, *Chase Me, Comrade!* (1964), by Ray Cooney, and *Come Spy with Me* (1966), by Bryan Blackburn—sufficed to keep the theatre open without a break. When in 1967 Rix opened a season of farces in repertory at the Garrick Theatre (q.v.), one, *Uproar in the House*, by Anthony Marriott and Alister Foot, was transferred to the Whitehall for a long run. In 1969 came *Pyjama Tops*, a comedy by Paul Raymond based on a French farce, *Moumou*.

WHITING, JOHN (1917–63), English dramatist and actor, who first came into prominence with *A Penny for a Song*, produced at the Haymarket in 1951. It was well received by the critics and the acting profession, but failed with the public. Rewritten and much improved, it was put on again at the Aldwych in 1962 by the Royal Shakespeare Company, who had previously staged Whiting's *The Devils* (1961), based on *The Devils of Loudun*, an historical work by Aldous Huxley. Whiting, who died just as his reputation in England was beginning to equal that which he had achieved on the Continent, particularly in Germany, was also the author of *Saint's Day* (1951), *Marching Song* (1954), and translations of Anouilh's *Madame de . . .* and *Le Voyageur sans bagage* (as *Traveller Without Luggage*) (both 1959). He was for a time drama critic of the *London Magazine*. After his death a play, *Conditions of Agreement*, was found among his papers and given its first performance at the Bristol Old Vic in 1965. In 1970 a volume of his collected notes and essays, edited by Ronald Hayman, was published under the title *The Art of the Dramatist*, and in the same year a play which had been seen on tour in 1956, but not in London, *The Gates of Summer*, was revived at the Tower Theatre (q.v.). *A Penny for a Song* was used in 1967 by Richard Rodney Bennett as the libretto of an opera. Two years after Whiting's death an award of £1,000 was instituted in his memory. It is given annually to a promising young playwright, and among the first recipients were Edward Bond, Tom Stoppard, and Peter Terson (qq.v.).

WHITLEY, James Augustus (c. 1724–81), see MANCHESTER.

WHITLOCK [née KEMBLE], ELIZABETH (1761–1836), see KEMBLE, ROGER.

Whitney Theatre, LONDON, see STRAND THEATRE (2).

WHITTY, DAME MAY (1865–1948), English actress, wife of Benjamin Webster (q.v.). In 1918 she was created D.B.E. for charitable work in connection with the First World War. She made her first appearance on the stage in Liverpool in 1881, and a year later was seen in London, spending some time at the St. James's Theatre. She then joined Irving (q.v.) at the Lyceum, and with his company made her first visit to America, where she later had a distinguished career, in 1895. Unlike her husband, she seldom appeared in Shakespeare, but was seen in a number of revivals and new plays, among them Anthony Wharton's *Irene Wycherley* (1907), Granville-Barker's *The Madras House* (1910), Lonsdale's *The Last of Mrs. Cheyney* (1925), Van Druten's *There's Always Juliet* (1931), in which she also appeared in New York in 1932, Ronald Mackenzie's *The Maitlands* (1934), and Emlyn Williams's *Night Must Fall* (1935), in which she also made her film début. In 1939 she went to New York with her husband and remained there until her death, playing the Nurse in *Romeo and Juliet* in 1940 and Madame Raquin in *Therese*, based on Zola's *Thérèse Raquin*, in 1945. There is an excellent account of her career in *The Same Only Different* (1969), a book of reminiscences by her daughter Margaret Webster (q.v.).

WHITWORTH, GEOFFREY (1883–1951), founder of the British Drama League (q.v.), which he directed from its inception in 1919 until 1948. He was also active in the cause of the National Theatre (q.v.), which formed the subject of two of his books—*The Theatre of My Heart* (1930) and *The Making of a National Theatre* (1951). He was for many years on the Executive Committee of Governors of the Shakespeare Memorial Theatre, Stratford-upon-Avon, and a member of the Critics' Circle. Although his work lay mainly among amateurs, it was of considerable benefit to the English theatre as a whole. His wife, PHYLLIS (née BELL), started in 1924 the Three Hundred Club for the production of distinguished but non-commercial plays, which in 1927 amalgamated with the Stage Society (q.v.).

WIETH, MOGENS (1920–62), Danish actor, who had been engaged to appear as Shakespeare's Othello and Ibsen's Peer Gynt with the Old Vic company in London when he died suddenly during the preliminary rehearsals. He occupied a unique position in the Danish theatre, where at an early age he established himself as a classical actor. Among his outstanding parts were Peer Gynt, the Narrator in Stravinsky's 'The Soldier's Tale', Jack Worthing in Wilde's *The Importance of Being Earnest*, and Higgins in the musical *My Fair Lady*. In 1948, during the celebrations held for the two-hundredth anniversary of the Royal Danish Theatre in Copenhagen, he played ten leading parts in eighteen days. He was invited to appear in London after attaining wide popularity through his films. He spoke six languages and was a man of great integrity, humility, and generosity, as well as being technically and artistically a fine actor.

WIGNELL, THOMAS (1753–1803), American actor of English extraction, who in 1774 joined the American Company (q.v.), quickly becoming its leading man. He was also instrumental in getting the first American comedy, Tyler's *The Contrast*, put on in New York in 1787, and in 1789 he played the comic doctor in *The Father*, by Dunlap (q.v.), to which he also spoke the prologue. In 1794 he opened the Chestnut Street Theatre (q.v.) in Philadelphia, for which he had recruited a good company during a visit to England, and remained there until his death, which took place seven weeks after his marriage to his leading lady, Mrs. Merry (q.v.).

WILDE, OSCAR FINGAL O'FLAHERTIE WILLS (1854–1900), Irish wit and dramatist, and the leader of a new aesthetic cult satirized in Gilbert and Sullivan's *Patience*, where he figures as Bunthorne. In 1882 he went to New York, where his play, *Vera*, was unsuccessfully produced. Even less successful was a blank-verse tragedy, *The Duchess of Padua*, also seen in New York in 1891, and it was with his light comedies that he ultimately achieved fame in the theatre—*Lady Windermere's Fan* (1892), *A Woman of No Importance* (1893), *An Ideal Husband* (1895), and finally, his most characteristic play, *The Importance of*

Being Earnest (also 1895). Though all his plays have been revived, *The Importance of Being Earnest* wears best and has proved the most consistently successful. It has twice been made into a musical—once as *Half in Earnest* (1957) and again as *Found in a Hand-Bag* (1968)—but neither production reached London. Wilde's one-act poetic play *Salome*, first produced in Paris by Sarah Bernhardt (q.v.), was banned by the censor and not seen in London until 1905, in which year it was set to music by Richard Strauss. Another one-act play, *A Florentine Tragedy*, which Wilde left unfinished, was completed by Sturge Moore and produced in 1906. In 1895 Wilde had been convicted of homosexuality and sentenced to two years' imprisonment with hard labour. When released he went to Paris, where he died. He was the subject of a play by Leslie and Sewell Stokes, produced in London in 1936 with Robert Morley (q.v.) as Wilde.

WILDER, THORNTON NIVEN (1897–1975), American novelist and dramatist, whose most important work for the theatre is found in his two stimulating and provocative plays, *Our Town* (1938; London, 1946), a picture of a small American community, and *The Skin of Our Teeth* (1942; London, 1945), a survey of man's hairbreadth escape from disaster through the ages, both of which were awarded the Pulitzer Prize for Drama. The latter provided, in Sabina, an excellent part for Tallulah Bankhead (q.v.) in New York and Vivien Leigh (q.v.) in London, where Laurence Olivier was responsible for its production. Among Wilder's earlier works for the theatre were *The Trumpet Shall Sound* (1927), a play about the American Civil War; a translation of Obey's *Le Viol de Lucrèce*, as *Lucrece* (1932), for Katharine Cornell (q.v.); a new version of Ibsen's *A Doll's House* (1937), for Ruth Gordon; and an adaptation of one of Nestroy's farces (*Einen Jux will er sich machen*, based on *A Day Well Spent* by John Oxenford) as *The Merchant of Yonkers* (1938). Rewritten and retitled *The Matchmaker*, this last was seen at the Edinburgh Festival in 1954 and later at the Haymarket in London. As a musical entitled *Hello, Dolly!* it had a spectacular success in New York in 1964 and in London a year later. Wilder's *Life in the Sun*, on the legend of Alcestis, was commissioned by Tyrone Guthrie (q.v.) for

the 1955 Edinburgh Festival, and was produced in the Assembly Hall there, but was not wholly successful, being rather three one-act plays, of which the second was the best, than a coherent whole. A trilogy of one-act plays, *Three Plays for Bleecker Street*, opened at the Circle-in-the-Square in New York in 1962. Wilder also wrote a number of other one-act plays, one of which, *The Long Christmas Dinner* (1931), provided the libretto for a short opera by Hindemith (1961), the text being adapted by Wilder himself.

WILKINSON, NORMAN (1882–1934), English artist, and designer of some outstanding settings and costumes for the theatre. He first worked for Charles Frohman at the Duke of York's in 1910, but sprang into prominence with his costumes and scenery for Granville-Barker's Shakespeare seasons at the Savoy, *A Midsummer Night's Dream* (1914) being particularly memorable, with its gilded fairies and 'magical iridescent forest'. His permanent set for *Twelfth Night* (1912) was also much admired. In the same year he designed the costumes and settings for a production of Euripides' *Iphigenia in Tauris*. He was with Playfair (q.v.) at the Lyric, Hammersmith, worked for C. B. Cochran (q.v.) and for the Phoenix and Stage Societies, and in 1932 designed *A Midsummer Night's Dream* for the Memorial Theatre at Stratford-upon-Avon, of which he was a Governor. To distinguish him from a marine artist of the same name he was usually referred to as Norman Wilkinson of Four Oaks.

WILKINSON, TATE (1739–1803), English actor and provincial theatre manager, who was engaged by Garrick (q.v.) for Drury Lane on the recommendation of Shuter (q.v.). He became well known for his imitations of living actors, particularly when Foote took him to Dublin, but failed to rouse much enthusiasm in London and eventually went into the provinces. There he took over the York circuit, which included also Hull and Leeds, and conducted it for about thirty years with conspicuous success, many well-known actors gaining their early experience under him. As he grew older he became very eccentric, and the elder Mathews (q.v.) used to do a charming monologue in imitation of him. Foote, after a violent but short-lived quarrel, satirized him as Shift in *The Minor* (1760), but in spite of his many foibles he was much loved and respected. He left an interesting account of his life in his *Memoirs* (1790) and *The Wandering Patentee* (1795).

WILKS, ROBERT (1665–1732), English actor, who to the end of his life retained the ability to play young men in high comedy. He was first engaged by Christopher Rich (q.v.) in 1692 to take the place of William Mountfort (q.v.), who had just been assassinated, and soon became popular with the public and his fellow-actors. When Rich left Drury Lane in 1709, Wilks took over the management with Cibber and Doggett (qq.v.), but although the theatre prospered, he found himself constantly at odds with the parsimonious Doggett, and harmony was not restored until the latter was replaced by Barton Booth (q.v.). Even then Wilks's imperious temper often led to trouble, and caused several actors to migrate to Lincoln's Inn Fields. But he was a conscientious, hard-working man, and the first to play the fine gentlemen in Cibber's plays and the heroes of Farquhar (q.v.), one of his best parts being Sir Harry Wildair in the latter's *The Constant Couple* (1699). He was not good in tragedy, but could always move an audience to tears in parts which, like Macduff in *Macbeth*, demanded pathos.

WILLARD, EDMUND (1884–1956), English actor, nephew of Edward Willard (q.v.), under whose management he appeared at the Tremont Theatre, Boston, and on tour. He made his first appearance in London in 1903, and after touring for many years in the provinces, played a series of Shakespeare parts at Stratford-upon-Avon in 1920 and 1921. He was at his best in strong dramatic parts, Macbeth, Othello, Jones in Galsworthy's *The Silver Box*, Lopakhin in Chekhov's *The Cherry Orchard*, Matvei in Afinogenov's *Distant Point*. One of his last and finest parts was the sinister Jonathan Brewster in the long run of Kesselring's *Arsenic and Old Lace* (1946) in London.

WILLARD, EDWARD SMITH (1853–1915), English actor, chiefly remembered for his villains in contemporary melodrama. He first attracted attention by his Clifford Armytage in Sims's *The Lights o' London* (1881), and enhanced his reputation by his playing of Captain Skinner in Jones and Herman's *The Silver King* (1882). Among his later successes were Charles Young's

Jim the Penman (1886) and Jem Dalton in a revival of Tom Taylor's *The Ticket-of-Leave Man* at the Olympic in 1888. In the following year he went into management at the Shaftesbury Theatre (q.v.), where he produced among other things Henry Arthur Jones's *The Middleman* (1889), himself playing Cyrus Blenkarn. He then appeared in America with such success that he returned there annually for some years, touring the United States and Canada with a repertory of successful plays. Among them was Barrie's *The Professor's Love Story* (1894), in which he made a great hit, thus proving that he could handle tenderness and emotion with the same skill as villainy. This had already been shown earlier in a revival of Tom Taylor's *Arkwright's Wife* and in his playing of Tom Pinch in Dickens's *Martin Chuzzlewit*. He retired in 1906.

WILLIAMS, BARNEY [really BERNARD O'FLAHERTY] (1824–76), American actor of Irish extraction, who with his wife MARIA PRAY (1826–1911), the sister-in-law of W. J. Florence (q.v.), toured the United States for many years, mainly in Irish comedies. He was seen in London in 1855 in Samuel Lever's *Rory O'More*, and remained there for four years, returning to New York to become manager of Wallack's old theatre, which he rechristened the Broadway (q.v.). But he soon found that touring was both pleasanter and more profitable than management and so took to the road again. He made his last appearance in 1875, after forty years in the theatre, and to the end remained not so much an actor as an entertainer, a much-loved, jovial, rollicking, drinking, stage Irishman on the boards and off.

WILLIAMS, BERT [really EGBERT AUSTIN] (c. 1876–1922), a Negro from the Bahamas who joined an American minstrel troupe. In 1895 he teamed up with George Walker, also a Negro comedian, and after perfecting a double act with him on tour, appeared in it with outstanding success at Koster and Bial's, New York. In 1903 he produced an all-Negro musical comedy, *In Dahomey*, which was given with much success in New York and London. It was followed by several others, but after the death of Walker in 1909 Williams gave up management and appeared as leading comedian in the *Ziegfeld Follies*, writing his own material. Off-stage he was a serious, scholarly man, light in colour, but for his performances he blacked himself and portrayed the shuffling, shiftless Negro of tradition. He had great gifts and might, had circumstances permitted, have become an outstanding actor. In his chosen line he did excellent work and was a pioneer for his race in the American theatre.

WILLIAMS, BRANSBY [really BRANSBY WILLIAM PHAREZ] (1870–1961), a top-line music-hall performer who for many years specialized in the presentation of characters from Dickens and Shakespeare, musical monologues, and imitations of famous actors. He was first with a provincial stock company, playing a variety of parts which laid the foundation of his excellent technique, but deserted the theatre for the music-hall in 1896, making his first appearance at Shoreditch, London. Shortly afterwards he deputized at short notice for Dan Leno at the Tivoli with such success that he was immediately engaged on his own account, and soon became one of the most popular entertainers of his day, both in England and America. He was a fine low comedian in pantomime and in his later years a star of radio and television. In 1954 he published a most interesting volume of reminiscences. Among his most famous recitations (to music) were Milton Hayes's 'The Green Eye of the Little Yellow God' and 'The Whitest Man I Know'.

WILLIAMS, (GEORGE) EMLYN (1905–87), Welsh actor, dramatist, and theatre director, who first appeared in London in 1927, and in 1933 made an adaptation of Fauchois's *Prenez-garde à la peinture* as *The Late Christopher Bean* which, with Edith Evans (q.v.) as Gwenny, ran for over a year. But his first outstanding success, both as actor and author, was scored with *Night Must Fall* (1935; New York, 1936). Among other excellent performances were his Angelo in *Measure for Measure* at the Old Vic in 1937 and Sir Robert Morton in Rattigan's *The Winslow Boy* in 1946. In 1962 he successfully took over the part of Sir Thomas More in the American production of Bolt's *A Man For All Seasons*, following Paul Scofield. He became widely known for his impersonation of Dickens in a 'one-man reading' from the latter's works, first seen in 1951, in which he toured the world, and also for *A Boy Growing Up* (1955), a reading from the works of his fellow-countryman, Dylan

Thomas. Some of his best work on the stage was done in his own plays, which include *Spring 1600* (1934); *He Was Born Gay* (1937) (which unfortunately 'died young'); *The Corn Is Green* (1938; New York, 1940), perhaps his best and certainly his most popular play, in which he played the young Welsh miner Morgan Evans, with Sybil Thorndike (q.v.) as his teacher, Miss Moffat; *The Light of Heart* (1940); *The Morning Star* (1941); *The Druid's Rest* (1944); *The Wind of Heaven* (1945); *Trespass* (1947); *Accolade* (1950); *Someone Waiting* (1953; New York, 1956); and, his last to date, *Beth* (1958). In 1961 he published *George*, a finely written account of his youth up to his first appearance on the stage. He was appointed C.B.E. in 1962 for services to the theatre.

WILLIAMS, (ERNEST GEORGE) HARCOURT (1880–1957), English actor and director, who celebrated his stage jubilee in 1948 while appearing as William the Waiter in Shaw's *You Never Can Tell*, in which he had appeared as Valentine in 1907. He made his first appearance in Belfast in 1898 under Benson, with whom he also appeared in London in 1900. He was with most of the leading players of the day, touring with Ellen Terry and George Alexander (qq.v.) and visiting America with H. B. Irving (q.v.), and was Count O'Dowda in the first production of Shaw's *Fanny's First Play* (1911). After serving in the First World War he reappeared on the London stage in 1919 in Drinkwater's *Abraham Lincoln*. Among his later parts were the Stranger in Chesterton's *Magic* (1923) and the Player King in *Hamlet* (1925), with John Barrymore (q.v.). From 1929 to 1934 he was at the Old Vic (q.v.), where his innovations in Shakespearian production were first criticized and later hailed as epoch-making, based as they were upon the ideas advanced by Granville-Barker (q.v.) in his *Prefaces to Shakespeare* and Williams's own love of and feeling for the swiftness and splendour of Elizabethan verse. He also introduced Shaw into the repertory with revivals of *Androcles and the Lion* and *The Dark Lady of the Sonnets* (1930), a precedent not often followed. In 1937 he gave a fine performance as William of Sens in Dorothy Sayers's *The Zeal of Thy House*, which he also directed, and some years later returned to the Old Vic company, with which he visited New York in 1946. In 1935 he published a volume of reminiscences, *Four Years at the Old Vic.* In 1908 he married JEAN STERLING MACKINLAY (1882–1958), who was prominently associated with the movement for a Children's Theatre in England and for twenty-seven years staged a unique series of children's matinées at Christmas-time.

WILLIAMS, PETER VLADIMIROVICH (1902–47), Soviet theatre designer, who in 1934 created some most original settings for *The Pickwick Club,* a dramatization of Dickens's novel produced at the Moscow Art Theatre. In 1946 he was equally acclaimed for his designs for Alexei Tolstoy's *Ivan the Terrible,* for which, rejecting the usual parade of sumptuousness and grandeur, he used a simple wooden structure whose severity served to intensify the harsh spirit of the time. One of his last décors was for Virta's *Great Days* (1947). His early death was a great loss to the Russian stage.

WILLIAMS, 'TENNESSEE' [really THOMAS LANIER] (1914–83), American playwright, whose outspoken plays caused much controversy. In 1939 he was awarded a Theatre Guild prize for four one-act plays entitled *American Blues,* but after this auspicious start his first full-length play failed to achieve Broadway, though *You Touched Me!,* written in collaboration with Donald Windham, ran at the Booth Theatre for several months in 1945. In the same year Williams scored an outstanding success with *The Glass Menagerie,* in which Laurette Taylor (q.v.) made her last appearance as the mother, the part played in London in 1948 by Helen Hayes (q.v.) with equal success. This was followed by the Pulitzer Prize-winner, *A Streetcar Named Desire* (1947), seen in London in 1949 with Vivien Leigh (q.v.) as Blanche du Bois, and by *Summer and Smoke,* first produced by Margo Jones (q.v.) in Dallas in 1947. It was seen in New York a year later and in London in 1951. Rewritten and retitled *The Eccentricities of a Nightingale,* it was revived at the Yvonne Arnaud Theatre (q.v.) in 1967. Williams's later plays, which usually reached London after a time-lag sufficient to soften their initial impact, include *The Rose Tattoo* (1951; London, 1959), banned in Dublin (q.v.) in 1957; *Camino Real* (1953; London, 1957), an unsuccessful essay in symbolism based on *Don Quixote*; *Cat on a Hot Tin Roof* (1955), which was awarded the Pulitzer

Prize for Drama but was banned in London and produced privately in 1958; *Orpheus Descending* (1957; London, 1959); *Garden District* (New York and London, 1958), a double bill consisting of *Something Unspoken* and *Suddenly Last Summer*; *Sweet Bird of Youth* (1959), which was given its first production in England by the Manchester Experimental Theatre Club in 1964 and revived at Watford in 1969; and *Period of Adjustment* (1960), which had a successful run in London in 1962. In 1961 *The Night of the Iguana* was seen on Broadway, and in 1965 was produced at the Ashcroft Theatre, Croydon, with Siân Phillips as Hannah Jelkes, the part played in New York by Margaret Leighton (q.v.). The Croydon production was subsequently transferred to the West End. Williams's next play, *The Milk Train Doesn't Stop Here Anymore,* was first seen at the Festival of Two Worlds, Spoleto, in 1962, and in New York a year later. In London it has so far been seen only in an amateur production by the Tavistock Repertory Company (q.v.). *Slapstick Tragedy* (1966), made up of two short plays, *The Gnädiges Fräulein* and *The Mutilated, The Seven Descents of Myrtle* (1968), and *In the Bar of a Tokyo Hotel* (1969), had only short runs in New York and have not so far been seen in London. Among Williams's other one-act plays, *Twenty-Seven Wagons Full of Cotton,* produced in London by the Quipu lunch-time players in 1966, was first seen in New York in 1955 as part of a triple bill, *All in One,* and has since been published, together with a number of other one-act plays and the full-length plays enumerated above.

Williamsburg, VIRGINIA, U.S.A., one of the first towns in the New World to have theatrical performances (see STAGG). In 1736 Addison's *Cato* was produced there, probably by a group of amateurs, also Mrs. Centlivre's *The Busybody* and, at a slightly later date, Addison's *The Drummer; or, the Haunted House.* It was at Williamsburg that a professional company headed by Hallam (q.v.) first played on their arrival from England, opening on 15 Sept. 1752 with Shakespeare's *The Merchant of Venice* and Ben Jonson's *The Alchemist.*

WILLIS, TED [really EDWARD HENRY; BARON WILLIS OF CHISLEHURST] (1918–   ), see UNITY THEATRE (2).

WILLS, IVAH (1882–1937), see COBURN, C. D.

WILSON, FRANCIS (1854–1935), an American actor, who at fourteen appeared in a black-face song-and-dance act in which he toured successfully for many years. He then worked at the Chestnut Street Theatre (q.v.) in Philadelphia, and subsequently appeared in a number of productions, making his reputation as Cadeaux in the musical play *Erminie* (based on Selby's *Robert Macaire*) at the Casino on 10 May 1886. From then until 1904 he appeared in musical comedy, and in 1907 was seen in Charles Marlowe's farce *When Knights Were Bold*. This was followed by his own play, *The Bachelor's Baby* (1909), which ran for three years and earned him a fortune. He retired in 1921.

WILSON, JOHN (1585–?1641), a member of Shakespeare's company who has been confused with the eminent lutanist and Oxford Professor of Music of the same name. He was evidently a musician, since a stage direction of *Much Ado About Nothing* puts 'Jacke Wilson' for Balthasar. He must therefore have been the original singer of 'Sigh no more, Ladies'.

WILSON, JOSEPHINE, see MILES, SIR BERNARD.

WILSON, ROBERT (?–c. 1600), an Elizabethan actor and playwright, who was originally one of Leicester's Men and joined the Queen Elizabeth's Men (q.v.) in about 1583. On the breaking-up of this company during the plague of 1592–3, Wilson probably gave up acting and devoted himself to playwriting, mainly for Henslowe's Admiral's Men (q.v.), and to extemporizing, a favourite Elizabethan pastime in which he is noted as having indulged at the Swan (q.v.) on Bankside.

WILSON, SANDY [really ALEXANDER] GALBRAITH (1924–), English dramatist and composer, who began his theatrical career by contributing material to such revues as *Oranges and Lemons* (1948), *Slings and Arrows* (1949), *See You Later* (1951), and *See You Again* (1952). In 1953 he scored an immense success with *The Boy Friend*, a parody of the type of musical popular in the 1920s. First produced as part of the nightly bill at the Players, this was expanded for production at the Embassy and then moved to Wyndham's, where it ran for five years. It was revived late in 1967, again with

great success, and has been seen at a number of suburban and provincial theatres throughout the country, including the Yvonne Arnaud at Guildford and the Northcott at Exeter. It also had a long run in New York in 1954, and was successfully produced in South Africa under the direction of the author. Wilson's later musicals, which were none of them as successful as *The Boy Friend*, include *The Buccaneer* (1953, revived 1955), *Valmouth* (1958), based on a novel by Ronald Firbank, and *Divorce Me, Darling!* (1965), a pastiche of the 1930s. He also contributed musical numbers to the revue *Pieces of Eight* (1959), and to the play *Call It Love* (1960), by Robert Tanich.

WILTON, MARIE (1839–1921), see BANCROFT, SIR SQUIRE.

Winchester, LONDON, see SURREY MUSIC-HALL.

Windmill Theatre, LONDON. This one-tier intimate playhouse, originally a cinema, was in Great Windmill Street (so called because a windmill stood there during the seventeenth and eighteenth centuries), off Shaftesbury Avenue. It opened on 22 June 1931 with Michael Barringer's *Inquest*, but the venture failed, and early in the following year Mrs. Laura Henderson, the owner of the theatre, and her manager, Vivian Van Damm, tried the experiment of non-stop revue, or 'continuous variety', which had already proved popular in Paris. This was successful; the Windmill Girls, in a show which ran from 2 p.m. to midnight, became a feature of London life. Many famous comedians, among them Jimmy Edwards, Harry Secombe, Eric Barker, and Tony Hancock, made their first successes on the small stage of the Windmill, and it was the only theatre to remain open during the bombing of London in 1941, adopting as its slogan 'We never closed'. After the death of Van Damm in 1960 the theatre continued for a time along the same lines but finally closed on 31 Oct. 1964 and became a cinema. The history of the Windmill was told by Vivian Van Damm in *To-night and Every Night* (1954).

Windsor Theatre, NEW YORK, see FORTY-EIGHTH STREET THEATRE.

Wing, a canvas-covered flat placed at the side of the stage, either facing or obliquely towards the audience, used in conjunction with a backcloth to mask-in the side of the set. There may be anything from one to eight rows on each side of the stage. Their use has been largely superseded by the closed-in box-set (q.v.), except in panto-mime and spectacular musical shows and in exteriors. To be 'in the wings' means to be standing in the space behind the wings, out of sight of the audience; here actors normally await their cues.

WINTER, WILLIAM (1836–1917), Ameri-can dramatic critic, whose conservatism made him the transatlantic counterpart of Clement Scott (q.v.). In 1861 he joined the staff of the *Albion*, and from 1865 to 1909 worked for the *New York Tribune*. He was the most powerful dramatic critic of his time in the United States, probably because he rarely committed himself to an opinion at variance with that of the great majority of his readers. He was undis-guisedly antagonistic to such foreign visitors as Duse, Bernhardt, and Réjane (qq.v.) and denounced both Ibsen and Shaw (qq.v.). After his retirement from the *Tribune*, he contributed articles on theatrical matters to *Harper's Weekly* and other periodicals and wrote biographies of a number of actors, including Irving, Jefferson, Booth, Mansfield, and Belasco. His books contain much valuable inform-ation, but they are so pompous that it is almost impossible to read them with any pleasure.

Winter Garden Theatre, NEW YORK, on the site of the American Horse Exchange, on the east side of Broadway between 50th and 51st Streets. This opened on 20 Mar. 1911 with a musical show and has been used mainly for musicals and revues. For some years it was a cinema but returned to live theatre in 1933. It was here that *West Side Story*, with music by Leonard Bernstein, began its long run on 26 Sept. 1957. In 1964 Barbra Streisand made a great success at this theatre in the musical *Funny Girl*.

(For an earlier Winter Garden Theatre in New York, see METROPOLITAN THEATRE; for the Winter Garden Theatre, London, see MIDDLESEX MUSIC-HALL.)

Winthrop Ames Theatre, NEW YORK, see LITTLE THEATRE (2).

WITKIEWICZ, STANISŁAW IGNACY (1885–1939), Polish artist, novelist, and dramatist, known as Witkacy. He led a stormy and unhappy life, in the course of which he travelled widely in Russia and also visited Australia, and committed suicide shortly after the division of Poland between Nazi Germany and Soviet Russia which preceded the Second World War. His plays, which form part of the *avant-garde* Expressionist movement which swept across Europe in the 1920s, were first performed only in small experimental theatres. They were rediscovered in 1956 and recognized not only as foreshadowing the work of Brecht (q.v.) but as contain-ing also the seeds of Beckett's and Ionesco's Theatre of the Absurd (q.v.). Many of them were revived, and in 1962 all his plays, numbering about thirty, were published in a two-volume edition. Two of them, as *Das Wasserhuhn* and *Narr und Nonne*, were published in a German translation in 1968. In the same year, as *The Waterhen* and *The Madman*, they appeared in an American edition, translated by D. C. Gerauld and C. S. Durer, with an introduction by the Polish theatre historian, Jan Kott (q.v.). The volume contained also *The Mother, The Crazy Locomotives, They,* and *The Shoe-makers. The Mother*, as *La Mère*, was pub-lished in a French translation in 1969, together with *La Metaphysique d'un veau à deux têtes.*

WOFFINGTON, PEG [really MARGARET] (c. 1718–60), a celebrated actress who first appeared on the stage as a child of twelve in Dublin, her birthplace, playing Polly in Gay's *The Beggar's Opera*. She was later engaged for the Smock Alley Theatre, Dublin, where she appeared in a wide range of parts, including Sir Harry Wildair in Farquhar's *The Constant Couple*, in which she was first seen in April 1740. She was then engaged by John Rich for Covent Garden, where the rest of her career was passed. As Sir Harry she became the toast of the town and the subject of a portrait by Hogarth. Al-though a certain harshness in her voice rendered her unfit for tragedy, she was excellent in such high-comedy parts as Millamant in Congreve's *The Way of the World*, Lady Townly in *The Provoked Husband* and Lady Betty Modish in *The Careless Husband*, both by Colley Cibber (q.v.). She was known as the most beautiful and least vain woman of her day, but her good nature did not extend to her fellow-actresses, and she was constantly at odds with them, particularly George Ann Bellamy (q.v.), whom she is said to have driven from the stage and wounded with a dagger in a fit of rage. She was for some years the mistress of Garrick (q.v.), who wrote for her the charming song 'My Lovely Peggy'. The last male part she appeared in was Lothario in Rowe's *The Fair Penitent*. She also played Lady Randolph in Home's *Douglas* when it was first seen in London in 1757, Spranger Barry (q.v.) playing Norval. She made her last appearance as Rosalind in *As You Like It* on 3 May 1757, being taken ill at the beginning of the Epilogue. She is the subject of the play *Masks and Faces* (1852), written by Charles Reade and Tom Taylor, on which Reade later based his novel *Peg Woffington*, and of a biography by Janet Dunbar, *Peg Woffington and Her World* (1968). Her younger sister Mary, known as Polly, was also on the stage for a short time, but left it to make a brilliant marriage with Robert, second son of the Earl of Cholmondeley.

Wolfenbüttel, a German town where at the end of the sixteenth century the reigning Duke of Brunswick, Heinrich Julius (1564–1613) (q.v.), had in his household a troupe of professional actors, mainly English, under the leadership of Thomas Sackville, who appeared in some of the plays written by the Duke in the 1590s, of which eleven are extant. Although the Duke adopted some of the stage conventions of the English Comedians (q.v.), recent research has shown that he was less under the influence of the Elizabethan dramatists, including Shakespeare, than had previously been supposed. About half the plays call for the old multiple set (q.v.), the others being in the new-style single set. There is unfortunately no record of the place and style of these Court presentations, and theatrical activities came to an end with the Duke's increasing involvement in politics. It was not until 1688 that a theatre was built near the castle by Duke Anton Ulrich (1633–1714), who took into his service a number of French and Italian dancers, singers, and musicians for whom he wrote the libretti of several operas. He also built an indoor theatre in his new château at Salzdahlum, near Wolfenbüttel, and an open-air theatre in the garden.

WOLFIT [really WOOLFITT], SIR DONALD (1902–68), one of the last English actor-managers, who made his first appearance on the stage in 1920 and four years later appeared in London in Temple Thurston's *The Wandering Jew*. He was at the Old Vic from 1929 to 1930, toured Canada as Robert Browning in Besier's *The Barretts of Wimpole Street* during 1931–2, and in 1933 was seen in London again as Thomas Mowbray in Gordon Daviot's *Richard of Bordeaux*. He was at Stratford-upon-Avon in 1936, and in the following year formed his own company, touring extensively in a Shakespearian repertory in which he also appeared for a season at the Kingsway in 1940. During the Battle of Britain he gave over one hundred lunch-time performances of scenes from Shakespeare, which were much appreciated by those whom the war and the black-out had deprived of theatre-going in the evening. He continued to tour in Shakespeare and other classics, two of his best performances being as Volpone in Ben Jonson's play of that name and Sir Giles Overreach in Massinger's *A New Way to Pay Old Debts*. He was excellent at the Old Vic in 1951 in the title-role of Marlowe's *Tamburlaine* and as Lord Ogleby in Colman's *The Clandestine Marriage*. In 1957 he appeared at the Lyric, Hammersmith, in two plays by Montherlant (q.v.), *The Master of Santiago* and *Malatesta*. He was the author of an autobiography, *First Interval*, and was knighted in 1957 for his services to the theatre, and to Shakespeare in particular. He married ROSALIND IDEN (1911–), daughter of B. Iden Payne (q.v.), who appeared as his leading lady in many of his Shakespearian and other productions.

WOOD, (GERALD) CHARLES (1932–), English dramatist, whose plays are mainly concerned with exploring military life and the military mind, as exemplified in the British army at its worst. His first work for the theatre—he had previously written for television—was *Cockade* (1963), a triple bill which included *Prisoner and Escort*, *John Thomas*, and *Spare*, all featuring aspects of army life. A further one-act play, *Don't Make Me Laugh* (1965), which shows the soldier at home, was followed by two full-length plays, *Dingo* (1967), set partly in a North African prisoner-of-war camp, and *H; Monologues at Front of Burning Cities* (1969), a savage indictment of Havelock's march to the relief of Lucknow during the Indian Mutiny. Wood's other and less successful plays include the farcical fantasy *Meals on Wheels* (1965), followed by *Fill the Stage with Happy Hours* (1966), *A Bit of a Holiday* (1969), and another triple bill called *Welfare* (1970), made up of the comic sketch *Tie Up the Ballcock*, a shortened version of *Meals on Wheels*, and *Labour*, which, like the other two, deals with the relationship between youth and age, pre- and post-Second World War. Wood has also to his credit a number of excellent film-scripts, and it remains to be seen whether the cinema will tempt him away from the theatre.

WOOD, MRS. JOHN [*née* MATILDA CHARLOTTE VINING] (1831–1915), a member of a well-known theatrical family, first cousin to Fanny Vining, the mother of Fanny Davenport (q.v.), and an actress and theatre manageress well known in England and the United States. She had already made a reputation for herself in the English provinces when in 1854 she went to America. Widowed in 1863, she took over the Olympic Theatre (q.v.) in New York, later to be made famous by Mitchell, and ran it successfully for three years, leaving to make her first appearance on the London stage in 1866 as Miss Miggs in a dramatization of Dickens's *Barnaby Rudge*. From 1869 to 1877 she was manageress of the St. James's Theatre in London, where she was highly respected by her company and popular with the public. She was at the Royal Court Theatre from 1883 to 1892, taking over the management in 1888 and appearing in the first productions of Pinero's *The Magistrate* (1885), *The Schoolmistress* (1886), and *Dandy Dick* (1887). A woman of liberal views, she spared no expense in the conduct of her affairs and ruled her actors kindly but firmly. She made her last appearance in New York under Daly (q.v.) in 1873, and thereafter was seen only in London, where she died.

WOOD, WILLIAM BURKE (1779–1861), the first American-born actor to hold a high place in the American theatre. With Warren (q.v.), he was for many years manager of the Chestnut Street Theatre, Philadelphia, and a diary which he kept from 1810 to 1833 contains much of interest on the history of the early American theatre. The list of plays given each season shows a marked preponderance of Shakespeare and of plays imported from England, but in later years more native offerings crept in. Wood's predilection for the English classics may have been due to his own admirable playing of polished comedy, but he was also good in

the lighter parts of tragedy. He married JULIANA WESTRAY, an actress, who with her two sisters had been at the Park Theatre, New York, and she appeared for many years under his management.

Wood's Broadway Theatre, NEW YORK, see BIJOU THEATRE (3).

Wood's Museum, NEW YORK, see DALY'S THEATRE (1).

WOODWARD, HARRY (1717–77), English actor, the last of the great Harlequins, before Grimaldi (q.v.) made Clown the central figure of the English harlequinade. He was on the stage as a child and in 1738 went to Drury Lane, where he remained for twenty years, writing many pantomimes for Garrick (q.v.), and playing Harlequin himself, being an excellent dancer and most expressive mime. He was also good as Mercutio (in *Romeo and Juliet*), as Touchstone (in *As You Like It*), as Petruchio (in Garrick's version of *The Taming of the Shrew*) to the Katharina of Kitty Clive (q.v.), as Bobadil (in Ben Jonson's *Every Man in His Humour*), and as Marplot (in his own adaptation of Mrs. Centlivre's *The Busybody*). In 1758 he went to Dublin as joint manager with Macklin and Spranger Barry (qq.v.) of the Crow Street Theatre, but their rivalry with Mossop (q.v.) at the Smock Alley Theatre resulted in the failure of both enterprises. Woodward returned to London in 1763 and joined the company at Covent Garden, where in 1775 he created the part of Captain Absolute in Sheridan's *The Rivals*.

WOODWORTH, SAMUEL (1785–1842), American dramatist, author of a domestic drama in the current European style, *The Deed of Gift* (1822); of an historical melodrama, *LaFayette*, played before Lafayette himself on his visit to New York in 1824; of *The Widow's Son* (1825), a tragedy based on an incident in the War of Independence; and of *The Forest Rose; or, American Farmers* (also 1825), featuring the popular Yankee character Jonathan Ploughboy, which later provided an excellent part for Dan Marble and Henry Placide (qq.v.). Woodworth, who was also a journalist, edited a Boston newspaper with John Howard Payne (q.v.).

WOOLGAR, SARAH JANE, see MELLON, MRS. ALFRED.

WOOLLCOTT, ALEXANDER HUMPHREYS (1887–1943), American dramatic critic, best remembered as the prototype of Sheridan Whiteside in *The Man Who Came to Dinner* (1939), by Kaufman and Hart. After working for several New York papers he retired in 1928 to devote himself to broadcasting, lecture tours, and the writing of magazine articles. As a dramatic critic his judgements were capricious in the extreme. He was more interested in players than in plays and missed or misjudged many important works of his time, including the plays of O'Neill (q.v.), which he dismissed as completely worthless. He himself turned playwright on two occasions, collaborating with George Kaufman on *The Channel Road* (1929) and *The Dark Tower* (1932), and appeared on the stage three times—in Behrman's *Brief Moment* (1932) and *Wine of Choice* (1938), and in the road company of *The Man Who Came to Dinner*. Though his criticism was ephemeral, he wrote engagingly, and his volumes of fugitive pieces were popular. They include *Shouts and Murmurs* (1922), *Mr. Dickens Goes to the Play* (1923), *Enchanted Aisles* (1924), *Going to Pieces* (1928), and *While Rome Burns* (1934). He also wrote a life of Mrs. Fiske (q.v.), published in 1917, and *The Story of Irving Berlin* (1925). An informative full-length biography of Woollcott himself was written by Samuel Hopkins Adams.

WORMS, GUSTAVE-HIPPOLYTE (1836–1910), French actor, who made his début at the Comédie-Française in 1858, playing young lovers in comedy and tragedy. He soon proved himself a good actor but, tired of waiting to be received as a member of the company, he left to go to Russia, where he spent several successful and profitable years. Back in Paris in 1877, the Comédie-Française asked him to return, which he did, making a great success as Don Carlos in a revival of Victor Hugo's *Hernani*, with Mounet-Sully (q.v.) in the title-role and Sarah Bernhardt (q.v.) as Doña Sol. He also appeared in several plays by the younger Dumas, but was at his best in heroic parts or in the elegant heroes of Old Comedy. For many years he was a professor at the Paris Conservatoire.

WYATT, FRANK (1852–1926), see MELNOTTE, VIOLET.

WYCHERLEY, WILLIAM (1640–1716), Restoration dramatist, whose comedies, though coarse and often frankly indecent, show so much strength and savagery in attacking the vices of the day that their author has been labelled 'a moralist at heart'. He was to some extent influenced by Molière (q.v.), but transmuted his borrowings by his own particular genius, and his style has an individuality seldom found in other writers of the time. His first play, *Love in a Wood; or, St. James's Park* (1671), was followed by *The Gentleman Dancing-Master* (1672), based on *El Maestro de danzar*, by Calderón (q.v.), and the least characteristic of his works. His best-known play is *The Country Wife* (1675), which was revived several times. In 1766 it was adapted by Garrick (q.v.) as *The Country Girl* and produced at Drury Lane, where the part of Peggy, the heroine, was a favourite with Mrs. Jordan (q.v.), who played it inimitably. It was not seen in London again until it was revived in its original form in 1924 by the Phoenix Society, as was *The Gentleman Dancing-Master* in 1925. Both have been seen in London since, *The Country Wife* at the Old Vic in 1936 and at the Royal Court in 1956 (it was also seen at the Chichester Festival Theatre in 1969), and *The Gentleman Dancing-Master* at the Gateway in 1950. Wycherley's last, and perhaps best, play was *The Plain Dealer* (1676). It was frequently revived up to the end of the eighteenth century, and in 1925 was produced at the Scala by the Renaissance Theatre company.

WYLIE [really SAMUELSON], JULIAN (1878–1934), English theatre manager. He was a theatrical agent in Manchester before going to London, where he added to his business an 'ideas department', advising the artistes he represented how best to use their talents and build up their acts. He was himself a very accomplished illusionist and invented a 'talking head', which, without any body attached, answered questions put to it by the audience. In addition to his mastery of stage magic he was well versed in theatre mechanics and was probably one of the best technical producers of his day. When pantomime (q.v.) was at a low ebb, he rescued it, producing *The Sleeping Beauty* at Drury Lane in Dec. 1929 after that traditional home of pantomime had been without one for ten years. He was also responsible for the production of the musical comedy, *Mr. Cinders*, with Bobby Howes, earlier in 1929, and of J. B.

Priestley's *The Good Companions* in 1931. He died suddenly while producing his second Drury Lane pantomime.

WYNDHAM [really CULVERWELL], SIR CHARLES (1837–1919), English actor-manager, who made his professional début in 1862 in London and then went to the United States, where, having trained originally as a surgeon, he served in that capacity in the Federal Army. He twice resigned to appear on the stage, playing Osric in the Hamlet of John Wilkes Booth (q.v.) in Washington in April 1863 and Thomas Brown in Barker's *The Indian Princess; or, La Belle Sauvage* with Mrs. John Wood (q.v.) at the Olympic in Oct. 1863. After an unsuccessful visit to London in 1864, he returned to the United States, where he became known as an excellent light comedian and from 1871 to 1873 headed the Wyndham Comedy Company on an extended tour of the Middle West. Back in London in 1874, he made a success with Bronson Howard's *Saratoga*, renamed *Brighton*, which he subsequently took to the Criterion (q.v.), thus inaugurating an association with that theatre which was to last for the rest of his life. He made it one of the foremost playhouses of London, and also built and managed the New Theatre and Wyndham's (qq.v.), making them equally successful. One of his best parts was David Garrick in T. W. Robertson's play of that name, but he was also good in the plays of Henry Arthur Jones—particularly *The Case of Rebellious Susan* (1894), *The Liars* (1897), and *Mrs. Dane's Defence* (1900), and in H. H. Davies's *The Mollusc* (1907). He was knighted in 1902 for services to the stage. He married as his second wife Mary Moore (q.v.), widow of the playwright James Albery.

WYNDHAM, R. H. (1817–94), see EDINBURGH.

Wyndham's Theatre, LONDON, in the Charing Cross Road. This was built by Charles Wyndham (q.v.), and opened on 16 Nov. 1899 with a revival of Robertson's *David Garrick*, in which Wyndham and his wife Mary Moore (q.v.) had already appeared with great success. A number of interesting plays followed, among them Henry Arthur Jones's *Mrs. Dane's Defence* (1900) and *Glittering Gloria* (1903), a farce by Hugh Morton which had James Welch and a bulldog in the leading

parts. Frank Curzon, who took over the management of the theatre in 1903, was equally successful with H. H. Davies's *Mrs. Gorringe's Necklace* (1903) and Charles Marlowe's *When Knights Were Bold* (1907). Two years later a play by Guy du Maurier dealing with the invasion of England, under the title *An Englishman's Home*, caused a sensation and materially increased the recruiting for the newly established Territorial Army. In 1910 Gerald du Maurier (q.v.) joined Curzon, and their joint management scored a number of successes, among them Barrie's *A Kiss for Cinderella* (1916) and *Dear Brutus* (1917); Sapper's *Bulldog Drummond* (1921); and *The Ringer* (1926), by Edgar Wallace, who was for a time manager of the theatre. Six of Wallace's plays had their first productions there, the last, *The Green Park*, in 1932, on the night before his death in Hollywood. Wyndham's son HOWARD (1865–1947) and SIR BRONSON ALBERY (1881–1971), son of Mary Moore by her first husband, then took over the theatre and inaugurated a long series of successful productions, among them Savory's *George and Margaret* (1937), and Esther McCracken's *Quiet Wedding* (1938) and its sequel, *Quiet Weekend* (1941). Among post-war successes have been *Deep Are the Roots* (1947), by Arnaud d'Usseau and James Gow, Bridie's *Daphne Laureola* (1948), in which Edith Evans (q.v.) gave a fine performance, Ustinov's *The Love of Four Colonels* (1951), in which he played a leading part himself, and four transfers from Theatre Workshop (q.v.)—Shelagh Delaney's *A Taste of Honey* and Brendan Behan's *The Hostage* in 1959, Stephen Lewis's *Sparrers Can't Sing* in 1961, and *Oh, What a Lovely War!*, by Charles Chilton and others, in 1963. In 1961 an American play on Helen Keller, *The Miracle Worker*, by William Gibson, had a long run. Later productions were a dramatization of Muriel Spark's novel, *The Prime of Miss Jean Brodie* (1966), Simon Gray's *Wise Child* (1967), and *The Italian Girl* (1968), by Iris Murdoch and James Saunders. This last was a transfer from the Bristol Old Vic, as was a comedy about contraception by Kevin Laffan, *It's a Two-Foot-Six-Inches Above-the-Ground World* (1970), which followed a successful American play about homosexuals, *The Boys in the Band*, by Mart Crowley. A further transfer from the Bristol Old Vic was Ronald Millar's play about a pair of star-crossed lovers, *Abelard and Heloise* (also 1970).

WYNYARD, DIANA [really DOROTHY ISOBEL COX] (1906–64), English actress of great personal beauty and charm, who appeared with equal success in a wide variety of Shakespearian and modern parts. She made her first appearance in London in 1925 and then went on tour. From 1927 to 1929 she was with the Liverpool Repertory Theatre, where she laid the foundations of her future outstanding career. After a visit to New York in 1932 she returned to London to make a great success as Charlotte Brontë in Clemence Dane's *Wild Decembers* (1933), and in 1939 played Gilda in Noël Coward's *Design for Living*—the part originally played in New York by Lynn Fontanne (q.v.). After the Second World War she spent two seasons (1948 and 1949) at Stratford-upon-Avon, and toured Australia with the Stratford company, appearing in Moscow as Gertrude to the Hamlet of Paul Scofield (q.v.). She then appeared in a succession of new plays, including Whiting's *Marching Song* (1954), Anderson's *The Bad Seed* (1955) and Hellman's *Toys in the Attic* (1960), Tennessee Williams's *Camino Real* (1957), and N. C. Hunter's *A Touch of the Sun* (1958). In 1953 she was created C.B.E. for services to the theatre.

WYSPIAŃSKI, STANISŁAW (1869–1907), Polish poet and playwright, director, and scene designer. The best of his poetic dramas, which are based on national themes interwoven with classical symbolism, are *The Wedding* (1901), *Akropolis* (1903), and *November Night* (1904), which deals with the Polish insurrection of 1830. Some of his works were translated into English in 1933. Considered as the successor of Mickiewicz (q.v.), he was the first to co-ordinate and stage the latter's vast poetic drama, *Forefathers' Eve*, in 1901. He made many innovations in stagecraft and envisaged a form of 'total theatre' which included a new architectural concept of the theatre building. Unfortunately his early death prevented the realization of his plans, but he had a great influence on his successors in the Polish theatre, notably Leon Schiller (q.v.). He had a wide knowledge of Shakespeare, and in a long introduction to a re-issue in 1901 of a translation of *Hamlet* by Paszkowski, first published in 1860, he put forward a new view of the play, making the Ghost the central character, which resulted in a most interesting production, first seen in 1901 and repeated in 1905. *Akropolis* was one of the plays chosen by the experimental producer Grotowski (q.v.) for his Laboratory Theatre's first appearance outside Poland in 1966.

Y

YABLOCHKINA, ALEXANDRA ALEXAND-
ROVNA (1868–1964), famous Russian
actress, who was on the stage as a child
at the Alexandrinsky (q.v.) in St. Petersburg (Leningrad), where her father was
stage manager. She made her adult début
in 1888 at the Maly Theatre in Moscow
(q.v.) where she remained until her death,
playing Miss Crawley in a dramatization
of Thackeray's *Vanity Fair* at the age of
ninety-four. During her long career she
appeared in a vast range of parts that included the heroines of Shakespeare, Oscar
Wilde, and Galsworthy and leading roles
in Russian plays from Griboyedov and
Gorky to Romashov and Korneichuk
(qq.v.). She devoted much of her time
under the Tsarist regime to theatrical
charities and was chairman of the All-
Russian Theatrical Society from 1916
until her death.

YAKOVLEV, ALEXEI SEMENOVICH (1773–
1817), Russian actor, who made his first
appearance on the stage in 1794 and,
thanks to his excellent presence and
powerful voice and the instruction given
him by Dmitrevsky (q.v.), was soon playing leading roles. His acting was mainly
intuitive, and his temperament rebelled
against craftsmanship and technical detail.
His performances were therefore very
unequal, but he had moments of greatness,
and was sufficiently interested in his
profession to try and initiate reforms
which were later carried out by Shchepkin
(q.v.). A heavy drinker, he died soon after
collapsing on stage while playing Othello.

Yale University, NEW HAVEN, CONN. This
American university had theatrical performances annually from as early as 1771.
Among the first productions were Steele's
The Conscious Lovers, Farquhar's *The
Beaux' Stratagem*, and in 1785 an original
play, *The Mercenary Match*, written by
one Bidwell, an undergraduate in his
senior year. There has now been for many
years an amateur dramatic society for the
students, and in 1925 a Drama Department was inaugurated. This has an excellent little experimental theatre built and
endowed by Edward Harkness, of which
Professor George Baker (q.v.) was the first
director. The curriculum comprises an

elaborate post-graduate course, with instruction in design, lighting, costuming,
and production, and provides opportunities for writing plays for subsequent production. There is also in the university
library a theatre collection, which houses
among other things a vast dossier of
photographs of theatrical material collected from all over Europe. This was
begun under the supervision of Professor
Allardyce Nicoll (q.v.) during his term of
office as head of the Drama Department,
and is constantly being added to.

YANSHIN, MIKHAIL MIKHAILOVICH
(1902–76), Soviet actor and director, who
became a member of the Moscow Art
Theatre company in 1924. One of the
most successful roles of his early career
was Lariossik in Bulgakov's *The Days of
the Turbins* (1926), in which he showed
warmth, intimacy, and a subtle sense of
humour. Among his later outstanding
classic parts were Gradoboyev in Ostrovsky's *Warm Heart*, Telyegin in Chekhov's
Uncle Vanya, and Sir Peter Teazle in
Sheridan's *The School for Scandal*. He was
artistic director of the Gypsy Theatre from
1937 to 1941, and in 1950 became chief
producer at the Stanislavsky Theatre in
Moscow, where under his direction many
new Soviet plays were produced, including
Yermolinsky's *Griboyedov* (1951), Simu-
kov's *Beauteous Maidens* (1952), and
Shcheglov's *The Dreaming Forest* (1955).

YATES, FREDERICK HENRY (1795–1842),
English actor, friend of the elder Charles
Mathews (q.v.), who persuaded him to go
on the stage. He was first seen in Edinburgh, and in 1818 went to London, where
he played Iago to the Othello of Charles
Mayne Young (q.v.) and, in the following
year, Falstaff to the Hotspur of Macready
(q.v.). Having no pretensions to be anything but a useful actor, he played everything that was offered to him and always
well, but he eventually deserted tragedy
for comedy, where his real talent lay. In
1825, with Daniel Terry (q.v.), he took
over the Adelphi Theatre and inaugurated
there a series of melodramas, farces, and
burlesques, being joined on Terry's death
in 1829 by Mathews. Some of the best
authors of the day wrote for him, and he

himself was excellent in such Dickensian parts as Fagin in *Oliver Twist*, Mr. Mantalini in *Nicholas Nickleby*, and the grotesque Miss Miggs in *Barnaby Rudge*. His wife, ELIZABETH BRUNTON (1799–1860), niece of the famous Mrs. Merry (q.v.), was a leading member of his company. Their son, EDMUND (1832–94), a well-known journalist, was the author of a number of ephemeral plays. It was in a dramatization of one of his novels, *Kissing the Rod*, as *A Millionaire* (1883), that Maud Holt, later the wife of Beerbohm Tree (q.v.), made her first outstanding success in London.

YATES, RICHARD (1706–96), English comedian, and almost as good a Harlequin as Woodward (q.v.). He was in Giffard's company at Goodman's Fields Theatre (q.v.) until 1737, and then went to Drury Lane, where he remained for many years, playing Sir Oliver Surface in the first production of Sheridan's *The School for Scandal* (1777). He was also good in Shakespeare's fools and was considered the only actor of the time to have a just notion of how to play them. Fine gentlemen and serious comedy, however, lay outside his range. His first wife having died in 1753 he married an actress, MARY ANN GRAHAM (1728–87), who in 1754 made her first appearance at Drury Lane, remaining there until 1785. Though deficient in comedy and pathos, she was considered the finest actress of the day in eighteenth-century tragedy.

YEATS, WILLIAM BUTLER (1865–1939), Irish poet and dramatist, co-founder with Lady Gregory (q.v.) of the Irish Literary Theatre in 1899, winner of the Nobel Prize for Literature in 1923. He was a director of the Abbey Theatre (q.v.) from its foundation in 1904 until his death, and all his plays were produced there. These, which show the influence of such diverse elements as Celtic legends and the Japanese *nō* play (q.v.), stand somewhat apart from the dramatic traditions of his time, during which the realistic plays of Ibsen (q.v.) reigned supreme, and are only now beginning to make themselves felt in a theatre which is perhaps more receptive to them. The earliest were poetic dramas in the style of Maeterlinck—*The Countess Cathleen* (1892), *The Land of Heart's Desire* (1894), and *Cathleen ni Houlihan* (1902). The last of these was written in collaboration with Lady Gregory, who was also part-author with him of *The Pot of Broth* (1904), and of two poetic plays dramatically more powerful than the earlier ones—*The King's Threshold* (also 1904) and *The Unicorn from the Stars* (1908). Other plays of this period were *On Baile's Strand* (1904), *Deirdre* (1907), *The Green Helmet* (1910), *The Shadowy Waters* (1911), and *The Hour-Glass* (1914). Originally written in verse, this last was produced at the Abbey Theatre, but for later productions elsewhere was rewritten in prose owing to the difficulty of finding verse-speakers who met with Yeats's approval. There are also two versions of *The Only Jealousy of Emer* (1919), the second version, in prose, being entitled *Fighting the Waves*. Together with *At the Hawk's Well* (1917), *The Dreaming of the Bones* (1919), and *Calvary* (1920), it forms part of a series of 'four plays for dancers' in which extreme simplicity of design and setting is matched by brevity of expression and serenity of thought. In the later plays, written after the First World War, this plainness and severity, noticeable also in Yeats's poetry, is very apparent, and the poet's thought and expression make increasing demands upon the concentration and imagination of his audience. This is particularly true of *The Player Queen* (1922), *The Words Upon the Window Pane* (1934), and *Purgatory* (1939). Yeats also made new versions of Sophocles' *King Oedipus* (1928) and *Oedipus at Colonus* (1934). His last play was *The Death of Cuchulain* (1939). (The dates of all the above are of publication, not performance.)

YERMOLOVA, MARIA NIKOLAIEVNA (1853–1928), tragic actress of pre- and post-Revolutionary Russia, considered by Stanislavsky (q.v.) the greatest actress he had ever known. She made her début in 1870 at the Maly Theatre (q.v.) in Moscow as Emilia Galotti in Lessing's play of that name. She soon proved herself a great tragic actress, outstanding in such roles as Lady Macbeth, Joan of Arc (in Schiller's *Die Jungfrau von Orleans*), Mary, Queen of Scots (in his *Maria Stuart*), and Phaedra (in Racine's *Phèdre*). Having weathered the storm of the October Revolution, she celebrated her stage jubilee in 1920. In 1930 a studio attached to the Maly was named after her which in 1937 became the Yermolova Theatre under the direction of Khmelev. One of his outstanding productions there was *As You Like It* (1939). This theatre later saw the first production of several important Soviet plays, including Surov's *Far From Stalingrad* in 1946 and Shteyn's *A Game Without Rules* in 1962.

YEVREINOV, NIKOLAI, see EVREINOV.

York. The first theatre in York, adapted from a tennis court, opened in 1734. The second, on a site adjoining the present Theatre Royal, was erected by Joseph Baker, who built a larger theatre in 1765. In the same year the provincial manager Tate Wilkinson (q.v.) took over the York circuit, comprising York, Hull, Leeds, Doncaster, Wakefield, and Pontefract. Under him an excellent company was maintained in which many players later famous in London gained their experience. Baker's second theatre was remodelled in 1822; further improvements were made in 1835, in 1875, in 1880, when the stock company was disbanded, and in 1901, when extensive rebuilding took place. In 1967 the theatre was extensively altered and redecorated, and now houses a successful repertory company. York came back into the mainstream of theatrical history with the revival in 1951 of the York Cycle of Mystery Plays as part of a York Festival which has since been held annually. Though centred round the Mystery Plays, performed by amateurs, this has now been enlarged to include concerts, operas, and professional performances of modern plays, including in 1969 the first English production of Pirandello's *Quando si è qualcuno* as *When One Is Somebody*.

York Cycle, see MYSTERY PLAY.

YOUNG, CHARLES (?–1874), see DUFF, MARY ANN and VEZIN, H.

YOUNG, CHARLES MAYNE (1777–1856), English actor, who in 1798, as Mr. Green, made his début in Liverpool. From there he went to Manchester and Edinburgh, and became an intimate friend of Sir Walter Scott. He was also friendly with the elder Mathews (q.v.), and with his help appeared at the Haymarket in London in 1807 as Hamlet, Mathews playing Polonius. Both actors appeared in the same parts when Young took his farewell of the stage in May 1832, with Macready (q.v.) as the Ghost. During his years in the London theatre the only new part of any importance which he created was the

title-role in Miss Mitford's *Rienzi* (1828), but he was good both in tragedy and comedy, particularly as Hamlet, Macbeth, Iago (in *Othello*), Falkland (in Sheridan's *The Rivals*), Sir Pertinax McSycophant (in Macklin's *The Man of the World*), and Macheath (in Gay's *The Beggar's Opera*).

YOUNG, STARK (1881–1963), American dramatic critic, generally accounted one of the most perceptive writers on acting of his time. He was on the staff of the *New Republic* from 1921 to his death, and from 1924 to 1925 also acted as drama critic of the *New York Times*. He reprinted a number of his critical articles in *Immortal Shadows* (1948). A good linguist, he translated Chekhov's main works and several plays from the Spanish and Italian. He was also the author of several plays in verse.

Young American Roscius, see COWELL, SAM; **Young Roscius,** see BETTY, W.

Young Vic, LONDON. The first theatre to be given this name was founded in 1945 as part of the new Old Vic Drama School, with the idea of presenting adult actors in plays suitable for young people. Under George Devine (q.v.) the company began operations in Dec. 1946 with Gozzi's *The King Stag*, but although this and some later productions were well received, lack of support and financial stringency caused it to disband in 1951. The second Young Vic opened in 1970 in a converted butcher's shop near the Old Vic (q.v.) with *Scapino*, an adaptation of Molière's *Les Fourberies de Scapin* which had already been seen at the Edinburgh Festival in 1967 and at the Jeannetta Cochrane Theatre in London earlier in 1970. The play, in *commedia dell'arte* style but in modern dress with many modern interpolations, was directed by Frank Dunlop, with Jim Dale as Scapino. Of the later plays performed by the Young Vic, in an informal atmosphere which encourages audience participation, the most popular so far with the new young audience has been Beckett's *Waiting for Godot*.

Youth Theatre, see NATIONAL YOUTH THEATRE.

YURKA [really JURKA], BLANCHE (1893–1974), American actress, who made her first appearance in New York in 1907, and was later with the stock companies of Buffalo, Dallas, and Philadelphia. She already had a long list of leading parts to her credit when in 1922 she played Gertrude to the Hamlet of John Barrymore (q.v.). Among her later parts were Gina in *The Wild Duck* (1928), Hedda in *Hedda Gabler* and Ellida in *The Lady from the Sea* (both 1929), and Hjordis in *The Vikings* (1930), in which she was outstanding. She was also much admired as Aristophanes' Lysistrata later in 1930 and as Sophocles' Electra in 1932. From 1936 to 1938 she toured the United States in a solo performance of scenes from great plays, and later toured as Mrs. Antrobus in Wilder's *The Skin of Our Teeth*, in a dramatization of Charlotte Brontë's *Jane Eyre* entitled *The Master of Thornfield* (1958), and as Miss Moffat in a revival of Emlyn Williams's *The Corn is Green* (1961). She is part-author of *Spring in Autumn* (1933), adapted from a play by Martínez Sierra, and author of *Dear Audience—A Guide to Greater Enjoyment of the Theatre* (1958). She made her only appearance in London in 1969 when she was seen in Giraudoux's *The Madwoman of Chaillot* at Studio '68.

Yvonne Arnaud Theatre, a small intimate playhouse in Guildford, Surrey, designed by John Brownrigg to fit an island site by the river Wey. This was donated by the local authority, who also gave a substantial sum towards the cost of the building, the rest being raised by private subscription. Named after the actress Yvonne Arnaud (q.v.), the theatre opened on 2 June 1965 under its first director Michael Redgrave (q.v.), who appeared in the initial productions, Turgenev's *A Month in the Country* and Milton's *Samson Agonistes*. Under its present director, Laurier Lister, the theatre continues to flourish and in 1969 staged the English première of Montherlant's *The Cardinal of Spain* (1960), with Max Adrian as Cardinal Cisneros and Siân Phillips as the mad queen Juana. A number of revivals, including plays by Somerset Maugham and Noël Coward, first seen at the Yvonne Arnaud, have subsequently been transferred to the West End.

Z

ZACCONI, ERMETE (1857–1948), Italian actor, child of strolling players, who made his first appearance on the stage at the age of seven. While still in his twenties he was recognized as one of the outstanding actors of his day, equalled only by Novelli (q.v.), and in 1884 he founded and directed his own company. With Duse (q.v.) he was mainly instrumental in introducing Ibsen (q.v.) to the Italian public, being the first Italian actor to play Oswald Alving in *Ghosts*, which he also directed, together with plays by Tolstoy, Hauptmann, and Strindberg (qq.v.). He appeared in a number of Italian plays and also in the great roles of Shakespeare. In 1899 he was with Duse, playing opposite her in D'Annunzio's *La Gioconda* and in the younger Dumas's *Le Demi-monde*; but he left her to tour again with his own company, going to Austria and Germany and as far afield as Russia, where he was well received. A versatile actor, he was particularly admired as Hamlet and in the title-role of Testoni's *Il Cardinale Lambertini* (1905), a comedy of intrigue based on the life of a seventeenth-century cardinal of Bologna.

ZAKHAVA, BORIS EVGENEVICH (1898–1976), Soviet actor and director, pupil and close collaborator of Eugene Vakhtangov, participating with him in many of his productions, notably *Turandot* (1922), by Gozzi (q.v.), in which he played Timur. After the death of Vakhtangov, Zakhava directed a number of Russian plays, of which the most important was Gorky's *Yegor Bulichev and Others* in 1935. He continued to act, however, and worked for two years under Meyerhold (q.v.) in order to study his methods. Among his later productions, which were sometimes controversial, were *Hamlet* and Dostoievsky's *The Idiot* (both 1958).

ZANGWILL, ISRAEL (1864–1926), Jewish author and philanthropist, who established his literary reputation with a fine novel, *The Children of the Ghetto* (1892). He also wrote some plays, of which *The Melting Pot*, a study of Jewish immigrant life in the United States, was the most important. Produced in New York in 1908, it was a great success and was

several times revived, being first seen in London in 1914.

Zany, the anglicized form of the Italian *zanni*, a term which covers all the male servant masks of the *commedia dell'arte* (q.v.). Among them were the prototypes of the English Harlequin (see ARLECCHINO) and Punch (see PULCINELLA), who have changed greatly in appearance and function; also of Scapin, Scaramouche, and Pasquin, who are perhaps better known under their French forms than their Italian—Scapino, Scaramuccia, and Pasquino (qq.v.). Pierrot (q.v.), who in France became a sad, solitary lover, and in England the gregarious member of a seaside concert party, is also distantly derived from a zany, Pedrolino. In Elizabethan times the word, which is now rarely used in England though still current in parts of America, always conveyed the idea of a 'clumsy imitator'.

Zarzuela, a Spanish musical play or operetta, which takes its name from the Palacio de la Zarzuela, a hunting-lodge in the woods not far from Madrid. Although many early Spanish plays contained a certain amount of music, the first true *zarzuela* was by Calderón (q.v.)—*El laurel de Apolo* (1658). The music for this and other early *zarzuelas* has been lost, but in 1933 that for the first act of Calderón's *Celos aún del aire matan* was found and published, followed in 1945 by that for the second act, and recently much of the music for Juan Vélez de Guevara's *Los celos hacen estrellas* has been identified. The *zarzuela* flourished as a courtly entertainment from 1660 onwards, its mythological or heroic plot being subtly designed to flatter its royal audience, but in the eighteenth century it suffered from the popularity of Italian opera. It was revitalized by Ramón de la Cruz (q.v.), who with *Las segadoras de Vallecas* introduced a new-style *zarzuela* with a plot drawn from daily life. His work was immensely successful during his lifetime but after his death was again eclipsed by Italian opera, until in the second half of the nineteenth century a new era began with Barbieri's *Jugar con fuego* (1851). This led to the opening in 1856 of a

Teatro de la Zarzuela in Madrid. The modern *zarzuela*, exemplified by the ever-popular *La verbena de la Paloma*, persisted well into the twentieth century and still exists, in a form strongly influenced by foreign revues and musicals.

ZAVADSKY, YURI ALEXEIVICH (1894–1977), Soviet actor and director, who began his career in 1915 as a pupil of Eugene Vakhtangov, appearing in his last production, Gozzi's *Turandot* (1922). In 1924 he opened his own studio, and was later appointed director of the Gorky State Theatre in Rostov. His early productions, among which were Alfred de Musset's *On ne badine pas avec l'amour* and Shaw's *The Devil's Disciple*, showed the influence of both Stanislavsky (q.v.) and Vakhtangov, but Zavadsky soon evolved a personal style, combining lyricism with excellent stagecraft, and giving a larger place than usual to music. He was with the Mossoviet Theatre (q.v.) in 1940, but returned to Rostov during the Second World War, where he directed Trenev's *Lyubov Yarovaya* and *On the Banks of the Neva*, Gorky's *Enemies* and *The Philistines*, and Shakespeare's *Othello*. Back at the Mossoviet after the war, his productions included Arkadevich's *The Brandenburg Gate* (1946), Surov's *Dawn over Moscow* (1950), a revival of Bill-Belotserkovsky's *Storm* (or *Hurricane*) (1951), Nazim Hikmet's *A Turkish Tale* and Virta's *Endless Distance* (both 1957). Zavadsky contributed not a little to the forward movement of the Soviet theatre during the 1950s, and held a high position in Russian theatrical life, many distinguished actors of today having been his pupils. He was twice awarded a Lenin Prize—in 1947 for a production of Shakespeare's *The Merry Wives of Windsor* and in 1965 for a revival of Lermontov's *Masquerade*. In 1967, on the occasion of the Festival of the Arts of the Russian Revolution held at Manchester University, he gave the inaugural lecture, taking the Soviet theatre as his theme.

ZEAMI (1363–1443), see NŌ PLAY.

ZEFFIRELLI, FRANCO (1923–), Italian director and scene designer, who first attracted attention in his own country with his sets for Visconti's productions of *Troilus and Cressida* in Florence in 1949 and Chekhov's *Three Sisters* in Rome in 1951. His work has since been seen at Covent Garden in London and the Metropolitan Opera House in New York, and in many other opera-houses throughout the world. Although mainly known for his designs for and productions of opera, he has directed a number of plays, notably *Romeo and Juliet* (1960), *Hamlet* (1964), and *Much Ado About Nothing* (1965) at the Old Vic, and *Othello* (1961) at the Royal Shakespeare Theatre, Stratford-upon-Avon.

ZENO, APOSTOLO (1668–1750), a writer of libretti for *melodramme*, or plays in which music and words were equally important. The first was *Gl'Inganni felici*, which, with music by Carlo Francesco Pollardo (1653–1722), was successfully performed at the Teatro Sant'Angelo in Venice in 1695. A year later *Lucio Vero*, with music by the same composer, was equally successful, and Zeno continued to write one or two pieces for Venice each year, fifteen of those after 1705 being written in collaboration with Pietro Pariati. Most of Zeno's libretti were based on stories from classical history or mythology and they were used by numerous composers, some being set as many as twenty times. He was Court poet at Vienna from 1718 to 1729, when he was succeeded by Metastasio (q.v.).

ZIEGFELD, FLORENZ (1867–1932), American theatre manager, who originated and perfected the American form of revue in a series of productions called the *Ziegfeld Follies*, which began in 1907 and continued annually until his death, being seen intermittently thereafter until 1957. Ziegfeld based his show on that of the Parisian Folies-Bergère (q.v.), with the emphasis on scenic splendour, comic sketches, vaudeville specialities, and beautiful girls, many of whom, like Marion Davies, Irene Dunne, and Paulette Goddard, later became film stars. He was also responsible for fostering the talents of such entertainers as Bert Williams (q.v.), and many foreign artistes appeared in New York under his management, among them Maurice Chevalier, Lupino Lane, and Evelyn Laye. Among the well-known designers, musicians, and librettists who worked for him were Joseph Urban, Irving Berlin and George Gershwin, and Oscar Hammerstein II. Apart from the *Follies*, he was responsible for a number of straight plays and musicals, of which the most successful was *Show Boat* (1927), based on Edna Ferber's novel. This was produced at the Ziegfeld Theatre (q.v.), and was equally successful in London a year later. Ziegfeld's second wife (his first was ANNA HELD, 1873–1918), whom he married in 1914, was the actress BILLIE [really ETHELBERT APPLETON] BURKE (1884–1970), who first appeared in a London music-hall in 1902, and in 1910 went to the United States, where she had a long and successful career as Daly's leading lady. In 1949 she published a volume of reminiscences entitled *With a Feather on My Nose*.

Ziegfeld Theatre, NEW YORK, on the north-west corner of 6th Avenue and 54th Street. Designed by the scene designer Joseph Urban for Florenz Ziegfeld (q.v.), it opened successfully on 2 Feb. 1927 with the musical *Rio Rita*, followed by *Show Boat*, based by Oscar Hammerstein on Edna Ferber's novel, with music by Jerome Kern. Further successes were Noël Coward's *Bitter Sweet* (1929) and the *Ziegfeld Follies of 1931*. After Ziegfeld died in 1932 his theatre became a cinema. It was reopened by BILLY ROSE (1899–   ) as a theatre, under its old name, on 7 Dec. 1944, with Beatrice Lillie (q.v.) in the revue *Seven Lively Arts*. From 1955 to 1963 it was used for television but returned to live theatre again on 29 Jan. 1963 with an evening of songs and sketches starring Maurice Chevalier (q.v.), followed by *Foxy* (1964), a musical based on Jonson's *Volpone* which starred Bert Lahr (q.v.). The building was demolished in 1967.

ZIEGLER, CLARA (1844–1909), German actress, who from 1867 to 1868 was in Leipzig and later went to Munich for some years as guest artist. At her best in tragic roles like Schiller's Joan of Arc or Euripides' Medea, she also, in the tradition of her day, played Romeo. She was the author of several plays and on her death left her house and library to the city of Munich as a theatre museum, together with money for the maintenance there of a theatre collection. The idea of such a museum first came to her in 1892 when visiting the International Music and Theatre Exhibition in Vienna, and it was formally opened in 1910. Its curator for many years was the famous German theatre historian Franz Rapp. Several other collections have been added to the original deposit, and in 1932 extra space

for display was acquired elsewhere, the house being used for books and catalogues.

ZOFFANY, JOHN (1733/5–1810), a painter of Bohemian extraction who in 1758 settled in London and remained there until his death. Among his works were many theatrical portraits, particularly of David Garrick (q.v.)—as Abel Drugger in Ben Jonson's *The Alchemist*, as Jaffier (with Mrs. Cibber) in Otway's *Venice Preserv'd*, as Macbeth (with Mrs. Pritchard), as Sir John Brute in Vanbrugh's *The Provoked Wife*, and so on. Zoffany also painted Samuel Foote, Shuter, King (qq.v.), and other actors, either singly or in groups from a particular play, as for example King and Mrs. Baddeley in Colman and Garrick's *The Clandestine Marriage* and a scene from Bickerstaffe's *Love in a Village*. Many of his paintings are in the possession of the Garrick Club (q.v.).

ZOLA, ÉMILE-EDOUARD-CHARLES-ANTOINE (1840–1902), French novelist and dramatist, who, though mainly remembered for his novels, in particular the twenty volumes of *Les Rougon-Macquart* (1871–93), had an important influence on the development of the French, and so of the European, theatre of his day. As the leader of the so-called 'naturalistic' school of literature, he much disliked the facile, optimistic works of such dramatists as Scribe (q.v.), and thought that a play should be a 'slice of life', thrown on the stage without embellishment or artifice. He set out his theories in a number of critical articles, later republished in two volumes, *Le Naturalisme au théâtre* (1878) and *Nos auteurs dramatiques* (1881), and exemplified them in his own plays, particularly *Thérèse Raquin* (1873), which he based on an earlier novel of the same name. In an English translation, this was seen in London in 1891 and has been several times revived, notably in 1938 as *Thou Shalt Not*. In 1945 it was produced in New York as *Therese*. Zola's other plays were less successful. The only other one to have been translated into English is a comedy, *Les Héritiers Rabourdin* (1874), which as *The Heirs of Rabourdin* was produced in 1894 by Grein's Independent Theatre Club. One of Zola's novels, *L'Assommoir*, was dramatized by Busnach and Gastineau, and in an English version, as *Drink*, by Charles Reade and Charles Warner (qq.v.), had a long run in London in 1879, Warner playing the chief part, Coupeau. It was subsequently revived several times. The original novel was also dramatized in English, less successfully, by Lacy, Callender, and Banks.

ZORRILLA, Francisco de Rojas, see ROJAS ZORRILLA.

ZORRILLA Y MORAL, José (1817–93), poet and dramatist of the Romantic movement in Spain. His best-known play is *Don Juan Tenorio* (1844), which added yet another version to the numerous interpretations of the legend of Don Juan (q.v.). It is still performed in Spain every year on 1 Nov. (All Saints' Day). Zorrilla was also the author of *El zapatero y el Rey*, written in two parts (1840 and 1841), of *El puñal del Godo* (1842), and of *Traidor, inconfeso y mártir* (1849), based on the life of a pretender to the throne of Portugal.

ZUCKMAYER, Carl (1896–1977), German dramatist who, under the influence of Expressionism (q.v.), wrote *Am Kreuzweg* (1920) and *Pankraz erwacht* (1925). They were unsuccessful, but his next play, a comedy entitled *Der fröhliche Weinberg* (also 1925), had an immediate success. Of his later plays, which included *Schinderhannes* (1927), *Katharina Knie* (1929), and *Der Schelm von Bergen* (1934), the most popular have been *Der Hauptmann von Köpenick* (1931), in which an unemployed ex-convict enforces obedience to his orders merely because he is wearing a military uniform—a satire which has much in common with *The Inspector General* of Gogol (q.v.)—and *Der Teufels General* (1946), a play with a Nazi background written after Zuckmayer, an anti-Nazi, had left Europe for the U.S.A. As *The Devil's General*, it was seen in London in 1953. Zuckmayer's later plays, none of which were completely successful, included *Der Gesang im Feuerofen* (1950), set in occupied France, *Das kalte Licht* (1956), based on the case of Dr. Fuchs, and *Die Uhr schlägt eins* (1961).

A GUIDE TO
FURTHER READING
ON DRAMA AND THE THEATRE

Compiled by Simon Trussler

In this classified guide to recommended reading on drama and the theatre, entries are arranged alphabetically by names of authors or editors within each subject heading. Brief descriptive notes have been added to entries whose titles or subject headings inadequately describe their contents, or whose reliability or scope requires comment.

No biographies of individuals have been included, but an attempt has been made to list the basic reference and source material on all subjects, thus enabling the interested reader to plot his own course of further study.

Each entry includes, besides author's or editor's name and title, brief particulars of the edition cited, its publisher, and date of publication. Place of publication is given in the entries for books originating outside London, if the name of the publishing house does not itself indicate its location.

An attempt has been made to note particulars of separate English or American editions where these are available, the publisher originating the book being noted first, and a second date of publication being given where this differs from the date of the original edition. Only a few foreign titles, notably those valuable for their illustrations, have been included, but out-of-print titles have been listed where these are fairly readily available from libraries. Many long out-of-print titles are now becoming available in photographic reprints, and, although these have been noted as fully as possible, the present boom in reprint publishing may well make many more works available in such editions during the currency of this *Concise Companion*.

REFERENCE WORKS

Encyclopedias

ADAMS, W. Davenport: *A dictionary of the drama.* Vol. I, A to G. New York: Franklin, 1964.
   First published in 1904. Although the work was never completed, this first volume remains a valuable guide 'to the plays, playwrights, players, and playhouses of the United Kingdom and America' up to the turn of the century.

ENCICLOPEDIA DELLO SPETTACOLO. 9 vols. Rome: Maschere, 1954–64. *Aggiornamento, 1955–1965.* Rome: Unione Editoriale, 1966.
   A comprehensive and profusely illustrated work, covering all the performing arts, and brought nearly up-to-date by its supplementary volume. Text in Italian.

GASSNER, John, and QUINN, Edward, eds.: *The reader's encyclopedia of world drama.* New York: Crowell, 1969. Methuen, 1970.
   A single-volume, alphabetically-ordered work on national dramas, playwrights, plays, and genres. Contains a supplement on dramatic theory, but limited to the study of drama as literature.

HARTNOLL, Phyllis, ed.: *The Oxford companion to the theatre.* 3rd edn. O.U.P., 1967.
   The full-length version of the present work. Includes articles on the theatrical history of particular countries, and a supplementary section of nearly 200 illustrations.

MELCHINGER, Siegfried: *Concise encyclopedia of modern drama.* New York: Horizon, 1966. Vision.
   Selective and sometimes confusing in arrangement, but strong in its treatment of dramatic theory and of modern theatrical movements. Well illustrated.

SOBEL, Bernard: *New theatre handbook and digest of plays.* 9th edn. New York: Crown, 1964.
>Useful for play synopses.

TAYLOR, John Russell: *The Penguin dictionary of the theatre.* Methuen, 1967. New York: Barnes and Noble.
>Convenient for quick reference, and good on the contemporary theatre.

Bibliographies

ARNOTT, J. F., and ROBINSON, J. W.: *English theatrical literature, 1559–1900.* Society for Theatre Research, 1970.
>Incorporates Robert W. Lowe's *Bibliographical account of English theatrical literature* (1888). A comprehensive and scrupulously researched guide to published material about the theatre prior to 1900, arranged chronologically within subject divisions.

BAKER, Blanch M.: *Theatre and allied arts.* New York: Blom, 1967.
>First published in 1952, this remains a useful annotated guide to some 6,000 books in English 'dealing with the history, criticism, and technique of the drama and theatre, and related arts and crafts'.

CHESHIRE, David: *Theatre: history, criticism, and reference.* Bingley, 1967. Hamden, Conn.: Archon.
>A fully descriptive and annotated guide, in narrative form, to the literature of the theatre. Sensible alike in selection and comment, but excludes studies of dramatic literature. Fully indexed.

LITTO, Fredric M.: *American dissertations on the drama and theatre.* Kent, Ohio: Kent State U.P., 1969.
>Covers all the performing arts, and includes author and key-word-in-context indexes.

LOEWENBERG, A.: *The theatre of the British Isles, excluding London.* Society for Theatre Research, 1950.
>Includes periodical articles as well as books on the theatre outside London. Arranged under place-names.

STRATMAN, C. J.: *A bibliography of American theatre, excluding New York City.* Chicago: Loyola U.P., 1965.
>Includes books, periodical articles, and theses. Arranged geographically, by state and city.

Dictionaries and Glossaries

BAND-KUZMANY, Karin R. M., comp.: *Glossary of the theatre in English, French, Italian, and German.* Amsterdam: Elsevier, 1969.

BOWMAN, Walter P., and BALL, Robert Hamilton: *Theatre language. A dictionary of terms in English of the drama and stage from medieval to modern times.* New York: Theatre Arts Books, 1961.

GRANVILLE, Wilfred: *A dictionary of theatrical terms.* Deutsch, 1952. New York: O.U.P., as *Theatre language.*

RAE, Kenneth, and SOUTHERN, Richard, eds.: *International vocabulary of technical theatre terms in eight languages.* Brussels: Elsevier, 1959. Reinhardt. New York: Theatre Arts.
>The languages are American, Dutch, English, French, German, Italian, Spanish, and Swedish. In other respects, the four works in this section fulfil the claims of their titles, but Bowman and Ball are particularly strong on historical terms, and Granville is good on stage jargon.

Biographical Dictionaries

NUNGEZER, Edwin: *A dictionary of actors and other persons associated with the public representation of plays in England before 1642.* New Haven, Conn.: Yale U.P., 1929. O.U.P.
>A scholarly study, but excludes playwrights.

PARKER, John, ed.: *Who's who in the theatre*. 11 edns. Pitman, 1912–52. 12th edn., ed. John Parker, Jr. Pitman, 1957. 13th and 14th edns., ed. Freda Gaye. Pitman, 1961 and 1967.

The fullest and most reliable reference work on the personnel of the English theatre. Each edition includes a cumulative index of names to be found in earlier editions, a long though sometimes arbitrary list of notable productions and revivals, and a comprehensive obituary. Since the 4th edition of 1922, detailed playbills of London productions have also been included, and these are cumulatively indexed in the 14th edition. John Parker's *Green Room Book*, published between 1906 and 1911, covered the first decade of the century on a less ambitious scale.

RIGDON, Walter: *The biographical encyclopedia and who's who of the American theatre*. New York: J. H Heineman, 1966.

This costly but compendious work includes over 3,000 biographies, a complete record of productions in the United States since 1900 (with full New York playbills since 1959), an international obituary, and a wealth of additional material.

Periodicals

DRAMA. Quarterly, 1919. In progress.

The journal of the British Drama League. Contents of general theatrical interest, variable in quality.

ENCORE. Bi-monthly, 1956–65.

The 'voice of vital theatre' during the period which saw the emergence of the new English dramatists. A tendency to polemics, but usually well-informed. Anthologized in *The Encore reader*, ed. Charles Marowitz *et al.* (Methuen, 1965).

PLAYS AND PLAYERS. Monthly, 1953. In progress.

Illustrated reviews of London and selected provincial productions. Critical quality much improved since 1960.

THE STAGE. Weekly, 1880. In progress.

The profession's own newspaper, providing full topical coverage of music hall, variety, and television, as well as the live theatre.

THEATRE ARTS. Monthly, 1919–64.

The only journal offering continuous coverage of the American theatre during its period of publication, it became more parochial and pictorially-oriented after 1948. Anthologized in *Theatre Arts anthology*, ed. Rosamond Gilder *et al.* (New York: Theatre Arts, 1950).

THEATRE QUARTERLY. Quarterly, 1971. In progress.

Lengthy studies of theatrical subjects past and present, backed up by useful reference material. Each issue contains a current bibliography of theatre studies.

THEATRE WORLD. Monthly, 1925–65.

Popular and pictorial reviews, mainly of the commercial London theatre.

TULANE DRAMA REVIEW. Quarterly, 1955. In progress, since 1967 as *The Drama Review*, New York.

In its early years a lively academic drama journal, but since about 1960 has become increasingly identified with the attitudes and aims of experimental and environmental theatre in America and abroad. Many valuable issues devoted to single countries or topics. Cumulative contents list in vol. xv, no. 4 (1971).

VARIETY. Weekly, 1905. In progress.

The professional journal of the performing arts in the United States. Commercially oriented, and self-conscious in vocabulary, but comprehensive and usually knowledgeable. Its history is traced in *Show-biz from vaude to video*, by Abel Green and Joe Laurie, Jr. (New York: Holt, 1951).

WORLD THEATRE. Quarterly, 1950–64. Bi-monthly, 1965–7.

Journal of the International Theatre Institute. Contents of wide and general interest, though sometimes synoptic in approach. Text in English and French, valuably illustrated. Cumulative indexes in vol. xiv, no. 4 (1964), and in vol. xvi, no. 6 (1967).

Periodical Guides and Indexes

BELKNAP, S. Y., ed.: *Guide to the performing arts*, 1957–   . In progress. Metuchen, N.J.: Scarecrow.
   Includes indexes to *New Theatre, Theatre Arts, Theatre Notebook, Theatre Research, Tulane Drama Review,* and *World Theatre.* From 1953 to 1956 appeared as a supplement to the same editor's *Guide to the Musical Arts.*

FAXON, F. W.: *Cumulated dramatic index.* 2 vols. Boston: Hall, 1964.
   Indexes theatre articles and illustrations from 1909 to 1949.

STRATMAN, C. J.: *American theater periodicals, 1798–1967: a bibliographical guide.* Durham, N. C.: Duke U.P., 1970.

STRATMAN, C. J.: *British dramatic periodicals, 1720–1960.* New York Public Library, 1968.
   Not an index, but a comprehensive chronological guide to British periodicals on drama and theatre, and to their location in libraries. Does not take into account the British Museum's wartime losses.

Guides to Libraries and Theatre Collections

BRITISH DRAMA LEAGUE, The: *The player's library.* Faber, 1950. First supplement, 1951. Second supplement, 1954. Third supplement, 1956.
   An alphabetical catalogue of plays, and classified catalogue of books on theatre, in the library of the British Drama League.

GILDER, Rosamond, and FREEDLEY, George: *Theatre collections in libraries and museums: an international handbook.* New York: Theatre Arts, 1936. Stevens and Brown.
   Still a useful guide, especially to illustrative rather than literary material.

KAHN, A. M. C., ed.: *Theatre collections: a symposium.* Library Association, 1955.
   A guide to collections in the greater London area

VEINSTEIN, André, *et al.*, eds.: *Performing arts libraries and museums of the world.* New edn. Paris: Editions du Centre National de la Recherche Scientifique, 1967.
   Public and private theatre collections in thirty-seven countries. Text in English and French.

GENERAL HISTORIES

ALTMAN, George, *et al.*: *Theater pictorial.* Berkeley: California U.P., 1953.
   A 'history of world theatre as recorded in drawings, paintings, engravings, and photographs'.

BROCKETT, Oscar G.: *The theatre: an introduction.* 2nd edn. New York: Holt, Rinehart, 1969.
   Deals successively with theatre as an art, its history, its modern development, and its present state in America.

FREEDLEY, George, and REEVES, John A.: *A history of the theatre.* 3rd edn. New York: Crown, 1968.
   A standard reference work, though not without inaccuracies. Non-evaluative, but comprehensive in scope, heavily factual, and fully illustrated.

GASCOIGNE, Bamber: *World theatre.* Ebury Press. Boston: Little, Brown, 1968.

HARTNOLL, Phyllis: *A concise history of the theatre.* Thames and Hudson. New York: Abrams, 1968.
   Both the above are sound and readable introductory surveys, with well-chosen illustrations, many in colour.

NAGLER, A. M.: *A source book in theatrical history.* New York: Dover, 1959.
   Over 300 documents illustrating world theatre history.

NICOLL, Allardyce: *The development of the theatre.* 6th edn. Harrap, 1966. *World drama from Aeschylus to Anouilh.* Harrap, 1952.
　　The first of these two works provides a personal and relatively concise account of the development of live theatre, the second a more detailed and objective view of the history of dramatic literature.

SOUTHERN, Richard: *Seven ages of the theatre.* 2nd edn. Faber, 1964.
　　An interpretative study, strongly influenced by its author's interest in theatre forms. Sound and often stimulating.

The Modern Drama and Theatre

BENTLEY, Eric: *The playwright as thinker.* New York: Meridian, 1955. Methuen.
　　A major interpretative study of the major modern dramatists.

BRUSTEIN, Robert: *The theatre of revolt.* Boston: Little, Brown, 1964. Methuen, 1965.
　　The concept of rebellion as expressed in the work of eight important playwrights.

CLARK, Barrett H.: *A study of the modern drama.* Rev. edn. New York: Appleton, 1938.
　　Remains of interest for its assessments of the less well-known Continental playwrights.

CLARK, Barrett H., and FREEDLEY, George, eds.: *History of modern drama.* New York: Appleton, 1947.
　　Twenty-four writers provide country-by-country summaries of modern theatre history since Ibsen.

ESSLIN, Martin: *The theatre of the absurd.* Eyre and Spottiswoode, 1962. Garden City, N.Y.: Doubleday, 1961.
　　A seminal study of the movement that traces its origins back to Jarry and has Beckett as its chief exponent.

GASSNER, John: *Directions in modern theatre and drama.* Rev. edn. New York: Holt, Rinehart, 1965.
　　The relationship between form and subject-matter in theatre and drama, with the emphasis on realism.

GORELIK, Mordecai: *New theatres for old.* Dobson, 1947. New York: Dutton, 1962.
　　A brilliant and far-reaching analysis, amply documented, of theatre in all its aspects.

ROOSE-EVANS, James: *Experimental theatre from Stanislavsky to Brecht.* Studio Vista, 1970.
　　The contributions of key figures to extending the range of theatre as an art.

WILLIAMS, Raymond: *Drama from Ibsen to Brecht.* Chatto, 1968. New York: O.U.P. 1969.

GENERAL CRITICAL AND CONCEPTUAL STUDIES

BENTLEY, Eric: *The life of the drama.* Methuen, 1965.
　　Deals both with constituent aspects of a play, and with the dramatic genres: especially good on melodrama and farce.

BROWN, John Russell: *Effective theatre: a study with documentation.* Heinemann, 1969.
　　Short but sensible introductory chapters on the various components of drama and theatre, supported by a wide range of documentary material.

FERGUSSON, Francis: *The idea of a theater.* Garden City, N.Y.: Doubleday, 1949. *The human image in dramatic literature.* Garden City, N.Y.: Doubleday, 1957.

MITCHELL, Roy: *Creative theatre.* 2nd edn. New York: D.B.S. Publications, 1969.
　　The relationship between the theatre, culture, and the community.

STYAN, J. L.: *The dramatic experience*. Cambridge U.P., 1965.
   An introduction to all the components of theatre and their relationships.

STYAN, J. L.: *The elements of drama*. Cambridge U.P., 1960.
   The elements which create the dramatic event on stage, the way they are organized,
   and how they can be judged in performance.

WILLIAMS, Raymond: *Drama in performance*. New edn. Watts, 1968. New York:
   Basic, 1969.
   The changing relationship between dramatic forms and methods of staging.

CLASSICAL DRAMA AND THEATRE

Ancient Greece

ARNOTT, Peter: *An introduction to the Greek theatre*. Macmillan, 1959. New York:
   St. Martin's.
   A good attempt to relate the written drama to conditions and techniques of stage
   performance.

BIEBER, Margarete: *History of the Greek and Roman theatre*. 2nd edn. O.U.P., 1961.
   Princeton U.P.
   A standard scholarly work. Well illustrated.

HAIGH, Arthur E.: *The Attic theatre: a description of the stage and theatre of the Athenians, and of the dramatic performances at Athens*. New York: Kraus Reprint, 1969.
   First published in 1907.

KITTO, H. D. F.: *Greek tragedy*. Methuen, 1961. New York: Barnes and Noble.

PICKARD-CAMBRIDGE, Arthur: *Dramatic festivals of Athens*. 2nd edn. O.U.P., 1968.

WEBSTER, T. B. L.: *Greek theatre production*. 2nd edn. Methuen, 1970. New York:
   Barnes and Noble.
   Scenery, staging, and costumes considered chronologically and geographically.

Ancient Rome

BEARE, W.: *The Roman stage: a short history of Latin drama in the time of the Republic*.
   3rd edn. Methuen, 1964. New York: Barnes and Noble, 1965.

DUCKWORTH, G. E.: *The nature of Roman comedy*. Princeton U.P., 1952. O.U.P.

BRITISH DRAMA AND THEATRE

Chronology

HARBAGE, A.: *Annals of English drama, 975–1700*. Rev. edn. Methuen, 1964. Philadelphia: Pennsylvania U.P.

General Histories and Studies

BRIDGES-ADAMS, W.: *The irresistible theatre*. First of 2 vols. Secker, 1957.
   A companionably-written introduction, the first volume ending at the Commonwealth. (No more published.)

CLUNES, Alec: *The British theatre*. Cassell, 1964. New York: Barnes.
   A brief but well-balanced study, fully illustrated.

EVANS, Ifor: *A short history of English drama*. 2nd edn. MacGibbon and Kee, 1965.
   Boston: Houghton Mifflin.
   An excellent short study, though confined to dramatic literature.

KNIGHT, G. Wilson: *The golden labyrinth: a study of British drama*. Phoenix House, 1962. New York: Norton.
　　A lively and provoking study, controversial alike in judgement and emphasis.

MANDER, Raymond, and MITCHENSON, Joe: *Picture history of the British theatre*. Hulton, 1957.
　　Over 500 illustrations, well selected and annotated.

NICOLL, Allardyce: *History of English drama, 1600–1900*. 6 vols. Cambridge U.P., 1952–9.
　　The fullest comprehensive study of the English drama, treated as theatre rather than literature. Like the handlists of plays which form the second part of each volume, its studies of particular periods are gradually being superseded by more definitive works, but the set remains valuable for its conciseness and easily located references.

Medieval and Tudor

BOAS, F. S.: *Introduction to Tudor drama*. O.U.P., 1933.

CHAMBERS, E. K.: *The medieval stage*. Two vols. O.U.P., 1903.
　　A comprehensive study in four parts—of the development of medieval drama, the folk play, religious drama, and the interludes.

ROSSITER, A. P.: *English drama from early times to the Elizabethans*. Hutchinson, 1966.

WICKHAM, Glynne: *Early English stages*. 2 vols. Routledge, 1959 and 1963. New York: Columbia U.P.
　　A lucid and authoritative study, fully documented, projected to continue to 1660. The first volume is concerned with the medieval dramatic tradition and forms of staging, the second with the sixteenth century.

Elizabethan and Jacobean

BRADBROOK, M. C.: *Themes and conventions of Elizabethan tragedy*. 2nd edn. Cambridge U.P., 1952. *The growth and structure of Elizabethan comedy*. Chatto, 1955.

CHAMBERS, E. K.: *The Elizabethan stage*. 4 vols. O.U.P., 1923.
　　The first volume considers the court and control of the stage, the second the companies and playhouses, the third techniques of staging and playwrights, and the fourth anonymous works.

GREG, W. W.: *Dramatic documents from the Elizabethan playhouses: stage plots, actors' parts, prompt books, reproductions and transcripts*. O.U.P., 1931.

KNIGHTS, L. C.: *Drama and society in the age of Jonson*. Chatto, 1957.
　　Economic and social influences on the plays and playwrights.

LAWRENCE, W. J.: *The Elizabethan playhouse, and other studies*. 2 vols. New York: Russell, 1963.
　　Reprint of collections which first appeared in 1912 and 1913. Much remains of value and interest.

WILSON, F. P.: *The English drama, 1485–1585*. O.U.P., 1969.
　　First part of a two-volume study in *The Oxford history of English literature* series. A sound short study, with chronology and bibliographies.

Shakespearian

No attempt has been made here to suggest more than a few representative works on the *staging* of the plays, and related practical problems. Halliday's *Shakespeare Companion*, fully cited below, includes a fuller but discriminating bibliography.

CAMPBELL, O. J., and QUINN, Edward, eds.: *The reader's encyclopedia of Shakespeare*. New York: Crowell, 1966. Methuen.

HALLIDAY, F. E.: *A Shakespeare companion, 1564–1964*. Penguin, 1964.
　　Both the above are standard, alphabetically-ordered reference works. The former is the fuller, but the latter more convenient for theatrically oriented studies.

HARBAGE, A.: *Shakespeare's audience*. New York: Columbia U.P., 1941. O.U.P.

ODELL, G. C. D.: *Shakespeare from Betterton to Irving*. 2 vols. New York: Blom, 1964. Constable.
    A standard work on the plays in performance, first published in 1920.

SPRAGUE, A. C.: *Shakespeare and the actors: the stage business in his plays*. Cambridge, Mass.: Harvard U.P., 1944. *Shakespearian players and performances*. Cambridge, Mass.: Harvard U.P., 1953. Black, 1954.

TREWIN, J. C.: *Shakespeare on the English stage, 1900–1964*. Barrie, 1964. New York: Humanities.
    Arranged chronologically rather than play-by-play, and thus a better guide to changing attitudes than to such details of interpretation as Sprague investigates for an earlier period.

WAIN, John: *The living world of Shakespeare: a playgoer's guide*. Macmillan, 1964. New York: St. Martin's.
    A critical study of the plays in groups, unusually responsive to the theatrical potential.

Caroline and Restoration

BENTLEY, G. E.: *The Jacobean and Caroline stage*. 7 vols. O.U.P., 1941–66.
    Intended to continue Chambers's *Elizabethan stage*, above, from 1616 to 1642. The first two volumes deal with theatrical companies and actors, the next three with plays and playwrights, and the sixth with playhouses. The last contains reference material serving the whole work.

HOTSON, Leslie: *The Commonwealth and Restoration stage*. Cambridge, Mass.: Harvard U.P., 1928. New York: Russell, 1962.

SMITH, Dane Farnsworth: *Plays about the theatre in England, 1671–1737*. O.U.P., 1936.
    Throws much incidental light on staging conditions and conventions.

SUMMERS, Montague: *The playhouse of Pepys, a description of the drama produced in the years 1660–82*. Routledge, 1935. New York: Humanities, 1964. *The Restoration theatre: an account of the staging of plays*. Routledge, 1934. New York: Humanities, 1964.
    Detailed studies of the playbills, audiences, scenery, and costumes of the period.

Eighteenth Century

BATESON, F. W.: *English comic drama, 1700–1750*. O.U.P., 1929. New York: Russell, 1963.

BERNBAUM, E.: *The drama of sensibility: a sketch of the history of English sentimental comedy and domestic tragedy*. Cambridge, Mass.: Harvard U.P. O.U.P., 1925.

CLINTON-BADDELEY, V. C.: *All right on the night*. Putnam, 1954.
    An account of the everyday life of the Georgian theatre, full of illuminating side-lights.

KRUTCH, Joseph Wood: *Comedy and conscience after the Restoration*. Rev. edn. New York: Columbia U.P., 1949.
    Remains the best account of the controversy surrounding Collier's *Short View*, and the alleged 'immorality' of the stage.

LOFTIS, John: *The politics of drama in Augustan England*. O.U.P., 1963.

ROSENFELD, Sybil: *Strolling players and drama in the provinces, 1660–1765*. Cambridge U.P., 1939.

SOUTHERN, Richard: *The Georgian playhouse*. Pleiades Books, 1948.
    A concise, well-illustrated account of the development of theatre forms from the Restoration to the Regency.

VAN LENNEP, William, *et al.*, eds.: *The London stage, 1660–1800.* Part I: 1660–1700. Part II, in 2 vols.: 1700–1729. Part III, in 2 vols.: 1729–1747. Part IV, in 3 vols.: 1747–1776. Part V, in 3 vols.: 1776–1800. Carbondale, Ill.: Southern Illinois U.P., 1960–8.
   A monumental work, containing a definitive record of performances in the London theatre, with full documentation and introductory material. The introductions to the five parts were published in separate volumes as Arcturus paperbacks in 1968.

Nineteenth Century

REYNOLDS, Ernest: *Early Victorian drama, 1830–70.* Cambridge: Heffer, 1936. New York: Blom, 1965.

ROWELL, George: *The Victorian theatre: a survey.* O.U.P., 1956.
   A study of the drama, the theatre, and their social context. A very useful introduction to a neglected period, with full play-lists and bibliographies.

SCOTT, Clement: *The drama of yesterday and today.* 2 vols. Macmillan, 1899.
   Often unreliable and idiosyncratic, but valuable as a personal account by a critic saturated in the theatre and thinking of his age.

SOUTHERN, Richard: *The Victorian theatre: a pictorial survey.* Newton Abbot: David and Charles, 1970.

Early Twentieth Century

AGATE, James: *A short view of the English stage, 1900–1926.* Herbert Jenkins, 1926. New York: Blom, 1969.

REYNOLDS, Ernest: *Modern English drama.* Harrap, 1949. Norman: Oklahoma U.P.

TAYLOR, John Russell: *The rise and fall of the well-made play.* Methuen, 1967. New York: Hill and Wang.

TREWIN, J. C., ed.: *Theatre programme.* Muller, 1954.
   A symposium of fifteen articles by specialist writers, which gives a clear view of the British theatre just before the emergence of the new generation of dramatists.

TREWIN, J. C.: *The theatre since 1900.* Dakers, 1951.
   An informed, chronological account of the period.

WILSON, A. E.: *Edwardian theatre.* Barker, 1951.

Contemporary

ARMSTRONG, William A., ed.: *Experimental theatre.* Bell, 1963.
   Ten reprinted lectures, of uneven quality.

KITCHIN, Laurence: *Drama in the sixties.* Faber, 1966. *Mid-century drama.* Faber, 1960.
   These two collections of miscellaneous essays and interviews deal with the theatre as well as the drama, and with interpretations of the classics and foreign dramatists in Britain as well as recent domestic developments.

MAROWITZ, Charles, and TRUSSLER, Simon, eds.: *Theatre at work.* Methuen, 1967. New York: Hill and Wang, 1968.
   A collection of interviews with dramatists and directors, and rehearsal logs of significant productions.

TAYLOR, John Russell: *Anger and after.* 2nd edn. Methuen, 1969. New York: Hill and Wang, 1969, as *The angry theatre.*
   A synoptic but comprehensive account of the new dramatists who emerged in the late nineteen-fifties.

IRISH DRAMA AND THEATRE

CLARK, William Smith: *The early Irish stage.* O.U.P., 1955. *The Irish stage in the county towns, 1720–1800.* O.U.P., 1965.
   The fullest accounts of the origins and early development of the Irish theatre.

ELLIS-FERMOR, Una: *The Irish dramatic movement*. 2nd edn. Methuen, 1954. New York: Barnes and Noble.
A critical study of Synge, Yeats, Lady Gregory, and the theatre in which they worked.

HOGAN, Robert: *After the Irish renaissance: a critical history of the Irish drama since 'The Plough and the Stars'*. Minneapolis: Minnesota U.P., 1967. Macmillan, 1968.

KAVANAGH, Peter: *The Irish theatre*. Tralee: Kerryman, 1946. New York: Blom, 1969.

ROBINSON, Lennox: *Ireland's Abbey Theatre*. Sidgwick, 1951.

EUROPEAN DRAMA AND THEATRE

Italy

DUCHARTE, Pierre Louis: *The Italian comedy: the improvisation, scenarios, lives, attributes, portraits and masks of the illustrious characters of the commedia dell'arte*. Harrap, 1929.

HERRICK, Marvin T.: *Italian comedy in the Renaissance*. Urbana: Illinois U.P., 1960. *Italian tragedy in the Renaissance*. Urbana: Illinois U.P., 1965.

KENNARD, Joseph S.: *The Italian theatre*. 2 vols. New York: Blom, 1964.
First published in 1932. The first volume describes the popular and court theatre till 1700, and the second ends at 1930.

McLEOD, Addison: *Plays and players in modern Italy: being a study of the Italian stage as affected by the political life, manners, and character of today*. Smith, Elder, 1912. Port Washington, N.Y.: Kennikat, 1970.

NAGLER, A. M.: *Theatre festivals of the Medici, 1539–1637*. New Haven, Conn.: Yale U.P., 1964.

SMITH, Winifred: *The commedia dell'arte: a study in Italian popular comedy*. New York: Columbia U.P., 1912. New York: Blom, 1964. *Italian actors of the Renaissance*. New York: Blom, 1968. (First published in 1930.)

Spain

CRAWFORD, J. P. W.: *Spanish drama before Lope de Vega*. 2nd edn. Philadelphia: Pennsylvania U.P., 1967.

DONOVAN, R. B.: *The liturgical drama in medieval Spain*. Toronto U.P., 1958.

PEAK, J. Hunter: *Social drama in nineteenth century Spain*. Chapel Hill: North Carolina U.P., 1965.

RENNERT, Hugo A.: *The Spanish stage in the time of Lope de Vega*. New York: Kraus Reprint, 1963.
First published in 1909. Fully documented, and containing a 'list of Spanish actors and actresses, 1560–1680'.

SHERGOLD, N. D.: *A history of the Spanish stage*. O.U.P., 1967.
A full account of the staging of plays from medieval times to the end of the seventeenth century. Useful glossary and bibliography.

France

CARLSON, Marvin: *The theatre of the French revolution*. Ithaca, N.Y.: Cornell U.P., 1966.

FOWLIE, Wallace: *Dionysus in Paris*. Magnolia, Mass.: Smith, 1961. Gollancz, 1961.
A 'guide to contemporary French theatre'. Mainly concerned with the drama.

FRANK, G.: *Medieval French drama*. O.U.P., 1954.

GUICHARNAUD, Jacques: *Modern French theatre, from Giraudoux to Genet*. New Haven, Conn.: Yale U.P., 1967.

HAWKINS, Frederick W.: *Annals of the French stage from its origin to the death of Racine*. 2 vols. Chapman and Hall, 1884. New York: Greenwood, 1969. *The French stage in the eighteenth century*. 2 vols. Chapman and Hall, 1888. New York: Greenwood, 1969.

HOBSON, Harold: *The French theatre of today: an English view*. Harrap, 1953. New York: Blom.
A detailed study of the dramatists to emerge since the war, with introductory theatrical background.

JEFFERY, Brian: *French Renaissance comedy, 1552–1630*. O.U.P., 1969.

KNOWLES, Dorothy: *French drama of the inter-war years, 1918–39*. Harrap, 1967. New York: Barnes and Noble, 1968.

LANCASTER, H. C.: *A history of French dramatic literature, 1610–1700*. 9 vols. Baltimore: Johns Hopkins, 1929–42. New York: Gordian, 1966. *Sunset: a history of Parisian drama in the last years of Louis XIV, 1701–1715*. Baltimore: Johns Hopkins, 1945. *French tragedy in the time of Louis XV and Voltaire, 1715–74*. 2 vols. Baltimore: Johns Hopkins, 1950. *French tragedy in the reign of Louis XVI and the early years of the French revolution, 1774–92*. Baltimore: Johns Hopkins, 1953.

LAWRENSON, T. E.: *The French stage in the seventeenth century: a study in the advent of the Italian order*. Manchester U.P., 1957.

LOUGH, John: *Paris theatre audiences in the seventeenth and eighteenth centuries*. O.U.P., 1957.

PALMER, John: *Studies in the contemporary theatre*. Secker, 1927. Freeport, N.Y.: Books for Libraries, 1969.

WICKS, C. Beaumont, ed.: *The Parisian stage*. 4 vols. University: Alabama U.P., 1950–60.
A comprehensive record of productions in the Parisian theatre during the nineteenth century.

WILEY, William: *The early public theatre in France*. Cambridge, Mass.: Harvard U.P., 1960.
A study of theatres, actors, and audiences from 1580 to 1630.

Germany and Scandinavia

BRAUN, Walter: *Theatre in Deutschland*. Munich: Bruckmann, 1956.
Text in German, but basically a pictorial account of the German theatre of its period.

BRUFORD, W. H.: *Theatre, drama, and audience in Goethe's Germany*. New York: Hillary. Routledge, 1950.

GARTEN, H. F.: *Modern German drama*. 2nd edn. Methuen, 1962. New York: O.U.P., 1964.
A sound and detailed study of the dramatic literature.

GAY, Peter: *Weimar culture: the outsider as insider*. Secker, 1969.
Not primarily concerned with theatre, but an enlightening view of an era neglected by writers in English.

GUSTAFSON, A.: *A history of Swedish literature*. Minneapolis: Minnesota U.P., 1961. O.U.P.

HEITNER, Robert R.: *German tragedy in the age of enlightenment, 1724–1768*. Berkeley: California U.P., 1963.

LUCAS, F. L.: *The drama of Ibsen and Strindberg*. New York: Macmillan, 1962. Cassell, 1963.

MCFARLANE, J. W.: *Ibsen and the temper of Norwegian literature*. O.U.P., 1960.

SHAW, Leroy R., ed.: *German theater today: a symposium*. Austin: Texas U.P., 1964.

SPALTER, Max: *Brecht's tradition*. Baltimore: Johns Hopkins, 1967.
  Detailed studies of Lenz, Grabbe, Büchner, Wedekind, and Kraus, besides Brecht himself.

Russia

CARTER, Huntley: *The new spirit in the Russian theatre, 1917–1928*. New York: Brentano's, 1929. Arno, Blom.

COLEMAN, Arthur P.: *Humour in the Russian comedy from Catherine to Gogol*. New York: Columbia U.P., 1925.

FÜLÖP-MILLER, René, and GREGOR, Josef: *The Russian theatre*. Philadelphia: Lippincott. Harrap, 1930. New York: Blom.

GORCHAKOV, Nikolai A.: *The theater in Soviet Russia*. New York: Columbia U.P. O.U.P., 1957.

MACLEOD, Joseph: *The new Soviet theatre*. Allen and Unwin, 1943.

SLONIM, Marc: *Russian theater from the Empire to the Soviets*. Cleveland: World, 1961. Methuen, 1963.
  The fullest and most impartial account yet published.

AMERICAN DRAMA AND THEATRE

ATKINSON, Brooks: *Broadway, 1900–1970*. New York: Collier, 1970. Cassell, 1971.

BIGSBY, C. W. E.: *Confrontation and commitment: a study of contemporary American drama, 1959–1966*. MacGibbon and Kee, 1967.

BLUM, Daniel, and WILLIS, John: *A pictorial history of the American theatre, 1860–1970*. 3rd edn. New York: Crown, 1969.

CLURMAN, Harold: *The fervent years*. 2nd edn. New York: Hill and Wang, 1957. MacGibbon and Kee.
  An account of the work and influence of the Group Theatre.

DOWNER, Alan S., ed.: *American drama and its critics: a collection of critical essays*. Chicago U.P., 1965.

DOWNER, Alan S.: *The American theatre today*. New York: Basic, 1967.

EWEN, D.: *The story of America's musical theatre*. New York: Chilton, 1968.

GASSNER, John: *Theatre at the crossroads: plays and playwrights on the mid-century American stage*. New York: Holt, Rinehart, 1960.

GOTTFRIED, Martin: *A theatre divided: the postwar American stage*. Boston: Little, Brown, 1969.
  An analysis of the schism between the Broadway stage and the resident companies and off-off-Broadway theatres.

HEWITT, Barnard, ed.: *Theatre U.S.A., 1668–1957*. New York: McGraw-Hill, 1959.
  A chronologically-arranged collection of contemporary accounts.

HUGHES, Glenn: *History of the American theatre, 1700–1950*. New York: French, 1951.

KERNAN, Alvin B., ed.: *Modern American theater: a collection of critical essays*. Englewood Cliffs, N.J.: Prentice-Hall, 1967.

KRUTCH, Joseph Wood: *The American drama since 1918*. 2nd edn. New York: Random House, 1957.

LITTLE, Stuart W., and CANTOR, Arthur: *The playmakers: Broadway from the inside.*
New York: Norton, 1970. Reinhardt, 1971.
Rather journalistic in approach, but highly revealing in its account of the mechanics and motives that generate the Broadway production system.

MCNAMARA, Brooks: *The American playhouse in the eighteenth century.* Cambridge, Mass.: Harvard U.P., 1969.

MESERVE, Walter, ed.: *Discussions of modern American drama.* Boston: Heath, 1966.

ODELL, G. C. D.: *Annals of the New York stage.* 15 vols. New York: Columbia U.P., 1927–49. A.M.S., 1970.
A detailed factual account, given lively narrative shape.

POGGI, Jack: *Theater in America: the impact of economic forces, 1870–1967.* Ithaca, N.Y.: Cornell U.P., 1968.

QUINN, A. H.: *History of the American drama from the beginnings to the Civil War.* 2nd edn. New York: Appleton, 1943. *History of the American drama from the Civil War to the present day.* 2 vols. in one. 2nd edn. New York: Appleton, 1936. Pitman, 1937.

TAUBMAN, Howard: *Making of the American theatre.* Rev. edn. New York: Coward, 1967. Longmans, 1967.

ASIAN DRAMA AND THEATRE

BOWERS, Faubion: *Theatre in the East: a survey of Asian dance and drama.* Nelson, 1956. New York: Grove, 1969.

BRANDON, James R.: *Theatre in Southeast Asia.* Cambridge, Mass.: Harvard U.P., 1967. O.U.P., 1968.

PRONKO, Leonard C.: *Theater East and West: perspectives towards a total theater.* Berkeley: California U.P., 1967. Cambridge U.P.

China

ARLINGTON, L. C.: *The Chinese drama from the earliest times until to-day.* Shanghai: Kelly and Welsh, 1930. New York: Blom.

CHEN, Jack: *Chinese theatre.* Dobson, 1949. New York: Dufour, 1950.

SCOTT, Adolphe C.: *The classical theatre of China.* Unwin, 1957. New York: Barnes and Noble. *An introduction to the Chinese theatre.* New York: Theatre Arts, 1959.

ZUNG, Cecilia S.: *Secrets of the Chinese drama.* Shanghai: Kelly and Welsh, 1937. New York: Blom, 1964.

Japan

ARNOTT, Peter: *The theatres of Japan.* Macmillan, 1969. New York: St. Martin's.
Besides studies of the *nō* and *kabuki* theatres, includes an analysis of western imitations of the Japanese tradition.

BOWERS, Faubion: *Japanese theatre.* Owen, 1959. New York: Hill and Wang.

ERNST, E.: *Kabuki theatre.* Secker, 1956. New York: O.U.P.

HACHIMONJIYA, Jisho: *The actors' analects.* New York: Columbia U.P., 1969.
A collection of notes and advice from *kabuki* players of the late seventeenth century.

SCOTT, Adolphe C.: *The Kabuki theatre of Japan.* New York: Collier, 1966.

India

GARGI, Balwant: *Folk theatre of India.* Seattle: Washington U.P., 1966. *Theatre in India.* New York: Theatre Arts, 1962.

KEITH, A. Berriedale: *The Sanskrit drama in its origin, development, theory, and practice.* O.U.P., 1924.

MATHUR, Jagdish C.: *Drama in rural India.* New York: Taplinger, 1964.

WELLS, H. W.: *The classical drama of India.* New York: Taplinger, 1963.

THEORIES OF DRAMA AND THEATRE

Anthologies

BENTLEY, Eric, ed.: *The theory of the modern stage.* Penguin, 1968.

CALDERWOOD, James L., and TOLIVER, Harold E., eds.: *Perspectives on drama.* New York: O.U.P., 1968.
    A collection of statements by practitioners and critics on dramatic forms, and on the elements of the drama.

CLARK, Barrett H., ed., rev. by Henry Popkin: *European theories of the drama, with a supplement on the American drama.* New York: Crown, 1965.
    A comprehensive collection of theoretical writings and extracts from more general works, arranged chronologically and by country. Full bibliography.

Studies

ELLIS-FERMOR, Una: *The frontiers of drama.* 2nd edn. Methuen, 1964.
    A study of the relation between content and form in drama.

NELSON, Robert J.: *Play within a play: the dramatist's conception of his art.* New Haven, Conn.: Yale U.P., 1958.
    Differing concepts of theatre defined from various dramatists' use of the play-within-a-play convention.

NICOLL, Allardyce: *The theatre and dramatic theory.* Harrap, 1962. New York: Barnes and Noble.
    A critical analysis of the development of dramatic theory since the sentimentalists.

Individual Theorists

ABEL, Lionel: *Metatheatre: a new view of dramatic form.* New York: Hill and Wang, 1963.
    The self-consciousness of modern theatre considered as the basis for a new concept of dramatic form.

ARISTOTLE: *Poetics,* translated by S. H. Butcher. New York: Hill and Wang, 1961.
    This edition has a valuable introductory essay by Francis Fergusson.

ARTAUD, Antonin: *Collected works.* Vols. I and II. Calder, 1968 and 1971. In progress.
    The first complete English edition of Artaud's works. *The theatre and its double,* containing the Theatre of Cruelty manifestoes, is available separately, translated by Victor Corti (Calder, 1970).

BARRAULT, Jean-Louis: *Reflections on the theatre.* Barrie and Rockliff, 1951.

BLAU, Herbert: *The impossible theater: a manifesto.* New York: Collier, 1965.

BRECHT, Bertolt: *Brecht on theatre.* Methuen, 1964. New York: Hill and Wang.
    A valuable collection of Brecht's theoretical writings, arranged chronologically, and fully annotated by John Willett, whose *Theatre of Bertolt Brecht* (Methuen 3rd edn., 1967) remains the best critical study.

BROOK, Peter: *The empty space*. MacGibbon and Kee, 1968. New York: Atheneum.

CRAIG, Edward Gordon: *On the art of the theatre*. 2nd edn. Heinemann, 1955. New York: Theatre Arts, 1958.

DRYDEN, John: *Of dramatic poesy, and other critical essays*. 2 vols. Dent, 1962. New York, Dutton.
  A comprehensive collection, including a glossary of key-words.

GRANVILLE-BARKER, Harley: *On dramatic method*. Sidgwick, 1931. New York: Hill and Wang, 1956.
  Dramatic theories throughout history shown to derive from usage rather than prescription.

GROTOWSKI, Jerzy: *Towards a poor theatre*. Methuen, 1969. New York: Simon and Schuster, 1970.
  Collection of essays and statements illustrating the theory and practice of the director of Poland's Laboratory Theatre.

IONESCO, Eugene: *Notes and counter-notes*. New York: Grove, 1964. Calder, 1965.
  A collection of essays, including the exchanges with Kenneth Tynan over the social responsibility of the playwright.

JARRY, Alfred: *Selected works of Alfred Jarry*. Methuen, 1965. New York: Grove.

MEYERHOLD, Vsevolod: *Meyerhold on theatre*. Methuen, 1969. New York: Hill and Wang.
  Writings covering the period 1902–39, interspersed with a full commentary by the translator, Edward Braun.

SHAW, Bernard: *Shaw on theatre*. New York: Hill and Wang, 1958.
  A selection by E. J. West of those of Shaw's writings which relate to dramatic art and theory.

TAÏROV, Aleksander: *Notes of a director*. Coral Gables, Fla.: Miami U.P., 1969.
  Practical and theoretical record of Taïrov's work during the first six years of the Moscow Kamerny Theatre.

WHITING, John: *The art of the dramatist*. London Magazine Editions, 1970.
  Includes some creative writing, but also important reflections on the role and art of the playwright.

DRAMATIC FORMS

Tragedy

CORRIGAN, Robert W., ed.: *Tragedy: vision and form*. San Francisco: Chandler, 1965.
  Collection of essays on the characteristics of the form.

LUCAS, F. L.: *Tragedy: serious drama in relation to Aristotle's Poetics*. Hogarth Press, 1927. New York: Macmillan, 1958.
  A standard study of Aristotle, which also relates his concept of tragedy to the work of later dramatists.

STEINER, George: *The death of tragedy*. Faber, 1961. New York: Knopf.
  Contends that there has been no true Western tragedy since Racine, and analyses the reasons for this.

STYAN, J. L.: *The dark comedy: the development of modern comic tragedy*. Cambridge U.P., 1962.

WILLIAMS, Raymond: *Modern tragedy*. Chatto, 1966.
  A general study of tragedy, followed by analyses of the work of modern writers in the form.

Comedy

BERGSON, Henri: *Laughter*. Garden City, N.Y.: Doubleday, 1956.
   Bergson's classic psychological study, together with George Meredith's *Essay on Comedy*, and a useful introductory essay.

CORRIGAN, Robert W., ed.: *Comedy: meaning and form*. San Francisco: Chandler, 1965.
   A symposium approaching the form from eight different aspects.

LAUTER, Paul, ed.: *Theories of comedy*. Garden City, N.Y.: Doubleday, 1964.
   A collection of essays including statements by Plato, Jonson, Molière, Hazlitt, Schiller, Freud, and others.

SEYLER, Athene, and HAGGARD, Stephen: *The craft of comedy*. 2nd edn. New York: Theatre Arts, 1957. Muller, 1958.
   An exchange of letters about the problems of playing comedy in general, and specific comic characters and scenes.

Other Forms of Drama and Theatre

BOOTH, Michael: *English melodrama*. Jenkins, 1965.
   An excellent study of the development of the form, and of its distinctive conventions.

CLINTON-BADDELEY, V. C.: *The burlesque tradition in the English theatre after 1660*. Methuen, 1952.

DISHER, M. Willson: *Blood and thunder: mid-Victorian melodrama and its origins*. Rockliff, 1949. *Melodrama*. Rockliff, 1954.
   The second is, in effect, a continuation of the preceding work, carrying the history of the form from 1850 to 1900.

GILBERT, Douglas: *American vaudeville*. New York: Dover, 1963. Constable.

GREEN, Stanley: *The world of musical comedy*. New York: Grosset and Dunlap, 1962.

HUGHES, Leo: *A century of English farce*. Princeton U.P., 1956. O.U.P.
   A study of the origins of farce, and of its development and theatrical history from the Restoration to the mid-eighteenth century.

MANDER, Raymond, and MITCHENSON, Joe: *British music hall*. Studio Vista, 1965.
   A valuable pictorial study.

OREGLIA, Giacomo: *The commedia dell'arte*. Methuen, 1968. New York: Hill and Wang.
   A concise but comprehensive study, well illustrated, and documented by several scenarios.

WILSON, A. E.: *The story of pantomime*. Home and Van Thal, 1949.

PLAYWRITING

ARCHER, William: *Play-making: a manual of craftsmanship*. Chapman and Hall, 1913. New York: Dover, 1960.
   A classic guide to the construction of the 'well-made' play.

COLE, Toby, ed.: *Playwrights on playwriting: the meaning and making of modern drama from Ibsen to Ionesco*. New York: Hill and Wang, 1960. MacGibbon and Kee, 1961.

ERVINE, St. John: *How to write a play*. Allen and Unwin, 1928.

MATTHEWS, Brander, ed.: *Papers on playmaking*. New York: Hill and Wang, 1957. MacGibbon and Kee.
   Statements by nineteenth-century playwrights, which together contrast with and interestingly complement Toby Cole's collection of more recent views, cited above.

PRIESTLEY, J. B.: *The art of the dramatist*. Heinemann. Boston: The Writer, 1957.

WAGER, Walter, ed.: *The playwrights speak.* New York: Delacorte, 1967. Harlow: Longmans, 1969.
A collection of interviews with major post-war dramatists about their careers and their craft.

ORGANIZATION AND ETHICS OF THE THEATRE

ARCHER, William, and GRANVILLE-BARKER, Harley: *A national theatre: schemes and estimates.* Rev. edn. Duckworth, 1907. Port Washington, N.Y.: Kennikat, 1970.
Long out of date in its economic arguments, this remains a pioneering and detailed 'feasibility study' into the possible workings of a true national theatre.

CHISHOLM, Cecil: *Repertory.* Davies, 1934.
Surveys the development of the movement, and its day-to-day organization.

ERVINE, St. John: *The organized theatre: a plea in civics.* Allen and Unwin, 1924. New York: Macmillan.

FINDLATER, Richard: *Banned.* MacGibbon and Kee, 1967.
An excellent history and critique of censorship in the theatre. The same author's *Comic Cuts* (Deutsch, 1970) revealingly anthologizes the actual deletions required by the censor.

FINDLATER, Richard: *The unholy trade.* Gollancz, 1952.
Though its artistic judgements are now out of date, this is still the most detailed account of the economics and administration of the British theatre.

FOWELL, Frank, and PALMER, Frank: *Censorship in England.* Palmer, 1913. New York: Blom, 1969.
A detailed historical study, amply documented.

GOLDMAN, William: *The season: a candid look at Broadway.* New York: Harcourt, 1969.
A detailed study of the inner workings and outward appearances of a single, representative Broadway season.

GRANVILLE-BARKER, Harley: *The exemplary theatre.* Chatto, 1922. Boston: Little, Brown.

LANDSTONE, Charles: *Off-stage: a personal record of the first twelve years of state sponsored drama in Great Britain.* Elek, 1953.

LEAPER, W. J.: *Copyright and the performing arts.* Stevens, 1957.

MACGOWAN, Kenneth: *Footlights across America: towards a National Theatre.* New York: Harcourt, 1929.
A full survey of the state of the 'art' and commercial theatre of its period, as well as a plea for the future.

MARSHALL, Norman: *The other theatre.* Lehmann, 1947.
A history and description of the activities of club and 'little' theatres in England.

PRIESTLEY, J. B.: *Theatre outlook.* Nicholson and Watson, 1947.

RENDLE, Adrian: *Everyman and his theatre.* Pitman, 1968.
History, development, and present state of the amateur theatre.

SWEETING, Elizabeth: *Theatre administration.* Pitman, 1969.

WHITWORTH, Geoffrey: *The making of a National Theatre.* Faber, 1950.

PLAYHOUSES AND FORMS OF STAGING

ALOI, Roberto: *Esempi architetture per lo spettacolo.* Milan: Hoepli, 1958. New York: J. H. Heineman, 1959.
   Text in Italian, but profusely illustrated. A comprehensive survey of modern theatre architecture.

BAUR-HEINHOLD, M.: *Baroque theatre.* Thames and Hudson, 1967. New York: McGraw-Hill.

BOYLE, W. P.: *Central and flexible staging.* Berkeley: California U.P., 1956.

BURRIS-MEYER, Harold, and COLE, Edward: *Theatres and auditoriums.* 2nd edn. New York: Reinhold, 1965.
   A detailed account of the relationships between architectural and artistic requirements in theatre planning.

CORRY, Percy: *Planning the stage.* Pitman, 1961.

HOWARD, Diana: *London theatres and music halls, 1850–1950.* Library Association, 1970.
   A comprehensive and authoritative factual and bibliographical survey.

JOSEPH, Stephen, ed.: *Actor and architect.* Manchester U.P., 1964.
   Six essays examining the relationship between actor, audience, and theatre designer.

JOSEPH, Stephen: *New theatre forms.* Pitman, 1968. New York: Theatre Arts.

MANDER, Raymond, and MITCHENSON, Joe: *The lost theatres of London.* Hart-Davis, 1968. New York: Taplinger. *The theatres of London.* Hart-Davis, 1961. New York: Hill and Wang.
   These two works are complementary surveys of the past and present playhouses of London, as much concerned with theatrical as architectural detail. *The lost theatres* is documented with a number of contemporary accounts.

SCHLEMMER, Oskar, *et al.*: *The theatre of the Bauhaus.* Middletown, Conn.: Wesleyan U.P., 1961.
   First English edition of *Die Bühne im Bauhaus* (1924).

SILVERMAN, Maxwell, and BOWMAN, M. A.: *Contemporary theatre architecture: an illustrated survey.* New York Public Library, 1965.
   More than forty recent playhouses studied in full architectural detail, with a comprehensive checklist of post-war publications on theatre architecture.

SOUTHERN, Richard: *Proscenium and sight lines.* 2nd edn. Faber, 1964. New York: Theatre Arts.
   A full survey of scenery and stage planning.

TECHNIQUES OF STAGECRAFT

Comprehensive Studies of the Production Process

CARTER, Conrad, *et al.*: *The production and staging of plays.* New York: Arc Books, 1963.

COTES, Peter: *A handbook for the amateur theatre.* Oldbourne, 1957.

COURTNEY, Richard: *Drama for youth.* Pitman, 1964.

FARBER, Donald C.: *Producing on Broadway: a comprehensive guide.* New York: D.B.S. Publications, 1969.

GASSNER, John: *Producing the play,* including *The new scene technician's handbook,* by Philip Barber. Rev. edn. New York: Dryden, 1953.
   Includes contributions, on all aspects of production technique, by Margaret Webster, Lee Strasberg, Mordecai Gorelik, and Robert Lewis.

GRUVER, Bert: *The stage manager's handbook.* New York: D.B.S. Publications, 1961.

HEFFNER, Herbert C., *et al.*: *Modern theatre practice: a handbook of play production, with an appendix on costume and makeup.* 4th edn. New York: Appleton, 1959.
Sections on directing, scenery, and stage lighting.

MELVILL, Harald: *Theatrecraft: the A to Z of show business.* Rockliff, 1954.

History and Technique of Directing

COLE, Toby, and CHINOY, Helen Krich, eds.: *Directors on directing.* 2nd edn. Indianapolis: Bobbs-Merrill, 1963.
An essay on the history of the director's role precedes this collection of personal statements by major figures, and documentation of their rehearsal methods.

FERNALD, John: *Sense of direction: the director and his actors.* Secker, 1968. New York: Stein and Day, 1969.
A well-grounded practical and artistic guide.

HUNT, Hugh: *The director in the theatre.* Routledge, 1954.
The rise of the director, and his relation to actors and playwrights.

MACGOWAN, Kenneth: *Continental stagecraft.* New York: Blom, 1964.
The methods and theories of Appia, Reinhardt, Craig, Stanislavsky, Jessner, and Copeau.

MARSHALL, Norman: *The producer and the play.* Macdonald, 1962. Chester Springs, Pa.: Dufour.
A history of the rise of the director and his influence, which includes studies of Irving, Tree, Craig, Barker, Komisarjevsky, Brecht, and Guthrie.

MCMULLAN, Frank: *The director's handbook: an outline for the teacher and student of play interpretation and direction.* New York: Shoe String Press, 1962.

ROOSE-EVANS, James: *Directing the play.* Studio Vista, 1968. New York: Theatre Arts.

History and Techniques of Stage Design

APPIA, Adolphe: *Music and the art of the theatre.* Coral Gables, Fla.: Miami U.P., 1962.
First English translation of the work which pioneered the freedom and basic principles of modern scenic and lighting design. Illustrated.

BURRIS-MEYER, Harold, and COLE, Edward C.: *Scenery for the theatre: the organization, processes, materials, and techniques used to set the stage.* Boston: Little, Brown, 1938. Harrap, 1939.
A comprehensive technical study.

FRETTE, Guido: *Stage design, 1909–1954.* Milan: G. G. Gorlich, 1955.

HAINAUX, René, ed.: *Stage design throughout the world since 1935.* New York: Theatre Arts, 1965. Harrap, 1957.
A valuable pictorial study, fully documented.

HAINAUX, René, and BONNAT, Y.-, eds.: *Stage design throughout the world since 1950.* Harrap, 1964. New York: Theatre Arts.

JOSEPH, Stephen: *Scene painting and design.* Pitman, 1964.

LAVER, James: *Costume in the theatre.* Harrap, 1964. New York: Hill and Wang.
The function of costume in the theatre from the earliest times.

SIMONSON, Lee: *The stage is set.* New York: Theatre Arts, 1963.
First published in 1932. A full and stimulating history of stagecraft, with a critical analysis of its importance and aesthetics.

SOUTHERN, Richard: *Changeable scenery: its origin and development in the British theatre.* Faber, 1952.
The use and development of stage scenery in England from the Restoration to the beginning of the present century.

Light and Sound in the Theatre

BENTHAM, Frederick: *The art of stage lighting*. Pitman, 1970.

BURRIS-MEYER, Harold, and MALLORY, V.: *Sound in the theatre*. New York: Theatre Arts, 1959.
    A concise, detailed guide.

CORRY, Percy: *Lighting the stage*. 3rd edn. Pitman, 1962.
    Particularly addressed to the amateur director or designer.

FUCHS, Theodore: *Stage lighting*. New York: Blom, 1963.
    First published in 1929. A classic in its field, though now outdated in many technical respects.

HARTMANN, Louis: *Theatre lighting: a manual of the stage switchboard*. New York: D.B.S. Publications, 1970.
    Reprint of the edition of 1930. An analysis by Belasco's lighting designer of both the practical and artistic aspects of lighting on the stage.

McCANDLESS, Stanley: *A syllabus of stage lighting*. 11th edn. New York: D.B.S. Publications, 1964.

PILBROW, Richard: *Stage lighting*. Studio Vista, 1970.

ACTING

History and Criticism

BRADBROOK, M. C.: *The rise of the common player*. Chatto, 1962. Cambridge, Mass.: Harvard U.P.
    The place of the actor in Elizabethan society. Detailed studies of Laneham, Tarlton, Wilson, and Alleyn.

DARLINGTON, W. A.: *The actor and his audience*. Phoenix, 1949.
    A study of the qualities that make for greatness in an actor.

GILDER, Rosamond: *Enter the actress: the first women in the theatre*. Harrap, 1931. New York: Theatre Arts, 1960.

JOSEPH, Bertram: *Elizabethan acting*. 2nd edn. O.U.P., 1964.
    A brief but well-documented study.

JOSEPH, Bertram: *The tragic actor*. Routledge, 1959. New York: Theatre Arts.
    A detailed study of the nature and conventions of tragic acting from Burbage to Irving.

WILSON, Garff B.: *A history of American acting*. Bloomington, Ind.: Indiana U.P., 1966.

Theory and Technique

ARCHER, William: *Masks or faces?* Longmans, 1888. New York: Hill and Wang, 1957.
    Diderot's anti-emotional views in *The Paradox of Acting* (reprinted in the Hill and Wang edition) answered by Archer on the basis of a questionnaire submitted to leading players of the day.

BLAKELOCK, Denys: *Advice to a player: letters to a young actor*. Heinemann, 1958.

BURTON, Hal: *Great acting*. B.B.C. Publications. New York: Hill and Wang, 1969.

COLE, Toby, ed.: *Acting: a handbook of the Stanislavski Method*. 2nd edn. New York: Crown, 1955.
    A collection of essays and notes by Stanislavsky and his associates.

COLE, Toby, and CHINOY, Helen Krich, eds.: *Actors on acting: the theories, techniques, and practices of the great actors of the world as told in their own words.* New edn. New York: Crown, 1970.
   A compendious anthology, extending from Thespis to the present day, with historical introductions to each of its fourteen sections.

COQUELIN, Constant: *The art of the actor.* Allen and Unwin, 1954.
   A translation of the classic study first published in 1894.

CORSON, Richard: *Stage make-up.* 3rd edn. New York: Appleton, 1960.

GIELGUD, John: *Stage directions.* Heinemann, 1963. New York: Random House.
   The actor's means of presenting character, mood, and emotion.

HAYMAN, Ronald: *Techniques of acting.* Methuen, 1969.
   A comparative study of different techniques of acting, and the requirements of the various performing arts.

HETHMON, Robert H., ed.: *Strasberg at the Actors' Studio: tape recorded sessions.* New York: Viking, 1965. Cape, 1966.

HODGSON, John, and RICHARDS, Ernest: *Improvisation.* Methuen, 1966.

MATTHEWS, Brander, ed.: *Papers on acting.* New York: Hill and Wang, 1958.

REDGRAVE, Michael: *The actor's ways and means.* Heinemann, 1953. New York: Theatre Arts.
   A survey of the literature of acting, and an outline of the author's own guidelines.

REDGRAVE, Michael: *Mask or face: reflections in an actor's mirror.* Heinemann, 1958. New York: Theatre Arts.
   A study of the acting profession, and of approaches to its theory and practice.

STANISLAVSKI, Constantin: *An actor prepares.* New York: Theatre Arts, 1936. Bles, 1937. *Building a character.* New York: Theatre Arts, 1949. Reinhardt, 1950. *Creating a role.* New York: Theatre Arts, 1961. Bles, 1963.
   The basic source books for the study of Stanislavsky's work. The first and second outline the substance of his theories, and how these are translated into technique, while in the third, a composite of several drafts assembled after the director's death, his ideas are applied to the realization of particular roles.

THEATRE CRITICISM

Studies

DOWNS, Harold: *The critic in the theatre.* Pitman, 1953.

HOBSON, Harold: *Verdict at midnight.* Longmans, 1952.
   First-night notices put to the test of time.

Anthologies

AGATE, James, ed.: *The English dramatic critics.* Barker, 1933. New York: Hill and Wang, 1958.

ROWELL, George: *Victorian dramatic criticism.* Methuen, 1971.

WARD, A. C., ed.: *Specimens of English dramatic criticism.* O.U.P., 1945.

Individual Critics

AGATE, James: *Brief chronicles.* Cape, 1943. *Immoment Toys.* Cape, 1945. New York: Blom, 1969. *Red Letter Nights.* Cape, 1944. New York: Blom, 1969.
   Personal selections from Agate's many volumes of collected reviews, surveying respectively Shakespearian and Elizabethan revivals, light entertainment, and post-Elizabethan drama.

ARCHER, William: *The theatrical world*. 5 vols., 1893–7. Walter Scott, 1894–8. New York: Blom, 1969.

BEERBOHM, Max: *Around theatres*. Hart-Davis, 1952. New York: Taplinger, 1969. *More theatres, 1898–1903*. Hart-Davis, 1969. New York: Taplinger. *Last theatres, 1904–1910*. Hart-Davis, 1970.

BENTLEY, Eric: *What is theatre?* New York: Atheneum, 1968. Methuen, 1969.

BROWN, John Mason: *Dramatis personae*. New York: Viking, 1963. Hamilton.

BRUSTEIN, Robert: *Seasons of discontent*. New York: Simon and Schuster, 1965. Cape, 1966. *The third theatre*. New York: Knopf, 1969. Cape, 1970.

CLURMAN, Harold: *Lies like truth*. New York: Macmillan, 1968.

DENNIS, Nigel: *Dramatic essays*. Weidenfeld, 1962.

GREIN, J. T.: *Dramatic criticism*. 5 vols., 1897–1904. Vol. I, J. Long, 1899. Vols. II and III, Greenwood, 1900 and 1902. Vols. IV and V, E. Nash, 1904 and 1905. Vols. I to V, New York: Blom, 1968.

HAZLITT, William: *Hazlitt on theatre*. Walter Scott, 1895. New York: Hill and Wang, 1957.

HOBSON, Harold: *Theatre*. Longmans, 1948. *Theatre 2*. Longmans, 1950.

JAMES, Henry: *The scenic art*. Hart-Davis, 1949. New York: Hill and Wang, 1957.

KERR, Walter: *Pieces at eight*. Reinhardt, 1958. *Thirty plays hath November*. New York: Simon and Schuster, 1969.

KOTT, Jan: *Theatre notebook, 1947–1967*. Methuen, 1968.

LEWES, G. H.: *On actors and the art of acting*. Smith, Elder, 1857. New York: Grove, 1957.

MACCARTHY, Desmond: *Theatre*. MacGibbon, 1954. Chester Springs, Pa.: Dufour.

McCARTHY, Mary: *Sights and spectacles, 1937–1958*. New York: Farrar, 1959. Heinemann.

MONTAGUE, C.E.: *Dramatic values*. Methuen, 1911. New York: Reprint House International.

NATHAN, George Jean: *Passing judgments*. New York: Knopf, 1935. New York: Johnson Reprint, 1969.

ROBINSON, Henry Crabb: *The London theatre, 1811–1866*. Society for Theatre Research, 1966.

SCOTT, Clement: *From The Bells to King Arthur: a critical record of the first-night productions at the Lyceum Theatre from 1871 to 1895*. John Macqueen, 1896. New York: Blom, 1969.

SHAW, Bernard: *Our theatres in the nineties*. 3 vols. Constable, 1932.

TYNAN, Kenneth: *He that plays the king*. Longmans, 1950. *Curtains*. Longmans, 1961. New York: Atheneum.

WALKLEY, A. B.: *Drama and life*. Methuen, 1907. Freeport, N.Y.: Books for Libraries, 1967.

WHITING, John: *John Whiting on theatre*. Alan Ross, 1966. Chester Springs, Pa.: Dufour.

YOUNG, Stark: *Immortal shadows*. New York: Scribner, 1947.

OXFORD

MORE OXFORD PAPERBACKS

Details of a selection of other Oxford Paperbacks follow. A complete list of Oxford Paperbacks, including The World's Classics, Twentieth-Century Classics, OPUS, Past Masters, Oxford Authors, Oxford Shakespeare, and Oxford Paperback Reference, is available in the UK from the General Publicity Department, Oxford University Press (RS), Walton Street, Oxford, OX2 6DP.

In the USA, complete lists are available from the Paperbacks Marketing Manager, Oxford University Press, 200 Madison Avenue, New York, NY 10016.

Oxford Paperbacks are available from all good bookshops. In case of difficulty, customers in the UK can order direct from Oxford University Press Bookshop, 116 High Street, Oxford, Freepost, OX1 4BR, enclosing full payment. Please add 10 per cent of the published price for postage and packing.

THE OXFORD SHAKESPEARE

General Editor: Stanley Wells

The Oxford Shakespeare offers new and authoritative
editions of Shakespeare's plays in which the early print-
ings have been scrupulously re-examined and interpreted
on freshly considered principles. An introductory essay
provides all relevant background information together
with an appraisal of critical views and of the play's effects
in performance. The detailed commentaries pay particular attention to language and staging. Reprints of
sources, music for songs, genealogical tables, maps, etc.
are included when necessary; many of the volumes are
illustrated and contain an index.

'This is now *the* paperback edition to have.' *Sunday
Times*

THE TWO NOBLE KINSMEN

Edited by Eugene M. Waith

The Royal Shakespeare Company's choice of *The Two Noble
Kinsmen* to open the Swan Theatre in 1986 demonstrated that
this long-neglected play is at last coming into its own as a
stageworthy, humorous, and moving dramatization of the conflicting claims of love and friendship. It was first published in
1634 as 'by the memorable worthies of their time, Mr John
Fletcher, and Mr William Shakespeare, Gent' and was probably
performed soon after the wedding of Princess Elizabeth, daughter of James I, to the Elector Palatine in February 1613.

The exceptionally full Introduction to this new edition
explains the relevance to the play of the ideas of chivalry and
of the classical idea of friendship. The edition (which is
illuminatingly illustrated) also offers a discussion of the cen-
turies-long debate about the play's authorship and a clarifica-
tion of its stage action.

Also available in the Oxford Shakespeare:

Hamlet
Julius Caesar
Henry V
The Tempest
The Taming of the Shrew

THE OXFORD AUTHORS

General Editor: Frank Kermode

The Oxford Authors is a series of authoritative editions of the major English writers for the student and the general reader. Drawing on the best texts available, each volume contains a generous selection from the writings—poetry and prose, including letters—to give the essence of a writer's work and thinking. Where appropriate, texts have been tactfully modernized and all are complemented by essential Notes, an Introduction, Chronology, and suggestions for Further Reading.

'The Oxford Authors series can always be relied upon to be splendid—with good plain texts and helpful notes.'
Robert Nye, *Scotsman*

OSCAR WILDE

Edited by Isobel Murray

The drama of Oscar Wilde's life has for years overshadowed his achievement in literature. This is the first large-scale edition of his work to provide unobtrusive guidance to the wealth of knowledge and allusion upon which his writing stands.

Wilde had studied Greek and Latin and was familiar with American literature, while he was as well read in French as he was in English, following Gautier and Flaubert as well as Pater and Ruskin. Through her Notes Isobel Murray enables the modern reader for the first time to read Wilde as such admiring contemporaries as Pater, Yeats, and Symons read him, in a rich, shared culture of literary and visual arts.

This edition underlines the range of his achievement in many genres, including *The Picture of Dorian Gray, Salome, The Importance of Being Earnest, The Decay of Lying,* and *The Ballad of Reading Gaol.* The text is that of the last printed edition overseen by Wilde.

Also in the Oxford Authors:

Sir Philip Sidney
Ben Jonson
Byron
Thomas Hardy

THE WORLD'S CLASSICS

The World's Classics Series makes available the greatest works of world literature at reasonable prices.

'An addition to the library of anyone setting out either to study or begin to read English literature.' *Times Educational Supplement*

COLONEL JACK

Daniel Defoe

Edited by Samuel Holt Monk
With a new Introduction by David Roberts

'Born a gentleman, put 'Prentice to a Pick-Pocket, was Six and Twenty Years a Thief, and then Kidnapp'd to Virginia. Came back a Merchant, married four Wives, and five of them prov'd Whores . . .'

Colonel Jack begins among the alleyways of London and ends in crime, marital disaster, political adventurism, and penitent prosperity. Its elusive hero has been compared to Oliver Twist, Lucky Jim, and to modern criminals who have made their fortune and escaped the law. Jack the occasional Jacobite suceeds almost in spite of himself in making his world conform to his highly individual ends. The result is a novel which subjects a vast range of eighteenth-century life to the scrutiny of an intriguingly unreliable narrator.

Samuel Holt Monk's Oxford English Novels text, the first to use the rare first edition of 1722, is here re-issued with a new introduction by David Roberts which shows why *Colonel Jack* increasingly commands the attention of modern readers.

Also available in the World's Classics:

Peregrine Pickle   Tobias Smollett
Castle Rackrent   Maria Edgeworth
Joseph Andrews and Shamela   Henry Fielding
Camilla   Fanny Burney